ALL ▪ IN ▪ ONE

CCNA

Certification

EXAM GUIDE

ALL ▪ IN ▪ ONE

CCNA
Certification
EXAM GUIDE

Robert E. Larson

Osborne / McGraw-Hill

New York • Chicago • San Francisco • Lisbon
London • Madrid • Mexico City • Milan • New Delhi
San Juan • Seoul • Singapore • Sydney • Toronto

Osborne/**McGraw-Hill**
2600 Tenth Street
Berkeley, California 94710
U.S.A.

To arrange bulk purchase discounts for sales promotions, premiums, or fund-raisers, please contact Osborne/**McGraw-Hill** at the above address. For information on translations or book distributors outside the U.S.A., please see the International Contact Information page immediately following the index of this book.

CCNA All-in-One Exam Guide

1234567890 DOC DOC 01987654321

Book p/n 0-07-212997-2 and CD p/n 0-07-212996-4
parts of

ISBN 0-07-212998-0

Publisher Brandon A. Nordin	**Technical Editor** Salvatore Collora
Vice President & Associate Publisher Scott Rogers	**Copy Editors** William McManus Stacey Sawyer
Acquisitions Editor Michael Sprague	**Compositor and Indexer** MacAllister Publishing Services, LLC
Project Editor Jennifer Malnick	
Acquisitions Coordinator Jessica Wilson	

DEDICATION

This book is dedicated to my CCNA students,
past and present, who have challenged me,
supported me, and brought much joy to my
life through their many successes.

ACKNOWLEDGMENTS

A book project of this size is always the culmination of many people's efforts, energies, and insights. It would be impossible to take credit for what is really a group effort.

To Paulden Rodriguez, CCNP, who is one of the most intelligent and articulate young minds in networking today—thank you. You helped me when I needed it most. Paulden wrote Chapter 11 and the WAN chapters.

To Salvatore Collora, CCIE, my technical editor—thank you for trying to keep me honest. Sal comes from the world of the huge-budget networks in California, and he continually pushed me to include latest technology and concepts.

To John Read, Michael Sprague, and Gareth Hancock at Osborne/McGraw-Hill— thank you for making this project available to me. To Neil J. Salkind, my agent at Studio B—thank you for helping me put this project together.

To the many Osborne/McGraw-Hill people, such as Jessica Wilson and Jennifer Malnick—thank you for your many helpful words and kindnesses along the way.

To my friend and traveling partner Dave Warner—it's past time to head to Texas to reacquaint ourselves with the river walk, beaches, border towns, and the most beautiful people in the world. I want to spend some time where "getting connected" means lining up a ride to hear Willie or any of the great Texas bands.

To my students, fellow instructors, my friend and peer Scott Wolfe, my parents, and most of all my wife and kids, all of whom I have neglected these past months—thank you for your patience, support, and interest.

—Bob Larson

ABOUT THE CONTRIBUTORS

Bob Larson lives in the Puget Sound area, 25 miles southeast of Seattle, with his wife, Jerri. Just as the four adult children, Brett, Chris, Jared, and Jade, move on to careers and lives of their own, the next generation, Iris Mae, keeps things from ever becoming truly peaceful.

On May 18, 1980, when Mt. St. Helen's volcanic eruption trapped him in his house for ten days with a brand-new computer, Bob decided to change careers. Over the next couple years, he went to grad school and started teaching computer applications. Since 1985, he's done nothing else. Bob Larson & Associates provides course development as well as networking and applications training. Bob provides network consulting through Lighthouse Consulting, Inc., owned by his son Brett. Since 1997, Bob has been involved with the Cisco Networking Academy Program at two area community colleges, offering both CCNA and CCNP training.

Bob has been fortunate to be able to provide training in 20 states and four countries. He was selected to teach the first Cisco Academy CCNA program on the African continent in 1999, graduating 18 top-flight CCNAs who are now making their mark in the new South Africa. He is hoping to have a reunion visit in Summer 2001.

Technical editor **Salvatore Collora** is a Systems Engineer for Cisco Systems. He holds a CCIE in Routing and Switching, and is currently involved in pre-sales engineering efforts in Los Angeles. He has designed several large networks for various enterprise customers including the Staples Center, the *Los Angeles Times*, and Children's Hospital Los Angeles. Prior to coming to Cisco, he was a weekly editorial contributor to *PC Week* magazine, and did systems design and support for Sony Pictures Imageworks.

Sal holds a Bachelors of Business Administration from Loyola Marymount University, and got his start in networking while on staff there. As he transitioned from LMU to Rubin Postaer and Associates in 1995 to bring Honda's first Web presence to fruition, he co-authored *Using Microsoft Exchange Server*, his first published work.

BRIEF CONTENTS

CONTENTS

INTRODUCTION

Welcome to *CCNA All-in-One Certification Exam Guide*. This book is here to help you prepare to take—and pass—Cisco Certification Exam 640-507, titled "Cisco Certified Network Associate," or CCNA. Even more important, it is here to share a pool of knowledge that should make you employable in the field. If you strive for knowledge and experience, the certification will come. In this section, we will discuss skill building and exam preparation alternatives, the certification exam situation itself, Cisco's certification programs in general, and how this book can help you prepare for Cisco's certification exams. We will look at the following:

- Things to do to prepare
- CCNA exam insights
- Cisco Certification Information

Things to Do to Prepare

I cannot emphasize enough how important it is to get some hands-on experience with Cisco routers and switches. The exam asks many questions involving the Cisco IOS command syntax and the proper mode for executing those commands. Experience configuring devices is the best way to become comfortable with the Cisco IOS features. I have tried to include enough screen captures to assist you if hands-on experience is not possible.

Unlike some other certification, memorizing a long list of facts is not necessarily the best approach for Cisco exams. You must be able to apply the information and see it from other perspectives. The following sections are a list of resources that can help you study and prepare.

What Is in This Book

Preparing for any Cisco certification exam (including the CCNA) requires you to obtain and study materials designed to provide comprehensive information about the subject matter that will appear on your specific exam. This book contains more than enough information to pass the exam. The task now is to apply and absorb that information and become comfortable with it. This will present different levels of challenges based on your experience with networking. Obviously, someone who has been working in the field for a period of time will have a base of knowledge and skills that they can build on. I think this book can be a good tool for that person.

The other type of CCNA student I find where I teach is the person interested in getting into the IT field but has little or no real network experience, maybe even limited computer experience. I have tried to write this book for that person—the student who may need some background material, who may need to look at things from two or more perspectives, the one who is willing to work and study but doesn't know what needs to be done. Note that I refer to networking experience, not computer experience. They are not the same thing.

Classroom Training

Whether you use this book or not, classroom training for many people is the preferred way to learn complex technologies. In this field, classroom training should be combined with hands-on experience with real routers and switches. There are several possible courses to follow:

Cisco Networking Academies   I believe in this program for the average person. Since 1987, Cisco Systems has set up Networking Academies in more than 6,400 locations around the world. Half are in high schools and the rest are primarily in community colleges and trade schools. A few are at universities and at service organizations. This highly developed multimedia curriculum combined with abundant hands-on experience offered part-time over a seven-month period can create a solid foundation. The academies offer CCNA and CCNP training and are now branching out to include non-Cisco technologies like UNIX and Web design. To learn more about the Academy Program or to locate one in your area, check the following Web site: **www.cisco.com/warp/public/779/edu/academy/.**

Cisco Training Partners   In larger cities, for the working administrator with solid foundation skills who truly meets the course prerequisites, these short, often five-day courses can be a quick way to fill in the gaps, gain limited hands-on experience, and move on to certification. I really like these programs for working professionals with a lot of experience. For them, this type of training can be an excellent value. On the other hand, if a person doesn't fit the target audience and can't keep up with the class, this can be a very expensive reality check. For more information, go to **www.cisco.com/** and click on the Training/Certification link.

Buying Equipment

Many students do particularly well if their long-term goal is CCNP or CCIE. Cisco vendors like Blackbox and **www.cdw.com** offer catalogs and knowledgeable support people. I have always had very good luck with eBay (**www.ebay.com**). Do a search on "Cisco" at the eBay site and there will be hundreds and some days thousands of items. The key is that you can't be in a hurry: Watch for the deal that you want and be ready to walk away.

There are two ways to use eBay. First, look at the people offering items. Many have Web sites linked to their auctions. See what kind of businesses they are and what other "deals" they have going. Second, if I'm buying a bigger item, I only buy from an auction that will take a credit card. I then use a card that guarantees my purchases. I've bought dozens of items and I don't feel that I've ever been hurt. I've never had an item fail to be delivered pretty much as advertised.

Virtual Labs and Simulators

One way to get a form of hands-on experience is through the use of router simulators or virtual labs. Some labs are real equipment scheduled for your use during a time period at an hourly rate. This method can be pretty expensive on a per-hour basis but a very good value when compared to the thousands of dollars it would take set up a similar lab. Other virtual labs are lab simulators that exist only in your computer or out on the Web. A Web site you might want to start with is **www.routersim.com**.

Practice Exams

I hate the thought of a person taking a test repeatedly until he knows enough of the questions to pass. This leads to what the industry refers to as "paper certifications" or, worse yet, "vapor certifications." It is bad for the industry and can't be all that great for the individual. What value is the certification if you get fired from the job because you can't do the work?

Having said that, I do believe in taking practice tests once you have trained and prepared yourself. This serves two purposes: First, it may point out gaps or weaknesses in your training plan; second, and more important, it helps to prepare you for the exam itself. Particularly for those students that have been out of school for a few years, the exam process can be a shock. Having gone through the MCSE, CCNA, and CCNP program plus many of the second-tier certifications out there, I suspect that Cisco exams are like none you've taken before. While they are fair and valid, they are not designed to pass a lot of students. They are designed to see if you know the exam material forward and backward. My students have found the exams at **www.boson.com** are both challenging and helpful.

Cram Sessions and Brain Dumps

There are Web sites called brain dumps, where test takers try to list as many test questions as they can remember. First, these are a waste of time and energy. Second, they violate the non-disclosure agreement that every test taker agrees to when they take the exam. In the end, you compromise your integrity for a bit of short-term memory fodder.

What time I've spent at the sites that I'm aware of, I've found a mix of good and bad questions, questions from old exams, questions from the wrong exams, and a small amount of mischief. There are better ways.

One site I like is **http://cramsession.brainbuzz.com/**. They have a series of study guides—usually 12 to 20 pages—for many exams that I recommend to all of my students. Although they do not give you questions, they give you lists of things to know. But this doesn't replace studying. The practice that I follow, and I recommend to my students, is that each night for the week before a scheduled exam, I read the Cram session just before bed. Typically, it will lead me to question some points and after researching, I put the results on the margins of the study guide. Their study guide is the only thing that I ever take to a test site. I try to review it once before going into the test site.

Do you need all of the things covered in this section? Probably not. But I've tried to offer a mix to helpful tools and suggestions.

CCNA Exam Insights

Once you have prepared for your exam, you need to register with a testing center. The computer-based CCNA exam costs $100 (North America), and if you don't pass, you may retest for an additional $100 each time. In the United States and Canada, tests are administered by Prometric Testing Centers.

You can sign up for a test through Prometric's Web site at **www.2test.com**, or you can register by phone at (800) 204-EXAM (within the United States or Canada). The Web site will not allow you to schedule exams within 48 hours, so use the phone registration for shorter scheduling intervals. It is often possible to take tests the same day. Be prepared to wait through voice messages.

To sign up for a test, you will need a valid credit card.

To schedule an exam, call the toll-free number or visit the Web page at least one day in advance. Before booking the exam, make sure that you understand the cancellation process and deadlines, currently before 7:00 P.M. Central Standard Time the day before the scheduled test time (or you will be charged, even if you don't appear to take the test).

When you want to schedule a test, have the following information ready:

- **Exam number (640-507) and title (CCNA)**
- **Your name**   Exactly the way that you want it to appear on your certificate
- **Your social security, social insurance, or Prometric number (SP)**
- **A method of payment**   Credit card
- **Contact telephone numbers**   In case of a problem so they can reach you
- **Mailing address**   Where you want your certificate mailed
- **E-mail address**   For contact purposes, you will get an e-mail confirmation

Once you sign up for a test, you will be informed as to when and where the test is scheduled. Try to arrive at least 15 minutes early—I tell students to show up an hour early, just in case. You can always relax and review your notes. I've sat in exams next to students who have showed up late for whatever reason. They seem miserable, and I suspect the stress and tension is reflected in the score.

Photo ID

You will need to bring two forms of identification to the testing site. One form must be a photo ID, such as a driver's license or a valid passport. The other must have a signature. The test cannot be taken without the proper identification.

Gum, Candy, and Cough Drops

Do yourself a favor and bring something with you. It can always just sit there ignored, but the last thing you want is a dry throat or coughing fit to disrupt your testing and the silence for your peers.

The Exam Process

When you show up at the testing center, you will need to sign in with an exam coordinator. They will ask you to show the two forms of signature identification. After you have signed in and your time slot arrives, you will be asked to deposit any items with you, such as books, bags, pagers, or calculators. Make sure that you know where the restrooms and drinking fountain are located. You will be escorted into a closed room.

All exams are closed-book. You will be furnished with one or two blank sheets of paper and a pen, or, in some cases, an erasable plastic sheet and an erasable pen. Before the exam, you should memorize as much of the important material as you can, so you can write that information on the blank sheet as soon as you are seated in front of the computer, before you start your exam. You can refer to this piece of paper any time you like during the test, but you will have to turn it in when you leave.

You will have some time to compose yourself, to record this information, and to take a sample orientation exam before you begin the real test. You will also be required to complete a computer-based survey to track demographics of the test candidates. Typically, if an exam has a 75-minute time limit, you will have 90 minutes to take the sample exam, complete the survey, and take the actual exam. Once you start the actual exam, you now have only the exam time limit. If this is your first Cisco exam, I suggest that you take the orientation test before taking your first exam.

Typically, the room will have up to a dozen computers. Each workstation will be separated from the others by dividers designed to keep you from seeing your neighbor's computer. Keep in mind that the people next to you could be taking a certification exam from an industry totally unrelated to yours, so don't be concerned if someone starts after you or finishes before you. Most test rooms use closed-circuit cameras. This permits the exam coordinator to monitor the room.

The exam coordinator will have preloaded the appropriate Cisco certification exam, which for this book is Exam 640-507. If there is a problem with the exam—such as the version number, the screen doesn't display all data, and so on—let the coordinator know right away. Do not put yourself at a disadvantage. You can start as soon as you are seated in front of the computer. I suggest that you sit back for a minute and relax. Take a deep breath. If the chair is adjustable, adjust it. Move your arms and legs to release any tension. You are going to be sitting there almost 90 minutes.

All Cisco certification exams allow a certain maximum amount of time in which to complete the work (this time is indicated on the exam by an on-screen counter/clock, so you can check the time remaining whenever you like). All Cisco certification exams are computer-generated and most use a multiple-choice format, often with six to eight choices. It is possible, if not likely, that several questions will refer to an exhibit containing dozens of commands from which you will be expected to select one as the answer to a specific question.

Although this may sound quite simple, the questions are not only constructed to check your mastery of basic facts and skills about the subject material, but they also require you to evaluate one or more sets of circumstances or requirements. Often, you are asked to give more than one answer to a question, although you will always be told how many to choose. *You get only one pass through the questions.* You cannot mark a question and return to it later.

When you complete the Cisco certification exam, the exam will tell you whether you have passed or failed. All test objectives are broken into several topic areas and each area is scored on a basis of 100 percent. Particularly if you do not pass the exam, select the option on the screen that asks if you want to print the report. The test administrator will print it for you. You can use this report to help you prepare for a second effort, if needed. Once you see your score, you have the option of printing additional copies of the score report. It is a good idea to print it twice.

Remember, if you need to retake an exam, you will have to schedule a new test with Prometric and pay another $100.

Exam Design

All Cisco tests use one of five basic question types:

- Multiple-choice with a single answer

- Multiple-choice with two or more answers (the question will indicate how many answers)

- Multipart with one or more answers (the question will indicate how many answers)

- CLI-based questions (many times, an exhibit will present a sample IOS configuration in which you are asked to choose the correct command or interpret the configuration's output, per the question's directions)

- A different format, such as fill in the blank, ordering, or matching

Take the time to read a question at least twice before selecting an answer, and pay special attention to words such as "not" that can radically change the question. If a question seems very simple, great—but read it over once more to make sure that you aren't missing something.

Always look for an Exhibit button as you examine each question. The Exhibit button brings up graphics used to help explain a question, provide additional data, or illustrate network design or program behavior.

NOTE: Before scheduling your test, make sure you understand the Windows interface—maximizing, restoring, moving, resizing, and tiling windows.

Cisco exams do not allow you to return to questions, so you must make sure to answer the question as best you can before proceeding to the next one. The exam will clearly state before you start whether you can mark answers and return.

Cisco's Testing Format

All Cisco exams are fixed-length with a fixed number of questions. Each candidate will get the same number of questions; the order of the questions can vary, as can the specific questions. If you retake an exam, assume there will be different questions. From time to time, questions are replaced and others may not be scored.

Cisco provides a counter in the upper-right corner (near the remaining time) showing the number of questions completed and the number outstanding. Monitor your time to make sure that you have completed at least one-quarter of the questions one-quarter of the way through the exam period and three-quarters of the questions three-quarters of the way through. Have the calculations done in advance, such as 16 questions by 18 minutes.

If you are not finished with ten minutes remaining, try to pick up the pace. When there are five minutes remaining, use the remaining time to guess your way through any remaining questions. Guessing is better than not answering—blank answers are always wrong, but a guess may turn out to be right. The important thing is to answer every question.

Some Basic Question-Handling Strategies

For those questions that take only a single answer, usually two or three of the answers will be obviously incorrect, and a couple of the answers will be plausible. Of course, only one can be correct. Unless the answer leaps out at you, begin the process of eliminating those answers that are most obviously wrong.

Many questions assume that the default behavior of a particular command or option is in effect. If you know the defaults and understand what they mean, this will help you with your choice.

Cisco exams are generally pretty straightforward and not intended to beat you out of your certification; but, then again, they are not designed to be easy. Pay attention, particularly with syntax. Knowing the difference between *access-list 1 deny any* and *access list 1 deny any* should be assumed (note the hyphen).

If the answer seems immediately obvious, reread the question to look for a trap; sometimes those are the ones you are most likely to get wrong.

Typically, at least one answer out of the possible choices for a question can be eliminated immediately because the answer does not apply to the situation or the answer describes a nonexistent issue or option.

If faced with guessing among two or more potentially correct answers, reread the question. Try to picture how each of the possible remaining answers would alter the situation. Be especially sensitive to terminology; sometimes the choice of words (such as "remove" instead of "disable") can make the difference between a right answer and a wrong one.

Cisco Certification Program

The Cisco Certification Program currently includes the following separate certificates with various specialty tracks. You should become familiar with and visit Cisco's Web site at **www.cisco.com/go/certifications/**.

The number of questions and time limits for the following exams were accurate at the time this book was written. Cisco reserves the right to change either as it sees fit. Cisco tries to keep this information confidential, although you can check either figure when you register for an exam.

The major certifications are:

CCNA (Cisco Certified Networking Associate)

Exam 640-507 is a 65-question, 75-minute exam. The cost is $100. The CCNA certification demonstrates the ability to install, configure, and operate simple-routed *local area network* (LAN), routed *wide area network* (WAN), and switched LAN. Topics include: Ethernet, Token-Ring, TCP/IP, IPX/SPX, IP RIP, IGRP, IPX RIP, access lists (ACLs), LAN switches, VLANs, Serial Communications, ISDN, Frame-Relay, and Point-to-Point Protocol (PPP).

The CCNA certification provides a foundation for pursuing advanced Cisco certifications. It is a prerequisite for the Cisco Certified Network Professional (CCNP) and Cisco Certified Design Professional (CCDP), and is suggested for the Cisco Certified Internetwork Expert (CCIE). The CCNA certification covers concepts and skills vital to the operation of modern computer networks, and would be valuable to network administrators, network engineers, and students preparing for these roles.

CCDA (Cisco Certified Design Associate)

Exam 640-441 is a 72-question, 120-minute exam. The cost is $100. The Cisco Network Design Career certification track is designed for people who want to design Cisco-based networks that predominantly include routed LAN, routed WAN, and switched LAN networks.

CCNP (Cisco Certified Networking Professional)

CCNP is a comprehensive internetworking skills certification that requires successfully passing four exams. Each exam is approximately 65 questions in 75 minutes. The cost of each exam is $100. The number of questions and time limit for each should be confirmed by checking with your testing center or by calling Prometric. The four exams are:

- BSCN (Building Scalable Cisco Networks)   Exam 640-503
- BCMSN (Building Cisco Multilayer Switching Networks)   Exam 640-504
- BCRAN (Building Cisco Remote Access Networks)   Exam 640-505
- CIT (Cisco Internetwork Troubleshooting)   Exam 640-506

CCDP (Cisco Certified Design Professional)

CCDP is a comprehensive internetworking design skills certification that requires successfully passing four exams. Each exam is approximately 65 questions in 75 minutes. The cost of each exam is $100. The number of questions and time limit for each should be confirmed by checking with your testing center or by calling Prometric. The four exams are:

- BSCN (Building Scalable Cisco Networks)   Exam 640-503
- BCMSN (Building Cisco Multilayer Switching Networks)   Exam 640-504
- BCRAN (Building Cisco Remote Access Networks)   Exam 640-505
- CID (Cisco Internetwork Design)   Exam 640-025

CCIE (Cisco Certified Internetwork Expert)

The CCIE certification is possibly the most influential in the internetworking industry today. It is famous (or infamous) for its difficulty and for how easily it holds its seekers at bay. The certification requires only one written exam (350-001); passing that exam qualifies you to schedule time at a Cisco campus to demonstrate your knowledge in a two-day practical laboratory setting. You must pass this lab with a score of at least 80 percent to become a CCIE. Recent statistics have put the passing rates at roughly 20 percent for first attempts and 35 to 50 percent overall. Once you achieve CCIE certification, you must recertify every two years by passing a written exam administered by Cisco.

Receiving Your Certificate

After passing the necessary certification exam(s) and agreeing to Cisco's nondisclosure terms, you will be certified. Official certification normally takes four to six weeks. The package includes a welcome kit that contains a number of elements:

- Official certificate (suitable for framing)

- A laminated wallet card

- A graduation letter

- A license to use the Cisco certification logo, in advertisements, promotions, documents, resumes, letterhead, business cards, and more

- Access to the online Tracking System

Tracking Cisco Certification Status

As soon as you pass any Cisco exam, you must complete a certification agreement. To do this, go to Cisco's Web site (**www.cisco.com/go/certifications/**) and select the Tracking System link, or go directly to the Certification Tracking Web site (**www. galton.com/~cisco/**). You can also mail a hard copy of the agreement to Cisco's certification authority. You will not be certified until you complete a certification agreement and Cisco receives it in one of these forms.

The Certification Tracking Web site also allows you to view your certification information. Cisco will contact you via e-mail and explain your certification and its use.

Recertification

Cisco requires three-year recertification for the non-CCIE programs. The best place to keep tabs on the Cisco Career Certifications program and its related requirements is on the Web, at **www.cisco.com/go/certifications/**.

About This Book

CCNA All-In-One Certification Exam Guide can provide you with the knowledge you need to study and prepare for CCNA Exam 640-507.

Cisco routers, LAN switches, firewalls, ATM switches, and so on, are at the heart of many of the world's networks, both large and small. The skills developed for this exam will help to make you a more useful and marketable member of the industry. If you know how to configure the de facto industry standard devices, then employers will know that you can work with any other technology—or learn the skills necessary to do so.

When you complete your CCNA, you will be at the threshold of a world of opportunities in the IT field. These opportunities are only limited by your ability to dream and then to act. Take the time while you are learning to see the opportunities in the field. Several of the people working for me wouldn't have bet they would be teaching a year or two ago. This is a rapidly advancing industry that offers ample opportunity for personal growth and for making a contribution to your business or organization. This book will provide the knowledge that you need today plus a sound basis for understanding the changes that you will encounter in the future. It also is intended to give you the hands-on skills you need to be a valued professional in your organization.

Without a doubt, this has been the best opportunity for people to make substantial changes in their lives. Most students are employed as they finish their training, move into other positions, or take positions with other companies.

What I have noticed is that although there are successes at every level, the ones who really seem to succeed are the ones that really apply themselves to learning their craft. They are the ones who use extra time to get more hands-on experience. If you have little or no experience, that doesn't have to remain a barrier. One of our greatest successes was stocking shelves at a Home Depot when he started CCNA training. Nine months later, he was moving halfway across the country for a new job and he has been on the fast track since—I imagine he will have his CCIE by the time you read this.

This is an exciting field with limitless opportunities for those who want to make the effort, take the setbacks (they happen too), and do the things necessary to prepare themself for the IT industry. Just reading this book won't do it all for you. It will help you develop your knowledge, but you need to do those things that will help you gather experience. Part of that is talking to people. Talk to anybody who will listen. Make sure they know what you are doing and why. Let them see that you are serious about this. You will be amazed where opportunities come from.

Let's get started!

Networking Introduction and Standards

This chapter will cover:

- **Computer hardware basics**

- **Workstations, servers, hosts, and nodes**

- **Peer-to-peer vs. server-based networks**

- **LANs, WANs, MANs, networks, and internetworks**

- **Communications media**

- **Industry standards**

- **OSI reference model**

- **Data encapsulation**

Before we get started working with networking technology and terminology, it is important to make sure we have a somewhat common point of reference on certain terms and concepts. The computer industry draws many of its terms from our common language, which makes getting started easier, but we need to make sure that we understand what these terms and phrases mean in the context of networking.

An extensive glossary appears at the back of the book, but here we are going to define some basic terms that we will use every day.

Later in the chapter, we will look at some of the key standards that allow so many companies from virtually every country in the world to build and integrate components into computer and network systems.

Computer Hardware Basics

It is not the purpose of this book to cover computer hardware in detail. In fact, there are many great books and courses that specifically cover computer hardware. From A+ training for the would-be PC technician to community college "Build Your Own PC" courses, there are ways to get the technical expertise and hands-on experience. Our goal here is to cover the basic concepts in order to make sure that you understand how computers fit into your networking model.

Whether working as a stand-alone computer, a single computer connected to the Internet, or a computer connected to a *local area network* (LAN), data or information is being converted to and from digital electrical patterns that move within the system to create screen images, sounds, data files stored on disks, documents to be printed, and data to be transmitted to others.

Whether browsing the Web, keeping the company's books, writing a novel, or doing any of the many other things that we use computers for, computers have become vital to our world economy, businesses of all sizes, and, in many cases, our own well being. Understanding the underlying concepts will help you when you need to connect your computers together.

Understanding the underlying concepts of the individual computer becomes even more important when you recognize that many of the devices that we will be talking about as network devices are themselves basically computers. From bridges and routers to access servers, when looked at "under the hood," these devices have much in common with the personal computer.

Bits and Bytes

Generally, data anywhere within an individual computer or network is digital binary, meaning it is a stream of electrical impulses that are represented as zeros and ones.

Actually, the data is more like a series of switches being either on or off, with the one representing on and the zero representing off. These individual ones and zeros are referred to as bits. *Bit* is short for binary digit and can be only a zero or a one. While bits can be interpreted in any quantity, we typically group 8 bits into a *byte* to create patterns that represent letters, numbers, punctuation, and computer control sequences. Figure 1-1 is a typical representation of data as a series of digital bits.

It is very important to recognize that a bit and byte are not the same thing. Although both are units of measurement, the byte is eight times as large as the bit. Mixing them up can greatly under- or overstate a situation and make you look somewhat foolish in the process.

Figure 1-1
Bits and bytes

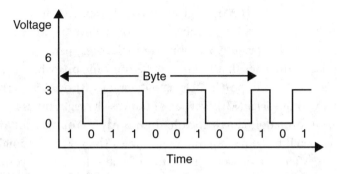

Table 1-1   Bit and Byte Increments

UNIT	DEFINITION	EXAMPLES
Bit (b)	0 or 1	0 or 1
Byte (B)	8 bits	10011010 or 11111111
Kilobyte (KB)	1,024 bytes	1KB or 256KB
Megabyte (MB)	1,024KB	1MB or 64MB
Gigabyte (GB)	1,024MB	1GB or 12.5GB
Terabyte (TB)	1,024GB	1TB or 7.3TB
Kilobit (Kb)	1,024b	1Kb or 56Kb
Megabit (Mb)	1,024 Kb	1Mb or 10 Mb

Simply stated, a byte (8 bits) equates to the binary storage of a single character. A kilobyte is generally 1,000 bytes, a megabyte is 1,000 kilobytes, a gigabyte is 1,000 megabytes, and so forth. This generalization is very adequate for most things, but a look at Table 1-1 shows that it isn't quite true—a kilobyte is not exactly 1,000 bytes. Since all digital data is stored as zeros and ones, there are only two possible numbers, and therefore every numeric value will generally be a power of two. The number 1,024 is two to the tenth power, or 2^{10}. This is why numbers like 32, 64, 128, and 512 keep popping up in measurements of computer resources, such as memory size.

Be sure to compare the bottom two items on the table with their larger siblings a few rows higher. There are also *Gigabit* (Gb) and *Terabit* (Tb) increments. When we talk about computer components, we often use byte increments, such as megabytes of *random access memory* (RAM) or gigabytes of disk space. When we talk about data transfer speeds on networks, it is more common to use bit increments, such as "56 Kb modems," which refers to 56 kilobits (not kilobytes) per second. To keep from sounding foolish, remember that the lowercase b means bits while the uppercase B means bytes and that it is important. Using *megabyte* (MB) or *kilobyte* (KB) when you mean *megabit* (Mb) or *kilobit* (Kb) overstates your case by eight times-8 bits to the byte.

If this information is new to you, do not panic. You will survive this, and in a few chapters, you'll be converting binary numbers (base 2) to decimal numbers (base 10) like a pro. After you are safely in control of that information, you will tackle hexadecimal (base 16) values. Many texts and courses deal with these conversions in the introductory phase but then do not use them until they get to network addressing and subnetting much later in the text or course. I prefer to introduce these conversions as we use them. It saves having to review them later, and I think it is easier for newer networkers to have a little of the big picture in place before they start dealing in the "math."

Major Computer Systems

The basic computer has a *central processing unit* (CPU) connected via a digital bus acting very much like your backbone or spine to connect memory, storage devices, and *input/output* (I/O) devices. To use an office analogy, the CPU is you, the thinker or thought processor. Memory is a work area or desktop that information is brought to so you can access it. Storage is the file cabinets or shelves where resources are kept until you need them. Then, they are moved to memory, the desktop, so that you can work with them. I/O devices are the many methods that the office uses to secure resources for your use, as well as the methods of distributing the results of your efforts. Figure 1-2 shows this basic computer process design.

Bus

A *bus* is a series of wire connections through which data is transmitted from one part of a computer to another. This bus is an integral part of the computer's main circuit board, often referred to as a *motherboard*. One measure of the bus is the number of wires that make up the data path. A 32-bit bus has 32 wires, which act very much like 32 lanes on a freeway. Obviously, a 32-bit bus will carry much more data than a 16-bit bus, but far less than a 64-bit bus. The bus capacity when talking about a motherboard is sometimes referred to as a 32-bit architecture or 64-bit architecture.

Many of the components we will discuss in the next few sections are permanently wired into this bus through the motherboard with gold connections to allow for maximum throughput speeds. Other components are connected through elongated sockets

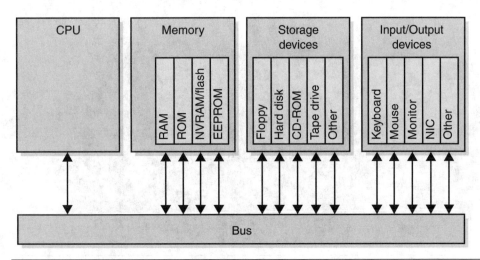

Figure I-2   Basic computer process design

that allow the many wires in the bus to each have direct contact with counterparts on the devices.

Central Processing Unit (CPU)

CPUs are silicon microprocessors that over the years have evolved to be able to perform the tasks of millions of transistors that would at one time have filled entire rooms. These CPUs easily fit in the smallest palm with a weight comparable to a few coins. They are manufactured by companies such as Intel, Motorola, and AMD and have names like Pentium, Xeon, Athlon, and others. While these processors get a lot of promotional hype when included in the marketing of a personal computer, they tend to be relegated to the small print when they are a part of a router or other network device. Figure 1-3 is a Pentium III CPU with heat sinks for cooling.

One characteristic that is used to differentiate CPUs is its speed rating in *megahertz* (MHz). One MHz represents one million instruction processing cycles per second. The higher the MHz rating of the CPU, the more instructions it can process per second and, therefore, the faster it is. Another unit of measure by which CPUs can be compared has to do with the number of wire connections a CPU has to plug into the bus. A 32-bit processor with a 32-bit bus can literally stage and process 32 instructions every time the CPU cycles. Therefore, a 500 MHz processor can process 32 simultaneous bit streams of data at a rate of 500 million instructions per second. With CPU speeds moving even higher and bus widths moving to 64-bit, the potential grows exponentially.

Figure 1-3 Pentium III CPU

Keep in mind that many of these speed ratings are compromised if other components on the system cannot handle the speed. Data, quite like drivers on the expressways, can only go as fast as the slowest devices. This is true *within* our computers, but it is even more important *between* our computers when we connect them together. Connecting two superfreeways with a long two-lane unimproved gravel road is a pretty good analogy of two modern computers sharing data over a telephone modem.

Memory

Memory in general refers to instructions and data that are located in silicon chips directly connected to the bus. As such, they can be accessed at the speed that electricity passes through a wire.

Compared to storage devices (discussed next), which are mechanical devices and therefore much slower, memory is the logical place to store the instructions and data that we are working with. Using our office analogy again, if we were calculating our taxes, we might bring our records, the government formulas (forms), and our calculator to the desk so that we can quickly access them as we need them. Each time we have to stop, go to a storage device, and return to work, our overall progress is slowed.

Memory comes in several forms, described next.

Random Access Memory (RAM)

RAM is a magnetic field maintained in a series of empty silicon chips directly connected, or socketed, to the bus. The bus then provides fast access to the CPU.

As the computer is started, the *operating system* (OS) is loaded into RAM. When you launch programs (software), the portions you are using currently are loaded into RAM, and then your data is moved into RAM. From time to time, you save your work, which copies the changes in the data to a storage device. RAM is very fast but disappears instantly if the power is interrupted for even a fraction of a second. This dynamic nature of RAM is also very handy when you are through working on one project and want to use another program. You can quickly dump the old program from RAM and load the new one in its place. If a computer has adequate RAM, multiple programs and associated data can reside in memory at the same time.

While the memory might physically reside in several or many silicon chips, the memory collectively creates a virtual workspace that the computer sees as a single area. If you remember that the chips can exchange data at the speed electricity travels through a very short wire, the separate chips presents no serious problem to the computer.

RAM in today's computers and network devices is generally measured in megabytes, such as 64MB or 128MB, but some network devices have smaller memories and still use kilobytes. Figure 1-4 shows a *dual inline memory module* (DIMM) memory stick on the top and a *single inline memory module* (SIMM) memory stick on the bottom that are used in the RAM for both PCs and many network devices.

Read-Only Memory (ROM)

ROM is a special type of memory chip that contains instructions "burnt in" at the factory that perform only a single set of instructions. A good example is the *basic input/output system* (BIOS) that performs the startup hardware check and the *power-on self test* (POST), which your computer goes through each time you turn it on.

Figure 1-4 DIMM and SIMM memory

Some early computers experimented with storing the operating system on ROM, which allowed for much quicker startups but made upgrading the OS more difficult. We will see later that some network devices, such as routers, do store a stripped-down version of the OS in ROM so that the unit cannot be rendered totally unable to function. Many of the palm-sized *personal digital assistant* (PDA) devices do that as well, allowing them to use less RAM and provide information quicker.

Nonvolatile Random Access Memory (NVRAM or Flash)

NVRAM is a type of memory that retains its contents when power to the unit is turned off. NVRAM may be memory chips within the device or it might be a magnetic card inserted into a slot in the device. PDAs, laptops, and many network devices use one form or the other to provide fast continuity between sessions. Some also store the OS, software, and data on flash cards.

NVRAM can be measured in kilobytes or megabytes.

Electrically Erasable Programmable Read-Only Memory (EEPROM)

EEPROM is a special type of ROM that can be erased and reprogrammed by exposing it to an electrical charge. EEPROM, like ROM, retains its contents when the power is turned off. Again like ROM, EEPROM is not as fast as RAM because it requires data to be written or erased one byte at a time. NVRAM or flash allows data to be written or erased in blocks, making it much faster.

Virtual Memory

Virtual memory is not really memory but disk storage space. Some operating systems temporarily offload data to disk when more memory space is needed. This disk space looks to the computer like additional RAM, thereby allowing a program or data set to be used that would not be able to fit in regular memory. The computer, when executing the program, copies into RAM those portions of the program needed at any given time. While this is not as fast as RAM, it is faster than loading and reloading a program or data from its normal storage area on the disk and, of course, it is preferable to not being able to run an application due to lack of memory.

To facilitate using virtual memory, the operating system divides virtual memory into pages, each of which contains a fixed number of addresses. Each page is stored on the disk until it is needed, and then the operating system copies the page from to RAM, translating the virtual addresses into real addresses. Translating virtual addresses into real addresses is called *mapping*, and copying virtual pages to RAM is known as *paging* or *swapping*.

We are addressing this topic to make sure every one knows that virtual memory is not real memory and also to indicate its importance particularly on network servers, which we will talk about later in this chapter. A server with too little virtual memory can become a bottleneck, undoing any performance gains that might have made elsewhere.

Virtual memory is usually measured in megabytes, although some servers might have gigabytes of virtual memory.

Storage Devices

Storage devices are the various types of magnetic or laser media that is used for non-volatile storage of your operating systems, software, and data. Floppy disks, hard drives, Zip drives, Jaz drives, tape units, and CD-ROM drives are all examples of storage devices. These devices and their removable media (where appropriate) are the file cabinets and bookshelves of your computer systems. Data stored on them is not impacted by loss of power and, with the exception of hard drives, they offer some level of portability and offsite backup of your data.

The storage capacity of these devices is measured in megabytes or, more often, gigabytes. Different types of data being stored require differing amounts of space. Generally, text and numbers store quite efficiently, whereas space requirements increase for artwork, photographs, video, and voice. At one time, we used to teach that a floppy disk (1.44MB) could store approximately 2,500 to 3,000 pages of text and numbers. A 10GB hard drive stores 6,700 times that amount. Even the basic home computer, if storing text documents, could easily store the equivalent of a nice-sized library.

Input/Output (I/O) Devices

I/O refers to any device, operation, or program that is used to enter data into a computer, modify data already in the computer, or extract data from the computer. The most obvious input devices are the keyboard and mouse. Similarly, the most obvious output devices are the monitor and printer. Some less-obvious input devices are scanners and barcode readers. Devices that may be considered both input and output are modems and *network interface cards* (NICs), as well as the serial, parallel, and *universal serial bus* (USB) ports. These devices all allow data to enter and exit the computer.

Other devices that would qualify as both input and output devices are the removable storage devices, such as floppy disks, Zip disks, and CD-ROMs. These have already been addressed under the "Storage Devices" section, but clearly they can both introduce and extract data from your computer.

Workstations, Servers, Hosts, and Nodes

Because the PC industry, and later PC networks, evolved from so many independent sources, which typically had their roots in the mythical "garage" rather than in a single megamanufacturer with a grand marketing plan, the terminology regarding this industry is inconsistent and tends to use many terms from common conversation.

Another reality in this business is that there are several very large players, such as Cisco, Microsoft, Intel, Hewlett-Packard (HP), IBM, Compaq, Lucent, Nortel, AT&T, and America Online (AOL). All of the key players tend to define terms and concepts as well as search for solutions to problems from within their own areas of strategic interests. So if you are familiar with TCP/IP from the Microsoft Certified System Engineer (MCSE) program, do not be surprised to see concepts in the Cisco environment redefined somewhat to reflect Cisco's position in the industry. Some of the key players originated as telephone companies, and their terminology and perspective reflects those roots. Others see software solutions to every problem, because they are in the software business, while others push hardware solutions. This is neither good nor bad; just be aware that when the terminology is at all ambiguous, it is natural to frame it to fit your own perspective.

In this section, we will attempt to establish a common set of terms to use as we start our journey.

Workstations

Workstation is a catchall phrase that includes any computer being used by individuals to do work-related tasks, play games, view entertainment, and so forth. From doing homework to monitoring stock portfolios over the Internet to listening to music, all of these activities are common uses for computers. Whether operating by itself in a den or dorm room or as part of a large corporate network, we refer to an individual's computer as a "workstation"—rather than as a "server," the meaning of which is discussed a bit later. If someone is sitting at a computer doing just about anything at all, it is a workstation.

Every computer small or large has an OS that provides the base-level functions and "intelligence" so that we can add programs (software) to help us perform our work or to provide entertainment. From the proprietary mainframe OSs to products like

Windows, Mac-OS, UNIX, and Linux, these products provide the basic functions of file access and storage, print management, security, and memory "workspace" so that your word processing software or Web browser doesn't need to deal with these tasks.

Sooner or later, you will discover that there are pools of users who are very passionate about their operating systems. The possible reasons and justifications are beyond the scope of this book. In most of our discussions, the particular OS of a computer is irrelevant. It does become an issue if you are building a network, small or large, based on, say, Windows or UNIX/Linux, and a group wants to use their iMac laptops. This will become a connectivity issue that you will need to deal with, and it will require some research on your part.

In today's world, workstations include any of the Intel Pentium-type computers running some version of a Windows OS. Workstations also include the Apple Macintosh and iMac lines of computers, as well as units running UNIX and Linux workstation software.

Workstations typically take the form of desktop machines, towers, and laptops. More and more, though, we are seeing new shapes, such as palm-sized computers and devices with integrated tools like barcode readers and cameras. Some of these devices have their own proprietary OS, such as the Palm units, while others use a variation of a larger operating system, such as Windows CE, which is used in many new devices. The one thing all workstations tend to have in common is the need to be integrated into computer networks so that they can share information and services, such as e-mail.

Servers

Once we start to connect computers together into networks, some computers are given the responsibility for sharing resources like printing or file storage to workstations. These machines are performing the functions of servers. The simplest definition of a *server* is any machine that is set up to share resources with other computers. In most environments, a server will be configured to share resources as its primary function and will even run a special OS, but a Windows 95 machine sharing files and/or a printer is still performing the functions of a server.

A concept we need to define is *sharing*. Consider the situation in which you bring a plate of cookies to work and your coworkers joyously indulge in "sharing" your cookies. From a computer perspective, the only one "sharing" in this situation is you. Everyone else eats your cookies, but they are not "sharing" anything. In computer terminology, they in fact are your clients. The term *client* traces back to the Roman concept wherein if you perform a service or favor for another person, that person is in your debt and becomes your client. So, "sharing a printer" means to make it available to others to use.

It becomes a network resource to the other computers, and they become clients if they use the printer.

Servers often run special versions of OSs that have been optimized to share resources. Common *network operating systems* (NOSs) are Windows 2000 Server, Windows NT Server, Novell NetWare, UNIX, and Linux. In addition to the ability to efficiently share resources, server OSs often offer other features, such as centralized security, dial-in capabilities, resource monitoring, management, and so on.

At one time, a very clear division existed between servers and workstations. A computer was either a workstation or a server, but not both. To a great extent, that is still true in the UNIX and NetWare worlds. A server shares resources and cannot really be used as a workstation. By the same token, the workstations use server resources but cannot share any resources they might have. The computers are said to have a client/server relationship. Workstations are often referred to as clients, client stations, or network clients.

The Microsoft Windows family has blurred this distinction somewhat. Windows for Workgroups (Win 3.11), Windows 95/98, Windows NT Workstation, and Windows 2000 Professional are all basically workstation OSs, but each has the ability to share disk space and printers with other computers. Using our simple definition of a "server" as any computer set up to share resources, these OSs can therefore be regarded as servers. They can be both client and server at the same time. A computer can be a client of one computer as it uses shared file storage, and can also be performing the functions of a server by sharing its printer to others.

Furthermore, nothing prevents a computer running any version of Windows Server software from being used as a workstation. While Windows NT Server and 2000 Server are optimized to be servers, they can still run user applications, browsers, and so forth. There are many good reasons, such as security concerns, not to do this in most cases, but in some small networks, the cost of having a separate dedicated server is just unacceptable. This probably will never be a concern of Fortune 500 businesses, but many small business servers work double-duty as the boss's or office manager's workstation.

Hosts and Nodes

Collectively, servers and workstations are often referred to as *hosts* on a network. Quite often, we are not as concerned about the function of the computer as we are about identifying them collectively. We will use the term *hosts* to refer to servers and workstations collectively. Occasionally, you will see the term *nodes* used to refer to computers on a network, and you might assume that it is interchangeable with hosts. This is not quite true in general usage. A *node* is any device that connects to the network, and may include computers as well other devices such as printers. So, while all hosts are nodes on a network, all nodes may not be hosts.

Peer-to-Peer vs. Server-Based Networks

The simplest definition of a *computer network* is two or more computers connected together to share a resource. This means connecting two computers in your home to share a single Internet connection or printer in fact creates a network. This type of network is typically referred to as a *peer-to-peer* network-a group of workstations connected together using an operating system like Windows to provide the ability to share resources. Figure 1-5 is a simple diagram of a peer-to-peer network using coaxial cable.

While Windows for Workgroups or programs like LANtastic introduced many people to peer-to-peer networking in the early '90s, the original Apple Macintosh had this capability back in 1985. A simple cable and a few setting changes, and two or more Macs could share files and printers. It was not fast but it was very easy, very reliable, and somewhat elegant even by today's standards. Today, all Windows versions support this feature but generally require a network card for implementation.

Once you add a computer to your network with a server OS such as Windows 2000 (or NT) Server or NetWare Server, you have a *server-based network*. While the server OS

Figure 1-5 Peer-to-peer network

will more efficiently share disk space and/or printers, particularly to a larger pool of users, there is usually some other feature of the server software that causes the organization to choose a server-based network.

Peer-to-peer networks tend to be less expensive and sometimes are easier to set up, but generally they're limited to small installations. You often hear that ten computers is the point at which an organization should move from a peer-to-peer network to a server-based network. The magic number ten probably comes from the fact that Windows NT Workstation was modified by Microsoft to allow sharing of a resource only to ten users. Windows 95/98 does not have that limitation. The decision of when to move to a server-based network should actually be driven by customer needs for network security, centralized administration, dial-in capabilities, and so forth. A very small organization with high security requirements may consider a server-based network, whereas an organization with a few dozen Windows 98 users but lower security requirements might stay with a peer-to-peer network. At one time, my training company ran multiple classrooms with 52 computers on a peer-to-peer network. We had no security concerns and used instructor workstations to download sample files and handle printing. While it was not elegant, it was thrifty, and we never lost a class to network failures. Figure 1-6 shows a simple server-based network.

The reality is that an organization needing a network administrator with the skills that you are developing is going to be using a server-based network.

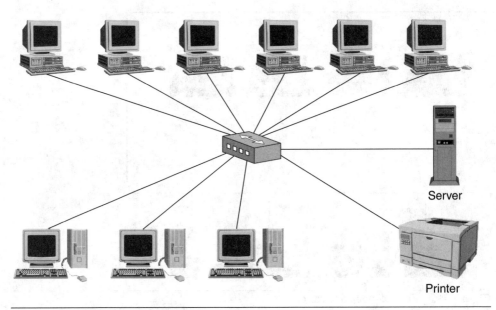

Server

Printer

Figure 1-6   Server-based network

NOTE: As you develop your skills and consider experimenting with some of the devices and concepts being discussed, you can implement them very easily with as few as one or two computers. You can configure one or more routers with a single computer. You can do the connectivity labs with a single computer connected to the Internet. You can access some pretty elaborate virtual router/switch labs over the Internet. Most of the technologies we will be covering do not require a particular NOS or type of host. If you decide to build a home test-bed network, it can grow incrementally with your experience, funds, and level of interest.

Servers

When an organization is small or just getting started with networking its computers, it may use a single server to provide the many services that it wants. That single server would provide network-wide security as well as e-mail, printing, and file storage services. It may also allow users to dial in from home or the road, and may host a small Web-based employee benefits information site.

As the organization grows, additional servers are added to split the workload and provide some level of redundancy if one of the servers fails. These new servers often become specialists, such as *file servers* to store employee and company data, *print servers* to manage the printers, *Web servers* for the Web-based activities, *access servers* to manage increasing volume of dial-in activity, *proxy servers* to secure the company from the Internet, and *domain controllers* to manage security. The larger the organization, the more likely it is to have multiple servers working on specific services to help meet the growing demands of employees, customers, the public, and perhaps even other servers.

I recently toured a facility with over 3,000 servers providing services to a worldwide company and its many constituencies. The control center looked very much like what you would expect at a nuclear facility or large utility. The building is a nondescript modern structure without signage sitting in a very large general-purpose office/industrial complex. Since there are few employees relative to the floor space, the parking lot appears empty. I suspect most of the neighbors think the business has fallen on hard times and would never guess that the world "visits" there hundreds of thousands of times per hour.

LANs, WANs, MANs, Networks, and Internetworks

Earlier we defined a network as two or more computers connected together to share resources. Technically, that is a *local area network* (LAN). A LAN is typically a single geographic location, but could include many users from various floors and/or departments within an organization. Since the organization owns the equipment and the connections, the network administrators are free to make the decisions about network speed, performance, technology, and design.

If we want to connect two or more geographically separated LANs, we create what is called a *wide area network* (WAN). A WAN typically involves one or more long-distance providers, such as a telephone company to provide the connections. While high-speed WAN services are becoming more common, the WAN connections tend to be slower than our LAN and usually more expensive. Since we are riding on someone else's network, we often may have to make compromises on our technology and design.

There are two networks types becoming common that are neither LANs nor WANs. When a company has multiple buildings on a single site that can be interconnected without an outside service provider, it is a *campus* network. Colleges are a common example, but more and more companies are building campuses, particularly in the suburbs. The other type of network is a *metropolitan area network* (MAN), where the buildings can be close enough geographically to create a campus network, but the space between the buildings is not under the control of the company, so a service provider must be used. Typically, relatively high-speed connections can be maintained on a MAN at a lower cost than on a WAN.

Working on a network is referred to as *networking*. Multiple networks connected together are referred to as *internetworks*. The largest and most famous internetwork is, of course, the Internet. The processes of getting multiple networks to work together is called *internetworking*.

Communications Media

Any network larger than the smallest LAN is a collection of servers, workstations, printers, and various networking devices such as hubs, LAN switches, routers, and ATM switches. To connect all of these devices, we use communications media that may consist of various types of copper wire, fiber-optic cables, radio waves, infrared light, microwave, and cellular signals. The communications media provides the vehicle to physically transmit the data signal from device to device. In your home, you might use a single media, such as twisted-pair copper wire or one of the new wireless technologies. But, the larger an organization grows, the more likely it is to need or want to use different media for different circumstances.

As a networker, you will want to be aware of as many of these technologies as possible, and may want to get some training in the more common ones. In both our MCSE and Cisco classes, we generally recommend that students consider getting certified in copper and maybe fiber-optic installation techniques. The manufacturers periodically put on classes locally in hotels, and some colleges are now offering these certification courses. There are many careers in this industry, and some students discover that their future is in cabling or fiber optics. Others find a way to pay their bills as they continue their network training.

Even if a person does not plan to do the actual cabling on the job, as a network administrator, they are usually responsible to specify and then verify that materials and installers have met the necessary installation standards to ensure that your network requirements can be met. In smaller organizations or startups, this is one area where we see network administrators stumble quite badly. As much as in any area of this business, the communications media and its connectors are critical to meeting the needs of our networks.

Recently, I had to break the news to a hospital network administrator that some of the shortcuts his staff made in a major rewiring project doomed the network to 10 Mbps throughput even though all of his new devices will support 100 Mbps. The next day, one of my students who works for Lucent Technologies took me on a tour of a new AT&T facility they were just finishing. The difference was like night and day. Everything was exactly to standard, but more importantly, someone who knew how things should be done and took considerable pride in attention to details did the installation. I have no trouble guessing which network will have the fewest problems from the start and be easiest to maintain, troubleshoot, and expand down the road.

Industry Standards

According to the International Organization for Standardization (ISO), "Standards are documented agreements containing technical specifications or other precise criteria to be used consistently as rules, guidelines, or definitions of characteristics, to ensure that materials, products, processes and services are fit for their purpose." In the computer and networking industry, these standards ensure interoperability of products from a variety of manufacturers, but it wasn't always this way.

With the development of the first computers in the late '40s and early '50s, manufactures developed systems based on proprietary standards that were protected by patent and copyright laws. This prevented competitors from being able to sell even accessories on that product. If an organization bought an IBM mainframe, for example, it would need IBM monitors, storage units, and printers, clear down to the cables and connectors. IBM was not alone in this approach, but it was the biggest player in the market.

While this type of single-source vendor may have had benefits, there were a few downsides. First, once the organization committed to a system and invested millions of dollars, it was very difficult to change vendors later. Doing so would involve either abandoning the current investment or maintaining two noncompatible systems, often requiring separately trained support staffs. Second, new technologies developed by the vendor's competitors were unavailable until the vendor developed a similar technology, if ever. This meant that a company could lose competitive advantage in its own industry simply because it aligned with a computer vendor that could not meet the changing needs. Third, the cost of support, upgrades, and supplies was very high because of the captive market. The organization could buy these items only from the original vendor, so the vendor had no competition and thus no incentive to contain prices.

In the '70s and '80s, government, military, education, and industry groups organized committees to develop and set standards for various aspects of the computer industry. These groups had counterparts in other fields, such as the telecommunications industry, that had successfully established international standards that allowed for connectivity between countries and encouraged interoperability between competing vendors.

Some of the standards evolving applied to data and protocol technologies such as TCP/IP, which led to computers from different vendors being able to share information and, ultimately, to the Internet, as we know it today. Others dealt with hardware standards, such as modems and NICs. The ultimate result was that the idea of a single vendor controlling all aspects of a network project became a thing of the past. Clearly, we still have some big players, but none can control the entire process in the way that existed in the first 30 years of this industry.

It could be argued that IBM saw the light of open standards when it released the first IBM *personal computer* (PC). A more cynical view is that IBM didn't believe in the PC industry, thought it was going to be a short-lived phenomena like CB radios and then disappear, and wanted to minimize its investment as it hedged its bets. Either way, the open standard led to many existing companies developing components and technologies as new companies sprang up to produce applications. For almost 20 years, we have watched the technology and productivity soar at the same time the purchase prices of PCs continue to drop.

This is an example of a de facto standard where IBM, by the power of its market position, was able to introduce a general standard that was not approved by any organization or governing body and yet was solid enough to encourage others to invest both time and capital. Standards have evolved over various aspects of the PC market, such as modems, connectors, and so forth, to add additional stability to the market.

Microsoft has shown that a company can create a product (Windows in this case) that becomes a de facto standard and provides the stability required for software developers to create and improve applications, while at the same time giving customers, particularly corporate buyers, the confidence to invest heavily in equipment and software.

I can clearly remember taking delivery of 125 DEC Rainbow personal computers the day before Digital Equipment announced that it was bailing out of the line. It wasn't much later that we learned Lotus Development was not going to release the next version of its 1-2-3 program in a DEC version. We weren't alone; they also weren't going to support Texas Instrument's version. This lack of a true standard in operating systems and underlying hardware relegated a lot of new hardware to the trash heap. It also scared many corporate purchasers.

Regardless of whether your feelings toward Microsoft are good, bad, or indifferent, Microsoft Windows, combined with evolving hardware standards, has brought stability and confidence while laying the foundation for ten years of rapid technological advancement at ever-declining prices. It can be argued that standards of any type may somewhat stifle some innovation and creativity, but when it comes to data networks, confidence, reliability, and stability often win out as arguments when looking for investment. Within a standards-based environment, innovation tends to be evolutionary rather than revolutionary.

Ask yourself this: If Cisco did not dominate an integral part of this industry, creating almost a de facto standard and therefore a stable demand for devices and people to support them, would you be studying for the CCNA certification? Would the publisher have invested in producing this book? Would I be spending a sunny Sunday afternoon sitting here writing? How many books do you find about the other players' technologies? With the implementation of standards, however developed, comes confidence and then investment.

Vendor-developed standards come with some risks. When a giant in an industry exercises its monopoly position, technically an oligopoly position, and attempts to change an existing standard or introduce a new standard, it still runs the risk that the world will not follow. IBM's attempts to introduce the microchannel architecture and OS2 in the mid '80s are both good examples. Of course, Microsoft's lawsuit with the U.S. Justice Department is another example of the risks faced by companies developing and implementing standards.

In the next few sections, we will look at some of the standards that have evolved from organizations formed specifically to create standards. These organizations are often international, made up of manufacturers, resellers, governmental representatives, researchers, and customers. Their decisions usually do not carry the weight of law, nor are their standards absolutely followed by all members. Their decisions tend to be derived through consensus-building processes that often take considerable time. They also often follow aggressive marketing campaigns of competing, incompatible technologies by the vendors until a standard evolves. The 56K modem standard is a good example of two technologies competing wildly in the market, each making claims and counterclaims until finally the v90 standard evolved and replaced both.

Many standards exist for computer hardware, for such things as CPU design, bus design, keyboards, printer communications, modem communications, network communications, as well as serial and parallel ports. We will concentrate on networking standards.

802 Standards

In February 1980, the Institute of Electrical and Electronics Engineers (IEEE) established a committee to develop networking standards particularly for cabling and transmission of data. The committee, which became known as the 802 committee (for 1980, second month), created subcommittees and standards that are referred to as the 802 standards, with specific standards having a decimal value, such as 802.3 and 802.5, that indicates the standard.

The following are the 802 committee's standards for LAN and MAN systems:

- **802** Standards for local and metropolitan area networks: Overview and Architecture. Describes the relationship of the 802 standards to the *Open Systems Interconnection* (OSI) basic reference model.

- **802.1** Standards for LAN/MAN bridging and management. Remote *media access control* (MAC) bridging.

- **802.2** Standards for *logical link control* (LLC) standards for connectivity.

- **802.3** Standards for *Carrier Sense Multiple Access with Collision Detection* (CSMA/CD) access method. This is basically the Ethernet standard.

- **802.4** Standards for token-passing bus access method.

- **802.5** Standards for Token Ring access method LAN/MAN.

- **802.6** Standards for information exchange between systems.

- **802.7** Standards for broadband LAN cabling.

- **802.8** Standards for fiber optics technologies.

- **802.9** Standards for integrated services like voice and data.

- **802.10** Standards for LAN/MAN security implementations.

- **802.11** Standards for wireless LAN connectivity. This is the technology behind Cisco and many other vendors' wireless network initiatives.

- **802.12** Standards for demand priority access method. Demand priority was an early 100 Mbps connectivity method that was neither Ethernet nor token-passing technology.

- **802.14** Standard for local and metropolitan networks: broadband cable access method.

- **802.15** *Wireless personal area network* (WPAN).

- **802.16** Fixed broadband wireless access.

Currently, the two standards we are most concerned about are the 802.3 (Ethernet) and, to a somewhat declining extent, 802.5 (Token Ring). These are the two most likely access methods we will use in our local area networks. As time goes on, and to meet particular requirements, others such as the broadband and wireless standards could become important to us.

Adding one or more letters after the decimal value further refines the preceding standards. For instance, the 802.3ab standard defines 1000Base-T gigabit Ethernet operation over category 5 twisted-pair wiring.

Recognizing at least the 802.3 and 802.5 standards will be important as you work in the industry, because those numbers are used on product descriptions and markings. It is not uncommon to find copper twisted-pair cable with 802.3 printed on the jacket, indicating it is suitable for Ethernet wiring. Many network devices will include these notations in the detailed product descriptions.

International Telecommunications Union (ITU)

Formerly the CCITT, this organization headquartered in Geneva, Switzerland, is an international organization comprised of governments and the private organizations developing standards for global telecom networks and services. CCITT sets standards for radio communications, modems, telephone systems, and international e-mail. For more information on the organization, you can check its Web site: www.itu.int/.

Internet Engineering Task Force (IETF)

The IETF is an organization operated under the auspices of the *Internet Society* (ISOC) that is responsible for developing Internet standards. The Internet standards are *Requests For Comments* (RFCs), a series of document used as the primary means for communicating information about the Internet. Some RFCs are designated by the Internet Architecture Board (IAB) as Internet standards, like protocol specifications such as Telnet and FTP. RFCs are available online from numerous sources including on the www.cisco.com site.

Internet Assigned Numbers Authority (IANA)

As a part of the Internet Architecture Board (IAB), IANA delegates authority for IP address-space allocation and domain-name assignment to Network Solutions (formerly InterNIC) and other organizations. IANA also maintains a database of assigned protocol identifiers used in the TCP/IP stack, including autonomous system numbers.

Telecommunications Industry Association (TIA) and Electronic Industries Association (EIA)

TIA/EIA are both located in Arlington, VA, and jointly develop and publish a series of standards covering structured voice and data wiring for LANs. The standards evolved after the U.S. telephone industry deregulation in 1984, which transferred responsibility for on-premises cabling to the building owner. Prior to that, AT&T used proprietary cables and systems in the U.S. TIA/EIA standards define uniform specifications for cabling commercial buildings and campuses.

While there are many standards and supplements to standards covering many types of communications media, grounding, data closet facilities, and so forth, the two we will be impacted the most by are probably the following:

- **TIA/EIA-568** Commercial Building Standard for Telecommunications Wiring. The standard specifies minimum requirements for telecommunications cabling, recommended topology and distance limits, media and connecting hardware performance specifications, and connector and pin assignments. There are several supplements covering some of the newer, faster copper media.

- **TIA/EIA-569** Commercial Building Standard for Telecommunications Pathways and Spaces. The standard specifies design and construction practices within and between buildings that are in support of telecommunications media and equipment. Specific standards are given for rooms or areas and pathways into and through which telecommunications equipment and media are installed.

We will look at these standards in more detail in Chapter 10 when we discuss structured cabling. If you are interested in getting more information, do a search on **TIA** on the Internet. Many cable manufacturers and resellers have sites summarizing and explaining the standards. Many also have structured cabling guides that they will mail to you if you fill out their questionnaire.

American National Standards Institute (ANSI)

ANSI, headquartered in Washington, D.C., serves as administrator and coordinator of the United States voluntary standardization system. The group is a private, nonprofit membership organization supported by almost 1,000 private, international, and government organizations. ANSI does not develop standards itself; rather, it facilitates development by establishing consensus processes among qualified groups. This is why you will see its acronym on many standards.

For more information, ANSI can be reached at its Web site: http://web.ansi.org/.

OSI Reference Model

The International Organization for Standardization (ISO), headquartered in Geneva, Switzerland, is a nongovernmental organization responsible for a wide range of standards, including those relevant to networking. ISO's work results in international agreements, which are published as International Standards.

In 1974, ISO developed the *Open Systems Interconnect* (OSI) reference model to establish networking standards that would allow different vendors to produce components and/or host systems and yet still be able to communicate. It is important to remember that the OSI model is a theoretical model and not a single component or software program.

The OSI model is a seven-layer model that breaks the networking process into functional layers. The layers are viewed as a stack. Starting from bottom, they are named as follows: physical, data link, network, transport, session, presentation, and application. Each layer has its own protocol or protocols that determine the layer's functions. Figure 1-7 depicts the layers in order from bottom to top.

Knowing the names and numbers of the layers as well as the devices, protocols, and functions of each layer will be a requirement of the CCNA certification exam and is important to understanding and troubleshooting networks. By midway through the book, you will be exposed to all of that information. For now, memorize both the name and the layer numbers. Make sure that you understand the order, because while the words "data link" may have a different meaning in other parts of the world, the concept of second layer (or Layer 2) will translate anywhere.

Figure 1-7
Seven OSI
model layers

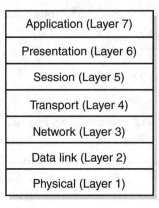

| Application (Layer 7) |
| Presentation (Layer 6) |
| Session (Layer 5) |
| Transport (Layer 4) |
| Network (Layer 3) |
| Data link (Layer 2) |
| Physical (Layer 1) |

A couple mnemonics that many people find useful for remembering the layers is "All People Seem To Need Data Processing" or "All People Seem To Need Double Pepperoni." Use either if it helps.

As you work with operating systems and network protocols, you will find that many of the developing organizations produce their own networking model. This model is almost always mapped to the OSI model to show where similar functions occur. We will do the same thing when we discuss TCP/IP and Windows NT/2000. While initially somewhat confusing, the practice of mapping network protocols to the OSI model demonstrates the importance of the OSI model as a point of reference.

Understanding this model is critical when troubleshooting networks. Without this knowledge and a systematic top-down or bottom-up methodology, troubleshooting problems is an aimless trial-and-error process at best.

Reasons to Use a Layered Model

To design and build all components, connectors, software, and accessories of a full computer network would be too complex for any but the largest organizations. The same could be said about building a house, and yet if we break down the tasks of building a house into functions, such as preparing the ground, building the foundation, building the floor and frame, doing the plumbing, doing the electrical, and so forth, the project starts to seem manageable. We might even start considering people who could help with each function, which makes the project seem even more manageable.

The reasons to use a layered model to define networking are as follows:

- It reduces the complexity of one large task into multiple smaller tasks.

- It facilitates modular development and engineering.

- It simplifies learning the functions and concepts.

- It allows for interoperability of vendor technologies. A vendor building a cabling system (Layer 1) component that complies with Layer 1 and any relative Layer 2 standards does not have to be concerned by the other layers.

- It can accelerate the evolution of development, because improvements in one layer may not have to wait for other layers to be implemented.

- It is critical for troubleshooting. When troubleshooting a problem, the engineer can group and identify symptoms as having the characteristics of a certain layer.

- It facilitates network design purposes. When designing a network, a Layer 1 and Layer 2 design is often completed before a Layer 3 design is complete.

We will look at each of the seven layers in detail in Chapters 2 through 7, but for now, a brief summary of each layer's functions is shown in Figure 1-8 and discussed in the next paragraphs.

The Seven-Layer Overview

If a computer sends data to another computer, the data passes down through the OSI layers on the sending computer, across the media, and then up through the OSI layers in reverse order on the receiving computer.

Before we discuss the layers, you need to understand that when two computers in a network are sharing data, the only method they have to communicate is through data

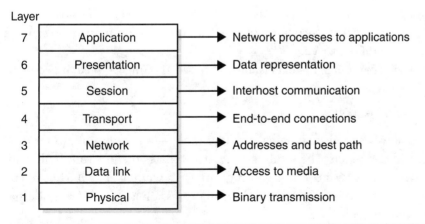

Figure 1-8 The OSI model with basic functions

packets that are sent from one machine to another. These packets go out onto the connection media alone and travel to the destination node.

These packets originate as the data from your network software applications, those programs that can use network services. E-mail is a good example of an application that wouldn't exist if it were not for networking. On the other hand, golf and solitaire games are local to your machine and do not use network resources. Products such as your word processor or spreadsheet might be working locally storing the document on the local hard drive and printing to a local (directly connected) printer. In this case, the OSI model layers are not involved, and the local CPU processes any requests. If the document is going to be stored on a server or printed on a network printer, the OSI model functions come into play.

When you set up your Windows software to be a network client, a feature was added called the *redirector,* which monitors all requests to determine whether they are local or network requests and directs the output accordingly.

Layer 7: Application Layer

The application layer interfaces with your application (software) to provide file and print access services to remote disk drives and printers. It can forward your output to remote servers for processing. E-mail is an example where your output is sent to the recipient's server for storage and notification. It can also perform file transfer and file management services on remote devices. We will see when we get to configure routers and switches that the application layer can also establish terminal sessions with remote devices that support that feature.

Layer 6: Presentation Layer

On the sending computer, this layer translates the data to a format appropriate for the receiving computer, adds any encryption required, and applies compression to squeeze out any extra spaces, if requested.

On the receiving computer, the data is uncompressed and unencrypted, if necessary.

Layer 5: Session Layer

This layer establishes and maintains an application-level communications link between the two computers. The sending computer initiates the link, but both computers maintain it. This layer controls which computer is sending and which is receiving at any given time. It disconnects the link when the session is over and reestablishes the link if it is accidentally broken.

Layer 4: Transport Layer

This layer on both machines ensures reliability of packet transmission between the computers. The sending computer sequences the packets (think of marking them 1 of 99, 2 of 99, and so on) and resends any packets not received by the receiving computer.

The receiving computer makes sure that the packets are resequenced and acknowledged by a special return packet if all are received. If any are missing, it requests a retransmission of those packets.

Layer 3: Network Layer

If the two computers are in different networks, then the sending computer determines the best route to that network and directs the packet to be delivered to the default gateway (a router), which can then forward the packets toward their destination. If the computers are on the same network, this layer supplies the local address to the data link layer.

On the receiving computer, this layer verifies the network addressing and forwards the packet on to the transport layer.

Layer 2: Data Link Layer

On the sending computer, this layer defines a data frame for the packet (think of it as a shipping envelope) that is in the appropriate format for the network. There are different formats for Ethernet and Token Ring. Think of it as using a FedEx envelope for FedEx deliveries and a UPS envelope for UPS deliveries.

The data link layer applies the appropriate local address to the frame to ensure proper delivery. Figure 1-9 is a generic view of a data frame. The destination address is the receiving machine's address, while the source address is the sending machine's address.

Layer 2 protocols create a quality-control check called a *Frame Check Sequence* (FCS), which is a calculation based on the entire packet, and stores the value at the end of the packet. This FCS allows recipient devices to quickly confirm that the packet received is the same as that shipped without having to analyze or even understand the contents of the packet. I have a client that sells meat to stores in bulk containers of varying weights.

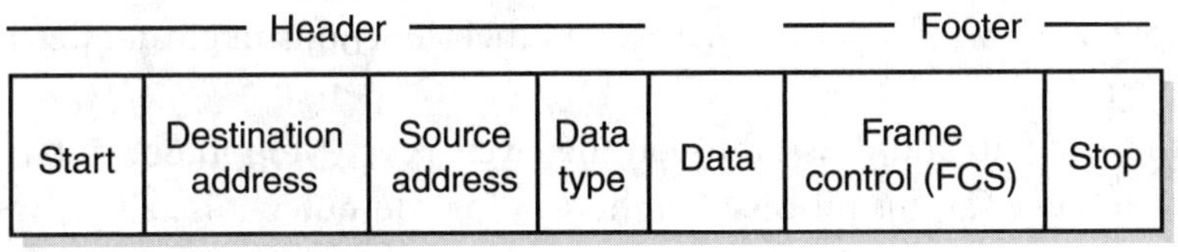

Figure 1-9 Generic data frame

Rather than invoice each box separately, he puts the number of boxes and total weight on the delivery slip and the customer's name on the boxes. As long as the total weight matches at delivery, the order is assumed to be complete.

Layer 2 protocols establish and maintain physical connectivity between the machines. The higher layers connect at different levels. Using a phone call as an analogy, this layer is like the dial tone, the ringing, and the connection—after which it's up to some higher layer to communicate.

The receiving computer monitors traffic passing by and copies only packets addressed to that computer. Layer 2 then recalculates the FCS entry and discards the packet as damaged if it doesn't match; otherwise, it forwards it up to the network layer. If the packet is discarded, its absence will be detected at the transport layer protocols and a retransmission will be requested.

When the transport layer sends an acknowledgment or retransmission packet to the sending computer, this layer builds the data frame and applies the local address, because it is now the sending computer.

Layer 1: Physical Layer

This layer defines the transfer medium, such as cable, fiber optic, or radio wave. It includes the physical shape or design (topology) of the network. It determines the voltage levels, wavelength, and so forth for signal transmission and synchronization. It translates the data into a signal appropriate for the transfer medium. At this point, the data is converted to a stream of binary ones and zeros on the sending computer and is converted back to data frames on the receiving computer.

Figure 1-10 shows the OSI process from top to bottom for the sending computer. Remember that the receiving computer will reverse the process to restore the text to its original form.

Data Encapsulation

We just looked at each layer of the OSI model and introduced the process of moving down through the OSI functions on the sending computer, moving through the communications medium, and then traveling up in reverse order through the OSI layers on the receiving computer. We will look at the layers and their functions in greater detail in Chapters 2 through 7.

This process of moving up and down through the layers is very important. In fact, each side has its own name for this process. On the sending computer, it is called *data encapsulation*, whereas on the receiving end, it is called *de-encapsulation*. Because the

Figure 1-10
Processing text
to binary

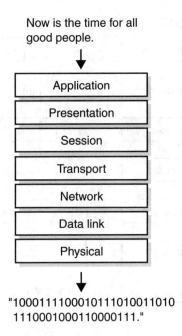

Now is the time for all
good people.

↓

| Application |
| Presentation |
| Session |
| Transport |
| Network |
| Data link |
| Physical |

↓

"100011110001011101001101010
1110001000110000111."

layers on each computer must communicate with their counterparts on the other
machine, and because they cannot just pick up the phone and dial, they communicate
by adding messages to the beginning (header) of the data. In essence, the application
layer's data becomes the data for the presentation layer. The presentation layer adds its
own message, and that becomes the data for the session layer. Each layer encapsulates
the previous layer. This continues until the data link layer, where the destination and
source addresses are added to the header, and the FCS is added to the footer for the
final encapsulation to create the data frame.

   The receiving device now strips off the encapsulation and appropriate messages at
each layer, using the messages to process or interpret the data. At the data link layer, the
destination address is confirmed to determine whether to accept or discard the data
frame. The FCS is confirmed and the Layer 2 data frame is stripped off, passing on to
the network layer exactly the packet that was passed out of the network layer on the
sending machine. This method of adding messages at each layer of encapsulation to be
used by the same layer on the receiving device allows layers to communicate without
generating additional traffic. It also makes it possible for the presentation layer to
encrypt on the sending side and make sure that the presentation layer on the receiving
side will know how to de-encrypt it. Figure 1-11 shows this encapsulation for the sending computer. The receiving computer would look the same, except the arrows would
be reversed.

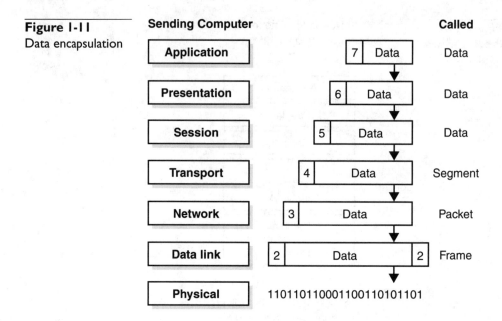

Figure 1-11
Data encapsulation

Note that the encapsulation changes names as it moves through some of the layers. You will need to know those four names and at which layer they apply.

The messages between the same layers on the sending and receiving computers are called *peer-level communications*. It is important to understand that a layer on the sending host can only communicate with the same layer on the receiving host.

Each layer can only talk to the layer immediately above and below it on its own OSI stack. The information passed between the adjacent layers are called *service data units* and are used to assist the next layer in doing its job. For example, the network layer will pass to the data link layer the appropriate MAC address of the destination host or next router so that it can be put on the frame. This is done at the same time the packet is sent.

Something else to understand is that each layer must accept without challenge or inspection the encapsulation from the layer above or below it. The assumption is that each layer performed up to the standard and therefore any delay would be pointless. For this reason, companies tend to not tolerate devices or software that do not follow the standards exactly.

Summary

In this chapter, we introduced many of the topics that we will look at in more detail in the rest of the book. We defined terms like workstations, servers, hosts, and nodes. We compared peer-to-peer to server-based networks in general terms and looked at why all but the smallest organizations use server-based networks.

We compared LANs, WANs, MANs, and Campus Networks. We created a simple definition for a network and discussed that combining networks creates internetworks.

We introduced the concept and importance of industry standards like those for various aspects of the networking industry We focused on the IEEE's 802 standards and the ISO's OSI reference model, which is generally accepted as the standard foe exchanging data within a computer network.

We introduced data encapsulation and de-encapsulation as a method of segmenting and packaging data for transmission and reassembly so that control can be transmitted within the data stream.

Practice Questions

Take a few moments and check your grasp of the concepts covered in this chapter. The answers are immediately following the questions.

Questions

1. How many bits make a byte?
   a. 7
   b. 8
   c. 10
   d. It depends

2. How many bytes make a kilobyte (KB)?
   a. 1,000
   b. 1,000,000
   c. 1,024
   d. 1,000,024

3. Which of the following are *not* correct? (Choose two)
   a. 1KB equals 1,024 bits
   b. 1,024MB equals 1GB
   c. 1TB equals 1,024GB
   d. 1,024K equals 1Mb

4. What is the unit of measure used to rate the speed of CPUs.
   a. Kbps
   b. Mbps
   c. MHz
   d. MB

5. If you have 100 workstations, 6 servers, and 4 printers on your network, how many hosts do you have?
   a. 100
   b. 110
   c. 106
   d. Not enough information given

6. Which of the following is not generally considered to be a benefit of a peer-to-peer network?
   a. Relatively easy to setup
   b. Requires less technical expertise to support
   c. Provides good network security
   d. Less expensive to setup

7. What do each of the following acronyms stand for?
   a. LAN
   b. WAN
   c. MAN
   d. OSI

8. Which of the following 802 standards defines the Ethernet transport method?
   a. 802.1
   b. 802.3
   c. 802.5
   d. 802.12

9. Which of the following 802 standards defines the Token Ring transport method?
   a. 802.1
   b. 802.3
   c. 802.5
   d. 802.8

10. What do the following acronyms stand for?
    a. IEEE
    b. ITU

   c. IANA

   d. IETF

11. List either of the mnemonics used to remember the layers of the OSI reference model.

12. What are the corresponding names of the following layers of the OSI model?
   a. Layer 7
   b. Layer 6
   c. Layer 5
   d. Layer 4
   e. Layer 3
   f. Layer 2
   g. Layer 1

13. In the encapsulation process, at which layer of the OSI reference model is data referred to as a segment?
   a. Layer 7
   b. Layer 6
   c. Layer 5
   d. Layer 4
   e. Layer 3
   f. Layer 2
   g. Layer 1

14. At which layer of the OSI reference model is the data referred to as a packet?
   a. Layer 7
   b. Layer 6
   c. Layer 5
   d. Layer 4
   e. Layer 3
   f. Layer 2
   g. Layer 1

15. At which layer of the OSI reference model is it decided that a data frame on the network is intended for this computer?
   a. Layer 7
   b. Layer 6
   c. Layer 5
   d. Layer 4
   e. Layer 3

f. Layer 2

g. Layer 1

Answers

1. **b.** 8 bits create a byte.

2. **c.** 1,024 bytes make up a kilobyte.

3. **a.** and **d.** 1KB equals 1,024 bytes (not 1,024 bits), and 1,024KB equals 1megabytes (not megabits). Humor me on this one, the point is to make sure they know the difference between bits and bytes

4. **c.** MHz **a.** Kbps and **b.** Mbps are data transfer rates, **d.** MB a unit of storage

5. **c.** There are 106 computers. While printers can be nodes, they cannot be hosts.

6. **c.** Provides good network security. Peer to peer networks lack centralized security. It is the security concerns that most often moves an organization to a server based network.

7. **a.** Local Area Network
   b. Wide Area Network
   c. Metropolitan Area Network
   d. Open Systems Interconnect

8. **b.** 802.3 *Carrier Sense Multiple Access / Collision Detection* (CSMA/CD) defines Ethernet.

9. **c.** 802.5 defines Token Ring

10. **a.** IEEE: Institute of Electrical and Electronics Engineers
    b. ITU: International Telecommunication Union
    c. IANA: Internet Assigned Numbers Authority
    d. IETF: Internet Engineering Task Force

11. All People Seem To Need Data Processing or All People Seem To Need Double Pepperoni

12. **a.** Layer 7: Application
    b. Layer 6: Presentation
    c. Layer 5: Session
    d. Layer 4: Transport

    e. Layer 3: Network

    f. Layer 2: Data link

    g. Layer 1: Physical

13. **d.** Layer 4: Transport

14. **e.** Layer 3: Network

15. **f.** Layer 2: The data link layer monitors network traffic for packets.

OSI Model–Layer 1

This chapter will cover:

- **Some basic electricity concepts**

- **Both analog and digital signaling methods**

- **Forces that threaten the data signals**

- **Communications media options**

- **Data collisions and collision domains**

- **Physical layer components and devices**

In this chapter, we will discuss communications media, Layer 1 devices and protocols, and Layer 1's characteristics. For example, we will discuss twisted-pair cable and its transmission capabilities, limitations, relative cost, and so forth. In Chapter 10, we will cover cabling standards and design considerations in more detail. The next eight chapters explain how to select your tools and building materials, which you will then implement in Chapter 10 to complete a LAN design.

Physical Layer: Layer 1

We are going to start our tour of the OSI reference model with a look at the physical layer, Layer 1. As we introduce technologies, protocols, and devices, we will approach them from somewhat of a historical perspective. In this industry, it is very easy to learn about the different devices or technologies from a functional perspective and not realize that they are part of a very rapid evolution. Without a historical perspective one might assume that two devices, or technologies, are just alternative choices to perform a task. The reality is that one device might be the most recent evolution of the other. For example, in Layer 1 a hub is an improved repeater. We will see in Chapter 4 that the Layer 2 switch is an improved hub. From a purely functional perspective, they each connect devices and networks together. The historical perspective tells us that repeaters have basically faded from the market; hubs are mature products and are enjoying their last days, while switches are the current standard and the future.

The historical perspective also explains why the "latest" features are on switches, and to a lesser extent hubs, but not on repeaters. *Research and development* (R&D) funds tend to be invested in new technologies, not fading classics. Just like less time, energy, and money went into developing buggies once automobiles became a reality. Figure 2-1 shows the OSI model with some of the devices and components that are used and defined in the physical layer.

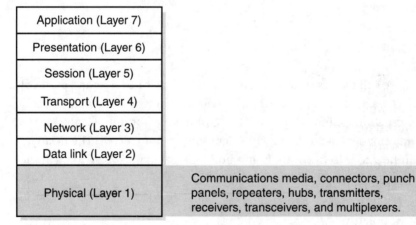

Figure 2-1 OSI Layer 1 devices and components

Electricity and Electronics

The physical layer's job is to transmit data by defining the energy specifications between the source and destination devices. Just as the electrical energy that powers our workstations, servers, and network devices travels within wires concealed in walls, floors, and ceilings, our network data is often either electrical pulses on copper conducting wires or light pulses in optical fibers traveling through the same spaces. Data can be such things as text, pictures, audio, or video.

In this chapter, we will cover enough basic energy theory to provide a foundation for networking at Layer 1, the physical layer, of the OSI reference model. We will look at the different technologies for transmitting data through physical media, such as cables and connectors. We will also look at the natural enemies, such as *electromagnetic interference* (EMI), found in Layer 1.

Terminology

We will start by defining some terms used to describe the physical layer environment and the processes that go on within it. Figure 2-2 is a simple electrical circuit demonstrating the terms to be defined in this section.

The upper example demonstrates an open circuit; the switch is open, and therefore current cannot flow. The lower example shows a closed circuit; current is flowing from the negative terminal toward the positive. The wire is the conductor, the light provides the resistance, and a battery supplies the voltage. A motor, meter, fan, or any other useful device that could be supported by the voltage could replace the light. Likewise, solar cells or a generator could replace the battery.

Electrical Current

Electrical current is the flow of charges created when electrons move through a closed loop, called a *circuit*, made up of conducting materials. Introduction of voltage causes the current to flow, while resistance and impedance oppose it. The electrons move from the negative terminal to the positive terminal.

Alternating current (AC) changes direction going first in one direction, and then reversing direction continuously. With AC voltage, the positive and negative terminals reverse polarity, causing the current to reverse direction.

Direct current (DC) charges always flow in the same direction, and the DC voltages maintain the same polarity. Current always flows from the negative terminal to the positive terminal.

Figure 2-2
Simple electrical
circuit

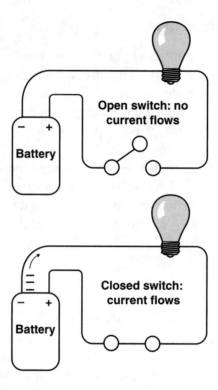

Open switch: no
current flows

Closed switch:
current flows

Voltage

Voltage is an electrical force, or pressure, that occurs when electrons and protons are separated. This separation pushes current toward the opposite charge and away from the like charge. This process can be generated by friction in static electricity, chemically in a battery, by magnetism in an electric generator, or by light in a solar cell.

Resistance

Resistance is a measure of a material's tendency to prevent, or resist, the movement of the electrons or current (DC). Substances with low, or no, resistance are called conductors, while those with high resistance to the current flow are called insulators. Resistance is measured in ohms.

Impedance

Impedance is a measure of a material's tendency to prevent, or resist, the movement of the electrons or current (AC). Like resistance, impedance is measured in ohms.

Ground

The word "ground" has several meanings in the electronics industry. A *ground* may be an electrical connection to the ground (earth) that is intended to carry current safely away from a circuit in the event of a fault, or it may refer to a wire that makes such a connection. The ground in a building can be traced to a cable that will eventually end up embedded in the ground. This ground should be the path of least resistance so that faults can be led safely away.

"Ground" may also be used as a verb, which refers to equipping an electrical circuit or appliance with a connection to the ground so that current is carried away safely in the event of a fault or short. On electric appliances in North America, the third prong is the ground, which provides a path to the building's grounding system and then to the earth. Figure 2-3 shows an example of a three-prong ground circuit common in North American homes and businesses.

Ground, or reference ground, can also mean a reference point—the 0-volts level—when making electrical measurements. A multimeter, a common instrument used to measure voltage, current, and resistance, has two wires, a red one and a black one. The black wire is referred to as the ground, or reference ground. The negative terminal on a battery is also referred to as 0 volts, or the reference ground. On computer circuit boards, this reference ground is built into the circuitry and connects to the device cabinet, and then reaches the ground circuit on the electrical plug-in.

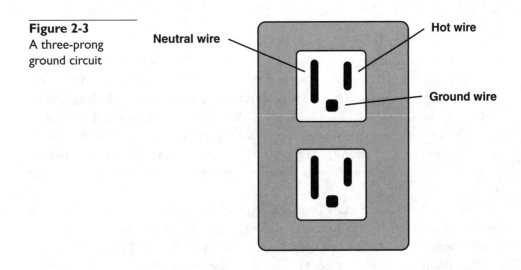

Figure 2-3
A three-prong
ground circuit

Insulators

Electrical insulators are very resistant to electron flows passing through them. The higher the insulator value, the less likely there is to be energy flow. Insulators include plastic, glass, rubber, paper, and dry wood. The chemical makeup of these materials makes them very stable and therefore resistant to electron flows.

Conductors

Electrical conductors are substances that allow electrons to flow easily through them. The better they flow, the better the conductor. Adding voltage to a conductor causes electrons to move, creating a current flow. Many substances are good conductors, including most metals and liquids. Unexpectedly, some of the best conductors are the higher-priced metals, such as gold, and are used internally in our electronic devices.

From a safety standpoint, you must recognize that the addition of a liquid can create a conductor where one did not exist before. For example, a rug or piece of clothing might be a good insulator, but get it wet and it becomes a good conductor. Be very careful with fluids anywhere around your networks.

Semiconductors

Semiconductors are substances that can be manipulated to precisely control electricity they conduct. Carbon and silicon are two examples of naturally occurring semiconductors that are used heavily in electricity and electronics technologies. Silicon is used to create computer main circuit boards (motherboards), CPUs, and microscopic-sized electronic circuits.

Electrostatic Discharge

Static electricity is unstable, negatively charged electrons that stay in one place, possibly building in volume. If a conductor moves close enough to this static charge, these electrons will jump to it, often causing a spark. This is called an *electrostatic discharge* (ESD). Most people have observed this situation by walking across a carpet and touching a doorknob or another person. While ESD is generally an irritant at most for humans, it can be disastrous for electronic equipment. If you can feel the spark, the destructive energy level is already many times that necessary to ruin electronic circuitry and devices.

ESD is a reality that can cause incredibly expensive problems for our networks. For this reason, it is essential to always use a grounding strap, usually worn on the wrist, when working inside our devices. We must also make sure that the building's and network's grounding features have not been compromised in any way.

Signaling

Layer 1 of a network segment uses established standards to generate and detect changes in data signals using electrical voltages, light patterns, or modulated electromagnetic waves. Each signaling method can carry networking data.

While each of these signaling methods can be used in a single network, devices to transfer the data from one communications media to another must convert them. A network device may be connected to a fiber-optic network yet distribute data to hosts on the network using copper wire. Similarly, it can transmit data from the hosts out onto the fiber network. The device is working as a *transceiver*.

Data signals are always binary, zeros, and ones, but there are two signal transmission methods, analog and digital. Like most of electronics, the computer industry is heavily committed to digital technology but still uses some analog devices, such as modems.

Analog

Analog signaling uses a very natural wave pattern that is typical of many found in nature. Light, sound, heat, and even the ripples on a pond caused by a stone are examples of wave patterns. In the case of analog transmissions, the sine wave pattern is generated by a pattern of positive and negative electrical voltages. Just like putting a message in a bottle and letting the waves of the ocean deliver it to a distant shore, we can use analog waves to deliver data between devices. Analog technologies, such as AM radio and most television and telephone communications, have been around for over 100 years. Figure 2-4 is representative of an analog sine wave pattern.

A principal feature of analog waves is that an infinite range of patterns can be created by varying the voltage to modify the *amplitude,* which is the height and depth of a wave,

Figure 2-4
Analog wave

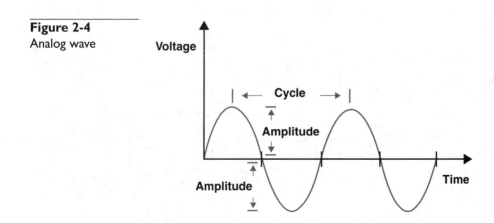

or by varying the *frequency,* which is the number of cycles per second. Binary data is then added to each cycle, creating our data signals.

While the infinite range of analog wave patterns allows for many shades of color or tones of sound, it introduced accuracy and reliability problems in building computer technologies. Virtually all computers are digital.

Digital

A digital signal has only two voltage states, one representing the number 1 and the other representing the number 0. The wave pattern produced is then jumpy, moving almost instantaneously from one state to the other. A good analogy of a digital signal is turning a light switch off and on. There must be a brief in-between time, but for all practical purposes, the light is either off or on. Figure 2-5 is a common representation of a digital signal.

The reality is not quite so pretty and precise. A relatively square digital wave signal is actually a combination of several sine wave signals, but like the light switch example, the in-between period really does not have any impact. It is either on or off, 1 or 0. Figure 2-6 is a truer representation of a digital signal.

Knowing about this truer representation may be useful in a few pages, when we talk about the forces that are at work to destroy our digital data. While the graphic may be a truer representation of a digital networking signal, we will use the traditional square model in future graphics. Notice that digital signals have single amplitude and that the pulse width can be increased to represent multiple 1's or 0's. Voltage sustained on for three time intervals would represent three 1's, whereas three time intervals off would represent three 0's.

Digital is not a typical state in nature. Humans experience sight, sound, warmth, and so forth in analog form with an infinite range of variations. Many of these experiences can be converted to digital for easy storage, rapid searching, and easy manipulation.

Figure 2-5
Simple digital
representation

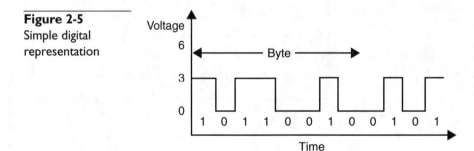

Figure 2-6
A truer digital signal representation

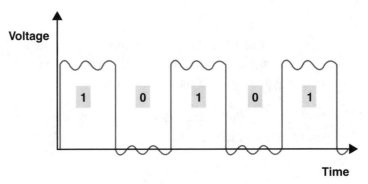

Digital synthesizers allow for easy storage of sounds, by overlaying multiple sound tracks, and yet can convert them to high-quality analog representations when we want to hear them. Photographs, when digitized, are converted to an array of dots. Under normal viewing, we do not see the dots, but upon closer inspection (often with a magnifying device) they become obvious. Digital manipulation techniques allow a photo's image to be changed to the point that people can be removed from group photographs. Recent movies have used similar techniques to insert actors into historical movies and to allow dangerous scenes to be captured (knowing, for example, that safety harnesses can be edited out and more flames can be edited in later).

The hard part is converting from analog to digital and back. But once accomplished, the data can be stored in forms that resist many of the elements and the ravages of time. The data can be transmitted around the world or deep into space for reliable conversion later. The implications for archiving, training, communications, and the free exchange of news and ideas are limited only by our imaginations.

Digital in Nonelectrical Media

The preceding discussion relates to electrical current moving through a copper media. In simplest optical signaling, the binary 0 could be represented as no light, or a low level of light, while binary 1 could be represented as a brighter light. Obviously, more complex patterns and colors could be used.

In wireless signaling, the binary 0 could be a short burst of waves, while binary 1 could be a longer burst.

Although using binary coding may be relatively new, these concepts are not. Samuel Morse created a pattern of electrical codes, Morse Code, that connected the world in the 19th century. Early Native Americans and probably many other primitive peoples used smoke signaling to communicate over great distances. If a media develops, someone will figure out how to use it for signaling.

Threats to Signaling

Even when the circuitry is right and everything seems to be working as designed, there are processes at work that can denigrate or destroy the data. In this section, we will look at the following potential threats to our signals:

- Collisions
- Propagation delay and latency
- Attenuation
- Noise
- Reflection

Collisions

A collision occurs when signals from two hosts are on a shared medium at the same time for whatever reason. The result is that the signal voltages are summed and values that are created cannot be recognized by the binary system, which only knows about two voltage levels. The resulting signals are corrupted and useless.

We will see later that network technologies such as Ethernet, Token Ring, and FDDI all have methods to deal with or prevent these collisions. For our purposes now, we need only recognize that when the data signal is involved in a collision, it must be discarded.

Propagation Delay and Latency

Propagation in this context refers to generating a signal and getting it across the network to its destination. In the case of electricity on a copper wire, we are talking about the time it takes between when current is applied and when it travels the length of the network. In a fiber-optic network, it would be the time it takes the light to travel through glass to the destination.

Visualize this scenario. I give you a piece of copper wire 100 meters long. You hold the bare wires of one end and I apply the other end to a car battery. How long do you have to release the wires before being stung? You cannot react quickly enough. The electricity travels at slightly slower than the speed of light (186,000 miles per second). Given this fact, it should be obvious that a greater distance will not require significantly longer times.

As we will see later in this chapter, in Ethernet networks, hosts "listen" to the wire for signals, or electrical current. If none is detected, the host is free to transmit its own signal. Therefore, if a host's signal is delayed, it is possible that another host will transmit, not knowing of the approaching signal, and a collision will occur. Since we pretty much ruled out the media as the source of delay, it must originate elsewhere. Many network devices actually capture a data frame, rebuild it much like an amplifier with filtering, and then forward it. This delay between the time when a device receives a frame and the time that frame is forwarded out the destination port is called *latency*. To some degree, there is delay for every device, component, and transistor that the signal must pass through. Some devices, such as switches and routers, have buffers to eliminate collision, but do so by increasing the latency.

Propagation delay is the time it takes to propagate a signal throughout the network. The propagation delay is the sum of the latency introduced by all devices. Without latency, the propagation time would be virtually instantaneous. Too much propagation delay can lead to increased data collisions.

Propagation delay and latency can be managed through network design and the choice of the devices and protocols used. This will become even more important as networks move toward gigabit speeds. Just like the freeways, accidents at high speeds tend to be messier and involve more devices.

Attenuation

Attenuation is the reduction of signal strength during transmission through a communications media. Attenuation is basically the opposite of amplification and is a normal and expected condition. If a signal attenuates too much, it becomes unintelligible to the hosts on the network. Attenuation is a fact on all communication media, whether copper, fiber-optic, or wireless.

All communication media have maximum-distance standards, such as 100 meters for copper twisted-pair cable for reliable Ethernet data transmission. This distance is a direct reflection of attenuation. If we stay within the distance limits and the environment is free of unusual amounts of other factors that degrade our signal, the signal should be readable by any host. We will see later in this chapter that networks can use repeaters at regular intervals to rebuild and amplify the signal to extend signaling distance. Attenuation is measured in *decibels*.

Noise

Noise, sometimes called *static*, is unwanted additions to the data signals from any source. This unwanted signal can come from a variety of sources and impact different signaling methods to different degrees. Some types cause serious problems for copper networks but have no impact on fiber-optic networks. The important thing is to keep the *signal-to-noise* (S/N) ratio as high as possible. If the noise level gets too high, the

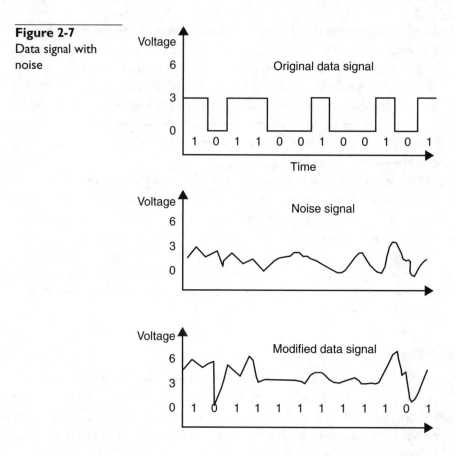

Figure 2-7
Data signal with noise

message signal, or part of it, can be destroyed. Figure 2-7 shows the result of noise on a data signal rendering it unintelligible to the hosts.

The top graphic shows a normal data signal, while the middle one shows a burst of noise across the media. The bottom image shows the result of the two being combined and the resulting loss of signal definition. It is questionable whether the signal could be interpreted at all, but clearly parts of it will not be correct.

To a great extent, our network cable acts like a long antenna that is susceptible to electrical signals from outside sources and even from other wires in the cable. The next sections will discuss common sources of noise.

EMI and RFI

Electromagnetic interference (EMI) and *radio frequency interference* (RFI) are two common sources of electrical impulses that can attack the quality of signals on the copper cable. Since fiber-optic circuits use light instead of electrical current, there is no EMI or RFI effect. Common sources of EMI are lighting fixtures such as fluorescent, mercury vapor, and sodium vapor. Technically, it is the ballasts that energize the gases in the lights that generate the EMI. Other sources are pumps, motors, vacuums, and any source of static electricity.

RFI can be generated by any radio systems, including commercial stations, radio-controlled devices such as cranes, and communications devices. RFI is a problem for data networks because they use frequencies in the 10 to 100 *megahertz* (MHz) range, which is where FM radio signals, TV signals, and many appliances operate.

There are a number of ways to limit EMI and RFI. One way is to increase the size of the conductor wires. Another way is to improve the type of insulating material used. However, such changes increase the size and cost of the cable faster than they improve its quality. Therefore, it is more typical for network designers to specify a cable of good quality, and to provide specifications for the maximum recommended cable length between nodes.

Shielding and *cancellation* are techniques used to reduce the impact of EMI and RFI. Shielded cable has a metal braid or foil around each wire pair to buffer against interfering signals. Figure 2-8 demonstrates a form of shielded cable. Adding shielding to cabling increases the cost substantially and often makes it a little more difficult to work with because it is both stiffer and slightly heavier than unshielded cable.

Cancellation is a technique that uses twisting pairs of wires around each other and that also twists multiple pairs of these twisted wires together to very exacting standards to effectively cancel noise from within and from outside the cable. Figure 2-9 shows an example of multiple twisted pairs.

Figure 2-8
Shielded cables

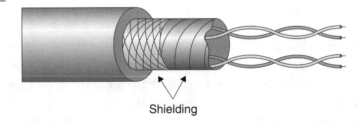

Shielding

Figure 2-9
Twisting pairs to
cancel noise

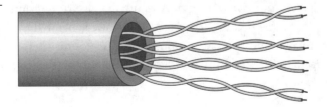

Electrical current passing through any wire generates a magnetic field around that wire that can be regenerated onto a second wire running parallel. This is the basic technology for a coil and transformer. In open areas of the country where very high-voltage lines pass overhead, a similar phenomena could occur if fences were allowed to run parallel to the transmission lines. If the two wires that make up an electrical circuit are placed together, their current flows are in opposite directions, meaning the resulting magnetic fields will also be in opposite directions, thereby canceling each other out.

Twisting the wires enhances this cancellation effect because the wires are no longer parallel but instead cut across each other at varying angles. The combination of twisting and cancellation can be engineered to provide noise-free media at much lower costs than shielding.

Crosstalk

Crosstalk is unwanted electrical noise on a cable originating from signals on other wires in the cable bundle. This is not unique to data networks; it also happens with telephone lines, in which case you can hear another conversation in the background. Crosstalk often occurs near connections where wires have been stripped and untwisted to apply a connector. There are several forms of crosstalk, but *NEXT,* or near-end crosstalk, is one that is often measured when certifying cable installations. Managing crosstalk is often a function of using quality materials, having good termination skills, and following TIA/EIA standards for pulling and terminating cable.

AC Power and Ground Noise

Electricity for our many machines and appliances runs through the walls, floors, and ceilings of our buildings and homes. *AC power line noise* is all around us. If treated with respect, it should not be a problem. The simplest rule is to keep your data cabling away from your electrical circuits, switches, and plug-ins as much as possible. Never bundle power cords and data jumpers together or run them in the same path.

Ground noise is another issue. Many of the other machines used around a business, particularly those businesses with machinery, can cause other problems. First, these devices tend to transfer considerable noise to the grounding circuits. Second, industrial areas may be more prone to faults or shorts and resulting spikes, which hopefully go to the grounding circuits for safe release into the ground.

Unfortunately, our computing devices use the electrical ground circuit as the signal reference ground (zero volts). Therefore, line noise generated by other devices, particularly machinery, can cause the computing devices to misinterpret data signals or miss them altogether. This type of problem can be very difficult to isolate and is often misdiagnosed.

If possible, the office should be on electrical and grounding circuits that are separate from areas with machinery. Furthermore, data networks should have their own additional power and grounding circuits. It could be argued that a *main data facility* (MDF) with servers and network devices should have two separate circuits and grounding paths so that backup power supplies are not plugged into the same circuit. In new structures or major remodels, consider putting in separate power distribution panels, or breaker boxes, for each office area and the MDF.

When working with maintenance personal, do not assume they will understand the significance of running a separate grounding circuit. To them, the purpose of the ground is to keep you safe, and they may not realize that your network can be far more vulnerable than you are. Also, when looking around for machinery, do not overlook items that may be in the office. We have had clients have problems from an in-wall vacuum system and from a popcorn popper added to a sales counter.

Reflection

Reflection is a wave bounce-back that can be caused by damage to the communications media, imperfections in the media itself, poorly terminated connections, and incorrect impedance (resistance) on the network. We have all seen examples of this wave characteristic in a swimming pool where even a gentle wave sent toward a wall "bounces" a smaller wave back. A portion of the wave's energy is being reflected back. Another example is seeing your reflection in a glass that is not a mirror; again, some portion of the light energy is reflecting back instead of moving through the glass.

It's easy to visualize this occurring with fiber optics, but it is also a problem in copper and wireless networks. If this reflection gets too great, reliability may suffer or normal media distance may not be attainable. Remember that our network only distinguishes between two signal strengths, and if the reflected value is added to the existing signal, it could be interpreted as an incorrect value or even a collision. If standards are observed, circuits are tested, and the communications media is protected from abuse, any reflection should be of minimal concern.

Communications Media

The cabling or wiring combined with the connectors and devices is often referred to as the network's *physical plant*. While generally "communications media" refers to some form of copper wire with electrical energy passing through it, it could also be fiber-optic cables with light passing through, or the open air with a variety of radio, light, and microwave energies creating connections between the devices.

In this section, we will look at the following communications media:

- Coaxial cable

- Shielded twisted-pair (STP) cable

- Unshielded twisted-pair (UTP) cable

- Fiber-optic cable

- Wireless technologies

As we look at each media, we will also consider any specifications, common connectors, termination methods, and standards that might apply. Each media will have different technologies and certifications based on its industry and the current products being used. For example, Category 5 standards have been common in copper twisted-pair discussions for the past several years to allow for either 10 or 100 Mbps transmission rates. Today, the emergence of Category 6 and 7, allowing up to gigabit transmission rates, means there is much more to know about copper to be effective in the workplace. It also means that continual training or, at least, awareness is necessary to keep your skills current.

Cable Jacket Material

There are three common jacket materials for copper and fiber cabling. *Polyvinyl chloride* (PVC), a plastic-like material, is the least expensive and is also the most common. The problem is that when PVC is in a fire, it gives off a deadly poisonous gas. In many LAN situations, this is not too serious a situation, the assumption being that you will know about the fire and be able to get away from it. However, in at least two situations, the use of PVC is not acceptable and is even banned under fire codes. These situations require plenum and riser-grade cable jacketing.

Plenum refers to the airspace above the ceiling or below the floor that is a part of the building's air circulation system. Not all such spaces are part of the circulation system, particularly in buildings with a cold-air return duct system, but if cabling must pass through any plenum space, PVC cannot be used. The jacket must be made of Teflon, which will still burn but does not give off poisonous gases. The fear is that a small fire in one part of a building could pull poisonous fumes into the circulation system and expel them in another part of the building where people who may not be aware of the fire or at risk from the flames could be killed.

Plenum cabling can cost more than twice the price of PVC and is designated on the jacket with either the word "plenum" or a coding such as CMP (for copper media plenum). Depending on local fire codes, failing to use plenum cabling where required could result in fines or the building being closed until the cabling is replaced.

Riser refers to another problem with fires. Any time a cable travels from one floor to another floor, the jacket must be riser-grade Teflon. Both PVC and plenum-grade cabling can burn, so the fear is that a flame will follow the cable from one floor into the air space of another floor, thereby spreading the fire. Riser-grade cable will melt but it will not carry a flame. Riser-grade cable costs more than plenum and will be designated on the jacket with a coding such as CMR (for copper media riser). Many organizations use orange-colored riser cable and do not use orange for any other cables, to make the riser cable easy to spot. Note that the standard for cabling between floors also calls for sealing any conduits with inert putty to further reduce the chances of fire moving from floor to floor.

Cable Nickname Conventions

A naming convention for cabling developed that was supposed to convey the general specifications in a compact, reliable form. It started with *10Base5*, the designation for ThickNet coaxial cable.

The *10* refers to the maximum throughput in megabits per second. Thus, 10Base5 supports up to 10 Mbps. *Base* indicates baseband transmission, as compared to broadband. In baseband, the entire media is used for a single transmission, somewhat like a single-lane roadway or trail. Broadband, on the other hand, allows several transmission channels at the same time, like a multilane one-way street. These channels could be different wave frequencies over copper media or different colors of light (different frequencies of light waves) over fiber optics.

The *5* is multiplied by 100 meters to give the maximum transmission distance without use of a repeater. Thus, 10Base5 is 10 Mbps media using a single transmission channel that can transmit data up to 500 meters—simple and compact. Unfortunately, the second effort, 10Base2, or ThinNet—a thinner, more flexible media—could not actually deliver data reliably for 200 meters, and the standard had to be redefined at 185 meters. Probably because both forms of coax were losing ground to twisted-pair and fading from the market, the name discrepancy was never dealt with. Twisted-pair uses a T instead of a number, such as 10BaseT.

The following table summarizes some of the more common designations:

NAME	MAXIMUM DISTANCE	MEDIA TYPE
10Base5	500 meters	Coaxial copper
10Base2	185 meters	Coaxial copper
10BaseT	100 meters	Twisted-pair copper

(continued)

NAME	MAXIMUM DISTANCE	MEDIA TYPE
10BaseFL	2,000 meters	Multimode fiber-optic
100BaseT	100 meters	Twisted-pair copper
100BaseFX	2,000 meters	Multimode fiber-optic
100BaseFX	10,000 meters	Single-mode fiber-optic
1000BaseCX	25 meters	Gigabit copper MDF/IDF
1000BaseT	100 meters	Cat 5 using four pairs

There are new gigabit versions of both copper and fiber being introduced and they will replace the "100" with "1000" in the names. Note the distances may change with the gigabit bandwidth.

Coaxial Cable

Coaxial cable, usually shortened to *coax,* is one of the older LAN cabling technologies, which was used extensively until the early to middle 1990s and can still be found in some installations today. Figure 2-10 shows an example of coaxial cabling.

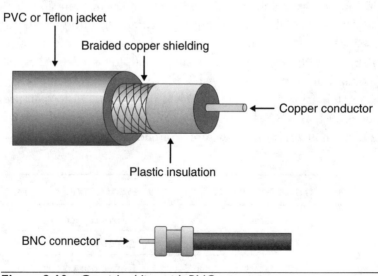

Figure 2-10   Coaxial cabling with BNC connector

Coax cable, the original PC network cable, has a copper conductor, solid or multi-strand, surrounded by a plastic insulator. This is wrapped in a copper mesh and possibly aluminum wrap, both of which provide shielding and grounding. The outer jacket is either PVC or Teflon.

Coax offers relatively easy installation, low cost, and reasonable distances (up to 185 meters). While very reliable, it is prone to corrosion within connectors, and debugging problems sometimes is difficult. There are two sizes of coax: ThickNet and ThinNet. While Coax installations still exist and need to be supported, new installations will generally use another media.

ThickNet, or 10Base5, was used for network backbone implementations to connect departments and floors. It was approximately one-half-inch thick, could carry data up to 500 meters, and supported up to 100 connections. *ThinNet*, or 10Base2, was about the size of TV cable, 0.25 to 0.35 inch, and was used to connect individual computers in a room or on a floor. The ThinNet literally ran from machine to machine like a long tether linking the devices, almost like a daisy chain. The actual connections were made with British Navel Connector (BNC) T-connectors. This connector allowed computers to be removed physically from the network without breaking the chain. The ThinNet became a backbone (bus) with devices attached at various points along the route. Each end had to have a thimble-like terminator to prevent signal reflection, or bounce-back, which would register as a data collision on the network. Figure 2-11 shows a BNC connector, T-connector, and terminator. Figure 2-12 shows a BNC T-connector connected to a network adapter.

Figure 2-11   BNC connector, T-connector, and terminator

Figure 2-12   BNC T-connector with network adapter

Coaxial cable was the original "shared" media in the Ethernet standard. Every device on the network was literally hard-wired together by a single cable, and all communication was carried over that single copper strand.

Coax has just about lost its position in LAN networks, but it is still used in other installations. Be aware that while the materials and components may look alike, other implementations for coax may have different standards. While LAN coax uses 50-ohm resistance connectors, cable TV uses 75-ohm connectors. One of our clients has a UNIX *computer aided design* (CAD) network that uses 90-ohm connectors. Mixing components from other implementations can lead to unreliable data transmission.

The following table summarizes coaxial standards for a single network segment (we will look at repeaters later in this chapter):

NAME	MAXIMUM NODES	MAXIMUM DISTANCE
10Base5	100	500 meters (1,650 feet)
10Base2	30	185 meters (610 feet)

This table shows that while coax has some nice distance capabilities, the number of nodes (computers, printers, and so forth) was going to become a serious problem in larger organizations. Other factors that lead to the demise of coax was the difficulty in troubleshooting line breaks, the 10 Mbps bandwidth limitation, and the fact that the new twisted-pair cable is easier to use, less expensive, and less obtrusive in most office installations. The serpentine nature of coax installations tended to use lots of unsightly wire, particularly in open-desk environments.

Twisted-Pair Cable

The two types of twisted pair cable are *shielded twisted-pair* (STP) and *unshielded twisted-pair* (UTP). As the name implies, STP has added a layer of metal shielding around the pairs, under the jacket, to fight the effects of EMI and RFI. This can almost double the cost and makes the cable a little stiffer and therefore a little more difficult to work with. The important thing to remember is that, in normal situations, STP does not give you any additional benefits such as increased bandwidth or distance. It does give you a better chance of a good signal in high EMI/RFI areas. In many cases, if the EMI/RFI are that high, you should consider using fiber-optic cable, which is immune to these attacks.

Another use for shielding is in high-security areas, because the shielding reduces the chances that a snoop could pull your data from the airways. Technically, devices exist that, if applied to a wall, can copy the signals from UTP running in the wall. Being realistic, however, if you are that concerned, fiber is probably your choice. So, the bottom line is that STP gives you a little more resistance to EMI, RFI, and spying at a lower cost than fiber. Figure 2-13 shows a twisted-pair cable and an RJ-45 connector. Figure 2-14 describes a twisted-pair cable.

Most twisted-pair cable is made up of four color-coded pairs of copper wire. The pairs are usually a solid-color wire matched with white wire that has the same color stripe on it. While the colors can vary, the four most common colors are brown/white with brown; blue/white with blue; orange/white with orange; and green/white with

Figure 2-13 Twisted-pair cable and RJ-45 connector

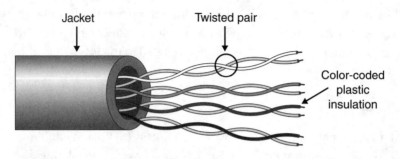

Figure 2-14 Unshielded twisted-pair (UTP) components

green. Depending on the standard used, two of the pairs will be used for data transmission and two will be used to reduce the impacts of EMI, RFI, and crosstalk.

Each pair is twisted around each other to exacting standards, and then the pairs are twisted together under the jacket. Both twist patterns are critical to maintaining bandwidth. Stretching a cable or bending it around a sharp corner could change the twist characteristics so that the Category 5 cable may not certify for 100 Mbps throughput. Consider that in the early to middle 1990s, twisted-pair cable was conducting up to 10 Mbps; by the last half of the 1990s, 100 Mbps was common; and now gigabit over copper, 1000BaseT, is defined in the IEEE 802-3ab standard. The difference is the twist patterns, the jacket design (some are loose, almost bag-like), and the precision of the connectors. In each case, like fine instruments, people that do not know how to handle them can ruin data cables.

The Telecommunications Industry Association and Electronic Industries Association (TIA/EIA) jointly has been the primary developer of standards for cabling. TIA/EIA designates twisted-pair cables using categories beginning with Category 1, which is voice-grade (telephone) wire. The following table summarizes the categories as they are today:

TIA/EIA CATEGORY	MAXIMUM TRANSMISSION
Category 3	16 Mbps
Category 4	20 Mbps
Category 5	100 Mbps
Category 6*	250 Mbps
Category 7*	1 Gbps

* Categories 6 and 7 are still in review and technically could change as this is being written.

Each category has its own standards for connectors, termination techniques, maximum distances, how it must be bundled, and how it is to be supported. Professional installers know this, and you should too. An ill-informed employee or contractor can turn some relatively expensive wire and connectors into junk suitable for performance that is one or more categories lower. I get installers in class who don't know that the maximum pull to be applied to Category 5 is 25 pounds, that it should only be bundled 40 cables to a bundle, or even that the maximum run is 100 meters.

The following table summarizes twisted-pair standards for a single network, assuming a central hub device of some type:

NAME	MBPS	MAXIMUM NODES	MAX. SEGMENT DISTANCE	MAX. DISTANCE ACROSS
10BaseT	10	1,024	100 meters (330 feet)	200 meters (660 feet)
100BaseT	100	1,024	100 meters (330 feet)	200 meters (660 feet)

A cruel irony is that cable is often put in place maybe months or years ahead of the devices that could take advantage of promised bandwidth. This is done in anticipation of future hardware upgrades. Only when the faster devices are added will it become clear that installation shortcuts may make the additional investment a waste. For example, if you are wiring a new building or addition, you might opt for Category 6 cable over Category 5, figuring a small increase in cost is a good investment in the future— good strategy. But if the job is not installed in compliance with standards throughout, tested and certified, it will probably still meet all of your current demands with ease. Only later when you try to add the new high-speed devices will you learn that corners that were cut or product abused during installation will not reliably support the new higher bandwidths promised.

Many companies are learning this lesson today with their investment in Category 5 cable installations over the past few years. When Category 5 was installed, the only devices the company was using were 10 Mbps, and they worked great. But now, as they try to update to 100 Mbps devices, which Category 5 is designed to support, they are discovering that installers used Category 3 connectors because they were cheaper or they stressed the cable beyond standards. Now it won't support 100 Mbps. The new Categories 6 and 7 promise to be even less tolerant of abuse than Category 5. For this reason, it makes good sense that all cabling should be certified at the time of installation, and even more important that network administrators know enough about cabling standards to insist on practices that conform with the desired standard. Figure 2-15 shows the punch tool and crimp tools used with Category 5 wiring.

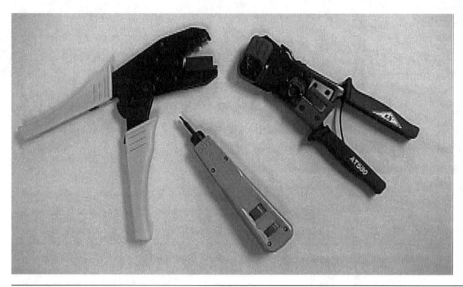

Figure 2-15   Punch tool and RJ crimp tools

While Category 3 is considered phone-grade wire, many companies are running multiple Category 5 or 6 wires to work stations or offices and then designating them for phone or data. If you put four cables into a faceplate, you can use any combination of data or telephone devices up to four. Technically, each Category 5 cable could support two telephone lines, if necessary. While Category 5 will carry data 100 meters and at 100 Mbps, it will carry voice almost 800 meters. Recognize that in the data facility (wiring closet), the voice circuits generally will need to be connected to the phone system, but with the introduction of the new Voice Over IP technology, it may not be long before those voice and data cables will all go to the same device for processing.

Fiber-Optic Cable

Fiber optics is one of the truly wondrous technologies of our age. The thought of moving digital forms of data, images, voice, and music as light through glass strands over very large distances almost seems like science fiction. Whether through deserts or under oceans, fiber technology can be applied where copper would succumb to the environment, and other technologies, such as microwave or satellite, would be too expensive. In this book, we deal with LAN uses of fiber optics, which often are baseband and matched to some existing copper standard, so while offering many advantages in this environment, we do not scratch the surface of the magic.

If you are interested, look into the WAN implementations and high-speed backbones that make up much of the country's data infrastructure, such as the Internet and

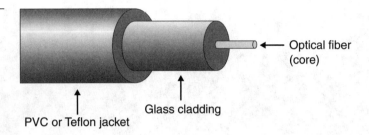

Figure 2-16
Fiber-optic cable

Optical fiber
(core)

Glass cladding

PVC or Teflon jacket

Internet 2. We are approaching technologies with which thousands of data streams can pass simultaneously through a single fiber-optic strand-television, music, heart telemetry, corporate data, thousands of Web surfers, and thousands of long-distance phone calls all moving through the same fiber. We will touch briefly on these capabilities in Chapter 17 when we address the WAN topics for CCNA.

Fiber-optic cable is a very pure glass strand running through a denser glass tube called cladding. That cladding is encased in a PVC or Teflon jacket much like copper. Figure 2-16 shows a diagram of a fiber-optic cable.

Fiber is often depicted as it is in Figure 2-16, but in reality it always requires at least two strands, one for each direction. It is typically bundled into cables that contain 12 to 48 separate fiber strands, meaning that a single cable may actually be carrying 6 to 24 pairs of fiber. These extra strands are often called *dark fibers*, referring to the fact that they are not being used, so no light is passing through them. The companies lay these extra lines in order to curb the costs of having to do it again in the future. In some cases, these dark strands can be leased to individuals or other companies who want to establish optical connections between their own locations. Apparently, some electrical utilities are doing this on their existing pole networks, opening new potential revenue streams using existing right-of-ways. Even very-high voltages do not impact fiber data transmissions. Figure 2-17 shows a photograph of a fiber-optic cable.

The following table summarizes fiber-optic LAN standards for a single network, assuming a central hub device of some type:

NAME	MBPS	MAXIMUM NODES	MAX. SEGMENT DISTANCE	MAX. DISTANCE ACROSS
10BaseFL	10	1,024	2,000 meters (1.2 miles)	4,000 meters (2-4 miles)
100BaseFX[1]	100	1,024	2,000 meters (1.2 miles)	4,000 meters (2-4 miles)
100BaseFX[2]	100	1,024	10,000 meters (6 miles)	20,000 meters (12 miles)

[1] Multimode   [2] Single-mode

Figure 2-17   Photo of a fiber-optic cable

Single-Mode Fiber (SMF) and Multimode Fiber (MMF)

Light travels through fiber in *modes*, or pathways of light. The mode is defined by the angle of the injecting signal. In single-mode cable, a laser injects the signal (light) directly down the center of the cable, thus the name. Multimode allows the signal to be injected at any number of angles, sending the light bouncing through the cable. This allows multimode optical fiber to propagate many signals simultaneously through the cable.

Multimode optical fibers have a much larger core than single-mode fibers, are easier to work with, are less expensive, and are used most often in LAN installations. Furthermore, multimode cable uses an LED instead of a laser to generate the signal, which allows MMF LAN components to be cheaper. It is the laser source that makes SMF perfect for longer-haul applications, because it degrades less due to its mode.

Advantages and Disadvantages

Compared to copper media, fiber is much more stable, immune to EMI and RFI, less susceptible to the elements, can carry data longer distances, extremely difficult to tap undetected, and can typically offer much greater bandwidth. Because fiber-optic cable carries light, not electricity, it can be used in environments where any risk of a spark is unacceptable, such as around fuels, paints, or solvents.

The disadvantages are primarily cost. Fiber can cost many times the price of copper to install, particularly the devices. Many companies can compare and choose copper installations because of price, but fiber's best features, such as distance, safety, and resistance to the environment, may cause price considerations to be secondary. Due to the difficulty and cost of terminating fiber, many people have dark fiber pulled, leaving many extra strands unterminated. They will invest the cost later if the circuits are needed.

Wireless Technologies

Wireless technologies use electromagnetic waves, thereby eliminating the need to cable devices together. There are many reasons this might be attractive to an organization, but mobility of users has to be one of the main forces behind wireless. People on the go, such as traveling to and from meetings, attending training, and so forth, can all remain connected. Even within the building, people moving around in a warehouse or on a sales floor can place orders, check an order's status, confirm inventory, or check e-mail.

Some organizations are located or have connectivity needs where adding physical cabling may be impossible. Many historical sites will not allow placing cables of any kind within the walls. We had one client who had an all-glass conference room looking out over the Puget Sound and the Olympic mountains. While incredibly beautiful, the only nonglass surfaces were the floors. Wireless technology prevented major structural and aesthetic changes to the room.

While undoubtedly some businesses are moving to all-wireless networks, probably a more typical implementation is to add wireless users to a traditional network. This can be as simple as giving them modems for their digital phones or even giving them the new wireless palm-size devices.

We will look at the following major wireless technologies, each of which has its strengths and weaknesses:

- Radio
- Infrared
- Microwave
- Cellular

Radio

Data signals are sent and received in much the same way as commercial radio signals are sent and received. The network may have one or more antennas located in the desired buildings or areas, and users have smaller transmitter/receiver units on their computers. PC card-sized units now are available that plug into a laptop with only a small antenna (2 to 3 inches) exposed. The Federal Communications Commission (FCC) closely regulates anything to do with airwaves. It allocates all transmission frequencies to various purposes and helps to make sure that users comply with all rules of operation so that individual users do not impact other groups. The freedom to innovate and generally run amok is somewhat limited in this area.

Without serious FCC licensing and rules, wireless radio systems are somewhat limited in transmission strength and speed, and may be limited to line-of-sight implementations. Data speeds are picking up, however; a Cisco unit I was looking at supports up to 11 Mbps. The IEEE 802-11b standard defines this type of wireless technology.

One consideration is that in these relatively unregulated frequency ranges, it's very difficult to keep another device using the same frequencies from coming into your area. Recall the problems with the first cordless phones for the home. Figure 2-18 shows a wireless implementation.

Infrared

One form of wireless network communications involves using the infrared light spectrum. There is even a standard called *IrDA*, which is short for *Infrared Data Association*, a group of device manufacturers that developed a standard for transmitting data via infrared light waves. IrDA ports are becoming very common on computers, particularly

Figure 2-18
Wireless devices

laptops, and other devices (such as printers). This technology enables data transfer from one device to another without any cables. For example, if both a laptop computer and printer have IrDA ports, it is possible to print without needing to connect the two with a cable.

While infrared supports roughly the same transmission rates as traditional parallel ports, the devices must have a clear line of sight between them and generally must be within a few feet. Infrared communications can also be impacted by bright lights outside the infrared spectrum. A stray bright light can blind an infrared port for a few minutes.

Infrared keyboards, mice, and palm-sized devices are becoming more common in the office environment. If you think you are unfamiliar with infrared, consider your remote control for your TV, VCR, or stereo, most of which are infrared. You have probably discovered that they must be able to see each other and may not work well in brightly lit rooms.

Microwave

Microwave is generally a high-cost solution that can be either terrestrial, point-to-point, or involve bouncing a signal off of a satellite. The terrestrial approach involves two dishes that are literally aimed at each. This line-of-sight approach can be across a parking lot or across a valley, as long as both dishes can "see" each other. Trees, new construction, and even bad weather can compromise or destroy the quality of the signal.

The second approach is the satellite system where all users have a dish pointed toward a satellite, which effectively bounces the sign between the users. This approach is impacted less by such considerations as curvature of the earth, landmarks, buildings, and trees. The small satellite dishes you see on some homes are a form of one-way satellite communications. For a two-way example, look at the roofline of the next Taco Bell you drive by, which will have a small dish aimed toward a satellite so that all the burritos can be accounted for.

Microwave technology generally requires FCC licensing and rules of operation. Its primary strength is that it can bounce data hundreds or thousands of miles if necessary. Microwave is subject to interference from EMI, weather, and atmospheric conditions. Figure 2-19 shows a satellite microwave implementation.

Cellular

A cellular network is an overlapping array of circular or hexagonal regions (cells) that can be reached by electromagnetic waves using land-based towers and remote mobile users. When a cellular connection is made, the mobile unit connects to the nearest tower, which then connects the user to the network. If the user stays in place, the communication continues unchanged until the link is broken. If the user is moving, as they

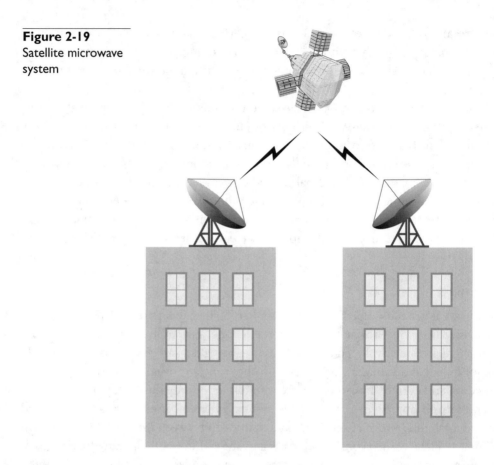

Figure 2-19
Satellite microwave
system

approach the edge of a cell, the tower will attempt to pass them off to the next cell. If there is an open connection in the new cell, everything is fine and the user may not sense the pass-off at all. On the other hand, if the next cell is busy and cannot free up a connection in time, the call will be broken (dropped). Figure 2-20 shows a cellular network.

Cellular can be relatively inexpensive compared to installing an infrastructure, allows for mobility, and is becoming somewhat universal, meaning you can use it anywhere in the country. The disadvantages are that it can be more expensive than existing land-based systems, may be subject to disruptions because of heavy telephone usage, and has security and privacy concerns because technology exists to capture this type of communications.

As a telephone system, it offers the option of modem communication for laptops and PDAs to a network or the Internet. Since many phones now have messaging and paging services, this capability can be incorporated into a strategy for notifying the remote user when important communications are needed.

Figure 2-20
Cellular network

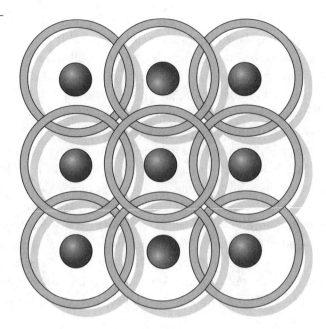

The evolving *Wireless Application Protocol* (WAP) is a secure specification that allows users to access information instantly via handheld wireless devices such as mobile phones, pagers, two-way radios, and communicators. WAP compliant devices can display and access the Internet by running what are called *microbrowsers* that can accommodate the low memory constraints of handheld devices and the low-bandwidth constraints of a wireless-handheld network.

Collisions and Collision Domains

LANs are often shared media environments, meaning that multiple hosts have access to the same communication media. This situation is common in copper-based networks but would apply as well to fiber and wireless networks. Originally on coaxial networks, all devices were literally connected to the same single wire. Today the networks may involve four wires on a Category 5 cable or a pair of fiber cables, but still the possibility exists of two devices transmitting at exactly the same time and creating a collision.

In the next few chapters, we will spend considerable time looking at protocols, access methods, and devices that reduce the possibility of collisions. But for the purpose of this section, we need to go back to the beginning, the original Ethernet networks defined by the original 802-3 standard.

The Ethernet standards and access methods recognized that several devices would be connected to the same wire and that occasionally a collision was bound to occur. There is actually a mechanism that defines how a host will monitor the wire and when it "hears" an opening in the signal, it is then free to transmit. The standard goes on to limit the size of data frames so that a single host cannot dominate the wire. We will look at Ethernet and the alternatives in detail in Chapter 3. For now, you just need to recognize what a collision is and what causes them.

The result of a collision is more voltage on the network wires than can be correctly interpreted by the hosts as either zeros or ones. The result is junk or scrap, much the same as many vehicles involved in collisions on our roadways are scrap. The network must be allowed to clear any signals, after which retransmission can occur.

Understanding how collisions occur will enable you to understand why the likelihood, and possibly the frequency, of collisions increases as more hosts are added to a network. As host computers become faster with better CPUs and more memory, it makes sense that they can react quicker and jump into gaps in traffic possibly at the expense of older and slower devices. This quicker response may also lead to increased collisions.

Any area within a network where the data packets originating from the hosts can collide is called a *collision domain*. In the simplest network of two computers, sharing a wire is a collision domain. As you will see in the next section, as you add computers to the network, the collision domain grows until at some point the frequency of collisions starts to negatively impact the network.

Layer 1 can do little to prevent collisions, because the technologies and devices are all "shared media" devices. However, as you will read in later chapters, Layer 2 and 3 devices can help you prevent collisions. One analogy is that Layer 1 technologies are like the roads, driveways, intersections, on-ramps to freeways, and freeways themselves. They are not the traffic-control devices, such as stop signs and stoplights. If for some reason all traffic lights and stop signs disappeared, traffic would still flow, because we have basic rules that apply, such as yielding the right of way and looking both ways before entering traffic. But misunderstandings could occur at intersections. As the number of vehicles increased, so would the misunderstandings and the collisions.

Fortunately, the network protocols at Layer 1 provide rules and methods that ensures that devices will wait until there is an opening in traffic, and they won't dominate the road, so collisions should not happen often. Note that collisions are not inherently evil; they are only a simple indicator of network congestion. Another nice factor that differentiates networks from human traffic is that computers don't get angry or impatient, so they don't make stupid mistakes. Add the incredible speeds they function at, and tremendous amounts of data is passed between collisions.

In the next section, we will look at network devices other than hosts and see how they impact collisions, collision domains, and the size of our networks. We will take a historical perspective that looks at the evolution of Layer 1 networks.

Layer 1 Components and Devices

We have discussed many of the components that make up Layer 1. They include the following:

- Cable media
- Cable connectors and terminators
- Patch panels

Together, these items make up the roads and on-ramps to the roads. In the next section, we will look at these devices:

- *Network interface cards* (NICs), transmitters, and receivers
- Transceivers
- Repeaters
- Hubs
- Multiplexers

Network Interface Cards, Transmitters, and Receivers

The NIC, sometimes called the network adapter, is actually a Layer 2 device but it has circuitry that is clearly a part of Layer 1. In fact, the connections on the NIC are in Layer 1 and must have already processed the data to make it suitable for transmission across the wires. The Layer 1 circuitry consists of those chips and connectors that convert and transmit the data in a form appropriate for the communications media and access method protocols being used. In other words, if we are using copper media and the Ethernet access method, the *transmitters* will put out electrical impulses appropriate for Ethernet (as compared to Token Ring). If we are using wireless, the transmitters will put out radio signals appropriate for the receiving stations.

On the receiving machine, the receiver circuitry will translate the signals into something the other layers can use. Figure 2-21 shows an example of a NIC.

It is possible that, particularly with wireless, the transmitter and receivers could be separate external devices, but it is becoming more common for them to be internal. This

Figure 2-21 Network interface card

reduces the desktop space requirements, eliminates the need for another power supply, and means that the unit can often be preconfigured at the factory or by a reseller.

Transceivers

Transceivers are devices that convert one media type into another. One of the most common connections is an *attachment unit interface* (AUI), originally a portion of the Ethernet standard that specified how a cable was to be connected to an Ethernet card. The transceiver plugs into a 15-pin AUI socket on the NIC and then allows coax, twisted-pair, or fiber-optic cable to be connected to the other end. Most transceivers only make one conversion, such as AUI to UTP or coax to UTP.

Transceivers typically require a power supply and vary in size depending on the conversion to be made. Any unit converting fiber optics will be larger and more expensive because of the internal circuitry required to change from electricity to light. Figure 2-22 shows an example of a transceiver.

Many equipment manufactures, such as Cisco, originally used AUI connectors so that they didn't have to produce multiple versions of the same device. The Cisco 2501 router is a good example. The AUI Ethernet could support UTP, coax, or fiber-optic

Figure 2-22   AUI to UTP Transceiver

cable with the appropriate transceiver. Over time, UTP using a RJ-45 connector has become the dominant Ethernet standard and most manufactures have replaced the AUI with 10BaseT or 10/100 interfaces.

Repeaters

In the days of coaxial cable, a ThinNet network was limited to 30 nodes and 2 of those nodes had to be terminators. This clearly was going to be a problem in larger organizations. The problem was that after passing through 28 T-connectors and traveling up to 185 meters, the signal had attenuated to the point that reliability was a concern.

Someone developed a device called a repeater to rebuild and filter the signal so that it could be retransmitted like new. This meant that another 28 nodes could be added and another 185 meters could be covered. The good news was that more employees could now share resources. The downside was that there were now twice as many computers, thereby increasing the potential for collisions. Since the repeater had no built-in intelligence, it could only retransmit everything that came to it, even if the destination was back on the originating segment.

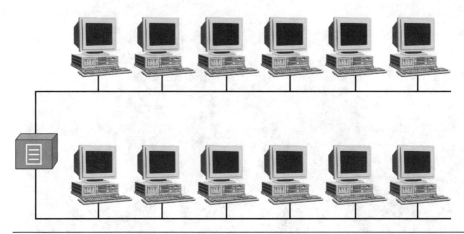

Figure 2-23 Repeater linking two networks

The *collision domain* just increased from 28 computers to 56 because any 2 computers could transmit simultaneously and therefore collide. If another repeater were added, the network and collision domain could grow by 28 more nodes. Figure 2-23 shows an example of a repeater being used to connect two floors.

Designers and engineers, being a clever lot, discovered ways to connect three or four networks to a single repeater. They now had a multiport repeater, which also became known as a hub or concentrator. At the same time this technology was evolving, twisted-pair cable was starting to gain a serious foothold in the industry. The smaller connector size and the larger number of computers that could be connected to hubs based on twisted-pair media quickly drew R&D funds away from coax.

While true repeaters still are available, and even some for twisted-pair, they tend to be specialty items and relatively expensive for their usefulness.

Four Repeater Rule

If repeaters rebuild the signal to original strength, we should be able to just keep adding repeaters until we have every one connected. Unfortunately, something we discussed earlier comes back to bite us here—propagation delay or latency. If we use more than four repeaters, the hosts on the ends will not hear each other in real time and can therefore generate collisions. The accumulative latency from being processed by so many repeaters will delay the signals long enough that one end can be transmitting but the other end will not hear it. Unfortunately, this is true of all Layer 1 devices, so hubs will have the same limitation.

If we were to put a repeater or hub on each of six floors, the users on the top and bottom floors would not be able to hear each other in real time and therefore could transmit on top of each other, only to collide somewhere midnetwork. We will look at this rule in more detail in later chapters, particularly in Chapter 10, when we look at LAN design.

Hubs

A *hub* essentially is a multiport repeater. A signal coming in one port is rebuilt and retransmitted out all other ports. Hubs quickly evolved with port densities of 24 to 48 interfaces, and since you could attach multiple hubs together, it was possible to develop even larger networks-up to 1,024 hosts, in theory. But what does this do to our collision domain? Doesn't it just continue to grow with each new device? Yes, as does congestion and the likelihood of collisions. Figure 2-24 shows an example of a network using a hub.

Figure 2-24 shows a small network in a department or classroom, but it is possible to connect multiple departments or classrooms to a single centrally located hub creating a larger network. It would take only a single cable from the central hub to each of the

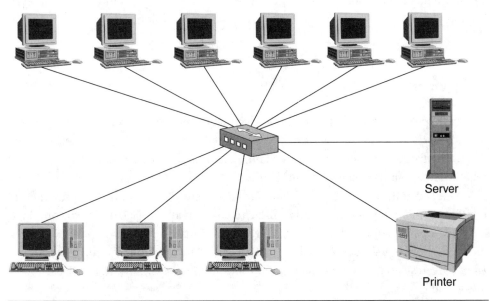

Figure 2-24   Hub-based network

Figure 2-25
Ethernet Hub

departments or classrooms and then use additional hubs to handle local distribution. Figure 2-25 shows an example of the front of a 12-port hub.

Multiplexers

A *multiplexer* is a device that can take signals from several devices and distribute those signals all onto a single data channel, like a "digital loop" (T1 or T3) line. At the other end, another multiplexer can break the data back out into the original number of connections. The phone company used this technology for years to keep from having to run so many phone lines to large office buildings. With two multiplexers and a T1 line, they could deliver 24 telephone connections, and with a T3 line, they could deliver 672 telephone connections.

More importantly, the companies could take part of those connections and use them as dedicated data lines. Figure 2-26 shows an example of using a multiplexer to consolidate data connections to run over a single connection. We will look at multiplexers in more detail in Chapter 17, while discussing WAN technologies.

Summary

In this chapter, we looked at some basic electricity concepts and terminology that will provide a basis for later discussions. We compared analog and digital signaling methods, recognizing that many things in nature are analog but that digitizing allows for reliable storage and efficient transmission.

We looked at the enemies of our data signals that are all too common in the environment. EMI, RFI, reflection, line noise, and crosstalk can all damage or destroy our data.

We compared copper, fiber-optic, and various forms of wireless communications media. Copper has some significant cost and ease of installation advantages over fiber. Fiber's greatest strengths are distance and minimal impact of EMI, RFI, reflection, line noise, and crosstalk.

We identified the physical layer components and devices as the communications media, connectors, fasteners, transceivers, hubs, and repeaters. Repeaters and hubs,

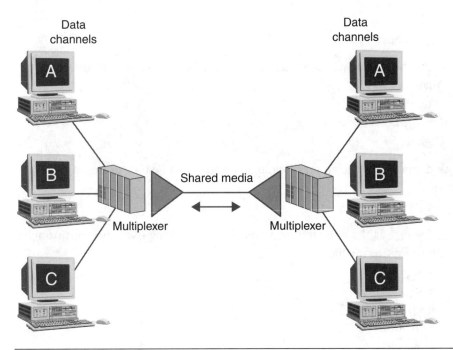

Figure 2-26   Multiplexer

which are multiport repeaters, regenerate the signal, allowing for greater distances and possibly more connections to the network.

A collision domain includes all devices that, if transmitting simultaneously, would result in a data collision. In a network made up of Layer 1 devices only, the entire network is a single collision domain.

Practice Questions

Take a few moments and check your grasp of the concepts covered in this chapter. The answers immediately follow the questions.

Questions

1. _____ is an electrical force, or pressure, that occurs when electrons and protons are separated.
    a. Resistance
    b. Circuit

      c. Voltage

      d. Impedance

2. What are the two signal-transmission methods discussed in this chapter?

      a. Analog

      b. Latency

      c. Propagation

      d. Digital

3. With digital signaling, an infinite range of values can be transmitted.

      a. True

      b. False

4. _____ is the reduction of signal strength during transmission through a communications media.

      a. Latency

      b. Noise

      c. Refection

      d. Attenuation

5. Which two of the following are not examples of noise, the unwanted additions to the data signals from any source?

      a. EMI

      b. AMI

      c. Crosstalk

      d. Resistance

      e. RFI

6. Define the three elements of the notation 10BaseT.

      a. 10

      b. Base

      c. T

7. What is the maximum bandwidth of Category 5 cable?

      a. 16 Mbps

      b. 20 Mbps

      c. 100 Mbps

      d. 100 MBps

8. What is the maximum distance for Category 5 cable?

      a. 100 feet

      b. 2,000 meters

    c. 100 meters

    d. 185 meters

9. Which one of the following is not a wireless technology?

    a. Radio

    b. Infrared

    c. Microwave

    d. Repeater

    e. Cellular

10. How many repeaters can you have in a Layer 1 network?

    a. 2

    b. As many as you need

    c. 4

    d. 5

11. Category 5 cable is an example of which one of the following?

    a. ThinNet

    b. ThickNet

    c. UTP

    d. Fiber optics

12. Which one of the following devices puts multiple signals on a single media?

    a. Hub

    b. Repeater

    c. Multiplexer

    d. Transceiver

13. Which of the following media coverings (ratings) is required by fire code when cable runs between floors?

    a. PVC

    b. Plenum

    c. Riser

    d. Fire retardant

14. Which of the following media coverings (ratings) is required by fire code when cable runs in the air circulation system of a building?

    a. PVC

    b. Plenum

    c. Riser

    d. Fire retardant

15. RJ-45 connectors are used in which of the following media?
    a. ThinNet
    b. ThickNet
    c. Fiber optics
    d. Category 5

Answers

1. **c.** Voltage is an electrical force, or pressure, that occurs when electrons and protons are separated.

2. **a.** and **d.** Analog and digital.

3. **b.** False. Analog allows an infinite range of values; digital only transmits zeros and ones.

4. **d.** Attenuation is the reduction of signal strength during transmission through a communications media.

5. **b.** and **d.** EMI, RFI, and crosstalk are all examples of noise.

6. **a.** 10 represents the maximum bandwidth, 10 Mbps
   b. Base represents baseband transmission
   c. T represents twisted-pair media

7. **c.** 100 Mbps

8. **c.** 100 meters

9. **d.** A repeater is a Layer 1 device, not a wireless technology.

10. **c.** You can have four repeaters in a Layer 1 network.

11. **c.** UTP. Both a and b are forms of coaxial cable.

12. **d.** Transceiver

13. **c.** Riser

14. **b.** Plenum

15. **d.** Category 5

Topology and Access Methods

3

This chapter will:

- **Introduce the basic network topologies**

- **Introduce the hierarchical network model**

- **Look at the Ethernet, Token Ring, and FDDI access methods**

- **Compare Ethernet and Token Ring data frames**

- **Discuss collisions and collision domains**

- **Discuss broadcasts and broadcast domains**

In designing or troubleshooting a network, the *topology*, the physical arrangement of network nodes and media, has a significant impact on your options. In looking at topologies, we first look at the more common options and then identify the strengths and weaknesses of each.

You can think of the *topology* of the network as the shape, or bird's-eye view, of the network's design. Keep in mind that the topology is really the map of how we plan to connect the devices in our network. The topology is operating system-independent, because Windows, NetWare, or UNIX/Linux will be able to function on it. For that matter, each topology could be used for a peer-to-peer network. So knowing the topology may indicate some of the strengths and weaknesses of a network design, but it does not include details like the operating system or even the specifics of the networking devices.

While the topology is generally what Layer 1 of your network looks like, not all devices that fit into the topology are Layer 1 devices, so this chapter will supplement the Level 1 discussion from the last chapter and prepare you to move on to other layers.

You will also discover that a larger network may contain segments of different topologies. This is not necessarily the result of planning, but could be the result of mergers and acquisitions as well as the different needs of departments within the organization. Quite often, linking to another network is easier than fully assimilating it into your design.

Topology Options

Depending on whom you talk to, you will get different names and numbers of topologies used in networking. In simplest terms, there are really only four basic topologies: bus, star, ring, and mesh. Everything else is just a variation or extension of one of the basic topologies. Figure 3-1 shows the four basic network topologies. The circles represent network nodes including computers and network devices.

Figure 3-1
The four basic topologies

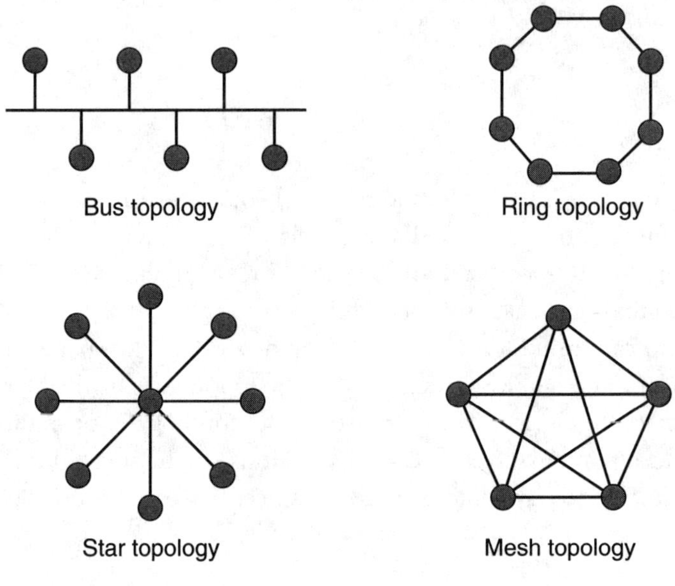

Bus topology

Ring topology

Star topology

Mesh topology

Physical vs. Logical Topology

In some cases, the access method for data signaling and the network devices create a situation where there are really two topologies for the same network design. The *physical topology* describes the plan for connecting the physical devices, and the *logical topology* describes how data actually flows in the network. This distinction should become clear when we discuss ring topologies.

Bus Topology

The bus topology is the original Ethernet topology that uses coaxial cable as the media. In ThinNet installations, each node is connected by a BNC T-connector directly to the backbone. If a ThickNet backbone is used, the nodes are connected with transceivers to an AUI connection to a section of ThinNet. The ThinNet is then connected to the backbone with another transceiver that contains a vampire-like clamp that literally bites into the ThickNet to make a connection. In either case, the bus backbone has to be terminated at each end to avoid signal reflection back onto the cable and a collision.

Since all hosts are wired directly, there is no need for any other devices to allow the hosts to communicate. If a node puts a data signal on the wire, all other nodes will see it almost instantaneously. The biggest disadvantage of this topology is that a break anywhere in the cable disconnects hosts from each other—creating two networks, each with an unterminated end. Figure 3-2 shows a simple example of a bus network.

Some organizations may still use a bus topology network, but realistically, the time of these networks is past because of the bandwidth limitations and relative difficulty of working with coaxial cable. We still have a machine shop client that maintains a bus network because of coax's resistance to EMI and RFI. The cost of upgrading to fiber is too high and the 10 Mbps throughput still meets their needs, although the office network segment was upgraded several years ago.

Server

Printer

Figure 3-2   Bus network topology

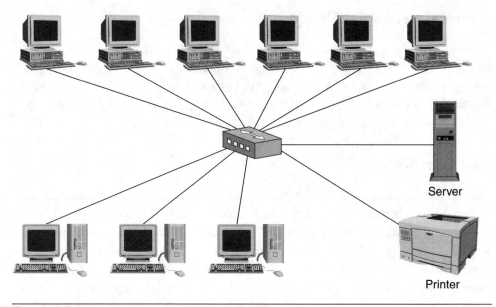

Figure 3-3 Star topology

Star Topology

The star topology has a central node, typically a hub or switch, with all links to other nodes radiating from it. The star topology with a hub at the center is the natural evolution from coaxial bus networks. Each device is still wired directly to all others, and every node hears every packet placed on the wire almost instantly.

The disadvantage usually associated with this topology is that the central node becomes a potential single point of failure that can bring down the entire network. It could be argued that a break in a bus backbone is only slightly better and could just as likely lead to a complete failure because of the unterminated ends. Figure 3-3 shows an example of a star topology.

Star-Bus Topology

A star-bus topology is really just a variation of a star topology. It is in fact two or more stars connected one to one with a bus link. Figure 3-4 shows an example of a star-bus topology that might be typical in a small organization on two floors of a building.

With hubs at the center of each star, all nodes are still directly connected together and all nodes hear every packet almost instantaneously. The entire network would still

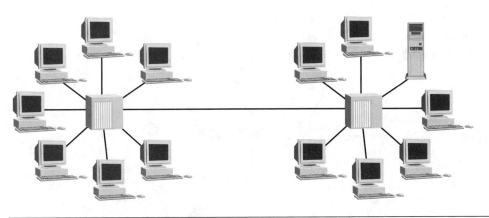

Figure 3-4   Star-bus topology

be a single collision domain—any two computers transmitting at the same time will result in a collision.

The link between the two hubs is self-terminating, the hub being the terminator. The link could be between two normal data ports or between two uplink ports. The difference is that a link between two data ports typically requires a crossover cable, where the send and receive pairs of the cable are reversed at one end, whereas a link between a normal port on one device and a uplink port on the other requires only normal cabling, because the crossover is handled internally in the first device. On some hubs, the uplink could be a different media, such as coax or fiber.

Extended Star Topology

An extended star topology LAN is often depicted diagrammatically and conceptually, as you see in Figure 3-5. The advantage to a centered device with hubs attached to the links is that it shortens the paths between any two nodes, thereby avoiding the four-repeaters rule discussed in the last chapter.

While the extended star topology might have some applications in large, single-floor organizations, such as some schools, a far more common implementation is in multi-floor buildings. You learned that with the star-bus topology, up to four floors can be connected to create a single network. Four floors is the maximum because going any higher would violate the four-repeater rule. Figure 3-6 represents a five-floor building using the star-bus topology that violates the four-repeater rule.

Figure 3-5
Extended star topol-
ogy, conceptually

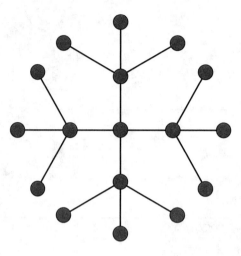

Any host on the bottom floor would need to pass through five hubs to get to any host on the top floor. The result would be an unacceptable number of collisions, because hosts on either end of the network would not hear the other end transmitting and, thinking the line was clear, would start transmitting their packets. This problem would only get worse with more floors.

If we were to add a centralized hub, thereby creating our extended star topology, we could cut the maximum number of repeaters to no more than three—well within the standard. Additional floors would still have no more than three hubs to pass though. This additional hub might be called a backbone hub, whereas the others would be called departmental or workgroup hubs. This design is often referred to as a collapsed backbone design. Figure 3-7 shows the multifloor building with a backbone device in place.

If we could flatten out our network looking at it in two dimensions by extending out the links from our backbone hub, we would have the extended star shown in Figure 3-5. We could add as many floors as we want and we would still have a maximum repeater path of only three repeaters. The actual backbone hub could be located in the data facility on any floor, but on taller buildings, it might make sense to place it near the center.

With hub technology, every node is directly connected to a single circuit, so as the network grows even more users are vying for access to a single shared media in a single collision domain. The extended star topology is very hierarchical in design, and lends itself to segmenting so that local data, perhaps local to each floor, could be kept separate—if we had some kind of device that was "smarter" than a hub for that backbone device. We will see in the next chapter when we look at Layer 2 devices that there are solutions that might help us with this problem.

Figure 3-6
Five-floor building
with network

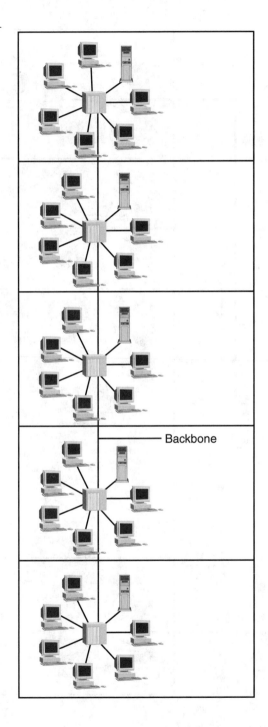

Backbone

Figure 3-7
Five-floor building
with backbone hub

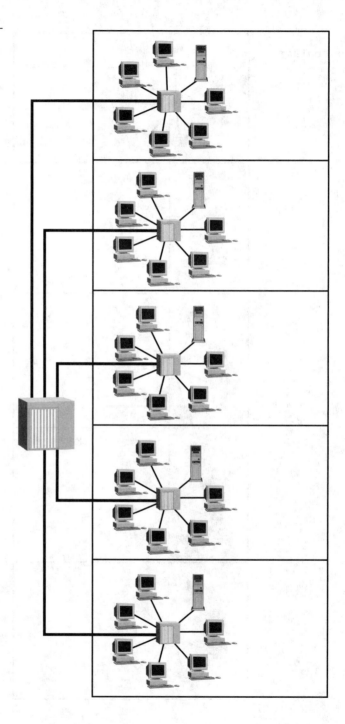

Tree Topology

The tree topology is really a variation of the extended star topology except that it does not usually use a single central node. This model is often used in depicting the hierarchical network model with Layer 1, 2, and 3 devices to represent a large network, including large campus networks. The primary benefit of this topology is that it is scalable (it can grow with the organization) and is able to incorporate redundancy to mitigate the results of a device failure. We will look at this model in more detail later in this section. Figure 3-8 shows a simple tree topology.

The top router, the round image, might be the organization's firewall between it and the Internet, providing security against hackers and unauthorized transmissions out of the organization.

Ring Topology

A ring topology is a single closed ring, or loop, with each node connected directly to the next until finally the ring is complete. This topology is used by the Token Ring access

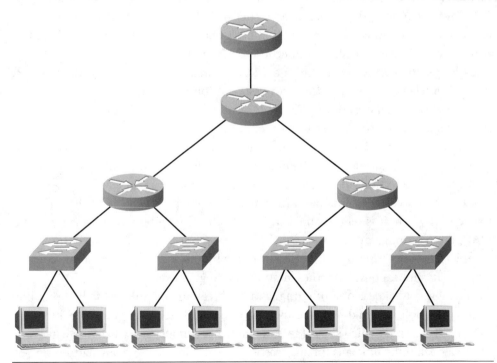

Figure 3-8   Tree topology

Figure 3-9
Token Ring logical
view

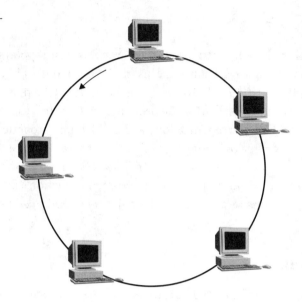

method (IEEE 802.5), which creates a single-direction flow from node to node. Figure 3-9 shows a logical representation of a ring network. This continuous loop is in contrast to the bus, which must be terminated at each end, and even the star topologies, in which the NIC terminates each connection to a hub or switch.

Each host then transmits data to the next in a circular pattern. Each host in essence becomes a relay agent. This process creates a collision-free environment, but any break in the circle stops all data flows. We will look at the actual process in more detail later in this chapter when we discuss access methods.

This topology is logically a ring and could be physically constructed as such, but far more common is the use of a *multistation access unit* (MAU or MSAU) that allows twisted-pair connections to run out to hosts much like a hub in the star topology except that the loop circuit is maintained within the MAU. A pair of wires takes the signal out to the host where it is rebuilt and sent back to the MAU after any processing. In the MAU, the returning circuit is forwarded to the next host, continuing until the loop is complete. In a star topology, data goes from the hub to the host but is never returned. Figure 3-10 shows a physical representation of a ring network.

The biggest weakness of a true ring is that a break in any link or the loss of a host brings the whole system down. The addition of the MAU technology actually helped in this area. Later units called smart MAUs actually have small gates where the wires head out to a host. If the link fails for any reason, the gate closes, effectively partitioning off that host and maintaining the logical ring intact.

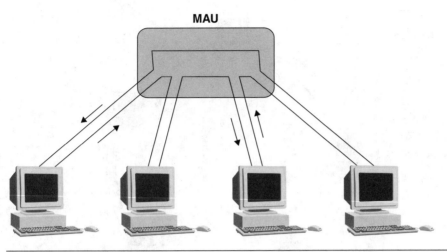

Figure 3-10 Token Ring physical view

 EXAM TIP: Remember that a ring topology is typically a logical ring within a physical star. The ring is maintained in the MAU.

Dual-Ring Topology

A dual-ring topology consists of two parallel closed rings, or loops, with each node connected directly to the next node on each ring until finally the rings are complete. This topology is used by the *Fiber Distributed Data Interface* (FDDI), a LAN standard for a 100 Mbps token-passing network using fiber-optic cable. It is capable of transmission distances of up to 2 km and uses the dual-ring architecture to provide redundancy. Figure 3-11 shows a dual-ring network.

The rings travel in opposite directions, with one ring being used for data while the other provides redundancy in case of a break in the circuit. We will look at this and other features of FDDI in more detail later in this chapter.

Mesh or Matrix Topology

In a fully meshed topology, every node is linked directly to every other node. Because most LAN hosts have only a single network interface this would not be a LAN topology

Figure 3-11
Dual-ring topology

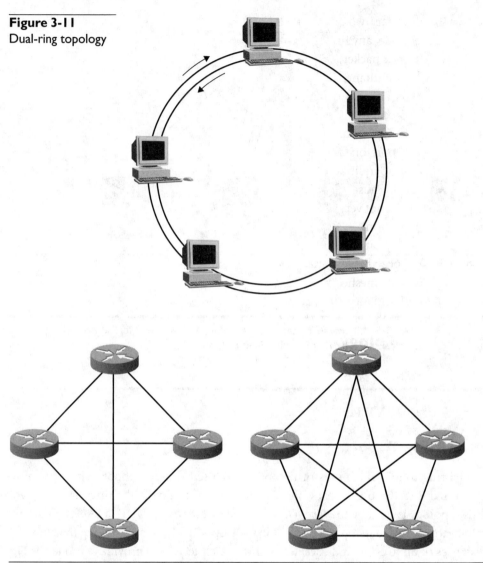

Figure 3-12 Two fully meshed networks

as much as it might be a WAN topology for connecting locations together. The devices that you see in the figure would then be routers or switches. It could also be implemented at what is called the distribution layer of a campus network, to connect buildings together. Again, the nodes would be routers. Figure 3-12 shows two fully meshed campus networks and the difference one node makes in the number of links.

This topology has two advantages. First, because every node is physically connected to every other node, any link failure should not prevent data from reaching its destination. Second, in a packet-switched network, this topology allows data to flow along multiple paths simultaneously to the destination.

This topology also has disadvantages. First, the number of wiring connections and links grows exponentially with new nodes. To calculate the number of links, the formula is $n*(n-1)/2$, where n is the number of nodes. Second, adding a new node requires a new port on every other device, which can be very expensive. Table 3-1 shows the increase in links and router ports required as nodes increase. Finally, while highly reliable because of the cabling requirements and ever-growing router port requirements, it is not very scalable, meaning that it cannot grow quickly and efficiently with the organization.

When you look at the cost and logistics of a fully meshed network, it generally becomes an unreasonable solution, but you may find that portions of an internetwork design are partially meshed, more than one link to each node, to meet some overruling reliability or redundancy requirement.

Cellular Topology

A cellular topology consists of overlapping rings of wireless communications. (Refer to Chapter 2 for more information regarding cellular technology.) Although this topology is viable for a cellular phone company, its only other potential use is as a method for connecting remote users to more traditional network topologies.

Table 3-1   Meshed Network Link and Port Requirements

NODES	LINKS	TOTAL ROUTER PORTS	PORTS PER ROUTER
3	3	6	2
4	6	12	3
5	10	20	4
6	15	30	5
7	21	42	6
12	66	132	11

Hierarchical Network Model

According to Microsoft's Encarta *World English Dictionary 2001*, the term "hierarchical" means "rigidly graded in order: relating to or arranged in a formally ranked order." The same source defines "hierarchy" as "formally ranked group: an organization or group whose members are arranged in ranks, for example, in ranks of power and seniority." As we go through the next paragraphs, we will see that both definitions help to understand the hierarchical model that is generally accepted as a requirement for designing scalable networks.

The hierarchical network model that has evolved is a three-layer model representing the core, distribution, and access layers or functions of a network. The core layer refers to site-to-site communications links, typically using WAN technologies. Depending on the size and design of the network, the distribution layer could be the links to departments within a building or possibly between buildings in a campus network. The access layer is where end users and workgroups are connected to the network. Many large campus networks today actually have their own three-layer model consisting of a LAN core that interconnects the buildings, distribution-layer switches in each building, and access-layer switches connecting to the distribution-layer devices. Figure 3-13 shows a very simple diagram of the three-layer model.

Each layer, and therefore each device in that layer, has a purpose and function. The better the integrity of each layer's purpose and function is preserved, the more scalable the network. The following are the five key requirements of a scalable network:

- Reliability and availability
- Responsiveness
- Efficiency

Figure 3-13
Hierarchical model

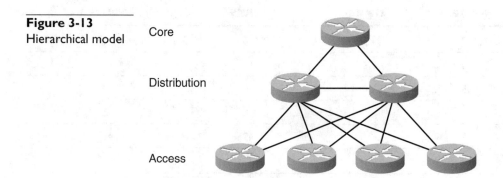

Core

Distribution

Access

- Adaptability

- Accessibility and security

"Scalable" means the network is able to grow and adapt rapidly to meet the changing organizational requirements. This change can be precipitated by increases or decreases in the number of users and/or user locations accessing the network, increases or decreases in the volume of transactions being processed by the existing users, or by the introduction of new technologies into the current networks. These new technologies could include such things as adding telephone communications to your data network (voice over IP), high-speed imaging capabilities, or adding Web-based applications for all phone-support personnel. Because many new technologies are developed in certain fields only to spring on the rest of the world almost fully developed, networking change can often be seen as revolutionary instead of evolutionary. This is why a networker would be wise to at least keep informed of related changes in telecommunications, WAN technologies, cabling, health care, and the graphic arts.

We will talk about this hierarchical model throughout most of the remaining chapters and use it as a guide in Chapter 10, when we look at LAN design. For now, it is important to recognize that the topologies discussed earlier could occur at various layers in the hierarchical model. Figure 3-14 demonstrates a hierarchical internetwork with various topologies included. Keep in mind that the more technologies added to a network, the greater the need for support and "spares" in case of component failure.

In looking at Figure 3-14, there are three ATM switches attached to the *Synchronous Optical Network* (SONET) "Core." Since each ATM represents a location, we can assume there will be that similar hierarchical network attached to each switch, giving us an extended start design.

Access Methods

Access methods are those combined standards and protocols that define how data signaling will be placed on and moved through Layer 1 of the network. The two most common LAN access methods are Ethernet and Token Ring, defined by IEEE standards 802.3 and 802.5, respectively. These general access methods are further refined within the standards to include Fast Ethernet and Gigabit Ethernet under 802.3, and FDDI under 802.5. Each access method and subset defines the data frame, how signaling will work, and how collisions are dealt with. We will see later, in Chapters 17 to 20, that many of the WAN protocols are also access methods residing only in Layers 1 and 2 of the OSI model.

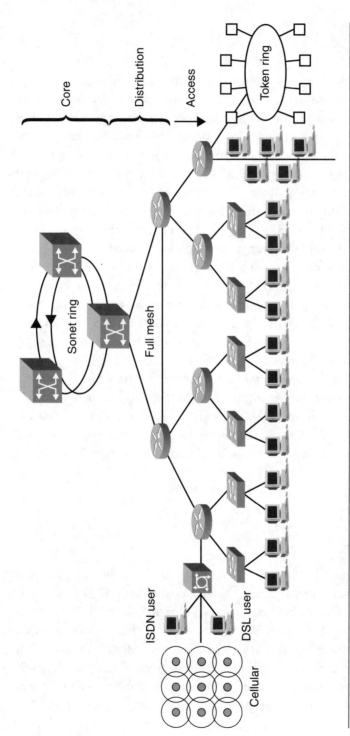

Figure 3-14 Network with multiple topologies

An access method, or access protocol, is the delivery system within or between our networks. Ethernet, Token Ring, Frame Relay, HDLC, and so forth are the equivalent to UPS, FedEx, or DHL in the networks. They are the Layer 1 and 2 protocols that apply the final data frame (shipping envelope), add the physical address for delivery, which they get from a higher-level protocol at Layer 3, and then put it on the road. Upper-level protocols, such as TCP/IP, IPX/SPX, and so forth, are the equivalent of the facilitators or project managers of the organization. They don't make the product, but they make sure that it gets delivered to the customer how, when, and in what form the customer wants.

These access protocols, such as Ethernet, at the data link layer (Layer 2) accept the data packet assembled at the network layer (Layer 3) along with the delivery (MAC) address of the destination. The access protocol is responsible for defining a package (frame) appropriate for the connection media.

Understanding that the OSI model does not map exactly to the other networking models that you will come across in networking helps you to accept some of the obvious discrepancies that occur when you try to make everything fit one model. Many texts in defining the OSI model and the devices associated with it include the NIC or network adapter in Layer 2. After all, the EEPROM that contains its MAC address for Layer 2 is on the NIC.

Yet, components such as the physical-layer termination (RJ-45, AUI, Fiber, or BNC) and the transmitter/receiver on the NIC, along with the protocols and technologies that control them, must by definition be a part of Layer 1. The OSI model was never meant to map to the physical world. We label things like switches, routers, load balancers, and so forth as Layer X devices because they perform a particular function characterized by a certain layer's functions.

IEEE's reason for grouping together the standards and protocols defining signaling and addressing makes sense, but how do we easily reconcile this structure with the OSI layer definitions? Figure 3-15 compares the IEEE networking standard and layers 1 and 2 of the OSI reference model.

We will see in later chapters that other networking models, such as the TCP/IP reference model, treat the OSI layers 1 and 2 as if they were a single layer, referred to as the *network interface layer*. This is why I have chosen to insert this chapter between the chapters covering Layer 1 and Layer 2.

Ethernet

Ethernet is a LAN transport protocol developed originally by Bob Metcalf and his colleagues at the Xerox Corporation at their *Palo Alto Research Facility* (PARC) in the early 1970s. Xerox originally registered the name Ethernet for the end product. It later

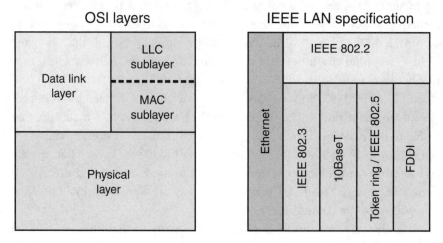

Figure 3-15   IEEE networking standard vs. OSI model

cooperated with Intel and *Digital Equipment Corporation* (DEC) in the early 1980s to develop the 10 Mbps shared-media protocol called the DIX (DEC, Intel, Xerox) standard, which later became the basis for the IEEE 802.3 standard that supported data transfer rates of 10 Mbps.

Fast Ethernet, defined later in the IEEE 802.3u standard, supports data transfer rates of 100 Mbps. In 1998, Gigabit Ethernet, supporting data rates of 1 Gbps in fiber-optic and copper media, was defined in IEEE 802.3z and 802.3ab, respectively. IEEE has chosen to not use the name Ethernet relative to the standard because of its policy against using commercial product names. It has continued this practice even though Xerox relinquished ownership of the name when it opened the standard in the 1980s. IEEE continues to refer to it as the 802.3 CSMA/CD standard.

As new technologies are added, such as 100 Mbps and 1 Gbps support, the standard is modified while retaining backward-compatibility. This allows networks to support all variations of the standard simultaneously and has lead to the Ethernet's wide acceptance as an access (delivery) method.

Today, Ethernet generally uses a variation of a star topology, but its original implementation was for a bus-type network using broadcasts over a shared media. Ethernet in one form or another is the most widely implemented LAN standard with probably a 90 percent or higher market share. The way Token Ring, the only other real LAN alternative, has been declining, this share percentage may even be understated.

Xerox's PARC Facility

While Xerox is best known for copier technology and document-management systems, its Palo Alto Research Center (PARC) facility is a research facility that did much "pure" research that greatly advanced the technologies we now take for granted. Developments at PARC and Xerox's somewhat cavalier attitude toward copyright and patents are the basis for many of our industries myths as well as some personal fortunes.

PARC was instrumental in developing technologies such as the mouse, *graphical user interface* (GUI), and networking protocols during the '70s and '80s. There are many famous stories about how Xerox's mouse and GUI became the heart and soul of the Apple Macintosh and ultimately the Microsoft Windows environment. While beyond the scope of this text, just about any good book about Apple Computer, Steve Jobs, or the computer industry in the mid-1980s should tell the tales well enough and provide useful background into why many things are the way they are today. If you are into used books and books written before the industry decided we needed to be taken so seriously, two of my favorites are *Steve Jobs: The Journey Is the Reward,* by Jeffrey S. Young (Scott Foresman and Company, 1988), and *Odyssey : Pepsi to Apple . . . a Journey of Adventure, Ideas, and the Future,* by John Scully and John A. Byrne (Diane Publishing). According to both of these sources, John Scully is the man who fired Steve Jobs from Apple.

Another protocol that you may come across when reading about TCP/IP and IPX/SPX is *Xerox Network Systems* (XNS), originally designed by PARC. Many early PC networking companies, such as 3Com, Banyan, Novell, and even Microsoft in its NWLink, used variations of XNS as their primary transport protocol.

Other research centers, such as AT&T's Bell Laboratories (now a part of Lucent Technologies) and IBM's research departments, have contributed significantly to the industry, but none probably so selflessly or colorfully as PARC.

Ethernet Signaling in 10 Mbps Ethernet

Ethernet is considered a *contention* system, because more than one host can be contending for access to transmit. No single node has transmission priority over any other. Ethernet uses the *Carrier Sense Multiple Access/Collision Detection* (CSMA/CD) protocol to determine how multiple hosts can have simultaneous access to the network media. CSMA/CD is one of those acronyms it would be wise to know and understand at least fundamentally. The easiest way to learn it is to break it up into three parts:

- **Carrier Sense**   Listen to the carrier or listen to the media for a carrier wave—when no signal is detected, any node can transmit.

- **Multiple Access** More than one host can be waiting to transmit.

- **Collision Detection** How do we know when a collision occurs and what do we do? Built into every Ethernet NIC is a collision-detection circuit that registers as a collision any voltage other than that specified for zero and one.

When a collision is detected, the transmitting nodes send out a long burst of binary ones (up to 48 bytes), called a *jam signal*, that notifies all nodes that a collision has occurred and to stop transmitting or receiving. Each transmitting node generates a random retransmission time that represents a "wait" interval. When the first unit reaches the wait interval, it starts to transmit. As the other units reach their wait interval, they must still listen to the media before transmitting. This should prevent back-to-back collisions.

Collisions

The word "collision" has a particularly negative connotation that overstates the severity of what has really happened. In Ethernet, a collision is a normal process, the result of two hosts transmitting at the same time. While an increasing number of collisions may reduce transmission efficiency, it is not like two produce carts colliding—nothing is lost and nothing is going to spoil. The Ethernet protocol is very efficient and can resolve collisions in microseconds (millionths of a second). If necessary, it can even change its backoff process if repeated retransmission collisions occur. In fact, data is not discarded unless 16 retransmission attempts fail.

10 Mbps, 100 Mbps, and 1 Gbps Ethernet

The 10 Mbps Ethernet protocol is a half-duplex, shared-media protocol designed for coaxial cable that relies on transmitting to all hosts and then trusting the destination host NICs to capture only frames addressed to them. Every host hears every frame. Half-duplex transmission refers to the fact that data frames can only travel in one direction at a time. This concept continued into 10BaseT, where twisted-pair copper is distributed by hubs, which are still shared-media devices.

Fast Ethernet (100 Mbps) or Gigabit Ethernet (1000 Mbps) require switches to eliminate collisions. We will discuss this technology in the next chapter. In these faster versions of Ethernet, CSMA/CD is disabled and full-duplex transmission is allowed because collisions have been virtually eliminated. This significantly increases throughput. Many devices are autosensing devices, which means if the entire circuit can support 100 Mbps, the interface will use the 100 Mbps, but otherwise it drops back to standard 10 Mbps Ethernet.

Ethernet Addressing

Ethernet uses *media access control* (MAC) addresses, which are defined by the IEEE standard, or Layer 2 of the OSI model. By definition, MAC addresses are 48 bits long, usually represented in hexadecimal, consisting of 24 bits identifying the manufacturer and 24 bits assigned by the manufacturer as a unique identifier. Therefore, no two nodes can have the same MAC address. If somehow it did happen, any network communication involving the two devices would be unreliable.

The MAC addresses are permanently imprinted in the circuitry of Ethernet devices, such as NICs, router Ethernet interfaces, and modems. Conceptually, MAC addresses are like social security numbers, because they are unique but are not hierarchical—the address can occur anywhere in the network. The MAC address is often referred to as the physical address of the device, as compared to the network or logical address, which we will discuss in Chapter 5.

To See Your MAC Address

To see your computer's MAC address, do one of the following:

For Windows NT/2000:

1. Open a Command window (Start | Programs | Accessories | Command Prompt).
2. Type ipconfig /all.
3. Press ENTER.
4. Look for the Physical Address. It will look similar to this: 00-10-5A-1E-86-40. Figure 3-16 shows what the result in Windows 2000 will look like.

For Windows 95/98 :

1. Use Start | Run from the taskbar.
2. Type **winipcfg** in the Open box.
3. Press ENTER.
4. Look for the Adapter Address. It will look similar to this: 00-00-86-54-9B-A6. Figure 3-17 shows what the result in Windows 98 will look like.

We will look at the other information displayed in these figures when we talk about IP addresses.

Ethernet Frames

There have been two Ethernet data frames: the original 802.3 frame specification, and the newer Ethernet II, modified slightly for the Internet and the world's evolving

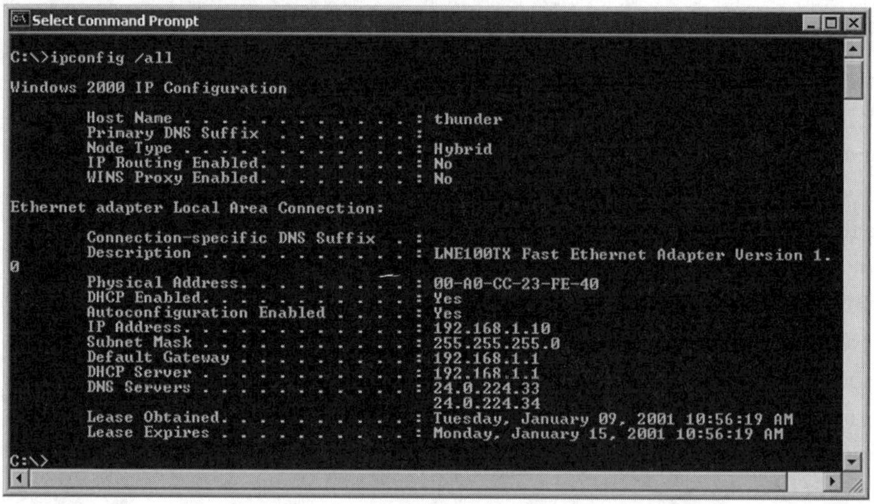

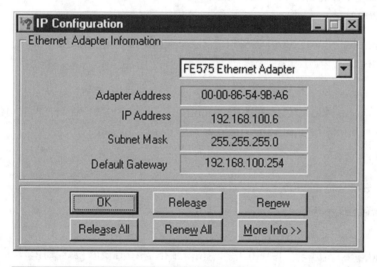

Figure 3-16   Windows 2000 ipconfig results

Figure 3-17   Windows 98 winipcfg results

reliance on TCP/IP as a network-addressing standard. A network should generally not have both types of frames at the same time. A NIC set up for one data frame will not be able to see the other one. Updating an older NIC's driver from the manufacturer's Web site will generally resolve this problem. There are two non-compatible versions of

Preamble 8 bytes	Destination 6 bytes	Source 6 bytes	Type 2 bytes	Data 46-1,500 bytes	FCS 4 bytes

Figure 3-18   Ethernet frame

Novel's IPX/SPX protocol that require special framing and configuration on routers, we will discuss these in Chapter 14.

The Ethernet data frame is a pretty simple design containing only six segments. Recall from Chapter 1's discussion of encapsulation that this frame is the final result of data progressing down through the OSI model processes. The packet created at the network layer is actually in the data segment in this final frame. Figure 3-18 represents an Ethernet II frame.

The Ethernet segments are as follows:

- **Preamble**   Field used for synchronization; 8 bytes. This unique pattern of bits identifies the beginning of an Ethernet data frame. While we refer to frames and packets, the network sees endless streams of 1's and 0's. This preamble allows the Ethernet interfaces to synchronize so that they know which bits are addressing, data, and so on. The preamble consists of alternating 1's and 0's but ends with two 1's. The idea is that the NIC will recognize the pattern, but if a few bits, or even bytes, have slipped by, it won't matter—the key is to be synchronized by the end of the preamble.

- **Destination**   Ethernet (MAC) address of the destination host; 6 bytes. The OSI network layer supplies this address when the packet is sent down for transmission. This segment could also contain a 48-bit broadcast address such as FF-FF-FF-FF-FF-FF.

- **Source**   Ethernet (MAC) address of the source host; 6 bytes. This address is furnished from the Ethernet interface (NIC) circuitry.

- **Type (or Length/Type segment)**   The type of data encapsulated in the Data segment; 2 bytes. While the data could be the output of some application, it can also be packets used by higher-level protocols such as IP, ARP, DHCP, RARP, and so on. A numerical value up to 1,518 in this segment indicates the length of data contained in bytes; for example, 512 would mean the data is 512 bytes long. If the value is greater than 1,535, it is a code indicating the type of higher-level protocol packet that is being transported.

- **Data**   Data storage area; 46 to 1,500 bytes. The 46-byte minimum is necessary to make sure that every node hears the signal within specified time limits. If for some reason the data generated is less than 46 bytes, padding will be added.

- **FCS**   The Frame Control Sequence contains the *Cyclical Redundancy Check* (CRC), 4 bytes used for error detection. This CRC, or checksum, is generated by the data link layer on the sending host and is confirmed by the same layer of the receiving host. Any discrepancy will indicate the packet has been corrupted.

We will look at the Layer 2 aspects of Ethernet in more detail in the next chapter.

Token Ring

Token Ring is an access method, or protocol, originally developed by IBM in the 1970s to connect its mainframes and minicomputers. This was a decade before the idea of LANs for personal computers was evolving. Token Ring uses a ring topology where data is passed in one direction only.

One of the hosts is designated as the *active monitor*. The active monitor's responsibility is to place a special frame (packet) on the media that has a bit pattern in its header that designates it as a token. The token passes from node to node until one host wants to transmit data. That node waits for the token and, instead of forwarding it, adds a fully loaded data frame to the token, addresses the frame to the destination node, and changes the token bits to indicate it is now a data packet. The frame then moves on to the next node.

Assuming that the next node is not the destination, this node captures the frame, recognizing that it is not addressed for it, rebuilds the frame, and retransmits it along the path to the next node. This continues until the frame arrives at the destination node. At this point, the host copies the data, sets the token bits to indicate the frame has been "received and copied," and then rebuilds the frame and places it back on the wire.

The frame continues like this until it returns to the sending host. At that point, after checking the token bits to see if it has been received and copied, the sending host removes the data, sets the token bits back to indicate it is again a token, and releases it back onto the wire. Another host can now use it. Or, when the frame returns, the original host can send more data. One analogy for a Token Ring network is a city with a single taxi driving a defined route with its "Available" light on until it picks up a fare, at which point it is no longer available until the fare is discharged.

IEEE 802.5 Standard

The IBM Token Ring technology became the basis for IEEE's 802.5 standard, which was a 4 Mbps single-token definition. Later, the standard was increased to 16 Mbps and two tokens. Since they travel at the same speed in the same direction, collisions are not a concern.

Each NIC for a Token Ring network rebuilds every frame and therefore is a repeater. This has several implications. The cards are more complex with more circuitry. This combined with a tiny market share means that large-scale manufacturing is not achieved, so they tend to be very expensive relative to their Ethernet counterparts. Second, each node adds latency or delays the packets, and since a frame may need to pass through many NICs to get to the destination, the networks are relatively slow at either 4 or 16 Mbps.

Priority System

Unlike Ethernet networks, in which every host has an equal opportunity to transmit, Token Ring networks implement a priority system that allows user-designated, higher-priority hosts to access the network more frequently. This priority system is implemented using two fields on the Token Ring frames, the *priority* and *reservation* fields.

Only a host with a priority rating equal to or higher than that contained in a token can capture the token. After the token has been captured and converted to a data frame, only hosts with a higher priority rating can reserve the token for the next network pass. After the data frame has completed its round, the token generated will contain the priority of the reserving host.

Ring Management

Token Ring networks use various processes for dealing with ring problems. Any host on the network can be designated as the active monitor. Its jobs will include generating new tokens as needed. It can watch for frames that are circling the ring continuously because the sending host has dropped from the network, thereby preventing other hosts from transmitting. Once detected, the active monitor removes the frame from the ring and generates a new token.

As we discussed in the last chapter, the IEEE 802.5 standard allows for a multistation access unit (MSAU) to work somewhat as a hub and allow the use of twisted-pair wiring in a star-like physical topology. Keep in mind that the actual circuitry is very different. Whereas a hub is a concentrator for a shared media, much like a very short bus, an MSAU maintains the loop circuitry so that the data travels sequentially past each node. The resulting star topology also contributes to the overall network reliability, since the MSAU can see all data and connection links on the network. The MSAU can monitor for problems and partition hosts from the ring, if necessary, using small electronic gates at the interfaces where the wires head out to a host. If the link fails for any reason, the gate closes, effectively partitioning off that host and maintaining the logical ring intact.

Linking MAUs

MAUs have a ring-in port and a ring-out port, which can be used to link together multiple MAUs by connecting the ring-out port on one device to the ring-in port on another device until a closed loop is created. Figure 3-19 represents a Token Ring network.

Figure 3-20 represents a Token Ring data frame, a Token Ring token frame, and the simpler Ethernet frame. Aside from the obvious additional segments in the Token Ring data frame, another difference is that the Token Ring data payload can be up to three times larger than that of an Ethernet network. This means that we have several problems when we try to mix Token Ring with Ethernet segments on a network. A device such as a router or bridge will be needed to connect Ethernet network segments to a

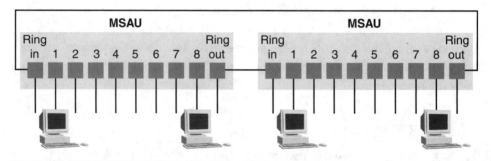

Figure 3-19 Token Ring network

Token ring data / Command frame

SD	AC	FC	DA	SA	Data	FCS	ED	ES
1 byte	1 byte	1 byte	6 bytes	6 bytes		4 bytes	1 byte	1 byte

Token frame

SD	AC	ED
1 byte	1 byte	1 byte

Ethernet frame

Preamble	Destination	Source	Type	Data	FCS
8 bytes	6 bytes	6 bytes	2 bytes	46-1,500 bytes	4 bytes

Figure 3-20 Token Ring frames vs. an Ethernet frame

Token Ring segment. The router or bridge will need to segment the larger Token Ring frame, sequence the new pieces to keep them in order, and build appropriate data frames to allow data to pass back and forth. We will discuss these devices in the next two chapters.

The following defines the segments of the Token Ring frame shown in Figure 3-20:

- **SD (Start Delimiter)**   Alerts the host that a frame or token is following (much like the preamble in Ethernet).

- **AC (Access Control)**   Contains the token bit that indicates the frame is a token rather than a data or command frame.

- **FC (Frame Control)**   Indicates whether the frame contains data or a command.

- **DA (Destination Address)**   MAC address of the destination host.

- **SA (Source Address)**   MAC address of the source host.

- **Data**   Contains upper-layer protocol information. Variable size.

- **FCS (Frame Control Sequence)**   Contains the CRC used for error detection. This CRC, or checksum, is generated by the data link layer on the sending host and is confirmed by the same layer of the receiving host. Any discrepancy will indicate the packet has been corrupted.

- **ED (End Delimiter)**   Indicates the end of the Token Ring token.

- **FS (Frame Status)**   Terminates data/command frame.

Unlike contention networks, such as Ethernet, Token Ring networks are *deterministic*, meaning you can calculate the maximum time until any particular node will be able to transmit. This predictability and the reliability of a collision-free environment make Token Ring networks perfect for some implementations. When comparing the maximum 10 Mbps Ethernet with the actual 4 Mbps of Token Ring, the speed difference may be minimal. But 100 Mbps Ethernet is just too much to pass up for many organizations, particularly when Fast Ethernet also overcomes the reliability and broadcast concerns.

FDDI

Fiber Distributed Data Interface is a dual-ring, 100 Mbps fiber technology standard developed by the *American National Standards Association* (ANSI) in the mid 1980s as a solution for connecting high-speed engineering workstations. Engineers needed a LAN solution that could support their workstations and applications but felt they had exceeded the capabilities of the existing Ethernet and Token Ring standards.

With the advent of 100 Mbps Ethernet and the promise of 1 Gbps Ethernet, FDDI LAN implementations are not as common as once predicted. FDDI is still used as LAN backbones and to connect high-speed mission-critical computers.

FDDI uses four specifications that translate approximately to the bottom one and a half layers in the OSI model.

- **Media Access Control (MAC)**   Defines how the medium is to be accessed.
- **Physical Layer Protocol (PHY)**   Defines data encoding/decoding signaling.
- **Physical Layer Media (PMD)**   Defines all properties of the transmission media.
- **Station Management (SMT)**   Defines the FDDI host configuration.

FDDI uses a token-passing strategy similar to that of Token Ring. Like Token Ring, FDDI moves a small frame, called a token, around the network. A token is a special frame (packet) that has a bit pattern in its header that designates it as a token. The token passes from node to node until one host wants to transmit data. That node waits for the token and, instead of forwarding it, adds a fully loaded data frame to the token, addresses the frame to the destination node, and changes the token bits to indicate it is now a data packet. The frame then moves on to the next node.

Assuming the next node is not the destination, this node captures the frame and, recognizing that it is not addressed for it, rebuilds the frame, and retransmits it along the path to the next node. This continues until the frame arrives at the destination node. At this point, the host copies the data, sets the token bits to indicate the frame has been "received and copied," and then rebuilds the frame and places it back on the wire.

If early token release is not supported, the token continues like this until it returns to the sending host. If early token release is supported, a new token can be released when the frame transmission has finished. At that point, after checking the token bits to see if the frame has been received and copied, the sending host removes the data, sets the token bits back to indicate it is again a token, and releases it back onto the wire. Another host can now use it. Or, when the frame returns, the original host can send more data.

The following are the strengths of FDDI networks:

- They are collision-free.
- They can carry a payload of up to 4,500 bytes, or three times that of Ethernet.
- They support real-time allocation of network bandwidth, making it ideal for a variety of different application types. FDDI provides this support by defining two types of serial traffic—synchronous and asynchronous.

- Unlike contention networks, such as Ethernet, Token Ring networks are deterministic, meaning that you can calculate the maximum time until any node will be able to transmit.

- They offer very high reliability because *dual-attached stations* (DASs), those that connect to both rings, can be used in case of a circuit interruption to reroute the circuit around themselves to join the two rings and maintain a single circuit. These DASs are also referred to as Class A stations, as compared to Class B stations, or *single-attached stations* (SASs), which are connected only to the primary ring and considered expendable. Figure 3-21 shows an FDDI ring resolving a link failure.

When a station detects a serious problem with the network (such as a cable break), it sends a special "beacon" frame that includes the station reporting the failure, its *nearest active upstream neighbor* (NAUN), and everything in between. Beaconing in turn initiates a process called autoreconfiguration, in which the nodes automatically perform diagnostics in an attempt to reconfigure the network around the failed areas. All nodes except A and B in Figure 3-21 would hear traffic on both rings. The A and B nodes would be able to determine that the disruption is between them, since they could only hear traffic coming from the other direction. Node B would then connect the two rings on its interface card, effectively cutting off A. Node A would do the same thing. Now,

Figure 3-21
FDDI ring with
link failure

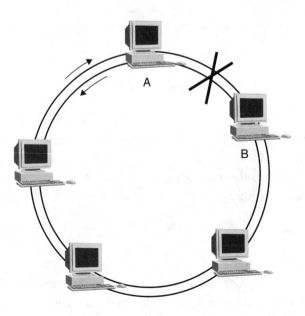

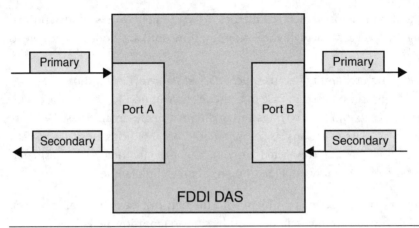

Figure 3-22 FDDI DAS port adapter

the outer and inner rings combine to create one rather long C-shaped loop or ring. Figure 3-22 represents an FDDI DAS port adapter with primary and secondary interfaces.

The data frame for FDDI is very similar to the data frame for Token Ring except that it uses a preamble to synchronize communications. I have not included it here, to avoid giving it too much importance. If you understand Token Ring and recognize that FFDI is a 100 Mbps reliable ring using multiple tokens, you can see why it was thought to be the future by many people, at least until Fast Ethernet hit the market. Today, FDDI is used on many campus networks to link buildings together. The ability to have 2,000 meters between nodes makes it very attractive for this type of application.

Broadcasts and Collisions

"Broadcast" and "collision" are two words that are often charged with a negative connotation that a little background information might help to alleviate. Both are natural occurrences in networks, particularly in 10 Mbps Ethernet. Clearly, an abundance of either broadcasts or collisions would impact the network's performance, but like salt or sugar in our diets, neither is inherently evil or destructive.

Broadcasts

As we progress through the chapters, we will see that many networking processes rely on broadcasts to perform their function, or at least to get started. We will see that a computer just being turned on and needing an IP address will have no choice but to perform a MAC layer broadcast in an effort to find a DHCP server. A similar process occurs when a host needs to resolve an IP address to a MAC address. There are many more examples.

The point is that a little bit of broadcast traffic per host is normal. But, as the number of hosts on a network segment increases, the total amount of broadcast traffic can get to be detrimental to the overall network performance. In the remainder of this book, we will look at several methods for managing the amount of broadcast traffic impacting the network as a whole.

You should understand a few things about packets and broadcast traffic. For purposes of this discussion, assume that the network is a 10 Mbps Ethernet shared-media network. If a host sends out a packet addressed to another host, that packet totally consumes the media until it has propagated throughout the network. No other host can transmit until that packet is off the network. Fortunately, this time is measured in microseconds. If the same host sends the same data as a broadcast, the result, as far as how long the network will be tied up, is exactly the same. So, why does it matter whether or not it is a broadcast?

With a unicast (to one address) and a multicast (to several addresses), the propagation time is the same as for a broadcast. While all hosts will have to read the destination address, only the host(s) associated with the destination address will copy the packet and process it any further. But in the case of a broadcast, every host will have to copy the packet and process it at least enough to recognize that it cannot do anything with it.

Think of a broadcast as being much like the junk mail you receive at home, to make it more like a broadcast assume that you have to open each piece of junk mail and read enough of the contents to determine that it is not intended for you or that you cannot use the data. A broadcast packet for a DHCP server must be accepted and quality-control checks must be performed at the data link layer of every host. The data link layer will then prepare and forward the packet up to the upper layers, which will discard it, assuming the host is not a DHCP server. Resources are consumed with no possibility of successful communications.

Furthermore, we will see in the next chapter that Layer 2 devices, such as bridges and switches, can selectively forward unicast or multicast frames based on the destination address. Unfortunately, a broadcast is in fact addressed to everybody on the network, so even bridges and switches cannot help in this area.

So, managing broadcasts and *broadcast domains*, the portion of a network covered by any broadcasts, will be important in our efforts to increase the network's efficiency. This will be particularly important in busy networks. A new smaller network with limited activity might not be impacted by broadcast traffic, but if you double or triple the number of users, or add applications that generate lots of broadcasts, broadcast traffic becomes a serious concern.

Too much broadcast activity can appear as slower response times to users or as applications that "time out" because they cannot connect or complete a process within a specified amount of time. A PC might appear "sluggish" on a network with excessive broadcasts because the PC's CPU is being interrupted to deal with network activity.

Broadcast Storms

In an Ethernet network, a malfunctioning NIC can generate unnecessary traffic and broadcasts. If ignored, this could literally bring down the entire network because, with the media being dominated by the out-of-control NIC, real traffic cannot gain access to the media. The good news is that, over the years, hub and switch technology has evolved that can literally monitor individual ports for this type of activity and partition, or shut down, the culprit. Even a simple $30 hub I bought recently has this capability. The hub will also check back on the partitioned port every 90 seconds to see if things are back under control. This means that a technician could replace the bad NIC and, within a minute or so, the host would be back online.

Collisions

You saw earlier that collisions in a 10 Mbps Ethernet network are a normal process, that these collisions are typically cleared in microseconds, and that in fact no data is lost—only delayed. Other technologies, such as 100 Mbps and 1 Gbps Ethernet as well as Token Ring, have gone to considerable lengths to try to reduce or eliminate collisions from the network.

The important thing to recognize is that some number of collisions will still be expected, possibly as systems first come up or when processes fail. Collisions may become indicators of growing congestion or component failures, but they are not themselves generally destructive to data and never harmful to components. Typically, a packet is quickly retransmitted and life goes on.

A *collision domain* is that area of a network that defines the hosts whose transmissions could collide if they were to transmit at the same time. In the original Ethernet network, the entire network was a collision domain. Today it could be as little as the segment between a switch port and its attached host, thereby virtually eliminating collisions.

Summary

In this chapter, we looked at the shape, or topology, of the network and how the topology impacts the scalability of the network. We looked at access methods, Ethernet, Token Ring, and FDDI and their interrelationship with topology.

We looked at the three-layer hierarchical network model and how it increases the scalability of the network. The three layers are access, distribution, and core. The access layer represents the point that the users connect to the network. The distribution layer, depending on the network design, could be those links to departments in a building or between buildings in a campus network. The core layer refers to site-to-site communications links, typically using WAN technologies.

Each layer, and therefore each device in that layer, has a purpose and function. The better the integrity of these layers and functions are maintained, the more scalable the network. The following are the five key requirements of a scalable network:

- Reliability and availability

- Responsiveness

- Efficiency

- Adaptability

- Accessibility and security

We compared Ethernet (CSMA/CD) and Token Ring methodologies for LAN access.

Practice Questions

Take a few moments and check your grasp of the concepts covered in this chapter. The answers are immediately following the questions.

Questions

1. The topology of a network can refer to which of the following?
   a. Physical design only
   b. Logical design only
   c. The metaphysical design only
   d. Physical and logical designs of the network
   e. None of the above

2. Coaxial networks use which topology?
   a. Dual ring
   b. Single ring
   c. Bus
   d. Star

3. Which of the following topologies can use hubs as concentrators?
   a. Dual ring
   b. Single ring
   c. Bus
   d. Star

4. Which two characteristics apply to a fully meshed network?
   a. Easy to configure
   b. Very reliable
   c. Doesn't scale very well
   d. Prone to failures

5. Which three of these are layers in the hierarchical network model?
   a. Distribution
   b. Network
   c. Access
   d. Transport
   e. Core

6. What are the five key requirements of a scalable network?
   a.
   b.
   c.
   d.
   e.

7. What are the two most common LAN access methods?
   a. TCP/IP
   b. IPX/SPX
   c. Ethernet
   d. Token Ring

8. What does the acronym CSMA/CD stand for?

9. What command do you issue in the command (MS DOS) window of a Windows NT or 2000 computer to see the MAC address?
   a. winipcfg
   b. ipconfig /all
   c. winipconfig
   d. ipconfig

10. The area that includes any hosts that will create a collision if they transmit simultaneously is called?
    a. LAN
    b. Broadcast domain
    c. Broadcast storm
    d. Collision domain

Answers

1. **d.** Topology can refer to both the physical and logical designs of the network.

2. **c.** Coaxial networks use a bus topology.

3. **d.** Any of the star topologies can use hubs.

4. **b.** and **c.** While very reliable, it does not scale well due to the number of connections.

5. **a., c.,** and **e.** The distribution, access, and core layers are in the hierarchical network model.

6. The answers in any order are:
   Reliability and availability
   Responsiveness
   Efficiency
   Adaptability
   Accessibility and security

7. **c.** and **d.** Ethernet and Token Ring are the two most common LAN access methods.

8. Carrier Sense Multiple Access/Collision Detection

9. **b.** ipconfig /all. Without the /all portion, you get only the IP info. winipcfg is a Win 95/98 command only.

10. **d.** A collision domain is the area that includes any hosts that will create a collision if they transmit simultaneously.

CHAPTER 4

OSI Model–Layer 2

This chapter will:

- **Look at Layer 2 processes and protocols**
- **Compare data link layer sublayers MAC and LLC**
- **Discuss Layer 2 devices NIC, bridges, and LAN switches**
- **Introduce switching methods**
- **Compare symmetrical and asymmetrical switching**

In the last chapter, we looked at topologies and access methods, because of their close relationship to the physical layer (Layer 1) as well as to the data link layer (Layer 2). In this chapter, we will look at processes and technologies of Layer 2. When the distinction between Layers 1 and 2 seems a little fuzzy, it can't hurt to keep in mind that some other protocols and organizations tend to see Layers 1 and 2 as a single process.

Data Link Layer: Layer 2

The data link layer—Layer 2—of the OSI reference model provides reliable transit of data across a physical link, physical addressing, network topology, line discipline, error notification, ordered delivery of frames, and flow control. The IEEE standard has divided this layer into two sublayers: the media access control (MAC) and the logical link control (LLC). Figure 4-1 shows the OSI model with IEEE sublayers in Layer 2.

We saw earlier that Layer 1 includes the communications media and the signals, or bit streams that travel on that media. It also includes those devices that put signals on media and those that connect the receiving host to the media. Their function is like that of UPS or FedEx to many businesses: they deliver the organizations' "stuff," but they cannot do it alone. Layer 2 can provide at least the basic missing pieces.

Layer 1 is great at transmitting bits through the appropriate media, but it cannot decide which host will transmit from a group of hosts waiting to send their data. Layer 2's MAC protocols know how to manage this and what to do in case two transmissions inadvertently collide.

Furthermore, the MAC protocols provide the necessary addressing to identify every node on the network so that Layer 1 can actually deliver its cargo to the desired destination. Regardless of the layer in the OSI model, the network's actual signal or data is always made up of streams of 0's and 1's. Layer 1 has no ability to interpret or use these 0's and 1's; it can only pass the signal on. In the case of a Layer 1 device, such as a repeater or hub, it can only rebuild the patterns of 0's and 1's and retransmit them.

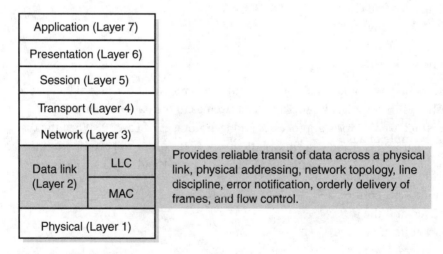

Figure 4-1   OSI model Layer 2 sublayers

A Layer 1 device cannot determine that the destination host has already received the packet, and any additional retransmission just wastes bandwidth. Layer 2 defines a framing template or mask that allows Layer 2 devices to synchronize and interpret the binary bits.

Layer 1 has no ability to communicate with its peers, let alone the upper layers of the network model. The LLC sublayer protocols allow information to be communicated between Layer 1 and the upper layers.

We will see that the MAC sublayer protocols tend to manage activities and processes relative to the physical layer, or layer 1, while the LLC sublayer protocols deal with the upper layers, particularly the network layer, Layer 3.

Network Interface Card

 NOTE: The NIC is generally considered a Layer 2 device and will be discussed later in the chapter, in the sections "NICs, Modems, and Network Devices" and "Network Interface Card." It is included here as well because it is so closely linked to Layer 2 processes, particularly the MAC sublayer processes.

The data link layer, and particularly the MAC feature set, is somewhat unique in the OSI model. All higher layers in the OSI reference model are theoretical, meaning that you have to grasp them conceptually without being able to open the computer and put your finger on a component and say this is it, this is the transport layer. Not so with the data link layer; the NIC or network adapter together with any drivers contain the data link layer. The card you choose and configure for your computer determines whether it is Ethernet, Token Ring, or FDDI. It also determines whether the media will be copper, fiber-optic, or something else. Even if you pick an Ethernet card with an RJ-45 adapter for copper twisted-pair, the specific model of that card will determine whether this link will be 10 Mbps, 100 Mbps, or maybe autosensing so that the card will decide after testing the connection. It will also determine whether this link can support full-duplex transmission. The card you choose and install will make that much difference. Figure 4-2 shows an example of a NIC for 10/100 Mbps Ethernet over copper.

A close scrutiny of the card will reveal chips and wires that run to the interface on the end. The chip set determines the interface itself-a chip set for copper means we will have an appropriate connector, such as an RJ-45. As discussed in Chapter 1, the transmitter, receiver, and the interface are actually a part of Layer 1, not Layer 2. But if you follow the circuits, they connect to other chip sets that must be providing Layer 2 features and services. The point is that those chips and circuits will be doing what we discuss in this section.

Figure 4-2   Ethernet NIC

Since the early 1990s, most NICs have the transceivers and interface connector built right into the card. It is cheaper and probably more reliable than when the transceiver was connected to the outside of the computer. It does rather blur our Layer 1/Layer 2 boundary. To go a step further, many computer manufactures no longer need separate NICs but instead add chip sets to the computer's motherboard and an RJ-45 connector to the case. This is one of the clear advantages of Ethernet over copper's tremendous market share.

Between these NIC chips, circuits, and device driver sets, the Ethernet or Token Ring technologies are installed and configured for your machine. Any computer can convert from being a client on an Ethernet or Token Ring network to a client on the other type by removing the card and installing the appropriate card and drivers. After attaching to and gaining access to an appropriate network, any new data frames will be of the right type and size. More importantly, neither the computer nor the user should have to change how they do business. It should be invisible to both.

Drivers

Drivers are software programs that supply feature sets to the computer when working with a particular device. There are drivers for just about any hardware component that can be added to a computer, including the mouse, video card, monitor, printer, and NIC. While most operating systems have the basic coding to work with many generic devices, they need driver files for the device to be able to take full advantage of the hardware's features.

In many cases, the user may not even be aware that a driver is being installed. The operating system detects the new item and retrieves an appropriate driver from a library of common devices that was installed on the computer. On the other hand, any time a very new technology or new model of a product is installed, the user may be asked to insert a disk or CD from which the computer will extract the drivers. It is possible that the user may be required to make a choice or two about features or local conditions, such as the default paper size for printers.

So, if installing drivers is so automatic, why are we discussing it at all? Particularly with NICs, it is not uncommon to want to use the latest driver set to make sure that you are getting all the features available from a device. If a NIC is not functioning as promised, you may want to download and install a newer version of the driver from the manufacturer's Web site. In the past year, I have added significant enhancements to a printer and an ISDN router by loading new drivers for each. Other times, mistakes occur undetected until a product ships, and a new driver set can resolve the problem. NICs tend to fall into this latter category.

NOTE: Being able to locate, download, and install new drivers for any of the many devices you might use on your computer or network is absolutely critical to being a networker. If you haven't mastered the skill, consider searching the Web for your printer manufacturer and downloading the latest driver. The following exercise should get you started.

Exercise: Downloading Drivers

Before we get started, keep the following points in mind:

- Web sites change often and these exact steps will not necessarily work in the future.

- If you understand the underlying process, you will be able to navigate the worst of sites like a pro and get what you need.

In this exercise, we will look for drivers for a printer and a NIC. The purpose of this exercise is to make sure you understand the process of downloading drivers. I am picking two common models to increase the chances this exercise will be useful for several years. I have no way of knowing which printer or NIC you have, so please do not install these drivers.

If you have only a modem connection to the Internet, you might want to stop short of actually downloading the drivers. I will remind you in the lab. From there on, just read along the remaining steps. A 4MB printer file can take an hour to download over a slow (28 Kbps) modem connection.

We will start by creating a folder on the computer called Drivers. If you are doing this in a classroom or library where you do not have permission to add items to the hard drive, use a floppy disk. If you use a floppy disk, you will not have enough room to download the printer driver, but you should have plenty of room for the NIC driver.

1. Open Windows Explorer using Start | Programs | Windows Explorer or Start | Programs | Accessories | Windows Explorer. It might be NT Explorer if you are using Windows NT.

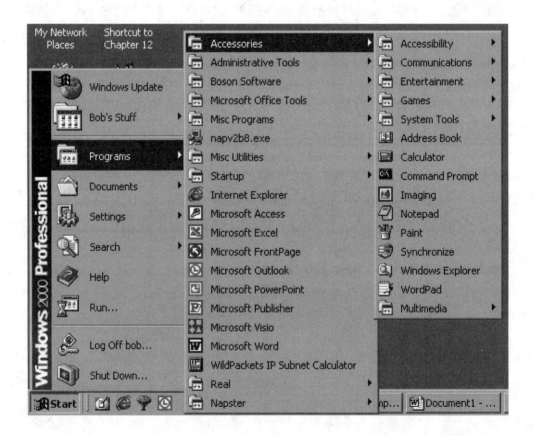

2. Select the C drive by clicking once on the Local Disk (C:) icon, or if you are using a floppy disk, insert the disk, and select the 3 1/2 Floppy (A:) icon.

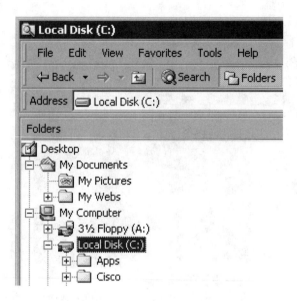

3. Choose File | New | Folder from the menu. Type **Drivers** to name the new folder. Minimize Windows Explorer using the leftmost of the three small buttons in the upper-right corner of the Explorer window; we won't need it for a while.

4. Open Internet Explorer or your browser.

5. In the Address box at the top of the screen, type **www.hp.com** and press ENTER. Although Hewlett-Packard's opening page will change over time, this illustration should be representative.

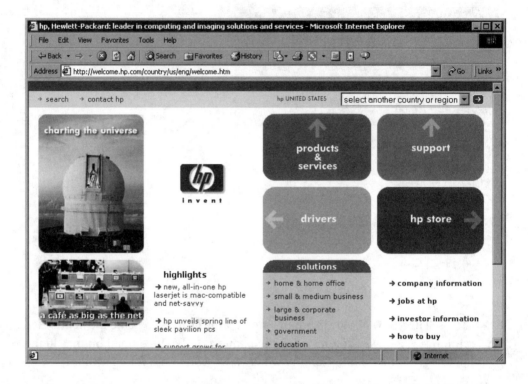

6. Scan the screen looking for the word "Support." In our example, it is the large blue rectangle in the upper-right corner. Click it to move to the next screen.

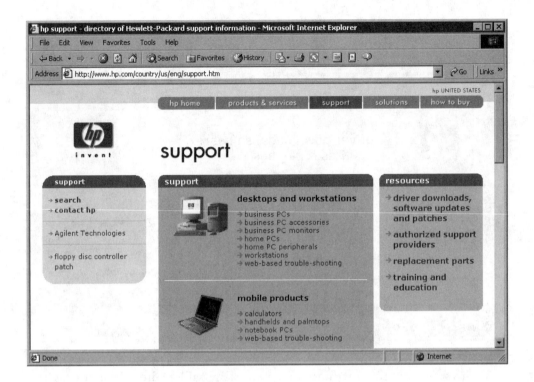

7. Typically, we are looking for a link labeled "Drivers" or "Driver Downloads." The latter is again in the upper-right corner. Click it to move to the product selection page.

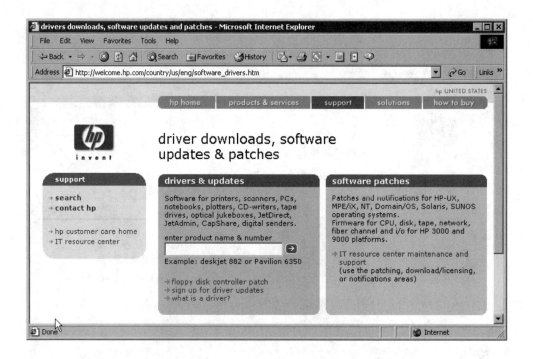

8. This screen varies from vendor to vendor. Many will use drop-down lists or have you pick a product family, like printers, and then have you choose from a list. If the screen looks at all like the preceding screen, type **Desk Jet 890C** and press ENTER.

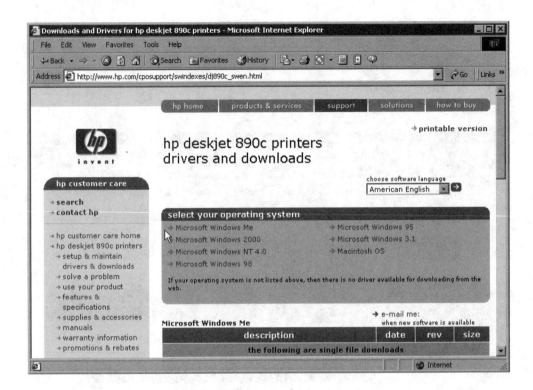

9. This is a pretty typical page to end up on. At this point, you pick your operating system. Remember, the whole purpose of a driver is to provide the necessary software so that your operating system can take advantage of the device's features. In my case, I selected Microsoft Windows Me (Windows 98 upgrade); the box is telling me that the file is 4.4MB, which will take hours to download at modem speeds.

NOTE: HP has added a link that will allow us to receive e-mail notification of further updates. If this is an important device to the organization or one of your standard devices used in many places, you definitely should use the service.

10. If you have a slow Internet connection, stop at this point; otherwise, click the link in the box to start the download.

11. The next screen typically has you verify your selection choices, displays the actual file name, displays any pertinent installation instructions, and offers a Download Now button.

12. Click Download Now.

13. Internet Explorer brings up a File Download screen that allows you to "run the program" or save the download file to a disk. With a driver, always save it to a disk, because you never know when you may need it again. Furthermore, when I download for an installation project, I often get drivers for several devices, so I prefer to do all of my downloading followed by my installation. It is particularly important if one of your updates knocks down your Internet connection—even temporarily.

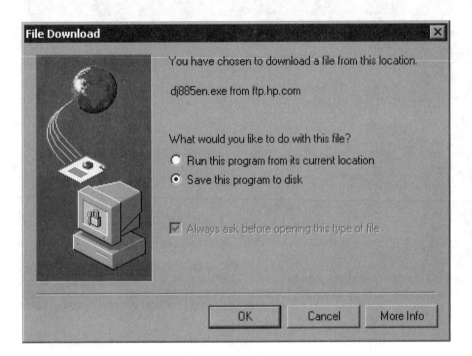

14. Make sure that your Drivers folder is displayed in the Save In box at the top of the Save As dialog box. In the following example, you would need to double-click the Drivers folder to move it up to the Save In box. If you are using the floppy disk, you need to use the drop-down arrow at the right end of the Save In box to select the 3 1/2 Floppy (A:) drive. When you are done selecting the location, click the Save button.

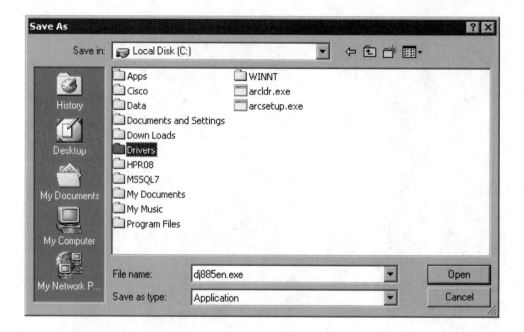

15. The next window tracks the progress of your download. On my ISDN service, which is 128 Kb, it takes about five to six minutes to download this driver.

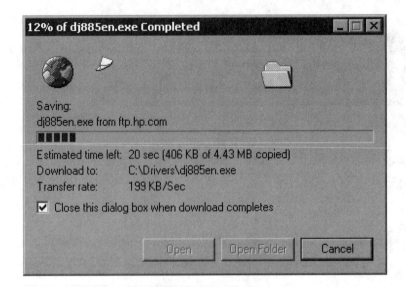

16. Open Windows Explorer again from the task bar. Select the Drivers folder on the left side of the Explorer window. The new driver installation file will appear in the right side of the Explorer window.

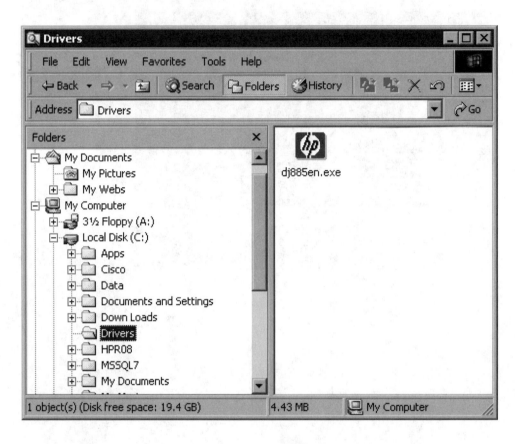

17. This file is typically a "zipped" file, and double-clicking it will expand it to create the actual driver and set up files that you need. We won't do that at this time—although it shouldn't hurt anything if you do. The worst that could happen is that your computer will think it has a new printer.

NOTE: You may need to go to www.winzip.com to get the latest copy of WinZip to be able to open the file. This wouldn't be a bad idea if you do not already have WinZip on your machine.

Use these skills to go to 3Com's site, www.3com.com, and download the latest NIC driver for the 3C590 NIC. Save the downloaded file in your Drivers folder. The file is about 756KB in size and should download in a few minutes on a modem connection. Figure 4-3 shows a product selection screen that is pretty common to help you find the right drivers.

Media Access Control

Media access control is usually represented as the lower of the two sublayers defined by the IEEE for the data link layer. This positioning is theoretical but generally makes sense, because the MAC sublayer functions provide Layer 1 services to handle access to communications media, a device address, and access method, such as whether to use token passing or Ethernet. In this section, we will look at these functions.

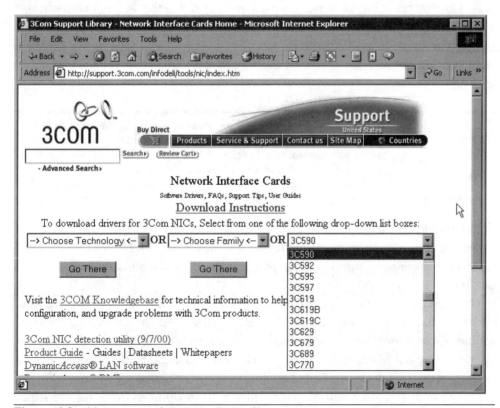

Figure 4-3   New printer driver installation file

MAC Addresses

Without physical addresses, we would have a number of "nameless" computers and devices on our LAN oblivious to the fact that a message system is available to them. Imagine if you took a trip to Africa or Europe without leaving any itinerary. How would your family reach you in case of an emergency? The most detailed and wonderful message is useless if it cannot be addressed to a destination.

MAC addresses are standards-defined 48-bit physical addresses that are required for every port or interface on any device that connects to a LAN that will be a source or destination for data. Other devices on the network use these addresses to locate specific interfaces in the network. They then use this information to create and maintain bridging or switching tables that can be used for forwarding data efficiently. MAC addresses are often called hardware addresses, MAC-layer addresses, Layer 2 addresses, burned-in addresses, or physical addresses (referring to a physical chip on the NIC, not to the physical layer).

Do not confuse MAC addresses with logical or network addresses, which are Layer 3 addresses. Whereas MAC addresses typically are assigned at the time of manufacturing and generally are changed only by replacing the interface, network addresses can be assigned by administrators or even by other devices, such as a DHCP server. With services like DHCP, the network address could technically change for a particular device on a regular basis.

 NOTE: Many Windows drivers make it possible to change the MAC address of a NIC. This is called spoofing and may be done to conceal the actual address from which a packet was actually sent. Spoofing is often used to skirt network security processes, such as filters and access lists. Cisco routers let you change interface MAC addresses using the "mac-address" interface configuration command.

Devices like repeaters, hubs, and bridges do not typically have MAC addresses associated with their interfaces, because they are *passthrough* devices. No frame is ever destined for or originates from these devices; it passes through them on its way to its destination.

One possible exception that might result in a pass-through device having a MAC address is that some of these network devices can be remotely monitored from a workstation. Those devices have management circuitry included and a MAC address so that the device can be "talked to." Without the circuitry and the MAC address, the requests for information would be forwarded on through with the rest of the 0's and 1's. In this case, the MAC address has nothing to do with the device doing its job; it has everything to do with that device's ability to report to management.

NICs, Modems, and Network Devices

We normally associate MAC addresses with a NIC. The address is in fact the NIC's address and would follow the NIC if it were moved to another computer. But, since any interface needing to be the source or destination for data frames must have a unique address, this really applies as well to routers with LAN interfaces, network printers with built-in interfaces, and any device that can be remotely administered on a LAN.

Ethernet and Token Ring MAC addresses are 48 bits long and typically expressed as 12 hexadecimal digits. The first 24 bits (6 hexadecimal digits) identify the manufacturer or vendor and are called the *Organizational Unique Identifier* (OUI). These OUIs are assigned and administered by the IEEE. The last 24 bits (6 hexadecimal digits) create the equivalent of the interface's serial number and are assigned and administered by the vendor. There are two formats for MAC addresses: 00-00-0c-12-34-56 or 0000.0c12.3456. We will learn to convert hexadecimal to decimal in Chapter 9, when we deal with binary conversions and IP addressing.

MAC addresses are "burned" into *read-only memory* (ROM) and are copied into the *random-access memory* (RAM) of the device when it initializes. It is important that these addresses are not easily modifiable by the end user; they represent the equivalent of a social security number (U.S.) and must be unique. No two devices can be on a network at the same time.

How NICs Use MAC Addresses

The MAC sublayer access method protocols determine how the NICs will use MAC addresses and which hosts will be able to transmit. For our example, assume the network is an 802.3 Ethernet access method LAN using half-duplex, hubs, and broadcast-like transmissions. All hosts will see all frames, and each host must examine every frame at least to check the destination address to determine whether they are the destination.

If a host wants to send data to another node, it can have its NIC create a frame with its own MAC address as the source and the MAC address of the intended recipient as the destination. As this data frame propagates through the network media, every NIC on the network checks to see if its MAC address matches the destination address. If there is no match, the frame is ignored or discarded. If a NIC's MAC address matches the destination address, the NIC makes a copy and forwards the frame to an upper-layer protocol.

In a *Token Ring network*, the packet would progress around the ring, being regenerated at every host, until a NIC MAC address and the destination address match. The frame would be regenerated and forwarded on toward the sender to confirm delivery and to release the frame back to the network.

We will see shortly that in a *switched Ethernet network*, switches would replace the hubs so that the data frame could be sent more directly to the destination without bothering the other hosts.

MAC Address Limitations

MAC addresses are critical to a well-run computer network, including the world's largest network, the Internet. MAC addresses provide an absolutely unique address for every host and device on the network. The good news is that, unlike IP addresses, there is no real shortage of MAC addresses. There are trillions of possible combinations.

The problem is that there is no hierarchy to MAC addresses. Knowing a machine's MAC address tells you nothing at all about its location in the network, or in the world for that matter. Knowing the MAC address is like knowing a person's social security number—unless you also have a home address, it won't help you find them. In the early days of LANs, when networks were small, a broadcast across the network would find the destination node.

As networks grew and broadcast traffic began to impact network performance, devices (routers) were placed in the networks that would not forward broadcasts. Performance improved, but if the destination MAC address was not on the same network segment as the source device, it was impossible for broadcasts to connect the two.

Another addressing system had to be developed that would indicate the network as well as the host name. Think of network addressing like the addressing on an envelope. The address allows the postal service to forward the item to the correct state. At that point, the item is sorted again using the "city" notation to get it routed to the correct city. Only once the envelope gets to the destination city is the street address finally checked to determine which mail carrier route to use. There is a hierarchy to the process. In fact, certain devices and services could specialize in delivering mail from city to city while others concentrate on local delivery.

Network layer addresses have a similar hierarchy to them with a network identifier and a separate node identifier. The network identifier is like the state and city on an envelope while the node identifier is like the street address. Just as the address "123 Main Street" has very little significance if you do not know which city it is in, network node identifiers are only relevant when you get to the correct network. Network addressing is covered in the next chapter.

Why Framing Is Necessary

Putting signals on any communications media representing 0's and 1's is in itself a major technological breakthrough. Unfortunately, without some method of synchronizing the sending and receiving devices, communications are difficult if not impossible. Think of the times you enter a room in the middle of a conversation or television show and are unable to pick up the intended message. Data framing provides the synchronization necessary to get the devices talking together.

From our discussion of digital data in earlier chapters, we know that our data is represented exclusively as patterns of 0's and 1's. With some limited technology, any device should be able to recognize the difference between them, and because there are no other options, communications should occur. If only it were that simple. If the sending and receiving devices are not synchronized right from the beginning of the communications, then it may be impossible to understand the message. If you have ever traveled to other parts of a country or to other nations that speak the same language, you may have noticed that you have trouble understanding conversations until your ear starts to recognize the cadence and inflection patterns of the region. If it takes too long to synchronize with the speaker, you may know that someone is in the hospital, but have no idea who since it was in the first part of the message. Data framing makes sure that the receiving device can synchronize with the message before important data is sent and then breaks the bits into recognizable patterns that can contain our valuable information. This framing gives us patterns that can be recognized as the following:

- Name (or address) of the source and destination devices
- A quality-control system (CRC) to test the reliability of the communication
- The length and/or type of the data payload
- Additional higher-level protocol communications between the two devices

Once an Ethernet NIC recognizes an extended pattern of 01 combinations (up to 62 bits) followed by two 1's, it knows the next 48 bits will be the destination MAC address. That will be followed immediately by a 48-bit source address. This is the Layer 2 data frame and is dependent upon the NIC and the associated access method-a Token Ring NIC would have a different pattern or framing. This difference in framing is what keeps different access methods, such as Ethernet and Token Ring, from residing on the same network segment.

This process is somewhat overwhelming when you try to think of it from a human perspective. Most of us wouldn't consider converting 208 bits, the size of an Ethernet frame without data, into bytes and then using the information to determine whether a piece of embedded data is intended for us. Ethernet interfaces do this tens of thousands of times per second for years at a time.

Data Frame Format

Figure 4-4 compares a Token Ring frame to an Ethernet frame in a pretty common display format. A difference clearly exists between the way our stream of 0's and 1's will be interpreted by these two different frames.

It is worth noting that the Token Ring payload can easily be three times the size of an Ethernet frame, which means that a Token Ring frame that is converted to Ethernet could require up to three frames, as well as some type of sequencing to make sure that they are reassembled later in the right order.

Frame Error Detection

As Chapter 2 explained, forces such as EMI, RFI, crosstalk, and so forth can attack our data. When you combine that these are unplanned voltages with the realization that the data is just voltages representing 0's and 1's, it should be obvious that it wouldn't be too difficult to change a bit or two from 0 to 1 or visa versa. Another possibility would be the loss of one or more bits for whatever reason. Since even a bit change will impact a byte and possibly a destination address or data element, it is important know how to detect these errors.

The *Frame Check Sequence* (FCS) field contains a number that is calculated by the data link layer of the source computer during the construction of the frame. When the frame arrives at the destination computer, its data link layer calculates the FCS number and compares it to the one stored in the frame. If the two numbers vary at all, it means something has changed-an error has occurred. The frame will be discarded.

There are several ways to calculate the FCS number, but using the *cyclic redundancy check* (CRC) is the most common. If a data frame is found to be defective, it is discarded. If appropriate, the transport-layer protocols will detect its absence and trigger a retransmission.

Token Ring data / Command frame

SD	AC	FC	DA	SA	Data	FCS	ED	ED
1 byte	1 byte	1 byte	6 bytes	6 bytes	Up to 4,500 bytes	4 bytes	1 byte	1 byte

Ethernet frame

Preamble	Destination	Source	Type	Data	FCS
8 bytes	6 bytes	6 bytes	2 bytes	46–1,500 bytes	4 bytes

Figure 4-4   Token Ring and Ethernet frames

Logical Link Control

Logical link control is usually represented as the upper of the two sublayers defined by the IEEE for the data link layer. This positioning is theoretical but generally makes sense, because the LLC sublayer functions perform services for the upper layers, such as error control, flow control, framing, and MAC sublayer addressing.

When the OSI model was developed, networks were typically small and made up of a single segment, or collision/broadcast domain. With the advent of segmenting and internetworking, it became apparent that more upper-layer protocol information would have to be communicated between the hosts. The LLC sublayer, defined by the IEEE 802.2 specification, actually created another layer within a layer. The new logical link sublayer would be able to function independently from the access technologies, such as Ethernet and Token Ring, which are now the domain of the MAC sublayer (the old data link layer).

This LLC sublayer provides this communications link for the upper-layer protocols (such as Layer 3) by being a part of the OSI model data-encapsulation process. The result effectively increases the OSI model to eight layers for some data. Figure 4-5 shows the traditional OSI encapsulation model.

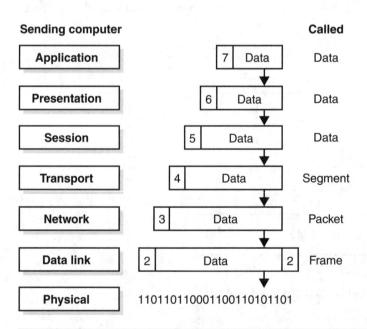

Figure 4-5   Traditional OSI encapsulation

Layer 3 packets are passed to the LLC sublayer, where additional addressing information is added to the header. The two addressing elements added are a *Destination Service Access Point* (DSAP) and a *Source Service Access Point* (SSAP). This new packet, sometimes called the LLC packet or PDU, is forwarded on to the MAC sublayer for encapsulation into the final frame specified by the access method technology (Ethernet, Token Ring, or FDDI).

LLC, as defined in the IEEE 802.2 standard specification, supports both the connectionless and connection-oriented communications used by higher-layer OSI protocols. We will cover both connectionless and connection-oriented communications when we get to Chapter 6 and talk about the transport layer. The standard defines a number of fields in the data link layer frames added by the LLC that allow multiple higher-layer protocols to share a single physical data link. Figure 4-6 shows the encapsulation model with the LLC sublayer. The figure shows only the bottom three OSI layers, because the others do not change.

Layer 2 Devices

In this section, we will look at the Layer 2 devices, which include NICs, bridges, and LAN switches. We will cover what separates them from Layer 1 devices and what benefits they can bring to a network.

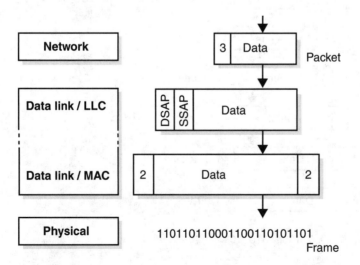

Figure 4-6 Encapsulation with LLC sublayer

Network Interface Card

We covered NICs pretty well earlier in this chapter and in Chapter 3's discussion of access methods, but NICs are Layer 2 devices, and it could be argued that Layer 2 wouldn't exist without them. A summary of the functions of the NIC and its related drivers include:

- **Logical link control** Communicates with upper-layer protocols and allows key upper-layer protocol information to be encapsulated with the data independent of the access method.

- **Device naming or addressing** Provides a unique MAC address identifier.

- **Data framing** Provides the Layer 2 header and trailer completing the encapsulation process involving packaging and defining the data bits for transport. The framing schema is defined by the access method.

- **Media access control** Provides structured access methods and protocols to shared communications media. This includes defining which host will transmit, for how long, and what to do if a collision occurs.

- **Signaling** Creates the appropriate signals and interface connection with the media by using built-in transceivers. Although this is a NIC function, it can be argued it is a Layer 1 activity.

Bridges

Let's look at Layer 2 devices from a historical perspective as we did with Layer 1 devices. When the first ThinNet coaxial networks were joined together using repeaters, the size of our networks doubled in both length and number of nodes. The downside is that there were also twice as many nodes to cause collisions or broadcasts—and thus network congestion increased. Figure 4-7 demonstrates two ThinNet networks joined by a repeater.

Whereas before users from Network A could not communicate with B, they can now; but everyone is noticing a slower performance than before. The problem is that if A26 sends a print job to A28, everyone has to wait until the packet is through, and if it is a large job with many pages and therefore many packets, there will be a sustained period of slower performance. While everyone will not actually have to wait until the entire print job is done because the network sharing is done on a frame-by-frame basis, it stands to reason that with one host transmitting a large number of frames, the delays could increase.

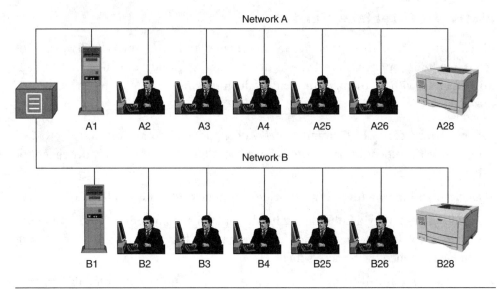

Figure 4-7 Using a repeater

This situation is even worse than it might appear on the surface insofar as the print job will probably go to the server and then travel right back on the same wire to get to the printer. We could literally have a host and a server competing for media access to carry the same print job. This is bad enough for Network A, but now the repeater is passing the problem into Network B, as well, because they are all now one big network.

Some sharp engineering-type person determined that if we could get the repeater to be selective as to what it passed through to the other network leg, then congestion could be reduced, collisions would be reduced, and performance could increase. It was determined that if a device knew which nodes were attached to which interface, it could choose to not forward frames with source and destination devices on the same side of the repeater.

Bridging Table

To accomplish this selective forwarding of packets, a bridging table was added to the device, as well as circuitry to read the MAC addresses of frames passing through the device. Conceptually, a network bridge works like a drawbridge on medieval castles. If the destination address is on the other side of the bridge, the frame is allowed to pass across the bridge. Otherwise, it is discarded. Now, traffic originating in Network A destined for a node on the same segment will be discarded when it reaches the bridge. The same would be true of Network B. We have now effectively "segmented" our network into two collision domains while still allowing traffic between the segments to cross over. Figure 4-8 demonstrates two ThinNet networks joined by a bridge.

Static vs. Dynamic

The earliest bridges used *static* MAC address assignment, meaning that a network administrator would configure the device by keying in the MAC addresses of all users and a reference to which interface they were connected to. There were several problems associated with this method:

- It was a terrible job. Imagine having to type even 50 MAC addresses each 48 bits long, or 24 hexadecimal values.

- A user moving from one segment to another would not receive data frames until the bridging table was rebuilt.

- New nodes or nodes with new NICs would not be recognized by the bridge until it had been reconfigured.

Later technologies were developed that allowed the bridge to *dynamically* configure its own table by reading the *source addresses* of packets arriving at the device. The source MAC address on a data frame is applied as the frame is being prepared for transmission,

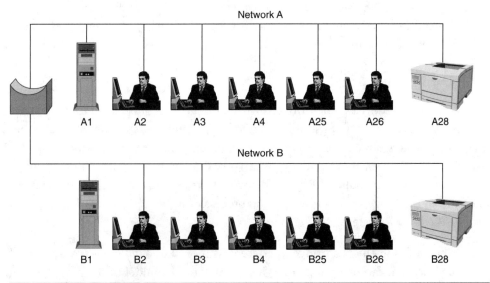

Figure 4-8 Using a bridge

and is taken directly from the circuitry of the sending NIC. It is therefore very reliable. The destination address could be wrong or unavailable (offline), and we really don't know which network segment it is on, so it is not stored. The bridge is said to be in *promiscuous mode* as it's reading these addresses.

Time To Live (TTL)

The bridging table stores three pieces of information: the MAC address of the node; the interface that the node is attached to; and the TTL, an increment of time that an entry will stay in the table before being automatically deleted. The TTL is like a countdown clock, and when the TTL reaches zero, the entry is removed. Each time a frame from a source arrives at the bridge, the TTL is reset. This mechanism clears old (in network terms) entries from the table.

If a bridging table has more entries than the memory will allow, the entries with TTLs closest to expiring will be dropped to make room for the new entries.

Broadcasts and Unknown Addresses

A bridge forwards broadcasts and packets with unknown destination addresses. While initially this may seem like a flaw, it is necessary, because so many processes, particularly computer startup processes, rely on broadcasts to get information needed to become a part of the network. Since bridges learn about nodes from source addresses, the bridge might not have an entry for a node. So, it forwards the frame out all interfaces, except the source interface, hoping that another segment can locate the destination.

Although bridges segment our network into separate collision domains, they do not help with broadcast domains or unknown destination addresses.

Bridging in More Detail

Although the preceding explanation tells what a bridge does, it is useful to understand the process it uses to accomplish this selective forwarding in greater detail. Remember that with repeaters, streams of 0's and 1's are rebuilt and forwarded on without any filtering; for that matter, they aren't even recognized as frames. So, a small amount of latency, or delay, is introduced. Bridges, being Layer 2 devices, can recognize data framing and can recognize MAC addresses. The process of forwarding a data frame would include the following steps:

1. When a frame enters a bridge interface, it is moved to a *buffer area*, a portion of memory that can be thought of as a parking lot or shoulder of the road. Moving it to the buffer pulls it out of the traffic lane in case other traffic needs to pass.

2. The bridge may run quality-control checks on the packet to determine if it has been damaged. If it has been, it is discarded. We will look at this process later in this chapter when we cover switching.

3. The source address is checked to see if it is in the bridging table. If it's not, it is added with a reference to the interface it came in on, and the TTL counter is started. If the source address is recognized, the table is updated with a new TTL entry.

4. The destination address is checked against the bridging table to see if it is known and also to see which interface it is attached to.

   If the destination is known and is from the same segment as the source, then the frame is discarded. This discarding of frames is sometimes referred to as sending them to the *bit bucket*. There is no physical "bit bucket" container, the bits are actually sent to the ground circuit where they disappear.

   If the destination is known, then the frame is forwarded to the interface that has that destination, which on a two-port bridge just means it is allowed to pass through.

   If the destination is unknown, then the frame is forwarded to all interfaces except the source interface. When the destination node responds to the frame, the bridge will capture its source address, and the table will be more complete.

5. Before the bridge moves the frame out of the buffer and onto the media, it checks for traffic on the media, thereby reducing the chances of a collision.

This last feature of bridges reduces intersegment collisions. A frame sent from a node on segment A to a node on segment B will be held by the bridge in the buffer until access to the media on segment B can be achieved without a collision. In this respect, the bridge's buffer works like railroad sidings where an eastbound train pulls off and waits for the westbound train to pass. When the track is clear, the eastbound train resumes its journey.

Bridges and Latency

A frame being processed by a bridge takes longer than if processed by a Layer 1 device, such as a repeater or hub. Latency or propagation delay can be increased by 10 to 30 percent by using a bridge. Bridges use store-and-forward switching, which is the slowest but most reliable method (see "Store-and-Forward," later in the chapter). Generally, the reduction in collisions and congestion and the provision of buffering between the segments are worth the increased latency.

Evolution of Bridges

Remember that this technology was evolving during the days when coaxial cable was still the primary media. The first bridges were typically one port in and one port out. They were very much like the medieval drawbridge. The decision was whether or not to allow the frame to pass through. Just as with early repeaters, somebody developed a method for connecting three and then four segments together to create a multiport bridge.

While the multiport repeater became known as a *hub*, the multiport bridge became known as a *switch*. At the same time, twisted-pair technology was beginning to be accepted for LAN wiring, so much of the hub and switch evolution occurred in twisted-pair devices rather than in coax-but both the hub and switch can trace their roots back to the repeater. You may hear people balk at the concept of a switch being a multiport bridge, because of the disparity of features and technology. It is really no different than other replacement technologies. The automobile clearly evolved from the buggy, and yet they share few similarities today, because there was no incentive for buggy manufacturers to continue to innovate.

There are new repeaters and bridges, but they are often at least as expensive as a hub or switch. Many administrators will put in a small switch where a bridge would work, or a hub where a repeater would work, figuring that the additional ports will be available for future expansion.

This part of the industry is further muddied by a lack of clearly defined names for devices. To some people, everything is a repeater. While this is true insofar as hubs, bridges, switches, and even routers all rebuild the signal before retransmission, this is a lot like lumping all vehicles together as cars or all canines together as dogs. To others, a distinction exists between hubs, intelligent hubs, and switching hubs. A cynical view is that marketing departments earn their keep by blurring the distinctions that could put their company's products at a competitive disadvantage. Keep it simple. If it is a multiport Layer 1 device, unable to differentiate MAC addresses, then it is a hub. If it is a multiport device that can forward frames based on MAC addresses, then it is a switch. Leave terms like "intelligent," "smart," and "switching" to the marketing people. There is enough ambiguity in this business as it is without you contributing to it.

NOTE: The early days of the PC industry met a lot of criticism about the heavy use of "buzz" words. One reaction has been a tendency to define devices and concepts using everyday terminology. Even simple words like "switch," which accurately describes what the Layer 2 device does, are often confusing because there are so many other unrelated common uses of the same word. We might have been better off to call it a "terklplat" and then define it as acting like a switch. Make sure you are comfortable with the terminology as used in this book. The exam will use these terms.

Repeaters, Hubs, Bridges, Switches, and Routers

In the next chapter, we will discuss routers and the "new" features they bring to the table. As we continue, keep in mind that much of the early evolution of these technologies occurred in a very short time during the 1980s, often by very different companies with different backgrounds and visions of the future. While the lowly repeater, a signal amplifier, evolved into a hub, it also evolved into the bridge. And while the bridge evolved into a switch, it also evolved into a router. The beauty of a standards-based technology using a layered model like the OSI model is that individuals and companies can pursue very different approaches to a problem. The market may reward those groups with insight while those without tend to end up like the buggy manufacturers.

While this evolution is important, the shift from coaxial cable to twisted-pair at the same time created another major difference between hubs and switches, when compared to their older counterparts, the repeater and bridge. The manufacturers of these multiport devices saw the opportunity of placing many more ports on hubs and switches with twisted-pair. While the RJ-45 connector is not significantly smaller than the coax connector, it requires much less "finger room" to install and remove it. It is much easier to fit 24 or 48 twisted-pair connectors on a much smaller device than with coax. With large companies needing rows of racks to house these devices, *port density* is a major design and sales feature. So, don't let the fact that hubs and switches tend to look very different from their predecessors blur their common past.

Cisco's Place in History

Cisco is one of the companies that dominate the router business. It offers products in many LAN and WAN categories and is one of the pioneer firms that figured out how to "bridge" networks together. This early work was done on university campuses in the San Francisco area. Cisco went on to develop a solid line of routers. Cisco is truly one of the "husband and wife" "started in an apartment" success stories that spawned all sorts of myths and urban legends. If you are interested, an excellent book on the subject is *Making the Cisco Connection: The Story Behind the Real Internet Superpower*, by David Bunnell (John Wiley & Sons, Inc., 2000).

Bridge Summary

Bridges work at the data link layer, Layer 2 of the OSI model, using MAC addresses with protocols such as Ethernet, Token Ring, and FDDI to manage access to the physical media segments and control data flow.

Bridges work best between segments where traffic is low. When traffic becomes heavier, the latency of bridges can cause them to become a bottleneck. Bridges split collision domains to one per port, or interface. So putting a bridge in the middle of a network creates two separate collision domains and reduces intersegment collisions by using buffers.

By segmenting the network, bridges increase the available bandwidth to each user as compared to before. The formula becomes bandwidth divided by users per segment, instead of bandwidth divided by number of network users.

Broadcasts and unknown addresses are forwarded by switches, so if either type of traffic increases, the bridge will not help and can even increase the problem because of the increased latency.

LAN Switches

First and foremost, LAN switches are multiport bridges, so most of what you learned in the last section applies to LAN switches as well. The most obvious difference is the fact that a switch having more ports will have more elaborate circuitry to connect the appropriate ports while the frame is forwarded. In this section, we will concentrate on the differences between bridges and LAN switches. Figure 4-9 is a simple single switch network with server and printer.

There are many types of switches, such as LAN switches, WAN switches, and telephony switches, and even routers perform a switching function. When it comes to communications switches, the switching function refers to the process of forwarding data arriving at one interface to another specific interface based on some type of address table. In bridges and LAN switches, the decision is based on MAC addresses. We will see in the next chapter that router-switching decisions are based on network addresses. WAN switches use the addresses appropriate to the particular WAN technology. For the purpose of this chapter, we will focus on LAN switches, and references to switches should be assumed to mean LAN switches.

Bridge vs. Switch Devices

LAN switches, much like bridges, connect LAN segments and use a MAC address table to make forwarding decisions. Switches can operate at much faster speeds than bridges,

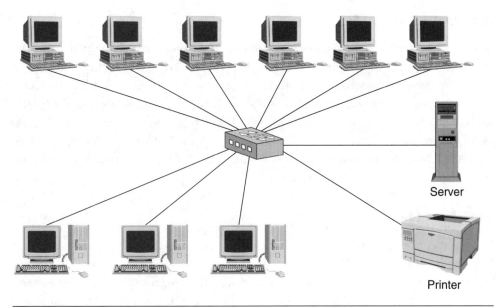

Figure 4-9   Server in a network

routinely supporting 10/100 Mbps autosensing capabilities and moving to 1 Gbps throughput. Switches tend to be less CPU-intensive than bridges, and they support new technologies such as *virtual LANs* (VLANs) and Layer 3 routing features. A reflection of these differences is that R&D investments are being directed at new switch technologies rather than at bridges, which clearly represent the past.

Many switches have now moved much of the switch processing from the CPU to the actual device circuitry to increase throughput speed. An *application-specific integrated circuit* (ASIC) is a chip designed for a particular application, such as switching. This moving the processing to the circuitry is sometimes referred to as "embedding it in the sand," a reference to the silica used to make the circuit boards. Another accurate phrase you will often hear about switches is that they are faster than bridges because they do their switching in hardware freeing up the CPU, while bridges switch in software, which is CPU intensive.

Switches, unlike most bridges, can interconnect segments with different bandwidths, such as a 100 Mbps Ethernet segment to a 10 Mbps Ethernet segment, by using internal buffering to balance the difference. See the section "Symmetrical and Asymmetrical Switches" later in this chapter.

Switches typically support higher port densities than bridges, which drives down the manufacturing cost, and thereby the selling price.

Incremental Upgrades

Both bridges and switches, particularly Ethernet devices, have benefited from the fact that they can be incorporated into existing LANs incrementally, allowing a phased conversion of departments and devices. A 10/100 Mbps switch can replace a hub with no other network changes. As the workstations are upgraded, using 10/100 Mbps NICs will allow those nodes to have faster access to the network resources. Furthermore, even before any workstations are upgraded, the network users may see significant performance improvements if collisions and congestion were the original problem.

Switching Methods

Latency was a concern with bridges and can be an even greater concern with switches because the port-selection decision is now more complex. Cisco and other switch manufactures offer several different switching methods to allow some control over latency. The names of these switching methods refer to how the frame is processed before forwarding. Three common methods you should be aware of are cut through, fragment free, and store-and-forward.

Cut Through

Sometimes called fast forward, this method moves the incoming frame to a buffer, checks the MAC destination address to see if it is in the switching table, and, if found, begins forwarding the packet to the outbound interface. If the MAC destination address is not found, the switch forwards the packet to all outbound interfaces. No quality control is performed and latency is minimized.

Fragment Free

Sometimes called modified cut through, this method moves the packet to a buffer and checks the size of the frame without the preamble to see if it falls within the specifications for the access method. For Ethernet, the specifications stipulate a frame size of 64 to 1,518 bytes. If the frame falls outside that range, it is a runt or giant and thus is considered defective and discarded. If the size is okay, the MAC destination address is checked to see if it is in the switching table. If the address is found, the switch forwards the packet to the outbound interface. If the address is not found, the switch forwards the frame to all outbound interfaces. There is greater quality control than the cut through method by catching the most common types of frame problems. Latency is somewhat increased over cut through.

Store-and-Forward

This method moves the packet to a buffer and checks the size of the frame, just like fragment free. It then performs Layer 2 quality control check and verifies the result against the value stored in the Frame Control Segment. If they do not match, the frame is discarded. If they do match, the MAC destination address is checked to see if it is in the switching table. If the address is found the packet is forwarded to the appropriate outbound interface. If it is not found, it is forwarded to all outbound interfaces. This forwarding method has the highest level of quality control and the highest latency.

Figure 4-10 represents the amount of a data frame that must be processed by each of the switching methods before the frame can be forwarded to the outbound interface.

Bridges typically only support store-and-forward switching, which reduces their ability to manage latency.

Many manufacturers' models of switches offer two or all of these methods, which can be configured by the administrator. Others offer technologies where a faster method like fragment free can be used until a defined percentage rate of defective frames causes the switch to revert automatically to store-and-forward until the failure rate falls back within tolerance.

Bandwidth Issues: Hubs vs. Switches

A hub is a shared media and therefore bandwidth is divided among the active ports. Think of a garden hose. If you put a "Y" splitter on the end of the hose, you get two streams of water but you don't get any more water. Likewise, if I take 12 wires and twist them together at one end so that the copper is now a single thick strand and then ask 12 people to hold the other end, one wire each, as I add the voltage of a battery to the common end, they won't each feel the full voltage of the battery. That's exactly how a hub works.

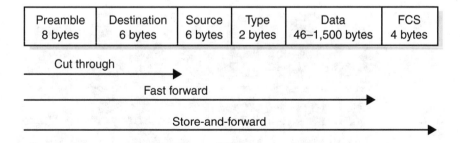

Figure 4-10 Switching methods compared

This means that if I have a 10 Mbps data connection to a 12-port hub, each user will actually receive 1/12th of the 10 Mbps, or about 0.8 Mbps. This assumes all ports are being used. What if I have a 24-port hub? Each user would receive 0.4 Mbps.

Some models of hubs can be "stacked" by connecting the hubs together using a special backbone cable, the result of which is that they are counted as only one hub for purposes of the "four repeaters" rule. When comparing hubs, the term "stackable" refers to this ability to connect the devices using technologies like "fire wire." The device specifications will define how many units can be stacked and the method of connection. This clever technique might allow five 24-port hubs to appear as a single 120-port hub to the network. I saw a similar arrangement in which five 48-port hubs created what appeared to the network to be a single 240-port hub.

Figure 4-11 demonstrates a typical stack unit. The good news is that we can have 240 users on a single segment. The bad news is that the available bandwidth would be split between the 240 users yielding 0.04 Mbps on a 10 Mb network. The point is that for this increased connectivity, bandwidth is split in more ways. By the way, a few years ago (pre-1995) when we were primarily passing text and numbers across our networks, this setup may have yielded an acceptable solution. However, when you add the Internet, intranets, Web-based business applications, live music and videos, desktop publishing, and so forth to the mix of network services, this scenario probably will not work today. Another issue is that there are now 240 users vying for the same common wire, meaning that congestion, collisions, and broadcast problems will all increase.

This is one area where switches clearly outperform hubs, because for that brief fraction of a second that the two nodes are passing the data frame, 100 percent of the bandwidth is dedicated to that connection. This means that any of the preceding scenarios could see significant improvement in resources to the end users by replacing the hubs with switches.

Figure 4-11
Stack unit

NOTE: As the price of switches drops, there is a definite move to replace hubs with switches in existing networks or to specify switches in new installations. These are probably sound decisions. Remember, however, that switches have higher latency than hubs, and therefore a small network with minimal traffic may actually perceive no improvement at all, and could actually sense that things are slower. In that scenario, don't be too quick to replace that hub.

Symmetrical and Asymmetrical Switches

When all interfaces on a switch are set to the same bandwidth, the switch is referred to as a *symmetrical* switch. When some interfaces can operate at higher bandwidths, then the switch is called an *asymmetrical* switch. This latter switch is commonly employed to provide faster connections to file and print servers, Web servers, engineering workstations, and power users. Figure 4-12 compares symmetrical and asymmetrical switches.

The asymmetrical approach makes sense when you think about the resources the network users are most likely to want. Although a network might include 100 users, they generally aren't communicating with or sharing data with each other. More likely, each is using the server's resources. Even when several users are working on a single project, often each user has a connection to common shared resources on the server(s). By providing one or more 100 Mbps connections between the switch and the server(s), you should reduce the time users have to wait for resources.

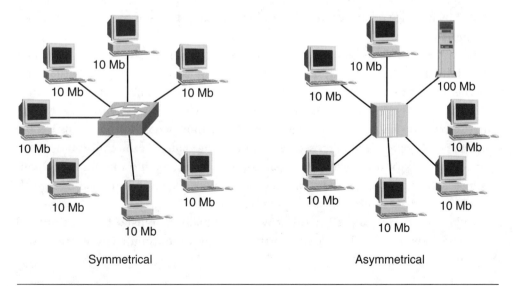

Symmetrical   Asymmetrical

Figure 4-12   Symmetrical vs. asymmetrical switches

EXAM TIP: Make sure you know the terms "symmetrical switch" and "asymmetrical switch" and the difference between them.

Simultaneous Communications

When you segment a LAN with a bridge, the buffers in the bridge allow two communications to occur simultaneously—one in each segment. The buffer will prevent the intersegment collision.

With a switch, technically this means that if the switch's buffers can handle the traffic, there could be a transmission on every segment, with the buffers preventing the collisions. When pricing switches, two of the variables to consider are the amount of memory for MAC addresses and the amount of and allocation of buffers to avoid this type of collision.

Collisions and Broadcasts

Switches, like bridges, create multiple LAN segments based on ports. A bridge that has two ports typically splits a network into two segments and two collision domains but still has only one broadcast domain. Figure 4-13 shows a network that has been segmented by a bridge to create two collision domains but that still has only one broadcast domain.

A switch, being a multiport bridge, creates a separate segment and collision domain for each interface. If it helps, think of each switch port as a microbridge. A twisted-pair Ethernet network with all switches instead of hubs would literally have a segment for every node or host. This is called *microsegmentation*, which when combined with full-duplex operation means that you have effectively eliminated collisions. Some people conclude that the result of microsegmentation is elimination of the collision domain; I prefer to think of it as segmenting our collision domains into one for every port. Because only one device can be connected to that port, the result is the same—no collisions. Figure 4-14 shows a switch segmenting a LAN.

While with an all-switched network we can virtually eliminate the collisions, all hosts are still in the same broadcast domain. A broadcast transmitted by any node will be seen by all other nodes.

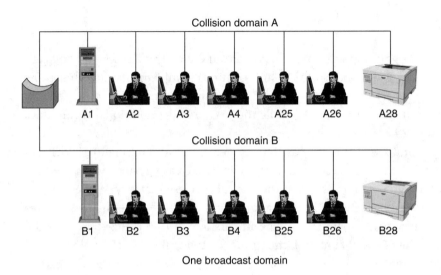

Figure 4-13 Using a bridge to segment a network

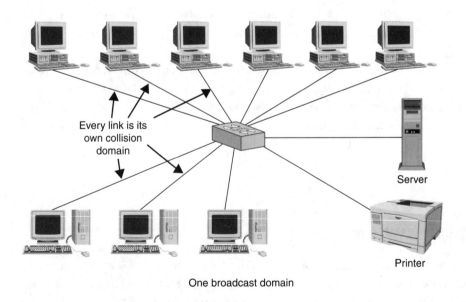

Figure 4-14 Segmenting with a switch

Summary

The NIC and its supporting software drivers determine the Layer 2 access method (Ethernet, Token Ring, FDDI, and so forth) and control its implementation. This implementation is split between two sublayers of the data link layer. The MAC tends to control layer features and protocols, while the LLC provides additional communications to the upper-layer protocols.

Both bridges and switches can be used to segment a network into multiple collision domains, thereby reducing network congestion while increasing bandwidth to individual users. This segmentation comes at the cost of increased latency. While there are many basic similarities between bridges and switches, switches offer many more features and enhancements that can best be understood if one realizes that switches evolved from bridges and that manufacturers are following the new technology.

Switches can segment a network into one segment per port. This is called microsegmentation, and when applied to the fullest extent (no hubs), we virtually eliminate the possibility of collisions.

There are two types of switching, symmetrical, and asymmetrical. Symmetrical switching occurs when all ports support the same bandwidth, just like bridges. Asymmetrical switching allows for ports with different bandwidths on the same switch. This arrangement can increase network performance by providing greater bandwidth to servers and power users.

There are three switching methods that determine the quality-control checking done by the switch and the related latency. Cut through (or fast forward) checks only the destination address. Fragment free (or modified cut through) also checks to see if the frame is between 64 and 1,518 bytes. Anything else is a runt or giant and is discarded. Store-and-forward, the default for most switches and the only method on some bridges, does the same thing as fragment free plus runs the CRC test.

Chapter Review

In this section, you will get an opportunity to check your grasp of the facts and concepts covered in the chapter. A small case study is included so that you can apply what you have learned to a specific scenario. A "Practice Questions" section follows that checks your grasp of the key points within the chapter.

Case Study: The Elm Park Elementary School

Your child's school is adding computers that have been donated by a local company. An extended star or star-bus topology has been suggested, using some hubs that are available. You are reviewing the design with an eye toward estimating whether collisions and bandwidth issues will cause potential problems. If you estimate potential problems, you will consider some Layer 2 devices and how they might help.

Scenario: For now, the very basic details are as follows: Elm Park Elementary is a four-year-old, single-level building with 12 classrooms and a library. Each classroom currently has 24 students but could possibly seat 32 students. There are currently no portable classrooms, but a student enrollment growth is just starting to hit the school.

Enough computers are available immediately for six classrooms and the library, and the goal is to outfit the remaining six classrooms next year. The plan is to make the Internet and some online services available to the students. The computers are current enough to be useful for at least two years.

The plan calls for using seven hubs daisy-chained (port to port) together, as shown in the following illustration. The library, which is somewhat centrally located, is where the server(s) will be connected. Assume that any distances fall well within the standards for Category 5 twisted-pair cable (100 meters). Assume that all rooms will have 24 computers and that a stackable hub solution will be used in each room that combines a 12-port hub and 24-port hub for 36 total ports. Being stackable units, the network will see each stack as a single 36-port device.

1. Will this design work? Do we comply with the four-repeaters rule for Layer 1 devices?

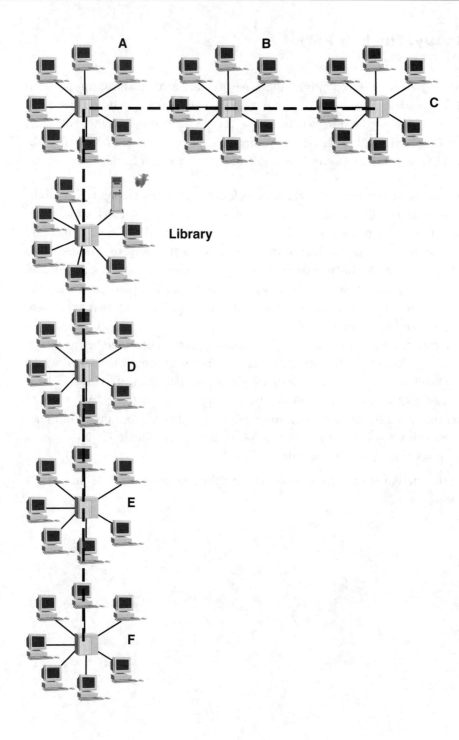

Library

2. Is there any single hub (12- or 24-port) that could be replaced with a switch to clear up this four-repeaters problem? Assume that you will not be changing the basic wiring from room to room.

3. The next illustration shows how a 12-port switch might be introduced to break of the four-repeaters rule. Notice that the hubs in each wing are still daisy-chained together. Assume that all hub and switch interfaces are 10 Mbps. Assume also that each room's hub has ports connected to 24 workstations plus the number of ports necessary to connect the other network hubs/switches. (A, B, D, and E would require two ports; C, F, and the library would need one port). What would be the bandwidth per user in each of the following rooms?
Library:
A:
B:
C:
D:
E:
F:

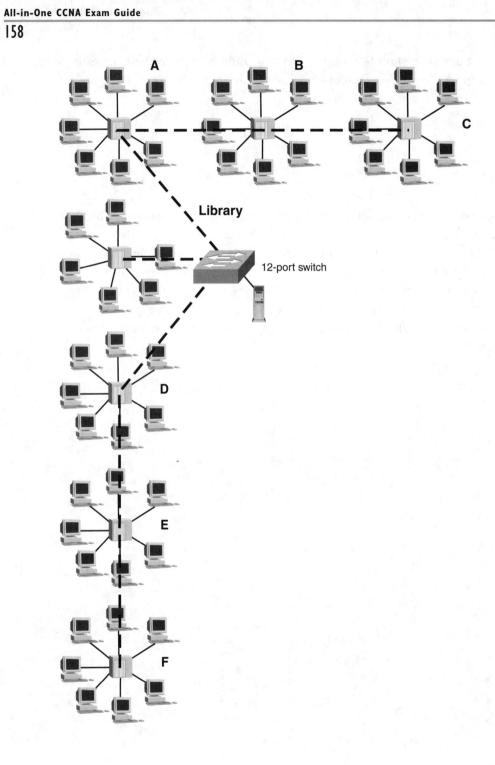

A

B

C

Library

12-port switch

D

E

F

4. Assuming that the bandwidth calculations are unacceptable, would anything help short of adding additional equipment? If so, what would be the new bandwidth allocations for each user?

   Library:

   A:

   B:

   C:

   D:

   E:

   F:

5. Assume that the school is open to other network devices; what might you suggest that would deliver 10 Mbps bandwidth to all users?

6. If you replaced all hubs in the original design with 10 Mbps switches, would this be a symmetrical or asymmetrical implementation?

7. Given our evolving design using switches instead of hubs, are there any links that if increased to 100 Mbps would reduce congestion and help assure 10 Mbps delivery to each user? After describing your changes, state whether the switches in each room would be symmetrical or asymmetrical?

   Library 12-port:

   Library 24-port:

   A:

   B:

C:

D:

E:

F:

8. Go to a Web site such as www.cdw.com or www.pcconnection.com and look up the prices of 12- and 24-port hubs and switches and do a ballpark estimate of what a couple of our proposed plans might cost just for the devices—do not worry about wiring. You may have to choose the "Networking" link on the Web site's main page to get started. If you aren't familiar with manufactures, try Cisco, 3Com, Nortel, D-Link, or Linksys.

Case Study Suggested Solution (Your solutions may vary)

1. It may work, but we violate the four-repeaters rule and must assume that there will be increased collisions. Nodes on the end hubs would not hear each other transmit and could therefore transmit at the same time.

2. You could replace the 12-port hub in the library with a 12-port switch. One port would go to the 24-port hub in the library; one port would serve classrooms A, B, and C; one port would serve classrooms D, E, and F; and any servers would be connected to the switch.

3. Library: $10/25 = 0.4$ Mbps

   A: $10/26 = 0.38$ Mbps

   B: $0.38/26 = 0.015$ Mbps

   C: $0.015/25 = 0.006$ Mbps

   D: $10/26 = 0.38$ Mbps

   E: $0.38/26 = 0.015$ Mbps

   F: $0.015/25 = 0.006$ Mbps

4. If we connected each room directly to the switch, we could preserve some bandwidth, particularly for classrooms B, C, E, and F.

   Library: $10/25 = 0.4$ Mbps (no change)

   A: $10/25 = 0.4$ Mbps

   B: $10/25 = 0.4$ Mbps

   C: $10/25 = 0.4$ Mbps

   D: $10/25 = 0.4$ Mbps

   E: $10/25 = 0.4$ Mbps

   F: $10/25 = 0.4$ Mbps

The following illustration shows a possible solution:

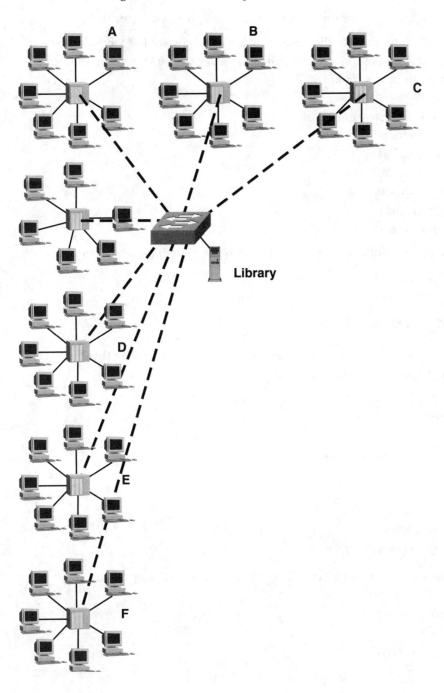

5. Replace all hubs with 10 Mbps switches.

6. When all interfaces are the same on your switch, it is symmetrical.

7. Make all connections to the 12-port switch in the library 100 Mbps. This will require that all other switch stacks have at least one 100 Mbps port to be implemented. All others could remain 10 Mbps.
Library 12-port: symmetrical
Library 24-port: asymmetrical
A: Asymmetrical
B: Asymmetrical
C: Asymmetrical
D: Asymmetrical
E: Asymmetrical
F: Asymmetrical

8. There are no right or wrong answers, and the prices will decrease over time.

Practice Questions

Take a few moments and check your grasp of the concepts covered in this chapter. The answers immediately follow the questions.

Questions

1. What are the two sublayers of Layer 2 of the OSI model?
   a. Physical
   b. Data link
   c. Transport
   d. Media access control
   e. Logical link control

2. Whether a network is Ethernet, Token Ring, or FDDI is determined by?
   a. Network layer
   b. MAC sublayer
   c. LLC sublayer
   d. Physical layer

3. The MAC address of a device is how long (choose two)?
   a. 32 bits
   b. 48 bytes
   c. 48 bits
   d. 6 bytes

4. Who creates the MAC address for a computer?
   a. Network administrator
   b. User
   c. NIC manufacturer
   d. Computer manufacturer

5. The MAC address is also referred to as which one of the following?
   a. Logical address
   b. Network address
   c. Physical address
   d. Memory address

6. Which of the following is not a benefit of segmenting a network with a bridge?
   a. Splits the collision domain into smaller sizes
   b. Increases bandwidth per user on each segment
   c. Filters data traffic moving from segment to segment
   d. Splits the broadcast domain into smaller sizes
   e. Regenerates any signal it sends on

7. What are the three switching methods for forwarding frames through a switch?
   a.
   b.
   c.

8. To change the MAC address of a network computer, you must do which of the following?
   a. Move it to another network segment
   b. Connect it to another port on the switch
   c. Change the network adapter (NIC)
   d. Assign it a new IP address

9. Look at the next illustration. What best describes the switches in the illustration?

   a. Both are symmetrical

   b. Both are asymmetrical

   c. Dept A is symmetrical while Dept B is asymmetrical

   d. Dept A is asymmetrical while Dept B is symmetrical

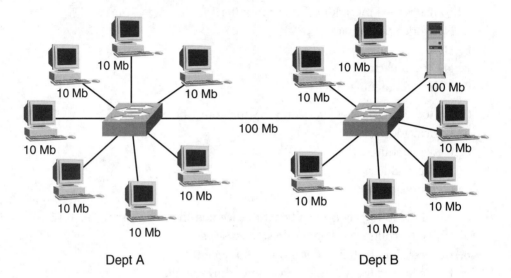

Dept A   Dept B

10. How many segments are in an all-switched network?

    a. Two

    b. One per port

    c. Two per port

    d. Not enough information

11. In an all switched network, how many collision domains are there?

    a. Two

    b. One per port

    c. Two per port

    d. Not enough information

12. In an Ethernet network with a 12-port hub, 11 users, and one server, how many simultaneous communications could go on?

    a. 11

    b. 12

    c. 1

    d. 2

13. In an Ethernet network with a 12-port switch, 11 users, and one server, how many simultaneous communications could go on?
    a. 11
    b. 12
    c. 1
    d. 2

14. If you were building a departmental network with 22 users, one department server, and a connection to the corporate switched network, which of the following might give the best performance?
    a. A 24 port/10 Mb hub
    b. A 24 port/10 Mb hub with two 10/100 ports
    c. A 24 port/10 Mb switch
    d. A 24 port/10 Mb switch with two 10/100 ports
    e. It doesn't make any difference

15. Using the data from question 14, if you chose answer d., which of the following would get the 10/100 connections?
    a. You
    b. The local power user
    c. The departmental server
    d. The corporate network
    e. It doesn't matter

Answers

1. **d.** and **e.** Media access control and logical link control.

2. **b.** MAC sublayer protocols determine access method.

3. **c.** and **d.** 48 bits or 6 bytes (8 bits to the byte).

4. **c.** and maybe **d.** Generally, it is the NIC manufacturer, but in the case of a PC manufacturer that puts the NIC on the motherboard, it could possibly be up to it, although it would probably buy someone else's chip set.

5. **c.** Physical address. Both the network and logical address refer to the Layer 3 (IP, or IPX possibly) address, and the memory address is a specific location in the device's memory.

6. **d.** Bridges cannot split the broadcast domains.

7. Cut through (or fast forward), fragment free (or modified cut through), and store-and-forward.

8. **c.** Change the network adapter (NIC). The MAC address is permanently assigned to the NIC at the time of manufacturing.

9. **b.** Both are asymmetrical.

10. **b.** One per port.

11. **b.** One per port. The segments and collision domains are the same. If this network is referred to as collision free, it is because we have microsegmented it so far that there are no two devices in a segment/collision domain to collide.

12. **c.** Only one communication at a time can occur on a hub network.

13. **b.** It is possible for all nodes to be transmitting if the switch's buffers can handle the load.

14. **d.** A 24 port/10 Mb switch with two 10/100 ports.

15. **c.** and **d.** The departmental server and the corporate network having the greater bandwidth would be able to more quickly meet the needs of the users (asymmetrical design).

CHAPTER 5

OSI Model–Layer 3

This chapter will:

- **Compare computer host names, MAC addresses, and network addresses**

- **Offer you a first look at the routing function**

- **Compare routable vs. nonroutable protocols**

- **Compare routable vs. routing protocols**

- **Introduce you to network protocols such as TCP/IP and IPX/SPX**

- **Show you IP addressing, including classful addressing, subnet masks, and default gateways**

- **Teach you how to perform addressing, connectivity, and ARP labs**

- **Tour the network client configuration process**

In the last chapter, we looked at how Layer 1 and Layer 2 processes and devices work within a network. We saw that Layer 1 technologies succumb to congestion-related problems as the number of users increases and the variety and complexity of applications change. With Layer 2 technologies, we were able to create separate collision domains but could not get around a single broadcast domain.

In this chapter, we will see how Layer 3 technologies allow us to split networks, creating both separate collision domains and separate broadcast domains. Layer 3 will enable us to create separate networks and yet provide a means for those networks to exchange data.

Network Layer: Layer 3

The network layer, Layer 3, is where internetworking occurs. As you saw earlier, Layer 1 technology and devices, such as repeaters and hubs, can facilitate data moving within a network. This is done using broadcast-like transmissions that are heard by every node and then copied by the NIC whose MAC address matches the destination address on the data frame.

Layer 2 devices, such as bridges and switches, enable us to reduce the congestion and collisions resulting from network growth by breaking the LAN up into collision domains. This brings order and increases performance, but it can't get around the fact that our networks are still single broadcast domains, meaning that every other node hears any device that puts out a broadcast. Remember too that any unknown destination addresses are also forwarded out every interface, creating broadcast-like traffic. As networks grow, this broadcast congestion impacts network performance.

Thus, we need a way to physically split networks into multiple collision and broadcast domains and yet provide a method for communicating between the networks when necessary. This means we need a different device and a different method of addressing, because we want to prevent broadcasts from traveling across this new device. If we were allowing broadcasts, then a switch would suffice.

The new device is called a router. It uses an addressing system that is hierarchical in design, indicating both the host identifier and a network identifier. The router, as its name implies, is also responsible for selecting (routing) the appropriate path that a data frame would travel to move between networks. Layer 3 is responsible for addressing and routing of frames moving through the network. Layer 2 addresses are "physical" addresses, providing only a unique identifier, Layer 3 addresses are considered "logical" or "software" addresses, because they are assigned by an administrator to allow for a hierarchical segmenting of a network. The *Internet Protocol* (IP) and *Internetwork Packet Exchange* (IPX) are Layer 3 network protocols.

Routers, like bridges, often are servers running software that enables them to do their jobs. Over time, routers and bridges have developed into specialty devices that may not look anything like their predecessors, but inside they still have components very similar to the PC (CPU, memory, circuitry, operating system, and a configuration program). Most network server operating systems, such as Windows NT/2000, Novell NetWare, and Linux, can and do still function as routers, particularly in small implementations.

Although the topic is beyond the scope of this book, once you understand using and configuring Cisco routers (and have your CCNA safely in hand), you might want to look at technologies such as Linux or Windows NT/2000 servers as routers, proxy servers, NAT servers, and firewall technologies. Each of these technologies is a router at its center. I'm not suggesting that these technologies are on par with dedicated devices, such as the Cisco products, but you may find them both interesting and educational—particularly if you do not have access to Cisco devices while you are learning. For more information, check **www.winroute.com** for one example of a low-cost tool.

Names and Addresses

When PCs were stand-alone devices, the concept of naming or assigning an address to that device was of little importance. As we started connecting PCs together with wires and fiber-optic cables, having a unique way of identifying each device started to become important. Whether you refer to the designation as a name or an address, it is still an identifier. In this section, we are going to compare three methods of naming or addressing that are associated with the devices on the network: the device name, the MAC address (Layer 2), and the network address (Layer 3).

Host Name or Computer Name

Network Basic Input/Output System (NetBIOS) is a software *application programming interface* (API) and device-naming convention used by applications on Microsoft and IBM LAN devices to request services from lower-level network processes. An API defines an interface to a service. These services might include session establishment and termination, and information transfer. The resulting name is often referred to as any of the following: NetBIOS name, host name, computer name, device name, or friendly name. Figure 5-1 shows a small network with the host names for the nodes.

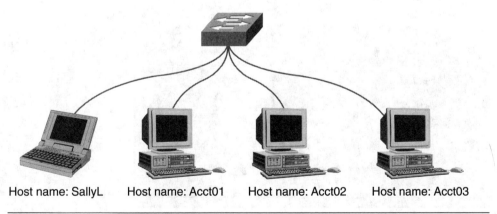

Host name: SallyL   Host name: Acct01   Host name: Acct02   Host name: Acct03

Figure 5-1   Network with host names

These NetBIOS names are assigned by the administrator or computer user and must be unique on the network. Each name can be up to 15 characters long, to which the operating system will append a single character indicating the type of device (such as server, printer, and so forth). If two devices have the same name, the second device to attempt to connect to the network will be rejected. Figure 5-2 shows the Network properties screen, which can be used to name or rename the computer.

The figure shows the host name for my laptop, which I personalized. In larger environments, a more common approach for naming desktop machines is something like NT211-07, where NT indicates the operating system, 211 indicates the room number, and 07 is the unique number of the PC within the room. A technician or administrator

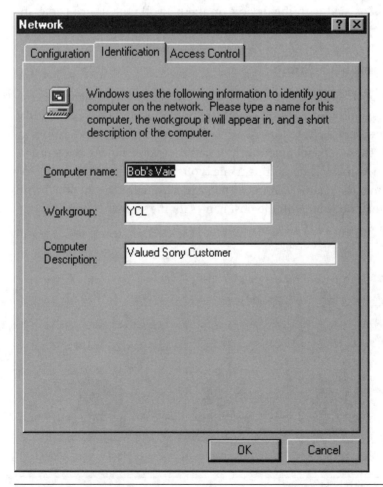

Figure 5-2   Network properties screen for changing the Computer name

can identify the machine by counting left to right from the front of the room, and confirm its identify by looking at a label on the system unit. We often use Network Neighborhood and this Host Name feature of encoding the location to detect machines with the power on prior to extended periods when our classrooms are unused, such as holiday breaks. These machines, which can be scattered throughout 20 rooms, can be detected on any host in the building.

Note that while my name is included in my host name, the host name actually identifies the computer on the network, not the user. The network's user authentication system (logon system) will identify the user. The same is true for the MAC and network addresses.

While a bit of an oversimplification, think of a small group of friends for which using first names only uniquely identifies each member. As the group grows, potential conflicts arise as new members have names that duplicate existing members. This leads to the use of nicknames and names like SallyL for the second Sally. At some point, using personalized names becomes unmanageable.

Although using host names is one of the earlier naming systems, the host name still plays a key role in *Transmission Control Protocol/Internet Protocol* (TCP/IP) networks. Host names are also instrumental in using shared resources on a network. We will revisit host names in Chapter 10. Other terms used for host name are computer name, device name, friendly name, and NetBIOS name. These "friendly" names are far easier to use or remember than MAC or network addresses. There are protocols that will resolve these names to MAC or network addresses in much the same way that domain names, such as **www.cisco.com**, are resolved to IP addresses.

In the exercises at the end of this chapter, we will look at assigning the host name, IP address and resolving IP to MAC addresses.

MAC Address

Chapter 4 pretty well defined MAC addresses, so at this point, we will limit our discussion to the fact that MAC addresses by their nature should be truly unique. Whereas a duplicate host name could easily occur if an organization does not have a structured naming system or when two networks are combined, the MAC addresses of all units should be unique. Because these addresses are permanently encoded on an interface during manufacturing, they are referred to as "physical" addresses. Much like *social security numbers* (SSNs), regardless of the size of the group, each MAC address is unique. Figure 5-3 shows a small network with the host names and MAC addresses for the nodes.

A MAC address would work fine within a single broadcast-type domain network, because all nodes hear the packets. Using our SSN analogy, if all students are in a single

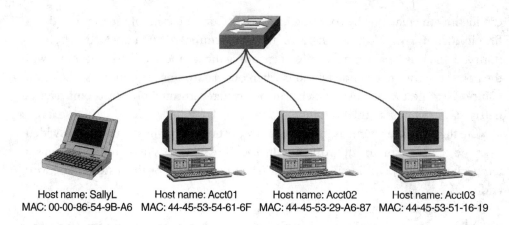

Figure 5-3 Network with MAC addresses

classroom, grades could be distributed by calling out SSNs. Even if two students are named Mary Barnes, each has a unique SSN.

The problem with MAC addresses is that they lack any type of network ID to help determine whether the destination is on the local network. If it's not, we would literally have to broadcast into every network to find a particular host. Imagine heading across the country to look for a relative if you only knew the person's SSN. Having only the host name (their name) would be as bad, or worse, because it is not unique.

Network Address

Network addresses are logical addresses that can be assigned by network administrators or even some network devices. The address contains two components: the network identifier and the node identifier. Network addresses are hierarchical in design, much like the U.S. telephone numbering system.

Assume we place a long-distance call to 1.509.555.1234. The first 1 tells the system that the call is a domestic (U.S.) long-distance call, as compared to 011 for South Africa, for example. The next three digits (509) identify the area code—a specific area of the country. The next three digits (555) identify a particular telephone exchange switch, and the last four digits (1234) identify the trunk and ultimately the particular connection on the system. Notice that the user-specific portion is closer to the right end, while the network portion proceeds from general to specific from the left side.

The upper-level protocols, such as Novell's *Internetwork Packet Exchange/Sequential Packet Exchange* (IPX/SPX) or the Internet's TCP/IP, will determine the structure of the address and the method of assignment.

Novell's IPX addressing method is very simple. A hexadecimal number identifying the network is followed by the MAC address, such as 201.0010.7B7F.948B, where 201 is the network identifier and 0010.7B7F.948B is the MAC address.

TCP/IP's IP addressing method uses a separate addressing system involving 32-bit binary values that are broken into four octets, each 8-bits long, and then converted to decimal equivalents, such as 201.116.14.23. In this case, the 201.116.14 represents the network, while the final octet, 23, is the host ID. IP uses a subnet mask to identify the network portion of the address; the subnet mask for this network is 255.255.255.0. Later in this chapter, when we look at TCP/IP in more detail, we will see how the subnet mask is used to derive the network and host IDs. Figure 5-4 shows a small network with the host names, MAC addresses, and both IPX and IP addresses.

The following are some things to note as you look over the figure:

- All the IPX addresses have 1 as the first element, representing the network ID. Each host is part of the 1 network. The MAC address portion of the IPX address uses an alternative way of displaying hexadecimal values. Instead of displaying them in pairs with a dash between, as in the MAC address, they are grouped in fours and separated with decimals (or periods). The decimals are only visual separators to make it easier for humans to see and recognize patterns, much the same as separators are used in phone numbers, such as (206) 555-1212 or 206.555.1212.

- The network is using a subnet mask of 255.255.255.0, which means that all the IP addresses have 192.168.3 as the first three octets representing the network ID. Each

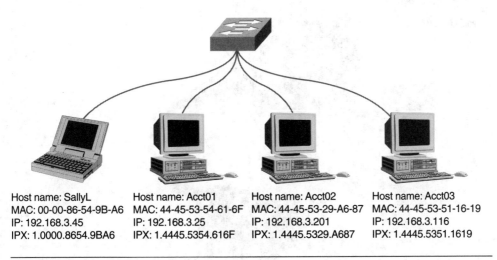

Host name: SallyL
MAC: 00-00-86-54-9B-A6
IP: 192.168.3.45
IPX: 1.0000.8654.9BA6

Host name: Acct01
MAC: 44-45-53-54-61-6F
IP: 192.168.3.25
IPX: 1.4445.5354.616F

Host name: Acct02
MAC: 44-45-53-29-A6-87
IP: 192.168.3.201
IPX: 1.4445.5329.A687

Host name: Acct03
MAC: 44-45-53-51-16-19
IP: 192.168.3.116
IPX: 1.4445.5351.1619

Figure 5-4 Network with all addresses

host is part of the 192.168.3.0 network. The gaps in the numbering of the last octet are not significant; they may represent machines that are not displayed or machines that are turned off.

Note also that the laptop, a portable device, must be a part of this network's addressing system if it is going to share resources with this group of computers. Unlike its MAC address, which cannot be changed, the IP address can be easily changed to make the laptop a part of another network.

- The first six hexadecimal bits of the MAC addresses are the same for the desktop computers. As described in the last chapter, this is the *Organizational Unique Identifier* (OUI) that identifies the manufacturer and model of the card. This simply means that the administrator uses a single manufacture's particular model of NIC. The last six digits are the unique ID for that specific card or interface, often all or part of the serial number of the unit. The variation in the last six digits is probably a function of the manufacturing, packaging, and distribution process.

Why is the MAC address of the laptop so very different from the desktop units? Even if the NICs are made by the same manufacturer, the desktop's NIC is the size of your hand, whereas the laptop's NIC is a flat, matchbook-sized card, which therefore has its own OUI number. Figure 5-5 shows a 10/100 Mbps PCMCIA card for a notebook computer with a "dongle" attachment for connecting to an RJ-45 connector.

Figure 5-5
PCMCIA NIC card

So, how does the picture change when we connect two networks? Figure 5-6 shows two LANs joined by a router. Note that the IP and IPX addresses, unlike the MAC addresses, both reflect that they are separate networks. Even the attempt to encode host names with a department code as a means of grouping users falls apart, because it isn't applied to the laptops.

Only the network addresses, IP and IPX, can identify both the unique node and the network it is a part of. Notice too that the interface on the router is also a part of each network, with its own network address and MAC address. In this simple example, the router is literally the connection between the two networks. Larger internetworks may have many routers between the LANs, but each end will always have a router with an interface that is a part of that "local" network.

Routing Data

A router, or Layer 3 device, must be able to perform two separate and distinct functions: switch frames through the router from an inbound interface to an outbound interface, and perform routing to create a table to be used by the switching function. Figure 5-7 shows a data frame being switched, or routed, across three routers toward its destination.

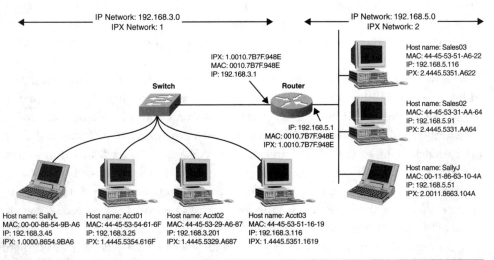

Figure 5-6   Two LANs joined by a router

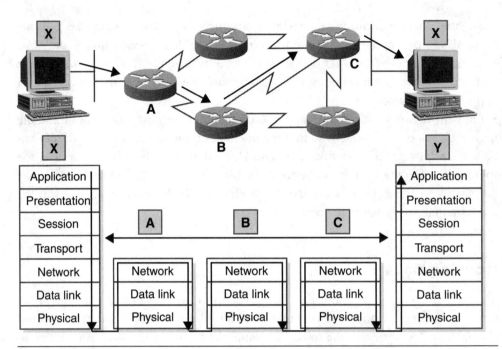

Figure 5-7 Frame forwarding across a network

Switching Function

Unlike Layer 2 switches, where the switching is based on a table of MAC addresses, Layer 3 devices (routers) use a table that contains only network addresses and associated next-hop interfaces. The next-hop interface refers to the router interface to which the data frame will be forwarded to continue it on its journey.

When a frame is received at a router, or at the destination host, the frame destination address (MAC) is verified by the data link layer before it is accepted, to verify that it is the correct destination. If the address matches, the frame control sequence calculation is performed and confirmed by comparing it to the value stored in the frame. If the two values match, it indicates that the frame that arrived has not changed since it was transmitted from the last device. It has not been corrupted. At this point, the Layer 2 frame is discarded so that the data segment can be passed up to the network layer. At this point, it should be the same as when the source host's network layer passed it down to the data link layer for preparation prior to transmission.

In the network layer, the subnet mask is used to determine the network ID portion of the destination address, which is then compared to the route table, and forwarding is based on finding the *most specific* match. If there is no match, the data packet is discarded and an ICMP message is sent to the original source. Figure 5-8 shows an Ethernet frame with the MAC destination and source addresses. The upper graphic shows the Data segment of the Ethernet frame, which was created at Layer 3 (network layer). This data contains the network (IP) destination and source addresses.

If a route exists, the next-hop interface is noted and data is returned to Layer 2 where the appropriate data frame is created, which includes rewriting the MAC header, updating the CRC, and decrementing the TTL.

Rebuilding the Data Frame

If the data needs to be forwarded (routed), the data frame is rebuilt by rewriting the MAC header using this router as the source address and the next device as the destination address. The next device will be the destination device if it is located on a network directly connected to this router; otherwise, it will be the next router, which will then repeat the process to continue forwarding the data. This next router is often called the next-hop device or next-hop router.

It is important to understand that while the original network layer header will always include the original source address (Layer 3) and destination address (Layer 3), the MAC header addresses (Layer 2) will be continually updated to reflect the immediate source and destination for each segment—where it is hopping from and where it is hopping to.

CRC Recomputed

The CRC is recomputed and added to the end of the new data frame. The original CRC was used to verify that the packet was undamaged when it arrived at the router interface and then discarded.

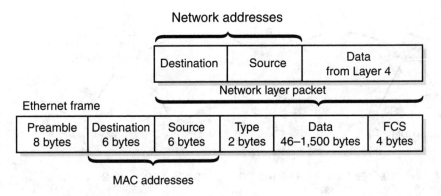

Figure 5-8   Ethernet frame with data defined

Time To Live (TTL)

TTL is a field in the IP header that indicates how long a packet is considered valid and can remain on the network. Every frame put on the network is assigned a TTL by the original source that identifies the maximum time (hops) in which the frame must complete its journey. When the data frame is being rebuilt for forwarding, the TTL is reduced (decremented) one second. If the TTL gets to zero, the next router will discard it and send an ICMP Time Exceeded message to the source. This process prevents frames from circulating indefinitely when data loops occur.

Routing Function

Layer 2 switches learn host addresses by monitoring frame traffic and pulling off source MAC addresses, whereas Layer 3 devices are configured by an administrator and then share their knowledge with other routers, thereby building a table of known networks. Figure 5-9 shows three routers and their connected networks.

When each router is configured, the administrator "tells" it about the locally connected networks. The original routing tables might look like this:

ROUTER A		ROUTER B		ROUTER C	
Network	Next hop	Network	Next hop	Network	Next hop
192.168.1.0		192.168.3.0		201.14.57.0	
192.168.2.0				201.14.58.0	

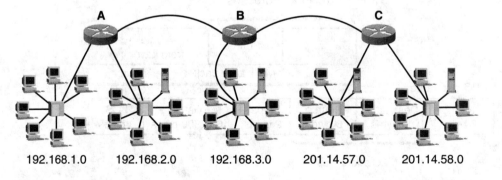

| 192.168.1.0 | 192.168.2.0 | 192.168.3.0 | 201.14.57.0 | 201.14.58.0 |

Figure 5-9   Three-router network

No Next Hop entries exist because the networks are all local to that router and therefore do not require being sent to another router.

In an order and method defined by the routing protocol, router A shares its routing information with router B. If we assume that no other updates have occurred, the routing tables would look like this:

ROUTER A		ROUTER B		ROUTER C	
Network	Next hop	Network	Next hop	Network	Next hop
192.168.1.0		192.168.3.0		201.14.57.0	
192.168.2.0		192.168.1.0	A	201.14.58.0	
		192.168.2.0	A		

Router B now "knows" that it can reach networks 192.168.1.0 and 192.168.2.0 by forwarding the frames to router A.

Router B will share all of this new information with router C. Likewise, router C will share with B, which will pass the information on to router A. The resulting router tables would look like this:

ROUTER A		ROUTER B		ROUTER C	
Network	Next hop	Network	Next hop	Network	Next hop
192.168.1.0		192.168.3.0		201.14.57.0	
192.168.2.0		192.168.1.0	A	201.14.58.0	
192.168.3.0	B	192.168.2.0	A	192.168.3.0	B
201.14.57.0	B	201.14.57.0	C	192.168.1.0	B
201.14.58.0	B	201.14.58.0	C	192.168.2.0	B

Best-Path Determination

When exchanging routes, it is possible with some network configurations to have two alternative routes to the same network. Path determination occurs at Layer 3, where the routing protocol enables a router to evaluate the alternative paths, and choose a best path, which will then appear in the routing table. Typically, the alternative path will not appear in the routing table unless something changes to make it the best path.

As we go along, we will add more detail to this simplified example, but for now, each router's switching function can forward data frames based on the routing table.

Routable vs. Nonroutable Protocols

Network protocols fall into two categories: routable (or routed), which are those that can be forwarded by a router from one network to another, and nonroutable (non-routed), which are those that cannot be forwarded. The *NetBIOS Extended User Interface* (NetBEUI) and *Data Link Control* (DLC) protocols are the two that are most often noted as being nonroutable. IPX, IP, and older protocols, such as *Xerox Network Systems* (XNS) and *Digital Equipment Corp Net/OSI* (DECNet), are all routable.

EXAM TIP: Know that NetBEUI is an example of a nonrouted or nonroutable protocol. DLC is getting a little too dated.

Routable vs. Routing Protocols

Network protocols such as IPX/SPX and TCP/IP, and older protocols such as XNS and DECNet, are all routable (or routed) protocols, meaning that they can be routed from one network to another.

We just saw that there is a whole other group of protocols, including RIP, IGRP, EIGRP, OSPF, and others, that have nothing to do with directly moving data frames. They are a parallel system that makes sure the routers have the information they need to be able to "route" your data. Their routing updates move through the circuits with your data (share bandwidth) much like cars and trucks share the roads. We look at these routing protocols in depth in Chapter 11 when we prepare to configure routers.

As if learning all of these protocols and acronyms weren't confusing enough, it is quite important to know whether they are network protocols (routable or non-routable) or routing protocols. The next table summarizes this for you.

Network Protocols

Protocols are agreed upon sets of rules and procedures that allow people, organizations, or devices to work together that are not particularly inclined to. The world of politics has many protocols that allow even nations at war to exchange representatives and conduct business. Often, what is thought of as a single protocol is actually a group or suite of protocols.

NETWORK PROTOCOLS (ROUTABLE/ ROUTED)	NETWORK PROTOCOLS (NONROUTABLE/ NONROUTED)	ROUTING PROTOCOLS
TCP/IP	NetBEUI	*Routing Information Protocol* (RIP)
IPX/SPX	DLC	*Enhanced Interior Gateway Routing Protocol* (EIGRP)
XNS (old)		*Open Shortest Path First* (OSPF)
DECNet (old)		*Border Gateway Protocol* (BGP)
AppleTalk		*NetWare Link Services Protocol* (NLSP - Novell)
		Routing Table Maintenance Protocol (RTMP - Apple)

This is true of network protocols as well. What we refer to as TCP/IP is an acronym for a protocol suite or stack made up of two major protocols: Transmission Control Protocol and Internet Protocol. But each of these protocols in fact includes other protocols. As we go along, these will be pointed out, because eventually you will need to know which are the IP or Layer 3 protocols as compared to, say, the TCP or Layer 4 protocols. This is not nitpicking for the exam; understanding what occurs at each layer of the OSI model, as well as what each protocol does, will make debugging your networks much easier. It separates systematic debugging from dumb luck.

The network protocol that we will spend the most time with is TCP/IP, because it's the networking protocol of the Internet, UNIX, and Windows NT/2000. Occasionally, we will return to IPX/SPX, not only because the exam objective requires, but also because a substantial installed base of IPX is still in place throughout the world.

There is a tendency for some students to frame this as a Microsoft vs. Novell issue. Whatever else may be going on, however, this issue has really been decided by the Internet's use of TCP/IP. If anything, it was almost Novell vs. the rest of the world until Novell came out with version 5 of its operating system, which now supports TCP/IP.

In this section, as we introduce network protocols, keep in mind that some are introduced for reference and to expose you to them in case you come across them in the workplace.

NetBEUI

NetBEUI was developed in the 1980s when small LANs were the norm. It conforms to the OSI model for Layers 1, 2, 4, and 5, but lacks the network (Layer 3) features that would allow it to be routed. There is not enough information in the NetBEUI frame to identify different networks.

So why not ignore it altogether? That day is coming, but NetBEUI is very easy to set up and use in a small LAN (up to 200 hosts). If it is activated on every host, and each device has a unique name, you can share folders and printers. What you cannot do is connect to other networks, such as the Internet, because that would require routing. At one time, NetBEUI was a natural starting point for connecting a few computers together in a home or a business. In the business model, the networks often grow. Now it is your job to switch them over to a TCP/IP network so that they can connect to the outside world.

The drawbacks to NetBEUI are that it's nonroutable, not compatible with the Internet, and isn't supported by non-Microsoft operating systems. Connecting a few PCs and a Mac computer (or UNIX box) cannot be done with NetBEUI.

IPX/SPX

IPX is the Layer 3 part of this Novell network protocol. This was one of the many derivatives of the XNS protocol developed in the early 1980s that went on to dominate LAN networking for over ten years.

While IPX is a routable protocol, unfortunately it is not directly compatible with the Internet or networks running TCP/IP's IP protocol. A "gateway" device is often required to fully integrate Novell servers and server resources into, say, a Windows NT network or visa versa. Figure 5-10 shows the IPX/SPX protocol suite mapped to the OSI model.

All the Layer 1 and 2 protocols shown are the same ones we've seen before in our earlier discussions. Like all network protocols, IPX/SPX is primarily concerned about Layers 3 to 7 and leaves the access method to the traditional Layer 1 and 2 protocols like Ethernet and Token Ring.

Notice also that IPX is at Layer 3, where TCP/IP's IP is found. Also, SPX is at Layer 4, where TCP is found. So while we won't talk as much about IPX/SPX, if similar functionality exists in both protocols, remembering this relationship will help you find the counterpart in IPX/SPX. Figure 5-11 shows the relationship.

Microsoft offers an IPX-compatible protocol for workstations that need to access IPX networks. This product is called NWLink, but it is often referred to as an IPX-compatible protocol. NWLink is another XNS derivative. We will look at setting up this feature in the labs at the end of this chapter.

Some things to know about IPX are that the addresses are up to 80 bits long and that the last 48 bits are always the MAC address. So, if you have the network address, you should be able to parse the network ID and the MAC address or host ID. Figure 5-12 shows several IPX addresses with the network ID and host ID (MAC address).

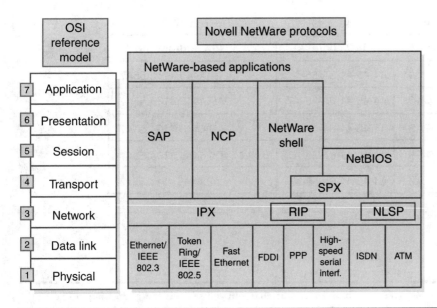

Figure 5-10   IPX/SPX vs. OSI model

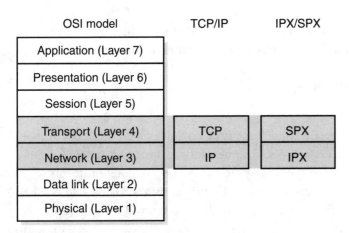

Figure 5-11   IPX/SPX vs. TCP/IP

Up to 32 bits	48 bits	Up to 80 bits
NETWORK ID	MAC address	IPX address
1	44-45-41-6A-55-A7	1.4445.416A.55A7
DAD	44-45-41-6A-55-A7	DAD.4445.416A.55A7
47AB	44-45-41-6A-55-A7	47AB.4445.416A.55A7
12A7.44E5	44-45-41-6A-55-A7	12A7.44E5.4445.416A.55A7
aa	44-45-41-6a-55-a7	aa.4445.416a.55a7

Figure 5-12   IPX addressing

 EXAM TIP: You have to assume that you will see this IPX addressing in one form or another. Make sure you understand the length is a maximum of 80 bits and that the last 48 bits are always the MAC address.

Table 5-1 contains some of the IPX/SPX acronyms that you will need to eventually become familiar with. We will look at these in greater detail in later chapters.

DLC, AppleTalk, XNS, DECNet, Banyan Vines, and so on

The exam should have no questions on these protocols. If you come across any old study materials, you may find references to some of these protocols. Except for DLC, which is not routable, you will find references to many of these older protocols when you actually start working with the routers and particularly the Help feature. Cisco evolved at the time many of these protocols were developing, and it chose to support them. So you will find features still supported today. Just because a protocol ceases to be popular does not mean that every customer that uses it will abandon it. It may be functioning just fine and, assuming it is not impacting network performance in other ways, can be left alone.

By default, all Macs still use AppleTalk. They do support TCP/IP, but AppleTalk is still pretty popular, because it is the default and generally just works. It is a very simple protocol to work with in an all-Mac network.

Table 5-1   IPX/SPX Acronyms to Know

ACRONYM	STANDS FOR	OSI LAYER	MEANS
GNS	Get Nearest Server		A request packet sent by a client on an IPX network to locate the nearest active server offering a particular type of service, such as printing or file storage. An IPX client issues a GNS request to get a response either from a local server or from a router that tells it where on the internetwork the service can be found.
IPX	Internetwork Packet Exchange	3	Novell NetWare network layer (Layer 3) protocol used for transferring data from servers to workstations. IPX is similar to IP and XNS, offering a connectionless internetwork service and features for addressing.
IPX/SPX	Internetwork Packet Exchange/ Sequential Packet Exchange		Common name for the suite of protocols used by Novell Netware until version 5 and Windows NT v3.51.
ODI	Open Data-Link Interface	2	Novell specification providing a standardized interface for NICs that allows multiple protocols to use a single NIC.
SAP	Service Advertisement Protocol	4-7	IPX protocol that provides a means for servers to inform network clients, via routers or directly, of available network resources and services.
SPX	Sequential Packet Exchange	4	Reliable, connection-oriented protocol that supplements the datagram service provided by IPX. Novell derived this protocol from the SPP of the XNS protocol suite.

TCP/IP

TCP/IP can trace its roots back to the 1960s when the U.S. *Department of Defense* (DOD) was concerned that during and in the aftermath of a nuclear attack, command and control of the military's many noncompatible computer systems could be lost. The research arm of the DOD, called the *Advanced Research Projects Agency* (ARPA), funded a large-scale research project to develop a packet-switched WAN technology that would be less vulnerable to a single point of failure.

The ultimate goal was to develop a robust transport protocol (ultimately IP) and a series of protocols that would allow computer systems from many manufacturers to share data (interoperability).

The original test of this new network, called ARPANET, included connecting three California and one Utah universities together with 50 Kbps phone lines. This test was successful in 1969. Over the next two decades, more universities and private research facilities got involved, if for no other reason than that ARPANET provided a "free" vehicle for sharing information with other researchers. Because the U.S. government was underwriting the network, the communication was free and the technology evolving became part of the public domain. In addition, it greatly increased the number of people who were developing tools and technologies to work in this new environment.

In 1985, I worked at the Academic Computing Center on the University of Washington campus, and I remember using this somewhat cryptic tool. More importantly, I remember other University employees developing Macintosh interfaces for ARPANET and other University mainframe systems. While I can't take any credit for the work, I clearly remember thinking that someday this funny little computer with icons and pointer device (mouse) would be the future of computing.

The huge academic interest in the protocols evolving was further advanced when TCP/IP was included in the Berkeley version of UNIX and became a protocol supported on mainframes, minicomputers, and personal computers.

The evolving TCP/IP networks were being referred to as the Internet or Net. Later, development of tools such as Web browsers and the World Wide Web brought all of this connectivity into our businesses and homes. Underneath it all is still TCP/IP.

Several TCP/IP protocols function at Layer 3, including ARP, DHCP, RARP, BOOTP, ICMP, IGMP, and IP. We will describe the function of these protocols in this section. Figure 5-13 compares the TCP/IP model to the OSI model and shows the Layer 3 protocols.

Internet Protocol (IP)

The IP protocol defines the logical or software addressing for every host on the network. That address includes both a network ID and a node ID. Recall that the MAC address provides the physical addressing. In addition to the address system, the network has a subnet mask that allows the network layer to quickly separate the network ID from the node ID. The network ID determines whether the address is local or must be sent to a

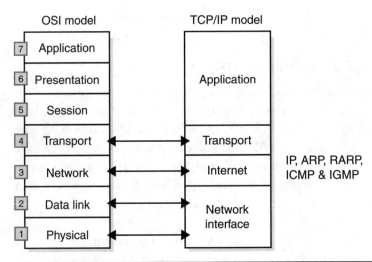

Figure 5-13   TCP/IP model vs. OSI model

router for forwarding. For example, assume the local host computer is configured with the following:

IP address: 192.168.1.177

Subnet mask: 255.255.255.0

Default gateway: 192.168.1.1

The mask tells us that the first three octets (192.168.1) identify the network, while the last octet (177) identifies the host. If we send any packets outside of this local network, they need to be forwarded (routed) through the default gateway (192.168.1.1), which is a router connected to this network. We will look at IP addressing and subnet masks in greater detail later in this chapter.

As the transport and higher layers are assembling the data segments, they are not concerned about the actual size of the final data frames. The IP protocol, if necessary, fragments these segments into packets suitable for transmission. It also applies sequencing numbers so that the packets can be reassembled into segments on the receiving device at Layer 3. Each of the packets has the IP address of the source and destination appended before it is passed on to the data link layer.

The IP protocol, having already determined whether the destination IP address is local (same network ID) or needs to be routed, goes to the ARP table and gets the MAC address of the destination if it is local or the default gateway router if the packet has to be forwarded. This MAC address is passed to the data link layer with the packet.

Dynamic Host Configuration Protocol (DHCP)

DHCP provides a mechanism for dynamically assigning IP addresses so that they can be automatically reused when hosts no longer need them. Instead of having to assign a static IP address, subnet mask, default gateway, and other resource addresses to each host, the DCHP server device can respond to a host request and furnish the information. The DHCP device could be a network server or a device such as a router. Many Cisco routers support the DHCP server service. This is also becoming a common feature on even the smallest of ISDN, DSL, and cable routers, allowing even small home networks to use DHCP technology.

We will discuss DHCP later in this section, and look at its implementation in Chapter 10 with regard to LAN design. At the same time, we will look at the IP Helper feature supported on many Cisco routers. We will also revisit DHCP in Chapter 21 when we cover Internet connectivity issues.

Address Resolution Protocol (ARP)

ARP maintains a table of IP and MAC address combinations, which IP address is associated with MAC address. ARP also has a mechanism to poll the local network if it needs a MAC address that it doesn't have. This table and process are accessed by the IP protocol as it is preparing a packet to be passed on to the data link layer for final framing. While Layer 2 builds the frame, it can pull the source MAC address from the NIC, but the destination MAC address is determined and supplied by Layer 3.

When a packet is being readied for transmission, the source and destination IP addresses must be attached at Layer 3, but when that packet is passed on to Layer 2 for the final framing, the destination hardware (MAC) address must also be supplied for the access protocols (Ethernet, Token Ring, and so on) to use. The IP protocol stack, the implementation of the protocol for any particular device, uses the subnet mask to derive the network ID of the destination and then determines whether the IP destination address is on the same network. If it is, we need the MAC address of the destination. If it's not, we need the MAC address of the default gateway. The default gateway is the router interface to which the local network is connected to provide connectivity with other networks. We need its MAC address because we are going to deliver the packet there and let the router forward it for us. Default gateways are discussed later in this section, and their implementation will be addressed in Chapter 10.

The first thing the source host does is check its own ARP table. This table is stored in the host's memory and contains the MAC and IP addresses of any host that the source has had recent communications with. If the MAC address is found, it is passed on with the packet to Layer 2. Figure 5-14 shows the laptop host A looking up host D's IP address in its ARP table. It won't be found.

If the MAC address is not found, the network protocol stack issues an ARP broadcast to the local network, asking for the MAC address of the host having the destination IP address. Only the host with that IP address can respond. It does so by sending a unicast back to the source; it does not need to broadcast because it has both the IP and MAC addresses of the source from the broadcast packet.

The source updates its ARP table and the MAC address is passed on with the packet to Layer 2.

Reverse Address Resolution Protocol (RARP)

Certain types of computers do not have storage disks for security or cost reasons. Such a computer therefore has no place to store its IP configuration when it is shut down. RARP allows a machine to broadcast its MAC address and a request for the necessary IP information. A RARP server on the network will respond with the information.

Whereas the ARP table is built and updated continually based on activity between hosts and is cleared of inactive entries to make sure that data frames aren't being sent to a shutdown workstation, the RARP table is configured by the administrator and remains indefinitely until changed. Dropping a RARP entry would mean that the host couldn't get an IP address the next time it started.

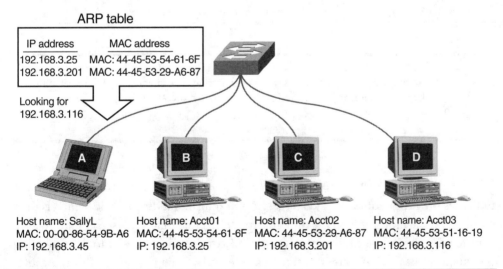

Figure 5-14   Sample network with an ARP table search

Very few networks use RARP anymore. Microsoft networks often use a DHCP server to perform RARP functions when needed.

Internet Control Message Protocol (ICMP)

ICMP (RFC 792) is a messaging service that allows a destination device or interim router to notify a source about various problems or conditions. These messages can be used for connectivity testing, flow control, or notification of discarded packets.

The following ICMP messages are samples of the types of messages and their purpose:

MESSAGE	PURPOSE
Echo	Sent by Ping command to verify connectivity.
Echo Reply	Response message from pinged host.
Time Exceeded	Packet took too long to be delivered. TTL dropped to zero. Discarding router sends message to source host.
Destination Unreachable	There are five messages for various packet-delivery problems.
Redirect	Router is notifying the source that another router would have been a better route.
Source Quench	Sent to the source because it is putting out packets faster than can be forwarded.
Parameter Problem	Notifies source that data parameter is wrong.
Timestamp/Reply	Used to measure round-trip time to a host.

 EXAM TIP: Being aware that the messages in the table are important when working with networks. You should assume that any of them could appear on the CCNA exam, although the first six are by far the most likely.

Echo, Echo Reply, and Ping

Ping uses the Echo request to ask a target host to transmit an Echo Reply, which is then reported on the monitor with the time information. Note that the Cisco enhanced Ping command allows some flexibility in testing the connectivity. We will look at the ping command in Basic Connectivity Exercise at the end of this chapter and in the router configuration coverage in Chapter 13.

Time Exceeded and TTL

As discussed earlier in this chapter, to prevent packets that get into a data loop from circulating forever, a header field is assigned a Time To Live by the source. This TTL is the
number of routing devices (hops) it can pass through before it is discarded. At each
device, the TTL is reduced by one second before forwarding. When it gets to zero, the
packet is discarded and the source is sent a Time Exceeded message.

The Cisco Trace and TCP/IP Tracert commands both use the TTL feature in a rather
clever way. The Trace (or Tracert) command sends three IP packets to the destination
with the TTL set to 1, three with the TTL set to 2, and so on. When the three packets with
the TTL set to 1 reach the first router, the 1 is decremented to 0 and the packet is discarded. A Time Exceeded message is sent to the source. The source now knows the IP
address of the first router from the message IP header. The packets with the TTL set to 2
are discarded by the second router and an ICMP message is sent. This continues until
there is a trail to the destination device. The following sample of the Cisco Trace command demonstrates the feature. The delivery times appear after the IP address.

```
lab-F#trace 192.168.93.2

Type escape sequence to abort.
Tracing the route to 192.168.93.2

  1 192.168.95.2 20 msec 20 msec 20 msec
  2 192.168.94.2 20 msec 16 msec 20 msec
  3 192.168.93.2 36 msec *  36 msec

lab-F#
```

Destination Unreachable

One of five different messages is sent, depending on the circumstances. In the ICMP
header, the Type field contains the code for Destination Unreachable, and the Code
field has a code to represent each of the following:

MESSAGE	SENT BY	PURPOSE
Network Unreachable	Router	No matching network for the packet is found in the routing table.
Host Unreachable	Router	Router connected to the destination network is not getting a response from the destination address; host might be off.
Can't Fragment	Router	Router needs to fragment the packet to forward it, but the Don't Fragment bit is set on.

MESSAGE	SENT BY	PURPOSE
Port Unreachable	Destination host	Requested port on destination host has not been opened by an application.
Protocol Unreachable	Destination host	The needed transport layer protocol is not available on the destination host.

IP Redirect

One of the functions of a router is to develop a routing table with a "best" route to each network. So it would seem that, under normal circumstances, this command shouldn't be needed. But if a local network is connected to more than one router—and one of the routers has been designated as the default gateway—then packets destined for outside the network will be sent by the hosts to the gateway for forwarding. What if the destination network is closer to the second router, possibly connected to it? The gateway can forward these packets, but it will send an ICMP Redirect message to the source host advising it to forward the remaining packets in this conversation directly to the other router.

Internet Group Management Protocol (IGMP)

As we have discussed, broadcasts can seriously impact the performance of our networks, because each host must process the frame at least far enough to recognize that it is of no interest. Routers then default to discarding broadcasts, thereby limiting their impact on the local network. So what do you do with network-based company announcements, press releases, training, and so forth? If we send them out using broadcasts, the routers will discard them. If we tell the routers to forward broadcasts, we have chaos.

Multicast routers send IGMP query messages to their attached local networks. Host members of a multicast group respond to a query by sending IGMP reports noting the multicast groups to which they belong. The multicast router takes responsibility for forwarding multicast datagrams from one multicast group to all other networks that have members in the group. The multicast packet is a single packet copied by the network and sent to a specific subset of network addresses. These addresses are specified in the destination address field.

Some routing protocols, such as OSPF and RIPv2, use multicasts so that routing updates go only to selected devices and are ignored by hosts, thereby reducing host CPU processing. Updates that are done with broadcasts must be processed at least to the point that they are determined to be irrelevant to the host.

> **NOTE:** It's still too early for this to appear in much detail on the exam, but you should at least recognize that ICMP and IGMP are not the same thing. In larger enterprises, router multicasts will be an important technology to be aware of. You should also know that any IP address with a first octet between 224 and 239, such as 224.0.0.9, is a multicast IP address. While it won't be on the exam, there are also multicast MAC addresses.

IP Addressing Basics

IP addresses are 32-bit binary values made up of four 8-bit values that are usually displayed in decimal form separated by decimal points. A few examples are 10.17.161.27 and 213.98.116.45. In Chapter 9, we will look at the binary numbers behind these decimal values, and work with calculating IP to decimal and decimal to binary. In this chapter we will look at some basic concepts without getting into the calculations.

The largest 8-bit value (11111111) is equal to 255 in decimal, which means the largest value that can appear in any octet of an IP address is 255. The smallest value is all 0's (00000000) and equates to 0, so the smallest value is 0. The range of possible values then is 0 to 255 for a total of 256 possibilities.

> **NOTE:** In computing, we will start our increments with 0—the exact center of the decimal numbering system. If we were to start at 1, we would skip all the valid decimal values between 0 and 1. This will take a little getting used to for some people. Another example involves 60-character documents or screens where character positions are identified as position 0 to 59.

Subnet Mask

A subnet mask, sometimes called the network mask or routing mask, is a tool used by the IP protocol to quickly identify the network portion of an IP address. Layer 3 looks only at that portion of the address to determine first whether the destination is local (in the same network) and, if not, where to forward the packet.

Technically, a subnet mask is a contiguous string of binary 1's starting at the left end of the address (higher-order bits), and the point at which the mask switches to 0's represents the border between the network ID and the host ID. If you recall that 255 is the decimal equivalent of eight 1's, or an octet of 1's, you should see that 255.0.0.0 indicates that only the first octet is the network ID, while the last three octets identify the host ID.

When configuring any device requiring an IP address and subnet mask, having the correct subnet mask is critical to reliable data flow.

Classful IP Addressing

The original group of people who developed TCP/IP did not envision its potential widespread use. They developed an addressing system in which the first octet was used to identify a local network, such as a university or branch of the military, which resulted in over 16 million host addresses available on that network. After all, there were over 250 unique first octets and only a few member organizations. So, they gave each member organization a unique first octet and continued to do that as new organizations wanted to connect to the growing internetwork.

As the number of schools and organizations wanting to participate grew, it was apparent that someday the number of IP network addresses would be exhausted. It was also recognized that giving every organization a network address with over 16 million host possibilities was a gross waste of addresses.

The various groups that governed the organization discussed and debated options and came up with a five-class system that would extend the life of the pool of IP addresses and somewhat more efficiently assign the remaining addresses. An organization called *Internet Assigned Numbers Authority* (IANA) was given the responsibility of assigning IP address pools. IANA delegated the task to *Network Information Center* (NIC), which later became InterNIC, and today is Network Solutions. Figure 5-15 shows the IP class addresses.

You will notice that the first octet alone determines the class. This is often called the "first octet rule." Whereas the original system could include a maximum of only 256

Class	Decimal value range	Maximum networks	Maximum hosts	Subnet mask
A	0–127	127	16,777,214	255.0.0.0
B	128–191	16,384	65,534	255.255.0.0
C	192–223	2,097,152	254	255.255.255.0
D	224–239			
E	240–255			

Figure 5-15   IP classful IP addresses

networks, this system allows for over two million. Also, the original system had over 16 million hosts in each network, whereas the new system allows for as few as 254 hosts in each network.

The subnet column indicates the default subnet mask for each class, and translates to class A networks having only their first octet assigned as a network ID, while class B networks have the first two octets assigned, and class C networks have the first three octets assigned. The remaining octet(s) can be assigned by the organization.

There are some important exclusions that you need to be aware of:

- Class D addresses are reserved exclusively for router multicasts, and class E is reserved for future expansion and research.

- First octet 0 (00000000) is not allowed.

- First octet 127 (01111111) is reserved for loopback and is used for internal testing. Using the ping command with the loopback address confirms a properly installed and functioning TCP/IP stack on the local machine (ping 127.0.0.1 at command line).

Private Addresses

The following IP address ranges are set aside as private addresses and can be used by any organization within its internal networks. While routers within your network will forward them normally, routers out in the Internet will drop them.

10.0.0.0 to 10.255.255.255: A full class A network

172.16.0.0 to 172.31.255.255: 16 contiguous class B networks

192.168.0.0 to 192.168.255.255: 255 contiguous class C networks

The first two are particularly useful for those organizations requiring a class B or A address pool, because none are left to be assigned. The drawback, of course, is that these addresses cannot be used directly on the Internet. The good news is that there are techniques, such as *Network Address Translation* (NAT), that will allow an organization to use the private addresses within their networks and a much smaller pool of public addresses from its ISP. It is not necessary or possible to register these addresses with any registration body, such as Network Solutions.

Default Gateway

If a network is connected to a single router, that connection interface is the default gateway for the local hosts on the network. This default gateway is the local network's portal to any other networks. If no default gateway is defined as part of the host configuration, communication is possible only with other hosts on the device's own logical (local) network segment.

Like the IP address and the subnet mask, an administrator can key this in as part of the host configuration, or a device performing DHCP services can assign it. Either way, the default gateway is the router interface that is a part of the local network and therefore shares the same network ID as the rest of the hosts. Figure 5-16 shows two networks connected by a router.

The router interface connected to the switch, 192.168.3.1, will be the default gateway for every host connected to that switch. The other router interface, 192.168.5.1, will be the default gateway for the other network.

This default gateway is used for data frames destined outside the local network for which there is no more specific route. In the case of a network with a single router connection, such as the one in Figure 5-16, the router interface would always be the default gateway.

It is possible, particularly for a large LAN, to have two or more router connections, in which case one would be designated as the default gateway. The second router would only be used for outgoing packets if an ICMP IP redirect message, as covered earlier in

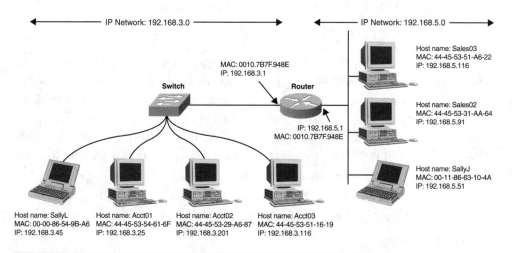

Figure 5-16 Two networks and a router

this chapter, is sent to the source by the default gateway, or if one or more hosts has a static route added to their routing tables.

In the example in Figure 5-16, if any host in the 192.168.3.0 network needs to get data to any host on the 192.168.5.0 network, it will have to do so via the default gateway. Let's look at the process for SallyL sending data to SallyJ on the other network.

First, as the packets are being assembled at Layer 3 of SallyL's laptop, her IP address is being applied as the source address, and SallyJ's IP address is going in as the destination address.

By now, the IP protocol knows they are not both in the local network. Using the default mask for a class C address (192) of 255.255.255.0 and performing a binary AND, it is determined that SallyL is in the 192.168.3.0 network while SallyJ is in the 192.168.5.0 network. (We look at the specifics of the binary AND in Chapter 9.)

We cannot get a MAC address for SallyJ for our Layer 2 destination address. Even if we tried to do an ARP broadcast, the router would kill it. We are stuck on opposite sides of the router.

SallyL's IP protocol goes to the ARP table and gets the MAC address of the default gateway. If for some reason it wasn't there, an ARP broadcast looking for the MAC address to go with IP address 192.168.3.1 would be answered by the router, and the ARP table would be updated. The MAC address for the default gateway will be forwarded with each packet to Layer 2 for final preparation.

The data link protocols will finish the frame and put SallyL's MAC address in as the Layer 2 source address and the default gateway's MAC address as the destination address. The frames are then put out on the network.

At the 192.168.3.1 interface of the router, the destination address will be confirmed as that of this interface. The frame will be moved into a buffer, and any quality control required by the access protocol will be performed. Conceptually, the frame will be removed and the data segment will be forwarded to Layer 3.

At Layer 3, the IP protocol will determine that it is not the intended destination because the IP address in the destination address doesn't match one of the router interfaces. So, it will determine that it has to forward the packet. It then checks the routing table for the network portion of the destination address and finds a matching directly connected route.

The IP protocol then checks the ARP table to get the MAC address for SallyJ based on her IP address and forwards that MAC address back down to Layer 2 with the packet. The data link protocols will finish the frame and put the router's MAC address in as the Layer 2 source address and SallyJ's MAC address as the destination address. The frames are then put out on the network for final delivery.

When SallyJ's machine receives the frames, Layer 2 will see the source as the router, while Layer 3 will see SallyL as the real source.

Layer 3 Devices

What is a Layer 3 device? The short answer is that any device with an IP address is a Layer 3 device, including any network hosts. Possibly a more complete definition would include any device that can route packets based on network addresses. This is also the definition of a router. A router is a Layer 3 device and, just like a PC, has Layer 1 and 2 components. While routing occurs at Layer 3, the terms "Layer 3" and "router" are often used as if they were synonymous. Much like a lion is always a cat, but all cats are not lions, the router is always a Layer 3 device, but not all Layer 3 devices are routers.

Today there are switches with Layer 3 modules that can perform Layer 2 switching, and the Layer 3 modules can also route data as needed. Several Cisco Catalyst switch models support L3 modules. The trend toward using more switches in our networks and the evolution of VLANs (covered in Chapter 16) make switches with Layer 3 capabilities very attractive. It is possible to have several similar-looking models of switches wherein some are strictly Layer 2 while others can also perform routing because of the Layer 3 module.

Keep in mind that in some networks, a server can be routing between networks. If you look at the function they are providing, you shouldn't have any trouble determining if it is working as a router. If there are two or more NICs, each in a different network, and data can be forwarded by the server from one network to another, then the server is routing and functioning at Layer 3. This is sometimes referred to as a multihomed server.

Remember also that while workstation hosts do not route between networks, they do perform some Layer 3 functions and use Layer 3 protocols when they process data both in- and outbound.

 EXAM TIP: For the exam, understand that a router is an example of a Layer 3 device and that routers function in Layer 3 of the OSI reference model.

TCP/IP Acronyms

Table 5-2 contains some of the TCP/IP-related acronyms that you need to eventually become familiar with. The various Internet organizations will not be tested, but you should at least recognize them. We will look at these in greater detail in later chapters.

Table 5-2   TCP/IP Acronyms to Know

ACRONYM	STANDS FOR	OSI LAYER	MEANS
ARP	Address Resolution Protocol	3	Internet protocol used to map an IP address to a MAC address.
DHCP	Dynamic Host Configuration Protocol	7	Provides a means for allocating IP addresses dynamically. Easier to implement than static addressing, and an address can be automatically reused if a host no longer needs it.
DNS	Domain Naming System	7	Internet process for translating names of network nodes into addresses.
FTP	File Transfer Protocol	7	Application layer protocol used for transferring files between network nodes. Part of TCP/IP protocol stack.
IAB	Internet Architecture Board		Board of internetwork researchers who oversee issues pertinent to Internet architecture. Responsible for appointing a variety of Internet-related groups such as the IANA, IESG, and IRSG. The trustees of ISOC appoint the IAB.
IANA	Internet Assigned Numbers Authority		The original authority for IP address-space allocation and domain-name assignment to InterNIC and other organizations. Also maintains a database of assigned protocol IDs used in the TCP/IP stack, including autonomous system numbers. Operates under the auspices of the ISOC as a part of the IAB.
ICMP	Internet Control Message Protocol	3	Network layer Internet protocol that reports errors and provides other information relevant to IP packet processing.
IESG	Internet Engineering Steering Group		Organization, appointed by IAB, that manages the operation of the IETF.
IETF	Internet Engineering Task Force		Consists of working groups responsible for developing Internet standards. Operates under the auspices of ISOC.
IGMP	Internet Group Management Protocol	3	Used by IP hosts to report their multicast group memberships to an adjacent multicast router.

Table 5-2 TCP/IP Acronyms to Know (continued)

ACRONYM	STANDS FOR	OSI LAYER	MEANS
InterNIC	Internet Network Information Center		Organization serving the Internet community by supplying registration service for Internet domain names, and other services. Formerly called *Network Information Center* (NIC) and now called Network Solutions.
IP	Internet Protocol	3	Network layer protocol in TCP/IP protocol stack that offers connectionless internetwork service. Provides features for addressing, *type-of-service* (TOS) specification, fragmentation and reassembly, and security.
IRSG	Internet Research Steering Group		Part of the IAB and oversees the activities of the IRTF.
IRTF	Internet Research Task Force		Network experts who consider Internet-related research topics. Governed by the IRSG and is a subsidiary of the IAB.
ISOC	Internet Society		International nonprofit organization that coordinates the development and use of the Internet. Delegates authority to other groups related to the Internet, such as the IAB.
NDIS	Network Device Interface Specification		A set of Microsoft standards for network drivers that define communication between the NIC and other protocols, allowing multiple protocols on a single NIC.
NIC	Network Information Center		*See InterNIC.* Old term. Don't confuse with network interface card.
RARP	Reverse Address Resolution Protocol	3	Protocol in the TCP/IP stack that provides a method for finding IP addresses based on MAC addresses.

Table 5-2 TCP/IP Acronyms to Know (continued)

ACRONYM	STANDS FOR	OSI LAYER	MEANS
RFCs	Requests for Comments		Series of documents used as the primary means for communicating information about the Internet. Some RFCs are designated by the IAB as Internet standards. Most RFCs document protocol specifications such as Telnet and FTP. Always followed by a number; e.g., RFC 791 defines IP.
SMTP	Simple Mail Transfer Protocol		Internet protocol providing electronic mail services.
SNMP	Simple Network Management Protocol		Network management protocol used in TCP/IP networks to provide a way to remotely monitor and control network devices, and to manage configurations, statistics collection, performance, and security.
TCP	Transmission Control Protocol	4	Connection-oriented transport layer protocol that provides reliable full-duplex data transmission.
TCP/IP	Transmission Control Protocol/ Internet Protocol		Suite of protocols developed for the U.S. DOD in the 1970s to support the construction of worldwide internetworks.
TFTP	Trivial File Transfer Protocol		Stripped-down version of FTP that allows files to be transferred from one node to another over a network.
UDP	User Datagram Protocol	4	Connectionless transport layer protocol that exchanges datagrams without acknowledgments or guaranteed delivery, relying on other protocols for error processing and retransmission if necessary.
URL	Universal Resource Locator		Standardized addressing scheme for accessing hypertext documents and other services using a Web browser.
WINS	Windows Internet Naming Service		Not a TCP/IP protocol, but a Microsoft technology that maps NetBIOS names to IP addresses.
WWW	World Wide Web		Large network of Internet servers providing hypertext and other services to users with Web browsers.

Optional Exercises

The following optional exercises are provided for those readers who may have limited hands-on experience with the features covered in this chapter. Each exercise is intended to demonstrate a topic covered in or related to the chapter as well as provide basic familiarity with the technology.

Address Exercise

The following lab assumes you are using any version of Windows. You will go out and see your host name, MAC address, and network address. This is a nondestructive lab and you should be able to do it with your home machine without concern of changing your system configuration.

Windows 95/98/Me

1. If you are doing this at home, establish a connection to your *Internet Service Provider* (ISP). This will connect you via your modem and make sure that you have an IP address. In a TCP/IP LAN, it shouldn't be necessary to do this step.

2. Using the taskbar, choose Start | Run. Type **winipcfg** and press ENTER. The following illustration shows the Run screen and the entry. Spelling winipcfg correctly is critical, although case is not. It is short for Windows IP Configuration.

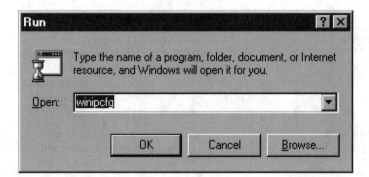

3. This first screen shows the adapter address (or MAC address), IP address, subnet mask, and the default gateway. Illustration 2 shows the basic IP Configuration screen.

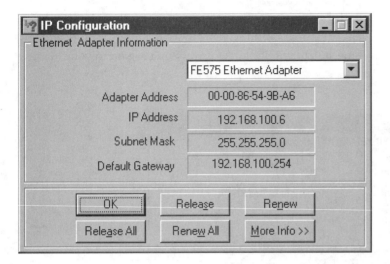

4. You should find that the IP address and the default gateway are in the same net-work or subnet; otherwise, this host wouldn't be able to communicate outside the network. In the previous illustration, the subnet mask tells us that the first three octets must be the same to be in the same network.

If you are on a LAN, you might not see the default gateway if you are running behind a proxy server.

If you are doing this on a LAN, compare the IP addresses of several machines. Are there any similarities?

What about the default gateways?

What about the adapter (MAC) addresses?

The IP addresses should share the same network portion. All machines in the LAN should share the same default gateway. While not a requirement, most LAN administrators try to standardize components such as NICS, so it would not be surprising to find all machines share the first three Hex pairs in the adapter address.

5. We also see our adapter model in the box at the top of the screen. Note what is displayed in that box.

Use the drop-down arrow in that box to see if there are any other configurations for this adapter (such as PPP). This could be true for a modem if you have AOL and another service provider. On a server, it is possible you might find another

NIC or a machine with both an NIC and a modem. The following illustration shows an AOL modem IP Configuration screen. Notice that there is no IP address. This is what your home system will look like if you don't log on to your Internet connection.

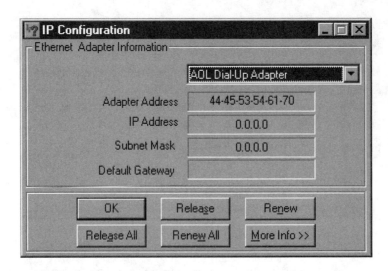

6. Be sure to return to the adapter that displays the NIC or modem data with an IP address.
   Write down both the IP address and the default gateway address.

7. Click the More Info button. Illustration 4 shows the detailed IP Configuration screen.

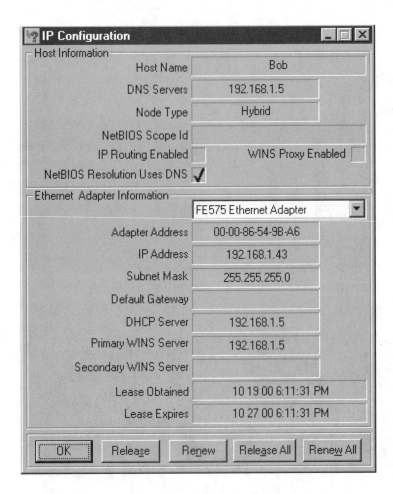

8. You should now see the host name (computer name, NetBIOS name), the DHCP server's address, if used, and the date the IP lease starts and ends. Look over the remaining information. You will probably see entries for DNS and WINS servers, which are used in name resolution.

Do all the servers share the same network portion of the IP address as your workstation? It would not be unusual for some or all to be in another network. It means that our default gateway is going to forward (route) our requests to the other network.

We will look at these servers in Chapter 10.

9. Write down the IP addresses of any servers listed. We will use these addresses in the ping exercise later.

10. Close the screen when you are through looking around.

Windows NT/2000

1. If you are doing this at home, establish a connection to your *Internet Service Provider* (ISP). This will connect you via your modem and make sure that you have an IP address. In a TCP/IP LAN, it shouldn't be necessary to do this step.

2. Use the Start menu to open the Command Prompt (MS-DOS-like) window (Start | Programs | Accessories | Command Prompt or Start | Programs | Command Prompt).

3. Type **ipconfig** and press ENTER. The following illustration shows the Command Prompt screen. Spelling ipconfig correctly is critical, although case is not.

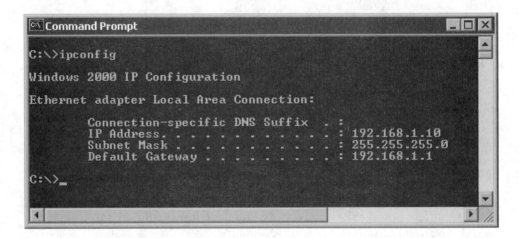

4. This first screen shows only the IP address, subnet mask, and default gateway. You should find that the IP address and the default gateway are in the same network or subnet; otherwise, this host wouldn't be able to communicate outside the network. In the previous illustration, the subnet mask tells us that the first three octets must be the same to be in the same network.

If you are on a LAN, you might not see the default gateway if you are running behind a proxy server.

If you are doing this on a LAN, compare the IP addresses of several machines. Are there any similarities?

What about the default gateways?

The IP addresses should share the same network portion. All machines in the LAN should share the same default gateway.

5. Write down both the IP address and the default gateway address.

6. To see more info, type **ipconfig /all** and press ENTER. The following illustration shows the detailed Command Prompt screen.

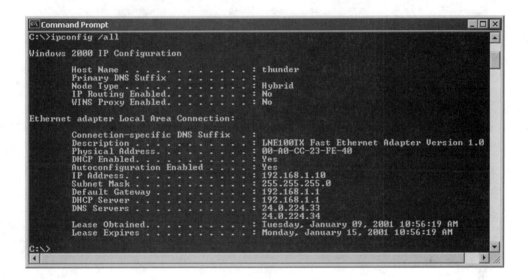

7. You should now see the host name (computer name, NetBIOS name), the DHCP servers address, if used, and the date the IP lease starts and ends. Look over the remaining information. You will probably see entries for a DNS server, which are used in name resolution.

Do all the servers share the same network portion of the IP address as your workstation? It would not be unusual for some or all to be in another network. It means that our default gateway is going to forward (route) our requests to the other network.

The previous illustration reveals that my router is also performing DHCP and DNS services for my small network—this is a *small office/home office* (SOHO) or small branch office implementation.

What about the adapter (MAC) addresses?

While not a requirement, most LAN administrators try to standardize components such as NICs, so it would not be surprising to find that all machines share the first three Hex pairs in the adapter address.

We will look at these servers in Chapter 10.

8. Write down the IP addresses of any servers listed.

9. Close the screen when you are through looking around.

Basic Connectivity Exercise

The following lab assumes you are using any version of Windows. This is a nondestructive lab and you should be able to do it with your home machine without concern of changing your system configuration. We will be looking at the Packet Internet Groper (Ping) and Trace Route (Tracert) commands.

1. If you are doing this at home, establish a connection to your ISP. This will connect you via your modem and make sure that you have an IP address. In a TCP/IP LAN, it shouldn't be necessary to do this step.

2. **Windows NT/2000 users:** Use the Start menu to open the Command Prompt (MS-DOS-like) window (Start | Programs | Accessories | Command Prompt or Start | Programs | Command Prompt).
   Windows 95/98/Me users: Use the Start menu to open the MS-DOS Prompt window (Start | Programs | Accessories | MS-DOS Prompt or Start | Programs | MS-DOS Prompt).

3. In the window, type **ping** followed by the IP address of your computer—you wrote it down on the last exercise. It might look like this: *ping 192.168.12.57.* Press ENTER. Ping uses the ICMP Echo Reply feature to test physical connectivity, and since it reports on four attempts, it gives us an indication of the reliability of the connection. The following illustration shows the possible results of pinging your own IP address. Look over your results.

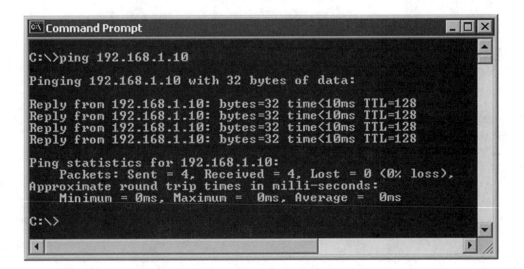

```
C:\>ping 192.168.1.10

Pinging 192.168.1.10 with 32 bytes of data:

Reply from 192.168.1.10: bytes=32 time<10ms TTL=128
Reply from 192.168.1.10: bytes=32 time<10ms TTL=128
Reply from 192.168.1.10: bytes=32 time<10ms TTL=128
Reply from 192.168.1.10: bytes=32 time<10ms TTL=128

Ping statistics for 192.168.1.10:
    Packets: Sent = 4, Received = 4, Lost = 0 (0% loss),
Approximate round trip times in milli-seconds:
    Minimum = 0ms, Maximum =  0ms, Average =  0ms

C:\>
```

4. Try pinging the default gateway's IP address, if one was listed in the last exercise. If you can ping it, it means you have physical connectivity to the router on your network and therefore the rest of the world.

5. Optional: If you are in a class or working with a second computer on the network, try pinging that IP address. Note the results. Try others.

6. Try pinging the IP address of the DHCP and/or any other servers listed in the last exercise. If it works for either server and they are not in your network, what does that tell us? It means our router is functioning as a default gateway to get us out.

7. Try pinging 127.0.0.1 (although it can be any 127 address). The 127 network is reserved for loopback testing. If you can successfully ping the loopback address, you know that TCP/IP is properly installed and functioning on your computer.

8. Try pinging your host name. The next illustration shows the possible result of pinging your host name. Look over your results. Notice that the first line of output shows us the host name followed by the IP address. This means our computer was able to *resolve* the host name to an IP address.

```
Command Prompt                                              _ □ ✕

C:\>ping m450

Pinging m450 [192.168.1.11] with 32 bytes of data:

Reply from 192.168.1.11: bytes=32 time<10ms TTL=128
Reply from 192.168.1.11: bytes=32 time<10ms TTL=128
Reply from 192.168.1.11: bytes=32 time<10ms TTL=128
Reply from 192.168.1.11: bytes=32 time<10ms TTL=128

Ping statistics for 192.168.1.11:
    Packets: Sent = 4, Received = 4, Lost = 0 (0% loss),
Approximate round trip times in milli-seconds:
    Minimum = 0ms, Maximum =  0ms, Average =  0ms

C:\>_
```

9. Optional: Try pinging the host name of another computer on your local network,
   if there are any. The following illustration shows the possible result. Notice that I
   had to put the name in quotes because the command language did not like the
   space in the name. This means I can test connectivity within the local network
   and discover the IP address if I have only a host name. Keep in mind that this may
   only work in Microsoft networks.

```
Command Prompt                                              _ □ ✕

C:\>ping "bob's vaio"

Pinging bob's vaio [192.168.1.12] with 32 bytes of data:

Reply from 192.168.1.12: bytes=32 time<10ms TTL=128
Reply from 192.168.1.12: bytes=32 time<10ms TTL=128
Reply from 192.168.1.12: bytes=32 time<10ms TTL=128
Reply from 192.168.1.12: bytes=32 time<10ms TTL=128

Ping statistics for 192.168.1.12:
    Packets: Sent = 4, Received = 4, Lost = 0 (0% loss),
Approximate round trip times in milli-seconds:
    Minimum = 0ms, Maximum =  0ms, Average =  0ms

C:\>
```

10. Try pinging www.lhseattle.com by typing **ping www.lhseattle.com** and pressing ENTER. The first line of output shows us the *Fully Qualified Domain Name* (FQDN) followed by the IP address. A DNS server was able to resolve the name to an IP address.

11. Try pinging www.microsoft.com and pressing ENTER. The following illustration shows the possible result. Notice that while DNS server was able to resolve the name to an IP address, we got no response. Microsoft routers have been configured to ignore these requests.

    Try other domain names you are aware of.

```
Command Prompt                                          _ □ X

C:\>ping www.microsoft.com

Pinging www.microsoft.akadns.net [207.46.230.219] with 32 bytes of data:

Request timed out.
Request timed out.
Request timed out.
Request timed out.

Ping statistics for 207.46.230.219:
    Packets: Sent = 4, Received = 0, Lost = 4 (100% loss),
Approximate round trip times in milli-seconds:
    Minimum = 0ms, Maximum =  0ms, Average =  0ms

C:\>
```

12. Try typing **tracert www.lhseattle.com** and pressing ENTER. Tracert is an abbreviation for Trace Route. The following illustration shows the possible result. The first line of output shows us the Fully Qualified Domain Name (FQDN) followed by the IP address. A DNS server was able to resolve the name to an IP address. A listing of all routers the command had to pass through to get to the destination follows.

```
Command Prompt                                                                        _ □ ×
C:\>tracert www.lhseattle.com

Tracing route to www.lhseattle.com [63.226.204.101]
over a maximum of 30 hops:

  1     10 ms     10 ms     10 ms  10.95.176.1
  2    <10 ms     10 ms     10 ms  r1-ge6-1.sttls1.wa.home.net [24.7.143.1]
  3    <10 ms     10 ms     10 ms  10.0.220.149
  4    <10 ms     10 ms     10 ms  c1-pos6-0.sttlwa1.home.net [24.7.74.81]
  5     30 ms     40 ms     30 ms  c1-pos3-0.lnmtco1.home.net [24.7.64.6]
  6     50 ms     50 ms     60 ms  c1-pos1-0.chcgil1.home.net [24.7.65.149]
  7     50 ms     50 ms     60 ms  ATM3-0.BR2.CHI2.ALTER.NET [137.39.52.105]
  8     60 ms     60 ms     50 ms  156.at-5-0-0.XR2.CHI2.ALTER.NET [152.63.67.246]
  9     50 ms     60 ms     50 ms  192.ATM3-0.TR2.CHI4.ALTER.NET [152.63.64.230]
 10     70 ms     80 ms     81 ms  106.ATM7-0.TR2.SEA1.ALTER.NET [146.188.136.170]
 11     70 ms     70 ms     70 ms  198.ATM7-0.XR2.SEA1.ALTER.NET [146.188.200.117]
 12     70 ms     70 ms     70 ms  194.ATM6-0.GW8.SEA1.ALTER.NET [152.63.105.229]
 13     71 ms     70 ms     70 ms  uswbel-oc3-1-gw.customer.alter.net [157.130.178.94]
 14     70 ms     81 ms    330 ms  gig0-0-0.sttl-agw2.sttl.uswest.net [206.81.192.249]
 15     70 ms     70 ms     70 ms  103.fa0-0-0.sttl-6400-gw5.sttl.uswest.net [207.224.249.101
]
 16     90 ms     80 ms     80 ms  63.226.204.102
```

13. Try a few more Tracert commands on any domain names or IP addresses that you are aware of. Try it on a local host name (yours if necessary). It shouldn't take long, because you don't pass through any routers.

14. If you find the Tracert command interesting, go to **www.neotrace.com/** on the Internet and download an evaluation copy of their NeoTrace program. The following illustration shows one of the four ways of viewing the results. The tool is pretty self-explanatory. It will give you some great insights into the Internet, and the Graph view will help you identify slow or erratic route segments.

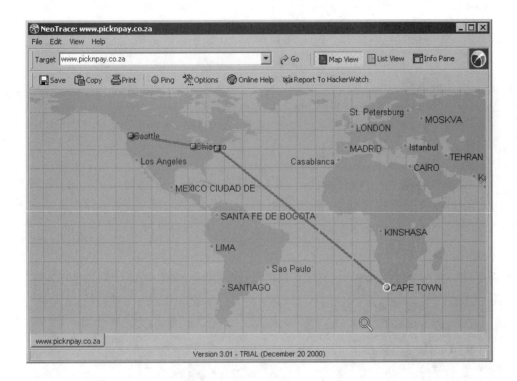

ARP Exercise

The following lab assumes you are using any version of Windows. This is a nondestructive lab and you should be able to do it with your home machine without concern of changing your system configuration. We will be looking at the ARP commands.

1. If you are doing this at home, establish a connection to your ISP. This will connect you via your modem and make sure that you have an IP address. In a TCP/IP LAN, it shouldn't be necessary to do this step.

2. **Windows NT/2000 users:** Use the Start menu to open the Command Prompt (MS-DOS-like) window (Start | Programs | Accessories | Command Prompt or Start | Programs | Command Prompt).
   Windows 95/98/Me users: Use the Start menu to open the MS-DOS Prompt window (Start | Programs | Accessories | MS-DOS Prompt or Start | Programs | MS-DOS Prompt).

3. In the window, type **arp -a** and press ENTER. Don't be surprised if there are no entries. The message would be No ARP Entries Found. Windows computers remove any addresses that are unused after a few minutes.

Try pinging a few local addresses and a Web site, and then rerun the command. The following illustration shows the result of the arp -a command. You won't get a MAC address for the Web site because it isn't local, but that will cause the default gateway to be listed.

This basically is the process the IP protocol goes through at Layer 3 to determine the MAC address of the next hop or destination so that it can forward that information to the data link layer.

Look over your results.

```
Command Prompt                                          _ □ X

C:\>arp -a

Interface: 192.168.1.10 on Interface 0x1000003
  Internet Address        Physical Address      Type
  192.168.1.1             00-20-78-d5-39-e7     dynamic
  192.168.1.11            00-10-5a-1e-86-40     dynamic
  192.168.1.12            00-00-86-54-9b-a6     dynamic

C:\>_
```

4. Try **arp -?** to see the help feature and look over the options.

Network Configuration Exercise

The following lab assumes you are using a version of Windows 95/98/Me; Windows 2000 or NT will have slightly different screens, but you should be able to adapt. We will not be making any actual changes during this tour, so it should be a nondestructive lab and you should be able to do it with your home machine without concern of changing your system configuration.

If you decide that you would like to perform these steps for real, consider using an extra machine the first time. Also assume that you might get asked for the CD-ROM that your Windows was installed from, and you might need to furnish a disk or CD-ROM with the drivers for your NIC. It is not necessary to connect to the Internet to perform these steps.

1. Close or minimize any open windows or programs.

2. Right-click the Network Neighborhood or My Network Places icon and choose Properties. If you do not have either icon on this machine, click the Start button (Start | Settings | Control Panel) and then double-click the Network icon. The following illustration shows the Network dialog box that opens.

    Notice that we are a Client for Microsoft Networks; there is a similar Client for Netware Networks. Choosing the right one installs and sets up any client services drivers that will be needed to access the network.

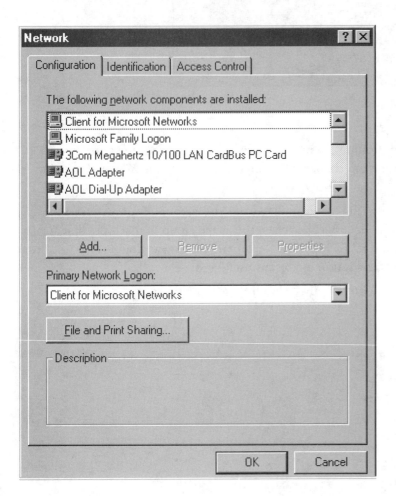

3. Click the File And Print Sharing button to open the dialog box shown in the following illustration. If you are a Windows client, selecting either of these boxes will allow this machine to share folders and/or printers with its neighbors. Note that on some networks, you, as a user, may not be able to change these features. Click the Cancel button to close the File And Print Sharing window.

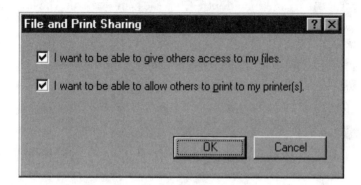

4. Click the Identification tab in the Network dialog box (see the next illustration). This is where you can change the Computer (Host) Name. You are limited to 15 characters.

The Workgroup, as the name implies, would be a group of computers (not users) that you want to identify collectively. This is the group of machines that appears in the first window of Network Neighborhood if you double-click the icon. The Computer Description can be any useful text.

Look over the options and then click the Configuration tab.

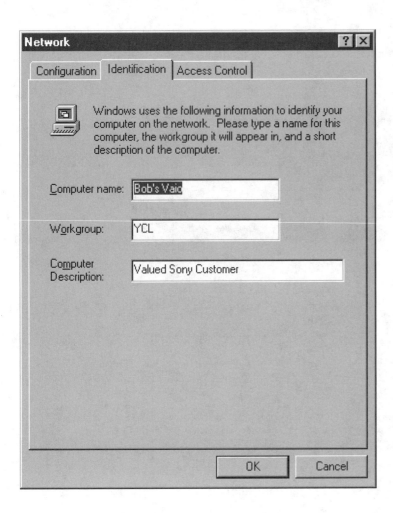

5. Using the Network Components Installed box, scroll until you can highlight the TCP/IP for your NIC—there may be other TCP/IP configurations. The following illustration is representative of the screen you might expect to see.

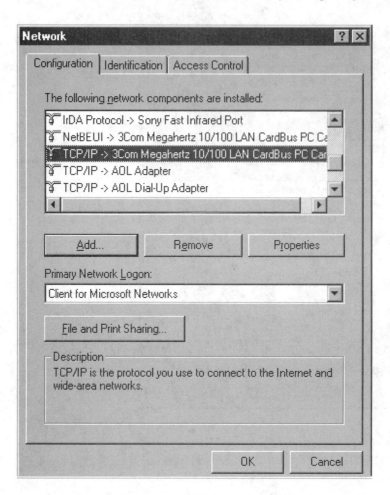

6. After you highlight the TCP/IP for your NIC, click the Properties button. Make sure that the IP Address tab is selected, as shown in the next illustration. Notice there is a choice between Obtain An IP Address Automatically, which would then rely on DHCP for configuration, and Specify An IP Address, which has you manually configure the card. In most networks, you would use the DHCP option for workstations but use the manual approach for servers so that their IP addresses remain constant.

If your machine is set to the automatic feature, it would not hurt to switch to manual and type in an IP address and subnet mask—type a period to move from octet to octet. Just remember to return to automatic when you are done.

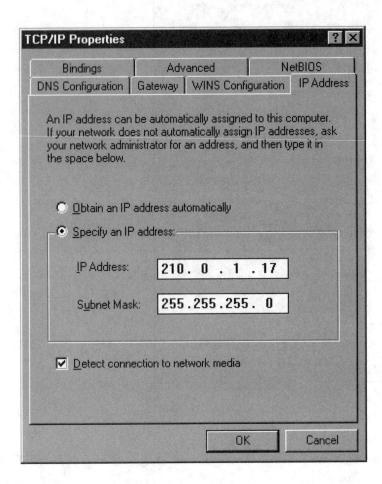

7. When you are done, click the Gateway tab, shown in the next illustration. If you are using the automatic IP address system, there is no need to worry about this setting, because the DHCP device will handle it.

If you manually configure the IP address, you need to enter the gateway address and then click the Add button. If you like, try it. It should end up in the Installed Gateways box. To remove any gateways from the box, click on them and then the Remove button until they are all gone.

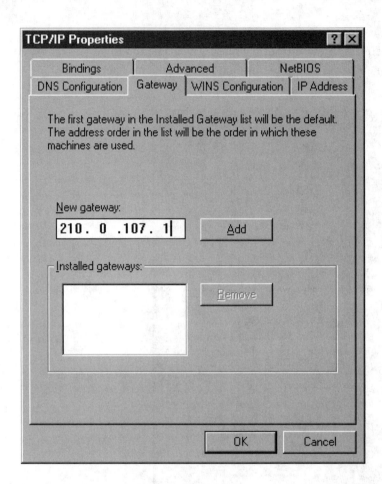

8. Take a few minutes and look over the other tabs. We can specify the addresses of WINS and DNS servers.

Click the Cancel button to close the TCP/IP Properties window.

To see how we might add a service, click the Add button on the Network window. The next illustration is representative of the screen you might expect to see. Select Client (as shown) and click the Add button.

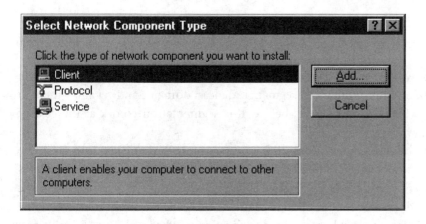

9. Select Client for Netware Networks and click Add. You should return to the Network window. We have added the client, but we have not configured it. With the new client highlighted, click the Properties button.

Look over the choices and look over any other features that catch your eye—just remember to use the Cancel button to get out of this screen so that you do not save any changes. You may have to click Cancel twice, depending on what screen you are looking at.

Summary

This chapter described Layer 3 protocols and how they function to facilitate addressing and route selection of our data frames.

We compared the host name, MAC address, and network address and saw that each plays a vital role in moving data within the network. The host name provides a friendly name that can be associated with a not-so-friendly MAC address. We saw that the MAC address is limited to but absolutely essential to delivery of all packets within the local network.

The network address allows for moving data between networks. Without it, we are left to the equivalent of trying to deliver a letter when all we have is a social security number.

We saw that while both bridges and switches can segment a network into multiple collision domains, only a router can segment broadcast domains and yet allow them to communicate when appropriate. As before, this segmentation comes at the cost of increased latency.

We saw that the subnet mask allows the Layer 3 protocols to quickly distinguish the network ID portion of an IP address. This is critical in determining whether a packet is for local delivery or needs to be routed to another network. If it needs to be routed, it is only the network portion of the address that is considered. The host portion is only important at the last router where the final connection will be local. The ARP table and process helps us determine the MAC address for that last segment.

We saw that default gateways are the router interfaces connected to a local network that facilitate forwarding packets out of the network.

Case Study: The Elm Park Elementary School

Your child's school is adding computers that have been donated by a local company. An extended star topology has been suggested, using some hubs that are available. The school agrees with your idea of adding a switch working as a backbone switch, as shown in the next illustration. The plan is to replace the classroom hubs as funds or donations allow.

Scenario: For now, the very basic details are as follows: Elm Park Elementary is a four-year-old, single-level building with 12 classrooms and a library. Each classroom currently has 24 students but could possibly seat 32 students. There are currently no portable classrooms but a student enrollment growth is just starting to hit the school.

Enough computers are available for six classrooms and the library immediately, and the intent is to outfit the remaining six classrooms next year. The plan is to make the Internet and some online services available to the students. The computers are current enough to be useful for at least two years.

The library, which is somewhat centrally located, is where the server(s) and router connecting the school to the Internet will be located. Assume that any distances fall well within the standards for Category 5 twisted-pair cable (100 meters). Assume that all rooms will have 24 computers and that each room will use a stackable hub solution

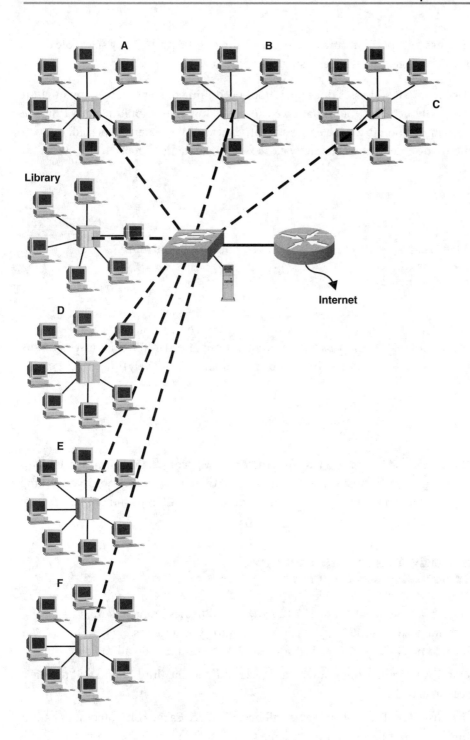

that combines a 12-port hub and a 24-port hub for 36 total ports. Being stackable units, the network will see each stack as a single 36-port device.

1. How many IP addresses does the school need immediately? How many might it eventually need for the initial seven rooms? How many could it need if it gets enough computers for the entire school? Exact numbers aren't expected, but you should be able to estimate pretty close from the data provided.

2. What class(es) of IP address do you need now and in the future?

3. The school district informs the group that it can afford 128 IP addresses from its allocation and no more. What will be the impacts (intuitively)?

4. Go to a Web site, such as **www.cdw.com** or **www.pcconnection.com**, and look up the prices of routers, cable, and DSL routers. You may have to choose Networking on the site's main page to get started. If you aren't familiar with manufactures, try Cisco, 3Com, Nortel, D-Link, and Linksys.

Case Study Suggested Solution (Your solutions may vary)

1. The school will need about 175 (25×7) IP addresses immediately.
   It could need 245 (35×7) IP addresses for the seven rooms.
   It could need 455 (35×13) IP addresses in the future to do all rooms.

2. Our first two milestones can use a class C address. The third option will require a second class C.

3. If we use TCP/IP, not all students will be able to access the computers at one time. Initially, about 65 percent of students will be able to access the computers simul-

taneously, but this figure will fall to 50 percent if the school experiences growth but acquires no more IP addresses.

4. There are no right or wrong answers, and the amounts will go down over time.

Practice Questions

Take a few moments and check your grasp of the concepts covered in this chapter. The answers are immediately following the questions.

Questions

1. What do each the following acronyms stand for?
   a. ARP
   b. DHCP
   c. ICMP
   d. IP
   e. IPX
   f. RARP
   g. RFC

2. How long is an IP address? (Choose 2)
   a. 32 bytes
   b. 4 bytes
   c. 32 bits
   d. Up to 80 bits

3. What two things does an IP network layer address identify?
   a.
   b.

4. Which two of the following are routing protocols?
   a. TCP/IP
   b. RIP
   c. IPX/SPX
   d. AppleTalk
   e. IGRP

5. How does an IPX address identify the host? (Choose all that apply)
    a. Uses three octets
    b. Uses the MAC address
    c. Uses the first 32 bits
    d. Uses the last 48 bits

6. Which one of the following identifies both the network and the specific host on the network?
    a. Host name
    b. MAC address
    c. Network address
    d. Physical address

7. What class of IP address is 191.17.205.99?
    a. Class A
    b. Class B
    c. Class C
    d. Class D
    e. Class E

8. What class of IP address is 101.17.205.99?
    a. Class A
    b. Class B
    c. Class C
    d. Class D
    e. Class E

9. What class of IP address is 224.0.0.9?
    a. Class A
    b. Class B
    c. Class C
    d. Class D
    e. Class E

10. What is the default subnet mask for 111.251.1.0?
    a. 255.0.0.0
    b. 255.255.0.0
    c. 255.255.255.0
    d. 111.251.0.0

11. Will the following work? Why or why not?

    IP address: 192.168.1.59

    Subnet mask: 255.255.255.0

    Default gateway: 192.168.5.1

    a. Yes or no?

    b. Why or why not?

12. Designate the class and default subnet mask for each of the following:

    a. 2.129.73.145

    b. 223.119.14.0

    c. 175.16.145.23

    d. 214.0.0.9

13. Which of the following are private addresses? (Choose all that apply)

    a. 10.100.100.1

    b. 172.32.0.1

    c. 191.168.1.121

    d. 172.17.178.123

    e. 192.168.1.121

14. NetBEUI is representative of which one of the following?

    a. A routing protocol

    b. A routable protocol

    c. A nonroutable protocol

    d. Layer 3 protocol

15. What command will display the IP address, subnet mask, and default gateway on a Windows 95/98 machine?

    a. ipconfig

    b. ipconfig /all

    c. arp -a

    d. winipcfg

Answers

1. a. ARP = Address Resolution Protocol

   b. DHCP = Dynamic Host Configuration Protocol

   c. ICMP = Internet Control Message Protocol

   d. IP = Internet Protocol

      e. IPX = Internet Packet Exchange
      f. RARP = Reverse Address Resolution Protocol
      g. RFC = Request for Comments

2. **b** and **c.** 4 bytes and 32 bits.

3. **a.** A network ID.
    b. A host ID.

4. **b.** and **e.** RIP and IGRP. The other three are routable network protocols.

5. **b.** Uses the MAC address.
    d. Uses the last 48 bits.

6. **c.** Network address. The others identify only a specific host.

7. **b.** Class B (1st octet between 128 and 191).

8. **a.** Class A (1st octet between 1 and 126).

9. **d.** Class D (1st octet between 224 and 239).

10. **a.** 255.0.0.0 is the default subnet mask.

11. **a.** No.
    b. The IP address and the default gateway are not in the same network.

12.

a.	2.129.73.145	Class A	255.0.0.0
b.	223.119.14.0	Class C	255.255.255.0
c.	175.16.145.23	Class B	255.255.0.0
d.	214.0.0.9	Class C	255.255.255.0

13.

a.	10.100.100.1	10.0.0.0 - 10.255.255.255
d.	172.17.178.123	172.16.0.0 - 172.31.255.255
e.	192.168.1.121	192.168.0.0 - 192.168.255.255

14. **c.** A nonroutable protocol.

15. **d.** winipcfg. Choices **a.** ipconfig and **b.** ipconfig /all display similar results on a Windows NT or 2000 machine. Arp -a displays the ARP table, which resolves IP and MAC addresses.

CHAPTER 6

OSI Model–Layer 4

This chapter will:

- **Compare connection-oriented vs. connectionless protocols**

- **Define reliability (error recovery)**

- **Look at data flow-control methods, including buffers and windowing**

- **Compare transport layer protocols: TCP and UDP**

- **Discuss the concept of port numbers and sockets**

- **Look at the TCP Layer 4 processes, including connection establishment, data transfer, and connection termination**

I n the last chapter, you saw that Layer 3 is responsible for delivering packets between hosts. To that end, the Layer 3 protocols provide network layer addressing and best-path delivery services for many, often-unrelated, communications sessions. In this chapter, you will see that Layer 4 is responsible for identifying and keeping the various communications separate, and that it regulates the flow of information from source to destination reliably and accurately.

TCP/IP is a combination of two protocols, TCP and IP, as well as a variety of supporting protocols. As Chapter 5 described, IP is a Layer 3 protocol that provides a connectionless, best-effort delivery service across the network. TCP is a Layer 4 protocol that provides a connection-oriented service with flow control and reliability. It is important to recognize that TCP cannot work on its own; ultimately, it must rely on IP packets for delivery. The TCP segment ultimately becomes the data for Layer 3 to encapsulate into an IP packet. Used together, the two protocols provide delivery services for the Internet, UNIX, Windows, and the latest version of NetWare networks.

Transport Layer: Layer 4

Layer 4's primary functions are to regulate the flow of information from source to destination, reliably and accurately. Using processes like sliding windows, sequencing numbers, and acknowledgements, Layer 4 provides this end-to-end control. The transport layer also provides delivery between the network layer and the upper layers of the OSI reference model.

As a simple analogy for reliability, consider a company shipping a seven-parcel order to a customer. The company could mark the parcels 1/7, 2/7, and so on, for 1 of 7, 2 of 7, and so on. The customer can verify reliability by confirming that all seven parcels arrive. If parcel four of seven is missing, requesting a replacement should be easy. An analogy of flow control is an assembly line on which the final stage, packaging, is having trouble keeping up, so packaging asks the line to be slowed.

Connection-Oriented vs. Connectionless Protocols

A critical concept to understand for the CCNA exam and in the field is the difference between connection-oriented and connectionless protocols. A *connection-oriented protocol* requires a setup sequence of data frames to be exchanged or a pre-established relationship between the hosts to be defined before any data can be transferred. TCP and SPX are examples of connection-oriented protocols that use a setup sequence. Frame Relay and ATM WAN technologies are examples of connection-oriented protocols that use a predefined circuit but do not require a startup sequence.

A *connectionless protocol* does not require either the setup exchange or the predefined relationship. Layer 3 protocols such as ICMP, as well as the 802.3 and 802.5 protocols, are examples of connectionless protocols.

Beware of the tendency to think of connection-oriented protocols as always having error recovery (reliability). Not all connection-oriented protocols provide error recovery, and some connectionless protocols provide error recovery. Again, Frame Relay and ATM WAN technologies are examples of connection-oriented protocols that do not provide error recovery. The next table demonstrates some combinations of connection and reliability features matched to common protocols.

CONNECTED?	RELIABLE?	EXAMPLES
Connection-oriented	Yes	TCP (TCP/IP), SPX (NetWare), S.25, and LLC type 2
Connection-oriented	No	ATM, Frame Relay, and *Point-to-Point Protocol* (PPP)
Connectionless	Yes	TFTP
Connectionless	No	UDP, IP, IPX (NetWare), Ethernet, and Token Ring

 NOTE: The word "reliable" is an emotionally charged term. To be tagged as "unreliable" carries more weight than should be applied in this context. Frame Relay and cell relay (ATM) are both designated as unreliable protocols simply because they do not rely on Layer 4 acknowledgments. This does not mean that reliability isn't monitored; it means that these protocols do not use Layer 4 technology for that purpose. By skipping this feature, overhead is reduced and delivery speed is increased. Other protocols do not use connection-oriented communications and/or acknowledgements because a single transmission is a part of a frequently reoccurring announcement or report that will be repeated in a few moments anyway.

Error Recovery (Reliability)

While the actual implementation may change with a particular protocol, reliability is basically a matter of numbering (sequencing) the data items, sending them out in order, and acknowledging them as they arrive. Any items that are discarded, for whatever reason, cannot be acknowledged and therefore need to be retransmitted. TCP numbers bytes, SPX numbers packets, and some other protocols number data frames.

Keep in mind that discarded packets are a normal event—not necessarily a desirable event, but normal just the same. Packets can be discarded if the sending host is transmitting faster than the receiving host can process them. Switches and routers can discard frames as they get backed up. We will look at flow control in the next section. Lower OSI layer processes in the receiving host can discard the packets if the various quality control checks fail. Packets can get discarded for physical reasons, such as line breaks, and for routing problems, such as loops.

A common method is to have sequence number and acknowledgement number fields in the Layer 4 header (see "Transmission Control Protocol" later in this chapter). A technique called *forward acknowledgement* involves sending an acknowledgement

Figure 6-1
Forward acknowl-
edgement sequence

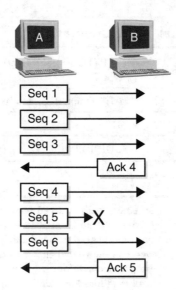

number one larger than the last sequence number received to indicate they are ready for that item. Figure 6-1 shows a simplified view of a forward acknowledgement exchange.

The figure shows that sequence items 1, 2, and 3 were sent and received, so an acknowledgement 4 was sent indicating that it is okay to send the next unit. When items 4, 5, and 6 were sent, something happened to cause 5 to be discarded. The receiving host then acknowledges 5, which in this case means item 5 needs to be retransmitted. The protocol determines whether just 5 is transmitted or 5 and 6 are transmitted. TCP resends just the one item and waits for an acknowledgement to see the status of 6; SPX would resend both.

Flow Control

One of the major repercussions of congestion is that data is discarded. This can occur at the receiving node, but can also occur at the routers and switches between the nodes. These discarded data items may be missed by a Layer 4 reliability check or a Layer 7 application and therefore may have to be retransmitted. If nothing has happened to resolve the congestion issue, these discards and retransmissions can actually make the situation worse—at least part of the system has to handle the same data twice.

The "bursty" nature of our data networks means that congestion is likely to happen in all networks from time to time. Sometimes it will be for just a few moments as a large database request is being processed. Congestion can also fall into predictable cycles, such as periods of the day (the start of a shift as people log on and check e-mail) or periods of the week, month, or year based on business process cycles. Clearly, congestion has to be monitored and resources may need to be added or reallocated to reduce the impact, but congestion generally is still a normal part of the network. It's worth noting that congestion can occur within the client or a server. In many cases, the network might not be the culprit; the problem could be slow server disk drives or inadequate server memory.

Flow control is a mechanism implemented by different protocols to attempt to deal with congestion by adjusting the transmission rates of the sending host, to reduce the amount of data discarded.

Buffers

Buffering applies to the sending and receiving nodes as well as to the intermediated devices (routers, switches, and bridges). *Buffer* is memory used for incoming data to be held until it can be processed. With adequate buffer space, no data should be discarded. If data starts to exceed the buffer space, the protocol determines what gets discarded. It could be as simple as the oldest data is the first to be discarded, or certain types of data may be discarded first.

When comparing network devices, the amount of buffer memory and how it is used may be a significant determinant in the cost and how useful the device is to the network. If a cheaper switch has little buffer space or poorly allocated buffer space, and therefore leads to an increase in discarded data and ultimately congestion, it may not be a particularly good value.

Routers, Switches, and Bridges

Some access method (Layers 1 and 2) protocols, such as Frame Relay, can send messages to the sending and/or receiving host when congestion causes the buffers to fill. If the network protocol can exercise flow control and can act on these messages, the transmission rate can be slowed. We will look at BECN and FECN packets when we look at Frame Relay in Chapter 20. This process is referred to as *congestion avoidance*.

Windowing

The earlier discussion of sending acknowledgements included an example in which three items were sent, followed by an acknowledgement allowing three more to be sent. The multiple-item interval is referred to as *windowing*. By allowing multiple transmissions between acknowledgements, we reduce bandwidth requirements and increase throughput. The actual number of items to be transmitted between acknowledgements is negotiated during the session setup.

If the receiving node becomes overloaded, it can request the sender to reduce the window size (see "Transmission Control Protocol").

Layer 4 Protocols

Each network protocol has its own unique Layer 4 protocols. TCP/IP actually uses two protocols: TCP, and its somewhat less famous sister, User Datagram Protocol (UDP). Figure 6-2 shows the OSI and TCP/IP reference models with Layer 4 protocols.

Transmission Control Protocol

TCP (RFC 793) is the connection-oriented transport protocol in the TCP/IP protocol stack that creates a virtual circuit between end-user applications to provide reliable full-duplex data transmission.

The following characteristics apply to TCP:

- Connection-oriented—requires circuit setup before data transfer

- Reliable—provides error recovery

- Splits outgoing upper-layer data into segments (sending host)

- Reassembles incoming segments into data (receiving host)

- Applies sequence numbers to outgoing segments (sending host)

- Uses sequence numbers to reorder incoming segments (receiving host)

- Acknowledges received segments (receiving host)

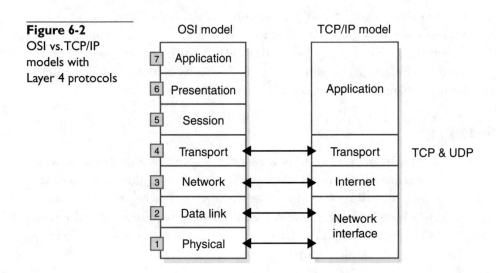

Figure 6-2
OSI vs. TCP/IP
models with
Layer 4 protocols

- Orders retransmission of missing incoming segments (receiving host)

- Retransmits any outbound segments not received (sending host)

- Uses windowing to manage flow control

Upper-layer protocols that use TCP include:

- **File Transfer Protocol (FTP)** Application layer protocol used for transferring files between network nodes

- **Hypertext Transfer Protocol (HTTP)** The protocol used by Web browsers and Web servers to transfer text and graphics files

- **Post Office Protocol (POP)** Common protocol used to retrieve e-mail from a mail server; POP3, the latest version, can be used with or without SMTP

- **Simple Mail Transfer Protocol (SMTP)** Internet protocol providing electronic mail services

- **Telnet** Terminal-emulation program used to run applications on some hosts; we will use it to configure Cisco routers and switches

Figure 6-3 shows a representation of the TCP segment format, including the TCP header and data. These segments are used to establish virtual circuits, carry acknowledgements, perform flow control, and transport upper-layer data.

The definitions of the fields in the TCP segment follow:

- **Source Port** Number of the sending port

- **Destination Port** Number of the receiving port

- **Sequence Number** Used to reconstruct data from incoming segments and trigger acknowledgements

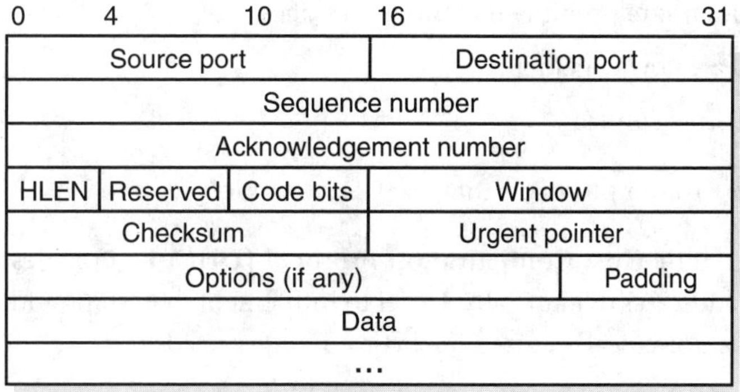

Figure 6-3
TCP segment
format

0	4	10	16		31
Source port			Destination port		
Sequence number					
Acknowledgement number					
HLEN	Reserved	Code bits	Window		
Checksum			Urgent pointer		
Options (if any)				Padding	
Data					
...					

- **Acknowledgment Number**   Next expected TCP segment

- **HLEN**   (offset) number of 32-bit words in the header

- **Reserved**   Set to zero

- **Code Bits**   (flags) control functions (like session setup SYN, acknowledgment ACK and termination FIN)

- **Window**   Number of bytes that the sender is willing to accept

- **Checksum**   Calculated checksum of the header and data fields

- **Urgent Pointer**   Indicates the end of the urgent data

- **Options (if any)**   Maximum TCP segment size

- **Padding**   Fill used to fill to bring segments up to minimum size

- **Data**   Upper-layer protocol data

User Datagram Protocol

UDP (RFC 768) is the connectionless transport protocol in the TCP/IP protocol stack that exchanges datagrams, without acknowledgments or assuring delivery. UDP does not use windowing or acknowledgments, so application layer protocols must provide reliability. Any error processing and retransmission of packets must be performed by other protocols. UDP is used by applications that do not require sequencing of segments. UDP applications are not slowed by the acknowledgement process, and the sending host's memory is freed up quicker.

The following characteristics apply to UDP:

- Transmits user datagrams

- Connectionless—does not requires circuit setup before data transfer

- Unreliable—provides no Layer 4 error recovery

- Does not reassemble incoming messages

- No acknowledgements

- No flow control

Upper-layer protocols that use UDP include:

- **Dynamic Host Configuration Protocol (DHCP)**   Provides a means for allocating IP addresses dynamically. Easier to implement than static addressing, the address can be automatically reused if a host no longer needs it.

- **Domain Naming System (DNS)** Internet process for translating names of network nodes into addresses.

- **Simple Network Management Protocol (SNMP)** Network management protocol used in TCP/IP networks to provide a way to remotely monitor and control network devices, and to manage configurations, statistics collection, performance, and security.

- **Trivial File Transfer Protocol (TFTP)** Stripped-down version of FTP that allows files to be transferred from one node to another over a network.

- Most video and audio streaming protocols, as well as Real Time Protocol (RTP) used in voice over IP. With these real-time protocols, acknowledgments, retransmissions, and resequencing would be counterproductive, leading to delayed packet delivery.

Figure 6-4 shows a representation of the UDP segment format, including the UDP header and data. These segments are used to transport upper-layer data.

The definitions of the fields in the UDP segment follow:

- **Source Port** Number of the sending port
- **Destination Port** Number of the receiving port
- **Length** Length of the header and data fields
- **Checksum** Calculated checksum of the header and data fields
- **Data** Upper-layer protocol data

Port Numbers

TCP and UDP both use port numbers to pass data to specific upper-layer applications. These port numbers are used as source and destination addresses in the TCP and UDP segment (refer to Figures 6-3 and 6-4). The two end systems use these port numbers to identify appropriate applications on each end so that the data can be used. Figure 6-5 shows a common figurative representation of port numbers.

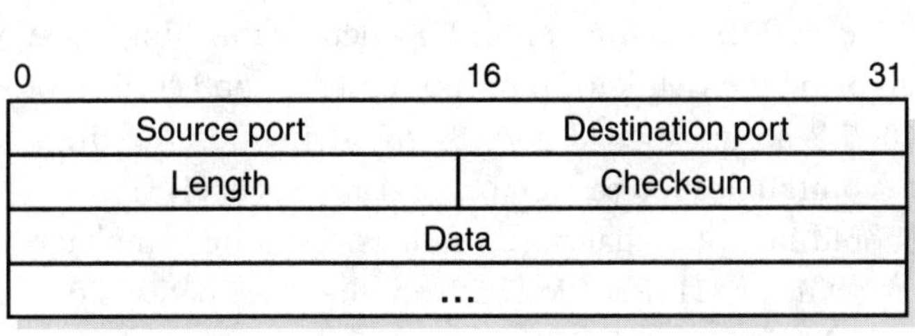

Figure 6-4
UDP segment format

Figure 6-5
Common port
numbers

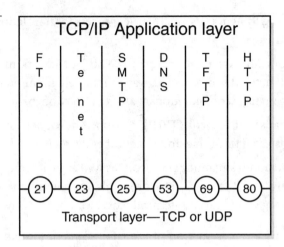

These port number combinations identify conversations that cross the network at the same time. Applications access TCP services by making software requests using the destination IP address, the port number that identifies the application to receive the data, and finally the data. The combination of the destination IP address, the port number, and the transport layer protocol (TCP or UDP) create a socket. A socket source/ destination pair identifies a unique communication between two hosts.

Application software developers and the industry have established what are called well-known port numbers (RFC 1700) that pertain to certain applications. Communications sessions that involve applications without well-known port numbers are assigned random port numbers within a specific range. Port numbers have the following assigned ranges:

- **0-255** Public applications
- **255-1023** For use by companies with marketable applications, like Microsoft
- **1024 and greater** Unregulated

Originating Source Port numbers are dynamically assigned by the source host, usually with a number larger than 1023. For example, a Web client might use a Source Port of 1025 and a Destination Port of 80 when establishing a session with a Web server—port 80 being the well-known port number for an HTTP server on the other machine. Port 1025 is an unassigned port. By specifying port 80, the sender also identifies the type of communication session being established, HTTP.

It should be noted that port numbers could be completely arbitrary. For example, you can set up an HTTP session with another Destination Port number (other than 80). Many applications use HTTP as a transport protocol, but the port number is determined by the specific application listening for the request. Many Cisco applications, like CiscoSecure ACS, put their administrative Web server on port 2002.

TCP Connection Establishment and Termination

The connection-oriented protocols involve three distinct phases:

- **Establishment (handshake)**   A single path (circuit) between the source and destination hosts is determined. Any required resources, including intermediate devices, are reserved to ensure service can be maintained. Figure 6-6 shows a connection established between Hosts 1 and 2 passing through Routers A, C, and E.

- **Data transfer**   Data is transmitted sequentially over the selected route. The data arrives sequentially except for any discarded by congested network devices. These discarded packets will be detected as missing by the receiving device and a request for retransmission will be sent.

- **Termination**   The connection is terminated and all resources are released to be available for other connections.

Positive acknowledgement and retransmission (PAR) is a technique used by many protocols, including TCP, to provide reliability. As the source sends an agreed-upon quantity of data (bytes), it starts a timer and waits for an acknowledgement before sending the next batch. If the timer expires before the acknowledgement is received, the source assumes the data was lost and retransmits the same data. It also starts the timer again.

TCP uses a numbered sequencing of segments with a forward reference acknowledgment, as described earlier, with increments in bytes. At the receiving node, TCP uses the sequence numbers to reassemble the segments into a complete message. If a sequence number is missing, that segment is retransmitted.

Establishment

TCP hosts use a three-way handshake to establish a connection-oriented session. This "handshake" establishes the port numbers that will be used for the session, thereby

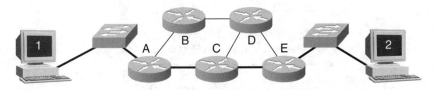

Figure 6-6   TCP connection circuit

indicating the type of communication. This connection process allows an exchange of sequence numbers that ensures retransmission of any data that is lost. Figure 6-7 shows connection establishment process.

The following are the steps for establishing a connection:

1. The initiating host sends a TCP packet indicating its initial sequence number (100—could be any number) and a proposed port to use for the session (1025), and one of the Code Bits (flags—refer to Figure 6-3) in the TCP header is set to indicate a connection request. The particular bit is the SYN bit, which stands for "synchronize the sequence numbers."

2. The other host receives the packet, records the sequence number, and issues a reply. The reply introduces its sequence number (500—could be any number), includes an acknowledgement number (one larger than the received sequence number), leaves the SYN bit set, sets a second Code Bit—the ACK (acknowledgement) bit—to on, and confirms the port numbers suggested. The SYN bit stays on until sequence number synchronization is complete, which cannot occur until this packet is delivered and processed. The ACK bit will remain on until the end of a termination sequence. Do not confuse this bit with the Acknowledgement Number, which is a separate field in the header.

3. The initiating host responds with its next sequence number (101) and includes an acknowledgement number (501), the ACK bit is on, and the SYN bit is off because synchronization is complete.

Different protocols use various units of measure in "windowing." TCP uses bytes in incrementing its windowing as well as the sequence and acknowledgement numbers. The preceding example assumes that no data is transferred during setup handshake so just a single byte increment has been used.

Figure 6-7
Connection
establishment

Seq = 100, SYN,
DesPort = 23, SrcPort = 1025

Seq = 500, ACK = 101, SYN,
ACK, DesPort = 1025, SrcPort = 23

Seq = 101, ACK = 501, ACK,
DesPort = 23, SrcPort = 1025

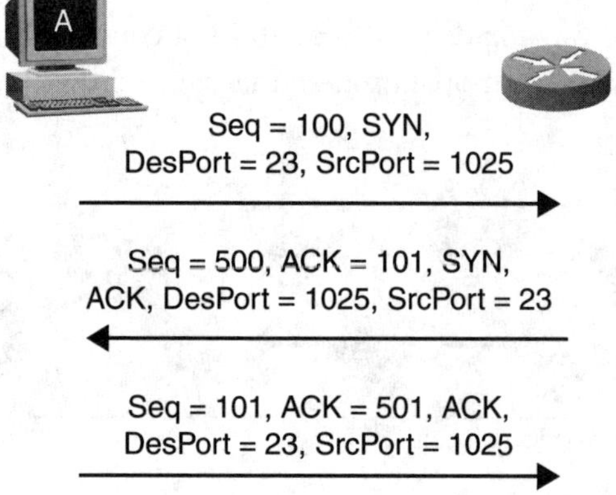

Data Transfer

Window size determines the amount of data that you can transmit at one time before receiving an acknowledgment from the destination. The larger the window size value (bytes for TCP) in the header, the greater the amount of data that the host can transmit at one time. After a host transmits the specified number of bytes, the host must receive an acknowledgment that the data has been received before it can send any more.

If the timer expires before an acknowledgement is received, the last data must be retransmitted and the transmission rate should be slowed. Adjusting the transmission rate uses the "sliding" aspect of windowing that allows the window size to be negotiated dynamically during the TCP session. The receiving end changes the value of the Window field in the TCP header of an acknowledgement packet. Figure 6-8 shows the windowing being increased from 3,000 bytes to 4,000 bytes.

Termination

TCP hosts use a four-way termination sequence to end a connection-oriented session. This sequence uses a FIN (finish) bit in the Code Bits field to indicate the end of the session. Figure 6-9 shows the connection-termination process.

This is pretty straightforward except that the host receiving the FIN packet notifies the application that the session is being terminated and waits for an acknowledgement from the application. It then sends the FIN packet back to the sender (step 3). The first acknowledgement (step 2) is needed because of the possible delay in getting an

Figure 6-8
Sliding window

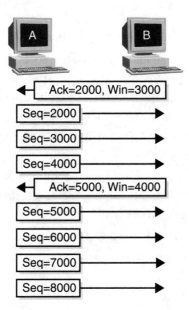

Figure 6-9
Connection
termination

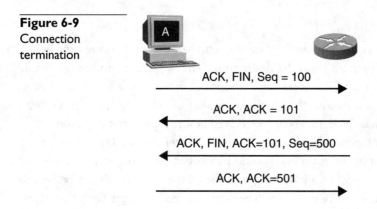

ACK, FIN, Seq = 100

ACK, ACK = 101

ACK, FIN, ACK=101, Seq=500

ACK, ACK=501

acknowledgement from the application. Its only purpose is to keep the sending device from assuming the packet was lost and retransmitting.

Summary

In this chapter, you learned about the transport layer as represented by the OSI and the TCP/IP reference models. Specifically, you learned that

- The transport layer protocols can regulate data flow, increase reliability or error recovery by providing acknowledgements for data received, and establish connection-oriented sessions.

- The TCP/IP protocol in Layer 4 has two protocols: TCP and UDP.

- TCP is connection-oriented, is reliable, splits outgoing upper-layer data into segments, reassembles incoming segments into data, applies sequence numbers to outgoing segments, uses sequence numbers to reorder incoming segments, acknowledges received segments, orders retransmission of missing inbound segments, retransmits outbound segments not received, and uses windowing to manage flow control.

- UDP transmits user datagrams, is connectionless, is unreliable (provides no Layer 4 error recovery), does not reassemble incoming messages, does not issue acknowledgements, and does not perform flow control.

- TCP and UDP both use port numbers to pass data to the upper layers and use sockets to keep track of different communication sessions running on the network at the same time.

- TCP uses a three-way handshake sequence to synchronize a connection between the sending and receiving hosts. During data transmission, TCP uses windowing for flow control. TCP uses a four-step connection-termination process.

Practice Questions

Take a few moments and check your grasp of the concepts covered in this chapter. The answers are immediately following the questions.

Questions

1. What do each the following acronyms stand for?
   a. TCP
   b. UDP
   c. SPX

2. Which two of the following protocols are connection-oriented?
   a. IP
   b. TCP
   c. IPX
   d. SPX
   e. Ethernet
   f. Token Ring
   g. UDP

3. What does "reliability" mean when used to define to a protocol?
   a. Uses connection-oriented sessions
   b. Uses best-effort delivery
   c. Uses windows to maintain reliability
   d. Uses acknowledgements to confirm delivered data
   e. Uses buffers

4. How many steps are involved in a TCP connection establishment?
   a. Two
   b. Three
   c. Four
   d. Five
   e. None

5. How many steps are involved in a TCP connection termination?
   a. Two
   b. Three
   c. Four
   d. Five
   e. None

6. How many steps are involved in a UDP connection establishment?
   a. Two
   b. Three
   c. Four
   d. Five
   e. None

7. What are the well-known port numbers for the following applications? Choose from this list: 21, 23, 25, 53, 69, 80, 101.
   a. FTP
   b. DNS
   c. http
   d. SMTP
   e. Telnet
   f. TFTP

8. If during the data transfer stage of a TCP session the windowing is changed from 4000 to 5000, it means the sending host can do what?
   a. Transmit 5,000 segments before getting an acknowledgement
   b. Transmit 5,000 packets before getting an acknowledgement
   c. Transmit 5,000 bytes before getting an acknowledgement
   d. Transmit 4,000 segments before getting an acknowledgement

9. Of the three Code Bits (Flags) FIN, SYN, and ACK, in which phase of the TCP connection process is each to be found?
   a. Establishment
   b. Data transfer
   c. Termination

10. TCP/IP transport layer protocols use what addresses to direct data to upper-layer applications?
   a. IP addresses
   b. MAC addresses
   c. Port numbers
   d. IPX addresses

Answers

1. **a.** Transmission Control Protocol
   b. User Datagram Protocol
   c. Sequenced Packet Exchange

2. **b.** and **d.** TCP and SPX are connection-oriented protocols.

3. **d.** A protocol that uses acknowledgements to confirm delivered data is reliable. Note: The use of best-effort delivery by a protocol means that the protocol is unreliable.

4. **b.** A three-step handshake is involved in a TCP connection establishment.

5. **c.** There are four steps in the TCP termination process.

6. **e.** None—there is no connection to establish with UDP.

7. **a.** FTP: 21
   b. DNS: 53
   c. HTTP: 80
   d. SMTP: 25
   e. Telnet: 23
   f. TFTP: 69

8. **c.** The sending host can transmit 5,000 bytes before getting an acknowledgement.

9. **a.** Establishment: SYN
   b. Data transfer: ACK
   c. Termination: FIN
   Note: ACKs will also appear in establishment and termination.

10. **c.** TCP/IP transport layer protocols use port numbers to direct data to upper-layer applications.

CHAPTER 7

OSI Model–
Layers 5, 6, and 7

This chapter will:

- **Discuss the session layer processes for session establishment and termination**

- **Discuss dialogue control and separation**

- **Cover session layer protocols such as NFS, SQL, and RPC**

- **Discuss presentation layer processes and protocols for data formatting, compression, and encryption**

- **Look at the application layer programs that provide network access for our network and standalone applications**

- **Look at the DNS name resolution process**

The CCNA exam deals with Layers 1 through 4 more than it deals with Layers 5 through 7. However, you do need to know and understand some basic concepts about Layers 5, 6, and 7, so we will deal with them in this chapter. This is also somewhat consistent with the TCP/IP's reference model, which sees everything above the transport layer as a single layer called the application layer. Figure 7-1 shows the OSI and TCP/IP reference models.

Figure 7-1
OSI and TCP/IP

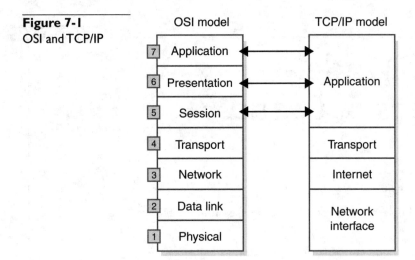

Session Layer: Layer 5

By the time the data gets to the receiving host's session layer in the OSI reference model or the application layer in the TCP/IP reference model, some pretty amazing things have happened. It has been encapsulated and de-encapsulated to add, use, and remove network addressing, physical addressing, as well as various levels of quality control. In the last chapter, we saw that the transport layer makes sure that the data is complete and properly reassembled before forwarding it to a port number (another address) for delivery to the proper application. So, how do these applications know what to do with the data, or even know that the data is coming? That is the function of the session layer.

The session layer establishes, manages, synchronizes, and terminates conversations, or sessions, between applications. These sessions can consist of many simultaneous conversations that occur between applications located in different network hosts. The session layer also has procedures for dealing with incomplete, or interrupted, communications.

With many applications, such as the Microsoft Office programs Word, Excel, and PowerPoint, limited application interaction occurs between the network hosts except for file handling. You typically launch Word locally, and then if you open a document on a server, it is transferred to your local machine and the copy on the server is locked so that others can only open "copies" of the document. When you are done, the revised document is stored to the server and is now available to others. Anyone who opens a copy of the document does not see your changes unless they open the revised file; similarly, any changes they make to the copy do not change your document.

There are client/server applications that allow client hosts to interactively manipulate data and initiate procedures that can immediately change data on a server. These applications typically allow multiple clients to make simultaneous changes to the same pool of data. These applications are often "front ends" for database programs like SQL (pronounced "sequel") that can distribute processing between one or more servers running the application software and possibly others storing the data.

Online banking is an example of a client/server application. As a user, you initiate a session using client software that's either loaded on your machine or accessible from the Internet. A bank's server, after authenticating you with a logon process, gives you access to various menus or features. Surely you are not the only one accessing the bank's computer at the moment, and locking the file, as in the case of products like Word or Excel, would be unacceptable. Somehow the system is able to separate your conversation from the many others accessing the system at that moment.

More importantly, suppose that you are transferring funds out of your account to make a house or car payment and the process is interrupted, and you lose your connection. At that point, you don't want the funds to be removed from your account if the information or final authorization for where they are to be transferred is incomplete. These client/sever features are application or session layer functions.

Session Establishment, Termination, and Reestablishment

Two important activities of the session layer are determining how to indicate the start and end of a communications session. In a telephone call analogy, this would be the hellos and goodbyes that indicate the beginning and end of a polite conversation. Cellular phones have made this an even better example insofar as it is not uncommon to lose a connection. My son, a network consultant and integrator, and I often talk to each other on cell phones. If one of us loses contact with a cell and disconnects without having said goodbye, we know it was a dropped call. This leads to another problem that needs to be resolved at the session layer: When a communication is dropped, who initiates the reconnection? Until my son and I worked out a "protocol," we would both dial each other and end up reaching each other's call waiting. A simple agreement to always have the original caller replace the call eliminated that confusion.

The session layer protocols exchange information during the initial communications setup that allows both sides to identify a particular communications session, how the session will be started, what coding will indicate the end of a session, a time-out period after which the connection will be interpreted as lost if no communication has been received, and what is to happen in case of a lost connection. The application involved with its security and accountability requirements often dictates whether a session can be reestablished without starting over.

Dialogue Control

When two hosts are communicating together, they alternate between which host is sending information and which is receiving—which one is talking and which is listening. It is up to the session layer protocols to define this process through dialogue control.

Dialogue control involves deciding whether to use *two-way simultaneous* (TWS) communication or *two-way alternate* (TWA) communication. With TWS communication, the session layer does not manage the conversation, leaving that to the other layers of the communicating hosts. Although session layer collisions can occur, they are different than Layer 1 collisions. They involve two messages passing each other and the resulting confusion that can result. An analogy is when two people talk at once on the phone without listening to the other person.

TWA communication is used if session layer collisions are not acceptable. TWA involves the use of a session layer data token that allows each host to take turns in much the same way a Layer 2 Token Ring handles Layer 1 collisions.

Dialogue Separation

In an important conversation, such as negotiating or reviewing a contract, the parties might stop periodically for what I call "reality checks" where they review what's been agreed to so far, who is doing what, and perhaps record or initial key points. It might even be appropriate to timestamp these activities. In the session layer, these reality checks are called checkpoints and they separate parts of a session.

This dialogue-separation process includes the orderly initiation, termination, and management of communication. At scheduled checkpoints, one host sends a synchronization message to the other host, which causes both hosts to perform the following steps:

1. Back up the particular files

2. Save the network settings

3. Save the clock settings—for synchronization

4. Make note of the end point in the conversation

This process would be repeated throughout the session. Figure 7-2 shows the checkpoints and synchronization process.

Figure 7-2
Dialogue separation

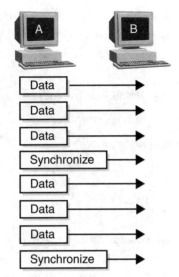

Layer 5 Protocols

The session layer has several protocols that you should be able to recognize as Layer 5 protocols for the exam:

- **Network File System (NFS)**   A distributed file system protocol suite developed by Sun Microsystems that allows remote file access across a network. NFS is one protocol in the suite that includes NFS, RPC, External Data Representation (XDR), and others.

- **Structured Query Language (SQL)**   A standardized query language for requesting information from a database, originally introduced by IBM's research program. In 1979, Oracle Corporation introduced a commercial implementation. While originally designed for database management systems running on mainframes and mini-computers, SQL is now supported by PC database systems such as Microsoft's SQL application because it supports distributed databases (databases that are spread out over several computer systems). This enables several users on a LAN to access the same database simultaneously.

- **Remote procedure call (RPC)**   Technological foundation of client/server computing. RPCs are procedure calls (requests) that are built or specified by clients and executed on servers. The results are returned over the network to the clients. Client/server computing describes distributed computing (processing) network systems in which transaction responsibilities are divided into two parts: client (front end) and server (back end).

- **X Window System** Distributed, network-transparent, device-independent, multi-tasking windowing and graphics system originally developed by MIT for communication between X terminals and UNIX workstations. *Do not confuse with Microsoft Windows.*

- **DecNet Session Control Protocol** Digital Equipment's session layer protocol.

- **AppleTalk Session Protocol (ASP)** Apple Computer's session layer protocol.

- **NetBIOS Names** NetBEUI's session layer protocol.

Presentation Layer: Layer 6

This layer allows communication between applications on diverse computer systems in a manner that's transparent to the applications. Simply, the presentation layer is responsible for preparing the format and representation of data so that it will be useful to the receiving host. If necessary, this layer can translate between different data formats using code formatting and conversion.

The presentation layer provides these three functions, if they are used:

- Data formatting (presentation)
- Data compression
- Data encryption

Data Formatting

It is the sending host's presentation layer that is responsible for encoding data in a form that the receiving device can understand. This pertains to text, pictures and images, as well as video and sound. It is up to Layer 6 to provide translation between these different codes.

Text Formats

Text files contain only character data and lack any of the formatting features, such as bold or italics, that we have become accustomed to in programs like Word and Excel. Notepad (accessed via Start | Programs | Accessories) can be used to create a text file, which will have .TXT as a file extension. Figure 7-3 shows a sample log file opened in Notepad. Many Windows applications, and even Windows' installation process, create many text files as a history file, with extensions such as .LOG and .INI. Next are the two text data formats:

- **American Standard Code for Information Interchange (ASCII)** Used by most PCs. The original ASCII used 7 bits and was limited to 128 character and symbol representations. The current (extended) ASCII uses 8 bits for 256 representations.

- **Extended Binary Coded Decimal Interchange Code (EBCDIC)** Used by IBM mainframe and minicomputers.

Figure 7-4 shows some common text file extensions and document icons when viewed in Windows Explorer.

An alternative to text formats is the binary format. Binary files contain specially coded data that can be viewed, modified, or printed only by specific software applications. Figure 7-5 shows what happens if you try to view a binary file using a text editor like Notepad.

Graphics Formats

Graphics and pictures are a special type of binary file format that allows images to be widely distributed over the Internet and other vehicles. Graphic files require reader software specifically designed to display an image file. Some reader programs support

Figure 7-3
Example of a
text file

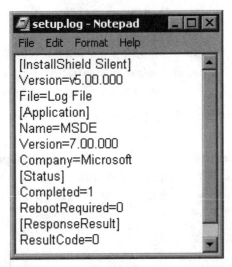

Figure 7-4
Common text
file icons

QUICKEN.INI   SchedLgU.Txt   setup.log

Figure 7-5
Binary file viewed
in Notepad

different image types and some can convert files from one type to another. Figure 7-6 shows a graphical representation of the image formatting process. The following are some of the standards for pictures and graphic images:

- **Graphics Interchange Format (GIF, pronounced "giff")**   A bit-mapped graphics file format used heavily on the Web. Supports color, various resolutions, and data compression. Files often have a .GIF extension.

- **BMP**   The standard bit-map graphics format for the Windows environment that stores graphics in a *device-independent bitmap* (DIB) format. Files have a .BMP extension.

- **Tagged Image File Format (TIFF)**   A format for high-resolution, bit-mapped images that can be black and white, grayscale, or color. Files often have a .TIF extension.

- **Joint Photographic Experts Group (JPEG, pronounced "jay-peg")**   A graphic compression technique for color images. It can reduce files sizes to about 5 percent of their normal size with only minor detail loss. Files often have a .JPG extension.

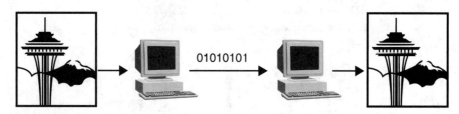

Figure 7-6   Image converted to digital and back

- **PICT**   A picture format used to transfer QuickDraw graphics between programs on the Apple MAC operating system.

Multimedia Formats

Another type of binary file is the multimedia file for video, music, and sounds. Depending on the format, these files can be fully downloaded and then played using reader (player) software. With newer formats, such as MP3, these files can be played while downloading, which is called streaming audio or streaming video. Streaming products require faster, more reliable connections. Figure 7-7 shows a graphical representation of the formatting process. Some of the standards for the presentation of sound and movies include:

- **Musical Instrument Digital Interface (MIDI)**   A format for digitized music.

- **Audio Video Interleave (AVI)**   Microsoft's video for Windows standard. While not adequate for full-screen or full-motion video, it does not require any special hardware or software. Files have an .AVI extension.

- **Motion Picture Experts Group (MPEG, pronounced "m-peg")**   Standard for a family of digital video compression standards and file formats. Achieves a high compression rate by storing only the changes from one frame to another, instead of each entire frame—generally the loss is imperceptible to the human eye. Two major MPEG standards exist:

  - **MPEG-1**   Provides video resolution of 352 × 240 at 30 *frames per second* (fps)— slightly below the quality of conventional VCR videos.
  - **MPEG-2**   Used by DVD-ROMs, provides video resolutions of 720 × 480 and 1280 × 720 at 60 fps—near full CD-quality audio. Meets the major TV standards like NTSC and HDTV. MPEG-4 will be based on the QuickTime file format.

- **MP3**   A standard for compressing audio signals, particularly music. MP3 is actually the file extension for MPEG, audio layer 3, one of three coding schemes (layers 1, 2,

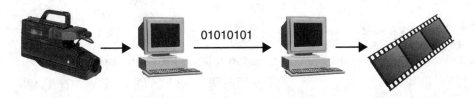

Figure 7-7   Video formatting

and 3—not OSI layers). Compression techniques reduce sound data-transfer rates to about 1/12 the number of bits per second required with minimal loss of sound quality.

- **WAV**   A Microsoft/IBM standard for storing sound data. Introduced in Windows 95 and supported by all later versions. Files have a .WAV extension.

- **QuickTime**   A standard that handles audio and video on the Apple MAC operating system.

Markup Language Formats

Another type of file format is markup language. Originally developed and standardized by the International Organization for Standards (ISO) in 1986, Standard Generalized Markup Language (SGML) is a system for organizing and tagging elements of a document. SGML does not itself contain any particular formatting; instead, it uses rules for tagging elements that can then be interpreted to format elements in different ways. Two common markup language formats include:

- **Hypertext Markup Language (HTML)**   Standard for electronically stored text that provides a set of directions for displaying a page and allows direct access to other text documents by way of encoded links. Hypertext documents created using HTML often integrate images, sound, and other media that can be viewed using a Web browser. HTML directions tell a browser whether to display text, display a graphic, or hyperlink to another URL. HTML, used widely on the Web and viewed on Web browsers, defines and interprets tags according to SGML rules. Figure 7-8 shows an example of an HTML file opened in a text editor—the text in < > are tags.

- **Extensible Markup Language (XML)**   Specification developed by the World Wide Web Consortium (W3C) as a subset of SGML that allows Web designers to create their own customized tags. It is hoped that these tags will expand on HTML's display capabilities to include definition, transmission, validation, and interpretation of data between applications and organizations primarily to facilitate e-commerce. W3C is the chief standards body for HTTP and HTML.

Data Compression

The presentation layer protocols are also responsible for the compression of files. For all practical purposes, compression is the equivalent of squeezing the unnecessary bits out of our data to reduce its transmission size. This recognizes that a smaller document (fewer bits) will transmit faster than a larger one.

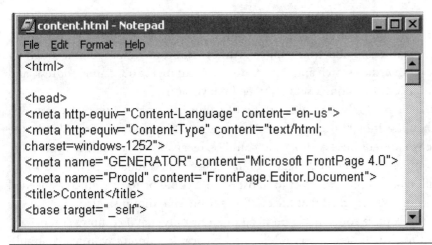

Figure 7-8   HTML as text

Data compression uses complex mathematical algorithms to identify repeated bit patterns that can be replaced by much smaller "tokens." At the receiving end, the tokens can be replaced to reconstitute the original data. In the last section, when we discussed graphic and multimedia formats, many of them included compression as part of their standard. Some do not use tokens but in fact just strip out permanently unneeded bit patterns that will go unnoticed by the human eye or ear. Figure 7-9 shows a graphical representation of data compression.

Figure 7-9
Data compression

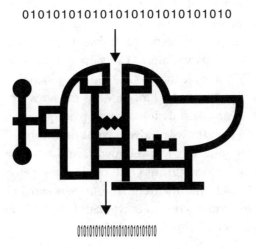

While not a great analogy, my company does a manual form of compression when we create original drafts of proposals and contracts. We type ***BLA** wherever we want our company name and address to appear. After the document has gone through all internal reviews, we do a search and replace on *BLA, supplying our name, address, and contact numbers. The customer sees only the final version.

Another analogy would be transporting 10 gallons of orange juice to a camping site versus hauling enough frozen concentrate to make 10 gallons of juice. Clearly, the concentrate would require less effort and could be reconstituted at the site with water. Another "compression" method creates orange juice concentrate in powdered form, which would require even less effort to transport and could be reconstituted as needed —although it might be argued that the quality is somewhat diminished.

As far as the exam is concerned, you need to know only that if compression occurs, the standard for it will be in Layer 6. From a practical standpoint, you really should have a working knowledge of what compression is and the benefits it can provide when transmitting data over links that can be very slow.

Many user applications today, such as Word, Excel, and PowerPoint, have compression built in because the developers understand the benefits of smaller file storage and shorter, often cheaper, data transmission times. The Microsoft Office training manuals that my company produces contain many graphics and screen captures. Until Office 97, it was not uncommon for these manuals to be 12 to 18MB in size for 100 pages. For years we used products like WinZip (**www.winzip.com**) to squeeze them down to around 10 percent of their original size before transmitting them by modem to printing companies. Today, those same documents stored as Office 97 or 2000 Word files take 1 to 2MB—virtually the same size we were getting from WinZip. This represents a substantial savings in disk space and means that we often transmit them now without further compression. We have discovered though that we can still zip these new document files to reduce their size by as much as 50 to 75 percent.

Many of the data compression standards are set by the International Telecommunication Union (ITU), formerly Comité Consultatif International Téléphonique et Télégraphique (CCITT). These are the people who developed the various "v" standards for modems, such as the v90 standard for 56 Kbps modems. They also developed the "Group 3" standard for FAX transmissions. For more information about data compression, consider checking this site: **www.advent.co.uk/ccitt.html**.

If the link is dead, try going to **www.webopedia.com** and do a search on "compression." There are many interesting links, although some get quite technical. There should be a link to WinZip information. If not, **www.winzip.com** has information screens as well as an evaluation copy to download. Everybody in this industry should understand how to use some form of zip technology.

Data Encryption

Data encryption enables you to secure your data before transmission by translating it into a secret code. This makes it more difficult, if not impossible, for someone to view your information. Like compression, encryption uses complex mathematical algorithms to encode your data. If encryption is going to be used to protect transmitted personal or credit card data, Layer 6 is responsible for ensuring that both the sending and receiving host are on the same page. If the data is to be used in any way by the receiving node, it must know how to decipher the incoming data.

Unencrypted data is called *plain text* while encrypted data is called *cipher text*.

As with compression, for the exam, you really only need to know that encryption, if it occurs as part of the data transmission processes, is the responsibility of Layer 6. But like compression, you probably ought to have at least a general understanding of encryption. You will run into it in many forms and as a feature of devices and software.

An encryption key is used to encrypt the data at its source, and then the same or another key is used to decrypt the data at its destination. While a bit of an oversimplification, the key is like a password that is used to "scramble" the bits, and without the same or a related password, it is impossible to unscramble them. Figure 7-10 shows a graphical representation of a key being used to encode the data.

The following are the two main forms of encryption:

- **Asymmetric encryption**   Uses two keys: one is the public key known to everyone, which is used to encrypt a message, and the second key, unique to the recipient, is used to decipher the message.

- **Symmetric encryption**   Uses the same key to encrypt and decrypt the message.

For more information, go to **www.webopedia.com** and do a search on "encryption."

Figure 7-10
Encryption key

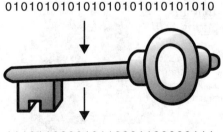

01010101010101010101010101010

1110110000101100011000000111

Format Exercise

The following lab assumes you are using any version of Windows. This is a nonde-structive lab and you should be able to do it on your home machine without concern of it changing your system configuration. This lab looks at your Web browser and image formats.

1. If you are doing this at home, establish a connection to your ISP. This will connect you via your modem and make sure that you have an IP address. In a TCP/IP LAN, it shouldn't be necessary to do this step.

2. Launch your Web browser. Any version of Internet Explorer or Netscape will work.

3. In the address box, type **www.cnn.com** and press ENTER. Look over the screen.

4. Place your mouse on any color photograph and click the right mouse button. Choose Properties from the pop-up menu. The following illustration shows the pop-up menu with Properties at the bottom.

   Near the top of the resulting window is the filename, and its extension should indicate the file format: a .JPG extension for JPEG.

5. Try the same thing on a piece of artwork or graphic and you may find it is a .GIF file. Try others.

6. If you right-click a photograph or graphic, the pop-up menu offers you the choice of Save Picture As, which will save the image as a file that can then be used in other programs like Word. Try it if you like.

   The pop-up menu also offers "Set As Wallpaper," which will make that picture the wallpaper for your computer desktop. If you choose to try this, when you return to the desktop (minimize all windows), you will see the results. Right-click the desktop and choose Properties | Background to change the image. Try the Center, Tile, and Stretch (not available on all versions) settings to see the results.

7. On the **www.cnn.com** site, scroll down to the Multimedia section and experiment with the video and audio options. While you probably won't see the format, you can see the results.

Application Layer: Layer 7

The application layer is the top protocol layer of the OSI or TCP/IP reference models. The application layer identifies and establishes the availability of potential communicating hosts, synchronizes applications, and establishes procedures for error recovery. It provides an interface to the presentation layer, and to all lower layers, as well as an interface to the applications using network services. In some cases, those applications (such as FTP, Telnet, and DNS) are actually a part of the TCP/IP protocol stack. In other cases, they are network-ready applications that could be used as stand-alone applications (such as like Word, Excel, or PowerPoint), or applications like e-mail and Web browsers that may not be all that useful without a network.

Network Applications

Some applications and protocols exist specifically because of networks. They are the natural extensions of providing various network services to end users. Most network applications are client/server applications—a distributed computing network system in which transaction processing responsibilities are divided into two parts: the client (front end) and server (back end). The client, located on the local host, requests services, and the server, remote host, furnishes resources (information). The client can also be an input device for the server, providing additional information, such as adding a new prospect to a customer database. Figure 7-11 represents a client/server application.

Figure 7-11
Client/server
application

Client

Server
Customer
Database

The following programs are examples of network applications:

- **Hypertext Transfer Protocol (HTTP)**   The protocol used by Web browsers and Web servers to transfer files, such as text and graphics files, from the many servers on the Internet.

- **E-mail**   Network application in which mail messages are transmitted electronically between end users over various types of networks using various network protocols.

- **Domain Name System (DNS)**   An Internet system that translates domain names of network nodes (such as **www.cisco.com**) into IP addresses so that the request can be forwarded.

- **Telnet**   A terminal client application that allows a host to remotely access other devices running Telnet server "daemon" applications. This terminal program can be used to configure and monitor the performance of routers and switches, and to log in to some Internet host devices and execute commands.

- **File Transfer Protocol (FTP)**   An application protocol used for transferring files between network nodes. FTP is part of the TCP/IP protocol stack.

The network applications like Telnet and FTP are discussed in greater detail at appropriate points in the book. Later in this chapter, we will look at an overview of HTTP, DNS, and e-mail as examples of network applications.

Standalone Applications

Software applications that can function on stand-alone devices are being designed to take better advantage of network services so that documents can be stored on network servers, printed on network printers, and forwarded as e-mail attachments from within the application. Programs such as word processors, spreadsheets, presentation software, small accounting packages, and so on all are examples.

Redirectors

A redirector is a protocol that works with computer operating systems and network clients, instead of with specific application programs, to provide network services to what would otherwise be stand-alone applications. Redirectors allow users to share documents, templates, databases, printers, and many other network resources.

When a host is set up as a network client, a redirector protocol is added that evaluates service requests to determine if network resources will be involved. If a stand-alone product such as Word is being used on a locally stored document and/or is being printed on a local printer, the redirector determines there is no network involvement and allows the local operating system to process the request.

If the client wants to save a Word document to a network server, the redirector reroutes the request to the proper network resource, while Word continues to treat it as a local process. At this point, the OSI model processes and protocols also come into play.

Some examples of redirectors are the following:

- Network File System (NSF)
- Novell's Netware Shell or Client32
- Windows Workstation and Server services on any Windows machine
- Apple File Protocol

The redirector and related protocols make network applications out of stand-alone applications that have at least minimal coding that would allow them to take advantage of network resources.

If you haven't been around long enough to remember installing old DOS applications, each with its own print drivers, fonts, screen drivers, mouse support, and so forth, you may not realize that Windows delivered us from tremendous frustration and relatively time-consuming installation processes. In Windows, we have an operating system that, while not perfect, takes responsibility for all of those functions. Once your fonts, monitor, printer, mouse, and so forth are set up, any applications you install can use those features. The applications companies were given specifications that, in essence, said "write to these standards and we [Microsoft] will handle the printing and so forth for you."

The redirector feature is a similar extension of networking services to the application community. Word doesn't have to have the network coding internally. It also doesn't become dependent on a particular network protocol; it can run on TCP/IP, NetBEUI, or IPX/SPX.

Application Layer Example

In this section, we are going to look at three Layer 7 applications, HTTP, DNS, and e-mail, as a way of summarizing much of what we have covered to this point in our discussion of the OSI model and to focus on the vital role DNS provides for many applications.

Domain Name System (DNS)

While IP addresses are hierarchical and reliably identify and locate hosts on the largest of internetworks, they tend to be very difficult for humans to remember and even more difficult to determine if unknown to you. Using friendlier text names that can be resolved to numeric addresses has been a well-established mechanism for networks like UNIX and NetBIOS. One solution is to have a local file on each host that is a table relating names to numeric addresses. The HOSTS file in UNIX and the HOSTS and LMHOSTS files in Microsoft networks are examples. Figure 7-12 is an example of a name resolution file. Since it will be searched by brute force (top to bottom), the most frequently used names should be at the top.

In the early days of the ARPANET, the predecessor of the Internet, Stanford Research Institute's Network Information Center (SRI-NIC) maintained a single master host file. Each host or network around the world would periodically use FTP to download the name resolution file. As time went on, the burden on a single site to provide the maintenance, the size of the download file, and the number of hosts downloading the data got to be unmanageable.

In the early 1980s, efforts to develop an alternative system of servers that could be maintained by more than one organization became the DNS standard. It is a distributed database that does not require a single host to contain all the data. Shortly after that, Sun Microsystems introduced the first commercial implementation of DNS for its operating system. While many DNS servers are UNIX devices, there are versions of DNS software that run on all network operating systems.

Figure 7-12
Name resolution file

198.137.240.92	www.whitehouse.gov
198.133.219.25	www.cisco.com
207.46.209.218	www.microsoft.com
198.41.0.6	internic.net
198.81.129.99	www.cia.gov

Today, the DNS that has evolved is a hierarchy of servers based on the Internet but extending in layers out to ISPs and corporate networks to provide name resolution services. If the first server that a host contacts does not have the appropriate name/address combination, it forwards the request to the next higher-level server.

To use DNS, each host must be configured with at least the IP address of one DNS server; it could be a corporate server or one located on the ISP's network. This configuration can be assigned manually by an administrator (static) or assigned as part of the DHCP process. If a host has not been given the address of a DNS server, it will not be able to resolve the domain names. In Chapter 5, we saw DNS work when we experimented with the Ping and Tracert commands. Typing **ping www.cisco.com** leads to a request to a DNS server that responds with the related IP address so that Ping can then continue.

Domain Name Space

To understand how DNS works, you need to look at domain name space and see that it looks very much like an organizational chart or inverted tree. At the top are the top-level domains, which now include over 200 designations. Figure 7-13 shows an example of the domain name space.

Each of the boxes represents a domain, with the upper-level domains containing any domains that are connected below it. BLA, Cisco, and Microsoft are all a part of the COM domain. These second-level domains are the domain names that are registered with organizations such as Network Solutions. At this level, there could be many thousands or even millions of unrelated domains that are all a part of the COM domain.

The sales and bob domains are subdomains that the BLA domain added to break up a large domain into easier-to-manage units. Small and medium-sized organizations

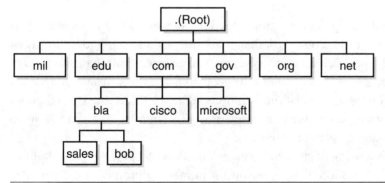

Figure 7-13   Domain name space

typically don't have subdomains, whereas large companies such as Cisco and Microsoft find the extra granularity to be worth the additional overhead.

The domain name significance is right to left, starting with the top-level domain and then the second-level domain. This right-to-left significance is used when the name is resolved.

How DNS Works

The DNS server software actually performs two functions: the server function, where it can reply to requests from its own database, and the resolver function that asks a higher-level DNS server to resolve the name when the name cannot be resolved locally.

If I type **www.bla.com** into my browser, the DNS server specified in my host configuration will be queried to resolve the name "www.bla.com" to an IP address. The DNS server checks its cache to see if it has a COM folder. If it does, it checks the COM folder for a BLA entry. If it finds BLA, it responds with the associated IP address. When the request can be supplied directly from the DNS server's cache, it is called an *iterative query*.

If the server has resolved the name recently, it will be available in cache. If the name has not been requested in a set amount of time (60 minutes on Windows DNS servers), the server will have discarded it to avoid supplying outdated information.

If the original DNS server does not find the name in its cache but does find the COM folder, the resolver sends out a query to the COM server to be resolved. When the name is resolved, the original DNS server is sent the information, which it uses to update its files and then responds to the original request. This type of query is called a *recursive query*. If for some reason the COM folder has not been accessed in cache before the entry expires, the query is sent to a root-level server, which furnishes the address of the COM server, and then the process continues. While this process seems complicated, it should only take a few seconds.

Domain Names

A domain, as originally intended, is a group of computers that are associated by their geographical location (using country designations such as .uk, .za, and so forth) or their organizational type (such as .com, .gov, and .edu). Since no mechanism exists to screen domain registrations to conform to the geographical or organizational type, all types of foreign and noncommercial organizations are using COM, the U.S. commercial domain, and nothing prevents a North American firm from registering a UK site to attempt to have greater access to British users.

A domain name is a string of characters and/or numbers (A-Z, a-z, 0-9, and dashes), usually a name or abbreviation, that represents the numeric address of an Internet site.

The actual domain name is typically the right most part of a fully qualified domain name. In our **www.cisco.com** example, cisco.com is the domain name, while .com indicates the top-level domain.

URLs and Domain Names

A Uniform Resource Locator (URL) address, like those used to find sites on your Web browser, is a standardized addressing scheme for accessing hypertext documents and other services using a browser. The URL can contain a domain name, separated by periods, and specify folders and documents on the server using entries following the domain code. For example, **www.mystuff.com/vacation/index.htm** is a .com domain, where *vacation* is a shared folder and *index.htm* is a specific document. While our example used the Web's http:// protocol, URLs can also be used with the other protocols, such as ftp://, news://, nfs://, and cifs://.

Top-Level Domain Names

There are more than 200 top-level domains on the Internet, examples of which include the following two-letter country codes:

.us	United States
.za	South Africa
.uk	United Kingdom
.br	Brazil

There are also organizational domains like these:

.com	Commercial sites
.gov	Government sites
.edu	Educational sites
.org	Nonprofit sites
.net	Network services

While .com was intended to be for U.S. commercial sites, many foreign companies and nonbusiness organizations register .com addresses to be easily accessible to the U.S. mass market. Other countries use different ways of identifying commercial sites, South Africa uses .CO.ZA as the common commercial extension creating names like www.itweb.co.za/.

Recently, Internet Corporation for Assigned Names and Numbers (ICANN), the Internet's managing authority, approved some additional top-level domains. They include the following:

.biz	Businesses
.info	International global option, similar to .com in the United States
.name	Individual names, like sally.larson.name
.pro	Professional registrations, like marysmith.law.pro or jowest.med.pro
.museum (or .mus)	For accredited museums worldwide
.air	The Societi Internationale de Tilicommunications Aironautiques (SITA), a cooperative organization of the air transport community for use in industry communications
.coop	For business cooperatives, such as credit unions and rural electric coops

In addition, several new country codes were added, such as .ps for the Palestinian Authority.

HTTP and the World Wide Web

HTTP and the way it works with the Web can probably claim credit for at least starting the tremendous public involvement with the Internet. Finally, the combination provided a relatively simple tool that was both visual and capable of bringing an extremely broad range of useful information into the classroom, office, and home.

The Web browser is a Layer 7 client/server application, requiring a client application on the local host and a server application on one or more remote hosts. The Web browser presents data in multimedia format on Web pages in a Layer 6 format language called Hypertext Markup Language (HTML). HTML can produce pages with text, graphics, and sounds that may be using other Layer 6 formatting protocols, and could include some Layer 6 encryption for secure data.

Once your Web browser is open, you see the default "home" page for the browser. It could be MSN, Yahoo, or any Web site of your choosing. At this point, you can type an IP address, or more likely a URL, in the browser's address bar and press ENTER. If a URL address is typed, the name is resolved using a DNS server and the appropriate server and document are found.

Another way of navigating the Web is to use hyperlinks that have been added to text or pictures on a page. The user can make choices by simply clicking on the hyperlink object. A hyperlink is any Web page object that contains a hidden URL address. Clicking the object triggers a request for the URL page. Figure 7-14 show a Web page with hyperlinks (underlined items).

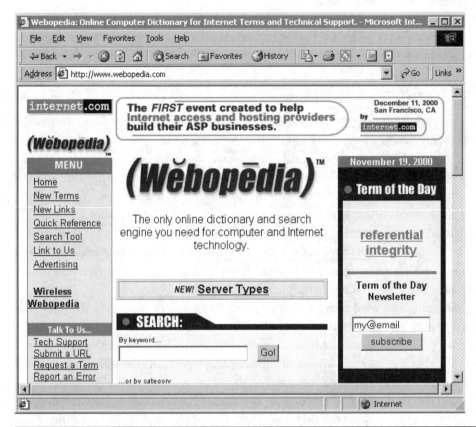

Figure 7-14   Web page with hyperlinks

In defining a URL address, we will use http://www.lhseattle.com. To better understand how the URL is read (right to left), we can read it backward, com.lhseattle. www//:http. The elements are described here:

- **www.lhseattle.com**   A *fully qualified domain name* (FQDN).

- **com**   The top-level domain.

- **lhseattle.com**   The domain name.

- **www**   A host name entry on the lhseattle.com DNS server that points to the IP address of the server.

- **http://**   Tells the browser which protocol and port to use for the communication, in this case the HTTP protocol and port 80 are used. Protocol designations such as ftp://, news://, nfs://, and file:// will do the same thing.

If the address is http://www.lhseattle.com/employment/, the employment/ portion indicates a particular folder on that server, allowing you possibly to bypass the site's home page and go to a temporary folder that may only be available with this full address.

E-Mail Service

E-mail programs use POP3, an e-mail client-access protocol, to retrieve e-mail, and the Simple Mail Transport Protocol (SMTP), a mail exchange protocol used between servers, to provide e-mail service. Another common client-access protocol called IMAP4 is backward-compatible with POP3, but has more of a server-based approach to mail whereby the mail and folders are kept on the server. Common e-mail programs include Microsoft Outlook, Microsoft Exchange Mail, Eudora, and Netscape Mail.

E-mail allows us to exchange text information with various types of attachments using one or more servers as "post offices." The sender forwards the e-mail to his/her e-mail server. That server forwards the mail to the recipient's e-mail server, and finally the document is delivered to the recipient.

In addressing an e-mail address such as mary@bla.com, the portion to the left of the @ (mary) indicates a username, while the information after the @ (bla.com) is the recipient's post office address (domain name). Note that the recipient's name is only important after the message arrives at the recipient's post office address. Figure 7-15 shows e-mail address and Subject boxes.

In order for mail to be delivered properly, the DNS server that houses the domain must be configured with a Mail Exchange (MX) record identifying the post office. If an MX record is present, the domain name portion of the address is resolved by the DNS server(s) using the same techniques covered earlier, and an IP address is returned. At this point, the e-mail is processed through the OSI layers as we've discussed in Chapter 1 as part of the encapsulation process before being transported to the recipient's post office server(s).

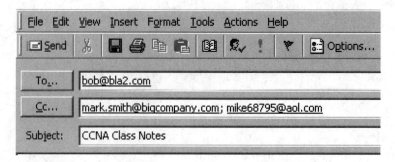

Figure 7-15 E-mail addresses

Once delivered to the recipient's post office server, the recipient's username becomes important. The server parses it from the e-mail address and checks to see whether it matches a client of its post office. If the recipient is a client, it stores the message in his or her mailbox until the user retrieves it using e-mail client software. If the recipient is unknown, the post office forwards the message to the postmaster (administrator of the post office) and generates an error message to the sender.

E-mail messages are normally sent as ASCII or plain text, but the attachments can be pictures, audio, video, or other types of data. For the attachments to be viewable, the encoding schemes must be the same on both the sending and the receiving systems. Multipurpose Internet Mail Extension (MIME) and UUencode (a UNIX utility program) are the two most common formats for e-mail attachments.

Hyperlinks Exercise

The following lab assumes you are using any version of Windows. This is a nondestructive lab and you should be able to do it on your home machine without concern of it changing your system configuration. This lab looks at your Web browser and hyperlinks.

1. If you are doing this at home, establish a connection to your ISP. This will connect you via your modem and make sure that you have an IP address. In a TCP/IP LAN, it shouldn't be necessary to do this step.

2. Launch your Web browser. Any version of Internet Explorer or Netscape will work.

3. In the Address box, type **www.msn.com** and press ENTER. Look over the screen. Notice how your mouse pointer changes as it moves over various objects on the screen. The underlined text often indicates a hyperlink, as does any spot over which your mouse pointer changes from an arrow to a hand with the index finger extended.

4. On the www.msn.com home page, find a link and click it.
   The resulting screen should have a box of choices on the left side of the screen. Internet is an option and a hyperlink. Click it.

   Near the top of the next page, find a link Check Your Speed and click it. In a few moments, you will get a report of your connection speed in kilobits per second and your download speed in kilobytes per second. You might want to add this to your Favorites or Bookmarks folder. It includes great information and links about bandwidth and modems.

   For the purpose of this exercise, we just used hyperlinks to navigate through several Web pages.

5. Open an MS-DOS window (NT/2000 users open a Command window) and then type **ping www.msn.com** and press ENTER. Notice that the first line of output shows the name resolved to an IP address—a DNS server somewhere provided that information. Write down the IP address to which it resolved.

   Try pinging **www.lhseattle.com** and **www.bla.com**. Write down the IP addresses of each.

6. Return to your Web browser and, in the Address box, type one of the IP addresses you just resolved and press ENTER. It should take you to its Web site. Try to remember one of the other IP addresses without looking at your notes. What about remembering the name?

   Try another if you like. Compare it to typing the domain name—the result should be the same.

   Another advantage to using the domain name is that many bigger sites can be using multiple servers with load balancing, meaning that your request will be forwarded to the server with the shortest queue. But, if you use the IP address, you go to that particular machine, which may or may not be busy.

7. Experiment with hyperlinks and the Back button on the toolbar until you are comfortable with the concepts.

HOSTS Exercise

The following lab assumes you are using any version of Windows. This is a nondestructive lab and you should be able to do it on your home machine without concern of it changing your system configuration.

1. If you are doing this at home, establish a connection to your ISP. This will connect you via your modem and make sure that you have an IP address. In a TCP/IP LAN, it shouldn't be necessary to do this step.

2. In this lab, we are going to look at the HOSTS file as a tool for resolving computer host and domain names to IP addresses. The HOSTS file is one method of resolving host names to IP addresses. In concept, this is somewhat similar to the file the ARPANET users had to download to resolve names.

3. Use the Start | Run *winipcfg* (NT/2000 users type **ipconfig** from the command window) from earlier to see your IP address.

   Note on a piece of paper your IP address and your default gateway. The following illustration shows the IP address and default gateway on my Windows 2000 machine.

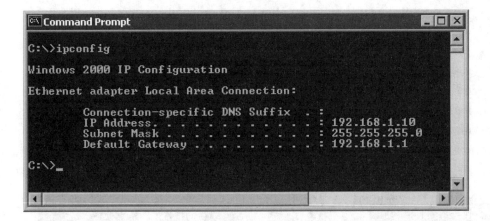

```
Command Prompt                                                    _ □ X

C:\>ipconfig

Windows 2000 IP Configuration

Ethernet adapter Local Area Connection:

        Connection-specific DNS Suffix  . :
        IP Address. . . . . . . . . . . : 192.168.1.10
        Subnet Mask . . . . . . . . . . : 255.255.255.0
        Default Gateway . . . . . . . . : 192.168.1.1

C:\>_
```

4. As long as we are here, Windows 95/98/Me users click the More Info button in the lower-right corner of the display to see the DNS server address (NT/2000 users type **ipconfig /all** from the command window).

5. Open an MS-DOS window (NT/2000 users open a Command window) and then type **ping www.cisco.com** and press ENTER. The following illustration shows the result of pinging the address. Notice that the first line of output shows the name resolved to an IP address—a DNS server somewhere provided that information.

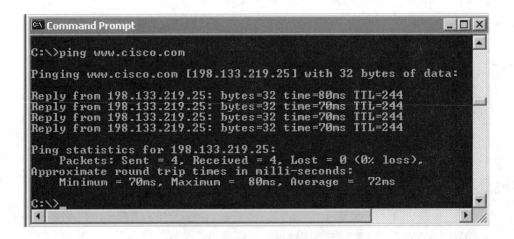

```
Command Prompt                                                    _ □ X

C:\>ping www.cisco.com

Pinging www.cisco.com [198.133.219.25] with 32 bytes of data:

Reply from 198.133.219.25: bytes=32 time=80ms TTL=244
Reply from 198.133.219.25: bytes=32 time=70ms TTL=244
Reply from 198.133.219.25: bytes=32 time=70ms TTL=244
Reply from 198.133.219.25: bytes=32 time=70ms TTL=244

Ping statistics for 198.133.219.25:
    Packets: Sent = 4, Received = 4, Lost = 0 (0% loss),
Approximate round trip times in milli-seconds:
    Minimum = 70ms, Maximum =  80ms, Average =   72ms

C:\>_
```

6. Try typing **ping seattle** and then **ping MyGatway**. Both attempts should fail. The names are not recognized.

7. Use the taskbar to choose Start | Search | For Files And Folders.
   Type **hosts** in the Search box and press ENTER or click the Search Now button. At least two files should appear: a HOSTS and a LMHOSTS file. The following illustration shows the result of searching for hosts. If multiple entries appear, we are interested in the set in your Windows folder. Note: You may not see the .SAM extension, depending on your Explorer settings.

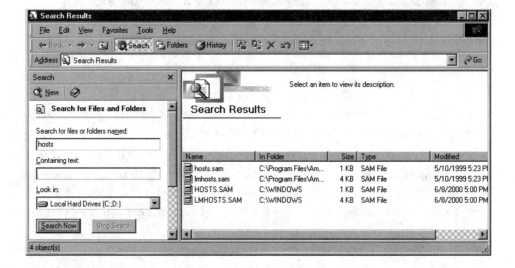

8. In the results window, double-click the HOSTS file. If the Open With window appears, choose Notepad and press ENTER. The following illustration shows the contents of the HOSTS file plus the three entries we will be adding in the next step. Read over the text and note there is probably a default entry for localhost.

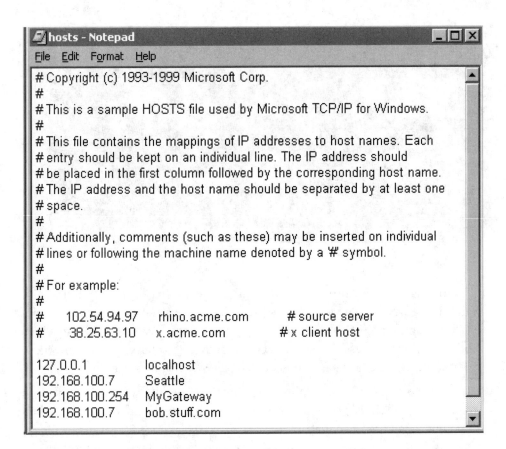

9. Move the cursor to the bottom of the screen, if necessary, and make the entries for Seattle and MyGateway, substituting the IP address for your computer in the Seattle entry and the IP address for your default gateway in the second entry. Use the TAB key to move to the hostname column. The final entry is your computer's IP address (or any IP address known to you—substitute your first name for mine. When you are sure that the IP addresses and spelling are correct, close the window and answer Yes when asked if you want to save the changes.

10. Return to the MS-DOS (or Command) window and ping both Seattle and MyGateway again. They are not case-sensitive. You should see that both names can now be resolved to addresses that you specified. The following illustration shows the result of resolving MyGateway.

```
Command Prompt                                          _ □ X

C:\>ping mygateway

Pinging MyGateway [192.168.100.254] with 32 bytes of data:

Reply from 192.168.100.254: bytes=32 time<10ms TTL=255
Reply from 192.168.100.254: bytes=32 time<10ms TTL=255
Reply from 192.168.100.254: bytes=32 time<10ms TTL=255
Reply from 192.168.100.254: bytes=32 time<10ms TTL=255

Ping statistics for 192.168.100.254:
    Packets: Sent = 4, Received = 4, Lost = 0 (0% loss),
Approximate round trip times in milli-seconds:
    Minimum = 0ms, Maximum = 0ms, Average = 0ms

C:\>_
```

11. Try to ping the final entry (bob.stuff.com) just as you typed it. It should resolve and succeed. Note that while we just created a .com entry and we can use it with TCP/IP commands like Ping and Tracert, an attempt to use it as a URL in a Web browser will fail unless there is a Web server at that IP address. It is far more likely that you will get a "The page cannot be displayed" error message.

12. Try pinging localhost. Remember it was in the hosts file with 127.0.0.1 as an address. You should see that it returns your computer's host name and a successful ping. Remember also that 127.0.0.1 is a reserved address for this type of loopback testing. The following illustration shows the result of resolving localhost.

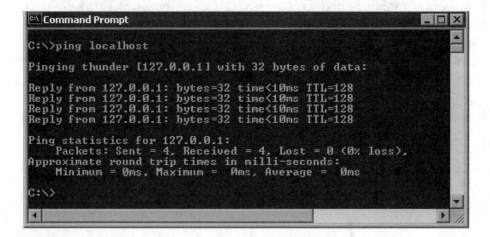

```
Command Prompt                                          _ □ X

C:\>ping localhost

Pinging thunder [127.0.0.1] with 32 bytes of data:

Reply from 127.0.0.1: bytes=32 time<10ms TTL=128
Reply from 127.0.0.1: bytes=32 time<10ms TTL=128
Reply from 127.0.0.1: bytes=32 time<10ms TTL=128
Reply from 127.0.0.1: bytes=32 time<10ms TTL=128

Ping statistics for 127.0.0.1:
    Packets: Sent = 4, Received = 4, Lost = 0 (0% loss),
Approximate round trip times in milli-seconds:
    Minimum = 0ms, Maximum = 0ms, Average = 0ms

C:\>
```

13. Either return to or redo your File search on hosts. When the lmhosts (or lmhosts.sam) file appears, double-click it and open it with Notepad as we did earlier with the hosts file.

We aren't going to use this one, but look it over. While the Hosts file resolves host names to IP addresses, this one maps NetBIOS names to IP addresses in Microsoft networks. If you choose to create an lmhosts entry to test it, the .SAM extension must be removed from the file before it will work properly.

Summary

In this chapter, you learned about the functions of the session layer and the different processes that occur as data packets travel through this layer. You saw that the session layer establishes, manages, and terminates sessions between applications. These sessions are multiple miniconversations between applications on different network devices

The session layer determines whether two-way simultaneous conversation or two-way alternate communication dialogue control is appropriate. Dialogue separation is used to initiate, terminate, and manage communication.

We saw that the presentation layer converts and translates between the different data formats to allow communications. The presentation layer provides data formatting, compression, and encryption as needed. We looked at some of the popular text, graphics, video, and audio formatting standards.

The application layer identifies and establishes the availability of potential communicating hosts, synchronizes applications, and establishes procedures for error recovery. It provides an interface to the presentation layer, and to all lower layers, as well as an interface to the applications using network services.

Practice Questions

Take a few moments and check your grasp of the concepts covered in this chapter. The answers are immediately following the questions.

Questions

1. What do each the following acronyms stand for?
   - a. NFS
   - b. SQL
   - c. RPC
   - d. ASCII
   - e. JPEG
   - f. MPEG
   - g. DNS
   - h. FTP
   - i. TFTP
   - j. HTTP
   - k. HTML

2. Next to each of the following, place the number 5, 6, or 7 to indicate which corresponding OSI layer each is associated with.
   - a. MIDI
   - b. GIF
   - c. RPC
   - d. ASCII
   - e. JPEG
   - f. HTTP
   - g. DNS
   - h. BMP
   - i. TFTP
   - j. MPEG
   - k. MP3
   - l. WAV
   - m. QuickTime
   - n. HTML
   - o. X Window System
   - p. NFS
   - q. TIFF
   - r. AVI
   - s. AppleTalk Session Protocol
   - t. EBCDIC
   - u. SQL
   - v. FTP

3. If you are at a cash machine withdrawing $300 and the transaction is interrupted before you get the cash, which OSI layer will hopefully prevent the amount from being debited from your account?
   - a. Presentation layer
   - b. Session layer
   - c. Application layer

4. List the seven OSI layers from seven to one.

   7.

   6.

   5.

   4.

   3.

   2.

   1.

5. *Two-way simultaneous* (TWS) communications and *two-way alternate* (TWA) communications are examples of which of the following?
   a. Dialogue control
   b. Dialogue separation

6. Which three of the following are the responsibilities of the presentation layer?
   a. User authentication
   b. Encryption
   c. End-to-end connectivity
   d. Data format
   e. Depression
   f. Compression

7. When you use a fully qualified domain name with Ping or as a URL on a Web page, which protocol resolves the name to an IP address?
   a. FTP
   b. NFS
   c. DNS
   d. SQL

8. In www.helpme.com, what part represents a fully qualified domain name?
   a. The whole thing
   b. .com
   c. helpme
   d. helpme.com
   e. www.helpme

9. In www.helpme.com, what part represents the top-level domain name?
   a. The whole thing
   b. .com
   c. helpme
   d. helpme.com
   e. www.helpme

10. In www.helpme.com, what part represents the domain name?
    a. The whole thing
    b. .com
    c. helpme
    d. helpme.com
    e. www.helpme

11. Which protocol determines whether a host process is a local or network activity?
    a. Requester
    b. Layer 5
    c. Redirector
    d. FTP

12. The TCP/IP reference model has only four layers from top to bottom. What are those four layers? List the OSI layer(s) that are comparable to each layer.
    a. _____   OSI layer(s): _____
    b. _____   OSI layer(s): _____
    c. _____   OSI layer(s): _____
    d. _____   OSI layer(s): _____

13. In www.helpme.com/inventory, what does /inventory represent?
    a. Top-level domain
    b. Host name
    c. Document
    d. Folder
    e. None of the above

14. What will be the result if a host is not configured with a DNS server address?
    a. Name resolution will take longer.
    b. It will have to rely on broadcasts to reach the DNS server.
    c. All applications will be unable to resolve names.
    d. None of the above.

15. Which two of the following are e-mail client-access protocols?

   a. SMTP

   b. POP3

   c. NFS

   d. IMAP4

Answers

1. **a.** Network File System

   b. Structured Query Language

   c. Remote procedure call

   d. American Standard Code for Information Interchange

   e. Joint Photographic Experts Group

   f. Motion Picture Experts Group

   g. Domain Name System

   h. File Transfer Protocol

   i. Trivial File Transfer Protocol

   j. Hypertext Transfer Protocol

   k. Hypertext Markup Language

2.

a. MIDI 6		**l.** WAV 6
b. GIF 6		**m.** QuickTime 6
c. RPC 5		**n.** HTML 6
d. ASCII 6		**o.** X Window System 5
e. JPEG 6		**p.** NFS 5
f. HTTP 7		**q.** TIFF 7
g. DNS 7		**r.** AVI 6
h. BMP 6		**s.** AppleTalk Session Protocol 5
i. TFTP 7		**t.** EBCDIC 6
j. MPEG 6		**u.** SQL 5
k. MP3 6		**v.** FTP 7

3. **b.** Session layer

4. 7. Application

   6. Presentation

   5. Session

   4. Transport

   3. Network

   2. Data link

   1. Physical

5. **a.** TWS and TWA are examples of dialogue control.

6. **b.** Encryption
    d. Data format
    f. Compression

7. **d.** DNS resolves the name to an IP address when you use a FQDN with Ping or as a URL on a Web page.

8. **a.** The whole thing, www.helpme.com, represents a FQDN.

9. **b.** .com represents the top-level domain name.

10. **d.** helpme.com represents the domain name.

11. **c.** A redirector protocol determines whether a host process is a local or network activity.

12. **a.** Application   OSI layer(s): Application, presentation, and session
    b. Transport   OSI layer(s): Transport
    c. Internet   OSI layer(s): Network
    d. Network interface   OSI layer(s): Data link and physical

13. **d.** In www.helpme.com/inventory, /inventory represents the folder.

14. **c.** If a host is not configured with a DNS server address, all applications will be unable to resolve names.

15. **b.** and **d.** POP3 and IMAP4. SMTP is a mail exchange protocol used between servers. NFS is Network File System, an open operating system designed by Sun Microsystems that allows all network users to access shared files stored on computers of different types.

CHAPTER 8

Servers and Network Operating Systems

This chapter will:

- **Look at Network Operating Systems like Windows NT/2000, UNIX/Linux, and NetWare**

- **Look at other services that often run on servers, such as DHCP, WINS, DNS, and RAS**

- **Observe the OS Network Security function**

- **Discuss fault tolerance issues relative to servers**

- **Compare several levels of RAID**

- **Discuss backup options for servers and workstations**

- **Look at uninterruptible power supplies and power grooming**

- **Introduce to the concept of a disaster recovery plan**

- **Review antivirus issues**

In earlier chapters and for most of the rest of this book, we limit our discussion to Layer 1, 2, and 3 issues, looking at the devices and the technologies in each layer. In most of the remaining chapters, we focus on using and configuring routers and switches. This chapter presents a brief overview of servers, network operating systems (NOSs), and some of the services provided by servers.

This material is important for those of you with limited experience in network administration; however, it is not covered on the CCNA exam. Without some understanding of network operating systems and the services they provide, I think it is possible to get a skewed view of the way networks work. Similarly, the administrator whose training is limited to server and OS (MCSE, CNE, UNIX) issues may get an unbalanced view. When it comes to network administration, particularly LANs, understanding both the "Cisco" material and the server capabilities is important in designing and troubleshooting the network. At least a minimal exposure to server OSs can also be helpful for the person looking for that first job. Your interests may be Layer 2 and Layer 3 devices, but there are many firms too small to require a person with skills only in those areas.

Network Operating Systems

In this chapter, we look briefly at *network operating systems* (NOSs) and the services that they provide to the network and its users. We look first at network type (peer-to-peer or server-based), operating system options, and common services provided by the NOS.

Peer-to-Peer Network or Server-Based Network

As we discussed in Chapter 1, there are two types of networks, peer-to-peer, also known as a workgroup network, and server-based (or client-server). In this section, we compare the two forms for background only. In reality, only server-based networks are used in networks large enough to be concerned about Layer 2 and 3 technologies, which are the primary focus of the CCNA exam.

Peer-to-Peer Networks

The simplest definition of a *computer network* is two or more computers connected together to share a resource. This means that connecting two computers in your home to share a single Internet connection or a printer is a network. This type of network is typically referred to as a *peer-to-peer network*, a group of workstations connected as equals using an operating system like Windows 95/98/Me to provide the ability to share resources. Figure 8-1 is a simple diagram of a peer-to-peer network using coaxial cable.

Peer-to-peer networks tend to be less expensive and sometimes easier to set up than server-based networks, but they are generally limited to small installations; Microsoft recommends no more that ten users in a peer-to-peer network. The significance of ten probably comes from the fact Windows NT Workstation was modified by Microsoft to allow sharing a resource by only ten users. Windows 9x-based workstations do not share that limitation. The peer-to-peer network allows users to control their own

Figure 8-1
Simple peer-to-peer
network

resources, does not require a dedicated server, and requires no additional software besides a suitable workstation operation system.

The disadvantages of peer-to-peer networks include these points: No centralized management exists, requiring each workstation to be administered and secured individually; shared resources have to be established and administered on each host; if a shared workstation is turned off or otherwise unavailable, its resources are not available; the network does not scale well as the organization grows; data security is limited and cumbersome to implement.

Peer-to-peer networks can use shared media like coaxial cable, hubs, and/or switches. While nothing inherently prevents the use of routers in a peer-to-peer network, generally the network shifts to being server-based long before that point.

Peer-to-peer operating systems include any version of Microsoft Windows after version 3.1, products like LANtastic, and the Apple Macintosh OS.

Server-Based Network

Once you add a computer to your network with a server operating system such as Microsoft Windows 2000 (or NT) Server, UNIX, or NetWare Server, you now have a *server-based network*. Operating systems like Linux, UNIX, and NetWare are client-server systems, meaning that each host is either a client or server but not both. Windows networks can be client-server if the network administrator disables the "sharing" features on the workstations. Otherwise, Microsoft Windows-based networks are a form of distributed network with workstations being able to provide limited "server" services like disk and printer sharing. Figure 8-2 shows the screens that turn on/off sharing on a workstation. This actually turns on/off the "server" services.

While the server operating system more efficiently shares disk space and/or printer resources, particularly to a larger pool of users, there are usually other features that make using a server-based model a more attractive solution. Features that appeal to network owners and administrators include centralized administration, centralized and more elaborate security including a single password to access any appropriate network resources, centralized data backup, and centralized resource administration (sharing). Figure 8-3 shows a simple server-based network.

Figure 8-2
Network
neighborhood
screen for sharing
resources

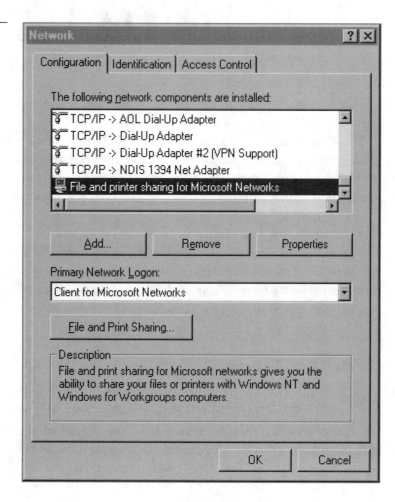

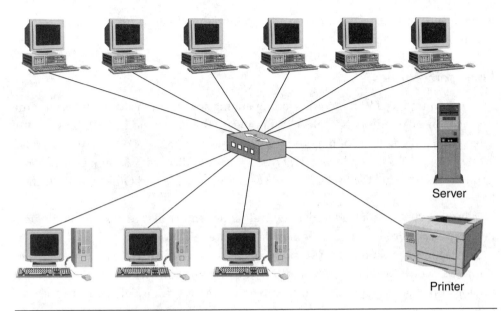

Figure 8-3 Simple server-based network

Some potential disadvantages of a server-based network include these points: Special network software (NOS) and hardware (server) add to the cost of building the network; NOS operation and maintenance often require specially trained personnel to administer the network. Another serious concern is that there can be a single point of failure in the network; if the server fails, all server resources are unavailable to the clients. In fact, the clients may not even operate without the server. This last concern can be mitigated with the same redundancy concepts that are used to reduce single-point-of-failure concerns about hubs, switches, and routers.

Even with the disadvantages, a client-server network is really the only choice for organizations with more than a few users.

NOS Choices

Regardless of the NOS used, its primary purpose is to control the network and to provide resources. This is accomplished by establishing a variety of services and features introduced in this section. Here we compare the backgrounds and basic features of the major operating system choices (Microsoft Windows, Novell NetWare, all flavors of UNIX/Linux). In the next section, we look at the major features supplied by NOSs in general, such as user security, passwords, and groups, along with system profiles and user profiles and policies.

Microsoft Windows

Microsoft introduced Windows network operating systems in the early 1990s with the first version of Windows NT (New Technology). The last version of NT, version 4.0, offers two configurations of the product, Windows NT Server (NTS) and Windows NT Workstation (NTW). Windows NT Server is also bundled with a variety of network applications to create the BackOffice Server Family and the BackOffice Small Business Server.

Windows 2000 was introduced at the end of the century in several server implementations plus the Professional version, which replaces NT Workstation.

The Windows NT and 2000 versions are separate from the consumer versions of Windows, which include 95, 98, and Me (Millennium Edition). While the consumer versions of Windows are not "full members" of the NT family of products, they are common workstations on most NT-based networks. This is an important distinction; the consumer versions cannot share fully in the security and file systems of the network versions. Many network monitoring and administration applications will not run on the consumer versions. When choosing an administrative workstation, one should consider Windows 2000 Professional or Windows NT Workstation.

The next version of Windows is currently scheduled to be released under the name Windows XP (eXPerience). There will be several releases under the Windows XP name including Professional, Personal replacing the current consumer versions of Windows, and three server versions: Server, Advanced Server, and Data Center Server.

One benefit of the Windows family of products is the common user interface across all Windows products making end-user training and support relatively easy and inexpensive.

The earliest version of Windows NT used IPX/SPX as the upper-level protocol suite. Beginning with version 4.0, Windows switched to and remains with TCP/IP. This was particularly fortuitous when the Internet caught fire shortly thereafter in both the consumer and commercial arenas.

Windows NT manages users and resources through a structure called a *Domain*. A domain is a logical grouping of users and resources under the administrative control of one server, the *primary domain controller* (PDC). For redundancy purposes, the PDC's primary duty of authenticating users can be shared with one or more secondary servers called *backup domain controllers* (BDCs). The PDC and BDC can both participate in network security and authenticate users allowing them access to the network resources. There is a third type of server called a *member server*, a stand-alone server, that does not play a security role in the network but is typically set up to support one particular application or service. Figure 8-4 shows a single domain with PDC, BDC, and member servers. The PDC and BDC share security and user-authentication responsibilities, while the member server provides a specialized service such as hosting an Intranet.

The presence of two domain controllers shown in Figure 8-4 signifies that there would be a significant number of networker hosts or severe intolerance to loss of the network resources. Figure 8-5 shows another use for multiple domain controllers where the users are separated by slow WAN links and one or more routers that do not forward broadcasts. Since many services that would possibly be housed on the domain controller—such as NetBIOS name resolution services (WINS), file and print sharing services, network resource browsing services, and user authentication—use broadcasts, the router would present an obstacle to the host connecting to the network and to user authentication.

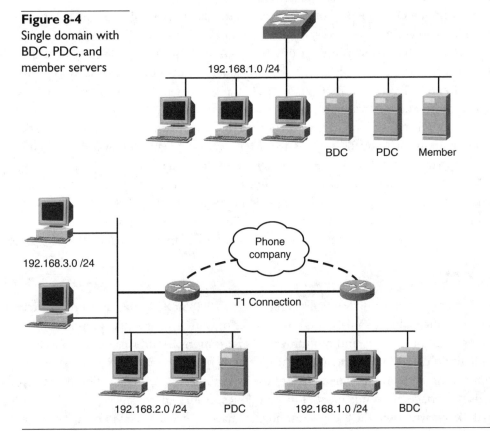

Figure 8-4
Single domain with BDC, PDC, and member servers

192.168.1.0 /24

BDC   PDC   Member

192.168.3.0 /24

Phone company

T1 Connection

192.168.2.0 /24   PDC   192.168.1.0 /24   BDC

Figure 8-5   Single domain separated by one or more routers

Users on each side of the WAN link use the local domain controller to authenticate. The PDC then updates the BDC on a scheduled basis. Network 192.168.3.0 still has a problem because the router separates it from a domain controller. The statement *IP helper address 192.168.2.5* configured on the LAN interface of the router would solve the problem (assuming the server address is 192.168.3.5). The IP helper command causes the interface to capture eight different types of broadcasts and converts them to unicasts to the specified server address. While the same logic could be applied to the 192.168.2.0 network directing the startup requests to the 192.168.1.0 network, it then makes the T1 connection the potential single point of failure for the network. The modem or ISDN backup link through the phone company could prove too slow for startup processes and authentication.

The Windows 2000 Server management structure changes the domains to an Active Directory Structure. In this structure, all domain controllers are peer controllers maintaining a distributed database for network security and user authentication. The peer controllers then use a multicast update system.

The Windows OSs support both the *file allocation system* (FAT) that originated in the DOS era and Microsoft's own file system, *new technology file system* (NTFS). With FAT, Windows NT—like all consumer versions of Windows—can provide only directory, or folder, level security. There is no mechanism for individual document security. NTFS for Windows NT and NTFS version 5 for Windows 2000 provide both directory level and document security and permissions. The consumer versions of Windows cannot use or recognize NTFS on their local hard drives but can share NTFS drive space over the network.

This support for both file systems is for backward compatibility and to allow the machine to dual boot. *Dual booting* basically means that two or more operating systems can coexist on the same machine with a choice required at startup. While the two OSs cannot run simultaneously and there is getting to be less value in this for regular users, it can be a handy feature for the struggling MCSE or CCNA student who would like to gain NT or 2000 server experience while still maintaining their normal OS.

UNIX / Linux

UNIX, pronounced *yoo*-niks, was developed in the 1970s at Bell Labs, the pure research facility for the Bell system. UNIX is a multi-user operating system that supports multitasking, multiprocessing, and multithreaded applications. UNIX was designed to be a small, flexible, and secure system to be used mainly by programmers. It is known for its cryptic commands and its general lack of user-friendliness. The introduction of graphical user interfaces may hide most of this quirkiness from end users.

UNIX was written in the C programming language, which allows it to be installed on any computer system for which a C compiler exists. This portability, combined with the fact that Bell Labs distributed the OS in its source-language form so that anyone who obtained a copy could modify and customize it for his or her own purposes, made it a popular choice among universities. By the end of the 1970s, dozens of different flavors of UNIX existed.

After the breakup of the Bell system in 1982, AT&T began to market UNIX. In addition to AT&T's efforts to develop a standard UNIX, the University of California at Berkeley has done considerable development. Commercial companies such as Sun Microsystems, IBM, Hewlett-Packard, and Santa Cruz Operation (SCO) all have their own versions of UNIX on the market. There are two free versions of UNIX, FreeBSD and Linux, the latter being the latest media "wunderkind."

Linux, pronounced *lee*-nucks, is a freely distributed, open-source implementation of UNIX that runs on a variety of hardware platforms, including Intel and Motorola microprocessors. As part of a grad student project, Linus Torvalds developed the original Linux. There are several commercial distributions of Linux that include drivers and documentation.

UNIX has a very large and committed following at universities and large organizations, in engineering and technology departments, and as secure servers at ISPs and large data installations. Many UNIX users hope that Linux will stimulate interest in the consumer and office application market, markets that have baffled and eluded UNIX for 30 years.

The UNIX operating system is kernel-based, isolating the hardware layer of the computer from improperly operating applications. UNIX uses the NFS (Network File System, Sun Microsystems's implementation), which supports both document- and directory-level security. UNIX maintains centralized user and resource control.

One of the many benefits that come with the freedom of "open system" OSs, such as UNIX/Linux that you don't hear too much about is that, because of all the variations and releases of this software, the clients and applications that work best with a particular version of UNIX are those specific to the developer of the operating system.

Novell NetWare

Developed by Novell Corporation in the early 1980s, NetWare was one of the first true server-based *local-area network* (LAN) operating systems. It was clearly the first big commercial success. NetWare runs on a variety of different types of LANs, including Ethernet and Token-Ring.

All versions prior to version 5.0 in 1999 used IPX/SPX as the upper-layer protocol. Version 5.0 introduces TCP/IP as an option.

As we will see in Chapter 14, NetWare has gone through several version changes without a completely clean upgrade history. This means that several major versions of

NetWare still need to continue to be supported on current networks. Part of the problem is due to noncompatible Ethernet frame types. NetWare versions up to and including 3.11 use Ethernet_802.3 frame encapsulation, while versions 3.12 up to 5.0 use Ethernet_802.2. Many applications written for the older 3.11 could not run on newer versions of NetWare, forcing companies to maintain dual systems. While these two frame types can coexist on the network, hosts configured to use one cannot recognize the other.

Another compatibility issue is the difference in Directory services used by NetWare versions 3.12, 4.11, and 5.0. NetWare 3.12 uses a feature called the Bindery to manage multiple users and resources, creating a server-centric network. This emphasis on the individual server as the point of control became a problem as multiple-server networks began to evolve.

Since version 4.11, NetWare uses NDS (Novell Directory Services) to manage users and resources. NDS creates a network-centric network, emphasizing the entire network as the point of control. This allows network management to be consolidated and allows the use of a single ID and password authentication system for users to access all network resources.

NetWare supports FAT and Novell's own DET (Directory Entry Table), which supports both file- and directory-level security.

NetWare clients include all versions of Windows, DOS, and Macintosh.

Server Services

In addition to the network security, user authentication, and system policies and profiles (which we look at in the next section) that are supported by network OSs, there are optional services that can also run on servers like Windows NT or Windows 2000. These services include but are not limited to DHCP, WINS, DNS, and RAS, which we will look at briefly in this section.

Dynamic Host Configuration Protocol (DHCP)

As we have seen, in the TCP/IP environment every host must have an IP address. Dynamic Host Configuration Protocol (DHCP) is a protocol for assigning IP addresses to network devices from one or more pools of available addresses. Dynamic assignment is a labor-saving alternative to having to create "static" addresses while configuring each network node. Using DHCP does not preclude using static addressing for key resources like routers, servers, Web sites, and so on that could disrupt network operations if they were to change. Router LAN interfaces become the default gateway for each workstation on that network; as such it would be disastrous if the interface IP address changed every time a router rebooted. Figure 8-6 shows a Windows DHCP server setup window indicating that the current server (Fife) has two IP pools of addresses (192.168.1.0 and 192.168.2.0).

There are two DHCP services. The DHCP server service is the ability to assign addresses; DHCP client service is the ability to accept an IP address from a DHCP server. Typically, the DHCP client receives the IP address, subnet mask, default gateway, and various critical server addresses at the same time. Some devices, such as the DSL / cable routers becoming common today, are both DHCP clients and servers. As clients, they accept the IP address and other information assigned by the ISP, and then they provide DHCP services for the hosts on the local network. In the process, they perform *network address translation* (NAT), providing at least some level of security by concealing internal addresses from the outside world. Figure 8-7 shows the IP address information supplied by my cable router to my laptop. DHCP client support is built into all Windows workstation OSs, while the Windows server products support both client and server services.

While DHCP server service is supported on routers, it is more common in Windows environments to make it a service offered on servers such as the domain controllers. In assigning an IP address to a host, the DHCP server "leases" it to the host for a specific amount of time. That lease period could be hours; however, the default is three days in NT and eight days in Windows 2000. At a point 50 percent of the way through the lease, the client will request an extension of the lease. Typically, if the DHCP server is

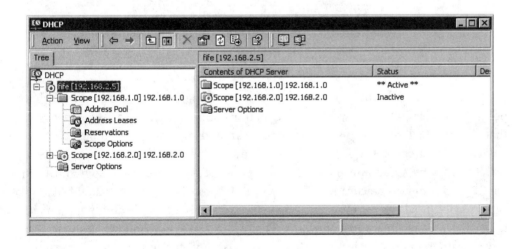

Figure 8-6 Windows 2000 DHCP setup window

Figure 8-7
DHCP information
supplied as viewed
with the *winipcfg*
(Win9x) command

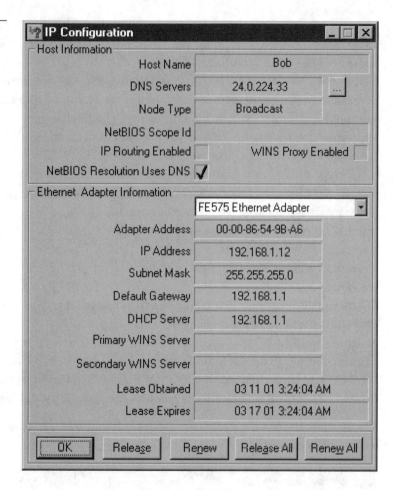

available, the lease will be extended—in essence starting the lease cycle again at that point. Longer leases mean fewer lease negotiations; shorter leases mean that a network that is short of addresses can salvage and lease unused addresses more quickly.

DHCP simplifies network administration by tracking the assigned IP addresses, thereby relieving an administrator of that task. Most IP networks use some form of DHCP. It is common practice for ISPs to use DHCP for dial-up users. Many DSL and cable service providers are moving toward DHCP because of the flexibility it offers in managing and reconfiguring networks. Figure 8-8 shows a Windows 2000 DHCP server's partial list of active leases. DHCP is not necessary on non-IP (pre-v5.0) versions of NetWare.

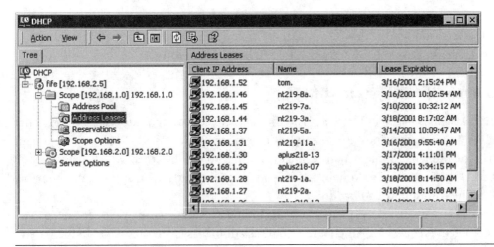

Figure 8-8 DHCP list of active IP leases

Windows Internet Naming Service (WINS)

Windows Internet Naming Service (WINS) is a system for determining the IP address associated with a particular network computer, or host, name. This name resolution supports all network client and server computers running any version of Windows. It can also provide name resolution for other computers with special configuration. Figure 8-7 showed that the host name for my laptop is Bob (not very original, I agree).

Using DHCP servers to dynamically assign IP addresses makes determining the IP address for a particular host computer a somewhat complex process. Since the IP address for a particular host can change, even to the extent of changing each time it accesses the network, we need to have some form of dynamic table that relates host names to their current IP address.

WINS performs this requirement using a database that is automatically updated with the names of computers currently available and the assigned IP addresses. There are three major drawbacks to WINS: (1) WINS stores all information is a single, flat database that must be parsed (read line by line) to find a match to a query; (2) The dynamic features of a WINS server can be utilized only by NetBIOS clients. Although many systems can use NetBIOS, WINS was designed for Microsoft clients; and (3) WINS requests, registrations, and releases use NetBIOS ports 137, 138, and 139 to communicate. These ports are usually disabled on routers for security purposes, thus limiting WINS services to the local subnet.

Non-NetBIOS devices and systems such as routers, UNIX/Linux, TCP/IP-based Novell servers, and remote devices use DNS (domain name system) instead of WINS.

Figure 8-9 shows the Windows 2000 WINS configuration screen.

Domain Name System (DNS)

The *Domain Name System* (DNS) is an Internet service that translates easy-to-remember text domain names into not-so-easy-to-remember IP addresses. While easy to remember for humans, domain names mean nothing to the Internet, which uses only IP addresses. Each time a domain name is used, a DNS service must translate the name into the corresponding IP address.

DNS is actually a network of servers including a local network or ISP server. If a DNS server gets a request for which it has no translation, it asks another server in the system, until the correct IP address is returned. In the process of resolving this address, the local DNS will store the information for a period of time in case another request comes up. Figure 8-10 shows the DNS configuration screen for Windows 2000.

The largest downside to DNS is that its database is static. An administrator must manually enter each entry into the DNS server. DNS is not suitable for environments that are constantly changing.

Newer implementations of DNS, such as the one used by Windows 2000, allow for dynamic updates to the DNS database. This technology is called *Dynamic DNS*, or *DDNS*. DDNS is likened to the marriage of the best of WINS and DNS. In a Windows 2000 environment, even non-Microsoft clients can utilize the features of DDNS.

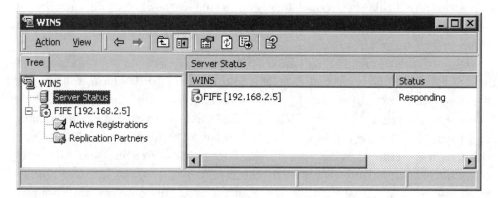

Figure 8-9   Windows 2000 WINS configuration screen

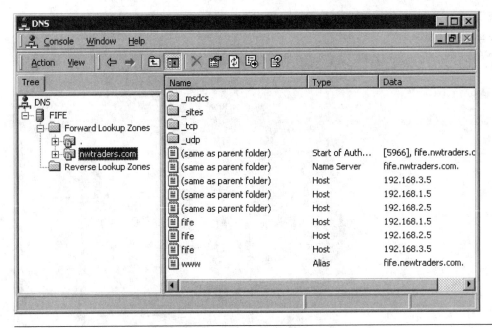

Figure 8-10 Windows 2000 DNS configuration screen

Remote Access Services (RAS)

Remote Access Services (RAS) is a service of Windows OSs that enables remote users to log into a Windows-based LAN using a modem, ISDN, or a WAN link. RAS on workstation software will allow a single caller to dial in to that workstation; on server versions of Windows, 256 users can dial in.

To use RAS three things have to be in place. First, the RAS server must be properly configured on the server. Second, the RAS client software, which is built into all current versions of Windows, or any PPP client software, must be installed and configured on the remote host. Third, and most important, the user account for the dialing-in party must be configured to allow dial-in access. If the first two are in place but the third is not (a common oversight since it is off by default), the user will get to log in successfully but then be told that the service is denied to their account.

Figure 8-11 shows the user account properties screen where the dial-in permission is granted on a Windows 2000 network. It also allows you to configure "call back" options for greater security. The call-back features mean that after authenticating, the server will hang up and then call either a user-supplied number or a preconfigured number.

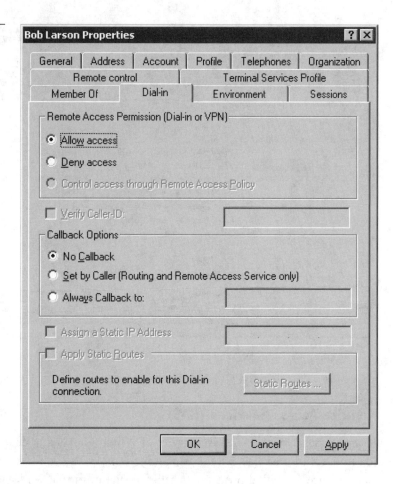

Figure 8-11
Setting permission
for dial-in
capabilities

Network Security

Probably the most important task of a network administrator is developing and implementing network security. Primary in that responsibility is the protection of all company network resources from loss or damage owing to any cause. The goal is making the network as secure as possible against unauthorized access or unauthorized use of network resources. In the next section, we look at ways to protect the network data from hardware failures. In this section, we look at securing the network resources from the intentional and unintentional damage or destruction by users.

A thought to ponder as we go through these next sections is this: The vast majority of network intrusions that lead to lost or stolen resources are perpetrated or facilitated by someone inside the organization.

Network Security Policies

Network security policies are decisions made by network administrators concerning such matters as minimum password length, maximum/minimum password age, uniqueness of passwords (whether the same password can be reused), what happens if a user unsuccessfully attempts to log in a certain number of times in a limited time frame (three failed attempts in ten minutes), and so on. These general policies apply to all user accounts. Figure 8-12 shows the Domain Security Policy screen that sets password length and age.

Other security features, such as the ability to access the network from dial-in connections and limiting user log-in to particular times of the day and/or days of the week, can be set by the network administrator when creating the User Account profile. The network operating system will then enforced these decisions.

Written Company Network Security Policies

The first step in establishing network security is the development of written company policies covering all aspects of network security. These policies need to include what is and is not acceptable use of computer resources and should cover hardware, software,

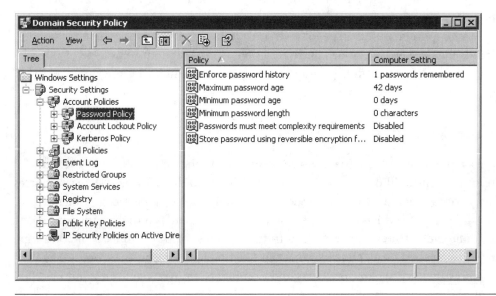

Figure 8-12 Domain Security Policy screen

and employee time. The policy should also delineate the consequences of violating user policies.

Some of these policies will outline basic things like rules surrounding passwords. How long must they be? Can they be reused? Don't use family, friends, or pet names. Don't write passwords anywhere in your work area. Don't share passwords with others, and so forth. Other policies will include statements about taking company software home to install on personal machines, as well as rules about logging out of the network and activating a password-protected screen any time a computer is unattended.

Some of these policies have to be created with the copyrights of software vendors in mind to protect the company from often-draconian "public" exposure. Software piracy is a reality and a crime. Piracy laws are enforced through fear and intimidation; you and your company do not want to become the next example. The people at the doors will be U.S. Marshals and a TV crew. Any official or semi-official sanctioning of software piracy must not be tolerated. Any disgruntled employee can place the call that gets the ball rolling.

A final note on piracy: If you receive a letter addressed to your firm from the SPA (Software Publishers Association), do not just assume it is a mass mailing. Take it as a reminder to recheck your software licensing.

To be effective, company management at all levels must buy into these network security policies and make a serious commitment to them. This is actually a pretty good filter to make sure that the policies meet the organization's security concerns without going too far and conflicting with other company policies or limiting users' access to necessary resources.

Most important, rules can be followed only if the user knows about them and understands them. They cannot be effectively implemented without some type of notification and explanation. While security and licensing concerns are burning issues to the IT department, most employees barely think about them.

User Accounts

A user, or log-in, account identifies a specific user to the network system. The network security feature will determine if the user has access to the network system's resources by checking the user ID with the user's password. If accepted, the user is authenticated. A valid user ID and password will not gain access if there is a time restriction on the account and the log-in attempt is outside that range of time. An example of a time restriction would be an employee that can only log in during business hours. Figure 8-13 shows the Active Directory Users and Computers setup screen from Windows 2000 with the current users accounts.

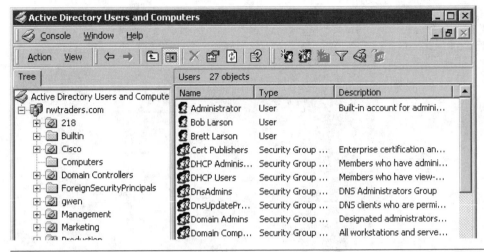

Figure 8-13 Active Directory Users and Computers setup screen from Windows 2000

The user ID also links the user to access privileges to specific network resources. User permissions are set by an administrator to permit or deny access to particular resources on the network. Printers, data folders, particular documents, program files, FAX systems, and even the ability to dial in to the system are all examples of network resources that can have access control based on user ID. If the user ID does not include the correct permission to access a printer or a document, nothing the user can do will gain them access except securing the correct permissions from the network administrator who will then update the account. Figure 8-14 shows the User Properties screen for a user account. On this screen, the User ID is established as well as the opportunity to require the password to have to be reset on the first log-in. Look over the tabs to see where limitations on dial-in permission, group membership, and so on can all be set.

Groups

Particularly in large organizations it becomes a monumental task to assign each and every resource to each and every employee. Add to that the need to remove employees that terminate or to change the permissions of employees that change positions within the company. The network includes "groups" that can be defined by the administrator based on department, job function, shift, or any other criteria. Groups are logical groupings of users on the network. The key is that users with similar requirements for access to resources can be added to a particular group. Permission to use a particular

Figure 8-14
User properties
screen for creating
user ID

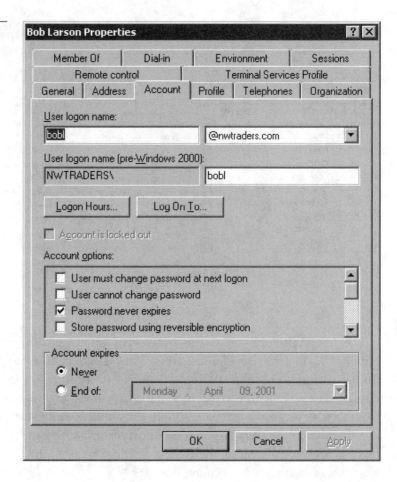

resource is then granted to the group. The user gains permission by his or her membership in the group. If the group's permissions to a resource are changed, that change will affect all group members. While individual permissions can still be assigned to individual users, it is more efficient to work with groups. Figure 8-15 shows the Windows 2000 screen for assigning users to groups.

We use this same grouping in our nonnetwork lives. If we get a ticket to a sporting event we become part of the group that will see the event live. By our membership in that group, we can access other resources at the facility, such as the concessions, which are closed to the nonticketed public. Other groups present include the team members, who, based on their group membership, get to wear the uniforms, use the locker rooms, and participate in the event. Game officials are yet another group, with specific permissions based exclusively on their being a member of that particular group.

Figure 8-15
Screen for assigning
users to groups

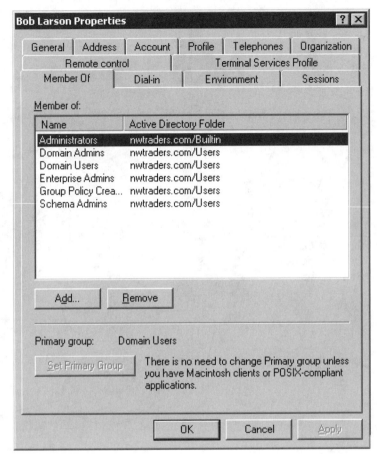

Figure 8-16 shows a new researcher added to the Research Group. As a member of the group, she has access to printers 2 and 4. The group was never granted permission to printer 1, so the researcher will not be able to use it. The group has also been specifically denied permission to use printer 3.

Figure 8-17 shows a common scenario: The researcher is added to a second group, the Budget Committee. As a member of this group, she has access to printer 1. While Budget Committee members have permission to use printer 3, this user still does not because of belonging to a group that has been denied access. As long as the user is part of a group explicitly denied access to a resource, no other permissions will get around that, even if her user account was given individual permission.

Being a network administrator is also being a member of a group. As a member of that group, the administrator can create or modify user accounts, modify system

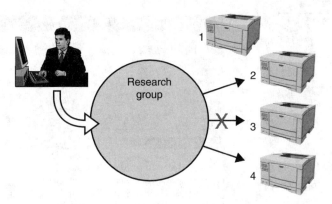

Figure 8-16
User groups and permissions

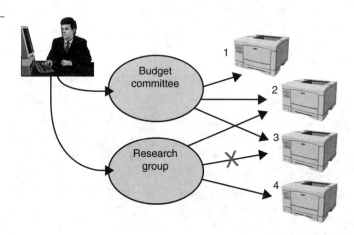

Figure 8-17
User as a member of two groups

settings, grant permissions to use network resources, modify user profiles, and create user policies.

User Profiles

With any Windows program, if changes are made to the user interface, the Desktop, such as adding a photograph to the wallpaper or repositioning the icons, then those changes will appear exactly that same way the next time that machine is started. On home machines, a person often inherits the desktop the way the previous user left it. In the work environment, or any time a unique log-in is required, it is possible to store the person's environment in something called a *user profile*. This means that two or more users sharing the same machine will each get his or her personal preferences at log-in. Figure 8-18 shows the part of my local profile that contains my Desktop items, shortcuts.

In a server-based network environment, it is possible to have these preferences follow the user to any computer that he or she can successfully log in to. This is called a "roaming" profile. Some of the features that make up the profile include desktop color scheme, wallpaper preference, Start menu items, and Desktop shortcuts. To the extent that software applications are installed in the same directories on the local machines and that shortcuts point to network resources, everything should work fine. But, if the user has Microsoft Office Professional with Access on his home machine, the Start menu in the profile will reflect that. If he logs in on a machine that does not have Microsoft Access installed, then the menu link will fail. As much as anything, this should be a reason to consider standardized software rollouts.

 NOTE: The Start Menu is nothing more than an organized collection of shortcuts. To look at your Start Menu options, right-click on the Start button and choose Explore. Experiment slowly.

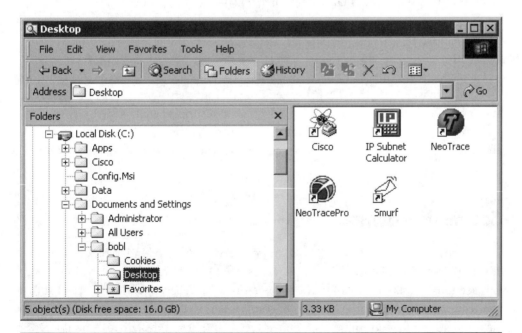

Figure 8-18   User profile showing Desktop shortcuts

The administrator can create a Mandatory Profile that would prevent user changes to the interface from being saved. The next time that the person logs in, he or she gets the original default screen. Mandatory Profiles can be assigned to individual users, or a group can share the same profile. In our classrooms, we use a common Mandatory Profile; thus we can ensure that every student gets exactly the same desktop and menus. While each student can customize the screen as desired during the session, any changes will be lost when he logs off or turns off the computer. This procedure means that many class- time catastrophes are only a reboot away from being fixed.

User Policies

Policies allow the administrator to take control over the activities of users, machines, and groups and regulate how they interact with resources on the local computer. Policy options include:

- Preventing a user from storing data on the workstation's local hard or floppy drive, thereby requiring them to use the network hard drives where backups are automated.

- Preventing a user from installing software to ensure that only legally obtained software is present on corporate computers.

- Preventing users from "sharing" resources such as a local printer.

- Preventing users from changing their system configuration, disk drive settings, sound or video card settings, NIC settings, and so on.

Generally, these are features of a company workstation that users shouldn't be changing anyway. When an inexperienced or malicious person modifies these settlings, it can often lead to extensive work for help desk and support staff.

Network permissions, log-in accounts, passwords, groups, profiles, and policies are the tools that the system administrator can use to control access to network resources.

Server Hardware

It is not my intention to suggest how to build a server or which kind to buy, but I would like to discuss some issues about network servers. Quite often, server performance can have serious effects on overall network operations. Each server, and computer for that matter, is made up of four major system components that need to be considered in the determination of a performance baseline: the CPU(s), RAM, disk drives, and the NIC.

Before we discuss each of these four components, we need to define a few key performance-monitoring terms:

- **Paging**   This term refers to the process of moving infrequently used instructions from active RAM to a temporary storage space on the hard disk. Paging enables computers to retrieve and manipulate data that would be otherwise too large for RAM to handle. However, it takes substantially longer to retrieve data from the page file than from RAM. Because paging depends on three of the four components to operate, excessive paging can considerably hurt system performance.

- **Queues**   This term refers to the number of instructions waiting to be executed by a particular device.

- **Usage**   This term refers to how much a particular device is being utilized at one time.

A quick note on usage: Measuring usage alone is not a valid performance baseline for a system. To accurately determine a device's performance, or lack thereof, we must also consider how many instructions are waiting to be executed, or the number of queues on a particular device.

Most important of the four components is RAM. If the server has too little RAM, the system will be constantly swapping information out to the disk drives. These page-file swaps tie up the disk drives and CPU cycles, so that they cannot be devoting that time to storing, processing, and retrieving information for the users. A simple rule on a production server is to take the manufacturer's recommended RAM figures and at least double or triple them. With Windows NT/2000 servers, you cannot have too much memory.

CPUs are the hardest component to size up or select because of all of the external factors that affect CPU performance, such as bus speed, cache memory, architecture, and so on. The application on the server greatly affects the type and number of CPUs you will need. For example, a server dedicated as a file server may perform satisfactorily with an older single-processor setup, whereas a data-center server designed to process thousands of data queries per minute may require as many as 32 processors. The easiest way to determine if your CPU is adequate is to measure the overall usage of the processor(s) and the number of queues on each processor. If the CPU usage is running at 70 percent or higher on a regular basis but has no queues, this may not be a problem. However, take the same processor and increase its usage to 80 percent and add two queue;, now it may be time to consider an upgrade. What might have been a perfectly acceptable departmental server last month may be driven into the ground by the local database application that has been added.

NICs are the server's connection to the network. Are you running more than one? If not, why? With a single NIC, you have a single point of failure and a potential bottleneck. Adding additional NICs will reduce the single-point-of-failure concerns. There are many multi-connection NICs on the market that increase the connection bandwidth but still don't eliminate the single-point-of-failure issue. (Be sure to check your operating system's documentation about adding a second NIC. In some instances, two NICs may actually degrade performance and create network accessibility problems.)

Disk drives are another performance issue. They have been getting bigger and faster. How do the ones in the server stack up? Using Performance Monitor to select the Physical Disk and then tracking % Disk Time and Current Disk Queue Length should give you an idea. If the Queue Length is 2 or greater, the disk is getting overloaded.

Performance Monitor

Performance Monitor comes with Windows NT and 2000. Other programs incorporate similar features, but this one happens to be free, if you have any package of NT or 2000. The tool itself is quite simple to use once you realize what you are looking for. While Performance Monitor can be used to monitor other systems in the network, my primary concern in this chapter is the server. Figure 8-19 shows what the Performance Monitor screen looks like in Windows 2000.

Clicking on the Add Counter button (the plus sign +) allows the user to specify which features are to be tracked. Figure 8-20 shows the Add Counters screen; I have selected Physical Disk as the Performance Object that I would like to track. The list at the bottom of the screen lets users choose the aspect of the Physical Disk they are interested in.

If a person does not have access to either NT or 2000, the other versions of Windows include a cousin to Performance Monitor called *System Monitor*. This tool can be accessed from the Start menu under Start | Programs | Accessories | System Tools. If it is not loaded, it will be necessary to use the control panel and add it under the Accessories option. Figure 8-21 shows the System Monitor screen running on my laptop with periods of pretty heavy CPU usage.

System Monitor does not have all the tracking and reporting capabilities of Performance Monitor, but it is worth spending a little time with as you run applications or browse the Internet.

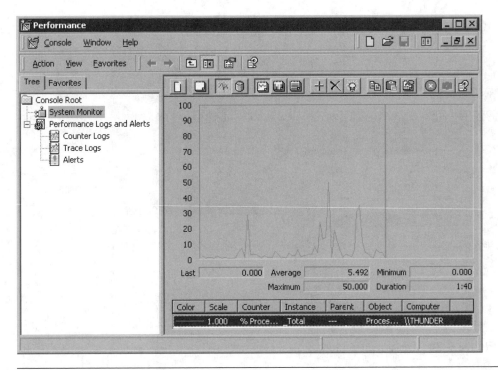

Figure 8-19   Windows 2000 Performance Monitor screen

Fault Tolerance

Fault tolerance refers to the ability of a computer or a network system to respond effectively to an unexpected hardware or software failure. The goal should be to eliminate or at least reduce the amount of downtime and any loss of data. Each organization will have its own approach to fault tolerance, often developed after the first catastrophe. The responsibility of developing and updating the company's plan for fault tolerance falls to the network administrator. Quite often the administrator will be telling management things they don't want to hear, looking for money for something that might not ever happen. However, even when management's support is not apparent, it is still the responsibility of the administrator to do the best he or she can with the resources available.

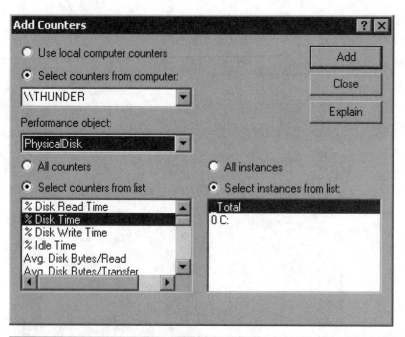

Figure 8-20   Performance Monitor Add Counters screen

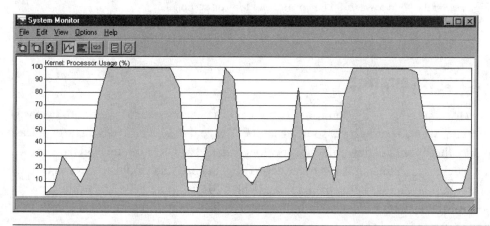

Figure 8-21   Windows Me System Monitor screen showing CPU usage

I know of one company whose tape backup system failed. The administrator researched a fine automated backup system. When management denied the expenditure for the new system, the administrator did nothing. A few months later, when a hard drive failed on a critical mailing-list system and there were no current backup tapes, the administrator was berated up one side and down the other. Attempts to point out management's earlier decision led to further rebukes about not being told "to do nothing at all, just not to buy that system." Right or wrong, it was a career-path killer at that firm.

This chapter covers several redundancy techniques that can be helpful in protecting network servers, but they also apply to all key network components. From designing redundancy into the network itself to maintaining spares, it all becomes part of the reliability planning for the network.

Before getting into redundancy, let's consider some other issues that should be understood in developing your approach to network reliability.

- Use high-quality, proven components. Corners cut here can lead to reliability problems and difficulties in troubleshooting. New technologies and new models of old technologies are exciting, but they stand a higher chance of having undetected bugs or problems. Always carefully test key components before adding them to the network.

- Use vendors that will stand behind you when things go wrong. No matter what precautions you have taken, things can still go wrong. Particularly for key components, make sure that you can get service and support when you need it. One law of the universe says that key components always fail at night and, if possible, right before a long weekend.

- Standardize key components to reduce the number of different spares that need to be maintained.

- Calculate and maintain an adequate inventory of spares. Have a system for spares replacement that ensures that you are never without spares of key components.

- The overall cost of implementing fault tolerance tends to be a fraction of the cost of losing essential systems for even one day; for some companies, that equates millions of dollars lost.

Redundancy

Redundancy, or duplication, is often the only solution for surviving a component or system failure. Redundancy can be applied at all levels within the network. Earlier, we discussed having a second domain controller in a Windows network, even though a single server could handle the load. With a single authentication server, the failure of that device can effectively prevent users from accessing the network.

In the case of a server fault tolerance, we need to look at both how to handle a power delivery failure to the building, such as "rolling blackouts," and to the failure of a power supply unit in a network device. From there, we can look at duplicating as many components as possible in the single device to literally having an entire mirror-image device.

There are many levels of fault tolerance, the lowest being the ability to continue operation in the event of a power supply failure. Many servers and network devices have two, or more, power supplies. Many fault-tolerant computer systems mirror all operations—that is, every operation is performed on two or more duplicate systems, so if one fails, the other can take over.

Redundant Array of Inexpensive Disks (RAID)

Redundant Array of Inexpensive Disks (RAID) is a technique of using two or more disk drives in combination for fault tolerance and/or to enhance performance. RAID disk drives are common on servers but generally are not cost effective on workstations. RAID can be supported in software, as in the case of Windows NT and 2000; there are also hardware only and hardware/software implementations.

There are many different RAID levels, but the three most common are 0, 1, and 5. RAID 0 is a performance-only implementation and provides no fault tolerance. The others provide fault tolerance and may provide enhanced performance.

In RAID 0 and 5, the RAID drives are formatted specially by the OS, or hardware-based RAID controller, to appear as a single drive to the system. The new data is applied in what are called *stripe sets*, whereby a block of data is placed on the first drive, then the second, and so on until the final drive. This process is repeated as needed until the data is stored. Any performance enhancements come from multiple controllers writing the data. The real throughput performance gain is from the multiple controllers being able to pull data faster from the drive set.

When you are striping drives with different-size partitions, the smallest partition determines the size of the set. If you have 3-, 6-, and 10-GB drives, the biggest stripe set you can make is 9 GB, or 3 GB per drive. The same would be true if you had four 10-GB drives, but 50 percent of one was already partitioned to another task. You would have 4×5, or 20 GB. In this case, you would be better off to stripe only the remaining three for 30 GB total (3×10).

Level 0

RAID level 0, referred to as *striping without parity*, uses 3-32 disk drives. The data is striped across all included drives. There is no redundancy. This level improves performance but does not deliver fault tolerance. Tape backups are important because, if one disk fails, then all data is lost. The drive will need to be replaced and the data loaded from the backup system. While initially this seems risky, consider what happens if you have a single 30-GB drive and it fails. You replace it and restore the data from backups. RAID level 0 allows us to combine multiple smaller drives into a single larger and more usable space.

One possible use for RAID 0 is content drives on Web servers or graphics libraries on desktop publishing systems where the content is not modified by the user. What you want is very fast throughput, and the total usable disk space is large. User data should be stored on other drives.

If you striped three 10-GB drives, you would have 30 GB total with 0 percent redundancy.

Level 1

RAID level 1, referred to as *disk mirroring*, uses an even number of disk drives in pairs. The content is written to both drives. This method tends to be used on smaller networks or where a high certainty of data recovery is required. RAID level 1 assumes a *single disk controller*, which could become a single point of failure.

A variant of RAID level 1, *disk duplexing*, uses an even number of disk drives in pairs. Again, the content is written to both drives. This method provides quicker downloads than disk mirroring. This variety of RAID level 1 assumes *two disk controllers*, avoiding the single point of failure and increasing output performance.

If you mirrored or duplexed two 10-GB drives, you would have 10 GB total usable storage with 50 percent redundancy. If more than two drives are to be mirrored, they are often paired so that you still end up with the 50 percent redundancy.

Level 5

RAID level 5, referred to as *striping with parity*, uses 3-32 disk drives. Assume that we have four 10-GB drives. On each stripe pass across the disks, three get data, but the fourth gets what is called a *parity block*. On the next pass, another drive gets the parity block and so on until the data is saved. If any one of the drives fail, the remaining drives can use the parity information to reconstruct the missing data.

The biggest advantage is that this system can often continue operating after a drive failure until the unit can be taken offline. With Windows NT, the system would have to be offline until the remaining drives were able to rebuild the data on the replacement drive. With Windows 2000, the unit needs to be offline only while the failed drive is replaced, and it will rebuild the new drive on the fly. Using Windows 2000's disk-administration tool, an administrator can manually attempt to perform error recovery on a failing drive while it continues to work. On a Windows system, the boot and system partitions cannot be located on a RAID 5 disk array.

If you striped three 10-GB drives, you would have 20 GB total usable storage with 33.3 percent redundancy. The formula for resulting capacity is $(n - 1) \times$ size per disk, while redundancy is $1/n$; in both cases n is the number of drives. So, ten 10-GB drives would yield 90 percent capacity and only 10 percent redundancy.

Volumes

Many server OSs allow the accumulation of small unused disk partitions to create what are called *volumes*. These volumes are in fact logical drives made from several physical drives. While somewhat useful for salvaging space, they provide no performance enhancement, and they provide NO data redundancy.

Back-Up Operations

To *back up* means to copy files to a second device (tape or disk) in case the first device fails and in some cases to provide auditable records. Any computer, or hard drive, can fail. The backup should be able to restore the data as quickly as possible. The frequency and method of backup will vary from organization to organization. I tell my small- and medium-size clients to keep one backup at a location different from where the computers are. Neither a fire nor a thief will have any more respect for your backups than they do for the computers themselves. Large accounts tend to have fireproof vaults and other facilities for securing the backups.

Backups can be done using operating system commands or special-purpose commercial backup programs. Backup programs often compress the data so that backups require less space.

Each file has an archive bit that, if set to off, means that it has already been backed up. If it is set to on, it means that the file is new or has been modified since the last backup. The five types of back up operations are as follows:

Full Backup

This is a complete disk backup. All files on the disk are stored to tape, and the archive bit for all files is set to off.

Incremental Backup

Backs up only the files that have been created or modified since the last full backup, and the archive bit for those files is set to off. If this method is used, all incremental backups since the last full backup, as well as the full backup, must be present to restore any data. If any tapes fail or are lost, you may lose a portion of your data.

Differential Backup

Differential backup is the same as incremental backup except that the archive bit for those files is NOT set to off. Any backup later will again copy these files. Using a full backup with a series of differential backups means that each differential backup includes all changes since the full backup. To restore the data, you now need only the full backup and the most recent differential backup.

Copy Backup

While part of the backup system, this is really a method of copying all or part of a drive without changing any settings between backups. This method backs up user-selected files to tape. It does not reset the archive bit to off.

Daily Backup

While part of the backup system, this is really a method of copying all or part of a drive without changing any settings between backups. This method backs up only the files that are modified on the day of the backup. It also does not reset the archive bit to off.

Do It Consistently

The frequency and type of backup depends on the organization and the nature of the data. My neighborhood drugstore does differential backups four times throughout the day. Our training site does a full backup of only the server data drive each day and performs a full system backup on Fridays. If tapes are to be reused, then a schedule must be followed, and tapes must be labeled and logged. If the backup task is assigned to a particular person, the process must be audited. Many small companies have learned the hard way that backups were stopped months earlier because no one ever "used" them or "asked about them." A good friend of mine had a database become corrupted only to find out that no one had taken the tape out of the backup unit for six months. Automated means different things to different people; don't assume the client knows what is important.

Keep it simple. If you want the data backed up each day and it can be done in a reasonable amount of time to a reasonable number of tapes, do a full backup each day. If the system fails, the most you should have to reconstruct is the current day's work. If the company is a Monday-to-Friday business, use five tapes. Each Monday, use the Monday tape. Do the same for each day of the week. If yesterday's backup is faulty, you have the previous day's backup. This could be done with four tapes, but in a five-day business, it's easier for the employees to follow and understand a five-tape rotation.

An example of a differential backup is as follows: First make a full backup on Friday; this would reset all the archive bits on the files. Label and store the disk. On Monday, do a differential backup to a separate tape; it won't reset their archive bit. Label and store the disk. Repeat this process until Friday, when a full backup is done. On Friday, a new set of disks is used; the first set isn't reused until the third or fourth week, depending on your level of risk aversion. The advantage is that this method requires only two tapes to restore the data. The disadvantage is that you use a lot of tapes.

Workstations

What about user workstations? When do they get backed up? The sad truth is that in many environments, they never get backed up. User policies could be created to force users to store work to the server drives; this is a good idea if the material is valuable to the company. Here are some other suggestions, all with varying advantages and disadvantages:

- You could add a tape unit or even a Zip drive to the workstation and then create a desktop icon that performs the necessary backup or copy commands. The advantage is minimal effect on the network. The downside is that it puts the backup responsibility on the user. It also assumes that the users won't change their data folder. They can create folders behind the data folder; they just shouldn't go anywhere else on the disk.

- Create a desktop icon that copies the contents of the data folder system to the user's home directory on the server. Encourage the user to perform the task on a schedule. The advantage is no new equipment. The downsides are that you are still relying on the users, and if enough of them started doing it at the same time, network traffic could suffer. I have some clients who, in addition to using the icon, have the Windows scheduler program run the program on a schedule, once per day or once per week.

Uninterruptible Power Supply

An *Uninterruptible Power Supply* (UPS) is a power supply that includes a battery to maintain power in the event of a power outage. The UPS, if it is an online UPS system, plugs into the wall; the computer, and/or the networking devices, plug into the UPS, and from then on the system is running off of the battery. The plug into the wall keeps the battery charged. Most UPSs emit a squeal if the power drops below a certain point even if for only a second.

Typically, a UPS will keep a computer running for several minutes after a power outage to allow the user to save her work and shut down the computer. Many UPSs offer software that performs automatic shut-down procedures after so many minutes following a power failure. This is critical for devices such as servers, switches, routers, and so on that may not have a user in attendance. If end users have UPSs and servers have UPSs, then any switches, hubs, routers, and so forth in-between need UPSs, or the user will be stranded in a power failure.

Many UPS systems work as surge protectors as well as against power drops. It is also common to have them create logs of the circuit's power activity. These logs are handy when you are talking to the power company and trying to convince them to deal with brownouts and regular power fluctuations. The APC units I use have a nice Web interface that allows me to configure features and monitor performance from anywhere I can get Internet access.

A second type of UPS system, *standby power systems* (SPSs), monitors the power line and switches to battery power as soon as it detects a problem. This switch to battery can require several milliseconds, during which your data is turning to ions and often the computers will perform a reboot. This is also called *Line-interactive UPSs*. For more info try **www.apc.com**.

Power Conditioning

To help protect your network equipment from problems in the building's electrical wiring, put the network equipment on separate circuits in the building. MDFs and IDFs, if they have servers and large important devices, should have at least two separate circuits. Ideally, these circuits should be from two different service panels. By having two circuits in the data facility, if a device has redundant power supplies, each could be connected to a different circuit. Other devices and technologies to consider:

- **Isolating transformer**   Surge suppresser for voltage spikes and high frequency noise.
- **Regulators**   Maintains constant output voltage despite changes in the power line's voltage. It handles such problems as brownouts and voltage surges.
- **Line Conditioner**   This is a regulator with an isolating transformer built in.

Disaster Recovery Plan

A disaster recovery plan is a series of worst-case scenarios with anticipated results and step-by-step instructions about what each person should do. This is a major project that requires some study and possibly some training.

A detailed plan for each facility should be developed to explain what needs to be done, who needs to be contacted both in the company and in emergency services, and so on for such things as fire, flood, tornado, hurricanes, and armed intruder. Clearly, not every business faces each of these threats, and fortunately those that do, do not experience them often.

If your data center is on the lower floors of a building or in the basement, a fire in the upper floors will result in flood-like conditions for you as the fire departments battle the flames.

Quite often when a catastrophe hits, no plan is in place, and the wrong people are on duty to figure things out. In your plan, be sure to include those things that you usually "never" do, such as turning off the mainframes, turning off the lights, and turning off the power to particular parts of the building. And how are you going to get all those data tapes down the stairs when the elevators are locked and the stairwells are full of people? These are not pleasant thoughts, but it is better to address them now than have people make catastrophic or life-threatening mistakes during an emergency.

Anti-Virus Protection

A virus is program or a piece of code that is loaded onto your computer without your knowledge and often performs unwanted tasks. Many viruses can also replicate themselves. The most recent ones use the host's e-mail system to mail themselves to everyone in the user's address book.

Viruses are intentional manmade creations and relatively easy to produce. Even the simplest virus can quickly use all available resources and bring the system to a halt. Obviously, there are even more dangerous types of virus out there.

Anti-virus programs are utilities that search a hard disk, memory, incoming e-mails, and so on for viruses and then remove any that are found. Most of these programs periodically recheck your computer system for the best-known types of viruses. Commercial anti-virus programs include an auto-update feature that enables the program to download profiles of new viruses so that it can check for the new viruses as soon as they are discovered. Always make sure that the anti-virus program will work with your OS; workstation anti-virus programs should not be used on servers.

Here are some steps to reduce the chances of getting a virus:

- Do not open e mail attachments from people you don't know. If you use Outlook, check Microsoft's Web site, **www.Microsoft.com**. They have a patch that will automatically block any executable attachments like EXE and VBA files. While this is restrictive on the user, it saves down time from viruses like the "I Love You" virus.

- Be careful about loading software, particularly games, without knowing exactly whom it comes from. This is a common host for virus distribution. Company policies should consider banning employees from loading any outside software.

- Don't let others use your computer with their disks. Any kind of file can carry a virus.

- Always use a current virus checker on all computers.

- Just because a disk comes from a vendor does not mean it is safe. During a client installation a few years ago, we found that the hardware driver disk was infected with a virus.

These are simple things that can be done to protect your computer from viruses. There are many other ways of detecting and preventing viruses that cannot be covered here. If you are worried about viruses, check the many articles and reports that can be obtained through the Internet.

Summary

This chapter provided a quick overview of servers and their key components in order to give a more complete view of networking. We saw that UNIX/Linux are the oldest kids on the block, with almost 30 years' experience as an OS. Linux is a low-cost alternative to UNIX. We saw the Novell's NetWare has been in the LAN environment for almost 20 years, dominating the industry for at least the first half of that time. Microsoft's Windows network OSs have been building a customer base for 10 years.

We looked at network security issues such as user accounts and user groups for assigning permission to network resources. We looked at topics such as user profiles and user policies as tools to assist users and at the same time keep them out of features that might interfere with the operations of their computers on the network.

Each OS supports multiprocessing, multitasking, and multithreaded applications, but the implementation is different. Novell and UNIX use a pure client-server model, whereas Windows distributes some server activities to workstations. This "server" capability is a feature that many network administrators disable. We saw how network servers also provide services like DHCP, WINS, DNS, and so on.

We looked at fault tolerance issues in servers, such as RAID, redundancy, backups, and UPS features. We also introduced the concept of the disaster recovery plan.

CHAPTER 9

IP Addressing and Subnetting

This chapter will:

- **Teach you how to convert between binary, decimal, and hexadecimal number systems**

- **Introduce classful IP addressing**

- **Teach you about default subnet masks and prefix masks**

- **Teach you how to calculate the number of subnets and host addresses for subnet masks**

- **Teach you how to create subnets of classful networks**

- **Introduce Classless Inter-Domain Routing (CIDR)**

- **Introduce Variable Length Subnet Masks (VLSM)**

- **Introduce Network Address Translation (NAT)**

As we saw in Chapter 5, where we introduced the OSI Layer 3, the network layer, TCP/IP uses 32-bit (binary) IP addresses to create a hierarchical network addressing system that identifies both the network and the specific host (node) on the network. TCP/IP is the protocol for the Internet, Windows NT/2000, Unix, and even Novell version 5.

The current version of IP, IPv4, usually displays network addresses as decimal values (for example, 207.161.57.143), called dotted decimal notation. This works well for end users who are more comfortable with base-10 numbers and symbols such as periods or commas as data separators. As an Internet worker, you need to understand how to convert decimal values to binary values and to hexadecimal values. Many processes covered later in this book and in future studies can be understood only if one recognizes that the devices use binary values to make decisions.

Before we look at IP addressing, IP address classes, and subnet masks, we investigate some simple techniques for converting decimal values (base-10) to and from both binary and hexadecimal values. Although the following discussion is quite basic, it is nevertheless critical to understanding how routers (OSI Layer 3) process addresses.

 EXAM TIP: More than any other chapter, this chapter covers processes and concepts that you must understand for the CCNA exam and to function intelligently in the field of networking. You may find that some concepts are hard to understand; revisit them as you work through the rest of the book. In addition to understanding the OSI model, you must know and be able to apply the principles of:
1. Binary-to-decimal and decimal-to-binary conversions
2. The five IP class address ranges and related subnet masks
3. The private IP address ranges and their purposes
4. Basic subnetting of Class C and B networks
5. Prefix notation as well as subnet masks
6. The basic concept behind supernetting
It will be important to not only recognize these items, but you must assume that you will have to understand them to the point that you can apply them as part of the solution to another problem.

Because of the number of calculations in this chapter, I'm going to include questions (with answers) throughout each section. Make sure you can do each exercise with confidence—if not today, then by the time you take your test.

Understanding the Numbers

Tools exist that can quickly and reliably convert decimal, binary, and hexadecimal values. Even the calculator tool that comes with Windows can do it. We will look at the Windows calculator and a subnet calculator in a lab at the end of this chapter. More than one student has argued that these tools suffice for this purpose; why bother with conversions and subnetting?

There are three important reasons:

1. The CCNA exam requires conversion skills and does not allow the use of a calculator.

2. Certain router processes are easier to understand if you understand binary.

3. If you know how to perform a task and then can work faster or more accurately using a tool, that's great. But far too many people are being taught to use tools

without understanding the underlying process. They can't tell when the tool indicates an absurd result. Worse yet, they are paralyzed if the tool fails.

With this in mind, we will start with some basics about decimal (base-10) numbers and then move on to binary and hexadecimal values.

Decimal Values

I know that decimal, or base-10, numbers have been a part of your life since before you started school. I want to introduce a table and a way of looking at these numbers. These should help later when we look at converting binary and hexadecimal numbers.

First, we need to recognize that the first number in the decimal series is zero (0). It is exactly in the middle of our numbering system, with as many numbers smaller (negative) than there are larger (positive). If we start counting with one, we effectively skip all the values between 0 and 1. The computer industry often includes 0 as the first numeral in many places. For example, when you map text on a screen or a document, a 65-character line usually includes positions 0 through 64. With 32-bit addresses, it is not uncommon for the positions to be identified as 0 to 31.

NOTE: Some parts of the world use this concept in numbering the floors of a building. You have the ground floor; above that is floor 1, and so on. I learned this somewhat abruptly when I was caught opening doors in a security area of a building while looking for the Copy Center that I had been told was on the first floor. Fortunately, a security official enlightened me before sending me on my way. He also pointed out some Dutch/Afrikaans signs that don't mean "Welcome! Come in."

If we use 0 as a starting point and include all single-digit numbers, we end up with 0 to 9, or a total of 10 possible values. This is where the term *base 10* comes from—there are 10 unique numerals. To get the next larger number, we return to 0 and put a 1 before it, giving us 10 more values, 10 to 19. We can return to 0 and put a 2 before it, giving us 10 additional values, 20 to 29; we can continue this process until we get to 99. To get the next larger number, we return to 0 and put a 10 before it, giving us 10 more values, 100 to 109. Figure 9-1 shows this progression of numbers.

If we look at these numbers, we can see that the right-most digits are all multiples of 1 ($7 \times 1 = 7$), whereas the second digits are multiples of 10 ($3 \times 10 = 30$), and the third digits are multiples of 100 ($5 \times 100 = 500$). Figure 9-2 gives an example of digit values and how they are calculated.

In the second-row calculation, the 10 comes from the number of unique digits (base 10), and the exponent represents the position, right to left or least to greatest significance.

One digit	Two-digit numbers									Three digits		
0	10	20	30	40	50	60	70	80	90	100	110	990
1	11	21	31	41	51	61	71	81	91	101	111	991
2	12	22	32	42	52	62	72	82	92	102	112	992
3	13	23	33	43	53	63	73	83	93	103	113	993
4	14	24	34	44	54	64	74	84	94	104	114	→ 994
5	15	25	35	45	55	65	75	85	95	105	115	995
6	16	26	36	46	56	66	76	86	96	106	116	996
7	17	27	37	47	57	67	77	87	97	107	117	997
8	18	28	38	48	58	68	78	88	98	108	118	998
9	19	29	39	49	59	69	79	89	99	109	119	999

Figure 9-1   Decimal number progressions

Position	3	2	1	0
Calculation	10^3	10^2	10^1	10^0
Value	1000	100	10	1
Digit	4	2	9	7
Equals	4000	200	90	7	= 4297

Figure 9-2   Decimal digit values: 4297

In the third row, the right-most value is always 1, because any positive number to the 0 power is always 1. Note that each value to the left is 10 times larger. We can pretty safely predict that the next value would be 10,000 and then 100,000.

Row four identifies the digits we are interested in, and row five multiplies each digit by its associated value. Since we are familiar with base-10 numbers, this calculation is unnecessary and trivial, but if we understand the concept, we can use a similar table for binary and hexadecimal conversions.

Reality Check

For many of us, it's been a long time since we worked with exponents in school, and we seldom if ever use them on the job. So, you need to take the time to relearn the math or develop a "shop aid" that is easy to remember and easy to use. Those of you who are gifted in math will have to humor those of us that are not. Figure 9-3 shows a "stripped down" table that gives us what we need to get by.

Position	4	3	2	1	
Value	1000	100	10	1	
Digit	8	6	2	7	
Equals	8000	600	20	7	= 8627

Figure 9-3   Simplified decimal table: 8627

Note that both the Position and Value rows begin on the right side with 1. The Position is labeling the digits by counting from right to left. Once you have the first value (always 1), the next value to the left is "this value" times "the number of unique digits"—in this case, 10. So, $10 \times 1 = 10$, $10 \times 10 = 100$, $10 \times 100 = 1000$, and so on.

Decimal Values in IP Addresses

As we discussed in Chapter 5, IP addresses are made up of four numbers separated by decimals. Often these numbers are displayed as decimal values—for example, 213.0.72.251. Each value represents the decimal equivalent of an 8-bit binary number, which is why they are referred to as *octets*. Four 8-bit numbers equal a 32-bit address.

We will see in the next section that the smallest 8-bit value is 0, and the largest is 255, meaning that the decimal values that can appear in each octet of an IP address must each fall within the range of 0 to 255. Therefore, 201.11.123.276 is erroneous—it cannot physically occur.

This leads to a relatively simple math concept that often gets overlooked. If you have an IP address of 12.1.2.221, the next address would be 12.1.2.222. Adding 10 to that would give us 12.1.2.232. Subtracting 5 from that would result in 12.1.2.227—all pretty straightforward, but what if the address is 12.1.2.255, and you want to add 1? That would result in a last octet of 256, which can't happen. So we need to think back to what we do with decimal values when we exceed 9—we place a 0 (or another value) and carry a 1 to the column to the left. Thus, our 12.1.2.255 plus 1 is 12.1.3.0; likewise, 12.1.2.255 plus 5 is 12.1.3.4.

A more important task would be determining the first value smaller than a network address like 12.1.2.0. If we take 1 from the third octet (leaving 1) and convert it to 256 in the last octet, we can now subtract our 1 and end up with 12.1.1.255. Similarly, subtracting 1 from 172.29.0.0 is 172.28.255.255. Take a few minutes to think this process through; it will be critical in subnetting. If you sketch out the table a couple times and do a few conversions, you will remember it. Take a moment to perform the following calculations:

a. 200.12.76.1 + 100   _____

b. 200.12.76.254 + 2   _____

c. 200.12.76.254 + 100   _____

d. 200.12.76.0 - 1   _____

e. 200.12.76.1 + 1000   _____

f. 200.12.76.1 - 1000   _____

Answers: a. 200.12.76.101, b. 200.12.77.0, c. 200.12.77.99, d. 200.12.75.255, e. 200.12.79.236 Hint: 1000/255 = 3 with 235 remaining. Add the 3 to the third octet and the remainder to the fourth. f. 200.12.72.21 Hint: First determine how many you must borrow from the third octet so that 1000 can be subtracted from the fourth. It must be 4 (4 × 255 = 1020). Subtract the 4 from the third octet and then subtract 1000 from 1021 (1020 + 1) for the fourth.

Binary to Decimal

Binary data is made up of 1's and 0's representing switches in the on and off (0) positions. Since there are only two possible numerals, it is a base-2 number system. Although binary data can be grouped in any increment, such as three or four digits (110 or 1011), in TCP/IP, it is usually grouped in 8-digit groups; each called a *byte* (equal to 8 bits). Thus, IP addresses are 32 bits, or 4 bytes, in length.

A byte can be any combination of eight 0's and 1's, ranging from 00000000 to 11111111, creating 256 unique combinations with decimal values ranging from 0 to 255. Figure 9-4 shows the 4-bit binary values that equal 0 through 8 in decimal values.

As before, we can build a simple table converting binary positions to decimal values. Each becomes an exponential power of 2. A summary of 8 bits numbered right to left beginning with 0, the formula for each position, and the resulting values are shown in Figure 9-5. This is exactly the way we calculated decimal values.

Note that in the digit row we entered the bit values 10101010; by using the same process as earlier of multiplying the digits by the values, we are able to convert 10101010 to 170 in decimal.

We can build a "job aid" similar to the simple table in Figure 9-8 that can be used to convert binary to decimal, decimal to binary, and even to assist in various subnet calculations. As we did earlier, we will number the positions right to left, but we will start with 1 and stop with 8.

Figure 9-4
4-bit binary
numbers

8	4	2	1

0	0	0	0	=	0
0	0	0	1	=	1
0	0	1	0	=	2
0	0	1	1	=	3
0	1	0	0	=	4
0	1	0	1	=	5
0	1	1	0	=	6
0	1	1	1	=	7
1	0	0	0	=	8

Position	7	6	5	4	3	2	1	0	
Calculation	2^7	2^6	2^5	2^4	2^3	2^2	2^1	2^0	
Value	128	64	32	16	8	4	2	1	
Digit	1	0	1	0	1	0	1	0	
Equals	128	0	32	0	8	0	2	0	= 170

Figure 9-5   8-bit binary number

Note that you can also number the top row 0 through 7 if you prefer. I use 1 through 8 because many students are familiar with that numbering and because it means you always start with 1 in both rows, making the process steps easier to remember for some. To calculate the values, start at the right with the same 1, and then double (2 × because it is base 2) the value of each position as you move left. The resulting two-row table is shown in Figure 9-6.

We build our table using only 8 bits because our IP addresses and subnet masks are broken into 8-bit increments (octets), but if we needed to work with any other number, we could just extend the table doubling the value each step.

If you have a binary number shorter than 8 bits, be sure to place it as far to the right as you can in the table, or you will get an erroneous number. The lower-order bits appear to the right, and the higher-order bits appear to the left. You always leave blank bits on the left end, or you can replace them with 0's.

To begin a conversion, enter the binary bits (for example, 11101001) in the third row on Figure 9-6. Now multiply the number in row 3 times the value in row 2. Finally, just sum the values in the fourth row. The result of converting 11101001 is shown in Figure 9-7.

Figure 9-6
Simple binary
conversion tool

Position	8	7	6	5	4	3	2	1
Value	128	64	32	16	8	4	2	1
Digit								
Equals								

Position	8	7	6	5	4	3	2	1	
Value	128	64	32	16	8	4	2	1	
Digit	1	1	1	0	1	0	0	1	
Equals	128	64	32	0	8	0	0	1	= 233

Figure 9-7   Sample conversion of an 8-bit binary number to decimal

EXAM TIP: At each Cisco exam, use one of the two sheets of paper and the pencil provided to sketch out the a table like the one in Figure 9-6 before you start the exam. You have up to 15 minutes to collect your thoughts, answer a survey, and take a sample test if you want. Even if you aren't asked to convert binary to decimal, the table will be useful in creating and/or verifying subnets, host numbers, and so forth. Even if you can "see" the correct answer, there is no excuse for math errors when it is so easy to check your work. During exams, I tend to write out only the two rows of numbers to save time, but add the labels if it helps to keep everything straight.

If you sketch out the table a couple times and do a few conversions, you will remember it. Take a moment to convert the following binary values to decimals:

a. 11010101 _____

b. 10000001 _____

c. 10001111 _____

d. 101 _____

e. 10000000 _____

f. 10100100.11101001.00011011.10000000 ____.____.____.____

g. 11100110.10101010.00110100. 00010111 ____.____.____.____

Answers: a. 213, b. 129, c. 143, d. 5, e. 128, f. 164.233.27.128, g. 230.170.52.23

Decimal to Binary

We can use our simple conversion table (Figure 9-6) and a series of simple divisions to help us convert decimal values to binary.

Assume we want to convert 207 to binary. The steps are shown in Figure 9-8:

1. Start with the left-most value (128) in the table and see if 207 can be divided by it. It will go once, so we put a 1 in the first box in row three of the bottom table. Calculate the remainder (79).

2. The remainder can be divided by the next value (64), so we put a 1 in the second box of row three of our table. Calculate the remainder (15).

3. Since the remainder is not divisible by either 32 or 16, we put 0's in boxes four and five of row three of our table.

4. Continue until there is no remainder. You can use row four to check your work.

NOTE: Steps 1–4 assume you are creating 8-bit numbers. When you are doing your divisions, the answer will always be 0 or 1. If you ever get a result larger than 1, you made a mistake in an earlier column. If your first calculation is greater than 1, then the value is larger than 255, the largest 8-bit number, and therefore cannot be a valid octet of an IP address or subnet mask.

Take a moment to sketch out the table and convert the following decimals values to binary:

a. 221 _____

b. 8 _____

Figure 9-8
Converting 207 to a binary value

```
128 | 207
      128
 64    79
       64
  8    15
        8
  4     7
        4
  2     3
        2
        1
```

Position	8	7	6	5	4	3	2	1
Value	128	64	32	16	8	4	2	1

Position	8	7	6	5	4	3	2	1	
Value	128	64	32	16	8	4	2	1	
	1	1	0	0	1	1	1	1	
	128	64			8	4	2	1	= 207

 c. 255 _____

 d. 127 _____

 e. 79 _____

 f. 116.127.71.3 ____.____.____.____

 g. 255.255.248.0 ____.____.____.____

Answers: a. 11011101, b. 00001000, c. 11111111, d. 01111111, e. 1001111, f. 01110100.01111111.01000111.00000011, g. 11111111.11111111.11111000.00000000

Working with the Table Relationships

The more you work with the table, the more you will see relationships within the table that can be used to speed up your calculations, and you will gain the ability to visualize the results without doing the calculations. The same process we used to build the 8-bit table can be extended, if necessary. A table extended to 12 bits is shown in Figure 9-9.

With binary numbers that are made up primarily of 1's, it may be quicker and easier to subtract the 0-bit values from 255. Converting the binary 11101101 is shown in Figure 9-10.

If you select any position in the value row, the sum of all the 1's to the right is the position value minus 1. Figure 9-11, for example, uses the 8-bit table and the value 64. Calculating the value of all 1's to the right yields 63.

Position	12	11	10	9	8	7	6	5	4	3	2	1
Value	2048	1024	512	256	128	64	32	16	8	4	2	1
Digit												
Equals												

Figure 9-9 A 12-bit conversion table

Position	8	7	6	5	4	3	2	1	
Value	128	64	32	16	8	4	2	1	
Digit	1	1	1	0	1	1	0	1	
Equals				16			2		255−18=237

Figure 9-10 Converting a binary number by subtracting the 0 values

Position	8	7	6	5	4	3	2	1	
Value	128	64	32	16	8	4	2	1	
Digit	0	0	1	1	1	1	1	1	
Equals	0	0	32	16	8	4	2	1	= 63

Figure 9-11   Value of all 1's to the right of a bit location

This method works for all positions. Looking at the first bit in our 8-bit table, we can see that having all 1's to the right of that position equals 127. We know this is true because all 8 bits set to 1 equal 255 (128 + 127).

Hexadecimal to Decimal

Hexadecimal is a base-16 numbering system that is used in computing. We saw it used earlier to represent MAC addresses. It is referred to as base 16 because it uses 16 unique symbols or numerals. Just like decimal and binary, combinations of these symbols can be used to represent all possible numbers.

Conversion is made a little more difficult because decimal numbering has only ten numerals (0 through 9). Since base 16 requires six more symbols, it also uses the letters A, B, C, D, E, and F. The letters are not case-sensitive. Figure 9-12 shows the hexidecimal and decimal equivalents.

Because there are 16 hexadecimal symbols, a binary byte can be represented by a combination of two symbols ranging from 00 to FF, creating 256 unique combinations with decimal values ranging from 0 to 255.

As before, we can build a table to convert binary positions to decimal values. Each becomes an exponential power of 16. A summary of four digits numbered right to left beginning with 0, the formula for each position, and the resulting values are shown in Figure 9-13. This is exactly the way we calculated decimal values.

Note that in the digit row we entered the digits 1234, and by using the same process as earlier of multiplying the digits by the values, we are able to convert 1234 in hexadecimal to 4660 in decimal. It gets a little more complicated if we use digits larger than 9. Figure 9-14 shows converting the number 1C3F to 7231 in decimal.

We have to remember the decimal value of the letter symbols, so I'll encode them, as shown in Figure 9-15.

To calculate the values, start at the right with 1, and then as you go to the left, multiply each value by 16 (base 16) to get the value of each position. The good news is that you won't use this calculation very often; typically we convert 32-bit binary values, so you will be using only two hex digits.

Hex.	0	1	2	3	4	5	6	7	8	9	A	B	C	D	E	F
Dec.	0	1	2	3	4	5	6	7	8	9	10	11	12	13	14	15

Figure 9-12   Decimal and hexadecimal values

Position	3	2	1	0	
Calculation	16^3	16^2	16^1	16^0	
Value	4096	256	16	1	
Digit	1	2	3	4	
Equals	4096	512	48	4	= 4660

Figure 9-13   4-digit hexadecimal

Figure 9-14
1C3F converted to decimal

Position	3	2	1	0	
Calculation	16^3	16^2	16^1	16^0	
Value	4096	256	16	1	
Digit	1	C	3	F	
Equals	4096	3072	48	15	= 7231

Figure 9-15
Conversion with values

Position	3	2	1	0	
Calculation	16^3	16^2	16^1	16^0	
Value	4096	256	16	1	
Digit	1	C(12)	3	F(15)	
Equals	4096	3072	48	15	= 7231

To begin a conversion, enter the hexadecimal digits (for example, FF) in the third row on Figure 9-15. Now multiply the number in row 3, or its decimal equivalent if a letter, times the value in row 2. Finally, just sum the values in the fourth row. The result of converting FF is shown in Figure 9-16.

Note that, just like in decimals and binary numbers, leading 0's are insignificant.

If you sketch out the table a couple times and do a few conversions, you will remember it. Take a moment to convert the following hexadecimal values to decimals:

Figure 9-16
Conversion of FF
to decimal

Position	4	3	2	1
Value	4096	256	16	1
Digit	0	0	f	f
Equals	0	0	240	15

= 255

a. 11 _____

b. 1C _____

c. C1 _____

d. DD _____

e. F0 CC 43 9A ____.____.____.____

f. 00-00-8C-47-6D-BF _____-_____-_____-_____-_____-_____

Answers: a. 17, b. 28, c. 193, d. 221, e. 240.204.67.154, f. 0-0-140-71-109-191

Decimal to Hexadecimal

We can use our simple conversion table (Figure 9-16) and a series of division calculations to help us convert decimal values to hexadecimal.

Assume we want to convert 191 to hexadecimal. The steps are shown in Figure 9-17.

1. Since 191 is smaller than 4096 and 256, we can skip the first two columns and start with 16 to see if the 191 can be divided by it. It will go 11 times, so we consult our hexadecimal-to-decimal conversion columns and see that 11 is B. We put a B in the box in row three of the table. Calculate the remainder (15).

2. The remainder 15 can be divided by the next value (1). It will go 15 times, so we consult our hexadecimal-to-decimal conversion columns and see that 15 is F. We put an F in the box in row 3 of the table. There is no remainder.

3. You can use row 4 to check your work.

Take a moment to sketch out the table and convert the following decimals values to binary:

a. 221 _____

b. 8 _____

c. 252 _____

Figure 9-17
Converting 191 to a
hexadecimal value

```
              11  = B
      16 [ 191
           176
       1    15  = F
```

Position	4	3	2	1
Value	4096	256	16	1
Digit	0	0	b	f
Equals	0	0	176	15

= 191

Hex.	Dec.
0	0
1	1
2	2
3	3
4	4
5	5
6	6
7	7
8	8
9	9
A	10
B	11
C	12
D	13
E	14
F	15

    d. 116.127.71.3   _____._____._____._____

    e. 255-255-255-255-255-255   _____-_____-_____-_____-_____-_____

Answers: a. DD, b. 8, c. FC, d. 74.7f.47.3, e. ff-ff-ff-ff-ff-ff

Hexadecimal and Binary Numbers

Converting between binary and hexadecimal can be simple if you remember that every
4 binary bits (digits) equal 1 hexadecimal digit. The conversion looks like this:

BINARY HEX	BINARY HEX
0000 = 0	1000 = 8
0001 = 1	1001 = 9
0010 = 2	1010 = A
0011 = 3	1011 = B
0100 = 4	1100 = C
0101 = 5	1101 = D
0110 = 6	1110 = E
0111 = 7	1111 = F

Until you become familiar with 4-bit binary values, you may find the conversion process easier by going binary first to decimal and then to hex. Whatever makes it work for you! Let's look at an example: We will convert 11100111 binary to hexadecimal:

1. We break it into two 4-bit numbers: 1110 and 0111.

2. The first value is 14 in decimal, or E in hexadecimal. The second value is 7 in both so, the result is E7.

This technique will work regardless of the size of the binary number. Start from the right end of the binary number and break it up into groups of four. When you get to the left end, if the number doesn't break evenly into 4 bits, add 0's to the left end until it does. Now convert each 4-bit value to its hex equivalent. Here is an example of a binary value we want to convert:
11001101001100011101010100101101101110
After breaking it up and adding two leading 0's to the left end, we get:
0011 0011 0100 1100 0111 0101 0100 1011 0110 1110
After we convert each 4-bit value to hexadecimal, we get:
3 3 4 C 7 5 4 B 6 E or 334C754B6E
To convert hexadecimal to binary, the steps are reversed. To convert DA hexadecimal to binary:

1. Convert each hex value to binary. D becomes 1101 binary, while A becomes 1010 binary. Make sure that each value is 4 bits long, supplying leading 0's as needed.

2. Combine the two values so that hex DA is 11011010 binary.

For larger hex values, just continue using the same process.
AD46BF hex converts to 101011010100011010111111 binary.
Take a moment to convert the following hexadecimal values to binary:

a. 23 _____

b. C1 _____

c. FF _____

d. 7c32a4b6 _____._____._____._____

Convert the following binary values to hexadecimal:

e. 11111100 _____

f. 011111111 _____

g. 101 _____

h. 11100110.10101010.00110100. 00010111 _____

Answers: a. 100011, b. 11000001, c. 11111111, d. 1111100.00110010.10100100.10110110, e. fc, f. 7F, g. 5, h. E6.AA.34.17

Many students tend to underestimate the importance of knowing how to do these conversions. Do yourself a favor and take the time to get it down. I see these same students struggle later with subnet masks, wildcard masks, and other relatively straightforward concepts—straightforward if you realize it is all done in binary, not decimal.

IP Classful Addressing

IP addresses are logical addresses of devices that operate at Layer 3 of the OSI network model. They were first defined in 1981 as 32-bit numbers. Because 32-bit numbers are intimidating even in decimal form, a dotted octet format was adopted. The common form is a set of four 8-bit numbers represented as decimal numbers separated by three periods—for example, 123.43.119.47. To the inexperienced, these numbers may seem random, much like Social Security Numbers. Nothing could be further from the truth.

As ARPANET evolved into the Internet, a system of assigning IP addresses developed. Originally, every organization got a unique first octet; there were then, after all, only a small handful of members. As requests to become a part of the network increased, the class system was developed to create three sizes of address groups that could be assigned to organizations, Class A, Class B, and Class C. In addition, Class D addresses were reserved exclusively for router multicasts, and Class E was reserved for future expansion and research.

It is common for networking students to memorize the three classes that are used for host connections: Class A comprises numbers 1 to 126; Class B, 128 to 191; and Class C, 192 to 223. Now that router multicast is becoming common, CCNAs also need to know that Class D is 224 to 239. But what happened to 127? And why not break the classes into increments of 25 to make them easier to remember? One of my early network instructors told me that each point was the number assigned when they decided they needed to refine the system. He was wrong, but it seemed reasonable at the time.

We need to look at the binary values of the first octet to see the reason for the break points. All Class A networks have a 0 as the first bit. All Class B networks start with 10 as the first two bits. Class C starts with 110, Class D 1110, and Class E 1111. Figure 9-18 shows the pattern and details for all five classes of addresses.

Class	Starts with	Binary range	Decimal Value range	Maximum subnets	Maximum hosts	Routing mask
A	0	00000000-01111111	0-127*	127	16,777,214	255.0.0.0
B	10	10000000-10111111	128-191	16,384	65,534	255.255.0.0
C	110	11000000-11011111	192-223	2,097,152	254	255.255.255.0
D	1110	11100000-11101111	224-239			
E	1111	11110000-11111111	240-255			

* The 0 octet is forbidden in the RFC, and 127 is reserved for loopback testing.

Figure 9-18   IP address class definitions and related properties

This method of determining IP address classes is referred to as the "first octet rule." In addition to defining the classes, it provides an efficient way for Layer 3 devices to start interpreting the address. Any address beginning with a 0 can be forwarded only to an interface that connects directly or indirectly to a Class A network.

Note the following important exclusions:

- Class D addresses, 224–239, are reserved exclusively for router multicasts. Some routing protocols—for example, RIPv2 and OSPF—use these addresses to communicate with other routers.

- Class E addresses, 239–254, are reserved for future expansion and research.

- First octet 0 (00000000 binary) is not allowed by the RFC. Specifically, the RFC forbids a network address to be either all 1's or all 0's. So, just as there cannot be a 0 network, there cannot be a 255 network.

- First octet 127 (01111111) is reserved for loopback and is used for internal testing. Using the ping command with the loopback address confirms properly installed and functioning TCP/IP on the local machine (for example, *ping 127.0.0.1* at the command line) without the need for a network connection.

Network/Host Relationships

In classful networks, the first octet defines the number of octets assigned to identify the network and the others define the host. These are always on an octet boundary. In a Class A network, only the first octet is registered as the network ID, and the remaining three octets represent the host addresses. This is sometimes represented as N.H.H.H, or net.host.host.host, to show the pattern. Figure 9-19 summarizes the relationship between class and the network/host boundaries.

Class	Octets registered	Notation	Example*	Routing mask
A	1	**N**.N.H.H	**117**.121.95.201	255.0.0.0
B	2	**N.N**.H.H	**161.45**.117.231	255.255.0.0
C	3	**N.H.H**.H	**207.113.91**.45	255.255.255.0

* Bold octets are the network ID. *Italics are the host portion.*

Figure 9-19   Class address network/host relationships

The default routing mask for each class indicates the host and network relationship. The number 255 (8 binary 1's) identifies the network, while the 0's identify the host portion. We will discuss these masks in the next section.

Take a moment to complete the following table. The first row is included as an example.

ADDRESS	CLASS	NETWORK ID	HOST PORTION
207.1.145.171	C	207.1.145.0	.171
189.7.7.7			
192.168.0.63			
224.0.0.6			
51.117.91.116			
127.123.95.14			
119.65.112.261			

Give me a ballpark answer. How many host addresses in:

a. Class A network   _____

b. Class B network   _____

c. Class C network   _____

d. Class D network   _____

Answers: a. 16 3/4 million, b. 65,000, c. 254 (know this one exactly), d. none—it's a multicast.

ADDRESS	CLASS	NETWORK ID	HOST PORTION
207.1.145.171	C	207.1.145.0	.171
189.7.7.7	B	189.7.0.0	.7.7
192.168.0.63	C	192.168.0.0	.63
224.0.0.6	D	N/A	None
51.117.91.116	A	51.0.0.0	.117.91.116
127.123.95.14	N/A	Loopback	
119.65.112.261		Invalid fourth octet	Greater than 255

Class Default Routing Masks

Routing masks allow the Layer 3 devices to quickly and efficiently separate the network portion of the address from the host portion. Remember that Layer 3 devices' routing masks are made up of a series of contiguous binary 1's beginning at the left, or higher-order bits. The point where the mask changes from 1's to 0's represents the boundary, or break point, between the network portion of the address and the host portion. Once the mask pattern changes to 0's, there can be only 0's to the 32nd bit.

All devices in the network will (must) share the same network portion of the address, but each must have a unique host portion. Only devices in the same network can communicate with one another without involving a router.

In the last section we saw that, in a classful network, you have to look at only the first octet to know both the class and therefore the default routing mask. Class default routing masks are even octets of eight 1's, which each equate to 255 in decimal values. For example, the IP address 171.15.12.112 falls in the Class B range (128–191), and therefore the default routing mask must be 255.255.0.0 (11111111.11111111.00000000.00000000 in binary), indicating that the 171.15 portion of the number is the network ID. The IP class address default routing masks are as follows:

DECIMAL FORM	BINARY FORM	PREFIX
255.0.0.0	11111111.00000000.00000000.00000000	/8
255.255.0.0	11111111.11111111.00000000.00000000	/16
255.255.255.0	11111111.11111111.11111111.00000000	/24

Prefix Notation

Another method of representing this address and routing mask is "prefix" notation. In this notation, the IP address is displayed like 171.15.12.112 /16, indicating that the mask is 16 bits long (or two octets). In a classful environment without subnetting, the only values that can appear after the IP address for default masks are /8, /16, and /24, representing full octets.

Calculating the Network ID

IP addresses and routing/subnet masks are numbers, and any analysis of those numbers involves some form of mathematical operation. In the decimal world, we are familiar with mathematical operations like addition, subtraction, multiplication, and division. These operations and their operators $(+, -, \times, /)$ indicate how we combine decimal values.

In the binary world, we use Boolean logic to work with the values. There are three Boolean operators:

• **AND** A form of multiplication

• **OR** A form of addition

• **NOT** Changes 0 to 1 and 1 to 0

The operator that we are interested in is the AND operator. Since there are only two digits in binary, all values and any resulting calculations have to be made up entirely of 1's and 0's. The comparison process is called a *bit-wise AND*, meaning it is done on a bit-by-bit basis. There are only two possibilities: 1 AND 1 results in 1; any other combination (1 AND 0, 0 AND 1, 0 AND 0) results in 0. Try it in your head substituting "times" for AND: $1 \times 1 = 1$, $1 \times 0 = 0$, $0 \times 1 = 0$, and $0 \times 0 = 0$.

To route a data packet, the router must first determine the destination network address by performing a logical AND using the destination host's IP address and the subnet mask. The result will be the network address. The following table demonstrates using the bit-wise AND to distill the network portion of the address.

BINARY FORM	DECIMAL FORM	DESCRIPTION
10110111.00110011.00011011.00011011	183.51.27.27	IP address
11111111.11111111.00000000.00000000	255.255.0.0	Routing mask
10110111.00110011.00000000.00000000	183.51.0.0	Network

What is the default routing (subnet) mask for each of the following addresses?

a. 161.85.6.112   255.255.0.0 (Class B)

b. 88.119.85.201   _____

c. 191.14.101.65   _____

d. 1.34.121.115   _____

e. 192.14.101.65   _____

f. 223.67.89.112   _____

Use prefix notation instead of the subnet mask for each of the following addresses.

g. 161.85.6.112   161.85.6.112/16

h. 88.119.85.201   _____

i. 191.14.101.65   _____

j. 1.34.121.115   _____

k. 192.14.101.65   _____

l. 223.67.89.112   _____

Answers: b. 255.0.0.0, c. 255.255.0.0, d. 255.0.0.0, e. 255.255.255.0, f. 255.255.255.0, h. 88.119.85.201/8, i. 191.14.101.65/16, j. 1.34.121.115/8, k. 192.14.101.65/24, l. 223.67.89.112/24

Private Addresses

Another group of IP address ranges is set aside as private addresses to be used by any organization within their internal networks. Early on it was relatively easy for an organization to secure a Class B network, thus allowing more than 65,000 host addresses to be allocated to a single company. It is easy to understand why addresses started to deplete so quickly. Few companies, even large ones, have a need for 65,000 hosts. So a substantial number of host addresses went allocated but unused.

Today all Class A and B addresses are committed. It is now possible to get blocks only of Class C addresses assigned. Yet large organizations still need large address pools for developing and scaling their Internetworks.

So, the Internet Assigned Numbers Authority (IANA) decided to allocate an entire Class A network, 16 Class B networks, and 256 Class C networks to private addressing. They documented this in RFC 1918 (February 1996). Essentially, these networks do not appear in any Internet routing table. Without an entry Internet routers will simply drop the packets. These addresses are as follows:

- **Class A (1)**   10.0.0.0 through 10.255.255.255
- **Class B (16)**   172.16.0.0 through 172.31.255.255
- **Class C (256)**   192.168.0.0 through 192.168.255.255

With these networks alone, an organization can implement a huge Internetwork without using a single public address, unless it wants to access the Internet. There are solutions such as *Network Address Translation* (NAT) that will allow an organization using private addresses internally to work with their ISP to use one or more public addresses to communicate with the rest of the world. This can even provide a layer of security to the network.

Determining the Number of Hosts

We often see tables with the classful address information including the number of host addresses. Figure 9-18 is an example. You should know how the number of hosts is calculated. If we look at the Class C address 211.9.21.0 and recognize that the first three octets are fixed, then it is pretty easy to see that the last octet could range from 0 to 255 for a total of 256 unique values. It isn't quite that simple.

All 0's and All 1's Rule

Just as the RFC does not allow a network ID to be made up of all 0's or all 1's, a host ID cannot be all 1's or 0's either. The all-0's address is reserved to identify the entire network, while the all-1's address is the network broadcast address.

CLASS	EXAMPLE	NETWORK	BROADCAST	HOST ADDRESSES
A	12.213.78.49	12.0.0.0	12.255.255.255	12.0.0.1–12.255.255.254
B	161.45.9.112	161.45.0.0	161.45.255.255	161.45.0.1–161.45.255.254
C	201.15.46.11	201.15.46.0	201.15.46.255	201.15.46.1–201.15.46.254

In each case we lose two addresses from each network to identify the network (all 0's) and the broadcast address (all 1's). The formula for calculating the number of hosts is $2^n - 2$ where n is the number of bits assigned to the host address. Since a Class C address uses 8 bits to identify the host, the result is $2^8 - 2 = 254$.

EXAM TIP: For nonmath majors: Just start with 2 and double it n times. For example, 2^4 yields 2, 4, 8, 16, with 16 being the right answer. Even 2^8, which might seem intimidating to some, yields 2, 4, 8, 16, 32, 64, 128, 256, with 256 being the right answer. Even if you are sure you know the right answer, it is a quick and reliable check—remember, it is foolish to blow a question if the math can be verified. Figure 9-20 shows the preceding power of 2 calculations up to 2^{15} (the second column is included here only for reference). This set of calculations is the second item I put on the sheets of paper at the test site—before I start the exam. The conversion table shown in Figure 9-20 is the other thing.

Similarly a Class B would be $2^{16} - 2 = 65,534$, and a Class A would be $2^{24} - 2 = 16,777,214$. While these latter examples become more difficult to do without a calculator, you should know the formula and the reason for subtracting the 2. This formula becomes more important when we get to subnetting our classful networks into subnetworks.

We will look at this topic in greater detail later in this chapter when we cover subnets.

Position	8	7	6	5	4	3	2	1
Value	128	64	32	16	8	4	2	1

2	2^1
4	2^2
8	2^3
16	2^4
32	2^5
64	2^6
128	2^7
256	2^8
512	2^9
1,024	2^{10}
2,048	2^{11}
4,096	2^{12}
8,192	2^{13}
16,384	2^{14}
32,768	2^{15}

Figure 9-20   Conversion table and powers of two (2^n)

Determining the Number of Classful Networks

The formula to calculate the number of classful network IDs is 2^n where n is the number of first octet bits used to identify the network. Since all Class A addresses must begin with a 0 bit, only 7 bits are left to identify the network. The result is $2^7 = 128$, or the range 0 to 127, but we have already seen that the Zero network is not allowed under the RFC, and the 127 is reserved for loopback testing. A summary of our network and host count calculations is represented in the following table.

CLASS	REQUIRED FIRST BIT(S)	NETWORK FORMULA	NETWORK COUNT	HOST FORMULA	HOST COUNT
A	0	2^7	128*	$2^{24}-2$	16,777,214
B	10	2^{14}	16,384	$2^{16}-2$	65,534
C	110	2^{21}	2,097,152	2^8-2	254

The Zero network is not allowed, and 127 is reserved for loopback, so 1-126.

Note that, with Class B, the exponent is the 6 bits remaining in the first octet plus the 8 bits from the second octet. Class C is the 5 bits remaining in the first octet plus the 8 bits from each of the second and third octets.

Things to Remember About Classful Addresses

Before we look at subnets and other topics, note that, both during the exam and on the job, as a CCNA, you must understand the preceding concepts forward and backward. You should be able to look at the these concepts from any angle and be able to make sense of them. Figure 9-21 shows a sample Internetwork made up of Class C networks from the private address series 192.168.0.0. The early points are general and would apply to any network and then progress to points specific to classful networks.

Some thoughts to consider:

- Each interface on a router must be connected to a different network.
- The router interface address must be a part of the local area network. That interface becomes the default gateway for the hosts on the local area network.
- Each host and the router interface on the local area network must share the same network portions of the IP address.

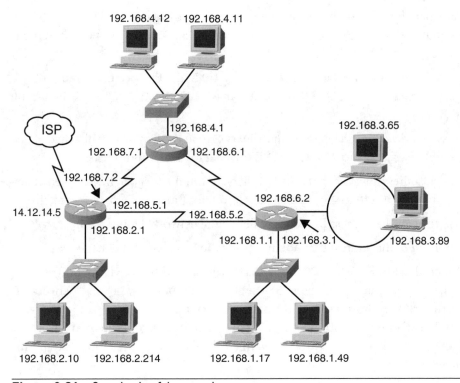

192.168.4.12   192.168.4.11

ISP

192.168.4.1   192.168.3.65

192.168.7.1   192.168.6.1

192.168.7.2

14.12.14.5   192.168.5.1   192.168.6.2

192.168.5.2

192.168.2.1

192.168.1.1   192.168.3.1   192.168.3.89

192.168.1.17   192.168.1.49

192.168.2.10   192.168.2.214

Figure 9-21   Sample classful network

- Each host and the router interface on the local area network must have unique host portions of the address.

- On a router-to-router connection, both interfaces must be in the same network.

- On a router-to-router connection, each interface must have a unique host portion of the address.

- No two of the local area networks, or router-to-router connections, can share the same network portion of the IP address. This is critical. Otherwise, once routing begins, it will appear to some or all the routers that there are two routes to the same network—one will receive all traffic. Another way of stating this point: The hosts in a network must not be separated by a router.

- A Class A address always begins with a binary 0 in the first octet. The range of network addresses is 0 to 127 with 0 prohibited by RFC and 127 reserved for loopback testing. The default mask is 255.0.0.0, and the default prefix is /8.

- A Class B address always begins with a binary 10 in the first octet. The range of network addresses is 128 to 191. The default mask is 255.255.0.0, and the default prefix is /16.

- A Class C address always begins with a binary 110 in the first octet. The range of network addresses is 192 to 223. The default mask is 255.255.255.0, and the default prefix is /24.

- A Class D address always begins with a binary 1110 in the first octet. The range of network addresses is 224 to 239. Class D is reserved for router multicasts.

- A Class E address always begins with a binary 1111 in the first octet. The range of network addresses is 240 to 255. Class E is reserved for future growth and research.

- The portion of the address that doesn't define the network defines the host.

- The portion of the address that doesn't define the host defines the network.

- Given an IP address such as 207.16.153.211, you should be able to identify its class (C), its default mask (255.255.255.0), its default prefix (/24), its network ID (207.16.153.0), its host ID (211), the network broadcast (207.16.153.255), the range of valid host addresses (207.16.153.1 to 207.16.153.254), and the number of host addresses ($2^8 - 2 = 254$). The same is true of any Class A or B address except that there would be many more hosts.

- Given an IP address (207.16.153.211), a subnet mask (255.255.255.0), and a default gateway (207.16.135.1), you should be able to determine if they will work together. These three will not. The third octet in the default gateway is different (possibly a transposition), but regardless it is now part of another network and therefore cannot communicate with our hosts and more importantly cannot work as a gateway to the router for our hosts.

- Know and recognize the private addresses: 10.0.0.0 (Class A), 172.16.0.0–172.31.255.255 (Class B), and 192.168.0.0 (Class C). Know that, while these addresses can be used by any organization without securing permission, they cannot be used to connect to the outside world, such as to the Internet. You should recognize that our Figure 9-20 will have problems with the ISP connection for this reason. Later in this chapter we will discuss Network Address Translation (NAT) as a solution to this problem.

Assume a classful network and default routing (subnet) mask for each of the following addresses and supply the missing information.

EXAMPLE	CLASS	NETWORK	BROADCAST	HOST ADDRESSES
12.213.78.49	A	12.0.0.0	12.255.255.255	12.0.0.1–12.255.255.254
207.15.23.19				
165.4.4.221				
201.0.0.1				
99.101.7.17				
130.19.100.1				

Assume a classful network for each of the following:

a. What is the Class C default network (subnet) mask? _____

b. What is the Class A default network (subnet) mask? _____

c. What is the Class B default network (subnet) mask? _____

d. What is an example of a Class C network address with prefix? _____

e. What is an example of a Class B network address with prefix? _____

f. What is an example of a Class A network address with prefix? _____

g. What is the formula to calculate the number of hosts in a Class C network?

_____

h. What is the formula to calculate the number of hosts in a Class A network?

_____

i. What is the formula to calculate the number of hosts in a Class B network?

_____

j. Use Figure 9-22 and the Class C private addresses to assign networks, interface addresses, and a sample of valid host addresses. Hint: Think about what portion of the address is the network ID and what part is the host ID.

k. Use Figure 9-23 and the Class B private addresses to assign networks, interface addresses, and a sample of valid host addresses. Hint: Think about what portion of the address is the network ID and what part is the host ID.

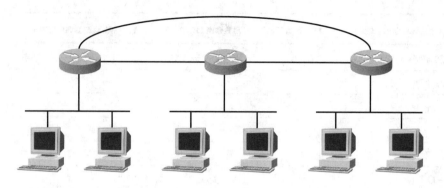

Figure 9-22 Class C private addresses

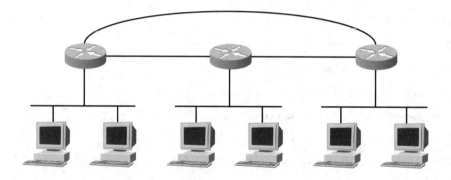

Figure 9-23 Class B private addresses

Answers:

EXAMPLE	CLASS	NETWORK	BROADCAST	HOST ADDRESSES
12.213.78.49	A	12.0.0.0	12.255.255.255	12.0.0.1–12.255.255.254
207.15.23.19	C	207.15.23.0	207.15.23.255	207.15.23.1–207.15.23.254
165.4.4.221	B	165.4.0.0	165.4.255.255	165.4.0.1–165.4.255.254
201.0.0.1	C	201.0.0.0	201.0.0.255	201.0.0.1–201.0.0.254
99.101.7.17	A	99.0.0.0	99.255.255.255	99.0.0.1–99.255.255.254
130.19.100.1	B	130.19.0.0	130.19.255.255	130.19.0.1–130.19.255.254

a. 255.255.255.0, b. 255.0.0.0, c. 255.255.0.0, d. 201.15.1.0 /24*, e. 169.54.0.0 /16*, f. 12.0.0.0 /8*, g. 2^{24} - 2, h. 2^{8} - 2, i. 2^{16} - 2, j. See Figure 9-24 for one solution. The third octet can be any number between 1 and 255. k. See Figure 9-25 for one solution. The second octet can be any number between 16 and 31. Because we are using classful masks, we cannot use the third octet to identify the network.

*The network address could be different, but the prefix must be the same.

In Figure 9-25, note the lower-right network addresses. All the hosts from 0.1 to 255.254 are valid—more than 65,000 possible. What will that do for congestion? We will address this concern in the next section on subnetworks.

IP Classful Subnets

Classful addressing, or using only the default classes, can lead to inefficiencies in the use of IP addresses. Few organizations can use a Class B address (65,500 hosts) fully, let alone a Class A with more than 16 million addresses. Yet all the Class A and B addresses are assigned. This means that, while we are conserving the relatively few Class C addresses remaining, literally millions of "dead" addresses are assigned to organizations that cannot use them.

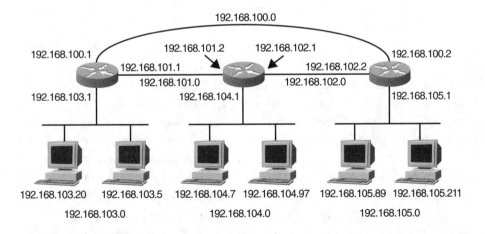

Figure 9-24   Class C private address solution

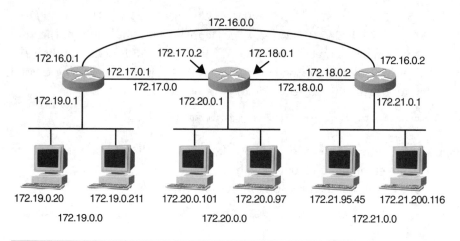

Figure 9-25   Class B private address solution

The most obvious solution of reclaiming these addresses and reassigning them doesn't work from several perspectives. First, with a classful system we can reassign them only in full units of A, B, or C. Even if we tried to break Class A's extra addresses into Class-B or -C-size units, the "first octet rule" stands in our way—the resulting addresses would begin with a 0 bit, which is by definition part of a Class A network.

Second, and even more important, if we could get around the preceding problem, we would start having what appears to be the same network showing up in multiple locations around the world. The Internet backbone routers would see this as two alternative routes to the same destination and start forwarding "all" traffic to the shortest route, resulting in misdelivered packets. Even if we could resolve this issue, we would dramatically increase the number of entries in the backbone router's routing tables. The Internet backbone routers already have 70,000+ entries, and any significant increase will reduce speed and efficiency and could threaten the integrity of the system.

Probably of more interest to us individually and the organizations we represent is the fact that this one-size-fits-all, technically three-sizes-fits-all, system can put too many users on the same network and lead to network congestion. It also means that users with different resource requirements, access to applications, bandwidth requirements, and security issues are all grouped together "side-by-side" on the same network.

Obviously, a 5,000-employee organization on a single network segment is pretty easy to visualize as a congestion problem—even with an all-switched network. But just as problematic could be a small training company with 15 employees and six classrooms open to the public. Does the company really want the students to have access to the business side of the network? Does it really want the student's Web-related or graphics activities dragging down the performance of the business network? Admittedly, the network operating system has features that can deal with part of this, but separating the classrooms on to one or more network segments can give us the best control and reduce bandwidth competition.

We now need to be able to create networks within networks, or subnetworks. We need to somehow be able to group users (host addresses) by location, resources required, access to software, and/or security requirements. We can increase the routing mask by adding more binary ones to the classful default mask. This effectively breaks up our network into subnetworks, or subnets. We can choose to break up a Class A, B, or C network into two or more subnets to suit our purposes.

Subnet masking was introduced in RFC 950 (August 1985), refined in RFC 1812 (June 1995), and was developed to add a level of hierarchy to an IP address. This level allows the extension of the number of addresses derived from a single IP address—that is the division of an address into a network portion and a host portion.

Simple Solutions

As we saw in Figures 9-23 and 9-24 in the last section, if we are using private addresses, we can just use multiple Class B or Class C private networks to segment our network hosts. Assuming you can get by with 16 Class B or 256 Class C networks, it is a pretty simple solution. Unfortunately, this probably will not work with real, legal IP addresses. We couldn't get multiple Class Bs or even a single one for that matter. While it might be possible to get a block of Class C network addresses, we wouldn't get enough for 5,000 hosts or 10,000 hosts.

There is a possibility that, if the organization has a Class B legal address, one could use a Class C mask, thereby creating 256 Class C networks that could be assigned as needed. To a great extent that is what the Community College system in Washington State does. They have a real Class B address pool, but they assign the equivalents of Class C networks to the individual colleges. By using the Class C mask, they have extended the default mask by 8 bits to 24 bits. What they have then is a 16-bit default mask plus an 8-bit subnet mask, and the routers and network administrators treat the resulting 24-bit network ID as if it were a true Class C address.

CLASS B NETWORK	172.16.0.0	NUMBER OF NETWORKS	NUMBER OF HOSTS EACH	TOTAL HOSTS
Default Mask	255.255.0.0	1	65,534	65,534
Default + Subnet Mask	255.255.255.0	256	254	65,024

Example networks are 172.16.1.0 /24, 172.16.100.0 /24, and 172.16.255.0 /24. I have used one of the Class B private address networks for demonstration purposes, but it would work the same for any real Class B network. Note that the total number of host addresses is reduced with subnets because we now have 255 more network and broadcast addresses (remember the −2 in our formula). Figure 9-26 demonstrates the default and subnet mask in binary form. Many people just refer to the combined mask as the subnet mask.

If an organization had a Class A address or was using the Class A private network, a similar masking would result in a series of Class B- or Class C-like networks. The following table summarizes an example.

CLASSFUL NETWORK	DEFAULT MASK	NUMBER OF NETWORKS	NUMBER OF HOSTS EACH	TOTAL HOSTS
Class A	255.0.0.0	1	16,777,214	16,777,214
Class B	255.255.0.0	256	65,534	16,776,704
Class C	255.255.255.0	65,536	254	16,646,144

This borrowing of another class's mask works, but it has somewhat limited application. You are still limited to basically two network sizes and have to segment your network to fit the mask rather than mask your network to match your host requirements.

Not-So-Simple Solutions

What if you need networks for 50 hosts, or 30? With classful addressing we would have to commit a minimum of 254 host addresses to each network, wasting more than 200 addresses per network.

A network mask comprises contiguous 1's that begin at the higher-order bits (left-most) and continue until the end of the network identifier. Default masks are always in full-octet

Figure 9-26
Subnet and default masks in binary

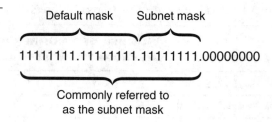

Default mask   Subnet mask

11111111.11111111.11111111.00000000

Commonly referred to
as the subnet mask

(8-bit) increments. A subnet mask extends from the default mask one or more bits into the host portion of the IP address, effectively extending the network mask one or more bits. Figure 9-27 shows an example of a Class C default mask with a 1-bit subnet mask.

If we use our earlier conversion table, we see that the single bit has a decimal value of 128, meaning that the new subnet mask is 255.255.255.128. Using our formula for calculating the number of subnets, we would have $2^1 = 2$ with 1 representing the 1 bit that identifies the network. Calculating the number of host addresses per subnet, we get $2^7 - 2 = 126$ where the 7 represents the number of bits that define the host address portion.

Before we get into the possible numbers of subnets and hosts, let us look just at how many possible subnet values there are. At first glance, it might seem that there could be dozens or even hundreds, but in fact there can be only eight. Sometimes realizing how few possibilities there really are helps to make this task seem less daunting. First, we need to remember that a subnet mask can be created only by adding contiguous 1's to the right end of a default routing mask. Each 1 we add to the routing mask reduces the number of 0's representing the host by 1 so that we stay within our 32-bit total. Second, each octet is only 8 bits long, so even if we want a subnet mask of 9 or 10 bits, we consider them only in groups of 8; that is, 10 bits become 8 bits plus 2 bits. In Figure 9-28, the upper sample shows us that adding a single 1 defines our first subnet mask, which is 128. The lower sample shows that adding a second 1 creates the next subnet mask, which is 192.

If we continue the process until all 8 bits are used, we see that the only possible subnet mask values are as shown in Table 9-1. For the purpose of this table, we will limit our interest to a Class C address.

Looking at the possible subnet values in Table 9-1, we see that the seventh and eighth values work only in subnetting a Class A from the default mask 255.0.0.0 to 255.254.0.0 or 255.255.0.0. It would also work in a Class B from the default mask 255.255.0.0 to 255.255.254.0 or 255.255.255.0. With a Class C, or the fourth octet,

Figure 9-27
Subnet mask

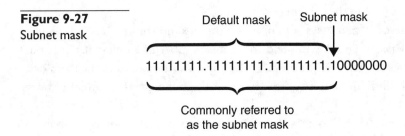

Default mask   Subnet mask

11111111.11111111.11111111.10000000

Commonly referred to
as the subnet mask

Figure 9-28
A single-bit and a
two-bit routing
mask

Position	8	7	6	5	4	3	2	1	
Value	128	64	32	16	8	4	2	1	
	1	0	0	0	0	0	0	0	
	128								= 128

Position	8	7	6	5	4	3	2	1	
Value	128	64	32	16	8	4	2	1	
	1	1	0	0	0	0	0	0	
	128	64							= 192

Table 9-1 Possible Subnet Mask Values Using up to 8 Bits (Class C)

BINARY FORM	DECIMAL FORM	EXAMPLE	SUBNETS	HOSTS / SUBNET
10000000	128	255.255.255.128	$2^1=2$	$2^7-2=126$
11000000	192	255.255.255.192	$2^2=4$	$2^6-2=62$
11100000	224	255.255.255.224	$2^3=8$	$2^5-2=30$
11110000	240	255.255.255.240	$2^4=16$	$2^4-2=14$
11111000	248	255.255.255.248	$2^5=32$	$2^3-2=6$
11111100	252	255.255.255.252	$2^6=64$	$2^2-2=2$
11111110	254	255.255.255.254	$2^7=128$	$2^1-2=0$
11111111	255	255.255.255.0*		

*255 can appear only in octets 2 and 3 because in the fourth octet it would be a broadcast address.

neither would leave any host addresses because we need to exclude the network and broadcast addresses (-2 in the formula).

One nice feature of IP addresses is that, if you understand subnetting options for a Class C address, Class B and A will yield the same number of subnets if the subnet involves only one octet. Table 9-2 shows that the same subnet values in the third octet of a Class B will result in the same number of networks, but a greater number of hosts, per network.

By now, you should be able to guess that a Class A network will look like Table 9-3.

Table 9-2 Possible Subnet Mask Values Using up to 8 Bits (Class B)

BINARY FORM	DECIMAL FORM	EXAMPLE	SUBNETS	HOSTS / SUBNET
10000000	128	255.255.128.0	2	$2^{15} - 2 = 32,766$
11000000	192	255.255.192.0	4	$2^{14} - 2 = 16,382$
11100000	224	255.255.224.0	8	$2^{13} - 2 = 8,190$
11110000	240	255.255.240.0	16	$2^{12} - 2 = 4,094$
11111000	248	255.255.248.0	32	$2^{11} - 2 = 2,046$
11111100	252	255.255.252.0	64	$2^{10} - 2 = 1,022$
11111110	254	255.255.254.0	128	$2^{9} - 2 = 510$
11111111	255	255.255.255.0	256	$2^{8} - 2 = 254$

Table 9-3 Possible Subnet Mask Values Using up to 8 Bits (Class A)

BINARY FORM	DECIMAL FORM	EXAMPLE	SUBNETS	HOSTS / SUBNET
10000000	128	255.128.0.0	2	$2^{23} - 2 = 8,388,606$
11000000	192	255.192.0.0	4	$2^{22} - 2 = 4,194,302$
11100000	224	255.224.0.0	8	$2^{21} - 2 = 2,097,150$
11110000	240	255.240.0.0	16	$2^{20} - 2 = 1,048,574$
11111000	248	255.248.0.0	32	$2^{19} - 2 = 524,286$
11111100	252	255.252.0.0	64	$2^{18} - 2 = 262,142$
11111110	254	255.254.0.0	128	$2^{17} - 2 = 131,070$
11111111	255	255. 255.0.0	256	$2^{16} - 2 = 65,534$

Calculating the Number of Subnets

Table 9-1 introduced the formula for calculating the number of subnets. The formula is 2^n, where n equals the number of bits beyond the default mask. Recall that we used a similar formula to calculate the number of classful networks.

Given a subnet mask of 255.255.255.240 for a Class C network, we can use our conversion table to determine that 240 requires 4 bits. We then calculate 2^4, which indicates 16 subnets created. Figure 9-29 shows the conversion for 240.

This becomes only slightly more difficult with longer subnet masks such as 255.255.255.192 on a Class B network. We know the third octet is eight 1's, and we can use our techniques from the last exercise to see that 192 requires 2 bits. Therefore, our mask requires 10 bits, or 2^{10}, yielding 1,024 subnets (2, 4, 8, 16, 32, 64, 128, 256, 512, 1,024). The next section deals with subnet masks larger than 8 bits.

Subnets Larger Than 8 Bits

Is it possible to have a subnet mask greater than 8 bits? It is in a Class A or B network. The good news it that, since 8 bits, or 255 decimal, is the largest possible value that can appear in an octet, we really need to work with only a minor variation of Tables 9-2 and 9-3. If we wanted to subnet a Class B network with 10 bits, the binary result would be 11111111.11000000, or 255.192, as in 255.255.255.192. The formula for the number of subnets is still 2^n where n is the number of bits in the subnet mask. The same process would work with additional bits up to subnetting a Class A with, say, 22 bits, which creates a binary subnet mask of 11111111.11111111.11111100, or 255.255.252. The resulting mask would be 255.255.255.252. Table 9-4 demonstrates subnet values greater than 8 bits.

If we compare Tables 9-1 and 9-4, we see that the number of subnets continues to double each time we add a bit to the mask, but the number of hosts is the same as if we were subnetting a Class C. There are only two formulas to remember: **subnets** = 2^n and **hosts** = $2^n - 2$ where n is the number of bits used to define each, respectively. In the next section we will look at *valid subnets*, which will add a slight variation to the formula.

The tables show that there are only eight possible subnet mask values: 128, 192, 224, 240, 248, 252, 254, and 255. Knowing how they are derived in binary prevents us from even considering a faulty decimal subnet mask. For example, the subnet mask 255.255.255.215 is clearly not valid when we convert the 215 to binary. Figure 9-30

Figure 9-29
Converting 240
to binary

Position	8	7	6	5	4	3	2	1	
Value	128	64	32	16	8	4	2	1	
	1	1	1	1	0	0	0	0	
	128	64	32	16					= 240

Table 9-4   Possible Subnet Mask Values Using More Than 8 Bits (Class B)

BINARY FORM	DECIMAL FORM	EXAMPLE	SUBNETS	HOSTS / SUBNET
11111111.10000000	255.128	255.255.255.128	$2^9=512$	$2^7-2=126$
11111111.11000000	255.192	255.255.255.192	$2^{10}=1,024$	$2^6-2=62$
11111111.11100000	255.224	255.255.255.224	$2^{11}=2,048$	$2^5-2=30$
11111111.11110000	255.240	255.255.255.240	$2^{12}=4,096$	$2^4-2=14$
11111111.11111000	255.248	255.255.255.248	$2^{13}=8,192$	$2^3-2=6$
11111111.11111100	255.252	255.255.255.252	$2^{14}=16,384$	$2^2-2=2$
11111111.11111110	255.254	255.255.255.254	$2^{15}=32,768$	$2^1-2=0$
11111111.11111111	255.255	255.255.255.255		

Figure 9-30
Converting 215 to binary to see if it is a valid subnet value

Position	8	7	6	5	4	3	2	1	
Value	128	64	32	16	8	4	2	1	
	1	1	0	1	0	1	1	1	
	128	64		16		4	2	1	= 215

shows that the resulting binary value will not work because routing masks must be contiguous 1's from left to right.

The 0 values of the third and fifth bits violate the rule of contiguous 1's, so 215 cannot be a valid subnet mask value. Being able to convert from decimal to binary kept us from accepting a bad default mask. In the field, you could use a PC-based subnet calculator or even the simple calculator that comes with all versions of Windows to quickly convert decimal to binary, but in most exams you won't have either tool.

Take a moment to calculate the number of subnets for each of the following examples:

a. 201.112.95.0 subnet mask: 255.255.255.128: _____

b. 201.112.95.0 subnet mask: 255.255.255.240: _____

c. 201.112.95.0 subnet mask: 255.255.255.252: _____

d. 101.202.95.0 subnet mask: 255.255.128.0: _____

e. 101.202.95.0 subnet mask: 255.255.224.0: _____

f. 161.92.115.0 subnet mask: 255.255.255.252: _____

Answers: a. $2^1 = 2$, b. $2^4 = 16$, c. $2^6 = 64$, d. $2^9 = 512$, e. $2^{11} = 2,048$, f. $2^{14} = 16,384$
Powers of 2 table: 2, 4, 8, 16, 32, 64, 128, 256, 512, 1,024, 2,048, 4,096, 8,192, 16,384

What About Valid Subnets?

Some vendors, and RFC 950 and 1878, use a different formula for calculating what are referred to as valid subnets. The formula $2^n - 2$ eliminates the first and last subnet because they are composed of all 0's or all 1's, respectively. The rule states that subnets cannot be made up exclusively of either 0's or 1's. This leads to significant losses of IP addresses from the invalid subnets. For example, a class C network with a subnet mask of 255.255.255.192 requires 2 bits, so $2^2 \times 2$ yields 2 subnets, and half the IP host addresses are lost. Figure 9-31 shows the possible bit combinations using 2 bits.

Note that the first value is 00, or the Zero subnet, and the last one is 11, or 192 (the subnet value). Under RFC 950 and 1878, these two and their host addresses would have to be discarded. Cisco IOS version 12 and beyond assumes that you will use these subnets, so no configuration is required. In versions 11.3 up to 12, IOS requires the *ip subnet-zero* command to use these subnets. We will look at this feature again in Chapter 13 when we look at router configuration.

Using the *ip subnet-zero* feature assumes that all Layer 3 devices in the network will also accept these subnets—one rationale for an all-Cisco network with current IOS versions. Routers in the Internet or *wide area network* (WAN) won't be an issue because they use only the network portion of the address to forward packets. The local routers, however, will need to agree to use these subnets. Figure 9-32 uses our earlier conversion table to compare the number of total subnets versus the valid subnets (before version 12).

Figure 9-31
Possible bit combinations using 2 bits

Position	8	7	6	5	4	3	2	1	
Value	128	64	32	16	8	4	2	1	
	0	0							= 0
	0	1							= 64
	1	0							= 128
	1	1							= 192

Figure 9-32
Comparing total subnets to valid subnets

Position	8	7	6	5	4	3	2	1
Value	128	64	32	16	8	4	2	1
Subnets 2^n	2	4	8	16	32	64	128	256
Subnets $2^n 2 - 2$	0	2	6	14	30	62	126	254

We revisit this topic later when we discuss *variable-length subnet masks* (VLSMs), but for now, assume we will use the Zero subnet features to maximize our IP address usage.

Number of Hosts per Subnet

There are several ways to figure out the number of addresses and hosts in a subnet, but it might be useful to look at what is happening in binary. Assume that we have a Class C network 201.11.92.0 with a subnet mask of 255.255.255.224. We determine that 224 will require 3 bits, and therefore we calculate the possible combinations of 3 bits. Figure 9-33 uses our conversion table to calculate the subnet combinations of 3 bits and their decimal values.

If we calculate the number of subnets using 2^n, or 2^3, we get 8, confirming that we have all the possible combinations. The decimal value for each then becomes the first IP address for each subnet.

Our second subnet then begins with 201.11.92.32. To get exactly 32 in the last octet, the 5 remaining bits for host addresses must all be 0's (00100000). But the RFCs say that we cannot have a host address of all 0's, so our first address is the subnet address identifying the entire subnet.

The largest value that can be created with the first 3 bits set to 001 is 00111111, or 63 in decimal form. Because the RFCs say that we cannot have a host address of all 1's, our last address is the subnet broadcast. Figure 9-34 shows a partial list of the binary values with the first three bits set to 001 (32).

A similar pattern appears if we look at each of the values created from our 3 bits; the first 1 is the subnet address (all 0's in the host), and the last 1 is the broadcast (all 1's in the host). Figure 9-35 summarizes the subnets using the first 3 bits.

Note that the broadcast address is always one less than the next subnet address. Recognizing this fact saves having to calculate it. The host addresses, then, are the range between the subnet and the broadcast addresses. The number of host addresses can then be calculated using $2^n - 2$, where *n* is the number of bits set aside for host addresses and the -2 subtracts the subnet and broadcast addresses.

Figure 9-33
Binary combinations
of subnet mask 224

Position	8	7	6	5	4	3	2	1
Value	128	64	32	16	8	4	2	1

0	0	0	=	0	201.11.92.0
0	0	1	=	32	201.11.92.32
0	1	0	=	64	201.11.92.64
0	1	1	=	96	201.11.92.96
1	0	0	=	128	201.11.92.128
1	0	1	=	160	201.11.92.160
1	1	0	=	192	201.11.92.192
1	1	1	=	224	201.11.92.224

Position	8	7	6	5	4	3	2	1
Value	128	64	32	16	8	4	2	1

0	**0**	**1**	0	0	0	0	0	=	32	Subnet Address
0	**0**	**1**	0	0	0	0	1	=	33	
0	**0**	**1**	0	0	0	1	0	=	34	
0	**0**	**1**	0	0	0	1	1	=	35	
0	**0**	**1**	1	1	1	0	1	=	61	
0	**0**	**1**	1	1	1	1	0	=	62	
0	**0**	**1**	1	1	1	1	1	=	63	Broadcast Address

Figure 9-34   Examples of binary values beginning with 001

Figure 9-35
Subnet details using
the first 3 bits

Position	8	7	6		Subnet	Broadcast	Host
Value	128	64	32		value	value	range

0	0	0	=	0	31	1-30
0	0	1	=	32	63	33-62
0	1	0	=	64	95	65-94
0	1	1	=	96	127	97-126
1	0	0	=	128	159	129-158
1	0	1	=	160	191	161-190
1	1	0	=	192	223	193-222
1	1	1	=	224	255	225-254

Subnet Increment

Figure 9-35 shows that the increment between subnets is 32. There are at least two simple ways to calculate this without having to build the table:

- If you know the decimal value of the subnet mask (for example, 224), subtract that value from 256. The result is the increment between subnets.

- If you know the number of bits used in the subnet, using our conversion table, take the value in the right-most bit location. Looking at Figure 9-36, we see that, with 3 bits used, the value of the third bit column is 32. That is the increment.

Either way, we now need only to start with 0 and continue to add the increment until the subnets have all been identified, stopping when we get to the subnet mask value (0, 32, 64, 96, 128, 160, 192, 224).

NOTE: If we are not using the Zero subnet feature (using valid subnets only), we would start with the increment value itself and stop excluding the subnet mask value (32, 64, 96, 128, 160, 192). The 0 and 240 subnets have to be discarded because of the all 0's and all 1's rule.

To summarize, the number of subnets equals 2^n, where n equals the number of bits used in the subnet. If we weren't using Zero subnets, it would be $2^n - 2$, to remove the first and last subnets, which are all 0's or all 1's, respectively. The number of host addresses is $2^n - 2$, where n is the number of bits set aside for the host address and the $- 2$ removes the subnet and broadcast addresses that cannot be assigned to a host. To determine the total number of hosts, multiply the number of subnets by the number of hosts in each subnet.

Extending our logic to Class A and B networks is pretty simple. Our formula of $2^n - 2$ still works, but in the case of 171.16.0.0 with 255.255.192.0, we are using 2 bits of the third octet for the subnet, leaving 14 bits for the hosts. Therefore, $2^{14} - 2$ would be

Figure 9-36

Calculating subnet increment

Position	8	7	6	5	4	3	2	1	
Value	128	64	32	16	8	4	2	1	
	1	1	1						
	128	64	32						= 224

16,382. We could use our doubling technique—2, 4, 8, 16—until we have the fourteenth 1. Figure 9-37 summarizes the subnets for a Class B network with a 3-bit subnet (224).

 NOTE: We know that in the real world you will use a subnet calculator or the calculator that comes with Windows or even Excel—but in the exam, none of those tools will be available to you.

Before dismissing the data in the table in Figure 9-37, look at the broadcast address for any subnet—it should be exactly 1 bit less than the next subnet address. The host range is 1 larger than the subnet address to 1 less than the broadcast address—just as in our Class C.

Determining the Subnet Mask

Typically, when determining the subnet mask, we will have a requirement for either a certain number of subnets or a required number of hosts in each subnet, sometimes both. Assume we want to create three Ethernet subnets on a new router, as shown in Figure 9-38.

The only tool we need is our powers-of-2 table we created earlier; eventually, we might want our conversion table, as shown in Figure 9-39.

To start with, let's assume a Class C network for simplicity. Assume also that we are using all available subnets (*ip zero-subnet*); then the table tells us it will take 2-bits to

Network: 171.16.0.0 with subnet mask 255.255.224.0

Position	8	7	6		Subnet value	Subnet address	Broadcast value	Host range
Value	128	64	32					
	0	0	0	=	0	171.16.0.0	171.16.31.255	171.16.1.1 = 171.16.31.254
	0	0	1	=	32	171.16.32.0	171.16.63.255	171.16.32.1 = 171.16.63.254
	0	1	0	=	64	171.16.64.0	171.16.95.255	171.16.64.1 = 171.16.95.254
	0	1	1	=	96	171.16.96.0	171.16.127.255	171.16.96.1 = 171.16.127.254
	1	0	0	=	128	171.16.128.0	171.16.159.255	171.16.128.1 = 171.16.159.254
	1	0	1	=	160	171.16.160.0	171.16.191.255	171.16.161.1 − 171.16.191.254
	1	1	0	=	192	171.16.192.0	171.16.223.255	171.16.192.1 = 171.16.223.254
	1	1	1	=	224	171.16.224.0	171.16.255.255	171.16.224.1 = 171.16.255.254

Figure 9-37   Class B network with a 3-bit subnet (224)

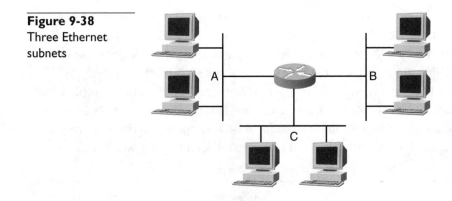

Figure 9-38
Three Ethernet
subnets

Position	8	7	6	5	4	3	2	1
Value	128	64	32	16	8	4	2	1

2	2^1
4	2^2
8	2^3
16	2^4
32	2^5
64	2^6
128	2^7
256	2^8
512	2^9
1,024	2^{10}
2,048	2^{11}
4,096	2^{12}
8,192	2^{13}
16,384	2^{14}
32,768	2^{15}

Figure 9-39   Conversion table and powers of 2

define our subnet. We can then use the conversion table if necessary to determine that
2 bits would be 192, yielding a subnet mask of 255.255.255.192, or prefix /26.

We also know that we have 6 remaining bits, so the number of hosts, from our
power-of-2 table, is 64 − 2, or 62 hosts. If this meets our requirements we are done.

Note that, if we were not using the Zero-subnet option, we would need 3 bits for the subnet mask (255.255.255.224 or /27). Two bits $(4 - 2 = 2)$ is too small, so we would need to use a third bit $(2^3 - 2 = 8 - 2 = 6)$—rather wasteful but the only option available to us. Using three bits for the subnet mask leaves only 5 bits for the host. From our power-of-2 table that would be $32 - 2$, or 30 hosts per subnet. This example should make it apparent why the Zero-subnet feature, while not covered in the RFC, is such an attractive feature to network administrators and bean counters. The following table summarizes the differences between all subnets and valid subnets when three subnets are required in a Class C network.

SUBNETS	BITS	SUBNET MASK	PREFIX	NUMBER OF SUBNETS	HOST BITS	NUMBER OF HOSTS EACH	TOTAL HOSTS USED
All	2	255.255.255.192	/26	$2^2 = 4$	6	$2^6 - 2 = 62$	$3{\times}62 = 186$
Valid	3	255.255.255.224	/27	$2^3 - 2 = 6$	5	$2^5 - 2 = 30$	$3{\times}30 = 90$

A Class A or B network would just have more hosts, but the percentage wasted (unavailable) would remain the same.

With a Given Number of Hosts

We could approach the calculation from the host requirements. Let's assume we have a series of classrooms that we want on separate subnets, and we need 25 host addresses in each subnet. Our powers-of-2 table tells us that the closest larger match is using 5 bits $(2^5 = 32) - 2$, or 30 hosts per subnet. This calculation is the same whether we are using all subnets or valid subnets only.

In a Class C network, that leaves 3 bits for the subnet. We could then have $2^3 = 8$ subnets, or $2^3 - 2 = 6$ valid subnets. Either way, our subnet mask is 255.255.255.224, or the prefix is /27.

With Both Host and Subnet Requirements

What if we need 500 hosts each in 50 subnets? First of all, it should be obvious that we are now talking about at least a Class B network. Our powers-of-2 table tells us that the closest larger match is using 9 bits $(2^9 = 512) - 2$, or 510 hosts per subnet. This calculation is the same whether we are using all subnets or valid subnets only.

The same powers-of-2 table tells us that the closest larger match for the subnets is using 6 bits $(2^6 = 64)$ subnets.

If we add the two octets together, we get only 15 bits. In a classful environment, we will need to add the extra bit to either the subnet or the hosts yielding either 1,022 hosts per subnet or 128 subnets. Either way, about half of the host addresses go unused.

Determining a Subnet Address

According to Figure 9-40, it should be pretty easy to assign a host address out of the second subnet for the network 201.17.100.0. It would be any unused address within 201.17.100.33 to 201.17.100.62. The network address would be 201.17.100.32 /27 or subnet mask 255.255.255.224. The broadcast address would be 201.17.100.63.

While it's not a rule, it would be common to reserve the first host address 201.17.100.33 for the router interface and default gateway for the other hosts. Figure 9-41 shows our three Ethernet Subnets example from earlier with the networks labeled and the router interface (default gateways) assigned. I use this technique in my example, but it is only an option. By always using the first host address, I'm better able to troubleshoot problems. It would actually be pretty common for us to reserve the first few addresses for devices that need static IP addresses, such as routers, servers, and printers, and for remote management of switches and hubs.

Figure 9-40
Subnet address and host addresses

Position	8	7	6		Subnet value	Broadcast value	Host range
Value	128	64	32				
	0	0	0	=	0	31	1-30
	0	0	1	=	32	63	33-62
	0	1	0	=	64	95	65-94
	0	1	1	=	96	127	97-126
	1	0	0	=	128	159	129-158
	1	0	1	=	160	191	161-190
	1	1	0	=	192	223	193-222
	1	1	1	=	224	255	225-254

Figure 9-41
Three Ethernet Subnets

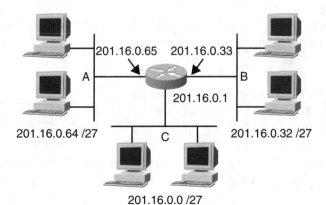

201.16.0.65   201.16.0.33

A   B

201.16.0.1

201.16.0.64 /27   C   201.16.0.32 /27

201.16.0.0 /27

A CCNA must be able to identify the network address and the broadcast address if given a host address and subnet mask (or prefix). For example, given 209.12.89.100 with a subnet mask of 255.255.255.240, we also need the network/subnet address and the broadcast address:

1. We can tell from the first octet and the subnet mask that the first three octets are the original Class C address 209.12.89.0. So we know that the subnet is in the fourth octet only—as compared to a Class B address with a subnet mask greater than 8 bits.

2. We need the subnet increment. The easiest way is to subtract the subnet mask from 256 (256 − 240) to get 16. Note that we could have used our conversion table to determine that 240 converts to 4 bits, and therefore the increment is 16 (value of the smallest bit). Figure 9-42 shows this method.

3. With the increment, we identify our subnet addresses (last octet): 0, 16, 32, 48, 64, 80, 96, 112, and so on.

4. We can now see that 209.12.89.100 must fall in the seventh subnet (it's bigger than 96 but less than 112). So the network address is 209.12.89.96.

5. The broadcast is always one smaller than the next subnet, so the broadcast address is 209.12.89.111.

I like this method, particularly when first starting out, because it is very visual. But there are other methods. One involves at step 3 dividing the host portion of the address (100) by the increment: (100 / 16 = 6.25). The network is the integer part of the answer (6) times the increment, or (6 × 16 = 96), giving us 209.12.89.96.

The broadcast address is the integer part of the answer (6) plus 1 times the increment minus 1 or [(6 + 1)(16) − 1 = 111] giving us 209.12.89.111. The 6 + 1, when multiplied by the increment, gets to the next subnet. The final −1 moves back to the broadcast address of the previous subnet. While initially this seems unnecessarily difficult, once you understand the simple principle behind it you can save some time with addresses such as 201.1.1.213/30, where the increment is going to be 4 (as in 0, 4, 8, 12 . . . 216, 220).

Figure 9-42
Calculating the increment

Position	8	7	6	5	4	3	2	1	
Value	128	64	32	16	8	4	2	1	
		1	1	1	1				
	128	64	32	16					= 240

Summarize Classful Subnetting

Creating subnets by extending the default routing mask allows us to segment our network and thereby reduce congestion, increase security, group users, and so forth. But this comes at the cost of lost host addresses. At a minimum, you lose the subnet and broadcast address for each subnet over the single network design. At worst, you can lose large numbers of hosts when you need a number of subnets that don't associate closely to a subnet mask, such as in our example of needing three subnets but having to set aside six valid subnets. With careful planning, we can manage this loss. We will also see that techniques such as variable-length subnet masks can help reduce this loss.

The subnet Zero feature on by default in IOS version 12 and optionally in older versions salvages two subnets of host addresses over the RFC standard for valid subnets. This is particularly critical when only a few subnets are required.

Assuming we will use all subnets (*ip zero-subnet*), take a moment to calculate the subnet mask and number of hosts for each of the following examples:

a. 201.112.95.0 with 2 subnets: Subnet mask: 255.255.255.128   Hosts: 126

b. 201.112.95.0 with 4 subnets: Subnet mask: _____   Hosts: _____

c. 201.112.95.0 with 6 subnets: Subnet mask: _____   Hosts: _____

d. 201.112.95.0 with 15 subnets: Subnet mask: _____   Hosts: _____

e. 179.4.0.0 with 4 subnets: Subnet mask: _____   Hosts: _____

f. 179.4.0.0 with 30 subnets: Subnet mask: _____   Hosts: _____

g. 179.4.0.0 with 10 subnets: Subnet mask: _____   Hosts: _____

h. 101.0.0.0 with 4 subnets: Subnet mask: _____   Hosts: _____

i. 101.0.0.0 with 12 subnets: Subnet mask: _____   Hosts: _____

Assuming we will use all subnets (*ip zero-subnet*), calculate the prefix mask and number of subnets for each of the following hosts per subnet-requirements examples:

j. 201.112.95.0 with 80 hosts: Prefix mask: /25   Subnets: 2

k. 201.112.95.0 with 14 hosts: Prefix mask: _____   Subnets: _____

l. 201.112.95.0 with 36 hosts: Prefix mask: _____   Subnets: _____

m. 201.112.95.0 with 10 hosts: Prefix mask: _____   Subnets: _____

n. 179.4.0.0 with 500 hosts: Prefix mask: _____   Subnets: _____

o. 179.4.0.0 with 1,000 hosts: Prefix mask: _____   Subnets: _____

p. 179.4.0.0 with 125 hosts: Prefix mask: _____ Subnets: _____

q. 101.0.0.0 with 4,000 hosts: Prefix mask: _____ Subnets: _____

r. 101.0.0.0 with 100,000 hosts: Prefix mask: _____ Subnets: _____

s. Assume you need at least 12 subnets with 3,500 hosts per subnet. You will be using one of the private network addresses. What is the main network address: _____, subnet mask: _____; prefix mask: _____; the first four subnet addresses: _____; and four host addresses from the sixth network: _____? (There are several possible solutions.)

Assume we will use all subnets (*ip zero-subnet*) for each of the following items and supply the missing information.

EXAMPLE	INCREMENT	NETWORK	BROADCAST	HOST ADDRESSES
200.15.7.85/28	16	200.15.7.80	200.15.7.95	200.15.7.81–200.15.7.94
207.15.3.191/26				
201.7.10.221/27				
199.101.7.17/25				
165.4.4.221/22				
113.19.100.1/12				

Answers: b. 255.255.255.192 / 62, c. 255.255.255.224 / 30, d. 255.255.255.240 / 14, e. 255.255.192.0 / 16,382, f. 255.255.248.0 / 2,046, g. 255.255.240.0 / 4,094, h. 255.192.0.0 / 4,194,302 i. 255.240.0.0 / 1,048,574

k. /28-16; l) /26-4; m) /28-16; n) /23-128; o) /22-64; p) /25-512; q) /20-4,096; r) /15-128; s). One possible solution: main network address 172.16.0.0; subnet mask 255.255.240.0; prefix mask /20, the first four subnet addresses; 172.16.0.0, 172.16.16.0, 172.16.32.0, and 172.16.48.0; and four host addresses from the sixth network: 172.16.80.1-4.

EXAMPLE	INCREMENT	NETWORK	BROADCAST	HOST ADDRESSES
200.15.7.85 /28	16	200.15.7.80	200.15.7.95	200.15.7.81– 200.15.7.94
207.15.3.191 /26	64	207.15.3.128	207.15.3.191	207.15.3.129– 207.15.3.190
201.7.10.221 /27	32	201.7.10.192	201.7.10.223	201.7.10.193– 201.7.10.222
199.101.7.17 /25	128	199.101.7.0	199.101.7.127	199.101.7.1– 199.101.7.126
165.4.4.221 /22	4	165.4.4.0	165.4.7.255	165.4.4.1– 165.4.7.254
113.19.100.1 /12	16	113.16.0.0	113.31.255.255	113.16.0.1– 113.31.255.254

Classless Inter-Domain Routing (CIDR)

The CCNA exam and the routing protocols you work with (RIP version 1 and IGRP) use only classful addressing. It is somewhat important to recognize that there is another approach that more efficiently allocates IP addresses. In this section we will discuss *classless inter-domain routing* (CIDR) only in enough detail to expose you to concepts and terminology. Particularly when combined with *variable-length subnet masks* (VLSM) (covered in the next section), it is possible to very efficiently allocate addresses and at the same time reduce the number of network addresses that must be maintained on the Internet routers.

For those of you going on to prepare for the Cisco Certified Network Professional (CCNP), CIDR is covered in more detail in the advanced routing exam (640-503) "Building Scalable Cisco Networks." More information can be found in many intermediate-level routing texts and by looking at RFCs 1518, 1519, 1817, and 2050.

Why do we need it?

- **Limited number of IP addresses**   As we have seen, there is a finite number of IP addresses. Assuming we do not count addresses that cannot be used for broadcasts, a 32-bit address represents at most 4,294,967,296 (2^{32}) unique addresses. While this may seem like a very large number of hosts, we must keep in mind that this pool is for the entire world, much of which is just discovering the Internet, and many addresses have been allocated inefficiently under the classful system, effectively trapping large pools of unusable addresses. One motivation for CIDR was to get away from the three-sizes-fits-all method of allocation.

- **Routing table growth**   In the year 2000 there were nearly 100,000 unique routes. For routers to efficiently pass packets from one network to another, they must compare destination addresses with this table. Think about how much processing is required to match each packet with a table of so many entries. The various Internet committees and organizations are working on ways to reduce the number of networks that must be stored on the Internet routers, thereby reducing processing time without sacrificing reliability. They are doing this using a process called *route summarization* (or *aggregation*) to consolidate routes. For this process to work, new network addresses must be assigned in such a way as to support this summarizing.

CIDR as Part of the Solution

At the heart of CIDR is the abandonment of the classful system and the assignment of addresses in quantities that better meet the organization's needs. Furthermore, to summarize addresses, ISPs are being assigned larger blocks of addresses, which they in turn assign to their clients. In the United States, the American Registry for Internet Numbers (ARIN) issues IP addresses.

At one time, an organization could "order" a Class C network address from ARIN, which would route packets to the company's selected ISP. This meant that two adjacent Class C addresses such as 210.100.1.0 and 210.100.2.0 could end up on opposite ends of the country, making it impossible to summarize them.

No longer so—as of May 2000, ARIN no longer issues IP addresses in blocks of fewer than 20 bits, or the size of 16 Class C networks. In 1995, when IANA was preparing to release the IP addresses 64.0.0.0 through 126.0.0.0, they directed ARIN and the other registry bodies to require that they be assigned only to organizations that fully support CIDR and CIDR—capable routing protocols.

A large ISP might secure the block of addresses 207.0.0.0 to 207.127.0.0, which would be identified on the Internet routers as 207.0.0.0 /9. Using the first octet rule we could assume that this is a Class C address, but the prefix doesn't match (subnet 255.128.0.0). But in reality what we have is a single pool of 8,388,608 (128 × 256 ×

256) addresses. This block will be allocated on a similar classless basis to match end-user requirements. One client could end up with 207.15.32.0 /22, a pool of 1,024 address (four Class Cs), while another might be assigned 207.6.101.96 /30, a pool of four IP addresses. Figure 9-43 shows a partial network for the ISP in the example.

Note that client A has 1,024 addresses (207.15.32.0 /22) that they could further break down to 207.15.32.0 to 207.15.35.0 /24. Client B 207.12.16.0 /20 has a pool of 4,094 addresses from B 207.12.16.1 to 207.12.31.254. Client C has a single Class C, and client D has a single IP address. While client D has four addresses, 207.6.101.96 is the network, 207.6.101.99 is the broadcast, and, of the remaining two addresses, the ISP will take one for their connection to the network.

The last paragraph mentioned classful networks in the discussion of CIDR. While the ISP must fully support CIDR and follow all addressing rules, many clients understand classes (even if just barely). There is no requirement that the end client use CIDR; as long as the ISP addresses are assigned properly, they will summarize in the ISP's network to become just a part of 207.0.0.0 /128 to the Internet routers. Once packets arriving from the Internet get to the ISP, it is their router's responsibility to get them distributed to the right client.

A pretty good analogy of how the system works is the five-digit ZIP code system in the United States' mail system. At least initially, the letter is routed only with reference to the first two digits, which gets it to the right state or part of a state. At that point, the regional center uses the last three digits to get it to the correct local post office. Only at the local post office does anyone look at the street address and then only to determine which route to assign it to.

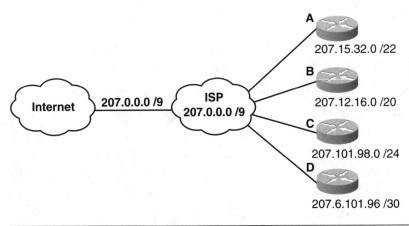

Figure 9-43   ISP with CIDR addressing

Prefix Notation

Identifying the subnet mask using the prefix mask is getting more common, and it has its roots in CIDR. You may even hear some people refer to it as CIDR notation. The important thing is to understand that both subnet masks and prefix notation identify exactly same thing—that portion of an IP address that identifies the network/subnet. Everything else identifies the unique host.

You will see when we get into configuring the routers that you must understand both methods of notation. Although it is now common to see prefix notation on instructions and network diagrams, many interfaces and processes will accept only subnet addresses.

Supernetting

To assign the equivalent of multiple Class C addresses or to summarize multiple Class C addresses to a single network address, a form of CIDR called *supernetting* is used. The network address 207.15.32.0 /22 is a pool of 1,024 addresses that include four Class Cs: 207.15.32.0 through 207.15.35.0.

For the CCNA exam, you need to know about supernetting. Just remember that, when the subnet mask or prefix extends a default class network you are subnetting, if the mask or prefix is shorter than the default mask you are supernetting, you need to be able to process "supernets" to identify the network address and the lesser Class (C) addresses.

Take a moment and assume that you work for an ISP with the block of IP addresses 207.11.0.0/16, which you are now assigning to clients. Specifically, you are working with the block that includes 207.11.101.0/18. Do you understand the addressing? What if they answer no?

a. What is your network address? _____. Hint: What is the increment used to create your block? _____

b. What is the range of addresses you have available? _____

c. A client wants four Class C networks. What would be the first address in your pool that would meet that requirement? _____/___ Which Class C networks are included? _____

d. Ignore the last question; a client needs 4,000 host addresses. What would be the first address in your pool that would meet that requirement? _____/___

e. Ignore the last question; a client needs a simple Internet network connection with only one IP address. They will use private addressing within the organization.

What would be the first address in your pool that would meet the requirement?

_____/___

f. You know that 207.11.118.0 was assigned as a part of a pool of 16 Class C networks. What was the network address of the pool? _____/___ What is the range of Class Cs included? _____

Answer:

a. 18 bits in the prefix means we are using 2 bits in the third octet. The increment is therefore 64. Given that, the possible networks are 207.11.0.0, 207.11.64.0, 207.11.128.0, and 207.11.192.0. Network 207.11.101.0 would fall in the second subnet, so 207.11.64.0 /18 is our network address.

b. The range of addresses then is 207.11.64.0 to 207.11.127.255. The host addresses would be the addresses between these addresses.

c. To get four Class C addresses, I need to "supernet" 2 bits from the default mask, meaning a subnet mask of 255.255.252.0, or prefix of /22. One bit to the left of the default would include two Cs, 2 bits is 4, and 3 bits would be 8 Cs—it's really no different from subnetting; you just going the other way. So, the first one in my pool that I could use would be 207.11.64.0 /22, which includes 207.11.64.0, 207.11.65.0, 207.11.66.0, and 207.11.67.0.

d. To get 4,000 addresses, I could give them 16 Class C addresses, which, according to the logic from the last exercise, would be supernetting 4 bits—meaning a subnet mask of 255.255.240.0 or a prefix of /20. So, the first one in my pool that I could use would be 207.11.64.0 /20, which includes 207.11.64.0 to 207.11.79.0.

e. The smallest network that will give them a single IP address would include four addresses: network, broadcast, ISP connection, and their connection. A check of our power-of-2 table indicates that it will take only 2 bits from the end of a Class C, a subnet mask of 255.255.255.252, or a prefix of /30. So, the first one in my pool that I could use would be 207.11.64.0/30, which includes 207.11.64.0 to 207.11.64.3.

f. If 207.11.118.0 was a part of a pool of 16 Class Cs, then the supernet had to be 4 bits, yielding a subnet mask of 255.255.240.0, or a prefix of /20. We know the increment is 16 (256 − 240), and we know that our subnets can't start at less than 64, so they are 64, 80, 96, 112, and 128 (128 won't work because it is outside our pool). The original network was 207.11.112.0 /20. The class Cs included are 207.11.112.0 to 207.11.127.0.

Variable-Length Subnet Masks (VLSM)

This section introduces the concept and usefulness of *variable-length subnet masks* (VLSM). As with CIDR, mastering VLSM is not a requirement of the CCNA exam or training, and also as with CIDR the routing protocols focused on in the CCNA program (RIP version 1 and IGRP) do not support VLSM. However, one still must be aware of the existence and need for this technology.

For those of you going on to prepare for the Cisco Certified Network Professional (CCNP), VLSM is covered in more detail in the advanced routing exam (640-503) "Building Scalable Cisco Networks." More information can be found in many intermediate-level routing texts.

Why Use Variable-Length Subnet Masks

Some routing protocols, primarily the distance vector protocols, such as RIP version 1 and IGRP, do not allow the use of different subnet masks within the network. The problem stems from the fact that these protocols do not include the subnet mask when they share routing information with their neighbor routers. They assume a classful environment and basically ignore any subnets summarizing everything to the default class address. Some of the routing protocols that support VLSM and CIDR are RIP version 2, OSPF, EIGRP, ISIS, and BGP. While subnetting itself is allowed, each subnet mask must be the same and therefore contain the same number of host addresses. Figure 9-44 presents a simplified view of the problem.

Figure 9-44
Simple network

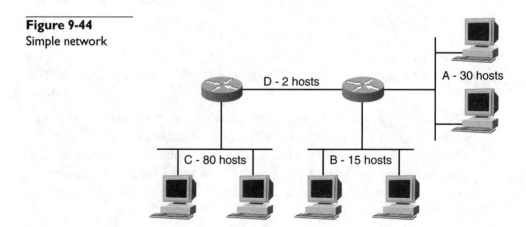

One non-VLSM solution would be to take four Class C networks from the private network 192.168.0.0 and assign one to each network. This would be wasteful on all networks but particularly on the connection between the two routers where 254 are committed and yet only two possible hosts exist. Waste is somewhat relative. Worrying about the waste of private addresses is a lot like worrying about wasting sunshine—it's a renewable source. But what if you have a Class C for which you will be paying your ISP each month? Now the situation becomes a little more serious.

From what we learned earlier, if we split our C into four subnets to cover the number of networks, they are too small to cover our largest network of 80 hosts. Four subnets would give us only 62 host addresses per network.

VLSMs provide the capability to include more than one subnet mask within a network and the capability to subnet an already subnetted network address. The benefits include:

• Efficient use of IP addresses

• Capability to utilize route summarization

Figure 9-45 shows subnetting our Class C into four different sized subnets, preserving almost 25 percent of the addresses (unassigned) for future use.

You'll recall that a /30 masking leaves 2 bits for the hosts, or a total of four addresses. But only two of these host addresses are usable, because the network address and the broadcast address take the upper and lower bounds. So even our router-to-router connection (subnet D) efficiently uses available addresses. Note also that network A and B have the same size subnet, because breaking it down one more bit would leave us with only 14 host addresses.

Figure 9-45
Variable-length
subnet masks

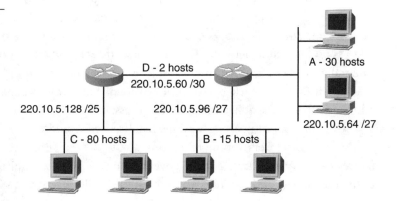

Network Address Translation (NAT)

For much of the business community, the Internet is a double-edged sword. One side offers tremendous opportunities for a relatively low price. The other side exposes businesses to the vulnerability of an attack in a brand new way—every bad guy in the world is standing virtually at the door. However, no matter what the security concerns are, companies do need to communicate on the public Internet. Following are a few examples of common business use of the Internet:

- Business-to-business (B2B) communication
- Electronic mail
- Marketing via a Web site
- Internetworking via a Virtual Private Network (VPN)
- Remote access to corporate resources
- Research and development

NAT allows a company to use an addressing scheme from a pool of private addresses, from a pool of legally licensed addresses, or from a pool of addresses legally registered to someone else. The router that connects the network to the outside world has one or more interfaces defined as internal, which means they are a part of the internal networking. They are the gateways for the internal networks. In addition, one or more interfaces are designated as external and connect only to the outside world. Quite simple, NAT, as defined in RFC 1631 (May 1994), allows a router to translate from private to public addresses. Packets arrive at an "internal" interface and are translated to the "external" interface. Figure 9-46 shows a network using the private address 192.168.0.0 internally and a NAT router supplying public addresses.

Packets traveling from a private network to a public network pass through the NAT router. The router then changes the source address to its public address on the public network and forwards it to its destination. The return address is, of course, the public address on the public network. The outside world sees only the public address, not the internal network. The NAT router must keep track of the outbound communication so that, when inbound packets return, it can then change the destination address to the address of the host that has the private address.

The public pool can be as few as one real licensed IP address, or it can be many. Even if more internal users routinely go out of the network than there are available IP addresses, NAT has a feature called "overloading" that allows multiple internal sources to use the same IP address. To keep the communications separate, the NAT router tracks

Figure 9-46
Network with NAT

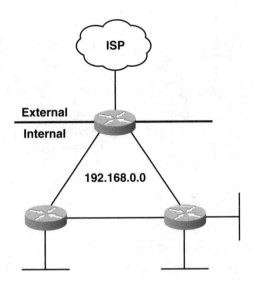

ISP

External
Internal

192.168.0.0

each communication using a combination of the IP address and the Layer 4 port number assigned to that session. This creates a temporary unique address that provides no long-term "trail of crumbs" back to the network. Because of the additional NAT-related tasks, to deliver best performance, this router has to have sufficient memory for route tables, as well as a fast CPU. Many companies use Cisco's PIX Firewall for this type of function.

In Figure 9-47 we have a simple NAT configuration. A workstation has an address of 192.168.10.1. To access a Web server on the Internet, it needs to pass packets through a series of routers—not only its perimeter NAT router, but also any routers within the Internet. Because 192.168/16 falls in the private Internet space, traffic from this address cannot pass. The NAT router changes the source address of the outgoing packet to its public address, 46.21.7.112, which it then passes to the Internet. It eventually will get to the destination server. When the server attempts to pass packets back to the workstation, it really passes it back to the NAT router—specifically the public address. When the NAT router receives the packet, it translates the destination address to 192.168.10.1 and forwards it onto the workstation within the private network.

It is not required for a NAT router to use private network addresses. They can be legally assigned IP addresses, or they can even be addresses that are assigned to another organization. The latter situation happens when a company changes ISPs but doesn't want to change their internal addressing scheme. NAT between private and public networks is the most common implementation and one of the functions of most firewalls

Figure 9-47
Simple NAT
network

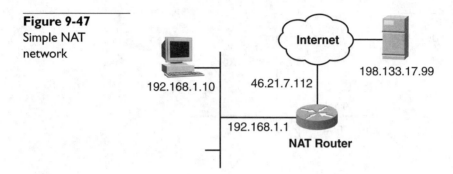

on the market. It should be noted that NAT by itself is not very secure. It is quite easy to spoof the NAT address and gain access to the inside network. Thus, it's important to have a firewall that inspects all packets.

Using the Windows Calculator

The following lab assumes you are using a version of Windows. This is a nondestructive lab, and you should be able to do it with your home machine without concern for changing your system configuration.

1. Using the taskbar, use Start | Programs | Accessories to select the calculator.

2. On the Calculator menu, choose View | Scientific. (See the following illustration.)

3. The Scientific calculator should look like the following illustration.

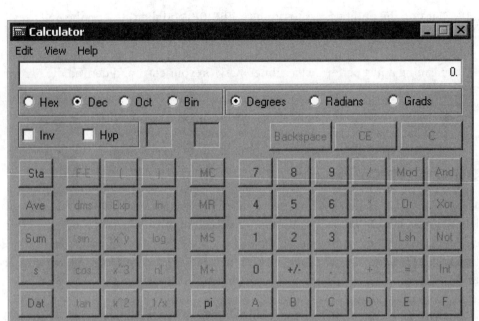

4. Make sure that decimal (Dec) is selected in the upper-left corner and type 123. Then select binary (Bin) and note the result.

5. After looking over the result, select the hexadecimal (Hex) option and note the result.

6. While still in the Hex mode, click on the clear (C) button in the upper-right corner.

7. Click twice on the C button near the bottom of the calculator, and then view the results as binary and then decimal. Is this easy or what?

8. Experiment with these features until you are comfortable that you can enter a number in one form and see it in the other two. Remember to clear between entries.

9. Clear any entries. Make sure that you are in the decimal mode.

10. Click once on the number 2 key on the calculator's keypad. Then click on the button to the left that has x^y on it. Now click on the number 6 and the equal sign (=) buttons. You should now have 2^6 or 64.

11. Calculate 2^{15} and 2^{24}. Continue until you are comfortable with the process.

12. Clear any entries. Make sure that you are in the binary mode.

13. Click on the number keys to produce 10101010 and then click on the AND key in the upper-right corner—nothing happens yet. Now click on the number keys to produce: 11111000 and then click on the equal (=) key. It should show 10101000, meaning it just performed a subnet mask on your entry and derived the network portion.

14. Continue until you are comfortable with the process. If you want, go back and redo some of the early conversion exercises.

Using an IP Calculator

The following lab assumes you are using a version of Windows. This is a nondestructive lab, and you should be able to do it with your home machine without concern for changing your system configuration. If you are doing this at home, establish a connection to your Internet Service Provider (ISP). In a TCP/IP LAN, it shouldn't be necessary to do this step.

1. Launch the Web browser on your machine to access the Internet.

2. We are going to download a nice demo calculator. Type **www.wildpackets.com** in the address bar and press ENTER. The site constantly changes, but look for a link to IP Subnet Calculator or Network Calculator. The latter is the $50 model, with many nice additional features you might want to consider. Even if you choose a link to or search for Network Calculator, there will be a link on that page for the IP Subnet Calculator.

3. At some point you will need to enter your name and e-mail address. Don't get cute with the e-mail address; they mail you a link to the download side.

4. The e-mail response is almost instantaneous. Download the file (550 K) and install it.

5. Launch the program. The following illustration shows what the calculator looks like.

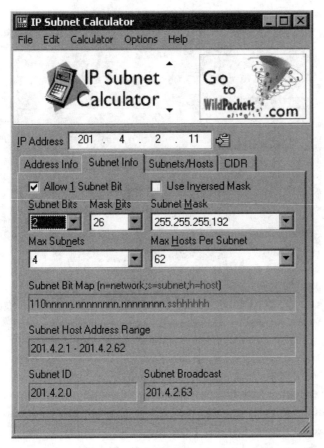

6. Make sure that the Subnet Info tab is selected, as in the picture. Try typing **204.4.2.11** in the IP Address box.

7. Note that the boxes Subnet Bits, Mask Bits, and so on all have drop-down arrow buttons. Use the drop-down arrow buttons to make changes in each box and note that the other boxes all update. Note also that the bottom of the screen shows the network address and the broadcast and host address range.

8. Set the Subnet Bits to 6 or the Mask Bits to 30 and note that the bottom box knows that this particular IP address is a part of the 201.4.2.8 network.

9. Note the Allow 1 Subnet Bit checkbox. Selecting it gives you all subnets, while removing the check gives you the "valid" subnets −2 fewer.

10. Experiment with the features on this tab until you are comfortable with them.

11. Try typing **192.168.1.0** and press ENTER. Set the Subnet Bits to 3 and look over the results. The following illustration shows the results.

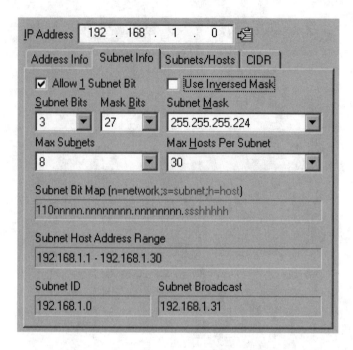

12. Note the checkbox Use Inverse Mask. Turn it off and on and watch the results in your subnet mask window. This won't mean anything to you today, but that is the mask used in Access Control Lists and other features on your router. You will return to this later. End up with the Inverse Mask off.

13. Click on the Subnets/Hosts tab; there are your subnets. If you wish, you can make the calculator wider by dragging the lower-right corner. Dragging the line in the column header can change the column width. You will get a two-headed arrow when the mouse is positioned properly. The following illustration shows the Subnets/Hosts information.

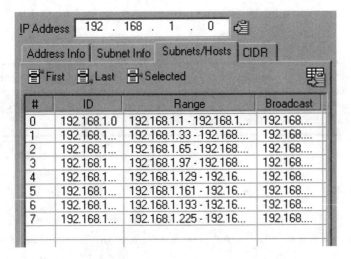

#	ID	Range	Broadcast
0	192.168.1.0	192.168.1.1 - 192.168.1...	192.168....
1	192.168.1...	192.168.1.33 - 192.168....	192.168....
2	192.168.1...	192.168.1.65 - 192.168....	192.168....
3	192.168.1...	192.168.1.97 - 192.168....	192.168....
4	192.168.1...	192.168.1.129 - 192.16...	192.168....
5	192.168.1...	192.168.1.161 - 192.16...	192.168....
6	192.168.1...	192.168.1.193 - 192.16...	192.168....
7	192.168.1...	192.168.1.225 - 192.16...	192.168....

14. Click on the CIDR tab. Set the Mask Bits to 22 and look over the results. Doesn't this look similar to the calculations we were just doing? The following illustration shows the CIDR calculations.

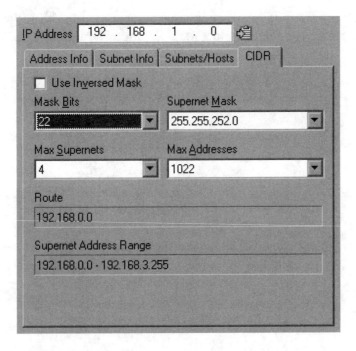

15. Experiment with all these features until you become familiar with the tool and its underlying concepts.

 WARNING: Do not let this tool distract you from learning the simple math techniques covered in this chapter. Use it to check your answers, or play with it to see the relationship between the components of subnetting—but you won't have this tool at the test.

RFC Search

The following lab assumes you are using any version of Windows. This is a nondestructive lab, and you should be able to do it with your home machine without concern for changing your system configuration. If you are doing this at home, establish a connection to your Internet Service Provider (ISP). In a TCP/IP LAN, it shouldn't be necessary to do this step.

1. Launch the Web browser on your machine to access the Internet.

2. Type **www.ietf.org/rfc** in the address bar and press ENTER. This will take us to the site where we can search for the RFCs we heard so much about. The following illustration shows the RFC search site.

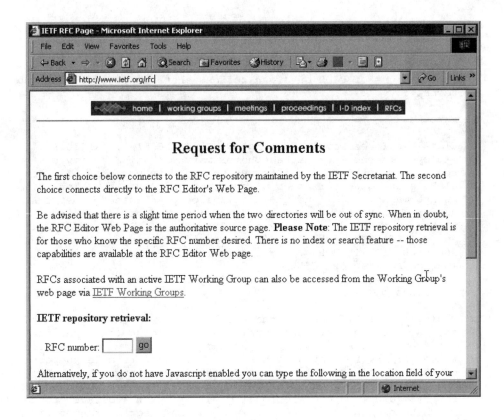

3. Type 1817 in the search box and press ENTER or click on the Go button. Look over the results (shown next). Note the references to other RFCs and the protocols that do not support CIDR.

4. Look over the results and use your Back button if you want to search for another RFC.

```
Network Working Group                           Y. Rekhter
Request for Comments: 1817                    cisco Systems
Category: Informational                         August 1995


                    CIDR and Classful Routing

Status of this Memo

   This memo provides information for the Internet community.
   This memo does not specify an Internet standard of any kind.
   Distribution of this memo is unlimited.


Abstract
```

Classless Inter-Domain Routing (CIDR) is used in the Internet as the primary mechanism to improve scalability of the Internet routing system. This document represents the IAB's (Internet Architecture Board) evaluation of the current and near term implications of CIDR on organizations that use Classful routing technology.

Background

Classless Inter-Domain Routing (CIDR) ([RFC1518], [RFC1519]) is deployed in the Internet as the primary mechanism to improve scaling property of the Internet routing system. Essential to CIDR is the generalization of the concept of variable length subnet masks (VLSM) and the elimination of classes of network numbers (A, B, and C). The interior (intra-domain) routing protocols that support CIDR are OSPF, RIP II, Integrated IS-IS, and E-IGRP. The exterior (inter-domain) routing protocol that supports CIDR is BGP-4. Protocols like RIP, BGP-3, EGP, and IGRP do not support CIDR.

Implications of CIDR

Deployment of CIDR has certain implications on the segments of the Internet that are still using routing technology that can not support CIDR. Existing sites that rely solely on a default route for their external connectivity may not require support of VLSM capable routing technology for their interior routing and CIDR for their exterior routing. All sites lacking support for VLSM and CIDR capable routing must rely on a default route, which consequently may result in a various degree of suboptimal routing. Organizations that operate as Internet Service Providers (ISPs) are expected to be able to support VLSM and CIDR.

Rekhter   Informational   [Page 1]
RFC 1817   CIDR and Classful Routing   August 1995

It is expected that in the near future the IANA will instruct the Internet Registries to begin allocating IP addresses out of the former Class A address space (64.0.0.0 through 126.0.0.0). The allocated blocks are going to be of variable size (based on the actual sites' requirements). Sites that will use these addresses will have to support CIDR-capable routing protocols. All the providers will be required to support CIDR-capable routing protocols as well. Sites that do not use these addresses would be required to continue relying on a default route, which in turn may result in a various degree of suboptimal routing. If a site wants to avoid the suboptimality (introduced by using default route), the site will need to transition to CIDR-capable routing protocols.

```
Security Considerations

    Security issues are not discussed in this memo.

Author's Address
    Yakov Rekhter
    cisco Systems
    170 West Tasman Drive
    San Jose, CA 95134

    Phone: (914) 528-0090
    EMail: yakov@cisco.com
```

Summary

This chapter extensively covered converting decimal, binary, and hexidecimal numbers so that you may better understand the principles of IP addressing, subnetting, and routing. We looked at a simple conversion table to assist conversion between decimal and binary and a technique for calculating powers of 2.

We looked at the five-level classful addressing system (A-E), how the ranges were determined, that the first octet determines the class, and how the class determines how the IP address is split between the network and host identifier. Class A networks have a first octet ranging from 1 to 126; only the first octet is assigned by the Internet registry agencies, and the first octet identifies the network. Class B networks have a first octet ranging from 128 to 191; the first two octets are assigned by the Internet registry agencies, and the first two octets identify the network. Class C networks have a first octet ranging from 192 to 223; the first three octets are assigned by the Internet registry agencies, and the first three octets identify the network. Class D, range 224 to 239, is reserved for router multicasts. Class E, range 240 to 255, is reserved for future growth and research.

Subnetting allows further segmentation of classful networks, providing congestion reduction, increased security, and bandwidth preservation. CIDR abandons the classful addressing system and, when combined with VLSM, allows additional levels of subnetting to provide a true hierarchical addressing system that can be summarized to reduce the size of routing tables. Supernetting is a method of summarizing a series of lower-level networks, often Class Cs, into a single upper-level network address.

NAT provides the bridge between networks using private addresses and the outside world.

Case Study: Tri-City Medical Group

Three medical clinics in the state have combined. Each has an Ethernet network with 75–100 hosts that is expected to grow to no more than 150–200 hosts over the foreseeable future. One location has a medical lab with an existing token ring network of 50 hosts that might double in size during the same time frame. The following illustration shows the proposed design. Assume that the WAN connections will be sufficient to allow one site to provide Internet connectivity to the others, as shown next.

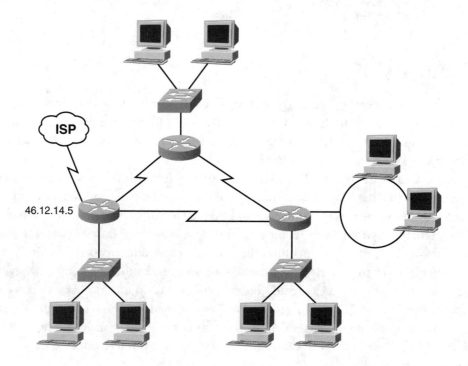

Scenario: Because none of the networks has connected to the outside in the past, there is a hodge-podge of IP addressing schemes, some of which are undoubtedly registered to others. Furthermore, two sites are moving from Netware to Windows and will now need IP addresses. After reviewing the cost with their ISP for enough IP addresses to handle their expected needs, Tri-City has opted to use private addresses within the organization and NAT to translate for the outside world. They haven't decided for sure, but it looks like they will be using RIP version 1 or IGRP for their internal routing protocol.

1. Is there a solution that does not require subnetting? If so, what is it? Demonstrate your solution on the preceding illustration by labeling the router interfaces and host addresses (sample).

2. One of the most influential members on the Tri-City committee just returned from a conference where John Chambers (CEO of Cisco) shared his vision of the future, including digital telephony, PDAs, and digital appliances yet to be designed that will all require IP addresses. This member is now suggesting that the expected long-term need for IP addresses should be more than quadrupled to about 1,000 per site, including the lab. His argument is that, since private addresses are free, why skimp? Nothing else is changing.

   Use the Class B private addresses to create subnets that will put as close to 1,000 host addresses as possible on each network.

   Demonstrate your solution on the preceding illustration by labeling the router interfaces and host addresses (sample).

Case Suggested Solution
(Your solutions may vary)

1. The Class C private addresses would not require subnetting. The following illustration demonstrates how the addresses might be applied. Note that the WAN connections all require a Class C network because our planned protocols are classful.

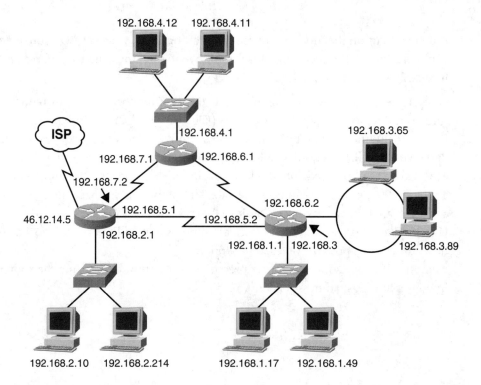

2. The Class B private addresses, 172.16.0.0 /22, would meet our requirements. The following illustration demonstrates how the addresses might be applied.

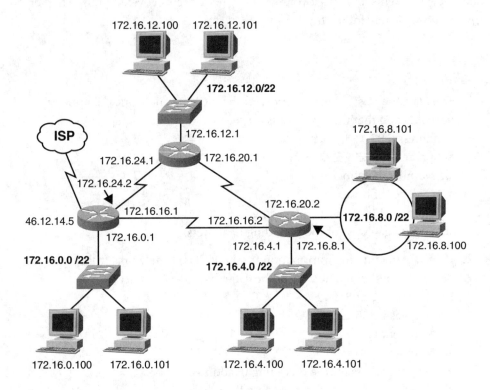

Practice Questions

Take a few moments and check your grasp of the concepts covered in this chapter. The answers immediately follow the questions.

Questions

1. Calculate the missing information for these Class C networks (assume valid subnets only and that the first host is for the gateway-router interface).
   IP address: 192.168.1.119
   Subnet mask: 255.255.255.224
   a. Number of subnets:
   b. Number of hosts:
   c. Subnet address for the preceding IP address:
   d. Default gateway for the preceding IP address:

2. Calculate the missing information for these Class C networks (assume all subnets and that the first host is for the gateway-router interface).
   IP address: 192.168.2.42
   Subnet mask: 255.255.255.252
   a. Number of subnets:
   b. Number of hosts:
   c. Subnet address for the preceding IP address:
   d. Default gateway for the preceding IP address:

3. Look at each of the following items and determine if the default gateway will work with the IP address and subnet mask (yes or no) _____.
   IP address: 192.168.119.125
   Subnet mask: 255.255.255.240
   Default gateway: 192.168.119.113

4. Look at each of the following items and determine if the default gateway will work with the IP address and subnet mask (yes or no) _____.
   IP address: 192.168.119.125
   Subnet mask: 255.255.255.248
   Default gateway: 192.168.119.120

5. Assume that router A has three Ethernet ports with the following IP addresses: port #1: 192.168.0.97; port #2: 192.168.0.129; and port #3: 192.168.0.161. The subnet mask for each port is 255.255.255.224.

    a. What is the network address for the subnet connected to Port 1?

    b. What is the network address for the subnet connected to Port 2?

    c. What is the network address for the subnet connected to Port 3?

    d. What is the default gateway for the subnet connected to Port 3?

    e. Should host 192.168.0.145 be able to ping host 192.168.0.131? Why or why not?

6. Assume:

   Host #1 IP Address: 208.17.16.165

   Host #2 IP Address: 208.17.16.185

   Subnet mask: 255.255.255.224

   Default gateway: 208.17.16.160

    a. Can host #1 ping (or communicate with) host #2?

    b. Host #2 cannot ping the DNS at 208.17.16.34. Why not?

    c. If the preceding statement is true, can host #1 reach the DNS?

    d. What single change will fix the problem in b?

7. What feature recaptures the subnets lost under the RFC?

    a. VLSM

    b. CIDR

    c. Supernetting

    d. IP Zero-subnet

8. What are the three private address ranges?

    a.

    b.

    c.

9. How many Class C networks are contained in the supernet address 201.1.16 /22?

    a. two

    b. four

    c. six

    d. eight

    e. What are the Class C networks?

10. Look at the following illustration. Assume that you have the Class C network 216.1.1.0 to work with, and you need to create the subnets shown. Assume that you are in a classful network with the IP Zero-subnet feature on.

    a. How many host addresses are in each subnet?

    b. What will be the subnet mask and the prefix mask?

c. Using the last three subnets, assign IP addresses to the router and hosts.

d. Label each subnet with the network address.

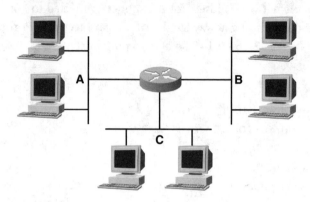

Answers

1. **a.** Number of valid subnets: $2^3 - 2 = 6$
   b. Number of hosts: $2^5 - 2 = 30$
   c. Subnet address: 192.168.1.96
   d. Default gateway: 192.168.1.97
      Increment: 32 (256 − 224), or third bit value from the conversion table.
      Subnets: 0, 32, 64, 96, 128, 160, 192, 224

2. **a.** Number of subnets: 64
   b. Number of hosts: 2
   c. Subnet address: 192.168.2.40
   d. Default gateway: 192.168.2.41

3. Yes

4. No. Gateway is the subnet address.

5. **a.** The network address for the subnet on port #1: 192.168.0.96
   b. The network address for the subnet on port #2: 192.168.0.128
   c. The network address for the subnet on port #3: 192.168.0.160
   d. The default gateway for the subnet on port #3: 192.168.0.161. Trick question.
   e. Host 192.168.0.145 should be able to ping host 192.168.0.131, assuming their default gateways are set properly, to the router port address. Router A will then connect the two subnets.

6. **a.** Both host #1 and #2 are in the same subnet (208.17.16.160). Therefore, they should both be able to ping each other.

   b. & c. Neither can ping out of the subnet because the default gateway is mistakenly set to the subnet network address, not a valid node address.

   d. Change the default gateway of both machines to 208.17.16.161.

7. **d.** IP Zero-subnet

8. **a.** 10.0.0.0, b. 172.16.0.0–172.31.0.0, c. 192.168.0.0

9. **b.** 4, **e.** 201.1.16 to 201.1.19

10. **a.** 62 hosts maximum, b. 255.255.255.192, or /26

    c. & d. See the following illustration for a solution. Although the last octet of each octet may vary, the network addresses should be the same (they can be assigned to A, B, and C in any order).

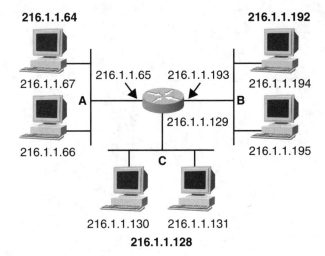

10

LAN Design

This chapter will:

- **Look at the hierarchical model for building scalable networks**

- **Look at design issues such as server placement, intranets, and segmenting**

- **Describe how to determine the various network requirements**

- **Work with the network design from the perspective of the bottom three OSI layers**

W̲e previously looked at the components and technologies that will become a part of the *local area network* (LAN) environment. In this chapter, we look at what steps we need to consider in designing a basic LAN. The remainder of the book introduces information about switching and *wide area network* (WAN) technologies that also needs to be considered in the final output.

For our purposes now, we are going to concentrate on pulling together the knowledge we have to create a basic LAN. In Chapter 21, we will revisit this topic and look at how WAN technologies can be incorporated into the design. A few of the topics in this chapter are repeated in Chapter 21, because they apply equally to the LAN and WAN design process.

Critical to ensuring a responsive and stable network is a network design that can change and grow with the organization, often in directions we can't even imagine today. This chapter provides an overview of the basic LAN design process.

LAN Design

A LAN is a collection of computing devices connected together to share resources. Typically, a LAN is a single geographical location that includes all computer resources for a small company, or just the resources of a single department, building, or floor within a larger organization.

Internetworking is the connection of two or more LANs to function somewhat as a single network. In addition to LANs and WANs, there is a growing number of *metropolitan area networks (MANs)* and campus networks, each with its own characteristics, strengths, and weaknesses. While our concern in this chapter is the LAN, it is crucial that our design will allow for growth to a larger entity or the assimilation of our LAN by another organization.

Even the smallest company can have WAN connections to support telecommuters, those employees who perform a portion of their work at home and connect to the Internet to access industry, vendor, and customer resources. Employee connections to the LAN may include, for example, telecommuters, sales representatives checking on inventory, a project leader downloading blueprints or a materials list at the job site, or management personnel wanting to track company activities from home or while on the road. By definition, WAN communication occurs between geographically separated areas. Routers, sometimes called *access routers,* provide the connection between the WAN links and the local network. These routers select the best path if more than one exists and they open any "on-demand" links as needed when working with ISDN and analog modem connections.

The network design must attempt to strike a balance between minimizing cost and maximizing bandwidth. Even if a company is not growing, the demand for increased bandwidth is escalating. To understand why, we must recognize that we are no longer dealing just with traditional data. Businesses of all sizes are moving toward including many of the following technologies, all of which use the same network as their data:

- Voice-over-IP for local and/or long-distance communication
- Video conferencing and collaborative work processes
- Client/server applications internally and with customers
- Multicasts for training and internal/external communications
- High-definition imaging for industries ranging from health care to publishing
- Telemetry to monitor critical processes and procedures
- Telecommuting employees working at home or in the field
- Various forms of e-commerce increasing the number of Internets and intranets

Many of these technologies also incorporate the use of the Internet as an alternative to the private and more traditional methods of connectivity. This blend of technologies, however, brings new concerns about, and new ways of securing, our data as well as our networks.

The increasing use of these technologies will mean that network administrators are going to be called on to provide ever-increasing levels of support for the following:

- **Greater overall bandwidth**   Provides enough network bandwidth to deal with any contingency.

- **Bandwidth on demand**   Technologies like Frame Relay where additional bandwidth can be made available on an as-needed basis at somewhat lower cost than trying to provide enough bandwidth to meet every contingency at all times.

- **Quality of Service (QoS)**   A standard for measuring performance of a transmission system that reflects its transmission quality, reliability, and service availability.

- **Class of Service (CoS)**   A prioritization system that includes a field within the Layer 2 header of an IP datagram that indicates how the datagram should be handled. A related feature is Type of Service (TOS), which is a series of bits in the Layer 3 header indicating how the packet should be handled.

NOTE: The implementation of features like QoS, CoS, and bandwidth on demand is the subject of other Cisco certifications, such as the CCNP Advanced Routing and Remote Access exams.

To be scalable, a network must be able to grow as the organization's requirements change with a minimum of disruption and loss of resources. The job of network administrators becomes one of trying to maximize requirements such as reliability, accessibility, and scalability while managing cost. Although a fully meshed network may provide high levels of reliability, it often cannot be expanded without considerable reconfiguration and resulting reductions in service. Carefully designing the LAN can reduce problems associated with a growing network. To design reliable, scalable LANs, network designers must keep in mind that each included technology has specific design requirements and limitations.

A network that is well designed, implemented, funded, and maintained should be able to grow, and contract, as quickly as needed to meet the changing requirements of the organization. The alternative is increased network congestion, which occurs when too much traffic exists for the available bandwidth. This is always inefficient, and in the worst case, it can mean a complete collapse in the data network and considerable losses in revenue, reputation, and future growth for the organization.

Design Goals

There is more to designing a network than just connecting computers together. The designer must realize that each major component and technology of the network presents unique problems and opportunities. The first step is to establish the goals of the design. The actual goals and objectives will vary somewhat from organization to organization, but the following are several universal goals common to most network design projects:

- **Functionality**   Does the network work? Can the users do their jobs? The network must provide acceptable and reliable connectivity to the organizational resources that users need.

- **Manageability**   Can the network be monitored and managed conveniently and efficiently by network professionals? If routine monitoring and maintenance is not convenient, it tends to be skipped.

- **Scalability**   Can the network expand and contract with changes within the organization? The original design should be able to adjust without having to be redesigned.

Different sizes and types of organizations will apply different weights to each of these goals, but generally each will be a part of the mix.

Network Scalability Requirements

Five requirements must be met in designing networks at all levels to ensure scalability in the future. The nature of the business and possibly its level of development will require assigning different levels of importance to each network. With some businesses, a loss of network resources (reliability) for a day would be an inconvenience, whereas with others, it could be a financial catastrophe from which recovery might be difficult.

These are the five key requirements to meet in designing networks:

- Reliability and availability

- Responsiveness

- Efficiency

- Adaptability

- Accessibility and security

Reliability and Availability

The reliability and availability requirement refers to the network's availability to users 365 days per year, around the clock, as advertised. Each business has to determine how important reliability is to it. Business size is not always a good predictor. A one-person ticket agency is out of business during the time its computer is offline.

The reliability and availability requirement is even more important for WAN connections between organization locations. Reduced reliability at this level will impact many users and significant portions of the network. It could mean that a manufacturing location cannot receive orders or design changes from other branches, thereby impacting overall company performance.

Responsiveness

Latency is a source of frustration for all users. The greater the latency, the greater the level of frustration. This is particularly true in time-sensitive transactions, such as stock purchases. As an example, although not exactly the same thing, remember the feeling the last time your credit card transaction was slow because the card reader couldn't connect to the host? The key is to strike a balance between QoS requirements and responding to user needs.

With today's switched 100-Mbps networks, typically the LAN connections and devices are *not* the bottleneck with regard to slow application performance. Most of the time, it is application design and server utilization that cause performance problems.

Efficiency

Designing a network to efficiently allocate resources often involves restricting unnecessary traffic to preserve bandwidth for the necessary traffic. Access lists and other technologies can be used to reduce the number and complexity of routing updates and other forms of broadcast traffic. At the extreme, entire types of services can be denied to preserve bandwidth. I recently worked at a site in Africa where 85 users had to share a single 64K ISDN connection to the Internet. Any reduction in efficiency literally meant total loss of service to everyone.

Adaptability

In addition to integrating different network technologies, protocols, and legacy systems, we must create an environment that can incorporate technologies that may be unknown today. Although we cannot always predict with great accuracy the course a network will take over the next few years, we should plan for many likely scenarios.

Beyond that, we need to incorporate a design and devices that increase our chances of responding to the unknown. By following accepted standards to devices and applications that support interoperability, we hedge our bets.

Accessibility and Security

A properly designed network must have capabilities to support the industry-standard WAN technologies efficiently and with a reliable level of security. As companies open their networks to remote users using dial-up services and to the two-way exposure of connecting to the Internet, it becomes increasingly important to be able to secure company resources.

The preceding five requirements represent the standard to which any network design must be held. While organizations will weight them differently, they must still be considered.

Hierarchical Network Model

Cisco recommends a three-layer hierarchical model to define the data distribution process. It maintains that even the largest networks can be reduced to these three layers. In some cases, this three-layer model can be applied at different levels within the network. The local network can use the three-layer model, which taken together becomes part of one layer in the enterprise network. The hierarchical model includes the following layers:

- Core layer
- Distribution layer
- Access layer

If properly implemented, this model allows for orderly address assignment, efficient transmission of data, increased scalability, and more structured device configuration. It simplifies device management and configuration because devices in the same layer perform the same tasks.

To understand the model, one must recognize that each layer represents a point in the network where a Layer 3 boundary occurs. This is where a router, Layer 3 switch, or other device separates the network into broadcast domains. An example of the three-layer model is shown in Figure 10-1.

The hierarchical design allows for modularity in network design, which allows for easier replication as the network grows. This same modularity can make it easier to implement phased software and hardware upgrades. The Layer 3 boundaries create transition points in the network and help to contain and identify failure points.

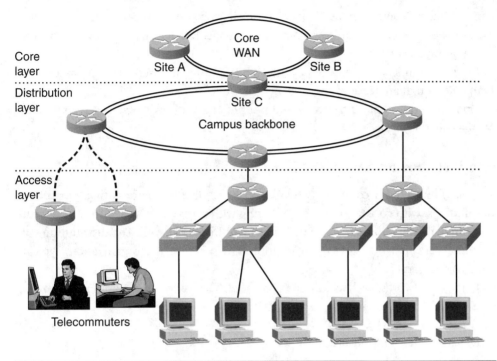

Figure 10-1   The Cisco three-layer hierarchical model

The hierarchical design works for smaller and medium-sized networks or even larger networks residing in several single-building locations. The growth of campus networks has actually pushed this entire three-layer model down into the MAN, where the core is actually the building-to-building connections, and the distribution layer is the in-building backbone. The building-to-building connections increasingly are incorporating switched devices such as ATM and other high-speed systems.

One of the drawbacks in describing these structures is that the organizations at both size extremes tend to make their own rules.

The Core Layer

The core layer represents the site-to-site WAN connections in a corporate or enterprise network. As such, it represents critical links that, if lost, would mean entire sites would be cut off from the rest of the organization. Therefore, at this layer, reliability and performance are most important. Although redundant links would be appropriate at this layer, filtering (ACLs) should be done at lower levels so that the core layer can concentrate exclusively on fast delivery. Load sharing and rapid convergence of routing protocols are also important design considerations. Efficient use of bandwidth in the core is always a concern.

Core WAN links are typically point-to-point and include services such as T1/T3 or Frame Relay that are leased from a service provider.

Good network design practice would not put end stations (such as servers) directly on the core backbone.

The Distribution Layer

The distribution layer connects network segments, possibly representing departments or buildings, with core layer services. Filtering with access lists is used to control traffic and implement QoS and CoS prioritization within the network. The distribution layer provides core network services to multiple LANs within the organization, typically using Fast Ethernet.

In larger networks, such as campus networks, this layer often includes the following:

- Address or area aggregation
- Departmental/building access
- Broadcast/multicast domain definition
- Virtual LAN (VLAN) routing
- Media transitions (such as fiber to copper)
- Internet and remote user access to the network
- Security for outside access (Internet/remote users)

Improved performance of Layer 2 and Layer 3 switches, as well as developing VLAN technologies, is pushing switches up into the distribution layer.

The distribution layer would include the campus backbone with all of its connecting routers and Layer 3 devices. The distribution layer can be summarized as the layer that provides policy-based connectivity, meaning that the routers are configured to allow only designated traffic on the campus backbone. Remember that in the larger campus networks, the core is the campus backbone and the distribution layer is the building backbone.

Good network design practice would not put end stations (such as servers) directly on the backbone. This allows the backbone to act as a high-speed path for traffic between workgroups or campus-wide servers.

The Access Layer

The workgroups and end users connect to the network in the access layer. The access layer is typically one or more LANs (Ethernet or Token Ring) providing users with access to network services. Filtering could be through the use of access lists or MAC layer filtering with bridges and switches. In smaller, noncampus networks, remote sites or users may connect at this layer, and then require the increased security of technologies such as user authentication and firewalls. The access layer is where almost all hosts are attached to the network, including servers of all kinds and user workstations.

In smaller, noncampus environments, the access layer can technically provide remote access to the corporate network for telecommuters via wide-area technology, such as Frame Relay, ISDN, or modem connections. Since these connections to telecommuters generally use router-to-router connections for the WAN and Internet, it's more likely to be a WAN distribution layer, rather than a LAN access layer.

Redundant Links

Each layer in the three-layer model should link only to the layer above or below it. Any links between devices in the same layer will compromise the hierarchical design and may make future expansion more difficult. An example of redundant links between layers is shown in Figure 10-2.

Smaller Networks

The three-layer model represents an enterprise-type network very well. However, not all environments require a full three-layer hierarchy, particularly in the early development stages of an organization. Smaller networks might use a one- or two-layer model until they

Figure 10-2
Redundant links
between layers

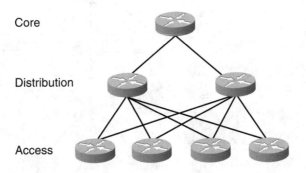

Core

Distribution

Access

grow or are assimilated by another organization. For this reason, the model should be considered in plans for even new startups, to avoid the inefficiency and disruptions that could occur during periods of rapid network growth or when the network is being assimilated into another, larger system. An example of the single-layer model is shown in Figure 10-3.

Figure 10-3 shows a small company with two types of remote users, including telecommuters, those people working at home, accessing the company through the Internet as they might with DSL or cable modem service. These users have high bandwidth access, but it comes at the cost of opening the network to the Internet. The dial-in users, who could be the sales or support staff using their laptops from various locations, such as client facilities or hotels, could dial directly into the company if the company supports the service. By the same token, they could access an Internet service and come through the same Internet access as the telecommuters. Company concerns about support, security, cost, and so forth could all impact the final decision regarding which way to go. While the company doesn't have multiple locations, these remote users put them in the WAN business.

Benefits of the Hierarchical Model

The benefits to using a hierarchical model include these:

- **Ease of implementation**   The modular nature of the hierarchical design and the clearly defined functionality of each layer make implementation and future expansion easier.

Figure 10-3
A single-layer
network model

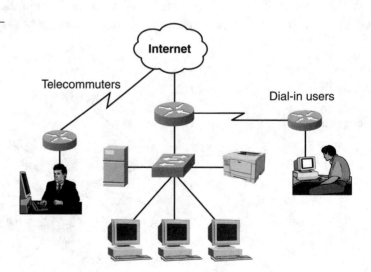

- **Ease of troubleshooting** The structure of the individual layers and their defined functionality make it easier to isolate problems.

- **Scalability** The modular nature of the hierarchical design allows the network to grow and, if necessary, contract as the business evolves.

- **Predictability** When change occurs in one layer, the structure of the functional layers makes the impact on other layers quite predictable. This helps to make capacity planning easier.

- **Protocol support** The modular nature of the hierarchical design facilitates supporting different protocols and even specialty applications within portions of the network or, if necessary, throughout the entire network.

- **Manageability** The structure of the hierarchical model, itself being like an organization chart, supports layering of network management. This allows departmental or workgroup administration of certain functions while also allowing higher-level control and monitoring.

LAN Design Issues

In the past few years, LANs have evolved from hub-based networks to the higher-bandwidth switch-based environments. Most recently, higher-bandwidth technologies like 100-Mbps switches, VLANs (see Chapter 16), and even Asynchronous Transfer Mode (ATM) switches are becoming a part of LAN architectures. To support scalability and the evolution of these faster high-speed technologies within the LAN, network designers need to address the following critical issues:

- Server function and placement
- Intranets
- Ethernet contention and congestion
- Segmentation
- Bandwidth versus broadcast domains

We will look at each of these issues in this section.

Server Function and Placement

Network servers provide the vast majority of network services and resources, which include user authentication; network security; remote network access; file sharing; printer and fax sharing; distributed databases and applications; communications services such as e-mail; and basic applications such as word processing, spreadsheets, and presentation programs. These servers typically run network operating systems such as Windows 2000/NT, NetWare, UNIX, and Linux.

The size, purpose, and resources of the organization determine whether a server performs a single function or multiple functions. In the smallest of networks, a single Windows 2000/NT server could provide all services and, in a stretch, might even double as a workstation. As the organization grows, the servers multiply into specialty devices and move into more secure placement, such as in a main data facility (MDF) or intermediate data facility (IDF) with climate control, restricted access, redundant power supplies, and support personnel. At the largest end of the spectrum, multiple servers may share the same task. One of my clients has 18 e-mail servers handling just one of its plant locations.

Servers can be divided into two categories: enterprise servers and workgroup servers. Enterprise servers support all the network users with services such as user authentication, network security, remote network access, e-mail, DHCP, WINS, DNS, and intranets. These services could include distributed databases and applications if most of the users need to access those services.

Workgroup servers, sometimes called departmental servers, support specific identifiable groups of users with services such as print sharing, file sharing, specialty databases, and applications. The engineering drawing database or purchasing database may be a workgroup service in many organizations, but may be an enterprise service in other organizations, depending on the percentage of users that needs to regularly access the resources. Just because a service is on a workgroup server does not necessarily preclude other users from accessing it, but, as we will soon see, if too many others are accessing it, maybe it should be moved to reduce outside traffic and possibly congestion within the workgroup.

Enterprise servers should be placed in the distribution layer of the hierarchical model and in the MDF within the building. By doing it this way, traffic to the enterprise servers has to travel only to the distribution layer and does not need to be transmitted into other network segments, which generates unnecessary congestion in those segments. Figure 10-4 shows the placement of an enterprise server (B) in the distribution layer and a workgroup server (A) in the access layer. If the enterprise server had been placed at A, then all enterprise traffic from Building A, and even the telecommuters, would travel down into and out of the network segment shown, creating additional congestion for the members of that segment.

Workgroup servers should be placed in the access layer as close to the end users as possible. That way, traffic to and from that workgroup server stays in the workgroup. Figure 10-4 shows that user 1, in Building A, can still access workgroup server A or

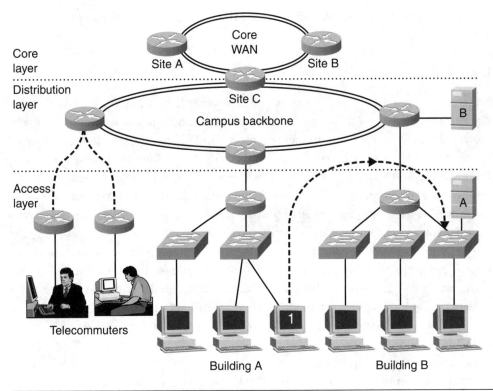

Figure 10-4 Placement of enterprise and workgroup servers

enterprise server B in Building B. If Building A and B users each need regular access to server A, then serious thought should be given to moving up with B in the distribution layer. One guide that is still used is that if 80 percent of the access to the server comes from one department or workgroup, then the server should be placed as close as possible to that department or workgroup. Keep in mind that this probably does not mean physically placing the server in among the users, but instead refers to connecting the server to the network at the same switch as the workgroup users.

In larger enterprise networks, there is an additional layer that we haven't spoken about. This is the enterprise server farm layer, which is generally Layer-3-connected to the core Layer 3 devices. In this model, all enterprise servers go there often in a mesh to ensure reliability. Departmental servers go into the distribution layer, where policy can be enforced. Given today's lightning-fast routers and switches, most companies find that keeping all of the departmental servers grouped together makes life easier than bridging VLANs all over the place just to have the servers live on the same switch/VLAN as the users.

Intranets

An increasing number of organizations are maintaining intranets as a source of information to employees. An intranet uses the same technologies as and may look very much like the company's Internet service, except, unlike the Internet sites, the intranet is only available to those users who can authenticate onto the corporate network. The Internet is typically open to the world, without a need for anything beyond a Web browser. The third type of Web exposure is the extranet that is open to inside users and those outside users who have been given user IDs and passwords. Typically, this group includes customers, vendors, and consultant-partners.

The target audience for an intranet may be the entire company, as in the case where benefit programs, employee forms, company-wide communications, and so on are delivered via Web browsers. By the same token, the target audience may be a workgroup or department if the content is intended for an identifiable subset of the employees.

If intranet Web servers are intended for the entire company, or a significant percentage of the employees, they should be placed at the distribution layer (B in Figure 10-4). If the target audience can be localized to a workgroup or department, then placement with the workgroup servers (A in Figure 10-4) would reduce backbone traffic.

Adding an intranet to a LAN is bound to increase the bandwidth requirements and potential for congestion-related problems within an existing network. Increasing backbone bandwidth and moving away from shared bandwidth devices (hubs) to switches will help. Depending on the amount of expected interaction with the intranet, extranet, and Internet desktop hosts should be upgraded to 10/100-Mbps NICs. The reality is that all hosts on any network typically have 10/100 NICs today.

Ethernet Contention and Congestion

Ethernet, by definition, is a contention system. All network devices are in contention for available openings on the media. Similarly, collisions that occur when the transmissions of multiple hosts collide are a normal part of Ethernet. While normal, collisions do lead to inefficient use of bandwidth, because the packets that collide are discarded and need to be retransmitted. It only makes sense that the higher the number of collisions, the greater the number of retransmissions, and therefore the less bandwidth available for transmitting new data. This can often lead to true available bandwidth usage of 35 to 50 percent on 10-Mbps Ethernet networks. Congestion is the point where network traffic approaches or exceeds network capacity.

Intuitively, the greater the number of hosts on a LAN, the greater the volume of traffic, the greater the number of collisions and retransmissions, and therefore the greater the network congestion. Not so intuitive, possibly, is the impact of your choices of network operating system (NOS), network applications, routing protocols, and server advertisements that use broadcasts to perform their functions. This contention and the resulting congestion relative to growth is Ethernet's Achilles' tendon when it comes to scalability.

In the Ethernet environment, congestion is reduced by segmenting the network by using bridges, switches, or routers to preserve bandwidth. Again, the preceding discussion is somewhat theoretical because so many LANs today are switched, using full-duplex, which provides a separate path for data in each direction. This means that, by definition, there are no collisions.

Segmenting Collision/Bandwidth Domains

In an Ethernet network, all devices on a shared media are part of a single collision domain insofar as simultaneous transmissions from any devices will collide. Similarly, they share the available bandwidth domain, meaning that a 10-Mbps segment with ten hosts effectively has 1 Mbps per host. The collision domain and bandwidth domain, while defined using different terms, refer to the same group of devices in an Ethernet network. *Segmentation* is the process of splitting a single collision, or bandwidth, domain into two or more domains using Layer 2 devices, resulting in more available bandwidth for individual stations. Figure 10-5 shows a simple LAN for a building on two floors. In the upper diagram, both floors are part of a single collision, or bandwidth, domain. The hubs broadcast traffic from each host so that every other host sees it.

In the upper diagram, assuming all devices are 10 Mbps, there are eight hosts sharing 10 Mbps; therefore, each host has available 10/8 or 1.25 Mbps. I know this is a very simple example, but the mathematics will translate to similar networks with dozens or hundreds of users per floor.

In the lower diagram, the bridge between the floors creates two collision domains by containing local traffic to each floor while still allowing users on each floor to access resources (server services) on the other floor. The result is that there should be less traffic on each floor, which translates to fewer hosts sharing the bandwidth on each segment, resulting in more bandwidth per host, less potential for congestion, and hopefully fewer overall collisions. The impact on bandwidth is that each floor's four hosts now split 10 Mbps, resulting in 2.5 Mbps available to each host (10/4 = 2.5).

Figure 10-6 shows using a single switch on the first floor to segment the network. The result for the second floor is the same as with the bridge insofar as all devices are still

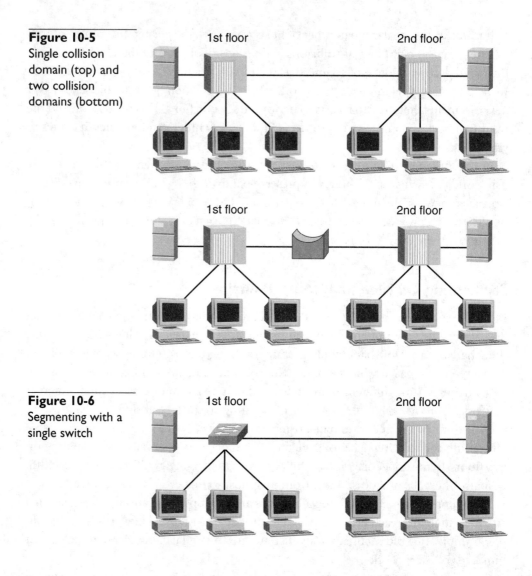

Figure 10-5
Single collision
domain (top) and
two collision
domains (bottom)

Figure 10-6
Segmenting with a
single switch

in a single collision domain. The first floor has been microsegmented so that each host is now in its own collision domain. The bandwidth implications are that each of the second-floor hosts still has 2.5 Mbps of available bandwidth ($10/4 = 2.5$), whereas each of the first-floor hosts has the full 10 Mbps available to it.

We have changed the collision/bandwidth domains using bridges or switches, but since both forward broadcast (FF-FF-FF-FF-FF) packets and unknown destination addresses each of our three diagrams is still a single broadcast domain. Since many of our network congestion sources are broadcasts (ARP, DHCP, some routing updates, Novell SAP, and so forth), segmenting with bridges or switches can only have limited impact.

Segmenting Broadcast Domains

All broadcasts from any host in a broadcast domain are visible to all other hosts in that broadcast domain. Broadcasts cannot be completely and arbitrarily eliminated, because many network processes (ARP, DHCP, user authentication, and so forth) rely on broadcasts to establish connectivity. While the scalability of a collision (bandwidth) domain depends on the total of all traffic, the scalability of a broadcast domain depends on only the broadcast traffic. Keep in mind that whereas bridges and switches forward broadcast traffic, routers typically do not. Figure 10-7 shows our two network diagrams with a router segmenting the floors into two broadcast domains.

In the upper diagram, we now have two broadcast domains and two collision/bandwidth domains with each host receiving 2.5 (10/4) Mbps of available bandwidth. The impact on the collision/bandwidth domains is the same as the earlier bridge example. In the lower diagram, collision/bandwidth domains remain the same, but now there are two separate broadcast domains.

Figure 10-7
Using a router to split a broadcast domain

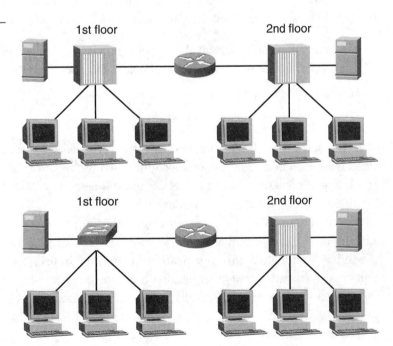

Other implications from Figure 10-7 include the following:

- There will now be different network addresses for each floor. Whether separate networks or two subnets, they must be different for the router to function. Two possible examples: the first floor's address is 192.168.1.0 /24 and the second floor's address is 192.168.2.0 /24; or the first floor's address is 192.168.1.0 /25 and the second floor's address is 192.168.2.128 /25. In all the other examples, both floors had to be in the same network or subnet.

- Each of the two floors has adequate resources, such as user authentication, DHCP, ARP, WINS, and so forth, to be able to function independently. Any process that requires broadcasts to complete or initiate will now be blocked at the router. An ip helper address command is available that can be configured on the router LAN interfaces to get around this problem, at least for those processes that are crucial for host startup processes. These solutions need to be addressed at the design phase. What you do not want is broadcast forwarding enabled on the router.

Gathering and Analyzing Requirements

For any network design project to succeed and meet the requirements of the organization and the users, it must follow a series of steps, including the following:

1. Gather information about the organizational and user requirements, including expectations for the new network. Review and document the current network.

2. Analyze the requirements.

3. Design and document the network.

In this section, we look at the first two items. The design and documentation functions will be addressed in the next section. Much of this information will be revisited in Chapter 22 when we look at WAN design. While the details and the end result will be different, the process is very similar.

In designing a LAN, it is necessary to gather information about the business structure, processes, and current technology. It is also necessary to gather information about the industry and where this organization fits into the industry. A "cutting edge" company may have very different requirements than a "market following" organization.

It is important to determine which employees and consultants (if any) will be working with you to design the network. What are their backgrounds? Where do they fit within the organization?

Much of business, technology, and organizational data can be gathered through interviews, focus groups, and surveys. While it is important to get management's view of the current situation and the expectations of the new system, it is equally important to get the views of the end users. Quite often, users and management have two very different views of how things are done and how they need to be done. An important component of the information-gathering phase is assessing the user requirements and expectations. A design that fails to furnish prompt and accurate information to end users in a form they can use is doomed.

When gathering user information, document their perceptions of the current system response time, reliability, and throughput. Try to determine volume and load patterns for WAN-dependent activities. If some aspect of an activity seems unusual, try to determine why it is currently done that way. Have they tried alternatives?

Every organization will tell you that reliability is important, but perceptions of reliability vary from organization to organization. Organizations providing financial services, securities sales, and emergency services require a high level of reliability. Determining the impact of downtime will be critical in justifying levels of redundancy that are higher than other organizations might require. While in many cases the impact might be measurable in dollars for some organizations, for a 911 system it could be the potential results of losing contact with police or fire resources.

Customer Requirements

To design a network that meets the customer's requirements, it is important to accurately understand its environment. This means knowing its business requirements, technical requirements, and organizational requirements (any limitations the organization might place on any project).

Business Requirements

This requirement looks only at the organization's business model to determine a solution, without great concern for the technological specifics of the implementation. A solution may be a technological marvel, but if it provides no business advantage over the current system, then it could be argued the expenditures are wasted. These are the questions to be answered here:

- Does the design benefit the company's business model?
- Does the design benefit or hinder the company's way of doing business?
- Does the design provide a competitive advantage, and if so, which costs are reduced and by how much?

- Is the business monitored, or audited, by others, and if so, has that been planned in?
- Does the design scale consistently with the organization's expected growth? This should be both a short- and long-term determination and should at least consider exceptional growth or decline.

Technical Requirements

Technical requirements include understanding the current technologies in use, the company's willingness to change, and the expected or current technologies that might be better. If a company is heavily invested in T1 lines and has long-term agreements in place, it may be less likely to consider a complete changeover but might consider alternatives for new links. The technical requirements fall into four categories:

- Performance requirements
- Application requirements
- Network management requirements
- Security requirements

The following questions will enable you to determine each of the four requirements for the organization. The results can then be weighted and used in developing the ultimate WAN design.

Performance Requirements

Are there any current network latency issues that need to be documented? Are current response times acceptable? How will the planned changes impact these issues? What are the requirements for WAN connection reliability? What will be the results of dropped links?

Application Requirements

Which centralized applications are currently used on the network? Who needs access to these applications and where are these users located? What new applications are being implemented with the new design or in the near future?

When the applications have been identified, determine the traffic patterns expected for each and the bandwidth requirements. In determining the traffic patterns, try to identify peak loads per day, per week, per month, and so forth. A high-bandwidth application that runs during the night won't have the same impact as one that runs during normal business hours.

Network Management Requirements

What network management systems are currently in place? How is the organization utilizing these systems? Will there be additional requirements when the project is done? Does the organization currently have the base-level skills? Will training or hiring be required?

Security Requirements

How is network security currently handled? Will there be additional exposure as a result of the new design? How will the additional security and related training be handled?

Organizational Requirements

The organizational requirements determine the organizational constraints, which can be identified through questions like these:

- Who has bought into this project? Is it supported high enough in the organization to make sure that resources and attention will be committed?
- Is there an existing budget, and if so, is it reasonable for what needs to be done?
- Who must approve of changes or budget increases?
- Is there an existing timeline for the project? Is the timeline reasonable? Is it dependent on business cycles, and if so, what are the implications of schedules sliding?

The first step in the LAN design process is to understand the business, technical, and organizational requirements for the project. The final design must "fit" within the various requirements and be acceptable to the organization.

Document the Current Network

An evaluation of the existing equipment must be made. How are these resources currently linked and shared? Will these resources be replaced or reused somewhere in the new design? Can the resources to be retained support the short- and long-term expectations for new services and features?

You should make sure you understand performance issues of any existing network. If possible, current network performance should be measured and documented. These performance indicators should try to identify or predict the average and peak requirements over time. There are many software tools available that can identify traffic patterns and volumes of different types of data. Some can be used to take current patterns and volumes and extrapolate the impact of various levels of increases.

Analyze Information

After gathering the various requirements and current inventory analysis, it is necessary to analyze the results to diagram company data flows, identify shared resources both in and out of the organization, identify which users access those resources, and identify current and planned WAN connections.

Before you can start the design, you must clearly identify which data and which processes are mission-critical. Mission-critical data and processes are those that are crucial to the day-to-day operations of the business. Whether a process or operation is mission-critical depends on the organization. Whereas the loss of the Internet connection to some companies may mean only that some employees have to play Solitaire to fill their day, at other companies, it may mean that orders can't be placed or tracked with vendors, customer support calls can't be handled, and so on.

Another component of the analysis phase is assessing the user requirements and expectations. A design that fails to furnish prompt and accurate information to end users in a form they can use is doomed.

Determining the Network Design

After analyzing all of the different requirements for the network and incorporating such factors as the current network, it is time to develop a LAN topology that will meet or exceed the various requirements. In many cases, the existing technologies and organizational constraints will limit the choices.

The CCNA exam and this book focus on Ethernet (CSMA/CD) technologies because they are the most frequently used today. The combination of Ethernet, Fast Ethernet, and Gigabit Ethernet offer the high-bandwidth opportunities to incorporate future technologies. We will continue to focus on Ethernet in this section, including the use of the star topology and extended star topology. If the client has invested heavily in Token Ring and is resistant to change, that would lead to other decisions.

One way of approaching the final LAN topology design is to break our task into three categories reflecting the bottom three layers of the OSI reference model. In addition to being a logical approach to the problem, it allows us to try to tie back in with our discussions of those layers in Chapters 1-5. Clearly, we do not have enough information to come up with a complete design that includes specific device models, routing protocols,

WAN technologies, and so on, but this process can give us a summary of where we are at this point. That summary also becomes a common point of reference for us to move on to the second half of the book, where the missing information will be addressed.

In this section, we will look at the network layer, the data link layer, and the physical layer components of our design.

Layer 1: Physical Layer

Since Layer 1 issues cause most network problems, the choice of physical cabling is probably one of the most important long-term decisions when designing a network. If a mistake is made in specifying a switch or server, it can be rectified by replacing the component, often with little or no downtime for users. If the wiring infrastructure is designed inadequately, or if the media is physically abused during installation, a reliability or low-bandwidth problem could be created that would not be so easy to resolve. In many cases, the wiring is "in the walls," placed there when the walls were open. Debugging problems and replacing major sections can be time-consuming, disruptive for users, and expensive. Furthermore, if a server, switch, or router has to be replaced because of deficient specifications, the device removed may still find a place in the network even if only as a "spare." But the bad wiring and the labor to replace it go only to the expenditures journal.

TIA/EIA Standards

The Telecommunications Industry Association and Electronic Industries Association (TIA/EIA) jointly has been the primary developer of standards for cabling and cabling installation. While TIA/EIA maintains several different standards, the two we are most concerned about here are the TIA/EIA-568 and TIA/EIA-569 standards. The elements of a cabling system are listed next with the related standard:

- Horizontal Cabling (568)
- Backbone Cabling (568)
- Work Area (568)
- Telecommunications Closet (569)
- Equipment Room (569)
- Entrance Facilities (569)

Network designs typically consist of fiber-optic cable in the backbone and between floors, with Category 5 UTP cable in the horizontal runs. The design and installation should conform to TIA/EIA-568 and TIA/EIA-569 standards. With the cost of replacement and the longer-term nature of cabling, it would be wise to consider selecting a contractor that can certify the circuits. While the upfront cost is higher, it typically comes with a manufacturer warranty that covers the cost of any circuit failures.

In conforming to standards, it is critical to comply with the distance limitations for each media and make sure that all components conform to the same standard. Putting Category 3 (16 Mbps) connectors on Category 5 (100 Mbps) cable creates a Category 3 network. This is not a factor that you can choose to ignore; many 10/100-Mbps interfaces test the circuit, and if they find anything less than Category 5, they will only function at 10 Mbps.

A worse situation is that, oftentimes, the devices will negotiate to 100 Mbps, not detecting the Cat 3 components, and then generate all kinds of errors. If the runs are Cat 3 or Cat 4, the administrator must lock down the switch interfaces to 10 Mbps so that this last situation cannot occur.

A complete cable audit of any existing circuits should be considered on projects that will be adding to existing infrastructure.

Other considerations, when it comes to wiring, include the following:

- Circuits running through air circulation spaces (plenum) must conform to state and national fire codes. Typically, this involves using plenum-rated cable.

- Circuits running between floors must conform to state and national fire codes. Typically, this involves using riser-rated cable.

- Many states and communities require licensing of cable installers at a level similar to that of electricians. In some communities, if the contractor or its employees are not licensed or bonded, the tenant assumes all liability. Know the appropriate regulations.

- Check the lease. If the space is rented, many leases include clauses that prevent the tenant from adding any network cabling without explicit written permission from the property management. In some cases, they will only grant that permission if their "people" do the work. I've seen leases that specify that only fiber-optic cable can be used in cabling between floors.

TIA/EIA-568-A vs. TIA/EIA-568-B Standards

The actual international standard for interior cabling is TIA/EIA-568-A. Like all standards in the industry, compliance is voluntary. Category 5 cable is made up of four pairs of color-coded wire. The TIA/EIA-568-A standard specifies which two pairs will be the transmit and receive pairs. Unfortunately, the two pairs selected by the standard are inconsistent with a very large installed base of network systems in the U.S. The TIA/EIA-568-B standard represents this group of systems.

TIA/EIA has been the primary developer of standards for cabling. It designates twisted-pair cables using categories beginning with Category 1, which is voice-grade (telephone) wire. The following table summarizes the categories as they are today.

TIA/EIA CATEGORY	MAXIMUM TRANSMISSION
Category 3	16 Mbps
Category 4	20 Mbps
Category 5	100 Mbps
Category 6*	250 Mbps
Category 7*	1 Gbps

*Categories 6 and 7 are still in review and technically could change as this is being written.

The way that this impacts you is that you must know which standard your patch panels (cross connects) and wall jacks use, and they must be consistent. Jumper cables, hubs, switches, and routers are not involved. Only the facility cabling is involved, and as long as both ends of the circuit use the same standard, there is no problem, but mixing the two standards cannot work.

Twisted-Pair Cable

There are two types of twisted-pair cable: shielded twisted-pair (STP) and unshielded twisted-pair (UTP). By far, the most common usage is UTP. STP has added a layer of metal shielding around the pairs, under the jacket, to fight the effects of *electromagnetic interference* (EMI) and *radio frequency interference* (RFI). This almost doubles the cost and makes the cable a little stiffer and therefore a little more difficult to work with. In many cases, if the EMI and RFI are high enough to be a concern, you should be considering using fiber-optic cable, which is immune to these attacks.

Fiber-Optic Cable

Fiber-optic cable is a very pure glass strand running through a denser glass tube called *cladding*. That cladding is encased in a PVC or Teflon jacket much like copper.

Fiber always requires at least two strands, one for each direction. It is typically bundled into cables that contain 12 to 48 separate fiber strands, meaning that a single cable may actually be carrying six to 24 pairs of fiber. In some cases, the extra strands are called *dark fibers*, referring to the fact that they are not currently being used, and hence are dark. In the LAN, these extra circuits are set aside for the future and generally are much less expensive to install than to have a contractor return in the future.

The following table summarizes some of the more common cable designations:

NAME	BANDWIDTH	MAXIMUM DISTANCE	MEDIA TYPE
10BaseT	10 Mbps	100 meters	Twisted-pair copper
100BaseT	100 Mbps	100 meters	Twisted-pair copper
100BaseFX	100 Mbps	2,000 meters	Multimode fiber-optic
100BaseFX	100 Mbps	10,000 meters	Single-mode fiber-optic
1000BaseCX	1 Gbps	25 meters	Gigabit copper MDF/IDF
1000BaseT	1 Gbps	100 meters	Cat 5 using four pairs

There are many gigabit media standards evolving, such as 1000Base-LX, 1000Base-SX, 1000Base-ZX, and 1000Base-LH. Note that the distances may change with the gigabit bandwidth as the standards are developed.

MDFs, IDFs, HCCs, VCCs, and POP

A *main data facility* (MDF) is the main data/wiring closet for a building. While its size and contents will vary based on the size of the organization and complexity of the network, in small to medium-sized organizations, it is where you are most likely to find the enterprise servers; major network devices such as routers, switches, and hubs; and possibly any network management stations. In a multifloor building, the MDF can be located on any floor. The MDF is usually climate controlled and secured from intrusion and mischief. Particularly in large organizations and campus networks, the actual MDF only houses cabling, not servers and switches. Those are kept in separate computer rooms.

In the case of a multifloor building, there will usually be an intermediate data facility (IDF) that contains the end connections to the workstation cabling. These connections are called *horizontal cross-connects* (HCCs), which usually consist of one or more rack-mounted patch panels. The IDF will be connected to the MDF via cabling called *vertical cabling*, or backbone cabling, which is often fiber-optic, but can be copper UTP if within distance limitations. Another rack-mounted panel, called a *vertical cross-connect* (VCC), terminates the vertical cabling. Figure 10-8 shows a four-floor building with an IDF on each floor. The MDF displayed to the left of the building would actually be incorporated on one of the floors, making that the MDF and the other three IDFs.

Figure 10-8
Four-floor building
with MDF and IDFs

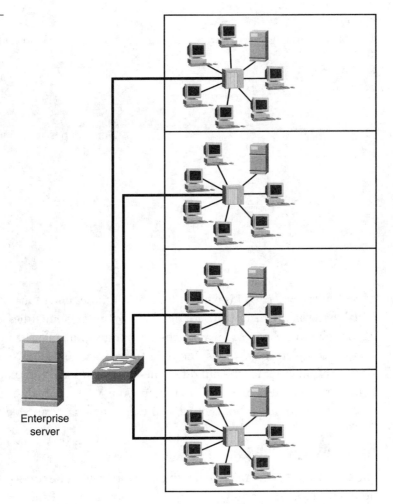

Enterprise
server

If a building is large enough that all users on a floor cannot be serviced by the MDF because of cable distance limitations (100 meters for Category 5 copper), then an IDF can be used to extend the reach. The cabling between the MDF and IDF is still referred to as "vertical" and the termination at both ends terminate at VCCs.

In addition to housing the ends of vertical and horizontal cabling runs, IDFs also contain the workgroup switches, hubs, and, in larger installations, routers. The larger the organization, the more likely you are to find workgroup servers in the IDF. Obviously, the more devices, the more security and climate control that will need to be provided. Figure 10-9 shows conceptually how the IDF connects the MDF, any workgroup servers, and the workstations.

Figure 10-9
IDF concept with MDF and workstation connection

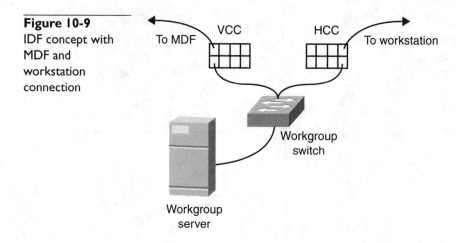

Point of presence (POP) is where the various utilities enter the building. This is often called the *demarc*, which stands for demarcation point. Sometimes, this is referred to as the phone room, because for years the telephone companies had this room to themselves to complete their voice communication circuits. Often, this is the entry point for electricity and water for the building. These two items and the general lack of security in these rooms is reason enough to not put your MDF, or anything else, there. A run of cable can run your telephone and data presence to a more suitable MDF location.

Horizontal Cabling

The TIA/EIA-568 standard specifies that network devices be connected to a central location with horizontal cabling. Figure 10-10 shows a simplistic view of a single-switch network using Category 5 cabling with a 100-meter maximum distance.

The reality is that the TIA/EIA-568 standard is a little more specific than this diagram as to how the 100 meters must be allocated. Figure 10-11 shows the allocation of the 100 meters in what is called the horizontal run. At one end is the user workstation, which is connected via a workstation cable (jumper cable) to a data-circuit wall jack. The wall jack is directly wired to a patch panel (HCC) in an MDF. The appropriate LAN switch or hub is connected to the HCC via a patch cable.

Some companies run fiber-optic cable to the desktop, in which case the horizontal distance is adjusted to match the media.

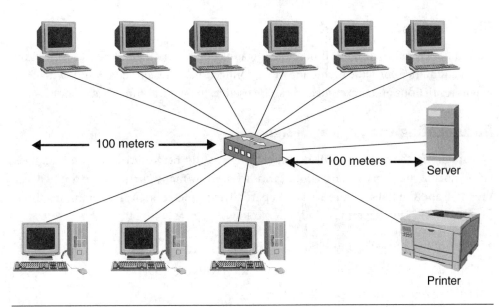

Figure 10-10   Simple single-switch network

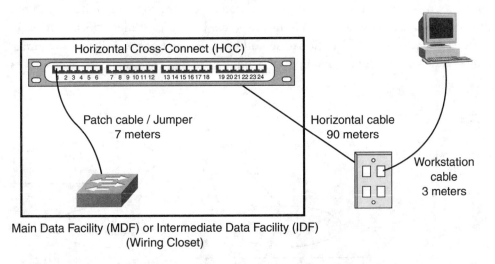

Figure 10-11   Horizontal cabling components

Gigabit Copper Ethernet

Currently, because of distance limitations, gigabit copper is used almost exclusively in the MDFs and IDFs to provide high-bandwidth connections between servers and switches. If length restrictions aren't exceeded, it can be used in the vertical runs (backbone).

Documenting the Logical Design

Documenting the network will become critical as the network evolves and changes. Good documentation can save a lot of trips to see how many circuits were run between the MDF and the IDFs. Figure 10-12 is a partially completed logical diagram of a three-floor network. The diagram includes the following:

- Locations of the MDF and IDFs

- Cabling "specs" used to interconnect the IDFs with the MDF

- Detailed documentation of all cable runs

Layer 2: Data Link Layer

For the purposes of our discussion in this chapter, LAN switches are limited to Layer 2 devices and therefore usually reside in the access layer of our hierarchical model. In Chapter 16, you will see additional capabilities, such as Layer 3 switches and *virtual LANs* (VLANs), that will expand upon the foundation that we create here. Figure 10-13

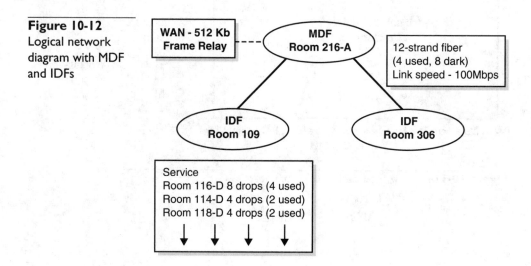

Figure 10-12
Logical network diagram with MDF and IDFs

WAN - 512 Kb
Frame Relay

MDF
Room 216-A

12-strand fiber
(4 used, 8 dark)
Link speed - 100Mbps

IDF
Room 109

IDF
Room 306

Service
Room 116-D 8 drops (4 used)
Room 114-D 4 drops (2 used)
Room 118-D 4 drops (2 used)

shows various implementations of switches in the access layer. The distribution layer shows a use for LAN switches connecting a group of servers to the router.

The primary purpose of Layer 2 bridges and LAN switches in the network is to segment the network to reduce congestion and preserve bandwidth. As we saw earlier in this chapter, both bridges and switches determine the size of collision and bandwidth domains, but in this section, we concentrate on LAN switches, reflecting their dominance of use in the market. We will look at issues to consider when implementing switches.

Asymmetric Switching

There are two types of switching: symmetric and asymmetric. A symmetric switch is one with all interfaces supporting the same bandwidth. Asymmetric switching involves being able to configure different bandwidths to each interface based on the purpose of connection. This allows using 100-Mbps interfaces for connections to servers, uplinks,

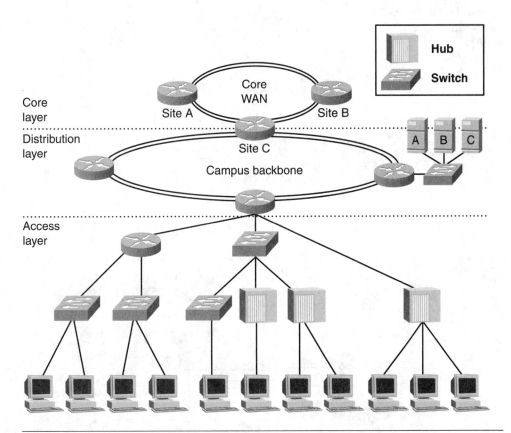

Figure 10-13   LAN with switch locations in distribution and access layers

vertical cabling, or even specific workstations requiring the extra capacity, while delivering 10 Mbps to regular users. Figure 10-14 shows a simple example in which 100-Mbps connections are configured to the server and to the uplink connection to another switch. The users are each allocated a 10-Mbps connection.

Bandwidth Impacts—Hubs vs. Switches

We discussed earlier that shared media, or Layer 1, devices such as hubs share the available bandwidth, whereas switches are able to deliver the full bandwidth to each host. When deciding between hubs and switches, it is important to understand the impact of shared bandwidth. The following figure and discussion will demonstrate why this is such an important issue. Figure 10-15 shows a four-floor structure with a hub or switch on each floor serving various sizes of workgroups.

Figure 10-14
Asymmetric switch
in LAN

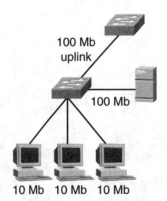

Figure 10-15
Four-floor network
with hubs

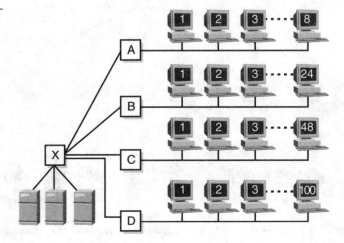

For our purposes, assume that device X is a switch providing 10 Mbps of bandwidth to each floor and that the devices A, B, C, and D are the 10-Mbps hubs. The following information summarizes the bandwidth available to each user on each floor:

HUB	NUMBER OF HOSTS	BANDWIDTH (MBPS/HOST)	FORMULA	COLLISION DOMAIN
A	8	1.25 Mbps	10/8	8 hosts
B	24	0.417 Mbps	10/24	24 hosts
C	48	0.208 Mbps	10/48	48 hosts
D	100	0.1 Mbps	10/100	100 hosts

If the switch and all hubs were 100-Mbps units, the results would get only slightly better, particularly as the number of interfaces (ports) increases. The following information summarizes the results for 100 Mbps:

HUB	NUMBER OF HOSTS	BANDWIDTH (MBPS/HOST)	FORMULA	COLLISION DOMAIN
A	8	12.5 Mbps	100/8	8 hosts
B	24	04.17 Mbps	100/24	24 hosts
C	48	02.08 Mbps	100/48	48 hosts
D	100	1.0 Mbps	100/100	100 hosts

In fairness, depending on the applications, these results might be entirely adequate, particularly in the near term. For perspective, a T1 connection is only 1.54-Mbps, so at the 100-user level, each user would get the equivalent of 2/3 of a T1. To really know whether it is a good deal financially, we would need to compare the cost of 100-Mbps hubs with 10-Mbps switches, which would deliver a full 10 Mbps to each user. I would speculate that you might do this last set of calculations if you already had the 100-Mbps hubs and were trying to determine whether to use them or scrap them. It would be hard to justify buying hubs in today's environment if bandwidth is one of the critical requirements.

Where the picture for hubs gets really ugly is if device X is also a hub. The following results assume that all devices are 10-Mbps hubs. Therefore, hub X is splitting bandwidth seven ways for a total of 1.43 Mbps to each port.

HUB	NUMBER OF HOSTS	BANDWIDTH (MBPS/HOST)	FORMULA	COLLISION DOMAIN
A	8	0.179 Mbps	1.43/8	180 hosts
B	24	0.060 Mbps	1.43/24	180 hosts
C	48	0.030 Mbps	1.43/48	180 hosts
D	100	0.014 Mbps	1.43/100	180 hosts

It should be obvious that even if you decide to keep hubs in the network, it would be best to keep them as close to the users as possible. A hub in the backbone can have a devastating impact on bandwidth. Even more important, all 180 users are now in the same collision domain competing for access to the media.

While switches are becoming common network devices, there are still many all-hub networks being used. If you are ever called upon to analyze a similar network and offer suggestions, it should be obvious that a single switch replacing hub X would have far greater impact than any upgrades that could be done at A, B, C, or D. Just replacing a hub with a switch may not yield the highest possible gain, if it replaces the wrong hub. Not understanding how switches work and the bandwidth-sharing characteristic of hubs has lead many companies to place the new switches close to the users. Unfortunately, by that point, there is little bandwidth left to preserve.

Cable Runs and Drops

The area served by an MDF or IDF is referred to as a *catchment area*. To determine the number of "cable drops" and device ports, we need to look at the floor and user requirements. It is important to understand the difference between the immediate requirements and "planned" requirements. While developing the design, we may know that the immediate requirements for a group of 20 offices in our catchment area is two 10-Mbps drops (circuits). We would probably opt to install Category 5e or the current highest standard for horizontal runs, anticipating that future requirements will exceed 10 Mbps. In many cases, this will be a relatively insignificant cost increase. With the explosion of digital devices, we would probably include more circuits (drops) than immediately required. We will put four drops in each office.

It is not a requirement of the CCNA exam, but we would probably be doing the voice drops at the same time, so we might schedule six Category 5e drops—four for data and two for voice. By using Category 5e throughout, we can change the ratio of data to voice at any time. We could choose to use one of our drops to support two phone circuits if we run short of voice circuits. When voice-over-IP becomes the norm, our telephone and data will come in on the same circuit.

To calculate the drops, we multiply 20 offices by 4 drops for a total of 80 circuits that need to be installed. Each will be finished off at the wall plate and on the punch panel in the wiring closet (MDF/IDF). Each end will be labeled and recorded in a log called a *cut sheet.*

Here is where we need to be careful. We need 80 circuits for future expansion, but we probably only need 40 switch (or hub) ports with an acceptable number of extras. This means that we also need to update our log to indicate which circuits are live and which are spares. It only takes a jumper and a switch port to make any jack live. So why not just order enough switches to make every port live? It would all depend on the expectations for growth within the organization. If the ports will be necessary in a year or so, then making every port live may not be a bad idea. But, if the growth is normal, the switches can be acquired as needed. The advantage is that switch prices on a per-port basis are declining quickly. At the same time, the standard has moved from 10 Mbps to 10/100 autosensing interfaces. By waiting, it is very likely that higher technology will be available for less money.

Vertical Runs

When working with an IDF, it is necessary to calculate the number of cable runs required from the MDF to the IDF, as well as the number of ports on the switch that will be needed for connecting to these vertical runs. With 10/100-Mbps asymmetrical switches and plans to provide 10-Mbps connections to the workstations, you would want to use 100-Mbps connections for the vertical runs. If you are going to have 40 live 10-Mbps circuits, that is 400 Mbps of potential draw on the system. You might want to consider connecting four 100-Mbps vertical circuits immediately, although the actual number would vary based on expectations about the users' network activities.

If 12 fiber strands connect the MDF and IDF, you would use eight to create four circuits (one fiber each in both directions). That would leave two circuits for future expansion.

Layer 3: Network Layer

Layer 3 devices, such as routers, are used to create separate LAN segments while still allowing communication between segments using Layer 3 addressing. In Figure 10-16, the hierarchical model uses routers at the transition point between the distribution and access layers to provide broadcast segmentation within the access layer. Routers also provide the connection to WAN links connecting one location of a business to another, or simply to provide an Internet connection.

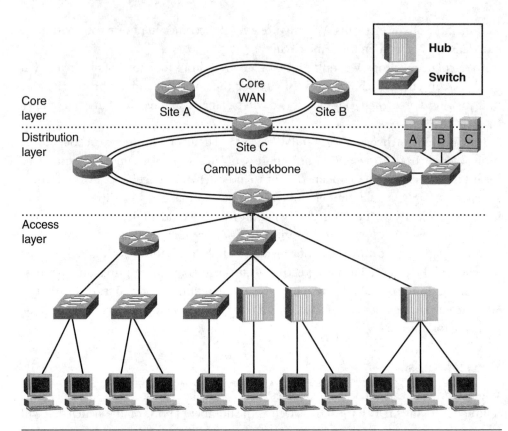

Figure 10-16 Layer 3 device placement throughout the network

The distribution layer router created three separate broadcast domains. The two on the right were then connected to the users with either switch or hub connections. The one on the left went to an access layer router that created two more broadcast domains. There is no reason that we couldn't have additional router layers within the access layer, except that advances in switching technologies, the drop in switch prices, and VLANs are all working together to move switches into broader roles. We will cover VLANs in Chapter 16.

Routers Within the Hierarchy

Following the model provides a topology with three distinct layers and distinct functionality for the routers in each layer. Layer 3 switching devices are becoming a consideration throughout the model. The routers in each layer provide the following functions:

- Core layer routers are responsible for site-to-site connectivity and must therefore be optimized for availability and reliability. Loss of service at this layer can be catastrophic. Maintaining connectivity of LAN and WAN circuits at this layer is critical.

- Distribution layer routers must implement QoS requirements through policy-based traffic control. Preserving bandwidth and maintaining network security need to be considerations at this level.

- Access layer routers, while not as common in today's switched networks as before, keep workgroup or departmental traffic from getting into upper layers. Routers at this level often need to manage access of dial-up users.

Logical and Physical Network Maps

After developing the IP addressing scheme, document it to include network addresses and site locations. You could add addresses of key devices such as servers, WAN connections, and so forth. The physical map helps to troubleshoot the network. Figure 10-17 shows a very simple form of a network map.

Summary

In this chapter, we saw how important having a good scalable network design from the very beginning is to facilitating growth and change. A poor design can lead to inability to meet the user and organizational needs and could lead to expensive down time.

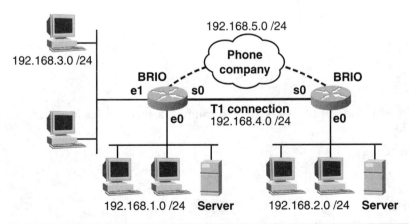

Figure 10-17 Network map with IP addressing

The requirements for scalability are reliability and availability, responsiveness, efficiency, adaptability, and accessibility and security.

Network design issues include server function and placement, intranets, Ethernet contention and congestion, segmentation, and bandwidth versus broadcast domains.

The design process includes the following: gathering and analyzing requirements, documenting and interpreting current data traffic patterns, projecting future requirements, and defining the Layer 1, 2, and 3 devices, along with the LAN and WAN topology.

To assist with future expansions and troubleshooting, be sure to document the physical and logical network.

Practice Questions

Take a few moments and check your grasp of the concepts covered in this chapter. The answers are immediately following the questions.

Questions

1. What are the three layers of the hierarchical model?
   a.
   b.
   c.

2. Which two TIA/EIA standards need to be followed in developing the Layer 1 aspects of your design and implementation?
   a. 658
   b. 566
   c. 568
   d. 569
   e. 596

3. According to the standards, what is the maximum transmission distance for Category 5 cable?
   a. 90 meters
   b. 90 feet
   c. 100 feet
   d. 100 meters

4. What does each of the following acronyms stand for?
   a. MDF
   b. IDF
   c. POP
   d. HCC
   e. VCC

5. Of the three layers of the hierarchical model, which one contains the bulk of the LAN technology?
   a. Core
   b. Distribution
   c. Redundant
   d. Access

6. The cabling that runs between the MDF and any IDFs is called what?
   a. Horizontal run
   b. Elliptical run
   c. Vertical run
   d. Horizontal cross-connect

7. What type of cable does Cisco recommend for the vertical runs of a network?
   a. Category 5
   b. Coaxial
   c. Fiber-optic
   d. UTP

8. In which layer of the hierarchical model would you expect to find workgroup servers?
   a. Core
   b. Distribution
   c. Access
   d. Support

9. If you have a network with a single 10-Mbps, 24-port hub, what is the available bandwidth per user?
   a. 0.417 Mbps
   b. 0.0417 Mbps
   c. 4.17 Mbps
   d. 10 Mbps

10. If you have a network with a single 10-Mbps, 24-port switch, what is the available bandwidth per user?
    a. 0.417 Mbps
    b. 0.0417 Mbps
    c. 4.17 Mbps
    d. 10 Mbps

Answers

1. The three layers of the hierarchical model are the core, distribution, and access layers.

2. **c.** and **d.** You must follow the 568 and 569 TIA/EIA standards in developing the Layer 1 aspects of your design and implementation.

3. **d.** For Category 5 cable, 100 meters is the maximum data run.

4. The acronyms represent the main data facility (MDF), intermediate data facility (IDF), point of presence (POP), horizontal cross-connect (HCC), and vertical cross-connect (VCC).

5. **d.** The access layer is were most LAN technology is.

6. **c.** The vertical run connects the MDF and IDF.

7. **c.** Fiber-optic cable is Cisco's preference. Each of the others could be used if necessary.

8. **c.** You would usually find workgroup servers in the access layer.

9. **a.** The available bandwidth per user on a network with a single 10-Mbps, 24-port hub is 0.417 Mbps (10 Mbps/24 ports = 0.417).

10. **d.** The available bandwidth per user on a network with a single 10-Mbps, 24-port switch is 10 Mbps.

Elements of Routing

This chapter will:

- **Describe the basic network layer functions of a router**

- **Identify the key pieces of information required before routing can occur**

- **Explain the differences between routed and routing protocols**

- **Discuss the nature of dynamic, static, and default routing**

- **Compare and contrast distance-vector, link-state, and hybrid routing protocols**

- **Identify the key elements of a routing table**

- **Describe how packets are forwarded through a routed domain**

This chapter presents a high-level overview of basic routing concepts, including routing requirements, methods of routing, and routing protocols. In this chapter, you will be introduced to the fundamental processes that a router goes through to forward packets from a source network to a destination network, and you will learn that there are various ways in which a router can learn the information required to accomplish this network layer task.

One of the ways in which a router learns the information required to route packets, called *dynamic routing,* uses routing protocols to discover the network topology, build routing tables, and communicate routing information to other routers. As you will no doubt come to realize, routing protocols are a tremendously crucial element to the successful design of most of today's data network infrastructures. A significant portion of this chapter is therefore devoted to introducing you to the fundamental characteristics of routing protocols, including their classifications, operation, and limitations. While specific routing protocols are introduced, their configuration is saved for Chapter 13.

Routing Fundamentals

What is routing? In the context of computers, routing basically is the process of determining where to forward information on a computer network. As you learned in Chapter 5, routers are the main devices responsible for determining the best path on which to forward packets of information that are destined for another computing device. To make this determination, however, a router must be capable of evaluating all possible paths to the destination and determining which of these paths is the best. This path determination function can be accomplished in a few different ways, but the most prevalent method is through the use of routing protocols, whose primary functions can be listed as follows:

• Acquire information on the network topology.

• Choose the best path to each network in the topology.

• Input information on the best paths into a routing table.

• Communicate routing information, including changes in the network topology, to other routers.

In addition to the router's path determination function, another fundamental task that it performs is *switching*. Switching is the process of taking a packet received on one interface and forwarding it out another interface based on the results of the path determination process. Switching is what physically moves the packet through the router onto the attached media. In the process of moving the packet to the outbound interface, the router does three things: rewrites the MAC address, decrements the TTL, and recomputes the FCS.

NOTE: Don't confuse this switching function with the switching that Layer 2 devices perform. While switching at both layers involves moving packets from one interface to another, Layer 2 devices use MAC addresses to determine the best path, whereas Layer 3 devices use network addresses to determine the best path.

To further learn how the network layer tasks of routing and switching occur, you must first understand how the router views network paths. This fundamental topic is introduced next.

How Addresses Represent Network Paths

For the router to be able to send a packet from one network location to another, it must have some way of being able to recognize where the packet is supposed to go. That is, the router must employ some type of addressing scheme to identify networks. This is accomplished via the packet's network layer address (see Figure 11-1).

As shown in Figure 11-1, the packet contains fields that include both a source and a destination address. These addresses are formatted in such a way that they convey two fundamental portions, namely, a network portion and a host portion. The network portion identifies the network segment on which the host device resides, whereas the host portion identifies the host device itself (see Figure 11-2).

Figure 11-1
Packets contain a
logical source and
destination address

Network
layer
packet

| Source: 3.5 | Destination: 11.2 | Data |

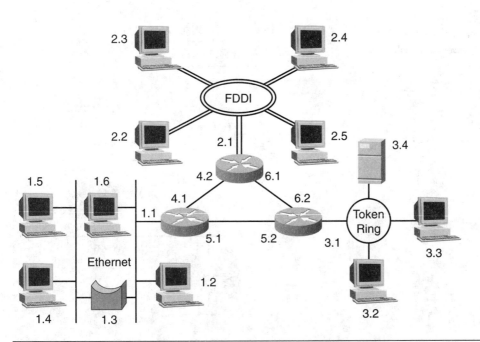

Figure 11-2 Logical addresses contain a network portion and a host portion

In Figure 11-2, for instance, there are six network segments, three of which are populated by host devices. The first number identifies the network and the second number the host. Host 2.3, for instance, resides on network 2 (which may also be referred to as 2.0) and is host number 3. Note also that the routers in this diagram are numbered with network addresses. Since the routers connect to multiple networks, they will have multiple network addresses, one for each interface.

Routers are therefore able to make their path determination based on a network layer address that contains both a network number and a host number. While the exact format for this address is a function of the network layer protocol that the packet is using (IP, IPX, AppleTalk, DECNet, and so forth), the principle to understand is that these addresses are used to get a packet from its source to its ultimate destination (see Figure 11-3).

While network layer addresses are used for getting packets from source to destination, it is important to understand that a different type of address is used to get packets from one router to the next, that is, from hop to hop. This address is called the *data link layer address*—also known as the *media access control (MAC) address* or *physical address*—and is used in conjunction with the network layer address. A data link layer address is

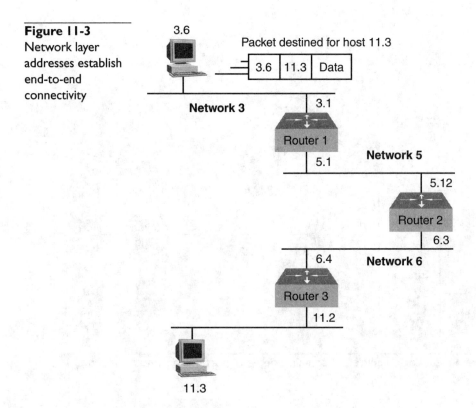

Figure 11-3
Network layer
addresses establish
end-to-end
connectivity

necessary because the source host—and intermediate routers—along a path must have a way of addressing the next-hop neighbors to which the packets are to be forwarded.

The not-so-desirable alternative is for these devices to simply just broadcast the packets toward the destination, but this would unnecessarily burden all devices along the way because they would all be forced to process the broadcasted packet. With data link layer addresses, on the other hand, the next-hop device along the path toward the destination can be explicitly addressed so that the packet can be sent directly to it without having to bother any other devices. Therefore, a physical address is used to specify the next-hop device along the path toward the destination host. Note that whereas network layer addresses remain constant throughout a packet's journey from source to destination, physical (data link layer) addresses change at each hop. This is the nature of data link layer addressing, because it allows each device along the path to specify the next hop (see Figure 11-4).

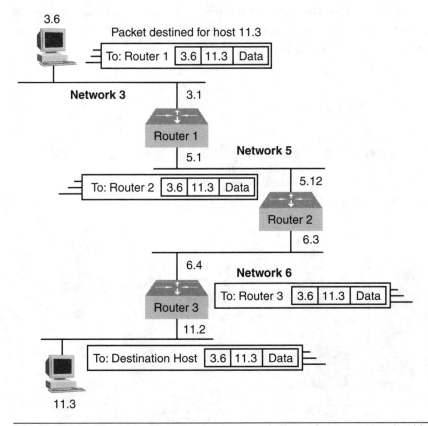

Figure 11-4 Physical addresses change at each hop, whereas network addresses remain the same from source to destination.

Routing Requirements

Now that the essential dynamics behind routing have been introduced, let's take a look at some of the specific requirements needed before routing can occur. These requirements entail having several key pieces of overhead information necessary for the router to be able to switch packets from source network to destination network. These key pieces of routing information are presented as follows:

- **Logical destination address**   The destination host is identified by a logical address (network address). The format of this address depends on the protocol suite running on the network, such as TCP/IP, IPX/SPX, AppleTalk, and so forth. Since routers are capable of supporting multiple protocol suites—a feature known as *multiprotocol routing*—they can understand multiple addressing formats (see Figure 11-5).

- **Routing information source**   Routing information includes data on how to best reach destination networks. The source of this information is typically a neighboring router. However, as will be seen in the next section, "Routing Methods," this information can be learned in a few other ways.

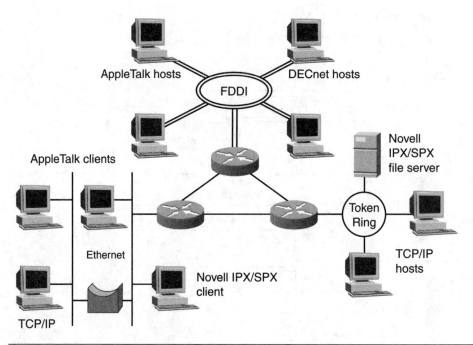

Figure 11-5   Multiprotocol network

- **Possible and best routes**   Many times, the router will have multiple ways to reach a destination. The router must in these instances choose only one route to use, the best route. In the case of routing protocols, "best" is generally defined as the route with the lowest metric. Metrics are introduced in an upcoming section, "Metrics."

- **Outbound interface**   The best path to a destination network is associated with an outbound interface on the router that will be used when forwarding to that destination. In addition, the router will have the network address of the next-hop router that can be reached out of this interface.

- **Verification of routing information**   Before packets can be routed, the router must lastly be able to verify that the routing information is valid and not outdated. If the router is not running a routing protocol, and is instead using static routing configurations, it is the network administrator's responsibility to make sure that the router's view of the network is accurate at all times, especially when topology changes occur. Static routing will be covered in an upcoming section, "Static Routing."

Expert Discussion

Understanding the Difference Between "Routed" and "Routing" Protocols

Sometimes "routing" protocols and "routed" protocols can be confused. Routing protocols learn the network topology and communicate routing information between routers, whereas routed protocols define the network layer packet formats and addressing schemes. Routing protocols are responsible for the path determination process, whereas routed protocols are responsible for being routed. Examples of routing protocols include RIP and OSPF; examples of routed protocols include IP and IPX.

While it helps to clarify the difference between the terms by comparing and contrasting their functions, it will also help, perhaps even more, to become familiar with how both types of protocols coexist and work with each other to accomplish their unique tasks. Further study of both protocols will gradually make these fundamentals intuitive to you.

Routing Methods

Because learning routing information is one of the router's most important duties, it is only natural that this device has the flexibility of being able to learn network routes in a variety of ways. One of the first ways in which a router becomes aware of a topology's networks is when the router is first configured with an *interface* network address. Being configured with an interface network address, such as an IP address (and, in this case, a subnet mask), makes a router immediately aware of its *directly connected* networks (see Figure 11-6).

In Figure 11-6, for example, the router has two attached networks that are defined when its interfaces are configured with an IP address and a subnet mask. Chapter 13 will introduce how to configure router interfaces.

In addition to learning of directly attached networks, a router is able to learn of nonattached (remote) networks. The following methods are available for learning remote networks:

- Dynamic routing

- Static routing

- Default routing

The next several sections will explore each of these learning methods in more detail.

Figure 11-6
A router discovers a directly attached network via the configuration of a network address on the network's interface

Router's interfaces configured with IP address and subnet mask

132.16.1.1
255.255.255.0

132.16.2.1
255.255.255.0

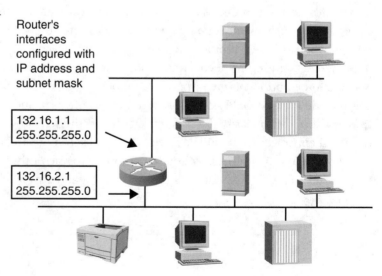

Dynamic Routing

Dynamic routing is an administratively enabled process in which routers exchange routing updates to learn of network routes and network topology changes. This dynamic process is carried out via the routing protocol, the primary responsibilities of which are to build the routing tables, determine the best paths to destination networks, communicate network information between routers, and respond automatically to topology changes (see Figure 11-7).

Routing Tables

An important element of dynamic routing (as well as static and default routing) is the routing table. It lists almost all the information necessary to forward packets from source to destination and is the routing protocol's "map" of the internetwork. The following information is listed on a per-entry basis in a router's routing table:

- **Routing information source**   If the information was learned dynamically, the source is the routing protocol.

- **Destination network address**   Either a network, subnet, or, in certain cases, a host address.

- **Administrative distance**   A measurement of the weight of the routing information source. (Administrative distance is covered in the next section.)

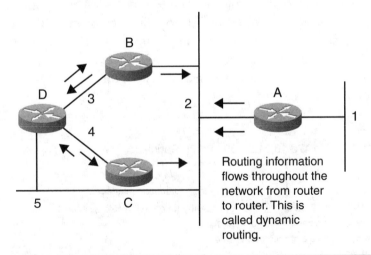

Figure 11-7   Dynamic routing involves the use of routing protocols to communicate routing information between routers.

- **Metric**   A measurement of how valuable the route is.

- **Next hop**   The logical address of the next hop along the route to the destination.

- **Age of routing information**   Indicates the amount of time the entry has been listed in the routing table.

- **Outbound interface**   The interface through which the destination can be reached. Figure 11-8 presents the format of a typical entry found within a routing table.

Administrative Distance

When routers are running multiple routing protocols at the same time, a situation occurs in which the same routing information is learned by multiple routing protocols. For example, in Figure 11-9, each router in the network is running two different routing protocols, Routing Information Protocol (RIP) and Open Shortest Path First (OSPF). Each router in this topology therefore acquires routing information from two separate and competing sources, RIP and OSPF. Running two protocols like this should be avoided in practice because of the extra overhead. It would typically occur during conversion from one protocol to another.

Now, because a router's internal logic prevents it from accepting each protocol source's best route for the same destination, the router is faced with a dilemma in which it must choose which routing protocol to accept the best route from. The answer to this dilemma is *administrative distance,* a simple numbering scheme for prioritizing IP routing protocols according to how sophisticated their metrics are. Protocols with more sophisticated or optimal metrics are preferred over routing protocols with less sophisticated or optimal metrics and are tagged with a *lower* administrative distance value. For example, RIP has an administrative distance of 120 whereas OSPF has an administrative distance of 110. Because OSPF's administrative distance is lower, a router would therefore prefer OSPF's routing information to the same routing information derived from RIP.

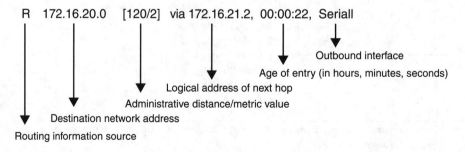

Figure 11-8   A sample routing table entry

Figure 11-9
Running multiple
routing protocols
creates a situation in
which routers learn
the same routing
information from
different sources

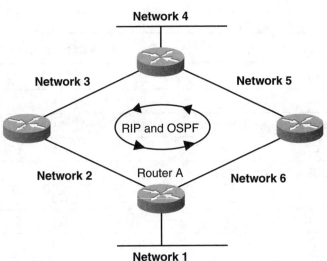

In situations where the same routing information is learned both dynamically and manually (configured), administrative distance will prefer the manually learned routes to the dynamically learned routes. The Table 11-1 presents default administrative distances for the most common sources of IP routing information.

Metrics

Routing protocols use what are known as *metrics* to determine the best route to a destination. Essentially defined as a quantifiable media characteristic, a metric is the routing protocol's criterion for evaluating just how good a given path (route) is. Typically, the path with the smallest metric value is considered the best path. The following list presents some of the more common metrics you will encounter:

NOTE: A link is equivalent to one network segment.

- **Hop count**   The number of routers that must be traversed to reach a destination. The path with the lowest hop count is preferred most.

- **Bandwidth**   The link speed (for example, 64 Kbps, 1.544 Mbps, and so forth). The path with the greatest bandwidth is preferred most.

Table 11-1 Default Administrative Distances for Common Sources of IP Routing Information

ROUTE SOURCE	DEFAULT DISTANCE
Connected interface	0
Static route	1
Enhanced IGRP summary route	5
External BGP	20
Internal Enhanced IGRP	90
IGRP	100
OSPF	110
IS-IS	115
RIP	120
EGP	140
External Enhanced IGRP	170
Internal BGP	200
Unknown	255

- **Delay** The amount of time (typically in microseconds) it takes for a packet to travel a link. The path with the least delay is preferred most.

- **Load** The amount of activity on a link. On Cisco routers, the value can typically range anywhere between 1 and 255, where 1 represents a link with the least load, and 255 a link with the most load. Paths with the smallest load are preferred most.

- **Reliability** The error rate on a link. On Cisco routers, the value can typically range anywhere between 1 and 255, with 255 representing a link with highest reliability. Paths with the greatest reliability are preferred most.

- **Ticks delay** Used by IPX RIP and represents the number of 1/18-second intervals required to forward a packet across a link. Paths with the lowest ticks delay are preferred most.

- **Maximum Transmission Unit (MTU)** The largest packet size (in bytes) allowed on a link. Paths with the highest commonly shared MTU are preferred most.

- **Cost** An administratively defined metric that typically is based on such factors as bandwidth or monetary expense. Least-cost paths are preferred most.

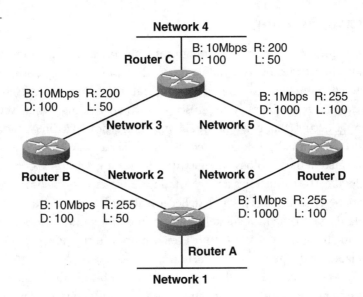

Figure 11-10
Metrics are used to calculate the best path to a destination

Network 4

Router C   B: 10Mbps   R: 200
            D: 100   L: 50

B: 10Mbps   R: 200
D: 100   L: 50

B: 1Mbps   R: 255
D: 1000   L: 100

Network 3   Network 5

Router B   Network 2   Network 6   Router D

B: 10Mbps   R: 255
D: 100   L: 50

B: 1Mbps   R: 255
D: 1000   L: 100

Router A

Network 1

To see how a routing protocol makes use of these metrics, consider the topology shown in Figure 11-10. Presented in this diagram are metric values for each link's bandwidth (B), delay (D), reliability (R), and load (L).

Assume for a moment that this internetwork is running a routing protocol, which uses only bandwidth as the criterion for selecting best paths. As a result, when Router A discovers that it has two possible paths to Network 3, it tallies up the bandwidth for each path's links and chooses the path that offers the most bandwidth. In the figure, you see that the path to Network 3 through Router B has a bandwidth of 30 Mbps, whereas the path through Router D offers only 12 Mbps. Router A would subsequently choose the path through Router B and would place this route in its routing table.

If Router A had based its path determination on, say, reliability, then it would have chosen the path to Network 3 going through Router D, since a reliability of 710 is better than a reliability of 655. And, conversely, if Router A had based its path determination on, say, delay, it would have then chosen the path through Router B, whose delay of 300 is better than Router D's delay of 2100. It is thus through adding up all the link metrics in a path and comparing the results to another path that the best path is found.

Most routing protocols calculate the best path to a destination by using only one metric. However, some routing protocols, such as Interior Gateway Routing Protocol (IGRP) and Enhanced Interior Gateway Routing Protocol (EIGRP), can use multiple metrics. To do so, the routing protocol takes a path's metric values, inputs them into a special formula, and then outputs a numeric result that is then associated with the path. Such metrics are known as *composite* metrics, and can be influenced through manual configuration.

Static Routing

While routers can employ routing protocols to learn and communicate routing information dynamically, routers also have the ability to use routing information that is entered manually by a network administrator (or, in many cases, by a specialized team of router technicians). With this approach to routing, whenever a *remote* topology change occurs (that is, a topology change that is not on a directly attached link), a router must be manually updated because there is no way the router could otherwise be informed of the topology change without running a routing protocol (see Figure 11-11).

Figure 11-11 illustrates a solely static routing environment in which one of the networks, Network 3, has just failed. Because Routers B and D are directly connected to this link, they become immediately aware of the link failure without having to be updated manually. Routers A and C, however, are not directly attached and must therefore be updated by the network administrator.

As you can imagine, with a network in which hundreds of routers are employing this routing method, the administrative burden of updating each router can be quite heavy! Which is why this feature in many cases is used *in conjunction with* dynamic routing instead of being used as a strict alternative. In fact, static routing is typically used only when it is needed to meet a certain technical requirement of the network. The following data points highlight what these requirements most often are:

• Reducing network overhead on links that connect stub networks

• Concealing networks for security purposes

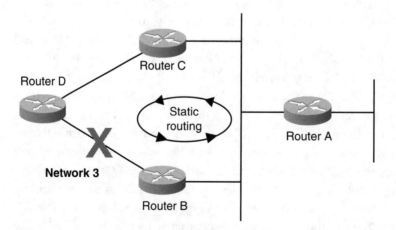

Figure 11-11 Static routing requires that routers be manually updated whenever topology changes occur

The next two sections demonstrate using static routing to meet these two require-ments.

Static Routing as a Security Solution

Sometimes a network's security policy mandates that certain network segments be kept hidden from other network segments that are running routing protocols. Consider Fig-ure 11-12, for example. In this diagram, Routers B and C are using RIP to communicate information about their directly attached networks. Router A, however, is not running a routing protocol but instead is programmed with information that lets it know of both neighboring routers' networks. Routers B and C therefore have no knowledge of Router A's Ethernet segment and consequently will not include this network in their routing updates. The Ethernet segment is hidden.

Be aware that this configuration assumes that the Ethernet hosts do not need to com-municate beyond Router A. While the Ethernet hosts can send packets out of the net-work, there will be no way for responses to come back because Routers B and C have no entries in their route tables for the Ethernet network. There are other means of hiding

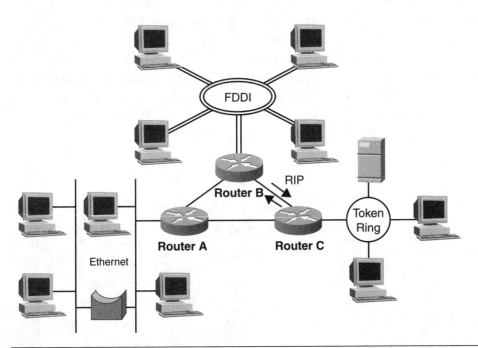

Figure 11-12   Routers B and C are unaware of Router A's Ethernet segment because Router A is using only static routing

network segments without resorting exclusively to static routing—for example, routers can employ a configuration feature called *passive interfaces*, which prevents routing updates from being sent out an interface—static routing is still a potently viable component for meeting a network's security requirements.

Static Routing as a Performance Optimization Solution

In addition to employing static routing for security purposes, this routing method can be used in instances where you have a stub network and a network performance policy that calls for minimizing the traffic that is sent to the stub network. As can be seen in Figure 11-13, a stub network is a segment that has only one connection to other networks. In the real world, these networks are typically branch offices that connect via a WAN link to corporate headquarters or to an ISP.

Using static routing on the router that connects to a stub network (in the case of Figure 11-13, Router A) and using either static routing or some other feature on the stub router's neighbor (in the case of Figure 11-13, Router B) prevents routing update traffic from crossing the link to the stub network. Since these links are most often WAN links in which available bandwidth is at a minimum, static routing offers an effective solution to reducing bandwidth consumption, by preventing potentially heavy routing protocol traffic from congesting the WAN link to the point where user traffic is dropped.

In Figure 11-14, for instance, the WAN link between Routers A and B is a 56 Kbps link. If Router B were to send routing information for hundreds or even thousands of networks to Router A, the link would likely overload, because this traffic would also have to compete with user data traffic. But if Router A were configured with static routes, and Router B were running a routing protocol that didn't send updates to Router A, the link could be saved this considerable bandwidth.

Figure 11-13
A stub network has only one connection to other networks

Network 1

Stub network

Router A

Router B

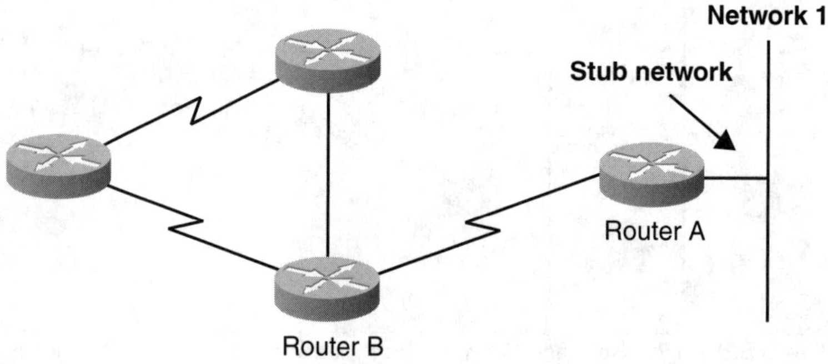

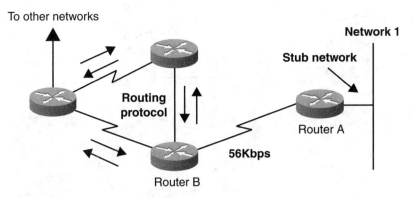

Figure 11-14 Preventing routing protocol traffic from crossing a slow-speed WAN link can prevent the link from becoming congested

While static routing is an effective means of reducing routing protocol overhead, there are also other means of accomplishing the same objective without having to sacrifice the functionality and convenience of dynamic routing. In reality, the decision to employ static routes is almost always a decision that is based on a specific technical goal and requirement for the network.

Default Routing

Default routing is another method that routers can use to determine where to forward packets. Like static routing, default routing requires that a network administrator make manual configurations. However, with default routing, instead of configuring actual networks, the administrator configures a *default route*, which is a routing table entry that specifies a network to forward any packets that have unknown destination addresses. Without a default route, when a router receives a packet that it doesn't know where to send, the router drops the packet.

For an example of how default routes can be used, consider Figure 11-15. In this scenario, Router B is configured with a default route that allows all unknown traffic it receives to be forwarded to the ISP and onto the Internet. This is an extremely useful feature because Router B would otherwise be required to maintain all Internet routes in its routing table, which is definitely not practical for a company that doesn't need to have explicit knowledge of every Internet route.

Typically, an administrator defines a default route on at least one router. The routing protocols can then be configured so that the static route is shared with other routers, thereby saving the labor of adding the route statically.

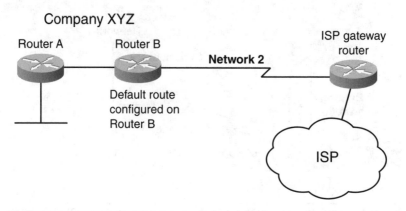

Figure 11-15 Default routes are used when the destination is not explicitly listed in the routing table

Routing Protocol Fundamentals

As mentioned earlier in this chapter, routing protocols are the elements responsible for such tasks as building the routing table and communicating routing information between routers. Upcoming sections continue that discussion by exploring the essential characteristics of routing protocols that are classified under the following three categories:

- **Distance-vector protocols**   RIP v1 and v2, IGRP, RTMP, and IPX RIP
- **Link-state protocols**   OSPF, IS-IS, and NLSP
- **Hybrid protocols**   EIGRP

Each of these categories relates essential features and functions that are shared by the majority of the traditional routing protocols within each category. The following sections explain.

Distance-Vector Protocols

Routers employing distance-vector routing algorithms (also known as Bellman-Ford algorithms) send periodic routing updates that contain complete routing tables. Upon first receiving a routing update from a distance-vector neighbor, the router examines the received routing table and places all the routes that it doesn't know about into its own routing table. At its next scheduled transmission, this new routing table is for-

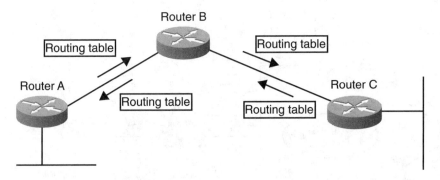

Figure 11-16 Distance-vector routers broadcast their routing tables to directly connected neighbors at periodic intervals

warded to all the router's distance-vector neighbors. These updates are transmitted
from router to router via broadcasts (see Figure 11-16).

Topology changes are handled in exactly the same way. That is, when topology
changes occur—such as when a network goes down or a new network comes online—
the router that first detects the topology change modifies its routing table and, upon its
next scheduled update, forwards the routing table to its directly connected neighbors.

Upon receiving this routing table, the neighbor routers subsequently incorporate the
new information into their own routing tables and, at the proper time, forward their
own routing tables to their respective neighbors.

When all routers have finally been notified of the topology change and are operating
with valid routing information, the network is said to have *converged*. It is thus in this
manner that distance-vector routers are informed of topology changes (see Figure 11-17).

Distance-vector protocols can choose from a variety of metrics to determine the best
path to a destination. IP RIP (versions 1 and 2), for instance, use hop count; IPX RIP
uses ticks delay (hop count is used as a backup metric); and IGRP uses a composite
metric based on bandwidth, delay, reliability, and MTU. Regardless of which metric is
used, each network listed in the distance-vector routing table is associated with a metric value (see Figure 11-18).

Figure 11-18 depicts how each router's routing table looks when a hop count metric
is used. Recall that hop count indicates the number of routers that are crossed to reach
a destination. Note that directly connected networks have a hop count of 0.

Now, when routers forward their routing tables to each other, they include the metric information so that, upon reception, the metric can simply be incremented by the
link's metric value.

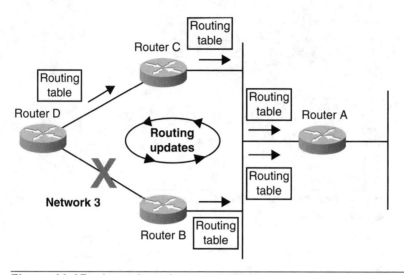

Figure 11-17 A topology change in a distance-vector environment requires routers to update each other with their complete routing tables

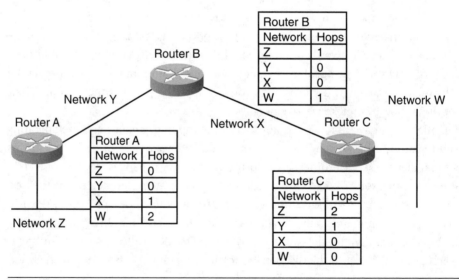

Figure 11-18 Networks are associated with metric values

In Figure 11-18, for instance, Router A advertised Network Z with a metric of 0. When Router B received this metric, it incremented it by one hop and then advertised this metric value to Router C, which incremented the hop count one more. This process of incrementing metric values is sometimes referred to as "accumulating distance vectors."

While accumulating distance vectors is a simple and efficient method of calculating best paths, it unfortunately means that a router's view of the entire network topology is not completely its own insofar as the router does not learn *first-hand* of network routes but rather has to rely upon routing information that it receives from its neighbors. Such a process of learning routing information is widely referred to as "routing by rumor."

Routing by rumor wouldn't be such a bad way of sending routing updates *if* the information contained therein could always be guaranteed to be valid *and* delivered expeditiously. However, the original nature of distance-vector operation militates against achieving both such goals, because of the following reasons:

- Routing updates are sent every 30 to 90 seconds, which means that topology changes are not immediately converged on. As described in the next section, this can lead to a problem called a *routing loop.*

- Routers accept routing information from neighbors without verifying whether the information they are receiving is accurate. As also described in the next section, this problem will lead to routing loops if not prevented.

Routing Loops in a Distance-Vector Environment

Distance-vector routing protocols were initially designed without safeguards for preventing routing loops. To see how routing loops occur in a distance-vector environment, consider Figure 11-19.

In Figure 11-19, Router A's link to Network 1 has just failed. Router A immediately removes the failed network from its routing table but has to wait until its next scheduled update before Router B can be notified. This delay in informing Router A allows Router B to send a normal routing update to Router A. Because the update contains Router B's

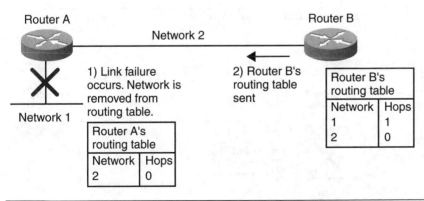

Figure 11-19   Router B's update is sent before Router A sends its topology change update

complete routing table-which contains an entry for Network 1-Router A thinks that it can now reach Network 1 through Router B. Router A's routing table is subsequently modified to include this new but incorrect information (see Figure 11-20).

What would happen if Router A were to send Router B a packet destined for Network 1? Router B would send it right back to Router A, because Router B's routing table still points to Router A as the next hop to this network. Note therefore that Router A never does send an update indicating Network 1's removal from its routing table. As a result, packets destined to Network 1 shuttle back and forth between the two routers: a situation that characterizes a routing loop (see Figure 11-21).

As the routing loop continues to exist, packets destined to Network 1 continue to be bandied back and forth. While a routing loop is in existence, an interesting side effect develops that involves the routing protocol's metric. Recall that metrics are incremented each time they are received in an update, a process that lets the router easily measure route viability from its own location. In a routing loop, however, this metric-incrementation process continues indefinitely as each router advertises the same looped network back and forth. Such a condition is commonly referred to as "counting to infinity."

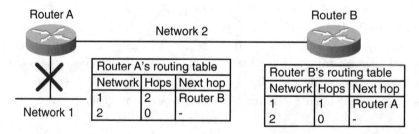

Figure 11-20   Router A believes that Network 1 is reachable through Router B

Figure 11-21
Packets are caught
in a routing loop

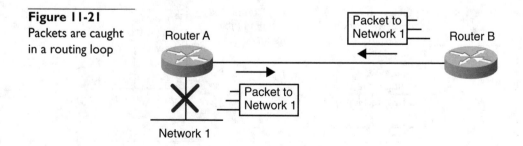

To see an example of how the counting-to-infinity problem manifests, let's go back to where we left off in our previous example, Figure 11-20. This figure shows us that Router A had just placed Network 1 back into its routing table. Note, at this point, that Network 1 is listed with a hop count of 2. Why? Because metrics for a network are incremented whenever they are received from the network's source. In our example, Router A learned of Network 1 from Router B, which had hence become the *source* for this network. Thus, when Router B advertised Network 1 with a hop count of 1, Router A proceeded to increment this hop count by one. While this was of course wrong, Router A cannot be faulted for having done this; it was simply following the rules of distance-vector operation.

When Router A next sends its routing table, Router B will likewise increment the hop count for Network 1, because, again, Router A is the source of information for Network 1, and Router B must therefore always increment the hop count whenever Router A sends an update for this network. As you can therefore see, this problem is perpetuated because each router considers the other to be the source of information for Network 1 (see Figure 11-22).

This situation characterizes the problem of counting to infinity.

So, what are the solutions to the problems of routing loops, accepting invalid routing information, and counting to infinity? Distance-vector algorithm designers have come up with several solutions:

- Defining a maximum
- Split horizon
- Poison reverse
- Hold-down timers

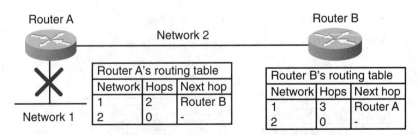

Figure 11-22 Hop counts for Network 1 continue to escalate as each router continues to update its source of information for this looped network

Defining a Maximum

Routing loops, and their concomitant side effect of counting to infinity, can be stopped at a certain point if a limit is placed on how high the metric for a looped network is allowed to increment. Once the metric limit is reached, the looped route is removed from the routing table and can't be reinstated until the route actually becomes available again. For example, if a maximum limit of 16 hop counts is set, each router involved in a routing loop is able to continue incrementing its hop count for the looped network until the number of increments reaches 16, at which point the network is removed from the routing table and advertised as unreachable.

To see how defining a maximum would apply to our previous example, consider Figure 11-23. This diagram shows that both routers have been incrementing the hop count for Network 1 for some time now, as Router A's hop count is at 14 and Router B's is at 15.

Router B is the next router to send its routing table to Router A. As usual, upon reception, Router A will increment the hop count by one. This time, however, Router A finds that incrementing the hop count of 15 will result in a maximum of 16. Router A subsequently removes Network 1 from its routing table and proceeds to update Router B with this new information at the proper time (see Figure 11-24).

Upon receiving Router A's routing table, Router B will notice that Network 1 has been removed. Router B will therefore proceed to remove this network from its own routing table. This last act finally ends the routing loop (see Figure 11-25).

NOTE: Defining a maximum is also referred to as defining "infinity." With RIP, for example, infinity is defined as 16 hops.

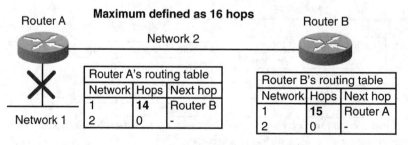

Maximum defined as 16 hops

Router A — Network 2 — Router B

Router A's routing table

Network	Hops	Next hop
1	14	Router B
2	0	-

Network 1

Router B's routing table

Network	Hops	Next hop
1	15	Router A
2	0	-

Figure 11-23   Both routers are nearing their maximum hop count of 16

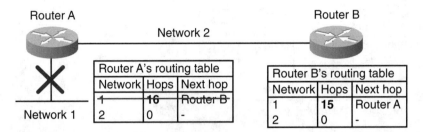

Figure 11-24   Router A's metric for Network 1 reaches its maximum

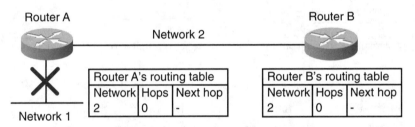

Figure 11-25   The routing loop is over once the looped network has been removed from the last routing table

Split Horizon

While defining a maximum brings an end to the problem of routing loops and counting to infinity, it does not prevent the routing loop from occurring in the first place. This is primarily due to the fact that defining a maximum is simply a damage-containment solution, as opposed to a prevention mechanism that can actually resolve the underlying issue causing the routing loop problem.

Enter split horizon.

Split horizon is a feature that prevents small routing loops by preventing routers from sending routing information back to the source from which that routing information was learned. In other words, a router will not advertise a network back to the router who told it about that network. Figure 11-26 shows how split horizon works.

This figure shows that routers employing split horizon do not advertise their neighbors' routes back to them. This means that when a router detects one of its links has failed, it won't receive an update a moment later from a neighbor indicating that the link is still reachable. Recall that routing loops initially begin when a router accepts

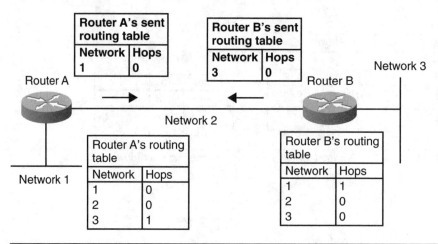

Figure 11-26 With split horizon, routing tables are sent to a neighbor without including that neighbor's routes

invalid routing information from a neighbor claiming that an unreachable network is reachable. Split horizon prevents exactly this from occurring (see Figure 11-27).

Hold-Down Timers

Although the split horizon mechanism is an effective means of preventing the occurrence of routing loops, it is not necessarily a cure-all. Consider Figure 11-28, in which

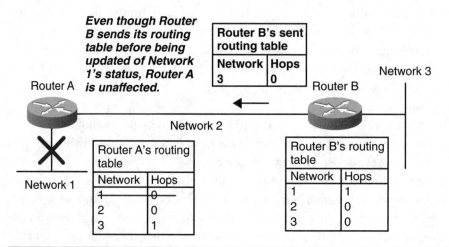

Figure 11-27 Split horizon prevents routing loops that are caused when invalid routing information is accepted

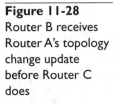

Figure 11-28
Router B receives
Router A's topology
change update
before Router C
does

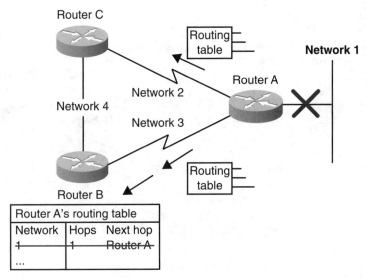

Router A's link to Network 1 has just failed. The following sequence of events outlines what occurs next:

1. Router A sends an update out to both Routers B and C. Router B receives the update and marks Network 1 as unreachable (see Figure 11-28).

2. Prior to receiving Router A's update, Router C sends out its regularly scheduled update to Routers A and B. Because split horizon is in effect, Router A is unaffected by this update. However, Router B *is* affected by this update because it now learns that Network 1 is reachable through Router C. Router B subsequently reinstates Network 1 back into its routing table, pointing to Router C as the next hop (see Figure 11-29). Router C, in the meantime, has processed Router A's update and has marked Network 1 as unreachable.

3. Router B sends an update to Routers A and C. Upon receiving the update, Router A notices that Network 1 is now reachable via Router B. Router A subsequently reinstates this network back into its routing table, pointing to Router B as the next hop (see Figure 11-30). Due to split horizon, Router C would still have Network 1 listed as unreachable. That would soon change when Router A sends out its next update indicating that Network 1 is now reachable via itself (see Figure 11-31).

A routing loop is now present in the network.

Why didn't split horizon prevent Router B from advertising Network 1 back to Router A? Because, at that point, Router A was no longer the *source* for Network 1, *Router C* was.

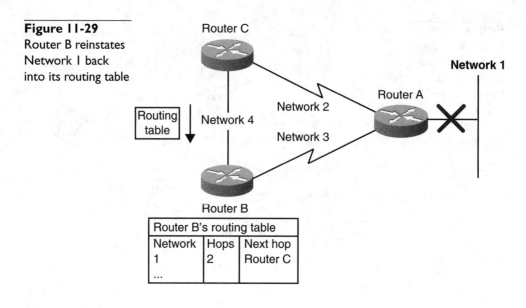

Figure 11-29
Router B reinstates
Network 1 back
into its routing table

Router C

Network 1

Router A

Network 2

Routing table

Network 4

Network 3

Router B

Router B's routing table		
Network	Hops	Next hop
1	2	Router C
...		

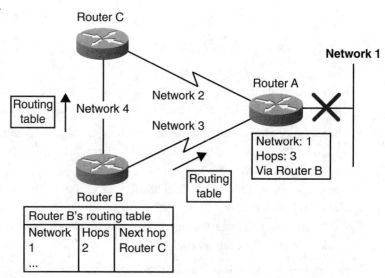

Figure 11-30
Router A rein-
states Network 1
back into its rout-
ing table

Router C

Network 1

Router A

Network 2

Routing table

Network 4

Network 3

Routing table

Network: 1
Hops: 3
Via Router B

Router B

Router B's routing table		
Network	Hops	Next hop
1	2	Router C
...		

Since split horizon only prevents information from being sent back to its source, Router B was free to advertise this network to Router A.

The problem, though, is not with split horizon. The problem is that unsynchronized convergence leads Router B to accept invalid routing information that overrides valid

Figure 11-31
Router C reinstates
Network 1 back
into its routing table

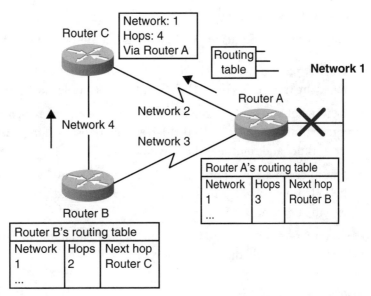

routing information. If Router B had simply rejected Router C's update indicating that Network 1 was reachable, the routing loop would never have occurred.

Enter hold-down timers. *Hold-down timers* are a feature that prevents routing loops by preventing normal routing updates from prematurely reinstating failed routes. When a router receives an update indicating a failed route, the router places a hold-down on the route for a certain period of time. This hold-down prevents the router from accepting any invalid information pertaining to the route for as long as the hold-down timer is in effect. The length of this timer is usually calculated to be just long enough for all routers in the network to be informed of the failed route.

NOTE: When the hold-down timer expires for a failed route, routers are once again susceptible to accepting misinformation pertaining to the route. This is why a network administrator will configure the hold-down timer to be long enough to allow updates for the failed route to reach the furthest routers in the network. It is also important to note that even though a route has been placed in hold-down, it will still be routed to. That is, traffic will still be sent to the network that has been placed in hold-down.

With the employment of hold-down timers in our previous example, Router B would not have accepted Router C's invalid information about Network 1. The routing loop therefore would have been prevented.

Hold-Down Timer Logic

The following data points highlight the logic behind how hold-down timers operate:

- If a routing update is received indicating that a network is inaccessible, the router marks the network as unreachable and begins a hold-down timer for it.

- If the neighbor from whom the failed network was learned reports back with an update indicating that the network has been reinstated, the router removes the hold-down timer and reinstates the network as reachable.

- If another neighbor reports with a better metric than the one originally recorded for the failed network, the hold-down timer is removed and the network is reinstated with the new, improved metric.

- If another neighbor reports with a metric worse than the one originally recorded for the failed network, the router ignores it.

Poison Reverse

The next solution to handling routing loops is a loop-prevention mechanism typically used in conjunction with hold-down timers. This solution is termed *poison reverse* or *route poisoning* and is a method of ensuring that failed routes get marked with an indicator that prevents the failed route from being improperly reinstated.

To see how route poisoning works, consider Figure 11-32. In this graphic, Router A's link to Network 1 has just failed. Instead of completely removing the route from its routing table, however, Router A proceeds to raise the route's *metric* to infinity. This signifies that the route is poisoned, or unreachable.

Figure 11-32
Route poisoning is a loop-prevention mechanism

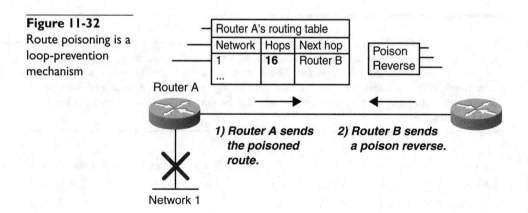

Upon receiving an update for this poisoned network from Router A, Router B will proceed to send a *poison reverse* back to Router A indicating that the network is poisoned. All this does is let Router A know that its neighbor has accepted the poisoned route. Router A is thus assured that Router B will not later be sending invalid routing information claiming that the poisoned route is reachable.

Triggered Updates (Flash Updates)

Triggered updates, also known as flash updates, are another loop-defense mechanism. However, instead of working to prevent the exchange of invalid routing information—one of the main causes of routing loops-triggered updates work by speeding up slow network convergence—one of the other main causes of routing loops. To accomplish this, triggered updates let routers inform their neighbors of a failed link without having to wait until their next scheduled update to do so. As a result, convergence is expedited and the window of opportunity for routing loops to develop is minimized substantially.

In Figure 11-33, for instance, triggered updates allow Router A to send out its routing table immediately after detecting its failed link to Network Z. Upon receiving this update, Router B likewise modifies its routing table and then sends it immediately to Router C. Convergence is consequently achieved with tremendous expediency.

Distance-Vector Protocols

With a solid understanding of the basic logic behind distance-vector algorithms, it is just a short step to understanding the unique features of each of the following distance-vector routing protocols:

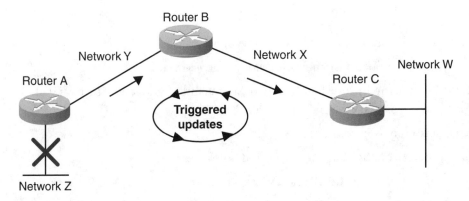

Figure 11-33   Triggered updates are sent immediately after the detection of a failed route

- Routing Information Protocol (RIP)
- Interior Gateway Routing Protocol (IGRP)

The following two sections highlight the main features of each of these two popular routing protocols.

RIP

RIP is a standard Internet routing protocol designed for small to medium-sized networks. The following data points highlight RIP's essential features:

- Sends periodic routing updates every 30 seconds.
- Sends triggered updates whenever topology changes occur.
- Uses a hop-count metric. Paths with the smallest hop count are the best.
- Defines a maximum hop count of 16. Packets are dropped if they require traversal of 16 or more hops to reach their destination.
- Allows up to 25 routes in a single routing update packet.
- Uses split horizon, hold-down timers, and poison reverse.
- Supports multiple routed protocols (versions for IP, IPX, and AppleTalk).
- Supports equal-cost load balancing.
- Comes in two versions. Version 2 supports additional features such as route authentication and Variable Length Subnet Masking (VLSM).

IGRP

IGRP is a proprietary routing protocol developed by Cisco. The following data points highlight some of IGRP's most salient features:

- Sends periodic routing updates every 90 seconds.
- Sends triggered updates whenever topology changes occur.
- Metric formula can include bandwidth, delay, reliability, and load. The path with the smallest composite metric is the best path.
- Has a maximum hop count of 255.
- Uses split horizon, hold-down timers, and poison reverse.
- Currently runs in only TCP/IP and OSI networks.
- Supports both equal cost and unequal cost load balancing.

In addition to these features, IGRP supports two types of routes in a TCP/IP environment: *interior* and *exterior*. Interior routes are routes within an autonomous system (AS), such as those shown in Figure 11-34.

Exterior routes are routes to networks outside the AS (see Figure 11-35). These routes are typically used as a gateway of last resort (a default route).

Link-State Protocols

Now that you have been introduced to some of the main features of distance-vector routing protocols, it is time to take a look at another class of routing protocol, called link-state.

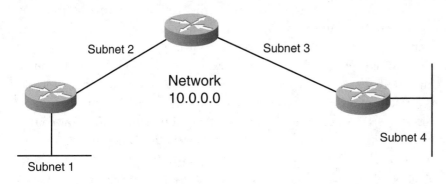

Figure 11-34 IGRP interior routes in AS

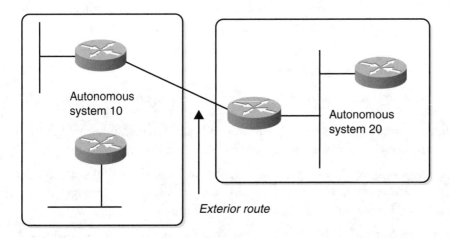

Figure 11-35 IGRP exterior routes are routes that lead outside the AS

Link-state routing algorithms, also known as *shortest path first (SPF)* algorithms, are quite unlike their distance-vector counterparts. For one, link-state routing protocols maintain not only routing tables but also comprehensive databases that contain information on how all routers in a network are interconnected. These databases, commonly referred to as *topological* or *link-state* databases, maintain not only the best routes but also all *possible* routes known of in the internetwork.

Also, link-state protocols don't send routing tables in their updates but instead send special routing updates called *link-state advertisements (LSAs)*, which are small-sized packets that link-state routers use to carry out the routing duties of discovering the network topology and informing the network of topology changes. In the event of a topology change, LSAs carry only the information that pertains to the topology change; they don't carry the routing table. Moreover, these link-state updates are quickly forwarded — "flooded" — to all routers in the known internetwork using special multicast addresses that target only routers, as opposed to using resource-intensive broadcasts that target every single network device (see Figure 11-36).

In addition, because these LSAs are flooded expeditiously to all link-state routers without being modified, each router always has a *first-hand* view of the entire network topology. As a result, many of the problems characteristic of the "routing by rumor" method of distance-vector routing algorithms (such as routing loops and slow convergence) are not a significant issue with link-state. However, this is not to say that link-state protocols don't have significant issues of their own, because, as you will soon learn, link-state protocols do in fact have certain performance issues that sometimes pose quite a threat to their integral operations.

The following sections explore just how link-state routing protocols operate. Also explored are some of the general performance issues that can arise when link-state routers are deployed in a network without due intelligence and forethought.

Stages of Link-State Operation

Link-state operation can best be characterized in a series of operational stages:

1. **Neighbor discovery**   Link-state routers establish and maintain formal neighbor relationships with each other via the use of what is called the *Hello* protocol.

2. **Topology discovery**   After forming neighbor relationships, link-state routers exchange LSA packets to build their link-state database. This storage element maintains information about all known routes within the entire network.

3. **Best path selection**   The SPF algorithm uses a metric (for example, cost) to calculate the best path for each destination listed in the link-state database. These

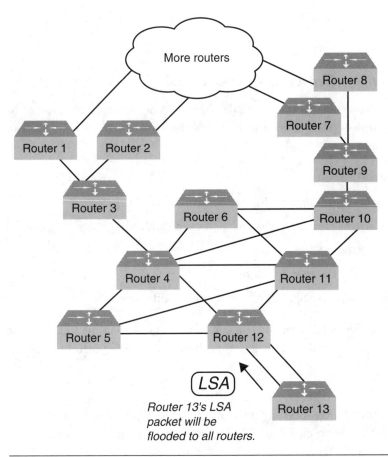

Figure 11-36 LSAs are flooded to all routers in the known internetwork

best paths are then ported to the routing table, which is what the router uses when it determines where to send packets.

4. **Route maintenance** Topology changes prompt the link-state router to generate an LSA packet that contains information pertaining only to the topology change. This LSA packet is flooded to all routers in the network.

Upon receiving an LSA, the router checks its validity to make sure that the packet is not outdated, or corrupted. If the packet is valid, the router proceeds to copy the LSA packet to its link-state database and then immediately forwards the packet out to its link-state neighbors. After the LSA has been forwarded, the router runs its SPF algorithm to recalculate its best routes. The results are placed in the routing table.

This maintenance process continues until all routers have converged on the topology change.

Route Maintenance—Convergence is the Goal

Once the routing tables for all devices are stable, the only time routing updates need to occur is when new devices or links are added, or when an existing route changes. The routing update steps are:

1. Topology change is detected.
2. Router that detects the change builds and sends LSA packet.
3. LSA is received by the Designated Router (DR) and validated.
4. LSA is copied to database.
5. LSA is flooded by the DR to network routers.
6. Routing table on each affected network router is modified.

In the absence of topology changes, link-state routing protocols send periodic routing updates at an interval that typically ranges anywhere between 30 minutes and two hours.

OSPF

OSPF is a link-state routing algorithm that was designed in 1988 as an open-standard solution to the scalability problems that RIP encounters in large internetworks.

Some of OSPF's essential features are presented as follows:

- Robust cost metric that bases path selection on link speed
- Supports up to 65,536 router hops
- Triggered LSA updates
- Periodic updates every 30 minutes (by default)
- Support for hierarchical routing features, including VLSM, multiarea routing, and route authentication, among others

Link-State Resource Issues

Link-state routing protocols are designed to be a powerfully scalable, efficient, and reliable means of addressing any network's dynamic routing goals and requirements. However, these tremendous design benefits are not had without a cost. In large, growing networks, link-state routers have the potential of consuming a significant amount of network bandwidth and router resources. The following bullets explain how these resource issues can manifest:

- **Increased CPU utilization** Link-state routers must be able to handle the increasing CPU load that results from processing traffic received from new network routers and newly installed network segments. As these new link-state devices begin sending Hello packets and LSA routing updates, and as their networks begin sending user application traffic, each link-state router in the network must subsequently establish new neighbor relationships, discover new networks, run the SPF algorithm to calculate new routes, and process and respond to all the traffic received from the new link-state routers and networks.

  All of these activities consume a router's CPU cycles. The more activities on which the router is working, the more CPU cycles that are consumed. Eventually, a router's performance will begin to buckle as a result of the increasing workload it is processing. Exactly when this performance degradation begins to occur is a function of the router's resource capacities—for example, its throughput and CPU speed—and of the traffic load placed on the router.

- **Decreased memory availability** A link-state router maintains comprehensive routing information databases, including the link-state database, routing table, and neighbor table. With large, growing networks, information on new neighbors needs to be entered into the router's neighbor table, new routes need to be entered into the topological database, and new optimal routing entries need to be listed in the routing table.

  All of these database entries consume a router's memory. The more neighbors and routes the router learns of, the more memory that is consumed. This results in the undesirable side effect of depleting the amount of router memory that is left available for other router processes besides those of the link-state routing protocol.

- **Increased bandwidth utilization** In large, growing link-state networks, the amount of routing protocol traffic required to maintain link-state operations can increase significantly, causing link-state protocol traffic to compete with user traffic for link bandwidth. Especially on slow links, the amount of congestion caused by this bandwidth shortage can result in packets being dropped for both user traffic and routing protocol traffic—definitely not a desirable situation.

Solutions to Link-State Resource Issues

Just as distance-vector protocols are able to offer solutions that let distance-vector networks effectively resolve the problems of routing loops and slow convergence, so too are link-state protocols able to offer solutions that let their associated networks adapt to the problems of heavy resource consumption. Link-state protocols have been designed with powerful hierarchical features that allow rapidly evolving networks to effectively balance resource costs with maximal routing performance and reliability. Such scalable link-state features include multiarea routing, route summarization, LSA routing optimization, and other features that let the link-state network scale with tremendous efficiency while maintaining a firm grip on increasing resource-consumption levels.

However, unlike the routing solutions of distance-vector algorithms, which are relatively easy to configure and maintain, the hierarchical solutions of link-state algorithms are in comparison rather complex and therefore require a complete, accurate understanding as to how their integration with the existing network infrastructure should be designed and deployed. Indeed, it cannot be stressed enough how critical it is that the design of a link-state network—or any network, for that matter—be done with utmost care and forethought. While this aspect of networking is outside the scope of this book, suffice it to say that no network in existence today can stand long without a scalable design and deployment. That includes the greatest network of them all, the Internet.

Summary of Distance-Vector and Link-State Protocols

Table 11-2 provides a short yet thorough summary of the main features of distance-vector and link-state routing protocols.

Hybrid Routing Protocols

Hybrid routing protocols (also known as *balanced hybrid* routing protocols) combine features of both distance-vector and link-state routing. Using sophisticated distance-vector metrics, and triggered updates, hybrid routing protocols offer fast convergence and other scalable features that offer a very attractive alternative to link-state routing solutions. Moreover, hybrid routing protocols don't have quite nearly the same concerns with resource-consumption issues as link-state protocols do.

The most popular hybrid routing protocol is Enhanced Interior Gateway Routing Protocol (EIGRP), which was developed by Cisco to be the scalable successor to IGRP. Simply, EIGRP is a distance-vector protocol with characteristics of a link-state protocol.

Interior vs. Exterior Routing Protocols

While routing algorithms can be classified according to whether they are distance-vector, link-state, or hybrid, they can also be classified according to whether they are

Table 11-2 Summary of Distance-Vector and Link-State Protocols

CATEGORY	DISTANCE-VECTOR	LINK-STATE
Examples of protocols	IP RIP, IPX RIP, RTMP, IGRP	OSPF, IS-IS, NLSP
Neighbor discovery	Doesn't have a formal way of learning about neighbors. Neighbors are discovered informally via periodic routing updates.	Establishes and maintains formal neighbor relationships via the Hello protocol.
Path discovery	Builds routing tables based solely on routing tables received from directly connected neighbors.	Builds link-state databases and routing tables based on LSA packets received from network area.
Best path selection	The path with the lowest metric is the best path. Metrics are incremented as they travel from router to router.	Runs the SPF algorithm to determine the best path, which is typically the path with the lowest cost.
Path maintenance	Complete routing tables are broadcast at fixed intervals that typically range between 30–90 seconds. Triggered updates occur when links fail. Convergence is still generally slow.	Periodic updates are flooded every 30 minutes to two hours. Topology changes cause triggered LSA updates to flood the entire area. Convergence is generally fast.
Network size	Suitable for small to medium-sized networks.	Suitable for large hierarchically designed networks.
Administration	Simple	Difficult
Issues	Routing loops and slow convergence. Solutions include defining a maximum, split horizon, hold-down timers, poison reverse, and triggered updates.	Increased bandwidth, memory, and CPU utilization. Solutions include hierarchical link-state features and scalable network design.

interior or exterior. The difference between interior and exterior routing protocols has to do with where they both operate in relation to an autonomous system. Recall from the discussion of IGRP that an AS is simply a collection of networks under common administration. It can be, for example, an ISP, a corporate network, or even a home business network (see Figure 11-37).

Basically, interior routing protocols are those that run *within* an AS, whereas exterior routing protocols are those that run *between* ASs (see Figure 11-38). Examples of the

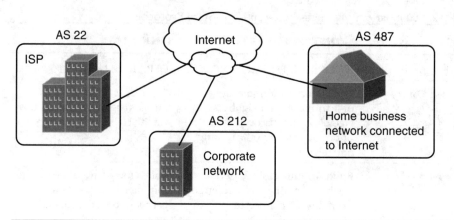

Figure 11-37   Examples of autonomous systems

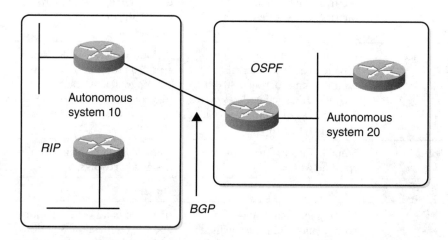

Figure 11-38   Interior routing protocols run *within* an AS, whereas exterior routing protocols run *between* ASs

former type include RIP and OSPF, whereas the most popular example of the latter type is Border Gateway Protocol (BGP).

 NOTE: Interior routing protocols are also known as **Interior Gateway Protocols (IGPs)**, and exterior routing protocols are also known as **Exterior Gateway Protocols (EGPs)**.

Concluding With the Switching Process

Now that you have learned the fundamentals behind routing, let's take a look at how the router's *switching process* uses the information derived from the routing process to actually get a packet from one network location to the next.

Consider Figure 11-39. This diagram depicts a TCP/IP network in which multiple types of LAN/WAN media have been interconnected and are all running IGRP. The network has been up for some time now, and all routers are aware of each other's network segments, which have all been identified with network addresses.

> **NOTE:** For simplicity, assume that the addresses in Figure 11-39 represent actual IP addresses. Assume the private address series 192.168.1.0 to 192.168.6.0. For simplicity, the 192.168 is not being displayed.

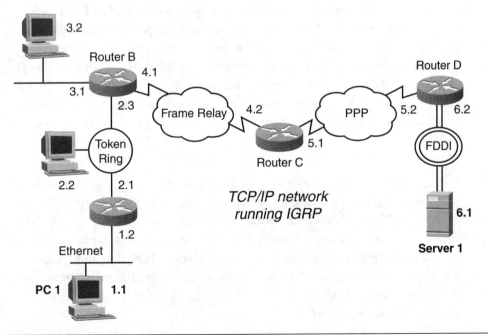

Figure 11-39   Diagram of a network topology

Now, assume that PC 1 (located on Ethernet network 1.0) has just opened a session with Server 1 (located on FDDI network 6.0) and is ready to begin sending data packets to this server. These data packets will go through the following stages to reach Server 1:

1. PC 1 builds the packet, which includes both an IP header (network header) and an Ethernet header (data link header). The IP header contains PC 1's network address of 1.1 as the logical source and Server 1's network address of 6.1 as the logical destination. The Ethernet header contains Router A's physical address as the data link destination (see the following illustration).

```
┌─────────────────────────────────────┐
│ Ethernet Header                      │
│ - - - - - - - - - - - - - - - - - -  │
│ Physical destination: Router A       │
├─────────────────────────────────────┤
│ Network (IP) Header                  │
│ - - - - - - - - - - - - - - - - - -  │
│ Source network address: 1.1          │
│ Destination network address: 6.1     │
├─────────────────────────────────────┤
│ Data                                 │
└─────────────────────────────────────┘
```

2. PC 1 sends the data packet to Router A. Upon receiving the packet, Router A looks first at the Ethernet data link header and sees that the packet is destined for one of its own physical addresses. Router A proceeds to then examine the packet's network header to see what network the packet is destined for. Upon looking in its routing table, Router A finds that the packet's destination network can be reached out its Token Ring interface. Router A proceeds to strip the Ethernet data link header from the packet and encapsulate the packet in a new Token Ring data link header that identifies Router B as its next physical destination. Before forwarding the packet, the router decrements the TTL and recomputes the FCS.

3. Router A sends the data packet to Router B. Upon receiving the packet, Router B goes through the same examination and encapsulation processes that Router A went through. That is, Router B examines the Token Ring data link header; examines the network header; determines that the destination network's outbound interface is its Frame Relay interface; strips the Token Ring data link header off; and encapsulates the packet in a new Frame Relay header that identifies Router C as the next physical hop. Before forwarding the packet, the router decrements the TTL and recomputes the FCS.

4. Router B sends the data packet to Router C. Router C goes through the same examination/encapsulation processes.

5. Router C sends the data packet to Router D. Router D also performs the same sequence of examination/encapsulation steps. This time, however, the destination physical address will be that of Server 1.

6. Router D sends the data packet to Server 1. Upon determining that it is the packet's logical destination, Server 1 strips the packet open and extracts the data.

The following illustration highlights the path that PC 1's packet takes to reach Server 1.

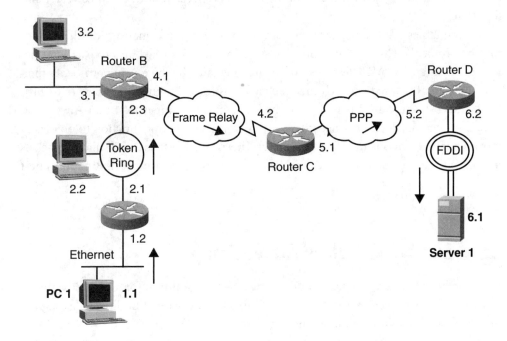

Note that during the packet's entire trip, its source and destination network (logical) addresses remain unchanged, whereas the data link (physical) addresses change at each hop.

This concludes our exploration of the router's switching function, and of the function responsible for the magic behind its motion-routing.

Summary

Routers are the key network layer devices responsible for routing, which is the process of determining where to forward information in a network. Routers support several different types of routing, including dynamic, static, and default routing. The first of these methods, dynamic routing, uses routing protocols to learn the network topology and to communicate this information between routers. The latter two methods use routing information that is configured on the router manually.

There are three main categories of routing protocols: distance-vector, link-state, and hybrid. Distance-vector routing protocols broadcast periodic routing updates that contain full routing tables, whereas link-state algorithms flood the entire network with LSAs. Hybrid routing algorithms combine the best aspects of both distance-vector and link-state.

Routing tables are the primary repositories of routing information for all types of routing protocols. The routing table always maintains the best routes to each destination in the internetwork. These best routes are calculated by the routing protocol's metric, which can be based on such media characteristics as bandwidth, delay, reliability, load, and cost. Typically, the path with the lowest metric value is the best path.

Besides the routing function, routers also perform a switching function to physically move a packet from one interface to another. This process entails encapsulating packets in data link headers and forwarding them to the next hop along a destination's best path.

Case Study: Xaliphor Advertising

You have been assigned the task of designing a routing solution for a local advertising company whose offices are located on all floors of a three-story building. As a diagram of this network's logical topology indicates (see Figure 11-40), each floor is equipped with a router that interconnects its respective network segment with the rest of the building in a triangle-shaped topology. In addition, the company is connected to the Internet via an ISP.

Directions: Now you will apply your new knowledge of routing protocols. Review the background information and network diagram (refer to Figure 11-40) for Xaliphor Advertising. Then review and pay close attention to the following technical requirements because, based on these network requirements, you will complete an analysis worksheet that will lead you through a simple step-by-step process for determining the right routing protocol category to use for Xaliphor Advertising.

Scenario: Xaliphor Advertising has recently hired you to devise a routing protocol solution that best fits its current network topology and routing protocol technical requirements. Your job is not to recommend a specific routing protocol, but instead to

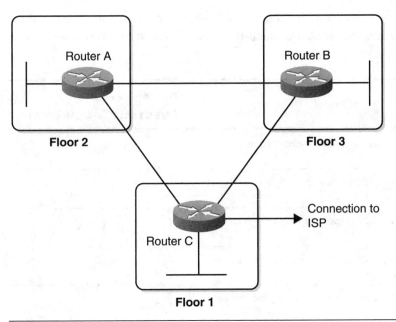

Figure 11-40   Logical topology of Xaliphor Advertising

determine which routing protocol *category* will satisfy Xaliphor's routing protocol requirements. Each of these technical requirements, listed as follows, has a number that weighs its relative importance on a scale from 1 to 10:

- The routing protocol must be able to support at least five routers (10)
- The routing protocol should be easy to configure and maintain (5)
- The routing protocol should respond quickly to network topology changes (8)
- The routing protocol should be able to support hierarchical features like route summarization (3)
- The routing protocol should only send routing updates on an hourly basis (4)
- The routing protocol should not have any routing loop issues (4)
- The routing protocol should be standard and not proprietary (2)

Xaliphor Advertising— Analysis Worksheet

In the following table, go through each routing protocol requirement and determine which routing protocol category, either distance-vector or link-state, meets the requirement's specification. Place the requirement's associated number under the routing protocol column that meets the requirement. If both routing protocol categories meet the requirement, place the number under *both* routing protocol columns. The first row has been filled in for you as an example.

REQUIREMENT	DISTANCE-VECTOR	LINK-STATE
The routing protocol must be able to support at least five routers (10)	10	10
The routing protocol should be easy to configure and maintain (5)		
The routing protocol should respond quickly to network topology changes (8)		
The routing protocol should be able to support hierarchical features like route summarization (3)		
The routing protocol should only send routing updates on an hourly basis (4)		
The routing protocol should not have any routing loop issues (4)		
The routing protocol should be standard and not proprietary (2)		

Total:

1. Add up all the numbers under each routing protocol column and place the totals in the last row.
2. Which routing protocol category has the highest total? This will be the routing protocol category that you recommend to Xaliphor Advertising.

Xaliphor Advertising—Analysis Solutions

REQUIREMENT	DISTANCE-VECTOR	LINK-STATE
The routing protocol must be able to support at least five routers (10)	10	10
The routing protocol should be easy to configure and maintain (5)	5	
The routing protocol should respond quickly to network topology changes (8)	8	8
The routing protocol should be able to support hierarchical features like route summarization (3)		3

The routing protocol should only send routing updates on an hourly basis (4)		4
The routing protocol should not have any routing loop issues (4)		4
The routing protocol should be standard and not proprietary (2)	2	2
Total:	25	31

    1. Total for distance-vector: **25**
       Total for link-state: **31**
    2. Link-state is the routing protocol category that you should recommend to Xaliphor Advertising.

Practice Questions

Take a few moments and check your grasp of the concepts covered in this chapter. The answers immediately follow the questions.

Questions

1. Which of the following are a router's two major network layer functions?
   a. Routing
   b. Name resolution
   c. Switching
   d. Addressing

2. Which of the following is *not* a function of a routing protocol?
   a. Acquire information on the network topology
   b. Choose the best path to each network in the topology
   c. Build the routing table
   d. Discover the physical address of the next hop

3. How do network addresses represent network paths?
   a. Network addresses specify the physical address of the next-hop device along a destination route.
   b. Network addresses include graphical pictures identifying network paths.
   c. Network addresses contain a network portion that identifies the destination route.
   d. Network addresses don't represent network paths, physical addresses do.

4. Which two of the following terms can be used interchangeably with the term *physical address*?

   a. MAC address

   b. Next-hop address

   c. Data link address

   d. Interface address

5. Which three of the following pieces of routing information are required before a router can route packets?

   a. Logical destination address

   b. Logical address of next-hop router

   c. A dynamic routing protocol

   d. An outbound interface

   e. The DNS name of the destination device

   f. A routing metric

   g. Verification of routing information

6. What is multiprotocol routing?

   a. Forwarding packets onto different data link media

   b. Forwarding packets between LANs and WANs

   c. Supporting multiple routed protocols in the same network

   d. Supporting multiple routing protocols in the same network

7. What is the primary difference between dynamic and static routing?

   a. Dynamic routing involves maintaining complete knowledge of the internet-work, whereas static routing maintains only limited knowledge of the network topology

   b. Dynamic routing involves the use of a routing protocol to discover and main-tain routing information, whereas static routing uses manually entered routes

   c. Dynamic routing is much more scalable than static routing because the for-mer type doesn't require as much manual administration to keep routers informed of network topology changes

   d. Dynamic routing uses routing tables, whereas static routing does not

8. Which two of the following pieces of information would *not* be found in the routing table?

   a. Routing information source

   b. Destination MAC address

   c. Administrative distance

   d. Metric

    e. Next hop

    f. Hold-down timer

    g. Age of routing information

    h. Outbound interface

9. True or False: When the same routing information is learned both dynamically and manually, administrative distance will by default prefer the manually learned routes to the dynamically learned routes?

    a. True

    b. False

10. Which three of the following are common metrics used by routing protocols?

    a. Hop count

    b. Interface type

    c. Next hop

    d. AS path

    e. Load

    f. Cost

11. For which two of the following are static routes most often used?

    a. To solve routing loops

    b. To reduce network overhead on links that connect to stub networks

    c. To hide networks for security reasons

    d. To support multiprotocol networks

12. In what way does static routing improve routing performance on slow-speed WAN links?

    a. By queuing traffic so that high-priority packets have priority access to the WAN link's bandwidth

    b. By forcing routing protocol traffic to slow down on the link

    c. The absence of routing protocol traffic leaves more bandwidth for user traffic

    d. Static routing offers no improvement in routing performance

13. Which of the following is not a routing protocol category?

    a. Distance-vector

    b. Link-state

    c. Autonomous system

    d. Hybrid

14. In which way do distance-vector routers determine the best path?
    a. They send a broadcast to neighbors asking them for their best routes
    b. They run the SPF algorithm to determine the best path
    c. They increment received metrics
    d. They try out each route to determine which is the best one.

15. In what way do distance-vector routing loops typically begin?
    a. High-bandwidth utilization causes routing updates to be dropped
    b. A router fails to learn the entire topology. Upon receiving a topology change update for an unknown route, the router sends the update back to the router from which the update was received
    c. A router detects a directly connected link failure, but fails to report this to other routers
    d. Slow convergence leads routers to accept invalid routing information.

16. Which one of the following does *not* help resolve the problem of routing loops?
    a. Defining a maximum
    b. Split horizon
    c. Route summarization
    d. Poison reverse
    e. Hold-down timers
    f. Triggered updates

17. What is split horizon?
    a. A method of stopping looped packets from being sent to the furthest routers in the network
    b. Marking a route as unreachable by raising its metric to infinity
    c. Removing invalid routing information from a network to prevent corrupted routing tables from being propagated
    d. A loop-prevention feature that prohibits routers from sending routing information learned from a source back to that source

18. Which of the following statements does *not* accurately describe hold-down timer operation?
    a. If a routing update is received indicating that a network is inaccessible, the router will mark the network as unreachable and begin a hold-down timer for it.
    b. If the neighbor from whom the failed network was learned reports back with an update indicating that the network has been reinstated, the router will ignore it.

c. If another neighbor reports with a better metric than the one originally recorded for the failed network, then the hold-down timer is removed and the network is reinstated with the new, improved metric.

d. If another neighbor reports with a metric worse than the one originally recorded for the failed network, the router will ignore it.

19. Which two of the following statements characterize RIP?

a. Sends periodic routing updates every 90 seconds

b. Sends triggered updates when failed routes are detected

c. Uses a metric based on bandwidth

d. Allows a maximum hop count of 16

e. Does not employ split horizon, hold-down timers, or poison reverse

f. Does not support multiple routed protocols

20. Which type of IGRP route is used as a default route to another AS?

a. Interior

b. System

c. Exterior

d. Gateway

21. Choose the two statements that best characterize link-state operation.

a. Establishes formal neighbor relationships via the Hello protocol

b. After forming neighbor relationships, link-state routers exchange routing tables with each other

c. The best path is typically the path with the smallest hop count

d. Topology changes result in the immediate flooding of LSA packets

22. Which of the following is not an issue with link-state routing protocols?

a. Increased CPU utilization

b. Decreased memory availability

c. Increased bandwidth utilization

d. Slow convergence

23. Which of the following is an example of a hybrid routing protocol?

a. RIP

b. OSPF

c. IGRP

d. EIGRP

e. IPX RIP

24. What is the simplest definition of an autonomous system?
   a. A network engaged in a business of some kind
   b. Any network that connects to the Internet
   c. A group of networks under common administration
   d. A collection of subnets

Answers

1. **a.** and **c.** Routing and switching are the router's two major network layer functions.

2. **d.** Routing protocols do not discover the physical address of the next hop. This function is accomplished by other means, such as ARP.

3. **c.** Network addresses represent network paths by containing a network portion that identifies the destination route.

4. **a.** and **c.** Physical addresses are also known as *MAC addresses* and *data link addresses*. The term *next-hop address* is not necessarily interchangeable with the term physical address because the former term can apply to both network addresses and physical addresses.

5. **a., d.,** and **g.** To be able to route, routers require a logical destination address, an outbound interface, and a means of verifying routing information, among other required items.

6. **c.** Multiprotocol routing involves the support of multiple routed (network layer) protocols in the same network.

7. **b.** The primary difference between dynamic and static routing is that the former routing method uses routing protocols, whereas the latter routing method uses manually configured routing information.

8. **b.** and **f.** The routing table does not contain either a destination MAC address or a hold-down timer.

9. **a.** It is true that manually learned routes are preferred to dynamically learned routes.

10. **a., e.,** and **f.** Common metrics include hop count, load, and cost.

11. **b.** and **c.** Static routes are most often used to reduce overhead on links that connect to stub networks and to hide networks for security reasons.

12. **c.** Static routing improves performance on slow-speed WAN links by preventing routing information from consuming unnecessary bandwidth.

13. **c.** Autonomous system is not a routing protocol category.

14. **c.** Distance-vector routers determine the best path by incrementing the metrics received from their distance-vector neighbors.

15. **d.** Distance-vector routing loops typically begin when slow convergence leads routers to accept invalid routing information.

16. **c.** Route summarization is not a technique used to resolve the problem of routing loops.

17. **d.** Split horizon is a loop-prevention feature that prohibits routers from sending routing information learned from a source back to that source.

18. **b.** This statement does not accurately describe hold-down timer operation.

19. **b.** and **d.** RIP sends triggered updates when failed routes are detected, and allows a maximum hop count of 16.

20. **c.** An IGRP exterior route is used as a default route to another AS.

21. **a.** and **d.** Link-state protocols establish formal neighbor relationships via the Hello protocol, and link-state topology changes result in the immediate flooding of LSA packets.

22. **d.** Slow convergence is not an issue with link-state routing protocols.

23. **d.** EIGRP is an example of a hybrid routing protocol.

24. **c.** The simplest definition of an autonomous system is a group of networks under common administration.

CHAPTER 12

Router Basics and Router Setup

This chapter will:

- **Analyze differences in router interfaces**

- **Describe three types of installation: telecommuter, remote office, and central office**

- **Discuss briefly some router models that might be used by each installation**

- **Examine the router startup sequence to clarify the difference between the IOS and the configuration**

- **Describe IOS version and feature differences**

- **Discuss setting up a console session**

- **Introduce the command-line interface (CLI)**

- **Introduce some basic commands to use when configuring a router**

- **Describe how to capture a configuration to a text file for later study or editing**

- **Look at the Cisco Setup application**

We are going to start configuring the router. First, we look at the router itself, focusing on some models and features you should be aware of. We cover some concepts that you should understand about router operations first, and then move on to discover the router's configuration. We look at some skills for capturing the configurations that will save you time later in both configuring and restoring a configuration.

At the end of the chapter, we look at the router setup feature, which you will probably never touch again. My personal feeling is that "setup" is a simple tool that a help desk person can use to walk a novice through over the phone. Once a basic configuration is created and network connectivity is established, the help desk person can then telnet in to finish the job.

Cisco Router Models

Cisco routers come in a variety of models, ranging from the 600 series to the 12000 series. For all practical matters, you can assume that the higher the router's model number, the more features it has and the higher its price is. Some models, like the 600 series, may only be available from service providers such as DSL providers. For the purposes of the CCNA exam and this book, we are going to concern ourselves only with those routers that use the Cisco Internetwork Operating System (IOS) software. This means that we will be looking at router models 800 and above on the current product line.

 NOTE: The Cisco switch line uses model numbers interspersed between the router models, making it a little more difficult to clearly separate routers from switches. One tip: if the word Catalyst appears in the name, it is a switch. Of course, it could be a Layer 3 switch, which means it can also perform routing. It is going to take some time to become comfortable with the many Cisco product models and what they do. Note also that some of the Cisco switches share the same IOS as the routers.

The fact that a *single operating system* (IOS) and basic command set runs through so much of the product line means that we do not have to concern ourselves too much at this stage about particular model differences for the certification exam. It also means that if you get experience on a smaller model, such as a 1600 or 1700, that experience will be applicable on larger units.

If the certification exam doesn't require model awareness, why are we discussing it? Since you are reading this book, we can assume that you have committed yourself to, or are considering committing yourself to, this industry. You should have at least a fundamental awareness of the manufacturers, products, pricing, and purchasing practices of the industry. The next time you see a farmer in a field (or on TV) with a piece of equipment attached to a tractor, ask yourself if you know what that machine does? How much does it cost? Where would you get one if you wanted one? Do you buy them or lease them? So, who cares? You would if you wanted to sell, install, or service farm equipment, or if you were the farmer. Eventually, you may want to sell, install, or service networking equipment, or become a LAN administrator who needs to purchase and administer network equipment.

If you are like most of my students—regardless of where you live in the world—it will be easier to learn about the farm equipment and the practices of that industry than Cisco routers and switches and their many applications. Routers are generally used in tight security environments. Even if you work for a firm with dozens or hundreds of devices, unless you are assigned to that area, you may not have access to them. The distribution (reseller) network is such that you typically cannot just go down to the showroom and browse through the inventory, gathering information.

At some point in the near future, you are going to want people to respect you for what you know about this industry. It isn't possible, or necessary, to know everything from the start. But it can't help if you are mixing up router and switch model numbers in an interview.

It isn't the purpose of this book, nor are there enough pages left, to introduce you to everything you will eventually want to know. What I hope to do is to lay a foundation and then point you in some directions where you can learn more of the basics for working in this industry.

To get more information on particular models of Cisco devices, or just to start to get a grasp of the huge array of products Cisco produces, go to the Web site at **www.cisco.com** and select the Products link and then Product Catalog. The Web site is huge and constantly updated, so be prepared to spend some time following links and retracing your steps. Be sure to add sites of interest to your Favorites list or bookmarked items. You should become familiar with the site anyway; it is a tremendous resource when confronted with a Cisco device you are not familiar with. On that site, you will find product features, model differences, configuration information, configuration tools, and so forth. If you are looking for a particular model or part number, you can use the search feature to quickly bring up related documents.

What you won't find there is pricing information. You need to get pricing from a Cisco reseller. If you followed my suggestion in the "Before You Get Started" section before Chapter 1 and ordered a Black Box (877-877-2269) catalog, you have a pretty good source of information and pricing on the lower end of the router and switch line (up to the 4xxx models of each). Another source for some pricing information would be the **www.cdw.com** Web site. Select the Brands link and then choose Cisco Systems.

Router Interfaces

The router interfaces or connections can vary significantly from model to model, but there are some basics you should be aware of. Most network routers will have a LAN side and a WAN side. Depending on the router model, there may be a single interface for each or multiple interfaces.

LAN Interfaces

The LAN side of the router includes one or more Ethernet or Token Ring interfaces. Earlier models used a 15-pin AUI connector for Ethernet access, providing 10 Mbps throughput. Later, an RJ-45 connector was added as twisted-pair cable became the dominant media standard. Figure 12-1 shows an AUI connector with an RJ-45 for 10 Mbps Ethernet connectivity. This is an either/or configuration where you choose one connection; it is actually a single interface with one address. Most devices now use only the RJ-45 for a 10 Mbps or 10/100 Mbps autosensing Ethernet connection. There might be a single Ethernet connection, or some models include a multiport hub. As a hub, there is only one LAN address, but it does facilitate a small network. We will see an example of this later in this chapter when we discuss then 700 and 800 series routers.

Figure 12-1   AUI and RJ-45 interface

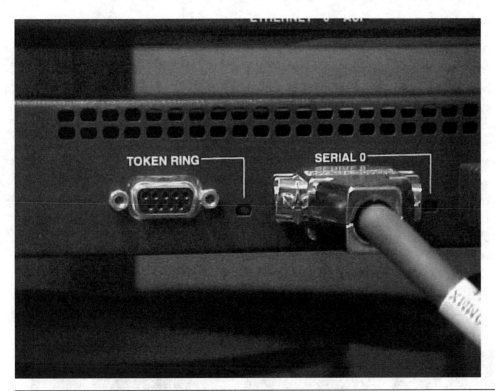

Figure 12-2   Token Ring interface

The Token Ring connector is a DB-9 and can be found individually or in multiples on some models. Figure 12-2 shows a Token Ring connector. There were some models of Cisco routers that incorporated a MAU into the same case, providing similar functionality as the Ethernet with hub units.

Together, the Ethernet and Token Ring interfaces represent the connections to the end users and any shared resources, such as servers and printers. Our LAN interfaces connect to hubs or switches for Ethernet or to a MAU unit for Token Ring, and from there are connected to our LAN host devices.

NOTE: In general, you would never connect an end user directly to a router except for those models with built-in hubs or MAUs. In the case of Ethernet routers and hubs or switches, a straight-through jumper cable is used for the connection. So, if for any reason you choose to connect your PC directly to a router while you are in a lab situation, use a cross-over cable to make sure that the TX and RX (transmit and receive) connections are connected properly.

WAN Interfaces

Although we cover WAN technologies in Chapters 17 to 22, we should at least discuss the connectors and identify them. The WAN connection(s) can take several forms. The basic serial interface can connect via a cable to another close router, or to a DSU/CSU device that provides the connection to leased lines, such as T1/T3 or Frame Relay networks. They could also connect to a modem for dial-up connections. The actual serial connector on the router has changed over the years, becoming smaller to allow multiple connections in the same space. This requires some attention to make sure that you have the right cables.

Some WAN connections have DSU/CSU circuitry and connections for 56K, 64K, or T1 connections. If the service provider will allow it, this saves the price, power connection, and configuration of another device. The connector is an RJ-45, although the wire combinations used for transmission may be different. Figure 12-3 shows a four-wire, 56K/64K, DSU/CSU connection.

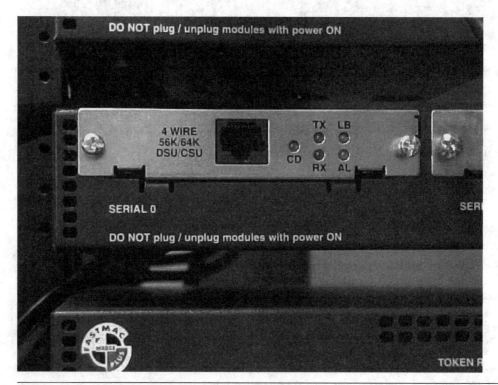

Figure 12-3 DSU/CSU interface

ISDN was once considered the digital dial-up replacement for the analog phone system. In its most common form, it provides up to 128 Kbps connections (two 64 Kbps channels) that are connected only as needed. ISDN connections can take several different forms depending on the service provider and the part of the world the device will be used in. *Basic Rate Interface* (BRI), the most common form of ISDN in North America, uses a built-in NT1 interface (U) that allows a cable to connect directly to the provider's network. In other parts of the world, ISDN can also use an RJ-45 interface (S/T) for connection to a vendor-supplied ISDN NT1 device. For the time being, all you really need to know is that, while the two connections look similar, they are not the same thing—*do not* mix them up. Plugging a cable from a S/T interface can do serious damage to a device expecting a U connector.

A *Primary Rate Interface* (PRI) ISDN connection allows for 24 64 Kbps channels (23 B channels and 1 D channel), which can be configured for different uses.

Some routers will have a single WAN and a single LAN connection providing remote connectivity to and segmentation from a single large network, such as a corporate network or an *Internet Service Provider* (ISP). The LAN connection allows local traffic to remain local only, while the WAN connection allows the local host(s) to access the larger network. Figure 12-4 shows a small remote connection, such as ISDN, with a direct dial-up connection to a corporate network.

End-user communications with the local server would not be transmitted to the corporate network. Similarly, the router on the corporate end would contain local communications, keeping it away from the remote site. A *digital subscriber line* (DSL) or

Figure 12-4
Single LAN and
WAN router

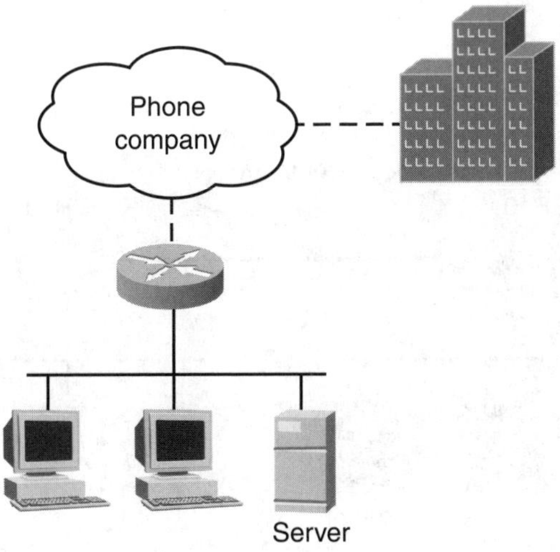

cable connection could provide similar connectivity, except that an ISP would replace the phone company.

Additional interfaces allow for both growth in the number of networks served and the ability to provide redundancy for critical connections. Figure 12-5 shows an example of routers with multiple interfaces. The network on the right has a second WAN connection, an ISDN interface, to provide a backup in case the T1 line fails. The network on the left has a similar ISDN interface plus a second LAN connection to support a second local network. The 128 Kbps bandwidth that the ISDN provides cannot fully replace the 1.54 Mbps that the T1 carried, but at least critical communications can be maintained.

Fixed vs. Modular Interfaces

Some models, particularly those at the lower end of the product line, have *fixed* interfaces, meaning that they cannot be modified after manufacturing. The advantage is that the fixed interface units may be manufactured in common configurations at large enough quantities to provide economies of scale and therefore lower selling prices. Figure 12-6 shows an example of fixed interfaces.

Many newer models and all higher-end units offer one or more bays that various interface modules can be plugged into. Each module can have one or more interfaces on it. The advantage is that functionality can be added or upgraded as needed without having to replace the basic unit. Figure 12-7 shows a router with modular interfaces and a module.

The modules on some routers are not fully interchangeable. On the Cisco 2524, the left two modules can be any combination of serial or DSU/CSU units. The third bay is

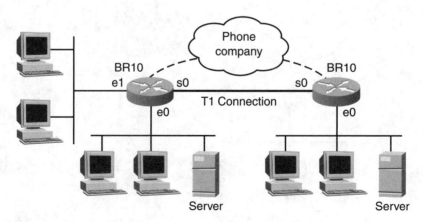

Figure 12-5   Routers with multiple LAN/WAN interfaces

Figure 12-6   Fixed interfaces

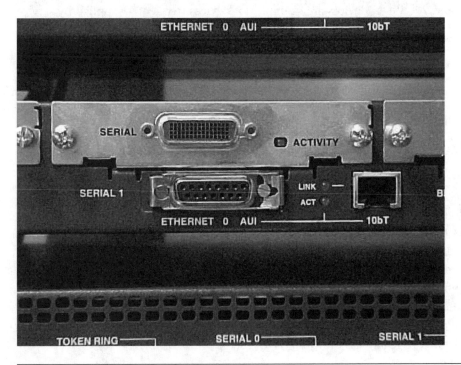

Figure 12-7   Modular interfaces

limited to a BRI interface. Likewise, some modules can only be used in a limited number of models, often within the same family. It's always a good idea to check the documentation before buying or installing modules.

Three Levels of Router Implementation

To help us define our discussion, let's think in terms of three basic levels of router implementation: the telecommuter, the remote site (branch office), and the central site (headquarters). These designations are not absolute and do in fact overlap at the edges.

Telecommuter

At the smaller end of three types of router installations is the telecommuter working at home but needing to access the company's network either directly or through the Internet. Originally, these were all dial-up modems, but the expanding availability of services such as DSL and cable Internet access have brought high-speed connectivity to the home. Traveling employees who need to check in from hotels and airports generally use analog dial-up connections.

Quite often, the types of service available in the area determine the device to be used. The service provider might furnish the devices, at least initially. The model 600 DSL devices and 700 ISDN devices are examples of devices frequently supplied by service providers. Since these devices have their own unique IOS, we will not discuss them in depth.

Expert Discussion

Service Provider's Interest vs. Personal Interest

If you are considering one of these high-speed services, or have clients using them, it is extremely important to keep in mind, particularly with consumer services (as compared to business services), that the service provider's interests are not likely to be the same as yours. The service providers are often looking for quick and cheap without introducing any possibility of additional support issues. Often, the service providers do not promise a higher level of security or functionality and therefore do not consider these to be relevant issues.

This manifests itself when the companies provide and support only a single model of a single vendor's products. You may even be told that you cannot use any other connection devices—regardless of who pays for them.

On a recent ISDN installation, the provider wouldn't consider a model of the same router family with a built-in -port hub. The hub would have provided easy access for the client's laptop and her daughter's computer. The service provider had no problems with hooking up a hub to the recommended unit to accomplish the same thing. Because the customer's company was buying the device, they wanted to step up from the 700 series to the 800 series (804); that was a no-go initially as well. There was no real explanation given, just that the number wasn't on the list—when we first started talking, the "list" only had one item on it. It took persistence and talking to several supervisors, but the customer ultimately got what she and her company wanted.

The development of and compliance with standards does not necessarily lead to interoperability in practice in the consumer services market.

The small *office/home office* (SOHO) model offers many benefits to both the employee and the company and should be considered a growth area. Particularly when connecting directly to the company's systems, using devices compatible with the company's features and security requirements will be important.

Even some individual high-speed Internet users are starting to have security concerns that are leading them to consider devices that would clearly fall into our telecommuter category. This is particularly true of those people managing their personal portfolios over the Internet. Similarly, it is easy to visualize a small remote office with a handful of staff being able to use some of these devices for their corporate or Internet connections.

The following router lines are generally considered the telecommuter or SOHO connections for ISDN, IDSL, ADSL, and cable Internet service. These are all fixed-interface devices configured with a single WAN connection and a single LAN interface, although the LAN interface may be a port hub on some models. They are stylish desktop units typically about the size of a textbook so that they can easily fit into the décor near a workstation. Typically, everything needed to get a user connected is in the package except a NIC. Units with built-in hubs require a straight-through jumper cable for any additional connections.

 NOTE: Although we discuss devices that can support cable Internet connections and xDSL service, they are not currently a part of the CCNA exam. They are included for reference and because of their increasing importance in the real world. Chapter 21 includes an introduction to cable and xDSL service.

The Cisco 700 Series

The 700 series, although it does not support the Cisco IOS, does provide ISDN service capabilities for IP and IPX protocols, DHCP service, and a form of NAT translation. The installation of the device is quite simple with the several handy tools included. This is a fixed interface router with a single ISDN and a single Ethernet interface. Some models include a built-in four-port hub. The IOS issue then is really more of a concern if the device is going to become part of a larger network, because of feature compatibility and the increase in the number of OSs the support personnel need to be familiar with.

The Cisco 800 Series

The 800 series includes the least expensive devices supporting the Cisco IOS. The 800 family currently includes the 801-805 models that provide ISDN/IDSL service or a serial interface, and the 826-827 units that provide ADSL service. There are some IDSL models that provide up to 144 Kbps bandwidth to sites too far from the telephone company's central office for regular DSL service. Each model supports the features of the 700 series plus additional features, increased performance, and security options such as firewall and IPSec versions of the IOS. Figure 12-8 shows a front and rear view of a model 804 router.

Some models offer two analog telephone connections (one for each 64 Kbps channel), meaning that a site could have a true 64 Kbps connection to the office or Internet

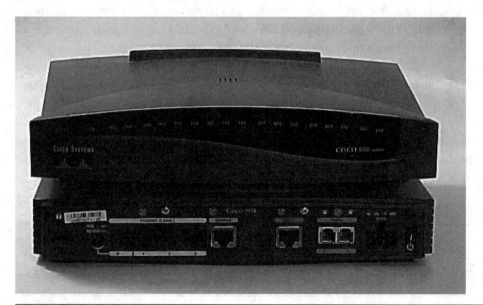

Figure 12-8 Model 804 front view

and still have telephone service. If the second 64 Kbps channel is multilinked, then the phone cannot be used while a data connection is going on.

These models are all fixed-interface units that have a WAN interface (ISDN, ISDL, or ADSL), either a single Ethernet interface or a four-port hub, and a console connection. So while these models could be used to get some exposure to working with the very basics of the IOS, they wouldn't generally be sufficient to cover the skills you will ultimately need for the exam. Figure 12-9 shows the four-port hub and analog phone connections on an 804 router.

The Cisco 900 Series

The 900 series provides router connectivity to cable Internet systems via an integrated DOCSIS (Data Over Cable Service Interface Specification) cable modem. Each model use the Cisco IOS. These products, with model numbers such as uBR905 and uBR924, are often supplied to service providers to enable them to offer expanded functionality and security to primarily commercial customers. The uBR924 offers *voice-over-IP* (VoIP) and *virtual private network* (VPN) solutions.

The Cisco 1000 Series

The 1000 series provides many of the same features as the 800 series (801-805 models) but does not support a built-in hub or analog phone lines. The 1000 series models have a PCMCIA flashcard slot so that IOS upgrades and configurations can be performed at

Figure 12-9   Model 804 back view

a central office and then delivered to the site. The 800 series will ultimately replace the 1000 line as it is phased out. If you go to Cisco's Web site for this line, it introduces the 800 series and then compares the two lines in a table that shows more features for the 800 line.

Remote Site

The remote site, or branch office, is an additional physical location of a business where company employees are able to serve local customers or have access to key resources. Several typical examples would be these:

- Branch locations of banks or credit unions
- Any location of a chain restaurant or chain retail store
- A components plant for a manufacturer
- A remote Buyers or Sales office of a manufacturer or retailer
- A hospital's remote clinic or lab
- An individual school in a school district

Remote locations then could range from being as small as some telecommuter locations to being larger than some communities—one of my company's clients has branch locations that often have 10,000 to 25,000 employees. The requirements will vary accordingly. For our purposes, we will assume that there are enough employees to require more than a couple workstations to have connectivity to the central office. While the branch office might be large enough to have its own network support, we will also assume that the central office sets the basic policies and direction. The larger branch locations with thousands of employees might require devices similar to a central location.

As with telecommuters, the type of WAN connections available locally drive the types of interfaces required. While services are expanding into new areas all the time, it is still very possible that some remote locations may not have access to their first choice of service, or the installation cost might be prohibitively high. The number of employees and the types of activities performed determine the number of LAN connections or whether additional routers are required locally. The following are typical remote site routers:

The Cisco 1600 and 1600R Series

The 1600s are small desktop units with a fixed single WAN, fixed single LAN interface, and a WAN slot. Most models have a single 10 Mbps Ethernet connection (the 1605 has two). Two models have fixed ISDN interfaces for their WAN connection, while the others can add ISDN via the WAN slot. The line supports synchronous and asynchronous connections.

NOTE: If you are looking for lower-cost devices to get hands-on experience with the IOS, the 1601 (one Ethernet and one serial interface) or the 1605 (two Ethernet and one serial interface) can be used. Add a WIC-1T module to get a second serial interface if you want. A pair of these would let you practice most of the skills required for the exam.

The Cisco 1700 Series

The 1700 series represents a step up from the 1600 series. The one fixed WAN/one fixed LAN/one WAN slot configuration is the same as the 1600, except that the 1700 has a 10/100 autosensing Ethernet interface. Another difference is that the 1700 line also supports VPNs and IPSec. The newest addition, the 1759, supports *Voice-over-IP* (VoIP).

The Cisco 2500 Series

This workhorse has been around for a long time and is probably reaching the end of its product life, but not its usefulness. Originally, the 2501 was a fixed-interface unit with one LAN (AUI) Ethernet and two serial interfaces. It has since been reborn in over two dozen configurations supporting a wide variety of connections including Ethernet, Token Ring, ISDN, DSU/CSU, an Ethernet hub, and a Token Ring MAU. The 2524/2525 models are Ethernet and Token Ring, respectively, and have three WAN slots. The 2500s are the first of the rack-mountable units.

NOTE: Models of the 2500 family are readily available on the used market. Because of the demand from CCNA and CCNP/CCIE candidates, the prices can fluctuate quite a bit from time to time and model to model. Make sure you check the Cisco site before purchasing a 2500 model so that you know which interfaces are present. The 2501 (one Ethernet interface) and the 2514 (two Ethernet interfaces) seem to demand higher prices because people are familiar with them, but some of the other models represent great buys—if you can use the interfaces.

The Cisco 2600 Series

The probable replacement for the 2500 series, each model in this family has at least one fixed Ethernet, Fast Ethernet, or Token Ring LAN connection. The model 2612 has one Ethernet and one Token Ring interface. Each unit also has two *WAN Interface Card* (WIC) slots, one Network Module slot, and an *Advanced Integration Module* (AIM) slot. These slots share more than 50 different modules from the Cisco 1600/1700/2600/3600 product lines.

The 2600 platform is the lowest-end model to support features such as inter-VLAN routing and the convergence of voice/fax/data over IP.

The Cisco 4000 Series

The Cisco 4000 series of modular routers, specifically the 4500 and 4700 models, offer connectivity to Ethernet, Token Ring, Fast Ethernet, ATM, *Fiber Distributed Data Interface* (FDDI), *High-Speed Serial Interface* (HSSI), ISDN, BRI, PRI, E1/T1 serial, and high-density, low-speed serial. The three module slots are specific to this series. This entire line is older and generally less technologically sophisticated than the 2600 and 3600 series. The 4500 and 4700 models are schedule for phase out.

 NOTE: For those looking for a used device to add to your practice lab, the model 4000 and 4000-M (increased memory) are the older original members of this family. They support the current IOS and the module features needed for CCNA and CCNP hands-on practice. With patience, the devices and modules are quite often available at very attractive prices.

The Cisco 3600 Series

The Cisco 3600 is a fully modular router platform. The third digit of the model number indicates the number of module slots—the 3620 has two slots, the 3640 has four, and the 3660 has six. The modules offer combinations of WAN connectivity, including ISDN, PRI, ISDN BRI, integrated digital and analog modems, very high-density asynchronous interfaces, two- and four-port voice/fax, ATM, OC-3, T1, low-speed asynchronous/synchronous serial, and hardware-compression-assisted network modules.

LAN connectivity includes Ethernet, autosensing Fast Ethernet, and Token Ring while supporting a variety of media. Voice and fax multiservice applications are also supported.

Central Site

The central site, or corporate headquarters, is typically where the company's shared resources are located. This could include company databases, e-mail systems, personnel/payroll data, and Web servers that need to be accessible throughout all sites. These resources will be connecting to the remote sites and probably are the most likely to grow and change quickly. For this reason, larger modular units are the most common.

Web servers, as they grow in number and the volume of transactions performed for the organization, can drive an organization to far larger devices than could be imagined just a few years ago. At the extreme are the Web-hosting sites located around the country with access to the high-speed fiber bacKbpsones. Whether servicing a single client or multiple clients, there can be literally thousands of servers and the router/switch infrastructure to support it.

The Cisco AS5000 Series

The Cisco AS5000 series of universal access servers offers a high concentration of circuit-switched WAN networks, modem, voice, and ISDN connections for large corporate networks, telephone companies, and large ISPs. There are four model lines in this family: the 5200, 5300, 5800, and new 5400 line.

The Cisco 7000 Series

There are three lines of routers that make up the 7000 series, including the 7100, 7200, and 7500. Each line has several models. These devices are designed for the enterprise backbone, high-end multifunction WAN edge, service provider *points-of-presence* (POPs), and mainframe data centers. All are modular devices that collectively provide support for VPN, high-density LAN and WAN interfaces, ATM and packet over SONET, ATM *Circuit Emulation Standard* (CES) connectivity for voice/data/video, T1/E1, T3/E3, *private branch exchange* (PBX) voice, and *video coder-decoder* (CODEC) connectivity.

The Cisco 12000 Series

The Cisco 12000 series *gigabit switch router* (GSR) is the current top-of-the-line family of devices, designed and developed for the core of service provider and enterprise IP backbones. The current models are 12008, 12012, and 12016, with the last two digits indicating the number of module slots. Modules can provide WAN connectivity to high-speed SONET/SDH fiber-optic rings up to 2.5 Gb, ATM up to 622 Mbps, and frame relay up to 45 Mbps. LAN modules support Gigabit Ethernet and 100 Mbps Fast Ethernet.

Hardware Basics

The router is basically a specialty computer that selects the best path (or route) and manages the switching of packets between two or more networks. The lower-end, fixed-interface routers share four of the five basic components of most PCs: a CPU, memory, input/output interfaces, and a bus connecting the components. The fifth basic component, a storage device, is unnecessary and too slow for use in routers. The inside of a lower-end Cisco router, such as the Cisco 2500 unit shown in Figure 12-10, looks very much like a simple computer. Many major components are absent because the router does not need to directly support monitors, keyboards, hard drives, and so forth.

The larger modular routers are more complex, with added processors, memory, and buffers for modules to assist with specific functions. These devices could be viewed as multiple specialty routers within a single case. As such, they can share resources, such as power supplies, management consoles, and configuration files, as well as have a

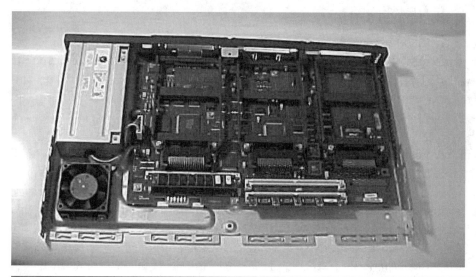

Figure 12-10   Cisco 2500 components

high-speed connection between the modules to facilitate forwarding packets between the modules. One module could manage one or more high-speed fiber-optic loop WAN connections while another module handles Fast Ethernet connections for the LANs.

The next few chapters discuss the router configuration: what it is, where it is stored, and how to create or modify it. You also need to understand the difference between the router's IOS and its configuration. As with all computers, routers have an operating system (OS) to provide basic-level functionality. We will look at the Cisco IOS in greater detail in the next section of this chapter. For now, you just need to recognize that the OS is furnished by Cisco as a part of the initial purchase or as an upgrade. The OS creates the basic platform that allows us to customize the router to behave, as we need it. This customization includes addressing interfaces, activating routing protocols, filtering packets, adjusting process timers, and so forth, all stored as part of the router configuration.

Simply, Cisco furnishes the IOS for a fee. The administrator creates and maintains the configuration to implement and customize IOS features.

Router Startup Sequence

In considering the basic components of a router (CPU, memory, I/O interfaces, and BUS), it is important to realize that there can be multiple interfaces, multiple CPUs, and four types of memory: ROM, RAM/DRAM, Flash, and NVRAM, each with its own

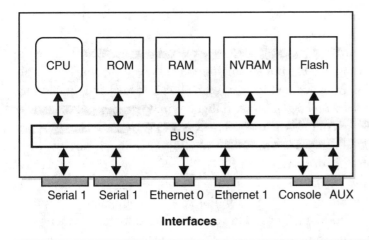

Figure 12-11   Basic router components

purpose. Figure 12-11 shows representations of the components. The diagram is intended only to show the interrelationships of the components and is not intended to be either a schematic or to scale.

The *interfaces* are network connections through which packets enter and exit a router. These interfaces can be directly connected to the router's motherboard, or they can be on a separate interface module, possibly with dedicated memory and a specialty processor to offload some of the CPU's burden.

The *CPU* (*central processing unit*) performs all processing, whether it is processing the startup self-test, the IOS, or the router configuration. Only the CPU has the ability to interpret instructions. The CPU processes only information that has been loaded, or moved, into RAM (random access memory).

ROM (*read-only memory*) is permanently encoded memory that contains power-on diagnostics and a bootstrap program that loads programs into RAM and starts the OS. ROM or flash also contains a stripped-down version of the operating system (IOS) software that can be used if a newer version is unavailable or corrupted. Without an OS, the router is unable to function at any level. At least with this limited version of the OS, a fully functional OS can be uploaded to Flash. Upgrading ROM requires replacing the chips in the router. ROM coding is not lost when the system powers down.

Flash (reprogrammable ROM) stores the current operating system (IOS) image and microcode that the router normally uses to function. At startup the IOS code is loaded into RAM to be available to the CPU. The advantage to flash over conventional ROM is that it can be upgraded without removing and replacing chips in the device. Flash coding is not lost when the system powers down. Flash is the storage device for router and switch devices.

NVRAM (*nonvolatile RAM*) stores the startup router configuration file. This file can contain interface addressing, feature implementation, access control lists, and so on. This startup configuration is loaded into RAM once the IOS is loaded and functioning, at which time it becomes the *running* or *active* configuration. Any changes made to the configuration by the administrator affect only the copy in RAM and will be lost if the power goes off unless specifically copied to NVRAM. NVRAM coding is not lost when the system powers down or performs a reload.

RAM/DRAM (*random-access memory/dynamic RAM*) stores any coding or data being processed by the CPU, including the IOS, the running or active configuration file, routing tables, ARP tables, and buffering for packets. You will see later that RAM can be allocated to provide advanced features such as fast-switching cache and packet hold queues. RAM coding is lost when the system powers down or performs a reload. Figure 12-12 is a representation of how the memory is allocated to tasks, with each area holding information that will be critical to the router performing its job.

The area marked as IOS in RAM has been loaded from Flash—it is not the Flash. Some models of Cisco routers run with the IOS fully in RAM, whereas others transfer only a portion into IOS and the rest remains in Flash.

The *command executive*, sometimes called a command interpreter, converts the text we type into the console or store in the configuration into coding that the CPU can understand. The *programs* are instructions loaded and started by the bootstrap routine in ROM. Basically, each time the power is turned on to a router, the device checks the integrity of each of its components, loads the OS, performs a self inventory, loads the

Figure 12-12
RAM allocation

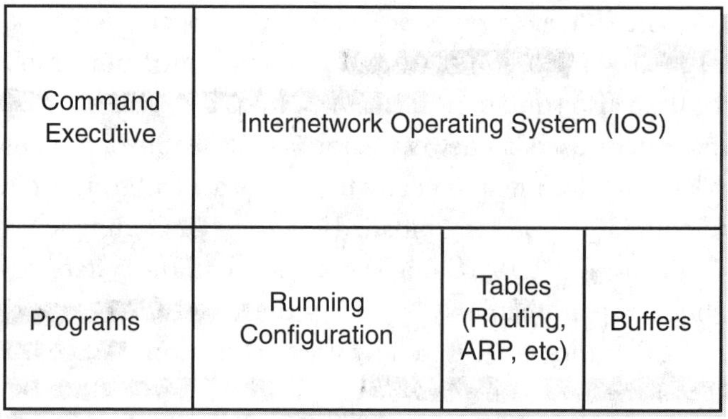

Command Executive	Internetwork Operating System (IOS)		
Programs	Running Configuration	Tables (Routing, ARP, etc)	Buffers

configuration file, and becomes operational. The startup steps in a little more detail are as follows:

The area of RAM in the figure labeled *Buffers* represent the portion of memory that data packets are moved into for processing before they are sent to the outbound interface.

1. **Power on and self-test (POST)**   The ROM programming performs the POST on each of the router components and then launches the bootstrap loader. The bootstrap is a set of instructions that causes procedures to run or programs to be loaded into RAM. The bootstrap loader is a part of a chain-reaction set of instructions, each of which launches the next level until the router is up and functioning.

2. **Load the IOS**   The operating system (Cisco IOS) must be located, loaded into RAM, and activated. The boot field of the configuration register tells the system where to find the IOS. Normally the IOS is stored in Flash, but it could be downloaded from a TFTP server, or the stripped-down version in flash or ROM, depending on the model, could be loaded.

3. **Self-inventory**   Once operational, the operating system inventories the hardware and software components of the router. If a console terminal is attached, the results are displayed on the monitor.

4. **Load the configuration**   The startup (backup) configuration file stored in NVRAM is loaded into main memory where it becomes the running configuration. As the startup configuration is loaded into RAM, the statements are executed sequentially. The configuration commands assign addresses to the interfaces, start routing processes, implement packet filtering, and so on. It is this configuration that we will be concerning ourselves with over the next chapters.

Note that if a good configuration file does not exist in NVRAM, the operating system starts a setup program, which is a series of questions that leads the administrator to supply the information required to create a router configuration. Once you understand how to modify (edit) the configuration, you won't use this somewhat cumbersome setup program. If a copy of the configuration file exists on a TFTP server, it could be copied from there. (We will look at the TFTP server in greater detail in Chapter 13.)

If you are familiar with the startup process that a PC goes through, this startup process is conceptually very similar. Whereas the PC uses a hard drive to store the OS and applications to be run, the router uses Flash ROM and NVRAM. In both cases, the code is loaded into RAM and then is available to the CPU for processing.

Cisco IOS

The Cisco Internetwork Operating System software, as with any OS, provides the basic level of functionality and security for the device. The common IOS for most Cisco routers and switches is part of the Cisco internetworking architecture that "fuses" together the scalability, stability, and security advantages of the latest routing technologies with the performance benefits of ATM and LAN switching, and the management benefits of VLANs (virtual LANs). To networkers, this move toward a common IOS means a common skill set is sufficient to configure and monitor a large portion of the Cisco product line of network devices.

Version Numbers

Conceptually, the IOS is to a Cisco router or switch what Windows 98 or 2000 is to the personal computer. The IOS provides the basic features and appropriate connectivity to all I/O interfaces. The whole-number changes in version numbers of the IOS, such as versions 11 and 12, are similar to the changes in Windows from version 95 to 98, and so on. The whole-number version changes represent significant changes but, like Windows, minor revisions also are released periodically. The decimal portions of version numbers, such as 12.1 or 12.7, are examples of these incremental changes. These decimal versions may represent bug fixes or the addition of what might be considered lesser features. The idea being that as problems are fixed and new feature sets are proven, they can be added to the product. New purchasers get the latest product, and existing users only need to upgrade if they are having problems or need a newly added feature.

Feature Packs

But even within the same version there are still differences. Unlike a PC workstation you purchase with Windows preinstalled, on which all the features are present for you to load (or not), the Cisco IOS has different releases with varying feature sets at different prices. The basic IP version does not support IPX or AppleTalk, but for an additional fee, you can buy a version that supports all three protocols. Some features, such as the Firewall feature, are available only on premium-priced versions of the IOS. The point is not to be judgmental, but rather to make sure that you realize that two routers running the same version number of the IOS may not support the same features. From another view, the solution to two very different problems might be the same device with different IOS feature sets.

To try to put this in proper perspective, if a user has a problem or requirement that only a router can solve, it will often be a version of the IOS that will actually solve the problem or meet that requirement, not the hardware. The device without the right IOS feature set is just silica, wires, and sheet metal.

One way to make the PC OS analogy more relevant to our router is to assume that you plan to assemble a good, solid computer from components or plan to buy one assembled to your specifications. Now you will need an operating system. For under $200, you could buy the latest consumer version of Windows 98/ME, or for about 50 percent more, you could choose Windows 2000 Professional and get a different feature set. For $600 to $800, you could step up to Windows 2000 Server. You could also opt for the features of Windows BackOffice for more money yet. Your choice should be based on what you plan to do with the computer. Each of the latter three choices might require you to increase resources on the computer, such as more memory or a faster CPU.

When selecting a router for a particular task, any interface modules and the IOS feature required can make a significant difference in pricing. A model 1601 router with the basic IP IOS and no extra interfaces might be purchased for under $1,200, but if you add an ISDN interface module and the IP/IPX/AT/IBM/Firewall Plus IPSec 56 Feature Pack, it can push the price over $3,000. The Cisco Web site, **www.cisco.com**, has tables with the features and the hardware requirements for the different features.

Features Exercise

This is a nondestructive exercise and you should be able to do it on your home machine without concern of it changing your system configuration. The purpose of this exercise is to see the variety of features available and to get some "ball park" idea about the costs of the lower-end models.

1. Launch your Web browser. Any version of Internet Explorer or Netscape will work.

2. In the Address box, type **www.cdw.com** and press ENTER.

3. Web sites are always changing, but the CDW site should have a link that says "Brands," indicating that you can list products by brand. After selecting Brands, you should get a list box where you can choose Cisco Systems. The following illustration shows a portion of what the screen might look like. Click Go.

4. On the next screen, choose All Cisco System Products and click Go.

5. That should bring up a series of pages with hundreds of items. You could scroll through them, but instead type **feature** in the Keywords box and click the Filter button. The following illustration shows what the filter screen might look like.

SMART SEARCH

973 product matches for your criteria
The following results sorted **by Group**

Filter your results below:

By Group:

View All Groups

Keywords:

feature

By Manufacturer:

View All Manufacturers

Sort By:

Group

☐ Show ready to ship products only (Shipping Definitions)

Page 1 of 20: **1** 2 3 4 5 6 7 8 9 10 Next >>

6. You should now be able to scroll through primarily IOS offerings for various models of routers. Clicking the hyperlinks often takes you to more information, or you may need to search the documents on **www.cisco.com**.

7. After looking over the results, change the Keywords box to **2621** and click the Filter button to get pricing for a model 2621 router.

8. Try the same thing with **3640** and **804**, or any other model numbers from the earlier sections. Keep in mind that it may not list devices higher than the 4000 series models.

What You Need for Hands-On Experience

Can you pass the CCNA exam without hands-on experience on the devices? Of course you can, and lots of people prove that every week. Is it easy? I don't think so. From my own test-taking experience, I found the CCNA exam to be as thorough and tough as any other vendor's certification exam and more thorough than most. All of the Cisco exams test your understanding of a concept, not whether you can identify a phrase that you read or memorized in preparation for the exam. Experience with devices makes the process of understanding and feeling confident easier.

One advantage to teaching a few dozen CCNA and CCNP students each week is that I get to see the results and compare them to the preparation techniques used. The ones who consistently do best are those who take every opportunity to work with the devices. They become familiar with the basic commands and the responses that the router will make to a specific command, and they develop a feeling for the process—what needs to be done to accomplish a particular result. They also have 30+ routers at their disposal.

So what do you do if you are not using this book as a part of a class with router and switch devices available? Obviously, financial circumstance and location in the world will have an impact on what you can do to get hands-on experience. Let's look at some options. We will start with the assumption that devices will be available, and move onto virtual labs, dial-up alternatives, and finally using this book by itself.

> **NOTE:** We are all motivated by different things and driven to different levels of achievement. Clearly, the CCNA certification by itself is a valid goal, but for many of you it is only part of the goal. You may want to work in the field working with Cisco devices, or you may view the CCNA certification as just a necessary first step toward higher certifications like CCNP, CCDP, or even CCIE. The more committed you are to working in the field or moving on to higher certifications, the more you should consider gaining access to devices. Whether by purchasing, partnering with someone having equipment, or renting lab time, the hands-on experience becomes more important at every new level.

What Equipment Do You Need?

Ideally, you have access to four or five routers, a similar number of switches and hubs, and a Token Ring MAU. We set up our CCNA classroom "pods" with four routers in the configuration you see in Figure 12-13.

To conserve space, we usually eliminate the second workstation attached to each hub or switch. The dashed line represents the console cable connection. The routers each have two serial interfaces and a single Ethernet interface, except Router A, which has two Ethernet interfaces. The hubs (four shown), a switch, or MAU could be interchanged as needed. The manufacturer and size of these devices are generally unimportant, but we use a Cisco switch for hands-on experience and to demonstrate switches and the common IOS in Chapter 16.

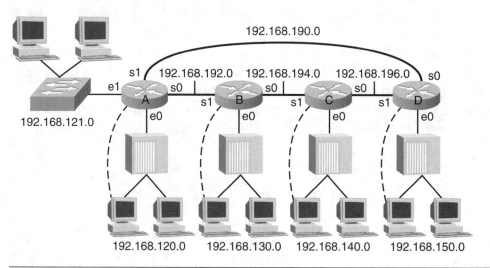

Figure 12-13   Four-router classroom lab

Smaller-Scale Options

Even one Cisco router that supports the IOS allows you to gain valuable experience with the command interface, the commands, and the features. What you cannot do with one device, however, is to test some of the processes, such as whether routing is occurring. Add a second router and you can accomplish most all of the features that you will be expected to understand or be aware of. Additional routers allow you to introduce features like Token Ring or alternative routes between networks.

A single 800 or 1000 model ISDN router can provide experience. But, because you must have an ISDN service provider to use the BRI interface, you want to be careful of paying too much for the experience. Also, adding a second device typically doesn't provide the connectivity that you would get from models with serial interfaces.

Model 1600, 2500, and 4000 units are readily available on the used market and can be acquired for reasonable prices. By careful attention to WAN interfaces, you can connect a mix of these devices together and use them as the start of your "lab" for higher Cisco certifications. Figure 12-14 shows a two-router lab configuration that minimizes other equipment.

The second hub and workstation could be eliminated if necessary and both networks could go into the remaining hub. While not a logical practice in the field, there is nothing in the CCNA requirements that would be impacted by two different networks using the same hub to save money and/or space. Figure 12-15 shows this as part of a three-router configuration incorporating a Token Ring LAN.

This figure also shows that, if necessary, you could get by with a single workstation as a part of one of the Ethernet networks and as the console machine for all three routers by moving the cable. Additional workstations and another hub or switch could be added.

Figure 12-14
Two-router lab

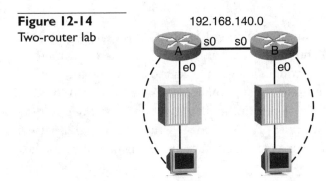

Figure 12-15
Three-router lab

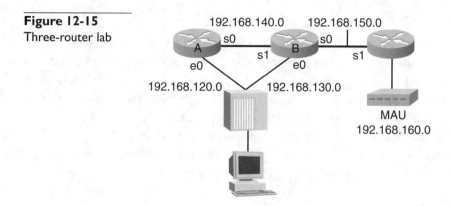

Hubs, Switches, MAUs, and Workstations

Any hubs, switches, and MAUs are basically included so that any link from a router interface plugs into a live device, allowing the circuit to "come up" and be worked with. You will learn later that there are ways to get around this, but I think there is a value in the cabling process and seeing the circuits work. That is also why I like to see two workstations, if at all possible, so that you can demonstrate user-to-user connectivity and not just router-to-router connectivity.

These workstations can be any PC, with a NIC, that supports Windows 95. In several of our labs, we use a line of 486-33 machines that take up a very small amount of space. The fact that they were virtually free was just a bonus. For our purposes, these workstations are only running HyperTerminal or the TCP/IP Telnet application, neither of which requires anything more than minimal memory, a CPU, and disk space.

I find that from a space and cost standpoint, four-port hubs work just fine, but any brand or size of hub or switch, new or used, will work. Given the decline in Token Ring technology, MAU units are incredibly cheap on the used market today. MAUs can be picked up on eBay for $5 to $30, often with cables.

Token Ring Devices

Hands-on experience with Token Ring is not critical for the CCNA exam, but there is still a lot of it in place, so it can't hurt to be familiar with it. One Token Ring router is nice to have for the experience, but you do not want to get too heavy into the technology, nor do you want to pay too much for any component. When I wanted to add a third router to my personal lab, I found that the model 2504 (one Token Ring, two Serial, and one BRI) was about half the price of a 2501 (one Ethernet and two serial); it was a no-brainer. The model 2513 router is a particularly nice unit in that it has an Ethernet, a Token Ring, and two serial interfaces and can often be purchased quite reasonably. Used Token Ring interfaces can often be added to a model 4000 router for under $100.

Where to Acquire Equipment

At the front of this book, in the section "Before You Get Started," are some contacts for used equipment. While I can't guarantee anything, I have purchased devices from each. Check out their Web sites and pay particular attention to any CCNA packages or specials they might be running.

If you have a Cisco reseller in your community, check with them about new and used equipment. It can't hurt to check with any other networking firms in the area. Businesses come and go, which means that liquidators occasionally end up with networking equipment.

If you can stand a little risk, eBay (**www.ebay.com**) can be a very good source. Typically there are over 1,000 Cisco items listed at any time. There are some suggestions about eBay in the "Before You Get Started" section as well. If nothing else, watching eBay for a week or two will give you some idea of what items sell for in that market. Check with your credit card company—some will now back your purchases against fraud—and then only buy from sellers that will take your card.

Cables

Cables, specifically serial cables, can be a challenge, particularly when you are mixing router models, which can have different connectors. Even if your router comes with a cable, it is often a DTE cable to be connected to a DSU/CSU device. So if you have two routers, you have two DTE cables and they won't connect together. You need a DCE cable for one of the routers, or there are some cables that are DTE on one end and DCE on the other. Another advantage to the DTE/DCE cables is that they often come in short sizes, such as 3, 5, or 10 feet, whereas the separate DTE and DCE cables are often each 10 feet long, giving you 20 feet of thick cable to deal with.

It is important to understand that even when two routers have the same size serial connector, if they are going to be connected directly together without any devices between them, then one must be the DTE connection (customer-premise equipment) and the other must be a DCE (service provider) connection.

There are lots of sources for cables, but I find that **www.pacificcable.com**/ has some nice tables telling you how to connect, for example, a serial port from a 4000 to a 2501. Dave can also help you with cables to connect a Token Ring interface to a MAU.

Ethernet connections on your router require standard straight-through Category 5 RJ-45 patch cables, which should be available anywhere. This cable then connects to a hub or switch. If you want to connect two routers together via their Ethernet interfaces, or if you want to connect a router directly to a workstation, you will need a Category 5 RJ-45 crossover cable. If your router has only an AUI connector, you need an AUI to RJ-45 transceiver.

Cisco Training Partners

One solution for getting hands-on experience is to take a class from one of the Cisco training partners. A portion of each class is dedicated to hands-on experience. The courses are typically one week long and offered in metropolitan areas. The Training/Certification link on the Cisco site, **www.cisco.com**, should give you information about pricing and schedules.

Cisco Networking Academies

Many communities have Cisco Networking Academies in their local college or trade school. The CCNA program is a six to nine month program with extensive hands-on experience as a major component. Use the Web site **http://cisco.netacad.net** and the Academy Locator link near the bottom of the screen to find the nearest Academy.

Rental Labs

At the front of this book, in the section "Before You Get Started," are some contacts for rental labs. Most are available over the Internet for a fee calculated on a per-hour basis. You may find that some enterprising CCNA or CCNP candidate in your community might rent time on their lab.

Virtual Lab Software

There are several sources for virtual labs on CD-ROM that can provide varying degrees of realism. I've included some sources in the "Before You Get Started" section. The Sybex CCNA Virtual Lab e-Trainer for under $100 has a three-router simulation that provides good experience with the commands and interface. The Web site **www.router-sim.com/** has several simulator programs available, including an upgrade for the Sybex e-Trainer.

Friends, Associates, and Employers

Don't overlook friends, family, associates, and employers when you are trying to get some time on a router. Be very clear that I am not suggesting that you should get your experience on someone's live production network. But let them know what you are studying and what you are trying to do. First of all, if you are going to be looking for work or a new job assignment, it can't hurt to let people know. You never know who may know someone that can help you.

Companies that you might not think of as technology companies but that have multiple locations may have routers. If they do, they may have a "spare" on the shelf or a unit that was replaced as part of an upgrade and is now collecting dust. As far-fetched as this may seem, I see students in almost every class have success obtaining a router in this way after we have this discussion. From grocery store to insurance agency to tent manufacturer, students have discovered units they can use. The Y2K upgrades in 1999 seem to have generated some of this.

Using this Book Without Hands-On Experience

Each of the chapters that involve configuring the routers are written assuming that you will try these commands and features on available equipment, a rental lab, or a virtual lab. In addition, the result of each command and feature is included in the text so that you can become familiar with the output. I also point out key information that you will want to remember.

Exploring a Router

In this section, we look at accessing the router. We start with connecting the console cable and setting up a HyperTerminal session to communicate with the device. This method bypasses any network interfaces and can be used either on a router that is configured and functioning on a network or a new router right out of the box. Later, we look at using telnet to access a functioning router on a network.

We will also cover the login process and the access levels within a router. We will look at basic commands for interacting with the router and getting help, and discuss the basic Setup feature. In the next chapter, we will look at configuring a router from "scratch."

Console Cable

The Cisco router does not have a monitor or keyboard so it relies on a workstation connection that will remotely execute commands and display output. This connection can be made using TCP/IP's Telnet application from any network workstation if the router has been configured to be a part of the network. The advantage to Telnet is that you do not have to be near the router; you could be in the next room or half way around the world. The drawback to Telnet is that if the router has not been configured or if the configuration is corrupted, you cannot get in. You have to have a functioning interface to come in over the network.

The console connection, on the other hand, plugs directly into a special port, the console port, on the router. This connection does not require that the router be configured or that the console station be a part of the network. I typically use my laptop for this purpose, which would not normally be a part of the client's network.

The *Cisco console cable* is a flat baby-blue (some are black) cable with RJ-45 connectors on both ends. The cable is called a *rollover* cable because the pin connections are exactly reversed from end to end. The wire to pin 1 on one end goes to pin 8 on the other end, 2 to 7, 3 to 6, and so on. You can verify this by looking at both connectors side by side with the clips away from you. Note this is not the same as a *crossover* cable, on which only two of the four pairs are crossed.

The router connection for the console cable plugs into an RJ-45 connector on the back of the router labeled as Console. Newer units have the label in the same baby-blue color as the rollover cable to facilitate making the right connection. Some older models, such as the 4000, require a DB-25 to RJ-45 connector (Cisco item CAB-5MODCM), which should come with the console cable. Figure 12-16 shows the DB-25 to RJ-45 connector. You should see that only seven of the pins are used and present.

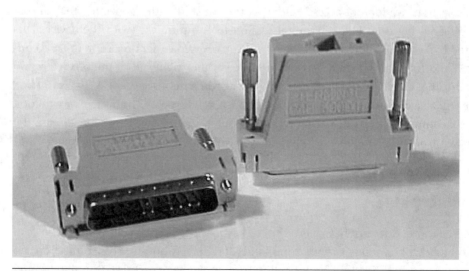

Figure 12-16   Router DB-25 to RJ-45 connector

The workstation connection is via a COM port, which means you need either a DB-9 or DB-25 to RJ-45 connector to make the connection. Most new computers use the smaller DB-9 (Cisco item 74-0495-01), but some older ones have the older DB-25 connection (Cisco item 29-0810-01). Note this is not the same DB-25 connector previously discussed; in fact, this one is the opposite connection and would plug into that connector. Figure 12-17 shows both connectors and the rollover cable attached.

When you connect to the COM port on the back of the computer, note any indication of whether it is COM port 1, 2, and so on. You will need that information when you set up your HyperTerminal session. If it isn't marked, we can determine it later.

Setting Up a HyperTerminal Session

The following discussion assumes that you are using a version of Windows and that HyperTerminal has been installed. HyperTerminal is a terminal emulation program that comes with all versions of Windows. It can be accessed from the Start button on the taskbar. The HyperTerminal session allows us to communicate with the router via the console connection discussed in the last section. The following exercise takes you through the steps of establishing and saving a HyperTerminal session.

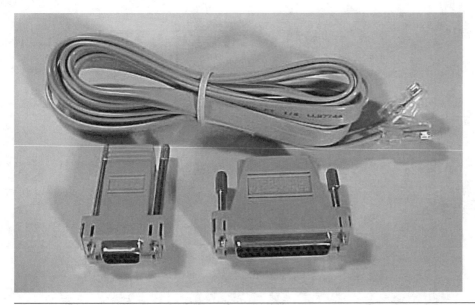

Figure 12-17   Workstation DB-9 and DB-25 connectors

HyperTerminal Exercise

1. After you connect your computer to the router (as covered in the last section) and make sure that the router is running, launch a new HyperTerminal session: Start | Programs | Accessories | Communications | HyperTerminalKbps. The following illustration shows the menu option under Windows 2000.

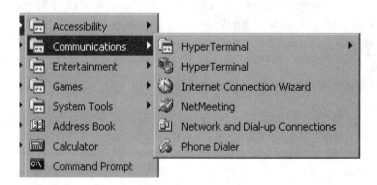

2. Note that the upper HyperTerminal icon with the folder contains any saved HyperTerminal setups. Since this is a first-time setup, use the second entry to launch the application. The following illustration shows the initial setup window with the HyperTerminal window in the background.

3. Type a name for the setup, select an icon, and then press ENTER or click the OK button. Type a name that makes sense to you. The following illustration shows the next screen, in which you select your COM port to configure.

4. You can see by this screen that HyperTerminal can also be used with a modem. For our purposes, we want to use the Connect Using list box and choose the COM port that you connected to. If you aren't sure, choose COM 1. You can change it later if it is wrong. After making the selection, press ENTER or click OK. The following illustration shows the Port Settings tab of the Properties dialog box.

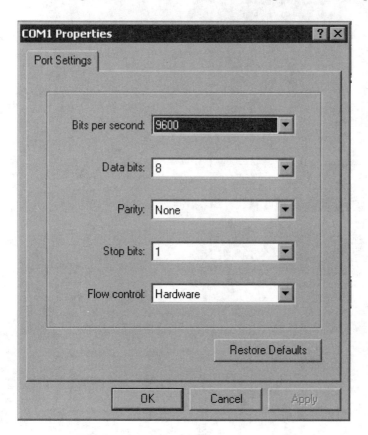

5. You probably only need to set the first entry to 9600. This sets the bit transfer rate between the workstation and router. If this is wrong, you will get gibberish on the screen. Make sure that your settings match those shown in the preceding illustration and then press ENTER or click OK. The setup window closes and leaves the HyperTerminal window open.

6. You may need to press ENTER a few times to get the router's attention. If the router is configured, it should prompt you for a password; otherwise, it will take you directly to the command line. The following illustration shows the password login screen.

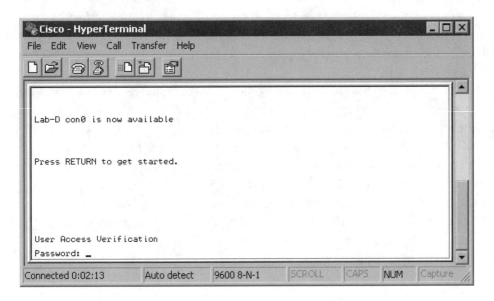

7. If the router cannot be reached, check all connections and that the router is running. If that is okay, then use File | Properties to change the port to COM 2 and try it again.

8. Once you have a connection, close the HyperTerminal window (File | Exit) and answer Yes when asked if you want to save your configuration settings.

9. To launch another session with that setup, return to step 1 and use the HyperTerminal folder option, which should have your setup name listed. Double-clicking it launches the session.

   If you are going to use the connection often, you should consider adding a shortcut to the desktop or drag your setup icon to the Start button to create an entry at the top of the Start menu.

These HyperTerminal settings should work with any Cisco router or switch. We will return to it often in the next few chapters as we look at exploring and configuring the router.

Command-Line Interface (CLI)

Cisco IOS uses a CLI to prompt you for input or requests. It is not a menu-driven program like most user applications today. Without a menu to work from, it is important that you understand the basic hierarchy and how to get help when you need assistance. It is essential for the CCNA exam and to work in the field that you be comfortable with this interface. Cisco sells some network management tools and some device configuration tools that can make many configuration tasks easier, but you must assume that you will have to deal with the CLI.

Throughout the next few chapters, we use the CLI to configure the router, to check on how it is performing, and to move to other routers. Figure 12-18 shows the CLI from the initial password to a command-line prompt.

The Lab-D portion of the prompt is the host name assigned to the router by the administrator. The name could be a location identifier such as SanteFe or Seattle, or it could be a department identifier such as Acctg3 or Sales. In the figure, the router used is a part of my personal lab and it is the fourth device in a series, hence the Lab-D.

The greater-than symbol (>) following the host name indicates that we are at the user mode of the router. Recognizing that symbol will eventually tell you what commands can or cannot be implemented at this level.

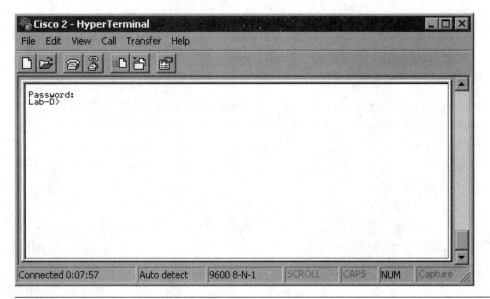

Figure 12-18   Command-line interface

Command lines are created by typing one or more words at the appropriate prompt. Some commands are very short, such as using the word **enable** to get to the privilege mode (see the next section), and some are very complex, such as those used in access control lists (ACLs), which we cover in Chapter 15. Many of the words can be abbreviated to save typing. For example, the enable command can be abbreviated to **en**. The abbreviations vary depending on the number of commands at a particular level that begin with the same letter(s). You can stop typing once you have typed enough letters to remove any ambiguity about which command you want.

After a period of inactivity on the keyboard, the IOS logs you out and closes the session, requiring you to press ENTER a few times to "wake" the interface and re-enter the password.

User and Privilege EXEC Modes

Assuming the router is configured properly and connected correctly, it functions without administrative interaction until a change needs to be made. It accepts packets and forwards them on their way efficiently and exchanges routing information with any appropriate routers on or added to the system.

When administrators needs to communicate directly with the router, they use the EXEC interactive command processor of the IOS. There are two basic levels to the EXEC mode that we need to concern ourselves with:

- **User mode**   Allows the user to look at a limited amount of information about the router, but makes no changes in the configuration or operation. User mode can be recognized by the greater-than symbol (>) at the end of the prompt.

- **Privilege mode**   Allows the user to see the configuration of the router and provides access to the configuration modes to make changes. The pound symbol (#) at the end of the prompt indicates privilege mode.

The enable command accesses privilege mode from user mode. The disable command returns you to user mode from privilege mode. Figure 12-19 shows the login process (password entries are not displayed) and the prompt changing at each level.

The second set of entries demonstrates reducing the enable command to the abbreviated form en. You can type more letters than needed but they must be spelled right. A few rows later, you see the result of shortening the disable command too far: The IOS cannot distinguish the command and displays an error message. The next line shows that the minimum abbreviation for the disable command is disa.

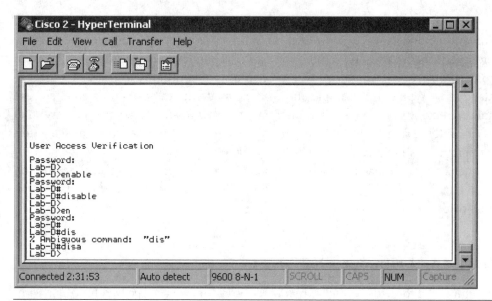

```
Cisco 2 - HyperTerminal
File   Edit   View   Call   Transfer   Help




User Access Verification

Password:
Lab-D>
Lab-D>enable
Password:
Lab-D#
Lab-D#disable
Lab-D>
Lab-D>en
Password:
Lab-D#
Lab-D#dis
% Ambiguous command:  "dis"
Lab-D#disa
Lab-D>

Connected 2:31:53     Auto detect     9600 8-N-1     SCROLL     CAPS     NUM     Capture
```

Figure 12-19   User and privilege modes

NOTE: It is important to understand that the screen output may vary a little with the specific version of the Cisco IOS software, the router configuration, and the model of device. It should not cause you any difficulty, but be tolerant of minor differences.

Each of the two modes can, and should, have unique passwords assigned to it to prevent unwanted guests from accessing the router. Recall that we could get here with a console cable and a laptop without being an authorized user of the network. The password system is part of the security from attack on this vital part of your network. It is only *part* of the security because the device itself should be stored in a secure place. Even if someone were to unplug it, you would have a serious disruption in your network until the unit could be plugged back in. If someone takes the device to sell on an online auction site, you have a major disruption that will be much more difficult to resolve.

Configuration Modes

To access any commands that can display the configuration or that enable you to make configuration changes, you must first be able to access privilege mode. This means you must know the second password (the enable password), if set. From privilege mode, you can display both the running (current) and the startup configurations.

If you want to make changes in the configuration, you must enter global configuration mode by typing **configure terminal**, or **conf t** for short. This mode allows changes that are router-wide, such as changing the host name. You also can enter specific configuration modes to make changes to a part of the router, such as a specific interface. Some of the other configuration modes, with examples of the tasks they can perform, include the following:

- **Interface**   Set IP addresses for the interface

- **Subinterface**   Create serial subinterfaces for a Frame Relay connection

- **Line**   See passwords for users telnetting in to the router

- **Router**   Set and define the routing protocol

There are other commands that you will be introduced to as we go along. The important thing is to understand the steps to get to the point of changing a configuration feature. For example, if you want to change the IP address or subnet mask on a router interface, you must access user mode (with password), privilege mode (with password), global configuration mode, and then interface configuration mode. Figure 12-20 demonstrates that set of steps without actually changing the IP address; we will do that in the next session.

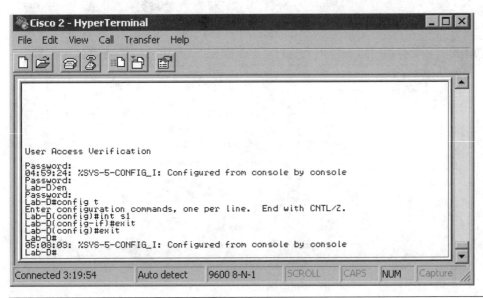

Figure 12-20   Steps to interface configuration mode

You should see that the command configure terminal was abbreviated to conf t, and that the prompt changed to Lab-D(config)#, with (config) indicating that you are now in global configuration mode.

In the next line, I abbreviated **Interface Serial 1** to **int s1** and the prompt again changed. This time to Lab-D(config-if)#, indicating interface configuration mode. Be aware that the prompt would be the same for any interface; it indicates the mode not the actual device.

The exit command is used to leave a mode and return to the previous mode. This example took two exit commands because we had gone two levels from privilege mode. The next section explains that I could have used CTRL-Z to exit directly back to privilege mode.

Router Help Feature

The Cisco IOS uses the question mark key (?) to bring up the help feature. It can be used to see which commands are available in any particular mode or to see what options exist for a command you have already started to type. Figure 12-21 shows the result of typing ? at the privilege mode prompt.

Figure 12-21 Help at privilege mode prompt

There are too many options to see on one screen, so it stops when the screen is full. "More" at the bottom of the screen indicates that there are more items to see. At this point, you can press any of the following keys:

- SPACEBAR to get another screen full of entries
- ENTER to get one more line to scroll up
- Any letter key to abandon the display

Looking at Figure 12-21, we see that the configure command is an option at this level. We also see that two commands begin with the letters con, so we need to type **conf** at least to avoid any confusion with the connect command.

Using TAB to Complete a Word

We saw earlier that we can abbreviate commands; another option is to type the unique characters for a command and then press the TAB key. The IOS will finish the word for you. The abbreviation identifies the command; the TAB key simply verifies that the router has understood the specific command. This has no impact on performance but sometimes makes for more meaningful recordings when you are capturing your steps for later study. We will look at capturing your work later in this chapter.

Figure 12-22 shows that after seeing the configure command in our earlier display with the ?, I typed a letter to abandon the help. I then typed **conf**, the fewest letters necessary, and pressed the TAB key. Notice that it completed the word on the next line. It also added a space, knowing that any additional text would require a space. By typing ? at this location, we now see the configure options, including the terminal command that we used earlier to get into global configuration mode.

Since only one option begins with the letter *t*, I typed **t** and pressed the TAB key. Trying the question mark on the next line showed that only <cr> or carriage return (ENTER) is available. Pressing ENTER put us in global configuration mode like earlier.

IOS Command History

The IOS records a history, or record, of the commands that you have entered at each mode or level. This record can be used to recall long or complex commands and thereby save typing. The CTRL-P keys bring up the previous command in the command history and can be repeated through the previous ten commands at that level. If you go past the command, CTRL-N will take you to the next command in the command history.

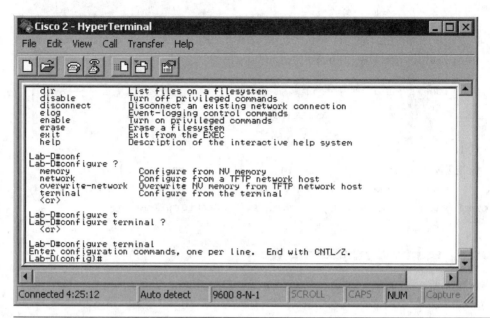

```
Cisco 2 - HyperTerminal                                           _ □ X
File  Edit  View  Call  Transfer  Help

  □ ☞  ☎ ☒   ▫ ☐   ☞

   dir              List files on a filesystem
   disable          Turn off privileged commands
   disconnect       Disconnect an existing network connection
   elog             Event-logging control commands
   enable           Turn on privileged commands
   erase            Erase a filesystem
   exit             Exit from the EXEC
   help             Description of the interactive help system

 Lab-D#conf
 Lab-D#configure ?
   memory             Configure from NV memory
   network            Configure from a TFTP network host
   overwrite-network  Overwrite NV memory from TFTP network host
   terminal           Configure from the terminal
   <cr>

 Lab-D#configure t
 Lab-D#configure terminal ?
   <cr>

 Lab-D#configure terminal
 Enter configuration commands, one per line.  End with CNTL/Z.
 Lab-D(config)#

Connected 4:25:12    Auto detect    9600 8-N-1    SCROLL   CAPS  NUM   Capture
```

Figure 12-22   Building commands using help

 EXAM TIP: Some versions of Windows let you use the up and down arrow keys to scroll through the command history. While this is a very friendly feature to use, it doesn't work in all cases and will not be an exam answer option.

Figure 12-23 shows that I exited out of configure terminal only to change my mind. A single ctrl-p brought back the command, so I only needed to press enter. I repeated the process again.

Be aware that each time you exit global configuration mode, you get a system message like the one that appears in Figure 12-23. It is just reporting to you that any changes made came from the console—you typed them.

In the next exercise, you will see that in addition to using the command history, you can change the size of the history file to as many as 256 commands, or you can disable the feature altogether.

IOS Editing Commands

The IOS supports a set of editing key functions that allow you to edit a command line rather than retype it. With some versions of Windows, you may be able to use your

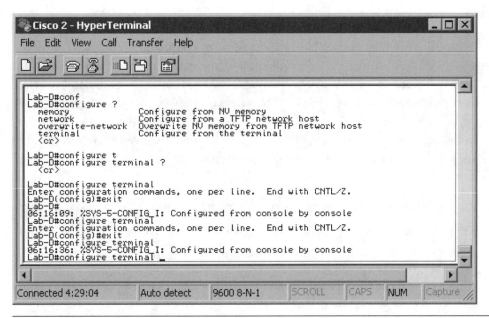

Figure 12-23   Command history

left/right arrow, HOME, and END keys to accomplish the same results. For your own good, make sure you remember at least the first four of these commands:

COMMAND	RESULT
CTRL-A	Move to the beginning of the line
CTRL-E	Move to the end of the line
CTRL-B	Move left (back) one character
CTRL-F	Move right (forward) one chARACTER
ESC-B	Move left (back) one word
ESC-F	Move right (forward) one word

The IOS performs a syntax check as you execute a command. If it finds an error or gets confused, it places a ^ where the error or confusion occurred. This error locator symbol used with the help system should allow you to quickly find and correct syntax errors.

Show Commands

Both user and privilege modes have a series of show command options that allow the user to look at specific parts of the configuration, the entire configuration, or the status of particular features, such as interfaces or access control lists. The command structure is simply the show command followed by what you want to look at. When first working with the feature, **show ?** is an easy way to see the options available at each level.

Show commands will become some of your most often used commands as you configure and debug the devices. In the following exercise, we will look at these show commands:

- **Show Running-config** Shows the current operating configuration in RAM.
- **Show Startup-config** Shows the contents of the startup configuration in NVRAM.
- **Show Interfaces** Shows the interface status and configuration.

While you will run into these commands again in later chapters, it is never too early to start to become familiar with them.

Basics Exercise

The following exercise include many of the features just discussed. The purpose of this exercise is two-fold: first to introduce the specific command or feature, and second to help you become familiar with the CLI.

1. If necessary, open your HyperTerminal session again and log in to user mode.

 NOTE: If you are asked "Would you like to enter the initial configuration dialog? [yes/no]:" answer no, and then when asked "Would you like to terminate autoinstall? [yes]:" just press enter to accept the default. This means your router isn't configured, but that won't hurt what we are going to do. It does mean you will not be asked to enter passwords, because none are set.

2. At the user mode prompt, type? but don't press ENTER.

When the screen stops filling, "More" tells us that we have more to view. Press ENTER a few times to see that it scrolls one new line.

Press the SPACEBAR to see the rest of the commands appear.

The result should look something like this:

```
Lab-D>?
Exec commands:
  access-enable    Create a temporary Access-List entry
```

```
access-profile    Apply user-profile to interface
clear             Reset functions
connect           Open a terminal connection
disable           Turn off privileged commands
disconnect        Disconnect an existing network connection
enable            Turn on privileged commands
exit              Exit from the EXEC
help              Description of the interactive help system
lock              Lock the terminal
login             Log in as a particular user
logout            Exit from the EXEC
mrinfo            Request neighbor and version information from a
multicast
                  router
mstat             Show statistics after multiple multicast
traceroutes
mtrace            Trace reverse multicast path from destination
to source
name-connection   Name an existing network connection
pad               Open a X.29 PAD connection
ping              Send echo messages
ppp               Start IETF Point-to-Point Protocol (PPP)
resume            Resume an active network connection
rlogin            Open an rlogin connection
set               Set system parameter (not config)
show              Show running system information
slip              Start Serial-line IP (SLIP)
systat            Display information about terminal lines
telnet            Open a telnet connection
terminal          Set terminal line parameters
traceroute        Trace route to destination
tunnel            Open a tunnel connection
udptn             Open an udptn connection
where             List active connections
x28               Become an X.28 PAD
x3                Set X.3 parameters on PAD
```

3. Type **show** followed by a space and a question mark (**show ?**) and see if running-config or startup-config are available. They shouldn't be. The result should look something like this:

```
Lab-D>show ?
  backup       Backup status
  cca          CCA information
  cdapi        CDAPI information
  cef          Cisco Express Forwarding
  class-map    Show QoS Class Map
  clock        Display the system clock
  compress     Show compression statistics
  diale        Dialer parameters and statistics
  exception    exception information
  flash:       display information about flash: file system
  history      Display the session command history
```

```
  hosts            IP domain-name, lookup style, nameservers, and
host table
  location         Display the system location
  modemcap         Show Modem Capabilities database
  policy-map       Show QoS Policy Map
  ppp              PPP parameters and statistics
  queue            Show queue contents
  queueing         Show queueing configuration
  radius           Shows radius information
  rmon             rmon statistics
  rtr              Response Time Reporter (RTR)
  sessions         Information about Telnet connections
  snmp             snmp statistics
  tacacs           Shows tacacs+ server statistics
  template         Template information
  terminal         Display terminal configuration parameters
  traffic-shape    traffic rate shaping configuration
  users            Display information about terminal lines
  version          System hardware and software status
```

4. After the commands have scrolled by, the command line should still say show followed by a space. Add the work **clock** and press ENTER.

   Do not be surprised if the date and time are wrong. Cisco routers do not use a battery to maintain the time, so if a unit is powered off, the clock starts again when the power comes back on.

5. Type **enable** to go to privilege mode and enter the password if prompted for one.

6. Use **?** and **show ?** to see what commands are available. Some will look familiar but there should be many more, including running-config and startup-config under the show option.

7. Once the commands have scrolled by, the word show should be left. Add characters so that the command says **show run** and press ENTER.

   This is the current configuration. It will vary from router to router but it should look something like this:

```
Lab-D#show run
Building configuration...
Current configuration:
!
version 12.0
service timestamps debug uptime
service timestamps log uptime
no service password-encryption
!
hostname Lab-D
!
enable secret 5 $1$U5M/$/Uw1RFSDZD1F5OhwWc0wC1
```

```
!
ip subnet-zero
ip host Lab-A 192.168.1.100 192.168.10.2 192.168.91.2
ip host Lab-B 192.168.20.1 192.168.30.1 192.168.91.1 192.168.92.2
ip host Lab-C 192.168.40.1 192.168.10.1 192.168.92.1 192.168.3.2
ip host Lab-D 192.168.50.1 192.168.93.1 192.168.94.2
ip host Lab-E 192.168.60.1 192.168.95.2 192.168.94.1
ip host Lab-F 192.168.70.1 192.168.95.1
!
interface Ethernet0
 ip address 192.168.94.2 255.255.255.0
 no ip directed-broadcast
!
interface Serial0
 no ip address
 no ip directed-broadcast
 no ip mroute-cache
 shutdown
!
interface Serial1
 ip address 192.168.93.1 255.255.255.0
 no ip directed-broadcast
 clockrate 56000
!
router rip
 network 192.168.93.0
 network 192.168.94.0
!
no ip classless
ip http server
!
line con 0
 password cisco
 logging synchronous
 login
 transport input none
line aux 0
 password cisco
 login
line vty 0 4
 password cisco
 login
!
end
Lab-D#
```

8. Look over your own result and my sample, which was just shown. Look particularly at the last few lines. It seems like the word password gets used a lot. Those
   are the user mode passwords for the console port and for people telnetting in
   through a network interface. Does it make sense now why user-level logins cannot
   view the running-config?

9. Up near the top there is this line:

   enable secret 5 1U5M/$/Uw1RFSDZD1F5OhwWc0wC1

   It is the privilege mode password, but it's nothing like what you typed, because it has been encrypted so that someone seeing the configuration cannot figure it out.

10. Try typing **sh star**, short for show startup-config. The result should look very much like the running-config. Unless someone has changed the configuration and has not saved the changes, it should be identical.

11. Note that the name in the prompt is the same as the hostname command near the beginning of the configuration.

    Type **config t** and press ENTER to go to global configuration mode.

    Note that the prompt has changed.

12. Type **hostname** followed by your first name, like **hostname bob**, and press ENTER. Note that the prompt has changed. It should be different.

13. Type **exit** to leave global configuration mode.

14. Show the **running-config** and note the hostname command. It should be what you typed:

```
bob#sho run
Building configuration...
Current configuration:
!
version 12.0
service timestamps debug uptime
service timestamps log uptime
no service password-encryption
!
hostname bob
!
```

15. Show the startup-config and note the hostname command. It should be the original.

    Our running-config (current) is now different than our startup. That means that if the router were rebooted, the hostname would revert back to the original.

16. Type **show int** and press ENTER. You should now get a display of the status of each interface. The result will look something like this:

```
bob#sho int
Ethernet0 is up, line protocol is up
  Hardware is Lance, address is 0010.7b3a.f5ba (bia
0010.7b3a.f5ba)
  Internet address is 192.168.94.2/24
```

```
   MTU 1500 bytes, BW 10000 Kbpsit, DLY 1000 usec,
      reliability 255/255, txload 1/255, rxload 1/255
   Encapsulation ARPA, loopback not set
   Keepalive set (10 sec)
   ARP type: ARPA, ARP Timeout 04:00:00
   Last input 00:00:10, output 00:00:07, output hang never
   Last clearing of "show interface" counters never
   Queueing strategy: fifo
   Output queue 0/40, 0 drops; input queue 0/75, 0 drops
   5 minute input rate 0 bits/sec, 0 packets/sec
   5 minute output rate 0 bits/sec, 0 packets/sec
      1822 packets input, 284714 bytes, 0 no buffer
      Received 1819 broadcasts, 0 runts, 0 giants, 0 throttles
      0 input errors, 0 CRC, 0 frame, 0 overrun, 0 ignored
      0 input packets with dribble condition detected
      5256 packets output, 598777 bytes, 0 underruns
      0 output errors, 0 collisions, 6 interface resets
      0 babbles, 0 late collision, 0 deferred
      0 lost carrier, 0 no carrier
      0 output buffer failures, 0 output buffers swapped out
Serial0 is administratively down, line protocol is down
   Hardware is HD64570 with 56k 4-wire CSU/DSU
   MTU 1500 bytes, BW 1544 Kbpsit, DLY 20000 usec,
      reliability 255/255, txload 1/255, rxload 1/255
   Encapsulation HDLC, loopback not set
   Keepalive set (10 sec)
   Last input never, output never, output hang never
   Last clearing of "show interface" counters never
   Input queue: 0/75/0 (size/max/drops); Total output drops: 0
   Queueing strategy: weighted fair
   Output queue: 0/1000/64/0 (size/max total/threshold/drops)
      Conversations  0/0/256 (active/max active/max total)
      Reserved Conversations 0/0 (allocated/max allocated)
   5 minute input rate 0 bits/sec, 0 packets/sec
   5 minute output rate 0 bits/sec, 0 packets/sec
      0 packets input, 0 bytes, 0 no buffer
      Received 0 broadcasts, 0 runts, 0 giants, 0 throttles
      0 input errors, 0 CRC, 0 frame, 0 overrun, 0 ignored, 0 abort
      0 packets output, 0 bytes, 0 underruns
      0 output errors, 0 collisions, 1 interface resets
      0 output buffer failures, 0 output buffers swapped out
      0 carrier transitions
      DCD=down  DSR=down  DTR=down  RTS=down  CTS=down
Serial1 is up, line protocol is up
   Hardware is HD64570 with 5-in-1 module
   Internet address is 192.168.93.1/24
   MTU 1500 bytes, BW 1544 Kbpsit, DLY 20000 usec,
      reliability 255/255, txload 1/255, rxload 1/255
   Encapsulation HDLC, loopback not set
   Keepalive set (10 sec)
   Last input 00:00:08, output 00:00:02, output hang never
   Last clearing of "show interface" counters never
   Input queue: 0/75/0 (size/max/drops); Total output drops: 0
```

```
     Queueing strategy: weighted fair
     Output queue: 0/1000/64/0  (size/max total/threshold/drops)
        Conversations  0/2/256 (active/max active/max total)
        Reserved Conversations 0/0  (allocated/max allocated)
     5 minute input rate 0 bits/sec, 0 packets/sec
     5 minute output rate 0 bits/sec, 0 packets/sec
        5228 packets input, 392068 bytes, 0 no buffer
        Received 5228 broadcasts, 0 runts, 0 giants, 0 throttles
        0 input errors, 0 CRC, 0 frame, 0 overrun, 0 ignored, 0 abort
        5250 packets output, 385381 bytes, 0 underruns
        0 output errors, 0 collisions, 4 interface resets
        0 output buffer failures, 0 output buffers swapped out
        12 carrier transitions
        DCD=up  DSR=up  DTR=up  RTS=up  CTS=up
bob#
```

17. Look over the sample output and compare it to yours. Looking at my Ethernet0 near the top, we see: Ethernet0 is up, line protocol is up. The first statement indicates that the physical link to the other device is good. The second statement indicates that the configuration on both sides is okay.

    Two lines down we can see the IP address and subnet mask for the interface. Farther down we can see some traffic statistics.

18. My Serial0 indicates it is not functioning and there is no IP address. If we were to look back at the running configuration, we would see that the interface isn't configured.

    The Serial1 interface should be up and running.

19. Look over your results, noting one of your interfaces, the type, and number.

20. At the privilege mode prompt, type **show int** but don't press ENTER.

    Press TAB to see the rest of the word interfaces appear.

Add a question mark to the end of the command to see the options. The following illustration should represent what you might find.

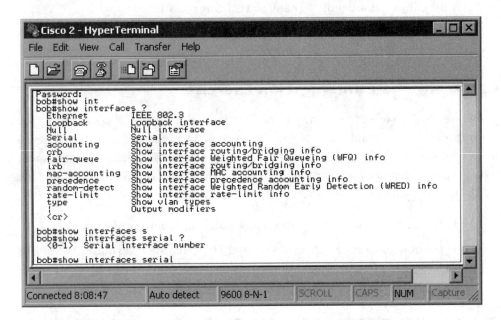

```
Cisco 2 - HyperTerminal
File  Edit  View  Call  Transfer  Help

Password:
bob#show int
bob#show interfaces ?
  Ethernet        IEEE 802.3
  Loopback        Loopback interface
  Null            Null interface
  Serial          Serial
  accounting      Show interface accounting
  crb             Show interface routing/bridging info
  fair-queue      Show interface Weighted Fair Queueing (WFQ) info
  irb             Show interface routing/bridging info
  mac-accounting  Show interface MAC accounting info
  precedence      Show interface precedence accounting info
  random-detect   Show interface Weighted Random Early Detection (WRED) info
  rate-limit      Show interface rate-limit info
  type            Show vlan types
  |               Output modifiers
  <cr>

bob#show interfaces s
bob#show interfaces serial ?
  <0-1>  Serial interface number

bob#show interfaces serial

Connected 8:08:47    Auto detect    9600 8-N-1    SCROLL    CAPS    NUM    Capture
```

21. Notice that there are many options that seem like accounting, but there should be an entry for each type of interface that you have.

    Add the first few letters of the interface type to the command and press the TAB key. In the last figure, note that I typed **s** for serial and pressing TAB finished the entry.

    Add a question mark to the command and it will tell you the choices. In the last figure, there is a 0 and a 1 serial interface.

    Add one of the numbers shown and press ENTER to see only the data on that interface.

    We just used the Help feature to walk us through building a command.

22. While this is helpful, if you are unfamiliar with a command or its options, it is also somewhat slow. Once you know the commands, typing **sho int s1** would have accomplished the same result.

23. At the privilege mode prompt, press CTRL-P a few times to see the command you just issued in reverse order.

    Try CTRL-N and CTRL-P to see that you can scroll up and down through the list.

    Try the **show history** command.

24. Experiment with the features covered until you get comfortable in the environment.

    Try the editing commands to change an existing command.

    Try any show command you like; it may not show anything, but it also can't hurt your configuration.

Capturing the Configuration Exercise

In this exercise, you learn to capture a HyperTerminal session as a way of capturing your efforts for later review and study. If you master these techniques, they will save you a tremendous amount of typing in later labs and on the job. The only equipment required is a single router, a workstation running a Windows operating system, and one 3 1/2-inch floppy disk with a label.

1. If necessary, return to privilege EXEC mode and show your configuration.

2. It is possible to capture the results of your HyperTerminal session in a text file, which can be viewed and/or printed using Notepad, WordPad, or Microsoft Word.

 NOTE: This feature captures your future screens—not what is currently on the screen. You are in essence turning on a recording session; you will later "stop" the session, at which time it will be written to a text file.

---

3. To start a Capture session, choose Transfer | Capture Text from the menu. A window similar to the following illustration will appear.

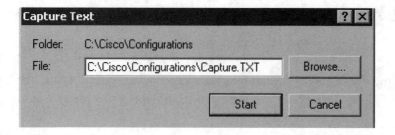

4. The default file name is CAPTURE.TXT and the data preceding it is the location of HyperTerminal on our disk. We don't want to use either. We want our results stored on our floppy disk.

   Make sure that your floppy disk is in the A drive. When the preceding box appears, change the File box to **A:\FirstTest**

   Then click the Start button. Anything that appears on the screen after this point will be copied to the file.

5. Do your **show run** command again using the SPACEBAR to advance through the display.

6. When the display is done, choose Transfer | Capture Text | Stop from the menu.

NOTE: This is probably one of the most important and most easily forgotten steps. If you forget it, your capture file will probably be empty.

7. Launch Windows Explorer utilizing the Start button. You will find Windows Explorer in Programs or Accessories, depending on your Windows operating system. Example: Use Start | Programs | Windows Explorer to launch the Explorer program with Windows 9*x*.

8. In the left-side pane, select the 3 1/2 Floppy (A:) drive. On the right side, you should see the file you just created.

9. Double-click the FirstTest document's icon. The result should look something like this:

```
Router#show run
Building configuration...
Current configuration:
!
version 12.0
service timestamps debug uptime
service timestamps log uptime
no service password-encryption
!
hostname Router
!
enable secret 5 $1$HD2B$6iXb.h6QEJJjtn/NnwUHO.
!
ip subnet-zero
no ip domain-lookup
!
```

```
interface Ethernet0
--More--                              no ip address
no ip directed-broadcast
shutdown
```

10. Note the word "More" and the gibberish appearing under the interface Ethernet0 line. That's where we had to press the SPACEBAR to see the rest of the list. Use basic word processing techniques to clean that up. Be sure the selection stops with the last box before deleting—the next space is the indent for that line. The result should look like this:

```
interface Ethernet0
no ip address
no ip directed-broadcast
shutdown
```

11. Continue cleaning up any more SPACEBAR debris.

12. Look over your results and then save them. This might not be such a bad starting point if you want to build a configuration for this router offsite.

13. Experiment with the capture feature until you are comfortable with it.

I suggest that you seriously consider capturing each router configuration for every exercise. They can be valuable as you prepare for the certification exam. If you ever need to quickly reconstruct a situation, these captured configuration files can be uploaded to the routers in less than five minutes, without typos. These text files are very small—hundreds would fit on a floppy disk.

Cisco Router Setup Feature

This is a feature that I really didn't care for in versions of the IOS prior to 12. It asked too many questions and seemed unnecessarily clumsy. The new version is much nicer and to the point, which is to give the router enough of a configuration so that you can then telnet in and finish the job. The downside that I still see is that you have to set up a console session to get to this point, so why use this tool when you could just go in and add it to the configuration? After the next chapter, you can decide for yourself.

The one value that I see to this routine is that a help desk person could walk someone through this process, putting in just enough information to get the device on the network. At that point, someone else could telnet in and finish the job.

Whenever possible, the Setup program default answers appear in square brackets [ ] following the question. Pressing ENTER accepts these defaults. If the device is already configured, the defaults are the currently configured values. This last feature allows you to go through setup several times if necessary without losing information already put in. For a new system, the factory defaults that exist will appear as the defaults.

If you make a serious mistake, you can always press CTRL-C to terminate the process and start over.

When you complete the setup process, the screen displays the configuration that you have just created. You are offered the following three choices:

- [0] Go to the IOS command prompt without saving this config.

- [1] Return back to the setup without saving this config.

- [2] Save this configuration to nvram and exit.

Setting Up Global Parameters

The first things the setup script asks you to define are the global parameters. This allows you to set the router host name and the various passwords used on the router.

When prompted with "Enter enable secret," the password that you type will be processed by a Cisco proprietary encryption routine and is never displayed in clear text. To anyone seeing the router configuration file, the enable secret password appears as a meaningless string of text and numbers.

The Setup program requires an entry for the clear-text enable password. If both an enable secret password and an enable password exist, only the enable secret will be used. Some people set both to the same word. The Setup program recommends that they be different but does not require it. While this may seem user-friendly, in your final configuration, both passwords are displayed together near the top. If I saw the encrypted password and right below it a clear-text password with the same name, I know what my first attempt would be.

Since you have to create an enable password, use one you will remember. I typically go back later and delete this entry from the final configuration. If you must use a clear-text enable password to work with devices using older versions of the IOS, consider a different password.

All passwords are case-sensitive and can be alphanumeric.

Sample Setup Session

The following is the text capture of a trip through the setup feature. The items in bold after the [ ] represent input from the user. Some extra blank lines and carriage returns have been removed to conserve space.

Would you like to enter the initial configuration dialog? [yes/no]: **yes**

At any point you may enter a question mark '?' for help. Use CTRL-C to abort configuration dialog at any prompt. Default settings are in square brackets '[]'.

Basic management setup configures only enough connectivity for management of the system, extended setup will ask you to configure each interface on the system

Would you like to enter basic management setup? [yes/no]: **yes**

Configuring global parameters:

Enter host name [Router]: **Test**

The enable secret is a password used to protect access to privilege EXEC and configuration modes. This password, after entered, becomes encrypted in the configuration.

Enter enable secret: **class**

The enable password is used when you do not specify an enable secret password, with some older software versions, and some boot images.

Enter enable password: **test**

The virtual terminal password is used to protect access to the router over a network interface.

Enter virtual terminal password: **cisco**

Configure SNMP Network Management? [yes]: **no**

Current interface summary

Any interface listed with OK? value "NO" does not have a valid configuration

(3) Interface	IP-Address	OK?	Method Status	Protocol
Ethernet0	unassigned	NO	unset up	up
Serial0	unassigned	NO	unset down	down
Serial1	unassigned	NO	unset up	down

Enter interface name used to connect to the management network from the preceding interface summary: **Serial0**

Configuring interface Serial0:

Configure IP on this interface? [yes]:

IP address for this interface: `192.168.111.1`

Subnet mask for this interface [255.255.255.0] :

Class C network is 192.168.111.0, 24 subnet bits; mask is/24

The following configuration command script was created:

```
hostname Test
enable secret 5 $1$IIVO$bQgwSqjYLhejECZFL4TOF1
enable password test
line vty 0 4
password cisco
no snmp-server
!
no ip routing
!
interface Ethernet0
shutdown
no ip address
!
interface Serial0
no shutdown
ip address 192.168.111.1 255.255.255.0
!
interface Serial1
shutdown
no ip address
!
end

[0] Go to the IOS command prompt without saving this config.
[1] Return back to the setup without saving this config.
[2] Save this configuration to nvram and exit.
Enter your selection [2]:
```

Summary

We looked at reducing router installations to three basic categories—telecommuters, remote offices, and central offices—and briefly looked at product lines that might work in each situation. We saw that modular interface units provide opportunity for growth without risking the existing investment in hardware.

We discussed Cisco's common IOS and the implications. We also discussed how version and feature set differences between routers can make a difference in whether a device is right for a job.

In preparation for configuring the router in the next chapter, we looked at the command line interface (CLI), the user and privilege modes, some of the configuration modes, the help feature, editing commands, the history feature, and a couple basic show commands.

We saw that the basic Setup program can be used to create enough of a configuration to allow for a management console or experienced person to access the device and finish the configuration.

Practice Questions

Take a few moments and check your grasp of the concepts covered in this chapter. The answers are immediately following the questions.

Questions

1. At what point in the router lines do all of the devices use the Cisco IOS?
   a. 900 series and above
   b. 700 series and above
   c. 800 series and above
   d. They all use it

2. Which two of the following are access modes on a Cisco router?
   a. User
   b. EXEC
   c. Enable
   d. Privilege

3. What do the letters CLI stand for?
   a.

4. How is the context-sensitive help system accessed?
   a. Type /H at the command line
   b. Press the help key
   c. Type ? at the command line
   d. Press f1

5. Which of the following is the correct command for going to global configuration mode?
   a. Router>config t
   b. Router#config t
   c. Router (Config)#config t
   d. RouterA>global config

6. What is the primary purpose of the Cisco Setup feature?
   a. To speed up configuration
   b. To allow anyone to configure Cisco devices
   c. To provide basic initial connectivity to the network management system
   d. To create foolproof configurations

7. Which command shows the active configuration?
   a. show start
   b. show run
   c. show ver
   d. show flash

8. When the show run command is used and it stops at a full screen, what key advances one line at a time?
   a. ENTER
   b. SPACEBAR
   c. TAB
   d. PAGEDOWN

9. Which cable is used to connect a workstation to the router console port?
   a. Straight-through RJ-45
   b. Crossover RJ-45
   c. Rollover RJ-45
   d. Serial cable

10. Which edit key moves the cursor to the beginning of the line?
    a. CTRL-B
    b. ESC-B
    c. CTRL-A
    d. CTRL-F

11. Which edit key moves the cursor to the end of the line?
    a. CTRL-E
    b. ESC-B
    c. CTRL-A
    d. CTRL-F

12. Which history key brings up the last command issued?
    a. CTRL-A
    b. ESC-B
    c. CTRL-P
    d. CTRL-N

13. What key will complete a partially typed command word?
    a. ?
    b. TAB
    c. SPACEBAR
    d. ENTER

14. Which configuration file is stored in NVRAM?
    a. Current Configuration
    b. Running-Config
    c. Startup-Config
    d. Interface Configuration

15. If the router cannot find an uncorrupted version of the IOS, it will get a stripped-down version from where as a last resort?
    a. RAM
    b. NVRAM
    c. ROM
    d. Internet

Answers

1. **c.** The 800 series and above use the Cisco IOS.

2. **a.** and **d.** User and privilege. The EXEC mode is the user and privilege modes together, and enable is the command to get to privilege mode.

3. **a.** Command-line interface

4. **c.** Type ? at the command line to access the context-sensitive help system.

5. **b.** Router#config t. You must be in privilege mode to go to global configuration mode. Only this prompt is in the privilege mode.

6. **c.** The Setup routine is intended to provide basic initial connectivity to the network management system.

7. **b.** show run. The running-config file is the active configuration loaded in RAM.

8. **a.** ENTER. The SPACEBAR advances an entire screen. Any other key stops the display.

9. **c.** A rollover RJ-45 cable provides the console connection.

10. **c.** CTRL-A moves the cursor to the beginning of the line.

11. **a.** CTRL-E moves the cursor to the end of the line.

12. **c.** CTRL-P brings up the last command issued.

13. **b.** TAB will complete a partially typed command word.

14. **c.** Startup-Config is stored in NVRAM.

15. **c.** ROM contains a stripped-down version of the IOS.

CHAPTER 13

Router Configuration

This chapter will:

- **Explain how to configure interfaces**

- **Describe how to set up and test routing protocols**

- **Review device naming and name resolution**

- **Show how to add labels and documentation to your configuration**

- **Describe how to work with router password security**

- **Examine how to perform configuration and IOS backups and loads**

- **Explain how to perform password recovery**

- **Explore how to use tools such as Cisco's ConfigMaker**

- **Describe how to use a Web browser to configure the router**

In the last chapter, we looked at the *command-line interface* (CLI) and some basic commands for viewing and editing the router configuration. In this chapter, we use those skills to configure a router, confirm connectivity, and perform configuration and IOS backup and restorations. We also look at tools such as Cisco's ConfigMaker and using a Web browser as tools to assist in router configuration.

Router Configuration

In this chapter, we cover both the basic configuration techniques required for the CCNA exam and those techniques necessary to be confident with your first router assignments at work. We will approach each step as if you have one or more routers and are following along. Also included are screen captures and results so that you can compare your results or, if you do not have access to a device, see what the results should look like. We will break the configuration process into sections, such as configuring interfaces. In each section, we look at the important options and then the troubleshooting or verification commands for that section.

In breaking the process into sections, I use the following sections to organize my thinking into the order I would follow if faced with this task:

1. Erasing or clearing the router configuration

2. Configuring the interfaces

3. Establishing connectivity, setting up the routing

4. Creating passwords and router security

5. Using labels, messages, and documentation

6. Working with name resolution

While the order is probably not critical, I find it logical. It helps me to focus on what is important in the process both for the exam and when faced with a real job. We use hands-on skills assessments in the Cisco Academies, and before we moved to teaching this sequence, too many students would get hung up on tasks that, although important, did not contribute to getting a router up and running.

After the basic configuration steps, we will look at the following related topics:

• Configuration and IOS back up, restore and upgrade options

• Password recovery techniques

• Alternative configuration tools, such as ConfigMaker and Web browsers

It is important to realize that the steps we are covering are basically the same for the entire line of Cisco router devices. Because of the common IOS throughout the product line, tasks such as configuring an interface or adding routing will be very similar, varying mostly in scale and numbers. As we go along, I will introduce the concepts necessary to apply these steps to larger modular devices.

This is not to say that if a production router failed, you would necessarily go through these steps on a replacement unit. In many organizations, it is more likely that a copy of the configuration would be loaded onto an identical replacement device, or the repaired device, from a TFTP server. It would be tested and installed. Similarly, new device configurations would be done in a test lab environment and thoroughly debugged before adding the device to a live system.

So, as we go through this chapter, we will concentrate on the skills required to do the job. We will use devices as examples that you might have access to for hands-on experience. The Cisco academies use a mix of five 1600 and 2500 units for all of the CCNA labs. Virtually all of the concepts could be done on as few as one or two 1601 or 2501 devices. The configuration steps could all be done on a single device, but we couldn't verify connectivity. Some concepts, such as configuring a Token Ring interface, will obviously only work if you have an appropriate device, but the steps will be similar enough to Ethernet that you will have no problems seeing what is required. Figure 13-1 shows a basic configuration with two 1601 or 2501 devices.

If necessary, the second hub and PC could be eliminated. The hub can be any size and from any manufacturer. While not a good practice in the field, both Ethernet interfaces could go to the same hub. Figure 13-2 shows the actual configuration that I will be using to demonstrate the different types of interfaces.

Figure 13-1
Two-router lab
configuration

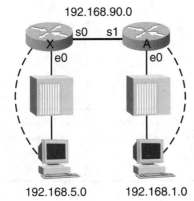

Figure 13-2
Three-router lab
configuration

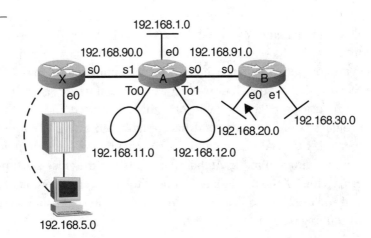

Most of our configuration in this chapter is done on Router X and assumes that Routers A and B are already configured. When we get to Token Ring interfaces, we will look at Router A. The only significance to the names is that a single letter is easy to apply as a label to a diagram; as you will see later, the routers could be named Seattle, Boston, and Paris.

Erasing or Clearing the Router Configuration

For the purpose of this chapter, we will assume that we will be adding Router X to an existing internal network that includes Router A and Router B. Each router represents a building on our growing campus. Building A and Router A are the original installations and support both Ethernet and Token Ring networks, which is a carryover from when the departmental LANs were integrated into a single network. All new installations and existing Ethernet networks are switched networks.

The new router we will be using has a single Ethernet interface and two serial interfaces, although we will initially be using only one of them. When the latest version of the IOS was loaded and the unit tested, some simple configuration was added. We will start by clearing the existing configuration, giving us a clean slate to work from.

NOTE: Using the latest IOS isn't always the best idea. You need to read the Release Notes for each version to ensure there are no caveats that apply to your configuration.

In earlier chapters, you learned that the configuration is stored in NVRAM and loaded into RAM as part of the router startup process. There is no command to directly erase the running configuration. This would be somewhat like sawing off a limb while you are standing on it. We need to erase the NVRAM copy, startup-config, and then perform a reload. The reload command is very much like a reset; it reloads the IOS and then the configuration. Since there will be no configuration in NVRAM to load, we will be taken to the autoinstall mode that we looked at in the last chapter.

We are using the flat Cisco console cable to connect our workstation's COM port to the router's "Console" port, and have established a HyperTerminal session with the router. Using the skills covered in the last chapter, we log in to the router and go into global configuration mode. At that point, we issue the **erase startup-config** command. Older versions of the IOS before 11.*x* used the write erase command, which is still supported and used by people in the field. The following code shows the results on a Cisco 2524 running version 12 of the IOS:

```
User Access Verification
Password:
Lab-AA>en
Password:
Lab-AA#erase start
Lab-AA#erase startup-config
Erasing the nvram filesystem will remove all files! Continue?
[confirm]
[OK]
Erase of nvram: complete
Lab-AA#show startup-config
%% Non-volatile configuration memory is not present
Lab-AA#
```

The prompt indicates this device has been named Lab-AA. We will see that this too will be eliminated. The **en** command is just the shortest number of keystrokes for "enable." The **erase start** command was completed to **erase startup-config** by pressing the TAB key. You are asked to confirm your intentions, and a "complete" message tells us that the NVRAM has been erased.

The **show startup-config** command was issued just so that you could see the resulting message when there is nothing stored in NVRAM.

The following display shows the **reload** command and the resulting output as the router resets itself and finds no configuration available. Notice that you are asked to confirm the reload, but that there is no severe warning, because the IOS does not know that you have erased the startup-config file. If you had made changes to the running-config, you would be asked if you want to save them. Answering yes would copy the running-config into NVRAM and thereby undermine our attempt to clear the configuration.

```
Lab-AA#reload
Proceed with reload? [confirm]

System Bootstrap, Version 11.0(10c), SOFTWARE
Copyright (c) 1986-1996 by cisco Systems
2500 processor with 14336 Kbytes of main memory

SERVICE_MODULE(1): self test finished: Passed
Notice: NVRAM invalid, possibly due to write erase.
F3: 7330424+102200+569972 at 0x3000060
                Restricted Rights Legend
Use, duplication, or disclosure by the Government is
subject to restrictions as set forth in subparagraph
(c) of the Commercial Computer Software - Restricted
Rights clause at FAR sec. 52.227-19 and subparagraph
(c) (1) (ii) of the Rights in Technical Data and Computer
Software clause at DFARS sec. 252.227-7013.

        cisco Systems, Inc.
        170 West Tasman Drive
        San Jose, California 95134-1706
```

```
Cisco Internetwork Operating System Software
IOS (tm) 2500 Software (C2500-I-L), Version 12.0(7)T
Copyright (c) 1986-1999 by cisco Systems, Inc.
Compiled Mon 06-Dec-99 14:50 by phanguye
Image text-base: 0x0303C728, data-base: 0x00001000

cisco 2524 (68030) processor (revision J) with 14336K/2048K bytes
of memory.
Processor board ID 08855309, with hardware revision 00000000
Bridging software.
X.25 software, Version 3.0.0.
1 Ethernet/IEEE 802.3 interface(s)
2 Serial network interface(s)
5-in-1 module for Serial Interface 0
56k 4-wire CSU/DSU for Serial Interface 1
32K bytes of non-volatile configuration memory.
16384K bytes of processor board System flash (Read ONLY)

          --- System Configuration Dialog ---
Would you like to enter the initial configuration dialog?
[yes/no]: n
Would you like to terminate autoinstall? [yes]:
```

The resulting messages tell us much about the router. The "Notice: NVRAM invalid, possibly due to write erase" message sounds scarier than it really is. It is telling us that the NVRAM is empty and it could be the result of us erasing the startup-config. The "write erase" portion of the message is a reference to an earlier-version command for erase startup-config. Commands such as write term and show config are older IOS alternatives to show run and show start. These commands are still supported for backward-compatibility.

The "IOS™ 2500 Software (C2500-I-L), Version 12.0(7)T" line tells us the feature set and version of the IOS. C2500-I-L indicates any model 2500 device and basic IP features only. Version 12.0(7)T indicates version 12 release 7. We will look at this coding information later in this chapter when we look at upgrading our IOS.

Looking over the rest of the output, you should be able to find the amount of RAM (DRAM actually), Flash, and the interfaces on the device. While it indicates two serial interfaces, it goes on to indicate that one is a standard "5-in-1 module for Serial Interface 0" while the other is a "56k 4-wire CSU/DSU for Serial Interface 1."

After we decline and confirm the invitation to the autoinstall, the following information appears before we are able to start to work:

```
Press RETURN to get started!
Passed
00:00:05: %LINK-3-UPDOWN: Interface Ethernet0, changed state to up
00:00:05: %LINK-3-UPDOWN: Interface Serial0, changed state to up
```

```
00:00:06: %LINK-3-UPDOWN: Interface Serial1, changed state to down
00:00:06: %LINEPROTO-5-UPDOWN: Line protocol on Interface Serial0,
changed state to up
00:00:31: %LINK-3-UPDOWN: Interface Ethernet0, changed state to up
00:00:32: %LINEPROTO-5-UPDOWN: Line protocol on Interface Ether-
net0,
changed state to up
00:00:44: %LINEPROTO-5-UPDOWN: Line protocol on Interface
Router> Serial0, changed state to up
00:00:59: %LINEPROTO-5-UPDOWN: Line protocol on Interface Serial0,
changed state to down
00:01:00: %LINK-5-CHANGED: Interface Serial0, changed state to
administratively down
00:01:00: %LINK-5-CHANGED: Interface Ethernet0, changed state to
administratively down
00:01:00: %LINK-5-CHANGED: Interface Serial1, changed state to
administratively down
00:01:01: %IP-5-WEBINST_KILL: Terminating DNS process
00:01:01: %LINEPROTO-5-UPDOWN: Line protocol on Interface Ether-
net0,
changed state to down
00:01:01: %LINEPROTO-5-UPDOWN: Line protocol on Interface Serial1,
changed state to down
00:01:07: %SYS-5-RESTART: System restarted ---
Cisco Internetwork Operating System Software
IOS (tm) 2500 Software (C2500-I-L), Version 12.0(7)T,
Copyright (c) 1986-1999 by cisco Systems, Inc.
Compiled Mon 06-Dec-99 14:50 by phanguye
Router>
```

Do not panic when you see the preceding system messages; the interfaces are attempting to "come up" and are discovering that the configuration is "incomplete." They then shut down. The prompt has been returned to the default.

We have cleared any configuration that has been added to this router, but it is not totally without a running configuration file. The next code segment shows the result of typing the show running-config command at this point:

```
Router>en
Router#show run
Router#show running-config
Building configuration . . .
Current configuration:
!
version 12.0
service timestamps debug uptime
service timestamps log uptime
no service password-encryption
!
hostname Router
!
ip subnet-zero
!
```

```
interface Ethernet0
 no ip address
 no ip directed-broadcast
 shutdown
!
interface Serial0
 no ip address
 no ip directed-broadcast
 no ip mroute-cache
 shutdown
!
interface Serial1
 no ip address
 no ip directed-broadcast
 shutdown
!
ip classless
no ip http server
!
line con 0
 transport input none
line aux 0
line vty 0 4
!
end
Router#
```

When we did our **reload**, we were returned to the user mode and therefore had to issue the **enable** command. Since the passwords were cleared with everything else, we aren't asked for a password. Note that the display gives us an inventory of our interfaces and shows that each has no IP address and has been explicitly shut down. It tells us the version of the IOS but not the feature set or release number. Some other commands that are added to the default command list in version 12.0(x) include the following:

COMMAND	RESULT
ip subnet-zero	Allows using the first subnet that is discarded under the RFC and in many CCNA texts. It refers to the network number where the subnet binary values are all zeros.
ip classless	Follows classless routing forwarding rules (CIDR). Not limited to classful routing. Since we will be using only RIP and IGRP, which are classful protocols, in the CCNA program, we won't see any benefit from this command.
no ip http server	Prevents Web browsers from accessing the router.
transport input none	No transport protocol for accessing the device through the console port is specified.
no ip directed-broadcast	The interface will not forward directed broadcasts.

The Copy Run Start Command

The copy run start command copies the running configuration to the startup configuration (NVRAM) so that the next time the device is started or reloaded, the changes will be available. As you are configuring your router, you may want to run this command periodically to save your work in progress. By the same token, if you mess up the running configuration with something you are trying, it is possible to restore from the last-saved copy by running a reload command. Keep in mind all changes since the last copy run start command will be lost.

EXAM TIP: For the CCNA exam, you really need to know the copy run start command. But, in practice, you may want to use an earlier-version command, write memory, which can be shortened to wri. While it provides no extra benefits, it is easier to type.

Commands Introduced in this Section

The following commands were introduced in this section:

- **copy run start**   Copies the current (running) configuration to NVRAM (startup configuration).

- **show running-config**   Shows the current or active configuration, the configuration controlling the device's operations.

- **show startup-config**   Shows the configuration file saved in NVRAM. This is the configuration file that is loaded into RAM when the router is started or a reload is executed.

- **erase startup-config**   Erases the contents of NVRAM. Following this with a reload command effectively erases the RAM.

- **Reload**   Reboots the router, reloading the IOS and the startup-config file into RAM.

Configuring the Interfaces

Interface configuration mode, designated by a prompt containing (config-if)#, is unique to each interface. To configure an interface, we first go to global configuration mode and then define the interface that we want to configure with a command like interface ethernet0 for the first Ethernet interface. There can be a space between the word "ethernet" and the number when you type the command, but the system will remove the space in any displays. Typically, we type the command in shorthand, like **int e0**, which accomplishes the same thing.

If you have fixed interfaces, it is pretty common to have them identified by type and then number, such as serial 0, serial 1, Ethernet 0, TokenRing 0, and so on, with 0 being the first interface of that type. This is also true of some of the older modular devices, such as the model 2524/2525 and the model 4000. Even though there may be multiple interfaces on a single module, they are still identified as serial 0 and serial 1, or Ethernet 0 and Ethernet 1.

The newer modular devices use a three-part identification that includes type, slot, and then number. On the 2600 series, there are two serial interfaces on a single module; they could be either serial 0/0 and serial 0/1 or serial 1/0 and serial 1/1, depending on the slot that they are in. Furthermore, the fixed Fast Ethernet interface uses the same identification, FastEthernet 0/0, even though it is not a part of a module. The value of this system becomes most pronounced when you get to the bigger devices that have multiple large modules, such as 4 to 16, and can have many interfaces per module, like 32. A notation like FastEthernet2/14 has an easier-to-identify location than, say, FastEthernet62.

To configure an interface on our device, we need to know the identification of that interface. The show running-config command we used earlier will supply the necessary information.

IP, IPX, or AppleTalk

Any of these network protocols, plus several others, can be configured on the same router and the same interface if the IOS feature set supports it. We will only be dealing with IP in this chapter. In the next chapter, we will look at configuring basic IPX. AppleTalk is no longer an exam objective and will not be addressed. If you understand configuring IP and IPX, the other protocols will not provide a great challenge if you need to deal with them.

Ethernet and Fast Ethernet

The original 10 Mbps Ethernet interface is rapidly being replaced by the newer 10/100 FastEthernet (note the words are run together when referring to the interface) interface on many devices. Configuring them is virtually the same once you get past the identification.

For either interface to "come up" and be functional or tested, it needs to be connected to either a switch or hub via a straight-through RJ-45 cable. As LAN interfaces, it would be a normal situation to connect to either device. In addition to its other functions, the switch or hub provides the Tx/Rx (send/receive) crossover necessary for the end user and the router to communicate. It is not necessary for any other devices to be connected to the switch or hub for the interface to "come up." If you choose to connect two routers via the Ethernet or FastEthernet ports, or to connect a workstation directly to a router, you need to use a crossover cable.

Although other options are available, all we initially configure on an Ethernet or Fast Ethernet interface are the IP address and subnet mask. Both are entered using dotted-decimal notation. Neither portion is optional.

The syntax is: ip address aaa.aaa.aaa.aaa mmm.mmm.mmm.mmm

Example: ip address 192.168.1.1 255.255.255.0

As we saw when we looked at our running configuration earlier in version 12 of the IOS, because all router interfaces are explicitly shut down, we need to issue a **no shutdown** command to open the interface. When we are through, the **exit** command takes us out of interface configuration mode and returns us to global configuration mode. Pressing CTRL-Z would take us clear back to privilege mode, in which we could save our work to NVRAM.

The following code shows an example of configuring an Ethernet interface with an IP address:

```
Router#conf t
Enter configuration commands, one per line.  End with CNTL/Z.
Router(config)#int e0
Router(config-if)#ip add 192.168.5.1 255.255.255.0
Router(config-if)#no shut
Router(config-if)#
00:09:16: %LINK-3-UPDOWN: Interface Ethernet0, changed state to up
00:09:17: %LINEPROTO-5-UPDOWN: Line protocol on Interface Ether-
net0, changed state to up
Router(config)#exit
Router#
00:09:28: %SYS-5-CONFIG_I: Configured from console by console
Router# copy run start
Destination filename [startup-config]?
Building configuration...
[OK]
Router#
```

The first two system messages (time stamped 00:09:16 and 00:09:17) indicate, respectively, that the physical link and the protocol are established. The third system message (time stamped 00:09:28) indicates that the configuration was changed from the console. These messages may appear while you are typing a command, causing the command to fragment across several lines. Ignore the interruption, and the command should run normally. We will look at a command later in this chapter that will make these messages less disruptive.

The **copy run start** command saves our changes. We had to press ENTER to confirm our intentions.

If we execute a **show running-config** command to see the results of our changes, the result would look like the following display. Notice that the abbreviations we used to create the commands are automatically replaced by the full terminology.

```
Current configuration:
Output omitted by author
!
interface Ethernet0
 ip address 192.168.5.1 255.255.255.0
 no ip directed-broadcast
!
Output omitted by author
```

Assigning a Second IP Address to an Ethernet Interface

It is possible to assign additional IP addresses to an interface by adding the *secondary* parameter to the entry. The following entries would add two additional IP addresses and the resulting configuration. While this is not the best solution for most circumstances, it does demonstrate the capability. The fifth line shows the ? being used to request the context-sensitive Help feature to show the options.

```
Router#
Router#conf t
Enter configuration commands, one per line.  End with CNTL/Z.
Router(config)#int e0
Router(config-if)#ip add 192.168.6.1 255.255.255.0 ?
  secondary  Make this IP address a secondary address
  <cr>
Router(config-if)#ip add 192.168.6.1 255.255.255.0 secondary
Router(config-if)#ip add 192.168.7.1 255.255.255.0 sec
Router(config-if)#^Z
Router#sho run
Building configuration...
Output omitted by author
interface Ethernet0
 ip address 192.168.6.1 255.255.255.0 secondary
 ip address 192.168.7.1 255.255.255.0 secondary
 ip address 192.168.5.1 255.255.255.0
 no ip directed-broadcast
!
Output omitted by author
```

Older AUI Interfaces

Some older router models have both an AUI and an RJ-45 connector for a single Ethernet connection. In some cases, you may have to designate the media type so that it knows which interface to use. The result would look like this example from a Cisco 4000M router:

```
!
interface Ethernet0
 ip address 192.168.1.100 255.255.255.0
 no ip directed-broadcast
 media-type 10BaseT
!
```

Adding Descriptions to Interfaces

It is a good idea to label the interfaces with descriptions that might help later when you are performing maintenance or updates on a router. In our example earlier, it is unusual to assign multiple IP addresses to the same Ethernet, so I've added a description (label) that reminds me or informs others of what I was doing. The command is **description**, followed by up to 80 characters. The following text shows the entries and the result of a **show run** command:

```
Router(config)#int e0
Router(config-if)#desc                             (pressed TAB)
Router(config-if)#description ?           (to see the options)
  LINE  Up to 80 characters describing this interface

Router(config-if)#Description - Classrooms A, B and C combined.
Router(config-if)#
!                                         (results of show run)
interface Ethernet0
 description - Classrooms A, B and C combined.
 ip address 192.168.6.1 255.255.255.0 secondary
 ip address 192.168.7.1 255.255.255.0 secondary
 ip address 192.168.5.1 255.255.255.0
 no ip directed-broadcast              (added by IOS default)
!
```

Token Ring

Configuring a Token Ring interface is very similar to configuring an Ethernet interface, except that you must also set the ring speed, which amounts to choosing between 4 and 16 Mbps. For the interface to "come up" and be functional or tested, it needs to be connected to a Token Ring MAU. The specific cabling will depend on the MAU unit. It could use Category 5 cabling with RJ-45 connectors or IBM type-1 connectors. Network host devices would then attach to the MAU using similar cabling and a Token Ring NIC. The following text shows typical entry commands and the resulting show run results:

```
Lab-A(config)#int to0
Lab-A(config-if)#Description - Accounting Department / 2nd Floor
```

```
Lab-A(config-if)#ip add 192.168.11.1 255.255.255.0
Lab-A(config-if)#rin                            (pressed TAB)
Lab-A(config-if)#ring-speed ?              (to see the options)
  16  Set the speed to 16Mbps
  4   Set the speed to 4Mbps

Lab-A(config-if)#ring-speed 4
Lab-A(config-if)#no shut
Lab-A(config-if)#
!                                          (results of show run)
interface TokenRing0
 description - Accounting Department / 2nd Floor
 ip address 192.168.11.1 255.255.255.0
 no ip directed-broadcast              (added by IOS default)
 ring-speed 4
!
```

Serial

The serial interfaces can be configured in many ways and can include many options, which we will look at later. For basic connectivity, we assign an IP address just like the other types and we issue the no shutdown command.

DTE vs. DCE Interfaces and Clock Rate

Typically, a Cisco router is considered a *data terminal equipment* (DTE) device, which connects to a *data communications equipment* (DCE) device, such as a DSU/CSU unit or modem.

The DTE represents the user side of the user-to-network interface, where the network could be the phone company or a WAN service provider. The DCE represents the network side of the same interface. The DCE provides a physical connection to the network and is responsible for providing the clocking. It doesn't matter whether the DCE device is physically on the customer premises or whether the customer or service provider owns it.

The clocking must be set with the clockrate command on the DCE interface. The choice of clockrate is impacted by distance and the communications standard used. Cisco recommends using the synchronous serial RS-232 signal at speeds of up to 64,000 bps. To permit a faster speed, use an RS-449 or V.35 standard. The clockrate can range from 300 bps to 4 million bps with specific values displayed if you type **clockrate ?** while in the interface configuration mode of a serial interface. The actual entry would be similar to **clockrate 64000**.

When we connect two Cisco routers together with a serial cable, one becomes the DCE, and that determination is made by the cable attached to the interface. The cable will be stamped, labeled, or otherwise marked indicating the DCE or DTE status. Any attempt to assign a clockrate to a DTE interface will fail and yield an error message.

Use the no clockrate command to remove the clock rate if you change the interface from a DCE to a DTE device.

The Bandwidth Command

The **bandwidth** command overrides the default bandwidth (T1/1.5 Mbps) that is used by some routing protocols, such as IGRP, for route determination metrics. The current bandwidth is displayed with the **show interfaces** command. The command is used in the interface configuration mode of a serial interface and the bandwidth value is entered in Kbps. For example *bandwidth 56* would indicate 56,000 bps.

The following serial interface configurations show both a DCE, serial 0, configuration and a DTE, serial 1, configuration. The bandwidth could have been applied to either a DTE or DCE interface.

```
!                                      (results of show run)
interface Serial0
 description DCE Connection to Building C
 bandwidth 64
 ip address 192.168.91.2 255.255.255.0
 no ip directed-broadcast             (added by IOS default)
 no ip mroute-cache                   (added by IOS default)
 fair-queue 64 256 0                  (added by IOS default)
 clockrate 56000
!
interface Serial1
 description DTE Connection to Building A
 ip address 192.168.90.1 255.255.255.0
 no ip directed-broadcast             (added by IOS default)
!
```

The DTE and DCE references in the descriptions are just reminders to me. The no ip directed-broadcast, no ip mroute-cache, and fair-queue 64 256 0 are default settings added by the IOS. The no ip mroute-cache command disables the switching cache for incoming multicast packets, and fair-queue 64 256 0 enables and configures fair queuing on the interface, which makes sure that all packets arriving are treated equally in cases of congestion. You will learn in later courses how to manipulate the queues to facilitate features like voice-over-IP.

Encapsulation

We saw in Chapter 4 that *encapsulation* is the wrapping, or embedding, of data in a particular protocol header. For example, IP data is wrapped in a specific Ethernet header before network transit. Serial interfaces support a variety of encapsulation methods. The following lines show the options supported on a 2600 router with the Basic IP feature set:

```
Router(config-if)#encapsulation ?
  atm-dxi          ATM-DXI encapsulation
  bstun            Block Serial tunneling (BSTUN)
  frame-relay      Frame Relay networks
  hdlc             Serial HDLC synchronous
  lapb             LAPB (X.25 Level 2)
  ppp              Point-to-Point protocol
  sdlc             SDLC
  sdlc-primary     SDLC (primary)
  sdlc-secondary   SDLC (secondary)
  smds             Switched Megabit Data Service (SMDS)
  stun             Serial tunneling (STUN)
  x25              X.25
Router(config-if)#
```

The default encapsulation is HDLC, which does not require any additional configuration. In the next chapter, we will look at IPX encapsulations, and in Chapter 18, we will look at PPP. If we had chosen to include the command, the syntax would be encapsulation hdlc.

In the next section, which covers the show interfaces command, the encapsulation method used for serial interfaces is shown.

The Show Commands

Several commands are very useful in troubleshooting our interface connections and seeing traffic statistics that are collected by the routers. The two basic commands are show interfaces and show ip interfaces. Each shows all interfaces in a long, scrolling output. Adding a specific interface to show just that interface can modify each of these commands. While the two commands show some common information, they are generally quite different.

In this section, we look at examples of each command and I point out pieces of information you should be able to identify and know which command provides it. As you learn more about the routers, more of the other information will start to make sense.

The Show Interfaces Command

The **show interfaces** command by itself shows all interfaces, or you can add an interface identifier and see just that one interface. The following display is for the Ethernet 0 interface and shares much of the same information as it would if we had chosen the serial or Token Ring interface. We will look at the differences after this display. Key things to look at are the following:

• Line one shows that the physical connection is up and that the protocol (configuration) is adequate to allow the connection to come up. It is possible that the first value would be up but the second down, indicating a possible configuration problem.

- Line two tells us the MAC address of the interface (0000.0c1b.0e02).

- Line three is the IP address and subnet mask in CIDR notation.

- Line four is the Maximum Transmission Unit (MTU)-maximum packet size, in bytes, for the interface. BW is bandwidth and DLY is delay.

- The rest of the lines report various statistics.

```
Lab-A#show int e0
Ethernet0 is up, line protocol is up
  Hardware is Lance, address is 0000.0c1b.0e02 (bia
0000.0c1b.0e02)
  Internet address is 192.168.1.100/24
  MTU 1500 bytes, BW 10000 Kbit, DLY 1000 usec,
     reliability 255/255, txload 1/255, rxload 1/255
  Encapsulation ARPA, loopback not set
  Keepalive set (10 sec)
  ARP type: ARPA, ARP Timeout 04:00:00
  Last input 00:02:03, output 00:00:04, output hang never
  Last clearing of "show interface" counters never
  Queueing strategy: fifo
  Output queue 0/40, 0 drops; input queue 0/75, 0 drops
  5 minute input rate 0 bits/sec, 0 packets/sec
  5 minute output rate 0 bits/sec, 0 packets/sec
     118 packets input, 15414 bytes, 0 no buffer
     Received 118 broadcasts, 0 runts, 0 giants, 0 throttles
     0 input errors, 0 CRC, 0 frame, 0 overrun, 0 ignored
     0 input packets with dribble condition detected
     2174 packets output, 233676 bytes, 0 underruns
     1 output errors, 0 collisions, 2 interface resets
     0 babbles, 0 late collision, 0 deferred
     1 lost carrier, 0 no carrier
     0 output buffer failures, 0 output buffers swapped out
Lab-A#
```

The following display is for the Token Ring 0 interface. Much of the information is similar to the Ethernet display. Key things to look at are the following:

- Line three shows the description line.

- Line five, the MTU, is almost three times as large as the Ethernet interface (4,464 vs. 1,500 bytes). What is the implication if a Token Ring interface passes packets to an Ethernet interface?
  The bandwidth is only 4 Kbps, but that shouldn't be surprising, because we set the ring speed to 4. The delay is 2 1/2 times that of Ethernet 0.

- A different encapsulation is used than on the Ethernet interface. Think back to the difference in the data frames.

```
Lab-A#sho int t0
TokenRing0 is up, line protocol is up
```

```
   Hardware is TMS380, address is 0000.30d8.7080 (bia
0000.30d8.7080)
   Description: - Accounting Department / 2nd Floor
   Internet address is 192.168.11.1/24
   MTU 4464 bytes, BW 4000 Kbit, DLY 2500 usec,
      reliability 255/255, txload 1/255, rxload 1/255
   Encapsulation SNAP, loopback not set
   Keepalive set (10 sec)
   ARP type: SNAP, ARP Timeout 04:00:00
   Ring speed: 4 Mbps
   Duplex: half
   Mode: Classic token ring station
   Single ring node, Source Route Transparent Bridge capable
   Group Address: 0x00000000, Functional Address: 0x08000000
   Ethernet Transit OUI: 0x000000
   Last input 00:00:00, output 00:00:07, output hang never
   Last clearing of "show interface" counters never
   Queueing strategy: fifo
   Output queue 0/40, 0 drops; input queue 0/75, 0 drops
   5 minute input rate 0 bits/sec, 0 packets/sec
   5 minute output rate 0 bits/sec, 0 packets/sec
      5632 packets input, 306060 bytes, 0 no buffer
      Received 4883 broadcasts, 0 runts, 0 giants, 0 throttles
      0 input errors, 0 CRC, 0 frame, 0 overrun, 0 ignored, 0 abort
      1519 packets output, 175570 bytes, 0 underruns
      0 output errors, 0 collisions, 3 interface resets
      0 output buffer failures, 0 output buffers swapped out
      8 transitions
```

Because the statistics portions of the interface output are not that different, I'm only including the first few lines each for the two serial interfaces in the following output. That is followed by just the first lines of an interface that is administratively down (shut down). Key things to look at are the following:

- No MAC address exists for either interface.

- Line 3 identifies whether the interface is a DCE or DTE connection.

- Line five, the MTU, is the same size as the Ethernet interface. The bandwidth for serial 0 is only 64 Kbps, which we set while serial 1 is the default 1.5 Mb (T1 equivalent). The delay is higher than either Ethernet or Token Ring.

- The default encapsulation for a serial interface is HDLC. We will discuss that more in the WAN Chapters 17-22.

- On serial 1, both the line and the protocol are down. It is connected to a router that is off. On the last entry, the interface is administratively down—a shutdown.

```
Lab-A#sho int s0
Serial0 is up, line protocol is up
   Hardware is MK5025
```

```
Description: DCE Connection to Building C
Internet address is 192.168.91.2/24
MTU 1500 bytes, BW 64 Kbit, DLY 20000 usec,
    reliability 255/255, txload 1/255, rxload 1/255
Encapsulation HDLC, loopback not set

Lab-A#sho int s1
Serial1 is down, line protocol is down
  Hardware is MK5025
  Description: DTE Connection to Building A
  Internet address is 192.168.90.1/24
  MTU 1500 bytes, BW 1544 Kbit, DLY 20000 usec,
      reliability 255/255, txload 1/255, rxload 1/255
  Encapsulation HDLC, loopback not set

Lab-A#sho int s0
Serial0 is administratively down, line protocol is down
  Hardware is MK5025
```

The Show ip Interfaces Command

The **show ip interfaces** command by itself shows all interfaces, or you can add an interface identifier and see just that one interface. The following display is for the Ethernet 0
interface and shares much of the same information as it would if we had chosen the serial or Token Ring interface. The other interfaces are similar enough that we will not display them here. Key things to look at are the following:

- The interface status, IP address, subnet mask, and MTU are about the only thing in
  common with the show interfaces command.

- The router is part of a multicast reserved group; note the address.

- The rest of the lines show the status of the various interface features.

```
Lab-A#sho ip int e0
Ethernet0 is up, line protocol is up
  Internet address is 192.168.1.100/24
  Broadcast address is 255.255.255.255
  Address determined by non-volatile memory
  MTU is 1500 bytes
  Helper address is not set
  Directed broadcast forwarding is disabled
  Multicast reserved groups joined: 224.0.0.9
  Outgoing access list is not set
  Inbound  access list is not set
  Proxy ARP is enabled
  Security level is default
  Split horizon is enabled
  ICMP redirects are always sent
  ICMP unreachables are always sent
```

```
ICMP mask replies are never sent
IP fast switching is enabled
IP fast switching on the same interface is disabled
IP Flow switching is disabled
IP Fast switching turbo vector
IP multicast fast switching is enabled
IP multicast distributed fast switching is disabled
Router Discovery is disabled
IP output packet accounting is disabled
IP access violation accounting is disabled
TCP/IP header compression is disabled
RTP/IP header compression is disabled
Probe proxy name replies are disabled
Policy routing is disabled
Network address translation is disabled
WCCP Redirect outbound is disabled
WCCP Redirect exclude is disabled
BGP Policy Mapping is disabled
```

The Show ip Interfaces Brief Command

The **show ip interfaces brief** command is probably one of the handiest commands, because it gives you a quick summary of the status of all interfaces plus the IP addresses. The result looks like this:

```
Lab-A#sho ip int brief
Interface       IP-Address      OK?   Method    Status    Protocol
Ethernet0       192.168.1.100   YES   NVRAM     up        up
Serial0         192.168.91.2    YES   NVRAM     up        up
Serial1         192.168.90.1    YES   NVRAM     down      down
TokenRing0      192.168.11.1    YES   NVRAM     up        up
TokenRing1      192.168.12.1    YES   NVRAM     up        up
Lab-A#
```

Interface Configuration Exercise

In this exercise, we will look at the basic steps for configuring the most common interface types.

1. If you have a single router, use the following illustration, the skills covered in this section, and the following information to configure the interfaces as shown on Router X. If you have two routers and a serial cable to connect them, configure the second one like Router A, shown as follows. Remember to make any allowances for different interface types or interface identification; such as Fast Ethernet 0/0 for the Ethernet 0 interface. Configure any additional interfaces as well.

ROUTER	INTERFACE	IP ADDRESS	CLOCKRATE	SUBNET MASK
X	Ethernet 0	192.168.5.1		255.255.255.0
X	Serial 0 (DCE)	192.168.90.2	56000	255.255.255.0
A	Ethernet 0	192.168.1.100		255.255.255.0
A	Serial 0 or 1	192.168.90.1		255.255.255.0

2. The following information and illustration represent the interface configurations for our expanded lab. If you have three or more routers and adequate cabling, consider building the expanded lab.

ROUTER	INTERFACE	IP ADDRESS	CLOCKRATE	SUBNET MASK
X	Ethernet 0	192.168.5.1		255.255.255.0
X	Serial 0 (DCE)	192.168.90.2	56000	255.255.255.0
A	Ethernet 0	192.168.1.100		255.255.255.0
A	Serial 1	192.168.90.1		255.255.255.0
A	Serial 0 (DCE)	192.168.91.2	56000	255.255.255.0
A (optional)	TokenRing 0	192.168.11.1		255.255.255.0
A (optional)	TokenRing 1	192.168.12.1		255.255.255.0
B	Serial 0	192.168.91.1		255.255.255.0
B	Ethernet 0	192.168.20.1		255.255.255.0
B (optional)	Ethernet 1	192.168.30.1		255.255.255.0

3. Be sure to try the various show commands when you complete your configurations.

4. Be sure to use **copy run start** on each router to save your configurations to NVRAM.

Commands Introduced in this Section

The following commands were introduced in this section:

- **bandwidth** *value* **(in Kbps)**   Sets the bandwidth value to be used by protocols such as IGRP that use bandwidth in determining the routing metrics. Example: bandwidth 56 or bandwidth 128.

- **clockrate** *value* **(in bps)**   Set on any serial DCE interface to establish clocking for the link. Example: clockrate 56000.

- **description**   Interface-specific description (up to 80 characters) on any interface.

- **interface** *type id*   Used to access a particular interface's configuration mode. Examples: interface Ethernet 0 (int e0), interface fastethernet0/0 (int fa0/0), and token-ring0/3 (int to0/3).

- **ip address** *aaa.aaa.aaa.aaa mmm.mmm.mmm.mmm*   Establishes the IP logical network address for an interface. Used to assign IP address and subnet mask to any IP interface. Example: ip address 210.1.1.17 255.255.255.0.

- **media-type** *type*   Sets interface media type on Ethernet interface with both AUI and RJ-45 interfaces. Choices are AUI and 10BaseT. Example: media-type 10BaseT.

- **no shutdown**   Attempts to manually force interface open (up), assuming a physical link and proper protocol configuration.

- **ring-speed** *(4 or 16)*   Sets the Token Ring speed (4 or 16 Mbps) on Token Ring interface.

- **secondary**   Optional parameter that allows additional IP addresses to be assigned to an interface. Example: ip address 210.1.2.18 255.255.255.0 secondary.

- **show interfaces id**   Shows interface status and various operational statistics. Example: show interfaces Fastethernet 0/0 (or sho int fa0/1).

- **show ip interfaces id**   Shows interface status and interface feature status. Example: show ip interfaces Serial 0/0 (or sho ip int s0/1).

- **show ip interfaces brief**   Summarizes interface status and shows IP addresses. Example: show ip interface brief (or sho ip int brie).

- **shutdown**   Forces interface to Administratively Down status.

Enabling IP Routing

Once we configure the interfaces with network addresses, we need to make sure the route table knows about any existing routes on the network. Initially, it only knows about those routes that are directly connected to interfaces on that router. Understand that we do not need to turn on IP routing. It is on by default on Cisco routers. If it were not, we couldn't configure IP addresses to interfaces or show the IP route table. What is missing is a method of adding unknown routes to that route table. In this chapter, we will look at several methods of adding those routes.

The Route Table

The route table shows the "best" route possible to any known networks. The route table is used by the router's "switching" function to know which interface and next-hop destination to use for forwarding any packets. A separate route table exists for each routable, or routed, protocol enabled on the router. As mentioned in the last section, IP routing is on by default but any other protocols, such as IPX or AppleTalk, need to be explicitly enabled.

The command to enable IPX routing will be covered in the next chapter. The command to enable IP routing is **ip routing**, which is issued in global configuration mode. Since it is on by default, we need to use it only if someone has issued a **no ip routing** command, which would turn the feature off.

The Show ip Route Command

To see the IP route table, use the **show ip route** command. The result on our X router would look as follows:

```
Router#show ip route
Codes: C - connected, S - static, I - IGRP, R - RIP, M - mobile, B
       D - EIGRP, EX - EIGRP external, O - OSPF, IA - OSPF inter
       N1 - OSPF NSSA external type 1, N2 - OSPF NSSA external
       E1 - OSPF external type 1, E2 - OSPF external type 2, E -
       i - IS-IS, L1 - IS-IS level-1, L2 - IS-IS level-2, ia - IS-
IS inter area
       * - candidate default, U - per-user static route, o - ODR
       P - periodic downloaded static route
Gateway of last resort is not set
C    192.168.90.0/24  is directly connected, Serial0
C    192.168.5.0/24  is directly connected, Ethernet0
Router#show ipx route      (Just to confirm IPX routing is not on)
              ^
% Invalid input detected at '^' marker.
Router#
```

The first seven lines are a legend to explain the codes in the first column of the route table. Following the legend, we see that our only two known networks are C networks, or directly connected networks. We also see the subnet mask in CIDR notation and the interface connected to that network. These are the networks we configured on our interfaces.

The following lines show the route table for the A router and, again, that the only known networks are those that we configured on the interfaces. Note that we have only one network in common with the X router, the 192.168.90.0 network.

```
Lab-A#sho ip route
Codes: C - connected, S - static, I - IGRP, R - RIP, M - mobile, B
       * - candidate default, U - per-user static route, o - ODR
       P - periodic downloaded static route
Gateway of last resort is not set
C    192.168.12.0/24  is directly connected, TokenRing1
C    192.168.91.0/24  is directly connected, Serial0
C    192.168.90.0/24  is directly connected, Serial1
C    192.168.11.0/24  is directly connected, TokenRing0
C    192.168.1.0/24   is directly connected, Ethernet0
Lab-A#
```

One of the commands we use extensively to confirm connectivity is the Cisco **ping** command, which is similar to the TCP/IP ping command that we looked at in Chapter 5. We will look at ping as well as the telnet and trace commands in more detail later in this chapter. First, we need to understand a few subtleties about our configuration thus far and how the ping command works.

If we ping our interfaces from the configuration console for Router X, we should confirm that they can be reached, which should be no surprise. What may come as a surprise is that we can also reach the serial interface of Router A, which shares a network with our serial 0 interface. The following lines demonstrate these results:

```
Router#ping 192.168.5.1            (our Ethernet Interface)
Type escape sequence to abort.
Sending 5, 100-byte ICMP Echos to 192.168.5.1, timeout is 2 sec-
onds:
!!!!!
Success rate is 100 percent (5/5), round-trip min/avg/max = 4/4/4
ms

Router#ping 192.168.90.2           (our Serial Interface)
Type escape sequence to abort.
Sending 5, 100-byte ICMP Echos to 192.168.90.2, timeout is 2 sec-
onds:
!!!!!
Success rate is 100 percent (5/5), round-trip min/avg/max = 68/122
/340 ms

Router#ping 192.168.90.1           (router A's Serial Interface)
```

```
Type escape sequence to abort.
Sending 5, 100-byte ICMP Echos to 192.168.90.1, timeout is 2 sec-
onds:
!!!!!
Success rate is 100 percent (5/5), round-trip min/avg/max = 32/37
/44 ms

Router#ping 192.168.5.10          (a host on our Ethernet LAN)
Type escape sequence to abort.
Sending 5, 100-byte ICMP Echos to 192.168.5.10, timeout is 2 sec-
onds:
!!!!!
Success rate is 100 percent (5/5), round-trip min/avg/max = 1/3/8
ms
Router#
```

The exclamation marks (!) indicate that we were successful on every effort, even in reaching a host attached to a switch on our Ethernet LAN. Apparently, we have connectivity between our two routers. Although a true statement, that connectivity may not be exactly as we deduce. Before elaborating, let's look at using the TCP/IP ping command from the host on Router X's Ethernet LAN to see if we can reach our routers. The following lines are the results:

```
C:\WINDOWS>ping 192.168.5.1          (Router X's Ethernet 0)
Pinging 192.168.5.1 with 32 bytes of data:
Reply from 192.168.5.1: bytes=32 time<10ms TTL=255
Reply from 192.168.5.1: bytes=32 time<10ms TTL=255
Reply from 192.168.5.1: bytes=32 time<10ms TTL=255
Reply from 192.168.5.1: bytes=32 time<10ms TTL=255
Ping statistics for 192.168.5.1:
    Packets: Sent = 4, Received = 4, Lost = 0 (0% loss),
Approximate round trip times in milli-seconds:
    Minimum = 0ms, Maximum =  0ms, Average =  0ms

C:\WINDOWS>ping 192.168.90.2          (Router X's Serial 0)
Pinging 192.168.90.2 with 32 bytes of data:
Reply from 192.168.90.2: bytes=32 time<10ms TTL=255
Reply from 192.168.90.2: bytes=32 time<10ms TTL=255
Reply from 192.168.90.2: bytes=32 time<10ms TTL=255
Reply from 192.168.90.2: bytes=32 time<10ms TTL=255
Ping statistics for 192.168.90.2:
    Packets: Sent = 4, Received = 4, Lost = 0 (0% loss),
Approximate round trip times in milli-seconds:
    Minimum = 0ms, Maximum =  0ms, Average =  0ms

C:\WINDOWS>ping 192.168.90.1          (Router A's Serial 1)
Pinging 192.168.90.1 with 32 bytes of data:
Request timed out.
Request timed out.
```

```
Request timed out.
Request timed out.
Ping statistics for 192.168.90.1:
    Packets: Sent = 4, Received = 0, Lost = 4 (100% loss),
Approximate round trip times in milli-seconds:
    Minimum = 0ms, Maximum =  0ms, Average =  0ms
```

We were able to reach Router X's Ethernet port, which shouldn't be a big surprise since it is by definition the default gateway for this host (refer to the lab figures, if necessary). We were then able to reach the serial 0 interface on Router X, which means the router had to have forwarded our packets from the Ethernet interface to the serial interface and then "routed" the replies back as well. This seems pretty easy.

Something went wrong when we pinged the serial interface on the other router. Our requests timed out, indicating that we could not reach the other router. Curiously, we were able to reach it just a few minutes ago when we pinged from the console. What's going on? Looking at the IP address of the other router's serial interface, 192.168.90.1, and seeing that it is in the same network as Router X's serial interface, 192.168.90.2, it seems that we should be able to reach both if we can reach one of them. The answer is that we did reach both, but when Router A was preparing the echo replies to send back, it had no entry in its route table for our Ethernet LAN, 192.168.5.0, so it could not reply. If necessary, check the route table for Router A, presented earlier in the "Show IP Route Command" section, to confirm that the route is missing. Figure 13-3 shows the basic lab design and the route tables of each router.

When the host's ping request for 192.168.90.1 reached Router X, there was a network entry in the route table, so the packets were forwarded to and out Router X's serial interface. Unfortunately, Router A had no idea where the pings came from since the 192.168.5.0 network is "unknown" to it, so the request could not be honored.

So why did the ping command work from the console connection, which is probably connected to the same computer? Remember that with the console cable, you bypass the Ethernet interface and go directly to the heart of the router. A ping, or any other command, issued from the console uses the IP address of the interface closest to the destination as the network source address. Therefore, when Router A received the request, it was from the 192.168.90.0 network, a known network, and so it was able to respond. This leads us to an important concept: Just because you have router-to-router connectivity does not mean that your end users necessarily have connectivity.

What we need to do now is get an entry in Router A's route table for Router X's Ethernet LAN. Looking at the lab figure, it's obvious that Router X would have a problem

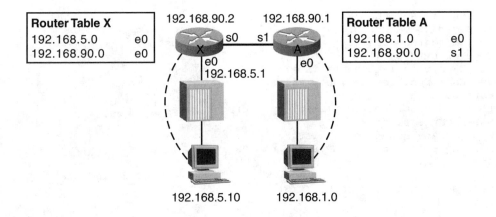

Figure 13-3   Basic lab with route tables

pinging Router A's Ethernet LAN as well. In the next section, we will look at several techniques for adding these routes.

Before we do, we should look at a feature of the Cisco ping (and trace) command that lets us specify a source address so that we can test connectivity from any interface. This is called the *extended ping feature* and works only in privilege mode. Basic ping will work in both user and privilege modes. The feature is implemented by typing **ping** at the prompt without a destination address. You then see a series of prompts offering choices. The following lines demonstrate the feature:

```
Router#ping 192.168.90.1             (just shows basic ping works)
Type escape sequence to abort.
Sending 5, 100-byte ICMP Echos to 192.168.90.1, timeout is 2 sec-
onds:
!!!!!                                   (5 successful pings)
Success rate is 100 percent (5/5), round-trip min/avg/max = 32/34
/36 ms
Router#ping
Protocol [ip]:
Target IP address: 192.168.90.1
Repeat count [5]:                       (Number of attempts)
Datagram size [100]:              (size of each test datagram)
```

```
Timeout in seconds [2]:
Extended commands [n]: y                    (most important choice)
Source address or interface: 192.168.5.1    (must be on the router)
Type of service [0]:
Set DF bit in IP header? [no]:
Validate reply data? [no]:
Data pattern [0xABCD]:
Loose, Strict, Record, Timestamp, Verbose[none]:
Sweep range of sizes [n]:
Type escape sequence to abort.
Sending 5, 100-byte ICMP Echos to 192.168.90.1, timeout is 2 sec-
onds:
 .....                                       (5 failed pings)
Success rate is 0 percent (0/5)
Router#
```

We just pressed ENTER for most commands, to accept the default options. The most important option is **Extended commands [n]:**. If you do not answer *y* for this one, you do not get the additional options, including the ability to specify a source address. The source address must be an interface on the router and not a network host.

Static Routes

A *static* route is one that is explicitly configured and entered directly into the route table. Static routes always take precedence over routes chosen by any dynamic routing proto-col. Static routes are created in global configuration mode and have the following syn-tax: ip route *network-address subnet-mask next-hop*; for example, ip route 192.168.5.0 255.255.255.0 192.168.90.2.

The following lines show the steps for adding the preceding static route to Router A and the resulting route table:

```
Lab-A#conf t
Enter configuration commands, one per line.  End with CNTL/Z.
Lab-A(config)#ip route 192.168.5.0 255.255.255.0 192.168.90.2
Lab-A(config)#^Z
Lab-A#show ip route
Codes: C - connected, S - static, I - IGRP, R - RIP, M - mobile, B
* - candidate default, U - per-user static route, o - ODR
        P - periodic downloaded static route
Gateway of last resort is not set
C    192.168.12.0/24  is directly connected, TokenRing1
C    192.168.91.0/24  is directly connected, Serial0
C    192.168.90.0/24  is directly connected, Serial1
```

```
C       192.168.11.0/24  is directly connected, TokenRing0
S       192.168.5.0/24   [1/0] via 192.168.90.2
C       192.168.1.0/24   is directly connected, Ethernet0
Lab-A#
```

There is now a route in Router A's route table for Router X's Ethernet LAN, so we should now be able to ping from either Router X's console or from the LAN host. The following lines confirm that the host can now reach Router A and, more importantly, that Router A can send replies back:

```
C:\WINDOWS>ping 192.168.90.1              (Router A's Serial 1)
Pinging 192.168.90.1 with 32 bytes of data:
Reply from 192.168.90.1: bytes=32 time=27ms TTL=254
Reply from 192.168.90.1: bytes=32 time=28ms TTL=254
Reply from 192.168.90.1: bytes=32 time=13ms TTL=254
Reply from 192.168.90.1: bytes=32 time=82ms TTL=254
Ping statistics for 192.168.90.1:
    Packets: Sent = 4, Received = 4, Lost = 0 (0% loss),
Approximate round trip times in milli-seconds:
    Minimum = 13ms, Maximum =  82ms, Average =  37ms
```

Similarly, Router A can now ping to the Ethernet interface on Router X and any host connected to that interface. The following lines confirm that Router A can, in fact, reach the host attached to Router X's Ethernet LAN:

```
Lab-A#ping 192.168.5.10                (a host on router X's LAN)
Type escape sequence to abort.
Sending 5, 100-byte ICMP Echos to 192.168.5.10, timeout is 2 sec-
onds:
!!!!!
Success rate is 100 percent (5/5), round-trip min/avg/max = 36/43
/64 ms
Lab-A#
```

Adding a static route to Router X's Ethernet LAN in Router A's route table was a pretty simple solution. One entry and the problem is solved. But, will Router X be able to access the Ethernet or Token Ring networks attached to Router A? If we look back at Figure 13-3, the answer has to be no, because there are no entries in Router X's route table to those networks. One solution would be to create static routes for each destination network. With the basic lab design, that would require only one entry for the Ethernet network on Router A, but on the extended lab design, we would need an additional entry for each Token Ring network. What about the networks on Router B?

Static routes work well for connecting a "stub" network, such as that served by Router X, to a larger network. Router A knows all it needs to know with a single entry (assuming only one LAN on the stub network). Creating the necessary static routes on the stub router could get cumbersome and could become outdated if more routes are added to the main network. An alternative is to use a default route, which is introduced in the next section.

Static Route Configuration Exercise

1. From Router X shown in the previous exercise, type **show ip route** to see the existing route table. You should only find the routes you configured in the last exercise.

2. If you have a second router configured as Router A, from Router X, try to **ping** the Ethernet interface on Router A (192.168.1.100). It should fail, because your route table does not include an entry for that network.

3. Use the preceding techniques to create a static route to the Ethernet interface on Router A.

4. Look at the route table to see if the route appears.

5. If you have a second router configured as Router A, try to **ping** the Ethernet interface on Router A (192.168.1.100) again. It should succeed this time. Try to use **extended ping** to the Ethernet interface on Router A (192.168.1.100) using Router X's Ethernet interface (192.168.5.1) as the source. It should fail, because although your route table does include an entry for that network, Router A's table does not know about Router X's Ethernet LAN.

6. If you have a second router (Router A), console into Router A and create a static route to Router X's Ethernet interface (192.168.5.1). Use **show ip route** to confirm the static route's presence.
   You should now be able to ping 192.168.5.1. Be sure to use **copy run start** to save your configurations to NVRAM.
   Console back to Router X and see that the extended ping should now work, because both route tables know about the routes.
   But, what if we want to ping any other networks attached to Router A, or those on Router B if a third router exists? They will be unreachable. Although we could

build static routes to each, it would become a burden, particularly as routes are added, removed, or changed. We will look at default routes in the next section.

7. Be sure to use **copy run start** to save your configurations to NVRAM.

Default Routes

A *default route* is a route table entry that is used to forward frames for which no network entry is explicitly listed in the route table. Loosely interpreted, if you don't find the network here, go to this address and that router will assist you. The syntax of the default route is ip route 0.0.0.0 0.0.0.0 *next-hop*. For example: ip route 0.0.0.0 0.0.0.0 192.168.90.1.

This entry, like the static route, is made in global configuration mode. The following lines demonstrate the steps and the result:

```
Router#ping 192.168.1.100          (pinging router X's Ethernet 0)
Type escape sequence to abort.
Sending 5, 100-byte ICMP Echos to 192.168.90.1, timeout is 2 sec-
onds:
. . . . ..                                  (5 failed pings)
Success rate is 0 percent (0/5)
Router#config t
Enter configuration commands, one per line.  End with CNTL/Z.
Router(config)#ip route 0.0.0.0 0.0.0.0 192.168.90.1
Router(config)#^Z
Router#ping 192.168.1.100          (pinging router X's Ethernet 0)
Type escape sequence to abort.
Sending 5, 100-byte ICMP Echos to 192.168.1.100, timeout is 2 sec-
onds:
!!!!!                                    (5 successful pings)
Success rate is 100 percent (5/5), round-trip min/avg/max = 36/49
/104 ms
Router#ping 192.168.11.1           (pinging router X's TokenRing 0)
Type escape sequence to abort.
Sending 5, 100-byte ICMP Echos to 192.168.11.1, timeout is 2 sec-
onds:
!!!!!                                    (5 successful pings)
Success rate is 100 percent (5/5), round-trip min/avg/max = 32/33
/36 ms
Router#show ip route
Codes: C - connected, S - static, I - IGRP, R - RIP, M - mobile, B
* - candidate default, U - per-user static route, o - ODR
       P - periodic downloaded static route
Gateway of last resort is 192.168.90.1 to network 0.0.0.0
C    192.168.90.0/24  is directly connected, Serial0
```

```
C    192.168.5.0/24   is directly connected, Ethernet0
S*   0.0.0.0/0  [1/0] via 192.168.90.1
Router#
```

The route appears with an *S** in the first column, indicating that it is "static" and "candidate default." Notice also that the "Gateway of last resort" is now set. This means that any unknown addresses will be forwarded to 192.168.90.1, and if the route table on that router has an appropriate entry, the packet will be forwarded on to its destination. This entry means that our hosts (users) on Router X's Ethernet LAN should have access to the networks (resources) on Router A. If Router A has appropriate routes to Router B and any other networks, such as the Internet, then Router X's users should be able to access those as well.

The drawbacks to static and default routes are that they are somewhat labor-intensive to set up, they may need to be updated if new routes are added, and they will not be able to indicate problems with a route. Dynamic routes, which we look at in the next section, offer an alternative to these problems. But, before we move on, it is important to realize that static and default routes can be very useful and important in the right circumstances. They require little router overhead and offer a level of security by not sharing the routes with others.

NOTE: Whether to use a static or a default route was a point of confusion for me when I first got started, and I see many students encounter the same confusion. The following thought has helped me to see the difference (remember this is not a rule): Static routes often point from a larger network into a smaller network, whereas default routes point from the smaller network into the larger network. An example would be a small business connected to an ISP (and therefore the whole world). To avoid having to have a router that could hold all the route entries for the Internet, the company would set up a default route to the ISP. This means that a user needing to access any address outside the company would be forwarded to the ISP. On the other hand, we would not want a default route from the ISP back to the small business, because it would then forward all "unknown" network packets into the small businesses network. Instead, one or more static routes would allow the ISP to forward only the appropriate packets. Figure 13-4 shows this relationship.

The Show ip Route Summary Command

There is an optional *summary* parameter for the **show ip route** command to summarize all routes and display the overhead and memory required. The following lines demonstrate the summary option from a router with RIP routing and a couple static routes to subnets:

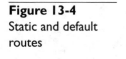

Figure 13-4

Static and default
routes

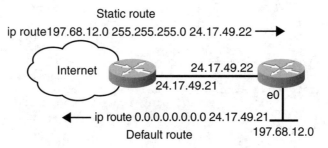

```
Static route
ip route197.68.12.0 255.255.255.0 24.17.49.22
Internet                24.17.49.22
                        24.17.49.21
                                          e0
ip route 0.0.0.0.0.0.0.0 24.17.49.21
Default route              197.68.12.0
```

```
Lab-A#show ip route summary
IP route table name is Default-IP-Routing-Table(0)
Route Source     Networks     Subnets     Overhead     Memory (bytes)
connected        5            0           260          700
static           0            3           156          420
rip              3            0           156          420
internal         1                                     1160
Total            9            3           572          2700
Lab-A#show ip route rip
R    192.168.30.0/24    [120/1] via 192.168.91.1, 00:00:13, Serial0
R    192.168.20.0/24    [120/1] via 192.168.91.1, 00:00:13, Serial0
R    192.168.5.0/24     [120/1] via 192.168.90.2, 00:00:25, Serial1
```

The word "summary" can also be replaced with connected, static, rip, igrp, and any
other protocol to limit the output to that technology. The following lines show the
options available:

```
Router#show ip route ?
  bgp          Border Gateway Protocol (BGP)
  connected    Connected
  egp          Exterior Gateway Protocol (EGP)
  eigrp        Enhanced Interior Gateway Routing Protocol (EIGRP)
  igrp         Interior Gateway Routing Protocol (IGRP)
  isis         ISO IS-IS
  list         IP Access list
  mobile       Mobile routes
  odr          On Demand stub Routes
```

```
ospf          Open Shortest Path First (OSPF)
profile       IP route table profile
rip           Routing Information Protocol (RIP)
static        Static routes
summary       Summary of all routes
supernets-only     Show supernet entries only
traffic-engineering  Traffic engineered routes
vrf                Display routes from a VPN Routing/Forward
|                  Output modifiers
<cr>
```

We will look at this command as we look at dynamic routing protocols in the next section.

Default Route Configuration Exercise

In the last exercise, we saw a limitation of static routes when there are multiple destination networks to be accessed or change occurs. In this exercise, we will remove the static route and replace it with a default route.

1. On Router X, copy the static route command from the running configuration.

2. In global configuration mode, type **no** and then paste the static route command. The result should be **no ip route 192.168.1.0 255.255.255.0 192.168.90.1**. Press ENTER.

3. Use the skills and information from this section to create a default route using 192.168.90.1 as the next-hop address.

4. Show the route table to confirm the changes.

5. If you have a second router configured as Router A, you should now be able to successfully ping any interface on Router A. The extended ping should work as well. We don't need to change the configuration of Router A because it already has entries in its route table for the only two routes on Router X. If we had a third network connected, extended pings from that interface would not work.

6. Be sure to use **copy run start** to save your configurations to NVRAM.

Dynamic Routing

Dynamic routing, once configured, adjusts automatically to network topology or traffic changes. This updating is accomplished by sharing route information with neighbor routers, as discussed in Chapter 11. The routing protocol determines the frequency and method of updating the route information. In this chapter, we will look at configuring the two distance-vector routing protocols that you will be expected to know for the CCNA exam. We will look first at the open standard RIP and then at the Cisco proprietary IGRP.

For routers to share information, they must be running the same routing protocol. Cisco routers support many routing protocols, each of which is enabled in global configuration mode using the **router protocol-name** command. To disable a routing protocol, type **no router protocol-name**, and any additional configuration will be removed.

It is possible, and often advantageous, to use dynamic routing protocols with static and default routing. It is important to keep in mind that when comparing a network route that was learned by a dynamic routing protocol versus one configured statically, the static route will always be selected. Therefore, if you are converting from static routes to a routing protocol, make sure that any static routes that are no longer wanted are removed.

RIP

RIP is the oldest of the routing protocols, dating back to the mid-1950s when it was first defined in academic texts. There are many flavors of RIP that are not necessarily compatible. We will concern ourselves with IETF RIP in this chapter, and look at Novell's RIP in the next chapter. IETF RIP comes in two versions, usually referenced as RIP, and RIPv2 for version 2. The biggest difference is that version 2 supports subnetting, VLSM, and CIDR. Version 1 accommodates subnetting by requiring a single subnet mask within the network.

For our purposes, you need only know how to specify version 2; if you do not specify, then version 1 is assumed and implemented. To implement version 1, type **router rip** in global configuration mode, which puts you in router configuration mode. Then, type the **network**, followed by the *network id* for each network attached to the router that you want shared with neighboring devices. The following lines reflect the entries necessary to set up RIP on our Router X. To implement version 2, just add the entry **version 2** once in router configuration mode. Version 2 and version 1 will not share information, so all routers that you want working together must be configured the same.

The next lines show the steps to remove our default route from the last exercises, and show the route table to confirm that only the configured routes appear:

```
Router#conf t
Router(config)#no ip route 0.0.0.0 0.0.0.0 192.168.90.1
Router(config)#^Z
Router#show ip route
Codes: C - connected, S - static, I - IGRP, R - RIP, M - mobile, B
            (legend lines omitted by author to conserve space)
Gateway of last resort is not set
C    192.168.90.0/24  is directly connected, Serial0
```

```
C    192.168.5.0/24  is directly connected, Ethernet0
Router#
```

The following lines reflect the entries necessary to set up RIP on our Router X, assuming that we want to "advertise" both the serial and Ethernet networks. Notice that I included the 192.168.96.0 network, which is on serial 1, but the router it is connected to is turned off.

```
Router#config t
Router(config)#router rip
Router(config-router)#network 192.168.5.0
Router(config-router)#network 192.168.90.0
Router(config-router)#network 192.168.96.0
Router(config-router)#^Z
Router#show ip route
Codes: C - connected, S - static, I - IGRP, R - RIP, M - mobile, B
              (legend lines omitted by author to conserve space)
Gateway of last resort is not set
C    192.168.90.0/24 is directly connected, Serial0
C    192.168.5.0/24 is directly connected, Ethernet0
Router#
```

When we do a **show ip route**, no new routes appear. Since we have not configured Router A yet, there is no one to share routes with. Second, even though we list the down 192.168.96.0 network, the route table will not include it. It also will not share this route with other routers as long as it is down. If and when it comes up, the route table will include it.

NOTE: Had we used host addresses on the network entries, the IOS would have converted them to the network addresses.

The following lines reflect the entries necessary to set RIP on Router A, assuming that we want to "advertise" all connected networks. There are three static routes to subnets that can be reached via 192.168.1.1. I will also remove, without displaying, the static route from the earlier exercise.

```
Lab-A#show ip route
Codes: C - connected, S - static, I - IGRP, R - RIP, M - mobile, B
              (legend lines omitted by author to conserve space)
Gateway of last resort is not set
C    192.168.12.0/24  is directly connected, TokenRing1
C    192.168.91.0/24  is directly connected, Serial0
```

```
C    192.168.90.0/24  is directly connected, Serial1
C    192.168.11.0/24  is directly connected, TokenRing0
     192.168.99.0/27  is subnetted, 3 subnets
S       192.168.99.0  [1/0] via 192.168.1.1
S       192.168.99.32 [1/0] via 192.168.1.1
S       192.168.99.64 [1/0] via 192.168.1.1
C    192.168.1.0/24  is directly connected, Ethernet0
Lab-A#config t
Lab-A(config)#router rip
Lab-A(config-router)#network 192.168.90.0
Lab-A(config-router)#network 192.168.1.0
Lab-A(config-router)#network 192.168.11.0
Lab-A(config-router)#network 192.168.12.0
Lab-A(config-router)#network 192.168.91.0        (serial link to
router B)
Lab-A(config-router)#^Z
Lab-A#sho ip rout
Codes: C - connected, S - static, I - IGRP, R - RIP, M - mobile, B
          (legend lines omitted by author to conserve space)
Gateway of last resort is not set
C    192.168.12.0/24  is directly connected, TokenRing1
C    192.168.91.0/24  is directly connected, Serial0
C    192.168.90.0/24  is directly connected, Serial1
R    192.168.30.0/24  [120/1] via 192.168.91.1, 00:00:24, Serial0
C    192.168.11.0/24  is directly connected, TokenRing0
     192.168.99.0/27  is subnetted, 3 subnets
S       192.168.99.0  [1/0] via 192.168.1.1
S       192.168.99.32 [1/0] via 192.168.1.1
S       192.168.99.64 [1/0] via 192.168.1.1
R    192.168.20.0/24  [120/1] via 192.168.91.1, 00:00:24, Serial0
R    192.168.5.0/24   [120/1] via 192.168.90.2, 00:00:05, Serial1
C    192.168.1.0/24  is directly connected, Ethernet0
Lab-A#
```

There are now three new routes "learned" by RIP. The *R* in the first column indicates the RIP routes. The line also tells us that two are from Router B, which must have RIP already configured, and that they can be accessed via Router A's serial 0 interface. Only one route comes from Router X, the Ethernet LAN. Router X does not share the down serial connection, and the serial route between Router X and this router was "bested" by the third entry, which is a directly configured route to the same network.

The RIP routes all have a [120/1] entry. The 120 is what is called an *administrative distance,* which is an indicator of the reliability of the information. RIP routes have an administrative distance of 120, IGRP is 100, static routes are 1, and directly connected networks are 0. When there are two or more routes to the same network, the one with the lower administrative distance will be selected for inclusion in the route table. Routes learned via IGRP will always dominate routes learned by RIP, but both will lose out to static routes.

The second element of the [120/1] entry is the hop count to that network. The 1 indicates that all of the RIP routes are one hop (router) away. The following lines are the route table for Router X and clearly show that the two RIP routes on Router B are two hops away:

```
Router#show ip route
Codes: C - connected, S - static, I - IGRP, R - RIP, M - mobile, B
            (legend lines omitted by author to conserve space)
Gateway of last resort is not set
R    192.168.12.0/24  [120/1] via 192.168.90.1, 00:00:06, Serial0
R    192.168.91.0/24  [120/1] via 192.168.90.1, 00:00:06, Serial0
C    192.168.90.0/24  is directly connected, Serial0
R    192.168.30.0/24  [120/2] via 192.168.90.1, 00:00:01, Serial0
R    192.168.11.0/24  [120/1] via 192.168.90.1, 00:00:06, Serial0
R    192.168.20.0/24  [120/2] via 192.168.90.1, 00:00:01, Serial0
C    192.168.5.0/24   is directly connected, Ethernet0
R    192.168.1.0/24   [120/1] via 192.168.90.1, 00:00:06, Serial0
Router#
```

The following lines demonstrate the show ip route summary option and the show ip route rip commands:

```
Lab-A#show ip route summary
IP route table name is Default-IP-Routing-Table(0)
Route Source    Networks    Subnets    Overhead    Memory (bytes)
connected       5           0          260         700
static          0           3          156         420
rip             3           0          156         420
internal        1                                  1160
Total           9           3          572         2700
Lab-A#show ip route rip
R    192.168.30.0/24  [120/1] via 192.168.91.1, 00:00:13, Serial0
R    192.168.20.0/24  [120/1] via 192.168.91.1, 00:00:13, Serial0
R    192.168.5.0/24   [120/1] via 192.168.90.2, 00:00:25, Serial1
Lab-A#
```

The routing entries become a part of the running configuration. The following lines show the appropriate lines from the show run command:

```
!
router rip
 network 192.168.5.0
 network 192.168.90.0
 network 192.168.96.0
!
```

The Debug ip RIP Command

To monitor RIP routing activity, use the **debug ip rip** command. A lot of activity will be scrolling on your screen, so you might want to use HyperTerminal's capture utility so that you can study the output later. To turn the debugging off, use the **undebug all** command, which can be shortened to **un all**. This command actually turns off all debugging, but it is easier to type than no debug ip rip, particularly with all the data scrolling by. The following lines represent the debug ip rip output for Router X:

```
Router#debug ip rip
RIP protocol debugging is on
Router#
10:47:09: RIP: received v1 update from 192.168.90.1 on Serial0
10:47:09:       192.168.1.0 in 1 hops
10:47:09:       192.168.11.0 in 1 hops
10:47:09:       192.168.12.0 in 1 hops
10:47:09:       192.168.20.0 in 2 hops
10:47:09:       192.168.30.0 in 2 hops
10:47:09:       192.168.91.0 in 1 hops
Router#
10:47:36: RIP: sending v1 update to 255.255.255.255 via Ethernet0
(192.168.5.1)
10:47:36: RIP: build update entries
10:47:36:          network 192.168.1.0 metric 2
10:47:36:          network 192.168.11.0 metric 2
10:47:36:          network 192.168.12.0 metric 2
10:47:36:          network 192.168.20.0 metric 3
10:47:36:          network 192.168.30.0 metric 3
10:47:36:          network 192.168.90.0 metric 1
10:47:36:          network 192.168.91.0 metric 2
10:47:36: RIP: sending v1 update to 255.255.255.255 via Serial0
(192.168.90.2)
10:47:36: RIP: build update entries
10:47:36:          network 192.168.5.0 metric 1
10:47:37: RIP: received v1 update from 192.168.90.1 on Serial0
Router#un all
All possible debugging has been turned off
Router#
```

At 10:47:09, RIP received an update from 192.168.90.1 on Serial0, which is Router A reporting in. The next six lines are the routes with a hop count (metric) that were received from Router A. Notice that the router does not advertise the route shared with Router X, 192.168.90.0. It knows that as a directly connected route, Router X will already know about it and have no interest in a "learned" listing.

At 10:47:36, RIP transmitted the route table out the Ethernet interface. It doesn't know that there are no routers on that network. We included it in the router rip configuration, so it advertises to that network. Notice that it added the 192.168.90.0 network to what it learned from Router A.

Also at 10:47:36, RIP transmitted to Router A the only route it hadn't learned from Router A, 192.168.5.0, the Ethernet LAN. In earlier chapters, when we discussed split horizon protocol as a method of preventing routing loops, this was an example of split horizon at work.

At 10:47:37, about 30 seconds later, the whole process started over again.

To demonstrate what a routing problem would look like, I've set Router X to use RIPv2 without changing the others. The following lines are the debug ip rip output. The 11:41:24 and 11:41:51 entries show that RIP is rejecting the updates from Router A. Since there are no updates from A, the routes being sent out the interfaces are limited to local routes.

```
Router#debug ip rip
RIP protocol debugging is on
Router#
11:41:24: RIP: ignored v1 packet from 192.168.90.1 (illegal ver-
sion)
Router#
11:41:35: RIP: sending v2 update to 224.0.0.9 via Ethernet0
(192.168.5.1)
11:41:35: RIP: build update entries
11:41:35:      192.168.90.0/24  via 0.0.0.0, metric 1, tag 0
11:41:35: RIP: sending v2 update to 224.0.0.9 via Serial0
(192.168.90.2)
11:41:35: RIP: build update entries
11:41:35:      192.168.5.0/24  via 0.0.0.0, metric 1, tag 0
Router#
11:41:51: RIP: ignored v1 packet from 192.168.90.1 (illegal ver-
sion)
Router#
```

RIP Version 1 vs. RIP Version 2

Compare the output of this last debug with the output of the one in the previous section for RIPv1. You should see that RIPv1 uses a broadcast address (255.255.255.255) to share routing, meaning all hosts will process it at least far enough to see that it is not applicable to them. RIPv2 uses a multicast of 224.0.0.9 (class D). If we look back at the show ip interface output earlier in this chapter, we see that these routers are part of "Multicast reserved groups joined: 224.0.0.9." This reduces the impact of routing updates on nonrouter devices.

The RIPv2 debug output also shows that RIPv2 transmits the subnet mask (/24 in the sample) with each network address update. This allows version 2 to support both CIDR and VLSM. The following lines compare a partial output of the version 1 and 2 updates sent out the Ethernet 0 interface:

```
RIP v1 example
10:47:36: RIP: sending v1 update to 255.255.255.255 via Ethernet0
(192.168.5.1)
10:47:36: RIP: build update entries
10:47:36:        network 192.168.90.0 metric 1
RIP v2 example
11:41:35: RIP: sending v2 update to 224.0.0.9 via Ethernet0
(192.168.5.1)
11:41:35: RIP: build update entries
11:41:35:        192.168.90.0/24  via 0.0.0.0, metric 1, tag 0
```

The "tag" on each RIPv2 update is a mechanism that allows RIP to pass on information learned through route redistribution from external networks.

The "via 0.0.0.0" in each update allows version 2 to advertise a route but direct the packet to another router on the subnet with a "better" route. This could occur in those circumstances in which two routers are connected to a network where the default gateway router is not the best route to a particular destination.

The Show ip Protocols Command for RIP

The **show ip protocols** command displays some useful information about the routing protocol. It tells both the update cycle (30 seconds) and how long until the next update. It shows that a route that has not been heard from in 180 seconds becomes invalid (but remains in the table) and is dropped if not heard from in 240 seconds. The hold-down timer is 180 seconds.

```
Lab-A#show ip protocols
Routing Protocol is "rip"
  Sending updates every 30 seconds, next due in 25 seconds
  Invalid after 180 seconds, hold down 180, flushed after 240
  Outgoing update filter list for all interfaces is
  Incoming update filter list for all interfaces is
  Redistributing: rip
  Default version control: send version 1, receive any version
    Interface       Send  Recv  Triggered RIP  Key-chain
    Ethernet0        1     1 2
    Serial0          1     1 2
    Serial1          1     1 2
    TokenRing0       1     1 2
    TokenRing1       1     1 2
  Routing for Networks:
    192.168.1.0
    192.168.11.0
    192.168.12.0
    192.168.90.0
    192.168.91.0
```

```
Routing Information Sources:
  Gateway            Distance      Last Update
  192.168.90.2          120        00:00:16
  192.168.91.1          120        00:00:21
Distance: (default is 120)
```

The output tells which interfaces can exchange routing information, which networks are being advertised by this router, and the address of other sources of routing information.

RIP Configuration Exercise

1. Use the same technique we used in the last exercise to remove any static or default routes.

2. Use the techniques from this section to add RIP routing to each router. Use version 2 if you like. Remember to include only those networks directly connected to each router in the network commands. It makes sense to include interfaces that you know are down, because when they come up, they will be automatically added to the route table and shared with other routers.

3. After all routers are configured with RIP, try each of the following commands and analyze the results:
   show ip route (should show all networks on all routers)
   show ip route summary
   show ip route rip
   show ip protocols
   debug ip rip (let this run a minute or two)
   undebug all
   Some of the commands will show little or no information if you have only one router.

4. Be sure to use **copy run start** to save your configurations to NVRAM.

IGRP

While RIP is the oldest and most widely implemented routing protocol, it has a couple serious drawbacks. First, it only uses hop count for route determination and therefore can choose a very slow path using a modem connection over a faster leased line based solely on hop count. Second, the 15-hop limitation of RIP presents a severe limitation as networks grow. Any device that is more than 15 hops (routers) away is by definition "unreachable" and therefore no packet will be sent. Figure 13-5 demonstrates this situ-

Figure 13-5
RIP vs. IGRP routing

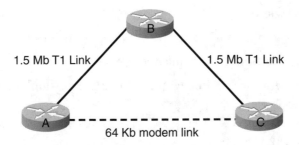

1.5 Mb T1 Link   1.5 Mb T1 Link

64 Kb modem link

ation. RIP would route packets directly from A to C even though ABC would be faster. IGRP using bandwidth and delay for metrics would choose the ABC route.

If we choose to use IGRP, the process is quite comparable to setting up RIP. The basic command is **router igrp** *autonomous-system-number*, such as router **igrp 100**. All routers in the network sharing the same autonomous system (AS) number would then share routing updates. Following the initial router igrp command would be a *network network-ID*, such as network 192.168.1.0, for each network configured on the router that you want shared with the outside world.

If we were upgrading from RIP to IGRP, we would want to turn RIP off after IGRP is functioning so that we are not using router overhead for two protocols to learn the same routes. To turn RIP off, we only need to issue a **no router rip** command in global configuration mode and all related lines will be removed. By the same token, we could use the existing lines to save us some typing. The following exercise demonstrates using Copy and Paste with Notepad to change from RIP to IGRP, although it would work both ways.

In a production environment, it would be very important to remove RIP after the upgrade to IGRP is complete on all routers so that you do not have a period of time without a routing protocol. If you are accessing the router using Telnet, removing a routing protocol before the replacement is up and functioning would cause you to lose your connection to the router with no way to reestablish the connection short of using a console connection.

Using Notepad to Assist Changing from RIP to IGRP Exercise

1. On Router X, do a **show run** and display the **router rip** output lines.

2. Select the router rip command and all network entries.

3. Copy the selection.

4. Use the Start button to open a blank Notepad document.

5. Paste the selection to the blank document.

6. Replace the router rip line with **router igrp 100** (don't press ENTER). The result should look like this:

   router igrp 100
   network 192.168.5.0
   network 192.168.90.0
   network 192.168.96.0

7. Select your results and copy them.

8. Use the Taskbar to return to your HyperTerminal session.

9. Go into global configuration (**config terminal**) mode and paste the results.

10. Show your configuration to see if it worked.

11. Do a **show ip route** to see if the new routes are showing up. They only appear when you have done the changeover on two adjacent routers, and then only if the new protocol has a better "administrative distance" rating.

12. Repeat the same process on the other router(s).

13. After all routers have been changed over, go back into global configuration mode on each and issue a **no router rip** command to remove RIP routing.

The following lines show the show ip route on Router A:

```
Lab-A#show ip route
Codes: C - connected, S - static, I - IGRP, R - RIP, M - mobile, B
          (legend lines omitted by author to conserve space)
Gateway of last resort is not set
C    192.168.12.0/24  is directly connected, TokenRing1
C    192.168.91.0/24  is directly connected, Serial0
C    192.168.90.0/24  is directly connected, Serial1
I    192.168.30.0/24  [100/8976] via 192.168.91.1, 00:01:08, Ser0
C    192.168.11.0/24  is directly connected, TokenRing0
     192.168.99.0/27  is subnetted, 3 subnets
S       192.168.99.0   [1/0] via 192.168.1.1
S       192.168.99.32 [1/0] via 192.168.1.1
S       192.168.99.64 [1/0] via 192.168.1.1
I    192.168.20.0/24  [100/8576] via 192.168.91.1, 00:01:08, Ser0
I    192.168.5.0/24   [100/8576] via 192.168.90.2, 00:00:06, Ser1
C    192.168.1.0/24  is directly connected, Ethernet0
Lab-A#
```

Three routes are "learned" by IGRP. The *I* in the first column indicates the IGRP routes. The line also tells us that two are from Router B, which must have IGRP configured, and that they can be accessed via Router A's serial 0 interface. Only one route comes from Router X, the Ethernet LAN. Router X does not share the down serial connection, and the serial route between X and this router was "bested" by the third entry, which is a directly configured route to the same network.

Earlier, we saw that the RIP routes all have a [120/1] entry, indicating an administrative distance of 120 as an indicator of reliability of the information. The IGRP routes are set to 100 so that they will take precedence over RIP routes, but will still lose out to static routes with 1 and directly connected networks with 0. Routes learned via IGRP will always dominate routes learned by RIP, but both will lose out to static routes.

The second element of the [100/8576] or [100/8976] entry is the metric to that network, which with IGRP is based on bandwidth and delay. The following lines are the route table for Router X and clearly show that the networks on Router B are farther away than those on Router A:

```
Router#show ip rout
Codes: C - connected, S - static, I - IGRP, R - RIP, M - mobile, B
           (legend lines omitted by author to conserve space)
Gateway of last resort is not set
I    192.168.12.0/24  [100/8726] via 192.168.90.1, 00:00:39, Ser0
I    192.168.91.0/24  [100/10476] via 192.168.90.1, 00:00:39, Ser0
C    192.168.90.0/24  is directly connected, Serial0
I    192.168.30.0/24  [100/10976] via 192.168.90.1, 00:00:39, Ser0
I    192.168.11.0/24  [100/8726] via 192.168.90.1, 00:00:39, Ser0
I    192.168.20.0/24  [100/10576] via 192.168.90.1, 00:00:39, Ser0
C    192.168.5.0/24   is directly connected, Ethernet0
I    192.168.1.0/24   [100/8576] via 192.168.90.1, 00:00:39, Ser0
Router#
```

The following lines demonstrate the show ip route summary option and the show ip route igrp commands:

```
Router#show ip route summary
IP route table name is Default-IP-Routing-Table(0)
Route Source    Networks    Subnets    Overhead    Memory (bytes)
connected       2           0          104         280
static          0           0          0           0
igrp 100        6           0          312         840
Total           8           0          416         1120
```

```
Router#show ip route igrp
I    192.168.12.0/24   [100/8726] via 192.168.90.1, 00:00:02, Ser0
I    192.168.91.0/24   [100/10476] via 192.168.90.1, 00:00:02, Ser0
I    192.168.30.0/24   [100/10976] via 192.168.90.1, 00:00:02, Ser0
I    192.168.11.0/24   [100/8726] via 192.168.90.1, 00:00:03, Ser0
I    192.168.20.0/24   [100/10576] via 192.168.90.1, 00:00:03, Ser0
I    192.168.1.0/24    [100/8576] via 192.168.90.1, 00:00:03, Ser0
Router#
```

The routing entries become a part of the running configuration. The following lines show the appropriate lines from the **show run** command:

```
!
router igrp 100
 network 192.168.5.0
 network 192.168.90.0
 network 192.168.96.0
!
```

The Debug ip IGRP Command

To monitor IGRP routing activity, use the **debug ip igrp** command, adding either the *events* or *transactions* parameters. The events option shows a history of the updates, whereas transactions shows the contents of the updates. A lot of activity will be scrolling on your screen, so you might want to use HyperTerminal's capture utility to study the output later. To turn the debugging off, use the **undebug all** command, which can be shortened to **un all**. The following lines represent the debug ip igrp events and transactions output for Router X:

```
Router#debug ip igrp events
IGRP event debugging is on
Router#
01:14:07: IGRP: sending update to 255.255.255.255 via Ethernet0
(192.168.5.1)
01:14:07: IGRP: Update contains 0 interior, 7 system, and 0 exte-
rior routes.
01:14:07: IGRP: Total routes in update: 7
01:14:07: IGRP: sending update to 255.255.255.255 via Serial0
(192.168.90.2)
01:14:08: IGRP: Update contains 0 interior, 1 system, and 0 exte-
rior routes.
01:14:08: IGRP: Total routes in update: 1
Router#
01:14:22: IGRP: received update from 192.168.90.1 on Serial0
```

```
01:14:22: IGRP: Update contains 0 interior, 6 system, and 0 exte-
rior routes.
01:14:22: IGRP: Total routes in update: 6
Router#
Router#un all
All possible debugging has been turned off
Router#debug ip igrp transactions
IGRP protocol debugging is on
Router#
01:16:51: IGRP: received update from 192.168.90.1 on Serial0
01:16:51:        network 192.168.12.0, metric 8726 (neighbor 2750)
01:16:51:        network 192.168.91.0, metric 10476 (neighbor 8476)
01:16:51:        network 192.168.30.0, metric 10976 (neighbor 8976)
01:16:51:        network 192.168.11.0, metric 8726 (neighbor 2750)
01:16:51:        network 192.168.20.0, metric 10576 (neighbor 8576)
01:16:51:        network 192.168.1.0, metric 8576 (neighbor 1100)
Router#
01:16:52: IGRP: sending update to 255.255.255.255 via Ethernet0
(192.168.5.1)
01:16:52:        network 192.168.12.0, metric=8726
01:16:52:        network 192.168.91.0, metric=10476
01:16:52:        network 192.168.90.0, metric=8476
01:16:52:        network 192.168.30.0, metric=10976
01:16:52:        network 192.168.11.0, metric=8726
01:16:52:        network 192.168.20.0, metric=10576
01:16:52:        network 192.168.1.0, metric=8576
01:16:52: IGRP: sending update to 255.255.255.255 via Serial0
(192.168.90.2)
01:16:52:        network 192.168.5.0, metric=1100
Router#un all
All possible debugging has been turned off
Router#
```

At 01:16:51, IGRP received an update from 192.168.90.1 on Serial0, which is Router A reporting in. The next six lines are the routes with the metric that were received from Router A. Notice that router does not advertise the route shared with Router X, 192.168.90.0. The routing protocol knows that as a directly connected route, Router X already knows about it and has no interest in a "learned" listing.

At 01:16:52, IGRP transmitted the route table out the Ethernet interface. It doesn't know that there are no routers on that network. We included it in the router igrp configuration, so it advertises to that network. Notice that it added the 192.168.90.0 network to what it learned from Router A.

Also at 01:16:52, IGRP transmitted to Router A the only route it hadn't learned from Router A, 192.168.5.0, the Ethernet LAN. In earlier chapters, when we discussed split horizon protocol as a method of preventing routing loops, this was an example of split horizon at work.

Approximately 90 seconds later, the whole process starts over again.

The Show ip Protocols Command for IGRP

The **show ip protocols** command displays some useful information about the routing protocol. It tells both the update cycle (90 seconds) and how long until the next update. It shows that a route that has not been heard from in 270 seconds becomes invalid (but remains in the table) and is dropped if not heard from in 630 seconds. The hold-down timer is 270 seconds. It shows that IGRP's maximum hop count is 100, compared to 15 for RIP.

```
Lab-A#show ip protocols
Routing Protocol is "igrp 100"
  Sending updates every 90 seconds, next due in 54 seconds
  Invalid after 270 seconds, hold down 280, flushed after 630
  Outgoing update filter list for all interfaces is
  Incoming update filter list for all interfaces is
  Default networks flagged in outgoing updates
  Default networks accepted from incoming updates
  IGRP metric weight K1=1, K2=0, K3=1, K4=0, K5=0
  IGRP maximum hopcount 100
  IGRP maximum metric variance 1
  Redistributing: igrp 100
  Routing for Networks:
    192.168.1.0
    192.168.11.0
    192.168.12.0
    192.168.90.0
    192.168.91.0
  Routing Information Sources:
    Gateway         Distance      Last Update
    192.168.90.2        100       00:00:46
    192.168.91.1        100       00:00:14
  Distance: (default is 100)
```

The output tells which interfaces can exchange routing information, which networks are being advertised by this router, and the addresses of other sources of routing information.

IGRP Configuration Exercise

1. If you didn't do the earlier exercise in this section, use the technique covered in this section to convert all RIP routing to IGRP 13, the 13 being the autonomous system number.

2. After all routers are configured with IGRP, try each of the following commands and analyze the results:

show ip route (should show all networks on all routers)

show ip route summary

show ip route igrp

show ip protocols

debug ip igrp events (let this run a minute or two)

debug ip igrp transactions

undebug all

Some of the commands will show little or no information if you have only one router.

3. Be sure to use **copy run start** to save your configurations to NVRAM.

Passive Interfaces

With both RIP and IGRP, we advertise all connected networks to neighbor routers by adding a **network net_address** command for each attached network. If we choose or fail to include a network in the routing configuration, two things will happen. First, that network will not be advertised to any other routers. Second, the router will neither send nor receive any routing updates on the associated interface.

An alternative is to use the passive-interface command in the routing configuration section. This command prevents outgoing routing updates over the associated interface. This feature is often used with interfaces connected to modems or ISDN connections so that the connection is not being opened or kept open just to exchange routing information.

The syntax of the command is: passive-interface *interface_ID*.

The following lines demonstrate the implementation of the command using RIP, but IGRP would be identical:

```
router(config)#router rip
router(config-router)#network 192.196.0.0
router(config-router)#network 192.196.1.0
router(config-router)#network 192.196.2.0
router(config-router)#network 192.196.3.0
router(config-router)#passive-interface serial0/0
```

The *interface_ID* could be any acceptable method of identifying an interface, such as s0, fa0/1, To3, and so on. If the word "default" is used instead of an interface_ID, updates on all interfaces will be suppressed.

The passive-interface command may have unexpected consequence with some routing protocols, such as EIGRP and OSPF, and often is replaced with an access control list in those cases.

EXAM TIP: For the CCNA exam, you should know what the passive-interface command does and that it is a part of the routing configuration.

Verifying Connectivity

Interface addressing problems constitute one of the most common problems that occur on IP networks. If the addressing (IP address and subnet mask, are wrong) connectivity with other hosts and networks might be impossible. Three Cisco IOS commands are used to verify address configuration and connectivity in our internetwork. Each has a TCP/IP counterpart that yields similar results from an MS-DOS or Command window. The Cisco commands are as follows:

- **Ping** Verifies Layer 3 connectivity between the source and destination host by using ICMP protocol features (we used this command earlier).

- **Telnet** Verifies Layer 7 connectivity between the source and destination host.

- **Traceroute** Similar to the TCP/IP Tracert command, extends the capabilities of ping by using TCP/IP's TTL values to create a path of routers between the source and destination.

When testing connectivity, you might try these commands in the following order: telnet, ping, and then traceroute. If telnet can establish a connection with a remote device, then we know that we have a physical connection and both devices are configured with TCP/IP. Cisco routers and switches can be configured to accept Telnet connections, and therefore remote configuration and/or administration. Many computer workstation OSs do not allow remote telnet access, but UNIX devices can.

If telnet is not possible, the ping command will test physical connectivity to Layer 3. If you cannot telnet to a router or switch but you can ping it, you know the upper-layer OSI functions of the device are not working properly. Rebooting the device and trying telnet again might resolve the problem. For the ping feature to work, the destination device must be within 15 hops (routers) of the source. While using Cisco's ping command from within a Cisco device, you also have access to the enhanced ping features we looked at briefly earlier.

If the ping command will not work, the traceroute command will test further (30 routers) and display a path of routers passed through to the destination. Even if we can't reach the destination, we can often identify the router just this side of the lost connection.

Ping

The ping command uses ICMP Echo packets and is supported in both user and privilege EXEC modes. In this example, one ping timed out, as reported by the dot (.), and four were successfully received, as indicated by the exclamation point (!). These are the results that may be returned by the ping test:

```
Router#ping 192.168.1.100
Type escape sequence to abort.
Sending 5, 100-byte ICMP Echos to 192.168.1.100, timeout is 2 sec-
onds:
.!!!!                                    (4 successful pings)
Success rate is 80 percent (4/5), round-trip min/avg/max = 36/49
/104 ms
```

In many cases, when you get the preceding response, the first dot is the delay while ARP resolution occurs. If we were to show the ARP table, we would see a very new entry. This is normal.

The following are the ping command response symbols:

EXAMPLE	DEFINITION
!	Successful ping
.	Ping timed out waiting for reply
U	Destination unreachable
C	Congestion-experienced packet
I	Ping interrupted (CTRL-SHIFT-6)
?	Packet type unknown
&	Packet TTL expired

The Cisco extended ping command is only available in privileged EXEC mode. The extended feature allows us to use the feature with other protocols or customize request options. The feature is implemented by typing **ping** at the prompt without a destination address. You will then see a series of prompts offering choices. The following lines demonstrate the feature:

```
Router#ping
Protocol [ip]:
Target IP address: 192.168.90.1
Repeat count [5]:
Datagram size [100]:
Timeout in seconds [2]:
```

```
Extended commands [n]: y                    (most important choice)
Source address or interface: 192.168.5.1        (must be on router)
Type of service [0]:
Set DF bit in IP header? [no]:
Validate reply data? [no]:
Data pattern [0xABCD]:
Loose, Strict, Record, Timestamp, Verbose[none]:
Sweep range of sizes [n]:
Type escape sequence to abort.
Sending 5, 100-byte ICMP Echos to 192.168.90.1, timeout is 2 sec.
.....                                             (5 failed pings)
Success rate is 0 percent (0/5)
Router#
```

We just pressed ENTER for most commands to accept the default options. The most important option is the Extended commands [n]:. If you do not answer *y* for this one, you do not get the additional options, including the ability to specify a source address. The source address must be an interface on the router and not a network host.

Specifying the source address is important, because it allows the administrator to test the routing function of the router. When you ping an address without using extended pings, it will use the address from which the route was learned (the one closest to the destination) as the source. In that case, there is no routing taking place on the source router. It is important to test the routing function, because often that's where the problem actually is.

Trace

The traceroute (or trace) command shows each router passed through on the way to the destination address. If a host name (see name discussion later in the "Device Names and Name Resolution" section) is associated with the address, it will be displayed in the results. In the following trace output, the times listed after the IP address represent the time required for each of three requests to return.

```
Router#trace 192.168.94.1
Type escape sequence to abort.                    (CTRL-SHIFT-6)
Tracing the route to Lab-E (192.168.94.1)
  1 Lab-A (192.168.90.1) 20 msec 16 msec 16 msec
  2 Lab-A (192.168.91.1) 36 msec 32 msec 32 msec
  3 Lab-C (192.168.92.1) 56 msec 48 msec 48 msec
  4 Lab-D (192.168.93.1) 68 msec 64 msec 64 msec
  5 Lab-E (192.168.94.1) 72 msec *   108 msec
Router#
```

The following are the traceroute command response symbols:

CHARACTER	DEFINITION
*	Time out
!H	Probe received by the router, but not forwarded, usually due to an access list
P	Protocol unreachable
N	Network unreachable
U	Port unreachable

The Cisco extended traceroute command is only available in privileged EXEC mode. The extended feature allows us to use the feature with other protocols or customize request options. The feature is implemented by typing **trace** or **traceroute** at the prompt without a destination address. You then see a series of prompts offering choices. The following lines demonstrate the feature:

```
Router#trace
Protocol [ip]:
Target IP address: 192.168.94.1
Source address: 192.168.5.1                    (changed source address
on router)
Numeric display [n]: Y              (y suppressed host name display)
Timeout in seconds [3]:
Probe count [3]: 4                  (changed number of probes sent)
Minimum Time to Live [1]:
Maximum Time to Live [30]:
Port Number [33434]:
Loose, Strict, Record, Timestamp, Verbose[none]:
Type escape sequence to abort.
Tracing the route to 192.168.94.1
    1 192.168.90.1 16 msec 16 msec 20 msec 20 msec
    2 192.168.91.1 36 msec 36 msec 32 msec 32 msec
    3 192.168.92.1 52 msec 48 msec 48 msec 48 msec
    4 192.168.93.1 68 msec 64 msec 64 msec 64 msec
    5 192.168.94.1 68 msec *   64 msec *

Router#
```

Telnet

The IOS telnet command opens a remote access session to a Cisco router or switch through one of up to five virtual terminal sessions. If a username and/or password are set up and a login is specified, the appropriate information must be entered before access is granted. The exit command closes a telnet session and returns the user to the previous device.

The following lines show the result of telnetting to Router A using a defined host name and then telnetting to Router B using the IP address:

```
Router#telnet lab-a
Trying Lab-A (192.168.90.1)... Open
User Access Verification
Password:
Lab-A>                           (if password entry is successful)
Lab-A>telnet 192.168.30.1
Trying 192.168.30.1... Open
User Access Verification
Password:
Lab-B>                           (if password entry is successful)
Lab-B>exit
  [Connection to 192.168.30.1 closed by foreign host]
Lab-A>exit
  [Connection to lab-a closed by foreign host]
Router#
```

The telnet command actually is not required. Typing the host name or IP address alone and pressing ENTER will accomplish the same result:

```
Router#lab-a
Trying Lab-A (192.168.90.1)... Open
User Access Verification
Password:
Lab-A>
Lab-A>192.168.30.1
Trying 192.168.30.1 ... Open
User Access Verification
Password:
Lab-B>
```

If a name or IP address is entered that cannot be interpreted as a telnet device, the following error message appears:

```
Lab-B>Router
Translating "Router"
Translating "Router"
% Unknown command or computer name, or unable to find computer
address
Lab-B>
```

Like the exit command, the CTRL-SHIFT-6, X sequence closes the current telnet connection and returns control to the previous device. The latter command has the additional advantage of being able to break out of a "hung" telnet session. This condition can occur if a user telnets to a router and shuts down the router or if a reload command is issued by another user logged on to the device.

The CTRL-SHIFT-6, X sequence is simply a terminal escape/break sequence that works in HyperTerminal and a Windows 95/98 Telnet session. Under other emulators, it could be a different key sequence.

Cisco Discovery Protocol (CDP)

CDP is supported on Cisco routers and switches to help determine device information about directly adjacent devices. It is a quick way to learn a Layer 3 address on a neighbor machine. CDP is a Cisco proprietary protocol that is enabled on each LAN, HDLC, ATM, and Frame Relay interface by default. CDP is a Layer 3-independent, Layer 2 protocol that multicasts CDP information every 60 seconds out each interface. It is possible to change the CDP multicast interval, and on specific interfaces, it can be disabled with the **no cdp enable** command. This latter option is frequently used on ISDN interfaces so that ISDN links aren't opened just to exchange CDP information.

The following lines show the result of the **show cdp neighbors** command executed on Router X. We can see that interface serial 0 is connected to a Cisco 4000 router at its serial 1 interface. We also see the host name for that router is Lab-A. Interface Ethernet 0 is connected to an unnamed Cisco 2924M switch on its interface 17. The "Capability" column indicates whether the device is a router (R) or switch (S).

```
Router#show cdp neighbors
Capability Codes: R - Router, T - Trans Bridge, B - Source Route
                  S - Switch, H - Host, I - IGMP, r - Repeater
Device ID    Local Intrfce Holdtme  Capability  Platform    Port ID
Lab-A        Ser 0            160        R       4000        Ser 1
Switch       Eth 0            168        T S     WS-C2924M   Fas 0/17
Router#
```

If we telnet over to Router A and run the **show cdp neighbors** command, we can see that it is connected to four Cisco devices, including our unnamed Cisco 2524 (we will learn how to name our device later in this chapter):

```
Lab-A#show cdp neighbors
Capability Codes: R - Router, T - Trans Bridge, B - Source Route
                  S - Switch, H - Host, I - IGMP, r - Repeater
Device ID    Local Intrfce  Holdtme  Capability  Platform  Port
ID
Lab-B        Ser 0            159         R        2500       Ser0
```

```
Lab-C          Tok 0          139          R          4000          Tok1
Lab-D          Tok 1          139          R          4000          Tok0
Router         Ser 1          149          R          2524          Ser0
Lab-A#
```

While this output tells us the type of devices and interfaces our router is connected to, it doesn't tell us much more. The show **cdp entry** *device-id* command gives us a more detailed look at a specific connected device. The following lines are the result of running the command from Router A. It gives us an IP address of the connected interface as well as the version and release of the IOS. This last information is very useful if you are trying to connect with a device running an older version of the IOS that may not understand newer commands.

```
Lab-A#show cdp entry lab-b          (shows device id is case sensitive)
Lab-A#show cdp entry Lab-B
-------------------------
Device ID: Lab-B
Entry address(es):
   IP address: 192.168.91.1
Platform: cisco 2500, Capabilities: Router
Interface: Serial0, Port ID (outgoing port): Serial0
Holdtime: 125 sec
Version:
Cisco Internetwork Operating System Software
IOS (tm) 2500 Software (C2500-I-L), Version 12.0(7)T,   RELEASE
SOFTWARE (fc2)
Copyright (c) 1986-1999 by cisco Systems, Inc.
Compiled Mon 06-Dec-99 14:50 by phanguye
advertisement version: 2                 (refers to version of CDP)
Lab-A#
```

The show cdp neighbors detail command gives us the same detailed look at all connected Cisco devices. The following lines are the result of running the command from Router X:

```
Lab-X#show cdp neighbors detail
-------------------------
Device ID: Lab-A
Entry address(es):
   IP address: 192.168.90.1
Platform: cisco 4000, Capabilities: Router
Interface: Serial0, Port ID (outgoing port): Serial1
Holdtime: 160 sec
Version:
Cisco Internetwork Operating System Software
IOS (tm) 4000 Software (C4000-JS-M), Version 12.0(5)T, RELEASE
```

```
SOFTWARE (fc1)
Copyright (c) 1986-1999 by cisco Systems, Inc.
Compiled Fri 23-Jul-99 13:02 by kpma
advertisement version: 2              (refers to version of CDP)
-------------------------
Device ID: Switch                     (the unnamed switch)
Entry address(es):
Platform: cisco WS-C2924M-XL,  Capabilities: Trans-Bridge Switch
Interface: Ethernet0,  Port ID (outgoing port): FastEthernet0/17
Holdtime: 169 sec
Version:
Cisco Internetwork Operating System Software
IOS (tm) C2900XL Software (C2900XL-C3H2S-M), Version 12.0(5)XU,
    RELEASE SOFTWARE (fc1)          (Cont. from previous line)
Copyright (c) 1986-2000 by cisco Systems, Inc.
Compiled Mon 03-Apr-00 16:37 by swati
Advertisement version: 2
Protocol Hello:  OUI=0x00000C, Protocol ID=0x0112; payload len=27,
value=00000000FFFFFFFF010121FF00000000000000216A7E140FF0001
VTP Management Domain: 'test'
Router#
```

The show cdp interface command displays the CDP configuration for each router
interface. It also reports the interface status (up/down) and the encapsulation method.
The following lines show the results of running the command on Router A:

```
Lab-A#show cdp interface
Ethernet0 is up, line protocol is up
  Encapsulation ARPA
  Sending CDP packets every 60 seconds
  Holdtime is 180 seconds
Serial0 is up, line protocol is up
  Encapsulation HDLC
  Sending CDP packets every 60 seconds
  Holdtime is 180 seconds
Serial1 is up, line protocol is up
  Encapsulation HDLC
  Sending CDP packets every 60 seconds
  Holdtime is 180 seconds
TokenRing0 is up, line protocol is up
  Encapsulation SNAP
  Sending CDP packets every 60 seconds
  Holdtime is 180 seconds
TokenRing1 is up, line protocol is up
  Encapsulation SNAP
  Sending CDP packets every 60 seconds
  Holdtime is 180 seconds
Lab-A#
```

Verifying Connectivity Exercise

1. Using the console connection, confirm that you can ping and trace from each router to every other interface on the router(s). If certain interfaces can't be reached, then check the connection, configuration, and routing.

2. Repeat the last exercise from the MS-DOS or Command window on your workstation. If you cannot ping any interfaces, check the TCP/IP setup for the workstation to confirm that the IP address, subnet mask, and default gateway are all configured properly.
   Remember that the TCP/IP trace command is Tracert. Compare the output to that of the Cisco command.

3. Because we haven't set passwords on the routers, it is necessary to wait until the next section to try the telnet command.

4. If you have more than one router configured, use the console ports on each of the routers and then use the show CDP commands to investigate the neighbor devices.

5. Be sure to use **copy run start** to save your configurations to NVRAM.

Commands Introduced in this Section

The following commands were introduced in this section:

- **debug ip rip**   Turns on the debug feature to report RIP activity.
- **debug ip igrp events**   Turns on the debug feature to report IGRP update occurrences.
- **debug ip igrp transactions**   Turns on the debug feature to report contents of IGRP updates.
- **undebug all**   Turns off all debug features.
- **ip route** *network-id subnet-mask next-hop*   Creates a static route.
- **ip route 0.0.0.0 0.0.0.0** *next-hop*   Creates a default route.
- **router rip**   Enables RIP routing.
- **router igrp** *autonomous-system-number*   Enables IGRP routing.
- **show ip route**   Displays route table.
- **show ip route summary**   Displays summary of the route table and resources used.
- **show ip route** *protocol*   Displays route table entries for the specified protocol.

- **telnet** *name or ip-address*   Opens a telnet session with the named device or using the IP address.

- **show ip protocols**   Displays the routing protocol current values.

- **passive-interface** *interface_ID*   Stops routing updates on the specified interface when included in the routing configuration.

- **show cdp neighbors**   Summarizes device information about neighbor devices.

- **show cdp neighbors detail**   Displays detailed device information about neighbor devices.

- **show cdp entry** *device-id*   Displays detailed device information about named device. The device-id is case-sensitive.

- **show cdp interface**   Displays interface configuration including CDP settings.

Passwords and Router Security

We saw in the last chapter that there are two access modes in the Cisco routers and switches: user mode and privilege mode. In addition, there are up to three methods for accessing the device: through the console port, by telnetting in through a virtual terminal, and via a modem using the AUX port, if available. Each of the three methods offers access to user mode from which the enable command can be used to access privilege mode.

Privilege Mode Password

Security for privilege mode involves being prompted for a password only if an enable password or an enable secret *password* has been previously defined in global configuration mode. If neither is set, there is no security for privilege mode, allowing a user to view and/or change the device configuration. They could even set a password and lock out other users.

The older enable password command followed by the desired password creates a clear-text entry in the running configuration that could be viewed by anyone seeing the configuration. The more secure enable secret command followed by the desired password creates an encrypted entry in the running configuration that cannot be understood by anyone seeing the configuration. The following lines demonstrate both entries followed by the lines created in a show run command display of the configuration. All passwords are case-sensitive and can be alphanumeric.

```
Router#conf t
Enter configuration commands, one per line.  End with CNTL-Z.
```

```
Router(config)#enable password test
Router(config)#enable secret cisco
Router(config)#^z
Router(config)#show run
!
enable secret 5 $1$lHIs$VWFifan./yutB/Stn4qbX1
enable password test
!
```

If both enable password and enable secret are created, the enable password will not work. Since the enable secret always takes precedence, it makes no sense to create a clear-text password. Once either enable password is created, everyone wanting access to the privilege mode is prompted and must supply the correct password.

User Mode Passwords

Security for user mode can and should be set up for each of the three access methods. There are several methods of authenticating users providing a range of security and administrative control. For the CCNA exam and to get started, you only need to know how to set basic passwords for each access method.

Since version 12 of the IOS, telnet access and AUX (modem) port access require a password. If no password is set, the user will be rejected with a message explaining that a password is required but none is set. The console port does not have this requirement, but it is a good idea to set a password so that anyone with a laptop and a console cable cannot access the device.

Password/Login

The following table shows each of the three access methods, the syntax, and an example using the same password for each method. It is possible to set different passwords for each access method if you like.

PASSWORD TYPE	ACCESS METHOD	SYNTAX	EXAMPLE
Console session	Console port	line con 0 password *password* login	line con 0 password *cisco* login
Telnet session	vty interfaces (sets all five virtual terminal interfaces)	line vty 0 4 password *password* login	line vty 0 4 password *cisco* login
AUX session	AUX port (if present can be accessed via a modem)	line AUX 0 password *password* login	line AUX 0 password *cisco* login

The login command requires each new access to be prompted for the password. In versions prior to 12 and for the console connection in 12, if the login command is omitted, only the first access might be prompted for a password. The login command used by itself expects the password to be defined as shown in the examples.

The following lines show the steps to add passwords to the three types of router access interfaces and the resulting show run lines:

```
Router#conf t
Enter configuration commands, one per line.  End with CNTL/Z.
Router(config)#line con 0
Router(config-line)#password cisco
Router(config-line)#login
Router(config-line)#line aux 0
Router(config-line)#password cisco
Router(config-line)#login
Router(config-line)#line vty 0 4
Router(config-line)#password cisco
Router(config-line)#login
Router(config-line)#^Z
Router#copy run start
Router#show run
!
line con 0
 password cisco
 login
line aux 0
 password cisco
 login
line vty 0 4
 password cisco
 login
!
```

Username/Password/Login Local

If you prefer to require both a username and a password to authenticate, as well as having the opportunity to have different username / password combinations for different users, there is another option. The following lines show creating three username/password combinations and the appropriate lines from a show run command:

```
Router#conf t
Enter configuration commands, one per line.  End with CNTL-Z.
Router(config)#username jerri password larson
Router(config)#username chris password larson
Router(config)#username dave password warner
Router#^z
Router#show run
!
username jerri password 0 larson
```

```
username chris password 0 larson
username dave password 0 warner
!
```

To finish the configuration, remove the password command on each access method you want to control and change the login command to **login local**. The following lines show the steps and the resulting show run lines:

```
Router#conf t
Enter configuration commands, one per line.  End with CNTL-Z.
Router(config)#line con 0
Router(config-line)#no password cisco
Router(config-line)#login local
Router(config-line)#line aux 0
Router(config-line)#no password cisco
Router(config-line)#login local
Router(config-line)#line vty 0 4
Router(config-line)#no password cisco
Router(config-line)#login local
Router(config-line)#^Z
Router#copy run start
Router#show run
!
line con 0
 login local
 transport input none
line aux 0
 login local
line vty 0 4
 login local
!
```

Now, only those three combinations of usernames and passwords can be used to access user mode. Like all passwords, these are case-sensitive and can include text and numerals. The usernames are not case-sensitive. The new access prompts will look like this:

```
User Access Verification
Username: Jerri
Password:
% Login invalid
Username: Jerri
Password:
Router>
```

The first attempt shows the result when I tried to use uppercase first letters for both entries. The second attempt shows that the login will accept a case difference in the username but not in the password. Any user that can access privilege mode will be able to see all username/password combinations by viewing the running configuration.

Password Exercise

1. On each router, in global configuration mode, type the following commands:
   Router#conf t
   Router(config)#enable secret cisco
   Router(config)#line con 0
   Router(config-line)#password cisco
   Router(config-line)#login
   Router(config-line)#line aux 0
   Router(config-line)#password cisco
   Router(config-line)#login
   Router(config-line)#line vty 0 4
   Router(config-line)#password cisco
   Router(config-line)#login
   Router(config-line)#^Z
   Router#copy run start

2. Use the **exit** command to leave user mode. When you press ENTER, you will be prompted for the password. Try leaving it blank or using the wrong word.

3. If you have more than one router configured, telnet between the routers to confirm that you can access both the user and privilege modes.

4. Be sure to use **copy run start** to save your configurations to NVRAM.

Commands Introduced in this Section

The following commands were introduced in this section:

- **enable password** *word*   Used on early versions of IOS to assign a password to privilege mode. The drawback is that the password is displayed in clear text any time the configuration is displayed or printed.

- **enable secret** *word*   Used on newer versions of IOS to assign an encrypted password to privilege mode. The password is not displayed in clear text when the configuration is displayed or printed.

- **Login**   Tells a device to display the login prompt for each user. The command assumes a password command will be in the same user mode access configuration commands.

- **password** *password*   The password that will be accepted by the IOS for the user mode access being configured.

- **username** *name* **password** *password*   Configured in global configuration mode to create valid username and password combinations to be used by the login local command.

- **login local**   Tells a device to prompt for both a username and password for each user.

Device Names and Name Resolution

So far, we have configured interfaces, set up routing, set up passwords, and used the tools ping, traceroute, and telnet to verify connectivity and our configurations. Many of the tools used IP addresses to identify a particular device. Just like using a Web browser, having to remember and type a large number of IP addresses can become difficult. It is possible to name devices and then use the name instead of the address in many situations.

In this section, we look at how to name devices and then how to resolve names to addresses.

The Hostname Command

One of the simpler and often one of the first basic tasks when configuring a router or switch is to assign it a name. This name is called the *host name* and is displayed by the system prompt. Many of our examples had names like Lab-A and Lab-B for the routers. The main router, being unnamed, continues to use the system default host name, Router. The router is named in global configuration mode using the syntax *hostname new-name*.

This host name becomes the device-ID for features like the CDP commands and is used by other commands in different ways. We will see later in this chapter that when using a Web browser to access a router, the host name is used for the username. The host name becomes the name of the device.

The command and result are demonstrated in the next lines. If I had wanted "seattle" capitalized, I would have needed to include it as part of the hostname command.

```
Router#conf t
Enter configuration commands, one per line.  End with CNTL-Z.
Router(config)#hostname seattle
seattle(config)#^Z
seattle#
```

The host name can be up to 29 characters long, containing letters, numbers, and many symbols. Long names may create their own problems when using them, so use caution.

I have intentionally withheld discussion of this command until this point so that it is very clear that the hostname command has nothing to do with configuring a functioning router. I typically assign a host name and the router passwords as one of the first configuration tasks. Having the host name appear in the prompt makes it easier to keep track of which device is being configured. This is particularly handy when frequently telnetting between devices.

The Prompt Command

There is a prompt *prompt-string* command that seems to have similar results to the hostname command in that it changes the prompt. It does not, however, change the host name of the device, so it cannot be used in those places where the host name becomes the device-ID, such as in the **show cdp entry device-id** command. It also only changes the prompt in user and privilege mode, but does not change it in any of the configuration modes. The following lines demonstrate the prompt command and its limitations:

```
seattle#config t                      (current host name and prompt)
seattle(config)#prompt Bellevue        (sets prompt to Bellevue)
seattle(config)#^Z                    (nothing has changed, yet)
Bellevue                    (prompt changes after exiting conf t)
Bellevuetelnet 192.168.90.1    (note: no > or # to indicate mode)
Trying 192.168.90.1...Open
User Access Verification
Password:
Lab-A>show cdp neighbors      (192.168.90.1 has been named Lab-A)
Capability Codes: R - Router, T - Trans Bridge, B - Source Route
Bridge
                  S - Switch, H - Host, I - IGMP, r - Repeater
Device ID    Local Intrfce    Holdtme   Capability  Platform  Port
ID
Lab-B         Ser 0            177          R         2500      Ser 0
Lab-A         Tok 0            145          R         4000      Tok 1
Lab-A         Tok 1            145          R         4000      Tok 0
seattle       Ser 1            174          R         2524      Ser 0
Lab-A>show cdp entry Bellevue         (doesn't recognize Bellevue)
Lab-A>
```

```
Lab-A>show cdp entry seattle            (still recognizes seattle)
-------------------------
Device ID: seattle
Entry address(es):
  IP address: 192.168.90.2
Platform: cisco 2524, Capabilities: Router
```

The command **no prompt** in global configuration mode removes the prompt feature.

Mapping Host Names to IP Addresses

In Chapter 7, when discussing Layer 7 applications and Web addresses, we discussed that it is difficult for humans to remember IP addresses, particularly a large number of them. We discussed features such as the Domain Name System (DNS) for resolving text names to IP addresses, and at one point looked at an LMHOSTS file as a local way of resolving computer names to IP addresses.

Similarly, we can associate, or map, text names to IP addresses when working with Cisco routers and switches. The Cisco IOS uses the word "host" when creating these mappings, but the mappings are not the same as the hostname command, which changes the device-ID of the device. These new "host" names have virtually nothing to do with the internal functions of the device. The hostname is easier for humans to remember and use. The "host" name can be used in place of the address when typing many commands.

The Cisco IOS maintains a cache in RAM of these "host" names and the associated IP address mappings for use by the various EXEC commands. This local cache speeds the process of resolving names to addresses.

The following are a few points to consider about host names that at first might seem contradictory:

• Each unique IP address can have a host name associated with it. This means that every interface can have a unique name if you so choose. For example, seattleE0 and seattleS0 could identify to interfaces on the "seattle" router.

• Each host name can have up to eight IP addresses associated with it. This allows the creation of a host name for a router and then associating multiple interfaces to that name. For example, ip host seattle 10.0.0.1 10.0.1.1 10.0.2.2 associates the three interfaces with the name "seattle."

• Some commands, such as ping, only use the first address assigned to a host name, while other commands, such as telnet, progress through the list until they find one they can access. Using "seattle" from the last paragraph, ping seattle would only try 10.0.0.1. If the interface is down, the ping will fail. On the other hand, telnet seattle would try 10.0.1.1 and then 10.0.2.2 if 10.0.0.1 is down.

- Host names created locally are locally unique. This allows the networker in Seattle to identify a network router in Cape Town as SA1, while that same router may have a host name such as Acct3rdFloor in Cape Town. SA1 could be used with commands such as ping and telnet from any Seattle device containing the mapping, but would have no meaning elsewhere in the network.

- A DNS server can be used to resolve host names if the ip name-server ip-address is used. The ip domain-lookup command that refers unknown names to the DNS server is on by default. Often, it is useful to perform a no ip domain-lookup command when working on lab routers, because typos result in an attempt at name resolution.

The ip Host Command (Local Name Resolution)

The ip host command issued in global configuration mode creates a static name-to-address entry in the router's configuration file. When the configuration is loaded, the name-to-address associations are cached in the device's RAM.

The following lines demonstrate the IP host entries for the sample lab. I chose to use the device-ID created for each device using the hostname command, but it isn't necessary. By using the device-IDs, I can create the IP host entries once and paste them into every device in the lab, thereby reducing my typing and the chances of typos.

```
Lab-X#show run
!
ip host seattle 192.168.90.2 192.168.5.1 192.168.96.2
ip host Lab-A 192.168.90.1 192.168.91.1 192.168.11.1 192.168.12.1
ip host Lab-B 192.168.91.1 192.168.92.2 192.168.20.1 192.168.30.1
!
```

Since some commands will only try the first associated address, it is somewhat important to order the entries for each name starting with the interface(s) most likely to be up, and then progress to those least likely to be up.

The **show hosts** command will display the mappings cached in RAM:

```
seattle#show hosts
Default domain is not set
Name/address lookup uses static mappings
Host            Flags      Age Type   Address(es)
Lab-B           (perm, OK)  2   IP     192.168.91.1
                                       192.168.20.1
```

```
Lab-A           (perm, OK)   1   IP    192.168.90.1
seattle         (perm, OK)   2   IP    192.168.90.2
seattle#
```

In the show hosts display, Age is the number of hours since the IOS referred to the name. Under Flags, "perm" means it is a static entry from the configuration, while "temp" would mean it came from a DNS server. OK means the entry is current, while EX would mean it had expired.

The next lines demonstrate using the host name in place of the IP address with the ping and telnet commands. Remember that some commands, such as ping, check only the first address associated with a name and fail if the interface is down. Others, such as telnet and trace, try the entries in sequential order until one works or the list is exhausted.

```
seattle#ping lab-b
Type escape sequence to abort.
Sending 5, 100-byte ICMP Echos to 192.168.91.1, timeout is 2 sec-
onds:
!!!!!
Success rate is 100 percent (5/5), round-trip min/avg/max =
64/68/72 ms
seattle#telnet lab-a                              (not case sensitive)
Trying Lab-A (192.168.90.1) . . .   Open
User Access Verification
Password:
Lab-A>
```

IP host names can be created on the fly if you are going to be interacting frequently with a particular device or interface on a device. These names do become a part of the running configuration but could be removed with a no ip host ip-address command after you are through. The next lines show a temporary name "Jerri" created to refer to an Ethernet interface on Router B. We already have a name, Lab-B, with that address, but the address we want is fourth in line and would never be used if the others are functioning normally.

```
seattle#conf t
seattle(config)#ip host Jerri 192.168.30.1
seattle(config)#^Z
seattle#show hosts   (there is now a Jerri in seattle's host table)
Default domain is not set
Name/address lookup uses static mappings
Host               Flags      Age Type   Address(es)
```

```
Jerri                  (perm, OK)   0   IP     192.168.30.1
Lab-B                  (perm, OK)   0   IP     192.168.91.1
192.168.92.2
                                                192.168.20.1
192.168.30.1
Lab-A                  (perm, OK)   0   IP     192.168.90.1
192.168.91.1
                                                192.168.11.1
192.168.12.1
                                                192.168.1.100
seattle                (perm, OK)   2   IP     192.168.90.2   192.168.5.1
seattle#ping jerri
Type escape sequence to abort.
Sending 5, 100-byte ICMP Echos to 192.168.30.1, timeout is 2 sec-
onds:
!!!!!                        (we confirmed that the interface is up)
Success rate is 100 percent (5/5), round-trip min/avg/max =
68/68/68 ms
seattle#jerri                          (telnetting to router B)
User Access Verification
Password:
Lab-B>show hosts            (there is no Jerri in Lab-B's table)
Default domain is not set
Name/address lookup uses static mappings
Host                   Flags       Age Type    Address(es)
Lab-X                  (perm, OK)   2   IP     192.168.90.2   192.168.5.1
   (Lab-B's table doesn't know I renamed Lab-X to seattle. Since
the entries are locally unique it won't matter. Ping Lab-X would
work on this machine.)
Lab-A                  (perm, OK)   2   IP     192.168.90.1
192.168.91.1
                                                192.168.11.1
192.168.12.1
                                                192.168.1.100
Lab-B                  (perm, OK)   2   IP     192.168.91.1
192.168.92.2
                                                192.168.20.1
192.168.30.1
Lab-B>exit
[Connection to jerri closed by foreign host]
```

The ip Name-Server Command

It is possible to use one or more DNS servers to resolve the host names in your network. To map domain names to IP addresses using a DNS server, in global configuration mode, specify a name server using the **ip name-server** command and enable DNS with the **ip domain-lookup** command. The ip domain-lookup command is on by default and has to be used only if the feature has been disabled. Any time the operating system software receives a host name it does not recognize, it refers to DNS for the IP address of that device. The IOS will also notify the DNS of new host names.

Examples of both entries and the appropriate lines from the show run command are displayed in the next lines:

```
seattle#conf t
Enter configuration commands, one per line.  End with CNTL/Z.
seattle(config)#ip name-server 192.168.1.254 201.17.24.56
seattle(config)#ip domain-lookup
seattle(config)#^Z
seattle#show run
!
ip name-server 192.168.1.254
ip name-server 201.17.24.56
!
```

The **ip domain-lookup** command does not appear in the running configuration because it is the default condition. If we had issued a no ip domain-lookup command, then it would appear.

Turning Off IP Domain Lookup

If the network is not using a DNS server, issuing a **no ip domain-lookup** command means that the router will not generate or forward name system broadcast packets. This has the additional benefit of reducing the delay the IOS goes through every time a command is misspelled. The device will attempt only to resolve the misspelling locally.

The next lines demonstrate a few characters of gibberish typed by accident that were sent four times, before finally giving up, to the DNS servers defined in the last section. The total time was probably a minute, but it seems like forever when you are watching it. After that, I turned off the ip domain-lookup and tried the same entry. It took only a second to return the message.

```
Lab-X#jhssg
Translating "jhssg"...domain server (192.168.1.254) (201.17.24.56)
Translating "jhssg"...domain server (192.168.1.254) (201.17.24.56)
Translating "jhssg"...domain server (192.168.1.254) (201.17.24.56)
Translating "jhssg"...domain server (192.168.1.254) (201.17.24.56)
% Unknown command or computer name, or unable to find computer
address
Lab-X#conf t
Enter configuration commands, one per line.  End with CNTL-Z.
```

```
Lab-X(config)#no ip domain-lookup
Lab-X(config)#^Z
Lab-X#jhssg
Translating "jhssg"
% Unknown command or computer name, or unable to find computer
address
Lab-X#
```

Names and Name Resolution Exercise

1. Use the techniques from the beginning of this section to create a host name for each router on your network. Use cities of your choosing for the names. You should see the prompt change immediately.

2. In one router, use the IP host techniques from this section to create IP host entries for each router on your network. Use the device hostname (cities from the last exercise) as the host entry and associate at least two addresses with each host, if possible.

3. Try the **show hosts** command to see the results.

4. Try the **ping** and **telnet** commands with the host names.

5. Copy the IP host lines from the running configuration and paste them into a second router to save having to retype them. You might want to use Notepad.

6. Be sure to use **copy run start** to save your configurations to NVRAM.

Commands Introduced in this Section

The following commands were introduced in this section:

- **hostname** *new-name*   Renames the device creating the device-ID. The defaults are either Router or Switch.

- **prompt** *prompt-text*   Changes the prompt in user and privilege modes but nothing else. The no prompt command will remove the feature.

- **ip host** *ip-address(es)*   Associates up to eight IP addresses with a host name. This name can be used instead of the IP address with commands such as ping, trace, and telnet.

- **show hosts**   Displays the cached host-to-address mappings created on the device.

- **ip name-server** *ip-address(es)*   Identifies up to six DNS servers that can be used to resolve host-to-address mappings.

- **ip domain-lookup**   Enables the use of DNS servers to resolve host-to-address mappings. This is on by default.

- **no ip domain-lookup**   Disables the use of DNS servers to resolve host-to-address mappings and can speed up recovery from misspelled commands. You use this only if you aren't using DNS servers to resolve network device host names.

Descriptions, Messages, and a Start File

In this section, we are going to review the description feature covered when we configured the interfaces, the "Message of the Day" banner, and a simple Start.txt file that you might find handy if you are going to be working much with practice router labs.

The Description Command

We looked briefly at adding descriptions to our interface configurations using the description command followed by up to 240 characters of information. This enables you to leave instructions or descriptions that might be useful in the future. The description command is created in interface configuration mode and should be considered as you configure the IP address and other options.

The following lines are an example of the entries and the resulting output of a show run command:

```
Lab-X#conf t
Lab-X(config)#int e0
Lab-X(config-if)Description: Connection to Sales Department. The
access list
prevents access to web and ftp servers.
Lab-X(config-if)#^Z
Lab-X#show run
!
interface Ethernet0
 description Connection to Sales Department. The access list pre-
vents access to
web and ftp servers.
 ip address 192.168.5.1 255.255.255.0
 !
```

Message of the Day (MOTD) Banner

It is possible to create a message that appears to everyone logging in to the user level. This message could be anything from a polite hello to a warning of company security policies for unauthorized access. To configure this message, use the banner motd command in global configuration mode. The syntax is a little unusual insofar as you type the command followed by a character you do not plan to include in the message. This character becomes a delimiter, in that everything you type after it until the character appears again will be part of the message. An example would be **banner motd *No Unauthorized Access***, where the asterisks indicate the beginning and end of the message. The asterisks will not appear in the message.

The following output demonstrates creating a banner MOTD:

```
Lab-X#conf t
Enter configuration commands, one per line.  End with CNTL-Z.
Lab-X(config)#banner motd *Unauthorized Access Could Result In
Termination*
Lab-X(config)#^Z
Lab-X#exit
Unauthorized Access Could Result In Termination
User Access Verification
Password:
Lab-X>
```

It is possible to make multiple-line messages by using SHIFT-ENTER at the end of the line and ignoring the warning message that appears the first time you try it. The following lines demonstrate this technique. Typing a new MOTD replaces the existing one.

```
Lab-X#conf t
Lab-X(config)#banner motd *If you have any trouble with this
device, call:
Enter TEXT message.  End with the character '*'.
(Ignore this)
Mark Smith in IT Tech Support
Phone: (555) 555-1111 ext 1234*
Lab-X(config)#^Z
Lab-X#exit                                    (To see the result)
If you have any trouble with this device, call:
Mark Smith in IT Tech Support
Phone: (555) 555-1111 ext 1234
User Access Verification
Password:
Lab-X>
```

Start File

This section is more of a suggestion for those of you contemplating continuing to work on router configurations in a lab setting where you will be configuring many devices from scratch. Create a simple text file with the password configuration and any other commands you routinely want added to the router configuration. You can then just copy and paste from this document into global configuration mode and you are off and running.

I particularly like this technique when I'm working as part of a team and we are telnetting between devices to check each other's work or troubleshoot a problem. It gets tiring when someone forgets to create passwords or misspells one.

The following lines are the bare minimum that I most often include. The text on the right side is for explanation only. Do not type it, because the IOS won't know what to do with it.

```
enable secret cisco      Sets secret password to cisco line con 0
 password cisco          Sets Console port access password to cisco
 login                 Requires each Console user to log in line aux 0
 password cisco Sets Auxiliary port (modem) access password to
cisco
 login                 Requires each Auxiliary user to login line vty 0 4
 password cisco  Sets all 5 (0-4) telnet sessions access password
to cisco
 login                   Requires each telnet user to login
```

To this I usually add some other useful commands. Here are some ideas you might find useful:

- **ip subnet-zero**   Makes sure that even older versions of the IOS recognize the first and last subnets, thereby salvaging most of the lost host addresses.

- **ip http server**   Lets us access our routers using Internet Explorer. While that may not be a big deal or even desirable on a production router, it gives us a series of HTTP sources in the lab if we want to work with access lists and demonstrate blocking HTTP access.

- **no ip domain-lookup**   Prevents the IOS from looking beyond the local router to resolve misspelled commands. Do not use this if your network devices use DNS to resolve names.

- **logging synchronous**   In the line con 0 configuration, redraws your command when system messages scroll through.

The result tends to look like this (again, don't type the explanations):

```
config t       Starts global configuration mode enable secret cisco
ip subnet-zero    Use of first/last subnets for IOS older than 12
ip http server                 Allows web browser access to the
router
no ip domain-lookup            Prevents DNS search when you make a
typo
```

```
line con 0
logging synchronous            Keeps your typed commands together
as you receive system messages to the console terminal.
 password cisco
 login
 transport input none
line aux 0
 password cisco
 login
line vty 0 4
 password cisco
 login
!
end                            Same as Ctrl-Z to end global configuration
copy run start                 Copies entries to NVRAM
```

Descriptions and Messages Exercise

1. Use the techniques from the "Description Command" section to create a description entry for each interface on at least one router. Use a message appropriate to your industry or just department names.

   Use the **show run** command to see the results.

2. Use the **banner motd** command to create a login banner that greets the user. Supply your own text.

3. Optionally, create a Start.txt file in Notepad and paste it to a router that you have erased the configuration from.

Commands Introduced in this Section

The following commands were introduced in this section:

- **description** *message* Created in interface configuration mode, this feature allows you to add up to 240 characters of label or messages that only appear when the configuration is displayed.

- **banner motd** *symbol message symbol* Banner that appears every time someone attempts to access user mode. The *symbol* is a character that is not in the message that indicates the beginning and end of the message text.

Cisco IOS

In this chapter, we have looked at the basics of router configuration without too much concern for the IOS. In this section, we look at the skills and techniques for checking the IOS, checking the memory, creating and using backup copies of the IOS, and, ultimately, upgrading the IOS. This section also describes how to set up and use a TFTP server as a source for IOS files for both backups and upgrades. We look at using TFTP as a vehicle to back up and restore configuration files.

The Show Version Command

The show version command displays detailed information about the Cisco IOS software version running on the router. The command also displays detailed information about the device, including the amount of RAM memory and Flash memory, the CPU model, and interfaces on the device. This is the only command that discloses the configuration register and the boot field setting that determines where the device will get the IOS.

In the following example, the third-line entry (C2500-D-L) indicates the IOS is for a 2500 series router, and D-L indicates the feature set, which is an IP/IPX feature set. Version 12.1(5)T is the version and "build" information. The version is 12.1, and the build is (5)T.

Line 12 indicates that the specific model is a 2524, with 16,384K of RAM (14336K/2048K). The two values need to be added together. Other features are annotated in parentheses in the output.

```
Lab-X#show ver
Cisco Internetwork Operating System Software
IOS(tm) 2500 Software (C2500-D-L), Version 12.1(5)T, RELEASE SOFT-
WARE (fc1)
Copyright (c) 1986-2000 by cisco Systems, Inc.
Compiled Sat 11-Nov-00 03:07 by ccai
Image text-base: 0x03050354, data-base: 0x00001000
ROM: System Bootstrap, Version 11.0(10c), SOFTWARE
BOOTFLASH: 3000 Bootstrap Software (IGS-BOOT-R), Version
11.0(10c),
RELEASE SOFTWARE (fc1)
Lab-X uptime is 2 hours, 1 minute
System returned to ROM by power-on
System image file is "flash:c2500-d-l.121-5.T.bin"
cisco 2524 (68030) processor (revision J) with 14336K/2048K bytes
of memory.
```

```
Processor board ID 08855309, with hardware revision 00000000
Bridging software.
X.25 software, Version 3.0.0.
1 Ethernet/IEEE 802.3 interface(s)
2 Serial network interface(s)
5-in-1 module for Serial Interface 0
56k 2-wire CSU/DSU for Serial Interface 1
32K bytes of non-volatile configuration memory.
16384K bytes of processor board System flash (Read ONLY)
(Flash memory)
Configuration register is 0x2102
Lab-X#
```

The Show Flash Command

The **show flash** command displays the contents of Flash memory, the IOS filename, the IOS file size, and available free memory. The **show flash summary** command summarizes the Flash memory information. The output of the show flash command will vary with different models. When planning an IOS upgrade, the show flash command is used to verify that sufficient system memory exists for the Cisco IOS software to be loaded. If there is insufficient Flash memory, a smaller Cisco IOS software image needs to be selected or the available memory on the router needs to be increased.

The following sample output indicates "read-only" memory, which indicates that this model transfers only a portion of the IOS to RAM for normal operations. Since part of the IOS is in Flash, it is necessary to reboot this device so that it can get the smaller "stripped-down" IOS from ROM before an upgrade can occur. The Cisco 1000, 1600, 2500, 4000, AS5200, and AS5300 series routers all fall into this category.

```
Lab-X#show flash
System flash directory:
File   Length    Name/status
   1   9960076   c2500-d-l.121-5.T.bin
[9960140 bytes used, 6817076 available, 16777216 total]
16384K bytes of processor board System flash (Read ONLY)
Lab-X#show flash summary
Partition  Size    Used    Free    Bank-Size  State      Copy Mode
   1        16384K  9726K   6657K   8192K      Read ONLY  RXBOOT-
FLH
16384K bytes of processor board System flash (Read ONLY)
Lab-X#
```

The next lines show the results of a show flash command on a model 2620 router. The output shows that the memory is (Read/Write), meaning that the IOS is loaded fully into RAM at startup. This will impact how we perform IOS upgrades. Models 1400, 1600-R, 1700, 2600, and 3600 routers all run fully from RAM.

```
2620-A#show flash
System flash directory:
File   Length    Name/status
  1    7175356   c2600-do3s-mz.120-5.T1
  2    745       a
[7176232 bytes used, 1212376 available, 8388608 total]
8192K bytes of processor board System flash (Read/Write)
2620-A#
```

Cisco IOS Naming Conventions

As covered in Chapter 12, there are many variations, or images, of the IOS to meet the many different customer requirements. These variations of feature sets have different version numbers and often have different requirements for both Flash and RAM. Cisco is constantly developing different IOS software images to accommodate the various platforms, available memory resources, and feature set needs customers have for their network devices.

The naming convention for Cisco IOS for Release 12.*x* has three parts:

1. Platform (model)

2. Letter(s) that identifies the feature sets:
   I IP
   d IP/IPX/AT/DEC
   js Enterprise Plus
   is56I IP Plus IPSec 56

3. Letter(s) that specifics where the image runs and if zipped or compressed:
   l Relocatable (RAM and Flash)/uncompressed
   mz RAM/compressed

EXAMPLES	PLATFORM	FEATURE SET	RUN/STORED
c2500-i-l.121-6.bin	2500	IP	Relocatable/uncompressed
c2500-d-l.121-6.bin	2500	IP/IPX/AT/DEC	Relocatable/uncompressed
c4500-d-mz.121-6.bin	4500	IP/IPX/AT/DEC	RAM/compressed
c2500-js-l.121-6.bin	2500	Enterprise Plus	Relocatable/uncompressed

EXAMPLES	PLATFORM	FEATURE SET	RUN/STORED
c2600-js-mz.121-6.bin	2600	Enterprise Plus	RAM/compressed
c4000-js-mz.121-6.bin	4000	Enterprise Plus	RAM/compressed
c7200-js-mz.121-6.bin	7200	Enterprise Plus	RAM/compressed
c3660-is56i-mz.121-6.bin	3660	IP Plus IPSec 56	RAM/compressed

It is important to recognize that the Cisco IOS software naming conventions are subject to change.

Using the TFTP Server

A TFTP server can be used for image and configuration uploads and downloads over the network. The TFTP server can be another router, or it can be a host system running TFTP server software. Trivial File Transfer Protocol (TFTP) is a stripped-down, simplified version of FTP that allows files to be transferred from one device to another over a network. TFTP, unlike FTP, does not allow for browsing or directory changing. The TFTP server application must be running on the network accessible from the device you want to back up or restore. You need to know the IP address of the TFTP server and the correct name of the file.

TFTP is very finicky about any kind of delay, so it tends to be best on point-to-point connections. Frame Relay connections tend to have delay problems causing TFTP to time out and stop transmitting.

Several freeware or shareware TFTP server programs are available for download from the Internet. Cisco has one on the **www.cisco.com** Web site and on the product documentation CD.

Configuring TFTP

Once the TFTP application has been installed, start the program, and a window similar to Figure 13-6 should appear.

By default, many TFTP programs store documents in the same folder that the program is installed in. I find it handy to create a separate folder that may not be buried so deeply in the computer's filing system. To change the default folder, it must be set in advance, because it is not possible to choose directories when you run the TFTP command. With the Cisco TFTP application, open the View menu and choose Options. A window similar to Figure 13-7 should appear.

The TFTP Server Root Directory box will be the destination and source for the file transfers. The Browse button can be used to find and select the folder. If you are going

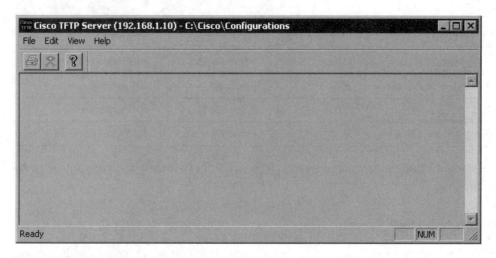

Figure 13-6   Cisco TFTP server

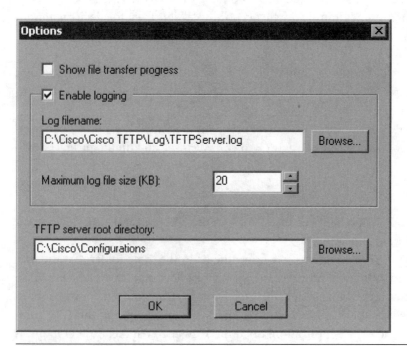

Figure 13-7   TFTP Options screen

to use Cisco's TFTP Server on the router console workstation, you must turn off the **Show File Transfer Progress** option. This is a graphical display, like Figure 13-8, on the TFTP server that shows the progress. This is particularly important if you're copying the IOS to or from the router console. The time it takes the Transfer Progress screen to update will cause the TFTP server to time out. This is not a problem, if you are using the TFTP Server on another machine.

The log file created using the Enable Logging option is a history of the TFTP transfers. Figure 13-9 is a sample of what a log file might look like.

TIP: The size of the organization and the network may impact placement and configuration of the TFTP server as well as how TFTP is used. I have a copy of TFTP installed and configured on my laptop, which I combine with a crossover cable so that I can do backups and upgrades with nothing more than a console cable and an Ethernet interface configured on the router or switch.

Preparing to Use the TFTP Server

To use a TFTP server in your network, make sure there is a good connection to the target device by pinging from the console connection for the device to the IP address of the TFTP server (workstation IP address not router IP address). The following lines show a successful ping from a 2620 router to the TFTP server at 192.168.1.12:

```
2620-A#ping 192.168.1.12
Type escape sequence to abort.
```

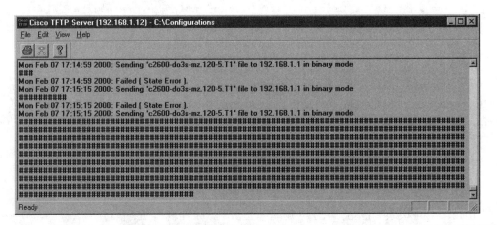

Figure 13-8   TFTP Server progress display

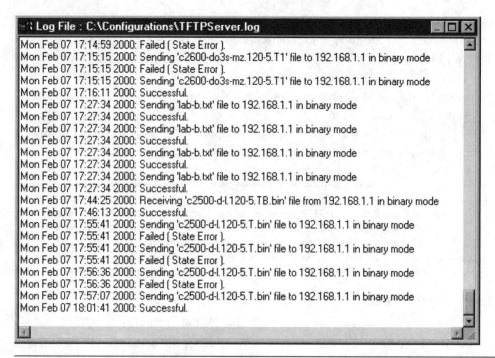

Figure 13-9 TFTP log file

```
Sending 5, 100-byte ICMP Echos to 192.168.1.12, timeout is 2 sec-
onds:
.!!!!
Success rate is 80 percent (4/5), round-trip min/avg/max = 1/1/1
ms
2620-A#
```

If the plan is to back up the current IOS, it will be necessary to have the name of the current IOS image. Since the name is both cryptic and case-sensitive, use **show flash** or **show version** to display the image name and copy the image name. The following lines show the output of both commands:

```
2620-A#show flash
System flash directory:
File  Length   Name/status
  1   7175356  c2600-do3s-mz.120-5.T1
  2   745      a
[7176232 bytes used, 1212376 available, 8388608 total]
8192K bytes of processor board System flash (Read/Write)
2620-A#
```

```
2620-A#show ver
Cisco Internetwork Operating System Software
IOS(tm) C2600 Software (C2600-DO3S-M), Version 12.0(5)T1
Copyright (c) 1986-1999 by cisco Systems, Inc.
Compiled Tue 17-Aug-99 13:18 by cmong
Image text-base: 0x80008088, data-base: 0x80CB67B0
ROM: System Bootstrap, Version 11.3(2)XA4, RELEASE SOFTWARE (fc1)
2620-A uptime is 19 minutes
System returned to ROM by power-on
System image file is "flash:c2600-do3s-mz.120-5.T1"
cisco 2620 (MPC860) processor (rev 0x102) with 26624K/6144K bytes
of memory
Processor board ID JAD04420CRR (4225611147)
M860 processor: part number 0, mask 49
Bridging software.
X.25 software, Version 3.0.0.
Basic Rate ISDN software, Version 1.1.
1 FastEthernet/IEEE 802.3 interface(s)
2 Low-speed serial(sync/async) network interface(s)
1 ISDN Basic Rate interface(s)
32K bytes of non-volatile configuration memory.
8192K bytes of processor board System flash (Read/Write)
Configuration register is 0x2102
2620-A#
```

At this point, connectivity is confirmed and the name of the image file is known so that the backup can be performed. We will look at that process in the next section.

Back Up and Restore the Configuration File

To create a backup of the configuration file, use the copy run tftp command. The running configuration is the current configuration and could include changes that haven't been saved to NVRAM (startup configuration). At that point, a series of prompts will ask for the IP address (192.168.1.12) of the TFTP server and the filename to be used (2620-A) for the saved document. Notice that there is no option for changing disk drives or folders. The next lines shows the **copy run tftp** process:

```
2620-A#copy run tftp
Address or name of remote host []? 192.168.1.12
Destination filename [running-config]? 2620-A
!!
1213 bytes copied in 1.936 secs (1213 bytes/sec)
2620-A#
```

The exclamation (!) marks indicate a successful copy. The number of exclamation marks indicates the size of the file. The two shown in the preceding example indicate a very small file.

The following lines use the help feature (?) to see the options for copying from the TFTP server. If we copy to the running configuration, the file in the TFTP folder will be merged with whatever is in the running configuration. This could result in a configuration that isn't exactly like the one in the TFTP folder. For this reason, it would be better to copy the configuration to the startup configuration (NVRAM). A reload would then clear the RAM and load the startup file into RAM.

```
2620-A#copy tftp ?
  flash:          Copy to flash: file system
  ftp:            Copy to ftp: file system
  lex:            Copy to lex: file system
  null:           Copy to null: file system
  nvram:          Copy to nvram: file system
  rcp:            Copy to rcp: file system
  running-config  Update (merge with) current system configuration
  startup-config  Copy to startup configuration
  system:         Copy to system: file system
  tftp:           Copy to tftp: file system
2620-A#copy tftp start
Address or name of remote host []? 192.168.1.12      (TFTP Server)
Source filename []? 2620-A
(Name of file)
Destination filename [startup-config]?         (ENTER to accept)
Accessing tftp://192.168.1.12/2620-A...
Loading 2620-A from 192.168.1.12 (via FastEthernet0/0): !
[OK - 1213/2048 bytes]
1213 bytes copied in 9.412 secs (134 bytes/sec)
2620-A#
```

The following lines show that copying to the running configuration requires about the same step. Notice that it does not warn you that the existing RAM entries are not erased before the new ones are added.

```
2620-A#copy tftp run
Address or name of remote host [192.168.1.12]?
Source filename [2620-A]?
Destination filename [running-config]?
Accessing tftp://192.168.1.12/2620-A...
Loading 2620-A from 192.168.1.12 (via FastEthernet0/0): !
[OK - 1213/2048 bytes]
1213 bytes copied in 1.232 secs (1213 bytes/sec)
2620-A#
```

Back Up and Restore/Upgrade the Cisco IOS

It is a good idea to back up the IOS image to a TFTP server so that it is available to restore later if the original is lost or corrupted. Another reason for this upload would be to provide a fallback copy of the current image prior to updating the image with a new version. Then, if problems develop with the new version, the administrator can download the backup image and return to the previous, reliable image.

The Cisco IOS is considerably larger than the configuration file and takes several minutes to transfer compared to the few seconds that the configuration file takes. Remember, if the TFTP server is running on the router console workstation, you must turn off the Show File Transfer Progress option (in TFTP Server, select View | Options). This is particularly true when copying the IOS to or from the router console. The time it takes the Transfer Progress screen to update will cause the TFTP server to time out. This is not a problem, if you are using TFTP Server on another network host.

To back up the IOS, type **copy flash tftp** and follow the prompts. It will be necessary to enter the IP address of the TFTP host and the Source filename (IOS name). The IOS name will look like c2600-do3s-mz.120-5.T1 and is case-sensitive. It might make sense to use the show flash command and copy the name. When asked for the Destination filename, press ENTER to use the same name as the source filename, or you can type a new name as shown in the next example:

```
2620-A#copy flash tftp
Source filename []? c2600-do3s-mz.120-5.T1          (case sensitive)
Address or name of remote host []? 192.168.1.12      (TFTP server)
Destination filename [c2600-do3s-mz.120-5.T1]? c2600-old-bob
!!!!!!!!!!!!!!!!!!!!!!!!!!!!!!!!!!!!!!!!!!!!!!!!!!!!!!!!!!!!!!!!!!!!!!!!
!!!!!!!!!!!!!!!!!!!!!!!!!!!!!!!!!!!!!!!!!!!!!!!!!!!!!!!!!!!!!!!!!!!!!!!!
!!!!!!!!!!!!!!!!!!!!!!!!!!!!!!!!!!!!!!!!!!!!!!!!!!!!!!!!!!!!!!!!!!!!!!!!
!!!!!!!!!!!!!!!!!!!!!!!!!!!!!!!!!!!!!!!!!!!!!!!!!!!!!!!!!!!!!!!!!!!!!!!!
!!!!!!!!!!!!!!!!!!!!!!!!!!!!!!!!!!!!!!!!!!!!!!!!!!!!!!!!!!!!!!!!!!!!!!!!
!!!!!!!!!!!!!!!!!!!!!!!!!!!!!!!!!!!!!!!!!!!!!!!!!!!!!!!!!!!!!!!!!!!!!!!!
!!!!!!!!!!!!!!!!!!!!!!!!!!!!!!!!!!!!!!!!!!!!!!!!!!!!!!!!!!!!!!!!!!!!!!!!
!!!!!!!!!!!!!!!!!!!!!!!!!!!!!!!!!!!!!!!!!!!!!!!!!!!!!!!!!!!!!!!!!!!!!!!!
!!!!!!!!!!!!!!!!!!!!!!!!!!!!!!!!!!!!!!!!!!!!!!!!!!!!!!!!!!!!!!!!!!!!!!!!
!!!!!!!!!!!!!!!!!!!!!!!!!!!!!!!!!!!!!!!!!!!!!!!!!!!!!!!!!!!!!!!!!!!!!!!!
!!!!!!!!!!!!!!!!!!!!!!!!!!!!!!!!!!!!!!!!!!!!!!!!!!!!!!!!!!!!!!!!!!!!!!!!
!!!!!!!!!!!!!!!!!!!!!!!!!!!!!!!!!!!!!!!!!!!!!!!!!!!!!!!!!!!!!!!!!!!!!!!!
!!!!!!!!!!!!!!!!!!!!!!!!!!!!!!!!!!!!!!!!!!!!!!!!!!!!!!!!!!!!!!!!!!!!!!!!
!!!!!!!!!!!!!!!!!!!!!!!!!!!!!!!!!!!!!!!!!!!!!!!!!!!!!!!!!!!!!!!!!!!!!!!!
!!!!!!!!!!!!!!!!!!!!!!!!!!!!!!!!!!!!!!!!!!!!!!!!!!!!!!!
7175356 bytes copied in 58.164 secs (123713 bytes/sec)
2620-A#
```

The version of the IOS used on this 2621 router is 7MB in size, which explains the large number of exclamation marks and the fact that it can take a few minutes to run.

Restoring a saved IOS or upgrading to a new IOS image using TFTP use exactly the same steps. The copy tftp flash command takes the IOS image in the TFTP folder and copies it to the device's Flash memory. After you enter the copy tftp flash command, the system prompts you for the IP address (or name) of the TFTP server. This could be another router working as a server for ROM or Flash images, or it could be a TFTP server like the one used in the other examples.

The 2600 router series is one of the models that runs the IOS fully from RAM so that the router does not have to be rebooted to run from the ROM image version before loading a new IOS image. We will see the difference later in this section.

The following output shows the steps for restoring an IOS from the TFTP server:

```
2620-A#copy tftp flash
Address or name of remote host [192.168.1.12]?
Source filename []? c2600-old-bob                    (case sensitive)
Destination filename [c2600-old-bob]?    (ENTER to accept default)
Accessing tftp://192.168.1.12/c2600-old-bob...
Erase flash: before copying? [confirm]
Erasing the flash file system will remove all files! Continue?
[confirm]
Erasing device . . .   eeeeeeeeeeeeeeeeeeeeeeeeeeeeeeee ...erased
Erase of flash: complete
Loading c2600-old-bob from 192.168.1.12 (via FastEthernet0/0):
!!!!!!!!!!!!!!!!!!!!!!!!!!!!!!!!!!!!!!!!!!!!!!!!!!!!!!!!!!!!!!!!!!!!!!!!
    (Output omitted by the author - same size as the copy earlier)
!!!!!!!!!!!!!!!!!!!!!!!!!!!!!!!!!!!!!!!!!!!!!!!!!!!!!!!!!!!!!!!!!!!!!!!!
[OK - 7175356/14350336 bytes]
Verifying checksum ... OK (0xEA37)              (verifying the image)
7175356 bytes copied in 58.204 secs (123713 bytes/sec)
2620-A#
```

There will actually be two IOS images in the machine at this point. The active IOS from RAM is still the original. The new image is not used until the next reload or the next time the router is restarted. The next lines show an abbreviated output from the show ver command that shows the old image is still running:

```
2620-A#show ver
Cisco Internetwork Operating System Software
IOS (tm) C2600 Software (C2600-DO3S-M), Version 12.0(5)T1
    (lines omitted by author)
System image file is "flash:c2600-do3s-mz.120-5.T1"
    (lines omitted by author)
8192K bytes of processor board System flash (Read/Write)
Configuration register is 0x2102
2620-A#
2620-A#show flash
System flash directory:
File  Length    Name/status
  1   7175356   c2600-old-bob                              (new image)
[7175420 bytes used, 1213188 available, 8388608 total]
8192K bytes of processor board System flash (Read/Write)
2620-A#reload
```

Some Cisco series routers run the IOS from Flash as well as RAM and therefore must be rebooted to run from the smaller ROM-based version of the IOS. The IOS image in Flash cannot be overwritten while it is in use. The next lines show the additional output and introduce a feature called "Flash load helper," which handles the reboot to ROM for use. The IOS image is c2500-d-l.120-5.T.bin and, with many screen fonts, can really cause some case-sensitivity problems. The "l" (as in d-l) is a lowercase *L* indicating that the image is "relocateable" and not compressed. Using a 1 prevents the copy, but no useful message appears to tell what went wrong.

```
Router#copy tftp flash
                    ****  NOTICE  ****
Flash load helper v1.0
This process will accept the copy options and then terminate
the current system image to use the ROM based image for the copy.
Routing functionality will not be available during that time.
If you are logged in via telnet, this connection will terminate.
Users with console access can see the results of the copy opera-
tion.
                ---- ******** ----
Proceed? [confirm]
Address or name of remote host [192.168.1.12]?        (TFTP server)
Source filename [Router#copy]? c2500-d-1.120-5.T.bin
```

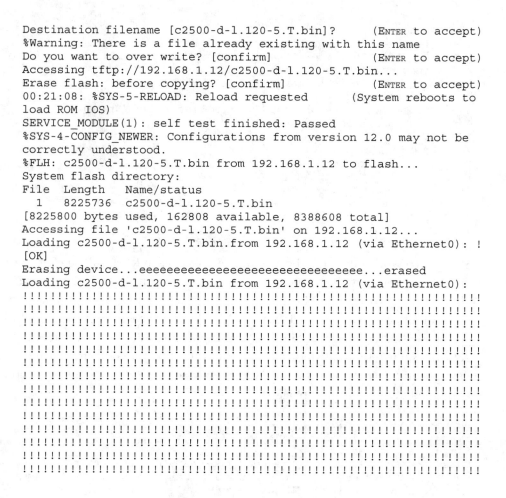

```
Destination filename [c2500-d-l.120-5.T.bin]?        (ENTER to accept)
%Warning: There is a file already existing with this name
Do you want to over write? [confirm]              (ENTER to accept)
Accessing tftp://192.168.1.12/c2500-d-l.120-5.T.bin...
Erase flash: before copying? [confirm]            (ENTER to accept)
00:21:08: %SYS-5-RELOAD: Reload requested      (System reboots to
load ROM IOS)
SERVICE_MODULE(1): self test finished: Passed
%SYS-4-CONFIG_NEWER: Configurations from version 12.0 may not be
correctly understood.
%FLH: c2500-d-l.120-5.T.bin from 192.168.1.12 to flash...
System flash directory:
File  Length   Name/status
  1   8225736  c2500-d-l.120-5.T.bin
[8225800 bytes used, 162808 available, 8388608 total]
Accessing file 'c2500-d-l.120-5.T.bin' on 192.168.1.12...
Loading c2500-d-l.120-5.T.bin.from 192.168.1.12 (via Ethernet0): !
[OK]
Erasing device...eeeeeeeeeeeeeeeeeeeeeeeeeeeeeeee...erased
Loading c2500-d-l.120-5.T.bin from 192.168.1.12 (via Ethernet0):
!!!!!!!!!!!!!!!!!!!!!!!!!!!!!!!!!!!!!!!!!!!!!!!!!!!!!!!!!!!!!!!!!!!!!!!
!!!!!!!!!!!!!!!!!!!!!!!!!!!!!!!!!!!!!!!!!!!!!!!!!!!!!!!!!!!!!!!!!!!!!!!
!!!!!!!!!!!!!!!!!!!!!!!!!!!!!!!!!!!!!!!!!!!!!!!!!!!!!!!!!!!!!!!!!!!!!!!
!!!!!!!!!!!!!!!!!!!!!!!!!!!!!!!!!!!!!!!!!!!!!!!!!!!!!!!!!!!!!!!!!!!!!!!
!!!!!!!!!!!!!!!!!!!!!!!!!!!!!!!!!!!!!!!!!!!!!!!!!!!!!!!!!!!!!!!!!!!!!!!
!!!!!!!!!!!!!!!!!!!!!!!!!!!!!!!!!!!!!!!!!!!!!!!!!!!!!!!!!!!!!!!!!!!!!!!
!!!!!!!!!!!!!!!!!!!!!!!!!!!!!!!!!!!!!!!!!!!!!!!!!!!!!!!!!!!!!!!!!!!!!!!
!!!!!!!!!!!!!!!!!!!!!!!!!!!!!!!!!!!!!!!!!!!!!!!!!!!!!!!!!!!!!!!!!!!!!!!
!!!!!!!!!!!!!!!!!!!!!!!!!!!!!!!!!!!!!!!!!!!!!!!!!!!!!!!!!!!!!!!!!!!!!!!
!!!!!!!!!!!!!!!!!!!!!!!!!!!!!!!!!!!!!!!!!!!!!!!!!!!!!!!!!!!!!!!!!!!!!!!
!!!!!!!!!!!!!!!!!!!!!!!!!!!!!!!!!!!!!!!!!!!!!!!!!!!!!!!!!!!!!!!!!!!!!!!
!!!!!!!!!!!!!!!!!!!!!!!!!!!!!!!!!!!!!!!!!!!!!!!!!!!!!!!!!!!!!!!!!!!!!!!
!!!!!!!!!!!!!!!!!!!!!!!!!!!!!!!!!!!!!!!!!!!!!!!!!!!!!!!!!!!!!!!!!!!!!!
```

```
!!!!!!!!!!!!!!!!!!!!!!!!!!!!!!!!!!!!!!!!!!!!!!!!!!!!!!!!!!!!!!!!!!!!!!!!
!!!!!!!!!!!!!!!!!!!!!!!!!!!!!!!!!!!!!!!!!!!!!!!!!!!!!!!!!!!!!!!!!!!!!!!!
!!!!!!!!!!!!!!!!!!!!!!!!!!!!!!!!!!!!!!!!!!!!!!!!!!!!!!!!!!!!!!!!!!!!!!!!
!!!!!!!!!!!!!!!!!!!!!!!!!!!!!!!!!!!!!!!!!!!!!!!!!!!!!!!!!!!!!!!!!!!!!!!!
!!!!!!!!!!!!!!!!!!!!!!!!!!!!!!!!!!!!!!!!!!!!!!!!!!!!!!!!!!!!!!!!!!!!!!!!
!!!!!!!!!!!!!!!!!!!!!!!!!!!!!!!!!!!!!!!!!!!!!!!!!!!!!!!!!!!!!!!!!!!!!!!!
[OK - 8225736/8388608 bytes]
Verifying checksum...OK (0xC662)           (verifying the image)
Flash copy took 0:04:46 [hh:mm:ss]            (almost 5 minutes)
%FLH: Re-booting system after download
```

Locating the Cisco IOS Software

Where a Cisco device looks for the IOS software at startup depends on the hardware platform, but most often it tries to use the boot system commands saved in Flash. If Flash is empty, the router loads a stripped-down version of the IOS from ROM. This is not intended to be used for production, but provides enough resources to allow for an IOS to be loaded.

It is possible to configure a series of contingency sources for the IOS to increase the chances that the device can boot to a usable image. This is particularly important in production environments where the cost of a "down" router could be substantial. The possible sources that routers can use to boot the Cisco IOS software from include the following:

- Flash memory (usually the default)

- TFTP server (must be preconfigured)

- ROM (not full Cisco IOS software)

You can use global configuration mode boot system commands to create a three-step fallback for loading the IOS. Create and save these statements to NVRAM with the copy run start command. The router follows the sequence until it finds a valid IOS each time it starts. The following configuration syntax would provide an example of three alternatives for the device:

```
Router#config t                                  (syntax)
Router(config)#boot system flash IOS_image_name
Router(config)#boot system tftp IOS_image_name tftp_IP_address
Router(config)#boot system ROM
Router(config)#copy run start
Router#config t                                  (example)
Router(config)#boot system flash c2500-d-l.120-5.T.bin
Router(config)#boot system tftp c2500-d-l.120-5.T.bin 192.168.1.12
Router(config)#boot system ROM
Router(config)#copy run start
```

Configuration Register Values

The order the router uses to look for system bootstrap instructions depends on the boot field setting in the configuration register. The configuration register is a 16-bit memory register in NVRAM containing instructions. The normal startup configuration register (address) is shown on the very last line of output of the show ver command. The following output is from a model 2621 router, but the last line is typical of the default configuration register:

```
2620-A#show ver
Cisco Internetwork Operating System Software
    (lines omitted by author)
8192K bytes of processor board System flash (Read/Write)
Configuration register is 0x2102
```

Under certain circumstances, such as password recovery (discussed in the next section), it may be necessary to change the default configuration register setting. The last 4 bits of the 16-bit binary configuration register (bits 3, 2, 1, and 0) are the boot field. This can be done with the config-register *mem_address* command while in global configuration mode. Rebooting the router will then implement the change:

```
Router#config t                                  (some examples)
Router(config)#config-reg 0x2101 (will boot from boot Flash - ROM)
Router(config)# config-reg 0x2102        (will boot from Flash)
```

If the last digit of the configuration register is 0, then the system boots to ROM Monitor (rommon) mode, which is a lower-level system language used by programmers and administrators when the IOS fails. (This sets the binary boot field bits to 0000.)

If the last digit of the configuration register is 1, then the system boots to the stripped-down version of the IOS stored in Flash or ROM depending on the model. (This sets the binary boot field bits to 0001.)

If the last digit of the configuration register is any HEX value but 0 or 1 (2 to F), then the system boots to Flash—normal startup mode. (This sets the binary boot field bits to a value from 0010 to 1111.)

Set the configuration register to any value from 0x102 to 0x10F to configure the system to use the boot system commands in NVRAM. This is the default. (These values set the boot field bits to 0-0-1-0 through 1-1-1-1.)

 EXAM TIP: For the exam, know that these configuration register settings will do the following: 0x100—launches ROM monitor (then use b command to launch IOS); 0x101—boots from IOS in ROM; 0x102 to 0x10F—boot from IOS in NVRAM.

Commands Introduced in this Section

The following commands were introduced in this section:

- **show ver** Displays a complete inventory of the device, including the amount of RAM and Flash; the name of the IOS image; and the configuration register setting.

- **show flash** Displays the contents of Flash memory, the IOS filename, the IOS file size, and available free memory.

- **show flash summary** Summarizes the Flash memory information.

- **config-register** *mem_address* Changes startup memory register.

- **copy run tftp** Copies the active configuration to a file on the TFTP server.

- **copy tftp run** Merges the configuration file on the TFTP server with the active configuration file. Be careful of this one, because the results may not be a clean copy of the TFTP file.

- **copy tftp start** Copies the configuration file on the TFTP server to NVRAM to become the startup configuration. This configuration will be used at the next reload command.

- **copy flash tftp** Creates a backup of the IOS image to the TFTP server.

- **copy tftp flash** Loads the IOS image on the TFTP server to Flash memory. This could be a restoration of an old image or an upgraded image.

Router Password Recovery

Securing our routers and switches with passwords is a reasonable security measure. What do you do if a password is forgotten, the administrator that set the password is gone, or a device is returned from a branch office with an unknown password set? There will always be circumstances where the password for a Cisco device needs to be reset.

The good news is that it is not very difficult to reset the password. The bad news is also that it is not very difficult to reset the password. Since the process is not secret information, it is very important that the devices themselves be physically secure. Password recovery does require physical access to the device, using a console cable to the console port.

Once the password recovery is underway, it is pretty consistent from model to model of router. The manner in which you start the process depends on which of two groups of routers the router model falls within: the newer model series, including the 1000, 1600, 1700, 2600, 3600, 4500, and 4700 models, or the older 2000, 2500, 3000, and 4000 series. Only steps 2 and 3 are different between the groups. When in doubt, always check the Web site **www.cisco.com** or the documentation that came with the device.

The steps are as follows:

1. Make sure that you have a console connection to the router and that the router is off.

2. Power the device up and, during the first 60 seconds, press the CTRL-BREAK keys at the same time—you may need to press CTRL-BREAK several times. On a standard keyboard, the BREAK key is typically in the upper-right portion of the keyboard and may also have the word PAUSE on the key cap. This will cause the router to interrupt its normal startup process. If the CTRL-BREAK doesn't work, check for the BREAK key sequence on your terminal emulator.
   Model 1000, 1600, 1700, 2600, 3600, 4500, and 4700 units will respond with: **rommon 1>**.
   Model 2000, 2500, 3000, and 4000 units will respond with:
   > (a greater-than symbol with no router name).

3. For model 1000, 1600, 1700, 2600, 3600, 4500, and 4700 units, carefully type **confreg 2142** at the rommon 1> prompt and press ENTER. Warning: If you incorrectly input these numbers, you could lose control of your router. A common mistake is to transpose the first two digits-resulting in the router producing only little white boxes on the screen.
   For model 2000, 2500, 3000, and 4000 units, carefully type **o/r 0x42** at the > prompt and press ENTER.

4. Everything from this point on is the same for all models.

   At the next prompt, type a lowercase **i** and press ENTER. The following shows the most common prompts you might expect:

   rommon 2>i (for model 1000, 1600, 1700, 2600, 3600, 4500, and 4700 units)

   >i (for model 2000, 2500, 3000, and 4000 units)

   This will cause the router to reboot and ignore its saved configuration in the NVRAM. The register changes we made in step 3 cause the router to ignore the startup config file.

5. Answer No if asked "Would you like to enter the initial configuration dialog? [yes/no]."

6. At the **Router>** prompt, type **enable** to get into Privilege mode.

   Note: The system will not ask for a password.

7. If you want to save the current router configuration, type **config mem** at the prompt. This will copy the startup-config file from NVRAM into the running configuration. If you do not want to keep the current configuration, you can skip this step.

8. Type **config t** to go to global configuration mode.

9. Type the following commands, using your new password(s) in place of the word "cisco":

   enable secret *cisco*

   line con 0

   password *cisco*

   login

   You could set the line vty 0 4 and aux 0 passwords, if you want.

   Warning: Remember passwords are case-sensitive!

10. Type **config-register 0x2102** and press ENTER. Be very accurate with this. This step is often forgotten and the next time the router is rebooted, it returns to password recovery mode. We are setting the memory register to return to normal on the next reload.

11. Press CTRL-Z to exit global configuration mode.

12. Type **copy run start** to save the new configuration with the passwords.

13. Type **show ver** and look at the very last line. It should tell you that the configuration register will change to 0x2102 on the next startup. The message should look like this: "Configuration register is 0x42 (will be 0x2102 at next reload)." If it does not, return to global configuration mode and start over at step 10.

14. Type **reload** to reboot the router.

ConfigMaker

Cisco ConfigMaker is an easy-to-use Windows 95/98/NT network drawing tool that configures a good selection of Cisco's small to medium-sized routers, switches, hubs, and other devices. While a limited number of switches and hubs is included, the greatest support is for routers (up through the 4700 model) and the technologies for connecting devices like Ethernet, ISDN, Frame Relay, and VPN. The product can be downloaded for free from the Cisco Web site, or it is included on some product documentation CDs. The easiest way to download ConfigMaker is to go to **www.cisco.com/warp/public/779/smbiz/service/index.html** to get to a site for small and medium-sized businesses, and then click the Tool Central button. Look for a ConfigMaker link. Figure 13-10 shows the site. You can also go directly to the **www.cisco.com** site and do a search on **ConfigMaker**.

The GUI and the very informative tutorial make this an excellent tool for configuring devices or for those who do not have hands-on access to devices. Once downloaded and ready, you draw your network, and then Cisco ConfigMaker creates the Cisco IOS configuration files for each device on your network. These configurations can be uploaded to the device if you have a console connection. Figure 13-11 shows Config-Maker and a simple ISDN connection between a Cisco 804 and 2524 router.

ConfigMaker is a network design program that can be used to configure the following features on virtual devices: Network Address Translation (NAT), voice-over-IP, firewalls, virtual private network (VPN), and much more. Once you place a device on the drawing, you are prompted with a series of screens that allow you to add passwords, choose device modules, add protocols, and define addresses to be used. If you have devices, Config-Maker can transfer configurations to and from the device via the console cable. Even if you have no equipment beyond a PC, download the tool and go through the tutorials. You can learn a lot about the technologies and the features of many Cisco devices.

Using a Web Browser

Since version 11.0 of the Cisco IOS, many Cisco routers and switches can be accessed via a Web browser such as Internet Explorer. The feature itself is somewhat limited and will not impress anyone for its elegance, but it does give access to the interfaces and the diagnostic log, and gives you the ability to launch a HyperTerminal session for more direct options. There are generally no graphics; instead, a series of text screens allows you to modify the configuration and view device information. Figure 13-12 shows the opening page for a Cisco 4000M. The mouse support and various links make it possible to perform some tasks with a limited knowledge of the CLI. The Cisco 1900 line of switches has a very nice graphical interface.

Figure 13-10   Sales Tools Central

Since most computers have Web browsers that could access the Cisco network devices and the limited added usefulness of using the browser many administrators choose to disable the router's ability to service HTTP requests. The idea being that the benefits do not outweigh the risks to network security. The command to turn the feature off is no ip http server, which is the default setting.

I agree with the security concerns in production settings, but in classrooms and practice labs, turning on the HTTP server means that we can test access control lists (ACLs) that block or modify Web access without having to be connected to the Internet or a functioning Web server. We will use this feature for exactly that reason in the next chapter.

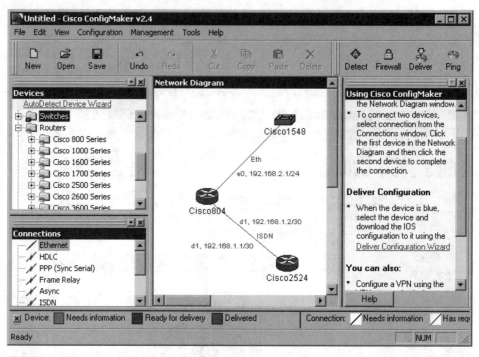

Figure 13-11 ConfigMaker interface

To use this feature, the router(s) needs to be set in global configuration mode to ip http server. Now, any workstation connected and configured to be a part of the network can use the Web browser to access the device's Web pages. Connection is established simply by typing the IP address in the Address line on the browser.

The login process uses the device's host name as the User Name, and the enable secret password as the Password. Figure 13-13 shows the login screen.

HTTP Server Exercise

1. On at least one router, in global configuration mode, type **ip http server** to enable the Web server access feature.

2. Open a Web browser on a workstation connected to the router network and type the IP address of the router.

3. Use the device's host name as the User Name and the enable secret password as the Password.

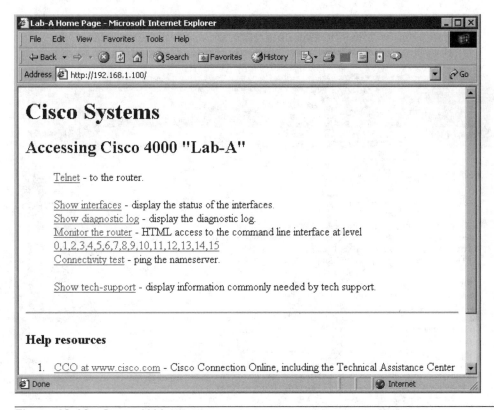

Figure 13-12   Router Web page

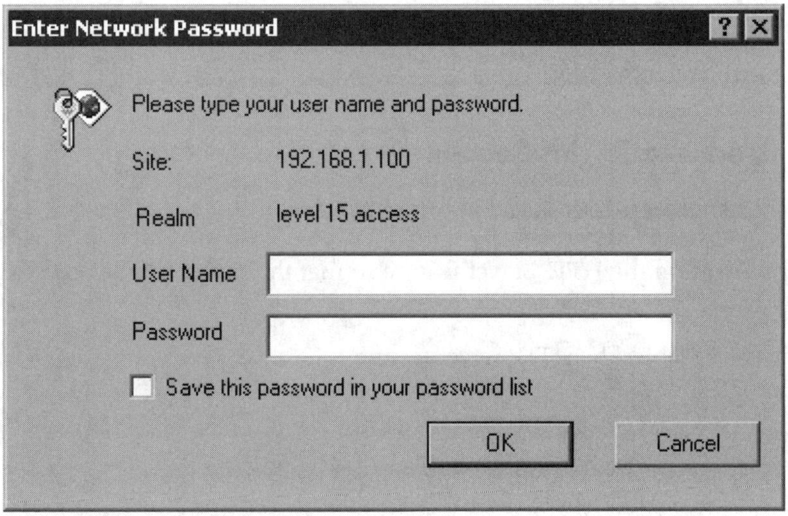

Figure 13-13   Access router login

4. Choose the "Choose the Show Interfaces link . . . " on the main page and look over the results. The following illustration shows the router interfaces.

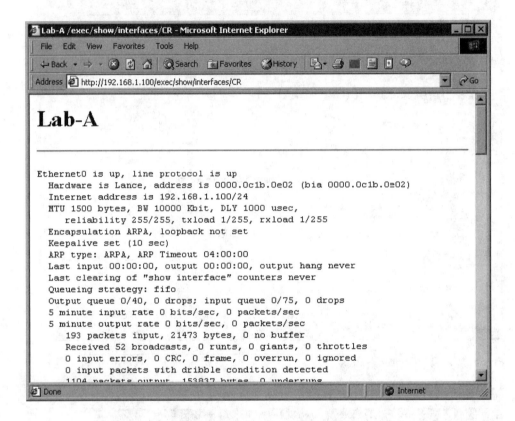

5. Experiment with any other links.

Commands Introduced in this Section

The following commands were introduced in this section:

- **ip http server** Turns on the HTTP server feature so that the router can be accessed from a Web browser.

- **no ip http server** Disables the HTTP server feature.

Summary

In this chapter, we looked at the basic techniques to configure a router to use IP. We started with assigning IP addresses to the various interface types using the IP address command. We also looked at how to set the clock rate on the DCE end of a serial connection and the ring speed on a Token Ring interface. We compared the show interface command to the show ip interface command.

We looked at adding both static and default routes directly to our route tables. We use one or more static routes to point to specific networks, while we use a default route as a route of last resort for unknown networks. We worked with enabling RIP and IGRP routing protocols. We used several debug commands and the show ip route command to troubleshoot and view the results of our routing. The passive-interface command can be used to restrict routing updates on a particular interface.

We used a variety of simple techniques to complete our router configuration. These techniques include using the hostname command to name our devices and the ip host command to map text names to up to eight IP addresses. We used the description command to document our interfaces, and the banner motd command to create an opening banner message. We also introduced ConfigMaker and the possibility of using a Web browser to view or edit our configurations.

We worked with a TFTP server to back up and restore configuration and IOS image files. The same techniques can be used to perform system IOS upgrades.

We looked at how to set up various passwords on a device, as well as basic password recovery techniques.

Practice Questions

Take a few moments and check your grasp of the concepts covered in this chapter. The answers are immediately following the questions.

Questions

1. Which two commands are used to clear the running configuration so that you can start a new configuration?
   a. erase run and reload
   b. reload and erase run
   c. erase start and reload
   d. clear start and reload

2. Which one of the following commands will set the IP address on a Fast Ethernet interface?
   a. router(config)# ip address 192.168.1.1
   b. router(config-if)#ip address 192.168.1.1
   c. router(config-if)#ip address 192.168.1.1 255.255.255.0
   d. router(config-if fa0/0)#ip address 192.168.1.1 255.255.255.0

3. Which answer choice accurately describes the following interface? (Which answer choice accurately describes what we know about the serial 0/0 interface?)
   interface serial 0/0
   ip address 192.168.1.145 255.255.255.192
   clockrate 56000
   no shutdown
   a. It is a DTE connection.
   b. It is a DCE connection.
   c. It is a passive interface.
   d. The bandwidth is 56K.

4. On a serial connection, what determines whether it is a DCE or DTE connection?
   a. Where the clockrate is set
   b. The cable connection
   c. The set dce command
   d. Administrator's choice

5. What is the following command: ip route 192.168.1.0 255.255.255.0 10.0.0.1?
   a. It is a default route
   b. It is a static route to host 192.168.1.0
   c. It is a static route to the 10.0.0.0 network
   d. It is a static route to the 192.168.1.0 network

6. Which of the following is a proper static route?
   a. router#ip route 192.168.1.0 255.255.255.0 10.0.01
   b. router(config)#ip route 192.168.1.0 255.255.255.0 10.0.01
   c. router#ip route 0.0.0.0 0.0.0.0 10.0.01
   d. router(config)#ip route 0.0.0.0 0.0.0.0 10.0.01

7. If there is a static route to a destination network, and the RIP routing protocol determines another route with the same hop count to the same network, what will appear in the route table.
   a. Both routes will appear
   b. The RIP route only
   c. The static route only
   d. Not enough information exists

8. What is the maximum reachable hop count for RIP routing?
   a. 100
   b. 15
   c. 16
   d. It can vary

9. What command enables RIP routing?
   a. route rip
   b. rip routing
   c. router rip
   d. enable rip

10. Which of the following commands would add the 192.168.1.0 network to either RIP or IGRP routing?
    a. router(config)#network 192.168.1.0
    b. router(config-if)#network 192.168.1.0
    c. router(config-router)#network 192.168.1.0
    d. router(config-network)#network 192.168.1.0

11. In the command router igrp 117, what is the 117?
    a. Network ID
    b. A sequence number
    c. Autonomous system number
    d. Asynchronous number

12. What does a passive interface do?
    a. Takes abuse well
    b. Sends routing updates only when asked
    c. Disables routing updates on that interface
    d. Blocks advertisements about the attached route to other routers

13. Which of the following is the command to name a device "seattle," setting the device ID?
    a. router#host name seattle
    b. router#hostname seattle
    c. router(config)#host name seattle
    d. router(config)#host-name seattle
    e. router(config)#hostname seattle
    f. router(config)#device-ID = seattle

14. What is the proper command to associate an IP address to a text name?
    a. router#hostname seattle
    b. router(config)#hostname seattle 192.168.1.1
    c. router(config)#ip host seattle 192.168.1.1
    d. router(config-if)#ip host seattle 192.168.1.1

15. Given the following two commands, what will happen?
    ip host central 192.168.1.1 192.168.2.1 192.168.3.1
    ping central
    a. A device named central will be pinged
    b. The 192.168.1.1 interface will be pinged
    c. All three interfaces will be pinged sequentially
    d. The 192.168.3.1 interface will be pinged

16. What command is used to create a security warning at the initial login screen?
    a. description
    b. banner motd
    c. login announce
    d. ip host

17. Given the next two commands, what will be the password to enter privilege mode?
    enable password seattle
    enable secret Vancouver
    a. Seattle
    b. seattle

    c. Vancouver

    d. vancouver

    e. Any of the above will work

18. Given the following commands, what will a user telnetting into a router be expected to provide to gain admittance to user mode?

    username scott password wolfeman

    line con 0

    login local

    line vty 0 4

    password cisco

    login

        a. scott & wolfeman

        b. wolfeman

        c. cisco

        d. wolfeman & cisco

19. Which two commands display the name of the IOS image?

        a. show IOS

        b. show interfaces

        c. show version

        d. show flash

20. What is the command to save a copy of the configuration file to the TFTP server?

        a. copy tftp run

        b. copy tftp start

        c. copy run tftp

        d. copt tftp flash

21. What is the command to load an upgrade of the IOS file from the TFTP server?

        a. copy tftp run

        b. copy tftp flash

        c. copy flash tftp

        d. copt tftp nvram

22. Which one of the following commands will tell you the IP address of a neighbor router?

        a. cdp neighbor

        b. cdp neighbor detail

        c. show cdp neighbor detail

        d. show cdp neighbor

23. Which two of the following will be detected by the cdp neighbor commands?
    a. All routers assigned IP addresses
    b. Cisco routers
    c. Cisco hubs
    d. Cisco switches
    e. All switches assigned IP addresses

24. What command has to be added to the RIP configuration to enable VLSM and CIDR?
    a. No special command
    b. version 2
    c. vlsm enable
    d. enable subnet-masks

25. What command turns off any debugging in progress?
    a. debug off
    d. disable debug
    c. undebug all
    d. stop debug

Answers

1. c. The erase start and reload commands are used to clear the running configuration so that you can start a new configuration; all of the other commands do not work.

2. c. The router(config-if)#ip address 192.168.1.1 255.255.255.0 command sets the IP address on a Fast Ethernet interface. IP addresses are defined at the configure interface mode. All of the other commands do not work. B needs a subnet mask.

3. b. The interface is a DCE connection. The clockrate command appears only on a DCE connection.

4. b. The cable connection determines whether a serial connection is a DCE or DTE connection. Only the interface with the DCE cable connection can set the clockrate. Answer c. is incorrect because no such command exists. Answer d. is incorrect, because although the administrator has the choice in connecting two internal routers, when connecting to an outside service, the router will always be a DTE.

5. **d.** The command is a static route to the 192.168.1.0 network.

6. **d.** router(config)#ip route 0.0.0.0 0.0.0.0 10.0.01 Answer a. is a static route issued at the wrong mode. Answer b. is a static route not a default route. Answer c. is a default route issued at the wrong mode.

7. **c.** The static route only appears in the route table because the administrative will always be deemed more reliable (lower administrative cost) than one learned from a routing protocol.

8. **b.** The maximum reachable hop count for RIP routing is 15; anything higher is by definition unreachable.

9. **c.** The router rip command enables RIP routing. All the other commands are not valid commands.

10. **c.** The router(config-router)#network 192.168.1.0 command would add the 192.168.1.0 network to either RIP or IGRP routing. Answers a. and b. are in the wrong mode. Answer d. is not a valid mode.

11. **c.** In the router igrp 117 command, 117 is the autonomous system number.

12. **c.** A passive interface disables routing updates on that interface. Answers a. and b. are nonsense. Answer d. is accomplished by not listing the network in the routing configuration.

13. **e.** The router(config)#hostname seattle command names a device "seattle," setting the device ID.

14. **c.** The router(config)#ip host seattle 192.168.1.1 command associates an IP address to a text name.

15. **b.** Given the two commands, the 192.168.1.1 interface will be pinged. Only the first associated address will be pinged.

16. **b.** The banner motd command is used to create a security warning at the initial login screen.

17. **c.** Given the two commands, the password to enter privilege mode is Vancouver. Passwords are case-sensitive, and whenever an enable secret is used, it takes precedence over the enable password.

18. **c.** Given the commands, a user telnetting into a router will be expected to provide **cisco** to gain admittance to user mode. The line vty 0 4 command sets the password to cisco.

19. **c.** and **d.** The show version and show flash commands display the name of the IOS image.

20. **c.** The copy run tftp command is used to save a copy of the configuration file to the TFTP server.

21. **b.** The copy tftp flash command is used to load an upgrade of the IOS file from the TFTP server.

22. **c.** The show cdp neighbor detail command tells you the IP address of a neighbor router.

23. **b.** and **d.** Only Cisco routers and switches will be detected by the cdp neighbor command.

24. **b.** The version 2 command has to be added to the RIP configuration to enable VLSM and CIDR. Only version 2 RIP supports VLSM and CIDR.

25. **c.** The undebug all command turns off any debugging in progress. It can be shortened to un all.

CHAPTER 14

Novell NetWare

This chapter will:

- **Discuss the recognition and use of IPX addressing**

- **Cover IPX encapsulation types**

- **Look at basic IPX workstation configurations**

- **Discuss the application and verification of basic IPX configurations to a router**

- **Cover the use and verification of IPX RIP routing**

- **Examine an IPX version of ping and the Cisco Discovery Protocol (CDP)**

- **Look at NetWare SAP and GNS features**

hapter 5 introduced Novell NetWare's IPX/SPX protocol and defined key terms. This chapter looks at configuring Cisco routers to use IPX.

Novell's NetWare is a network operating system (NOS) similar to Microsoft's Windows NT and 2000 products, as well as Linux and the many flavors of UNIX. Netware is like Linux and UNIX in that it is true client/server architecture. As such, NetWare hosts can be either workstations (clients) or servers, but they cannot be both, as in Windows. Netware servers provide all the typical server functions including print and file sharing, network-centralized security, centralized databases, and remote access authentication. While not the fastest-growing or -selling NOS on the market, Novell has the largest installed base of network installations in many parts of the world.

Although industry groups and vendors use many ways to measure and rank NOSs, one must be objective in viewing the results. Having the largest installed base and being third in sales may be more of an indicator of past activity than future business. But, because NetWare's installed base is large, you will likely have to support it in the field.

Too many companies, vendors, and customers delude themselves with installed base rankings to reassure themselves that the world of technology isn't passing them by. Lotus 1-2-3, WordPerfect, dBase, and Paradox are famous giants of the past. NetWare is probably joining that group. Of course, each of these "old" technologies was great in its time; each was on magazine covers, each made millionaires of many people, but each lost track of the business they were in and ignored changes in technology that moved too fast for a second chance. It can be argued that one of Novell's biggest mistakes was ignoring TCP/IP for way too long.

Until NetWare 5.0 was released in late 1998, all NetWare networks used one or more versions of IPX. Until 1995, with the release of Windows NT 4.0, the Microsoft used IPX as well. Each company's product, along with Apple's AppleTalk, eventually migrated to IP.

 NOTE: For ten years I was a commercial photographer. One day I was talking to one of the leaders in the field, and I commented that I was lusting after a particular model of camera that had been a traditional favorite in the industry. He told me to get over thinking of your tools as if they were kittens. You don't want to fall in love with them. They are tools, nothing more. Eventually something better will come along, and if you remain objective you will recognize it and move on. Otherwise, you become one of the old guys hanging around the fringes talking about how great things used to be. The computer industry is full of people of all ages who have fallen in love with their tools.

Novell IPX/SPX Protocol Suite

In the early 1980s, Novell, Inc. introduced the first version of NetWare, a derivative of Xerox's XNS. NetWare was an immediate market success. As it did with other early network vendors—for example, Apple and Dec—Cisco worked with Novell to support and extend their technologies. A look at the Help feature of a Cisco router using a feature set supporting IPX/SPX reveals extensive support for NetWare features. Figure 14-1 shows the IPX/SPX protocol suite, the MAC protocols that both Cisco and NetWare support, and the relationship among IPX, TCP/IP, and the OSI reference model.

Novell Netware, IPX/SPX, is a proprietary suite that includes the following protocols:

- **Internetwork Packet Exchange (IPX)**   A connectionless Layer 3 protocol that does not use acknowledgments and that defines the network and node address scheme; Novell's equivalent to IP

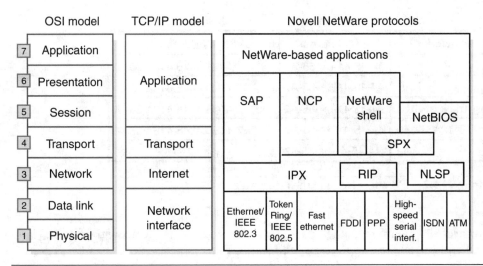

Figure 14-1 IPX/SPX, TCP/IP, and the OSI reference model

- **Sequenced Packet Exchange (SPX)** Layer 4 connection-oriented services conceptually comparable to TCP

- **Novell Routing Information Protocol (IPX RIP)** A distance vector protocol conceptually comparable to but noncompatible with IP RIP

- **NetWare Link Services Protocol (NLSP)** Link-state routing protocol based on DEC's IS-IS

- **NetWare Core Protocol (NCP)** Protocol that provides client-to-server connections and applications

- **Service Advertising Protocol (SAP)** A broadcast method of advertising network services

In addition, Cisco supports a Netware version of their proprietary EIGRP, a hybrid routing protocol.

IPX Addressing

IPX addresses are up to 80 bits long, and the last 48 bits always constitute the MAC address of the device. If you have the network address, you should be able to parse the network identifier and the MAC address or host identifier. Configuring a device, whether it is a router or a computer, amounts to assigning the network identifier; the

Up to 32 bits	48 bits	Up to 80 bits
Network ID	**MAC Address**	**IPX Address**
1	44-45-41-6A-55-A7	1.4445.416A.55A7
DAD	44-45-41-6A-55-A7	DAD.4445.416A.55A7
47AB	44-45-41-6A-55-A7	47AB.4445.416A.55A7
12A7.44E5	44-45-41-6A-55-A7	12A7.44E5.4445.416A.55A7
aa	44-45-41-6a-55-a7	aa.4445.416a.55a7

Figure 14-2 IPX addresses and their derivations

protocol will combine that with the MAC address to create the network address. Figure 14-2 shows some IPX addresses and how they were derived.

This simple addressing scheme requires little effort on the part of network administrators and eliminates IP features like DHCP and ARP.

Since IPX addressing is organization-specific, the network administrator must ensure that the network IDs are unique. Because of the uniqueness of MAC addresses, two networks using the same network ID would not create duplicate node addresses, but this arrangement can cause problems with any routers that see the situation as two alternative paths to the same network.

In a multi-protocol environment, it would seem logical for router interfaces to have both IP and IPX configurations. Even in an all-IPX environment, IP configurations are common on router interfaces to enable routers to use features like telnetting, a TCP/IP application. Workstations may also have both configurations to access the various servers and services on the network. Figure 14-3 shows our two-router lab network from the last chapter with IPX network IDs.

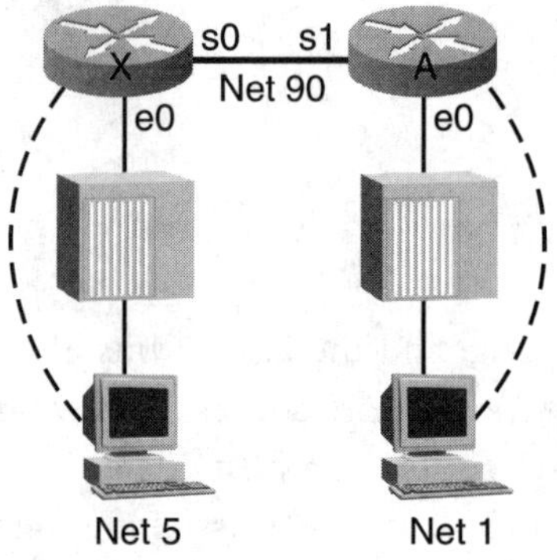

Figure 14-3
Two-router IPX lab

Net 5   Net 1

Figure 14-4
Three-router
IPX lab

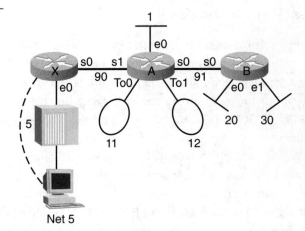

Figure 14-4 shows our three-router lab network from the last chapter with IPX network IDs.

Both address schemes are simple and probably wouldn't be suitable for a larger network. I used the unique octet from the IP network address as the IPX network address, which helps to relate the segments. Since the network portion can be up to 32 bits long using the Hex values 0 to F, it would be possible to develop much more elaborate naming schemes. Figure 14-5 gives another example that keys off of the router, possibly a building, and creates a map that ties networks to routers. Even the networks between routers describe their connections.

Figure 14-5
Another three-
router naming
scenario

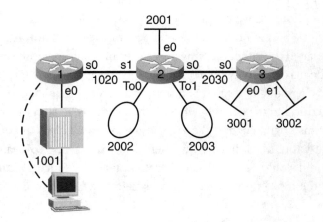

Encapsulation Methods

Chapter 1 covered encapsulation, the process of adding header information at each layer of the OSI model to communicate with the corresponding layers on the destination host. *Frame encapsulation* refers to the data-link layer header created by the routing process. As the frame moves through a router, the data-link header is stripped away after being checked at the inbound interface, and a new one appropriate to the outbound interface is added.

So far we haven't had to think much about encapsulation, although it has been occurring all along, because we have been using the default encapsulation for our interface/protocol combination. The only time we had a frame change was when we passed to a different type of interface, such as Ethernet to Token Ring or serial. Ethernet to Ethernet or Token Ring to Token Ring would not normally involve a different frame type in the IP world.

However, life just got a little more complicated. NetWare supports four different frame types for Ethernet and five for FDDI or Token Ring. If all NetWare workstations and servers are using the same version of NetWare, there will likely be just a single encapsulation, and configuring will be comparable to that for IP. But if any workstations and servers are using different versions of NetWare, then the connectivity between those devices will probably have to be maintained with another frame type.

How does this happen? Version incompatibility. NetWare versions up to and including 3.11 used Ethernet_802.3 frame encapsulation. Versions 3.12 to 5.0 used Ethernet_802.2. The solution seems simple enough: Make the entire network upgrade at one time. The problem is that early versions of NetWare allowed programmers to put "hooks" into the NOS source code, "tweaking" NOS features. The upgraded versions of NetWare did not support those "hooks," so applications written for the older NOS could not be moved onto the newer versions without reprogramming. Some of the original applications were very expensive, as were the upgrades. In some cases, the original developers were no longer in business or they were not interested in performing the necessary fixes. It then became an issue of maintaining both versions of NetWare, as well as the necessary network configurations to support multiple frame types.

I had a client that had spent $85,000 for a warehouse management program that was mission critical to the small business. When the new version of NetWare came out, the network was upgraded, and the warehouse software failed. In going back to the company that wrote the software, the client learned that the software upgrade would be $50,000 and would be months away from availability. Since the current version worked fine and the new improved version was neither available nor offering any significant benefits, the company opted to configure a single server and a few workstations that ran only the old NOS and the warehouse software. It was a textbook case on how not to upgrade a network, and it came almost at the cost of a small business and the families dependent on it. A few years later, when the system was upgraded again, no NOS, vendor, consultant, or software involved in the earlier upgrade was even considered in the choice.

Encapsulation Choices

To further complicate the issue of encapsulation, the Cisco name for each encapsulation is different from the names used by Novell. Figure 14-6 shows the encapsulations for each of the common LAN access protocols and the corresponding Cisco name.

Fortunately the Cisco Help feature shows the options and both the Cisco and Novell names. The following lines show the Help information.

```
Lab-X(config-if)#ipx network 5 encapsulation ?
  arpa          IPX Ethernet_II
  hdlc          HDLC on serial links
  novell-ether  IPX Ethernet_802.3
  novell-fddi   IPX FDDI RAW
  sap           IEEE 802.2 on Ethernet, FDDI, Token Ring
  snap          IEEE 802.2 SNAP on Ethernet, Token Ring, and FDDI
```

It is important to understand that each header does not just represent a bit-setting difference on a single field but that each one is a different header with varying numbers of fields. Figure 14-7 shows a simplification of the headers and data.

Encapsulaton Type	Novell IPX Name	Cisco IOS Name
Ethernet	Ethernet_II Ethernet_802.3 [Def thru v3.11] Ethernet_802.2 [Def v3.12+] Ethernet_SNAP	arpa novell-ether sap snap
Token Ring	Token-Ring Token-Ring_SNAP	sap snap
FDDI	FDDI_SNAP FDDI_802.2 FDDI_RAW	snap sap novell-fddi

Figure 14-6   Encapsulation choices: Novell and Cisco

Novell name	Cisco name	Data frame				

Ethernet_II	ARPA	Ethernet	IPX	DATA		
Ethernet_802.3	Novell-ether	802.3	IPX	DATA		
Ethernet_802.2	SAP	802.3	802.2	IPX	DATA	
Ethernet_SNAP	SNAP	802.3	802.2	SNAP	IPX	DATA

Figure 14-7 Encapsulation types with header

Configuring a Workstation

The following setup description assumes you are using Windows Me on the workstation. Other versions of Windows, including NT or 2000, should be close enough to allow you to figure out the setup from these steps. If the Windows CAB files have not been installed on the workstation, you will probably need the installation CD.

At the Windows Desktop, right-click on Network Neighborhood and choose Properties. Figure 14-8 shows the Network Properties screen that should appear.

On the configuration tab, if Client For NetWare Networks is not present, click on the Add . . . button. If Client For NetWare Networks is present, the service is installed but it will not hurt to complete the rest of these steps. Figure 14-9 shows the Select Network Component Type screen that appears. Choose Client and click on the Add . . . button.

Figure 14-10 shows the Select Network Client screen. Choose Client For NetWare Networks, and then click on the Add . . . button.

You should have returned to the original Network screen. Some older versions may take you to the Select Network Component Type screen—just click on the Cancel button to return to the Network screen.

If you scroll through the listings in the window, you see that IPX/SPX has been added for each of the connection types. We need to configure the NIC, so scroll through the options until you are sure that you can see the appropriate one. Figure 14-11 shows the choice for my 3Com PCMCIA NIC.

Either double-click on the entry or select it and then click on the Properties button, which will bring up a window with several tabs at the top. Figure 14-12 shows the Advanced tab selected and the Frame Type option highlighted. I also opened the drop-down list of choices for the frame type. If you leave the default as Auto, the system chooses a frame type based on the first IPX packet it receives. If you must configure for a specific server OS and multiple frame types, choose the frame type from this list.

Figure 14-8
Network Properties
screen

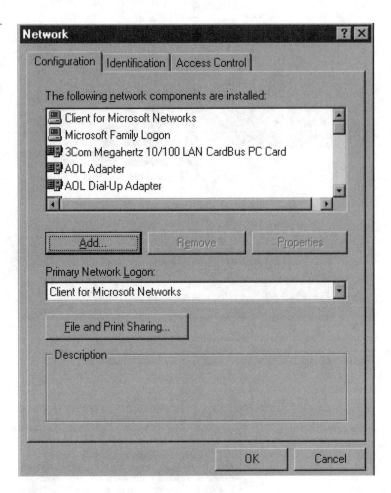

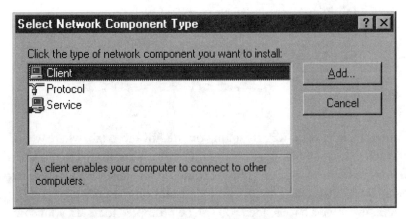

Figure 14-9   Select Network Component Type screen

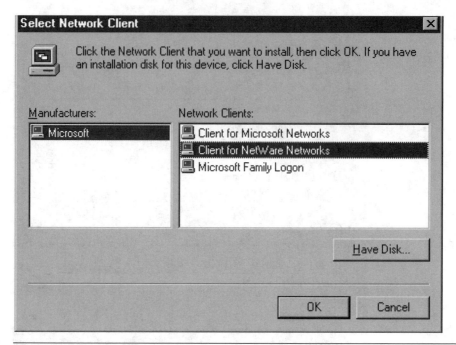

Figure 14-10 Client For NetWare Networks screen

Figure 14-11
Selecting IPX for
the NIC

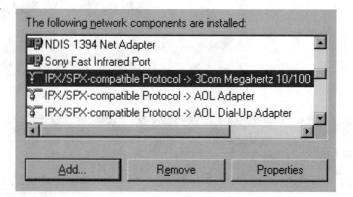

Figure 14-13 shows the Network Address setting on the Advanced tab, where we tell the workstation which network it belongs in. Since my laptop is connected to the number 1 network, I've typed that in, but the address could be any legal IPX network ID. After making the address entry, click on OK and then again on the OK button on the Network screen. After the drivers have loaded you will be prompted to restart your computer so the features can take effect.

Figure 14-12
Advanced tab
with Frame Type
selections

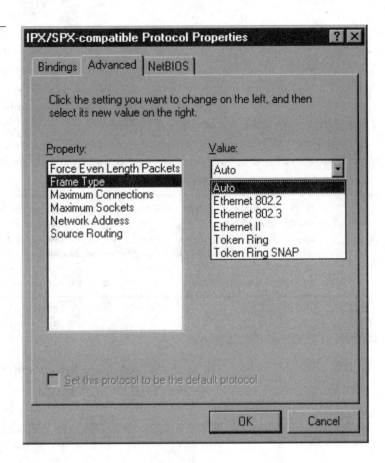

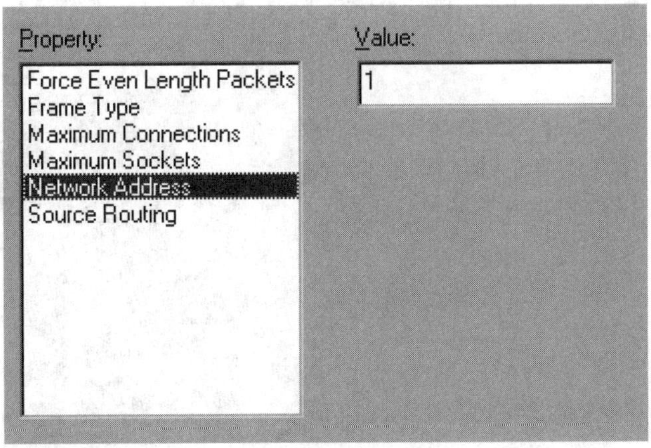

Figure 14-13
Setting the Network
Address

Unfortunately, no simple command like winipcfg (or ipconfig) allows us to see the new network address, but we can figure it out. If the workstation is running Windows 95/98/Me, use Start | Run, type *winipcfg* in the Open box, and press the enter key. Windows NT and 2000 users will need to open a Command window and type *ipconfig/all*. Figure 14-14 shows what I get on my laptop connected to the number 1 network.

The Adapter Address (MAC address) is the host portion of the IPX address. Generally the IPX address will be stated as three groups of four HEX numbers separated by decimals. Since I identified this network as 1, my IPX address would be 1.0000.8654.9BA6.

 NOTE: If this were a true NetWare network with one or more servers, it wouldn't be necessary to manually configure the network ID on the host. Manually configuring the network address is much the same as Static configuration of hosts in IP in that it is labor intensive and creates potential configuration problems when hosts are moved to other networks. The configuration process is included here so that you can see it and configure a host or two on the sample network.

Configuring a Router

Multiple network protocols can be configured on the same router and the same interface if the IOS feature set supports them. The last chapter covered IP; this chapter looks at IPX. AppleTalk is no longer an exam objective and will not be addressed. If you understand configuring IP and IPX, you will be able to deal with other protocols.

Figure 14-14
Winipcfg shows the adapter (MAC) address

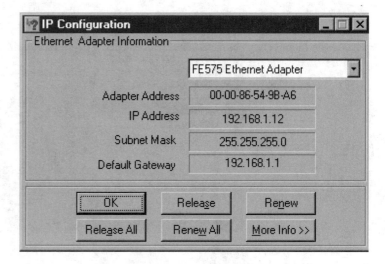

Configuring a router for IPX is a fairly simple two-part process. First, the IPX routing is enabled at global configuration mode and then the interfaces are configured for network address(es) and, optionally, an encapsulation method.

Global Configuration

Two global configuration commands should be considered. First, the *ipx routing* command enables IPX RIP routing, SAP broadcasts (covered at the end of this chapter), and the interfaces to accept IPX configuration commands. Unlike the *router rip* command in the IP world, in this situation there are no network commands required to include networks and specify interfaces that will share routing information. IPX RIP, once enabled, automatically includes any attached networks and uses all interfaces configured for IPX.

The second global configuration command is *ipx routing [node]* examples *ipx routing* or *ipx routing 1234.1234.123,4* where the node is a unique MAC identifier for the device. This node identifier, if supplied, is used on serial interfaces, which do not have MAC addresses on their own. Without the node identifier, the serial interface will use the MAC address of the first LAN interface. Since the node address is HEX, it can be made up of the digits 0-9and the characters A-F. If IPX was enabled on the A router with the command *ipx routing AAAA.AAAA.AAAA*, the 55 network attached to serial 0 interface would have a network address of 55.AAAA.AAAA.AAAA. We will look at this in more detail in the interface section.

To create a node address, the device uses the LAN interfaces, looking first to the Ethernet, then Token Ring, and finally the FDDI interfaces. If there are no LAN interfaces, the node portion of the command is no longer optional but must be supplied.

IPX does not support load balancing by default but can be told to do so using the *ipx maximum-paths 2* command. If you do not use this command, the default is 1. The acceptable entries are 1 to 64.

The following lines show the commands entered in global configuration mode and the resulting show run lines. Note that, since no node entry was made, the show run command reveals that IPX pulled the MAC address from Ethernet 0—the first LAN interface.

```
Lab-X#conf t
Lab-X(config)#ipx routing
Lab-X(config)#ipx maximum-paths 2
Lab-X(config)#^Z
Lab-X#
Lab-X#show run
!                                   (lines omitted)
ipx routing 0010.7b3a.3dd5 (0010.7b3a.3dd5 MAC of the 1st LAN int)
ipx maximum-paths 2
!                                   (lines omitted)
```

The following lines show the same configuration for router A where the node was defined using the HEX digits AAAA.AAAA.AAAA.

```
Lab-A#conf t
Lab-A(config)#ipx routing aaaa.aaaa.aaaa
Lab-A(config)#ipx maximum-paths 2
Lab-A(config)#^Z
Lab-A#
Lab-A#show run
!                                        (lines omitted)
ipx routing aaaa.aaaa.aaaa
ipx maximum-paths 2
!                                        (lines omitted)
```

Configuring the Interfaces

Interface configuration is accomplished with a single command that can be entered two ways. Getting into interface configuration mode is exactly the same as in IP. The syntax is *ipx network* network-address [*encapsulation* type] [*secondary*]. The simplest example would be *ipx network a*, in which case the default encapsulation for the interface type is used.

If two or more encapsulation types are used on the same link, there are two ways that they can be applied to the interface. They can be added using the secondary option on the *ipx network* command for any networks after the first one, or subinterfaces can be created, each assigned its own address and encapsulation type. We will look at both techniques in the next sections.

If the interface has not been previously fully configured for IP, it will be necessary to add the clock rate to DCE connections and the ring speed to Token Ring interfaces.

The following lines show first the encapsulation options via the Help feature and then the error message that occurs if you attempt to assign an IPX address to an interface without first using the *ipx routing* command.

```
Lab-X#conf t
Lab-X(config)#int e0
Lab-X(config-if)#ipx network 5 encapsulation ?
  arpa          IPX Ethernet_II
  hdlc          HDLC on serial links
  novell-ether  IPX Ethernet_802.3
  novell-fddi   IPX FDDI RAW
  sap           IEEE 802.2 on Ethernet, FDDI, Token Ring
  snap          IEEE 802.2 SNAP on Ethernet, Token Ring, and FDDI
Lab-X(config-if)#ipx network 5
%Must give "ipx routing" command first          (error message)
Lab-X(config-if)#
```

The next lines show configuring the IPX interface with the encapsulation command as a second line. It also shows the encapsulation options for serial interfaces.

```
Lab-X#conf t
Lab-X(config)#int s0
Lab-X(config-if)#ipx network 90
Lab-X(config-if)#encapsulation ?
  atm-dxi       ATM-DXI encapsulation
  frame-relay   Frame Relay networks
  hdlc          Serial HDLC synchronous
  lapb          LAPB (X.25 Level 2)
  ppp           Point-to-Point protocol
  smds          Switched Megabit Data Service (SMDS)
  x25           X.25
Lab-X(config-if)#encapsulation hdlc
Lab-X(config-if)#^Z
Lab-X#show run
!
interface Serial0
 ip address 192.168.90.2 255.255.255.0
 ipx network 90
 clockrate 56000
!
```

Assigning a Second IPX Address to an Ethernet Interface

The following lines show enabling the IPX routing and assigning two IPX addresses to the Ethernet interface using the *secondary* option. The *secondary* option can be used only if a different encapsulation type is chosen. There cannot be two IPX networks with the same encapsulation assigned to an interface. While the example shown is not the best method to use in most situations, it does demonstrate the capability.

```
Lab-X#conf t
Lab-X(config)#ipx routing
Lab-X(config)#ipx maximum-paths 2
Lab-X(config)#int e0
Lab-X(config-if)#ipx network 5
Lab-X(config-if)#ipx network 6 encapsulation sap secondary
Lab-X(config-if)#^Z
Lab-X#show run
!
ipx routing 0010.7b3a.3dd5
ipx maximum-paths 2
!
interface Ethernet0
 ip address 192.168.5.1 255.255.255.0
 ipx network 5
 ipx network 6 encapsulation SAP secondary
!
```

Figure 14-15
Two versions of
NetWare servers

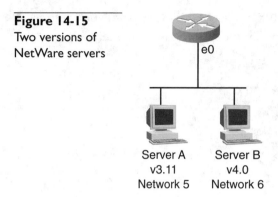

Server A   Server B
v3.11   v4.0
Network 5   Network 6

Figure 14-15 shows an Ethernet network segment with two servers running two versions of NetWare requiring different encapsulation types. The configuration lines and *show run* output in the previous section could be the configuration for this Ethernet interface.

The process of choosing the correct encapsulation is simple: If the destination address is Server A, then it is on Network 5 and the default Novell-ether encapsulation will be used; if the destination is Server B, then it is on Network 6, and the newer SAP encapsulation will automatically be used.

Split Horizon and the Secondary Option

The problem with applying additional addresses to a single interface is its effect on routing updates for any networks on that interface. Figure 14-16 shows two networks configured on one interface of router X. If the status of network A1 were to change, router A would notify router X. The split-horizon protocol that prevents routing loops does so by not allowing routing updates of information learned from one interface from being sent back out that same interface. This means that router B has no way of learning about the A1 network, or even that router A exists. Likewise, router A would have no way of knowing about network B1 or router B.

Figure 14-16
Split-horizon
implications

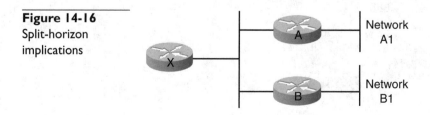

Network
A1

Network
B1

If the interfaces use different encapsulations, the A and B routers would not "hear" each other's updates even though they might share a common interface on router X.

> NOTE: Not hearing each other's updates is not unique to IPX. IP supports the secondary option for LAN interfaces; the same result could occur.

Subinterfaces

One way to solve the split-horizon dilemma is to use subinterfaces. IPX supports subinterfaces, which are logical interfaces associated with a physical interface. Subinterfaces are also used extensively in Frame Relay connections. The router treats each subinterface as if it were a separate physical interface. While each subinterface can have its own network address and must have a unique encapsulation, it still shares the bandwidth capacity of the physical interface. This means that a Fast Ethernet interface with four subinterfaces does not produce 400 Mb of capacity but shares the 100 Mb of the original interface.

The subinterface can be created in global configuration mode using the *interface type-ID* command and adding a decimal to the type-ID designation. Instead of *interface fastethernet0/0* it could be *interface fastethernet0/0.1*. Since the decimal value can be up to 10-digits long and the digits need not be sequential, it is possible to use the network number or DLCI number in Frame Relay, such as *interface fastethernet0/0.71126*.

The following lines show the configuration steps and *show run* output of creating two Ethernet subinterfaces on router X for networks 5 and 6. The running configuration output clearly indicates that the router sees the two subinterfaces as real and separate interfaces. Note that even though the encapsulation type was specified for network 5, it is excluded in the *show run* output because it was the default option. The aborted attempt to create 0.7 interface was done just to show that you cannot have two subinterfaces with the same encapsulation.

```
Lab-X#conf t
Lab-X(config-if)#int e0.5
Lab-X(config-subif)#ipx network 5 encapsulation novell-ether
Lab-X(config-subif)#int e0.6
Lab-X(config-subif)#ipx network 6 encapsulation sap
Lab-X(config)#int e0.7
Lab-X(config-subif)#ipx network 7 (attempt to use same
encapsulation)
%Encapsulation already in use by IPX network 5, on interface
Ethernet0.5
```

```
Lab-X(config-subif)#^Z
Lab-X#show run
!
ipx routing 0010.7b3a.3dd5
ipx maximum-paths 2
!
interface Ethernet0
 ip address 192.168.5.1 255.255.255.0
!
interface Ethernet0.5
 ipx network 5
!
interface Ethernet0.6
 ipx network 6 encapsulation SAP
!
```

The next lines indicate that the route table also sees the interfaces as two separate entities, each with a directly connected primary network. We will look at the *show ipx route* command in greater detail in the next section.

```
Lab-X#show ipx route
Codes: C - Connected primary network,    c - Connected secondary
network
       S - Static, F - Floating static, L - Local (internal),
W - IPXWAN
       R - RIP, E - EIGRP, N - NLSP, X - External, A - Aggregate
       s - seconds, u - uses, U - Per-user static
9 Total IPX routes. Up to 2 parallel paths and 16 hops allowed.
No default route known.
C          5 (NOVELL-ETHER),  Et0.5
C          6 (SAP),           Et0.6
C         90 (HDLC),          Se0
R          1 [07/01] via      90.aaaa.aaaa.aaaa,   13s, Se0
R         11 [07/01] via      90.aaaa.aaaa.aaaa,   13s, Se0
R         12 [07/01] via      90.aaaa.aaaa.aaaa,   13s, Se0
R         20 [13/02] via      90.aaaa.aaaa.aaaa,   13s, Se0
R         30 [13/02] via      90.aaaa.aaaa.aaaa,   13s, Se0
R         91 [07/01] via      90.aaaa.aaaa.aaaa,   13s, Se0
Lab-X#
```

The *show IPX interface* command, which we will look at in greater detail, indicates two separate interfaces. Note that the node portion of the network address for both interfaces is the same (0010.7b3a.3dd5) because they both are using the MAC address of the Ethernet 0 interface.

```
Lab-X#show ipx interface
Ethernet0.5 is up, line protocol is up
  IPX address is 5.0010.7b3a.3dd5, NOVELL-ETHER [up]
  Delay of this IPX network, in ticks is 1 throughput 0 link
delay 0
            (output omitted)
```

```
Ethernet0.6 is up, line protocol is up
  IPX address is 6.0010.7b3a.3dd5, SAP [up]
  Delay of this IPX network, in ticks is 1 throughput 0 link
delay 0
          (output omitted)
```

While the Secondary feature is supported on IP interfaces, the Subinterface option for IP is allowed only in specific implementations like VLANs. An interface can be configured once for each protocol enabled on the router, so using IP addressing does not interfere with the ability to use IPX subinterfaces or AppleTalk configuration.

Token Ring

Configuring a Token Ring interface is similar to configuring an Ethernet interface except that you must also set the ring speed, which amounts to choosing between 4 and 16 Mbps. Ring speed needs to be set only once. If it was configured for IP, it doesn't need to be done again. For the interface to "come up" and be functional or tested, it will need to be connected to a Token Ring MAU.

Show Commands

Several commands are useful in troubleshooting interface connections and seeing traffic statistics that are collected by the routers. The two basic commands are *show ipx interfaces* and *show ipx interfaces brief*. These commands show all interfaces in a long scrolling output. However, the *show interfaces* commands, while useful, do not show ipx protocol information.

Show IPX Interfaces

Unmodified, this command shows all interfaces; you can also add an interface identifier and see just that one interface. The following display is for the Ethernet 0 interface. It shares much information with the serial and token ring interfaces; we will look at the differences shortly. Key things to look at:

1. Line one shows that the physical connection is up and that the protocol (configuration) is adequate to allow the connection to come up. It is possible that the first value would be up but the second down, indicating a possible configuration problem.

2. Line two indicates the IPX address and the encapsulation type.

3. Line three shows the metric for IPX delay and the delay for this interface.

4. Line five shows the secondary IPX address and the encapsulation.

5. The rest of the lines report various statistics.

```
Lab-X#show ipx int e0
Ethernet0 is up, line protocol is up
  IPX address is 5.0010.7b3a.3dd5, NOVELL-ETHER [up]
  Delay of this IPX network, in ticks is 1 throughput 0 link
delay 0
  IPXWAN processing not enabled on this interface.
  Secondary address is 6.0010.7b3a.3dd5, ARPA [up]
  Delay of this IPX network, in ticks is 1
  IPX SAP update interval is 60 seconds
  IPX type 20 propagation packet forwarding is disabled
  Incoming access list is not set
  Outgoing access list is not set
  IPX helper access list is not set
  IPX helper access list is not set
  SAP GNS processing enabled, delay 0 ms, output filter list is
not set
  SAP Input filter list is not set
  SAP Output filter list is not set
  SAP Router filter list is not set
  Input filter list is not set
  Output filter list is not set
  Router filter list is not set
  Netbios Input host access list is not set
  Netbios Input bytes access list is not set
  Netbios Output host access list is not set
  Netbios Output bytes access list is not set
  Updates each 60 seconds aging multiples RIP: 3 SAP: 3
  SAP interpacket delay is 55 ms, maximum size is 480 bytes
  RIP interpacket delay is 55 ms, maximum size is 432 bytes
  RIP response delay is not set
  IPX accounting is disabled
  IPX fast switching is configured (enabled)
  RIP packets received 0, RIP packets sent 42, 0 Throttled
  RIP specific requests received 0, RIP specific replies sent 0
  RIP general requests received 0, 0 ignored, RIP general replies
sent 0
  SAP packets received 0, SAP packets sent 2, 0 Throttled
  SAP GNS packets received 0, SAP GNS replies sent 0
  SAP GGS packets received 0, 0 ignored, SAP GGS replies sent 0
Lab-X#
```

Because the statistics portions of the output are not that different, I'm including only
the first few lines for a Token Ring and serial interface.

```
Lab-A#show ipx int t0
TokenRing0 is up, line protocol is up
  IPX address is 11.0000.30d8.7080, SAP [up]
  Delay of this IPX network, in ticks is 1 throughput 0 link delay
0
  IPXWAN processing not enabled on this interface.
  IPX SAP update interval is 60 seconds
  IPX type 20 propagation packet forwarding is disabled
```

```
Lab-X#show ipx int s0
Serial0 is up, line protocol is up
  IPX address is 90.0010.7b3a.3dd5 [up]
  Delay of this IPX network, in ticks is 6 throughput 0 link
delay 0
  IPXWAN processing not enabled on this interface.
  IPX SAP update interval is 60 seconds
```

Show IPX Interfaces Brief

Like its IP counterpart, this is probably one of the handiest commands because it gives you a quick summary of the status of all interfaces, the encapsulation type used, plus the IPX network IDs. The result looks like this:

```
Lab-A#show ipx int brief
Interface       IPX Network Encapsulation Status     IPX
State
Ethernet0       1           NOVELL-ETHER  up         [up]
Serial0         91          HDLC          up         [up]
Serial1         90          HDLC          up         [up]
TokenRing0      11          SAP           up         [up]
TokenRing1      12          SAP           up         [up]
Lab-A#
```

Show Protocols

The *show protocols* command simply displays the protocols running on the device, the status of each interface, and the network addresses associated with each interface.

```
Lab-A#show protocols
Global values:
  Internet Protocol routing is enabled
  IPX routing is enabled
Ethernet0 is up, line protocol is up
  Internet address is 192.168.1.100/24
  IPX address is 1.0000.0c1b.0e02
Serial0 is up, line protocol is up
  Internet address is 192.168.91.2/24
  IPX address is 91.aaaa.aaaa.aaaa
Serial1 is up, line protocol is up
  Internet address is 192.168.90.1/24
  IPX address is 90.aaaa.aaaa.aaaa
TokenRing0 is up, line protocol is up
  Internet address is 192.168.11.1/24
  IPX address is 11.0000.30d8.7080
TokenRing1 is up, line protocol is up
  Internet address is 192.168.12.1/24
  IPX address is 12.0000.30d8.7020
Lab-A#
```

Interface Configuration Exercise

Use the network lab figure 3 or 4, and add the IPX network addresses to the interfaces. In each case, use the default encapsulation, but use ? to see the options for each type of interface.

Commands Introduced in this Section

This section covered the following commands:

- **ipx routing [node]**   Enables IPX RIP and allows IPX networks to be assigned to the interfaces. (example: *ipx routing A100.AAAA.AAAA*). The optional node assigns an ID to the device; if one was not supplied, the MAC address of the first LAN interface will be used.

- **ipx maximum-paths paths**   Enables IPX load balancing, which is off by default. The paths value can be set to any number between 1 and 64 (example: *ipx maximum-paths 2*).

- **ipx network network [Encapsulation type] [secondary]**   Assigns a network address to the interface. The network address is combined with the MAC address to create a network address (example: *ipx network 12* or *ipx network 12 encapsulation arpa*).

- **Secondary**   Optional parameter that allows additional IPX addresses and encapsulations to be assigned to an interface (example: *ip address 210.1.2.18 255.255.255.0 secondary*).

- **show ipx interfaces id**   Shows interface IPX status and interface feature status. (example: *show ipx interfaces Serial 0/0 or sho ip int s0/1*).

- **show ipx interfaces brief**   Summarizes interface status and shows IPX network addresses (example: *show ipx interface brief or sho ipx int brie*).

- **show protocols**   Displays the protocols running on the device, the status of each interface, and the network addresses associated with each interface.

IPX Routing

The *IPX routing* command automatically enables IPX RIP without further configuration. It is important to understand that IPX RIP is not compatible with its IP cousin. Both are distance vectors, but the IPX version uses a 60-second update schedule, compared to 30 seconds for IP RIP. IPX RIP uses ticks and hop count as the routing metric. A [6/1] metric indicates 6 ticks and 1 hop. Route choices are based on ticks, and, when a tie occurs, the hop count is used. A tick is a measure of delay, with each tick equal to 1/18 of 1 second. The Cisco default tick values links are 6 for WAN interfaces and 1 for LAN interfaces. A [6/1] metric indicates that the network is 1 hop away over a WAN interface. IPX RIP, like its IP counterpart and the RIP standard, has a maximum hop count of 15.

Each routing packet can contain up to 50 routes; if there are more than 50 routes then additional packets, each with 50 routes, will be added.

Novell's NLSP is a link-state protocol that can be used in place of RIP to reduce routing overhead. Configuring NLSP is not a requirement of the CCNA exam, but recognizing it as an alternative—like OSPF or IS-IS in the IP world—is useful.

The Routing Table

The routing table shows the "best" route possible to any known networks. The routing table is used by the router's "switching" function to determine which interface and the next hop destination to use for forwarding packets. There will be a separate route table for upper-level network protocol enabled on the router. As mentioned in the last chapter, IP routing is on by default, but any other protocols, such as IPX or AppleTalk, need to be explicitly enabled.

Show IPX Route

To see the IPX route table, use the *show ipx route* command. The result on our X router would look like the following lines.

```
Lab-X#show ipx route
Codes: C - Connected primary network,    c - Connected secondary
network
       S - Static, F - Floating static, L - Local (internal),
W - IPXWAN
       R - RIP, E - EIGRP, N - NLSP, X - External, A - Aggregate
       s - seconds, u - uses, U - Per-user static
9 Total IPX routes. Up to 2 parallel paths and 16 hops allowed.
No default route known.
C         5 (NOVELL-ETHER),   Et0
c         6 (ARPA),           Et0
C        90 (HDLC),           Se0
R         1 [07/01] via       90.aaaa.aaaa.aaaa,    20s, Se0
R        11 [07/01] via       90.aaaa.aaaa.aaaa,    20s, Se0
R        12 [07/01] via       90.aaaa.aaaa.aaaa,    20s, Se0
R        20 [13/02] via       90.aaaa.aaaa.aaaa,    20s, Se0
R        30 [13/02] via       90.aaaa.aaaa.aaaa,    20s, Se0
R        91 [07/01] via       90.aaaa.aaaa.aaaa,    20s, Se0
Lab-X#
```

The first four lines act as a legend to explain the codes in the first column of the routing table. The two networks with uppercase Cs are directly connected primary networks, while the one with the lowercase c is a secondary network.

The R in the first column of the routing table, as in IP routing tables, indicates RIP protocol. The second column shows the network number. The third indicates the ticks/hops metrics used for route selection or the encapsulation type for connected networks. In the last six entries, we see that the information came from the serial interface connected to router A and network 90. The 20s mean that the data was updated 20 seconds ago.

The following lines show the routing table for the A router. We see that RIP learned about two routes from router B (91.bbbb.bbbb.bbbb) and two routes from router X. Because no node option was added to router X's ipx routing command, the next hop address (90.0010.7b3a.3dd5) includes a MAC address taken from one of the LAN interfaces.

```
Lab-A#show ipx route
Codes: C - Connected primary network,    c - Connected secondary
network
       S - Static, F - Floating static, L - Local (internal),
W - IPXWAN
       R - RIP, E - EIGRP, N - NLSP, X - External, A - Aggregate
       s - seconds, u - uses, U - Per-user static
9 Total IPX routes. Up to 2 parallel paths and 16 hops allowed.
No default route known.
C        1 (NOVELL-ETHER),   Et0
C        11 (SAP),           To0
C        12 (SAP),           To1
C        90 (HDLC),          Se1
C        91 (HDLC),          Se0
R        5 [07/01] via       90.0010.7b3a.3dd5,   47s, Se1
R        6 [07/01] via       90.0010.7b3a.3dd5,   47s, Se1
R        20 [07/01] via      91.bbbb.bbbb.bbbb,   27s, Se0
R        30 [07/01] via      91.bbbb.bbbb.bbbb,   27s, Se0
Lab-A#
```

Router B's routing table shows that all "learned" routes came from router A, which shouldn't be any surprise.

```
Lab-B#show ipx route
Codes: C - Connected primary network,    c - Connected secondary
network
       S - Static, F - Floating static, L - Local (internal),
W - IPXWAN
       R - RIP, E - EIGRP, N - NLSP, X - External, A - Aggregate
       s - seconds, u - uses, U - Per-user static
9 Total IPX routes. Up to 2 parallel paths and 16 hops allowed.
No default route known.
C        20 (NOVELL-ETHER),  Et0
C        30 (UNKNOWN),       Lo1
C        91 (HDLC),          Se0
R        1 [07/01] via       91.aaaa.aaaa.aaaa,   59s, Se0
R        5 [13/02] via       91.aaaa.aaaa.aaaa,   59s, Se0
```

```
R           6 [13/02] via      91.aaaa.aaaa.aaaa,    59s, Se0
R          11 [07/01] via      91.aaaa.aaaa.aaaa,    59s, Se0
R          12 [07/01] via      91.aaaa.aaaa.aaaa,    59s, Se0
R          90 [07/01] via      91.aaaa.aaaa.aaaa,    59s, Se0
Lab-B#
```

Show IPX Traffic

The *show ipx traffic* command displays statistics about the numbers and types of IPX packets being moved through the device. The sample display shows mainly RIP broadcast traffic, reflecting that this sampling was taken from a classroom lab rather than a production network.

```
Lab-A#show ipx traffic
System Traffic for 0.0000.0000.0001 System-Name: Lab-A
Time since last clear: never
Rcvd:    1051 total, 0 format errors, 0 checksum errors, 0 bad hop
count,
         546 packets pitched, 505 local destination, 0 multicast
Bcast:   502 received, 1385 sent
Sent:    1386 generated, 0 forwarded
         0 encapsulation failed, 0 no route
SAP:     1 Total SAP requests, 0 Total SAP replies, 0 servers
         1 SAP general requests, 0 ignored, 0 replies
         0 SAP Get Nearest Server requests, 0 replies
         0 SAP Nearest Name requests, 0 replies
         0 SAP General Name requests, 0 replies
         0 SAP advertisements received, 0 sent, 0 Throttled
         0 SAP flash updates sent, 0 SAP format errors
RIP:     1 RIP requests, 0 ignored, 1 RIP replies, 9 routes
         503 RIP advertisements received, 1330 sent 0 Throttled
         23 RIP flash updates sent, 0 atlr sent
         0 RIP format errors
Echo:    Rcvd 0 requests, 0 replies
         Sent 0 requests, 0 replies
         0 unknown: 0 no socket, 0 filtered, 0 no helper
         0 SAPs throttled, freed NDB len 0
Watchdog:
         0 packets received, 0 replies spoofed
Queue lengths:
         IPX input: 0, SAP 0, RIP 0, GNS 0
         SAP throttling length: 0/(no limit), 0 nets pending lost
route reply
         Delayed process creation: 0
EIGRP:   Total received 0, sent 0
         Updates received 0, sent 0
         Queries received 0, sent 0
         Replies received 0, sent 0
         SAPs received 0, sent 0
Trace:   Rcvd 0 requests, 0 replies
         Sent 0 requests, 0 replies
Lab-A#
```

Debug IPX Routing Events

The *debug ipx routing events* command reports when a routing has occurred. The first routing update at 03:57:16 tells us that the routing update was a broadcast to network #1. The ffff.ffff.ffff node address is the layer 2 broadcast. We also see that the broadcast to network #1 was done again 60 seconds later at 03:58:16. We can see that there was a routing broadcast made outbound on each interface, so in this case, if an adjacent router is not getting updates, it isn't because this router isn't sending them.

To turn the debugging off use the *undebug all* command, which can be shortened to *un all*. This command turns off all debugging, and it is easier to type than *no debug ipx routing events*, particularly with all the data scrolling by. The following lines represent the *debug ipx routing events* output for router A.

```
Lab-A#debug ipx routing events
IPX routing events debugging is on
Lab-A#
03:57:16: IPXRIP: positing full update to 1.ffff.ffff.ffff via
EthernetO (broadcast)
Lab-A#
03:57:18: IPXRIP: positing full update to 11.ffff.ffff.ffff via
TokenRing0 (broadcast)
Lab-A#
03:57:26: IPXRIP: positing full update to 12.ffff.ffff.ffff via
TokenRing1 (broadcast)
Lab-A#
03:58:10: IPXRIP: positing full update to 90.ffff.ffff.ffff via
Serial1 (broadcast)
03:58:11: IPXRIP: positing full update to 91.ffff.ffff.ffff via
Serial0 (broadcast)
Lab-A#
03:58:16: IPXRIP: positing full update to 1.ffff.ffff.ffff via
EthernetO (broadcast)
Lab-A#
03:58:18: IPXRIP: positing full update to 11.ffff.ffff.ffff via
TokenRing0 (broadcast)
Lab-A#
03:58:26: IPXRIP: positing full update to 12.ffff.ffff.ffff via
TokenRing1 (broadcast)
Lab-A#
```

Debug IPX Routing Activity

The *debug ipx routing activity* command displays details of the routing process. While the *events* option showed only the outgoing routing updates, this command shows the inbound updates as well. At 04:03:15, an update was sent out to the #1 network. The second line at that time shows the source and destination addresses, and the next lines show the shared route information.

At 04:03:22, a routing update was received from router X. It contained only two net-works—both of the IPX configurations that we applied to the Ethernet interface. The following lines represent the *debug ipx routing activity* output for router X.

```
Lab-A#debug ipx routing activity
IPX routing debugging is on
04:03:15: IPXRIP: positing full update to 1.ffff.ffff.ffff via
Ethernet0 (broadcast)
04:03:15: IPXRIP: Update len 96 src=1.0000.0c1b.0e02,
dst=1.ffff.ffff.ffff(453)
04:03:15:      network 5, hops 2,   delay 8
04:03:15:      network 6, hops 2,   delay 8
04:03:15:      network 30, hops 2,   delay 8
04:03:15:      network 20, hops 2,   delay 8
04:03:15:      network 12, hops 1,   delay 2
04:03:15:      network 11, hops 1,   delay 2
04:03:15:      network 90, hops 1,   delay 2
04:03:15:      network 91, hops 1,   delay 2
04:03:16: IPXRIP: positing full update to 11.ffff.ffff.ffff via
TokenRing0 (broadcast)
04:03:16: IPXRIP: Update len 96 src=11.0000.30d8.7080,
dst=11.ffff.ffff.ffff(453)
04:03:16:      network 5, hops 2,   delay 8
04:03:16:      network 6, hops 2,   delay 8
04:03:16:      network 30, hops 2,   delay 8
04:03:16:      network 20, hops 2,   delay 8
04:03:16:      network 12, hops 1,   delay 2
04:03:16:      network 90, hops 1,   delay 2
04:03:16:      network 91, hops 1,   delay 2
04:03:16:      network 1, hops 1,   delay 2
Lab-A#
04:03:22: IPXRIP: update from 90.0010.7b3a.3dd5
04:03:22:      6 in 1 hops, delay 7
04:03:22:      5 in 1 hops, delay 7
Lab-A#
04:03:24: IPXRIP: positing full update to 12.ffff.ffff.ffff via
TokenRing1 (broadcast)
04:03:24: IPXRIP: Update len 96 src=12.0000.30d8.7020,
dst=12.ffff.ffff.ffff(453)
04:03:24:      network 5, hops 2,   delay 8
04:03:24:      network 6, hops 2,   delay 8
04:03:24:      network 30, hops 2,   delay 8
04:03:24:      network 20, hops 2,   delay 8
04:03:24:      network 11, hops 1,   delay 2
04:03:24:      network 90, hops 1,   delay 2
04:03:24:      network 91, hops 1,   delay 2
04:03:24:      network 1, hops 1,   delay 2
Lab-A#
04:03:43: IPXRIP: update from 91.bbbb.bbbb.bbbb
04:03:43:      20 in 1 hops, delay 7
04:03:43:      30 in 1 hops, delay 7
Lab-A#
04:04:08: IPXRIP: positing full update to 90.ffff.ffff.ffff via
```

```
Serial1 (broadcast)
04:04:08: IPXRIP: Update len 80 src=90.aaaa.aaaa.aaaa,
dst=90.ffff.ffff.ffff(453)
04:04:08:      network 30, hops 2,  delay 13
04:04:08:      network 20, hops 2,  delay 13
04:04:08:      network 12, hops 1,  delay 7
04:04:08:      network 11, hops 1,  delay 7
04:04:08:      network 91, hops 1,  delay 7
04:04:08:      network 1, hops 1,  delay 7
04:04:09: IPXRIP: positing full update to 91.ffff.ffff.ffff via
Serial0 (broadcast)
04:04:09: IPXRIP: Update len 80 src=91.aaaa.aaaa.aaaa,
dst=91.ffff.ffff.ffff(453)
04:04:09:      network 5, hops 2,  delay 13
04:04:09:      network 6, hops 2,  delay 13
04:04:09:      network 12, hops 1,  delay 7
04:04:09:      network 11, hops 1,  delay 7
04:04:09:      network 90, hops 1,  delay 7
04:04:09:      network 1, hops 1,  delay 7
Lab-A#un all
All possible debugging has been turned off
Lab-A#
```

Connectivity

The IPX feature sets include a version of the ping command for verifying connectivity.
The Cisco Discovery Protocol (CDP) supports IPX to help identify and develop information about adjacent devices.

Ping for IPX

The ping command is a TCP/IP command; however, the Cisco IOS has an IPX version
that allows you to ping IPX addresses. Both the basic and extended versions of the
command work just like the IP counterpart. The following lines show the use of ping to
test connectivity to the serial interface on router B from router X. Remember: This will
not work from the workstation MS-DOS or Command window.

```
Lab-X#ping 91.bbbb.bbbb.bbbb
Translating "91.bbbb.bbbb.bbbb"
Type escape sequence to abort.
Sending 5, 100-byte IPX Novell Echoes to 91.bbbb.bbbb.bbbb,
timeout is 2 seconds:
!!!!!
Success rate is 100 percent (5/5), round-trip min/avg/max =
72/78/104 ms
Lab-X#
```

The ping command response symbols areas follows:

EXAMPLE	DEFINITION
!	Successful ping
.	Ping timed out waiting for reply
U	Destination unreachable
C	Congestion-experienced packet
I	Ping interrupted (CTRL-SHIFT-6)
?	Packet type unknown
&	Packet TTL expired

The Cisco extended ping command is available only in the privileged EXEC mode. The extended feature allows us to use the feature with other protocols or to customize request options. The feature is implemented by typing ping at the prompt without a destination address. You will then see a series of prompts offering choices. The following lines demonstrate the feature.

```
Lab-X#ping
Protocol [ip]: ipx
Target IPX address: 91.bbbb.bbbb.bbbb
Repeat count [5]: 7
Datagram size [100]:
Timeout in seconds [2]:
Verbose [n]:
Type escape sequence to abort.
Sending 7, 100-byte IPX Novell Echoes to 91.bbbb.bbbb.bbbb,
timeout is 2 seconds:
!!!!!!!            (7 because I changed the repeat count above)
Success rate is 100 percent (7/7 ), round-trip min/avg/max =
64/70/88 ms
Lab-X#
```

We just pressed ENTER for most commands, accepting the default options.

Commands Introduced in this Section

This section covered the following commands:

- **debug ipx routing events** Turns on the debug feature to report RIP update occurrences

- **debug ipx routing activity**   Turns on the debug feature to report contents of RIP updates

- **undebug all**   Turns off all debug features

- **show ipx route**   Displays IPX routing table

- **show ipx traffic**   Displays summary of all IPX packet traffic

Cisco Discovery Protocol (CDP)

The CDP commands we used earlier in IP also work in IPX. There are no special IPX options. The *show cdp neighbor* identifies the neighbor directly adjacent to the device. The *show cdp neighbor detail* command displays the IPX address and the IOS information. The following lines show both commands from router A in our lab network. We should see router X and B on either side.

```
Lab-A#show cdp neighbor
Capability Codes: R-Router, T-Trans Bridge, B-Source Route Bridge
                 S - Switch, H - Host, I - IGMP, r - Repeater
Device ID    Local Intrfce  Holdtme  Capability  Platform  Port ID
Lab-B        Ser 0          124         R         2500      Ser 0
Lab-X        Ser 1          162         R         2524      Ser 0
Lab-A#
Lab-A#show cdp neighbor detail
-------------------------
Device ID: Lab-B
Entry address(es):
  IP address: 192.168.91.1
  Novell address: 91.bbbb.bbbb.bbbb
Platform: cisco 2500,  Capabilities: Router
Interface: Serial0,  Port ID (outgoing port): Serial0
Holdtime : 143 sec
Version :
Cisco Internetwork Operating System Software
IOS (tm) 2500 Software (C2500-D-L), Version 12.0(5)T,  RELEASE
SOFTWARE (fc1)
Copyright (c) 1986-1999 by cisco Systems, Inc.
Compiled Fri 23-Jul-99 03:53 by kpma
advertisement version: 2
-------------------------
Device ID: Lab-X
Entry address(es):
  IP address: 192.168.90.2
  Novell address: 90.0010.7b3a.3dd5
Platform: cisco 2524,  Capabilities: Router
Interface: Serial1,  Port ID (outgoing port): Serial0
Holdtime : 177 sec
```

```
Version :
Cisco Internetwork Operating System Software
IOS (tm) 2500 Software (C2500-D-L), Version 12.1(5)T,  RELEASE
SOFTWARE (fc1)
Copyright (c) 1986-2000 by cisco Systems, Inc.
Compiled Sat 11-Nov-00 03:07 by ccai
advertisement version: 2
Lab-A#
```

Commands Introduced in this Section

This section introduced the following commands:

- **ping ipx-address**   IPX version of ping and extended ping feature to test connectivity

- **show cdp neighbors**   Summarize device information about neighbor devices

- **show cdp neighbors detail**   Display detailed device information about neighbor devices

IPX SAP and GNS

All versions of NetWare use Service Advertisement Protocol (SAP) broadcasts for servers to notify network hosts about services available. These SAP broadcasts occur every 60 seconds, in addition to any routing updates. Each server and any Cisco routers keep a complete database of services learned from SAP broadcasts so that they can respond to a host's request for information. Cisco routers forward their SAP table to other routers so that they can update their database of services. Using a router greatly decreases the amount of SAP traffic on a network because it "eats" the SAPs on the local interfaces and sends out only one summarized SAP to its neighbors. SAP services use a numbered code, such as 4 for file server or 7 for print server.

Host devices use a Get Nearest Server (GNS) request broadcast to find a server offering the service needed. A NetWare server on the network will respond with the information, and a client/server relationship will be established. If no NetWare server responds to the GNS request, a Cisco router can respond from its SAP table to direct the host to resource.

Because of the frequency of IPX routing updates and SAP broadcasts, Access Control Lists (ACLs) are commonly used to block IPX/SAP traffic into any network segments that do not need or use NetWare resources. These filters will be covered in the next chapter.

Show IPX Servers

For both the CCNA exam and in the field, you must be able to display a list of server resources available on a network. The command is *show ipx servers*. The following output approximates the result. Note that you will not get any results if there are no NetWare servers on your network.

```
Lab-X#show ipx servers
Codes: S - Static, P - Periodic, E - EIGRP, N - NLSP,
H - Holddown, + = detail
U - Per-user static
3 Total IPX Servers
Table ordering is based on routing and server info
     Type Name           Net     Address      Port   Route Hops Itf
P      4 ServerA          5.0000.0000.0001:0452    8/02    2  et0.5
P      7 ServerA          5.0000.0000.0001:0452    8/02    2  et0.5
P      7 ServerB          6.0000.0000.0001:0452    8/02    2  et0.6
```

Debug IPX SAP Activity

The *debug ipx sap activity* command shows the detailed results of the SAP broadcasts occurring every 60 seconds. The following lines show the output for one interface.

```
Lab-A#debug ipx sap activity
IPX service events debugging is on
Lab-A#
04:46:54: IPXSAP: Response (in) type 0x2 len 288 src:
91.aaaa.aaaa.aaaa
dest: 91.ffff.ffff.ffff(452)
04:46:54:   type 0x4, "ServerA", 5.0000.0000.0001(452), 2 hops
04:46:54:   type 0x7, "ServerA", 5.0000.0000.0001(452), 2 hops
04:46:54:   type 0x7, "ServerB", 6.0000.0000.0001(452), 2 hops
04:47:02: IPXSAP: positing update to 1.ffff.ffff.ffff via Ether-
net0 (broadcast)
(full)
Lab-A#
```

On production networks, any debug command can have a serious effect on performance because of the volume of output generated. Avoid using this command on an IPX production network because the volume of debug output could kill the router in some cases.

Commands Introduced in this Section

This section introduced the following commands:

- **show ipx servers**   Generates a list of all server resources on the network
- **debug ipx sap activity**   Turns on the debug feature to report contents of SAP updates

Summary

This chapter covered the basic techniques of configuring a router to use IPX. We started by looking at IPX's simple method of creating network addresses from a network ID assigned by an administrator and having the device adding a MAC address from an interface. We saw that the main "show" and "debug" commands from the IP feature set have IPX counterparts.

While encapsulation type is fairly routine in the IP environment, the NetWare version differences may require multiple encapsulation types on a single device and may require additional planning and design to ensure connectivity.

We worked with configuring IPX on a Windows workstation and the basic router configuration steps. We saw that a form of ping can be used in the IPX routers and that the *show cdp neighbors detail* command will reveal the IPX address of neighbor devices.

We looked at the concept of using server broadcasts (SAP) to announce resource availability within the network. The GNS request is a way for a host to request services that will result in a GNS reply from a server or, if one isn't available, from a Cisco router.

Practice Questions

Take a few moments and check your grasp of the concepts covered in this chapter. The answers are immediately following the questions.

Questions

1. Which one of the following is a valid IP network host address?
   a. 202.16.123.4
   b. 123A.2563.A6A9
   c. 0600.4231.5561.6C6C
   d. 600

2. Which global configuration enables both IPX routing and SAP exchanges?
   a. Router IPX
   b. IPX routing
   c. IPX maximum paths 6
   d. Enable IPX routing

3. Which one of the following commands will set the IP address on a Fast Ethernet interface?
   a. router(config)# ipx address 6.0010.7b3a.3dd5
   b. router(config-if)#ipx address 6.0010.7b3a.3dd5
   c. router(config-if)#ipx network 6
   d. router(config)# ipx network 6

4. Which statement applies best to the following three interfaces?
   interface serial 0/0, ipx network 88 encapsulation arpa secondary, no shutdown
   a. This is the 88th network segment.
   b. There is at least one other IPX configuration on this interface.
   c. There is no such encapsulation type.
   d. The IP address is missing.

5. What is the maximum reachable hop count for IPX RIP routing?
   a. 100
   b. 15
   c. 16
   d. It can vary

6. Which of the following commands would add the 12 network to IPX RIP routing?
   a. router(config)#network 12
   b. router(config-if)#ipx network 12
   c. router(config-router)#ipx network 12
   d. router(config-network)#ipx 12

7. In the command ipx routing cccc.cccc.cccc, what is the cccc.cccc.cccc?
   a. Network ID
   b. optional node identifier
   c. Autonomous System Number
   d. Asynchronous Number

8. Which two commands give the IPX address of an interface?
  a. show ipx interfaces brief
  b. show interfaces
  c. show ipx interfaces
  d. show protocols

9. Which of the following commands will tell us the IPX address of a neighbor router?
  a. cdp neighbor
  b. cdp neighbor detail
  c. show cdp neighbor detail
  d. show cdp neighbor

10. Which command will display all IPX server resources?
  a. show ipx servers
  b. show cdp neighbors servers
  c. show ipx sap
  d. show ipx resources

11. Which command enables detailed IPX RIP debugging?
  a. debug ipx routing events
  d. debug ipx routing transactions
  c. debug ipx routing activities
  d. debug ipx sap

12. What protocol or process is used for servers to broadcast to hosts about the services that they offer?
  a. SAP
  b. GNS
  c. IPX RIP
  d. NLSP

13. What distance vector feature makes secondary IPX addresses less attractive than subinterfaces?
  a. poison reverse
  b. split horizon
  c. slow convergence
  d. too many updates

14. Which one of the following will create an IPX subinterface?

    a. subinterface Fa0/0.1

    b. int Fa0/0.1

    c. ipx interface Fa0/0.1

    d. int Fa0/0

15. Which one of the following is not a Cisco IPX encapsulation type?

    a. ARPA

    b. Novell-ether

    c. SAP

    d. Ethernet_802.3

    e. SNAP

16. What two possibilities could explain why you cannot assign a proper primary IPX address to a LAN interface?

    a. IPX has not been enabled with the IPX routing command.

    b. There is already an IP address assigned to that interface.

    c. There is no MAC address for the interface.

    d. The IOS feature set does not support IPX.

Answers

1. **c.** 0600.4231.5561.6C6C is correct, with 0600 for the network and the rest for the MAC address of the interface or device. a. 202.16.123.4 is an IP address. b. 123A.2563.A6A9 is too short; it is only the MAC address. d. 600 is only the network ID portion.

2. **b.** IPX routing enables IPX and SAP. a. and d. No such commands. c. IPX maximum paths 6 enables load balancing.

3. **c.** *router(config-if)#*ipx network 6. While in interface configuration mode, you need to assign only the network ID.

4. **b.** There is at least one other IPX configuration on this interface. a. is wrong because network numbers do not need to be sequential c. is wrong; the earliest encapsulation type was arpa. d. is wrong because an IP address is not required.

5. **b.** 15 is the maximum hop count.

6. **b.** *router(config-if)#*ipx network 12. Configuring the network on an interface automatically adds the network to IPX RIP routing.

7. **b.** Optional node identifier. This becomes the MAC address for serial interfaces. Can be any valid HEX address.

8. **c. and d.** *show ipx interfaces* and *show protocols* both show the IPX address. a. *show ipx interfaces brief* shows the interface status but not the address. b. *show interfaces* includes only any IP addresses.

9. **c.** *show cdp neighbor detail*

10. **a.** *show ipx servers*

11. **c.** *debug ipx routing activities*

12. **a.** SAP service advertising protocol. b. GNS is just the opposite; it is a host requesting the address of a server. c. IPX RIP is a routing protocol; it does not forward SAP info to hosts d. NLSP is Novell's link-state routing protocol.

13. **b.** Split horizon prevents the additional networks associated with an interface from receiving updates about the other networks on that interface.

14. **b.** *int Fa0/0.1*

15. **d.** Ethernet_802.3 is Novell's name for Cisco's SAP.

16. **a. and d.** IPX has not been enabled with the IPX routing command, and the IOS feature set does not support IPX.

CHAPTER 15

Access Control Lists— Managing Network Traffic and Resources

This chapter will:

- **Teach you the structure and significance of access list numbering**

- **Show you how to create and implement IP standard access lists**

- **Introduce you to creation and implementation IP extended access lists**

- **Show you how to create and implement IP named access lists**

- **Give an overview of IPX standard, extended, and SAP filter access lists**

- **Teach you how to verify and monitor access lists**

- **Teach you how to apply access lists to interfaces and virtual terminal sessions**

- **Show examples of using ACLs to manage different types of network traffic**

- **Look at the basic principles behind firewall systems**

In the last chapters, we've looked at techniques for configuring routers to provide connectivity and access within our Internetwork. Probably as important is how we secure this same Internetwork and control access of individuals and networks that have no business being there or that present a risk to the network. Network operating systems provide a level of control and security with user-level security and passwords on devices; of course, physically securing key components to the extent possible is still our first responsibility.

Routers provide another tool that allows data filtering and allows or denies access based on a predefined list of criteria. At the heart of this filtering is a router feature called *access control lists* (ACLs) or often just *access lists*. Access lists can block a single host's access to a resource, or it can selectively provide filtering to a variety of IP resources. Access lists are a starting point for adding security and traffic management to your network, but they cannot protect your network by themselves. Devices like firewalls and proxy servers, as well as password management, physical security, and solid administrative policies, should be used to augment them.

ACLs are powerful tools but are understood fully by few people; take the time necessary to master the skills involved. Proficiency in building and debugging access lists is one of the skills that can distinguish you from the masses.

 NOTE: ACLs use a feature called wildcard masks that will be considerably easier to understand if you have mastered IP addressing and subnet masks. If you are not comfortable with subnet masks, you might want to review this topic first—or at least review it if you get stuck.

Access Control Lists (ACLs)

ACLs are a series of sequentially processed permit or deny statements that can be used to filter data traffic for many purposes. Each ACL statement includes a criterion definition that is used to determine whether the permit or deny statement is implemented. This criterion could be as simple as a source address for the packet, or it could be an elaborate combination based on data frame segments such as the source address, destination address, protocol used by the source and/or destination, and/or the TCP/UDP port number used. Since version 12.0, such criteria can also be time and date sensitive.

With skill, planning, and practice we should be able to define very specific limited criteria. For example, we can block all access to a network by a host or group of hosts based exclusively on their source address. Or, we could choose to limit Web browsing to selected servers during certain hours while still allowing unlimited FTP and e-mail access.

We have examples of similar processes in our noncomputer lives. Filing income taxes in the United States is one example. If you look at the "Who must file?" information on the cover of any of the tax-form instructions, you will see a list of conditions. If you meet any one of the conditions, you must file a report. Each condition is very specific; if you match one or more criteria, you are in. In Washington State, a jury summons has a short access list that asks four questions. If you answer no to any one, you are excluded from the pool. Your desire or interest in participating is not one of the questions.

Why Use ACLs

We will start by looking at ACLs from the perspective of limiting access to an interface and therefore resources beyond that interface. This is probably the most common type of ACL and is often where users are first introduced to the concepts and technology. As you continue in the field, you will discover that some form of access list is used for many other things. Some of the uses for ACLs include:

- **Managing routing traffic** ACLs can be used to filter routing updates. They can block entire protocols from updating over an interface, or they can selectively filter the contents of a routing update limiting information about certain networks.

- **Adjusting the routing metric** ACLs can be used to adjust the routing metric for particular routes, thereby changing the likelihood that a route will be used.

- **Determining "interesting" traffic** In *Dial on Demand Routing* (DDR) ACLs are used to determine what is "interesting" traffic that will cause a modem or ISDN device to open a connection with another device. This interesting traffic could be defined by an ACL as a protocol, such as IP, or it could be a specific application, such as e-mail. The designated interesting traffic will cause the link to open and remain open as long as interesting traffic is present. This can greatly reduce the use and cost of metered services.

- **Defining traffic** ACLS can be used to define the traffic that another command will use. For example the *debug IP packet* command monitors all IP traffic on the device. If a reference to an ACL is added, then the ACL can specify which IP traffic to monitor.

- **Priority queuing** ACLs can be used to create priority queuing for processing packets, thereby giving preference to certain types of traffic based on protocol or application.

- **Limiting access** ACLs can provide the base-level security for network resources by limiting access to parts of the network. This security aspect could apply to keeping outside hosts out of the network entirely or preventing certain network hosts from accessing specific network segments. An ACL applied to the interface connecting the network to the Internet might block all access into the network that does not originate from within the network. This allows local users to browse the Internet but does not allow outsiders to initiate a connection into your network.

In each case, the basic ACL itself will be the same and use the same structures that we are going to cover. What will vary in each case is how and with which commands the ACLs are implemented.

Keep in mind that, like all good things, access lists can be overused, and they can be used incorrectly, causing more harm to the network's performance than you might imagine. Since ACLs have to be processed by the CPU on every packet, good minimalist design is essential to accomplish the goal while preserving router resources. A poorly designed access list can hurt network performance and still fail to meet the original objective.

Note that devices like the Catalyst 6500 process ACLs in hardware, and therefore, the device incurs no loss of performance whatsoever.

ACLs and Network Protocols

ACLs are network-protocol specific. Each upper-level protocol (IP, IPX, AppleTalk) has its own access list structures and options, but if you understand one, you should not have a difficult time with another. Just as running multiple protocols requires more resources, such as memory and CPU usage, multiple access lists will affect those same resources. Some protocols, like IPX, refer to ACLs as filters, particularly in output displays such as *show IPX interfaces.*

ACLs are numbered or named. If numbered, the number indicates the protocol used; if named, the ACL explicitly identifies the protocol supported. It is possible to have multiple ACLs per protocol on a particular router, each with its own unique number or name. In the case of IP and IPX ACLs, it is possible to apply up to two ACLs on a particular interface: one inbound and one outbound. With other protocols, you apply only one ACL to an interface, which filters both inbound and outbound packets.

For the CCNA exam, you will need to be familiar with the basics of IP access lists, so we will concentrate on those. But in the initial discussions of general topics, such as naming and numbering access lists, we will discuss IP and IPX together. As we develop our skills, we will concentrate on IP features.

Access List Basics

There are two types of access lists: standard and extended. Standard access lists are the simpler of the two and use only the source addresses as the criteria to make decisions about whether a packet will be permitted or denied access. Extended access lists do exactly what the name implies: They extend the capabilities of the access list by using several criteria in the decision process.

We will start our coverage by looking at some access list basics that apply to both standard and extended lists. We will then look at the specifics of the standard access list and move on to the more complex extended lists. Much of the basic "why" and "how" of access lists will be covered in this section or in the next section, where we expand on the standard list. Subsequent sections will cover extend lists.

Access List Numbering

Initially, access lists were numbered to allow multiple lines to be grouped together even if they were entered at different times. The number also created a short and specific reference to the list that could be used when the list was implemented. Each access list must have a unique number, and all lines within the access list must use that same number. Figure 15-1 shows our test lab from Chapters 12-14 with a host added to the Ethernet LAN of router A. The next few paragraphs describe a simple standard access to prevent that host from reaching the Ethernet LAN on router X, 192.168.5.0.

The following lines show a simple two-line standard access list that prevents a particular host, 192.168.1.10, from accessing any devices on the 192.168.5.0 network. Both lines were created in global configuration mode and are the appropriate lines from the *show run* output.

```
!
access-list 50 deny 192.168.1.10
access-list 50 permit any
!
```

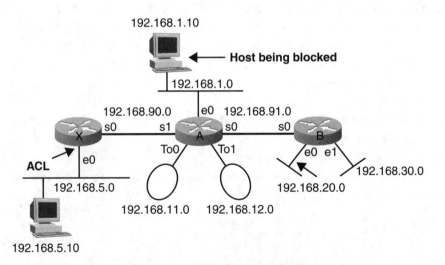

Figure 15-1   Practice lab with ACL on Router X

Both lines contain the number 50, indicating they are from the same list. This number also groups the commands if there were other access lists on the router. The lines are entered and processed sequentially, so we know that "access-list 50 deny 192.168.1.10" was entered first; and it will be processed before the second command. The next lines are the *show run* output for the same router, showing how the access list is applied to the Ethernet 0 interface.

The hyphen between "access" and "list" appears because all ACL objects and command verbs (action words) are single words. By using a hyphen, one converts two words into a one-word object name. This is the same reason the space is removed from "Fast Ethernet" and "Token Ring" when they are referenced as interfaces. It also explains why we can name our router Router-X, RouterX, or Router_X, but we cannot name it Router X (with a space). Understanding this concept will be critical on the CCNA and future Cisco exams; you will have to select the correct command for a task, and the only difference between two choices will be the hyphen.

```
interface Ethernet0
 ip address 192.168.5.1 255.255.255.0
 ip access-group 50 out
 !
```

The "50" indicates that access list 50 is to be used; "out" indicates that it is the outbound traffic that will be filtered; that is, traffic passing from the router out into the 192.168.5.0 network will be processed using the access list. Traffic from the network inbound to the router are not affected at all.

The "IP" indicates that an IP access list is being applied to the interface. There can be only one access list applied in each direction per protocol used. So, while we could have another IP access list applied inbound, and we could have AppleTalk and IPX access list for both directions, the only way that we can have more filtering outbound on this interface is to edit this list. Adding a new outbound IP access list would automatically remove this one.

Access-group is the special command word used to apply an access list to an interface. We will see that, while the access lists themselves do not change from application to application, the command to implement them does.

The following lines show the result when host 192.168.1.10 tries to ping a workstation on the 192.168.5.0 network:

```
C:\>ping 192.168.5.10
Pinging 192.168.5.10 with 32 bytes of data:
Reply from 192.168.90.2: Destination net unreachable.
Reply from 192.168.90.2: Destination net unreachable.
Reply from 192.168.90.2: Destination net unreachable.
Reply from 192.168.90.2: Destination net unreachable.
```

```
Ping statistics for 192.168.5.10:
    Packets: Sent = 4, Received = 4, Lost = 0 (0% loss),
Approximate round trip times in milli-seconds:
    Minimum = 0ms, Maximum =  0ms, Average =  0ms
C:\>
```

The following lines are included only to show that 192.168.1.10 was able to successfully ping 192.168.5.1 before the access list was implemented. Attempts to Telnet or use a Web browser to access that network would also be rebuffed.

```
C:\>ping 192.168.5.10
Pinging 192.168.5.10 with 32 bytes of data:
Reply from 192.168.5.10: bytes=32 time=30ms TTL=254
Reply from 192.168.5.10: bytes=32 time=20ms TTL=254
Reply from 192.168.5.10: bytes=32 time=20ms TTL=254
Reply from 192.168.5.10: bytes=32 time=20ms TTL=254
Ping statistics for 192.168.5.10:
    Packets: Sent = 4, Received = 4, Lost = 0 (0% loss),
Approximate round trip times in milli-seconds:
    Minimum = 20ms, Maximum =  30ms, Average =  22ms
C:\>
```

The next lines show that Router B in our test lab is still able to access 192.168.5.10, because the access list was specific to only one host, 192.168.1.10. Even other workstations on the 192.168.1.0 network can access the 192.168.5.0 network.

```
Lab-B>ping 192.168.5.10
Type escape sequence to abort.
Sending 5, 100-byte ICMP Echos to 192.168.5.10, timeout is 2 sec-
onds:
!!!!!
Success rate is 100 percent (5/5 ), round-trip min/avg/max = 72/79
/108 ms
Lab-B>
```

The following lines show the access-list number ranges that have been defined by Cisco. The access-list number is actually more than a grouping tool or a name; it also indicates the protocol used. For the CCNA exam, you will be expected to know at least the first two IP and the three IPX number ranges that I annotated. The last two are relatively new and indicate the importance of ACLs by adding huge pools of numbers to the system.

```
Lab-X(config)#access-list ?
    <1-99>        IP standard access list          (know for sure)
    <100-199>     IP extended access list          (know for sure)
    <200-299>     Protocol type-code access list
    <300-399>     DECnet access list
    <600-699>     Appletalk access list
    <700-799>     48-bit MAC address access list
```

```
<800-899>   IPX standard access list          (know for sure)
<900-999>   IPX extended access list          (know for sure)
<1000-1099> IPX SAP access list               (know for sure)
<1100-1199> Extended 48-bit MAC address access list
<1200-1299> IPX summary address access list
<1300-1999> IP standard access list (expanded range)   (new)
<2000-2699> IP extended access list (expanded range)   (new)
```

The Permit and Deny Commands

Every access list is made up of one or more access-list lines or statements. Each statement contains the *permit* or *deny* command. Following is the basic syntax of all access-list lines.

router(config)#access-list acl-number {permit|deny} . . .

The *permit* command allows packets matching the criteria on that line to be accepted for whatever the access list is being used for. In the case of our earlier example, a permit statement allows qualifying packets to pass out into the 192.168.5.0 network.

The *deny* command discards packets matching the criteria on that line. In the case of our earlier example, the deny statement caused packets from 192.168.1.10 to be discarded and therefore be unavailable to the 192.168.5.0 network.

Implied Deny Statement

In many implementations of access lists, such as those used with interfaces, the creation of an access list changes the environment to "deny everything" except that which is specifically "permitted" by the ACL. By default, interfaces are wide open to any packets traveling in either direction. But, once an ACL is applied to an interface and defined, that interface is then absolutely closed to all traffic in the direction of the access list except that traffic specifically allowed by the ACL statements.

This is often represented as an implied "deny everything" statement as the final statement in the access list. The statement is not actually present, but its effect is. The following single-line access list clearly denies packets from host 192.168.1.10.

```
Router(config)#access-list 75 deny 192.168.1.10
```

But what is not so clear is that all other traffic will be discarded as well, as if the list looked like the following lines:

```
Router(config)#access-list 75 deny 192.168.1.10
Router(config)#access-list 75 deny any            (implied)
```

The word "any" is an ACL keyword used to mean any host in any network. To prevent all other traffic from being discarded, most access lists have a special permit statement as the last statement. The result looks like this:

```
Router(config)#access-list 75 deny 192.168.1.10
Router(config)#access-list 75 permit any
```

The implied "deny any" is still in effect, but since all remaining packets have been permitted by the "access-list 75 permit any" statement, the implied deny statement will never be reached.

At Least One Permit Statement Required

There is no requirement that an ACL have a deny statement. If nothing else, the implied "deny any" statement takes care of this need. But, if there are no "permit" statements, the effect will be same as if there were only a single "deny any" statement. Look at the following lines:

```
Router(config)#access-list 75 deny 192.168.1.10
Router(config)#access-list 75 deny 192.168.17.123
Router(config)#access-list 75 deny 192.168.100.5
Router(config)#access-list 75 deny 192.168.63.21
```

While it looks like the preceding statements will block four hosts if applied to an interface, the implied "deny any" statement combined with these lines mean that all packets will be discarded.

ACL Statement Order

ACLs are simple but powerful tools. Each ACL statement is added to the access list in the order in which it is created. It is not possible to add a new statement anywhere except at the bottom. When the access list is used, each statement is processed by the IOS in the order in which it was created. If a statement's criteria is met, then the permit or deny statement is applied to that packet, and no further statements are checked. The next packet to be filtered starts again at the top of the list.

```
Router(config)#access-list 75 deny 192.168.1.10
Router(config)#access-list 75 deny 192.168.17.123
Router(config)#access-list 75 permit any
Router(config)#access-list 75 deny 192.168.63.21
```

In the preceding example, a packet from host 192.168.63.21 is checked by the first statement and passed over as not meeting the criteria. The same thing happens with the second statement. The third statement, matching packets from any host in any network, permits the packet to pass. The packet never sees the fourth statement; in fact, no packet would ever see the fourth statement.

It is not possible to reorder the list, skip statements, edit statements, or to delete statements from a numbered access list. With numbered access lists, any attempt to delete a single statement will result in the entire list being deleted. We will see in the "Named Access Control List" section, later in this chapter, that named ACLs do allow for deleting individual statements.

For all these reasons, it makes sense to create access lists in a text processor such as Notepad and either paste them while in global configuration mode or use a TFTP server to add them to the running configuration. Even if you choose to build the access lists directly in terminal configuration mode so that you have access to the online Help features, you may want consider using Copy and Paste with Notepad for editing.

Top-Down Processing

ACLs are processed in a top-down manner, meaning that the first statement is processed fully; if there is no match, then the next statement is processed until all statements are completed, at which point the implied "deny any" will discard the packet. This concept is critical to understanding and building reliable ACLs that conserve router resources. Remember to organize your access-list statements so that specific criteria involving a specific network or subnet appear before general criteria. In other words, deny the single host or subnet before issuing a "permit any" statement. Look at the following example:

```
Lab-X(config)#access-list 13 deny 192.168.1.10
Lab-X(config)#access-list 13 deny 192.168.2.0 0.0.0.255
Lab-X(config)#access-list 13 permit any
Lab-X(config)#access-list 13 deny 192.168.3.16 0.0.0.15
```

The last statement can never be processed, because the third statement has allowed everything to be permitted. While this may seem nonsensical, it happens when a third network, 192.168.3.0, is added to an existing router, and the administrator attempts to add the new line to an existing ACL. Look at the *show run* and *show access-list* commands covered in this chapter as a way of catching this problem.

Whenever possible, place frequently occurring conditions near the top of the ACL and less frequently occurring conditions farther down to increase router performance. Keep in mind that every packet using the feature involving the ACL, such as one passing through an interface, will be tested one statement at a time. If a high percentage of packets predictably fall into one or two criteria, try to get those criteria as high in the list as prudent so that those packets do not need to be tested any more than necessary. Conversely, if you have a worst-case scenario criterion that you hope will never or seldom occur, try to put it near the bottom. Obviously, this organization method has to be coordinated with the "specific before general" guideline just mentioned.

Editing Work-Arounds

While it is not possible to reorder or edit existing ACL statements, some work-around methods can be used to deal with production routers that cannot be down any more than absolutely required.

Use a text editor to create a copy of the ACL. Make the desired changes and then change the ACL number of the new list. After pasting or copying the new ACL into the router, use the *ip access-group* command to apply the new access-list number to the router interface. Since there cannot be two ACLs on the interface using the same protocol, the new ACL will replace the old one. There will be a few fractions of a second with no protection on the interface while the router replaces the old access list with the new one.

What also often works well is doing a "show run" and copying the access list into an editor. Assume that the access-list is 15. Create a few spaces, insert "no access-list 15" at the top of the new section, paste again, and then proceed to edit the statements as needed. Then just copy and paste the results right back into the router. In essence, you remove an ACL and then immediately create a new ACL using the same number. This way the access-group command does not have to be changed. It is only a fraction of a second that passes without security, and, if anything goes wrong, you have a copy of the original ACL. The following lines are one example of the resulting commands starting with the original ACL:

```
access-list 15 deny 192.168.1.10
access-list 15 deny 192.168.2.0 0.0.0.255
access-list 15 permit any
```

After the edits, the result might look like this:

```
no access-list 15
access-list 15 deny 192.168.1.0 0.0.0.255
access-list 15 deny 192.168.2.0 0.0.0.255
access-list 15 deny 192.168.3.16 0.0.0.15
access-list 15 permit any
```

In some environments, even this brief security lapse is unacceptable. A solution is to shut down the interface while the changeover occurs. If the router is supporting multiple protocols, use the *ip shutdown* command rather than the *shutdown* command we are familiar with. The *ip shutdown* command disables the interface only for IP packets. The following lines show an example of the changeover commands that could be quickly implemented by creating the commands in a text editor and pasting it into global configuration mode:

```
Lab-X(config)#interface fastethernet 0/1
Lab-X(config)#ip shutdown
Lab-X(config)#ip access-group 85 in
Lab-X(config)#no ip shutdown
```

IP Access Lists

In this section, we look at the implementation of ACLs in an IP environment. While many of the concepts apply to other protocols, the implementation may be unique to IP because of the addressing used. At the "IPX Access List section" later in this chapter, we will look at IPX ACLs.

Wildcard Masks

In identifying IP addresses, ACLs use a wildcard mask instead of a subnet mask. Initially, they may look like the same thing, but closer observation reveals that they are basically opposites. Whereas a subnet mask is a 32-bit value made up of contiguous 1's and then 0's, a wildcard mask 32-bit value begins with 0's indicating a "must match" and 1's meaning "either value is okay." Some examples might help.

IP ADDRESS	SUBNET MASK	WILDCARD MASK
192.168.1.15	255.255.255.255	0.0.0.0
192.168.1.0	255.255.255.0	0.0.0.255
192.168.0.0	255.255.0.0	0.0.255.255
192.168.1.16	255.255.255.240	0.0.0.15
192.168.96.0	255.255.224.0	0.0.31.255

As with subnet masks, the comparisons are all being done in binary, not decimal. Consider the values in the fourth row in the table in binary form. The number 16 in binary is 00010000. The number 15 is the largest value that can be created with 4 bits, 00001111—it is also the wildcard mask. Remembering that the 0's must match but the 1's need not, the mask is telling us that any value from 00010000 (16) to 00011111 (31) is acceptable. The following lines should make this situation easier to see:

Last octet value 00010000 16
Wildcard mask 00001111 15

We see from the mask that the first 4 bits must be 0001; therefore, we cannot have a value greater than 31 because that would make the third bit a 1 and probably the 4th bit a 0.

The fifth row in the table is the supernet 192.168.96.0/19, which includes all addresses between 192.168.96.0 and 192.168.127.255.

The term *wildcard* used for the mask-bit matching process is undoubtedly a reference to the wildcard in many card games; that card can stand for any other card.

Thinking of subnet masks and wildcard masks as opposites may make it easier to grasp the implementation of wildcard masks initially, but remember that they have two different purposes. The subnet mask determines the network portion of an IP address by using the contiguous 1's in the mask. From the boundary where 1's change to 0's, the rest of the value is the node identifier. The pattern according to the standard is all 1's and then all 0's.

With wildcard masks, the 0's and 1's determine whether the bits must be matched or can be ignored, respectively. There is no corresponding all-0's and then all-1's rule.

Implicit Masks

Implicit masks can be implied from the current mask or the lack of a mask. Implicit masks reduce typing and simplify configuration. The following line is an example of an implicit mask.

Access-list permit 192.168.1.10

Listing a valid host address with no wildcard mask is interpreted as having a mask of 0.0.0.0. The implicit mask makes it easier to create statements for multiple hosts. When the keyword "any" is used, the mask 255.255.255.255 is implied. The preceding example is the equivalent of either of the following statements:

Access-list permit 192.168.1.10 0.0.0.0

Access-list permit host 192.168.1.10

Another example is when you permit one (host or network) and thus have implied that you deny all others. This is the basis for making sure that you specifically "permit" any nodes or traffic that you want; otherwise, it is assumed that you meant to deny them. Once an access list is configured and applied, the assumption is that you will now explicitly define what is to be permitted.

Following are two common mistakes made with implicit masks:

- *Access-list permit 0.0.0.0* Probably meant to mean that everything or possibly the wildcard mask 255.255.255.255 was overlooked. Unfortunately, it is an illegal address by itself and results in blocking all traffic from getting through. The keyword "any" would have worked better.

- *Access-list permit* **192.168.0.0** This is a network address, not a host address, and, as such, no packet will ever have this address as the source address (it will have a host address). No packet will ever meet the criteria, and thus no packets will be permitted. This was probably meant to be 192.168.0.0 0.0.255.255.

While the last example may obviously seem to be a network address, what about 192.168.1.64? If it is 192.168.1.64/24, it is a host address (192.168.1.1 to 192.168.1.254). However, if it is 192.168.1.64/26 (or greater), it is a subnet address and again cannot appear as a source address on a packet. The host addresses for 192.168.1.64/26 are 192.168.1.65 to 192.168.1.126.

The "Any" and "Host" Keywords

A keyword is a special word that the IOS interprets as meaning something special. In dealing with IP addresses, we use two keywords, "any" and "host." As we saw earlier in our example, the keyword "any" means any host on any network, or in IP / wildcard notation, it would be 0.0.0.0 255.255.255.255. While the IP / wildcard notation works, it is time consuming and opens the door to typos. The keyword "any" can be used any time to mean any IP address.

The second keyword, "host," recognized by the Cisco IOS, can be used with an IP address to indicate a single host address. The syntax is *host ip-address*—for example, *host 192.168.1.10*. This combination will be treated exactly the same as 192.168.1.10 0.0.0.0, where the wildcard mask indicates that all octets must match exactly. Statement one, which follows, demonstrates the "host" keyword.

```
Router(config)#access-list 75 deny host 192.168.1.10
Router(config)#access-list 75 deny 192.168.17.123
Router(config)#access-list 75 permit any
```

Statement two does not have either the "host" keyword or a wildcard mask. On version 12 of the IOS, an entry made with an IP address but no mask will be assumed to be a host address. The newer IOS prefers this method and drop the host reference in the running configuration. The following lines show the running configuration after the last three entries:

```
!
access-list 75 deny    192.168.1.10
access-list 75 deny    192.168.17.123
access-list 75 permit any
```

How ACLs Work

There are two parts to building ACLs: creating the access-list statements in global configuration mode and applying the list to the purpose it will be used for. Since version 11.2 of the IOS, it doesn't matter in which order you do these two steps.

A set of access-list statements that have not been applied will have no effect on the processing of the router. Similarly, applying an access list to a task, such as applying an ACL to an interface with the access-group command when there are no access-list statements will have no effect. It hasn't always been this way. Before version 10.3, applying an access group to an interface without supporting access-list statements effectively closed that interface in the specified direction.

Processing an ACL

An ACL is a series of statements that must be processed sequentially until one of the statements matches the packet. If one of the statements matches the packet, then the permit or deny statement determines whether the packet is forwarded or discarded. If none of the ACL statements matches the packet, then the implied "deny any" statement will cause the packet to be discarded. Unless a permit statement matches the packet, it will be discarded. Figure 15-2 shows the flow of a packet through an ACL.

Let's consider applying an ACL to an interface. It could be applied inbound or outbound on a particular interface. If you do not specify a direction, the default is outbound. When you are trying to determine if it should be in or out on an interface, visualize the direction from the center of the router—is the packet coming into the router or moving out of the router? This is a relatively easy distinction but one that is often confused by students. They want to block traffic from coming into a LAN so they apply the ACL on the Ethernet interface inbound. The problem is that traffic into the LAN is outbound on the router's Ethernet interface. Figure 15-3 shows this situation.

In Figure 15-3, we are trying to protect the LAN users from something on the Internet. If we apply the ACL inbound on e0, that would block the users' access to the router and anything beyond. Outbound, from the perspective of the router, would be the correct direction. We should see that if we applied the ACL to s0 inbound, we would prevent the packets from reaching the LAN. We would want to be careful with this latter approach because we would also block the packet from anything on interface s1, which may not be desirable. It's generally better to be conservative and not secure more than your original objective.

It is possible to apply an ACL to more than one interface on the router. Figure 15-4 shows a variation on the last example in which it makes sense to apply the ACL to both LAN interfaces as outbound filters.

Figure 15-2
Flow diagram of
ACL statements

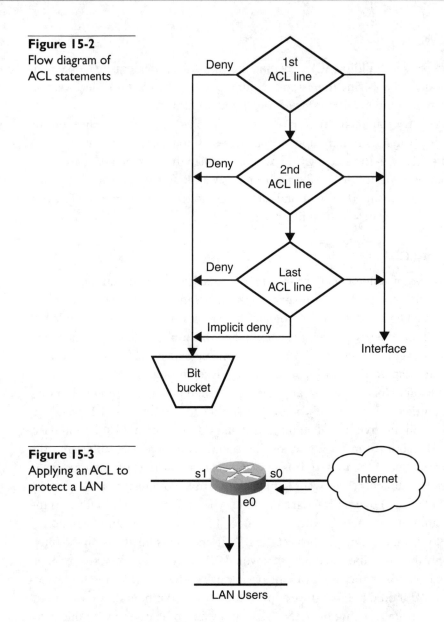

Figure 15-3
Applying an ACL to
protect a LAN

From a performance perspective, it makes more sense to block packets on ingress. By blocking outbound packets, the router will have to switch the packet from one interface to the other and then apply the ACL and discard the packet, thus wasting CPU resources. Unfortunately, with standard ACLs, it isn't always possible to filter on the inbound interface. We will compare standard and extended ACLs in this chapter.

Figure 15-4
Applying an ACL to
two LAN interfaces

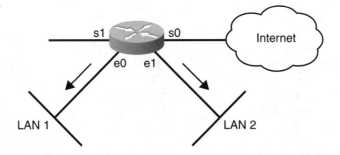

The ACL statements can be applied only on the router that contains the ACL. If you need the ACL on a second router, it will need to be added to that router's configuration. This could be done with a TFTP server or by using Copy and Paste. While two ACLs on the same router cannot use the same number or name, there is no problem with using the same number on multiple routers.

Figure 15-5 shows the process faced by a packet passing through a router with ACLs. There could be an inbound ACL on the receiving interface and an outbound ACL on the interface that used to exit the router. Failing either ACL, or not being "permitted" by either ACL, would cause the packet to be discarded. The ACL processing is in addition to all interface and route processing.

By matching the first test, a packet is denied access to the destination. It is discarded and dropped into the bit bucket, and it is not exposed to any ACL tests that follow. If the packet does not match the conditions of the first test, it drops to the next statement in the ACL.

Standard ACLs

Standard ACLs are the simplest to create because the only criterion is the source address specified in each access-list statement. A standard ACL is similar to a security guard at a gate; if you don't have the correct pass (source address), you don't get through—your purpose and ultimate destination address are irrelevant.

Based on the wildcard mask, if any, Standard ACLs can be used to permit or deny all traffic from a host, a network, or a subnet. Standard ACL numbers must be between 1 and 99. The full syntax of the command is as follows:

Router(config)# access-list acl-number {deny | permit} source [source-wildcard] [log]

There is no way to remove just one line of an ACL. If you want to remove the entire list of statements, use the "no" form of this command and identify only the acl-number. Here is the full syntax:

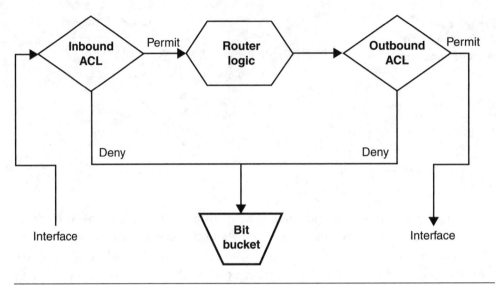

Figure 15-5 Inbound and outbound ACLs in the router

Router(config)# no access-list acl-number

Examples of both commands would look like the following lines:

```
Lab-X#conf t
Lab-X(config)#access-list 90 deny 192.168.1.0 0.0.0.255
Lab-X(config)#access-list 90 deny 192.168.2.0 0.0.0.255
Lab-X(config)#access-list 90 deny 192.168.3.128 0.0.0.127
Lab-X(config)#no access-list 90
Lab-X(config)#^Z
Lab-X#
```

Using the *show run* command gives no sign of the ACL 90 because the last command removes the whole thing. The result would have been exactly the same had I typed:

Lab-X(config)#no access-list 90 deny 192.168.3.128 0.0.0.127.

It is not possible to selectively remove a single numbered ACL statement.

The Log Option

The Log option causes message to be printed to the console screen the first time that the ACL is activated and then every five minutes while the ACL is still being used. The first report indicates only the first packet, but the subsequent reports summarize the number of occurrences. The following output lines show the result of adding "log" to our earlier ACL that blocked host 192.168.1.10's access to the 192.168.5.0 network. While it was not necessary to reapply the ACL to the interface, I include it to show the two-step process of creating the list and then assigning it to a task, an outbound interface filter in this example.

```
Lab-X(config)#access-list 50 deny    192.168.1.10 log
Lab-X(config)#access-list 50 permit any
Lab-X(config)#int e0
Lab-X(config-if)#ip access-group 50 out
Lab-X(config-if)#^Z
Lab-X#Lab-X#
11:29:37: %SEC-6-IPACCESSLOGS: list 50 denied 192.168.1.10 1
packet
Lab-X#
11:34:53: %SEC-6-IPACCESSLOGS: list 50 denied 192.168.1.10 27
packets
Lab-X#
```

Once the ACL was created with the Log option, I went to the workstation and attempted to ping host 192.168.5.1 seven times from the MS-DOS window. The first packet was recorded in the first log entry. The other 27 packets, 4 per ping, were reported five minutes later. Because I made no further attempts, the log did not report again.

The "logging" command in global configuration mode can be used to modify the Log options, including specifying a host address to which to forward all log entries.

Show Run Command

One way to see your access lists and how they are applied is to use the *show run* command to see the active configuration. The following lines show the output of a *show run* command with some of the unrelated lines removed:

```
Lab-X#show run
version 12.1
hostname Lab-X
enable secret 5 $1$VAM7$Q9ml7Dm.YlostltOdzfWt1
ip host Lab-X 192.168.90.2 192.168.5.1
ip host Lab-A 192.168.90.1 192.168.91.1 192.168.11.1
ip host Lab-B 192.168.91.1 192.168.92.2 192.168.20.1
!
ipx routing 0010.7b3a.3dd5
ipx maximum-paths 2
!
interface Ethernet0
 ip address 192.168.5.1 255.255.255.0
 ip access-group 50 out
!
interface Serial1
```

```
 ip address 192.168.96.2 255.255.255.0
 ip access-group 75 in
 ipx network 96
!
access-list 50 deny    192.168.1.10 log
access-list 50 permit any
access-list 75 deny    192.168.17.123
access-list 75 deny    192.168.1.10
access-list 75 permit any
!
```

We should see that ACL 50 is applied to Ethernet 0 as an inbound access list, and ACL 75 is applied to Serial 1 as an inbound list. This display also shows us the order of our commands.

Show Access-Lists Command

The *show access-lists* command displays all access lists on the router but does not show if or where they are applied. The command *show ip access-lists* includes only IP access lists, which in this case would be exactly the same display. Both commands allow you to specify an ACL number or name after the command to display just that ACL.

```
Lab-X#show access-lists
Standard IP access list 50
    deny    192.168.1.10 log
    permit any
Standard IP access list 75
    deny    192.168.17.123
    deny    192.168.1.10
    permit any
Lab-X#
```

Show IP Interfaces Command

The *show ip interface* command that we looked at in Chapter 13 will tell us if an inbound or outbound access list has been applied to an interface. Rows 9 and 10 of the following output contain the information. The rest of the lines do not pertain to ACLs, so they have been omitted. You will recall that the *show ip interface* command displays all interfaces, but adding the interface ID, *show ip interface s0/0*, to the end of the command limits the output to that interface.

```
Lab-X#show ip interface
Ethernet0 is up, line protocol is up
  Internet address is 192.168.5.1/24
  Broadcast address is 255.255.255.255
  Address determined by non-volatile memory
  MTU is 1500 bytes
  Helper address is not set
  Directed broadcast forwarding is disabled
```

```
Multicast reserved groups joined: 224.0.0.9
Outgoing access list is 50
Inbound  access list is not set
Proxy ARP is enabled
```

Denying a Specific Host

Figure 15-6 shows a network like our two-router sample lab. The following example shows how to use a standard ACL to block traffic to Router X's LAN from a single specific host, 192.168.1.10 on Router A. We apply our rule about placing standard ACLs close to the destination to router X's interface Ethernet 0 so that we do not interfere with 192.168.1.10's ability to get to any other networks in the future.

```
Lab-X(config)#access-list 50 deny host 192.168.1.10
Lab-X(config)#access-list 50 permit 0.0.0.0 255.255.255.255
Lab-X(config)#interface ethernet 0
Lab-X(config-if)#ip access-group 50 out
```

The second access-list line shows using wildcard notation (0.0.0.0 255.255.255.255) to represent any host on any network. It could, and probably should, have been replaced by the keyword "any"—"access-list 50 permit any." The statement prevents any packet that does not match the first line of the ACL from being discarded by the implicit "deny any" statement (not shown).

If this ACL were configured on a lab like our example lab, you could test the result by going to 192.168.1.10 and trying to ping 192.168.5.10, which should fail. Not quite so obvious is that an attempt to ping the other way, 192.168.5.10 to 192.168.1.10, would also fail. The original ping, echo request, would go out normally, but the echo replies would be stopped by the ACL. The echo requests are inbound on the Ethernet interface and so are unaffected by the ACL, but the replies pass out of the Ethernet interface and therefore would be checked. Since the source address for the replies would be

Figure 15-6
2-Router example
to block a single
host

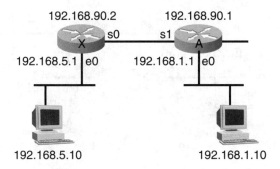

192.168.90.2   192.168.90.1

s0   s1

192.168.5.1 e0   192.168.1.1 e0

192.168.5.10   192.168.1.10

192.168.1.10, the packets will be denied and discarded. This would be true of telnet, http, ftp, and any requests from 192.168.5.10 to 192.168.1.10 that require a response. This is an important consideration with standard ACLs; without exception, they block everything meeting the criteria.

Denying a Network

Using Figure 15-6 from the last example, the following example shows how a standard ACL can be used to block the entire LAN network, 192.168.1.0 on Router A. In the first line of the ACL, the wildcard mask zeros in 0.0.0.255 indicate that the first three octets must match exactly while the last octet comprises all 1's, any value from 0-255.

```
Lab-X(config)#access-list 60 deny 192.168.1.0 0.0.0.255
Lab-X(config)#access-list 60 permit any
Lab-X(config)#interface ethernet 0
Lab-X(config-if)#ip access-group 60 out
```

Denying a Subnet

Figure 15-7 shows a network similar to the one in our two-router sample lab with Router A having three LANs using subnet addressing. The following example shows how use a standard ACL to block traffic to Router X's LAN from the second subnet only, 192.168.1.64 255.255.255.192 on Router A.

```
Lab-X(config)#access-list 70 deny 192.168.1.64 0.0.0.63
Lab-X(config)#access-list 70 permit any
Lab-X(config)#interface ethernet 0
Lab-X(config-if)#ip access-group 70 out
```

The first access-list line shows wildcard notation, 0.0.0.63, to represent a subnet on the 192.168.1.0 network. The IP address 192.168.1.64 indicates the second subnet. If

Figure 15-7
2-Router lab to
block a subnet

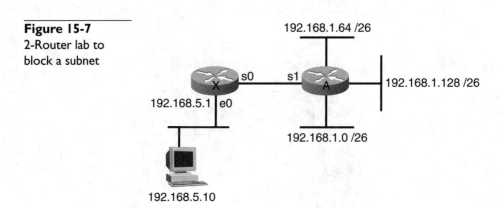

you are having trouble visualizing this, convert the 64 to binary, 01000000. The 63 in the wildcard mask indicates the acceptable values: 0-63. When these values are added to our starting value of 64, we get 64-127, which is the second subnet of 192.168.1.64 255.255.255.192. If it helps, identify your subnets using the skills covered in Chapter 9.

Filtering Telnet Access

Using Figure 15-7 from the last exercise, let's assume that we want to limit Telnet access to Router X to users on Router A's third subnet, the network administration department. Just as we can filter the physical interfaces, such as Ethernet 0 and serial 1, we can use access lists to filter the virtual ports, thereby limiting Telnet access to our routers.

There are five virtual ports, or vty lines, designated as vty 0 through vty 4, allowing up to five Telnet sessions to be established. Since we cannot control which virtual port will be accessed (first available), we will set identical restrictions on all vty lines at one time.

An inbound access list, 15, will limit access to that particular router. An outbound access list, 16, will prevent users that have successfully telnetted into the router from being able to use it as a platform to access other devices.

```
Lab-X(config)#access-list 15 permit 192.168.1.128 0.0.0.63
Lab-X(config)#access-list 16 deny any
Lab-X(config)#line vty 0 4
Lab-X(config-line)#access-class 15 in
Lab-X(config-line)#access-class 16 out
Lab-X(config-line)#password cisco
Lab-X(config-line)#login
```

The important command here is *access-class*. It is used in place of access-group when we are applying an ACL to a virtual terminal. This command is not a requirement of the CCNA exam; however, it is included here to show how ACLs can be used for more than filtering physical interfaces. As you continue your Cisco training, you will learn about other implementations.

The following code shows the result when another router, or a host on any other subnet / network, tries to telnet into Router -X. This would include our host 192.168.1.10. This implementation of the access-list applies to the entire router not just one direction on an interface.

```
Lab-A>telnet 192.168.5.1
Trying Router-A (192.168.5.1) . . .
% Connection refused by remote host
```

The following lines show the result of a permitted user (who cleared access list 15 and supplied the password) trying to telnet on to another router. The output assumes that an IP HOST table was set up with three IP addresses associated with the name Lab-B. Telnet attempts all three interfaces but blocks each attempt.

```
Lab-X>telnet Lab-B
Trying Lab-B (192.168.91.2)...
% Connections to that host not permitted from this terminal
Trying Lab-B (192.168.20.1) . . .
% Connections to that host not permitted from this terminal
Trying Lab-B (192.168.30.1) . . .
% Connections to that host not permitted from this terminal
Lab-X>
```

Show Line VTY Command

The following output demonstrates that the *show line vty* command lists the access lists that are applied to the virtual terminals. Run this command to verify that your access lists are, in fact, applied to all virtual terminals.

```
Lab-X#show line vty
 Tty Typ    Tx/Rx   A Modem   Roty AccO AccI Uses  Noise  Overruns
   2 VTY             -   -       -   16   15    0      0     0/0
   3 VTY             -   -       -   16   15    0      0     0/0
   4 VTY             -   -       -   16   15    0      0     0/0
   5 VTY             -   -       -   16   15    0      0     0/0
   6 VTY             -   -       -   16   15    0      0     0/0
```

Extended Access Control Lists

Standard access lists are relatively easy to configure, and they use minimal CPU resources because each list is based on a single criterion—the source address of the packet. Extended access lists provide a higher level of control by being able to filter based on the transport-layer protocol, source and/or destination IP address, and application port numbers or application keywords. For example, this makes it possible to limit HTTP traffic from a network while still allowing e-mail and FTP activity. Figure 15-8 shows an IP header and data segment.

With the standard access list, we can block all IP traffic based only on the IP source address segment (B) and the wildcard mask. With an extended access list, segments A, B, and C can be used. If segment A indicates IP, then all traffic matching any criteria based on B and/or C will be permitted or denied. But, if segment A indicates TCP, UDP, or ICMP, then additional coding in the segment(s) following "options" will determine specifically what is being filtered. For example, a TCP packet would have source and destination port numbers. We will look at the specific types of packets in a few minutes.

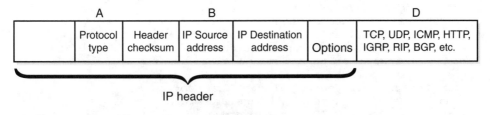

Figure 15-8   IP header and data segment

Creating an Extended Access List

As with standard lists, the access-list command is used to create each condition of the list-using one condition per line. The lines are processed sequentially and cannot be reordered once in place. The IOS version 12.x syntax for each line in the list is as follows:

access-list access-list-number {permit | deny} {protocol | protocol keyword} {source | any} [source-wildcard] [source port] {destination | any} [destination-wildcard] [destination port] [options]

Example:

```
Lab-X(config)#Access-list 101 deny tcp 192.168.1.0 0.0.0.255 any
eq http
Lab-X(config)#Access-list 101 deny tcp any eq ftp 192.168.1.25
Lab-X(config)#Access-list 101 permit ip any any
```

The access-list keyword must be hyphenated and must begin each statement. The access list-number range for IP extended access lists is 100 to 199. The permit or deny option determines whether the list allows or discards the packet; because there is no default, you must choose one.

The protocol entry defines the protocol to be filtered, for example, IP, TCP, UDP, or ICMP. Because IP headers transport TCP, UDP, and ICMP, it is important to specify the protocol or you could end up inadvertently filtering more than you want to. The following lines show the protocol keywords that could be included. Note that many routing protocols are included, meaning that we could block routing updates in or out on an interface. RIP is an option under the UDP protocols.

```
Lab-X(config)#access-list 101 permit ?
  <0-255>  An IP protocol number
  ahp      Authentication Header Protocol
  eigrp    Cisco's EIGRP routing protocol
  esp      Encapsulation Security Payload
  gre      Cisco's GRE tunneling
  icmp     Internet Control Message Protocol
  igmp     Internet Gateway Message Protocol
  igrp     Cisco's IGRP routing protocol
  ip       Any Internet Protocol
  ipinip   IP in IP tunneling
  nos      KA9Q NOS compatible IP over IP tunneling
  ospf     OSPF routing protocol
  pcp      Payload Compression Protocol
  pim      Protocol Independent Multicast
  tcp      Transmission Control Protocol
  udp      User Datagram Protocol
```

The source address functions the same as for standard access lists, including the keywords "host" and "any." The optional source port can be specified as a port number, such as 80, or as a mnemonic or acronym, such as HTTP. The choices for TCP, UDP, and ICMP are covered in the following sections.

The destination address feature functions the same as the source address, including the keywords "host" and "any." The optional destination port can be specified as a port number, such as 80, or as a mnemonic or acronym, such as HTTP. The choices for TCP, UDP, and ICMP are covered in the following sections.

The optional "options" parameter includes the log feature discussed earlier in the standard access lists section. TCP ACLs offer another option, "established," which restricts traffic to that originating in the protected network.

Processing Extended ACLs

In the processing of extended ACLs, every condition listed in each access-list statement must match for the statement to match and the permit or deny condition to be applied. As soon as one condition (segment) fails, the next line in the access list is compared. Figure 15-9 shows how each line of an extended access list is processed.

Many options are available for filtering with extended access lists; use the question mark (?) feature to look at all the possibilities. We cover the most common ones in the next sections.

Avoiding the Implicit "Deny Any"

A concept that you really need to understand about extended ACLs is that a simple statement, such as ACL 101 as follows, implicitly denies all other IP traffic, not just all other TCP traffic. A common mistake many people make is assuming that, since they

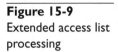

Figure 15-9
Extended access list
processing

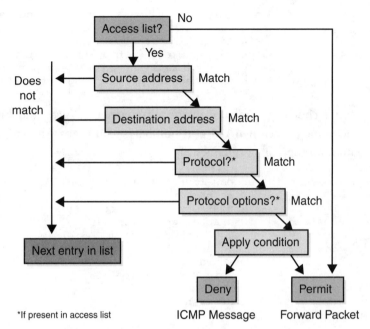

specified TCP only in the main statement(s), then they need to refer to TCP only in the final "permit any" statement, such as 102 as follows. The unplanned result would be that all ICMP and UDP traffic matching the address / protocol criteria would be blocked.

```
Lab-X(config)#Access-list 101 deny tcp any 192.168.1.25 eq ftp
Lab-X(config)#Access-list 101 permit IP any any
Lab-X(config)#Access-list 102 deny tcp 10.0.0.0 0.255.255.255
192.168.1.15 eq ftp
Lab-X(config)#Access-list 102 permit TCP any any
```

The second "any" is required because of the source and destination address requirement of extended ACLs.

TCP Syntax

The access list TCP protocol option supports both source and destination ports. You can access each by using either the port number or a mnemonic or acronym. Keyword relational operators such as those shown in the following code output precede these.

```
Lab-X(config)#access-list 101 deny tcp any ?
  A.B.C.D  Destination address
  any      Any destination host
```

```
eq         Match only packets on a given port number
gt         Match only packets with a greater port number
host       A single destination host
lt         Match only packets with a lower port number
neq        Match only packets not on a given port number
range      Match only packets in the range of port numbers
```

After choosing a relational operator (eq, gt, lt, neq, and range), you specify a mnemonic (or acronym) or port number, such as those shown in the following code output for the TCP port names:

```
Lab-X(config)#access-list 101 deny tcp any eq ?
  <0-65535>    Port number
  bgp          Border Gateway Protocol (179)
  chargen      Character generator (19)
  cmd          Remote commands (rcmd, 514)
  daytime      Daytime (13)
  discard      Discard (9)
  domain       Domain Name Service (53)
  echo         Echo (7)
  exec         Exec (rsh, 512)
  finger       Finger (79)
  ftp          File Transfer Protocol (21)
  ftp-data     FTP data connections (used infrequently, 20)
  gopher       Gopher (70)
  hostname     NIC hostname server (101)
  ident        Ident Protocol (113)
  irc          Internet Relay Chat (194)
  klogin       Kerberos login (543)
  kshell       Kerberos shell (544)
  login        Login (rlogin, 513)
  lpd          Printer service (515)
  nntp         Network News Transport Protocol (119)
  pim-auto-rp  PIM Auto-RP (496)
  pop2         Post Office Protocol v2 (109)
  pop3         Post Office Protocol v3 (110)
  smtp         Simple Mail Transport Protocol (25)
  sunrpc       Sun Remote Procedure Call (111)
  syslog       Syslog (514)
  tacacs       TAC Access Control System (49)
  talk         Talk (517)
  telnet       Telnet (23)
  time         Time (37)
  uucp         Unix-to-Unix Copy Program (540)
  whois        Nicname (43)
  www          World Wide Web (HTTP, 80)
```

Using the ? in place of the port number in the command allows you to verify the port number associated with a protocol name. Other port names can be found in RFC 1700. The numbers in parentheses in the preceding code are the port numbers.

Denying Telnet While Permitting All Other Traffic

The following example using Figure 15-10, denies Telnet traffic using the port number (eq 23) from the LAN on Router X while all traffic from any other source to any destination is permitted, as indicated by the keyword "any." The ACL is applied to interface E0, which kills off any Telnet requests before any router resources are expended.

```
Lab-X(config)#access-list 101 deny tcp 192.168.5.0 0.0.0.255 any
eq 23
Lab-X(config)#access-list 101 permit ip any any
Lab-X(config)#interface ethernet 0
Lab-X(config-if)#ip access-group 101 in
```

The first statement could have used the mnemonic "telnet" in place of 23 with exactly the same result. The one advantage to using the mnemonic is that it is more intuitive to anyone having to support the device. Clearly an admin should know the key port numbers by heart, but I also know that in cases of stress and fatigue, mistakes happen.

Limiting Access to Hypertext Transfer Protocol

Using Figure 15-10 as an example, let us assume we want to block network 192.168.5.0 from being able to surf the Web while we still want to allow other services such as FTP. We also do not want to interfere with network 195.168.1.0 users in any way. The code would be the following:

```
Lab-X(config)#access-list 106 deny tcp 195.168.5. 0 0.0.0.255 any
eq www
```

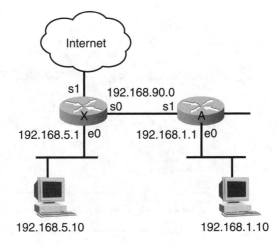

Figure 15-10
Blocking Telnet
from LAN

```
Lab-X(config)#access-list 106 permit ip any any
Lab-X(config)#interface ethernet 0
Lab-X(config-if)#  ip access-group 106 in
```

Using TCP's Established Option

The Established option is available only with TCP because it uses the connection-oriented attributes of the TCP. The Established option is true only when the TCP, ACK, or RST bits are set. Because the established option only allows an already established connection, the communication session must have been precipitated by an internal host, not an outsider. With the established option, it is possible that SYNchronize messages used to establish a new connection from the outside can then be explicitly or implicitly denied, thereby helping to reduce a common type of hacker attack that buries a host in SYN requests, preventing the host from handling normal business.

Consider the three-step "handshake" that TCP uses to establish a connection. Figure 15-11 demonstrates this process, which was detailed in Chapter 6.

Assume that the objective is to stop Host B from initiating a TCP connection with Host A while still permitting A to initiate connections with B. If you create a standard access list to block IP packets from B, it will in fact stop B from initiating a TCP session, but it will also block any TCP session initiated by A because the acknowledge (ACK SYNchronize) from B will never be allowed back.

Because the packet being blocked is coming from Host B, it isn't possible for the router to send an ICMP message to Host A. Host A will then appear to hang until it gets a TCP time-out.

Figure 15-11
Establishing a TCP
connection process

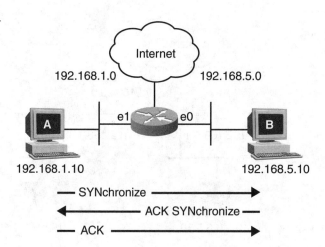

A possible solution using the Established option might look like this:

```
access-list 150 permit tcp host 192.168.5.10 host 192.168.1.10
established
access-list 150 deny tcp host 192.168.5.10 host 192.168.1.10
```

The "established" keyword permits sessions to be initiated in one direction but not the other—without it, TCP time-outs may occur. Since Cisco IOS version 10.3, the "established" option can be configured on statements with ports specified. Earlier versions allowed only the established option on TCP access list statements without specific port numbers.

NOTE: Source-port filtering, the process of filtering data on the source port of a packet, is not secure because a hacker could change a source port. A hacker could easily create a packet with a different source port that could pass through the filter.

UDP Syntax

The access list UDP option (RFC 768), like TCP, supports both source and destination ports. Using either the port number or a mnemonic (or acronym) can access each. Keyword relational operators such as those shown in the following code output precede these.

```
Lab-X(config)#access-list 101 permit udp any ?
  A.B.C.D   Destination address
  any       Any destination host
  eq        Match only packets on a given port number
  gt        Match only packets with a greater port number
  host      A single destination host
  lt        Match only packets with a lower port number
  neq       Match only packets not on a given port number
  range     Match only packets in the range of port numbers
```

After choosing a relational operator (eq, gt, lt, neq, and range), you specify a mnemonic (or acronym) or port number such as those shown in the following code output for the UDP port names.

```
Lab-X(config)#access-list 101 permit udp any eq ?
  <0-65535>   Port number
  biff        Biff (mail notification, comsat, 512)
  bootpc      Bootstrap Protocol (BOOTP) client (68)
  bootps      Bootstrap Protocol (BOOTP) server (67)
  discard     Discard (9)
  dnsix       DNSIX security protocol auditing (195)
```

```
domain          Domain Name Service (DNS, 53)
echo            Echo (7)
isakmp          Internet Security Association and Key Management
Protocol (500)
mobile-ip       Mobile IP registration (434)
nameserver      IEN116 name service (obsolete, 42)
netbios-dgm     NetBios datagram service (138)
netbios-ns      NetBios name service (137)
netbios-ss      NetBios session service (139)
ntp             Network Time Protocol (123)
pim-auto-rp     PIM Auto-RP (496)
rip             Routing Information Protocol (router, in.routed,
520)
snmp            Simple Network Management Protocol (161)
snmptrap        SNMP Traps (162)
sunrpc          Sun Remote Procedure Call (111)
syslog          System Logger (514)
tacacs          TAC Access Control System (49)
talk            Talk (517)
tftp            Trivial File Transfer Protocol (69)
time            Time (37)
who             Who service (rwho, 513)
xdmcp           X Display Manager Control Protocol (177)
```

Blocking RIP Routing Updates

One example of using ACLs with UDP packets would be to block RIP routing updates from passing out a particular interface using an ACL like the following:

```
Lab-X(config)#access-list 150 deny udp any any eq rip
Lab-X(config)#access-list 150 permit ip any any
Lab-X(config)#int e0
Lab-X(config-if)#access-group 150 out
```

ICMP Syntax

The access list ICMP option (RFC 792) allows filters on icmp-type, icmp-code, and icmp-message. After designating permit/deny and the source and destination addresses, include the ICMP code or type (numbers 0 to 255). Since Cisco IOS version 10.3, you can use symbolic names to make configuration and understanding complex lists easier. You no longer need to use cryptic message numbers such as 0 to filter the ping echo-reply.

The following code includes the symbolic names you can use:

```
Lab-X(config)#access-list 101 permit icmp any any ?
  <0-255>                     ICMP message type
  administratively-prohibited Administratively prohibited
```

alternate-address	Alternate address
conversion-error	Datagram conversion
dod-host-prohibited	Host prohibited
dod-net-prohibited	Net prohibited
echo	Echo (ping)
echo-reply	Echo reply
general-parameter-problem	Parameter problem
host-isolated	Host isolated
host-precedence-unreachable	Host unreachable for precedence
host-redirect	Host redirect
host-tos-redirect	Host redirect for TOS
host-tos-unreachable	Host unreachable for TOS
host-unknown	Host unknown
host-unreachable	Host unreachable
information-reply	Information replies
information-request	Information requests
log	Log matches against this entry
log-input	Log matches against this entry,
include input	
	interface
mask-reply	Mask replies
mask-request	Mask requests
mobile-redirect	Mobile host redirect
net-redirect	Network redirect
net-tos-redirect	Net redirect for TOS
net-tos-unreachable	Network unreachable for TOS
net-unreachable	Net unreachable
network-unknown	Network unknown
no-room-for-option	Parameter required but no room
option-missing	Parameter required but not present
packet-too-big	Fragmentation needed and DF set
parameter-problem	All parameter problems
port-unreachable	Port unreachable
precedence	Match packets with given precedence
value	
precedence-unreachable	Precedence cutoff
protocol-unreachable	Protocol unreachable
reassembly-timeout	Reassembly timeout
redirect	All redirects
router-advertisement	Router discovery advertisements
router-solicitation	Router discovery solicitations
source-quench	Source quenches
source-route-failed	Source route failed
time-exceeded	All time exceededs
timestamp-reply	Timestamp replies
timestamp-request	Timestamp requests
tos	Match packets with given TOS value
traceroute	Traceroute
ttl-exceeded	TTL exceeded
unreachable	All unreachables
<cr>	

Blocking Ping Requests and Replies

If you want to prevent users from pinging one or more of your router interfaces, you can use the ICMP echo and echo-reply ports on an extended access list. The following commands demonstrate this feature; you would undoubtedly want to add other features:

```
Lab-X(config)#access-list 101 deny icmp any any echo
Lab-X(config)#access-list 101 deny icmp any any echo-response
Lab-X(config)#access-list 101 permit ip any any
Lab-X(config)#int s1
Lab-X(config-if)#ip access-group 101 in
```

The result of pinging the interface from another router is as follows:

```
Lab-A>ping 192.168.5.1
Type escape sequence to abort.
Sending 5, 100-byte ICMP Echos to 192.168.5.1, timeout is 2 sec-
onds:
U.U.U
Success rate is 0 percent (0/5 )
```

The result of pinging the interface from a workstation at the command or DOS prompt is as follows:

```
ping 192.168.5.1
Pinging 192.168.5.1 with 32 bytes of data:
Reply from 192.168.5.1: Destination net unreachable.
Reply from 192.168.5.1: Destination net unreachable.
Reply from 192.168.5.1: Destination net unreachable.
Reply from 192.168.5.1: Destination net unreachable.
Ping statistics for 192.168.5.1:
    Packets: Sent = 4, Received = 4, Lost = 0 (0% loss),
Approximate round trip times in milli-seconds:
    Minimum = 0ms, Maximum =  0ms, Average =  0ms
```

RFC 1812 specifies that traffic denied by filtering (ACL) will display an ICMP "Administratively Prohibited" message to the sender, using the sender's address as destination and the filtering router as source address. This may not always be good security practice. It might be better not to send this message back to external users because of the implication that when there is filtering, there is something worth protecting or hacking, depending on your point of view. You might want to deny ICMP Administratively Prohibited messages outbound at the external interface. The host attempting to ping the site will be a "timed-out" message instead of destination unreachable. If you ping **www.Microsoft.com,** you should see this policy in effect.

Limiting Debug Output

When you are first learning to work with routers and packets, the various debug commands allow you to watch activities and processes in real time. While debug traffic can have devastating effects on production networks, it is a valuable tool when you can use it. The *debug ip packet* command, which outputs information about IP packets sent and received by the router, is particularly useful. An example might be when you try to ping a site but you are not getting any replies. It might be interesting to see if the pings are getting to the target. This command will tell show you if the requests are arriving. The problem is often too much traffic being displayed including routing updates, and so on.

If you telnet to the target router, you probably will not see the debug output. To display the debug results during a Telnet session, you will need to issue a *terminal monitor* command from the privilege mode.

The following lines record the steps to see if ping requests from host 192.168.1.10 are arriving at Router-B in our example lab:

```
Lab-X#telnet 192.168.30.1
Lab-B#
Lab-B#terminal monitor
Lab-B#debug ip packet
IP: s=192.168.91.2 (Serial0), d=255.255.255.255, len 132, rcvd 2
IP: s=192.168.20.1 (local), d=255.255.255.255 (Ethernet0), len
172, sending broad/multicast
IP: s=192.168.30.1 (local), d=255.255.255.255 (Loopback1), len
172, sending broad/multicast
IP: s=192.168.91.1 (local), d=255.255.255.255 (Serial0), len 72,
sending broad/multicast
IP: s=192.168.30.1 (Loopback1), d=255.255.255.255, len 172,
unroutable
IP: s=192.168.1.10 (Serial0), d=192.168.30.1, len 60, rcvd 4
IP: s=192.168.30.1 (local), d=192.168.1.10 (Serial0), len 60,
sending
IP: s=192.168.1.10 (Serial0), d=192.168.30.1, len 60, rcvd 4
IP: s=192.168.30.1 (local), d=192.168.1.10 (Serial0), len 60,
sending
IP: s=192.168.1.10 (Serial0), d=192.168.30.1, len 60, rcvd 4
IP: s=192.168.30.1 (local), d=192.168.1.10 (Serial0), len 60,
sending
IP: s=192.168.1.10 (Serial0), d=192.168.30.1, len 60, rcvd 4
IP: s=192.168.30.1 (local), d=192.168.1.10 (Serial0), len 60,
sending
Lab-B#u all                    (undebug all - to turn debug off)
```

We are seeing too much detail—both the send and receive pings plus any routing updates. What we are interested in is whether the ping requests are getting here reliably.

We use the following lines to demonstrate filtering to include only ICMP packets from the specific host. We could easily add a second line and add the replies if we chose to.

```
Lab-B(config)#access-list 171 permit icmp host 192.168.1.10 any
Lab-B(config)#^Z
Lab-B#debug ip packet ?                    (to see the options)
  <1-199>      Access list
  <1300-2699>  Access list (expanded range)
  detail       Print more debugging detail
  <cr>
Lab-B#debug ip packet 171        (to specify our access list)
Lab-B#
01:40:45: IP: s=192.168.1.10 (Serial0), d=192.168.30.1, len 60,
rcvd 4
01:40:46: IP: s=192.168.1.10 (Serial0), d=192.168.30.1, len 60,
rcvd 4
01:40:47: IP: s=192.168.1.10 (Serial0), d=192.168.30.1, len 60,
rcvd 4
01:40:48: IP: s=192.168.1.10 (Serial0), d=192.168.30.1, len 60,
rcvd 4
```

The filtered output shows us only the packets received from the specified host, 192.168.1.10.

Placing an Extended Access List

Because extended access lists can filter on more than the source address, placing them is much more flexible than standard ACLs. Placement can now be dictated by network strategy and performance objectives. Moving the placement closer to the source will minimize traffic congestion and maximize performance by reducing the use of router resources.

Consider these guidelines in determining placement of extended access lists:

• Keep denied traffic, or traffic to be inevitably denied, off the network backbone.

• Place access list as close to the source as possible to reduce the effect on such network resources as router CPU usage and network bandwidth. Why route a packet through an entire network (maybe over large geographical area) only to kill it and then send an ICMP message back?

Show Access-List

The *show access-list* command is used to display any access lists from all protocols. The following display shows a standard and extended access list. You will note that this command displays the number of filtered packets for each line.

```
show access-lists
xtended IP access list 145
```

```
    deny tcp any host 192.168.5.1 eq telnet (7 matches)
    deny tcp any host 192.168.1.100 eq telnet (4 matches)
    permit ip any any (317 matches)
show access-list
Standard IP access list 50
    deny   192.168.1.10 (2 matches)
    permit any (91 matches)
```

Show IP Access-List

The *show ip access-list* command displays only the IP access lists. Adding the optional access-list-number displays only the one list; without it, all IP access lists are displayed. Note that the display information is identical to the *show access-list* display.

```
show ip access-list 145
xtended IP access list 145
    deny tcp any host 192.168.5.1 eq telnet (7 matches)
    deny tcp any host 192.168.1.100 eq telnet (4 matches)
    permit ip any any (317 matches)
```

Clear Access-List Counters

The system automatically counts how many packets meet the condition for each line of an access list; the counters are displayed with the *show access-list* command. Use the *clear access-list counters* command in EXEC mode to clear the counters of an access list so you can start fresh after making changes. Adding the optional access-list-number will clear only the one counter; without it, all counters are cleared.

Named Access Control Lists

The Cisco IOS supports using named access lists instead of using the traditional number designations. This ability to name a list makes ACLs easier to recognize and can make them easier to debug. An access list named "AccessToDenver" conveys more to most people than the number 147. Another advantage of named ACLs is that it is possible to delete individual entries from a specific ACL rather than erase the entire list. This enables you to modify your ACLs without deleting and then reconfiguring them.

Here are two things to consider when you are implementing named ACLs:

- Names like numbers must be unique on each router.
- Named ACLs are not compatible with Cisco IOS releases earlier than Release 11.2.

Once you are comfortable working with them, named ACLs are actually easier to create. The first step is to create the ACL using the following syntax:

Router(config)#ip access-list {standard | extended} name

Example:

Lab-X(config)#ip access-list extended BlockInternet

You explicitly indicate the protocol and whether the list is a standard or an extended ACL. This puts you in ACL configuration mode, very much like "router rip" puts you in routing configuration mode. At this point, you create separate lines to specify one or more conditions permitted or denied to determine whether the packet is passed or dropped. The syntax is as follows:

Router(config {std- | ext-}nacl)# {deny | permit}(appropriate criteria)

Example:

Lab-X(config ext-nacl)#deny any any eq http

The following example shows both a standard and an extended ACL being created as well as the *show run* and *show access-list* output:

```
Lab-X#conf t
Lab-X(config)#ip access-list ?                    (to see the options)
  extended    Extended Access List
  log-update  Control access list log updates
  logging     Control access list logging
  standard    Standard Access List
Lab-X(config)#ip access-list standard ProtectLAN
Lab-X(config-std-nacl)#deny 192.168.20.0 0.0.0.255
Lab-X(config-std-nacl)#deny 192.168.30.0 0.0.0.255
Lab-X(config-std-nacl)#permit any
Lab-X(config-std-nacl)#exit
Lab-X(config)#ip access-list extended FilterOutside
Lab-X(config-ext-nacl)#permit tcp any 192.168.5.0 0.0.0.255 estab-
lished
Lab-X(config-ext-nacl)#deny icmp any 192.168.5.0 0.0.0.255
Lab-X(config-ext-nacl)#permit ip any any
Lab-X(config-ext-nacl)#^Z
Lab-X#show run
!                                               (output edited & omitted)
ip access-list standard ProtectLAN
  deny   192.168.20.0 0.0.0.255
  deny   192.168.30.0 0.0.0.255
  permit any
!
ip access-list extended FilterOutside
  permit tcp any 192.168.5.0 0.0.0.255 established
  deny   icmp any 192.168.5.0 0.0.0.255
```

```
    permit ip any any
!
Lab-X#show access-list
Standard IP access list ProtectLAN
    deny   192.168.20.0, wildcard bits 0.0.0.255
    deny   192.168.30.0, wildcard bits 0.0.0.255
    permit any
Extended IP access list FilterOutside
    permit tcp any 192.168.5.0 0.0.0.255 established
    deny icmp any 192.168.5.0 0.0.0.255
    permit ip any any
Lab-X#
```

The following example shows how easy it is to delete a row from an existing named ACL. We have decided we no longer want to block network 192.168.30.0's access to the LAN on Router X.

```
Lab-X#conf t
Lab-X(config)#ip access-list standard ProtectLAN
Lab-X(config-std-nacl)#nodeny192.168.30.0 0.0.0.255 (copy n paste)
Lab-X(config-std-nacl)#^Z
Lab-X#
Lab-X#show access-list
Standard IP access list ProtectLAN
    deny   192.168.20.0, wildcard bits 0.0.0.255
    permit any
Extended IP access list FilterOutside
    permit tcp any 192.168.5.0 0.0.0.255 established
    deny icmp any 192.168.5.0 0.0.0.255
    permit ip any any
Lab-X#
```

Although this named ACL provides some significant improvements in creating, understanding and editing ACLs, it is not universally supported throughout the IOS. Commands such as *debug ip packet* that we looked at earlier use numbered ACLs only. If you are going to use ACLs for interface filtering, named ACLs will always work. For other tasks, be sure to try a short sample before you invest a lot of time in building the ACLs.

EXAM TIP: Make sure that you understand the mechanics of named lists and that they may be more intuitive and get around the limited number of ACL numbers. This last point is less of an issue with the new numbers above 1100. I think you will find named lists easy to use and a blessing when you need to delete mistakes.

Commands Introduced in this Section

The following commands were introduced in this section:

- *show access-lists acl-num*   Shows all ACLs and a summary of how many times each criteria row has been used. If you add an ACL number (or name) to the end of the command, it will limit the output to that ACL.

- *show ip access-lists acl-num*   Same as *show access-list* except that it limits output to IP ACLs.

- *clear access-list counters acl-num*   Clears the summary counters for all ACLs or just the one specified.

- *show line vty*   Lists the access lists that are applied to the virtual terminals.

- *access-list*   ACL statements.

- *access-group*   Applies an ACL to a physical interface.

- *access-class*   Applies an ACL to a virtual (vty) interface.

IPX Access Lists

The IPX requirement for the CCNA exam is quite small, but as you read through this section, you'll see that IPX ACLs are not radically different from creating and using IP ACLs. The continuing longevity of the IPX installed base, particularly supporting specific applications, means that you are somewhat likely to need to understand how IPX works and how to filter it to preserve bandwidth in your non-IPX network segments.

We have 12 computer and networking classrooms at my satellite campus. We are connected to our main campus by a T1 line that is committed 50 percent to telephones and 50 percent to data and Internet connectivity. In monitoring traffic on that link, we routinely find that 60 percent of the traffic is IPX traffic even though we have no IPX servers or clients at our site. While we can filter that traffic out on our end to keep it out of our LANs, it is taking up bandwidth on the slowest link in our system. Concern about this is apparently dependent on which end of the link you are on.

There are four basic IPX access list types, each with its own number range. If you cannot remember the IPX access-list number ranges, the Help feature will give them to you. For the CCNA exam, you should know the first three, but don't be surprised if you don't get asked directly.

```
Lab-B(config)#access-list ?
  <800-899>    IPX standard access list
  <900-999>    IPX extended access list
```

```
<1000-1099>  IPX SAP access list
<1200-1299>  IPX summary address access list
```

Standard IPX Access Lists

Standard IPX access lists vary from their IP cousins in that we have both source and destination addresses to work with instead of just the source address. Figure 15-12 shows our example network for this discussion. If you configured any of the IPX networks from earlier chapters. they should match these numbers. The syntax for an IPX standard ACL is as follows

access-list number {permit | deny} source destination

Example:

```
Lab-B#config t
Lab-B(config)#access-list 850 deny 5 30
Lab-B(config)#access-list 850 permit -1 30
Lab-B(config)#int e1
Lab-B(config-if)#ipx access-group 850 out
```

Our first access-list command starts a list #850 that denies network 5 access to network 30. The second line allows traffic from any other network, thereby avoiding the implicit "deny any." The "-1" is IPX's equivalent to IP's "any."

The IPX access-group statement is virtually identical to the IP implementation. It applies the access list to the Ethernet1 interface (of Lab-B) for outgoing traffic—traffic into network 30.

Figure 15-12
Example IPX
network

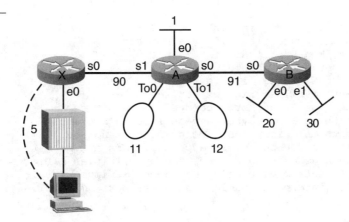

Show Access-List and Show IPX Access-List

The *show access-list* command displays any existing ACLs mixing both IP and IPX. The *show ipx access-list* command displays only the IPX ACLs. As with IP, the ACL number can be added to the end of the command to further refine the output.

```
Lab-B#show access-list
Extended IP access list 171access-list 171
    permit icmp host 192.168.1.10 any
Standard IPX access list 850
    deny 5 30
    permit -1 30
```

Show IPX Interface

Like its IP counterpart, the *show IPX interface* command lists any ACLs that have been applied. You will notice that in the IPX output, the Cisco IOS programmers tend to use the word *filter* instead of *access list,* although that is not absolutely consistent. I'm including the entire output so that you can see the number of filtering possibilities in IPX.

```
Lab-B#show ipx interface e1
Ethernet1 is up, line protocol is up
  IPX address is 30.0050.7338.ba14, NOVELL-ETHER [up]
  Delay of this IPX network, in ticks is 1 throughput 0 link delay
0
  IPXWAN processing not enabled on this interface.
  IPX SAP update interval is 1 minute(s)
  IPX type 20 propagation packet forwarding is disabled
  Incoming access list is not set
  Outgoing access list is 850
  IPX helper access list is not set
  SAP GNS processing enabled, delay 0 ms, output filter list is
not set
  SAP Input filter list is 1050
  SAP Output filter list is not set
  SAP Router filter list is not set
  Input filter list is not set
  Output filter list is not set
  Router filter list is not set
  Netbios Input host access list is not set
  Netbios Input bytes access list is not set
  Netbios Output host access list is not set
  Netbios Output bytes access list is not set
  Updates each 60 seconds, aging multiples RIP: 3 SAP: 3
  SAP interpacket delay is 55 ms, maximum size is 480 bytes
  RIP interpacket delay is 55 ms, maximum size is 432 bytes
```

Extended IPX Access Lists

Extended IPX access lists are similar to their IP cousins in that they have both source and destination addresses, and you can specify a protocol and a socket (IP ports). Syntax:

> access-list number {permit | deny} source socket destination socket

In the following example, we use a series of Help screens (?) to create an extended IPX ACL to block other networks from using the Cisco IPX ping in network 30. Note the structural similarities to IP with any unfamiliarity limited to the protocol and service names.

```
Lab-B(config)#access-list 950 ?           (choose permit or deny)
   deny     Specify packets to reject
   permit   Specify packets to permit

Lab-B(config)#access-list 950 deny ?    (choose the protocol - RIP)
   <0-255>   Protocol type number (DECIMAL)
   any       Any IPX protocol type
   ncp       NetWare Core Protocol
   netbios   IPX NetBIOS
   rip       IPX Routing Information Protocol
   sap       Service Advertising Protocol
   spx       Sequenced Packet Exchange

Lab-B(config)#access-list 950 deny rip ?   (specifying the source)
   <0-FFFFFFFF>  Source net
   N.H.H.H       Source net.host address
   any           Any IPX net             (note the keyword any)
   log           Log matches against this entry
   <cr>

Lab-B(config)#access-list 950 deny rip any ?   (source socket)
   <0-FFFFFFFF>  Source Socket HEXIDECIMAL
   all           All sockets
   cping         Cisco ipx ping
   diagnostic    Diagnostic packet
   eigrp         IPX Enhanced Interior Gateway Routing Protocol
   log           Log matches against this entry
   ncp           NetWare Core Protocol
   netbios       IPX NetBIOS
   nlsp          NetWare Link State Protocol
   nping         Standard IPX ping
   rip           IPX Routing Information Protocol
   sap           Service Advertising Protocol
   <cr>
```

```
Lab-B(config)#access-list 950 deny rip any cping ? (select desti-
nation)
  <0-FFFFFFFF>  Destination net
  N.H.H.H       Destination net.host address
  any           Any IPX net
  log           Log matches against this entry
  <cr>

Lab-B(config)#access-list 950 deny rip any cping any
Lab-B(config)#access-list 950 permit any
Lab-B(config)#int e1
Lab-B(config-if)#ipx access-group 950 out
```

Our first access-list command creates a list #950 that denies RIP protocol from any network to cping (Cisco IPX ping command) any other network. The second line allows any other IPX traffic, thereby avoiding the implicit "deny any." Since our ACL was applied to the interface for network 30, it will block Cisco ping traffic into the LAN.

If we run a *show access-list* command, we get the following output. The IOS substituted the number 2 for the cping you chose from the list. If you look back at the example, you will see that cping was the second option on the list. For those not familiar with IPX, this use of codes makes interpreting the configuration and some command results a little more complicated.

```
Lab-B#ipx access-list
IPX access list 950
    deny rip any 2 any
```

Configuring IPX SAP filters

IPX access lists allow us to block access to a network much the same as IP access lists do. In IPX, if we can block a node or a network from receiving SAP packets for a particular service (or all services), we can effectively prevent them from using that service; if you don't know about a service, you can't ask for it. In this section, we will look at filtering SAP traffic for printing services on a server in network 30 from being used by any other network while allowing any other SAP traffic through. The syntax for a SAP filter is as follows:

access-list number {permit | deny} source service-type

We need to use a number between 1000 and 1099 for SAP filters.

```
Lab-B#config t
Lab-B(config)#access-list 1050 deny 30.0000.0000.0001 7
Lab-B(config)#access-list 1050 permit 30.0000.0000.0001 0
Lab-B(config)#int e1
Lab-B(config-if)#ipx input-sap-filter 1050
```

The first *access-list* command starts a list #1050 that denies server 30.0000.0000.0001 (MAC portion is made up because we have no server) from advertising its print service. The second line allows service from that server to be advertised, thereby avoiding the implicit "deny any." The last two lines apply the ACL to the Ethernet1 port (of Lab-B) for accepting print server SAPs from our server.

Four common IPX service codes that we could have used are these:

0—all services

3—print queue

4—file server

7—print server

If we use the *show run* and *show access-list* commands, a partial result would look like this:

```
interface Ethernet1
 ip address 192.168.30.1 255.255.255.0
 ipx input-sap-filter 1050
 ipx network 30
!
access-list 1050 deny 30.0000.0000.0001 7
access-list 1050 permit 30.0000.0000.0001 0
!
Lab-B#show access-list
IPX SAP access list 1050
    deny 30.0000.0000.0001 7
    permit 30.0000.0000.0001 0
```

Commands Introduced in this Section

The following commands were introduced in this section:

- *show access-lists acl-num*   Shows all ACLs and a summary of how many times each criteria row has been used. If you add an ACL number (or name) to the end of the command, it will limit the output to that ACL.

- *show ipx access-lists acl-num*   Same as *show access-list* except that it limits output to IPX ACLs.

ACLs and Firewall Routers

Border routers, those on the edge of a network, are often charged with the responsibility of providing network security from potential attacks from outside the network.

Figure 15-13 shows the simplest situation where the border router becomes the clear demarcation between the network and the rest of the world. Typically, intruders come from the global Internet and the thousands of networks connected to it.

The situation depicted in the picture is probably typical only of the smallest of companies and the many home users that have connected to DSL and cable networks. With only a modem connection to these outside systems, there is no security between the user's network and the outside world. Much like leaving your doors unlocked, you are trusting that no problems will find you. Even the simplest of routers between the internal network and the outside world provides some level of security. Typically, network address translation (NAT) is implemented to conceal the internal IP addresses. Some systems offer varying degrees of filtering for additional security. These measures are considerably better than nothing at all but generally present very little challenge to a serious hacker.

The preceding model was the norm for business until the expansion of e-commerce and the marketing of products and services over the Internet. If Web servers, FTP servers, and so on were placed on the internal network, security was seriously compromised. The problem became how to allow the public to access the servers without giving them access to the local network. Figure 15-14 shows a single router implementation that,

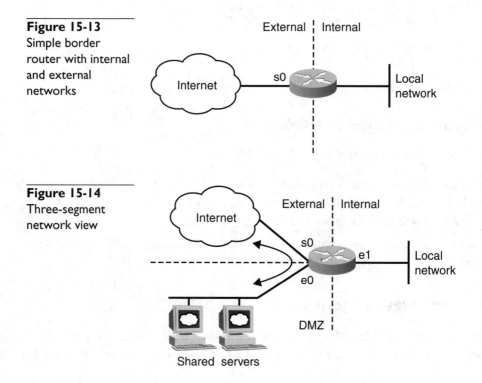

Figure 15-13
Simple border router with internal and external networks

Figure 15-14
Three-segment network view

when combined with NAT and ACLs, presents about the same level of security as the earlier model.

The border router is split three ways. The Internal network hasn't changed much but could obviously include quite a large structure of routers and switches or could be as simple as a single Ethernet LAN. The external network is still the Internet. The DMZ (demilitarized zone) is basically outside the internal network but still needs some levels of security from attacks from the outside. The DMZ needs to have relatively free availability to and from the outside world but still be accessible with increased security by internal users.

This single-router design would probably still use NAT and would definitely use some form of access control lists. The servers in the DMZ would include any that need to be accessed by the outside world. A special type of device called a *content server* could reside out there to cache information pulled down from outside resources to be more quickly available to internal users. As a Web site or other resource is accessed, the content is cached and future requests are filled from the cache, if only until the latest data can be downloaded.

Proxy servers, such as Microsoft's Proxy Server, are designed to be this router with the caching stored on board. The MS Proxy implementation uses menu-driven techniques for building filters. My intent is not to recommend this over other implementations but to point it out so that you know that it exists and where it fits in the grand scheme of things.

Figure 15-15 shows a third type of firewall implementation that uses two or more routers to provide the security. The border router, A, is ultimately responsible for securing the LAN(s) and could run NAT and would typically use ACLs. Of particular importance would be ACLs to protect the LAN from attack from hackers that have compromised the shared servers in the DMZ. The firewall router, F, is responsible for protecting both the shared servers and the internal networks from attack from outside.

Figure 15-15
Two-router firewall implementation

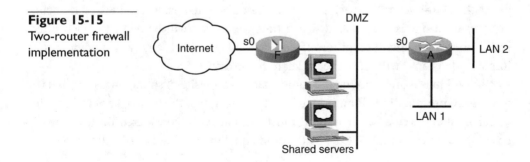

In an optimal solution, this would be a specialty device like Cisco's PIX box, which combines hardware and software to secure the connection. Whether a specialty device or a router with the Firewall feature set, ACLs will be a part of the solution.

Other implementations of firewalls include specialty servers—gateways that exist between the two routers. These servers process all packets coming from or going to the internal network. The firewall router makes sure that only the types of packets allowed inside the internal network are forwarded to the Gateway server(s).

Depending on the size and the complexity of the DMZ implementation, there could be other devices out there providing load balancing and route redundancy. Faced with the complexity, cost, and security concerns of a large implementation, many companies opt to use Web host sites that combine tremendous bandwidth with security, and support services.

Summary

This chapter covered two types of *access control lists* (ACLs) for both IP and IPX. Standard lists use a less sophisticated set of criteria, such as source addresses, to determine whether to permit or deny packets to be used by a router process or interface. Extended lists allow filtering on multiple criteria, including source and destination addresses as well as protocol and protocol features used.

ACLs can be used to filter data traffic on interfaces, for routing updates, to implement security procedures, and with other IOS features, such as filtering debug commands.

The most common protocols, IP and IPX, can have up to two ACLs applied to an interface: one inbound ACL and one outbound ACL to control traffic flow.

ACLs are a series of criteria statements that must be created sequentially and that are processed sequentially without any mechanism to skip or change the order of statements. Numbered ACLs cannot be edited; attempts to delete a single statement will delete the entire access list. Each packet processed is tested against the ACL statements in order until one is matched, at which time the packet will be denied or permitted based on the statement definition. If a packet fails to match any ACL statement, the implicit "deny any" will cause the packet to be discarded.

Wildcard masks are conceptually somewhat the opposite of subnet masks in that 0's mean the corresponding bit must match and 1's mean that the bit need not match. The actual masking occurs in binary and must ultimately be considered on a bit-by-bit basis. The subnet mask 255.255.255.0 would equal the wildcard mask 0.0.0.255.

ACLs can make up a portion of the network's security. Firewall IOS feature-sets in border routers and specialty firewall devices like Cisco's PIX devices typically use some type of ACL as part of the security defense barrier between the internal network and an external network (Internet).

Practice Questions

Take a few moments and check your grasp of the concepts covered in this chapter. The answers immediately follow the questions.

Questions

1. What is the range of valid IP standard access list numbers?
   a. 1–100
   b. 101–199
   c. 1–299
   d. 1–99
   e. 100–199

2. What is the range of valid IP extended access list numbers?
   a. 1–100
   b. 101–199
   c. 1–299
   d. 1–99
   e. 100–199

3. The entries 255.255.255.0 are an example of:
   a. Subnet mask and a wildcard mask
   b. Subnet mask
   c. Wildcard mask
   d. Class E IP address

4. The entries 0.0.0.255 are an example of:
   a. Subnet mask and a wildcard mask
   b. Subnet mask
   c. Wildcard mask
   d. Class E IP address

5. True or false? Subnet masks and wildcard masks are basically opposites. The first identifies the network portion of an IP address while the latter identifies the hosts.

   a. True

   b. False

6. Look over the following statements. What do they do?

   int e0

    ip access-group 50 out

   !

   access-list 50 deny 192.168.1.0 0.0.0.255

   access-list 50 permit any

   !

   a. Block all outbound traffic to network 192.168.1.0

   b. Block all outbound traffic to host 192.168.1.10

   c. Block all outbound traffic from network 192.168.1.0

   d. Block all outbound traffic from host 192.168.1.10

7. Look over the following statements. What do they do?

   Int e0

    ip access-group 50 out

   !

   access-list 50 deny 192.168.1.0 0.0.0.255

   access-list 50 deny 192.168.2.0 0.0.0.255

   access-list 50 deny 192.168.3.0 0.0.0.255

   access-list 50 permit any

   !

   a. Deny traffic from three subnets through the router

   b. Deny traffic from three networks outbound on Ethernet 0 only

   c. Block all traffic outbound on the Ethernet 0 interface

   d. Block all traffic through the Ethernet 0 interface

8. Look over the following statements. What do they do?

   int s0

    ip access-group 50 out

   !

   access-list 50 deny 192.168.1.0 0.0.0.255

   !

   a. Block all traffic to network 192.168.1.10

   b. Block all traffic to host 192.168.1.10

   c. Block all traffic from network 192.168.1.10

   d. Block all traffic from host 192.168.1.10

   e. Block all outbound traffic on the first serial interface

   f. Block all inbound traffic on the first serial interface

9. What are the two steps in implementing an access list?

   a. Create the filter using one or more access list statements

   b. Create the filter using one or more access-list statements

   c. Apply the list using the *ip access group* command while configuring the interface

   d. Apply the list using the *ip access-group* command while configuring the interface

   e. Apply the list using the *ip access-group* command in global configuration mode

10. With numbered access lists, in which configuration mode are the list statements created?

   a. User mode

   b. Privilege (Enable) mode

   c. Global configuration mode

   d. Interface configuration

11. With numbered access lists, is the order in which the statements are created important?

   a. Yes, put the most important ones first.

   b. Yes, put the least important ones first.

   c. Yes, create them in the order you want them processed.

   d. No, the program will sort them as needed.

   e. No, you can move them around later.

   f. No, the IOS processes them all anyway.

12. Generally speaking, a standard access list should be applied to an interface considering which of the following situations?

   a. Close to the destination

   b. Close to the source

   c. On any interface you want

   d. Close to both the source and destination

13. True or false? An access list must always contain at least one deny statement.

   a. True

   b. False

14. True or false? An access list must always contain at least one permit statement.
    a. True
    b. False

15. Look over the following statements. What is wrong?
    int s0
     ip access-group 50 out
     ip access-group 60 out
     !
    access-list 50 deny 192.168.1.0 0.0.0.255
    access-list 50 permit any
    !
    a. There are no access list statements for access list 60.
    b. It is not possible to assign more than one access list to an interface in the same direction for the same protocol.
    c. The access list 60 having no statements will block all outbound traffic.
    d. The access list 60 having no statements will allow all outbound traffic.

16. Look over the following statements. What is wrong?
    int s0
     ip access-group 50 out
     ip access-group 60 in
     !
    access-list 50 deny 192.168.1.0 0.0.0.255
    access-list 50 permit any
    access-list 60 deny 192.168.1.0 0.0.0.255
    access-list 60 deny 192.168.2.0 0.0.0.255
    access-list 60 deny 192.168.3.0 0.0.0.255
    !
    a. Nothing. The lists will work fine.
    b. It is not possible to assign more than one access lists to an interface for the same protocol.
    c. The access list 60 will block all inbound traffic.
    d. The access list 60 will allow all inbound traffic.

17. Look over the following statements. What two things do they do?

int e0

 ip access-group 50 out

!

access-list 50 deny 192.168.1.16 0.0.0.15

access-list 50 permit any

!

   a. Deny outbound traffic from the 192.168.1.0 network

   b. Deny outbound traffic from the hosts 192.168.1.16 through 192.168.1.31

   c. Block all traffic outbound on the Ethernet 0 interface

   d. Block all traffic through the Ethernet 0 interface

   e. Block outbound traffic from the second subnet of the 192.168.1.0 with subnet mask 255.255.255.240

18. The keyword "any" is the equivalent of which of the following access list items?

   a. 255.255.255.255 255.255.255.255

   b. 255.255.255.255 0.0.0.0

   c. 0.0.0.0 255.255.255.255

   d. 0.0.0.0 0.0.0.0

19. Which of the following is a literal interpretation of the keyword "host"?

   a. 192.168.112.19 0.0.0.0

   b. 192.168.112.19 255.255.255.0

   c. 192.168.112.19 255.255.255.255

   d. 192.168.112.0 0.0.0.0

   e. 0.0.0.0 0.0.0.0

20. Look over the following statements. What do they do?

int s0

 ip access-group 50 out

!

access-list 50 deny 192.168.10.0 0.0.0.0

access-list 50 permit any

!

   a. Deny outbound traffic from the 192.168.10.0 network

   b. Deny outbound traffic from the host 192.168.10.0

   c. Permit all outbound traffic on the serial 0 interface

   d. Block all outbound traffic through the serial 0 interface

21. Look over the following statements. What do they do?

    int s0

     ip access-group 50 out

     !

    access-list 50 deny host 192.168.10.77

    access-list 50 deny host 192.168.10.85

    access-list 50 deny host 192.168.10.121

    access-list 50 permit any

     !

    a. Deny outbound traffic from three host addresses
    b. Deny outbound traffic from the network 192.168.10.0
    c. Permit all outbound traffic on the serial 0 interface
    d. Block all outbound traffic through the serial 0 interface

22. Look over the following statements. What do they do?

    int s0

     ip access-group 50 out

     !

    access-list 50 permit 192.168.10.0 0.0.0.255

    access-list 50 deny host 192.168.10.77

    access-list 50 deny host 192.168.10.85

    access-list 50 deny host 192.168.10.121

    access-list 50 permit any

     !

    a. Deny outbound traffic from three host addresses
    b. Deny outbound traffic from the network 192.168.10.0
    c. Permit all outbound traffic on the serial 0 interface
    d. Block all outbound traffic through the serial 0 interface

23. You have four routers A, B, C, and D connected sequentially A to B to C to D using the serial interfaces. Each has one Ethernet interface with a single Class C network attached. You want to use a standard access list to block the hosts on D's Ethernet interface from accessing the hosts on the Ethernet interface on B. Which router do you create the access list on?

    a. A
    b. B
    c. C
    d. D
    e. B and D

24. Based on question 23, which interface do you apply the access-group to?

   a. Serial 0

   b. Serial 1

   c. Ethernet 0

   d. Ethernet 1

   e. Token Ring 0

25. The only criterion considered in standard access lists is which?

   a. Destination address(es)

   b. Source address(es)

   c. Source host address

   d. Source network address

   e. Destination network address

26. True or false? Look over the following statements. They will block the outbound traffic from the 192.168.10.0 network.

int s0

 ip access-group 101 out

!

access-list 101 deny 192.168.10.0 0.0.0.255

access-list 101 permit any

!

   a. True

   b. False

27. You have four routers A, B, C, and D connected sequentially A to B to C to D using the serial interfaces. Each has one Ethernet interface with a single Class C network attached. You want to use a standard access list to block the all hosts on D's Ethernet interface from accessing a single server on the Ethernet interface of B while allowing access to other hosts on that LAN. Which router do you create the access list on?

   a. A

   b. B

   c. C

   d. D

   e. None. It won't work.

28. Look over the following statements. What three things do they do?

int s0

 ip access-group 150 out

 !

access-list 150 deny tcp 192.168.10.0 0.0.0.255 any eq http

access-list 150 deny tcp 192.168.10.0 0.0.0.255 any eq ftp

access-list 150 permit tcp any any

 !

   a. Deny outbound Web traffic from the 192.168.10.0 network to any destination

   b. Deny all udp and icmp outbound traffic on serial 0

   c. Permit all outbound traffic on the serial 0 interface

   d. Block all outbound traffic through the serial 0 interface

   e. Deny outbound FTP traffic from the 192.168.10.0 network to any destination

29. Look over the following statements. What three things do they do?

int s0

 ip access-group 150 in

 !

access-list 150 deny tcp any host 192.168.10.125 eq http

access-list 150 deny tcp any host 192.168.10.125 eq ftp

access-list 150 permit ip any any

 !

   a. Deny inbound Web traffic from the 192.168.10.0 network to any destination

   b. Deny all UDP and ICMP outbound traffic on serial 0

   c. Deny inbound Web traffic from any host to server 192.168.10.125

   d. Deny inbound FTP traffic from any host to server 192.168.10.125

   e. Deny inbound FTP traffic from the 192.168.10.0 network to any destination

   f. Permit any other inbound traffic

30. Generally speaking, an extended access list should be applied to an interface considering which of the following situations?

   a. Close to the destination

   b. Close to the source

   c. On any interface you want

   d. Close to both the source and destination

31. You have four routers A, B, C, and D connected sequentially A to B to C to D using the serial interfaces. Each has one Ethernet interface with a single Class C network attached. You want to use an extended access list to block all the hosts on D's Ethernet interface from accessing a single server on the Ethernet interface of B while allowing access to other hosts. Which router do you create the access list on?

a. A

b. B

c. C

d. D

e. None. It won't work.

32. Based on question 31, which interface do you apply the access-group to?

a. Serial 0

b. Serial 1

c. Ethernet 0

d. Ethernet 1

e. Token Ring 0

33. You have four routers A, B, C, and D connected sequentially A to B to C to D using the serial interfaces. Each has one Ethernet interface with a single Class C network attached. You want to use an extended access list to block the hosts on A's Ethernet interface from accessing any Web servers on any of the other routers. Which router do you create the access list on?

a. A

b. B

c. C

d. D

e. A and B

34. Assuming the information from the last question, which interface do you apply the access-group to?

a. Serial 0

b. Serial 1

c. Ethernet 0

d. Ethernet 1

e. Token Ring 0

35. Look over the following statements. What three things do they do?

    int s0

     ip access-group 150 out

     !

    access-list 150 deny icmp any any

    access-list 150 permit ip any any

     !

    a. Deny all outbound ICMP traffic to any destination
    b. Permit all outbound TCP traffic to any destination
    c. Deny inbound ICMP traffic from any host
    d. Permit all outbound UDP traffic to any destination
    e. Permit any other inbound traffic

36. True or false? Named access lists can be either standard or extended.

    a. True
    b. False

37. True or false? Named access lists can allow more standard or extended access lists than the numbered lists.

    a. True
    b. False

38. Look over the following statements. What do they do?

    int e0

     ip access-group 50 out

     !

    access-list 50 deny 192.168.1.0 0.0.0.127

    access-list 50 permit any

     !

    a. Deny traffic from the first subnet of 192.168.1.0 /25 through the router
    b. Deny traffic from the first subnet of 192.168.1.0 /25 outbound on Ethernet 0 only
    c. Block all traffic outbound on the Ethernet 0 interface
    d. Block all traffic through the Ethernet 0 interface

39. Look over the following statements. What do they do?

    int e0

     ip access-group 50 out

     !

access-list 50 deny 192.168.1.0 0.0.0.31
access-list 50 deny 192.168.1.96 0.0.0.31
access-list 50 deny 192.168.1.160 0.0.0.31
access-list 50 permit any
!

   a. Deny traffic from three subnets through the router

   b. Block all traffic through the Ethernet 0 interface

   c. Block all traffic outbound on the Ethernet 0 interface

   d. Deny traffic from three subnets outbound on Ethernet 0 only

40. Look over the following statements. What do they do?

int e0
 ip access-group 50 out
!
access-list 50 deny 192.168.1.30 0.0.0.1
access-list 50 deny 192.168.1.32 0.0.0.8
access-list 50 permit any
!

   a. Deny e0 outbound traffic for hosts 192.168.1.30 to 192.168.1.40

   b. Block all traffic outbound on the Ethernet 0 interface

   c. Deny traffic from two subnets outbound on Ethernet 0 only

   d. Block all traffic through the Ethernet 0 interface

41. Look over the following statements. What do they do?

int e0
 ip access-group 50 out
!
access-list 50 deny 192.168.1.40 0.0.0.7
access-list 50 deny 192.168.1.96 0.0.0.15
access-list 50 deny 192.168.3.168 0.0.0.31
access-list 50 permit any
!

   a. Deny traffic from three subnets through the router

   b. Deny traffic from three networks outbound on Ethernet 0 only

   c. Deny e0 outbound traffic for hosts 192.168.1.40 to 192.168.1.48, 192.168.1.96 to 192.168.1.111, and 192.168.1.168 to 192.168.1.199

   d. Block all traffic through the Ethernet 0 interface

Answers

1. **d.** 1–99

2. **e.** 100–199

3. **b.** Subnet mask

4. **c.** Wildcard mask

5. **a.** True

6. **c.** Block all outbound traffic from network 192.168.1.0

7. **b.** Deny traffic from three networks outbound on Ethernet 0 only

8. **e.** Block all outbound traffic on the first serial interface

9. **b.** and **d.** Create the filter using one or more access-list statements / Apply the list using the *ip access-group command* while configuring the interface

10. **c.** Global configuration mode

11. **c.** Yes, create them in the order you want them processed.

12. **a.** Close to the destination

13. **b.** False. They generally must have one permit statement.

14. **a.** True

15. **b.** It is not possible to assign more than one access list to an interface in the same direction for the same protocol.

16. **c.** The access list 60 will block all inbound traffic. No permit statement.

17. **b.** and **e.** Deny outbound traffic from the hosts 192.168.1.16 through 192.168.1.31 and block outbound traffic from the second subnet of the 192.168.1.0 with subnet mask 255.255.255.240. The two identify the same hosts.

18. **c.** 0.0.0.0 255.255.255.255

19. **a.** 192.168.112.19 0.0.0.0

20. **c.** Permit all outbound traffic on the serial 0 interface. The 192.168.10.0 0.0.0.0 cannot be a host; it is a network address.

21. a. Deny outbound traffic from three host addresses.

22. c. Permit all outbound traffic on the serial 0 interface. The first access-list statement permits the three hosts before the next three statements are processed.

23. b. B; since as a standard ACL it has to be applied close to the destination, it must be created on B.

24. c. Ethernet 0; since as a standard ACL, it has to be applied close to the destination, it must be applied to the interface. Since there is only one it is Ethernet 0.

25. b. Source address(es)

26. b. False. The list number is for an extended list.

27. e. None. It won't work. Standard access lists filter only on the source address(es) so they cannot allow traffic to some hosts but block others.

28. a., b., and e. Deny outbound Web traffic from the 192.168.10.0 network to any destination. / Deny all UDP and ICMP outbound traffic on serial 0 (the permit any statement permits only TCP packets) / Deny outbound FTP traffic from the 192.168.10.0 network to any destination.

29. c., d., and f. Deny inbound Web traffic from the 192.168.10.0 network to any destination. / Deny inbound FTP traffic from any host to server 192.168.10.125. / Permit any other inbound traffic.

30. b. Close to the source—to save router resources if you are going to kill the packet.

31. d. D; since as an extended ACL, it can be applied close to the source to save router resources, it must be created on D.

32. c. Ethernet 0; to save router resources if you are going to kill the packet.

33. a. A; since as an extended ACL it can be applied close to the source to save router resources, it must be created on D.

34. c. Ethernet 0; to save router resources if you are going to kill the packet.

35. a., b., and d. Deny all outbound ICMP traffic to any destination. / Permit all outbound TCP traffic to any destination / Permit all outbound UDP traffic to any destination.

36. a. True. Named access lists can be either standard or extended.

37. **a.** True. Basically, you can have an unlimited number.

38. **b.** Deny traffic from the first subnet of 192.168.1.0/25 outbound on Ethernet 0 only; *tip*: Convert to binary to see why this works.

39. **d.** Deny traffic from three subnets outbound on Ethernet 0 only; *tip*: Convert to binary to see why this works.

40. **a.** Deny e0 outbound traffic for hosts 192.168.1.30 to 192.168.1.40; *tip*: Convert to binary to see why this works.

41. **c.** Deny e0 outbound traffic for hosts 192.168.1.40 to 192.168.1.48, 192.168.1.96 to 192.168.1.111, and 192.168.1.168 to 192.168.1.199; *tip*: Convert to binary to see why this works.

CHAPTER 16

LAN Switching

This chapter will:

- **Identify common performance issues with legacy Ethernet environments**

- **Compare half-duplex and full-duplex transmission**

- **Explore LAN switching operation**

- **Compare Layer 2 and Layer 3 switching**

- **Discuss the benefits of microsegmentation**

- **Characterize the various switching methods**

- **Compare symmetric and asymmetric switching**

- **Describe memory buffering in switches**

- **Explain how VLANs work**

- **Explore the benefits of VLANs**

- **Compare common VLAN implementation methods**

- **Address STP fundamentals**

The explosive growth currently being experienced by networks all over the e-world has led to an unprecedented demand for networking technologies, products, and services that are capable of solving specific networking needs and problems. One such problem has been the need for networks to cost-effectively scale their LAN's bandwidth capacity to support a growing number of users and new bandwidth-hungry applications such as high-speed Web access, IP telephony, IP multicasting, and high-capacity file transfers. It has been in response to these types of needs that *LAN switching* has subsequently emerged as one of the most resourceful networking technologies capable of delivering growing numbers of users the bandwidth they require to support their increasingly bandwidth-intensive applications while at the same time minimizing such factors as cost, delay, and unreliable service.

This chapter presents the fundamentals behind LAN switching and discusses how LAN switching can be used to cost-effectively scale legacy Ethernet architectures. Technologies such as full-duplexing, microsegmentation, Fast/Gigabit Ethernet, and *virtual local area networks* (VLANs) are introduced. This chapter also presents a short discussion of the Spanning Tree Protocol (STP).

Legacy Ethernet

One of the more common LAN architectures currently in use is Ethernet, which is a desktop technology that allows interconnected devices such as computers, printers, and servers to communicate with each other over a shared medium (see Figure 16-1). These devices are typically attached to a Layer 1 hub via *unshielded twisted-pair* (UTP) cable. Recall that hubs are unintelligent devices that simply receive a signal and broadcast it out all interfaces. This means that devices connected to the same hub see each other's transmissions every time a transmission occurs.

To prevent two devices from transmitting at the same time on a shared medium, Ethernet 802.3 has defined the Carrier Sense Multiple Access/Collision Detection (CSMA/CD) access method. With CSMA/CD, a device that wishes to transmit must first detect whether any other devices have just transmitted. When the medium is clear, the device can transmit.

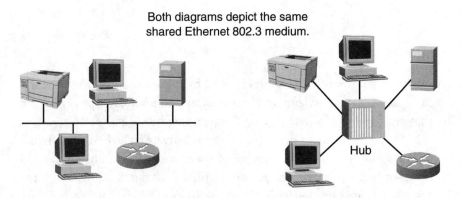

Both diagrams depict the same shared Ethernet 802.3 medium.

Hub

Figure 16-1 Shared Ethernet medium

Often, however, two devices will both detect that the medium is clear and then transmit (see Figure 16-2). This event results in a *collision* and requires that all devices on the medium hold off from transmitting for a certain interval of time. When transmissions are allowed to begin again, the two devices involved in the collision have to retransmit their collided packets. This has the subsequent effect of consuming bandwidth and adding additional *latency,* which is the amount of time it takes to transmit a frame from source to destination.

The extent to which collisions are propagated is known as the *collision domain.* All devices that are attached to the same shared medium, as in Figure 16-2, are said to be in the same collision domain.

Collisions have the potential of causing significant performance problems in shared Ethernet environments. For one, this situation can be a problem for hosts using applications that are sensitive to delay. Because collisions add latency to the transmission, delay-sensitive traffic that gets involved in too many collisions may cause errors to occur on the receiving end. In addition, collisions can be a problem when available bandwidth is scarce. Because collisions result in retransmissions, extra bandwidth is consumed, potentially leading to increased congestion and dropped packets. And lastly, if a host experiences too many collisions, it will just stop transmitting the packet altogether.

Such problems with latency, bandwidth, and congestion are magnified substantially when more users are added to the shared LAN medium. Besides increasing the potential for more collisions, devices must spend more time trying to gain access to the increasingly busy CSMA/CD medium in order to transmit. After spending too much time trying to access the shared Ethernet segment, many devices simply give up and drop the packet, figuring that they'll never gain transmission access.

The problems with shared Ethernet networks have subsequently forced network designers to deploy networking technologies that are better equipped to handle the

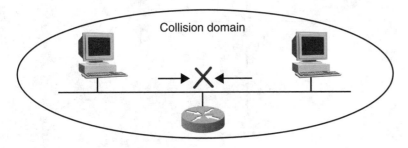

Figure 16-2   Packet collision

significant performance, reliability, and scalability issues related to legacy networks. One of the best networking solutions to have sprung onto the networking scene to tackle these issues has been the LAN switch. As the following sections will explain, LAN switches are highly flexible devices that play a crucial role in the success of today's modern network infrastructures.

LAN Switching Fundamentals

In Chapter 4, you learned that switches are essentially multiport bridges that forward frames based on MAC addresses. When a bridging or switching device receives a frame, it looks in its bridging table (also called content addressable memory, or CAM) to determine the outbound port associated with the frame's destination MAC address. If the destination host's MAC address is found, the frame is forwarded out the appropriate port. If, however, the destination MAC is not found in the CAM table, or has the broadcast address of FFFFFFFFFFFF, the frame is forwarded out all ports except the port on which the frame was received (see Figure 16-3). This event is referred to as *flooding*.

At the same time that the CAM table is referenced to determine the associated outbound port of a destination address, the frame's source MAC address is examined to determine if there is an entry for it in the CAM table. An entry would indicate that the

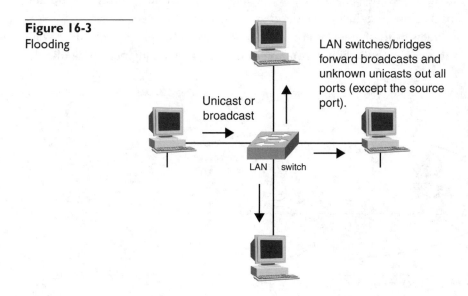

Figure 16-3
Flooding

LAN switches/bridges forward broadcasts and unknown unicasts out all ports (except the source port).

Unicast or broadcast

LAN   switch

switch has learned of the source's MAC address and associated port. If an entry were not present, the switch would simply create an entry that included the source frame's MAC address and port of entry. It is through this process that MAC addresses are learned.

In addition to learning the source address, the switch also maintains an *aging timer* for it in the CAM table. Every time a packet is received from the source, the aging timer is reset. If the switch doesn't hear from the packet before the aging timer expires, the entry for that source is removed from the CAM table. Typically, the aging timer is set to five minutes, but a network manager can modify it to suit the network's unique requirements.

Layer 2, Layer 3, and Upper-Layer Switching

The process of learning and switching a packet based on its MAC address is referred to as *Layer 2 switching*, and is to be distinguished from *Layer 3 switching*. With the latter type, packets can be forwarded based not only on their Layer 2 addresses but also on their Layer 3 addresses (for example, IP address). This added functionality, referred to as *routing*, allows a Layer 3 device such as a router to take advantage of an extra level of hierarchical network addressing so that instead of having to maintain the MAC address of every device in the entire network (which is what bridges and switches do), the router is able to utilize a Layer 3 address format that identifies a packet's destination network and host number (see Figure 16-4). Because hosts residing on a network share the same network number, the router only has to keep track of which network numbers are being used in its routing table. Chapter 11 explores the routing process in further detail.

As you learned in Chapter 11, routing or Layer 3 switching is essential to maintaining flexible, high-performance traffic flows. While this degree of functionality is enough for most network designs, there are also higher levels of switching that allow for even greater flexibility and efficiency in forwarding packets. Referred to as *Layer 4* and *Layer 5 switching*, these approaches allow packets to be forwarded based not only on their MAC and network layer addresses, but also on their Layer 4 transport information, such as their TCP and UDP port numbers. As explained in Chapter 5, Layer 4 port numbers are used to identify specific services running on a machine, such as FTP (ports 20 and 21), Telnet (port 23), and the Web (port 80), among others. Occasionally, this is referred to as Layer 5 and Layer 7 switching, particularly in marketing pieces, but you are actually using Layers 4 and 5. With Layer 4 and Layer 5 switching, the ability to make forwarding decisions based on port numbers can be of significant use to such applications as security and *Quality of Service* (QoS).

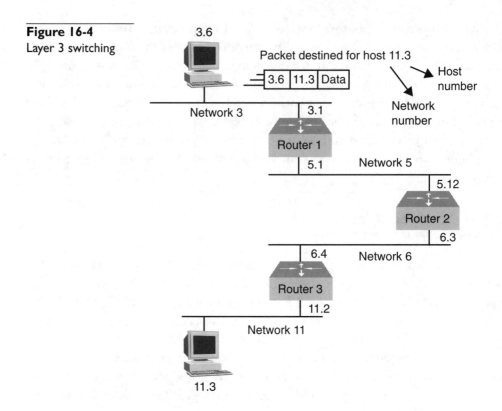

Figure 16-4
Layer 3 switching

LAN Switching Advantages

While bridges and switches both share the same two functions of switching data frames and maintaining CAM tables, switches have several technical advantages over their Layer 2 cousins:

- **Lower latency**   LAN switches offer lower latency than LAN bridges.

- **Switching methods**   The ability to choose a switching method, such as store-and-forward or cut-through (see the next section), enables network managers to balance network performance with reliability.

- **Microsegmentation capability**   Devices directly attached to a switch can experience full-media bandwidth. Concurrent transmissions through the switch are enabled.

- **Full-duplexing**   Devices attached directly to full-duplex-capable ports can transmit and receive at the same time.

- **Media-rate adaptation** With media-rate adaptation, a LAN switch is capable of supporting a mix of 10, 100, and 1000 Mbps ports.

- **Memory buffering methods** Two buffering options give network planners the flexibility of choosing a switching device that is best suited for their network's infrastructure.

The following sections explore these features in greater detail.

Lower Latency

As mentioned earlier, *latency* (also referred to as *propagation delay*) is the amount of time it takes a frame, or packet, to travel from its source to its destination. Latency is typically affected by the following factors (see Figure 16-5):

- **Distance** This is simply the distance required to travel from source to destination.

- **Cable type** Some cable types add more latency than others. Fiber-optic cable, for instance, has less cable delay than copper wire.

- **Type and number of intermediate devices** A packet, on its journey through a network, passes through intermediate devices such as repeaters, switches, or routers. Depending on which networking device the packet travels through, a certain amount of latency is added to that packet's journey due to the time it takes to travel from the device's source port to and out its destination port.

Figure 16-5
Latency factors

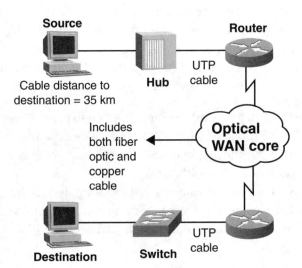

Bridges add more latency than switches, primarily because bridges must receive and store a packet before forwarding the packet out an interface (an event that adds an estimated 10 to 30 percent increase in network latency), whereas switches have the capability of forwarding a frame *as* it arrives. The ability to forward frames out a switched port as they arrive is referred to as *cut-through switching*, discussed in the next section.

Switching Methods

A frame can be forwarded through a LAN switch using various methods:

- **Store-and-forward**   An entire frame is received and stored before it is forwarded out an interface. Latency is highest with this method. However, error detection is best because the entire frame can be checked for errors.

- **Cut-through**   An incoming frame is forwarded as it arrives. This method results in the least amount of latency. However, in comparison to store-and-forward switching, error detection is worse because the entire frame cannot be checked for errors. Two forms of cut-through switching exist:

    - **Fast-forward**   Forwards an incoming frame as soon as the *destination address* has been read (see Figure 16-6). Of all the switching methods, fast-forward delivers the least latency. However, because it does not check for frame errors once the destination address has been read, error detection is poorest with this switching method.

    - **Fragment-free**   Forwards an incoming frame as soon as its first 64 bytes have been checked for errors (see Figure 16-7). In a network that is abiding by distance-limitation and media-repeater rules, most frame errors that the switch detects are the result of collisions. These collisions create fragments that are generally smaller than 64 bytes. Therefore, with fragment-free switching, the frame is checked for collision fragments and then forwarded out. Latency with this method is higher than that of fast-forward switching.

When error rates on a network are high, it is best to employ either store-and-forward switching or fragment-free switching. When errors are not an issue, fast-forward switching can be used. Note, though, that when frames containing errors are forwarded, the receiving devices have to deal with them.

Cisco Catalyst LAN switches are store-and-forward devices, but they forward at wire rate with low latency due to the use of synergy and index bus features. Where bridges use the CPU for switching decisions, Catalyst switches use ASICs (Application-Specific Integrated Circuits).

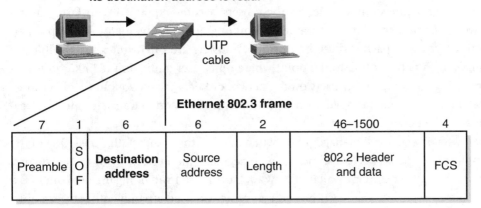

**With fast-forward switching,
a frame is forwarded as soon as
its destination address is read.**

UTP
cable

Ethernet 802.3 frame

7	1	6	6	2	46–1500	4
Preamble	S O F	**Destination address**	Source address	Length	802.2 Header and data	FCS

SOF = Start-of-Frame Delimiter
FCS = Frame Check Sequence
Note: Units are in bytes

Figure 16-6   Fast-forward switching

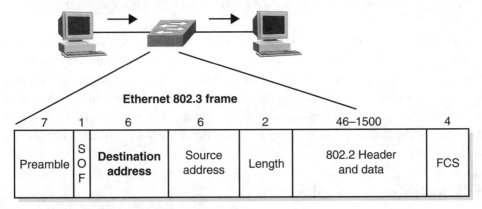

**With fragment-free switching, a frame is
forwarded as soon as its first 64 bytes have
been determined to be error free.**

Ethernet 802.3 frame

7	1	6	6	2	46–1500	4
Preamble	S O F	**Destination address**	Source address	Length	802.2 Header and data	FCS

SOF = Start-of-Frame Delimiter
FCS = Frame Check Sequence
Note: Units are in bytes

Figure 16-7   Fragment-free switching

Microsegmenting

As the number of users in a network grows, so does their need for more bandwidth. The need is tremendously intensified as these users become equipped with faster, more-powerful computers that are capable of handling applications that gobble up a network's carrying capacity. These bandwidth monsters are often times responsible for congesting a network link to the point where other user traffic on the link grinds to a screeching halt, forcing the users on the network to delay their work until a later time. The end result is lost productivity, which in the final end often translates into lost revenue for the network's company.

So what is a network manager to do when faced with a bandwidth crisis? One of the simplest and most effective solutions is to segment the network with LAN switches. This technique maximizes available network bandwidth by dividing the network into a number of segments that each has access to the full media bandwidth. For example, consider Figure 16-8.

In Figure 16-8, the before scenario shows a shared 10 Mbps network in which all devices are interconnected via Layer 1 hubs. Because this is a shared network, no device has complete access to the full 10 Mbps. The after scenario, on the other hand, shows what occurs when these hubs are replaced with Layer 2 switches equipped with dedicated 10 Mbps ports. The result is that each device attaches to the switch at 10 Mbps! And this bandwidth isn't shared; rather, each device has a dedicated 10 Mbps connection to the switch. Furthermore, each link that attaches to the switch is in its own collision domain, which means that collisions that occur on the switched link do not affect any other network devices besides the device and switch port involved in the collision (see Figure 16-9).

The technique of attaching one device to a dedicated switch port is known as *microsegmenting*. While traditional multiport bridges also have the capability of microsegmenting, they don't have a switch's capability of supporting *concurrent transmissions*. With concurrent transmissions, multiple devices each attached to dedicated switch ports can communicate with each other simultaneously (see Figure 16-10). This is in contrast to traditional bridges, which can support only one communication session at a time.

Half-Duplex vs. Full-Duplex

With legacy Ethernet architectures, all devices residing on the shared media must use the CSMA/CD access method to prevent more than one device from transmitting at the same time. If two devices transmit at the same time, a collision occurs. As a result, any given device on a shared network is only allowed to either transmit or receive; it cannot do both of these tasks at the same time. Such a process is referred to as *half-duplex*.

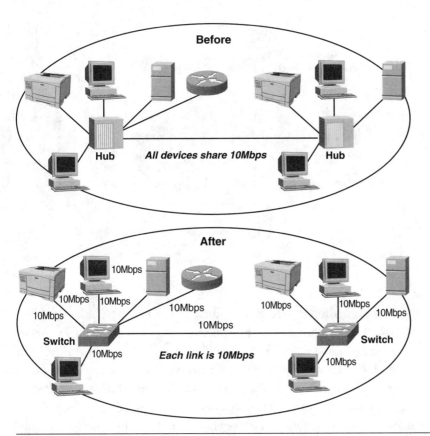

Figure 16-8   Before and after LAN switch segmenting

Figure 16-9
Switched links are
separate collision
domains

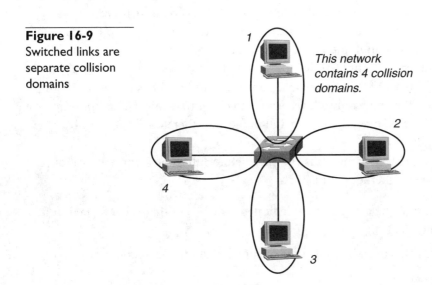

Figure 16-10
LAN switches
support concurrent
transmissions

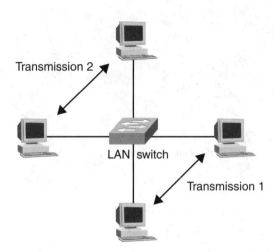

While half-duplex transmission is necessary for shared Ethernet LANs, it is not necessary for *switched* Ethernet LANs, because switched Ethernet networks can deploy switches that connect devices on dedicated links—a process referred to as microsegmenting. With microsegmenting, each device attached to the switch is on a dedicated point-to-point link and is in its own collision domain. This means that instead of being required to operate in half-duplex mode, stations can now operate in *full-duplex mode,* which allows them to transmit *and* receive at the same time (see Figure 16-11). As two stations are subsequently allowed to transmit and receive at the same time, there is no chance that their transmissions will result in a collision. Consequently, full-duplex stations no longer have a need to detect collisions or abide by the CSMA/CD access method.

In addition to the benefit of eliminating the need to detect for collisions before transmitting to another full-duplex station, full-duplex transmission allows for stations to transmit and receive at full bandwidth in each direction. For example, a full-duplex device running on a 10 Mbps link would transmit at 10 Mbps *and* receive at 10 Mbps. In contrast, half-duplexing only allows devices to either transmit at 10 Mbps or receive at 10 Mbps. The advantage here with full-duplexing, therefore, is up to a two-fold increase in bandwidth.

The following requirements must be met before full-duplex communication can occur between two Ethernet stations:

- Each station must be attached to a dedicated switch port that is configured in full-duplex mode.

- Each station's NIC must be configured to support full-duplex mode.

Figure 16-11
Full-duplex
communications

*Full-duplex communication allows
two stations to transmit and receive
at the same time.*

Host A   LAN switch   Host B

- The media must meet appropriate Ethernet specifications. In addition to meeting distance limitations, this requirement also entails using a cable type that is capable of supporting full-duplex communication. Supported cable types include 10BaseT, 10BaseFL, 100BaseT, 100BaseFX, 100BaseT, 1000BaseLX, 1000BaseSX, and 1000BaseT, among others. Unsupported cable types include 10Base2, 10Base5, and 100BaseT4, among others.

NOTE: Many of today's Ethernet NICs (and most of today's switch ports) support a feature called autonegotiation. This feature allows a station's NIC to negotiate with the switch port to determine a compatible duplex mode (either full- or half-duplex), cable type, and link speed. Because autonegotiation is a dynamic feature, configuration management has the potential of being simplified in large growing networks. Since there is no IEEE standard for autonegotiation, it sometimes causes problems because vendors do it differently.

Media-Rate Adaptation

Switches can support a variety of link speeds, ranging from half-duplex 10 Mbps to full-duplex Gigabit Ethernet (1,000 Mbps). When a switch is provisioned with ports that are of uniform bandwidth, such as when all ports are, say, 10 Mbps, the switch is considered to be *symmetric*. In Figure 16-12, for instance, the switch in Network 1 is a symmetric switch because all of its ports are 10 Mbps.

On the other hand, switches that are equipped with a mixture of port speeds are known as *asymmetric* switches. In Figure 16-12, the switch in Network 2 is an asymmetric switch because it has both 10 Mbps and 100 Mbps ports.

EXAM TIP: While the difference between symmetric and asymmetric switching is a simple concept, understand it and be able to recognize it. Also recognize that it is a common technique used for adding a server to a LAN using a higher bandwidth interface.

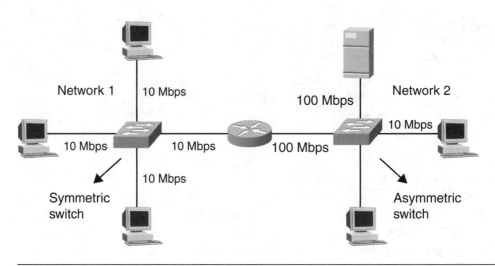

Figure 16-12 Asymmetric vs. symmetric switches

Fast Ethernet, Gigabit Ethernet, and Beyond

The flexibility of being able to provision a LAN switch with enough ports to support increasing numbers of users and with bandwidth capacities tailored to meet the performance needs of high-speed workstations and applications is absolutely critical to a network's current and future ability to adapt to network growth and modification. To support these needs, switch engineers have worked hard to deliver LAN switching equipment and technologies that are geared toward providing cost-effective, high-performance LAN switching solutions that can keep pace with a network's burgeoning traffic demands while also leveraging the network's current infrastructure so as to ease the integration process.

One of the first LAN switching solutions that switch developers seized upon was Fast Ethernet, a 100 Mbps media specification standardized by the IEEE. This copper media option allowed a network to scale its bandwidth from 10 Mbps to 100 Mbps without the need of having to upgrade the network's existing cabling infrastructure. However, while this tenfold increase in bandwidth may have been enough for some networks, other networks were still besieged by congested links that were often high-traffic backbone links or links to centralized server farms. Due to the critical importance of these heavily utilized areas, solutions developers once again had to come up with higher-speed links and higher-capacity LAN switches.

The result was Gigabit Ethernet, a 1,000 Mbps media option (specified in IEEE 802.3z and 802.3ab) that allows enterprise and service provider networks to scale their backbones, data centers, and wiring closets and at the same time preserve their existing copper cabling and legacy networking equipment (see Figure 16-13). Specifically instrumental to the evolution and acceptance of this technology was the relative simplicity with which networks could integrate copper-based Gigabit Ethernet switching into their existing Fast Ethernet switched networks. Due to media distance limitations, 1000BaseT, or GE over copper, is generally used in server farms only and in short cable lengths.

Now, with the coming demise of traditional, slow-speed, less-scalable LAN architectures such as 4/16 Mbps Token Ring and 100 Mbps FDDI, and with the demise of ATM in the LAN, Fast and Gigabit Ethernet are poised to carry today's high-powered switched networks in only one direction: forward. Indeed, work is already underway to introduce the next phase of Gigabit Ethernet, called 10 Gigabit Ethernet, which is a 10 Gbps media option that could see deployment as early as 2002 (see Figure 16-14). Furthermore, there is already discussion of 40 Gigabit Ethernet and even 100 Gigabit Ethernet.

While some estimates suggest that switched Ethernet speeds will be able to top out at terabit speeds (trillions of bits per second), which is the theoretical maximum speed allowed on a copper wire, the fact that the laws of physics place an ultimate limit as to

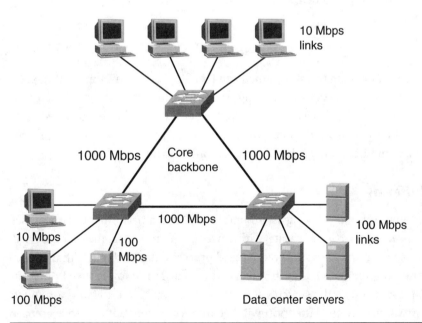

Figure 16-13   Gigabit Ethernet in the LAN

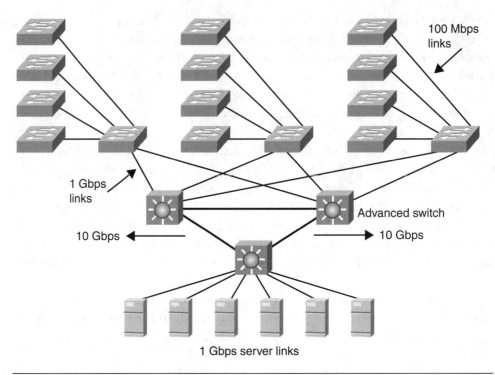

100 Mbps links

1 Gbps links

10 Gbps

Advanced switch

10 Gbps

1 Gbps server links

Figure 16-14   Future Gigabit Ethernet

how fast any information can travel on a medium (on fiber-optic, this limit is the speed of light) means that other ways of addressing bandwidth limitations once these extra-ordinary rates of transmission have been reached eventually need to be explored if, of course, there will ever be a need to communicate at such rates. Considering present trends, there just might be. But, as the cliché goes, only the future will tell.

Memory Buffering

In an Ethernet environment utilizing asymmetric switching, a performance issue arises when higher-speed ports communicate with lower-speed ports on the same device. Because higher-speed ports are able to receive and process data much faster than lower-speed ports, the potential exists for a bottleneck to occur at the lower-speed ports. In Figure 16-15, for example, if the switch's 100 Mbps port attempts to forward too much traffic to the 10 Mbps port, the latter port will become congested as it fails to keep pace with the increased traffic load.

To help prevent this type of event from destabilizing a network's performance, switches are designed with internal memory buffers that serve as holding facilities for received packets. The packets are stored in these memory buffers for just as long as it takes the switch to forward them out the destination interfaces. There are two methods of buffering packets in a switch:

- **Port-based memory buffering** Packets are stored in *queues* (memory buffers) that are associated with specific incoming ports (see Figure 16-16). A packet is transmitted once all other packets ahead in the queue have been successfully transmitted. As a result, however, a single packet that cannot be transmitted because of a busy destination port can end up blocking all packets in the queue behind it even if other destination ports are completely free. This condition is commonly referred to as "head-of-line blocking" because the packets behave as if they are in a single-file line that is being held up by one packet (see Figure 16-17).

- **Shared memory buffering** Allows all packets coming into the switch to be deposited into one super-sized queue that is shared by all ports. Each packet that gets deposited into this memory buffer is then queued for delivery to its respective destination port(s) (see Figure 16-18). To prevent too many packets from being queued

Figure 16-15
Bottleneck on low-speed port

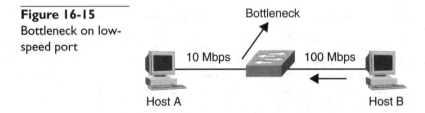

Figure 16-16 Port-based memory buffering

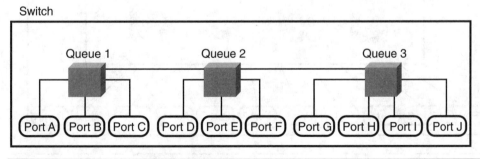

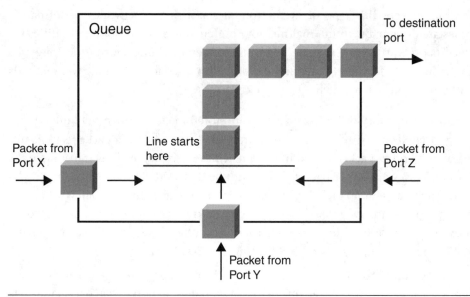

Figure 16-17   Packets queued single-file

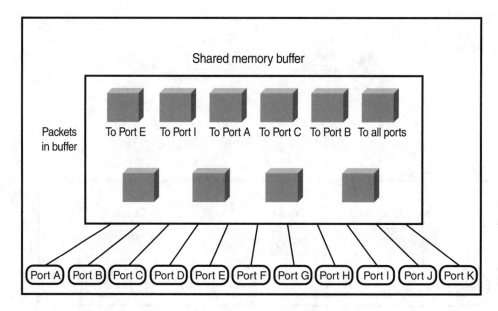

Figure 16-18   Shared memory buffering

for a specific outbound port, the switch places a limit on how many packets and bytes can be queued for any destination port in the switch. Note, though, that there is no limit as to how many packets or bytes can be deposited into the memory buffer—other than the limit imposed by the buffer's own capacity and availability.

Shared memory buffering doesn't suffer the same line-blocking problem that port-based memory buffering does, because the shared memory buffering doesn't use receive queues; packets are deposited into the shared memory buffer and then mapped to their destinations *in parallel*. As a result, there is no way that a packet destined to a congested port could delay forwarding for all other packets in the buffer. This is not to say, though, that switches employing shared memory buffering are totally immune to becoming congested. In fact, packets are dropped when destination queue thresholds are reached, signifying that congestion is causing the problem.

Virtual Local Area Networks

With traditional LAN architectures, switches only have the capacity to create separate collision domains; they aren't able to create separate broadcast domains, because all ports on the switch are automatically relegated to the same Layer 2 broadcast domain, which means that switches are always required to flood broadcasts out all interfaces. In these environments, the only device that has the capability of defining broadcast domain boundaries is the router. The router automatically creates broadcast domains by preventing broadcasts from being propagated across its routed interfaces (see Figure 16-19). Each routed interface therefore defines the broadcast domain's physical boundary.

With VLAN technology, switches are endowed with this router-like capability to create broadcast domains. However, instead of being required to have one broadcast domain per port (like a router), switches can be configured with broadcast domains on whichever ports the network manager chooses. As a result, a broadcast received on one port will only be forwarded to other ports in the same broadcast domain. For example, the switch in Figure 16-20 has been configured with four broadcast domains, each of which has been assigned specific ports. When, say, the host on Port 6 transmits a broadcast or an unknown unicast, the switch forwards the broadcast only to Port 2, because this is the only other port in Broadcast Domain 3.

These switch-created broadcast domains are called VLANs. VLANs can be created either on one switch or on multiple switches. When created on multiple switches, the same VLAN is subsequently able to span across multiple switches. However, traffic from

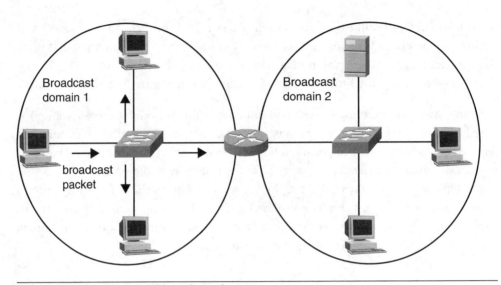

Figure 16-19   Traditional broadcast domains

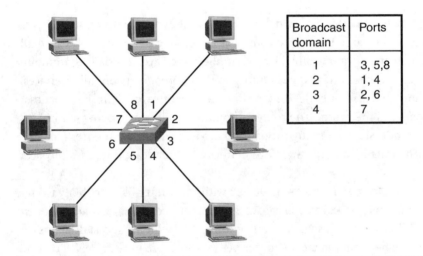

Broadcast domain	Ports
1	3, 5,8
2	1, 4
3	2, 6
4	7

Figure 16-20   Creating broadcast domains on switches

one VLAN cannot communicate with another VLAN without going through a Layer 3 device, such as a router. The router logically interconnects the VLANs to enable inter-VLAN communication (see Figure 16-21).

Figure 16-21
VLANs

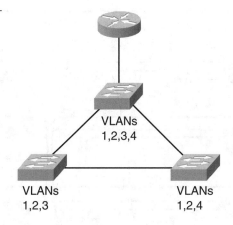

VLANs
1,2,3,4

VLANs
1,2,3

VLANs
1,2,4

The Practical Side to VLANs

Thus far, you have been introduced to the technical definition of a VLAN, which is a Layer 2 broadcast domain created on a switch or multiple switches. The practical definition of a VLAN, on the other hand, takes into account the fact that there is a purpose for applying VLANs in a switched network. With the practical definition, VLANs become an instrument for organizing users and devices into logical workgroups or communities of interest. All users within the logical group (VLAN) share a common function or characteristic. For example, a VLAN can be created based on department; all users and devices residing in a certain department belong to the same VLAN (see Figure 16-22). Or, as another example, VLANs can be defined based on application; all users and devices using the same application belong to the same VLAN. Yet another example would be grouping users based on their particular function. Furthermore, users and devices that are in the same VLAN can be spread across the entire network. They can reside on separate building floors, or between buildings, or even across WANs while still belonging to the same Layer 2 broadcast domain.

This type of mobility and organizational flexibility is in stark contrast to traditional switched networks, which must abide by physical constraints when grouping users and devices together. Typically, these types of networks employ Layer 3 router segmentation when attempting to group users and devices into logical workgroups. However, this method does not scale as cost-effectively as switched VLAN networks. Note also that while routers can accomplish VLAN segmentation without the help of switches, it would most likely be cost prohibitive for any network to replace switches with routers that had the same high port densities.

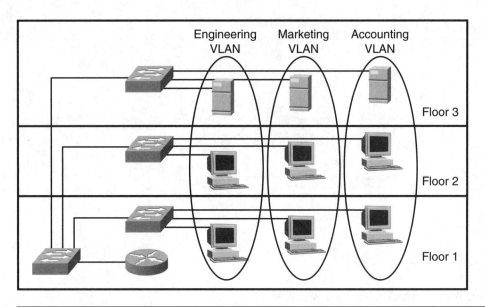

Figure 16-22   Grouping users into VLANs based on departmental association

VLAN Implementation Methods

Cisco switches can associate ports to a VLAN. Any device that attaches to a VLAN port is automatically placed in that port's VLAN. If a shared hub is attached to the port, then all devices attached to the hub will belong to the same VLAN. This method of VLAN association is referred to as the *port-centric* approach to VLANs.

There are two ways in which ports can be assigned to VLANs. The first method is simply by *statically* assigning a port to a VLAN. With this method, a network manager configures the switch port with the appropriate VLAN number. Any device that attaches to the port will belong to that VLAN. In the event that a device needs to change its VLAN membership, the network manager must reassign the device's port to the new VLAN. This VLAN implementation approach is generally used in networks that require simplified configuration management and high control over user moves and changes.

The other way in which ports can be assigned to VLANs is through dynamic assignment. With dynamic VLANs, a port automatically learns its VLAN assignment when a device attaches to the port and sends a packet. Based on the device's MAC address, network layer address, or network layer protocol, the device's port is associated with the proper VLAN. For this dynamic process to work, the network manager creates a VLAN management database that contains a static mapping of VLANs to MAC addresses (or whichever associated feature is being used). This is how the switch knows which VLANs are to be associated with which ports. Dynamic VLANs offer several benefits, including greater flexibility in determining VLAN assignments, improved security, and less administration in the wiring closet when users are moved.

NOTE: This is not meant to be an exhaustive representation of VLAN technologies. Other, evolving VLAN methodologies are easier to set up and troubleshoot. For the CCNA exam, you need to know what a VLAN is and the benefits, but the technologies are covered in greater detail in the CCNP "Switching" exam materials.

VLAN Communication

For communication to occur between all devices in a switched VLAN environment, switches must have a way of being able to determine how a packet is to be dealt with in light of its new VLAN association. Specifically, the switch must make forwarding and filtering decisions based upon the VLAN information configured by the network manager and must then be able to communicate this information to other switches and routers across the network. There are two different approaches that a switch can take to accomplish these tasks: *frame filtering* and *frame tagging* (also called frame identification).

With frame filtering, the switch builds a filtering table that is based upon such information as device MAC addresses, network layer protocol types, or application types, as determined by the network manager. Upon receiving a packet, the switch examines the packet's frame and compares it to the filtering table to determine what action to take. The switch then filters the packet, forwards it out an interface, or broadcasts it.

While frame filtering has the benefit of allowing users to be grouped with a high level of administrative control, this approach doesn't scale well because each packet that the switch receives must be processed with a filtering table; this adds latency and increases switch utilization levels. As a result of this disadvantage, most of today's switched VLAN architectures employ the second method of VLAN communication, frame tagging.

With frame tagging, each frame that the switch receives gets tagged with a unique VLAN identifier before being forwarded to another switch or router on the network backbone. When the destination switch or router receives the frame, it removes the VLAN identifier before sending the frame to the destination end station.

In switched Ethernet VLANs using Cisco equipment, this identifier is generally an *Inter-Switch Link* (ISL) header that encapsulates the frame and identifies the source frame's VLAN. This ISL encapsulation is important because it allows traffic from multiple VLANs to cross the same link, a process referred to as *trunking* (see Figure 16-23).

NOTE: For the CCNA exam, you must recognize ISL, but be aware that more and more people are using the standards-based 802.1q approach, which is based largely on Cisco's ISL.

VLAN Benefits

VLANs help to resolve several important issues related to traditional switched network architectures. For one, VLANs simplify the administrative cost and burden of dealing with user moves, adds, and changes. In addition to reduced administrative load, VLANs also have the benefits of optimizing bandwidth utilization, addressing network security, controlling broadcast activity, and leveraging existing equipment. The sections that follow examine these VLAN implementation benefits.

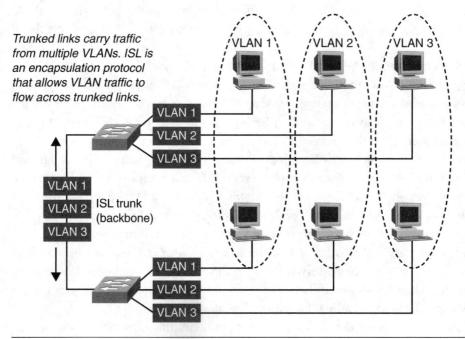

Figure 16-23 Trunking

Reduced Administrative Load

Moving users from one location to another, setting up new users, and dealing with changes to existing users are all significant undertakings for many of today's traditional switched networks. This is in large part due to the fact that a considerable amount of time and expense must go into planning the technical logistics behind the implementation, provisioning the necessary products and services, and then deploying the changes—which involves installation, configuration, testing, potential troubleshooting, and, lastly, documentation. While an analysis of all of these issues is beyond the scope of this book, it would be insightful to look at some of the technical logistics that are involved with managing user moves, adds, and changes. Table 16-1 therefore presents a quick overview of some of these concerns and identifies the OSI layers at which these concerns occur.

VLANs eliminate all Layer 3 issues when moving a user from one network location to another. As long as the user stays within their original VLAN, they will be in the same broadcast domain. This means that the user can keep the IP address and network layer configurations left intact, and the router and firewall can keep the configurations intact as well.

While Layer 3 issues are no longer a concern in switched VLAN networks, Layer 1 and 2 issues are still a concern, because a user who is relocating to another location still needs to be hooked up at that location and the necessary Layer 2 configurations still need to be made. For example, a switch port at the new location must be available and must be configured (whether statically or dynamically) with the user's associated VLAN.

NOTE: If a user is changing **VLAN** membership (that is, joining a new **VLAN**), then Layer 3 issues are a concern. However, the benefit of using VLANs means that the user does not have to physically relocate to join the new **VLAN**.

In addition, depending on the nature of the user's relocation, upper-layer issues can still be a concern as well. That is, application configurations may still need to occur and resource consumption issues may still need to be taken into consideration. However, with proper deployment, VLANs have the capacity of helping to resolve the latter of these two issues, resource consumption. Specifically, VLANs address *bandwidth utilization* by allowing users to be placed on dedicated collision-free segments with full access to the link's bandwidth for sending and receiving traffic, without being affected by broadcasts from neighboring devices residing in other VLANs (see Figure 16-24).

Table 16-1   Issues with Managing User Adds, Moves, and Changes

LOGISTICS ISSUE	DESCRIPTION
	LAYER 1
Device/port availability	There must be a port available to connect the new user; otherwise, a new switch or hub might need to be installed.
Cable compatibility	The cable type (for example, Category 5, fiber-optic, or wireless) at the user's new location must be compatible with the user's NIC.
Link speed	The new link to which the user attaches must be of sufficient speed.
Distance limitations	The user must be able to reach from its new location to the switch/hub without violating the cable's distance limitation.
	LAYER 2
Access method compatibility	If the new user attaches to a different media type (for example, Ethernet, Fast Ethernet, Token Ring, or FDDI), the NIC needs to be replaced to match the new media. The *drivers* for the new NIC must also be compatible with whichever upper-layer protocols the user has installed on his or her machine.
Switch/bridge configurations	The new switch (or bridge) to which the user attaches may need to be configured with the appropriate settings.
	LAYER 3
Workstation configurations	If the network is IP, and DHCP isn't running, the user's station may need to be assigned an IP address, default gateway, DNS server, and so forth.
Router and firewall configurations	Access lists and firewall configurations may need to be modified to allow the new user to access the network and appropriate services.
	LAYERS 4–7
Applications	The user may need to install new software and applications that allow the user to access new products, services, and technologies.
Resource availability	The network must be able to support the user's bandwidth requirements; the user must be able to support any increase in workload.

Network Security

With shared networks, traffic sent from one station is seen by all devices on that same network. The security problem with this is that any station using a software package to monitor network traffic can capture confidential, mission-critical data. Figure 16-25, for instance, shows a user attached to a shared hub who is secretly monitoring traffic sent from the accounting department to the sales department. Clearly, this is not a desirable situation.

VLANs would immediately resolve this security problem by allowing each department to be placed on its own VLAN, including the department on which the curious

Figure 16-24
VLANs optimize
switched bandwidth

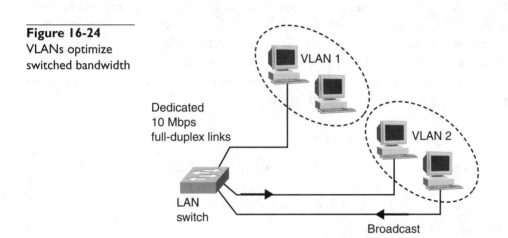

Figure 16-25
Security breach

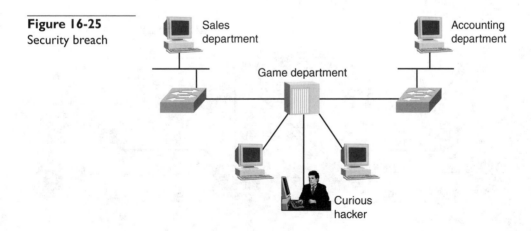

hacker resides. As a result, traffic from the accounting VLAN heading to the sales VLAN would not pass through the hacker's VLAN without being specifically addressed to it. While simply replacing the shared hub in Figure 16-25 with a switch would also resolve this problem, the deployment of VLANs would allow users from different departments to reside on the same switch without having to worry about their broadcast traffic being looked at covertly (see Figure 16-26).

Besides benefiting security by automatically containing the flow of traffic within administratively defined broadcast domains, VLANs also allow an administrator to configure the switch to restrict which users may join the VLAN. Only users with the appropriate permissions, which can be based on station address, network layer protocol type, or application type, can join the secured VLAN. If an unknown user attempts to plug into a port on the VLAN, the switch rejects the connection.

In addition to controlling which users can join a VLAN, a network manager can also use router access lists to restrict communicating between VLANs. These access lists filter the traffic flowing between VLANs to deny those users who don't have the appropriate permissions. Access lists are covered in Chapter 15.

Leveraging Existing Investments

Companies looking to upgrade their shared LAN architectures to high-performance switched VLANs will already have an investment placed in existing hubs, cabling, switches, and other networking equipment. VLANs preserve this investment by allow-

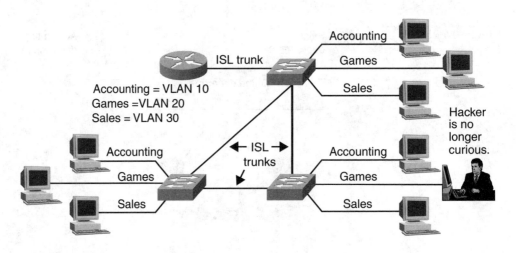

Figure 16-26   VLANs add security

ing the company's existing network infrastructure to cost-effectively integrate with the deployment of new networking equipment, such as routers and VLAN-capable switches (see Figure 16-27).

Hubs in the VLAN

Hubs are legacy technologies that still have a broad base in many of today's modern networks. While hubs are being increasingly phased out of the network backbone as demands skyrocket for high-performance switches that can deliver dedicated bandwidth to the desktop, these legacy devices still find application in areas of the network where performance and service demands aren't critical enough to warrant their replacement. For example, many companies that are migrating to VLAN architectures are leveraging their hub investments by connecting VLAN-capable switches to the backplanes of hubs.

There are a couple different ways in which this hub/switch integration can occur. If the hub is not modular and has only one backplane, all devices that attach to the hub will belong to the same VLAN. But for those hubs that provide multiple backplanes, VLAN assignments can be unique to each backplane connection from the hub to the switch. As a result, devices that attach to different backplane modules on the hub would belong to separate VLANs (see Figure 16-28).

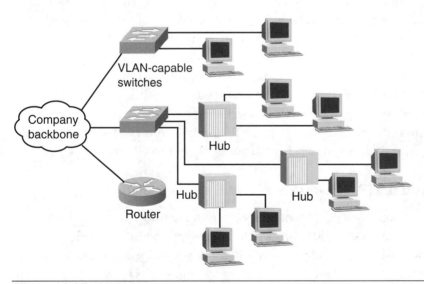

Figure 16-27 VLAN integration

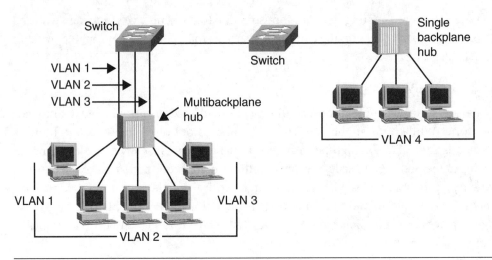

Figure 16-28   VLANs with hubs

Overview of the Spanning Tree Protocol

All bridged and switched environments run a Layer 2 protocol called the Spanning Tree Protocol (STP). STP is basically a loop-prevention feature that allows bridges and switches to communicate with each other to discover Layer 2 loops. This communication occurs via special frames called *bridge protocol data units* (BPDUs). Once these BPDUs are exchanged, bridges and switches are then able to calculate a loop-free logical topology. Figure 16-29 shows an example of a physically looped Layer 2 network that has been detected and dealt with by STP.

As indicated in the illustration, all ports are allowed to forward traffic except for one of the ports on Switch B. STP has closed, or blocked, this particular port to break the physical loop that exists. In the event that another port fails anywhere in the network, STP will reactivate the blocked port. Hence, STP also functions as a redundancy mechanism by allowing bridges and switches to converge on a Layer 2 port failure.

Steps to Initial STP Convergence

STP calculates a loop-free logical topology by determining which ports on a switch will be allowed to forward traffic and which will be allowed *not* to forward traffic. The communication and decision-making processes that bridges and switches go through to accomplish this task of calculating a loop-free logical topology is referred to as *STP convergence.* Just as routers initially go through a series of steps to converge on a network topology (that is, discovering network routes, building a routing table, and exchanging

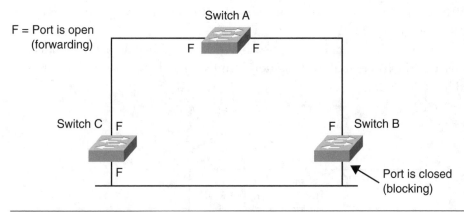

F = Port is open
(forwarding)

Switch A

F   F

Switch C   F

F

F   Switch B

Port is closed
(blocking)

Figure 16-29   Layer 2 loop

routing information with other routers), so also do bridges and switches go through a sequence of steps to converge on a loop-free topology. These steps can be outlined as follows:

1. **Elect a Root Bridge**   When all the bridges and switches in a network are first powered up, they all exchange BPDUs with each other. These BPDUs contain STP information that allows one bridge or switch in the network to be the designated Root Bridge. Whichever device gets elected the Root Bridge is automatically able to forward on all of its ports.

2. **Elect Root Ports**   Once the network's Root Bridge has been determined, all other bridges and switches will each elect a Root Port, which is basically the port through which the bridge's or switch's own *best path* to the Root Bridge can be reached. (The Spanning Tree Algorithm defines "best" according to a special decision sequence.) The Root Ports are able to forward.

3. **Elect Designated Ports**   The last step in initial STP convergence requires that each bridge and switch (except the Root Bridge) in the network elect one Designated Port for each bridged segment. This means that when two bridges are connected via one link, both bridges must determine which side is going to have the Designated Port. In general, the best port through which the Root Bridge can be reached is elected the Designated Port. ("Best" is once again based on the Spanning Tree Algorithm's decision sequence.) The Designated Ports are able to forward.

Once elections are over, any port that is *not* either a Root Port or a Designated Port is considered a *blocking port*. Blocking ports are not allowed to forward any traffic at all, whether it is user traffic, routing protocol traffic, VLAN information, STP BPDUs, or so forth. Therefore, the only ports that are allowed to forward and receive traffic are Root Ports and Designated Ports.

Figure 16-30 shows an example of a network that has finished the steps to initial STP convergence. The letters in this illustration identify the STP *port states*, which are presented in Table 16-2.

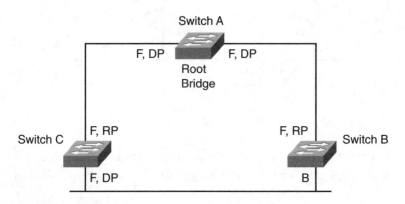

Figure 16-30   Results of STP convergence

Table 16-2   STP Port States

STP PORT STATE	ABBREVIATION	DESCRIPTION
Blocking	B	No traffic is being forwarded. Only STP BPDUs can be received.
Listening		Port is going through the steps of STP convergence. Only STP BPDU traffic is currently being forwarded.
Learning		Port has been elected Root Port or Designated Port. Port is now receiving traffic and is building bridging table, but is not yet forwarding traffic.
Forwarding	F	All traffic is being received and forwarded.
Disabled	D	Port has been administratively disabled. No traffic can be received.
Designated Port	DP	Allowed to send and receive traffic to and from a segment.
Root Port	RP	Allowed to send and receive traffic to and from a segment. Is the port on the bridge/switch that has the best path to the Root Bridge.

EXAM TIP: Designated Port and Root Port are not technically considered port states. They are actually just labels used to designate a port's STP function. Know the five states and what is happening during each state.

Cisco Catalyst switches employ a Spanning Tree for each VLAN, rather than a single physical Spanning Tree. This allows trunk ports to be forwarding for some VLAN interfaces and blocking for others. This leads to VLAN load balancing across trunks.

Summary

Legacy Ethernet networks use shared hubs to segment the network. Besides creating collision and broadcast issues, shared architectures pose significant limitations to scaling user bandwidth and performance. To meet these requirements, LAN switches were designed with capabilities that allow network managers to cost-effectively migrate their shared LANs to high-performance switched architectures that can provide such scalable features as dedicated bandwidth to user end stations, full-duplex communication, support for Gigabit speeds, reduced latency, and the ability to create VLANs.

With switched VLAN architectures, network managers are able to assign users and devices that share a common function, department, application, or protocol to separate broadcast domains. The benefits of deploying VLANs include reduced administrative costs associated with managing user moves, adds and changes, maximum control over broadcasts, improved network security, increased bandwidth, and the ability to leverage the network's existing infrastructure.

In conclusion, the flexibility afforded by today's LAN switching products, technologies, and services allows network planners to provision custom-tailored switching solutions that are more than capable of adequately addressing a network's specific requirements for performance, reliability, and scalability, all at minimal cost and with maximal effectiveness.

Case Study: Atlantis College

Now you will apply your knowledge of LAN switching. Review the following background information on Atlantis College and examine its current logical topology (shown in the following illustration). After reviewing the requirements for this network's LAN infrastructure, answer the questions that follow about which LAN switching technologies would best meet the requirements set forth.

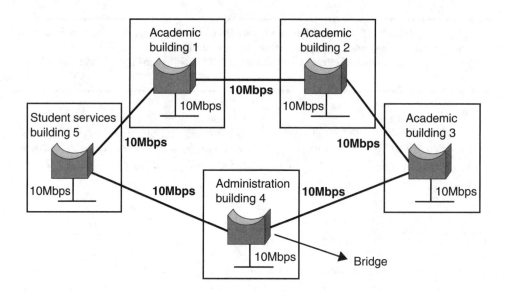

Background: Atlantis College (AC) has five building that are all located within a few hundred meters of each other. The first building houses the Math, Science, and Engineering departments; the second building houses the Language, Social Science, and Business departments; and the third building houses the Arts and Vocational departments. The fourth building on AC's campus is the administration building, which holds various departments, including Student Admission/Registration, and faculty and staff offices. The last building contains all the student resource departments, such as the library, bookstore, and counseling center.

AC's current network is a flat, bridged Ethernet network, where each building contains a bridge and shared hubs that connect users, servers, and networking equipment. Each bridged segment on the TCP/IP network has a 10 Mbps capacity. Because the entire network is using bridges, there is only one broadcast domain.

Recently, AC's traffic levels have been increasing due to a growing number of users who are using bandwidth-intensive applications. This situation is causing bottlenecks on bridged segments and is thereby creating the need for links that can deliver more bandwidth. In addition, the network is experiencing heavy broadcast traffic that is leading to increased congestion on the bridged network backbone.

Besides resource-consumption issues, AC is also concerned about security issues, because broadcast packets can be seen by all users and devices connected to the network.

Scenario: Atlantis College is seeking a complete redesign of its network. The following list sets forth what the technical requirements are for this redesign:

- Bridges and shared hubs must be leveraged with any new LAN architecture that is implemented.

- Due to the high number of packets that contain errors, the new LAN architecture must address reliability issues.

- Bandwidth capacities on the network backbone need to scale from 10 Mbps to 100 Mbps.

- No user on the network requires more than 10 Mbps bandwidth capacity.

- Student users should not be able to access restricted areas of the network, including the administration and faculty departments.

- If VLANs are used, each department should be placed in its own VLAN.

As the network design consultant for AC, it is your task to devise a basic LAN switching solution that is scalable, reliable, and cost-efficient. The following worksheet questions provide you with a guide for choosing the solution that best meets these goals and requirements.

Design Worksheet for Atlantis College

1. Explain how switches can be used to help resolve the performance and scalability issues that Atlantis College is currently facing? How could existing bridges and hubs be used in the switched architecture?

2. What type of switching method should be used to help deal with AC's high error rates? How does this switching method work?

3. How could VLANs be deployed to address broadcast activity and security issues on AC's network?

4. Based on AC's requirements and existing network infrastructure, sketch a diagram of a network topology that incorporates department-based VLANs and asymmetric LAN switches.

Case Study—Suggested Solutions (Your solutions may vary)

1. The bridges that are currently interconnecting AC's buildings can be replaced with high-speed LAN switches. These asymmetric switches would offer high-density ports capable of providing 100 Mbps bandwidth links between backbone links and 10 Mbps links to intrabuilding segments. Existing hubs and bridges could be

used to attach user segments to ports on the switch. Although each user attached to a shared hub would be affected by traffic from other users on the same hub, the number of users that attach to the hub can be limited so that sufficient bandwidth is provided. If necessary, users can be placed on their own dedicated 10 Mbps switch ports. In addition, full-duplex communication can be enabled between the 100 Mbps backbone links to effectively double throughput to 200 Mbps. This switching solution is scalable because it allows the network to efficiently adapt to future performance and service requirements, and it is cost-effective because the switches can be provisioned and integrated into the existing LAN infrastructure with minimal time and expense.

2. Store-and-forward would be the appropriate switching method to use to help resolve high error rates in the network. Although in reality it would be best to resolve the underlying issue causing the errors to occur, store-and-forward switching would be an acceptable solution for the interim. This method works by storing received packets in the switch's memory buffer and examining the frame for errors before forwarding the frame out to its destination. The alternative solution would be fragment-free switching, which examines the first 64 bytes of an incoming frame (checking for collision fragments) before forwarding the frame out to its destination.

3. VLANs could be deployed in AC's network based on department. Each department within a building would be placed in its own VLAN, thereby creating separate broadcast domains within each building. For example, the Math department would be placed in one VLAN, the Language department in another, the Vocations department in another, and so on. This allows increased mobility for VLAN users, because a user is no longer impaired by the physical constraints that are characteristic of shared LAN architectures; the user can be anywhere in the network and still belong to the same VLAN. The problem with security would also be addressed by VLANs, because traffic from one VLAN could be restricted from accessing another secured VLAN (for instance, the Administration department). The following illustration is one possible topology for Atlantis College.

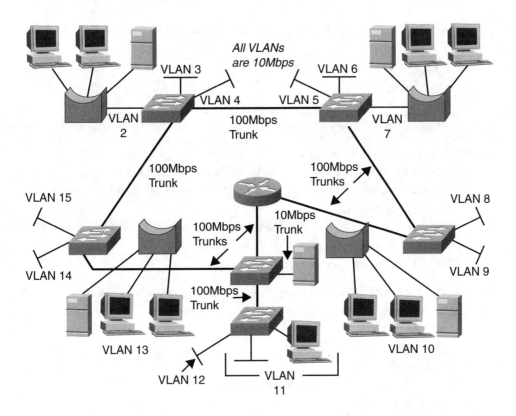

Practice Questions

Take a few moments and check your grasp of the concepts covered in this chapter. The answers are immediately following the questions.

Questions

1. Which of the following issues is *not* a problem commonly associated with shared Ethernet LANs?
   a. Increased latency
   b. Increased bandwidth utilization
   c. Congestion
   d. Broadcasts
   e. Collisions
   f. Slow STP convergence

2. Which three of the following elements would be found in a switch's CAM table?
   a. MAC address
   b. IP address
   c. Port number
   d. Aging timer
   e. Next-hop information

3. How does Layer 4 switching work?
   a. Packets are forwarded based on MAC address and protocol type.
   b. The switch forwards the packet based on its network layer address and TCP or UDP port numbers.
   c. A packet is forwarded based on MAC address, network layer address, and TCP or UDP port numbers.
   d. There is no such thing as Layer 4 switching.

4. What three of the following factors influence propagation delay (latency)?
   a. Access method
   b. Cable distance
   c. Cable type
   d. Application
   e. Type and number of intermediate devices
   f. CPU speed
   g. Memory availability

5. How does fast-forward switching work?
   a. The switch forwards an incoming frame after examining its first 64 bytes.
   b. The switch forwards an incoming frame after examining its destination MAC address.
   c. The switch forwards an incoming frame after storing it and checking it for errors.
   d. The switch forwards an incoming frame after checking its first 128 bytes.

6. How does microsegmenting optimize available bandwidth?
   a. By reducing the workload of a station attached to the switch.
   b. Microsegmenting allows a user to attach to a switch port and experience full media bandwidth.
   c. Groups of users and devices that attach to a switch port can experience full-duplex communication on a dedicated segment.
   d. Microsegmenting raises a port's speed from 10 Mbps to 100 Mbps.

7. What's the primary difference between full-duplex and half-duplex?
   a. Half-duplex stations cannot send and receive traffic at the same time, whereas full-duplex stations can.
   b. Half-duplex stations can send and receive traffic at the same time, whereas full-duplex stations cannot.
   c. Full-duplex is a switching technique that allows a switch to forward its complete CAM table to neighboring switches, whereas half-duplex cannot.
   d. Full-duplex is a switching technique that allows a switch to carry multiple VLANs on a link, whereas half-duplex does not.

8. What's the primary difference between a symmetric and an asymmetric switch?
   a. A symmetric switch has half of its ports configured with the same speed and the other half of its ports configured with a mix of speeds, whereas an asymmetric switch has all of its ports configured with a mix of speeds.
   b. A symmetric switch supports only store-and-forward switching, whereas an asymmetric switch supports all switching methods.
   c. All ports on a symmetric switch are of the same speed, whereas all ports on an asymmetric switch are not of the same speed.
   d. Symmetric switches have a fixed configuration architecture, whereas asymmetric switches are modular.

9. Which two of the following statements are true about port-based memory buffering?
   a. Incoming packets are stored in queues that are associated with specific incoming ports.
   b. All incoming packets are deposited into one large memory buffer that is shared by all ports on the switch.
   c. A packet is transmitted after all other packets ahead in the queue have been successfully transmitted.
   d. It doesn't have the problem of head-of-line blocking

10. Which two of the following describe a VLAN?
    a. A Layer 2 broadcast domain created by switch configuration
    b. A Layer 3 broadcast domain created by router configuration
    c. A group of users and devices configured on a switch to be in the same logical workgroup
    d. A group of users and devices attached to the same collision domain

11. Which two of the following statements do not characterize VLANs?
   a. Provide organizational flexibility.
   b. Allow users in one broadcast domain to communicate with users in another broadcast domain without going through a router.
   c. Users belonging to the same VLAN can reside anywhere in the network, as long as they are connected to a switch port that has been assigned to that user's VLAN.
   d. Do not support large growing networks.

12. How does frame filtering allow VLAN communication to occur?
   a. Frames are tagged with an ISL header that identifies the source station's VLAN.
   b. Frames are compared against a filtering table to determine where the frames are to be forwarded.
   c. Frames must travel to the router in order to be filtered against access lists.
   d. An incoming frame is stored in a memory buffer until the switch learns about the VLAN in its CAM table.

13. Which two of the following are not benefits of VLANs?
   a. Eliminate all Layer 1 and Layer 2 issues associated with moving users from one location to another.
   b. Broadcasts can be contained with maximum control.
   c. Eliminate the need for Layer 3 devices such as routers.
   d. Reduce administrative costs associated with managing user moves, adds, and changes.

14. Which two of the following are Layer 3 issues associated with moving users in a network?
   a. The compatibility of the NIC
   b. Firewall configurations
   c. Workstation DNS configuration
   d. Hub/switch port availability

15. Which two of the following are functions performed by the Spanning Tree Protocol?
   a. Removes physical loops in a Layer 2 bridged/switched network
   b. Determines the best path to destination networks
   c. Uses VTP packets to communicate topology information
   d. Determines which ports can and cannot receive and forward traffic

Answers

1. **f.** Slow STP convergence is not a problem commonly associated with shared Ethernet LANs.

2. **a, c, d.** A MAC address, port number, and aging timer would all be found in a switch's CAM table.

3. **c.** Layer 4 switches forward packets based on MAC address, network layer address, and TCP or UDP port numbers.

4. **b, c, e.** Propagation delay is influenced by cable type, cable length, and the number and type of intermediate devices.

5. **b.** Fast-forward switching works by forwarding a frame immediately after examining the frame's destination MAC address.

6. **b.** Microsegmenting optimizes available bandwidth by allowing a user to attach to a dedicated switch port and access the full media bandwidth.

7. **a.** The primary difference between full-duplex and half-duplex is that the former type allows stations to transmit and receive simultaneously, whereas the latter type only allows a station to either transmit or receive at one time.

8. **c.** The primary difference between a symmetric and an asymmetric switch is that the latter type contains different speed ports, whereas the former type contains only ports that are of the same speed.

9. **a, c.** With port-based memory buffering, incoming packets are stored in queues that are associated with specific incoming ports, and a stored packet is only transmitted after all other packets ahead in the queue have been transmitted.

10. **a, c.** A VLAN is both a switch-configured Layer 2 broadcast domain and a group of users and devices configured to be in the same logical workgroup.

11. **b, d.** VLANs *do* require Layer 3 devices such as routers, and VLANs *do* support large growing networks.

12. **b.** With frame filtering, packets are compared against a filtering table to determine where the packets are to be forwarded.

13. **a**, **c.** VLANs do *not* eliminate Layer 1 and Layer 2 issues associated with user relocation, and VLANs do *not* eliminate the need for Layer 3 devices such as routers.

14. **b**, **c.** Firewall and DNS configurations are two Layer 3 issues associated with moving users in a network.

15. **a**, **d.** STP removes physical loops in a bridged/switched network and determines which ports can and cannot receive and forward traffic.

CHAPTER 17

Introduction to Wide Area Networks

This chapter will:

- **Discuss the differences between a LAN and a WAN**

- **Cover the common devices that make up a WAN infrastructure**

- **Look at the three approaches to WAN connectivity**

- **Examine the various WAN encapsulation methods, including HDLC, PPP, LAPB, Frame Relay, and ISDN**

- **Explore dial-on-demand routing (DDR)**

This chapter presents you with a broad overview of wide area networks (WANs) by introducing you to the fundamental concepts, technologies, and terminology used in WAN communications. WANs provide the means for interconnecting local area networks (LANs) over broad geographic regions using a variety of connectivity options, networking equipment, and protocols. Later chapters further explore individual WAN communication strategies, including Point-to-Point Protocol (PPP), Frame Relay, and Integrated Services Digital Network (ISDN).

WAN Overview

A WAN is a communications network that connects users and LANs across a broad geographic area. WANs are typically used by enterprise companies to connect their branch offices and telecommuters to company headquarters or to other remote offices served by the company headquarters. Because it's not generally economically feasible to build a

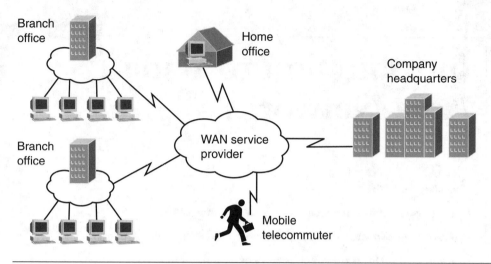

Figure 17-1   The function of a WAN service provider

leased-line network to reach all remote locations, companies usually subscribe to a WAN service provider, such as a regional Bell operating company (RBOC), whose internetworks provide the interconnection of central and remote sites (see Figure 17-1).

To connect to the WAN provider, a customer can choose from a variety of WAN access services and protocols. Some of the most common of these WAN access methods and protocols include PPP, Frame Relay, ISDN, Asynchronous Transfer Mode (ATM), dial-up, cable modem, and Digital Subscriber Line (DSL), among others. Each of these WAN technologies uses specific equipment and protocols that operate at the bottom three layers of the OSI model. Figure 17-2 shows the WAN protocols that we explore in this chapter and in following chapters.

NOTE: The CCNA exam does not cover ATM, cable modems, or DSL. Chapter 21 includes background coverage for cable modems and DSL because of their growing influence in Internet connectivity.

Terminology

Following are several key components of an end-to-end WAN infrastructure.

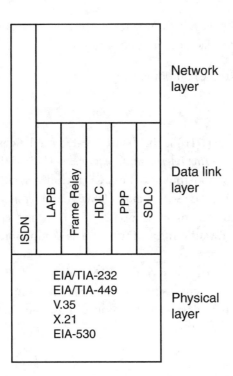

Figure 17-2
WANs and the
OSI model

Network layer

Data link layer

ISDN · LAPB · Frame Relay · HDLC · PPP · SDLC

Physical layer

EIA/TIA-232
EIA/TIA-449
V.35
X.21
EIA-530

- **Customer premises equipment (CPE)** The CPE comprises equipment that is located on the WAN subscriber's premises. This equipment includes devices that are owned by the subscriber and/or leased to the subscriber by the WAN service provider.

- **Demarcation (demarc)** This is the point at which the CPE ends and the local loop begins. Generally, the demarc is located at the subscriber's *point of presence* (POP), which is the point at which the subscriber wiring ends and the service provider wiring begins.

- **Local loop (last mile)** This portion of the WAN includes the cabling that stretches from the demarc to the service provider's *central office* (CO) or POP. The local loop cabling is typically copper wire, but it can also be fiber optic.

- **Central office (CO)** This location describes the service provider's local facility. It includes the telecommunications and networking equipment, such as WAN switches and routers, that terminates the local loop. The CO connects to other central offices located within the toll network.

- **Toll network** The toll network comprises all the switching and routing equipment and telecommunications facilities located within the WAN service provider cloud.

Figure 17-3 illustrates these components.

DTE and DCE

The *data terminal equipment* (DTE) is the device located on the customer premises that communicates with the *data circuit terminating equipment* (DCE). The DTE includes such devices as PCs, terminals, and routers. The DCE includes such devices as modems, *channel service units* (CSUs), *data service units* (DSUs), and *terminal adapters* (TAs). The DCE is responsible for connecting the subscriber's DTE to the service provider's facility by converting the DTE traffic into a form that is compatible with the provider's equipment.

As shown in Figure 17-4, each end of the WAN link has a DTE/DCE connection. In this figure, for instance, the connection is between the router and the CSU/DSU. Because the CSU/DSU is a device that connects the router (DTE) to the service

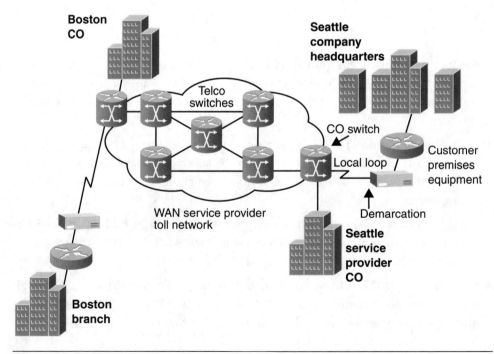

Figure 17-3 WAN components

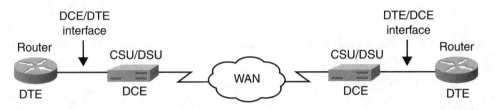

Figure 17-4 The DTE/DCE interface

provider's CO, the CSU/DSU is responsible for converting the router's traffic into a format that the CO switch will understand and, on the reverse end, for reconverting traffic from the provider's switches back into its original format.

Note that there are physical layer protocols that define how the DCE/DCE interface operates. These protocols will be explored later in the section, "WANs at the Physical Layer."

 EXAM TIP: **A WAN link is between two end-to-end DTEs.**

SVCs and PVCs

Another element common to the WAN infrastructure is the virtual circuit, which is defined as a logical circuit established between two network devices. The two types of virtual circuits are explained as follows:

- **Switched virtual circuit (SVC)**   SVCs are temporary connections that are established dynamically and torn down once a communication session has ended. SVCs go through three stages: link establishment, data transfer, and link termination.

- **Permanent virtual circuit (PVC)**   PVCs are permanently established connections. Unlike SVCs, once established PVCs are not torn down after communication has ended.

SVCs are generally used with WAN connections in which traffic is sent periodically. In this case, traffic doesn't require a costly always-on connection and is therefore well suited to utilizing virtual circuits that exist only for the duration of a transmission session. PVCs, in contrast, are well suited to carrying frequent high-volume traffic.

WAN Devices

The devices found in a WAN architecture can vary according to the type of WAN technology being used and the services and protocols being employed. The most common of these devices are these:

- Routers
- Access servers
- WAN switches
- Modems
- CSUs/DSUs

Routers in the WAN

In a WAN environment, routers are responsible for connecting the customer's network to the WAN service. With a modular construction that supports a broad range of media capabilities, link speeds, network layer protocols, and application services, routers are critical to meeting the scalability, performance, and management requirements of a network infrastructure seeking WAN connectivity.

Access Servers in the WAN

Access servers are basically gateway routers that provide a concentration point for dial-up users. For example, access servers can be equipped with internal or external modems that can terminate 56 Kbps calls from remote users and provide dial-out capabilities for local users. Figure 17-5 shows an example of how this dial-up concentration can occur.

WAN Switches

WAN switches are multiservice networking devices commonly deployed in service provider backbones. These devices are capable of supporting a wide variety of WAN technologies, including ATM, Frame Relay, and broadband services. Figure 17-1 illustrated a WAN service provider backbone that connects a corporate network's headquarters with a branch office using WAN switches.

Modems

Modems are devices that convert analog signals to digital, and vice versa. You are most likely familiar with modems because they often connect home computers to the Inter-

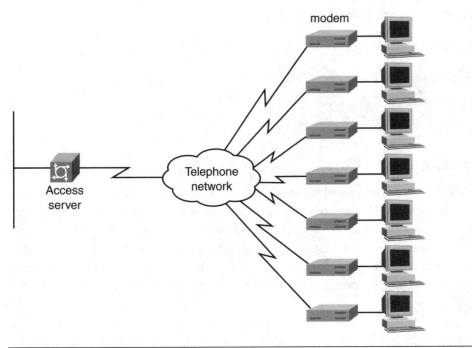

Figure 17-5   Access server concentrating dial-up users

net. Yet, in addition to being used as Internet access devices for the home consumer, modems are also used by many companies to connect telecommuters to the company office. Figure 17-5 illustrated how this remote-access solution works.

CSUs/DSUs

A channel service unit/data service unit is a device that adapts the physical interface on a DTE device, like a router, to the interface on a DCE device, like a WAN switch, residing in the CO. For example, in Figure 17-1, the routers at both ends of the WAN link each connect to a CSU/DSU that is located on the customer premises, and the CSU/DSU connects to the CO switch.

The CSU/DSU is also responsible for providing the clocking signal for communication between the DTE and the DCE.

WAN Connectivity Approaches

There are three major types of WAN connections (see Figure 17-6).

- Dedicated leased lines
- Packet-switched connections
- Circuit-switched connections

Dedicated Leased Lines

A dedicated leased line provides an always-on point-to-point WAN link from a customer site through a carrier network to a remote site. This connection is pre-established and is permanently fixed for each remote location that is reached through the carrier network. Because these lines are physically dedicated, they cannot be dynamically torn down to reach new locations, as is possible with virtual circuits. In addition, the leased line is private, which means that the link's bandwidth is not shared with other service provider customers.

Dedicated leased lines are used in the WAN to carry voice, video, and data traffic at speeds typically ranging between 64 Kbps and 45 Mbps. These types of links are therefore well suited to networks that have high bandwidth requirements and a need to support diverse traffic types.

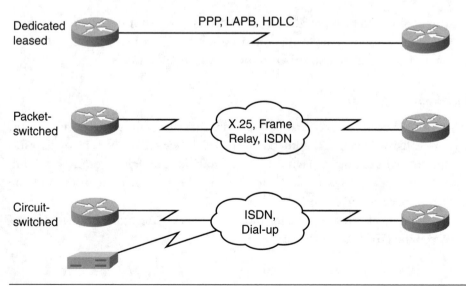

Figure 17-6   WAN connection types

Some common examples of WAN protocols used on dedicated leased lines include PPP, High Level Data Link Control (HDLC), and Link Access Procedure, Balanced (LAPB).

Provisioning Bandwidth

When a subscriber orders the leased connection, the subscriber has the option of choosing the link's bandwidth capacity. In North America and in many other parts of the world, WAN bandwidth for copper links is provisioned according to the guidelines set forth by the North American Digital Hierarchy, which defines standard rates of transmission for user-to-network copper cabling.

The hierarchy begins by defining one 64 Kbps channel as a digital stream level 0 (or DS0). Higher rates of transmission are simply multiples of the basic DS0 rate. For example, 1.544 Mbps (DS1) is a standard rate of transmission that comprises 24 DS0 channels. Table 17-1 shows some of the most common capacity rates specified by the hierarchy.

Note that each capacity listed in the hierarchy can also be referred to by its T designation. T1 and T3 are the most commonly used capacities.

Europe has its own digital transmission standard, called the *E system*. Defined by the Committee of European Postal and Telephone (CEPT), the E system is similar to that of the North American T system. Table 17-2 shows the European E system.

For fiber optic cabling, the standard transmission rates are defined by the Synchronous Digital Hierarchy (SDH), which is a system based on multiples of a 51.84 Mbps rate, called Synchronous Transport Signal level 1 (or STS-1). The STS rates correspond to SONET Optical Carrier (OC) levels, the more common of which are presented in Table 17-3.

Table 17-1   North American Digital Hierarchy

DIGITAL STREAM	CAPACITY	NUMBER OF DS0S	COMMON TERM
DS0	64 Kbps	1	Channel
DS1	1.544 Mbps	24	T1
DS1C	3.152 Mbps	48	T1C
DS2	6.312 Mbps	96	T2
DS3	44.736 Mbps	672	T3
DS4	274.176 Mbps	4032	T4

Table 17-2   CEPT Hierarchy

SIGNAL	CAPACITY	NUMBER OF EIS	NUMBER OF DSOS
EO	64 Kbps		1
E1	2.048 Mbps	1	32
E2	8.448 Mbps	4	132
E3	34.368 Mbps	16	537
E4	139.264 Mbps	64	2176

Table 17-3   Synchronous Digital Hierarchy

STS RATE	SONET OC LEVEL	CAPACITY
STS-1	OC-1	51.84 Mbps
STS-3	OC-3	155.52 Mbps
STS-9	OC-9	466.56 Mbps
STS-12	OC-12	622.08 Mbps
STS-24	OC-24	1.244 Gbps
STS-48	OC-48	2.488 Gbps
STS-96	OC-96	4.976 Gbps
STS-192	OC-192	9.952 Gbps

Circuit-Switched Connections

With circuit switching, a dedicated physical connection is established from a customer premise through a carrier network to a remote network location. Once the communication session has ended, the circuit-switched link is terminated. One of the most common examples of this type of connection is the telephone call, which is a dedicated link that goes through an establishment phase, a maintenance phase, and a termination phase. Another example would be an ISDN connection (see Figure 17-7).

Circuit switching is generally used when WAN bandwidth requirements are low and when traffic is transmitted only on a periodic basis, as opposed to on a constant basis. For instance, many small companies have an ISDN Internet connection that they use only for sending e-mail and small file transfers and for surfing the Web. And many

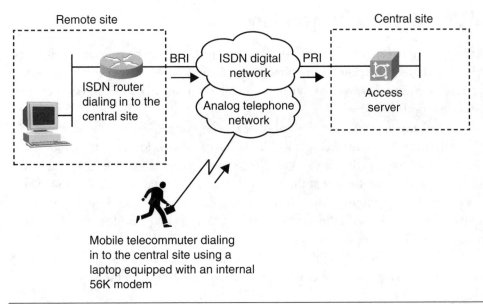

Figure 17-7   Circuit switched connections

companies also connect small branch offices and mobile telecommuters to the company's central site using dial-up 56k modems. In both cases, bandwidth requirements and usage patterns are so low that it would not be cost-effective to choose remote access technologies that offered always-on, dedicated connections.

Packet-Switched Connections

Packet-switched connections transport packets from a source to a destination through a carrier network using virtual circuits, which can either be SVCs or PVCs. Packets transported across the carrier network are switched according to the information contained in the their headers, for example, destination address.

Like dedicated leased lines, packet-switched connections are capable of supporting speeds of up to T3/E3 rates (44.736 Mbps/34.368 Mbps). However, unlike dedicated leased lines, where the bandwidth is not shared, packet-switched lines are shared among the carrier network's customers. Although this has the benefit of lowering connection costs, performance and availability issues become a concern because traffic from one customer has the potential of negatively affecting the traffic flow from another customer. To address these concerns, service providers now allow subscribers to sign contracts called *service level agreements* (SLAs) that specify minimum levels of performance and/or availability that the service provider is required to deliver.

WANs at the Physical Layer

As you learned in Chapter 2, the physical layer of the OSI model is concerned with specifying standards that relate to the physical characteristics of the network cabling and networking equipment, such as transmission rates, cabling distances, physical connectors, signal timing, and so forth.

In a WAN environment, the physical layer also describes the connection between the DTE and the DCE. As you read earlier, the DCE is a device (for example, a modem or CSU/DSU) whose function is to convert the signals received from the DTE (such as a PC or a router) into a form that the CO switch can understand. Typically, the DCE is located on the customer premises in the wiring closet or telecommunications closet, but it can also be located at the service provider CO. It is also possible for the CSU/DSU to be an interface on a Cisco router.

Several standardized physical layer protocols define the interface between the DTE and DCE. Following are the ones most commonly used by Cisco equipment.

- **EIA/TIA-232** This specification defines the DB-25 connector and supports unbalanced circuits at signal speeds of up to 64 Kbps. Formerly known as RS-232, this standard has undergone development by both the Electronic Industries Association (EIA) and the Telecommunications Industries Association (TIA).

- **EIA/TIA-449** Developed by the EIA and TIA, this standard supports balanced and unbalanced circuits, speeds of up to 2 Mbps, transmissions over longer distances than EIA/TIA-232, and defines the DB-37 connector. Intended as a replacement for the EIA/TIA-232 standard, EIA/TIA-449 was not widely accepted because of the large installed base of DB-25 hardware.

- **V.35** Developed by the International Telecommunication Union-Telecommunication Standardization Sector (ITU-T), the V.35 standard supports speeds of up to 48 Kbps (practically, however, speeds of up to 4 Mbps are allowed; 8 Mbps for short distances).

- **X.21** Developed by the ITU-T, the X.21 standard supports balanced circuits and uses a DB-15 connector. This standard is most commonly used in Europe and Japan to connect network devices to public data networks.

- **EIA-530** This standard essentially defines the EIA/TIA-449 standard for the DB-25 connector, which was originally supported only by EIA/TIA-232.

WANs at the Data Link Layer

WAN data link layer protocols are responsible for encapsulating user traffic for transport across WAN media. These protocols define such data link characteristics as physical addressing, error detection, sequencing, flow control, and network layer protocol identification.

In general, the encapsulation protocol that is used depends on which *WAN technology* the subscriber has provisioned and what *equipment* is being used to provide the WAN communication, as well as the services that the protocol will need to support. For example, if a customer orders a dedicated leased line, some of the protocols that are available include PPP, HDLC, Frame Relay, and LAPB. And, if the customer is using Cisco equipment, there is the added option of using Cisco's proprietary version of the standard HDLC protocol. The choices are then narrowed down based on the specific services that are required for the WAN protocol.

Following are some of the WAN encapsulation protocols that we will cover in the rest of this chapter and throughout the rest of the book:

- **High-level Data Link Control (HDLC)**   HDLC is a standardized bit-oriented synchronous data link layer WAN protocol that is typically used on dedicated leased lines or on circuit-switched links. Cisco has developed its own proprietary version of the standard HDLC protocol.

- **Point-to-Point Protocol (PPP)**   PPP is a standardized data link layer WAN protocol that is most commonly employed on dedicated and circuit-switched links. It supports various physical interfaces, including synchronous, asynchronous, *high-speed serial interface* (HSSI), and ISDN interfaces and allows the simultaneous transport of various network layer protocols over the same PPP link. PPP also supports a variety of link configuration options, including link authentication, packet compression, and frame field negotiations, among others.

- **Link Access Procedure, Balanced (LAPB)**   LAPB is a standardized data link layer WAN protocol used in the encapsulation of X.25 traffic. As a reliable, connection-oriented protocol, LAPB is most commonly used in packet-switched X.25 networks and is occasionally used on dedicated leased lines to provide robust reliability features.

- **Frame Relay**   Frame Relay is a WAN technology typically used on packet-switched infrastructures. With virtual circuits to connect devices in multipoint, point-to-multipoint, or point-to-point configurations, user traffic can be encapsulated in either a standard frame or a frame that's proprietary to Cisco.

- **Integrated Services Digital Network (ISDN)**   ISDN is a circuit-switched WAN technology capable of transporting digitized voice, video, and data over the existing telephone infrastructure. ISDN specifies two types of service interfaces: *basic rate interface* (BRI) and *primary rate interface* (PRI).

- **Dial-on-demand routing (DDR)**   DDR is not a WAN encapsulation protocol but is instead a technique that allows WAN circuits to be used only when traffic that has been deemed "interesting" is received for transport across the WAN connection. DDR is most commonly used with ISDN.

HDLC

HDLC was originally developed by the International Organization for Standardization (ISO—Note that ISO is not an acronym; instead, the name derives from the Greek word *iso*, which means equal.) and is derived from the Synchronous Data Link Control (SDLC) protocol. The HDLC standard does not support multiple network layer protocols on the same link. However, Cisco has adopted its own proprietary version of HDLC, which *does* allow multiple network layer protocols to share the same point-to-point link. This support is made possible by inserting a proprietary *protocol type* field in the HDLC frame format, as shown in Figure 17-8.

The fields in the HDLC frame are explained as follows:

- **Flag**   The flag field is a single byte and indicates the beginning or end of a frame. This field consists of the binary sequence 01111110.

- **Address**   The address field is one or two bytes in length and is usually set to the binary sequence 11111111, which denotes the standard broadcast address.

- **Control**   The control field is one or two bytes in length and is used to indicate the frame type, which can be an information frame, a supervisory frame, or an unnumbered frame.

- **Protocol type**   The protocol field is two bytes long and is used to identify the upper-layer protocol encapsulated in the data field.

- **Data**   The data file is variable in length and contains the upper-layer information.

Figure 17-8
Cisco HDLC
frame format

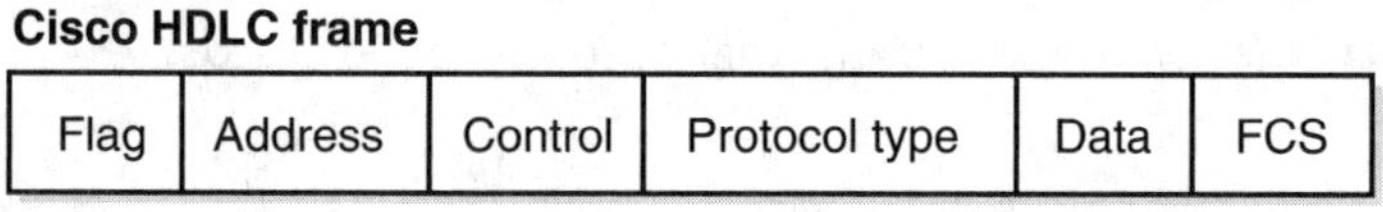

Cisco HDLC frame

Flag	Address	Control	Protocol type	Data	FCS

- **FCS**   The *frame check sequence* (FCS) field is two bytes long and is used to calculate whether any bit errors occurred during frame transmission. This error-checking procedure ensures the integrity of received data.

Expert Discussion

Understanding the Difference Between Error Detection and Error Recovery

With respect to data link layer protocols, error detection is a process that involves identifying bit errors in the frame of a received packet. Specifically, a frame field called the Frame Check Sequence (FCS) or Cyclical Redundancy Check (CRC) is used to perform a calculation on the received frame to determine if any bit errors occurred during transmission. If an error is detected, the frame is discarded.

Error recovery is the process that involves *retransmission* of the discarded frame.

All WAN data link layer protocols perform error detection. However, not all WAN data link layer protocols perform error recovery. In the latter case, it would be up to a higher-layer protocol to provide the error-recovery mechanism. Examples of WAN data link layer protocols that do and do not provide error recovery are listed in the following table:

WAN DATA LINK PROTOCOL	ERROR RECOVERY?
Frame Relay	No
HDLC	No
LAPB	Yes
LAPD (Link Access Procedure on the D Channel)	No
PPP	Optional
SDLC	Yes

Cisco's HDLC is the default encapsulation used by Cisco routers over synchronous serial links. As a proprietary protocol, Cisco's HDLC may not work other vendor's HDLC implementations. A network manager will therefore need to make sure that both devices at each end of the HDLC link are compatible before traffic can be allowed to flow across the link (see Figure 17-9). When the compatibility can't be established between devices from different vendors, then PPP can be used.

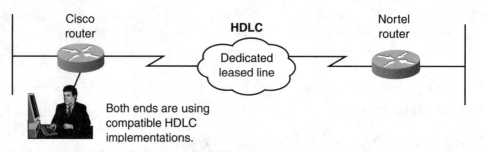

Figure 17-9 HDLC link device compatibility

HDLC's Predecessor: SDLC

HDLC is derived from the SDLC protocol, which was developed by IBM during the mid-1970s for use in IBM's Systems Network Architecture (SNA) networks. As a bit-oriented synchronous WAN data link layer encapsulation protocol, SDLC was designed to support various types of WAN topologies and link types, including point-to-point and multipoint links, and circuit-switched and packet-switched connections. The protocol was also designed with full-duplex and error-recovery capabilities.

Traditional SDLC architectures define two network node types: primary stations and secondary stations. Primary stations (or primaries) are responsible for controlling the operations of secondary stations (or secondaries). This includes polling the secondaries to determine if they need to transmit and establishing, maintaining, and terminating circuit-switched connections. Because they are under the control of the primary, secondaries are allowed to transmit to the primary only when granted permission (that is, when polled by the primary).

HDLC Transfer Modes

Transfer modes define how stations access the WAN media. HDLC supports the following transfer modes:

- **Normal Response Mode (NRM)**   Under this transfer mode, secondary stations are not allowed to communicate with a primary until being granted permission by being polled. NRM is the transfer mode used by SDLC.

- **Asynchronous Response Mode (ARM)**   Under this mode, secondaries can communicate with primaries at any time; they do not have to be polled.

- **Asynchronous Balanced Mode (ABM)**   Under ABM, a station can be either a primary or a secondary. As a result, stations employing this transfer mode can communicate with one another at will. On Cisco routers, ABM is the default transfer mode on HDLC links.

PPP

The Point-to-Point Protocol is a standardized data link layer WAN encapsulation that supports multiple interface types and multiple network layer protocols. Using the Link Control Protocol (LCP), PPP supports a wide variety of link-control features that allow both ends of a PPP link to negotiate how data transfer will occur on the link. PPP is explored further in Chapter 18.

LAPB

The Link Access Procedure Balanced protocol is a standardized data link layer WAN encapsulation most commonly found in X.25 networks. In an X.25 environment, LAPB's responsibility is to ensure that packets are sequenced and received error free, which makes this protocol well suited to unreliable analog media. LAPB also features link compression and support for dedicated serial lines.

LAPB's robust reliability features are built in to the fields of its frame header. Because LAPB's frame format is based on HDLC's format, the fields in an LAPB frame are structured similar to HDLC's fields (see Figure 17-10). However, unlike HDLC, which does not support reliability mechanisms such as windowing, flow control, or error recovery, LAPB's frame types have been tweaked to support these types of reliability features. Following are the LAPB frame types that have been tweaked to provide these added reliability features:

- **Information frame (I-frame)**   This LAPB frame type transports upper-layer information and some control information. I-frames are responsible for sequencing, flow control, and error detection and recovery.

- **Supervisory frame (S-frame)**   This frame type carries control information. S-frames are responsible for such tasks as requesting and suspending transmission, reporting frame status, and acknowledging the receipt of I-frames.

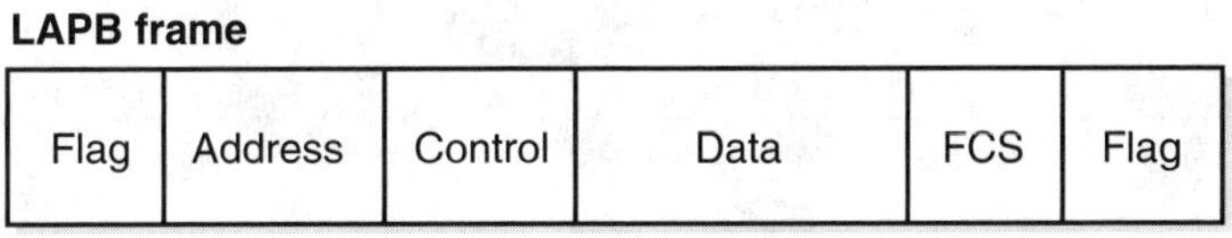

Figure 17-10
LAPB frame format

LAPB frame

Flag	Address	Control	Data	FCS	Flag

- **Unnumbered frame (U-frame)** This frame carries control information and is responsible for such tasks as link setup and termination, and reporting frame errors.

Frame Relay

Frame Relay is a WAN data link layer encapsulation used widely in packet-switched infrastructures. Standardized by the ITU-T, Frame Relay supports the interconnection of multiple network devices over a variety of link configurations, including point-to-point links and numerous multipoint link configurations (see Figure 17-11). In a packet-switched environment, these links are typically PVCs.

Frame Relay defines the interface between user devices (for example, routers and PCs) and carrier-owned network equipment (for example, CO packet switches). User devices are known as DTEs, and the network equipment to which the DTE attaches is known as the DCE. Although Frame Relay is most often provisioned from a service provider, it can also be implemented within an enterprise's own private network.

When interfaced to a North American *packet-switched telephone network* (PSTN), Frame Relay access speeds generally range between 56 Kbps and 44.736 Mbps (T3), while in Europe and other parts of the world, speeds of up to 34.368 Mbps (E3) are

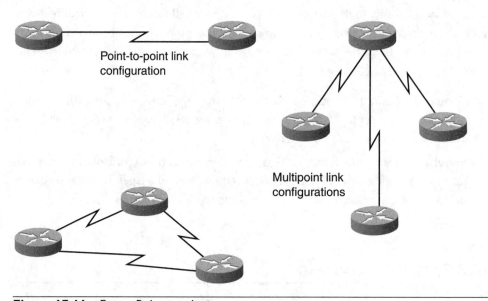

Figure 17-11 Frame Relay topologies

common. Note that Frame Relay's bandwidth capacity offers a significant advantage over traditional X.25 packet-switched connections, which are typically able to offer only up to 128 Kbps transmission rates.

In addition to offering increased bandwidth for WAN access, Frame Relay connections are often able to take advantage of the service provider's reliable, high-performance fiber optic and digital backbone networks. Not only does this benefit transfer rates, it also has the effect of minimizing transmission errors, which is important because Frame Relay does not offer error recovery.

Although Frame Relay does not offer error recovery, it does implement basic flow control. This flow control process is made possible by the use of special frame bits called *backward explicit congestion notification* (BECN) and *forward explicit congestion notification* (FECN). Both bit mechanisms allow for the notification of network devices on detection of congestion within the Frame Relay network.

Frame Relay will be explored in greater detail in Chapter 20.

ISDN

ISDN is a communication technology designed to carry digitized voice, video, and data traffic across the existing telephone network. Because ISDN communication occurs over the telephone network, ISDN is a circuit-switched transmission method, which means that ISDN calls go through an establishment phase, a maintenance phase, and a termination phase.

ISDN services can be provisioned over two types of links: basic rate interface (BRI) and primary rate interface (PRI). The first of these service types, BRI, provides two 64 Kbps B (bearer) channels for transmitting user traffic and one 16 Kbps D (delta) channel for transmitting signaling and control information. Considered relatively low speed, BRI offers a total bandwidth capacity to the users of 128 Kbps. With the 16 Kbps signaling channel and 48 Kb of framing bits, ISDN actually uses 192 Kbps.

The second ISDN service, PRI, delivers 23 64 Kbps B channels and one 64 Kbps D channel for a combined bit rate of up to 1.544 Mbps. This bit rate applies primarily to North America and Japan; in Europe, Australia, and many other parts of the world, ISDN PRI delivers 30 B channels and one 64 Kbps D channel for a combined bandwidth capacity of up to 2.048 Mbps.

ISDN Elements

As part of the circuit-switched ISDN architecture, ISDN specifies a variety of network components, the most common of which can be summarized as follows:

- **Terminal Equipment Type 1 (TE1)**   A TE1 is an ISDN-compatible device that connects to either an NT1 or an NT2. Such devices include PCs, telephones, and routers that are equipped with ISDN interfaces.

- **Terminal Equipment Type 2 (TE2)**   A TE2 is a non-ISDN-compatible device. To connect to the ISDN network, a TE2 connects to a *terminal adapter* (TA).

- **Network Termination Type 1 (NT1)**   An NT1 connects the four-wire ISDN subscriber wiring to the two-wire local loop.

- **Network Termination Type 2 (NT2)**   An NT2 concentrates all subscriber ISDN devices and connects them to the NT1. Besides serving as a concentration device, the NT2 also switches user traffic.

- **Terminal Adapter (TA)**   A TA provides the ISDN interface for non-ISDN-compatible devices. A TA is sometimes referred to as an ISDN modem.

In addition to the preceding components, ISDN also defines specific reference points that are used to identify the interfaces between ISDN devices. These reference points are as follows:

- **R reference point**   Defines the interface between a TE2 and a TA.

- **S reference point**   Defines the interface between an NT2 and a TE1 or a TA.

- **T reference point**   Defines the interface between an NT1 and an NT2. If no NT2 is being used, then the R reference point is located between the NT1 and the TE1 or the TA.

- **U reference point**   Defines the interface between the NT1 and the CO ISDN switch.

Figure 17-12 presents an example of how all these components and interfaces fit together.

Chapter 19 explores ISDN in greater detail.

DDR

Dial-on-demand routing is a feature that allows WAN links to be used *selectively*. That is, by defining traffic as interesting, a network manager has the ability to select which traffic will be allowed to initiate a circuit-switched WAN connection, such as an ISDN call. As a result, a router will, on receiving traffic that has been defined as interesting, allow the traffic on-demand access to the WAN circuit.

The ability to send prioritized traffic on an as-needed basis is important for links that are charged based on how often they are utilized. With these types of connections, it is not cost-effective to allow nonpriority user traffic to bring up WAN links on an

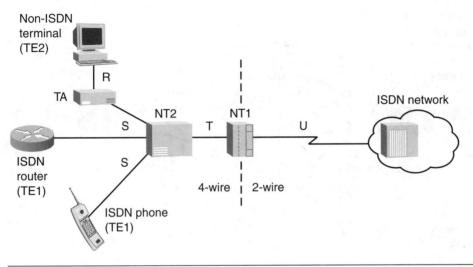

Figure 17-12   ISDN

as-requested basis. For example, a network manager may deem that WWW traffic is not important enough to bring up the network's ISDN connection but that e-mail traffic is important and should thus be granted unrestricted access to the costly ISDN connection.

This does not mean, though, that non-interesting traffic is never allowed access to the WAN media. It simply means that this type of traffic is not allowed to *bring up* or *establish* the WAN connection; this traffic can still be transmitted when a link has been activated for interesting traffic. In conclusion, therefore, non-interesting traffic can access the WAN link only when the link has already been established for interesting traffic.

The administrator can also configure the link to close after a set period of time if no interesting traffic has been transmitted. While non-interesting traffic can travel across the open connection, it cannot keep it open.

DDR Benefits

DDR is commonly used as a cost-effective alternative to dedicated leased lines or Frame Relay links. In these situations, user traffic is of such low volume and of such short duration that the need for expensive dedicated connections can be waived, thus potentially minimizing WAN expenditures to a tremendous extent.

In addition to being used as a cost-effective alternative to dedicated WAN links, DDR also provides redundancy. Specifically, DDR can be used as a backup to a primary WAN connection (such as a leased line) and/or as a load sharing mechanism. In the latter case, DDR would be used to bring up a second WAN link whenever the primary one

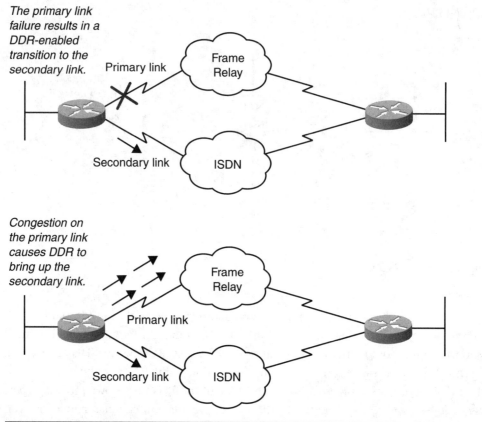

The primary link failure results in a DDR-enabled transition to the secondary link.

Primary link

Frame Relay

Secondary link

ISDN

Congestion on the primary link causes DDR to bring up the secondary link.

Frame Relay

Primary link

Secondary link

ISDN

Figure 17-13   DDR and redundancy

reached a certain level of congestion. Figure 17-13 illustrates how redundancy may occur in a DDR environment.

ISDN Uses

While the data requirements and services available in a location have a major impact on a business's WAN choices, it is pretty safe to say that few medium to large enterprises choose to use ISDN as their primary WAN technology. It provides a very cost-effective backup to other technologies, but its use as a primary connection is appropriate for small single-site businesses and small branch locations. However, DSL and Cable service with higher bandwidth and often considerably lower cost are both cutting severely into ISDN's market.

Summary

WANs are communications networks that connect users and LANs across wide geographic areas. Typically ordered from a service provider, WAN connectivity is of three types: dedicated leased lines, packet-switched connections, and circuit-switched connections. Dedicated leased lines are private always-on links that support only permanent point-to-point connections. Packet-switched connections use virtual circuits to establish either permanent or temporary connections between remote locations through a packet-switched carrier network. Circuit-switched connections use physical dedicated links that remain active throughout the duration of a communication session, but then are torn down once communication has ended.

A number of WAN devices can be found in a WAN infrastructure, including routers, access servers, CSUs/DSUs, WAN switches, modems, terminal adapters, NT1s, and NT2s.

At the physical layer, WAN protocols define the interface between the DTE and DCE. The DCE is the device (for example, a CSU/DSU, modem, or WAN switch) that connects the DTE (for example, a router, PC, or terminal) to the CO switch. Examples of physical layer WAN protocols that define the interface between the DTE and DCE are EIA/TIA-232, EIA/TIA-449, and V.35.

At the data link layer, WAN protocols define the encapsulation method used on the link between two end-to-end DTE devices. The WAN protocol that is chosen for the link depends on the WAN connectivity option and devices that are being used. Examples of data link layer WAN encapsulation protocols are HDLC, PPP, Frame Relay, and ISDN.

Case Study: Tuvix IT Solutions

Now you will apply the knowledge you have gained from this chapter's discussion of WANs. Review the following background information on Tuvix IT Solutions and examine its proposed WAN topology (shown in next illustration). After reviewing the requirements for this network's WAN infrastructure, answer the questions that follow about which WAN technologies, equipment, and protocols would best meet the requirements set forth.

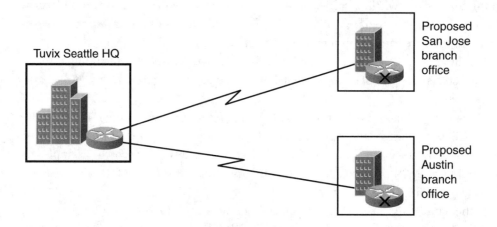

Scenario: Tuvix is a small IT solutions company that provides network consulting and training services to small and medium-sized businesses. With offices currently located only in Seattle, Tuvix is looking to expand its services nationwide by establishing new offices in San Jose and Austin.

The first of these new locations, San Jose, will house an estimated 50-75 employees and will be required to access the central Seattle site for long periods of time each day. The bandwidth requirements for this site will require a WAN link that can provide *at least* 30 Mbps transfer rates. In addition, this link must be private and dedicated.

For the Austin site, which will hold around 25 employees, WAN traffic is projected to be low-volume and periodic. A WAN link that can provide at least 64 Kbps will suffice. Although this site is projected to undergo increased traffic levels as more users are added, current plans will address only the site's temporary needs.

In addition, Tuvix will have mobile telecommuters dialing in to the company's central and remote offices from remote locations throughout the country. Because these users are mobile, they will need to use dial-up 56K modems.

Directions: As the network planner for Tuvix, you have been assigned the task of outlining a simple WAN design that can address the company's requirements for cost, performance, availability, and scalability. The WAN solution must include the appropriate WAN connectivity methods—that is, dedicated leased lines, packet-switched connections, or circuit-switched connections—for each location and must specify which WAN encapsulation protocols—that is, HDLC, PPP, LAPB, Frame Relay, or ISDN—are to be used for each proposed WAN connection.

To select the best WAN solution for meeting Tuvix' business and technical needs, you gathered the following additional information:

- CPE devices will be from multiple vendors. Any protocols that are chosen must be standardized.

- Multiprotocol traffic will be supported on the WAN infrastructure.

- Other than general security, there are no traffic restrictions placed on users.

- The prospective WAN service providers are using reliable, high-performance media and networking equipment within their facilities.

Now that you've learned what you need to know to begin your WAN design task, the following worksheet questions will guide you through the process of selecting the appropriate technologies and protocols for Tuvix IT Solutions.

Design Worksheet for Tuvix IT Solutions: San Jose WAN Design

1. Which WAN connectivity approach—dedicated leased line, packet-switched, or circuit-switched—should be used for the link between the Seattle and San Jose sites? How much bandwidth should be provisioned (use appropriate digital hierarchy standard)?

2. Based on the chosen WAN connectivity option for the San Jose site, identify which WAN devices—CSUs/DSUs, modems, routers, access servers, or WAN switches—would be located at the San Jose premises, and describe what functions these devices would serve.

3. Based on the WAN connectivity option and devices chosen for the San Jose site, and based on the network's other requirements, which WAN data link layer protocol should be used? Why?

Austin WAN Design

4. Which WAN connectivity approach—dedicated leased line, packet-switched, or circuit-switched—should be used for the link between the Seattle and Austin sites?

5. Based on the chosen WAN connectivity option for the Austin site, identify which WAN devices—CSUs/DSUs, modems, routers, access servers, or WAN switches—would be located at the Austin premises.

6. Based on the WAN connectivity option and devices chosen for the Austin site, and based on the network's other requirements, which WAN data link layer protocol should be used? Why?

WAN Topology

7. Sketch a diagram of your proposed WAN topology. Be sure to indicate all the WAN devices that will be used in your design (represent the service provider with clouds).

Case Study Suggested Solution
(Your solutions may vary)

1. The link between the Seattle and San Jose sites should be a dedicated leased line. This meets the requirements for constant usage and private connection. To be able to provide at least 30 Mbps transfer rates, the WAN link between these two sites should be T3 (44.736 Mbps).

2. The WAN devices that will be used at the San Jose site will include a router and a CSU/DSU. The router will connect the San Jose LAN to the CO switch using the CSU/DSU, which will provide the signal conversion and clocking.

3. The WAN data link layer protocol that should be used on the dedicated leased line is PPP. PPP provides support for multiple network layer protocols and multiple vendor implementations. In addition, PPP provides link authentication procedures using PAP or CHAP. These features satisfy Tuvix's requirements.

   Although HDLC (Cisco version) supports multiple network layer protocols, it should not be used because network requirements specify that the protocol should be standardized. LAPB should not be used because it does not support multiple network layer protocols (refer to Figure 17-10). As a result, PPP is the best option for the WAN link between Seattle and San Jose.

4. The WAN connection used between the Seattle and Austin sites should be a circuit-switched connection like ISDN. The connection is dynamically established

and torn down to accommodate calls that don't require full-time dedicated sessions. It would be wise to compare the projected prices of the ISDN service and a Frame Relay link. Frame Relay might be cheaper in the long run, more reliable, easier to manage, and can expand as more users are added.

5. The WAN devices used at the Austin site will depend on which WAN technologies are being employed. For a circuit-switched connection, the devices can include modems, a router or access server, and ISDN equipment such as TAs, NT1, NT2, TE1s, and TE2s. For packet-switched connections, the devices may include a router and CSU/DSU.

6. The WAN data link layer protocol chosen for the link between Seattle and Austin will depend on which WAN technology is used, among other requirements. For a circuit-switched connection, the WAN link should be ISDN BRI. This service addresses the link's bandwidth requirement by providing two 64 Kbps data channels, and it allows a connection to be terminated when its communication session has ended.

For a packet-switched connection, the WAN data link layer protocol could be Frame Relay.

7. See the following illustration.

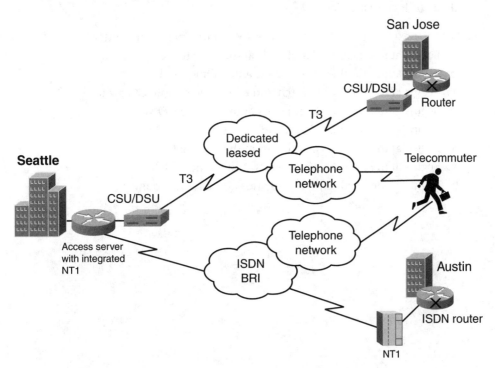

Practice Questions

Take a few moments and check your grasp of the concepts covered in this chapter. The answers follow the questions.

Questions

1. Which three layers of the OSI model can WANs operate at?
   a. Physical
   b. Data link
   c. Network
   d. Transport
   e. Session
   f. Presentation
   g. Application

2. Which of the following statements does *not* accurately characterize the CPE?
   a. Located on the WAN subscriber's premises
   b. Includes devices that may be leased to the WAN subscriber
   c. Includes all DTE devices
   d. Includes all DCE devices

3. See the next illustration. Where does a WAN link begin and end?
   a. Begins at the local DTE and ends at the remote DCE
   b. Begins at the local DCE and ends at the remote DTE
   c. Begins at the local CO switch and end at the remote CO switch
   d. Begins at the local DTE and ends at the remote CO switch
   e. Begins at the local DCE and ends at the remote CO switch
   f. Begins at the local DTE and ends at the remote DTE
   g. Begins at the local DCE and ends at the remote DCE
   h. Begins at the local demarc and ends at the remote demarc

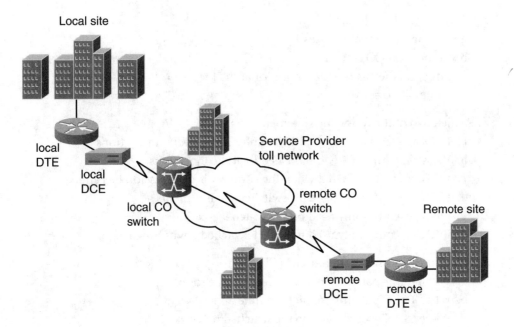

Local site

local DTE

local DCE

local CO switch

Service Provider toll network

remote CO switch

Remote site

remote DCE

remote DTE

4. Which two of the following are functions of the CO?

   a. Contains the CPE

   b. Terminates the local loop

   c. Contains the customer's DTE and DCE

   d. Contains toll network switching equipment

5. Which five of the following are typical examples of DCE devices?

   a. Routers

   b. Modems

   c. CSUs/DSUs

   d. TE1s

   e. NT1s

   f. CO switches

   g. Terminals

   h. PCs

   i. Tas

   j. LAN switch

6. Where is the DCE located?
   a. On the customer premises
   b. At the local CO
   c. Either on the customer premises or at the local CO
   d. None of the above

7. Which two of the following statements characterize PVCs?
   a. PVCs are permanently established physical, private connections
   b. PVCs are permanently established logical connections
   c. PVCs can be terminated when the communication session has ended
   d. PVCs are used only in circuit-switched environments
   e. PVCs are commonly used on dedicated leased lines
   f. PVCs are commonly used in packet-switched environments.

8. When are SVCs most often used? (Choose two)
   a. When traffic patterns are low-volume and periodic
   b. When traffic patterns are high-volume and frequent
   c. When ISDN is used over circuit-switched networks
   d. In packet-switched environments

9. Which of the following devices is used to concentrate dial-up users?
   a. Modem
   b. CSU/DSU
   c. WAN switch
   d. Access server
   e. NT1
   f. TA

10. How are analog modems commonly used? (Choose two)
    a. To connect telecommuters to their work
    b. To connect high-traffic LANs to the Internet
    c. To connect routers to WAN service providers
    d. To connect home users to the Internet

11. What are the three WAN connectivity options?
    a. Analog
    b. DSL
    c. Packet-switched
    d. Cable modem
    e. Circuit-switched
    f. Frame Relay
    g. Dedicated leased line

12. What are three common examples of WAN data link layer protocols used on dedicated leased lines?
    a. LAPB
    b. LAPD
    c. PPP
    d. Frame Relay
    e. HDLC
    f. ISDN

13. Which of the following statements does *not* characterize a circuit-switched connection?
    a. A dedicated physical connection that lasts for the duration of a call
    b. A temporary logical connection used in packet-switched networks
    c. Example of a circuit-switched connection includes telephone calls
    d. None of the above

14. What is the difference between a dedicated leased line and a packet-switched PVC connection? (Choose two)
    a. A dedicated leased line is shared, whereas a packet-switched PVC connection is private
    b. A dedicated leased line is private, whereas a packet-switched PVC connection is shared
    c. Packet-switched PVC connections support rates only up to T1, whereas dedicated leased lines support rates up to T4
    d. Packet-switched PVC connections are logical circuits, whereas dedicated leased lines are physical circuits.

15. What do WAN physical layer protocols define?
    a. The interface between the DCE and the DTE
    b. The data link layer encapsulations that are allowed on the WAN link
    c. The network layer IP address of the remote DTE
    d. The applications supported between the DTE and the DCE

16. What is the most common physical connector used by the EIA/TIA-232 standard?
    a. DB-37
    b. DB-25
    c. EIA/TIA-449
    d. Winchester

17. Choose four of the features that correctly describe Cisco's HDLC.
    a. Supports multiple network layer protocols
    b. Supports flow control, error recovery, and sequencing
    c. Is a bit-oriented synchronous protocol
    d. Was derived from the SDLC protocol
    e. Is supported by all vendors
    f. Typically used in packet-switched networks
    g. Is the default encapsulation on Cisco serial links

18. Which three of the following WAN data link layer protocols are capable of performing error recovery?
    a. Frame Relay
    b. HDLC
    c. LAPB
    d. LAPD
    e. PPP
    f. SDLC

19. Which of the following statements best describes the HDLC ABM transfer mode?
    a. A secondary station is allowed to communicate with a primary only when granted permission by being polled
    b. Secondaries can communicate with primaries at any time
    c. Stations in this transfer mode can communicate with one another at will
    d. A station can access the WAN media at any time but only when its status changes to mainframe

20. Which two of the following statements best characterize LAPB?

    a. Proprietary to Cisco

    b. Commonly used in packet-switched X.25 networks

    c. Is a WAN network layer protocol

    d. Performs error recovery, flow control, and sequencing

    e. Is the most popular WAN protocol used on dedicated leased lines

21. Which of the following statements does *not* accurately describe the Frame Relay protocol?

    a. Standardized

    b. WAN data link layer protocol used widely in packet-switched networks

    c. Supports point-to-point and multipoint link configurations

    d. Supports transfer rates up to T3/E3 speeds

    e. Basic flow control is implemented via FECN and BECN bits

    f. Does not support SVCs

22. Characterize ISDN?

    a. ISDN is a communication technology designed to carry analog traffic at high speeds over traditional packet-switched networks

    b. ISDN supports packet-switched communication over dedicated, private leased lines

    c. As a circuit-switched transmission method, ISDN calls go through an establishment phase, a maintenance phase, and a termination phase

    d. ISDN does not support DDR

23. Which four of the following are ISDN reference points?

    a. U

    b. F

    c. R

    d. P

    e. S

    f. V

    g. T

24. What is DDR?

    a. A WAN data link layer encapsulation protocol that carries ISDN traffic

    b. A technique for determining which traffic is not ISDN traffic

    c. A technique that allows WAN links to be established only when ISDN traffic is received for transport across a backup link

    d. A technique that allows WAN links to be established only when interesting traffic is received for transport across the WAN link

25. What are two common applications of DDR?
   a. Backup for a primary WAN connection
   b. Load balancing
   c. User authentication
   d. QoS

Answers

1. **a., b., c.** WANs operate at the bottom three layers of the OSI model.

2. **d.** The CPE does not include all DCE devices, because the DCE may be located at the CO.

3. **f.** WAN links begin at the local DTE and end at the remote DTE.

4. **b., d.** The CO terminates the local loop and contains toll network switching equipment.

5. **b., c., e., f., i.** DCE devices include modems, CSUs/DSUs, NT1s, CO switches, and TAs.

6. **c.** The DCE is located either on the customer premises or at the local CO.

7. **b., f.** PVCs are permanently established *logical* connections commonly used in packet-switched environments.

8. **a., d.** SVCs are most often used when traffic patterns are low-volume and periodic and in packet-switched environments.

9. **d.** Access servers are used to concentrate dial-up users.

10. **a., d.** Analog modems are commonly used to connect telecommuters to their work and to connect home users to the Internet.

11. **c., e., g.** The three WAN connectivity options are dedicated leased lines, packet-switched connections, and circuit-switched connections

12. **a., c., e.** Common examples of WAN data link layer protocols used on dedicated leased lines include LAPB, HDLC, and PPP.

13. **b.** A circuit-switched connection is not a temporary logical connection used in packet-switched networks; instead, it's a *physical* connection used in circuit-switched networks.

14. **b., d.** The first difference between a dedicated leased line and a packet-switched PVC connection is that the former connection is private, whereas the latter connection is shared. The second difference is that the former connection is a physical connection, whereas the latter connection is logical.

15. **a.** WAN physical layer protocols define the interface between the DCE and DTE.

16. **b.** The DB-25 connector is the most common physical connector used by the EIA/TIA-232 standard.

17. **a., c., d., g.** Cisco's HDLC supports multiple network layer protocols, is a bit-oriented synchronous protocol, is derived from SDLC, and is the default encapsulation on Cisco serial interfaces.

18. **c., e., f.** LAPB, PPP, and SDLC perform error recovery. In PPP's case, error recovery is optional.

19. **c.** Stations operating under the ABM transfer mode can communicate with one another at will.

20. **b., d.** LAPB is commonly used in X.25 packet-switched networks and performs flow control, error recovery, and sequencing.

21. **f.** Frame Relay *does* support SVCs.

22. **c.** ISDN is a circuit-switched transmission method in which calls go through an establishment phase, a maintenance phase, and a termination phase.

23. **a., c., e., g.** ISDN reference points include the R, S, T, and U reference points.

24. **d.** DDR is a technique that allows WAN links to be established only when traffic that has been defined as interesting is received for transport across the WAN link.

25. **a., b.** Link backup and load balancing are two common applications of DDR.

CHAPTER 18

PPP

This chapter will:

- **Identify the main components involved in PPP communication**

- **Identify and describe the five stages of PPP operation**

- **Describe how link authentication occurs with PAP and CHAP**

- **Configure and verify basic PPP operation**

In Chapter 17, you learned that various data link layer protocols are involved in WAN communications. One of the protocols you were introduced to in that chapter is the Point-to-Point Protocol (PPP), which you learned is a WAN encapsulation method used for transporting multiprotocol traffic across point-to-point serial links. This chapter continues that discussion of PPP by exploring the protocol's essential components, including its Link Control Protocol (LCP) and Network Control Program (NCP), and its stages of operation, which, as you will soon discover, comprise functions such as link configuration, authentication, and network layer protocol encapsulation. Lastly, this chapter presents you with some of the basic Cisco IOS commands used for enabling PPP and verifying its operation in a production environment.

PPP Overview

The Internet Engineering Task Force (IETF) developed PPP in the late 1980s as a replacement for the Serial Line Internet Protocol (SLIP). Designed to be a standard data link layer protocol for transporting multiprotocol traffic across serial point-to-point links, PPP is most often used to connect remote dial-up users to a central site and for router-to-router connectivity between remote locations (see Figure 18-1). The following data points highlight some of PPP's more salient features:

- **Support for multiple network layer protocols** PPP uses the NCP protocol to encapsulate traffic from multiple upper-layer protocols, including IP, IPX, AppleTalk, DECNet, and the Open Systems Interconnect/Connectionless Network Protocol (OSI/CLNS).

- **Support for various link configuration features** Through the use of its LCP protocol, PPP is able to support features such as error recovery, loop detection, authentication with the Password Authentication Protocol (PAP) and Challenge Handshake Authentication Protocol (CHAP), data compression, and load balancing (multilink PPP), among others.

- **Support for a variety of WAN technologies and interfaces** PPP can be used on ISDN links, dial-up analog lines, and dedicated leased lines. Supported interfaces include synchronous, asynchronous, and High Speed Serial Interface (HSSI) interfaces.

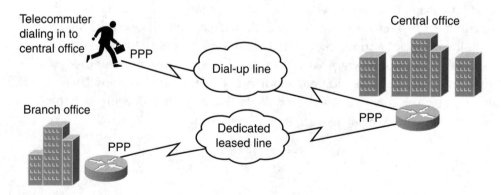

Figure 18-1   PPP implementations

PPP and the OSI Model

While PPP is considered a data link layer protocol, it does offer both physical and network layer services.

PPP at the Physical Layer

At the physical layer, PPP is associated with the protocols that define the interface between the *data terminal equipment* (DTE) and the *data circuit-terminating equipment* (DCE), as depicted in Figure 18-2. Recall from last chapter's discussion on WAN physical layer protocols that the DTE/DCE interface is concerned with specifying media characteristics such as transmission speed, cabling lengths, physical connectors, electrical signaling, and clocking.

You may also recall that the organizations responsible for defining the DTE/DCE protocols include the Electronics Industries Association (EIA), Telecommunications Industries Association (TIA), and International Telecommunication Union-Telecommunication Standardization Sector (ITU-T), among others. It is these agencies that have standardized the physical layer protocols that are used today throughout the world in a wide spectrum of network infrastructures. Some examples of DTE/DCE protocols that are supported by PPP are listed as follows:

- EIA/TIA-232

- EIA/TIA-422

- ITU-T V.24

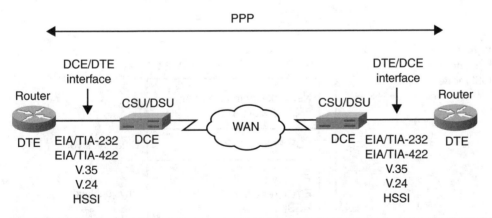

Figure 18-2   The DTE/DCE interface

- ITU-T V.35

- HSSI

PPP at the Network Layer

At the network layer, PPP is responsible for encapsulating application traffic from various network layer protocols. This encapsulation process is accomplished through the use of NCP, which is actually a family of protocols responsible for choosing and configuring various network layer protocols such as IP, IPX, and AppleTalk.

Each network protocol is encapsulated in its own NCP. Some examples of common NCPs are listed as follows:

- Internet Protocol Control Protocol (IPCP)

- Internetwork Packet Exchange Control Protocol (IPXCP)

- AppleTalk Control Protocol (ATCP)

 NOTE: NCPs do not just encapsulate network layer protocols; they also carry data link layer protocols, such as the Cisco Discovery Protocol (CDP) and the Spanning Tree Protocol (STP).

Figure 18-3 illustrates PPP's relation to the OSI model layers.

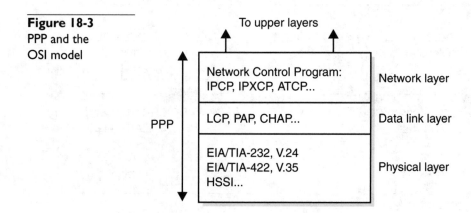

Figure 18-3
PPP and the
OSI model

PPP Framing

It is important to recognize that PPP is defined by its frame format. That is, the frame format contains fields that specify how PPP operation occurs. Figure 18-4 presents PPP's frame format.

Table 18-1 describes each field's purpose in the PPP frame.

It is important to note that PPP's LCP is able to make modifications to the standard PPP frame format, an event that would occur during PPP's first stage of operation. This stage, and others, is covered next.

1	1	1	2	Variable	2 or 4
Flag	Address	Control	Protocol	Data	FCS

Field length, in bytes

Figure 18-4   PPP frame format

Table 18-1   Fields of the PPP Frame

FIELD	DESCRIPTION
Flag	A single byte consisting of the binary sequence 01111110 (hexadecimal 7E). PPP frames always begin and end with this field.
Address	A single byte consisting of the binary sequence 11111111 (hexadecimal FF), the standard broadcast address. Because PPP's Address field is always set to broadcast, it does not support unicast addressing at the data link layer.
Control	A single byte consisting of the binary sequence 00000011 (hexadecimal 03).
Protocol	Consists of two bytes that identify the protocol carried in the Data field. Examples of protocol field values are listed as follows: 8021 (IPCP) C021 (LCP) 8029 (ATCP) C023 (PAP) 802B (IPXCP) C223 (CHAP)
Data	Field consisting of up to 1,500 bytes (negotiable through LCP). Also referred to as the Information field, the Data field contains the upper-layer traffic specified in the protocol field.
FCS	Frame Check Sequence. A 2-byte field used for detecting errors in the frame. LCP can negotiate a 4-byte FCS for improved error detection.

Note: A complete up-to-date listing of protocol field values can be obtained in RFC 1700.

PPP Stages of Operation

PPP operation can be characterized by a series of stages in which PPP links are established, configured, tested, authenticated, and terminated. These stages may be presented as follows:

1. **Link establishment and configuration negotiation** In the initial stage of PPP operation, a point-to-point link is established between two sites and LCP frames are exchanged to negotiate various link configuration parameters.

2. **Link-quality determination (optional)** This is an optional stage in which LCP tests the link to determine if the link is of sufficient quality to carry multiprotocol traffic.

3. **Authentication (optional)** This is an optional stage in which either PAP or CHAP authentication occurs.

4. **Network layer protocol configuration negotiation** During this stage, both sides of the PPP link exchange NCP frames to choose and configure the network layer protocols that will be transported across the link.

5. **Transmission and link termination** Packets from each network layer protocol are transmitted across the PPP link for as long as the link remains active.

The following sections explore each of these PPP stages of operation in fuller detail.

Link Establishment and Configuration Negotiation

When a PPP link is first established between two peers, LCP frames are sent to negotiate data link layer configuration parameters. Some examples of data link layer parameters that are negotiated by LCP include the following:

NOTE: Aside from the authentication protocol parameter, the following LCP features are not CCNA exam objectives.

- **Maximum receive unit (MRU)** This parameter specifies the largest acceptable frame size on the PPP link. The default MRU is 1,500 bytes.

- **PPP compression** Using a compression algorithm such as *Stacker* or *Predictor*, data in a PPP frame can be compressed before being transmitted. This procedure has the benefit of improving throughput on the PPP link.

- **Multilink PPP**   PPP allows multiple point-to-point links leading to the same destination to be bundled together into one logical link. Packets that are sent across the bundled link are chopped into little fragments, sequenced, load-balanced across each of the individual links in the bundle, and then recombined at their destination (see Figure 18-5). This process has the benefit of maximizing available bandwidth and reducing latency between end devices.

- **Authentication protocol**   During PPP's initial stage of operation, LCP negotiates and chooses which (if any) authentication protocol, either PAP or CHAP, will be used to authenticate both ends of the PPP link. If an authentication protocol is chosen, the actual authentication process occurs in PPP's authentication stage of operation.

- **Looped link detection**   Using the *Magic Number* protocol, both sides of a PPP link can detect whether a physical loop exists on the link. If a loop is detected, LCP can be configured to take the link down.

Not all of the preceding configuration features are required to be used on a PPP link; they are all optional. This in fact is why each side of a PPP link sends LCP frames to the other side: to negotiate which options will be used and which options will be rejected. Once an option has been either accepted or rejected, an acknowledgement frame is sent to indicate that the option is no longer negotiable.

Link-Quality Determination

After the link has been established and configuration parameters have been negotiated, LCP has the option of testing the link to assess whether or not the link is good enough to bring up the soon-to-be-configured network layer protocols. If this option is selected, protocol transmission typically will not begin until after LCP has finished testing the link.

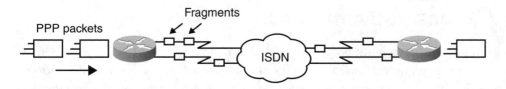

Figure 18-5   Multilink PPP example

Authentication

Authentication is a security feature that prevents unauthorized peers from establishing a communication session with each other. The following protocols may be involved in PPP authentication:

- **PAP**   A simple authentication method that uses a two-way handshake to authenticate users based on username and password.

- **CHAP**   A strong authentication method that uses a three-way handshake to authenticate users based on username and password. CHAP offers a more secure authentication scheme than PAP offers.

PPP authentication is covered in greater detail in the upcoming section "PPP Link Authentication."

Network Layer Protocol Configuration Negotiation

Once the link has been optionally tested and authenticated, both sides of a PPP link exchange NCP frames to choose and configure the network layer protocols (such as IP, IPX, AppleTalk, and so forth) that are to be encapsulated for transport across the link. Each protocol that is to be encapsulated is associated with its own NCP.

Transmission and Link Termination

Once the appropriate network protocols have been chosen and initialized, packets from each protocol can then be transmitted across the PPP link.

Transmission can be terminated at any time. Typically, LCP will terminate a link at the request of a user, but link termination may also occur when the carrier signal is lost or when the link's idle timer expires. If LCP closes the link, it informs the NCP so that the upper-layer protocols can be prepared for link termination.

PPP Link Authentication

PPP allows point-to-point peers to be authenticated using either PAP or CHAP. Or, no authentication may be chosen at all. The choice is based on the peers' configurations, which indicate the authentication scheme and other related configuration parameters. Depending on which parameters are configured and what types of peers (whether routers or dial-in users) are being authenticated, the authentication process can proceed in a variety of ways. However, no matter which type of configuration or peer is involved, the process can still be summarized in a series of steps. The flowchart presented in Figure 18-6 illustrates the following steps in PPP authentication:

1. **An incoming PPP connection request is received**   This event characterizes the initial two stages of PPP operation.

2. **The authentication method is determined**   Authentication options include PAP, CHAP, or none (no authentication). If no authentication has been configured on the receiver, the PPP session is *allowed* to commence.

   If authentication has been configured successfully on both peers, the following steps ensue.

3. **The authentication process occurs**   The nature of this authentication depends on which protocol, either PAP or CHAP, is used.

4. **Authentication succeeds or fails**   If successful, the PPP session is allowed to commence. Otherwise, the connection is terminated immediately.

You can view the debug output of the process by issuing a **debug ppp auth** statement on the router. It is always good to see this kind of output so you know what's going on.

PAP

PAP is an authentication method that involves a simple two-way handshake between two peer routers. As illustrated in Figure 18-7, the first handshake occurs when the remote router sends its username and password to the central site router. The second

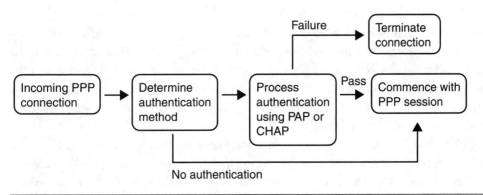

Figure 18-6   The PPP authentication process

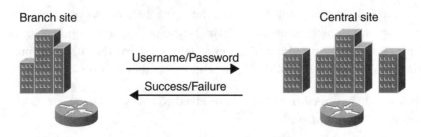

Figure 18-7   PAP two-way handshake

handshake occurs when the central site router sends a message indicating that authentication succeeded or failed.

With PAP, authentication occurs only upon initial link establishment. During this period, the peer attempting to establish a PPP session sends its username and password repeatedly over the link until the receiving peer either acknowledges the connection or terminates the link. The peer logging in determines the timing and frequency of these repeated login attempts.

PAP typically is not considered a secure authentication method, primarily because user passwords are sent over the link unencrypted and in clear text, which allows anyone with a protocol analyzer or software package to capture the password while it is in transit and use it to authenticate their way into the network—definitely not a desirable situation.

As the next section points out, CHAP offers a more secure, more sophisticated way to authenticate users attempting to access a central site's network.

CHAP

CHAP is an authentication method that involves a three-way handshake between two peer routers. As illustrated in Figure 18-8, the first handshake occurs when the central site router receives the connection request (not shown) and sends a challenge to the branch router. The second handshake occurs once the branch router has processed the challenge and sent its response. The third handshake occurs once the central site router has processed the response and sent a message to the branch router indicating success or failure.

Unlike PAP, in which authentication occurs only upon initial link establishment, CHAP authentication occurs also during normal transmission, at periodic intervals. That is, every so often, the three-way handshake between the central and remote router will repeat itself, with the timing and frequency of the repeated login sessions being

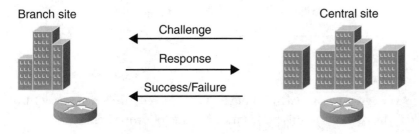

Figure 18-8 CHAP three-way authentication

determined by the central site router. This is a security feature that is intended to ensure the continued authenticity of both sides of the link while the link remains active. It also prevents hackers from using brute-force attacks to authenticate their way into the network.

Encrypted passwords are another security feature employed by CHAP. Unlike PAP, which sends passwords over the network in clear text, CHAP sends passwords that have been encrypted using the Message Digest 5 (MD5) algorithm. This procedure ensures that passwords captured by a protocol analyzer or software package cannot be read, at least not without going through a sophisticated decryption process.

Expert Discussion

CHAP Authentication

In this section (which is not an exam objective and is optional), we explore exactly how the three-way handshake occurs between two peer routers using CHAP authentication. As you just learned, this handshake procedure comprises three steps:

1. Receiving a login attempt and sending the CHAP challenge

2. Responding to the challenge

3. Accepting or rejecting the login attempt

Receiving a Login Attempt and Sending the CHAP Challenge

In the next illustration, Router ABC is attempting to establish a communication session with Router XYZ.

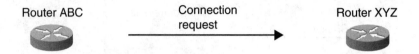

After both peers agree to use CHAP, Router XYZ proceeds to generate a CHAP challenge packet. The contents of this packet includes the following items:

- CHAP packet type 01 (challenge)
- Challenge ID number
- Random number
- Username of challenger (Router XYZ)

The following illustration shows the challenge packet being sent to Router ABC:

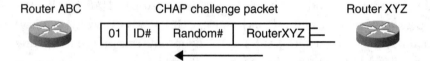

Responding to the Challenge

Upon receiving the challenge from Router XYZ, Router ABC proceeds to process the challenge by using the MD5 algorithm. Specifically, items from the CHAP challenge packet, along with the password associated with Router XYZ, are fed into the MD5 algorithm's *hash generator*. The result is an MD5-hashed CHAP value. The next illustrates how the MD5 process occurs.

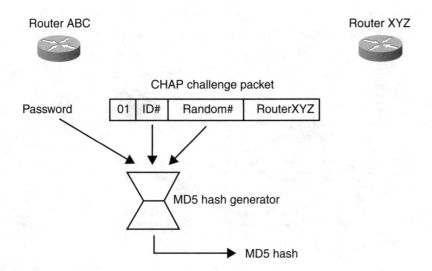

After generating the MD5 hash, Router ABC will proceed to construct a CHAP *response* packet that includes the following items:

- CHAP packet type 02 (response)
- Response ID number
- MD5 hash
- Username of challenged peer (Router ABC)

The following illustration shows the CHAP response packet being sent to Router XYZ:.

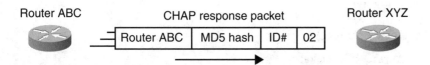

Accepting or Rejecting the Login Attempt

Upon receiving the response, Router XYZ will proceed to process the CHAP response packet using the MD5 algorithm. Specifically, Router XYZ will gather the ID number and random number from the original CHAP challenge packet and will toss these items, along with the password it has configured for Router ABC, into the MD5 hash generator (see the following illustration). The result is another MD5 hash value, which

Router XYZ then uses to compare with the hash received from Router ABC. If the two hash values are equal, CHAP authentication is successful.

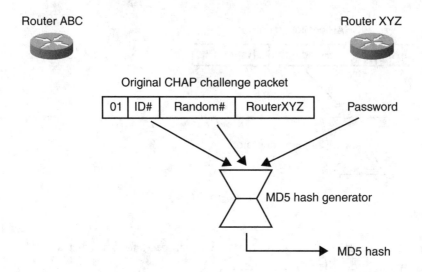

If Router ABC's login attempt is successful, Router XYZ sends a CHAP success packet that contains the following items:

- CHAP packet type 03 (success)
- ID number from response packet
- Text message indicating that authentication was successful

If on the other hand the login failed, Router XYZ sends a CHAP failure packet that contains the following items:

- CHAP packet type 04 (failure)
- ID number from response packet
- Text message indicating that authentication failed

The CHAP success or failure packet is subsequently sent to Router ABC.

Basic PPP Configuration

Configuring basic PPP operation is essentially a matter of enabling PPP encapsulation on the router's interface and specifying the parameters for authentication.

PPP Configuration Tasks:

1. Enable PPP encapsulation on the appropriate interface
2. Enable PAP or CHAP authentication

PPP Encapsulation Configuration

To enable PPP encapsulation on a Cisco serial interface, issue the **encapsulation ppp** command in interface configuration mode.

This command must be issued on both ends of the PPP link. Otherwise, if one side is using PPP encapsulation and the other side is configured with another encapsulation, such as HDLC, communication will not occur over the link.

PAP Configuration

To enable PAP authentication, you must first specify a username and password. In global configuration mode, issue the following command:

```
Router(config)#username username password password
```

The *username* is the host name of the router on the opposite end of the link, and the *password* is anything you choose.

 NOTE: The username and password are case-sensitive and the password on both peers must match. After specifying the username and password in global configuration mode, go into the appropriate interface and issue the ppp authentication pap command. You also need to issue the following command:

```
Router(config-if)#ppp pap sent-username username password
password
```

The *username* you specify here is your router's host name, and the *password* is the same one you configured previously using the username password command.

Router_B(config)#username Router_A password one2
Router_B(config)#interface serial 0
Router_B(config-if)#encapsulation ppp
Router_B(config-if)#ppp authentication pap
Router_B(config-if)#ppp pap sent-username Router_B
password one2

Router A

Router B

Router_A(config)#username Router_B password one2
Router_A(config)#interface serial 0
Router_A(config-if)#encapsulation ppp
Router_A(config-if)#ppp authentication pap
Router_A(config-if)#ppp pap sent-username Router_A
password one2

Figure 18-9 PPP configuration with PAP

Figure 18-9 presents an example configuration for two peer routers using PAP authentication.

CHAP Configuration

CHAP configuration is pretty straightforward. Issue the **ppp encapsulation chap** command in interface configuration mode and issue the **username password** command in global configuration mode. As was the case with PAP, the username specified in the latter of these two commands is the host name of the peer router on the opposite end of the link. In addition, passwords must again be identical at both ends, and the username and password are again case-sensitive.

Figure 18-10 presents an example configuration for two peers using CHAP authentication.

Router A   Router B

Router_A(config)#username Router_B password one2	Router_B(config)#username Router_A password one2
Router_A(config)#interface serial 0	Router_B(config)#interface serial 0
Router_A(config-if)#encapsulation ppp	Router_B(config-if)#encapsulation ppp
Router_A(config-if)#ppp authentication chap	Router_B(config-if)#ppp authentication chap

Figure 18-10 PPP configuration with CHAP

Verifying PPP

There are a variety of IOS commands you can use to verify and troubleshoot PPP configuration and operation. For the purposes of the CCNA exam, you only need to be familiar with one, the show interfaces command.

The show interfaces command, displayed in Figure 18-11, indicates that PPP is the encapsulation protocol configured on the interface. It also indicates the status of LCP and which network layer protocols the NCP has encapsulated.

```
Router# show interfaces
Serial0 is up, line protocol is up
  Hardware is HD64570
  Description: connects to Router_B
  Internet address is 172.21.10.10/8
  MTU 1500 bytes, BW 1544 K bit, DLY 20000 usec, rely 255/255, load 1/255
  Encapsulation PPP, loopback not set
  LCP Open
  Open: IPCP, CDP
  Last input 00:00:18, output 00:00:08, output hang never
  Last clearing of "show interface" counters never
  Input queue: 0/75/0 (size/max/drops); Total output drops: 0
  Queueing strategy: weighted fair
  Output queue: 0/64/0 (size/threshold/drops)
    Conversations 0/1 (active/max active)
    Reserved Conversations 0/0 (allocated/max allocated)
  5 minute input rate 3000 bits/sec, 4 packets/sec
  5 minute output rate 3000 bits/sec, 7 packets/sec
    1365 packets input, 107665 bytes, 0 no buffer
    Received 0 broadcasts, 0 runts, 0 giants, 0 throttles
    0 input errors, 0 CRC, 0 frame, 0 overrun, 0 ignored, 0 abort
    2064 packets output, 109207 bytes, 0 underruns
    0 output errors, 0 collisions, 4 interface resets
    0 output buffer failures, 0 output buffers swapped out
    4 carrier transition
    DCD=up  DSR=up  DTR=up  RTS=up  CTS=up
```

Figure 18-11   The show interfaces command

Summary

PPP is a data link layer WAN encapsulation protocol for point-to-point serial links and is commonly used to connect remote telecommuters to the corporate LAN and for router-to-router connectivity between remote locations.

PPP supports a variety of link configuration features through the use of its LCP, which is the protocol responsible for negotiating which configuration parameters are used on a PPP link.

PPP stages of operation include link establishment and configuration negotiation, link-quality determination (an optional stage), authentication (an optional stage), network layer protocol configuration negotiation, and transmission and link termination.

PPP authentication may use either PAP or CHAP. With PAP, the authentication process is a two-way handshake that uses username/password login information to authenticate a remote peer. With CHAP, authentication involves a three-way handshake in which the remote peer is challenged to provide a response that the local peer will use to base its authentication decision on.

PAP is typically considered less secure than CHAP because CHAP, unlike PAP, uses repeated challenges throughout the duration of a communication session, as well as encrypted passwords.

Case Study: Deus Institute

Now you will apply your knowledge of PPP and CHAP. Review the following background information on Deus Institute. After reviewing the requirements, answer the questions that follow about implementing PPP.

Background: The Deus Institute is a private research foundation dedicated to the exploration and advancement of public policy issues. Research conducted by the organization's resident scholars and fellows encompasses a broad range of fields, including economics, foreign relations and diplomacy, health and welfare, education, science and technology, and culture and religion.

Currently headquartered in Washington, D.C., the Deus Institute recently established a branch location in New York City. Because the Institute requires dedicated full-time connectivity between both of these sites, a dedicated leased line was ordered from the local service provider. PPP was chosen as the WAN encapsulation protocol.

Scenario: As the lead network manager for the new branch site, it is your task to configure the new router for PPP encapsulation and Challenge Handshake Authentication Protocol (CHAP) authentication. You also are required to verify your configuration to ensure that both sites are able to communicate successfully over the PPP link.

The next several sections will provide you with the knowledge you need to accomplish this task of implementing PPP for the Deus Institute.

Directions: Now you will apply the knowledge you have gained from this chapter to configure the PPP link for the Deus Institute. After examining the WAN topology for the organization's network, shown in the following illustration, fill out the configuration worksheet that follows.

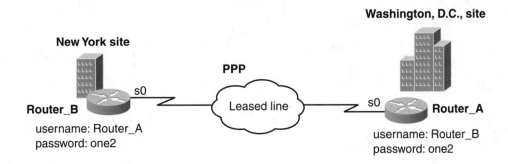

Configuration Worksheet for the Deus Institute

On Router B (the New York router):

1. Write down the correct command to configure the appropriate username and password. In which configuration mode would you issue this command?

2. Write down the correct command for enabling PPP encapsulation. In which configuration mode would you issue this command?

3. Write down the correct command for enabling CHAP authentication. In which configuration mode would you issue this command?

4. Which show command would you use to verify PPP operation?

Case Study-Suggested Solutions
(Your solutions may vary)

1. Use the following global configuration command to configure the username and
   password on Router B:

   ```
   Router_B(config)#username Router_A password one2
   ```

2. Use the following interface configuration command to configure PPP encapsulation on Router B's serial 0 interface:

   ```
   Router_B(config-if)#encapsulation ppp
   ```

3. Use the following interface configuration command to configure CHAP authentication on Router B's serial 0 interface:

   ```
   Router_B(config-if)#ppp authentication chap
   ```

4. You would use the show interfaces command to verify PPP operation.

Practice Questions

Take a few moments and check your grasp of the concepts covered in this chapter. The
answers are immediately following the questions.

Questions

1. Which of the following types of connections does PPP *not* support?
   a. ISDN
   b. HSSI
   c. Synchronous
   d. Asynchronous
   e. None of the above

2. Which two of the following are functions of LCP?
   a. Establishing and configuring network layer protocols
   b. Negotiating PPP data link layer configuration parameters
   c. Authenticating users using a three-way handshake
   d. Terminating the link

3. Which of the following is not one of the five stages in PPP operation?
   a. Link establishment and configuration negotiation
   b. Looped-link detection
   c. Network layer protocol configuration negotiation
   d. Authentication

4. How does PAP authentication occur?
   a. A remote peer sends a challenge to the local peer, who authenticates the remote peer based on its username and password.
   b. A remote peer sends its username and password to the local peer, who authenticates the remote peer based on this information.
   c. The remote peer uses the MD5 algorithm to authenticate its way into the network.
   d. The remote peer sends its username, password, ID number, and a random number to the local peer, who authenticates the remote peer based on this information.

5. Which two of the following are reasons why CHAP is a more secure alternative than PAP?
   a. Unlike PAP, CHAP sends passwords over the network encrypted.
   b. Unlike PAP, CHAP uses repeated challenges throughout the duration of a communication session.
   c. Unlike PAP, CHAP doesn't allow dial-in modem users to log in.
   d. Unlike PAP, CHAP sends usernames over the network encrypted.

6. When does the link-quality determination stage of PPP operation begin?
   a. After the network layer protocol configuration negotiation stage
   b. After authentication
   c. Right after the first stage of PPP operation
   d. Immediately before the last stage of PPP operation

7. True or False: PPP supports individual station MAC addressing in its frame.
   a. True
   b. False

8. What command is used to enable PPP encapsulation?
   a. encapsulation ppp
   b. ppp encapsulation
   c. ppp
   d. configure ppp encapsulation

9. Which command is used to enable CHAP authentication?
   a. ppp chap authentication
   b. ppp authentication chap
   c. ppp chap sent-username password
   d. enable chap authentication

10. Which two of the following statements about the username password global configuration command are true?
   a. The username specified in the command identifies the host name of the router on the opposite end of the PPP link.
   b. The username specified in the command identifies the router's own host name.
   c. The username and password are *not* case-sensitive
   d. The passwords configured on both ends of the PPP link must match.

Answers

1. **e.** PPP supports all the specified connection types.

2. **b.** and **d.** Two of LCP's functions are to negotiate PPP configuration parameters and to terminate the PPP link.

3. **b.** Looped-link detection is not a stage in PPP operation.

4. **b.** A remote peer sends its username and password to the local peer, who authenticates the remote peer based on this information.

5. **a.** and **b.** CHAP is more secure than PAP because the CHAP uses encrypted passwords and repeated challenges.

6. **c.** The link-quality stage of PPP operation begins immediately following the first stage of PPP operation.

7. **b.** False. PPP's frame only supports the broadcast address.

8. **a.** The encapsulation ppp command is used to enable PPP encapsulation on the interface.

9. **b.** The ppp authentication chap command is used to enable CHAP authentication on the interface.

10. **a.** and **d.** When using the username password command, you must ensure that the username you specify is the host name of the router on the opposite side of the PPP link. You must also ensure that the passwords on both routers match.

CHAPTER 19

ISDN

This chapter will:

- **Explain what ISDN is used for**

- **Describe ISDN components and reference points**

- **Analyze the differences between ISDN BRI and PRI**

- **Identify ISDN protocols**

- **Describe DDR**

- **Explain how to configure basic ISDN BRI**

- **Explain how to configure basic DDR**

- **Examine how to verify and troubleshoot ISDN**

This chapter presents a high-level overview of Integrated Services Digital Network (ISDN). Topics that will be explored in this chapter include ISDN services, components, protocols, and fundamental configuration commands. This chapter also explores *dial-on-demand routing* (DDR), specifically its operation and configuration over ISDN Basic Rate Interface (BRI). Lastly, this chapter presents some of the basic commands used in verifying and troubleshooting ISDN and DDR connectivity.

ISDN Elements

ISDN is a collection of communication protocols that provide end-to-end digital connectivity between customer sites using the existing telephone network infrastructure. As a digital WAN technology, ISDN allows companies to transport a variety of traffic types, including voice, video, data, text, graphics, and music, across the telephone network using high-speed digital equipment and a broad assortment of standardized ISDN protocols and interfaces.

Examples of ISDN applications include videoconferencing, high-speed image and file transfers, telecommuter access, and high-speed Internet access. Coupled with DDR, ISDN is also commonly used for *small office/home office* (SOHO) and telecommuter connectivity and for redundancy purposes either as a backup to a leased line or as a means for providing extra bandwidth when a primary line reaches capacity (see Figure 19-1).

ISDN works very much like an analog telephone call in that ISDN calls go through a setup and termination phase. However, unlike analog calls, which are made over an analog local loop and must be modulated at the local *central office* (CO) for transmission through the carrier's facilities, ISDN calls are digital and are therefore made over a digital local loop. The benefits to this type of connection are highlighted in the following data points:

- The use of digital signaling from end to end allows telephone networks to deliver digital services that support a variety of voice, video, and data applications.

- Compared to analog dial-up modems, ISDN dial-up offers a considerable improvement in bandwidth. In addition, ISDN allows customers the flexibility to choose the service level that will provide the customer's network the necessary bandwidth.

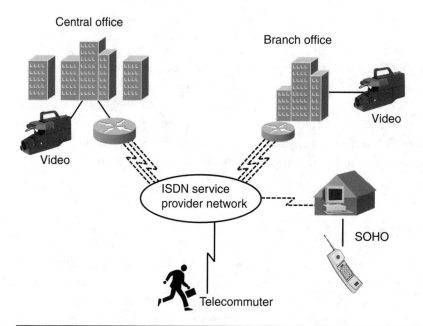

Figure 19-1 ISDN Network

- Unlike analog modems, which typically require over half a minute to establish a connection, ISDN devices can establish a call in under a second.

ISDN Services

ISDN lines consist of three primary channels: B channels, D channels, and synchronization channels. The B channel (also referred to as the *bearer* channel) carries the voice or data traffic encapsulated in data link layer frames. The D channel is an out-of-band signaling channel and is responsible for carrying messages involved in call setup, maintenance, and termination. And, lastly, the synchronization channel handles traffic synchronization and framing for ISDN traffic.

The quantity and bit capacity of channels in an ISDN line depend on the type of ISDN service implemented (see Figure 19-2). ISDN currently offers the following two services:

- **BRI** A BRI line consists of two 64 Kbps B channels and one 16 Kbps D channel, as well as 48 Kbps worth of framing and synchronization. The total capacity of a BRI line is therefore 192 Kbps.

- **PRI** In North America and Japan, PRI service comprises twenty-three 64 Kbps B channels and one 64 Kbps D channel, as well as 8 Kbps of synchronization and framing, which results in a total bit rate of up to 1.544 Mbps.

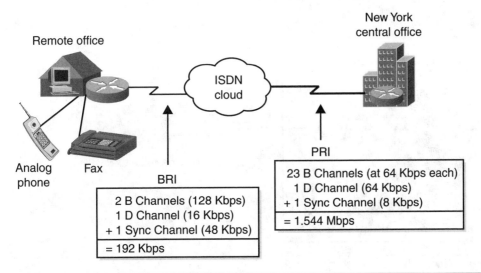

Figure 19-2 ISDN BRI and PRI

In Europe, Australia, and other parts of the world, PRI service includes thirty 64 Kbps B channels and one 64 Kbps D channel, as well as 64 Kbps of synchronization and framing, resulting in a total bit rate of up to 2.048 Mbps.

Both ISDN BRI and PRI services allow each B channel to be used for separate applications. For example, with BRI, the first B channel can be used for, say, browsing the Internet, while the second B channel is used at the same time for, say, connecting to a corporate LAN (see Figure 19-3). Moreover, both services allow individual B channels to be aggregated together into a single logical pipe in order to increase available throughput and reduce latency on the ISDN connection.

ISDN Components

ISDN standards specify a broad range of communication devices, known as *function groups*. The most common ISDN function groups are illustrated in Figure 19-4 and explained here:

- **Terminal Equipment 1 (TE1)**   This type of device is compatible with the ISDN network. Examples of TE1s include ISDN telephones, ISDN fax machines, and routers with ISDN interfaces.

- **Terminal Equipment 2 (TE2)**   This type of device is not compatible with the ISDN network. To connect to the ISDN network, a TE2 requires a Terminal Adapter. Examples of TE2s include terminals, PCs, and routers without ISDN interfaces.

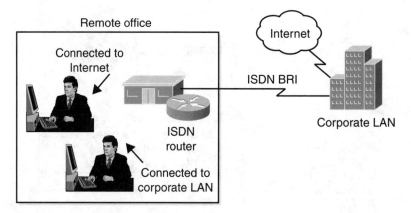

Figure 19-3   BRI connectivity example

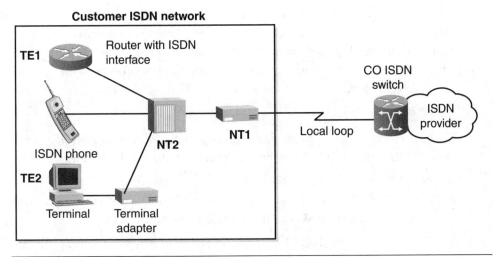

Figure 19-4 ISDN components

- **Terminal Adapter (TA)**   The TA connects the non-ISDN-compatible equipment (TE2s) to the ISDN network. TAs can be devices that are either standalone or integrated onto the TE2's motherboard.

- **Network Termination Type 1 (NT1)**   The NT1 is the device that connects the customer's ISDN network with the CO ISDN switch.

- **Network Termination Type 2 (NT2)**   The NT2 is the device that connects all the customer's TE1s, TE2s, and TAs to the NT1. A PBX is an example of an NT2.

NOTE: Devices that combine the functionality of both an NT1 and an NT2 are sometimes referred to as NTUs.

ISDN Call Setup

The ISDN local loop terminates at the CO or, in ISDN terms, the local exchange. The local exchange facility contains the telecommunications equipment that connects the customer's ISDN network with the ISDN provider's carrier network. This equipment consists largely of telephone company (telco) switches that serve the function of relaying the customer's ISDN traffic to destination networks.

In a BRI or PRI environment, the first telco switch to which the customer's NT1 (BRI environment) or channel service unit/data service unit (PRI environment) connects is responsible for intercepting the customer's ISDN call and establishing a communication path through the carrier network to the called device. The sequence of events listed next and depicted in Figure 19-5 presents a basic explanation of how this call setup process occurs.

1. The Boston router dials the Seattle router by signaling the local ISDN switch located at the Boston CO. The signaling occurs over the BRI D channel.

2. The local ISDN switch receives the called number and proceeds to use the *Signaling System 7* (*SS7*) protocol to set up a path through the carrier network and pass the called number to the ISDN switch located at the Seattle CO.

3. Upon receiving the called number, the Seattle ISDN switch signals the Seattle customer's router. The signaling occurs over the PRI D channel.

4. Once the Seattle router answers the Boston router's signal call, call setup is complete and communication between both routers then occurs over the B channel.

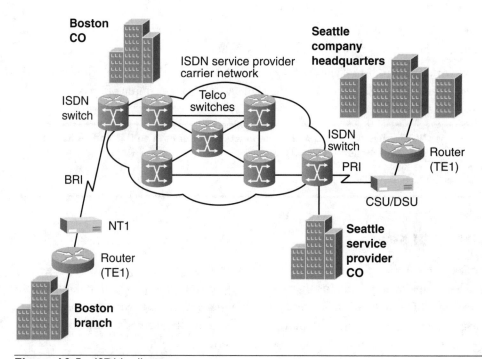

Figure 19-5   ISDN call setup

NOTE: ISDN is an access technology that operates only up to the ISDN switch. Inside the carrier network, telco switches don't use ISDN; they instead use the SS7 signaling protocol.

ISDN Switch Types

As previously mentioned, the ISDN switch is located at the CO and is responsible for providing the customer access to the service provider network. Service providers use a wide variety of ISDN switch types to deliver ISDN access and ISDN services. The switch type used by a provider generally depends on the provider's geographic location. Table 19-1 presents some of the more common switch types that are used throughout the world.

Each switch type has slightly different signaling requirements. To ensure compatible signaling between the customer router and ISDN switch, it is necessary that the ISDN router be configured with the switch type used at the CO. In a later section on ISDN configuration, you will learn which Cisco IOS command is used to accomplish this task.

ISDN Reference Points

So far, you have been introduced to the various ISDN services (BRI and PRI), components (TE1s, NT2s, and so forth), and switch types involved in ISDN communications.

Table 19-1   ISDN Switch Types

SWITCH TYPE	GEOGRAPHIC LOCATION
AT&T 5ESS and 4ESS	United States
Northern Telecom DMS-100	North America
National ISDN-1 and ISDN-2	North America
1TR6	Germany
VN2, VN3	France
Net3, Net5	United Kingdom
Net3	Europe
TS013, TS014	Australia
NTT	Japan

Another element involved in ISDN communications is the *reference point*, which essentially is an ISDN connection or interface between two ISDN devices, such as a TE1 and an NT2. As shown in Figure 19-6, there are different types of reference points, all of which are standardized by the International Telecommunication Union Telecommunication Standardization Sector (ITU-T).

The standard ISDN reference points are explained as follows:

- **R** Defines the connection between the TE2 (non-ISDN-compatible equipment) and the TA. This connection uses a physical layer interface specified by such standards as EIA/TIA 232-C, V.24, V.35, and so forth.

- **S** Located between the NT2 and the TE1 or TA, and is electrically similar to the T reference point.

- **T** Located between the NT1 and NT2, and is electrically similar to the S reference point. When no NT2 device is present (as is often the case in small ISDN implementations), the T reference point defines the connection between the NT1 and TE1 or TA.

- **U** Defines the two-wire local loop connection between the NT1 and ISDN switch.

As indicated in Figure 19-6, an ISDN network contains both four-wire and two-wire subscriber wiring. The two-wire subscriber wiring extends from the NT1 to the ISDN switch, and the four-wire subscriber wiring connects the subscriber ISDN equipment with the NT2 and NT1.

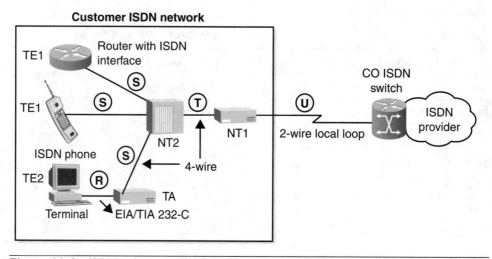

Figure 19-6   ISDN reference points

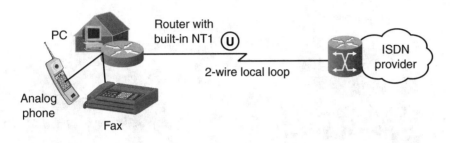

Figure 19-7   Router with built-in NT1

In North America, routers can be provisioned with a built-in NT1. In this instance, the two-wire subscriber wiring connects directly to the router's U interface, as illustrated in Figure 19-7.

NOTE: In Europe, the NT1 is located at the CO.

ISDN Solutions

ISDN is a versatile technology that offers corporate customers a variety of high-performance, cost-effective solutions for connecting telecommuters and remote branch offices to the corporate LAN or to the Internet and for providing redundancy options such as dial backup and load balancing. Although telecommunication providers are beginning to roll out powerful new broadband services such as xDSL and cable—two technologies that are quickly driving the home market away from ISDN en route toward faster, cheaper, and simpler access solutions—ISDN still has a broad user base in the business sector, which typically uses ISDN PRI over T1/E1 lines to connect remote BRI offices and carry high-volume traffic to and from these locations (see Figure 19-8).

Typical applications for ISDN are summarized as follows:

- High-speed access to corporate servers and databases
- Sharing and transferring large files/images
- Point of sale transactions

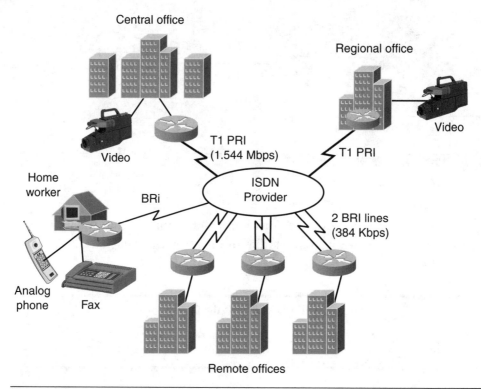

Figure 19-8   ISDN business implementation

- Teleconferencing
- Voice
- Remote LAN/telecommuter access
- Redundancy

ISDN Remote Connectivity Methods

Remote ISDN connections can be grouped into three different categories:

- Remote access
- Remote node
- Small office/home office

The following sections explore each of these remote connectivity methods.

Remote Access Connections

Remote access connections allow remote users to access the corporate LAN via dial-up connections using either an analog or ISDN modem/router. Users that are mobile generally use laptops equipped with internal V.90 modems to dial in to their company's main offices to retrieve e-mail and transfer files to and from the company's servers. This type of access solution is the least costly and most widely available because it uses the *plain old telephone service* (POTS).

Alternatively, remote users that are stationary have the option of connecting to the company's main offices via ISDN. Typically, such users are located at either their home or a small office and require access to speeds and services that are unavailable with traditional analog dial-up.

Figure 19-9 depicts two remote users, one using analog and one using ISDN, connecting to the corporate LAN.

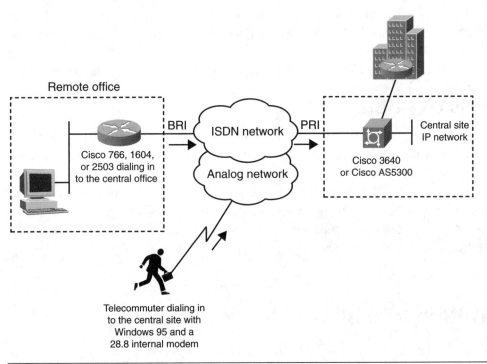

Figure 19-9 Remote access

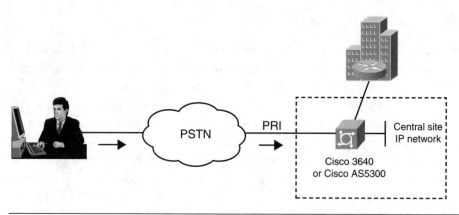

Figure 19-10   Remote node

Remote Node Connections

Users who are remote nodes are able to connect to the central site and have the same access as if they were local users, only with lower speeds. With this type of setup, the remote node is equipped with client software and a modem for connecting to the corporate access server, which, as you learned in Chapter 17, is a routing device that concentrates dial-up users.

Figure 19-10 shows a remote node using an ISDN router to access the central site.

SOHO Connections

The small office/home office, or SOHO, contains one to a few users. Because SOHOs generally require more bandwidth than is available from analog dial-up service, these locations implement ISDN BRI for digital dial-up connectivity to the corporate LAN or to the Internet (see Figure 19-11). In addition, because SOHOs typically use an ISDN router, such as the Cisco 800 series router, SOHOs have the capability to take advantage of advanced features like *virtual private networks* (VPNs) and *Network Address Translation* (NAT), among others.

ISDN Protocols

Various ISDN protocols have been developed and standardized by the ITU-T. These protocol standards have been organized and grouped into three different *series*, presented as follows:

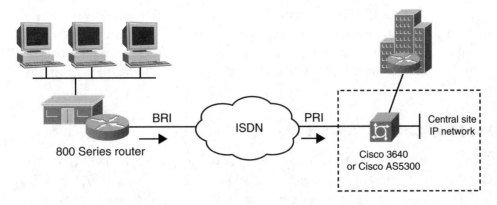

Figure 19-11 ISDN SOHO

- **E-series protocols** Specify telephone network standards for ISDN. E.164, for example, specifies international ISDN addressing.

- **I-series protocols** Specify ISDN concepts and interfaces. I-series protocols comprise the following subcategories:

  I.100 series Specify ISDN concepts and structures

  I.200 series Deal with ISDN service aspects

  I.300 series Deal with network layer aspects

  I.400 series Deal with the *user network interface* (UNI)

- **Q-series protocols** Specify standards for ISDN switching and signaling. Q.921, for example, describes Link Access Procedure on the D Channel (LAPD). An additional Q standard, Q.931, defines Layer 3 features. A simple way to tell these protocols apart is the second digit-2 for Layer 2, and 3 for Layer 3.

Protocols defined by the ITU-T operate at the physical, data link, and network layers of the OSI reference model. The following sections explore these protocols in further detail.

Physical Layer ISDN Protocols

At the physical layer, ISDN BRI is defined by the ITU-T I.430 protocol (ISDN PRI is defined by the ITU-T I.431 protocol). Because it is a part of the I.400 series, I.430 describes how the physical connection occurs between the ISDN *customer premises equipment* (CPE) and the ISDN local exchange.

In addition, I.430 defines the ISDN physical layer frame format. ISDN specifies two types of frame formats: inbound frame formats (frames that travel from the local exchange to the ISDN customer) and outbound frame formats (frames that travel from the ISDN customer to the local exchange). Both frame formats are illustrated in Figure 19-12.

ISDN at the Data Link Layer

At the data link layer, ISDN specifies the LAPD signaling protocol. Defined by ITU-T Q.920 (BRI) and Q.921 (PRI), LAPD is responsible for transmitting control and signaling information over the D channel between the ISDN CPE and local exchange.

The LAPD frame format is similar to that of the ISO HDLC frame format. Like HDLC frames, LAPD frames include a Flag, Address, Control, Information (Data), and Frame Check Sequence (FCS) field. Figure 19-13 presents the LAPD frame format.

 NOTE: LAPD is not to be confused with Link Access Procedure, Balanced (LAPB), which is the data link layer protocol used in X.25 networks. For more information on LAPB, refer to Chapter 17.

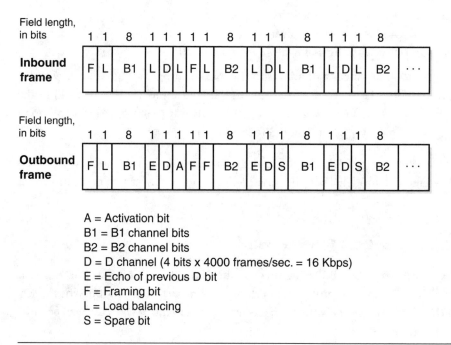

A = Activation bit
B1 = B1 channel bits
B2 = B2 channel bits
D = D channel (4 bits x 4000 frames/sec. = 16 Kbps)
E = Echo of previous D bit
F = Framing bit
L = Load balancing
S = Spare bit

Figure 19-12 ISDN physical layer frame formats

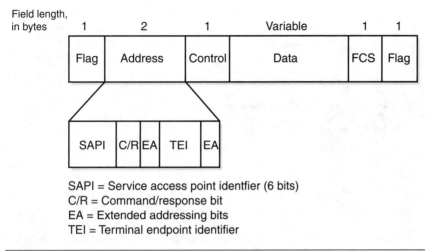

SAPI = Service access point identfier (6 bits)
C/R = Command/response bit
EA = Extended addressing bits
TEI = Terminal endpoint identifier

Figure 19-13 LAPD frame format

ISDN at the Network Layer

At the network layer, ISDN is responsible for specifying the switching and signaling protocols involved in end-to-end ISDN communication over the D channel. These protocols include ITU-T I.450 (also referred to as ITU-T I.930) and ITU-T I.451 (also referred to as ITU-T Q.931).

 NOTE: There are two useful ISDN setup debug commands: debug isdn q921, which helps troubleshoot L2 connectivity to the switch, and debug isdn q931, which helps troubleshoot call processing.

DDR Overview

One of the benefits to using ISDN is the ability to send traffic on an as-needed basis through the application of a feature called dial-on-demand routing. With DDR, ISDN links are established only when the router receives traffic that has been defined as "interesting." The network administrator, using router IOS commands, defines the interesting traffic that will trigger a DDR call (see Figure 19-14).

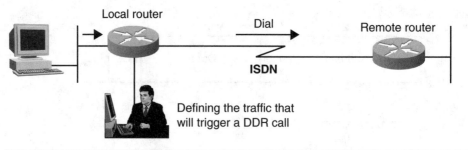

Figure 19-14 DDR

DDR operation involves several steps, listed next:

1. Upon receiving traffic that is to be sent to a remote device, the router looks in its routing table to find the destination route and the associated outbound interface. If the outbound interface is configured for DDR, the router then determines whether the traffic is interesting.

2. The router locates the dialing instructions for the destination and checks to see whether the outbound interface is currently connected to the destination.

    If the interface is already connected to the destination (meaning that the link is already established from a previous session), traffic is sent as usual—whether it is interesting or not.

    If the interface is not currently connected to the destination, the router establishes a connection—but only if the traffic is interesting; if the traffic isn't interesting, it is dropped.

3. While the link to the remote destination is up, both interesting *and* uninteresting traffic can be sent.

    There is, in addition, an idle timer placed on the link that begins ticking whenever interesting traffic is not sent. As soon as the router detects interesting traffic, it resets the timer. If the timer expires, the link is disconnected.

 NOTE: Only interesting traffic can reset the idle timer.

In a later section, "DDR Configuration," you will learn some of the basic IOS commands used in enabling this feature.

ISDN BRI Configuration

The most basic ISDN configuration involves specifying the following parameters:

- Switch type
- *Service profile identifiers* (SPIDs)
- Encapsulation protocol

Setting the ISDN Switch Type

As mentioned earlier in the chapter, various types of ISDN switches are used in different regions of the world. In the United States, for instance, the most common switch types used in service provider networks are the AT&T basic-rate switches, the Nortel DMS-100 switch, and the National ISDN-1 switch.

Because these switches operate slightly differently, the router must be configured with the correct switch type in order to ensure compatible operation. The switch type can be configured with the following global configuration command:

```
Router(config)#isdn switch-type switch-type
```

Available values for the *switch-type* parameter in the command are specified in Table 19-2.

A switch type configured in global configuration mode applies to all interfaces. To accommodate multiple switches on different interfaces, the preceding command may be used in interface configuration mode, as follows:

```
Router(config)#interface bri number
Router(config-if)#isdn switch-type switch-type
```

The BRI interface number identifies the interface to which the ISDN BRI line is attached. The *switch-type* can be any of the values listed in Table 19-2.

Setting the SPID

The ISDN CO needs to have a unique identification number for each BRI B channel that it assigns to its customers. This identification number is referred to as a service profile identifier, or SPID, and is sent to the ISDN switch during call setup.

Depending on which switch type the ISDN service provider uses, the customer may be provided with SPIDs that need to be inputted into the router. In North America, for example, only the National ISDN-1 and DMS-100 ISDN switches require SPID configuration; the AT&T-5ESS switch does not.

Table 19-2
Values for the *switch-type* Parameter

Switch-type VALUE	DESCRIPTION
basic-16r6	Switch type for Germany
basic-5ess	AT&T switch type for the U.S.
basic-dms100	Nortel switch type for North America
basic-net3	Switch type for the U.K. and Europe
basic-ni1	Switch type for North America
basic-nwnet3	Switch type for Norway
basic-nznet3	Switch type for New Zealand
basic-ts013	Switch type for Australia
ntt	Switch type for Japan
vn2	Switch type for France
vn3	Switch type for France

When assigned SPIDs by your ISDN service provider, use the following BRI interface configuration commands:

```
Router(config-if)#isdn spid1 spid# [ldn]
Router(config-if)#isdn spid2 spid# [ldn]
```

The following briefly explains the parameters used in the two commands:

- *spid#*   A string of numbers that the ISDN service provider uses to identify the ISDN subscriber's services. There is one SPID number for each B channel on the BRI interface.

- **ldn**   The local directory number, a seven-digit string assigned by the ISDN service provider and delivered by the ISDN switch in the incoming call setup message.

Setting the Encapsulation Protocol

When configuring ISDN, you have the option of specifying which data link layer encapsulation protocol to use on the ISDN interface. The two most common encapsulations used on ISDN interfaces are the High-Level Data-Link Control (HDLC) and Point-to-Point Protocol (PPP), with the HDLC being the default encapsulation used on Cisco interfaces. Other supported encapsulations include Frame Relay (used if ISDN traffic crosses a Frame Relay network), LAPB (used if ISDN traffic crosses an X.25 network), and LAPD.

The recommended encapsulation for ISDN is PPP, primarily because this protocol provides robust features such as CHAP authentication, multilink PPP, and standardized support for multiple network layer protocols, among other scalable, attractive features. Refer to Chapter 18 for more information on PPP.

If using PPP as the encapsulation protocol for the BRI interface, you issue the following interface command:

```
Router(config-if)#encapsulation ppp
```

In addition to the preceding command, you may also issue other PPP configuration commands, such as link authentication with PAP or CHAP.

DDR Configuration

DDR configuration involves three main tasks:

1. Defining interesting traffic

2. Specifying static routes

3. Configuring dialer instructions on the BRI interface

The following sections cover each of these DDR configuration steps.

Defining Interesting Traffic

As you learned earlier in this chapter, ISDN traffic that is defined as interesting is allowed to bring up a DDR link. This traffic is defined using the following global configuration command:

```
Router(config)#dialer-list dialer-group# protocol protocol-name
[permit|deny|list] access-list#
```

The parameters in the command are explained as follows:

- *dialer-group#*   A numeric value that is associated with an interface using the dialer-group interface configuration command.

- *protocol-name*   The protocol traffic involved with DDR. Options include IP, IPX, AppleTalk, DECNet, and Vines.

- **permit|deny**   Permits or denies the aforementioned protocol traffic. If neither parameter is used, all traffic is permitted (defined as interesting) by default.

- **list** *access-list#*   Specifies an access list to use to test traffic to determine whether the traffic is interesting. Traffic permitted by the access list is deemed interesting, whereas any traffic that is denied by the access list is deemed uninteresting.

 NOTE: Omitting the access list parameters permits all traffic from the specified protocol by default.

The ability to use an access list in the dialer-list command gives the network manager finer control when establishing the criteria that determines what traffic will be allowed to trigger a DDR call.

Figure 19-15 presents an example of a scenario in which an access list is used together with the dialer-list command to specify interesting traffic. In this scenario, the dialer list indicates that access-list 100 will be applied to all IP traffic destined for a remote device that the router receives. The first access list statement indicates that RIP packets are to be denied, which means that RIP packets will constitute uninteresting traffic. The second access list statement denies World Wide Web (WWW) packets from being considered interesting. The third access-list statement indicates that all other IP traffic is permitted and, hence, deemed interesting. This last statement is necessary because there is an *implicit deny any* at the end of the access list.

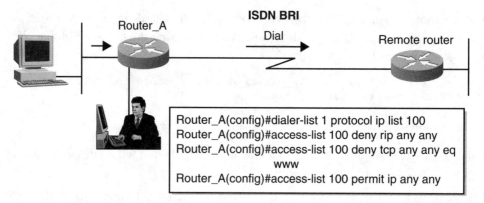

Figure 19-15   Defining interesting traffic

NOTE: Refer to Chapter 15 for more information on access-list configuration.

Specifying Static Routes

If you will not be running a routing protocol across the ISDN DDR link, you need to define static routes. The following global configuration command is used for this purpose:

```
Router(config)#ip route prefix mask [next-hop|outbound interface]
```

The parameters in the command are explained as follows:

- *prefix*   The destination network or subnet
- *mask*   The destination network/subnet mask
- *next-hop*   The logical address of the next-hop router
- *outbound interface*   Interface used to reach the destination

In Figure 19-16, for example, Router A is configured with static routes leading to subnets 172.16.3.0 and 172.16.4.0.

When configuring static routes, keep in mind that you will most likely need to specify static routes for all remote networks and subnets that your router would have learned of automatically had it been running a routing protocol. While configuring

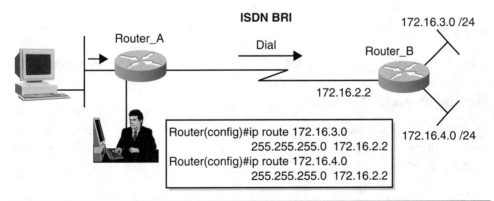

Figure 19-16   Defining static routes

these routes may not be too much of a burden for small-sized networks with few routes, the administrative burden can be an issue for larger-sized networks with numerous routes. In this latter case, a *default route* could be used in lieu of defining static routes.

Configuring Dialer Instructions

The router must be instructed how to dial remote sites. For a BRI interface, this basically entails specifying the service and dialer parameters that will be used to reach a called device. The following interface configuration commands can be used to specify this information:

- dialer map
- dialer-group

The dialer map Command

The dialer map command is used to specify the destination's called number, IP address, and host name, among other information. The abbreviated syntax for this command is presented as follows:

```
Router(config-if)#dialer map protocol next-hop [name hostname]
called#
```

A brief explanation of the parameters in the command is given next:

- *protocol*   Network layer protocol used to reach the called device; for example, IP.
- *next-hop*   Logical address of next-hop router along the path to the destination.
- **name** *hostname*   Host name of the called device. If using PPP encapsulation, this name is used for PAP or CHAP authentication.
- *called#*   Number to call to reach the destination device.

Figure 19-17 illustrates an example of how the dialer map command is used.

The dialer-group Command

Recall for a moment that the first step in configuring DDR on a BRI interface involves defining interesting traffic using the dialer-list global interface command. The syntax for this command is repeated here:

```
Router(config)#dialer-list dialer-group# protocol
[permit|deny|list]              access-list#
```

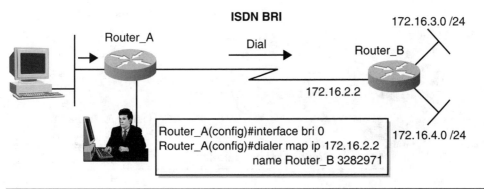

Figure 19-17   The dialer map

In this command, the *dialer-group#* parameter is used to link an interface to the dialer list. The command used on the interface to create this link is the dialer-group command, presented next:

```
Router(config-if)#dialer-group dialer-group#
```

The *dialer-group#* specified in the command is the same one specified in the dialer-list command.

Example BRI DDR configuration

Figure 19-18 presents a sample configuration for a router using DDR over ISDN BRI to dial a remote router.

Verifying and Troubleshooting ISDN and DDR

To verify that the ISDN interface is configured and operating correctly, and to verify that DDR is functioning properly on the ISDN interface, use the IOS commands listed in Table 19-3.

To troubleshoot basic ISDN and DDR connectivity problems, use the debug commands listed in Table 19-4.

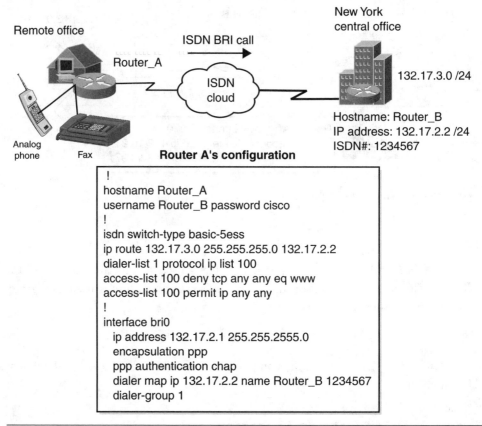

Figure 19-18   Example BRI DDR connectivity

Table 19-3
Verifying ISDN BRI and DDR

COMMAND	EXPLANATION
show dialer interface bri *number*	Provides general DDR statistics for the BRI interface, including dialed numbers, whether the dialed numbers have been successfully configured, and current information for each BRI B channel, including the number to which the interface is currently connected and the idle time for the connection.
show isdn active	Displays the called number(s) to which the router is currently connected.
show isdn status	Displays status information on the physical, data link, and network layers of the ISDN connection.

Table 19-4
ISDN Debug Commands

COMMAND	EXPLANATION
debug isdn q921	Displays real-time data link layer signaling events occurring between the router and local ISDN switch over the D channel.
debug isdn q931	Displays real-time network layer call setup and teardown events occurring between the router and remote networks.
debug dialer	Shows the progress of dial attempts.

Summary

ISDN is a digital WAN access technology that connects users over the existing telephone infrastructure via either BRI or PRI service. BRI service consists of two 64 Kbps B channels and offers a bit capacity of 192 Kbps, whereas PRI service consists of either twenty-three or thirty 64 Kbps B channels and offers a bit capacity of either 1.544 Mbps (T1) or 2.048 Mbps (E1).

There are various ISDN components and reference points involved in ISDN architectures. Examples of ISDN components (also called function groups) include TE1s, TE2s, NT1s, NT2s, and TAs. Examples of ISDN reference points include the R, S, T, and U reference points, which define the interfaces between ISDN component devices.

ISDN is used for a variety of reasons, including connecting remote users to the corporate LAN or Internet, providing high-speed file transfers between local and remote sites, and providing redundancy. Because ISDN supports high-speed digital connections using a variety of protocols, devices, and services, ISDN is well suited to carrying voice, video, and data traffic across the service provider network.

Case Study: Remote Connectivity with ISDN and DDR

As you will discover in this chapter, ISDN is commonly used as a means for connecting remote offices with the corporate LAN. Because this is a widely configured function of ISDN, the case study will present you with the task of configuring a remote office for basic ISDN and DDR connectivity. You will also be required to verify the connection to ensure that communication can occur successfully between both sites.

Directions: Now you will apply the knowledge you have gained from this chapter. After reviewing the diagram (see the following illustration) and scenario for the case study network, proceed to answer the questions in the following case study worksheet.

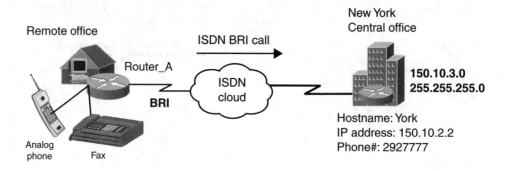

Scenario: Your task is to configure the remote office router in Figure 19-19 for ISDN BRI connectivity and basic DDR, and to verify proper operation of the connection.

Configuration Worksheet for Remote Office Router

In global configuration mode:

1. Specify the basic-5ess switch type.

2. Specify a static route for network 150.10.3.0/24.

3. Define all IP traffic as interesting except Web traffic.

In BRI interface configuration mode:

4. Go into the BRI 0 interface and specify PPP encapsulation.

5. Configure a dialer map using the information shown in the network diagram.

6. Assign the dialer list to the BRI 0 interface.

In privileged exec mode:

7. Issue the command you would use to verify the ISDN connection's status at the physical, data link, and network layers.

8. Issue one of the commands that allows you to see what number the router is currently connected to.

Case Study-Suggested Solutions
(Your solutions may vary)

1. Use the following command to specify the 5ess switch type:

```
Router_A(config)#isdn switch-type basic-5ess
```

2. Use the following command to specify a static route for 150.10.3.0:

```
Router_A(config)#ip route 150.10.3.0 255.255.255.0 150.10.2.2
```

3. Use the following commands to define all IP traffic as interesting except Web traffic:

```
Router_A(config)#dialer-list 1 protocol ip list 100
Router_A(config)#access-list 100 deny tcp any any eq www
Router(config)#access-list 100 permit ip any any
```

4. Use the following commands to specify PPP encapsulation on the BRI 0 interface:

```
Router_A(config)#interface bri 0
Router_A(config-if)#encapsulation ppp
```

5. The following dialer map is appropriate for the case study network:

```
Router_A(config-if)#dialer map ip 150.10.2.2 name York 2927777
```

6. Use the following command to associate the preceding dialer list with BRI 0:

```
Router_A(config-if)#dialer-group 1
```

7. Issue the following command to verify the remote office router's physical, data link, and network layer ISDN status:

```
Router_A#show isdn status
```

8. Issue the following command to view the number to which the router is currently connected:

```
Router_A#show dialer
```

Practice Questions

Take a few moments and check your grasp of the concepts covered in this chapter. The answers are immediately following the questions.

Questions

1. Which of the following does *not* describe a benefit that ISDN has over analog modems?
   a. ISDN can reliably carry voice, video, and data.
   b. ISDN doesn't use dial-up connections.
   c. ISDN call setup occurs much faster.
   d. Transfer rates are significantly improved with ISDN.

2. In North America, what is the function of the NT1?
   a. Designates a device that is compatible with the ISDN network
   b. Designates a device that is not compatible with the ISDN network
   c. Concentrates different subscriber devices
   d. Connects the four-wire ISDN subscriber wiring to the two-wire local loop

3. What does a non-ISDN-compatible device attach to in order to access the ISDN network?
   a. TE2
   b. TE1
   c. NT2
   d. NT1
   e. TA

4. In which two of the following places can the S reference point occur?
   a. Between the NT2 and the TE1
   b. Between the NT1 and the ISDN switch
   c. Between the TA and the NT1
   d. Between the TE2 and the NT2
   e. Between the NT1 and the NT2

5. What are ISDN Q-series protocols concerned with?
   a. How switching and signaling occurs
   b. Telephone network standards
   c. ISDN service aspects
   d. ISDN concepts and structures

6. What is the primary difference between an ISDN B channel and an ISDN D channel?

    a. The B channel carries the LAPD protocol, whereas the D channel specifies the UNI

    b. The B channel carries user traffic, whereas the D channel carries mainly control and signaling information

    c. The D channel operates at the OSI physical layer, whereas the B channel operates at the OSI data link layer

    d. The D channel operates at 64 Kbps, whereas the B channel operates at 16 Kbps

7. Which is the standard data link layer signaling protocol for ISDN?

    a. Q.931

    b. ITU-T I.450

    c. LAPD

    d. LAPB

8. What is the purpose of the ISDN SPID?

    a. Identifies a subscriber's services to the local ISDN switch

    b. Negotiates call authentication features

    c. Sends signaling and control information to the local ISDN switch

    d. Allows uninteresting traffic to trigger a DDR call

9. Which two of the following are functions of the CO ISDN switch?

    a. Authenticates users based on either PAP or CHAP

    b. Establishes a path through the carrier network and passes the ISDN call to the remote ISDN switch

    c. Terminates the local loop

    d. Defines the traffic that is allowed to trigger a DDR call

10. What is a SOHO?

    a. A standard device that allows home users to access the corporate LAN

    b. A protocol that is used by PPP to negotiate ISDN call parameters

    c. A type of user that can access the corporate LAN and appear as a local network node

    d. A small office or home office consisting of a few users

11. How many B channels does a T1 PRI in North America have?

    a. 2

    b. 23

    c. 1544

    d. 46

12. Which command is used to specify the ISDN switch type to which the router attaches?

   a. Router#switch-type isdn

   b. Router(config)#isdn switch-type

   c. Router(config-if)#basic-5ess

   d. Router(config)#config switch

13. What is the primary function of ISDN DDR?

   a. Determining which number to use to dial a remote device

   b. Preventing routing updates from crossing the ISDN link

   c. Allowing only interesting traffic to bring up an ISDN link

   d. Configuring BRI

14. Which of the following would not be an application for DDR?

   a. Connecting remote users on an as-needed basis

   b. Providing redundancy

   c. Preventing routing updates from clogging up slow-bandwidth links

   d. Preventing uninteresting traffic from *ever* gaining access to the ISDN link

15. What are the three steps to configuring basic DDR?

   a. Defining static routes

   b. Configuring QoS

   c. Specifying interesting traffic

   d. Enabling PPP authentication

   e. Specifying the ISDN switch type

   f. Configuring the dialer instructions

16. What is the dialer-list command used for?

   a. Identifying the calling parameters used to reach the destination

   b. Configuring the ISDN SPIDs

   c. Specifying the idle time before a call is disconnected

   d. Specifying interesting traffic

17. Which of the following commands successfully configures the dialing parameters used to reach a remote device?

   a. Router(config)#dialer isdn ip 100.20.20.10 2375555 Router_B

   b. Router(config-if)#dialer map ip 100.20.20.10 name Router_B 2375555

   c. Router(config-if)isdn dialer ip 100.20.20.10 name Router_B 2375555

   d. Router(config)#dialer map 2375555 Router_B ip 100.20.20.10

18. Which ISDN device performs switching and concentrating functions?

   a. TE2

   b. TE1

   c. NT2

   d. NT1

19. Which reference point occurs between the NT1 and the NT2?

   a. R

   b. S

   c. T

   d. U

20. Which command would you use to verify the physical, data link, and network layer status of an ISDN connection?

   a. show dialer

   b. show isdn active

   c. show isdn status

   d. debug isdn q921

Answers

1. b. ISDN *does* use dial-up connections.

2. d. In North America, the NT1 connects the four-wire ISDN subscriber wiring to the two-wire local loop.

3. e. Non-ISDN-compatible devices must attach to a TA (Terminal Adapter) before they can access the ISDN network.

4. a. and c. The S reference point can occur between the NT2 and the TE1, and between the TA and NT1 (this latter connection would occur when the NT2 is absent).

5. a. ISDN Q-series protocols are concerned with how switching and signaling occurs.

6. b. The primary difference between an ISDN B and D channel is that the B channel carries user traffic, whereas the D channel carries mainly control and signaling information.

7. c. The standard data link layer signaling protocol for ISDN is LAPD.

8. **a.** The ISDN SPID identifies a subscriber's services to the local ISDN switch.

9. **b. and c.** The CO ISDN switch establishes a path through the carrier network and passes the ISDN call to the remote ISDN switch, and terminates the local loop.

10. **d.** A SOHO is a small office or home office consisting of a few users.

11. **b.** A T1 PRI contains 23 B channels.

12. **b.** The isdn switch-type global configuration command specifies the CO ISDN switch to which the router attaches.

13. **c.** The primary function of ISDN DDR is to allow only interesting traffic to bring up (establish, trigger, set up, and so forth) an ISDN link.

14. **d.** DDR *does* allow uninteresting traffic to cross the ISDN link whenever the link is already established. Therefore, preventing uninteresting traffic from *ever* gaining access to the ISDN link would not be an application of DDR.

15. **a., c., and f.** The three main steps to configuring DDR are defining static routes, specifying interesting traffic, and specifying the dialer instructions.

16. **d.** The dialer-list command is used for specifying interesting traffic.

17. **b.** Router(config-if)#dialer map ip 100.20.20.10 name Router_B 2375555 successfully configures the dialing parameters used to reach a remote device.

18. **c.** The NT2 is an intelligent device that performs switching and concentrating functions.

19. **c.** The T reference point occurs between the NT1 and NT2.

20. **c.** The show isdn status command is used to verify the physical, data link, and network layer status of an ISDN connection.

Frame Relay

20

This chapter will:

- **Discuss how Frame Relay operates in a multiprotocol WAN environment**

- **Cover the essential functions of the Frame Relay LMI**

- **Look at the purpose of the Frame Relay DLCI**

- **Discuss how Frame Relay address mapping occurs**

- **Describe Frame Relay connectivity issues in an NBMA environment**

- **Discuss how Frame Relay point-to-point subinterfaces resolve NBMA issues**

- **Cover various Frame Relay topologies and subinterface types**

- **Show you how to configure the basic Frame Relay operation**

- **Discuss verification and troubleshooting of Frame Relay operation and configuration**

The dramatic growth being experienced by today's enterprise networks has resulted in a tremendous demand for *wide area network* (WAN) services and technologies that can provide scalable network bandwidth, high-performance links, and flexible remote connectivity solutions all at an efficient cost to the enterprise customer. One such WAN technology that has developed to meet these business needs is Frame Relay, which is the subject of this chapter.

In this chapter, we begin exploring Frame Relay technology by focusing on its characteristic features and operation in multiprotocol environments. We will cover specific Frame Relay components, such as *local management interface* (LMI), *data link connection identifier* (DLCI), and Inverse Address Resolution Protocol (Inverse ARP), as well as Frame Relay subinterfaces, such as the point-to-point and multipoint subinterfaces.

Then we will look at some of the fundamental Cisco Internetwork Operating System (IOS) commands that can be used to configure, verify, and troubleshoot basic Frame Relay operation in an enterprise customer network.

Frame Relay Elements

Frame Relay is a packet-switched WAN technology used for transporting data across connection-oriented virtual circuits using the *public data network (PDN)*, a standardized data-link layer protocol that was developed by the International Telecommunication Union Telecommunication Standardization Sector (ITU-T) and the American National Standards Institute (ANSI). It is intended to be a high-performance alternative to the overly reliable, slow-speed X.25 WAN protocol.

Expert Discussion

Frame Relay and Reliability

The Frame Relay protocol was built without robust reliability and must therefore rely on upper-layer protocols and services to implement general reliability features like error correction and flow control. While the absence of these reliability features would generally be undesirable in a data link layer protocol, particularly one used in a WAN environment, Frame Relay is commonly deployed over reliable, high-speed optical and digital service provider network infrastructures, which means that transmission errors and bottlenecks are kept at a minimum. In addition, with regard to flow control, most Frame Relay implementations are able to take advantage of traffic-shaping policies that control the rates at which Frame Relay traffic is transmitted. As a result of not being encumbered with reliability overhead, Frame Relay supports data transfer rates of up to T3 speeds (44.736 Mbps).

As a WAN access technology, Frame Relay defines the connection between the *customer premises equipment* (CPE) and the service provider's *data-circuit terminating equipment* (DCE). Typically, the CPE is a device such as a router, an access server, or a Frame Relay access device (FRAD; a device that connects terminals to the Frame Relay network), while the DCE is a Frame Relay switch located at the service provider's local *central office* (CO). It is the CPE's responsibility to connect the attached customer LAN to the Frame Relay switch, the device responsible for providing the link through the service provider's carrier network to connect remote sites (see Figure 20-1).

 NOTE: Frame Relay operates only between the CPE and the Frame Relay switch. It does not define communication within the service provider network. In the cloud the service provider could be using a leased line, ATM, or SONET circuits, to name a few.

The end-to-end Frame Relay link established between two CPEs is referred to as a *virtual circuit* (VC). This is a logical connection that is either permanently established (PVC) or temporarily established (SVC).

In a Frame Relay environment, multiple virtual circuits can be statistically multiplexed over the same physical interface on the router to allow access to multiple remote locations without having to use separate individual physical interfaces. In Figure 20-2, for example, the New York router uses a single interface to reach three remote locations via VCs, instead of using a separate interface for each connection.

 NOTE: While Frame Relay provides support for SVC communication, most Frame Relay implementations use only PVCs. In this chapter, we will be discussing PVC implementations only.

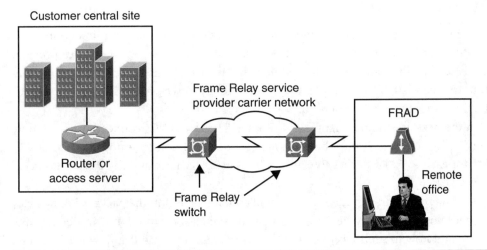

Figure 20-1 Frame Relay network

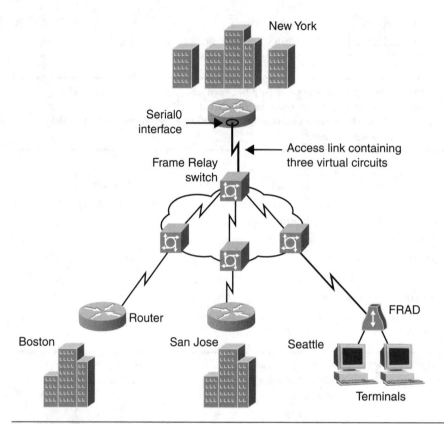

Figure 20-2   Frame Relay virtual circuits

DLCI

Frame Relay virtual circuits are identified by what's known as a data link connection identifier, or DLCI. It is assigned to the Frame Relay customer by the service provider and is used by the router to address which virtual circuit to use to reach a remote location. In Figure 20-3, for example, the number that you see next to Router A is a DLCI that identifies the PVC to Router B.

In the next illustration, Figure 20-4, Router A has two PVCs connecting two remote sites. Because each PVC must be associated with a DLCI, Router A now has two DLCIs, one for each PVC: Router A's PVC to Router B uses DLCI 30, and the PVC to Router C uses DLCI 40.

All data packets transmitted on a VC will contain a DLCI in the packet's Frame Relay header. This is necessary because Frame Relay switches use the DLCI in determining where and how to send received packets. Whenever the Frame Relay switch receives a

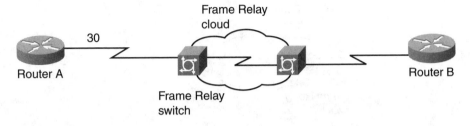

Figure 20-3 One DLCI

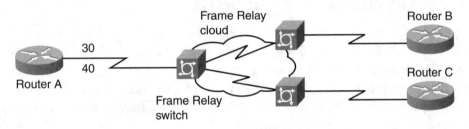

Figure 20-4 Multiple DLCIs

packet, it will look in its switching table (covered later) to determine where the packet should be sent based on the DLCI. In the preceding example, for instance, if Router A transmits a data packet containing DLCI 30, on receiving the packet, the local Frame Relay switch will subsequently know that the packet is destined for the circuit leading to Router B. One way to think of a DLCI is as being analogous to a MAC address in Ethernet or Token Ring.

Understanding Locally Significant DLCIs

Although the previous illustrations show DLCIs being used on only one end of the PVC (Router A's end), the remote sites will also be using DLCIs as well. The remote ends will use the DLCIs for the exact same purpose of VC identification.

Typically, the remote end of a VC will use the same DLCI number that the opposite end uses. However, this is not a requirement. Both sides of a VC can use a different DLCI to refer to the same VC, as shown in Figure 20-5.

The ability to use either the same or different DLCIs to refer to the same VC means that DLCIs have local significance. All the DLCI examples we have studied thus far use locally significant DLCIs.

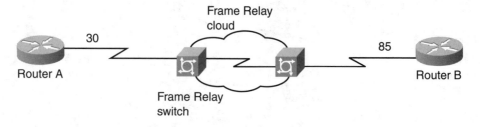

Figure 20-5   Different DLCIs at each end of the same connection

Understanding Globally Significant DLCIs

Locally significant DLCIs are the standard convention for VC identification. However, DLCIs can also be globally significant. With global significance, each end of a VC is uniquely identifiable by a DLCI, similar to how an interface IP address is uniquely identifiable in an IP network. In this environment, a router that wishes to communicate with a peer must use the remote peer's DLCI number, similar to how you would use a telephone number to call somebody.

Figure 20-6 shows a Frame Relay implementation that is using globally significant DLCIs. When Router A wishes to communicate with Router B, Router A will place DLCI 200 in its transmitted packets. Likewise, to communicate back to Router A, Router B will place DLCI 100 in its transmitted packets.

 NOTE: Although the DLCI convention of global significance may seem more intuitive and less confusing than that of local significance, the rest of the diagrams presented in this chapter use locally significant DLCIs, which is the standard convention on Cisco routers.

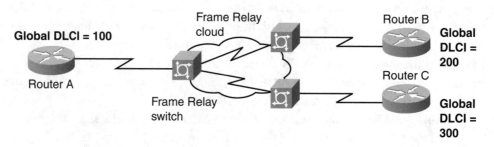

Figure 20-6   Globally significant DLCIs

Later in this chapter, you will learn how the router discovers DLCIs, and you will learn more about how the Frame Relay switch uses DLCIs to establish connectivity between Frame Relay sites.

Frame Relay Frame Format

Let's now take a look at the frame used to carry Frame Relay traffic. Figure 20-7 introduces the standard Frame Relay frame format. Table 20-1 explains what each field in the frame is used for.

LMI

In 1990, Cisco teamed up with three other networking companies (Stratacom, Northern Telecom, and Digital Equipment Corporation) and worked on developing

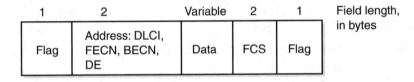

Figure 20-7   Frame Relay frame format

Table 20-1   Fields in a Frame Relay Frame

FIELD	EXPLANATION
Flag	The flag field delimits the beginning and end of a frame.
Address	A 16-bit field that consists of the following items: 10-bit DLCI. Forward explicit congestion notification (FECN) bit—Indicates to the receiver that there is congestion in the network. Backward explicit congestion notification (BECN) bit—Indicates to the sender that there is congestion in the network. Discard eligibility (DE) bit—Set by the router to indicate that the frame can be discarded if the network is congested.
Data	Contains the upper-layer information. This field is variable in length.
FCS	Frame check sequence. The FCS is used to ensure the integrity of transmitted and received frames. Error frames are discarded but are not retransmitted unless the upper-layer protocol requests retransmission.

extended features for the basic ITU-T/ANSI Frame Relay specifications. The result of this combined effort produced the *local management interface* (LMI) signaling protocol.

The essential purpose of the LMI signaling protocol is to manage the link between the CPE and the Frame Relay switch (see Figure 20-8). This management task involves the following signaling functions:

- **Status signaling** A router sends LMI messages to the local Frame Relay switch to report on the router's status and to ask the switch which DLCIs the router can use reach remote destinations.

- **Keepalive signaling** LMI keepalive messages are exchanged between the router and Frame Relay switch to prevent the link's idle timer from expiring.

- **Multicast signaling** The LMI provides a multicasting mechanism that allows DLCIs to have global rather than local significance. In addition, the LMI allows multiple destinations to be grouped together using special multicast DLCIs.

There are three LMI types supported by Frame Relay switches and Cisco routers: *cisco*, *ansi*, and *q933a*. With IOS release 11.2 or later, a router will be able to automatically detect which LMI type the local Frame Relay switch is using. Once the LMI type has been learned, the router is able to exchange the various LMI management messages with the local Frame Relay switch.

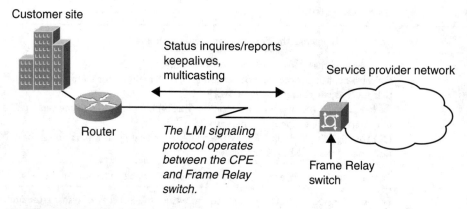

Figure 20-8   Frame Relay LMI signaling

LMI Extensions

As previously mentioned, the LMI was designed as an added feature to the basic Frame Relay specification. Specifically, the protocol defines several extensions, which can be summarized as follows:

- **PVC status messages (common)**   Routers and Frame Relay switches exchange various status messages to report on which PVCs are available.

- **Global addressing (optional)**   DLCIs can be given global significance. With globally significant DLCIs, VCs are uniquely addressable within the Frame Relay network.

- **Multicasting (optional)**   One packet containing a multicast address can be sent and delivered to multiple devices. The alternative is to send packets to each individual device, a situation that would subsequently require increased bandwidth.

- **XON/XOFF flow control (optional)**   This is a basic flow control mechanism suited for devices that aren't capable of responding to the Frame Relay congestion notification bits (covered later).

NOTE: Common LMI extensions are supported by all compliant Frame Relay implementations, whereas optional LMI extensions may or may not be supported.

LMI Frame Format

The LMI has its own frame format, as shown in Figure 20-9.

One of the more important fields in the LMI frame to take note of is the *message type* field. LMI frames can contain one of two message types: status and status inquiry. The

Field length, in bytes

1	2	1	1	1	1	Variable	2	1
Flag	LMI DLCI	Unnumbered information indicator	Protocol discriminator	Call reference	Message type	Information elements	FCS	Flag

Figure 20-9   LMI frame format

latter message type is what the router sends to the Frame Relay switch after initializing to discover which DLCIs are available. The former message type is sent by the Frame Relay switch in response to the status inquiry message.

In addition to being used as a response to status inquiry messages, status messages are also used as keepalives. These messages are exchanged every 10 seconds (by default) between the router and the switch for the purpose of keeping the link's idle timer from expiring. If the idle timer should for some reason expire, for example because of a failed interface, then the link enters an *inactive* state and is no longer able to support traffic.

Figure 20-10 illustrates the various LMI message types.

LMI connection states

LMI connection states are summarized as follows:

- **Active** Indicates that the connection between two routers is up and capable of transmitting data.

- **Inactive** Indicates that the connection between the local router and the local Frame Relay switch is operational, but the remote router's link is not operational.

- **Deleted** Indicates a failed connection between the local router and the local Frame Relay switch.

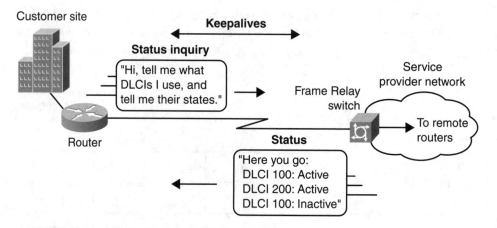

Figure 20-10 LMI messages

Inverse ARP

When a router first initializes, it transmits an LMI *status inquiry* message to the local Frame Relay switch to discover which DLCIs the router can use to communicate with remote routers in the Frame Relay network. At this stage, the router has no knowledge of which DLCIs lead to which remote routers (assuming that the router has not been manually preconfigured with this information). Because the router must know which DLCIs to use to establish connections with remote peers, the router must somehow be able to learn the mapping between the local DLCIs and the network addresses of the remote peers (see Figure 20-11).

One way to accomplish this task of mapping remote routers to local DLCIs is to use Inverse ARP, a dynamic protocol that resolves DLCIs to network-layer addresses. A router that uses this method will send Inverse ARP messages to remote peers, asking

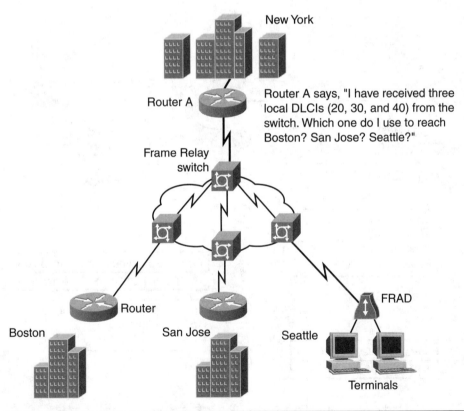

Figure 20-11 Router A requires a mapping between local DLCIs and remote routers.

them to respond with their network address. Based on the responses, the router will construct a table that contains a mapping of network addresses to DLCIs.

Figure 20-12 shows the steps involved in the Inverse ARP process. The list that follows details each of these steps.

1. The local router sends an LMI status-inquiry packet to the local Frame Relay switch, notifying the switch of its status and asking for the status of local DLCIs.

2. On receiving the status-inquiry packet, the local switch does a lookup in its switching table to determine which local DLCIs are available to the local router. Available DLCIs are placed in a status-response packet and forwarded to the local router.

3. On receiving the status-response packet, the local router proceeds to construct an Inverse ARP packet for each received local DLCI that is active. The Inverse ARP

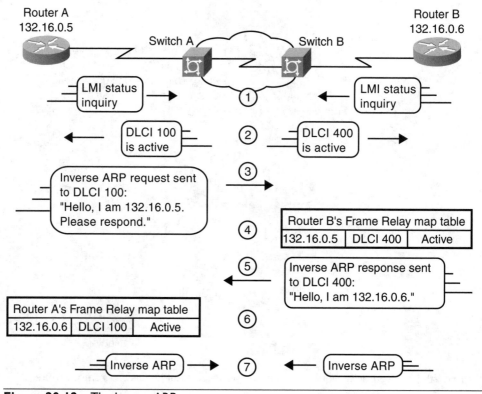

Figure 20-12 The Inverse ARP process

packet contains such items as the local router's network address and the DLCI to be resolved.

The Inverse ARP packets are transmitted to the local Frame Relay switch, whose responsibility it is to deliver the packets to their appropriate destinations (in the section "Frame Relay Switching Table," we will explore how the switch makes the forwarding decision).

4. On receiving the Inverse ARP packet, the remote router creates an entry in its Frame Relay map table that contains the source router's network address and local DLCI. (Note that the remote router is the first to take advantage of Inverse ARP's resolution function.)

5. The remote router then responds by transmitting an Inverse ARP response packet to the source router.

6. On receiving the Inverse ARP response, the source router creates an entry in its Frame Relay map table.

7. Every 60 seconds (by default), routers exchange Inverse ARP messages.

Swapping the DLCI

As you have already learned, the local DLCI indicates which VC the router will use to reach a remote destination. This numeric value is always placed in a Frame Relay frame by the router before the frame is transmitted.

What you may not know, however, is that the DLCI sent by a router is often *not* the same DLCI received by a remote router. To explain how and why this situation occurs, look at Figure 20-12 again.

In step number three of Figure 20-12, Router A sends an Inverse ARP request packet containing DLCI 100 (the VC used to reach Router B) to the local Frame Relay switch, Switch A. The packet is subsequently forwarded through the Frame Relay service provider cloud toward the remote switch, Switch B, who, on receiving the Inverse ARP packet, does the following:

1. Tears the packet open

2. Replaces DLCI 100 with DLCI 400

3. Delivers the packet to Router B

Why does Switch B swap the DLCIs? The answer to this question is found when we reexamine local significance. Recall that, with this convention, the DLCI is a router's *own* indication as to the VC used to reach a remote router; both routers on a VC have their own DLCI that they use to refer to the VC. Because both routers on a VC use their own DLCI, neither router needs to know what DLCI the other is using. As a result, whenever a remote switch receives a Frame Relay packet, the switch swaps the DLCIs so that the destination router's DLCI is received instead of the source's DLCI.

NOTE: With local significance, both peers on a VC are allowed to use the same DLCI to refer to their VC. Consequently, the remote switch doesn't have to swap the DLCIs.

Frame Relay Switching Table

You may be wondering how the Frame Relay switches know which DLCIs map to which routers. The answer is that Frame Relay switches are programmed with the DLCIs of customer links. When a customer orders Frame Relay from a service provider, the customer is assigned the DLCI numbers for the WAN. This information is programmed into the switches' switching table, which contains entries that map DLCIs to port numbers on the switch. Specifically, each entry contains four items:

- **Inbound port number** This identifies the switch interface on which a Frame Relay packet is received.

- **Inbound DLCI** This is the DLCI contained in the received Frame Relay packet. Frame Relay packets contain only one locally significant DLCI.

- **Outbound DLCI** This is the DLCI that the Frame Relay packet contains when it is delivered to the destination. The remote Frame Relay switch swaps a packet's inbound DLCI with this value.

For an example of how Frame Relay switching tables work, look at Figure 20-13. In this example, Router A has transmitted a Frame Relay packet that is addressed to DLCI 20, Router A's VC to Router C. On receiving the packet from Switch A on Port 0, Switch C looks in its switching table and sees that, whenever a packet is received on Port 0 with a DLCI of 20, it should be forwarded out Port 2 with a DLCI of 40. Subsequently, Switch B modifies the packet so that it is delivered to Router C with a DLCI of 40.

Frame Relay Traffic Control

In the following sections, we will examine how Frame Relay deals with the traffic-control functions of error control and flow/congestion control.

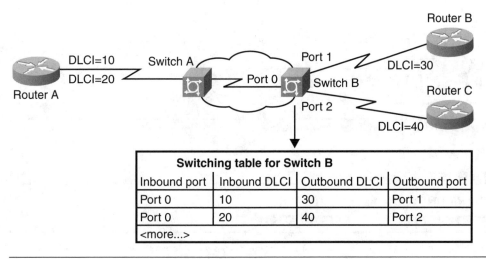

Figure 20-13   Frame Relay switching table

Error Control with Frame Relay

Frame Relay is a streamlined protocol intended for use over reliably built service provider networks, such as those that use high-performance equipment and optical/digital transmission media. As a result, Frame Relay does not provide any built-in error-correction capability (other than the typical error-detection feature that all WAN protocols use, but this is not *error correction*; see Chapter 17 for a technical discussion on the difference between error detection and error correction). This means, consequently, that Frame Relay must rely on upper-layer protocols to provide retransmission of erroneous or missing frames.

Flow/Congestion Control with Frame Relay

While Frame Relay error control is lacking for the most part, Frame Relay does offer a pseudo-flow-control capability via the FECN and BECN bits contained in the protocol frame's address field (see Figure 20-14). (It is not true flow control because upper-layer protocols are still required to carry out the task of reducing transmission rates.) Also offered in the protocol frame's address field is a congestion control mechanism called discard eligibility, or DE.

Table 20-2 explains how each of these flow/congestion control bits works.

In addition to the preceding flow-control and congestion-control mechanisms, a Frame Relay router can be configured with specific traffic-shaping capabilities that give the router more power and flexibility in helping regulate transmission rates and

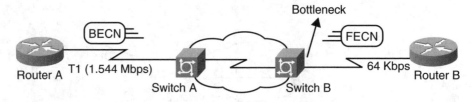

Figure 20-14   Frame Relay flow control

Table 20-2   Congestion Control

FLOW/CONGESTION CONTROL BIT	EXPLANATION
FECN	Whenever the Frame Relay switch detects congestion in the Frame Relay network, it sends a FECN packet to the destination router. On receiving the FECN packet, the router's upper layer protocols will (if they are reliable) implement appropriate flow-control measures.
BECN	Whenever the Frame Relay switch detects congestion in the Frame Relay network, it sends a BECN packet to the source router. On receiving the BECN packet, the source router is instructed to reduce its rate of transmission.
DE	When a router detects congestion in the Frame Relay network, for example, during oversubscription, it can set the DE bit on a frame before transmitting the frame into the congested network. The Frame Relay switch is able to discard frames that are set with the DE bit.

combat congestion-related problems in the Frame Relay network. These additional traffic control features are beyond the scope of this book.

Additional Traffic Control Terminology

Other Frame Relay traffic control terms that you might want to be familiar with include:

- **Local access rate**   This is the physical speed of the physical link attached to the router's physical Frame Relay interface. It is to be distinguished from a logical connection rate that identifies the speed of one of the interface's VCs. Common local access rates include T1 (1.544 Mbps) and 56 Kbps.

- **Committed information rate (CIR)**   The CIR is the rate at which the Frame Relay provider guarantees transmission without frame drop. Any frames exceeding this rate get a DE bit set, which allows them to be dropped if congestion occurs. CIRs can be provisioned for individual VCs.

- **Committed burst** This defines the maximum number of bits that the Frame Relay switch agrees to transfer during any committed rate measurement interval. This term, while probably in most contracts, generally isn't used much. The value is in bits per second.

- **Excess burst** This defines the maximum number of uncommitted bits that the Frame Relay switch attempts to transfer beyond the CIR. The excess burst will not exceed the local access rate.

- **Oversubscription** An access link is oversubscribed when the combined traffic rate on all VCs coming into the router's interface exceeds the access link's speed. Although the router's access link is typically provisioned with enough bandwidth to support the CIRs of all incoming VCs, the router may not be able to additionally support the bursting capacities of the VCs, which is generally the condition in which oversubscription occurs.

- **Port speed** The maximum burst rate in bits per second. Basically, CIR is what you're guaranteed, port speed is what you can burst up to, and local access rate is the physical interface to the cloud.

Figure 20-15 presents a Frame Relay network in which the central site is using a T1 access link (1.544 Mbps) to connect three remote sites via PVCs. Two of the remote sites are equipped with a 768 Kbps access link and a CIR of the same rate, while one of the remote sites uses a 56 Kbps access link with a CIR of the same rate.

Frame Relay Topologies

One of the benefits to using Frame Relay is the ability to interconnect LANs in a variety of ways. As shown in Figure 20-16, Frame Relay supports the following topologies:

- Star topology
- Full mesh topology
- Partial mesh topology

Star Topology

In a star topology, remote sites have point-to-point links to a central site. Remote sites cannot communicate with one another without going through the central site.

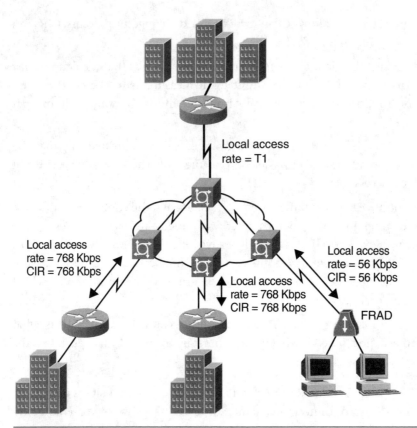

Figure 20-15   CIRs and local access rates

Star topologies are the least expensive to implement and maintain because they use the least number of VCs.

Full Mesh Topology

In a full mesh, all sites are interconnected. With this type of configuration, all sites are able to communicate directly with one another.

There are several benefits to using a full mesh topology:

- **Decreased latency**   Point-to-point links between sites result in expedited communication.

- **Load balancing**   Traffic can be sent to a single destination simultaneously over multiple links.

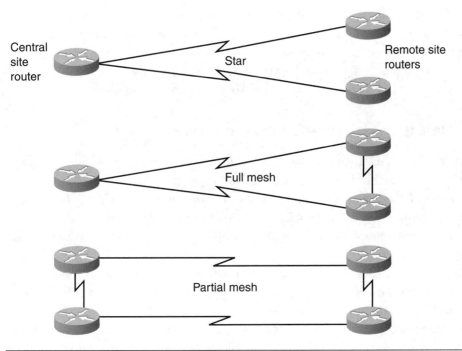

Figure 20-16 Frame Relay topologies

- **Backup redundancy** If a router's link fails, other links can take its place to preserve reachability.

There are a couple major disadvantages, however: increased cost and lack of scalability. The cost of having to deploy and maintain a full mesh can be significant, especially in large internetworks. Because they are cost-prohibitive, fully meshed designs are not often considered scalable solutions.

NOTE: The number of links in a full mesh can be calculated with the formula $n(n - 1)/2$, where n is the number of fully meshed routers.

Partial Mesh Topology

In a partial mesh topology, not all sites have direct connectivity with one another. This type of configuration offers the greatest flexibility for a Frame Relay network designer, because of the ability to tailor a design that meets the exact connectivity requirements of the network. This topology is used most often because most companies use the "double-home" approach, where, say, LA and NY are the bigger sites, and all spokes "home" (or originate) back to both of the these hubs. Generally, there is a PVC, a physical circuit, or ISDN—or any combination—between the two big sites.

Reachability Issues with Frame Relay

Before we get into discussing some of the connectivity problems encountered in Frame Relay networks, we need to cover the classification of Frame Relay connections.

A router's Frame Relay connection can be classified as either *point-to-point* or *multipoint*. A point-to-point connection involves a single VC to another router. For example, as seen in the star topology in Figure 20-17, Routers B, C, and D each have a point-to-point VC to Router A.

However, a router with a multipoint connection has multiple point-to-point VCs leading to other routers. In Figure 20-17, Router A has a multipoint connection to Routers B, C, and D.

In a Frame Relay environment using multipoint connections, indirectly connected routers may encounter communication problems owing to an inherent Frame Relay feature called *nonbroadcast multiaccess* (*NBMA*). In an NBMA network, received broadcasts cannot be forwarded across a multipoint connection. In Figure 20-18, for example, any broadcasts that Router A receives from Router B cannot be forwarded to Routers C and D (and, likewise, broadcasts received from Router C or D cannot be forwarded either) because of the NBMA nature of Frame Relay.

The reason for this broadcast inability is a rule known as *split horizon*. The rule says that a broadcast (such as a routing update, for example) cannot be forwarded out the

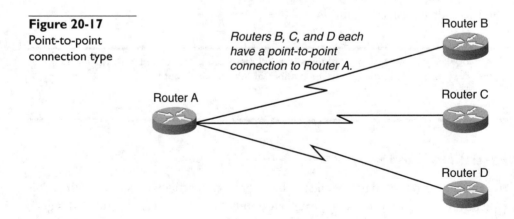

Figure 20-17
Point-to-point
connection type

*Routers B, C, and D each
have a point-to-point
connection to Router A.*

Router A

Router B

Router C

Router D

Figure 20-18
NBMA Frame
Relay network

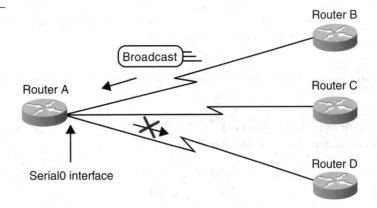

same interface that received it. Thus Router A in Figure 20-18 is unable to forward broadcasts across its serial 0 interface, because, even though multiple individual PVCs terminate on this interface, split horizon does not recognize that fact and must as a result prevent broadcast communication between the remote routers.

NOTE: The purpose of split horizon is to prevent routing loops, which is typically an issue only in environments that are using distance vector routing protocols. For more information on split horizon and routing loops, please refer to Chapter 11.

Resolving Frame Relay Reachability Issues by Disabling Split Horizon

One way of solving the problem of incomplete broadcast connectivity in an NBMA Frame Relay environment is to disable split horizon on the router's multipoint interface. While this is perhaps the simplest and easiest method of dealing with the debilitating effects of split horizon, it is often not recommended because, without this mechanism, there is an increased chance that the network will encounter routing loops, particularly when the network is using a distance vector routing protocol (such as RIP or IGRP) that depends on split horizon to help prevent this problem. In addition, another reason why disabling split horizon may not a viable option is because some network protocols, such as Internetwork Packet Exchange (IPX) and AppleTalk, do not allow split horizon to be disabled. Internet Protocol (IP) does allow it to be disabled.

> **NOTE:** To disable split horizon on an IP interface, use the no ip split horizon interface configuration command.

Resolving Frame Relay Reachability Issues by Using Subinterfaces

While disabling split horizon may or may not be a sufficient option for resolving broadcast connectivity issues in an NBMA Frame Relay environment, the recommended solution is to configure subinterfaces on the multipoint interface. Subinterfaces are logical interfaces that are configured on a physical interface, like the router's serial interface. In Figure 20-19, for example, Router A has been configured with two subinterfaces (s0.1 and s0.2) on its serial 0 interface.

With subinterfaces, each VC coming into the router's physical interface can connect to its own subinterface. By associating VCs with individual subinterfaces, as opposed to using a VC for each physical interface, the router is able to support a larger number of connections without having to use additional router interfaces. As a result, subinterfaces are a cost-effective solution to scaling a Frame Relay network.

So how do subinterfaces resolve split horizon issues, though? The answer is that split horizon sees the subinterface—specifically, a *point-to-point* type (more on this classification in the next section—in exactly the same way it sees a physical interface. Because it regards the subinterface as if it were a regular physical interface, broadcasts received on one subinterface can be sent out another subinterface without violating split horizon issues.

In Figure 20-20, for instance, Router A receives a broadcast on its serial 0.2 subinterface and forwards it out its serial 0.1 interface to Router B. This situation is identical to

Figure 20-19
Subinterfaces

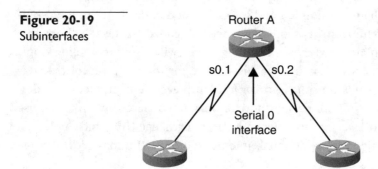

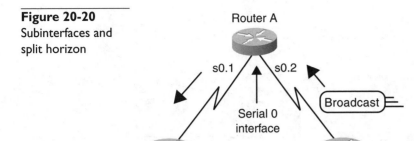

Figure 20-20
Subinterfaces and
split horizon

receiving a broadcast on one physical interface and forwarding it out another. In both instances, split horizon sees that the broadcast is not being forwarded out the same interface or subinterface from which the broadcast was received.

As a result, with subinterfaces configured on a multipoint interface, broadcast connectivity between indirectly connected peers is permitted in an NBMA Frame Relay network.

Subinterface Types

Two subinterface types are supported on Cisco routers:

• Point-to-point subinterfaces
• Multipoint subinterfaces

Point-to-Point Subinterfaces

Point-to-point subinterfaces behave like leased lines in that a PVC associated with a point-to-point subinterface connects two sites via a dedicated connection that is on its own IP subnet (or IPX network, AppleTalk network, and so forth). In Figure 20-21, for example, Router A's serial 0 interface is configured with two point-to-point subinterfaces (s0.1 and s0.2) that are each on different subnets (132.16.1.0/24 and 132.16.2.0/24).

Subinterfaces can connect to an interface of any type. In the preceding example, Router A's s0.1 subinterface connects to a physical interface (serial 1) on Router B, and Router A's s0.2 subinterface connects to a subinterface (s0.1) on Router C.

Because subinterfaces attach to individual VCs, a point-to-point subinterface attaches to only one VC. As a result, each subinterface is associated with its own local DLCI. If an interface is configured with multiple subinterfaces, the interface will consequently have multiple VCs and multiple DLCIs.

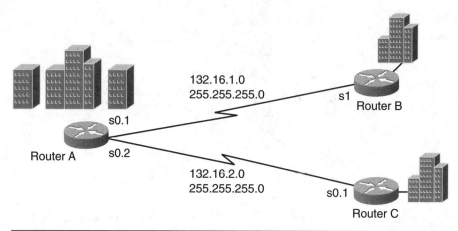

Figure 20-21 Point-to-point subinterfaces

> **NOTE:** Although a physical interface can have multiple subinterfaces, each of which attaches to separate VCs, don't confuse this configuration with a multipoint subinterface. Multipoint subinterfaces are covered in a later section, "Multipoint Subinterfaces."

As another example, Figure 20-22 presents a star topology in which Router A's serial interface is configured with three subinterfaces (s0.1, s0.2, and s0.3). Each subinterface is on its own subnet, attached to its own VC, and associated with its own DLCI. Although not shown in the diagram, Router A's s0.1 subinterface is on subnet 132.16.1.0, its s0.2 subinterface is on 132.16.2.0, and its s0.3 subinterface is on 132.16.3.0.

Note that since this is a star topology the Seattle and San Jose sites can reach one another only by going through the New York site; that is, traffic transmitted between the Seattle and San Jose routers must travel through the New York router. Figure 20-23 presents another depiction of this same network.

Split Horizon and Point-to-Point Subinterfaces

Although split horizon is enabled by default on point-to-point subinterfaces, broadcast connectivity is not an issue because split horizon treats this type of subinterface as a single physical interface. Point-to-point subinterfaces are therefore a solution to broadcast connectivity in an NBMA Frame Relay network; they are the types of subinterfaces that we used in a previous section to show how subinterfaces resolve Frame Relay reachability issues ("Resolving Frame Relay Reachability Issues by Using Subinterfaces").

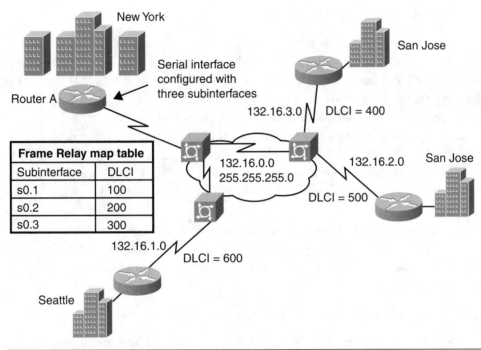

Figure 20-22   Subinterfaces and DLCIs

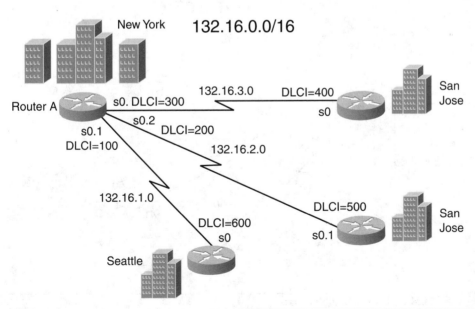

Figure 20-23   Frame Relay Network with DLCIs

Multipoint Subinterfaces

Unlike a point-to-point subinterface, which can connect only one VC, a multipoint subinterface can connect multiple VCs. Although each VC is still associated with its own DLCI, all VCs on the same multipoint subinterface are in the same IP subnet (or IPX network, AppleTalk network, and so forth). As shown in Figure 20-24, for example, all VCs attach to the same subinterface on the same subnet (132.16.1.0 /24).

Just like their point-to-point cousins, multiple multipoint subinterfaces can be configured on the same physical interface. In this configuration, all VCs that attach to the same subinterface are again in the same subnet. In Figure 20-25, for example, the Hub router has three multipoint subinterfaces (s0.1, s0.2, and s0.3), each of which attaches three VCs.

In Frame Relay, a multipoint subinterface is used similarly to a physical interface; that is, both interface types support multiple VCs in a configuration in which all VCs belong to the same network. The only major difference is that one type is logical and the other is physical.

Split Horizon and Multipoint Subinterfaces

Split horizon is disabled by default on multipoint subinterfaces, which means that, although broadcast connectivity issues are no longer present, routing loops may be an

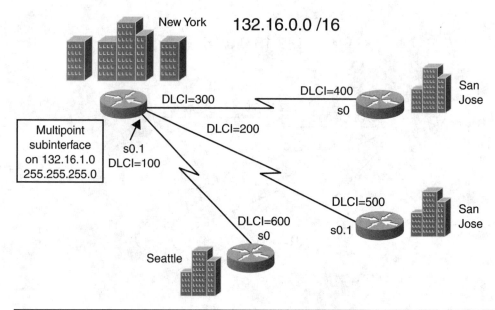

Figure 20-24   Multipoint subinterface

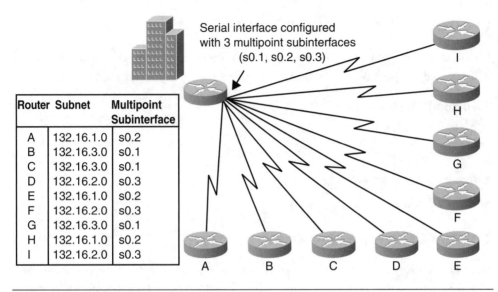

Router	Subnet	Multipoint Subinterface
A	132.16.1.0	s0.2
B	132.16.3.0	s0.1
C	132.16.3.0	s0.1
D	132.16.2.0	s0.3
E	132.16.1.0	s0.2
F	132.16.2.0	s0.3
G	132.16.3.0	s0.1
H	132.16.1.0	s0.2
I	132.16.2.0	s0.3

Serial interface configured with 3 multipoint subinterfaces (s0.1, s0.2, s0.3)

Figure 20-25 Multiple multipoint subinterfaces

issue, depending on which routing protocol the Frame Relay network is using. (Refer to the section "Resolving Frame Relay Reachability Issues by Disabling Split Horizon.")

Summarizing the Frame Relay Subinterfaces

Table 20-3 summarizes the major features of the Frame Relay point-to-point and multipoint subinterfaces and the Frame Relay physical interface.

Table 20-3 Summary of Frame Relay Interfaces

POINT-TO-POINT SUBINTERFACE	MULTIPOINT SUBINTERFACE	PHYSICAL INTERFACE (NO SUBINTERFACES)
Attaches to only one VC	Can attach to multiple VCs	Can attach to multiple VCs
Each VC is in its own subnet	All VCs attached to the same subinterface are in the same IP subnet	All VCs attached to the same interface are in the same IP subnet
Supports all Frame Relay topologies	Supports all Frame Relay topologies	Supports all Frame Relay topologies
Split horizon is enabled by default	Split horizon is disabled by default	Split horizon is disabled by default

Frame Relay Configuration

Initial basic configuration of an enterprise customer's router for Frame Relay operation will generally require the use of one or several of the following Cisco IOS commands:

- encapsulation frame-relay
- frame-relay lmi-type
- bandwidth
- frame-relay inverse-arp
- frame-relay map

Enabling Frame Relay Encapsulation

Basic Frame Relay configuration on a Cisco router begins with enabling the serial interface for Frame Relay encapsulation. On the interface on which you want to enable Frame Relay, enter the following command:

```
Router(config-if)#encapsulation frame-relay [cisco|ietf]
```

Use the *cisco* keyword if the router(s) to which the interface connects to is a Cisco router. If the remote router is a non-Cisco router, use the *ietf* keyword. The default encapsulation type is *cisco*.

The following example shows how to enable Frame Relay with the default Cisco encapsulation on the serial 0 interface:

```
Router(config)#interface serial0
Router(config-if)#encapsulation frame-relay
```

Specifying the LMI type

If you are using IOS version 11.1 or earlier, you will need to specify the LMI type used by the local Frame Relay switch. In interface configuration mode, enter the following command:

```
Router(config-if)#frame-relay lmi-type [ansi|cisco|q933a]
```

The default LMI type is *cisco*.

As an example, the following command was issued to specify the ANSI LMI type:

```
Router(config-if)#frame-relay lmi-type ansi
```

The *frame-relay lmi-type* command is not required with IOS version 11.3 or later, because in these later IOS releases, the router is able to dynamically acquire the LMI type from the local Frame Relay switch.

Configuring the Link Bandwidth

You have the option of specifying the speed of a Frame Relay interface by using the following interface configuration command:

```
Router(config-if)#bandwidth kbps
```

The kbps parameter identifies the speed (bandwidth) of the interface. The default bandwidth for serial lines operating at E1 rates (2.048 Mbps) and below is 56 Kbps.

For example, the following command configures a bandwidth of T1 (1.544 Mbps):

```
Router(config-if)#bandwidth 1544
```

NOTE: The bandwidth command does not set the rate at which traffic is transmitted across the interface. In fact, the command is generally used only by a router's routing protocol, for example, Interior Gateway Routing Protocol (IGRP) and Enhanced Interior Gateway Routing Protocol (EIGRP), solely for the purpose of calculating how much of the interface's bandwidth should be used for routing protocol traffic.

Enabling Inverse ARP

Inverse ARP, you will recall, is the protocol used to dynamically resolve DLCIs to IP addresses.

Inverse ARP is enabled by default (except on point-to-point subinterfaces, where it is not needed because there is only one possible destination that can map to the link's DLCI). In cases where you had to disable Inverse ARP for some reason, you can use the following command to re-enable it:

```
Router(config-if)#frame-relay inverse-arp [protocol] [dlci#]
```

You can re-enable Inverse ARP either for all protocols and DLCIs used on the interface or for just a specific protocol and DLCI. Omit the *protocol* and *dlci#* parameters when you want to accomplish the former task.

The following command was issued to enable Inverse ARP for all protocols and DLCIs on the router's serial interface:

```
Router(config-if)#frame-relay inverse-arp
```

Configuring a Static Map

If you will not be using Inverse ARP to dynamically map DLCIs to protocol addresses, then you will likely need to create a static mapping. Use the following command in interface configuration mode to accomplish this task:

```
Router(config-if)#frame-relay map protocol protocol-address dlci#
[broadcast] [ietf|cisco]
```

Table 20-4 explains the parameters used in the preceding command.

Figure 20-26 presents an example of a Frame Relay configuration in which static mapping is used instead of Inverse ARP to map DLCIs to next-hop protocol addresses.

Configuring Subinterfaces

This section covers the configuration of point-to-point and multipoint subinterface types. Following sections present configuration examples showing how subinterfaces are implemented in various Frame Relay topologies, including full mesh and partial mesh topologies.

Table 20-4 Explaining the *frame-relay map* Command

PARAMETER	EXPLANATION
protocol	Protocol used on the interface. Supported protocols include: *appletalk, decnet, dlsw, ip, ipx, llc2, rsrb, vines,* and *xns*
protocol-address	Protocol address of remote router interface
dlci#	Local DLCI used to reach the remote router
broadcast	Permits the forwarding of broadcasts when multicasting is not enabled
ietf|cisco	Frame Relay encapsulation type. Overrides the encapsulation type specified in the *encapsulation frame-relay* command

Router A's Frame Relay configuration

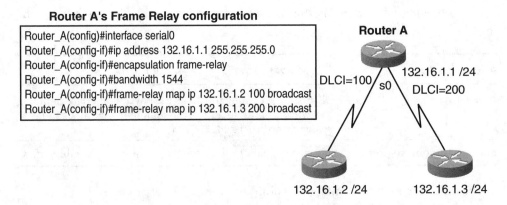

```
Router_A(config)#interface serial0
Router_A(config-if)#ip address 132.16.1.1 255.255.255.0
Router_A(config-if)#encapsulation frame-relay
Router_A(config-if)#bandwidth 1544
Router_A(config-if)#frame-relay map ip 132.16.1.2 100 broadcast
Router_A(config-if)#frame-relay map ip 132.16.1.3 200 broadcast
```

Figure 20-26   Frame Relay Static mapping example

Steps to Configuring Subinterfaces

Subinterface configuration involves a series of steps:

1. Enter the physical interface on which you want to create the subinterface.

   Example: `Router(config)#interface serial0`

2. If the interface has a network address, remove it. This step is necessary because you will instead be configuring a network address on the subinterface.

   Example: `Router(config-if)#no ip address 132.16.1.1 255.255.255.0`

3. Configure Frame Relay encapsulation on the physical interface.

   Example: `Router(config-if)#encapsulation frame-relay`

 NOTE: By default, the Frame Relay encapsulation type (cisco or ietf) that is chosen will apply to all the subinterfaces you configure on the physical interface. If a subinterface connects to a remote router that uses a differing Frame Relay encapsulation type, the subinterface can be configured with its own overriding encapsulation type.

4. Enter the subinterface on which you want to configure Frame Relay. Do this by using the following command:

```
Router(config-if)#interface serial#.subinterface#
multipoint|point-to-point
```

The following table explains the parameters associated with the preceding command.

PARAMETER	EXPLANATION
#.subinterface#	The value preceding the dot is the physical interface number. The *subinterface#* identifies the subinterface number and is a value from 1 to 4,294,967,293.
multipoint|point-to-point	Designates either a multipoint or point-to-point subinterface

The following example configures a point-to-point subinterface on serial 0:

```
Router(config-if)#interface serial0.1 point-to-point
```

5. Configure a network address on the subinterface.

Example: `Router(config-subif)#ip address 132.16.1.1 255.255.255.0`

NOTE: Configure a network address for each protocol that will be running on the subinterface.

6. Link a PVC to the subinterface by using the following command:

```
Router(config-subif)#frame-relay interface-dlci dlci# [ietf|cisco]
```

The *dlci#* identifies the DLCI that will be used to reach the remote destination. The *ietf* or *cisco* keyword can be used to override the Frame Relay encapsulation type specified on the physical interface.

The *frame-relay interface-dlci* command is necessary because, even though the router receives the local DLCIs from the Frame Relay switch (remember, the router learns local DLCIs from the Frame Relay switch), the router has no way of knowing which DLCI belongs to which subinterface unless this command is used to apprise the router.

In fact, the only times the *frame-relay interface-dlci* command is not required is when one is configuring multipoint subinterfaces with static mappings or using physical interfaces without subinterfaces.

Subinterface Configuration Examples

The following sections provide examples of Frame Relay subinterface configurations that have been applied on various Frame Relay topologies. Specifically, we will be taking a look at the following examples:

- Point-to-point subinterface over star topology

- Point-to-point subinterface over full mesh topology

- Multipoint subinterface over star topology

- Multipoint subinterface over full mesh topology

- Hybrid subinterface (point-to-point and multipoint) over partial mesh topology

Point-to-Point Subinterface Over Star Topology

In Figure 20-27, Router A is a central site router using point-to-point subinterfaces to connect remote routers B and C. Router C's Frame Relay configuration is on a point-to-point subinterface, and Router B's Frame Relay configuration is on a physical interface.

Note that Router B has a static mapping configured on its physical interface. This is necessary because Router B is not running Inverse ARP with Router A, whose point-to-point subinterfaces automatically disable Inverse ARP. (The reason why a point-to-point subinterface does not need a mapping is because there is only one possible destination with which the subinterface's DLCI can be associated.)

Point-to-Point Subinterface Over Full Mesh Topology

In our next example, all routers are linked together in a full mesh topology via point-to-point subinterfaces. Figure 20-28 presents the diagram and router Frame Relay configurations for this network. Note that each router on the same subinterface link uses the same DLCI. As mentioned before in the section, "Understanding Locally Significant DLCIs," this is permissible with the DLCI convention of local significance. In fact, it is the most common way to use locally significant DLCIs.

Router A's configuration

```
Router_A(config)#interface serial0
Router_A(config-if)#no ip address
Router_A(config-if)#encapsulation frame-relay
Router_A(config-if)#interface serial0.1 point-to-point
Router_A(config-subif)#ip address 132.16.1.1 255.255.255.0
Router_A(config-subif)#bandwidth 768
Router_A(config-subif)#frame-relay interface-dlci 30
Router_A(config-subif)#interface serial0.2 point-to-point
Router_A(config-subif)#ip address 132.16.2.1 255.255.255.0
Router_A(config-subif)#bandwidth 768
Router_A(config-subif)#frame-relay interface-dlci 40
```

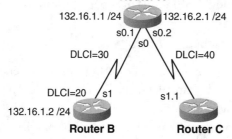

Router B's configuration

```
Router_B(config)#interface serial1
Router_B(config-if)#description my Frame Relay link to Router A
Router_B(config-if)#ip address 132.16.1.2 255.255.255.0
Router_B(config-if)#encapsulation frame-relay
Router_B(config-if)#bandwidth 368
Router_B(config-if)#frame-relay map ip 132.16.1.1 20
```

Router C's configuration

```
Router_C(config)#interface serial1
Router_C(config-if)#no ip address
Router_C(config-if)#encapsulation frame-relay
Router_C(config-if)#interface serial1.1 frame-relay
Router_C(config-subif)#description my Frame Relay link to Router A
Router_C(config-subif)#ip address 132.16.2.2 255.255.255.0
Router_C(config-subif)#bandwidth 368
Router_C(config-subif)#frame-relay interface-dlci 40
```

Figure 20-27   Star topology with point-to-point subinterfaces

Router A's configuration

```
Router_A(config)#interface serial0
Router_A(config-if)#no ip address
Router_A(config-if)#encapsulation frame-relay
Router_A(config-if)#interface serial0.1 point-to-point
Router_A(config-subif)#description my Frame Relay link to Router B
Router_A(config-subif)#ip address 132.16.1.1 255.255.255.0
Router_A(config-subif)#frame-relay interface-dlci 20
Router_A(config-subif)#interface serial0.2 point-to-point
Router_A(config-subif)#description my Frame Relay link to Router C
Router_A(config-subif)#ip address 132.16.2.1 255.255.255.0
Router_A(config-subif)#frame-relay interface-dlci 40
```

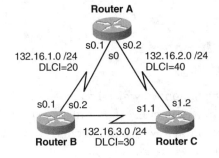

Router A

s0.1   s0.2
s0

132.16.1.0 /24   132.16.2.0 /24
DLCI=20   DLCI=40

s0.1 s0.2   s1.1   s1.2

132.16.3.0 /24
Router B   DLCI=30   **Router C**

Router B's configuration

```
Router_B(config)#interface serial0
Router_B(config-if)#no ip address
Router_B(config-if)#encapsulation frame-relay
Router_B(config-if)#interface serial0.1 point-to-point
Router_B(config-subif)#description my Frame Relay link to Router A
Router_B(config-subif)#ip address 132.16.1.2 255.255.255.0
Router_B(config-subif)#frame-relay interface-dlci 20
Router_B(config-if)#interface serial0.2 point-to-point
Router_B(config-subif)#description my Frame Relay link to Router C
Router_B(config-subif)#ip address 132.16.3.1 255.255.255.0
Router_B(config-subif)#frame-relay interface-dlci 30
```

Router C's configuration

```
Router_C(config)#interface serial1
Router_C(config-if)#no ip address
Router_C(config-if)#encapsulation frame-relay
Router_C(config-if)#interface serial1.1 frame-relay
Router_C(config-subif)#description my Frame Relay link to Router B
Router_C(config-subif)#ip address 132.16.3.2 255.255.255.0
Router_C(config-subif)#frame-relay interface-dlci 30
Router_C(config-subif)#interface serial1.2 point-to-point
Router_C(config-subif)#description my Frame Relay link to Router A
Router_C(config-subif)#ip address 132.16.2.2 255.255.255.0
Router_C(config-subif)#frame-relay interface-dlci 40
```

Figure 20-28   Full mesh with point-to-point subinterfaces

Multipoint Subinterface Over Star Topology

Figure 20-29 depicts a central site router, Router A, using a multipoint interface to connect remote routers B and C, which are both using physical interfaces to connect to Router A. In addition, static mappings are being used in lieu of Inverse ARP.

Multipoint Subinterface Over Full Mesh Topology

Our next example presents a configuration in which all routers are using multipoint subinterfaces in a full mesh (see Figure 20-30). Because Inverse ARP is used, no static mappings are required.

Point-to-Point and Multipoint Subinterface Over Partial Mesh (Hybrid) Topology

So far, you have seen examples of configurations in which Frame Relay point-to-point and multipoint subinterfaces have been used in either star or full mesh topologies. In our next example, we examine a configuration in which both Frame Relay subinterface types are used in a partial mesh topology, where all sites are not directly connected. Because this type of topology typically combines the features of both a full mesh configuration and a star configuration, there are a number of ways in which the subinterfaces can be applied.

Figure 20-31, for example, presents but one way of how point-to-point and multipoint subinterfaces can be applied on one router, Router A. In this figure, Router A's serial0 interface is configured with one multipoint interface (connecting Router B and C) and two point-to-point interfaces (connecting Router E and F, respectively). As a result, Router A's serial interface uses three subnets: 132.16.1.0/24, 132.16.2.0/24, and 132.16.3.0/24. No static mappings are used in the network.

Router A's configuration

```
Router_A(config)#interface serial0
Router_A(config-if)#no ip address
Router_A(config-if)#encapsulation frame-relay
Router_A(config-if)#interface serial0.1 multipoint
Router_A(config-subif)#description my Frame Relay links
Router_A(config-subif)#ip address 132.16.1.1 255.255.255.0
Router_A(config-subif)#bandwidth 1544
Router_A(config-subif)#frame-relay map ip 132.16.1.2 30
Router_A(config-subif)#frame-relay map ip 132.16.1.3 40
```

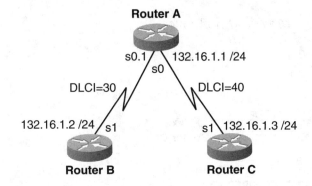

Router B's configuration

```
Router_B(config)#interface serial1
Router_B(config-if)#ip address 132.16.1.2 255.255.255.0
Router_B(config-if)#bandwidth 768
Router_B(config-if)#encapsulation frame-relay
Router_B(config-if)#frame-relay map ip 132.16.1.1 30
```

Router C's configuration

```
Router_C(config)#interface serial1
Router_C(config-if)#ip address 132.16.1.3 255.255.255.0
Router_C(config-if)#bandwidth 768
Router_C(config-if)#encapsulation frame-relay
Router_C(config-if)#frame-relay map ip 132.16.1.1 40
```

Figure 20-29   Star topology using multipoint subinterface

Router A's configuration

```
Router_A(config)#interface serial0
Router_A(config-if)#no ip address
Router_A(config-if)#encapsulation frame-relay
Router_A(config-if)#interface serial0.1 multipoint
Router_A(config-subif)#ip address 132.16.1.1 255.255.255.0
Router_A(config-subif)#frame-relay interface-dlci 30
Router_A(config-subif)#frame-relay interface-dlci 40
```

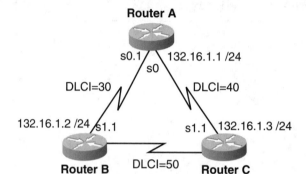

Router B's configuration

```
Router_B(config)#interface serial1
Router_B(config-if)#no ip address
Router_B(config-if)#encapsulation frame-relay
Router_B(config-if)#interface serial1.1 multipoint
Router_B(config-subif)# ip address 132.16.1.2 255.255.255.0
Router_B(config-subif)#frame-relay interface-dlci 30
Router_B(config-subif)#frame-relay interface-dlci 50
```

Router C's configuration

```
Router_C(config)#interface serial1
Router_C(config-if)#no ip address
Router_C(config-if)#encapsulation frame-relay
Router_C(config-if)#interface serial1.1 multipoint
Router_C(config-subif)# ip address 132.16.1.3 255.255.255.0
Router_C(config-subif)#frame-relay interface-dlci 40
Router_C(config-subif)#frame-relay interface-dlci 50
```

Figure 20-30 Multipoint subinterface over full mesh

Router A's configuration

```
Router_A(config)#interface serial0
Router_A(config-if)#no ip address
Router_A(config-if)#encapsulation frame-relay
Router_A(config-if)#frame-relay lmi-type ansi
Router_A(config-if)#interface serial0.1 multipoint
Router_A(config-subif)#description my links to routers B and C
Router_A(config-subif)#ip address 132.16.1.1 255.255.255.0
Router_A(config-subif)#bandwidth 1544
Router_A(config-subif)#frame-relay interface-dlci 20
Router_A(config-subif)#frame-relay interface-dlci 30
Router_A(config-subif)#interface serial0.2 point-to-point
Router_A(config-subif)#description my link to router E
Router_A(config-subif)#ip address 132.16.2.1 255.255.255.0
Router_A(config-subif)#bandwidth 1544
Router_A(config-subif)#frame-relay interface-dlci 40
Router_A(config-subif)#interface serial0.3 point-to-point
Router_A(config-subif)#description my link to router F
Router_A(config-subif)#ip address 132.16.3.1 255.255.255.0
Router_A(config-subif)#bandwidth 1544
Router_A(config-subif)#frame-relay interface-dlci 50
```

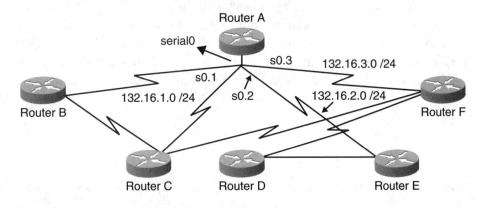

Figure 20-31   Hybrid interface configuration

Monitoring, Verifying, and Troubleshooting Frame Relay

Basic monitoring, verification, and troubleshooting of Frame Relay operation and configuration involve several Internetwork Operating System (IOS) commands, the more common of which are as follows:

- show interfaces serial
- show frame-relay lmi
- show frame-relay pvc
- show frame-relay map
- debug frame-relay lmi

The next sections explore these commands in detail.

The show interfaces serial Command

Use the *show interfaces serial* command to verify that the physical interface is up and running and that the encapsulation used on the interface is Frame Relay. When Frame Relay is enabled, you can use this command to view such information as which DLCIs the interface is using (as well as their status), various LMI statistics, and the keepalive interval. The following code presents sample output from this *show* command.

```
Router#show interfaces serial
Serial 2 is up, line protocol is up
   Hardware type is MCI Serial
   Internet address is 131.108.122.1, subnet mask is 255.255.255.0
   MTU 1500 bytes, BW 1544 Kbit, DLY 20000 usec, rely 255/255 ,
load 1/255
   Encapsulation FRAME-RELAY, loopback not set, keepalive set (10
sec)
   multicast DLCI 1022, status defined, active
   source DLCI   20, status defined, active
   LMI DLCI 1023, LMI sent 10, LMI stat recvd 10, LMI upd recvd 2
   Last input 7:21:29, output 0:00:37, output hang never
   Output queue 0/100 , 0 drops; input queue 0/75 , 0 drops
   Five minute input rate 0 bits/sec, 0 packets/sec
   Five minute output rate 0 bits/sec, 0 packets/sec
       47 packets input, 2656 bytes, 0 no buffer
       Received 5 broadcasts, 0 runts, 0 giants
       5 input errors, 0 CRC, 0 frame, 0 overrun, 0 ignored, 57
abort
       518 packets output, 391205 bytes
```

```
        0 output errors, 0 collisions, 0 interface resets, 0
restarts
        1 carrier transitions
```

Table 20-5 explains a few of the Frame Relay fields in the preceding output.

The show frame-relay lmi Command

Use the *show frame-relay lmi* command to display information about the LMI, including the LMI type, and the number and type of LMI messages sent and received. The following sample output was gathered from this command:

```
Router# show frame-relay lmi

LMI Statistics for interface Serial1 (Frame Relay DTE) LMI TYPE =
ANSI
    Invalid Unnumbered info 0        Invalid Prot Disc 0
    Invalid dummy Call Ref 0         Invalid Msg Type 0
    Invalid Status Message 0         Invalid Lock Shift 0
    Invalid Information ID 0         Invalid Report IE Len 0
    Invalid Report Request 0         Invalid Keep IE Len 0
    Num Status Enq. Sent 9          Num Status msgs Rcvd 0
    Num Update Status Rcvd 0        Num Status Timeouts 9
```

Table 20-5   Explaining the *show interfaces serial* Command

FIELD	EXPLANATION
keepalive set (10 sec)	This is the keepalive interval, which identifies how often the interface sends keepalive messages to the local Frame Relay switch.
source dlci 20, status defined, active	This is the local dlci used on the serial interface. Its status is currently active.
multicast DLCI 1022, status defined, active	This is the multicast dlci used on the serial interface. Its status is currently active.
LMI DLCI 1023	The local management interface (LMI) uses its own DLCI to communicate with the Frame Relay switch. The default LMI DLCI is 1023.
LMI sent 10	This indicates that 10 status inquiry messages have been sent.
LMI stat recvd 10	This indicates that 10 status messages have been received.
LMI upd recvd 2	This indicates that 2 status updates have been received.

The show frame-relay pvc Command

Use the *show frame-relay pvc* command to view PVC status and traffic statistics, including the DLCI, DLCI status, and type and number of Frame Relay packets sent and received on the PVC. If you do not include any optional parameters with this command, the output displays information for all PVCs that are on all interfaces. It is therefore best to specify either the exact PVC or the exact interface you want to obtain information for. The following *show frame-relay pvc* command presents the options you may use for this purpose:

```
show frame-relay pvc [interface interface [dlci]]
```

For example, the following output is for the PVC associated with DLCI 100:

```
Router# show frame-relay pvc 100

PVC Statistics for interface Serial5/1   (Frame Relay DTE)
DLCI = 100, DLCI USAGE = LOCAL, PVC STATUS = ACTIVE, INTERFACE =
Serial0.1
     input pkts 9           output pkts 16        in bytes 154
     out bytes 338          dropped pkts 6        in FECN pkts 0
     in BECN pkts 0         out FECN pkts 0       out BECN pkts 0
     in DE pkts 0           out DE pkts 0
     out bcast pkts 0       out bcast bytes 0
     pvc create time 00:35:11, last time pvc status changed
00:00:22
     Bound to Virtual-Access1 (up, cloned from Virtual-Template5)
```

As you can see, the *show frame-relay pvc* command can display counters for inbound and outbound data, FECN, BECN, DE, and broadcast packets, as well as a counter for the number of inbound and outbound data packets that have been dropped (owing to errors in the Frame Relay frame, for example).

The show frame-relay map Command

Use the *show frame-relay map* command to view the Frame Relay map table, which shows the DLCI-to-protocol address mapping. The following output displays this mapping:

```
Router#show frame-relay map

Serial 1 (up): ip 131.108.177.177
dlci 177 (0xB1,0x2C10), static, broadcast, CISCO
```

The preceding output shows that DLCI 177 maps to the destination address 131.108.177.177. Other fields in this command are as follows:

- **static**   Indicates that the map entry was statically configured (for example, via the *frame-relay m*ap command)

- **broadcast**   Indicates that the associated VC supports broadcasts

- **CISCO**   Indicates the Frame Relay encapsulation type (that is, cisco or ietf)

NOTE: If Frame Relay is configured on a point-to-point subinterface, then the show frame-relay map command will display the subinterface in place of the protocol address.

The debug frame-relay Command

When you need to analyze the packets that are being transmitted and received on the router's Frame Relay interface, use the *debug frame-relay* command. Sample output from this troubleshooting command is displayed as follows:

```
Router# debug frame-relay

Serial0(i): dlci 500(0x7C41), pkt type 0x0800, datagramsize 24
Serial0(i): dlci 1023(0xFCF1), pkt type 0x309, datagramsize 13
Serial0(i): dlci 500(0x7C41), pkt type 0x0800, datagramsize 24
Serial0(i): dlci 1023(0xFCF1), pkt type 0x309, datagramsize 13
Serial0(i): dlci 500(0x7C41), pkt type 0x0800, datagramsize 24
```

Look at the first line of this output. It indicates that the router's serial 0 interface received (i) a 24 byte packet on DLCI 500 (which, in hexadecimal, is 7C41) and that the packet's code type is hexadecimal 0800, which identifies an IP packet.

NOTE: For a listing of decoded packet types, consult Cisco's online documentation.

Summary

Frame Relay is a WAN data-link layer protocol that encapsulates data traffic for transport across packet-switched virtual circuits. As an access technology that supports speeds ranging from 56 Kbps to T3 (44.476), Frame Relay is generally ordered from a

WAN service provider, whose Frame Relay switches are used to establish connectivity through the carrier network between remote Frame Relay sites.

There are a variety of protocols and protocol-related elements used in a Frame Relay implementation. The following protocol elements are common:

- **LMI** The local management interface, or LMI, was developed in part by Cisco as a signaling protocol for managing the link between the router (CPE) and the Frame Relay switch (DCE).

- **DLCI** The data link connection identifier, or DLCI, is used by the Frame Relay switch and router to identify the VC. DLCIs can have either local or global significance.

- **Inverse ARP** Refers to a protocol used to dynamically map DLCIs to protocol addresses.

Frame Relay also supports a variety of topologies, including star, full mesh, and partial mesh, as well as a couple of subinterface types, including point-to-point and multipoint. Frame Relay topologies are typically configured using subinterfaces.

Case Study: Zahandra Communications

Background: Zahandra Communications is a publishing, marketing, and production company specializing in the development of educational materials—like books, audio CD-ROMs, CD-ROMs, and videos. Headquartered in a suburb of Denver, Zahandra Communications has remote offices in Los Angeles and San Francisco.

Currently, the company's offices are all interconnected via slow-speed X.25 links. Because the company wants to upgrade its network with a WAN technology that offers higher transmission rates over dedicated links at an affordable price, it was decided that Frame Relay would be deployed to replace the X.25 network.

Directions: Now you will apply the knowledge you have gained from studying this chapter's presentation of the Frame Relay protocol. After examining the scenario and accompanying diagram (shown in the next illustration) for Zahandra Communications, fill out the configuration worksheet that follows.

Scenario: Zahandra Communications has just ordered Frame Relay from the local Frame Relay service provider. As the network planner/manager, it is your task to configure the company's routers, shown in Figure 20-32, using a design that meets the following requirements:

- The Denver site router must use point-to-point subinterfaces to connect the Los Angeles and San Francisco site routers, which will also use point-to-point interfaces to connect to the Denver site.

- The Los Angeles and San Francisco sites do not require direct connectivity with each other.

- Local significance will be the convention of choice for DLCIs.

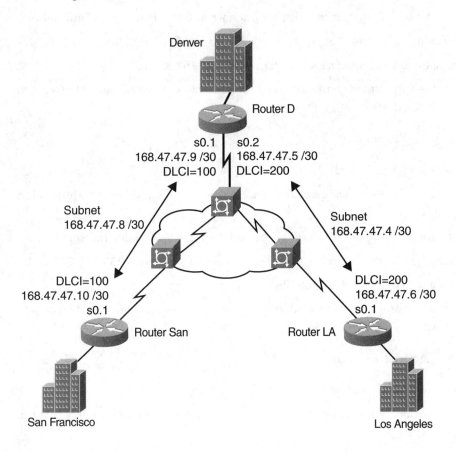

Configuration Worksheet for Zahandra Communications

On the Denver router:

1. Enter the serial 0 interface.

2. Enable Frame Relay encapsulation (use the default Frame Relay encapsulation type of Cisco).

3. Enter the serial0.1 point-to-point subinterface and specify a description for it (use any description you'd like).

4. Configure a subinterface address of 168.47.47.9 255.255.255.252.

5. While still in subinterface configuration mode, specify a bandwidth of 768 Kbps.

6. Issue the appropriate command to let the router know that this subinterface is to be associated with DLCI 100.

7. Enter the serial0.2 point-to-point subinterface and configure a description for it.

8. Specify the IP address 168.47.47.5 255.255.255.252

9. Configure the subinterface with a bandwidth of 768 Kbps.

10. Issue the appropriate command to let the router know that this subinterface is to be associated with DLCI 200.

On the Los Angeles router:

1. Enter the serial 0 interface.

2. Enable Frame Relay encapsulation (use the default Frame Relay encapsulation type of Cisco).

3. Enter the serial0.1 point-to-point subinterface and specify a description for it.

4. Configure the subinterface with an IP address of 168.47.47.6 255.255.255.252.

5. Configure a bandwidth of 768 Kbps.

6. Issue the appropriate command to let the router know that this subinterface is to be associated with DLCI 200.

On the San Francisco router:

1. Enter the serial 0 interface.

2. Enable Frame Relay encapsulation (use the default Frame Relay encapsulation type of Cisco).

3. Enter the serial0.1 point-to-point subinterface and specify a description for it.

4. Configure the subinterface with an IP address of 168.47.47.10 255.255.255.252

5. Configure the subinterface with a bandwidth of 768 Kbps.

6. Issue the appropriate command to let the router know that this subinterface is to be associated with DLCI 100.

Verifying your configurations:

1. On the Denver router, issue the Frame Relay *show* command that will allow you to view the traffic statistics for all PVCs.

2. On the Denver router, issue the Frame Relay *show* command that will allow you to view the Frame Relay map.

Case Study Suggested Solutions
(Your solutions may vary)

On the Denver router:

```
 1. Router_D(config)#interface serial0
 2. Router_D(config-if)#encapsulation frame-relay
 3. Router_D(config-if)#interface serial0.1 point-to-point
    Router_D(config-subif)#description my Frame Relay link
 to Frisco
 4. Router_D(config-subif)#ip address 168.47.47.9 255.255.255.252
 5. Router_D(config-subif)#bandwidth 768
 6. Router_D(config-subif)#frame-relay interface-dlci 100
 7. Router_D(config-subif)#interface serial0.2 point-to-point
    Router_D(config-subif)#description my Frame Relay link to LA
 8. Router_D(config-subif)#ip address 168.47.47.5 255.255.255.252
 9. Router_D(config-subif)#bandwidth 768
10. Router_D(config-subif)#frame-relay interface-dlci 200
```

On the Los Angeles Router:

```
 1. Router_LA(config)#interface serial0
 2. Router_LA(config-if)#encapsulation frame-relay
 3. Router_LA(config-if)#interface serial0.1 point-to-point
    Router_LA(config-subif)#description my Frame Relay link to
 Denver
 4. Router_LA(config-subif)#ip address 168.47.47.6 255.255.255.252
 5. Router_LA(config-subif)#bandwidth 768
 6. Router_LA(config-subif)#frame-relay interface-dlci 200
```

On the San Francisco Router:

```
 1. Router_San(config)#interface serial0
 2. Router_San(config-if)#encapsulation frame-relay
 3. Router_San(config-if)#interface serial0.1 point-to-point
 Router_San(config-subif)#description my Frame Relay link to Denver
 4. Router_San(config-subif)#ip address 168.47.47.10
 255.255.255.252
 5. Router_San(config-subif)#bandwidth 768
 6. Router_San(config-subif)#frame-relay interface-dlci 100
```

Verifying your configurations:

```
 1. Router_D#show frame-relay pvc
 2. Router_D#show frame-relay map
```

Practice Questions

Take a few moments and check your grasp of the concepts covered in this chapter. The answers follow the questions.

Questions

1. What does the DLCI identify?
   a. The router's subinterface type
   b. The LMI signaling protocol type
   c. The VC between the source and destination
   d. The rate at which the switch agrees to transfer data to and from the router

2. Which three of the following functions are handled by the LMI?
   a. Determining PVC status
   b. Transmitting Inverse ARP messages
   c. Transmitting keepalive messages
   d. Configuring point-to-point subinterfaces
   e. Multicasting
   f. Defining which Frame Relay topology is used

3. What does the address field in a Frame Relay frame contain? (Choose four)
   a. LMI type
   b. DLCI
   c. Next-hop address
   d. Protocol type
   e. FECN
   f. FCS
   g. BECN
   h. DE

4. What is the main difference between DLCIs that are locally significant and those that are globally significant?
   a. Locally significant DLCIs can be automatically discovered, whereas globally significant DLCIs must be manually configured
   b. Locally significant DLCIs are supported by all standard Frame Relay implementations, whereas globally significant DLCIs are supported only by Cisco
   c. Locally significant DLCIs are used on point-to-point subinterfaces, whereas globally significant DLCIs are used on multipoint subinterfaces that disable Inverse ARP
   d. Locally significant DLCIs are significant only relative to each router, whereas globally significant DLCIs have unique significance within the entire Frame Relay network.

5. What does Inverse ARP do?
   a. Discovers the local Frame Relay LMI type
   b. Determines whether the remote router is available
   c. Dynamically maps DLCIs to protocol addresses
   d. Gives DLCIs global rather than local significance

6. On initializing, how does a router typically discover which DLCIs are available?
   a. The router sends an Inverse ARP message to the local Frame Relay switch
   b. The router sends a status inquiry message to the local Frame Relay switch
   c. The router must wait until a remote router initiates communication
   d. The router is always configured with its DLCIs

7. What is the major difference between a point-to-point and multipoint subinterface?
   a. A point-to-point subinterface requires Inverse ARP, whereas with a multipoint subinterface it is optional
   b. A point-to-point subinterface attaches to only one VC, whereas a multipoint subinterface can attach to multiple VCs
   c. A point-to-point subinterface supports only star topologies, whereas a multipoint subinterface supports all types of topologies
   d. A point-to-point subinterface supports only locally significant DLCIs, whereas a multipoint subinterface supports either locally significant or globally significant DLCIs

8. What is the best definition of a subinterface?
   a. A logical subdivision of a physical interface
   b. An interface that supports VCs
   c. An interface that can be either point-to-point or multipoint
   d. A logical interface that uses a separate subnet for each attached VC

9. What is the major reachability issue in an NBMA Frame Relay environment?
   a. Split horizon protocol that prevents broadcast connectivity between indirectly connected routers is not supported
   b. Full mesh topologies allow only multipoint connectivity between directly connected routers
   c. Split horizon prevents routing updates from being transmitted between any two point-to-point routers
   d. Lack of broadcast support causes routing loops that bring down the Frame Relay network.

10. What command would you use to enable Frame Relay encapsulation?
    a. *frame-relay encapsulation*
    b. *encapsulation frame-relay*
    c. *configure frame-relay*
    d. *enable frame-relay*

Answers

1. **c.** The DLCI identifies the VC between the source and destination.

2. **a., c., e.** The LMI handles PVC status messaging, multicasting, and keepalives, among other functions.

3. **b., e., g., h.** The address field in a Frame Relay frame contains the DLCI, FECN, BECN, and DE bits.

4. **d.** The major difference is that locally significant DLCIs are significant only relative to each router, whereas globally significant DLCIs have unique significance within the entire Frame Relay network.

5. **c.** Inverse ARP dynamically maps DLCIs to protocol addresses.

6. **b.** The router discovers DLCIs by sending an LMI status inquiry message to the local Frame Relay switch, which responds with the DLCIs in a status message.

7. **b.** The major difference between a point-to-point and multipoint subinterface is that a point-to-point subinterface attaches to only one VC, whereas a multipoint subinterface can attach to multiple VCs.

8. **a.** A subinterface can best be defined as a logical subdivision of a physical interface.

9. **a.** The major reachability issue in an NBMA Frame Relay network is that split horizon prevents broadcast connectivity between indirectly connected routers.

10. **b.** *encapsulation frame-relay*

Evolving Internet Connectivity

This chapter will:

- **Look at cable modem service**

- **Look at DSL service**

- **Cover several emerging wireless Internet access services**

- **Look briefly at wireless LAN technology and standards**

In all chapters except Chapter 8, we have been looking at technologies and standards that are covered on the CCNA exam. This chapter looks briefly at new or emerging technologies that may dramatically change the way parts of the networking industry works and thinks. Cisco is involved in many of these technologies and will undoubtedly include at least the main ones, such as cable modems, DSL, and wireless LANs, in future exam requirements.

Cable Modems

Cable modems provide high-speed data connection to the Internet using the same coaxial cable that already brings television into many homes and businesses. Older cable installations often reach data speeds much faster than T1 leased lines. In our area in 2000, my neighbors were reporting access speeds up to 8 Mbps using MSN.COM's "Bandwidth Speed Test." After six months, enough new customers were added so that 1-2 Mbps during nonbusiness hours was common and often 500 to 800 Kbps during afternoons and evenings. As I write this on a Sunday afternoon, my connection is 1.063 Mbps.

 NOTE: These numbers relate to the Seattle metropolitan area using AT&T@Home service. My experience seems to be pretty consistent with others in the area and with colleagues I've discussed this with from California, Texas, and the east coast.

Even at its slowest, cable is 10 to 20 times faster than a standard analog modem connection and 4 to 7 times faster than ISDN for downloading. This makes cable a very attractive medium for browsing the Web and for downloading large video clips, audio files, and data files. Transfers that take minutes to download using ISDN can be done in seconds using a cable-modem connection. And ISDN is 3 to 5 times faster than most analog modems.

The biggest advantage of cable-modem access over leased lines, Frame Relay, or even ISDN is significantly lower costs. Cable-modem service in our area is about $40 per month, or $30 if you have your own modem. That is about 35 percent of the cost of 128 Kbps ISDN service and a much smaller percentage of the monthly fee for leased lines or Frame Relay. Cable service can be month-to-month in many places or at most a one-year commitment. Most leased-line and Frame-Relay setups are long-term commitments.

If you have TV cable service, installation amounts to an installer putting a splitter on the line and placing a special connection near where you want your service. Because of the splitter, the subscriber can continue to receive cable television service while simultaneously receiving data on a cable modem. Multiple users in the same household can create a small LAN to share the cable modem data connection.

I have several students who have cable-modem service but do not have cable TV service. In our area, the two services are packaged and billed separately. Since the service does not involve the telephone company at all, you can use your telephone while you browse the Internet. Our cable provider, AT&T, is already offering local and long-distance telephone service over that same cable in some areas. It looks like the convergence of voice, video, and data may make it to our cable TV before it becomes common in our data networks.

In many respects, cable-modem service is an Ethernet shared media network similar to the coaxial data networks of the mid-1980s and early 1990s. Figure 21-1 shows the similarities between the two.

To connect to the cable service, you need a modem that meets *Data Over Cable Service Interface Specification* (DOCSIS). This standard was developed by CableLabs and approved by the ITU in March 1998. It defines interface standards for cable modems and supporting equipment. With licensing from CableLabs, companies like Cisco will be able to produce cable modems and routers with built-in modems for retail sale, so consumers have a choice beyond that offered by their cable providers.

HDTVs and Web-enabled set-top boxes for regular televisions also recognize and support the DOCSIS standard.

While most communities have cable TV service in North America, and almost 85 percent of homes are wired for cable, very few office buildings have currently been outfitted for cable connections. This is somewhat of an immediate barrier to wide acceptance of cable service by businesses, but I suspect that the cable companies' biggest initial interest may be high-speed service at the homes of telecommuters and key employees. While retrofitting any building with any cable can be a major task, we are talking only about running a single connection to each business for a connection to the LAN and letting the LAN do the local delivery.

Cisco Cable Devices

Cisco's 900 series devices are for the cable industry. The Cisco uBR904 universal broadband router cable modem is like the 804 ISDN router mentioned in Chapter 12 in that it includes a built-in 4-port hub. It is a fully functional Cisco IOS router. Particularly for

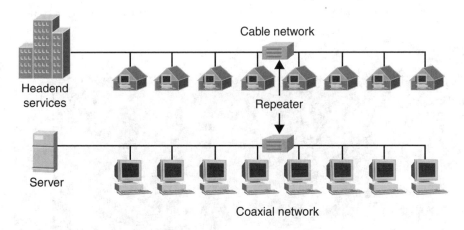

Figure 21-1   Cable network compared to coaxial Ethernet network

telecommuters, individuals, and small branch locations, this product offers simple installation and a greater level of security than a cable modem by itself. Figure 21-2 shows the front and rear view of a Cisco uBR904 router.

In December 2000, I could not get my cable service provider to accept a Cisco uBR904 as an acceptable connection to their system. While both companies claim to support and comply with the "standards," AT&T apparently doesn't. I spent about 10 hours trying to run down various contacts within AT&T to get this approved. At each level, I was initially told simply no. As I persisted, I was able to build up a growing list of approved devices, but the 904 was not on it. Some day when I'm feeling flush, I'll just hook one up and see if it works. My interest in this project included being able to show CCNA students a way to have a Cisco IOS router for hands-on configuration experience.

The uBR904 supports the latest versions of the IOS and does have different feature sets offering IP Security (IPSec) and firewall capabilities. With these features the unit can provide virtual private network (VPN) tunneling, with authentication and encryption.

Cable modems provide a full-time connection. As soon as users turn on their computers, they are connected to the Internet. This setup eliminates the time and effort of dialing in to establish a connection. The "always-on" cable connection also means that a company's "information pipe" is open at all times. This implementation increases the vulnerability of data to hackers and is a good reason to install firewalls and configure cable routers to maximize security. Fortunately, the industry is moving toward the standardization of cable modems, and the move is likely to address encryption needs.

Always-On Technology

In most instances, the cable modem and the connection remain live all the time, regardless of whether the computer is off or on. This means that the user has very fast

Figure 21-2
Front and back of
a Cisco uBR904
router

connection times, typically before the OS has finished all its startup processes. A cable connection is a permanently established connection to an ISP. It is not possible to use it as a point-to-point connection to different networks or locations. This means that telecommuters will be able to use cable service only if the company network supports connections to the Internet. This may introduce security concerns for the company that will need to be resolved with devices like Cisco's uBR904, with which higher levels of security and the ability to remotely administer the device are options.

When combined with the computer being left on and the relative lack of security features on a modem-only installation, this always-on feature may create opportunities for hackers to a home system to launch denial-of-service attacks on Web sites. This exposure is probably no greater for cable modems than for DSL service when similar customer premise devices are used. Either service is more at risk when used with a modem, less at risk when used with a router; the more security features supported by the router the better.

How Cable Connections Work

DOCSIS external cable modems provide IEEE 802.1d bridging to the customer network. The PC can attach indirectly to the cable modem through a network adapter (NIC) or through a USB port. There is no phone number to dial and therefore no call setup delay. The cable modem can be connected to a device that supports *network address translation* (NAT) and DHCP server services, such as a router, which can then be connected to an Ethernet hub for distribution to multiple LAN users. The other alternative is the "all-in-one" type device like uBR904, which combines the modem, the router, and the hub into a single device.

Like analog modems, cable modems modulate and demodulate the data signal into a stream of data. Analog modems operate on a circuit reserved for them, but cable modems must also be able to separate data traffic from the many other types of traffic sharing the wire. To do this, cable modems have a tuner that allows them copy the data traffic while ignoring the TV and pay-per-view data. The cable modem contains network-management software agents that allow the cable company to control and monitor the modem and user operations. There is also encryption circuitry for privacy.

Downstream versus Upstream Traffic

With analog modems, 56 Kbps applies only to downloading rates (traffic from the ISP to the user's machine). This is called *downstream traffic* and *downstream rate. Upstream traffic* is the opposite and is set at 28 Kbps. With cable modems, these rates vary considerably more. More important, both rates are adjustable and set at the "headend" of the connection, the service provider's end of the connection.

The DOCSIS standard specifies downstream traffic transfer rates between 27 and 36 Mbps over a *radio frequency* (RF) path in the 50 MHz to 750+ MHz range, and upstream traffic transfer rates between 320 Kbps and 10 Mbps over a RF path between 5 and 42 MHz.

For all practical purposes, a cable modem is a 64/256 QAM (Quadature Amplitude Modulation) radio frequency (RF) receiver capable of downloading up to 27 to 36 Mbps of data using one cable channel.

Upstream traffic depends on the cable system. Some older cable systems are one-way only, meaning the return stream is accomplished using a telephone line and a standard analog modem. This type of system is called a *telephony return interface* (TRI) system. This is the same type of service some satellite systems use. The download (downstream) service uses the high-speed technology, but the return (upstream) service uses plain old analog modems. This, of course, has implications about phone availability while you are on the computer. Figure 21-3 illustrates using a single cable channel for downstream traffic and an analog modem for upstream.

Fortunately, many cable service providers have been upgrading their systems to allow two-way high-speed connections using a QPSK/16 QAM transmitter with data rates from 320 Kbps up to 10 Mbps to send data upstream on a second cable channel. Figure 21-4 shows conceptually the two cable channels providing different downstream and upstream rates.

Cable systems use the Ethernet frame format for data-transmission data channels. The downstream data channels and the associated upstream data channels on a cable network basically form an Ethernet WAN. Because cable data uses shared media such as the old coaxial data networks, individual subscribers will see rates drop as more users are added to the system. What you end up with is downlinks varying from 500 Kbps to 30 Mbps and uplinks ranging from 96 Kbps to 10 Mbps.

Figure 21-3
Single cable channel
with telephony
return

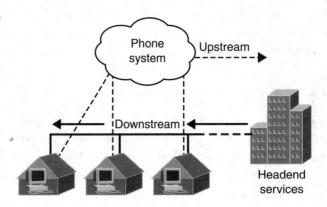

Figure 21-4
Two cable channels providing different upstream and downstream bandwidths

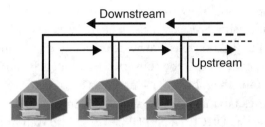

In addition to the number of users affecting transfer rates, headend (service provider) can further adjust these rates. This means that a business service willing to pay a premium rate can be configured (provisioned) to transmit and receive at relatively high rates. A residential user, however, who is receiving what the service provider calls "best effort" service, can have his downstream service configured to receive higher bandwidth for fast access to the Internet while severely limiting the upstream bandwidth to the network.

In our area, the service provider has capped residential upstream service to a maximum rate of 128 Kbps ostensibly to prevent people from setting up Web servers on these connections. The result for me is that my cable connection downstream (from the Internet) is significantly better than my ISDN service even in a high-traffic time period. Upstream is another matter. In theory, I have the same 128 Kbps upstream as with ISDN, but the actual speed is considerably slower at any time of the day. While many Web surfers probably would not be affected, I send a fair number of large files out as e-mail attachments each day so I can see the difference. While I haven't been able to verify it, I suspect it is just slightly better than a modem connection.

Internet Service on Cable

The cable system has lots of experience receiving signals from many sources and combining them over their cable channels to offer variety to the end users and additional revenue streams to the service provider and the content providers. Adding data services is really different only because of the two-way nature of the communications.

Currently, headends receive television programming, such as NBC, CBS, FOX, and the many cable networks (VH1, ESPN, Comedy Central, QVC, and so on). In some markets, additional channels of music-only content are added. These inputs are converted to separate channel frequencies and scrambled if necessary for the premium channels and pay-per-view. These frequencies are all combined onto a single, broad-band analog channel using *frequency-division multiplexing* (FDM).

The Internet and other computer downstream services are really nothing more than additional channels of content to be converted to frequencies and then multiplexed in with the rest. Assuming the cable service provider is going to work as its own ISP, then a regional site will need to maintain the server farms necessary to support the data and Internet services such as DHCP, DNS, FTP, TFTP, SNMP, Web hosting (HTTP), e-mail, news, chat, caching, and streaming-media servers. Figure 21-5 shows how a regional service center can support multiple cable service providers.

Current plans for some cable service providers include the addition of local and long-distance telephone service channels. The resulting combined analog signal is broadcast downstream to subscribers. When the combined signal arrives at the user's site, the television converter box on the TV separates and processes the television portions of the signal, and the cable modem or router separates and processes the user data.

The Cable Network

A *cable modem terminal server* (CMTS) at the headend communicates with the individual cable modems to enforce the Media Access Control (MAC) protocol and RF control functions. This CMTS provides data switching necessary to route data between the Internet and cable-modem users. This CMTS is the key for cable companies who have

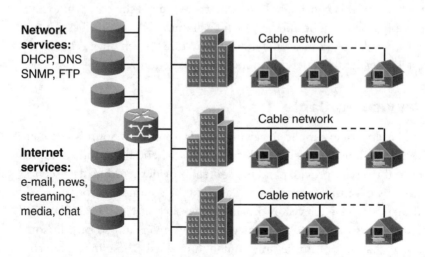

Figure 21-5   Regional service center with cable service providers

been traditionally content-delivery-only (downstream) services to be able to integrate upstream and downstream communications. The number of channels in either direction for a CMTS can be designed and adjusted as the number of users and data rates offered to each user changes. Security features allow a CMTS to link cable-modem identities to subscriber identities and manage access to the appropriate network services.

The *element management system* (EMS) is an operations system used specifically to monitor, configure, and manage multiple CMTSs and the cable-modem subscribers served by each. These operations include provisioning the accounts, day-to-day network administration, monitoring network performance, troubleshooting network alarms, and testing system components. From a *Network Operations Center* (NOC), a single EMS can support many CMTS systems in a particular geographic region. The NOC operations closely resemble the same facility in a large enterprise network or at a large Web hosting site.

Shared Bandwidth Concerns

The common argument that cable-modem connections are inferior to DSL connections because the bandwidth on a cable link is "shared" is suspect at best. The entire Internet is based on shared bandwidth. While an individual user's DSL connection may not be shared, the DSL connection ultimately ends up at an Internet router, at which point the many streams from other users are merged into one or more shared links. Internet backbone links are shared by thousands of ISPs and millions of users.

The issue really isn't whether or not a particular link is shared as much as whether or not there is enough bandwidth on the shared link(s) to serve all users at that particular time. My particular concern with cable has less to do with shared bandwidth and more to do with their ISP services and whether or not resources will be allocated to meet the growing service demands. Unfortunately, the cable industry's track record on customer service and commitment to quality is somewhat less than stellar.

Digital Subscriber Line (DSL)

Most DSL that you hear about uses the existing copper telephone network to connect to the Internet. But DSL, like Frame Relay, ATM, and the other technologies can be incorporated in the enterprise network. An organization can literally use DSL as their connectivity between buildings or to connect remote users. Cisco is a prime example in San Jose; they use a private DSL network to connects users to Cisco. So a better definition might be that DSL uses the existing copper telephone network to connect to a network.

This use of existing telephone circuits is a major benefit to service providers trying to quickly and economically meet the growing demand for fast, reliable digital service as well as competing with alternative access providers like cable modem and wireless services. The various forms of DSL (or xDSL) provide, or offer the promise of, high-speed Internet access, voice communications, television programming including high definition TV (HDTV), interactive activities, online services and secure Virtual Private Networks (VPNs) for consumers, small office/home offices (SOHOs), telecommuters, and branch location connections. Obviously, using the existing copper network is considerably less expensive than implementing full fiber to the home.

How DSL Works

DSL is a family of "last mile" or "local loop" solutions providing point-to-point digital access between the *network service provider's* (NSP's) central office (CO) and the customer location. DSL technology uses the existing copper-wire telephone delivery system to transport data, voice, and video to a Digital Subscriber Line Access Multiplexer (DSLAM) unit located at the service provider's CO. At the CO any voice data, which is below 4 KHz frequency on the circuit, is split off and forwarded to the NSP's phone network. All other data, above 4 KHz, is multiplexed for transmission over a fiber-optic connection to an ISP. Figure 21-6 shows a simplified basic DSL implementation.

DSL is actually stumbling over some compromises the telephone companies made in the past to save money while meeting the growing need for telephone service. As cities expanded to the suburbs, the need for telephone services increased beyond the limits of the *incumbent local exchange carrier's* (ILEC's) local loop-delivery systems. Rather than build additional COs, the companies ran fiber loops out to the develop-

Figure 21-6
A basic DSL
implementation

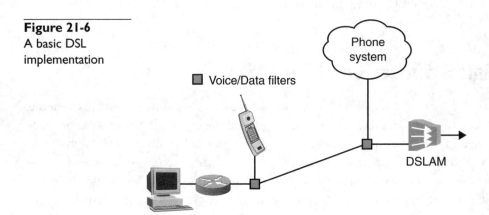

ment and then used switch stations to create the copper local loops that extended to the individual sites. The local loop has a fiber segment.

The problem is that DSL service cannot travel across fiber links, at least until it has been multiplexed by the DSLAM unit. This is why many homes that are actually within the distance limits from the COs are unable to get DSL service. This leaves the companies with the choice of not offering services to what is quite often a growing, high-income area or the prospect of having to place expensive DSLAM units in areas that may not be able to use the full capacity of the DSLAM. While this might seem like a simple cost-benefit problem, it is actually more complex than that. The catch is that the switching stations tend to be small. Even if they could house a DSLAM unit, they clearly are too small to provide co-location space to the *competitive local exchange carriers* (CLECs) that are entitled under court order to share such access.

While it is still very early in the implementation cycle, industry groups have developed and are expanding DSL standards to deal with interoperability issues providing an increased confidence level for suppliers, service providers, and consumers.

Different Flavors of DSL Service

DSL is offered in a variety of formats to meet the requirements of different markets. The "x" in the common xDSL reference refers to the whole family of offerings, which include ADSL, ADSL Lite, R-ADSL, HDSL, VDSL, and IDSL. The main variable is length of the copper connection and therefore the bandwidth available. Generally, the fastest services can be attained only close to the CO or DSLAM unit—the greater the distance, the lower the bandwidth. Another difference between DSL service offerings involves asymmetric or symmetric delivery. Asymmetric service allocates higher bandwidth to downstream transmissions than to upstream, whereas symmetric is equal in both directions. From the perspective of the user, downstream refers to data traffic from the service provider to the user, and upstream refers to traffic from the user to the provider.

The asymmetric service works well for consumers and business accounts that are primarily interested in browsing the Internet or working with online services where much more data is coming in than going out. Businesses or individuals offering content servers with more than minimal activity will find this configuration inappropriate and will opt for one of the symmetric service options or at minimum increased upstream bandwidth commitment.

Other issues that can affect service availability and quality are wire gauge and quality, the presence of bridged taps (remnant of party line era), cross-talk interference from other lines, and numerous or poor quality splices.

The major different services are discussed in the following paragraphs and summarized in Table 21-1.

Table 21-1   DSL Service Comparison

SERVICE	DOWNSTREAM RATE	UPSTREAM RATE	PAIRS	DISTANCE
ADSL	1.5–8 Mbps	Up to 1.544 Mbps	1	18,000 ft
R-ADSL	1.5–8 Mbps	Up to 1.544 Mbps	1	18,000 ft
ADSL Lite	Up to 1.5 Mbps	Up to 512 Kbps	1	18,000 ft
HDSL (DS1)	1.544 Mbps	1.544 Mbps	2	12,000–15,000 ft
HDSL (E1)	2.048 Mbps	2.048 Mbps	3	12,000–15,000 ft
SDSL (DS1)	1.544 Mbps	1.544 Mbps	1	10,000 ft
SDSL (E1)	2.048 Mbps	2.048 Mbps	1	10,000 ft
VDSL or symmetrical	13–52 Mbps up to 34 Mbps	1.5–2.3 Mbps up to 34 Mbps	11	1,000–4,500 ft
IDSL	144 Kbps	144 Kbps	1	18,000 ft

Asymmetric Digital Subscriber Line (ADSL)

ADSL is an asymmetrical technology allowing more bandwidth downstream than upstream. This configuration, combined with the always-on status, eliminating call setup, is ideal for consumers and businesses primarily interested in Internet/intranet access, telecommuting, or remote LAN access. They typically receive far more content than they transmit on a regular basis. The upstream rate is still adequate for periodic file uploads. The upstream rate can be 640 Kbps to 1.54 Mbps, while the downstream rate is 1.5 to 8 Mbps. While ADSL supports local loop distances up to 18,000 feet (3.5 miles), the speed is distance-dependent, with the fastest speeds attainable at less than 10,000 feet. The drop off is nonlinear, as shown in Table 21-2.

ADSL can share the same line as a voice connection for plain old telephone service (POTS), which can represent a significant benefit to end users-no extra line cost and they can use their phones while they are on the computer. The ADSL data frequencies (above 4 KHz) do not interfere with the telephone service frequencies (below 4 KHz). The voice service is added and eventually separated from the ADSL modem circuits using POTS splitters. Depending on the provider, this might involve a service installation or a user-installable filter at the customer premises. Since ADSL can support voice

Table 21-2 Distance Implications for ADSL

CO TO CUSTOMER DISTANCE	DOWNSTREAM SPEED
Up to 5,000 feet	8 Mbps
Up to 8,000 feet	7 Mbps
Up to 10,000 feet	5 Mbps
Up to 12,000 feet	3 Mbps

and requires only a single copper pair, the customer does not need to install additional lines or give up an existing service such as a children's line or a FAX line.

The International Telecommunications Union (ITU), the international standards body (formerly CCITT), has developed a standard called ITU-T Recommendation G.992.1 to cover ADSL technology. This standard is often referred to as G.dmt.

Rate-Adaptive Asymmetric Digital Subscriber Line

R-ADSL is a rate-adaptive (adjustable) version of ADSL offering the same possible transmission capabilities but allowing the actual connection speed to be determined at the time of connection or to be controlled via a signal from the central office.

Asymmetric Digital Subscriber Line Lite (ADSL Lite)

ADSL Lite, sometimes called G.Lite, is a standards-based simplified DSL technology that should allow faster DSL deployment by standardizing customer premises equipment (CPE), allowing ADSL Lite to be distributed through retail channels and reducing the requirements for NSP installers.

The actual standard is ITU-T Recommendation G.992.2 and is referred to as G Lite. The standard allows voice and data transmission without the need for a POTS supplied and installed splitter at the customer site. It is common for vendors to use inline *low-pass filters* (LPFs) at each telephone, FAX, or other non-DSL device to prevent transmission interference with the DSL signal. Similarly, *high-pass filters* (HPFs) are being built into the DSL modem to prevent data from "leaking" into voice frequency.

While not offering the higher speeds of ADSL, the Lite implementation is supposed to be able to support greater distances and therefore reach more users. The standard allows for an upgrade path to full ADSL.

High Bit-Rate Digital Subscriber Line (HDSL)—North America

HDSL is a symmetrical technology offering the same upstream and downstream bandwidth using two copper pairs to achieve the 1.544 Mbps capacity. HDSL's operating distance of 12,000 to 15,000 feet is somewhat less than ADSL; but it is possible with repeaters to extend the range. This technology does not currently support POTS.

HDSL has been in use for some time by ILECs as an alternative to T1 (1.544 Mbps) in servicing campus networks, long-distance service providers, Internet servers, and business clients.

A new HDSL 2 standard, when implemented, will provide HDSL service up to 18,000 feet over a single copper pair.

High Bit-Rate Digital Subscriber Line— Europe / International (HDSL-EI)

This version of HDSL uses three copper pairs to achieve full duplex bandwidth of 2.048 Mbps, matching the European E1 standard.

Single-Line Digital Subscriber Line (SDSL)—North America

SDSL is a predecessor of HDSL offering symmetrical bandwidth. Unlike HDSL, it uses a single copper pair and can support T1 bandwidth (1.544 Mbps) only up to about 9,500 feet from the CO. Bandwidth drops sharply to 416 Kbps at 18,000 feet and 160 Kbps at 22,000 feet. This technology does not currently support POTS. Many of the CLECs are aggressively deploying SDSL service particularly for videoconferencing and Internet server access.

An evolving standard, S.shdsl, will replace the current SDSL as a rate-adaptive form of HDSL. The standard should extend the coverage distance.

Single-Line Digital Subscriber Line— Europe / International (SDSL-EI)

This version of SDSL uses a single copper pair to achieve full duplex bandwidth of 2.048 Mbps, matching the European E1 standard.

Very High Bit-Rate Digital Subscriber Line (VDSL)

VDSL is capable of supporting very fast symmetrical or asymmetrical DSL service to those customers located close to the CO or to an optical network unit located on a fiber-optic link to the CO. In asymmetrical configuration, VDSL touts downstream bandwidths of 13 to 52 Mbps with upstream rates of 1.5 to 2.3 Mbps while still supporting POTS. The 52 Mbps rate is attainable only within about 1,000 feet of the CO. Bandwidth drops to 26 Mbps at 3,000 feet and to 13 Mbps at 4,500 feet (less than one mile).

DSL can also be configured symmetrically offering full duplex bandwidth of up to 34 Mbps for installations close to the CO.

ISDN Digital Subscriber Line (IDSL)

IDSL is an always-on alternative to the existing ISDN technology. It supports distances up to 36,000 feet from the CO and can be used in areas with *digital loop carriers* (DLCs)—a fiber loop from the CO to, say, a suburb and then distributed over copper.

IDSL's main attraction to users is that it can be used in areas excluded from DSL because of fiber digital loops; it may be less expensive than traditional service in some areas where rates are metered; existing customer ISDN equipment may be used for the connection; and there may be a slight increase in bandwidth because IDSL is 144 Kbps full-duplex, while ISDN is 128 Kbps. The extra 16 Kbps is recovered from D channel, which is used in call setup in ISDN.

IDSL's main downside, beyond relatively low bandwidth, is that it is not scalable. If faster DSL service becomes available, the customer will need to upgrade their entire service, including modems.

Always-On Technology

In most instances, the DSL device and the connection remain live all the time, regardless of whether the computer is off or on. There is no session setup time as there is with a modem and to a lesser extent ISDN. A DSL connection is a permanently established connection to an ISP. Larger companies will be able to use DSL as a point-to-point connection to different company networks. For others, DSL means that telecommuters will only be able to access the company network through the Internet.

This may introduce security concerns that will need to be resolved with devices like Cisco's line of DSL routers, with which higher levels of security and the ability to remotely administer the device are options. Some DSL service providers are implementing on-demand services that will have a connection setup time.

As with cable modems, when combined with the computer being left on and the relative lack of security features on a modem-only installation, this always-on feature may create opportunities for hackers to a home system to launch denial-of-service attacks on Web sites. This exposure is probably no greater for DSL service than for cable modems when similar customer premise devices are used. Either service is more at risk when used with a modem and less at risk when used with a router; the more security features supported by the router, the better.

Wireless Network Access

In spite of the lower cost and higher bandwidth of wired networks, wireless networks at all levels are popular with consumers. Cellular telephones and paging services are obvious examples. But even basic broadcast television is a wireless service that is expense to install, expensive to maintain, and expensive to repair compared to faster and less expensive wired services.

There are other wireless technologies providing services primarily to consumers that are aggressively developing Internet access solutions. These technologies include:

- Direct Broadcast Satellite (DBS)
- Multichannel Multipoint Distribution Services (MMDS)
- Local Multipoint Distribution Services (LMDS)

The network architecture of these wireless networks includes beaming the content off a satellite or ground-based station to a receiving antenna at the end -user's location. Unfortunately, each of these is a one-way technology, which means that any return-path traffic must travel through wired or wireless networks. This, of course, means that some technology must merge the downstream and upstream traffic to provide any control over downstream data flows. This is a problem similar to that of some older cable service providers who haven't upgraded their systems to two-way communication. This is not a problem with television or radio, because everything gets beamed down together and the receiver is used to tune to the desired channel.

My imagination just runs wild when I try to visualize controlling high-speed data downloading (or Web browsing) by using an analog modem. On a recent conference call with five other people, I lost my voice connection. I could hear but not be heard. After several attempts to re-establish, I contacted the others by e-mail. The others suggested that since we were on a deadline that we try to "wing it" using e-mail as the final leg. What a joke. Fortunately, the destiny of mankind did not hang in the balance.

Direct Broadcast Satellite (DBS)

DBSs are satellite competitors to the cable companies; they have had varying degrees of success selling television service to those customers that can't receive cable or can't stand the cable operators. The companies are Primestar, DirecTV, and United States Satellite Broadcasting (USSB), all of whom have been around since the mid-1990s.

The reality is that these firms aggressively market a wide variety of programming using the same model as do cable companies.

DBS Architecture

The system operators receive analog content from wide range of sources, including many of the same sources as cable, at a single giant headend. This analog content is encoded into Motion Picture Experts Group (MPEG) format for digital retransmission and multiplexed together. It is then converted to the uplink frequency and beamed to the appropriate North American geosynchronous satellites for remodulation to the designated spectrum for DBS. DBS satellites broadcast at a high enough bandwidth to enable reception on small satellite dishes. The higher-powered transmission and smaller dish distinguish DBS from other forms of satellite reception. The DBS can achieve nearly 1 GB of bandwidth.

Data Service

Early Internet delivery efforts amounted to broadcasting content from 200 popular Web sites to be cached on the hard drive in the user's PC. The user then browsed through the cached material. Additional content like weather, stock quotes, and AgCast could be either continuous feeds or by using the caching technique. There was no ability to expand your search beyond the selected content or to change the choice of sites because there was no return-path connection to the system. Figure 21-7 represents the centralized content and telephony return path.

DirectPC, owned by DirecTV and Hughes Network Systems, supplies access to the Internet using a telephone line as a return path. DirectPC offers up to 400 Kbps of downstream service to their two-way users. The upstream rate is limited to 56 Kbps modem speeds.

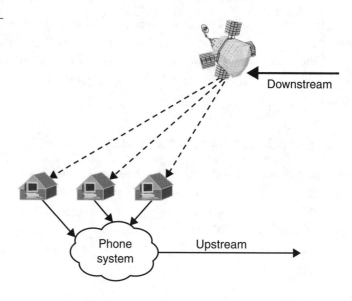

Figure 21-7
DBS with telephone
return

Multi-Channel Multipoint Distribution Services (MMDS)

There are two major distinctions between DBS and MMDS. First, MMDS uses local land-based microwave transmitters instead of satellite-based units so its range is relatively limited compared to DBS. Second, it is locally mixed and can contain both local content and local advertising. DBS, being broadcast from one central location, cannot do either. MMDS can achieve nearly 1 GB of bandwidth. While the content may be TV or movies in many areas, it is possible to also include Internet connectivity.

The telephone companies are often the providers. They are motivated by the success of DBS operations and they view microwave as a fast-start, lower-overhead service that allows them to distribute video to compete against cable and DBS. The microwave transmission technology is known as wireless cable, which is used to deliver analog television service to rural areas that cannot be served economically by wired cable.

The local content is combined with regional and national content. It is then multiplexed and encoded before transmission from a tower on a high elevation. At the user's location, a small microwave-receiving dish receives the signals. A decoder processes the TV images and forwards them to the TV set. For those network systems offering data service or Internet connectivity, another decoder can process the data for PC users. The return-path data uses telephone networks, although digital PCS connections are being developed. Figure 21-8 shows a MMDS network using a tower.

Figure 21-8
MMDS network
with telephone
return

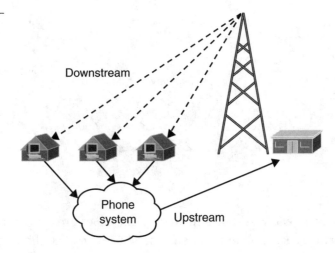

Downstream

Phone
system   Upstream

MMDS is a line-of-sight technology, so coverage is limited by the unevenness of the terrain and the ability to get the transmitter to a high elevation point. In some areas, a mountain range or tall building will work, but in others a tower is the only option. While it is easy to think of this technology as a blessing for the flat, rural areas of the country, it is not limited to these areas. Approximately 75 percent of homes Los Angeles and Orange County can receive MMDS signals reliably. It is hard to envision MMDS as a data service in Los Angeles, where both cable and DSL are prevalent.

Local Multipoint Distribution Services

Local Multipoint Distribution Service (LMDS), or, as it is known in Canada, *Local Multipoint Communication Service* (LMCS), is conceptually a cable-modem-type network using MMDS distribution technology. The difference is that this service is committed to providing an inband return path, rather than telephone return, and sufficient bandwidth to compete with cable's channel capacity.

This is a technology in development with significant technological hurdles to overcome. The plan is to offer more spectrum (bandwidths up to 155 Mbps) from smaller, cheaper transmitters placed very much like cellular telephone antennas. Each LMDS is a small-cell technology, with each cell having about a 2- to 4-mile radius. The signal modulation would be the same QPSK/QAM modulation used by cable service providers. Figure 21-9 shows LMDS with two-way local communications.

Figure 21-9
LMDS with two-way
communications

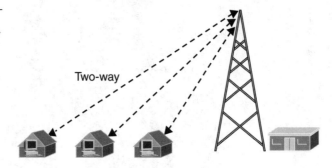

Two-way

At the user's end would be a small dish capable of two-way communications. If the two-way high-speed communications can occur, then the technology will literally be a wireless cable network.

Ricochet

I've included the Ricochet, by Metricom, here because it is a relatively low-cost wireless Internet connection. For all practical purposes, it is an always-on modem for a laptop or handheld device that uses the Ricochet network. In the markets in which it is available, it is a reliable, easy-to-use, mobile method of access to the Internet and thereby the world.

Ricochet is available at 128 Kbps in the following markets: Atlanta, Baltimore, Dallas/Fort Worth, Denver, Detroit, Houston, Los Angeles, Minneapolis-St. Paul, New York City, Philadelphia, Phoenix, San Diego, and the San Francisco Bay Area. Washington, D.C., and Seattle are still at 28.8 Kbps. Coverage is scheduled to reach 46 markets in 2001.

My experience with Ricochet is relatively good. I open my laptop anywhere in the Seattle metropolitan area, and, by the time Windows Me has loaded, the Internet is up and waiting for me. As an always-on system, there is no connection setup time. While 28.8 Kbps is terrible by DSL and cable-modem standards, it is a pretty true 28.8. My company uses Ricochets to download drivers and access online support when a client's network can't reach the Internet.

Network Architecture

The Ricochet network is a combination of subscriber devices, microcell radios, wired access points, network interconnect facilities, gateways, name server, and a network operations center.

The microcell radios are intelligent routing, self-contained, shoebox-sized radio transceivers typically mounted to streetlight or utility poles, approximately five per square mile, in a mesh network. The microcell radios communicate with users' laptops or handheld devices through Ricochet wireless modems. Each microcell is configured to route incoming packets to the optimal wired access point.

Wired access points (WAPs) are strategically placed within a 10- to 20-square-mile area. Each WAP collects and converts the radio frequency packets for transmission on a local wired IP network using fiber and T1 links. Ricochet Gateways are designed to connect the Ricochet network with other networks.

Two Network Operations Centers (NOCs) located in Dallas and Houston split the network support load for the country.

Wireless Local Area Networking

While not technically an Internet access technology, wireless LANs are growing, which means that more and more users will be accessing company networks and/or the Internet from mobile devices. The *wireless local area network* (WLAN) provides the features and benefits of traditional LAN technologies without the restrictions of cables. Possible WLAN applications include:

- Mobility within the organization for support personnel, sales people, executives, and others

- Areas of the company where frequent remodels and redesigns mean constant rewiring—for example, product show rooms, meeting rooms

- Any site where traditional LAN wiring may be banned, such as historical registry sites

WLAN technology can work alone or with the traditional wired network to extend its reach and capabilities. WLAN equipment includes two components: a client adapter and an access point. A client adapter can be a PC Card laptop or a handheld device, or a NIC-sized device for desktop machines. Each client adapter will have a small antenna. The access points act somewhat like the hubs and switches in a wired network. Proper placement of the access points will help ensure maximum flexibility for the mobile users.

Wireless LAN standard

In 1997, the IEEE released the 802.11 standard for wireless LANs. The 802.11 WLAN standard provides for transmission over different media. Media include infrared light and two types of radio transmission within the unlicensed 2.4-GHz frequency band: *frequency hopping spread spectrum* (FHSS) and *direct sequence spread spectrum* (DSSS). The more recent 802.11b standard specifies a data rate of 11 Mbps throughput over DSSS. FHSS does not support data rates higher than 2 Mbps.

As the standards create stability in the market, data rates have increased from 1 to 11 Mbps, and prices have dramatically decreased. The future holds promise that this trend will continue. Cisco has devices that will support 22 Mbps in the works; however, governmental regulation issues need to be resolved. While they will undoubtedly be pricey, the 802.11a devices operating at 5 GHz will support speeds up to 54 Mbps.

The Cisco Aironet series of *wireless LAN* (WLAN) products provides a standards-based, field-proven, high-speed wireless networking solution for both in-building and building-to-building WLAN applications. The Cisco Aironet series products are easy to manage and deliver a complete solution to customers who require the mobility, flexibility, and freedom of a WLAN to complement or replace a wired LAN. Cisco's Aironet products are being used by many enterprise networks to free their workers from their network tethers.

Security

Any wireless technology stimulates customer concerns about security; after all, the data is just floating around in the air. The *wired equivalent privacy* (WEP) option to the 802.11 standard begins to address these concerns. Both 40- and 128-bit encryption and authentication options are a part of the 802.11 standard. With WEP each client and access point has up to four keys. These keys are used to encrypt the data before transmission. The 128-bit WEP isn't a standard yet.

Summary

This chapter looked at cable modems as vehicles for high-speed Internet access for the home user, the telecommuter, and small businesses. Unless an organization can negotiate a service agreement with the cable service provider, the relatively low upstream speed precludes using cable service for anything but the most limited shared server.

The shared-media nature of cable service means that downstream bandwidth will fluctuate throughout the day and possibly degrade as additional users are added to the network segment. Our knowledge of shared bandwidth Ethernet networks, particularly coaxial networks, help us understand the mechanics of a cable network. It may be that this bandwidth issue isn't as big of a deal as bottlenecks elsewhere in the system, including capacity of the ISP services.

DSL service, which is not available everywhere, uses the existing copper local loop from the telephone company's CO to the site. As such, it is more like a switched network. While a DSL network isn't prone to loss of bandwidth in direct proportion to the number of users, there is still the concern about the capacity of the ISP and the connections from the DSLAM to the ISP.

Security concerns for both cable modems and DSL seem to be somewhat similar. A modem connection to either system makes you a part of their network and possibly more vulnerable. Placing a router between the modem and the local network and using what security features it offers should improve your chances of remaining secure. If security is a significant concern, then one of the Cisco routers with appropriate feature sets would be in order.

The various wireless Internet access systems are still works in progress, and none would compare favorably to cable or DSL service.

CHAPTER 22

WAN Design

This chapter will:

- **Review network scalability requirements**

- **Discuss LAN/WAN integration issues**

- **Identify WAN design issues and requirements**

- **Describe how to identify and gather customer requirements**

- **Discuss how to use the three-layer hierarchical model in WAN design**

- **Compare WAN technology options**

- **Identify which router CPU features to consider in selecting a WAN device**

I n Chapters 17 to 20, we looked at the WAN technologies that are covered on the CCNA exam. In Chapter 21, we looked at some of the other technologies, such as cable, DSL, and wireless, that will play a role in networks of the future. Network administrators are often called on to develop and manage more and more complex WANs.

In this chapter, we will look at WAN design methods to follow to ensure scalable and reliable networks to support the growing demands of the organization.

WAN Design Considerations

Chapter 1 defined *internetworking* as the connection of two or more LANs to function somewhat as a single network. Internetworking was probably never really as simple as that implies, and it clearly isn't getting simpler today. We now need to consider connecting not only LANs and WANs, but also the growing numbers of MANs and campus networks, each with its own characteristics, strengths, and weaknesses. The task becomes one of connecting these elements together to equitably and reliably share resources.

By definition, WAN communication occurs between geographically separated areas. Routers, sometimes called *access routers*, provide the connection between the WAN links and the local network. These routers select the best path if more than one exists, and they open any "on-demand" links as needed when working with ISDN and analog modem connections.

WAN communication typically involves a network service provider who charges fees for the WAN services it provides. This service provider may broker the services of other providers to complete a particular connection.

WAN technology is constantly improving, and faster services are becoming more broadly distributed across the country and around the world. Particularly when compared to LAN technologies at any point in time, WAN links are generally expensive, have relatively low bandwidth, are delay-prone, and have higher error rates. The cost issue is substantial and reflects the fact that there is a service provider in the mix. In building LANs, generally any cost in getting a necessary bandwidth and reliability is the acquisition cost of the equipment and media. It is a capital cost associated with letting users do their "real" business, whatever that happens to be.

For the WAN service provider, this connection that you want to create *is* its business. It is not a sideline, it's what they do. Furthermore, while it may have competitors, you generally cannot create this connection without a WAN provider. Stringing a cable for just a few miles through public and private property is virtually impossible for most companies. Issues such as rate of return, fair market value, competitive pressures, and the degree of regulatory involvement all go into determining the monthly "rate" to be paid for WAN connections.

WAN bandwidth is getting cheaper due to technology options such as IP+ Optical ATM and VPN services. The importance of competition cannot be underestimated. In many parts of the world, WAN services need to be secured from a government-approved, if not -owned, monopoly. Even in countries like the United States, where deregulation in the communications field has been evolving since the mid-1980s, tremendous barriers to entry still exist for new competitors, which Economics 101 tells us tends to keep prices high.

Even if a company is not growing, the demand for increased WAN bandwidth is escalating. To see why, we must recognize that we are no longer dealing just with traditional data. Businesses of all sizes are moving toward including many of the following technologies, all of which use the same network as their data:

- Voice-over-IP for local and/or long-distance communication
- Video conferencing and collaborative work processes
- Client/server applications internally and with customers
- Multicasts for training and internal/external communications
- High-definition imaging for industries ranging from health care to publishing
- Telemetry to monitor critical processes and procedures
- Telecommuting employees working at home or in the field
- Various forms of e-commerce increasing the number of Internets and intranets

Many of these technologies also incorporate the use of the Internet as an alternative to the private and more traditional methods of WAN connectivity discussed in the last few chapters. This blend of technologies, however, brings new concerns about, and new ways of securing, our data as well as our networks.

The increasing use of these technologies means that network administrators are going to be called on to provide ever-increasing levels of support for the following:

- **Greater overall bandwidth** Providing enough network bandwidth to deal with any contingency.
- **Bandwidth on demand** Technologies like Frame Relay where additional bandwidth can be made available on an as-needed basis at somewhat lower cost than trying to provide enough bandwidth to meet every contingency at all times.
- **Quality of Service (QoS)** A standard for measuring performance of a transmission system that reflects its transmission quality, reliability, and service availability.
- **Class of Service (CoS)** A prioritization system that includes a Layer 2 field within an IP datagram that indicates how the datagram should be handled. This is similar to a Layer 3 field for Type of Service (TOS).

 NOTE: The implementation of features such as QoS, CoS, and bandwidth on demand are the subject of other Cisco certifications, such as the CCNP Advanced Routing and Remote Access exams. I've chosen to reference them here because they are often critical in choosing some WAN technologies. Lack of or limited support for features such as QoS, CoS, and security protocols (such as VPN and IPSec) may make some low-cost alternatives such as cable service and DSL less attractive.

To be scalable, a network must be able to grow as the organization's requirements change with a minimum of disruption and loss of resources. The job of network administrators becomes one of trying to maximize requirements such as reliability, accessibility, and scalability while managing cost. Although a fully meshed network may provide high levels of reliability, it often cannot be expanded without considerable reconfiguration and resulting reductions in service. Carefully designing WANs can reduce problems associated with a growing network. To design reliable, scalable WANs, network designers must keep in mind that each WAN technology has specific design requirements and limitations.

A network that is well designed, implemented, funded, and maintained should be able to grow, and contract, as quickly as needed to meet the changing requirements of the organization. The alternative is increased network congestion, which occurs when too much traffic exists for the available bandwidth. This is always inefficient, and in the worst case, it can mean a complete collapse in the data network and considerable losses in revenue, reputation, and future growth for the organization.

Network Scalability Requirements

Five requirements must be met in designing networks at all levels to ensure scalability in the future. The nature of the business and possibly its level of development will require assigning different levels of importance to each requirement. With some businesses, a loss of network resources (reliability) for a day would be an inconvenience, whereas with others, it could be a financial catastrophe from which recovery might be difficult.

The five key requirements in designing a network are as follows:

- Reliability and availability
- Responsiveness
- Efficiency
- Adaptability
- Accessibility and security

Reliability and Availability

The reliability and availability requirement refers to the network's availability to users 365 days per year, around the clock, as advertised. Each business has to determine how important reliability is to it. Business size is not always a good predictor. A one-person ticket agency is out of business during the time its computer is offline.

The reliability and availability requirement is even more important for WAN connections between organization locations. Reduced reliability at this level will impact many users and significant portions of the network. It could mean that a manufacturing location cannot receive orders or design changes from other branches, thereby impacting overall company performance.

Responsiveness

Latency is a source of frustration for all users. The greater the latency, the greater the level of frustration. This is particularly true in time-sensitive transactions, such as stock purchases. The key is to strike a balance between QoS requirements and responding to user needs. WAN links, which typically are slower than LAN links can become network bottlenecks.

Efficiency

Designing a network to efficiently allocate resources often involves restricting unnecessary traffic to preserve bandwidth for the necessary traffic. Access lists and other technologies can be used to reduce the number and complexity of routing updates and other forms of broadcast traffic. Due to the monthly service charges associated with WAN connections, efficient use of available bandwidth becomes very important.

Adaptability

In addition to integrating different network technologies, protocols, and legacy systems, we must create an environment that can incorporate technologies that may be unknown today. Although we cannot always predict with great accuracy the course a network will take over the next few years, we should plan for many likely scenarios. Beyond that, we need to incorporate a design and devices that increase our chances of responding to the unknown. From following accepted standards to using only devices and applications that support interoperability, we hedge our bets.

New WAN access technologies, such as DSL, cable, and wireless, will offer opportunities and challenges in the near future.

Accessibility and Security

A properly designed network must have capabilities to support the industry-standard WAN technologies efficiently and with a reliable level of security. As companies open their networks to remote users using dial-up services and to the two-way exposure of connecting to the Internet, it becomes increasingly important to be able to secure company resources.

The preceding five requirements represent the standard to which any network design must be held. While organizations will weight each requirement differently, they must still be considered.

LAN/WAN Integration

Until recently, LAN and WAN communications remained logically separate. In the LAN, bandwidth is considered basically free and connectivity is limited only by hardware and implementation costs. In the WAN, bandwidth's monthly cost is the overriding issue. Until recently, delay-sensitive traffic such as voice has remained on its own network.

Distributed applications are generally database implementations. There has been a tremendous explosion in database awareness and skills throughout the user community. Prior to the early 1980s, any database applications were limited to the largest of organizations with mainframe computers and the support resources to develop and maintain the applications. Even the simplest mailing lists were often so complicated that they were relegated to specialists and print shops.

The introduction of dBASE II by Ashton-Tate in the early 1980s led to growing user interest in having control and access of their organization's data. By the end of the decade, Borland's Paradox, with its simpler approach, was catching the imagination of businesses of all sizes. When Microsoft introduced Access, the world was ready for easy-to-use, attractive, department-wide (LAN) databases. Throughout the 1990s, Access training has grown and extended through all levels of small and large organizations.

As WAN connectivity has become more common, many organizations and individuals have learned the hard way that a great LAN-based database application can be a real "dog" when run over much slower, bandwidth-limited WAN links. Products such as SQL and Web-based database "front ends" have found a market that understands the benefits and underlying concepts of database-driven technology. Entire industries are now built around converting companies' ways of doing business to Web-based applications. These distributed applications need increasingly more bandwidth.

In many organizations, voice communications and voice messaging are now being combined with paging features and e-mail to connect workers to their customers. The fact that many of these technologies are being added to the data network's infrastructure is making the network a mission-critical tool for information flow.

Other Internet applications, such as voice, music, and real-time video, are pushing the customers' expectations about reliable and predictable LAN and WAN performance. These multimedia applications have moved beyond amusement to becoming critical components of many businesses' communications, training, public relations, vendor relations, and personal productivity business plans. I have a client that has a Web camera mounted on the monitor of every employee in several departments and has outfitted each of its vendors with a similar setup. The company's estimates in savings of time and money are staggering. In areas of the country where a 15-minute meeting with a vendor can be a three-hour process involving transportation, construction delays, parking, security passes, and so on, these systems can greatly increase worker productivity.

Companies motivated by promised increases in productivity are moving ahead with implementation plans, often without fully considering the impact on existing LAN and WAN infrastructures. Concepts such as QoS and the technologies that support them are going to become increasingly important as IT departments are called on to deliver increasing forms of multimedia traffic to the desktop without killing the business-critical data traffic. Network designers are going to need far greater training, exposure to emerging technologies, and increased flexibility in dealing with these multimedia networks.

User Perceptions of LAN/WAN Technologies

At one time, the WAN connections between sites were accepted as slow and costly. Businesses often performed timed updates between local and central computers at specific times during the day or night. It was accepted that you couldn't get data more recent than the last update. Even early client/server applications were text-based technologies that allowed for local updating and retrieval of data. There tended to be a limited number of terminals, which generally were used only for that centralized task.

Since the early 1980s, the PC has become a staple in the office. More recent PC designs encourage it to be taken home and into the field, and, in the case of the smallest units, it has even become a part of the "uniform" of the day for many. While the mobility of laptops and palm-sized devices adds new pressures on the corporate network, the PC itself has changed the world's perception of what data is and how it should be viewed. No more text and numbers on bland plain screens; the data must be able to be formatted, in color, accompanied by music and images of the company's product line, or the latest sports celebrity.

As the standards for what the data should look like have escalated, so have the expectations for how quickly that data should be gathered and from how many sources. I can remember in the mid-1980s, when an MBA who knew Lotus 1-2-3 could write their own ticket. They would be given exciting tasks, such as summarizing worldwide production for a specific product, and could then spend a week or more pouring over printouts, making calls, and maybe flying to sites to gather the necessary data. Today, that same person had better have an Excel VBA script that will pull the data through a

LAN connection from the company's seven worldwide data centers and display it in both tabular and graph form on a PowerPoint slide before the next agenda item, or someone else will be doing it next week.

The PC and the software that runs on it combine to create the perfect technology-age product. Together, they simultaneously increase the expectations of the users and provide the solution for a relatively low cost. At least it was a relatively low total cost when the devices were all stand-alone devices, or even when the data could be pulled from the local network. Now it is common to want to incorporate data from remote branches and possibly distribute printing to each site. Now we have to get a service provider involved.

Today's users, and to a great extent management, do not see a distinction between LANs and WANs. It is just the network to them. The fact that a forecast is being statistically validated in Germany as the raw data streams out of Singapore is irrelevant to them. They just want the information that they requested. There seems to be a general lack of awareness of the complexity and cost of WAN connections among users. Probably the fact that most of us have never had to secure WAN services, such as Frame Relay, may account for the ignorance of the cost. The proliferation of services such as DSL and cable Internet connections with high-bandwidth connections for relatively small monthly fees may further reduce perceptions about the cost of WAN services.

User Perceptions of LAN/WAN Costs

As I have been writing this book, this issue has been on my mind, so I've made a conscious effort to talk to the people I come in contact with in business, at schools, and in government. In each case, I asked the person that I was dealing with what kind(s) of WAN data connection their organization used and approximately what it cost per month. Not one could give me any real estimate about the monthly cost, and by far most had no idea whether they used T1/T3 lines, Frame Relay, modems, and so forth. I am discounting estimates such as "a ton of money" and "it would scare you" to be euphemisms for "I don't know."

To be clear, I did not search out the person in the organization who would know about these issues. Obviously, each organization has staff that manages and monitors these issues. I just asked everyday users, albeit what used to be called "power users." Several of my informal sample group include top management or business owners. The point is that, collectively, they don't know what technologies their organizations have and they have even less idea what it costs. In one case, two network administrators knew they had a T3 line to San Francisco. One thought it cost $10,000 per month while the other was sure it cost $40,000 per month. Either way, the number was totally irrelevant to both of them in the performance of their jobs.

The combination of the increased user expectations and the addition of so many new technologies sharing the company data networks is putting greater pressure on LAN and WAN administrators. Networks are being required to cost less, while supporting the increasing number of new technologies, software applications, and users with increased performance.

WAN Design Issues

Designing a WAN and calculating the traffic requirements can be a complex job. In this section, we look at things that need to be understood when planning a WAN implementation. The concepts and steps described here can lead to improved WAN performance with control over costs. Most WAN networking projects can be boiled down to two issues:

- **Resource availability** The network's function is to connect the users with the resources they need to do their jobs. That resource could be a company database or it could be a voice and data connection over a single cable. If the user cannot get to the resource they need to do their job, the network is not doing its job.

- **Managing costs**   It is a given that technology costs money and that many services and devices cost large sums. It is the responsibility of the designer to meet the requirement for providing resources while providing cost-effective use of existing and future network resources. Quite often this involves working well ahead of a project's acceptance to predict the impact on existing resources and the need for any capital expenditures.

The need to access resources drives a project. Whether the project is cost effective has to be weighed after considering the company's attitudes about requirements for reliability and availability, responsiveness, efficiency, adaptability, and accessibility. The lowest-cost solution may fail the reliability and availability test and therefore be unacceptable.

WAN Design Requirements

Due to the ongoing monthly expenditures to service providers, a successful WAN design should meet each of the following requirements:

- Provide reliable service
- Minimize the cost of bandwidth
- Use the available bandwidth efficiently

Provide Reliable Service

Reliability of service requirements will vary from organization to organization. The way the network is used within the company and the "cost" to the company of network downtime will drive their reliability requirements. WAN reliability is the result of redundancy of links. The topology of the WAN portion of the network will determine the reliability. Figure 22-1 shows a simple star topology that, while efficient, provides no redundancy at all. Every location is served by a single link, so a failure of any link means that one location is no longer connected. In some business models, this might be an inconvenient but nonfatal weakness, but for others, it could be a disaster. A far bigger problem with the star topology is that there is a single failure point that could disrupt the entire network.

On the other extreme, full-mesh WAN topologies are very reliable but become very expensive as the number of locations increases because of the number of links that must be maintained. Two locations require two links, possibly a Frame Relay link and an ISDN backup connection. But as the number of locations grows, the number of links goes up dramatically. The formula is $n*(n-1)/2$, where n is the number of locations. In our example shown in Figure 22-2, that means we have 5*4/2, or 10, links. It also means that we need secure routers that can support that many interfaces. Very few organizations use fully meshed circuits anymore. Frame Relay and ATM PVCs generally provide redundancy in the service provider cloud.

In many cases, some form of partial mesh, where each location has at least two connections, provides an adequate level of redundancy and therefore reliability. Figure 22-3 shows our example WAN with a partial-mesh topology. Additional links can then be weighed based on a reliability versus costs analysis.

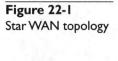

Figure 22-1
Star WAN topology

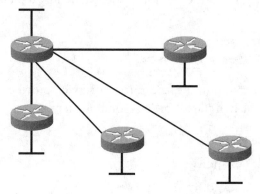

Figure 22-2
Full-mesh WAN
topology

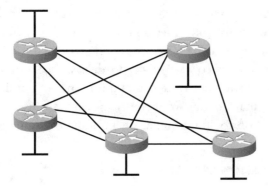

Figure 22-3
Partial-mesh WAN
topology

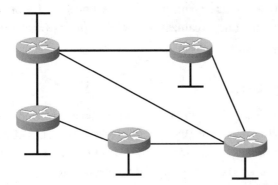

Minimize the Cost of Bandwidth

Minimizing bandwidth cost is going to occur if the correct WAN technology is implemented. Determining which is the best is a matter of determining the volume and pattern of expected traffic, the requirements for availability, and the services available in the market. Just because ISDN may be cheaper than Frame Relay or fractional T1 service doesn't make it the best choice if it cannot deliver the required bandwidth. Long-term consistent usage levels would recommend leased lines or Frame Relay, whereas fluctuating low-volume usage might indicate that ISDN would be a better alternative.

Use the Available Bandwidth Efficiently

Multiplexing services over the same bandwidth can improve the efficiency of bandwidth usage. Video conferencing or voice-over-IP running on the data networks could coexist with the data. The bursty nature of data transmissions and the improvements in compression technology for both video and voice make this an attractive combination, particularly if you are able to save long-distance charges on the voice communications.

Because of voice and video's sensitivity to delays, QoS technologies need to be implemented to make sure that voice communications are not delayed. While a two-second delay in an e-mail arriving would be unknown to the user, a similar delay or gap in a phone conversation could mean that key information is missed.

Customer Requirements

To design a network that meets the customer's requirements, it is important to accurately understand its environment. This means knowing its business requirements, technical requirements, and organizational requirements (any limitations the organization might place on any project).

Business Requirements

This requirement looks only at the organization's business model to determine a solution, without great concern for the technological specifics of the implementation. A solution may be a technological marvel, but if it provides no business advantage over the current system, then it could be argued the expenditures are wasted. The questions to be answered here are the following:

- Does the design benefit the company's business model?
- Does the design benefit or hinder their way of doing business?
- Does the design provide a competitive advantage, and if so, which costs are reduced and by how much?
- Is the business monitored, or audited, by others, and if so, has that been planned in?
- Does the design scale consistently with the organization's expected growth? This should be both a short- and long-term determination and should at least consider exceptional growth or decline.

Technical Requirements

Technical requirements include understanding the current technologies in use, the willingness to change, and the expected or current technologies that might be better. If a company is heavily invested in T1 lines and has long-term agreements in place, it may be less likely to consider a complete changeover, but might consider alternatives for new links. The technical requirements fall into four categories:

- Performance requirements
- Application requirements
- Network management requirements
- Security requirements

The following questions will enable you to determine each of the four requirements for the organization. The results can then be weighted and used in developing the ultimate WAN design.

Performance Requirements

Are there any current network latency issues that need to be documented? Are current response times acceptable? How will the planned changes impact these issues? What are the requirements for WAN connection reliability? What will be the results of dropped links?

Application Requirements

Which centralized applications are currently used on the network? Who needs access to these applications and where are those users located? What new applications are being implemented with the new design or in the near future?

When the applications have been identified, determine the traffic patterns expected for each and the bandwidth requirements. In determining the traffic patterns, try to identify peak WAN loads per day, per week, per month, and so forth. A high-bandwidth application that runs during the night won't have the same impact as one that runs during normal business hours.

Network Management Requirements

What network management systems are currently in place? How is the organization utilizing these systems? Will there be additional requirements when the project is done? Does the organization currently have the base-level skills? Will training or hiring be required?

Security Requirements

How is network security currently handled? Will there be additional exposure as a result of the new design? How will the additional security and related training be handled?

Organizational Requirements

The organizational requirements determine the organizational constraints, which can be identified through questions like these:

- Who has bought into this project? Is it supported high enough in the organization to make sure that resources and attention will be committed?

- Is there an existing budget, and if so, is it reasonable for what needs to be done?

- Who must approve of changes or budget increases?

- Is there an existing timeline for the project? Is the timeline reasonable? Is it dependent on business cycles, and if so, what are the implications of schedules sliding?

- Will existing equipment be replaced or reused somewhere in the new design?

The first step in the WAN design process is to understand the business, technical, and organizational requirements for the project. The final WAN design must "fit" within the various requirements and be acceptable to the organization.

Gathering Information

In designing a WAN, it is necessary to gather information about the business structure, processes, and current technology. It is also necessary to gather information about the industry and where this organization fits into the industry. A "cutting edge" company may have very different requirements than a "market following" organization.

It is important to determine which employees and consultants (if any) will be working with you to design the network. What are their backgrounds? Where do they fit within the organization?

Much of business, technology, and organizational data can be gathered through interviews, focus groups, and surveys. While it is important to get management's view of the current situation and the expectations of the new system, it is equally as important to get the views of the end users. Quite often, users and management have two very different views of how things are done and how they need to be done.

When gathering user information, document their perceptions of the current system's response time, reliability, and throughput. Try to determine volume and load patterns for WAN-dependent activities. If some aspect of an activity seems unusual, try to determine why it is currently done that way. Have they tried alternatives?

Every organization will tell you that reliability is important, but perceptions of reliability vary from organization to organization. Organizations providing financial services, securities sales, and emergency services require a high level of reliability.

Determining the impact of downtime is critical in justifying levels of redundancy that are higher than other organizations might require. Whereas the impact of downtime might be measurable in dollars for some organizations, for a 911 system, for example, the impact could mean loss of contact with police or fire resources.

Analyzing Information

After gathering the information outlined in the previous section, it is necessary to analyze the results to diagram company data flows, identify shared resources both in and out of the organization, identify which users access those resources, and identify current and planned WAN connections.

If possible, current network performance should be measured and documented. These performance indicators should try to identify or predict the average and peak requirements over time. There are many software tools available that can identify traffic patterns and volumes of different types of data. Some can be used to take current patterns and volumes and extrapolate the impact of various levels of increases.

Hierarchical Network Model

The three-layer hierarchical model introduced in Chapter 10 has many implications for WAN design and implementations. The hierarchical model includes the following layers:

- Core layer
- Distribution layer
- Access layer

If properly implemented, this model allows for orderly address assignment, efficient transmission of data, increased scalability, and more structured device selection and configuration. It simplifies device management and configuration because devices in the same layer perform the same tasks. To understand the model, one must recognize that each layer represents a point in the network where a Layer 3 boundary occurs. This is where a router, Layer 3 switch, or other device separates the network into broadcast domains. An example of the three-layer model is shown in Figure 22-4.

The hierarchical design allows for modularity in network design, which allows for easier replication as the network grows. This same modularity can make it easier to implement phased software and hardware upgrades. The Layer 3 boundaries create transition points in the network and help to contain and identify failure points.

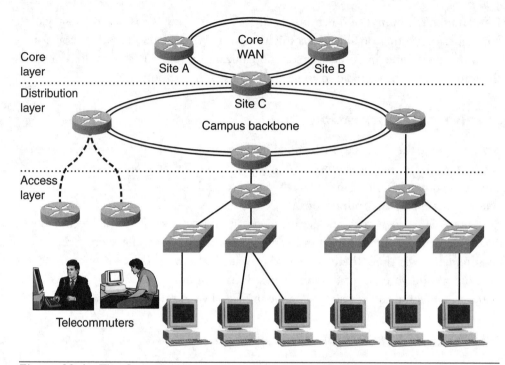

Figure 22-4   The Cisco three-layer hierarchical model

The Core Layer

The core layer represents the site-to-site WAN connections in a corporate or enterprise network. As such, it represents critical links that, if lost, would mean entire sites would be cut off from the rest of the organization. Therefore, at this layer, reliability and performance are most important. Although redundant links would be appropriate at this layer, filtering (ACLs) should be done at lower levels so that the core layer can concentrate exclusively on fast delivery. Load sharing and rapid convergence of routing protocols are also important design considerations. Efficient use of bandwidth in the core is always a concern.

Core WAN links are typically point-to-point and include services such as T1/T3 or Frame Relay that are leased from a service provider.

Good network design practice would not put end stations (such as servers) directly on the core backbone.

The Distribution Layer

The distribution layer connects network segments, possibly representing departments or buildings, with core layer services. Filtering with access lists is used to control traffic and implement QoS and CoS prioritization within the network. The distribution layer provides core network services to multiple LANs within the organization, typically using Fast Ethernet.

In larger networks, such as campus networks, this layer often includes the following:

- Address or area aggregation

- Departmental/building access

- Broadcast/multicast domain definition

- Virtual LAN (VLAN) routing

- Media transitions (such as fiber to copper)

- Internet and remote user access to the network

- Security for outside access (Internet/remote users)

Improved performance of layer 2 and layer 3 switches, as well as developing VLAN technologies, is pushing switches up into the distribution layer.

The distribution layer would include the campus backbone with all of its connecting routers and Layer 3 devices. The distribution layer can be summarized as the layer that provides policy-based connectivity, meaning that the routers are configured to allow only designated traffic on the campus backbone.

Good network design practice would not put end stations (such as servers) directly on the backbone. This allows the backbone to act as a high-speed path for traffic between workgroups or campus-wide servers.

The Access Layer

The workgroups and end users connect to the network in the access layer. The access layer is typically one or more LANs (Ethernet or Token Ring) providing users with access to network services. Filtering could be through the use of access lists or MAC layer filtering with bridges and switches. In smaller, noncampus networks, remote sites or users and the Internet may connect at this layer, and then require the increased security of technologies such as user authentication and firewalls. The access layer is where almost all hosts are attached to the network, including servers of all kinds and user workstations.

In noncampus environments, the access layer can provide remote access to the corporate network via wide-area technology, such as Frame Relay, ISDN, or leased lines.

Routers Within the Hierarchy

Following the model provides a topology with three distinct layers and distinct functionality for the routers in each layer. Layer 3 switching devices are becoming a consideration throughout the model. The functions of the Layer 3 devices in the hierarchical model include the following:

- Core layer routers are responsible for site-to-site connectivity and must therefore be optimized for availability and reliability. Loss of service at this layer can be catastrophic. Maintaining connectivity of LAN and WAN circuits at this layer is critical.

- Distribution layer routers must implement QoS requirements through policy-based traffic control. Preserving bandwidth and maintaining network security need to be considerations at this level.

- Access layer routers keep workgroup or departmental traffic from getting into upper layers. Routers at this level often need to manage access of dial-up users.

Redundant Links

Each layer in the three-layer model should link only to the layer above or below it. Any links between devices in the same layer will compromise the hierarchical design and may make future expansion more difficult. An example of redundant links between layers is shown in Figure 22-5.

Server Placement

Server placement can have significant impacts on network traffic patterns and accessibility for users. Enterprise servers are those with resources that need to be accessible

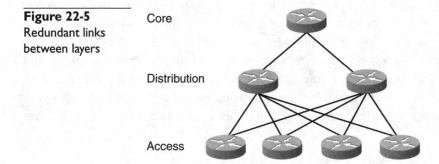

Figure 22-5
Redundant links
between layers

Core

Distribution

Access

throughout the network, such as login authentication, e-mail, and order entry/tracking systems.

Placing an enterprise server in the access layer of a network forces departmental or workgroup devices and links to support heavier traffic requirements than otherwise. If nothing else, it could lead to inefficient purchasing and installation of resources to support traffic that should be in the distribution layer. In Figure 22-6, if server A is an enterprise server, then all departments and even remote users must use the links from X to Y and from Y to Z. The problem becomes even more serious if the connection between X and Y is a slower WAN link. Most server requests to A would have to traverse the link between X and Y twice, thereby compounding the mistake.

By moving the enterprise server to position B, those two links and the extra router (Y) and switch (Z) are relieved of the extra traffic.

On the other end of the spectrum are those servers that are typically only accessed by users from a single workgroup or department. The network will still allow others to access workgroup or departmental servers, but if 80 percent or more of the expected traffic is from an identifiable group in the access layer, it only makes sense to connect

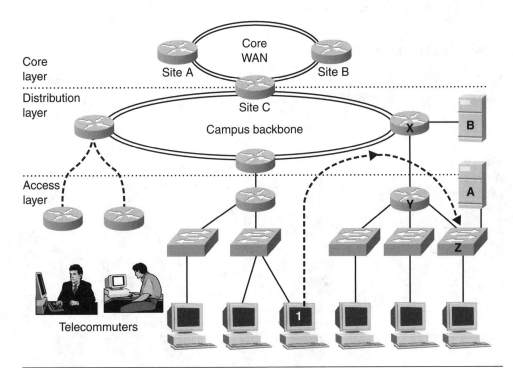

Figure 22-6 Three-layer network with server placement

that server as close to the users as possible. Server A's placement would be particularly suitable for a workgroup attached to switch Z, or departmental users attached to Y.

Smaller Networks and the Hierarchical Model

The three-layer model represents an enterprise-type network very well. However, not all environments require a full three-layer hierarchy. Many smaller networks use a one- or two-layer model until they grow or are assimilated by another organization. For this reason, the model should be considered in plans for even new startups, to avoid the inefficiency and disruptions that could occur during periods of rapid network growth or when the network is being assimilated into another, larger system. An example of the single-layer model is shown in Figure 22-7.

A one-layer design can be implemented if there are only a few remote locations and access to any server services is done mainly via the local LAN server. Each site is a separate broadcast domain. While primary connectivity is via a Frame Relay connection, a backup ISDN link has been established in case the primary link fails.

Figure 22-8 shows an example of a two-layer network design. In the two-layer design, multiple LANs in the building connect to the site router C, which has WAN connections to the company's other two locations.

WAN Options

In choosing the appropriate WAN technology, many factors need to be considered, and no one solution is right for all cases. While a company might use leased lines

Figure 22-7
A single-layer
network model

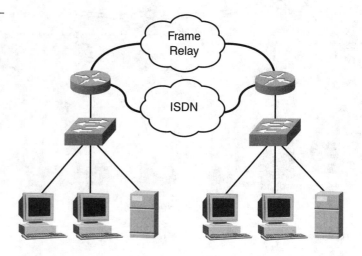

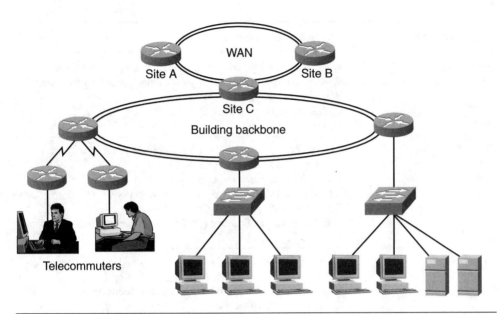

Figure 22-8   A two-layer network model

(T1/T3) to connect business locations, that probably wouldn't be an appropriate technology for telecommuters. A more cost-effective solution could be dial-up service like
ISDN or even analog modem service, depending on the frequency of the connection,
the length of each connection, and the volume of data transmitted. In some cases, a
Frame Relay connection might be appropriate for the telecommuter with frequent
connections and long duration transmissions. Today, of course, we would also want to
look at cable and DSL as alternatives for the telecommuter in those markets where service is available.

The following table compares the WAN technologies covered in this course and on
the CCNA exam:

WAN TECHNOLOGY	USE AND CONSIDERATIONS
Leased line	Common for business connections, including Internet connections Fractional T1 (up to T1), T1 (1.544 Mbps), and T3 (44.736 Mbps) Long-term solution with expected high-traffic volumes Rates tend to be fixed whether capacity is used or not Dedicated (nonshared) link

WAN TECHNOLOGY	USE AND CONSIDERATIONS
Frame Relay	Alternative to leased line with comparable bandwidth options Charges can reflect usage charges, including bandwidth fluctuation Both private and service provider networks Circuit maintenance is provider's responsibility Packet-switched link
ISDN (BRI)	64 Kbps or 128 Kbps bandwidth (can use 64 K voice/64 K data) Good for small branch or telecommuters Supports voice, video, and data Ideal for less frequent, lower volume connections Good low-cost backup to other services Use dial-on-demand routing (DDR) to limit time to important data Circuit-switched link
Analog modem	Lowest-cost option for very low frequency and volume connection Connections up to 56 Kbps (typically 28–45 Kbps) Can be used as a backup for other types of connections Circuit-switched link (nondigital solution)
X.25	Packet-switched with Layer 3 functions and reliability Not used much in North America Up to 128 Kbps connections
ATM (not on CCNA exam)	Supports very high bandwidth requirements Supports voice, video, and data Connects to T3 and SONET links (45–622 Mbps) Supports QoS and ToS for applications with varying requirements Charges based on dedicated line connection (T3 to SONET) Cell-switched link

Two-Location Considerations

If the WAN includes two locations, offering a level of reliability requires a 100 percent redundancy in circuits. After analyzing the company's bandwidth requirements for normal operation, a second calculation of "worst case" bandwidth requirements will indicate whether the second link could be a dial-on-demand technology such as ISDN or even analog modem. Figure 22-9 shows an example of using ISDN to back up a leased-line or Frame Relay primary connection.

ISDN could be the primary link and an analog modem could be used as the backup link in a very small branch office, or telecommuter situation. In a larger situation, the primary link might be a T3, with a T1 as the backup when higher minimum bandwidth is required.

Figure 22-9
Using ISDN to back
up a leased-line or
Frame Relay
connection

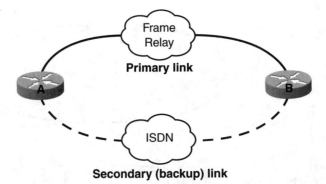

Another possibility that should be considered based on the requirement for flexible bandwidth is to use two T1, T3, or Frame Relay links and then use load balancing. If one circuit fails, the other carries the load. In this scenario, it is important to make sure that both circuits are not in the same trench (or cable bundle). In that case, you have additional bandwidth but somewhat limited redundancy, because a single backhoe operator can bring down both circuits.

Multilocation Considerations

If the WAN includes more than two locations, establishing a level of reliability requires weighing the need for connectivity versus the cost of maintaining additional circuits. Even full mesh would be less than the 100 percent redundancy required for two locations. Figure 22-10 shows an example of connecting three locations using combinations of leased-line or Frame Relay connections.

Each of the three connections could be an ISDN, T1, T3, or Frame Relay link. With two connections per location, it would take two link failures to strand a site.

Figure 22-11 shows a possible WAN using ATM devices connected to one or more SONET rings providing very high site-to-site bandwidths. OC3 (155.54 Mbps) to OC12 (622 Mbps) would be possible if the links exist in each area. Particularly in MANs involving certain regions of North America, this could be accomplished. Not only could voice, video, and data be supported, but so could broadcast-quality television.

In the example in Figure 22-11, additional links (cross ring) could be established for higher levels of redundancy.

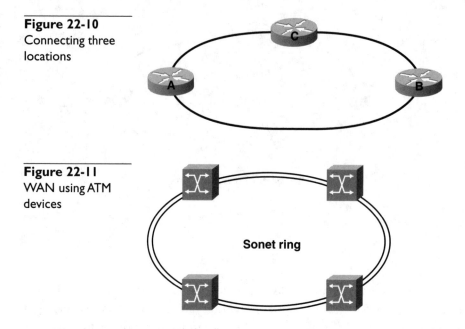

Figure 22-10
Connecting three
locations

Figure 22-11
WAN using ATM
devices

Sonet ring

Selecting the Router

Another consideration is determining the appropriate router to use with the new WAN connection. Interface and IOS feature set options are important in selecting a device. While beyond the scope of the CCNA exam and this book, it is also important to recognize that different models of devices have different CPUs and switching technologies for moving packets through the router. If we look only at the "fast switching" performance figures for a few devices, you will see what I mean. The 2500 series can process 6,000 packets per second (pps), while the 2600 series varies from 15,000 to 37,000 pps. The soon to be retired 4700 model can process 50,000 pps. If this is going to be a high-volume connection, you do not want to underpower the Layer 3 device.

A Cisco dealer or the Cisco Web site, **www.cisco.com**, could be used to compare the feature and performance options available.

Summary

In this chapter, we reviewed the five key requirements for scalability of any network design project: reliability and availability; responsiveness; efficiency; adaptability; and accessibility with security.

WAN design includes gathering and analyzing various requirements, such as business, technical, and organizational requirements. Technical requirements include performance, application, network management, and security requirements. A WAN design should meet three requirements: provide reliable service, minimize the cost of bandwidth, and use the available bandwidth efficiently.

The three-layered hierarchical model provides scalability for WAN implementations by using each layer to perform a particular function. The three layers are the core, distribution, and access layers.

A variety of factors, such as bandwidth requirements, frequency, and duration of communications sessions, contribute to determining the appropriate WAN technology for both the primary and secondary links between locations. These technologies include leased lines, Frame Relay, ISDN, and analog modem connections.

Practice Questions

Take a few moments and check your grasp of the concepts covered in this chapter. The answers are immediately following the questions.

Questions

1. Which of the following is not a requirement of a WAN design?
    a. Reliability of service
    b. Minimize the cost of bandwidth
    c. Lowest possible cost
    d. Efficient use of the available bandwidth

2. While each of the three layers of the hierarchical model can have WAN connections, in which one is it most important to have unrestricted, unfiltered WAN service?
    a. Core
    b. Distribution
    c. Access

3. True or False: The more redundant links within a network layer the better.
    a. True
    b. False

4. Which layer of the hierarchical model is most likely to have users in it?
   a. Core
   b. Distribution
   c. Access

5. Which two of the following need to be considered when designing a WAN implementation?
   a. Microsoft Word
   b. Distributed applications
   c. Internet access
   d. Printing

6. Of the following choices for WAN connection, which will most likely provide the greatest bandwidth options?
   a. Analog modem
   b. X.25
   c. ISDN BRI
   d. Frame Relay

7. If the WAN requirements called for dial-on-demand routing (DDR) as a backup link, which two technologies could be considered for the backup links?
   a. Analog modem
   b. X.25
   c. ISDN BRI
   d. Frame Relay

8. Using the three-layer hierarchical model, in which layer would departmental servers normally be placed?
   a. Core
   b. Distribution
   c. Access

9. True or False: Layer 3 devices are not necessary in the hierarchical model except in the core layer.
   a. True
   b. False

10. Which one of the following is generally referred to as a leased or dedicated line?

   a. Analog modem

   b. x.25

   c. ISDN BRI

   d. Frame Relay

   e. T1 line

Answers

1. **a**, **b**, and **d**. A WAN design should meet three requirements: provide reliable service, minimize the cost of bandwidth, and use the available bandwidth efficiently.

2. **a.** The core layer connecting sites should have unfettered traffic as much as possible. Any filtering should be done at lower layers.

3. **b.** False. Any links between devices in the same layer will compromise the hierarchical design and may make future expansion more difficult.

4. **c.** The access layer is where users and workgroups access network services.

5. **b** and **c.** Distributed applications and Internet access need to be considered when designing a WAN implementation. Microsoft Word is typically a local application, and printing is typically a local service.

6. **d.** Frame Relay supports up to T1 bandwidth (T3 in some areas). Analog modem supports up to 53 Kbps, x.25 supports up to 128 Kbps, and ISDN BRI supports up to 128 Kbps.

7. **a** and **c.** Both analog modems and ISDN can be used with DDR.

8. **c.** Placing departmental servers in the access layer keeps heavy departmental traffic out of the higher layers.

9. **b.** False. Pretty much by definition, each layer represents a point in the network where a Layer 3 boundary occurs.

10. **e.** Both T1 and T3 lines are considered leased (or dedicated) lines.

Router Configurations

Chapter 13

Figure A-1
Chapter 13 Basic IP
Lab Configuration

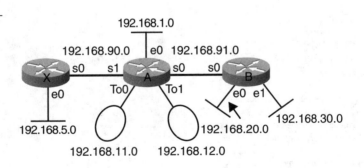

Lab A: Basic Configuration

```
Lab-A#sho run
Building configuration...

Current configuration:
!
version 12.0
service timestamps debug uptime
service timestamps log uptime
no service password-encryption
!
hostname Lab-A
!
enable secret 5 $1$9slc$ElvLM8zTnaoRqPbxk1uad/
!
!
ip subnet-zero
no ip domain-lookup
ip host Lab-B 192.168.91.1 192.168.92.2 192.168.20.1 192.168.30.1
ip host Lab-A 192.168.90.1 192.168.91.2 192.168.11.1 192.168.12.1
192.168.1.100
ip host Lab-X 192.168.90.2 192.168.5.1
!
cns event-service server
!
process-max-time 200
!
interface Ethernet0
 ip address 192.168.1.100 255.255.255.0
 no ip directed-broadcast
 media-type 10BaseT
!
interface Serial0
 ip address 192.168.91.2 255.255.255.0
 no ip directed-broadcast
 no ip mroute-cache
 no fair-queue
 clockrate 56000
!
interface Serial1
 ip address 192.168.90.1 255.255.255.0
 no ip directed-broadcast
!
interface TokenRing0
 ip address 192.168.11.1 255.255.255.0
 no ip directed-broadcast
 ring-speed 4
!
interface TokenRing1
 ip address 192.168.12.1 255.255.255.0
 no ip directed-broadcast
 ring-speed 4
!
```

```
router rip
 network 192.168.1.0
 network 192.168.11.0
 network 192.168.12.0
 network 192.168.90.0
 network 192.168.91.0
 !
ip classless
ip http server
!
line con 0
 password cisco
 logging synchronous
 login
 transport input none
line aux 0
 password cisco
 login
line vty 0 4
 password cisco
 login
!
end

Lab-A#
```

Lab B: Basic Configuration

```
Lab-B#show run
Building configuration...

Current configuration:
!
version 12.0
service timestamps debug uptime
service timestamps log uptime
no service password-encryption
!
hostname Lab-B
!
enable secret 5 $1$FqmS$lReFkab49nT.gBSSc2.z3.
!
!
ip subnet-zero
no ip domain-lookup
ip host Lab-B 192.168.91.1 192.168.92.2 192.168.20.1 192.168.30.1
ip host Lab-A 192.168.90.1 192.168.91.2 192.168.11.1 192.168.12.1
192.168.1.100
ip host Lab-X 192.168.90.2 192.168.5.1
!
process-max-time 200
!
interface Loopback1
```

```
   ip address 192.168.30.1 255.255.255.0
   no ip directed-broadcast
 !
 interface Ethernet0
   ip address 192.168.20.1 255.255.255.0
   no ip directed-broadcast
 !
 interface Serial0
   ip address 192.168.91.1 255.255.255.0
   no ip directed-broadcast
   no ip mroute-cache
   no fair-queue
 !
 interface Serial1
   ip address 192.168.92.2 255.255.255.0
   no ip directed-broadcast
 !
 router rip
   network 192.168.20.0
   network 192.168.30.0
   network 192.168.91.0
   network 192.168.92.0
 !
 ip classless
 ip http server
 !
 line con 0
   password cisco
   logging synchronous
   login
   transport input none
 line aux 0
   password cisco
   login
 line vty 0 4
   password cisco
   login
 !
 end

 Lab-B#
```

Lab X: Basic Configuration

```
 lab-X#show run
 Building configuration...

 Current configuration : 972 bytes
 !
 version 12.1
 no service single-slot-reload-enable
 service timestamps debug uptime
 service timestamps log uptime
```

```
no service password-encryption
!
hostname Lab-X
!
enable secret 5 $1$xdaP$oLUxyR/0MHUyw4LVZh/AY.
!
ip subnet-zero
no ip finger
no ip domain-lookup
ip host Lab-B 192.168.91.1 192.168.92.2 192.168.20.1 192.168.30.1
ip host Lab-A 192.168.90.1 192.168.91.2 192.168.11.1 192.168.12.1
192.168.1.100
ip host Lab-X 192.168.90.2 192.168.5.1
!
!
interface Ethernet0
 ip address 192.168.5.1 255.255.255.0
!
interface Serial0
 ip address 192.168.90.2 255.255.255.0
 no fair-queue
 clockrate 56000
!
interface Serial1
 ip address 192.168.96.2 255.255.255.0
!
router rip
 network 192.168.5.0
 network 192.168.90.0
 network 192.168.96.0
!
ip classless
ip http server
!
line con 0
 password cisco
 logging synchronous
 login
 transport input none
line aux 0
 password cisco
 login
line vty 0 4
 password cisco
 login
!
end

lab-X#
```

Chapter 14

Figure A-2
Chapter 14 Basic
IPX Lab
Configuration

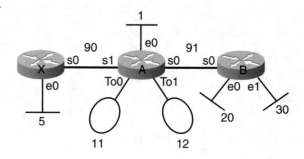

Lab A: Basic IPX Configuration

```
Lab-A#show run
Building configuration...

Current configuration:
!
version 12.0
service timestamps debug uptime
service timestamps log uptime
no service password-encryption
!
hostname Lab-A
!
enable secret 5 $1$XYjo$Uoo/ZPVg7RpPMUqyBfW1i1
!
!
ip subnet-zero
!
ipx routing aaaa.aaaa.aaaa
ipx maximum-paths 2
cns event-service server
!
process-max-time 200
!
interface Ethernet0
 no ip address
 no ip directed-broadcast
 media-type 10BaseT
 ipx network 1
!
interface Serial0
 no ip address
 no ip directed-broadcast
 no ip mroute-cache
 ipx network 91
 clockrate 56000
```

```
!
interface Serial1
 no ip address
 no ip directed-broadcast
 ipx network 90
!
interface TokenRing0
 no ip address
 no ip directed-broadcast
 ipx network 11
 ring-speed 4
!
interface TokenRing1
 no ip address
 no ip directed-broadcast
 ipx network 12
 ring-speed 4
!
ip classless
no ip http server
!
line con 0
 password cisco
 logging synchronous
 login
 transport input none
line aux 0
 password cisco
 login
line vty 0 4
 password cisco
 login
!
end

Lab-A#
```

Lab B: Basic IPX Configuration

```
Lab-B#show run
Building configuration...

Current configuration:
!
version 12.0
service timestamps debug uptime
service timestamps log uptime
no service password-encryption
!
hostname Lab-B
!
enable secret 5 $1$2.Uy$/KhpYAbQfi9ulzJ/FRbj10
!
```

```
!
ip subnet-zero
!
ipx routing bbbb.bbbb.bbbb
ipx maximum-paths 2
!
process-max-time 200
!
interface Loopback1
 no ip address
 no ip directed-broadcast
 ipx network 30
!
interface Ethernet0
 no ip address
 no ip directed-broadcast
 ipx network 20
!
interface Serial0
 no ip address
 no ip directed-broadcast
 no ip mroute-cache
 ipx network 91
 no fair-queue
!
interface Serial1
 no ip address
 no ip directed-broadcast
 ipx network 92
!
ip classless
no ip http server
!
line con 0
 password cisco
 logging synchronous
 login
 transport input none
line aux 0
 password cisco
 login
line vty 0 4
 password cisco
 login
!
end

Lab-B#
```

Lab X: Basic IPX Configuration

```
Lab-X#show run
Building configuration...
```

```
Current configuration : 721 bytes
!
version 12.1
no service single-slot-reload-enable
service timestamps debug uptime
service timestamps log uptime
no service password-encryption
!
hostname Lab-X
!
logging rate-limit console 10 except errors
enable secret 5 $1$M5yp$r1wUExZednUKstEbsdDgl.
!
ip subnet-zero
no ip finger
!
ipx routing 0010.7b3a.3dd5
ipx maximum-paths 2
!
interface Ethernet0
 no ip address
 ipx network 5
!
interface Serial0
 no ip address
 ipx network 90
 no fair-queue
 clockrate 56000
!
interface Serial1
 no ip address
 ipx network 96
!
ip classless
no ip http server
!
line con 0
 password cisco
 logging synchronous
 login
 transport input none
line aux 0
 password cisco
 login
line vty 0 4
 password cisco
 login
!
end

Lab-X#
```

Chapter 16

Cisco 2924-M Switch: Basic Configuration

```
Switch#show run
Building configuration...

Current configuration:
!
version 12.0
no service pad
service timestamps debug uptime
service timestamps log uptime
no service password-encryption
!
hostname Switch
!
ip subnet-zero
!
interface FastEthernet0/1
!
interface FastEthernet0/2
!
interface FastEthernet0/3
!
interface FastEthernet0/4
!
interface FastEthernet0/5
!
interface FastEthernet0/6
!
interface FastEthernet0/7
!
interface FastEthernet0/8
!
interface FastEthernet0/9
!
interface FastEthernet0/10
!
interface FastEthernet0/11
!
interface FastEthernet0/12
!
interface FastEthernet0/13
!
interface FastEthernet0/14
!
interface FastEthernet0/15
!
```

```
interface FastEthernet0/16
!
interface FastEthernet0/17
!
interface FastEthernet0/18
!
interface FastEthernet0/19
!
interface FastEthernet0/20
!
interface FastEthernet0/21
!
interface FastEthernet0/22
!
interface FastEthernet0/23
!
interface FastEthernet0/24
!
interface FastEthernet1/1
!
interface FastEthernet1/2
!
interface FastEthernet1/3
!
interface FastEthernet1/4
!
interface FastEthernet2/1
!
interface FastEthernet2/2
!
interface FastEthernet2/3
!
interface FastEthernet2/4
!
interface VLAN1
 no ip directed-broadcast
 no ip route-cache
!
line con 0
 transport input none
 stopbits 1
line vty 0 4
 login
line vty 5 15
 login
!
end

Switch#
```

Chapter 19

Lab A: Basic ISDN Configuration

```
Lab-A#sho run
Building configuration...

Current configuration:
!
version 12.0
service timestamps debug uptime
service timestamps log uptime
no service password-encryption
!
hostname Lab-A
!
enable secret 5 $1$9slc$ElvLM8zTnaoRqPbxk1uad/
!
!
ip subnet-zero
no ip domain-lookup
ip host Lab-B 192.168.91.1 192.168.92.2 192.168.20.1 192.168.30.1
ip host Lab-A 192.168.90.1 192.168.91.2 192.168.11.1 192.168.12.1
192.168.1.100
ip host Lab-X 192.168.90.2 192.168.5.1
!
isdn switch-type basic-ni
username Lab-A password cisco
!
process-max-time 200
!
interface Ethernet0
 ip address 192.168.1.100 255.255.255.0
 no ip directed-broadcast
 media-type 10BaseT
!
interface bri 0
 ip address 192.168.93.1 255.255.255.0
 isdn switch-type basic-ni
 isdn spid1 51055540000001 5554000
 isdn spid2 51055540010001 5554001
 dialer-group 1
 encapsulation ppp
 ppp authentication chap
 dialer idle-timeout 60
 dialer map ip 192.168.93.2 name Lab-X 5551234
!
interface Serial0
 ip address 192.168.91.2 255.255.255.0
 no ip directed-broadcast
 no ip mroute-cache
 no fair-queue
```

```
 clockrate 56000
!
interface Serial1
 ip address 192.168.90.1 255.255.255.0
 no ip directed-broadcast
!
interface TokenRing0
 ip address 192.168.11.1 255.255.255.0
 no ip directed-broadcast
 ring-speed 4
!
interface TokenRing1
 ip address 192.168.12.1 255.255.255.0
 no ip directed-broadcast
 ring-speed 4
!
router rip
 network 192.168.1.0
 network 192.168.11.0
 network 192.168.12.0
 network 192.168.90.0
 network 192.168.91.0
 network 192.168.93.0
!
dialer-list 1 protocol ip permit
ip classless
ip http server
!
line con 0
 password cisco
 logging synchronous
 login
 transport input none
line aux 0
 password cisco
 login
line vty 0 4
 password cisco
 login
!
end

Lab-A#
```

GLOSSARY

A

Access class   A method of restricting Telnet access to and from a router using access lists.

Access group   When an access list is created, it must be associated with a physical interface. Access-group associates the access list to the interface.

Access layer   In the Hierarchical Network Model, the layer where the users connect to the network. It is here that hubs and LAN switches reside. Where workgroups access the network.

Access list   Access Control Lists (ACL). List of comparison statements used by Cisco routers to control access (permit / deny) to or from a router interface for a number of services (for example, to prevent packets with a certain IP address from leaving a particular interface on the router). A two-part process: The access list contains the statements then access-group applies it to an interface and specifies in or out bound traffic.

Access method   The standards that control the way in which network devices access the network medium.

Access router   Any router that exists at the lowest levels of a network hierarchy.

Access server   Communications device that connects asynchronous devices to a LAN or WAN through network and terminal emulation software. Performs both synchronous and asynchronous routing of supported protocols—such as modems, TA (ISDN) and T1 lines. Sometimes called a network access server. See *Communication Server*.

ACK   See *Acknowledgment*.

Acknowledgment   A transport layer response to the successful receipt of one or more data packets that triggers the next scheduled transmission of packets in a connection-oriented protocol network. TCP and IPX both use acknowledgements. It is sometimes referred to as its IEEE signal as ACK.

Active hub   A network device (multiport repeater) that amplifies LAN transmission signals, can increase the overall length of the network and the number of nodes.

Adaptive routing   See *Dynamic Routing*.

Address   A set of numbers, usually expressed in binary format, used to identify and locate a resource or device on a network.

Address mask The address mask for an IP address is used to identify the boundary between the network portion of the address and the host portion. For example ,the IP address 161.150.23.157 and address mask 255.255.0.0 indicates that the first two octets 161.150 are the network and the last to identify the host. Another notation would be 161.150.23.157/16 indicating the mask and therefore the network is the first 16 bits or two octets.

Address resolution The process of determining one address type, such as IP, from another type, such as MAC. The discovery can be done by broadcast packets and the result is stored for future reference. See *ARP, RARP,* and *WINS.*

Address Resolution Protocol (ARP) A method for finding a host's physical address from its IP address. An ARP request is sent to the network, naming the IP address; then the machine with that IP address returns its physical address so it can receive the transmission.

Administrative distance A reliability rating of the method a router used to learn about a route. It is one of the factors used in selecting a best path. The smaller the administrative distance ,the more attractive the method of learning about a route. Directly connected routes have no administrative distance. Cisco routers use administrative distance values between 0 and 255.

Administrator Person responsible for the control and security of the user accounts, resources, and data on a network.

ADSL See *Asymmetric Digital Subscriber Line.*

Advertising Router process in which routing or service updates are sent at specified intervals to other routers on the network so they can update lists of usable routes.

Algorithm A well-defined rule or method for determining a solution to a problem. In networking, algorithms are commonly used to determine the best path for traffic between a source to and destination or to prevent looping within the network.

American National Standards Institute (ANSI) An organization that develops standards for many things, only some having to do with computers, such as programming languages, properties of diskettes, etc. ANSI is the U.S. member of the International Standards Organization (see *International Standards Organization*).

American Standard Code for Information Interchange (ASCII) A code in which each alphanumeric character is represented as a number from 0 to 127, translated into a 7-bit binary code for the computer. ASCII is used by most microcomputers and printers, and because of this, text-only files can be transferred easily between different kinds of computers. ASCII code also includes characters to indicate backspace, carriage return, and other control characters.

Analog transmission Wave-like signal transmissions over wires or through the air in which information is conveyed through varying some combination of signal amplitude, frequency, and phase.

ANDing The binary process of comparing the bits of an IP address with the bits in the subnet mask to determine the boundary between the network portion and the host portion of the address.

ANSI See *American National Standards Institute.*

Anti-virus A type of software that detects and removes virus programs.

Any In access lists, a keyword used to specify the permission or denial of traffic no matter the source, destination, protocol, or port.

AppleTalk A LAN protocol suite developed by Apple Computer for communication between Apple Computer products and other computers. There are implementations of AppleTalk. Phase

1 supports a single physical network that can have only one network number and be in a single zone. Phase 2, the more recent version, supports multiple logical networks on a single physical network and allows networks to be in more than one zone.

Application layer   The layer of the OSI model that provides support for end users and for application programs using network resources.

ARCnet   Token bus LAN (802.4) technology used in the 1970s and 1980s.

ARP   See *Address Resolution Protocol*.

ARPANET   Advanced Research Projects Agency Network. Packet-switching network established in 1969 and developed in the 1970s by BBN—funded by ARPA (and later DARPA). Evolved into the Internet.

AS   See *Autonomous System*.

ASCII   See *American Standard Code for Information Interchange*.

Asymmetric Digital Subscriber Line (ADSL)   A service that transmits digital voice and data over existing (analog) phone lines. It is differentiated from other digital subscriber line technologies in that the transmit speed is often different from the receive speed. Typically, the uplink speed is smaller than the downlink speed.

Asynchronous Transfer Mode (ATM)   International standard used in high-speed transmission media—such as E3, SONET, and T3—for cell relay in which multiple service types (such as voice, video, or data) are conveyed in fixed-length, 53-byte cells.

Asynchronous Transmission Synchronization (ATS)   A process used in serial data transfer in which a start bit and a stop bit are added so the receiving station can know when a particular bit has been transferred. Also known as bit synchronization.

Attachment Unit Interface (AUI)   IEEE 802.3 specification used between an MAU (Multistation Access Unit) and a network interface card.

Attachment Unit Interface (AUI) connector   A 15-pin D-type connector sometimes used with Ethernet connections.

Attenuation   The loss of signal that is experienced as data is transmitted across network media.

Authority zone   The authority zone is associated with DNS, It is a section of the domain-name tree for which one name server is the authority. See also *DNS*.

Autonomous switching   Cisco-specific feature that allows faster packing processing. The CiscoBus handles the packets independently, thus freeing the system processor to handle other tasks.

Autonomous System (AS)   A group of networks under a common administration sharing a common routing strategy. Autonomous systems are subdivided into areas. Each autonomous system must be assigned a unique 16-bit number by the IANA.

Average rate   The average rate, in kilobits per second (Kbps), at which a given virtual circuit will transmit.

B

B channel   In ISDN, a single 64 Kbps link. In BRI implementations, there are two such B channels. In PRI, there are 23.

Backbone   A high-capacity infrastructure system that provides optimal traffic between separated network segments.

Backoff   The retransmission delay introduced by MAC protocols. When a collision occurs between two transmitters, both "backoff" for a random time period thus encouraging the line to be free for transmission, assuming that there is no interference from a third party.

Backplane   The physical connection between boards, whether processor-based, memory-based or I/O-based. It is often a chassis with individual slots to handle each device. The chassis may also provide power to all devices.

Backward Explicit Congestion Notification (BECN)   A Frame Relay network device detecting congestion can set a single address bit in frames traveling in the opposite direction (toward the source of the data). A DTE receiving frames with the BECN bit set to one can forward the info on to higher-level protocols to exercise flow control. Compare with *Forward Explicit Congestion Notification (FECN)*.

Bandwidth   The rated throughput capacity of a given network protocol or medium. Compare with *Throughput*.

Base bandwidth   The difference between the lowest and highest frequencies available for network signals. The term is also used to describe the rated throughput capacity of a given network protocol or medium.

Baseband   A communications strategy that uses a single carrier frequency over a medium. Ethernet is such an example of baseband signaling. Baseband is often called narrowband. Compare with *Broadband*.

Basic Rate Interface (BRI)   An ISDN digital communications line that consists of three independent channels: two Bearer (or B) channels, each at 64 Kbps, and one Data (or D) channel at 16 Kbps. ISDN Basic Rate Interface is often referred to as 2B+D.

Baud rate   Named after a French telegraphy expert named J. M. Baudot, this term is used to define the speed or rate of signal transfer.

Bc   See *Committed Burst*.

Be   See *Excess Burst*.

BECN   See *Backward Explicit Congestion Notification*.

Bellman-Ford algorithm   The process by which distance-vector routing protocols exchange updates on a periodic timer. This process is generally characterized by low memory utilization and slow convergence time. It is also known as routing by rumor. The algorithm itself iterates on the number of hops in route to find a shortest-path spanning tree. It is computationally simpler than a link state routing algorithm, but is prone to problems such as routing loops.

Best-effort delivery   A network system that does not use an acknowledgment system to guarantee reliable delivery of data.

BGP   See *Border Gateway Protocol*.

BGP4   BGP Version 4. Version 4 of the predominant interdomain routing protocol used on the Internet. BGP4 supports CIDR and uses route aggregation mechanisms to reduce the size of routing tables.

Binary   A Base2 numbering system used in digital signaling, characterized by 1's and 0's.

Binding   The process of associating a protocol and a network interface card (NIC).

Bit   An electronic digit used in the binary numbering system.

Bit rate   The speed at which bits and transmitted—usually in bits per second (bps).

Bit-oriented protocol   Class of communications protocols that can transmit frames independent of the frame content. Bit-oriented protocols provide full-duplex operation and are more efficient and reliable than byte-oriented protocols. Bit-oriented protocols live at the data link layer of the OSI model. See also *Byte-Oriented Protocol.*

Blackout   A total loss of electrical power.

BOOTP   A protocol used in resolving an IP address based on a Layer 2 MAC address.

Border Gateway Protocol (BGP)   An interdomain routing protocol (RFC 1163) that replaces EGP. Exchanges reachability status only with other BGP systems.

Bottleneck   Any point in an internetwork where the amount of data being received exceeds the data-carrying capacity of the link. See also *Congestion.*

BPDU   See *Bridge Protocol Data Unit.*

BRI   See *Basic Rate Interface.*

Bridge   A device that connects and passes packets between two network segments that use the same communications protocol. Bridges operate at the data link layer of the OSI Reference Model. A bridge filters, forwards, or floods an incoming frame based on the MAC address of that frame.

Bridge group   In transparent bridging, the designation given to a physical interface (usually Ethernet) to initiate its participation in bridging functions.

Bridge priority   The criterion on which a root bridge is elected. The bridge with the lowest priority becomes the root bridge.

Bridge Protocol Data Unit (BPDU)   A spanning tree protocol update entity used in path determination between bridges.

Bridged Virtual Interface (BVI)   In IRB, an interface used to translate between routed and bridged traffic. This interface has both a protocol address for the protocol to be routed and a MAC address on which to base bridging decisions.

Bridging address table   A list of MAC addresses kept by bridges and used when packets are received to determine which segment the destination address is on before sending the packet to the next interface or dropping the packet if it is on the same segment as the sending node.

Broadband   A communications strategy that uses signaling over multiple communications channels. Cable television and cable modems are such an example of putting multiple signals onto a single wire. Compare with *Baseband.*

Broadcast   A packet delivery system in which a copy of a packet is given to all hosts attached to the network.

Broadcast address   A special address reserved for transmitted messages to all hosts on a network. Compare with *Multicast Address* and *Unicast Address.*

Broadcast domain   The collective group of devices that are the designated recipients of a broadcast. The broadcast domain is usually limited to a single segment bounded by a router. This is because routers do not forward broadcasts. However, bridges do forward broadcasts and therefore the domain usually includes both sides of a bridge.

Broadcast storm   An undesirable condition in which broadcasts have become so numerous as to bog down the flow of data across the network.

Brouter   A device that can be used to combine the benefits of both routers and bridges. Its common usage is to route routable protocols at the Network layer and to bridge nonroutable protocols at the data link layer.

Brownout   A short-term decrease in the voltage level, usually caused by the startup demands of other electrical devices.

Buffer   Storage space allocated to deal with the inconsistent nature of incoming versus outgoing data. If data comes in faster than a device can push it out, then the data must be stored in a buffer.

Bus mastering   A bus accessing method in which the network interface card takes control of the bus in order to send data through the bus directly to the system memory, bypassing the CPU.

Bus topology   A path used by electrical signals to travel between the CPU and the attached hardware.

BVI   See *Bridged Virtual Interface*.

Byte   A set of bits (usually 8) operating as a unit to signify a character.

Byte-oriented protocol   Class of communications protocols that uses a specific character from the user character set to delimit frames. As such, more processing is required and parallel processing is much more difficult. Bit-oriented protocols have pretty much replaced byte-oriented protocols because they are more efficient. Byte-oriented protocols live at the data link layer of the OSI model. See also *Bit-Oriented Protocols*.

C

Cable   Transmission medium of copper wire or glass fiber encased in a protective cover (PVC or Teflon).

Cable modem   A modem that provides Internet access over cable television lines.

Caching-only server   A server that operates the same way as secondary servers, except that a zone transfer does not take place when the caching-only server is started.

CAM   See *Content-Addressable Memory*.

Carrier   An entity that delivers items from one location to another. In telephony, a carrier is referred to as a third party organization that provides the means to deliver voice and data.

Carrier Sense Multiple Access with Collision Avoidance (CSMA/CA)   A contention media-access method that uses collision avoidance techniques (Ethernet).

Carrier Sense Multiple Access with Collision Detection (CSMA/CD)   A contention media-access method that uses collision detection and retransmission techniques (AppleTalk).

Category 1 cabling   The lowest of the five grades of UTP cabling described in the current EIA/TIA-568 standard. Used for telephone communications and is not suitable for transmitting data.

Category 2 cabling   One of five grades of UTP cabling described in the current EIA/TIA-568 standard. Capable of transmitting data at speeds up to 4 Mbps.

Category 3 cabling   One of five grades of UTP cabling described in the current EIA/TIA-568 standard. Used in 10BaseT networks and can transmit data at speeds up to 10 Mbps.

Category 4 cabling   One of five grades of UTP cabling described in the current EIA/TIA-568 standard. Used primarily in Token Ring networks to transmit data at speeds up to 16 Mbps.

Category 5 cabling   One of five grades of UTP cabling described in the current EIA/TIA-568 standard. Used for Ethernet and Fast Ethernet installations and can transmit data at speeds up to 100 Mbps. Pending the new standards, this is the typical "spec" for data and often phone to allow maximum flexibility down the road.

CCITT   Consultative Committee for International Telegraph and Telephone. International organization based in Switzerland that is responsible for the development of communications standards. Now called the ITU-T.

CD Carrier Detect. A signal indicating that an interface is active. Also, a modem signal indicating that a call has been connected.

CDDI Copper Distributed Data Interface. Implementation of FDDI protocols over STP and UTP cabling. CDDI transmits over relatively short distances (up to 100 meters), providing data rates of 100 Mbps using a dual-ring architecture to provide redundancy. Based on the ANSI Twisted-Pair Physical Medium Dependent (TPPMD) standard.

CDP Cisco Discovery Protocol. Media- and protocol-independent device-discovery protocol that runs on all Cisco-manufactured equipment including routers, access servers, bridges, and switches. With CDP, a device can advertise its existence to other devices and receive information about other devices on the same LAN or on the remote side of a WAN. Runs on all media that support SNAP, including LANs, Frame Relay, and ATM media.

Cell A fixed-size data unit for ATM switching and multiplexing. Cells include identifiers that specify the data stream to which they belong. Each cell consists of a 5-byte header and 48 bytes of payload.

Cell relay Network technology based on the use of small, fixed-size packets, or cells. Because cells are fixed-length, they can be processed and switched in hardware at high speeds. The basis for such high-speed network protocols as ATM, IEEE 802.6, and SMDS.

Central Processing Unit (CPU) The device that executes machine instructions is called the central processing unit, or CPU. All computing devices have a CPU although some are more general purpose than others. Cisco routers have general purpose CPUs but run a specific operating system, IOS.

Challenge Handshake Authentication Protocol (CHAP) Security feature supported on lines using PPP encapsulation that prevents unauthorized access to a network by identifying the remote end. The router or access server can then decide whether to allowed access. An improvement over the earlier PAP.

Channel A communications path used for data transmission. Several channels can be multiplexed using several techniques to pass simultaneously through a single media.

Channelized E1 Access link operating at 2.048 Mbps that is subdivided into 30 B-channels and 1 D-channel. Supports DDR, Frame Relay, and X.25. A European contemporary of the North American T1.

Channelized T1 Access link operating at 1.544 Mbps. It can be subdivided into 24 channels (fractional T1s) of 64 Kbps each. The individual channels or groups of channels can be connected to different destinations. Supports DDR, Frame Relay, and X.25.

Channel Service Unit (CSU) A digital device that connects end-user equipment to the local digital telephone loop. Often referred to together with DSU, as CSU/DSU. See *DSU*.

CHAP See *Challenge Handshake Authentication Protocol*.

Checksum Technique for verifying the integrity of received data. A checksum is a value calculated by the receiving node and compared to one calculated by the sending node and then stored in the frame. There can be a separate checksum for the header and data fields.

CIA See *Classical IP over ATM*.

CIDR See *Classless Interdomain Routing*.

CIR See *Committed Information Rate*.

Circuit A communications path between points. Most circuits involve two endpoints.

Circuit switching A telephony term indicating the physical switching of a path connecting endpoints of a "call."

Cisco IOS software   The operating system that runs on Cisco equipment is called Cisco IOS or *Internetworking Operating System*. Most Cisco hardware loads the IOS into flash memory so that the operating system is retained even during power outages. The IOS is easily updated to new revisions as they are released.

CiscoView   A GUI-based device-management software to provide dynamic status, statistics, and configuration information for Cisco devices. In addition to displaying a physical view of Cisco chasses, it can also provide device monitoring functions and basic troubleshooting. CiscoView can also integrate with other SNMP-based network management devices.

Class A network   A TCP/IP network that uses addresses starting between 1 and 126 and supports up to 126 subnets with 16,777,214 unique hosts each.

Class B network   A TCP/IP network that uses addresses starting between 128 and 191 and supports up to 16,384 subnets with 65,534 unique hosts each.

Class C network   A TCP/IP network that uses addresses starting between 192 and 254 and supports up to 2,097,152 subnets with 223 unique hosts each.

Class D network   Any IP address with a first octet value that is between 224 and 239. This class of address is used for multicast operations.

Class E network   Any IP address with a first octet value that is between 240 and 247. This class of address is used for research purposes only and is not currently deployed in existing internetworks.

Classful routing   Routing based on information derived from the natural boundaries of the different classes of IP addresses. Routing table information for networks that are not directly connected is kept only based on that natural network because the subnet masks of those remote networks are not contained in the routing update.

Classless Interdomain Routing (CIDR)   Classless Interdomain Routing. Technique supported by BGP4 based on route aggregation that allows routers to group IP networks together under a single address thereby reducing the number of entries stored in core routers.

Classless Routing   Routing based on information derived from routing updates that includes subnet mask (such as prefix) information. Routing table information shows all known networks and their accompanying prefix information.

Command Line Interface (CLI)   The basic interface for Cisco devices.

Client   A node that requests a service from another node on a network.

Client/server networking   Networking architecture utilizing front-end "clients" nodes that request and process data stored by the back end or "server" node.

Clock source   The specification of the party responsible for providing clocking for synchronization of a circuit.

CO   Telephone company Central Office. Many services, such as ISDN and DSL, are available only within certain distances from the CO.

Coaxial cable   Data cable, commonly referred to as *coax*, made of a solid copper core, which is insulated and surrounded by braided metal and covered with a thick plastic or rubber covering. This is the standard cable used in cable TV and in older bus topology networks.

CODEC   A device that typically uses pulse code modulation to transform analog signals into digital signals and digital signals back into analog signals is called a coder-decoder, or CODEC for short.

Coding   Coding is the electrical process that is used to convey digital information.

Collapsed backbone   A non-distributed backbone in which all network segments are interconnected by a single internetworking device. Hubs, routers, and switches are examples of devices that collapse a virtual network segment.

Collision   The result of two frames transmitting simultaneously in an Ethernet network and colliding, thereby destroying both frames.

Collision domain   Segment of an Ethernet network between managing nodes where only one packet can be transmitted at any given time. Switches, bridges, and routers can be used to segment a network into separate collision domains.

Committed burst (Bc)   The maximum amount of data that a Frame Relay network is committed to accept and transmit at the committed information rate. This is a negotiated tariff metric. See also *Committed Information Rate* and *Excess Burst*.

Committed Information Rate (CIR)   The rate, measured in bits per second, which a Frame Relay network agrees to make available to transfer information under normal conditions, averaged over a minimum increment of time. CIR and "burst" rates (Bc) are used in negotiating rates.

Common carrier   Supplier of communications utilities, such as phone lines, to the general public.

Communication   The transfer of information between nodes on a network.

Communication port (COM port)   A connection used for serial devices to communicate between the device and the motherboard. A COM port requires standard configuration information, such as IRQ (interrupt request), I/O (input/output) address, and COM port number.

Communication server   Communications device that connects asynchronous devices to a LAN or WAN through network and terminal emulation software. Performs only asynchronous routing of IP and IPX. See *Access Server*.

Compression   The process of converting a data set or a data stream that reduces the storage or bandwidth requirements, respectively, is called compression. Typically, in order to evaluate the data, an reverse process called expansion occurs. See *Expansion*.

Concurrent routing and bridging   A technology that allows the mixing of routing and bridging on a single device. However, data that arrives at the router through a bridged interface can be dispatched only via another bridged interface. The same is true for routed traffic.

Configuration register   Cisco hardware has a 16-bit *configuration register* that describes how the router behaves when it is powered-up. Typical examples are console baud rates, OEM identification, etc.

Congestion   A condition that arises when the data being passed across a circuit exceeds the data-carrying capacity of that circuit.

Congestion avoidance   An ATM network can control traffic entering the network to minimize delays via a mechanism called congestion avoidance. Lower priority traffic can be discarded at the edge of the network if the conditions dictate that it cannot be delivered.

Connectionless-oriented communication   Refers to packet transfer in which the delivery is not guaranteed.

Connection-oriented communication   Refers to packet transfer in which the delivery is guaranteed.

Connectivity   The linking of nodes on a network in order for communication to take place.

Console   A physical port used in the configuration of a router. The console is the default source for configuration information.

Content-addressable memory   Memory that is accessed based on its contents, not on its memory address.

Contention   The access method in which network devices compete for permission to access a physical medium is called contention.

Convergence   The exchanging of routing updates by routers that participate in dynamic routing protocol activities to form a consistent perspective of the network. When all routers know of all possible destinations in the network, the network has converged.

Copper Distributed Data Interface (CDDI)   The implementation of the FDDI standard using electrical cable rather than optical cable.

Core gateway   Primary routers in the Internet.

Core layer   In the Hierarchical Model, it is the backbone of the network, designed for high-speed data transmission.

Core router   Any router attached to the highest level of network hierarchy, usually the core backbone of the network.

CoS   Same as Type of Service (ToS)

Cost   In OSPF, the metric used for route calculation. This calculation is based on the bandwidth of the link in question.

CPE   See *Customer Premise Equipment*.

Cps   Cells per second.

CPU   See *Central Processing Unit*.

CRB   See *Concurrent Routing and Bridging*.

CRC   See *Cyclic Redundancy Check*.

Crosstalk   Electronic interference caused when two wires get too close to each other.

CSMA/CA   See *Carrier Sense Multiple Access/Collision Avoidance*.

CSMA/CD   See *Carrier Sense Multiple Access/Collision Detection*.

CSU   See *Channel Service Unit*.

Customer Premise Equipment (CPE)   Terminating equipment, such as terminals, telephones, modems, TA and CSU/DSUs supplied by the telephone company, installed at customer sites, and connected to the telephone company network.

Custom queuing   A Cisco proprietary strategy for prioritizing traffic output from a router interface, usually a low-speed Serial interface.

Cut-through packet switching   A switching method that does not copy the entire packet into the switch buffers. Instead, the destination address is captured into the switch, the route to the destination node is determined, and the packet is quickly sent out the corresponding port. Cut-through packet switching maintains a low latency.

Cyclic Redundancy Check (CRC)   Error-checking technique in which a frame recipient performs a calculation on the frame contents and compares the result to a value stored in the frame by the sending node. If the values are different then the frame has been corrupted.

D

D channel   A digital subscriber service channel to facilitate communication between an ISDN-capable router and the switch to which that router is connected.

D connectors   Connectors shaped like a "D" that use pins and sockets to establish connections between peripheral devices using serial or parallel ports. The number that follows is the number of pins they use for connectivity. For example, a DB-9 connector has 9 pins, and a DB-25 has 25.

Data Communications Equipment (DCE)   An EIA term referring to the network end of a communications channel. The other end, DTE, refers to the user end of the communications channel. The DCE provides a physical connection to a network, forwards traffic, and provides a clocking signal used to synchronize data transmissions. Modems and interface cards are typical DCE devices whereas computers, multiplexers, and protocol translators are DTE devices.

Data field   In a frame, the field or section that contains the data.

Data Link Connection Identifier (DLCI)   A value that specifies a permanent virtual circuit (PVC) or a switched virtual circuit (SVC) in a Frame Relay network.

Data link layer   The layer in the OSI Model at which hardware signals and software functions are converted. This is also known as Layer 2 of the OSI Model. This layer is logically subdivided into two parts: the MAC sublayer and the Logical Link Control (LLC) sublayer. The MAC portion is where the burned-in hardware address is stored. The LLC discriminates between protocols to ensure proper passage of various network-layer protocol traffic types.

Data Service Unit (DSU)   Device used in digital transmission that adapts the physical interface on a DTE device to a transmission facility such as a T1 or an E1. The DSU is also responsible for such functions signal timing. Often referred in conjunction with a CSU.

Data Terminal Equipment (DTE)   Device, used at the user end of a user-network interface, that serves as a data source, a destination, or both. These devices include computers, protocol translators, and multiplexers. See also *Data Communications Equipment.*

Datagram   Information groupings that are transmitted as a unit at the network layer.

DB-9   This connector has 9 pins and is used for serial-port or parallel-port connection between PCs and peripheral devices.

DB-25   This connector has 25 pins and is used for serial-port or parallel-port connection between PCs and peripheral devices.

DCE   See *Data Communications Equipment.*

DDP   See *Database Description Packet.*

DDR   See *Dial On-Demand Routing.*

Debug   Any of the many commands used in diagnosing router problems, or simply watching router operation processes.

DECnet   Group of communications protocols developed and supported by Digital Equipment Corporation (now Compaq Computer Corporation). It supports both OSI protocols and proprietary Digital protocols.

Decryption   The process of taking an encrypted stream of information and un-encoding it, making it understood by the existing application, or a downstream application. See also *Encryption.*

Dedicated LAN   A network segment dedicated or allocated to a single device. Data collection devices make use of these, as do LAN switching devices.

Dedicated line or **dedicated circuit**   Usually used in WANs to provide a constant connection between two points.

De facto standard   Standard that exists because of its widespread use, not necessarily because it is a standard approved by any particular governing body. See also *De jure Standard.*

Default gateway   Normally a router or a multihomed computer to which packets are sent when they are destined for a host that's not on their segment of the network.

Default route   A route that signifies a gateway of last resort for traffic destined for remote networks for which a router does not have specific reachability information.

De jure standard Standard that exists because of approval by an official standards body. See also *De facto Standard*.

Delay A calculation based on bandwidth of the link to determine the amount of time it takes to transmit data from across that link. This value is an amount of time expressed in milliseconds.

Demarc See *Point of Demarcation*.

Deny The process of prohibiting the passage of specific traffic.

Destination address The network address where the frame is being sent. In a packet, this address is encapsulated in a field of the packet so all nodes know where the frame is being sent.

Destination protocol address The Layer 3 address of the intended recipient of a specific packet.

DHCP See *Dynamic Host Configuration Protocol*.

Dial backup A DDR technology used to provide redundancy for a primary circuit to compensate for overload and/or failure of that circuit.

Dialed number identification service The method for delivery of automatic number identification using out-of-band signaling.

Dialer group A designation that specifies the association of a dialer-list with a specific router interface. A dialer-group is usually used in the definition of interesting traffic.

Dialer interface A logical interface used in the creation of rotary groups. A dialer interface is generally in charge of one or more physical interfaces.

Dialer list A designation used to define interesting traffic that should be allowed to initiate a DDR call to a specific destination.

Dialer pool A group of physical interfaces ordered on the basis of the priority assigned to each physical interface.

Dialer profile A configuration of physical interfaces to be separated from a logical configuration required for a call. Profiles may also allow the logical and physical configurations to be bound together dynamically call by call.

Dialer string A telephone number associated with a particular destination.

Dial on-demand routing A technology generally associated with ISDN in which a data connection is established on an as needed basis. When not in use, the link automatically disconnects and returns to an idle state.

Dial-up line A communications circuit that is established by a switched-carrier connection using the network of a telephone company.

Dial-up networking Refers to the connection of a remote node to a network using POTS. Also the name of temporary networking under the Microsoft Windows family of operating systems.

Digital In networking technologies, a string of electrical signals that take on the characteristics of one of two discrete binary states.

Digital Network Architecture (DNA) A network architecture developed by Digital Equipment Corporation (now Compaq Computer Corporation). The products that embody DNA (including communications protocols) are collectively referred to as DECnet.

Digital Subscriber Line (DSL) A public network technology that delivers high bandwidth over conventional copper wiring at limited distances.

Directed broadcast A Layer 3 term for a data transmission destined to all hosts in a specific subnet.

Discard eligible (DE) ATM cells that have their cell loss priority (CLP) bit set to 1. If the network is congested, discard eligible traffic can be dropped to ensure delivery of higher-priority traffic. It is also called *Tagged Traffic*. See also *CLP*.

Distance vector routing algorithm See *Bellman-Ford Algorithm*.

Distance vector routing protocol Any dynamic routing protocol that uses of the Bellman-Ford Algorithm for routing update exchange that employs the use of metric addition to derive a measurement of a route to a particular destination network. Commonly referred to as "routing by rumor."

Distributed Update Algorithm (DUAL) An EIGRP finite state machine that performs all route computations and allows all EIGRP routers involved in a topology change to synchronize near-instantaneously on a loop-free topology. Using a composite metric based on such media properties as bandwidth and delay, the DUAL calculates successors and feasible successors for each destination listed in the topology table. Whenever the router detects that a successor has become unavailable for a certain destination, the DUAL performs a route evaluation and possibly a route recomputation. See also *Route Evaluation* and *Route Recomputation*.

Distribution layer In the Hierarchical Model, this layer functions as the separation point between the Core and Access layers of the network. The devices in the Distribution layer implement the policies that define how packets are to be distributed to the groups within the network.

Distribute list A configuration option that allows the filtering of reachability (such as routing) information using access-list commands to permit and/or deny routes.

Distribution router Any router in your internetwork hierarchy that connects lower-level access routers to the higher-level core routers.

Djykstra Algorithm The process that many link-state routing protocols employ to keep reachability information in a current state. Generally characterized by high memory usage and very fast convergence time.

DLCI See *Data-Link Connection Identifier*.

DNA See *Digital Network Architecture*.

DNS See *Domain Naming System*.

Domain Networking system used worldwide on the Internet and in Windows NT networks to identify a controlled network of nodes that are grouped as an administrative unit.

Domain Name Service (DNS) The part of the distributed database system responsible for resolving a fully qualified domain name into the four-part IP (Internet Protocol) number used to route communications across the Internet. DNS can also stand for domain name server. See also *Domain Name System*.

Domain Name System (DNS) A hierarchical client/server based database management system. The DNS was created and is operated by the InterNIC to provide alpha-based names for numeric-based IP addresses. See also *Domain Name Service*.

Dot address A dot address refers to the 32-bit IP address in decimal form. It consists of 4 octets that are 8 bits in length each and converted into decimal. It does *not* refer to a domain name.

DRAM See *Dynamic Random Access Memory*.

DS-0 A single 64,000-bit-per-second timeslot, usually associated with a T1 or fractions thereof.

DS-1 A grouping of 24 DS0s, DS1 refers to the framing methodology of T1 transmissions. However, DS1 is often incorrectly considered to be synonymous with T1. T1 refers to the Line Coding Methodology.

DS-1/DTI An interface circuit used for DS-1 application with 24 trunks.

DS-3 Framing specification for transmitting digital signals at 44.736 Mbps on T3 equipment.

DSL See *Digital Subscriber Line*.

DSU See *Data Service Unit*.

DTE See *Data Terminal Equipment.*

DUAL See *Distributed Update Algorithm.*

Dumb terminal A keyboard/monitor combination that accesses a mainframe computer for data but provides no processing at the local level.

Dynamic Host Configuration Protocol (DHCP) A greatly expanded implementation of the BootP protocol used for dynamic assignment of IP addresses on the network. DHCP also provides for gateway, DNS servers, WINS servers, and a myriad of other network elements.

Dynamic address resolution The use of an address resolution protocol (ARP) to acquire and store information as needed. See also *Address Resolution Protocol.*

Dynamic routing The routing process the adjusts itself according to routing conditions, congestion, and other factors. In this fashion, packets make take different routes from source to destination at different points in time. Also called *Adaptive Routing.*

Dynamic Random Access Memory (DRAM) Variable state memory that stores information using capacitors. Because capacitors drain, they must be continually be "refreshed." DRAMs cannot be accessed during refresh cycles and therefore are slower than SRAMs. SRAMs require no refresh cycle as they maintain information as long as power is applied.

Dynamic window Used in flow control as a mechanism that prevents the sender of data from overwhelming the receiver. The amount of data that can be buffered in a dynamic window varies in size—hence its name.

E

E1 Wide-area digital transmission scheme used predominantly in Europe that carries data at a rate of 2.048 Mbps. E1 lines can be leased for private use from common carriers. Compare with T1.

E3 Wide-area digital transmission scheme used predominantly in Europe that carries data at a rate of 34.368 Mbps. E3 lines can be leased for private use from common carriers. Compare with T3.

EBGP See *External Border Gateway Protocol.*

EEPROM An EPROM that can be erased electronically (instead of using Ultra-violet light) is called an Electrically erasable programmable read-only memory. See also *EPROM* and *PROM.*

EGP See *Exterior Gateway Protocol.*

EIA See *Electronics Industry Association.*

EIA/TIA-232 The official name for RS-232 (which has been officially dropped), or physical layer for the transmission of serial information. The original TIA-232 was far more ambitious than the minimal 3-pin usage, or even the 8-pin usage. Maximum transmission speed in this specification is 64 Kbps. The most common usage is for terminals, modems, and console devices.

EIGRP See *Enhanced Interior Gateway Routing Protocol.*

Electromagnetic Interference (EMI) The term used for the external interference of electromagnetic signals that causes reduction of data integrity and increased error rates in a transmission medium.

Electronic mail The application level form of messaging for end-users. By far the most prevalent protocol for the transmission of electronic mail is SMTP. However, large organizations use more enterprise-based protocols. See *Simple Mail Transfer Protocol.*

Electronics Industries Association (EIA) The group that specifies electrical transmission standards. Responsible for many common signaling specifications such as EIA RS-232, EIA-RS-422, etc.

Encapsulation   The technique used by layered protocols in which a layer adds header information to the protocol data unit (PDU) from the layer above.

Encapsulation bridging   The encapsulation of transparently bridged frames into the framing type of a Serial link (HDLC, Frame Relay, and so on) in order to cross a WAN.

Encryption   The modification of data for security purposes prior to transmission so that it is not comprehensible without the decoding method. See also *Decryption.*

End system   A end-user device on a network.

Enhanced Interior Gateway Routing Protocol (EIGRP)   A Cisco proprietary dynamic routing protocol that attempts to combine the positive traits of distance-vector and link-state protocols. EIGRP is sometimes referred to as a hybrid routing protocol or an advanced distance-vector routing protocol.

Enterprise network   The collective set of computing and networking devices that provide for the needs of an entire organization. It likely consists of many networking technologies from assorted vendors. Although the desire to standardize on a minimum number of vendors is a goal, it is often unachievable because of the diverse number of platforms.

EPROM   See *Read-Only Memory.*

Error control   A process or technique to detect and in some cases correct errors in the transmission of data.

ES   See *End System.*

Ethernet   A framing convention used in CSMA/CD networks.

Excess burst (Be)   The amount of data that a Frame Relay internetwork will attempt to transmit after the committed burst (Bc) is accommodated. In general, the data from excess burst is delivered at a lower probability than the data from committed burst because excess burst data can be marked as discard eligible (DE). See also *Committed Burst* and *Discard Eligible.*

Exchange state   An OSPF state which indicates that two OSPF routers are exchanging link-state advertisements (LSAs) to discover the link-state topology.

EXEC   The interactive command line processor in Cisco IOS.

Expansion   The process of running a compressed data set or compressed data stream through an algorithm to derive an original data set or data stream that is larger or requires more bandwidth. See also *Compression.*

Explorer   An SRB term that refers to frames dispatched from a source device in order to locate a suitable pathway to a specific destination device.

Extended access list   Any access list that is meant to employ more than basic functionality of traffic filtering. In IP, an extended access list can filter on source address, destination address, protocol, and port.

Extended superframe   A T1 framing convention that employs the transmission of 24 T1 frames.

Exterior gateway protocol   Any generic internetworking protocol that exchanges routing information between two or more autonomous systems. EGP is a specific instance of an exterior gateway protocol, even though they have the same name. The distinction is the same as for *internet* and *Internet.*

Exterior Gateway Protocol (EGP)   An Internet protocol that exchanges routing information between two or more autonomous systems as defined in *RFC 904*. It has been replaced by BGP. See also *BGP.*

External Border Gateway Protocol (EBGP)   A BGP implementation that connects external ASs. EBGP peers are usually directly connected physically.

External Gateway Protocol (EGP)   A dynamic routing protocol that connects two external ASs.

External route   In OSPF, a route received from any source outside of the local area.

F

Fast Ethernet   IEEE 802.3 specification for data transfers of up to 100 Mbps.

Fast switching   A Cisco feature used to expedite packet switching through a router by means of a route cache. Compare with *Process Switching*.

Fault tolerance   This is a theoretical concept defined as a resistance to failure. It is not an absolute and can be defined only in degrees.

FCS   See *Frame Check Sequence*.

FDDI   See *Fiber Distributed Data Interface*.

Feasible distance   In EIGRP, the metric associated with each piece of routing information entered into the routing table.

Feasible successor   In EIGRP, the second best route to a particular destination network. The feasible successor is selected only if the advertised distance of the second best route is lower than the feasible distance of the best route. The feasible successor also refers to the next-hop router along the alternative path to a destination.

FECN   See *Forward Explicit Congestion Notification*.

Fiber channel, fibre channel   This technology defines full gigabit-per-second data transfer over fiber-optic cable.

Fiber Distributed Data Interface (FDDI)   A high-speed data-transfer technology designed to extend the capabilities of existing local area networks using a dual-rotating ring technology similar to token ring.

Fiber optics   The transmission of energy by light through glass fibers for communication and signaling.

Fiber-optic cable   Also known as fiber optics or optical fiber, this is a physical medium capable of conducting modulated light transmissions. Compared with other transmission media, fiber-optic cable is more expensive, but is not susceptible to electromagnetic interference and is capable of higher data rates.

FIFO   See *First-In First-Out*.

File Transfer Protocol (FTP)   The set of standards or protocols that allow you to transfer complete files between different computer hosts.

Filter   A process or a device that screens and separates items. A router, for instance, will filter packets according to a set of rules and allow or deny forwarding accordingly.

Firewall   A generic term for a device that filters network traffic. On the low end it can be a simple router with an access list. On the high end, it can be a device that opens up packets and evaluates it high on the OSI network model.

Firmware   Code that is typically embedded into a ROM, PROM, or EPROM and delivered with a hardware device. Typically, firmware is the code that the device executes upon power-up. In general, it is not changeable without physically removing and/or replacing the ROM.

First-In First-Out (FIFO)   A queuing strategy that dispatches traffic in the order in which it was received. In other words, FIFO is the absence of queuing.

Flapping   A problem with routing where an advertised routes keeps switching, or flapping, between two or more paths due to an intermittent network failure.

Flash memory   A form of non-volatile memory. It can sustain its contents without power. It is therefore suitable to use flash memory to deliver changeable code, such as Cisco's IOS as well as store configurations.

Flash update   The writing of code or data to flash memory. A flash update occurs when you upgrade the Cisco IOS from 11.2 to 12 on a router, for example. An update occurs also when you save a configuration, although it is not necessarily viewed as a flash update.

Flat addressing   A method of addressing that doesn't use any sort of hierarchy to determine location. MAC addresses are flat because there is nothing embedded in the address itself— bridges must broadcast or flood packets to all network segments to deliver any packets to their destinations. Compare with *Hierarchical Addressing.*

Flooding   The process of distributing routing information throughout the network.

Flow control   A method used to control the amount of data that is transmitted within a given period of time. There are different types of flow control. See also *Dynamic Window* and *Static Window.*

Forward Explicit Congestion Notification (FECN)   A method for the frame relay network to deal with congestion. The network can set a single address bit in frames traveling toward their destination. A DTE receiving frames with the FECN bit set to one can forward the info on to higher-level protocols to exercise flow control. Compare with *Backward Explicit Congestion Notification (BECN).*

FRAD   See *Frame Relay Access Device.*

Fragment-free   A fast packet-switching method that uses the first 64 bytes of the frame to determine if the frame is corrupted. If this first part is intact, then the frame is forwarded.

Frame   Grouping of information transmitted as a unit across the network at the data link layer.

Frame Check Sequence (FCS)   A function performed on inbound frames to determine whether or not they are valid entities and are worthy of further processing.

Frame Check Sequence field   This field performs a cyclic redundancy check (CRC) to ensure that all of the frame's data arrives intact.

Frame forwarding   The method that frame traffic traverses an ATM network.

Frame length field   In a data frame, the field that specifies the length of a frame. The maximum length for an 802.3 frame is 1,518 bytes.

Frame relay   Data link layer switching protocol used across multiple virtual circuits of a common carrier, giving the end user the appearance of a dedicated line.

Frame Relay Access Device (FRAD)   Device that provides access to frame relay networks with support for a variety of LAN and Legacy protocols. FRADs often include an integral CSU/DSU or high speed serial network interface and comply with industry standard RFC1490 for internetworking with routers.

Frame type field   In a data frame, the field that names the protocol that is being sent in the frame.

Frequency   Expressed in hertz, it's the number of cycles of an alternating current signal over a unit of time.

Frequency Division Multiplexing (FDM)   This technology divides the output channel into multiple, smaller bandwidth channels, each using a different frequency range.

FTP   See *File Transfer Protocol.*

Full-duplex   The transmission of data in two directions simultaneously.

Full mesh   A network topology where each device in the network has a physical or virtual connection to every other device in the network (or mesh). It is extremely efficient as a delivery mechanism in that there is a route to each device, minimizing any propagation delay. However, it is costly from a growth standpoint as the number of links grows exponentially with each device that is added to the system.

G

Gateway   A hardware and software solution that enables communications between two dissimilar networking systems or protocols. Gateways usually operate at the upper layers of the OSI protocol stack, above the Transport layer.

GB   Gigabyte.

GBps   Gigabyte per second.

Gb   Gigabit.

Gbps   Gigabit per second.

Generic Routing Rencapsulation (GRE)   A tunneling protocol developed by Cisco to encapsulate a number of protocol packet types inside an IP tunnel. This creates virtual point-to-point links to Cisco routers at remote points over an IP network.

Giant   An Ethernet frame in excess of the maximum transmittable unit size of 1,518 bytes.

Gigabit (Gb)   Term used to specify one billion bits or one thousand megabits.

Gigabit Ethernet   IEEE specification for transfer rates up to one gigabit per second.

Gigabits per second   One billion bits per second.

Gigabyte   One billion bytes.

Gigabytes per second   One billion bytes per second.

Graphical User Interface (GUI)   An interface that uses a graphics subsystem instead of a character generator to provide visual display. Modern GUIs use mice, menus, and virtual windows to separate and select content.

GRE   See *Generic Routing Encapsulation.*

Group-membership-LSA   See *LSA Type 6.*

GUI   See *Graphical User Interface.*

H

Half-duplex   A circuit designed for data transmission in both directions, but not simultaneously.

Handshaking   The initial communication between two modems, during which they agree upon protocol and transfer rules for the session.

HDB3   See *High Density Bipolar Level Three.*

HDLC   See *High Level Data Link Control.*

Header   Control information placed at the beginning of a data stream.

Hello interval   The time that elapses between the transmission of two consecutive hello packets. In OSPF, the default hello interval is 10 seconds; in EIGRP, the default hello interval is 5 seconds. Sometimes referred to as the keepalive interval. Compare with dead interval.

Hello packet   A packet used by some routing protocols to discover and maintain neighbor relationships.

Hello protocol A means of communication between two hosts on a network that require constant and continued connectivity to each other. The two devices exchange these Hello messages at a specified interval.

Helper address An address used to forward selected broadcasts by converting them to unicasts or directed broadcasts.

Heterogeneous network A network that consists of dissimilar devices using dissimilar protocols that may provide or support dissimilar functions and/or applications.

Hierarchical addressing An addressing scheme that incorporates contiguous addressing and tools like VLSM in accordance with a hierarchically designed network.

High Density Bipolar Level Three (HDP3) A line-coding technique employed by users of E1 technologies.

High-Level Data Link Control (HDLC) A Cisco proprietary Serial framing convention that allows the use of multiple protocols across a Serial link. This is the default encapsulation for Serial interfaces on Cisco routers.

High-Speed Serial Interface (HSSI) The network standard for high-speed serial communications over WAN links. It includes frame relay, T1, T3, E1, and ISDN.

Holddown The state entered in by a router that has just received a routing update indicating a failed route. The holddown prevents a router from accepting routing information for the failed route for a predetermined amount of time.

Holdtime A general term that refers to how long a device waits before purging an entry in a routing table, neighbor table, topology table, and so on. Once the HoldTime expires, the entry, whatever the type, is purged. In EIGRP, the default HoldTime is 15 seconds; in BGP, the default HoldTime is 180 seconds. Also referred to as the holdtime and hold-time.

Hop The crossing of a router in an internetwork.

Hop count The number of routers or hops between a source and a destination.

Host Used generically for any system on a network. In the Unix world, used for any device that is assigned an IP address.

Hostname The NetBIOS name of the computer or node, given to the first element of the Internet domain name. It must be unique on your network.

Host number In IP, the decimal number that identifies the host portion of an IP address.

HOSTS file Similar to LMHOSTS except that the HOSTS file is most commonly used for TCP/IP name resolution of domain names.

Hot Standby Routing Protocol (HSRP) Allows redundant default gateways.

HSSI A Serial interface that must be employed in order to transmit and/or receive at a rate greater than 2 Mbps, up to 52 Mbps.

HTTP Hyper-text transfer protocol.

HTML Hyper-text markup language.

Hub Also known as a concentrator or multiport repeater, this is a hardware device that connects multiple independent nodes.

Hybrid network A network made up of more than one type of networking technology.

Hybrid routing protocol A routing protocol that employs the characteristics of both distance-vector and link-state protocols to attempt to exploit the positive aspects of each.

HyperTerminal A Windows-based communications program that allows you to establish Host/Shell access to a remote system.

Hypertext Transfer Protocol (HTTP)   A protocol used by Web browsers to transfer pages and files from the remote node to your computer.

I

IANA   See *Internet Assigned Numbers Authority*.

IBGP   See *Internal Border Gateway Protocol*.

ICMP   See *Internet Control Message Protocol*.

IEEE   See *Institute of Electrical and Electronics Engineers*.

IEEE 802.1   Standard that defines the OSI model's physical and data link layers. This standard allows two IEEE LAN stations to communicate over a LAN or wide area network (WAN) and is often referred to as the "internetworking standard." It also includes the Spanning Tree Algorithm specifications.

IEEE 802.2   Standard that defines the LLC sublayer for the entire series of protocols covered by the 802.x standards. This standard specifies the adding of header fields, which tells the receiving host which upper layer sent the information. It also defines specifications for the implementation of the Logical Link Control (LLC) sublayer of the data link layer.

IEEE 802.3   Standard that specifies Physical-layer attributes, such as signaling types, data rates and topologies, and the media-access method used. It also defines specifications for the implementation of the physical layer and the MAC sublayer of the data link layer, using CSMA/CD, This standard also includes the original specifications for Fast Ethernet.

IEEE 802.4   Standard that defines how production machines should communicate and establishes a common protocol for use in connecting these machines together. It also defines specifications for the implementation of the physical layer and the MAC sublayer of the data link layer using token-ring access over a bus topology.

IEEE 802.5   Standard often used to define token ring. However, it does not specify a particular topology or transmission medium. It provides specifications for the implementation of the physical layer and the MAC sublayer of the data link layer using a token-passing media-access method over a ring topology.

IEEE 802.6   Standard that defines the distributed queue dual bus (DQDB) technology to transfer high-speed data between nodes. It provides specifications for the implementation of metropolitan area networks (MANs).

IEEE 802.7   Standard that defines the design, installation, and testing of broadband-based communications and related physical media connectivity.

IEEE 802.8   Standard that defines a group of people who advise the other 802-standard committees on various fiber-optic technologies and standards. This advisory group is called the Fiber Optic Technical Advisory Group.

IEEE 802.9   Standard that defines the integration of voice and data transmissions using isochronous Ethernet (IsoEnet).

IEEE 802.10   Standard that focuses on security issues by defining a standard method for protocols and services to exchange data securely by using encryption mechanisms.

IEEE 802.11   Standard that defines the implementation of wireless technologies, such as infrared and spread-spectrum radio.

IEEE 802.12   Standard that defines 100BaseVG-AnyLAN, which uses a 1,000 Mbps signaling rate and a special media-access method allowing 100 Mbps data traffic over voice-grade cable.

IETF   See *Internet Engineering Task Force.*

IGP   See *Interior Gateway Protocol.*

IGRP   See *Interior Gateway Routing Protocol.*

Industry Standards Architecture (ISA)   The standard of the older, more common 8-bit and 16-bit bus and card architectures.

Infrared (IR)   Wavelength of light (longer than light visible to the naked eye) that is used in many wireless data transmission technologies.

Init state   An OSPF state which specifies that a neighbor received a valid hello packet and added the sender's router-ID to its neighborship database.

Institute of Electrical and Electronics Engineers (IEEE)   A standards body comprised of electronic and electrical engineers charged with creating physical- and data link-layer standards.

Interdomain routing   Routing that occurs between autonomous systems. Also called inter-autonomous system routing.

Integrated Routing and Bridging (IRB)   Integrated routing and bridging is used in Cisco IOS to route a given protocol between routed interfaces and bridged interfaces within a single router.

Integrated Services Digital Network (ISDN)   An internationally adopted standard for end-to-end digital communications over PSTN (Public Switched Telephone Network) that permits telephone networks to carry data, voice, and other source traffic.

Intelligent hubs   Hubs that contain some management or monitoring capability.

Inter-area route   In OSPF, any route to a destination outside of the local area.

Interesting traffic   In DDR, the specific traffic types that can initiate an ISDN connection to connect two remote sites.

Interface   A device, such as a card or a plug, that connects pieces of hardware with the computer so that information can be moved from place to place (for example, between computers and printers, hard disks, and other devices, or between two or more nodes on a network).

Interface processor   The I/O processor for any of the media and protocol adapter boards that operate in the Cisco 7000 series routers.

Interference   An entity that delays, prohibits, or otherwise prevents a process from performing its function or within its specified parameters. Electrical interference, for example, may prevent radio signals or wired signals from maintaining their patterns, thus preventing transmission of information.

Intermediate System-to-Intermediate System (IS-IS)   An OSI link-state hierarchical routing protocol based on DECNet routing where routers exchange routing information based on a single metric to determine network topology.

Internal Border Gateway Protocol (IBGP)   An implementation of BGP between routers inside the same AS. IBGP peers do not have to be directly connected physically with each other, so long as they can reach each other via an IGP or static route.

Interior Gateway Protocol (IGP)   Any routing protocol employed within an AS.

Interior Gateway Routing Protocol (IGRP)   A Cisco proprietary routing protocol that functions on a 90-second update timer.

Internal loopback address   Used for testing with TCP/IP, this address—127.0.0.1—allows a test packet to reflect back into the sending adapter to determine if it is functioning properly.

Internal router   In OSPF, any router in which all interfaces configured for OSPF operation are in the same area.

International Standards Organization (ISO) A voluntary organization founded in 1946, comprised of the national standards organizations of many countries, and responsible for creating international standards in many areas, including computers and communications. ANSI (American National Standards Institute) is the American member of ISO. ISO produced OSI (Open Systems Interconnection), a seven-layer model for network architecture.

Internet A public IP-based internetwork that facilitates communications on a global scale.

Internet Short for internetwork.

Internet Assigned Numbers Authority (IANA) The organization responsible for Internet protocol addresses, domain names, and protocol parameters.

Internet Control Message Protocol (ICMP) Network-layer internet protocol, documented in RFC 792, that reports errors and provides other information relevant to IP packet processing.

Internet domain name Name used on the Internet. Made up of three elements: the computer name, the top level domain to which your machine belongs, and the root-level domain.

Internet Engineering Task Force (IETF) A group of research volunteers responsible for specifying the protocols used on the Internet and for specifying the architecture of the Internet.

Internet Group Management Protocol (IGMP) Protocol responsible for managing and reporting IP multicast group memberships.

Internet layer In the TCP/IP architectural model, this layer is responsible for the addressing, packaging, and routing functions. Protocols operating at this layer of the model are responsible for encapsulating packets into Internet datagrams. All necessary routing algorithms are run here.

Internet Network Information Center (InterNIC) The group that provides Internet services, such as domain registration and information, directory, and database services.

Internet Protocol (IP) Network-layer protocol, documented in RFC 791, that offers a connectionless internetwork service. IP provides features for addressing, packet fragmentation and reassembly, type-of-service specification, and security.

Internet Research Task Force (IRTF) The research arm of the Internet Architecture Board, this group performs research in areas of Internet protocols, applications, architecture, and technology.

Internet Service Provider (ISP) A company that specializes in providing individuals, companies, and corporations with access to the public Internet.

Internetwork A group of networks that are connected by routers or other connectivity devices so that the networks function as one network.

Internetwork Operating System (IOS) Cisco's router operating system software that provides the intelligence and functionality of Cisco routers.

Internetworking The process of interconnecting network devices, protocols, and technologies for the purpose of communicating information.

InterNIC See *Internet Network Information Center.*

Interoperability The capacity for different devices, protocols, or technologies to work together.

Inverse ARP Method of building dynamic routes in a network. It allows an access server to discover the network address of a device associated with a virtual circuit.

IOS See *Internetwork Operating System.*

IP See *Internet Protocol.*

IP address 32-bit number representing a unique designation for a network device. An IP address is represented in decimal dotted octets (i.e., 8 bits separated by dots with each octet represented as a decimal number).

IPCONFIG   Windows NT command that provides information about the configuration of the TCP/IP parameters, including the IP address.

IP multicast   A routing technique that allows IP traffic to be propagated from once source to many destinations, or from many sources to many destinations. One packet is sent to a multicast group, which is identified by a single IP destination group address.

IPSec   A protocol designed for virtual private networks (VPNs). Used to provide strong security standards for encryption and authentication.

IP Spoofing   The process of substituting the source IP address on a packet or set of packets to fool a device into allowing it to be forwarded.

IPX address   The unique address used to identify a node in the IPX network. An IPX address is an 80-bit number, 48 of which identify the MAC address and 32 of which identify the network number.

IPv6   The next generation of IP. Supports a 128-bit address, CIDR, and authentication.

Internetwork Packet Exchange (IPX)   Connectionless network-layer protocol from Novell.

IR   See *Infrared.*

IRB   See *Integrated Routing and Bridging.*

ISDN   See *Integrated Services Digital Network.*

IS-IS   See *Intermediate System-to-Intermediate System.*

ISO   See *International Standards Organization.*

Isochronous transmission   A method of asynchronous transmission requiring a node other than the sender or receiver to provide the clock signaling.

ISP   See *Internet Service Provider.*

ITU-T   The International Telecommunications Union-Telecommunications Standards Sector. A body that formally sets standards, specifications, and recommendations, it used to be known as the CCITT, or the Consultative Committee on International Telegraphy and Telephony.

J

Jabber   An error condition in which a network device continually transmits random, meaning-less data onto a network. Under 802.3, it's a data packet whose length exceeds what is prescribed in the standard.

Jam   Describes the collision reinforcement signal output by the repeater to all ports. The jam signal consists of 96 bits of alternating 1's and 0's. The purpose is to extend a collision sufficiently so that all devices cease transmitting.

Jitter   The fluctuation of the data packet in respect to a standard clock cycle. Jitter is undesirable and must be minimized.

JPEG   A file format for compressing photo-realistic images. Compression yields are often 10 percent of original size. For compressing non-photo-realistic images, GIF is the preferred format. It is also a very common type of data found in HTTP streams.

K

K Values   In IGRP and EIGRP, the values of bandwidth, delay, reliability, load, and MTU.

K56flex technology   One of the original two 56 Kbps data-transfer technologies designed for modems. They were both replaced by the V.90 standard.

KB Kilobyte.

Kb Kilobit.

KBps Kilobytes per second.

Kbps Kilobits per second.

Keepalive interval A routing protocol term that refers to how often keepalive messages are sent to a router to determine if the router is still active and to keep the connection from timing out.

Keepalive message A message passed across a link in order to keep an active, constant conversation with a node on the remote end.

Kerberos A standard for authenticating network users. Passwords are not transmitted across the network and therefore cannot be decrypted.

Kermit Kermit is a file transfer protocol first developed at Columbia University in New York City in 1981 for the specific purpose of transferring text and binary files without errors between diverse types of computers over potentially hostile communication links, and it is a suite of communications software programs from the Kermit Project at Columbia University. Kermit software offers a consistent approach to file transfer, terminal emulation, script programming, and character-set conversion on hundreds of different hardware and operating system platforms, using diverse communication methods.

L

L2F Protocol Layer 2 forwarding protocol. A protocol that supports the use of virtual private dial-up networks over the Internet.

LAN See *Local Area Network*.

LAN Switch A high-speed switch that forwards packets between data link segments.

LAPB See *Link Access Procedure Balanced*.

LAPD See *Link Access Procedure D Channel*.

Laser A laser is an acronym for *light amplification by stimulated emission of radiation*. A narrow beam of coherent light that is modulated into pulses to carry data. SONET is a form of networking based on laser technology. See also *Synchronous Optical Network*.

LAT See *Local Area Transport*.

Latency The time used to forward a packet in and out of a device. Commonly used in reference to routing and switching.

Layer 1 See *Physical Layer*.

Layer 2 See *Data Link Layer*.

Layer 3 See *Network Layer*.

Layer 4 See *Transport Layer*.

Layer 5 See *Session Layer*.

Layer 6 See *Presentation Layer*.

Layer 7 See *Application Layer*.

Layer 2 Forwarding Protocol (L2F) A dial-up VPN protocol designed to work in conjunction with PPP to support authentication standards, such as TACACS+ and RADIUS, for secure transmissions over the Internet.

Layer 2 Tunneling Protocol (L2TP) A dial-up VPN protocol, it defines its own tunneling protocol and works with the advanced security methods of IPSec. L2TP allows PPP sessions to be tunneled across an arbitrary medium to a "home gateway" at an ISP or corporation.

Learning bridge   A bridge that builds its own bridging address table, rather than requiring you to enter information manually.

Leased line   A transmission line provided by a communications carrier for private and exclusive use by a customer.

Link Access Procedure Balanced (LAPB)   A Layer 3 technology associated with X.25 implementations.

Link Access Procedure D Channel (LAPD)   A technology that allows the use of a separate access path for ISDN signaling and call requests.

Link state   In OSPF, the status of a link between two routers.

Link-state database   See *Topological database.*

Link-State Advertisement (LSA) packet   An OSPF packet that describes link-state information, such as the router's operational interfaces, the cost used to send traffic out an interface, the next hop router-ID, and advertised routes. There are several types of LSAs.

Link-state database   See *Topological database.*

Link-State Request (LSR) packet   An OSPF packet used to request missing or outdated LSA information.

Link-state routing algorithm   See *link-state routing protocol.*

Link-state routing protocol   Any dynamic routing protocol that employs the Djykstra Algorithm for passing and maintaining routing information.

Link-state update packet   An OSPF packet that contains the LSA packet. Sent when a topology change occurs or in response to an LSR packet.

LLC   See *Logical Link Control.*

LLC2   See *Logical Link Control, Type 2.*

LMHOSTS file   A text file that contains a list of NetBIOS host-name-to-IP-address mappings used in TCP/IP name resolution.

LMI   See *Local Management Interface.*

Load   A value between 1 and 255 that specifies the saturation level of a link.

Load balancing   In routing, the ability of a router to distribute traffic across all of its interfaces that are the same distance from the destination address. Effective load balancing occurs when the maximum number of factors (including cost) are built into the equation and that links are used to their fullest extent.

Loading state   In the loading state, an OSPF router sends a link-state request (LSR) packet to request missing or outdated LSA information. The router receiving this request responds by sending the information in a link-state update (LSU) packet.

Local Area Network (LAN)   A high-speed computer network limited to a relatively small geographic area—typically a small building or floor of an office tower. LANs typically connect workstations, servers, printers, and other office productivity appliances. LAN standards specify signaling and cabling at the physical and data link layers of the OSI networking model. Token Ring, Ethernet, and FDDI are the most common LAN technologies.

Local Area Transport (LAT)   A Layer 2 protocol developed by the Digital Equipment Corporation (now Compaq Corporation).

Local broadcast   A broadcast on the local network, looking for the IP address of the destination host.

Local preference   A well-known discretionary path attribute that provides an indication to routers in the AS about which path is preferred to exit the AS. Paths with highest local preference are always preferred. This attribute is propagated within the AS but is not propagated outside the AS.

Local Management Interface (LMI) An interface that provides an ATM end-system user with network management information. It is defined by the ITU-T.

Logical addressing scheme Refers to the addressing method used in providing manually assigned node addressing.

Logical AND The process of deriving an IP network address by associating the address with a subnet mask and performing this Boolean function on the pair.

Logical channel A communications path between two or more network nodes that is packet-switched and non-dedicated. Because packet-switching is used, multiple logical channels may exist simultaneously on a single physical channel.

Logical Link Control (LLC) Sublayer of the data link layer of the OSI reference model. Provides an interface for the Network-layer protocols and the media access control (MAC) sublayer, also part of the data link layer.

Logical Link Control, Type 2 (LLC2) Connection-oriented OSI LLC-sublayer protocol. See also *LLC*.

Longest match The methodology behind route selection and data forwarding decisions within the router. The more bits a router can match when comparing the destination address and the routing table, the better the chance of reaching that destination.

Loop A continuous circle that a packet takes through a series of nodes in a network until it eventually times out.

Loopback plug A device used for loopback testing.

Loopback testing A troubleshooting method in which the output and input wires are crossed or shorted in a manner that allows all outgoing data to be routed back into the card.

M

MAC See *Media Access Control*.

MAC address See *Media Access Control Address*.

MAC address learning Function performed by a learning bridge. The source address and also interface of each received packet is stored for future delivery of packets by the learning bridge. Unless the MAC address is known, a bridge must forward packets to every interface instead of the known interface. This enables the bridge to operate efficiently as traffic does not go to unintended locations.

MAN See *Metropolitan Area Network*.

Management Information Base (MIB) A network information database installed on an end station that is used and maintained by a network management protocol such as SNMP or CMIP.

Mark In T1/E1 implementations, a binary value of 1. T1-capable devices use 1's to maintain proper clocking.

Master name server The supplying name server that has authority in a zone.

Match condition A route-map command used to match a routing update with based on specified conditions. See also *Set Action*.

Maximum Transmittable Unit (MTU) The largest entity that can be forwarded by any given layer 2 encapsulation.

MB Megabyte. One million bytes. Usually refers to file size.

Mb   Megabit. One million bits. Term used to rate transmission transfer speeds (not to be confused with megabyte).

Mbps   Megabits per second.

MD5   Authentication protocol.

Media   Various physical environments where data transmission occurs. This is the plural form of *medium.*

Media Access Control (MAC)   In the OSI model, the lower of the two sublayers of the data link layer. Defined by the IEEE as responsible for interaction with the physical layer.

Media access control address   A six-octet number that uniquely identifies a host on a network. It is a unique number, burned into the network interface card, so it cannot be changed.

Media Access Unit (MAU)   IEEE 802.3 specification referring to a transceiver. Not to be confused with a token ring MAU (Multistation Access Unit), which is sometimes abbreviated MSAU.

Media rate   The maximum transmission rate that can occur over a specific media type. Often specifications are less than the maximum so as to give headroom for manufacturing or installation defects.

Memory address   Usually expressed in binary, this is the label assigned to define the location in memory where the information is stored.

Mesh   A connection, can be either partial or full.

Message   A portion of information that is sent from one node to another. Messages are created at the upper layers of the OSI Reference Model.

Metric   A unit of measure to facilitate the selection of the best route to a given destination. In BGP, the metric is an optional non-transitive path attribute also known as the MED.

Metropolitan Area Network (MAN)   An internetwork implementation that spans across a city, not necessarily large geographic spans.

MIB   See *Management Information Base.*

Microsegmentation   The process of using switches to divide a network into smaller segments.

Microsoft Point-To-Point Encryption (MPPE)   Microsoft's proprietary, point-to point, secure data-encryption method, designed for use with PPTP (Point-To-Point Tunneling Protocol).

Microwaves   Very short radio waves used to transmit data over 890 MHz (megahertz).

Modem   A device used to modulate and demodulate the signals that pass through it. It converts the direct current pulses of the serial digital code from the controller into the analog signal that is compatible with the telephone network.

MTU   See *Maximum Transmittable Unit.*

Multiaccess network   Any network that allows multiple devices to communicate simultaneously.

Multicast   A single packet transmission from one sender to a specific group of destination nodes. In OSPF, the means by which routing updates are passed. Only OSPF routers respond to OSPF multicasts.

Multicast Open Shortest Path First (MOSPF)   An intradomain multicast routing protocol use in OSPF networks. MOSPF adds extensions to base the OSPF unicast protocol to support IP multicast routing.

Multiplatform   Refers to a programming language, technology, or protocol that runs on different types of CPUs or operating systems.

Multicast address   An address that specifies a subset of devices on the network—or a group of addresses. Compare with *Broadcast Address* and *Unicast Address.*

Multicast group   A group of devices that are identified by a multicast address. Network devices join a multicast group when they wish to receive the group's transmissions.

Multicast router   A router that is running a multicast routing protocol and configured to receive multicast traffic.

Multihoming   The process of connecting an AS to multiple ISPs.

Multilayer switch   A switch that operates at different layers of the OSI model. The most prominent multilayer switches operate at Layers 2 and above. Examples of multilayer switches include switch-routers and router- switches.

Multilink PPP   A standardized implementation of PPP that allows for the bonding of multiple B channels to aggregate bandwidth for the duration of a specific call.

Multimode fiber   Fiber-optic cabling that supports the propagation of multiple light frequencies. Compare with *Single-Mode Fiber*.

Multiplexing   Method of transmitting multiple logical signals across the same channel at the same time.

Multiring   In bridging, the use of a bridged network to forward traffic between two layer 3 networks.

Multistation Access Unit (MAU or MSAU)   A hub used in an IBM token-ring network. It organizes the connected nodes into an internal ring and uses the RI (ring in) and RO (ring out) connector to expand to other MAUs on the network.

Multivendor network   A network that is comprised of not only products from different manufacturers but of different protocols or protocol standards.

Mux   A multiplexing device. A mux combines individual signals into a single signal for transmission over a medium. At the other end, a demux, separates the signal back into its original signals.

N

Name caching   The storage of name-to-network addresses so that future lookups are not necessary. Name caches are always accompanied with a timeout period wherein future lookups are compulsory.

Name resolution   The process of resolving network names to network addresses.

Name servers   These contain the databases of name resolution information used to resolve network names to network addresses.

NAP   See *National Access Provider*.

NAT   See *Network Address Translation*.

National Access Provider (NAP)   A corporation responsible for larger portions of the public Internet. NAPs are in charge of providing public Internet access to ISPs and to efficiently manage scarce IP address space.

NBMA   Nonbroadcast multiaccess. Refers to multiaccess networks that do not by default support broadcast/multicast traffic. Examples include Frame-Relay, SMDS, and ISDN PRI.

NBTSTAT   A command-line utility that displays protocol statistics and current TCP/IP connections using NBT (NetBIOS over TCP/IP).

Neighbor   Two routers that exchange routing information with each other are neighbors. In OSPF, neighbors are routers that have established bi-directional communication. In BGP, neighbors are routers that have established a TCP BGP connection. See also *Neighborship* and *Adjacency*.

Neighborship   A condition in which routers have established a neighbor relationship with each other. In OSPF, neighborship refers to the relationship formed between two routers that have established bi-directional communication with each other; this includes the relationship between directly connected non-DR/BDR neighbors, as well as the relationship between DRs/BDRs and directly connected neighbors. Compare with adjacency.

Neighborship database   An OSPF data repository that contains all of a router's known neighbors within the area. Also called a neighbor database.

Neighbor table   In non-distance-vector routing protocols, a listing of routers that share directly connected links. In EIGRP, the neighbor table stores information about adjacent neighbors, including the neighbor's address and local router's outbound interface for the neighbor. The EIGRP neighbor table also stores information required by the reliable transport protocol (RTP), including the transmission list. There is a topology table for each network-layer protocol that EIGRP supports.

Neighbor database   See *Neighborship Database*.

Neighborship database   An OSPF data repository that contains all of a router's known neighbors within the area. Also called a neighbor database.

NetBEUI   See *NetBIOS Extended User Interface*.

NetBIOS   Network Basic I/O System. A connectionless, data link-layer protocol that utilizes broadcasts for communications.

NetBIOS Extended User Interface (NetBEUI)   A nonroutable, Microsoft-proprietary networking protocol designed for use in small networks.

NetBIOS Name Server (NBNS)   A central server that provides name resolution for NetBIOS names to IP addresses.

Netstat   A command-line utility that displays protocol statistics and current TCP/IP network connections.

Network   A network is a term used to describe the interconnectivity of computing devices: workstations, servers, printers, routers, etc.

Network address   A network address is a logical or physical number or name used for identification purposes. In order for a device to properly communicate with a different device, they must agree and cooperate using a common protocol. A network address is one such element of this protocol and is used to establish identity amongst devices so that they can ultimately communicate.

Network Address Translation (NAT)   A technology that allows the static and/or dynamic mapping of private, internal IP addresses to registered public IP address for communication via the public Internet.

Network administrator   The role of a network administrator is complicated. At one level it is to organize and implement the care and feeding of a network—to ensure that the network devices can competently, efficiently, and consistently communicate with each other. At another level, it is to plan growth and adjust for impending changes as well as to implement any changes.

Network analyzer   A network analyzer is a device that resides on a network and watches packets as they travel "on the wire." It is used for diagnostics as well as statistical purposes. Sophisticated analyzers are aware of higher level application protocols and can peel off network layers easily. Originally, network analyzers were single-purpose devices. However, most network analyzers are often very fast PC devices that are able to keep up with gigabit traffic.

Network down A term used when the clients are unable to utilize the services of the network. This can be administrative, scheduled downtime for upgrades or maintenance, or the result of a serious error.

Network ID The part of the TCP/IP address that specifies the network portion of the IP address. This is determined by the class of the address, which is determined by the subnet mask used.

Network Information Services (NIS) The user, group, and security information database utilized in a Unix internetwork.

Network interface A logical device for the purpose of receiving and transmitting information. Most network interfaces map directly to physical interfaces such as an Ethernet or serial port. However, network interfaces are often used to distinguish DLCIs in a single physical port into a frame relay network or an encrypted tunnel in a virtual private network.

Network Interface Card (NIC) Also known as a network adapter, this is the hardware component that serves as the interface, or connecting component, between your network and the node. It has a transceiver, a MAC address, and a physical connector for the network cable.

Network interface layer The bottom layer of the TCP/IP architectural model. Responsible for sending and receiving frames.

Network jordanism Any broadcast protocol that artificially sets ToS for its own packets to something with an elevated level of service in the network, in order to gain greater access for low priority traffic, usually succeeding only in adversely affecting all other traffic flows.

Network layer The third layer of the OSI Reference Model, this is where routing based on node addresses (IP or IPX addresses) occurs.

Network management The entire concept of maintaining, configuring, troubleshooting and scaling a computer network. Often hardware and software tools are employed to provide feedback.

Network News Transfer Protocol (NNTP) An Internet protocol that controls how news articles are to be queried, distributed, and posted.

Network number Part of an IP address that specifies the network to which a particular host belongs.

Network Operating System (NOS) An operating system for a computer that provides resources to other entities on a network. Novell Netware, Linux, and Microsoft Windows NT are examples of general purpose operating systems that provide file and printing resources (as well as others) to workstations on a computer network.

Network Termination 1 (NT1) An ISDN device that connects the point of demarcation to the CPE.

Network Termination 2 (NT2) An ISDN device that performs Layer 2 and 3 protocol functions and concentration services.

NIC See *Network Interface Card.*

Node The endpoint of a network connection. Nodes can be processors, controllers, or a workstation. It's also a generic term for a participant on a computer network, or a device that can transmit or receive information utilizing a computer network.

Noise Also known as EMI. See *Electromagnetic Interference.*

NOS See *Network Operating System.*

Notification message A BGP message sent to inform peers that an error occurred with a routing update. The BGP connection is closed immediately after sending this message.

NT1 See *Network Termination 1.*

NT2 See *Network Termination 2.*

Null interface   A logical software interface in a router used as an alternative to access lists to deny traffic. Traditionally, a static route is configured to specify the null interface as the outbound interface for traffic destined for the denied network.

NVRAM   Non-volatile Random Access Memory. Static memory space in the router where the router's configuration is stored. NVRAM, as the name implies, does not require power to keep its contents in storage.

O

Octet   One of four 8-bit divisions of an IP address.

Open architecture   Any architecture specification that lies within the public domain. Third-party develops are mandated to license the architecture for their products to any body. However, there are usually strict rules about making modifications.

Open Data Link Interface (ODI)   These drivers, heavily used in both Novell and Appletalk networks, allow the NIC (network interface card) to bind multiple protocols to the same NIC, allowing the card to be used by multiple operating systems. Similar to NDIS.

Open message   A BGP message that is sent to open up a BGP connection between two neighbors that have just established a TCP connection with one another. The open message contains negotiable parameters, such as the holdtime, and other introductory information, such as the sender router-ID.

Open Shortest Path First (OSPF)   A standardized dynamic-link state routing protocol designed to overcome the limitations of RIP by utilizing a hierarchical area structure.

Open Systems Interconnection (OSI) reference model   A seven-layer model created by the ISO to standardize and explain the interactions of networking protocols. In reality, there are very few implementations of OSI. The prevalent models, IP, IPX, AppleTalk, etc., span the various layers differently.

OSI   Open Systems Interconnection. See *Open Systems Interconnection (OSI) Reference Model.*

OSPF   See *Open Shortest Path First.*

P

Packet   A logical piece of information that contains control information as well as data. Control information is usually in the header or a trailer (less frequent).

Packet InterNET Groper (PING)   A TCP/IP protocol-stack utility that works with Internet Control Message Protocol and uses an echo request and reply to test connectivity to other systems.

Packet-Switched Network (PSN)   A network that utilizes packet-switching technology for data transfer. Sometimes called a packet-switched data network (PSDN).

Packet switching   Networking method where nodes share bandwidth by dividing the multiple information streams into smaller, more manageable packets. The packets are then transmitted mixed across a medium mixed in with packets from other nodes.

PAP   See *Password Authentication Protocol.*

Parallel transmission   Method of data transmission where bits of data are transmitted simultaneously over a number of channels. Compare with *Serial Transmission.*

Partial mesh   A physical configuration in which not all routers are directly connected.

Passive state An EIGRP router's state for a destination that is not in the route recomputation process. This is the normal state for a route. Compare with active state.

Password A set of characters used with a username to authenticate a user on the network and to provide the user with rights and permissions to files and resources.

Password Authentication Protocol (PAP) An authentication method that utilizes clear text usernames and passwords to permit and deny access to remote users and/or routers.

Patch panel A device where the wiring used in coaxial or twisted-pair networks converge in a central location and are then connected to the back of this panel.

Path attributes Metrics used by BGP to enforce policy-based routing. Path attributes can fall into four separate categories, including well-known mandatory, well-known discretionary, optional transitive, and optional non-transitive. Example of path attributes include weight, as-path, next-hop, origin, local preference, atomic aggregate, aggregator, communities, and Multi-Exit-Discriminator.

Payload The data portion of a packet (i.e., without the control information). See also *Packet*.

PBX See *Private Branch Exchange*.

PDM See *Protocol Dependent Module*.

PDN See *Public Data Network*.

Peak rate The maximum rate that a virtual circuit can transmit data.

Peer A neighbor router. In BGP, a peer is a neighbor that has established a TCP BGP connection with another neighbor. Peers do not have to be directly connected physically in order to exchange routing information.

Periodic update A routing update dispatched at a specified interval.

Permanent Virtual Circuit (PVC) A logical path—established in packet-switching networks—between two locations. Similar to a dedicated line. Known as a *permanent virtual connection* in ATM terminology. (Not to be confused with Private Virtual Circuit, also known as a PVC.)

Physical addressing scheme Refers to the MAC address on every network card manufactured. Cannot be changed.

Physical layer Bottom layer (Layer 1) of the OSI Reference Model, where all physical connectivity is defined.

Ping A utility that issues ICMP (Internet Control Message Protocol) packets to a host for acknowledgement of receipt. It is one of the most common (though not necessarily the most robust) utilities available to determine connectivity between hosts. See also *Packet Internet Groper*.

Plain Old Telephone System (POTS) The current analog public telephone system.

Point of demarcation In telecommunications, the point at which responsibility for the Serial link changes from the customer to the telco and vice versa.

Point of Presence (POP) Physical location where a long-distance carrier or a cellular provider interfaces with the network of the local exchange carrier or local telephone company.

Point-to-multipoint connection A partial mesh.

Point-to-point connection A connection between two routers.

Point-to-Point Protocol (PPP) A common dial-up networking protocol that includes provisions for security and protocol negotiation and provides host-to-network and switch-to-switch connections for one or more user sessions. The common modem connection used for Internet dial-up.

Point-to-Point Tunneling Protocol (PPTP) A protocol that encapsulates private network data in IP packets. These packets are transmitted over synchronous and asynchronous circuits to hide the underlying routing and switching infrastructure of the Internet from both senders and receivers.

Poison reverse updates   A routing update that explicitly indicates that a network or subnetwork is not reachable. Poison reverse updates are sent to default routing loops.

Polling   The media-access method for transmitting data, in which a controlling device is used to contact each node to determine if it has data to send.

POP   See *Point-of-Presence* or *Post Office Protocol.*

Port number   In IP, a service access point between the transport layer and the upper application layers.

POST   Power-On Self Test.

Post Office Protocol (POP)   A protocol for the delivery and retrieval of electronic mail. In most implementations it is merely a services for the retrieval of electronic mail, whereas SMTP is used for delivery. See also *Simple Mail Transfer Protocol.*

POTS   See *Plain Old Telephone Service.*

PPP   See *Point-to-Point Protocol.*

PPP Multilink   See *Multilink PPP.*

PPTP   See *Point-to-Point Tunneling Protocol.*

Prefix   The bits in an IP address that comprise the network portion.

Presentation layer   Layer 6 of the OSI Reference Model. Prepares information to be used by the Application layer.

PRI   See *Primary Rate Interface.*

Primary Rate Interface (PRI)   A higher-level network interface standard for use with ISDN. Defined at the rate of 1.544Mbps, it consists of a single 64-Kbps D channel plus 23 (T1) or 30 (E1) B channels for voice or data.

Print server   A network device that intercepts print requests, stores (or spools) the data to local storage, thus freeing the transmitting device from managing and maintaining a connection to a physical printer. The print server is then free to re-transmit the printing stream to any number of devices at any specified time in any quantity.

Priority queuing   A Cisco queuing strategy that allows the prioritization of various traffic based on its importance in the network.

Private Branch Exchange (PBX)   An analog or digital switchboard for telephones located on subscriber premises to connect private and public telephone networks.

Private internetwork address space   Any IP addresses that exists in space defined by RFC 1918 (consisting of network 10.0.0.0 through 10.255.255.255, 172.16.0.0 through 172.31.255.255, and 192.168.0.0 through 192.168.255.255).

Private virtual circuit (PVC)   Provides a logical connection between locations through a Frame Relay/ATM cloud. Example: A company has three branch offices. Each location physically connects to the Frame Relay provider's network through a series of switches, but it appears to the end users as if the three branch offices are directly connected to each other, as if it were an unbroken circuit. (Not to be confused with Permanent Virtual Circuit, also known as a PVC.)

Process switching   Packet processing without the use of a route cache. Therefore, performance is limited by process level speeds. Compare with *Fast Switching.*

Profile   A template for a user account.

PROM   See *Read-Only Memory.*

Propagation delay   The amount of time that it takes information to reach its destination or to reach multiple destinations. It is often related to control information and synchronizing rather than raw data.

Proprietary   A standard or specification that is created by a single manufacturer, vendor, or other private enterprise.

Protocol   A set of rules or standards that control data transmission and other interactions between networks, computers, peripheral devices, and operating systems.

Protocol address   A network-layer address that consists of a network and a host portion.

Protocol converter   A device or procedure to change the language of one system to the language of another system.

Protocol Dependent Module (PDM)   Responsible for EIGRP multi-protocol support. PDMs are responsible for supporting network-layer, protocol-specific requirements.

Protocol identification field   In a frame, a five-byte field used to identify to the destination node the protocol that is being used in the data transmission.

Protocol stack   Also known as a protocol suite, it's two or more protocols that work together, such as TCP and IP or IPX and SPX.

Protocol translator   A device or software that converts one protocol to another. The protocols are often at the same or span the same OSI layer. Otherwise, there would be little equivalency between the protocols and translation would be difficult or impossible.

Proxy   An entity or device that performs a function on behalf of another device.

Proxy ARP   Variation of the ARP protocol in which an intermediate device such as a router sends an ARP response on behalf of an end node to a requesting host. See also *Address Resolution Protocol*.

Proxy server   A program that makes a connection and retrieves information within a computer network on behalf of a client.

PSDN   Packet-switched data network. See *Packet-Switched Network*.

Pseudo ring   In source-route translational bridging, the method used to portray an Ethernet segment to token ring hosts as simply another token ring.

PSN   See *Packet-Switched Network*.

PSTN   See *Public Switched Telephone Network*.

Public Data Network (PDN)   A network offered to the public, usually for a fee. PDNs enable small organizations to extend their networks to remote locations without having to purchase long-distance point-to-point links.

Public internetwork address space   Any IP addresses that exist outside of the private address space. Public address space is normally under the control of a registration authority in charge of assigning these addresses to companies and/or individuals that require them.

Public Switched Telephone Network (PSTN)   A general term referring to all of the telephone networks and services in the world. The same as POTS, PSTN refers to the world's collection of interconnected public telephone networks that are both commercial and government owned. PSTN is a digital network, with the exception of the connection between local exchanges and customers, which remains analog.

PVC   See *Permanent Virtual Circuit*.

Q

Q.920/Q.921   The ITU-T (formerly the CCITT) specifications for ISDN UNI data link layer.

Q.931   An ISDN call setup protocol that deals with the ISDN network layer between the terminal and switch.

QoS   See *Quality of Service*.

QoS parameters   The ATM parameters including cell loss ratio (CLR), cell error rate (CER), cell misinsertion rate (CMR), cell delay variation (CDV), cell transfer delay (CTD), and average cell transfer delay.

Quality of Service (QoS)   The measurement of performance for a transmission system. This involves both availability of devices or links as well as the ability to perform within specified parameters. In the specific sense, it refers to ATM performance over a virtual circuit.

Queue   A first-in first-out list.

Queuing   The process of prioritizing traffic output on a Serial interface.

Queuing delay   The amount of time that an entity enters a queue and when it is released.

R

R Interface   In ISDN, the interface between the TE2 and TA.

RAM   See *Random Access Memory*.

Random Access Memory (RAM)   Volatile memory space in a router in which the running configuration is stored. Without power applied, the contents of RAM will be lost.

RARP   See *Reverse Address Resolution Protocol*.

Read-Only Memory (ROM)   Read-only memory is a hardware device that can store code and/or data. ROMs cannot be written to by the device that they're installed on, hence the term, read-only. However, programmable read-only memory (PROM) can be programmed using a separate special device. Erasable programmable read-only memory (EPROM) can be written to and erased multiple times.

Redistribution   The process of translating routing information from one protocol into another and advertising the translated information to the network. See *Route Redistribution*.

Redundancy   The process of providing fail-safe connectivity for hardware and/or software.

Reliability   A measurement of dependability of a link on a scale of 1 to 255, with 255 being highly dependable.

Reliable Transport Protocol (RTP)   Responsible for the guaranteed, ordered delivery of EIGRP packets to all neighbors. The reliable transport protocol uses a transmission list to keep track of all neighbors to which reliable packets have been sent; each neighbor is expected to respond with an acknowledgement.

Remote bridge   A bridge that unifies a network via WAN links.

Remote node   A node or computer that is connected to the network through a dial-up connection. Dialing in to the Internet from home is a perfect example of the remote node concept.

Repeater   A device that regenerates and retransmits the signal on a network. Usually used to strengthen signals going long distances.

Request for Comments (RFC) Method used to post documents regarding networking or Internet-related standards or ideas. Some have been adopted and accepted by the Internet Architecture Board as standards.

Resource Reservation Protocol (RSVP) A protocol that supports the reservation of resources across an IP network.

Reverse Address Resolution Protocol (RARP) A process that dynamically provides addressing information to end clients that know only their MAC address. This process is similar to BootP and/or DHCP.

RFC See *Request for Comments.*

RI See *Ring In.*

Ring In (RI) A connector used in an IBM token-ring network on a Multistation Access Unit (MAU) to expand to other MAUs on the network. Counterpart to the RO (Ring Out), the ring-in connector on the MAU connects to the media to accept the token from the ring.

Ring group In source-route bridging, the definition of logical ring that exists inside the bridge to act as a destination ring for a multiport SRB.

Ring Out (RO) A connector used in an IBM token-ring network on a Multistation Access Unit (MAU) to expand to other MAUs on the network. Counterpart to the RI (Ring In), the ring-out connector on the MAU connects to the media to send the token out to the ring.

Ring topology A LAN topology that implements a unidirectional closed-loop among nodes. Each node is connected to two and only two neighbors.

RIP See *Routing Information Protocol.*

RJ-11 connector This connector is used with telephone systems and can have either four or six conductors. A red/green pair of wires is used for voice and data; a black/white pair is used for low-voltage signals.

RJ-45 connector An Ethernet cable connector, used with twisted-pair cable, that can support eight conductors for four pairs of wires.

RMON The remote monitoring standard established in 1992 by RFC 1271 for its usage in Ethernet networks. It provides network administrators with comprehensive network fault diagnosis and performance information.

RO See *Ring Out.*

ROM See *Read-Only Memory.*

Root bridge A bridge in the internetwork that has been configured with the lowest bridge priority value, to make it the highest-priority bridge. All other bridges in the internetwork base path-determination decisions on the cost related to forwarding traffic to the root bridge.

Rotary group In DDR, a number of physical interfaces that have been associated and are under the control of one or more logical dialer interfaces.

Route Information in a router regarding reachability of a particular destination network.

Route evaluation An EIGRP process that occurs whenever an EIGRP router detects a topology change. In this process, the DUAL evaluates the topology table to discover whether there are any new best routes for a given destination. If the topology change was the result of a failed successor for a certain destination, the DUAL would try to find a feasible successor for that destination. If no feasible successor could be found in the topology table, the DUAL would enter route recomputation. See also *Route Recomputation* and *Distributed Update Algorithm.*

Route filter   A configuration, employing access lists, used to control the networks being advertised out of or into a router.

Routed protocol   Any of the Layer 3 protocols that can be implemented on a routed interface. Examples of routed protocols are IP, IPX, AppleTalk, DECnet, and VINES.

Route-map   An IOS feature used to control routing information received from or sent to a neighbor router.

Route recomputation   An EIGRP process that occurs whenever the DUAL fails to find a feasible successor in the topology table after a topology change. During this process, the router sends out query packets to ascertain whether EIGRP neighbors have an alternative route for the destination in question. The route recomputation process ends once all neighbors have replied to the router and the router has finished either 1) adding an alternative route for the queried destination to its topology and routing tables, or 2) removing the queried destination from its topology and routing tables. See also *Route evaluation* and *Distributed Update Algorithm*.

Route redistribution   The sharing of routing information between two separate routing protocols. Redistributed routes are propagated throughout the network as routes derived by the protocol receiving the shared information.

Route summarization   The process of consolidating a range of contiguous network numbers into a single route and advertising it on the network. Requires VLSM.

Router   A device that works at the Network layer of the OSI Reference Model to control the flow of data between two or more network segments.

Router-LSA   See *LSA Type 1*.

Routing   The concept of delivering objects from a source to a destination and includes the learning of routes to a destination.

Routing domain   Group of nodes and intermediate systems that agree on a set of administrative rules for routing. Each domain has a unique addressing scheme.

Routing information field   In token ring implementations, a field that consists of route control and route descriptor fields that provide pathway information for SRB hosts.

Routing Information Protocol (RIP)   Protocol that uses hop count as a routing metric to control the direction and flow of packets between routers on an internetwork.

Routing metric   A quantitative value assigned to a route by an algorithm that indicates reachability. The routing metric is then stored in a routing table. Routers can make decisions to forward packets to a destination by comparing these metrics and choosing the route that has the best value. Some metrics that contribute to a routing metric include bandwidth, communications cost, hop count, delay, MTU, reliability, and load.

Routing protocol   Any protocol that builds and maintains network reachability information in a routing table.

Routing table   A listing of destination networks, metrics necessary to reach those networks, a next hop address, and an outbound interface through which to depart the router to reach that destination network.

RS-232   The communications standard that defines the flow of serial communications and the particular functions.

RSVP   See *Resource Reservation Protocol*.

RTP   See *Reliable Transport Protocol (RTP)*.

Runt   Any frame transmitted that is smaller than the minimum transmittable unit.

S

Sample   In T1 technologies, a measurement of the height of an analog wave at 125-microsecond intervals, represented by an 8-bit code word.

SAP   See *Service Access Point* and *Service Advertisement Protocol.*

Scalable internetworks   Networks connected together by interconnectivity devices that are reliable, secure, accessible, and adaptable to the evolving needs of the network.

SDLC   See *Synchronous Data Link Control.*

Seed router   A router within a network that has fixed addressing rather than dynamic addressing. This allows other routers within the same network to establish network addressing for themselves based on the seed router's address(es). The AppleTalk suite of protocols makes use of seed routers.

Segment   A section of a network that is bounded by a router, a bridge, or a switch.

Serial interface   Any interface designed to access WAN services. Typical Serial interfaces include V.35, EIA/TIA 232, EIA/TIA 449, and so on.

Serial Line/Internet Protocol (SLIP)   A method of encapsulation that allows the TCP/IP protocol to be used over asynchronous lines, such as standard telephone lines. Previously used for most Internet access, it has been replaced by PPP because of SLIP's lack of error-checking capabilities.

Serial transmission   Method of data transmission where bits of data are transmitted one-by-one over a single channel. Compare with *Parallel Transmission.*

Server   A node that fulfills service requests for clients. Usually referred to by the type of service it performs, such as file server, communications server, or print server.

Server-based application   An application that is run off of a network share, rather than from a copy installed on a local computer.

Server-based networking   A network operating system that is dedicated to providing services to workstations, referred to as clients. See *Client/Server Networking.*

Service Access Point (SAP)   This field in a frame tells the receiving host for which protocol the frame is intended.

Service Advertisement Protocol (SAP)   An IPX protocol that provides network clients information about network resources such as file servers or print servers.

Service Profile Identifier (SPID)   A number that identifies the service to which you have subscribed. This value is assigned by the ISDN service provider and is usually a 10-digit telephone number with some extra digits. The SPID can consist of 1 through 20 digits.

Session   Term used referring to the dialog that exists between two computers.

Session layer   The fifth layer of the OSI Reference Model; it establishes, manages, and terminates sessions between applications on different nodes.

Set action   A route-map command used to control routing updates. In BGP, the set action specifies how matching routes are to be preferred, accepted, advertised, or redistributed. See also *Match Condition.*

SF   See *Superframe.*

Shared systems   The infrastructure component routed directly into the backbone of an internetwork for optimal systems access. Provides connectivity to servers and other shared systems.

Shielded Twisted-Pair (STP)   Twisted-pair network cable that has shielding to insulate the cable from electromagnetic interference.

Shortest-path routing   Routing that minimizes distance or path cost.

Silicon switching   Switching using a silicon-switching engine or processor rather than via embedded software and the main process. The end result is that routing decisions occur much faster.

Silicon Switching Engine (SSE)   Routing and switching mechanism that compares the header of an incoming packet to a silicon-switching cache and forwards the packet to the appropriate interface. Since the SSE is embedded in the hardware of the Silicon Switch Processor (SSP) of a Cisco 7000, it can perform switching independently of the system processor. Execution of routing decisions occur much faster than in software.

Single-mode fiber   Fiber-optic cabling that operates with a very narrow spectral width. It supports very high bandwidth but requires a light source to operate at the specified frequency. Compare with *Multimode Fiber.*

Single point of failure   Any point in the network that exists without redundancy. If this point fails, much, or all, of the network suffers an outage as well.

Simple Mail Transfer Protocol (SMTP)   An Internet protocol used for the transfer of messages and attachments.

Simple Network Architecture (SNA)   A non-routable IBM protocol usually associated with mainframe connectivity.

Simple Network Management Protocol (SNMP)   A protocol used almost exclusively in TCP/IP networks to do several things: to provide network devices with a method to monitor and control network devices; to manage configurations, statistics collection, performance, and security; and to report network management information to a management console.

Simple Network Management Protocol Trap (SNMP Trap)   An SNMP protocol utility that sends out an alarm notifying the administrator that something in network activity differs from the established threshold, as defined by the administrator.

S Interface   See *Subscriber interface.*

Sliding window flow control   Method whereby a receiver allows a transmitter to transmit information until a specific window is full. When the window is full, then the transmitter must stop until the receiver advertises a larger window.

SLIP   See *Serial Line/Internet Protocol.*

Small Computer System Interface (SCSI)   A technology defined by a set of standards originally published by ANSI for use with devices on a bus known as a SCSI bus.

Smart bridge   Also known as a learning bridge, it builds its own bridging address table, rather than requiring you to enter information manually.

SMDS   See *Switched Multimegabit Data Service.*

SMP   See *Symmetrical Multiprocessing.*

SMTP   See *Simple Mail Transfer Protocol.*

SNA   See *Simple Network Architecture.*

SNAP   See *Subnetwork Access Protocol.*

Snapshot client   A DDR-capable device that runs a distance-vector routing protocol that has frozen its routing table for a specified duration known as a quiet period. Once the quiet period has expired, the client dials the server router and exchanges routing updates.

Snapshot routing   A DDR feature that allows distance-vector routing tables to be frozen for long periods of time known as quiet periods. When the quiet period expires, a client router dials a server router to initiate a period of active routing update exchange.

Snapshot server   The router that receives the snapshot call to initiate routing update exchange.

SNMP   See *Simple Network Management Protocol*.

SNMP Trap   See *Simple Network Management Protocol Trap*.

Socket   A logical interprocess communications mechanism through which a program communicates with another program or with a network.

Socket identifier   Also known as a socket number, this is an 8-bit number used to identify the socket. It is used by IPX when it needs to address a packet to a particular process running on a server. The developers and designers of services and protocols usually assign socket identifiers.

SONET   See *Synchronous Optical Network*.

Source address   The address of the host who sent the frame is contained in the frame so the destination node knows who sent the data.

Source protocol address   The Layer 3 address of the originating host.

Source-route bridges   Used in source-route bridging, these bridges send the packet to the destination node through the route specified by the sending node and placed in the packet.

Source-Route Translational Bridge (SR/TLB)   A bridge that is capable of forwarding traffic between Ethernet and token ring clients by converting the frame type from one to the other and back again.

Source-Route Transparent Bridge (SRT)   A Token Ring implementation of bridging between hosts that utilize a RIF and those that do not. The source-route transparent bridge adds or removes the RIF according to the end station's needs.

Source Service Access Point (SSAP)   This one-byte field in the frame combines with the SAP to tell the receiving host the identity of the source or sending host.

Spanning Tree Algorithm (STA)   Defined by IEEE 802.1 as part of the Spanning Tree Protocol to eliminate loops in an internetwork with multiple paths.

Spanning Tree Protocol (STP)   Protocol developed to eliminate the loops caused by the multiple paths in an internetwork. Defined by IEEE 802.1.

SPID   See *Service Profile Identifier*.

Spike   An instantaneous, dramatic increase in the voltage output to a device. Spikes are responsible for much of the damage done to network hardware components.

Split-horizon updates   A technique used by routers whereby route propagation does not exit an interface where it was learned. This helps eliminate routing loops.

Spoofing   The process of representing false information to show connectivity when there is none. In DDR with IPX, spoofing of watchdogs and SPX Keepalives is done to simulate client/server connectivity.

SRAM   See *Static Random Access Memory*.

SRB   See *Source-route bridge*.

SRT   See *Source-Route Transparent Bridge*.

SR/TLB   See *Source-Route Translational Bridge*.

SSAP   See *Source Service Access Point*.

SSE   See *Silicon Switching Engine*.

Standard   Any agreed upon specification is a standard. Standards may be *de facto* or *de jure*. See *De Facto Standard* and *De Jure Standard*.

Standard area   In OSPF, an area that accepts all types of OSPF traffic. Also referred to as a non-stub area.

Standard access-list An access list of limited functionality, generally used to permit or deny access to/from hosts and networks.

Star topology A LAN topology where nodes on the network are connected to a common central switch using point-to-point links. Compare with *Bus Topology* and *Ring Topology*.

Static IP addresses IP addresses that are assigned to each network device individually, often referred to as hard-coded.

Static Random Access Memory (SRAM) *See Dynamic Random Access Memory.*

Static route A route that an administrator places in the routing table to override or augment the dynamic routing process.

Station IPX address A 12-digit number that is used to uniquely identify each device on an IPX network.

Store-and-forward A fast packet-switching method that produces a higher latency than other switching methods because the entire contents of the packet are copied into the onboard buffers of the switch, and the Cyclical Redundancy Check (CRC) calculations are performed before the packet can be passed on to the destination address.

STA *See Spanning Tree Algorithm.*

Statistical multiplexing A specific case of multiplexing whereby bandwidth can be dynamically allocated according to need. This makes better use of the bandwidth and it also allows streams to be multiplexed. See also *Multiplexing*.

STP *See Spanning Tree Protocol.*

Subinterface A logical or virtual interface assigned to a single physical interface.

Subnet A logical Layer 3 network.

Subnet address The part of an IP address that defines the subnet. It is revealed from the IP address by logically ANDing the IP address with its subnet mask.

Subnet mask A 32-bit address that is used to mask or "screen" a portion of the IP address to differentiate the part of the address that designates the network and the part that designates the host.

Subnetting The process of dividing your assigned IP address range into smaller clusters of hosts.

Subnetwork In an IP network, a subnetwork is part of an existing subnet. Subnetworks provide network administrators with a multilevel, hierarchical routing structure—effectively shielding the entire network structure from other networks.

Subnetwork access protocol (SNAP) An Internet protocol that specifies a standard method of encapsulating IP datagrams and ARP messages on a network.

Subscriber interface In ISDN, the connection between the customer equipment (BRI interface or TA) and an NT1.

Superframe (SF) In T1 technology, an entity that consists of 12 T1 frames.

Supernetting The aggregating of IP network addresses and advertising them as a single classless network address.

Supernetting mask Mask—similar to the subnet mask—used in supernetting.

Surge The opposite of a brownout. A surge's voltage increase is less dramatic than that of a spike, but it can last a lot longer.

Surge protectors Also known as surge suppressers, these are inexpensive and simple devices that are placed between the power outlet and the network component to protect the component from spikes and surges.

SVC   See *Switched Virtual Circuit.*

Switch   A Layer 2 networking device that forwards frames based on destination addresses.

Switch type   In ISDN, the model of switch to which the CPE is connected.

Switched LAN   A LAN that takes advantage of LAN switches or frame switches.

Switched Multimegabit Data Service (SMDS)   Defined by IEEE 802.6, it is the physical-layer implementation for data transmission over public lines at speeds between 1.544Mbps (T1) and 44.736Mbps using cell relay and fixed-length cells.

Switched Virtual Circuit (SVC)   A virtual circuit that is established dynamically on demand to form a dedicated link and is then broken when transmission is complete. Known as a *switched virtual connection* in ATM terminology.

Symmetrical Multiprocessing (SMP)   The utilization of multiple processors on a single system.

Synchronization   The agreement of data between two or more devices. In communications, an important synchronization element or data point is common timing.

Synchronous Data Link Control (SDLC)   An IBM proprietary Serial encapsulation that is capable of transporting only a single protocol. SDLC is usually associated with mainframe connectivity.

Synchronous Optical Network (SONET)   An ANSI standard for broadband public networks using fiber optics, initiated by the regional Bell operating companies. With SONET it is possible for telecommunications products from different vendors to communicate over networks, with data transmission rates from 51.84Mbps to 48Gbps.

Synchronous transmission   Digital signal transmission method using a precise clocking method and a predefined number of bits sent at a constant rate.

T

T1   Digital WAN carrier facility that transmits DS-1-formatted data at 1.544Mbps through the telephone switching network, using AMI or B8ZS coding.

T1 frame   One sample from each of 24 T1 timeslots placed end to end, with one additional bit added for framing.

T3   Digital WAN carrier facility that transmits DS3-formatted data at 44.736Mbps through the telephone switching network.

TA   See *Terminal Adapter.*

Tagged traffic   See *Discard Eligible.*

TCP   See *Transmission Control Protocol.*

TCP/IP   See *Transmission Control Protocol/Internet Protocol.*

TDI   See *Transparent Driver Interface.*

TDR   See *Time Domain Reflectometry.*

TE1   See *Terminal Equipment 1.*

TE2   See *Terminal Equipment 2.*

Telco   Short for telephone company.

Telecommunications   Communications over a telephony network. See also *Telephony.*

Telecommunications Industry Association (TIA)   An organization that develops standards—with the EIA (Electronics Industries Association)—for telecommunications technologies.

Telephony The science and industry devoted to the transmission of sound between endpoints-often substantial distances. The transmission of data has built upon telephony standards that have existed for decades, which is why telephone companies are the primary implementers of network transport equipment.

Telnet Standard terminal-emulation protocol in the TCP/IP protocol stack. It is used to perform terminal emulation over TCP/IP via remote terminal connections, enabling users to log in to remote systems and use resources as if they were connected to a local system.

Terminal A physical device used to control and/or communicate with a host computer. In early computing it was always a character-based device such as a cathode ray tube (CRT) and keyboard or a teletype (tty). Also a program, process, or other device that emulates a physical terminal.

Terminal adapter An adapter used in connecting non-native interfaces to ISDN facilities.

Terminal Equipment 1 (TE1) A native ISDN-capable router interface.

Terminal Equipment 2 (TE2) A non-native ISDN interface that must be attached to a TA for ISDN connectivity.

Terminal emulator A character-based program that will mimic the behavior of other terminals, often industry standard hardware devices. The most common emulators are ANSI, VT100, and 3270.

Terminal server A network device that connects physical terminals (See *Terminal*) or other asynchronous serial devices to a LAN or WAN often using TCP/IP, X.25, or LAT protocols.

TFTP See *Trivial File Transfer Protocol*.

Throughput The rate at which information passes through a juncture or a device in a network. Compare with *Bandwidth*.

Thicknet coaxial Thick cable most commonly used as the backbone of a coaxial network. It usually comes about .375 inch in diameter.

Thinnet coaxial Thinner than thicknet but still about .25 inch in diameter, it is commonly used in older bus topologies to connect the nodes to the network.

TIA See *Telecommunications Industry Association*.

Time-To-Live (TTL) Field in an IP header that indicates how long a packet is considered valid. It is also a generic term meant for caches and other temporary storage areas.

T Interface See *Trunk Interface*.

Time domain reflectrometry Method for locating cable lengths, or cable interfaces by sending a signal down the wire and watching for the faint reflections returned at each anomaly in the cable including the large reflection from the end. Using the known propagation speed in the wire media (approximately 0.7 c for instance in 10Base2 cable) and timing the reflections yields the distances to each of the sources of reflection. Commonly used for finding cable breaks and length of wire loop in telephony.

Timeslot The space available for a single piece information from a particular channel in time division multiplexing.

Token A frame that provides controlling information. In a token-ring network, the node that possesses the token is the one that is allowed to transmit next.

Token ring IBM proprietary token-passing LAN topology defined by IEEE standard 802.5. It operates at either 4 or 16Mbps in a star topology.

Token ring adapters Traditionally ISA or Microchannel devices with 4 or 16Mbps transfer capability, they are used to connect nodes to a token-ring network.

Topological database   An OSPF data repository that stores all known routes in the OSPF inter-network and indicates how these routes are interconnected. All routers in the same area maintain identical topological databases. Also called a link-state database.

Topology   Defines the shape or layout of a physical network and the flow of data through the network.

ToS   See *Type of Service.*

Traffic management   Any methods employed to avoid congestion in a network. Management also involves the use of hardware and software tools to provide feedback as to the status of specific links as well as their performance.

Traffic policing   A process used to measure traffic flow across a connection to determine whether or not action should occur. Where configured limits are breached, then an action such as discarding discard eligible (DE) frames is employed. This occurs in ATM and Frame Relay networks as well as other similar technologies. See also *Discard Eligible.*

Traffic prioritization   The process of configuring the router to treat differing traffic types as more or less important in consideration for output priority.

Trailer   Any control information that is at the end of a data stream or packet. Compare with *Header.*

Transceiver   A coined word that combines *transmitter* and *receiver.*

Transmission Control Protocol (TCP)   Part of the TCP/IP protocol stack, it's a connection-oriented, reliable data-transmission communication service that operates at the Transport layer of the OSI model.

Transmission Control Protocol/Internet Protocol (TCP/IP)   The suite of protocols combining TCP and IP, developed to support the construction of worldwide internetworks. See *TCP* and *IP.*

Transmission Control Protocol/Internet Protocol (TCP/IP) sockets   A socket, or connection to an endpoint, used in TCP/IP communication transmissions.

Transmission list   See *Reliable Transport Protocol.*

Transmit   The process of sending data using light, electronic, or electric signals. In networking, this is usually done in the form of digital signals composed of bits.

Transparent bridging   A situation in which the bridges on your network tell each other which ports on the bridge should be opened and closed, which ports should be forwarding packets, and which ports should be blocking them—all without the assistance of any other device.

Transport Driver Interface (TDI)   A kernel-mode network interface that is exposed at the upper edge of all Windows NT transport protocol stacks. The highest-level protocol driver in every such stack supports the TDI interface for still higher-level kernel-mode network clients.

Transport layer   Layer 4 of the OSI Reference Model, it controls the flow of information.

Triggered update   A routing update spawned as a result of a topology change. These updates are not sent out regularly. They go out on an as-needed basis only.

Trivial File Transfer Protocol (TFTP)   A connectionless file-sharing protocol that requires no authentication for uploading and/or downloading of files.

Trunk   The physical and logical connections between switches enabled for network traffic.

Trunk interface (T interface)   In ISDN, this is usually coexistent with the S interface between the NT1 and the customer equipment.

TTL   See *Time-To-Live.*

Tunnel   A logical configuration of the encapsulation of one Layer 3 protocol inside the payload of another layer 3 protocol. Tunnel configuration requires the configuration of the source, destination, and encapsulation mode of the tunnel as well as encapsulated protocol attributes on the logical tunnel interface.

Tunnel destination   The termination point of a logical tunnel.

Tunnel interface   A logical interface to which encapsulated protocol attributes are assigned. The tunnel's source, destination, and mode are defined here as well.

Tunnel mode   The encapsulation method used for a tunnel configuration. The default is **gre-ip.**

Tunnel source   The origination point of a logical tunnel.

Twinaxial   A type of coaxial cable more commonly found in IBM mainframe environments or used with AppleTalk networks. Contains two insulated carrier wires twisted around each other.

Twisted-pair   A type of cable that uses multiple twisted pairs of copper wire.

Two-way state   An OSPF state which specifies that two neighboring routers have seen each other's hello packet and established bi-directional communication.

Type of Service (ToS)   Single-byte field in the IP header that defines the abstract parameters precedence, delay, throughput, and reliability. This field is used to manage the priority of any single packet in a network, such that in comparison to other ToS values, it is delivered appropriately. ToS is defined in *RFC 791*.

U

UART   See *Universal Asynchronous Receiver/Transmitter.*

U Interface   In ISDN, the connection between the NT1 and the demarc.

Universal Asynchronous Receiver/Transmitter (UART)   A chip that's responsible for communications carried over a serial port, converting between data bits and serial bits.

UDP   See *User Datagram Protocol.*

Unicast   A message sent to a single address or network node.

Unicast address   The network address of a single network node. Compare with *Broadcast Address* and *Multicast Address.*

Universal Resource Locator (URL)   Standardized addressing scheme for accessing network resources. *De facto* standard has made it synonymous with web addresses, although it can refer to protocols other than http.

UNIX   An operating system in wide use, with more than 100 variations.

Unshielded Twisted-Pair (UTP)   A type of cable that uses multiple twisted pairs of copper wire in a casing that does not provide much protection from EMI. The most common network cable in Ethernet networks, it is rated in five categories.

Update message   A BGP message that contains network reachability information for a single path with either one or several associated networks; multiple paths require multiple update messages. This message also contains path attributes and paths that have been withdrawn.

User Datagram Protocol (UDP)   A communications protocol that provides connectionless, unreliable communications services and operates at the transport layer of the OSI model. It requires a transmission protocol such as IP to guide it to the destination host.

URL   See Universal Resource Locator.

UTP   See *Unshielded Twisted-Pair.*

V

V.90 standard   The standard that replaced both the K56flex technology and the x.2 technology as the standard for 56K serial data transfer over phone lines.

Variable Length Subnet Mask (VLSM)   A subnet mask that does not remain constant throughout the internetwork for a given classful network.

Variance   A multiplier value that allows a router to perform unequal cost load balancing. In IGRP and EIGRP, load balancing can only occur over paths whose cost is smaller than the cost of the best path multiplied by the variance.

Versatile Interface Processor (VIP)   An interface card designed for the Cisco 7000 and Cisco 7500 serious routers and enables the use of multilayer switching.

VIP   See *Virtual IP* or *Versatile Interface Processor.*

Virtual circuit   A logical connection setup across a network between a source and destination. The route is fixed and bandwidth is dynamically allocated. See also *Permanent Virtual Circuit.*

Virtual connection   A connection established between a source and a destination where packets are forwarded along the same path. Bandwidth is not permanently allocated until it is used.

Virtual IP (VIP)   A Cisco Catalyst 5000 running Virtual Networking Services can create logically separated switched IP workgroups across switched ports. This feature is called virtual IP.

Virtual LAN (VLAN)   Group of devices located on one or more different LAN segments whose configuration is based on logical instead of physical connections so that they can communicate as if they were attached to the same physical connection. See also *Local Area Network (LAN).*

Virtual link   In OSPF, a link that must be configured when a non-Area 0 must be connected directly to another non-Area 0. The virtual link transits the non-Area 0 that is connected to Area 0 to create a logical connection of the new area to Area 0.

Virtual Private Network (VPN)   A network that uses a public network such as the Internet as a backbone to connect two or more private networks. Provides users with the equivalent of a private network in terms of security.

Virtual ring   The configuration of a logical ring for implementations of multiport SRBs. The virtual ring must be specified as the destination ring in the SRB configuration of each interface.

Virtual Terminal (VTY)   A logical port to provide a means of accessing a router through the use of a Telnet session.

VLAN   See *Virtual LAN.*

VLSM   See *Variable Length Subnet Mask.*

VTY   See *Virtual Terminal.*

W

WAN   See *Wide Area Network.*

Wide Area Network (WAN)   Data communications network that serves users across a broad geographical area. Often uses transmission devices such as modems or CSUs/DSUs (Channel Service Units/Data Service Units) to carry signals over leased lines or over common carrier lines.

Weighted Fair Queuing (WFQ)   A Cisco queuing strategy employed to give low-volume traffic the priority for output consideration. Also called Last-Bit-In-First-Out (LBIFO).

WFQ   See *Weighted Fair Queuing.*

Wildcard mask   A four-octet mask used in the configuration of access lists to specify addresses for permission and/or denial. Also used in defining OSPF area membership.

Windows 2000   Equivalent of Windows NT 5.0.

Windows 95/98   Ubiquitous client operating systems enabling a friendly graphical interface. It has applications in consumer and small business environments but is often unsuitable for corporate networks due to its lack of unified security controls.

Windows Millennium Edition (ME)   The successor to Windows 98.

Windows NT   Ubiquitous corporate network operating system with graphical user interface.

Wiring closet   A location within a building, floor, or other convenient place to put cross-connect panels. It is also a place for small network devices, access devices, and remotely managed equipment. It is often not climate controlled and is therefore not suitable for servers or other temperature- and humidity-sensitive equipment.

Workgroup   A small group of machines that participate in a logical network. Network service broadcasts are often limited to those participants both to minimize network traffic and to narrow choices for workstations.

World Wide Web   The collective client/server process for retrieving documents that consist of text, graphics, sound, and video over the public Internet. Many of the standards are defined at the W3C consortium (http://www.w3c.org), although many large corporations have done their own standardization.

WWW   See *World Wide Web*.

X

x.2 technology   Developed by US Robotics in 1997, one of the original two 56Kbps data-transfer technologies that were replaced by the V.90 standard.

X.21bis   This Physical-layer communications protocol used in X.25 supports synchronous, full-duplex, point-to-point transmissions with speeds up to 19.2Kbps.

X.25   A WAN technology used in many parts of the world. X.25 is generally a very low-bandwidth Serial technology.

Xmodem   One of the most popular file-transfer protocols. It sends data in blocks along with a checksum and waits for an acknowledgment of receipt by the receiver.

XNS   Xerox Network System. Early predecessor of IPX/SPX and NWLink.

X terminal   A character-based virtual terminal session within the X-Windows environment. Sometimes referred to as x-term.

X Window System   A client/server model to enable graphical users applications on UNIX and UNIX-like operating systems. The server is the graphical system and has been adapted for multiple operating systems. The client is almost always UNIX or a UNIX derivative.

Z

Zmodem   A communications protocol similar to Xmodem. However, Zmodem provides better transfer rates and error checking. It achieves faster transmission by allowing larger blocks of data to be transmitted.

Numbers

10Base2   10Mbps baseband Ethernet specification using 50-ohm thin coaxial cable. Part of the IEEE 802.3 specification and has a distance limitation of 185 meters per segment. It is sometimes referenced as Thinnet or cheapernet.

10Base5   10Mbps baseband Ethernet specification using 50-ohm thick coaxial cable. Part of the IEEE 802.3 specification and has a distance limitation of 500 meters per segment.

10BaseFx   10-Mbps baseband Ethernet specification for Ethernet over fiber-optic cabling (IEEE). The x would indicate a particular variation of the Fiber-optic standard; variations include 10BaseFB, 10BaseFL and 10BaseFP.

10BaseT   The IEEE 802.3 specification for running Ethernet at 10Mbps over shielded or unshielded twisted-pair wiring. The maximum length for a 10BaseT segment is 100 meters (328 feet).

100BaseFX   The IEEE specification for running Fast Ethernet over fiber-optic cable.

100BaseTX   The IEEE 802.3u specification, also known as Fast Ethernet, for running Ethernet at 100Mbps over shielded or unshielded twisted-pair.

100BaseT4   This technology allows the use of Fast Ethernet technology over existing Category 3 and Category 4 wiring, utilizing all four pairs of wires.

100BaseVG (Voice Grade) AnyLAN   The IEEE 802.12 specification that allows data transmissions of 100Mbps over Category 3 (data grade) wiring, utilizing all sets of wires.

1000BaseX   This IEEE 802.3z specification, known as Gigabit Ethernet, defines standards for data transmissions of 1,000Mbps Access Control List (ACL)

56K technology   The serial transfer of data over analog modems at rates of up to 56Kbps. Although 56K technology started as two competing technologies, the x.2 and the K56flex, eventually the V.90 standard was established. Due to telephone industry standards limiting throughput to 53Kbps, the transfer rate of 56Kbps is theoretical and is not a reality in any of these technologies.

INDEX

INTERNATIONAL CONTACT INFORMATION

AUSTRALIA
McGraw-Hill Book Company Australia Pty. Ltd.
TEL +61-2-9417-9899
FAX +61-2-9417-5687
http://www.mcgraw-hill.com.au
books-it_sydney@mcgraw-hill.com

CANADA
McGraw-Hill Ryerson Ltd.
TEL +905-430-5000
FAX +905-430-5020
http://www.mcgrawhill.ca

**GREECE, MIDDLE EAST,
NORTHERN AFRICA**
McGraw-Hill Hellas
TEL +30-1-656-0990-3-4
FAX +30-1-654-5525

MEXICO (Also serving Latin America)
McGraw-Hill Interamericana Editores S.A. de C.V.
TEL +525-117-1583
FAX +525-117-1589
http://www.mcgraw-hill.com.mx
fernando_castellanos@mcgraw-hill.com

SINGAPORE (Serving Asia)
McGraw-Hill Book Company
TEL +65-863-1580
FAX +65-862-3354
http://www.mcgraw-hill.com.sg
mghasia@mcgraw-hill.com

SOUTH AFRICA
McGraw-Hill South Africa
TEL +27-11-622-7512
FAX +27-11-622-9045
robyn_swanepoel@mcgraw-hill.com

**UNITED KINGDOM & EUROPE
(Excluding Southern Europe)**
McGraw-Hill Publishing Company
TEL +44-1-628-502500
FAX +44-1-628-770224
http://www.mcgraw-hill.co.uk
computing_neurope@mcgraw-hill.com

ALL OTHER INQUIRIES Contact:
Osborne/McGraw-Hill
TEL +1-510-549-6600
FAX +1-510-883-7600
http://www.osborne.com
omg_international@mcgraw-hill.com